My Country
My Life

My Country
My Life

L.K. Advani

RUPA

Published by
Rupa Publications India Pvt. Ltd 2008
7/16, Ansari Road, Daryaganj
New Delhi 110002

Sales centres:
Bengaluru Chennai Hyderabad
Jaipur Kathmandu Kolkata
Mumbai Prayagraj

Copyright © L.K. Advani 2008, 2010

The views and opinions expressed in this book are the author's own and the facts are as reported by him which have been verified to the extent possible, and the publishers are not in any way liable for the same.

All rights reserved.
No part of this publication may be reproduced, transmitted, or stored in a retrieval system, in any form or by any means, electronic, mechanical, photocopying, recording or otherwise, without the prior permission of the publisher.

P-ISBN: 978-81-291-1654-3
E-ISBN: 978-81-291-2528-6

Second impression 2024

10 9 8 7 6 5 4 3 2

The moral right of the author has been asserted.

Printed in India

This book is sold subject to the condition that it shall not, by way of trade or otherwise, be lent, resold, hired out, or otherwise circulated, without the publisher's prior consent, in any form of binding or cover other than that in which it is published.

Dedicated to

all my fellow Indians

✸

my party colleagues and *karyakartas*, of today and yesteryears
*whose cooperation, support and affection has given me
strength in my public life*

✸

Rajpalji Puri and Pandit Deendayal Upadhyaya
*two great souls whose soaring idealism and patriotism shaped
my thinking and personality*

✸

and
my family,
Kamla, Jayant, Geetika
and
Pratibha
*whose limitless love and care has sustained me
through all the ups and downs in life*

Bharat Mata

Contents

Acknowledgements — ix
Foreword by Atal Bihari Vajpayee — xvii
Prologue — xxiii

Phase One

1. Triumph of Freedom, Tragedy of Partition — 2
2. Sindh and India: An Unbreakable Bond — 13
3. My First Twenty Years in Sindh — 27
4. Partition: Who Was Responsible? — 52

Phase Two

1. Migration from Sindh to Rajasthan — 62
2. My Work as a RSS *Pracharak* — 66
3. Mahatma Gandhi's Tragic Assassination — 71
4. Dr Mookerjee and Formation of the Bharatiya Jana Sangh — 83
5. The Thrill of Participating in the First General Elections — 91

Phase Three

1. Moving from Rajasthan to Delhi — 100
2. The *Organiser* Years — 108
3. The Bliss of Family Life — 119
4. My Entry into the Delhi Metropolitan Council — 128
5. Pandit Deendayal Upadhyaya — 137
6. The Beginning of My Parliamentary Career — 155
7. The Journey from Kanpur to Kanpur — 175
8. Two Events that Changed History — 193
9. Emergency: Democracy Imprisoned — 201

Phase Four

1. The End of the Darkest Period in India's History — 256
2. My Stint in the Information & Broadcasting Ministry — 267
3. The People Betrayed: The Fall of the Janata Government; Return of Indira Gandhi — 286
4. The Lotus Blooms — 306
5. The 1980s: The BJP's Phoenix-like Rise — 320
6. The Ayodhya Movement — 341
7. The Trauma and Triumph of Punjab — 422
8. The Entry and Exit of Two Prime Ministers in Two Years — 439
9. Five Years of P.V. Narasimha Rao's Government — 453
10. Three Prime Ministers in Two Years — 476
11. The Swarna Jayanti Rath Yatra: *A Patriotic Pilgrimage* — 490

Phase Five

1. The Beginning of a New Era — 528
2. The Kargil War: A Decisive Victory for India — 561
3. The NDA Returns to Power — 578
4. Review of the Working of the Indian Constitution — 587

5.	At the Helm of the Home Ministry	600
6.	Cross-Border Terrorism	620
7.	Pakistan's Proxy War	643
8.	Dealing with the Kashmir Issue	665
9.	Vajpayee-Musharraf Summit in Agra	694
10.	Securing Assam and the North-East for the Future	711
11.	Naxalism, other Challenges and Initiatives	734
12.	Communal Violence in Gujarat: Propaganda versus Reality	751
13.	Defeat in Polls, Turmoil in the Party	761
14.	My Pakistan Yatra	783
15.	'I Have No Regrets'	824
16.	Atal Bihari Vajpayee: A Statesman with a Poetic Soul	833
17.	Reminiscences and Reflections	847
18.	In Pursuit of Meaning and Happiness in Life	875

Epilogue — 893

Appendices

    Appendix I: Free India's Message to the World by Maharshi Aurobindo — 902

    Appendix II: Swami Vivekananda and the Future of India by Swami Ranganathananda — 905

    Appendix III: A Tale of Two Emergencies by L.K. Advani — 916

    Appendix IV: BJP's Palampur Resolution on Ayodhya — 931

    Appendix V: Speech by L.K. Advani at a function organised by The Karachi Council on Foreign Relations, Economic Affairs & Law, June 2005 — 934

    Appendix VI: Statement by L.K. Advani at the BJP's National Executive Meet, Chennai, 18-19 September 2005 — 941

References — 943

Glossary — 955

List of Acronyms — 959

Index — 964

Acknowledgements

My Country My Life is not only the memoir of one person; it is essentially a political autobiography that narrates the journey of my life and my party, the Bharatiya Janata Party (BJP), in the larger context of the march of modern India. Thus, I realised as soon as I began working on it—and the realisation became stronger as the work progressed—that many people would join this book's steady journey from idea to print. This journey could not have been successfully traversed without the generous help, active support, constant encouragement and creative contribution of those very people. It is my duty to acknowledge them all.

I express my deepest gratitude to Atal Bihari Vajpayee—Atalji, for me and his countless admirers—for writing the *Foreword*. As this book chronicles, we have been working together for a common goal since 1951. What he has written about me, and what I have written about him in this book, is a tribute to our close association, which I deeply cherish. I wish and pray for his good health, and both my party and I will continue to seek his wise guidance.

I sincerely thank Dr A.P.J. Abdul Kalam, the hugely popular President of India (2002-07), for consenting to launch the book. To say 'thank you' to Bhairon Singh Shekhawat, Vice President of India (2002-07), for agreeing to preside over the function to launch the book, would sound formal. He is my dear and longtime colleague, and I have fond memories of our close association.

As I have alluded to in the *Prologue*, I am immensely proud of my active association with the Rashtriya Swayamsevak Sangh (RSS), which I joined at the age of fourteen. I am what I am today principally because of the *samskaras* (values and traditions) that I acquired from this nationalist organisation. It is, therefore, naturally my duty to express my gratitude to Shri K.S. Sudarshan, *Sarsanghchalak* of the RSS, Shri Mohanrao Bhagwat, *Sarkaryawah* (General Secretary) of the RSS, and all its other senior functionaries on the occasion of the publication of this book.

I thank my colleague Jaswant Singh, who, besides providing initial encouragement, regularly inquired about the progress of the book. 'We all would be poorer without your memoirs,' he had said. That, surely, was an exaggeration. Nonetheless, coming from a fine and prolific writer, who has penned several books despite his preoccupation with political work, the comment prompted me to stay right on course.

My sincere appreciation and thanks are due to my publishers R.K. Mehra and Kapish G. Mehra of Rupa & Co. Their experienced hand guided this project at every stage. Sanjana Roy Choudhury and her team, Milee Ashwarya, Trisha Bora, Pushpanjali Barooah and Barnasha Baruah had to cope with impossible deadlines, and so did those working in the production department. But cope they did with admirable professionalism. Sanjana, Peali Dutta-Gupta and Shamik Kundu who handled the cover design and other aesthetic aspects of the book with great aplomb, made numerous visits to my residence, often at short notice. This collaborative effort brought me much joy. My best wishes to one and all at Rupa & Co. My thanks to the printers Gopsons Papers Ltd.

A book of this nature, in which I have narrated my own life story in the context of the journey of modern India, perforce required considerable research and reference work. I had to consult several people, both in and out of government. I cannot mention them all, since some of them are still in service. Nevertheless, I wish to sincerely acknowledge the assistance rendered by Kamal Pande, former Cabinet Secretary who worked with me as Home Secretary; Ajit Doval and K.P. Singh, both former Chiefs of the Intelligence Bureau; and Satish Chandra, former deputy National Security Advisor.

A highly useful source of information pertaining to the history of the Bharatiya Jana Sangh and, later, the BJP was the compendium (consisting of seven volumes of the former and ten volumes of the latter) published on the occasion of the Rajat Jayanti (silver jubilee) of the BJP in April 2005. The Party Documents Committee, headed by the late Vishnukant Shastri, and executed by its Working Chairman, Dinanath Mishra, had accomplished a stupendous job. I take this opportunity to once again commend all those who were associated with this project. In doing so, I also fondly remember my dear colleague, the late Rajendra Sharma, who served as our parliamentary Party Secretary for several decades. It was he who had first conceived of meticulously documenting all party-related literature.

I am especially beholden to my very close friend and colleague, Sudheendra Kulkarni, for the invaluable assistance he has given me in writing these memoirs. It is he who has been working with me tirelessly from the day I decided to pen such a book. Again, it is Sudheendra who has organised all the research work necessary for the book.

The final stages of the book, in particular, involved a number of painstaking tasks requiring multiple skills. This was done with commendable dedication by a small team comprising A. Suryaprakash, a veteran journalist; Zorawar Daulet-Singh, a young researcher; journalists Rajkumar Sharma and Ravindra Dani, who made many a helpful comment; and Prodyut Bora, a young BJP activist. Another person who made valuable contribution to this effort was Sadhvi Bhagwati of Parmarth Niketan, Rishikesh.

I also wish to thank my colleagues S. Gurumurthy and Balbir Punj for their insightful comments on the manuscript.

Collecting, and selecting, photographs for this book proved to be a substantial task. Here again, the photographic archives of the Jana Sangh and the BJP, produced by the Party Documents Committee, proved very helpful. Rohit Puri, son of Rajpalji Puri, gave us a much-cherished photograph of his father. My sister Sheela, in Mumbai, discovered some rare photographs of my childhood in Karachi. Tarun Vijay, former Editor of *Panchajanya*, and R. Balashankar, Editor of *Organiser*, provided both photographic and documentary material. Rajkamal Jha, Executive Editor of the *Indian Express* and Sanjay Malik, head of the newspaper's archives, were generous in making available almost their entire photo collection for this project. The same generosity was also shown by photographers Subhash Chander and Khadak Singh. Sanjay Gupta and his colleague Raj did the formatting of the book admirably. I would like to thank Nalini Bansal for the index. The photo section of this book carries my portrait, which is a creation of Krishn Kanhai, a *chitrakar* belonging to Kanhai tradition of Krishna art, based in Vrindavan. My sincere thanks to all of them.

I am grateful to my office staff—headed by Deepak Chopra, my Private Secretary for over two decades and Prakash Chander, Additional Private Secretary, for their devoted and diligent service, which I relied upon at every stage of the project. Incidentally, the cover photo was taken by Deepak when I had gone on an official visit to Andaman & Nicobar Islands in 2002.

The Hindi edition of this book will be published by Prabhat Prakashan, which has earned a well-deserved reputation for promoting nationalist literature of high quality in Hindi. Its owner, Shyam Sunder, and his sons Prabhat Kumar and Piyush Kumar, have been the family's friends for many years. They provided useful assistance in this project as well.

*

In my long political career there have been several instances when I have had to face prosecution at the hands of the government. On a few occasions, as for example, in the Bangalore High Court, at the very outset of the Emergency, I argued my own case. But, in most cases, many eminent lawyers have defended me very ably. As I mention in the chapter on the Emergency, the Counsel who appeared on behalf of Atalji and myself in Bangalore were a formidable galaxy—M.C. Chagla, Shanti Bhushan, K.K. Venugopal, Rama Jois and Santosh Hegde.

A case was filed against me in Gwalior against registration of my name in the voters list. In this case, I was ably represented on different occasions by Ram Jethmalani, Sushma Swaraj and Mahesh Jethmalani.

In the 'Hawala' case, it was Arun Jaitley and Ram Jethmalani who argued my case. A lot of analytical groundwork was done by S. Gurumurthy.

Kamla's meticulous maintenance of my personal accounts was of immense help to Gurumurthy in his work.

In matters relating to Ayodhya, two lawyers who have helped me immensely at all stages of the numerous cases instituted by the government have been K.K. Sood and Mahipal. When during my Somnath to Ayodhya Rath Yatra, I was arrested at Samastipur (Bihar) and then detained at Massanjore, Ravi Shankar Prasad had come to argue the case against my detention and secured quick relief for me.

Arun Jaitley, Ravi Shankar Prasad and Sushma Swaraj have been following up all Ayodhya matters involving me whenever they have come up for hearing in any Delhi Court. On several occasions it has been two very eminent lawyers, Fali Nariman and Harish Salve, who have defended the cases instituted against me. Throughout the period I was testifying before the Liberhan Commission, it was Satyapal Jain of Chandigarh who assisted me.

I wish to record my deep gratitude to all these lawyers.

*

George Santayana, an American philosopher, describes the family as one of Nature's masterpieces. I experience the truth of this description each day of my life. I did so yet again during the course of writing this book, the very idea of which, as I mention in the *Prologue*, came from my wife, Kamla, and daughter, Pratibha. There was hardly a day when Kamla did not ask me about the progress made in accomplishing the work she had 'assigned' to me. Pratibha, in fact, pleasantly surprised me with the talent and meticulousness she brought to bear on the various tasks associated with the book's production—checking facts, suggesting re-ordering and reformulation of the narrative, giving design inputs, reading the proof copies and, above all, in selecting both the title and the cover photo of this book. I am proud of you, Pratibha.

Foreword

I am pleased to write this *Foreword* to the memoirs of my longtime friend and colleague Shri Lal Krishna Advani. Advaniji's autobiography, aptly titled *My Country My Life*, closely follows the defining moments of Independent India, including the tragedy of Partition that accompanied the joy of freedom from the British rule, allowing readers to learn both about him and, to some extent, also about the extraordinary times he has lived in.

Advaniji was born in Karachi and lived in Sindh for the first twenty years of his life. Like millions of people on both sides of the bloodied border between India and Pakistan, he too was uprooted from his home and became a refugee. It is a testimony to the innate strength of his personality and character that he surmounted this adversity, just as he would overcome many other adversities in his life, to relentlessly pursue his chosen path. Even before this great tragedy struck he had devoted his life to the selfless service of our Motherland by becoming a *pracharak* of the Rashtriya Swayamsevak Sangh (RSS). It is these qualities of commitment, devotion, and determination to face all odds in the course of serving the nation, which have characterised Advaniji's life.

Advaniji has been my friend and comrade-in-arms ever since he started working for the Bharatiya Jana Sangh over fifty years ago. When I look back, I see him in a multitude of roles as the young secretary of the fledgling parliamentary wing of our party when I was first elected to the Lok Sabha in 1957; as a disciplined organiser of the party's Delhi unit where it achieved some of its initial successes in the country; as an erudite journalist with *Organiser*; as one who assisted Pandit Deendayal Upadhyaya and, later, me, in building the party in a most difficult period in its history; as a crusader for democracy and fellow-prisoner during the Emergency; as an associate who, along with me, experienced both, the joy of the formation of the Janata Party government, and the frustration of its early fall; as one who helped me found the Bharatiya Janata Party (BJP), which grew from strength to strength to become a viable alternative to the Congress party; as one who assisted me in forging the National Democratic Alliance (NDA); and as my able deputy in steering the ship of the nation for six years.

Yes, we have had our differences on issues and approaches during the course of our long association as it is not possible for two individuals to always have an identical response while working together for over a half century within an organisation. However, it is not the differences, but the unity of purpose and action, that marked our relationship. Divergence of viewpoints never led to discord; neither did they become a cause for division. This is because our party, both as the Jana Sangh and the BJP, was rooted in the ethos of working together for a larger common objective. I consider that philosophy to be the primary reason why the BJP has remained united, an exception in India, where organisational fissures have sadly been a regular feature.

This ethos of camaraderie is something that, according to me, needs to be zealously preserved and further strengthened in the BJP, as it charts its future course of development. The self-imposed discipline of never taking differences beyond the *Laxman Rekha* in matters of what is good for the party and the nation is the most reliable guarantor of success in the long-term. Indeed, going a step further, I would add that the philosophy of working together needs to be imbibed by all our political and non-political organisations and inculcated as a strong cultural trait of our national life. It has become a fundamental requirement for strengthening our proudly cherished democratic system and making it immune to the often debilitating pulls and pressures of politics in the era of coalitions. It is also an imperative for fully realising India's potential in socio-economic development, so that the needs and aspirations of each member of our billion-plus population can be fulfilled.

India is a vast nation with immense diversities. We must accept and respect these diversities in both our social and political lives. However, India's progress, and its ability to successfully confront the challenges of the present and the future, depend crucially on the degree to which we are able to construct a unity that transcends diversity and, indeed, transforms it into a source of vitality. Our national unity should not be weakened by following a flawed concept of secularism. Advaniji has made an enduring contribution to a vigorous public debate on genuine secularism and the main roots of our nationhood.

During the course of his long, and inarguably eventful, political life, Advaniji has, at times, been misunderstood and as a result become a victim of the dichotomy between image and reality. But those who have worked or interacted with him closely know him as a man who has *never* compromised on his core belief in nationalism, and yet has displayed flexibility in political responses whenever it was demanded by the situation. Above all, he has an open mind that always absorbs new ideas from diverse sources, a quality that has been nurtured by his lifelong love for books. I have always been amazed at how he manages to keep this hobby alive, in spite of devoting so much time to public life. Even at this age, he travels tirelessly, addresses party and public forums, campaigns, reads voraciously and writes.

Through this book, Advaniji has now added another special accomplishment to his life. In India, we do not have a deep-rooted tradition of prominent figures in public life writing their autobiographies. I am certain that *My Country My Life* will be read widely, and with keen interest, by people from diverse backgrounds. For mirrored in this book is the remarkable journey of a sensitive human being and an outstanding leader whose best, I hope and pray, is yet to come.

Atal Bihari Vajpayee
Prime Minister of India (1998-2004)

A close and unbroken partnership of fifty-six years, unparalleled in India's political history:
1952: Atal Bihari Vajpayee, Lal Krishna Advani and Bhairon Singh Shekhawat as young activists of the Bharatiya Jana Sangh, photographed at a party meeting in Kota, Rajasthan

2003: Bhairon Singh Shekhawat, Vice President of India, Prime Minister Atal Bihari Vajpayee and Deputy Prime Minister Lal Krishna Advani photographed at the Prime Minister's residence on Atalji's birthday on 25 December

Prologue

India celebrated the sixtieth year of its independence on 15 August 2007. Independence Day is, indeed, a special day for each one of us. Every year, I have two fixed morning engagements on that day. The first is to attend the official function at Red Fort, the majestic sandstone structure of the Mughal era where the Prime Minister unfurls the national flag and addresses the nation. It is in this fort, built by Emperor Shah Jahan in AD 1638, and in its historic environs that one can still see the footprints of many crucial developments in our Motherland's journey from the ancient era to the modern, including those of India's First War of Independence in 1857. It is a significant coincidence that the 60th anniversary of India's Independence also marked the 150th anniversary of that glorious uprising in which India united—Hindus and Muslims, as well as kings, queens and commoners—and fought as one against foreign rule.

My second engagement of the day, upon arriving home, is to join my family, colleagues, friends and office staff, in hoisting the tricolour and singing the national anthem, on the lawns of my residence. Although the programme is simple and away from the public glare, it gives me immense personal satisfaction, because it is my own special way of paying tribute to our Motherland. If Mother India is divine, as I indeed believe she is, then my faith teaches me that both individual and collective veneration of the divinity has its own significance.

In 2007, after concluding the two engagements, I spent most of the latter half of the day watching various television channels and reading newspapers, all of which had special stories on the sixtieth anniversary. One TV channel carried a feature called the 'Ten Defining Moments in Independent India'. It presented my views, taken in an interview conducted earlier, on a couple of them—namely, the Emergency Rule in 1975-77; and the Ram Janmabhoomi movement in the late 1980s and early 1990s.

Similar programmes were featured by other TV channels and newspapers. Some of the other 'defining' political developments that the media talked about included the Partition of India in 1947; Mahatma Gandhi's assassination in 1948; integration of 562 princely states by Sardar Vallabhbhai Patel, India's first Home Minister; first general elections in 1952, pursuant to the declaration of India as a Republic; the Chinese aggression in 1962; split in the Congress party in 1969; the India-Pakistan war in 1971 leading to the liberation of Bangladesh; the first ever defeat of the Congress party in parliamentary elections, followed by the formation of the Janata Party government in 1977; Indira Gandhi's assassination in 1984, followed by the gruesome anti-Sikh riots in the national capital; the Bofors scandal and Rajiv Gandhi's defeat in the 1989 elections; India becoming a nuclear weapons state with Atal Bihari Vajpayee's government conducting nuclear tests at Pokharan in May 1998; and the first non-Congress government, that of the Bharatiya Janata Party (BJP)-led National Democratic Alliance (NDA), to rule India for six years (1998-2004).

What struck me, as I watched this 15 August special feature, was that I had either been a participant in, or a ringside viewer of, almost all the above-mentioned seminal developments in independent India.

Along with my senior colleagues Atal Bihari Vajpayee and Bhairon Singh Shekhawat, I feel fortunate to be one of the few persons in Indian politics to have participated in every single general election since 1952—either as a campaigner or as a candidate. Even today, in 2008, I am an active participant in the debate, both within and outside Parliament, on the major issues facing the nation, including the Indo-US nuclear deal and its negative implications for our strategic defence and foreign policy.

My life, in a nutshell, has been an active one. The journey from 1947 to 2007 is a very short one in a nation's history, especially a nation as ancient as ours. But it is quite considerable in an individual's life. In my case, independent India's political voyage has subsumed my own, giving me an opportunity to both observe, and in my own humble way contribute to the many momentous developments along the way. It has also been a fairly eventful life—brimming with activity, and full of vicissitudes—however, in totality, highly satisfying. Indeed, it is filled with more satisfaction than I had ever anticipated. It has taught me innumerable lessons, helping me evolve into the person I am today.

I believe I have something to communicate to my fellow citizens and hence the thought of writing my memoirs began crystallising in my mind some time back. I admit that I am neither a historian nor a scholar of political science. However, as someone who has devoted all of his adult life in the service of the nation and amassed a wealth of experience, I *can* claim to have the practical and contemplative understanding that comes to a dedicated, longstanding and goal-oriented practitioner of politics. I felt it was time for me to share my experiences and understanding with my fellow Indians; and also to share, especially with the youth, my dreams and concerns, my aspirations and apprehensions, about tomorrow's India.

As a political activist, I have used the art of communication to propagate ideas, promote ideals, support or criticise policies, and to highlight my party's programmes. But I have seldom spoken or written about my *own* life. I might have done so, occasionally, in a fragmented way during an interview or in an article, but never in a comprehensive and organised manner. I was not alone in my thinking. The thought was echoed, with a mounting degree of insistence, by my wife Kamla and daughter Pratibha. Quite often, it was as if they were keener than I that I should write my memoirs. 'You have experienced so much in life. People should know about it,' Kamla had said to me on several occasions. I knew that she was only articulating a thought that had been taking shape in my own mind.

Every significant event has its own predestined time of occurrence. The arrival of 2007 provided a compelling context for many reasons. Firstly, the sixtieth anniversary of India's Independence also marks six decades of my life after I migrated from Sindh. Secondly, I turned eighty in November 2007. God has been kind in blessing me with a long and healthy life. Besides marking my fifty-five years in political life, the year 2007 also marked sixty-five years of my active and continuous association with the Rashtriya Swayamsevak Sangh (RSS) as a *swayamsevak*, an association I am immensely proud of. Kamla turned seventy-five in 2007 and Pratibha celebrated her fortieth birthday. They, along with my son Jayant and daughter-in-law Geetika, are very dear to me. Whatever I have been able to do for my country is primarily because of the limitless and unconditional love, affection, support and care I have received from my family.

Soon the idea of the book began taking concrete shape. Now it is in your hands, esteemed readers.

*

A brief introduction to the contents of this work would be in order.

In Chinese script, I am told, the word 'crisis' is written as a compound of two characters, one denoting 'danger' and the other 'opportunity'. My own life has recurrently brought home to me the fact that there is an immense truth in the interrelationship of these two concepts. Both for an individual and a community, conditions of adversity pose a challenge. And a challenge brings out the best in each one of us.

My first experience of the validity of opportunity being the flipside of crisis came in 1947, a life-transforming year both for my country and for me. It appeared as a dividing line in India's history, as well as in my own life. I spent one-fourth of my life, the first twenty years, in Sindh, which is now a part of Pakistan. I was born in Karachi, the capital of Sindh, in 1927. In 1942, when I had just turned fourteen, I joined the RSS, a nationalist organisation dedicated to uniting Hindu society across the dividing lines of caste, language and region, and bringing about India's national renaissance on the basis of her cultural and civilisational heritage.

Motherland. Freedom. A bright new future for India. These concepts had taken hold of my youthful imagination with the power of idealism, which is a wonderful boon of that age. Patriotism was palpable in the air.

However, as the years passed, there was another reality, an alarming reality, which gripped the minds of my fellow *swayamsevaks* and me—indeed, the minds of all Hindus in Karachi. Clouds of partition had begun to hover over the sky in Sindh. Even though I knew very little about the politics of the day, whatever I knew was sufficient enough to cause concern. Fear and uncertainty had gradually begun to spread amongst the Hindus, who were a minority in Sindh. A strange phrase 'Two Nation Theory', and an unfamiliar name 'Pakistan', were being talked about in hushed and anxious tones. Rumours were rife that a new Muslim nation was being created. Would Karachi and Sindh cease to be in India? Would we have to leave our city, our beloved Sindh? Even the thought of it was menacing.

The thought turned into a violent reality on 15 August 1947.

Our Motherland was partitioned. India's freedom and Pakistan's creation were heralded by unprecedented mass killings and the largest ever cross-border human migration in history. Nearly a million people died in the inferno of communal riots, and approximately fifteen million people became refugees. I was one of them. I left Karachi for good on 12 September 1947. Uprooted from our home, and escaping the flames of Partition, my family and I found protection and solace in the bosom of Mother India. Though herself mutilated and truncated, she made us feel at home.

For Hindus living in those parts of undivided India, which later became Pakistan, Partition was a terrible calamity. Apart from the North-West Frontier Province (NWFP) and Baluchistan, the other main provinces affected were Punjab, Bengal and Sindh. But while Bengal and Punjab were divided and so provided a natural home to the uprooted Hindus from these two provinces, Sindh became a part of Pakistan in its entirety. There were districts in Sindh contiguous to Rajasthan, like Tharparkar, which had a Hindu majority. A more assertive leadership could perhaps have succeeded in bringing these districts to India, in which case India's western boundary could have stretched right upto the sacred Sindhu river. Sadly, that did not happen.

For the Hindus in Sindh, Partition has meant not only being uprooted from their hearths and homes, but also a tragic distancing from their culture and language. It may surprise many to know that at the time of Partition,

Hindus constituted more than half of Karachi's population of four lakhs. Out of Sindh's population of about forty lakhs, Hindus numbered thirteen lakhs. Of these, approximately eleven lakhs migrated to the Indian side. The migration from Karachi was almost total. Although a majority of the Sindhi refugees, constituting mainly the trading community, went to Gujarat, Maharashtra, Rajasthan and Madhya Pradesh, they settled down in almost all parts of the country.

For most migrant families, Partition was both a psychological and economic catastrophe. It was a common sight those days for children from erstwhile affluent families of Sindh to be forced to sell sweets, combs, key chains, etc., in trains and at bus stations. In spite of these privations, Sindhis not only survived, but also thrived. Like the phoenix rising from the ashes, the community has risen from being down and out, to people who took the lead in commerce, arts, medicine, engineering and a variety of fields. Even among the NRIs, Sindhis have carved out a very distinctive place for themselves. The community has also made major contributions to philanthropic activities aimed at the promotion of education, healthcare, and care of destitute children and senior citizens. Above all, it has supported various religious projects, especially at pilgrimage centres. Thus, in a very short span, Sindhis who came here as *sharanarthis* (refugees) earned acclaim for being both *purusharthis* (achievers owing to their own hard work) and *paramarthis* (generous patrons of spiritual activities).

Political analysts have often wondered why the Hindus and Sikhs who came from Sindh and Punjab so were quickly and easily integrated into free India and why, on the other hand, the Muslims who went from this part of India to West and East Pakistan were treated as unwelcome *muhajirs* for many decades. The only answer that comes to my mind is the age-old sense of cultural unity that binds Indians of diverse castes, communities and regions into a natural national entity. In the decade of the 1980s and '90s, I developed this theme as 'cultural nationalism' and made it the subject of a countrywide debate on what defines Indian nationhood. Explication of this theme is an important aspect of the *raison d'etre* of this book.

My first experience of 'cultural nationalism' occurred when my family was about to leave Sindh, and was deliberating on which part of India to go to. I remember my eighty-year-old grandmother telling my father, 'Take me to Kashi. I want to live my remaining years, and breathe my last, on the banks of the Holy Ganga'. My father fulfilled her wish. Thus, when we were forced to leave our home near the Sindhu, it was Mother Ganga, who quintessentially symbolises Mother India, wholeheartedly accepted us.

*

The second major challenge I would like to recall in this context is the one that came in 1975, that is, almost midway between the advent of Independence, and today. Once again, an adversity turned into an opportunity. On, 11 June, the Congress party's supposedly invincible citadel of Gujarat crumbled when the Opposition alliance under the banner 'Janata Morcha', led by Morarji Desai, trounced the Congress (I) in the state assembly elections. On the same day, the Allahabad High Court pronounced its verdict on the election petition filed by Raj Narain, an important Opposition leader, against Prime Minister Indira Gandhi. The court accepted the election petition alleging corrupt electoral practices, annulled Indira Gandhi's election and disqualified her from Parliament for six years.

These two events together caused the equivalent of a political earthquake in the government and the Congress party. Its tremors set off a sequence of events, the climax of which was the promulgation of an Emergency under Article 352 of the Indian Constitution. While this Article had been invoked earlier during the wars with China (1962) and Pakistan (1965 and 1971), this was the first time it was being used to deal with 'internal disturbance'. Tens of thousands of leaders and activists belonging to Opposition parties, including a large number of Members of Parliament (MPs) and state legislators were put into prison. These included the venerable Lokanayak Jayaprakash Narayan. Along with my senior colleague Atalji, I was imprisoned in Bangalore Central Jail, where I spent nineteen months. Stringent press censorship was imposed and even the coverage of parliamentary proceedings became subject to censorship. For over nineteen months democracy was eclipsed.

At one point of time, during this period, it seemed as if multi-party democracy would never again return to our country. The Congress party's *National Herald* wrote gushing editorials on the virtues of a one-party system like that of Tanzania. Prime Minister Indira Gandhi declared that 'the nation was more important than democracy'. The entire network of mass media, including the all-pervasive All India Radio (AIR), was harnessed with the primary objective of brainwashing people into believing that liberty, civil rights, press freedom and judicial independence were all elitist concepts which had nothing to do with the common man's welfare, and that the nation should show gratitude to the Congress government for the transformation wrought by Emergency.

When the opportunity eventually came in March 1977 for testing how effective the mendacious campaign had been, political pundits were astounded. Even the unlettered elector was not taken in by the propaganda. Indira Gandhi and her Emergency was rejected. A neat ballot-box coup was effected, an electoral massacre of her men took place, and the Janata Party was installed in New Delhi. The danger to democracy had been averted, and the crisis got converted or rather, transformed itself into an opportunity. I am proud that I could play a role in this transformation. As Minister of Information & Broadcasting in Morarji Desai's government, it was principally my task to dismantle the elaborate and legally sanctified edifice of a shackled press, which was one of the most hated aspects of the Emergency. This book describes, at considerable length, the sad saga of the Emergency and the thrilling tale of the triumph of democracy. It also demonstrates how the Congress leadership tried to destroy the basic structure of the Constitution, a wrongdoing which the party has never honestly debated or apologised for. This is not surprising since the culture of dynastic rule in the Congress leaves no scope for introspection and self-correction on the many blunders committed by the Nehru-Gandhi family, for which India continues to pay a heavy price. Indeed dynasticism is now part of the 'basic structure' of the Congress.

※

In the post-Emergency era, I was called upon to lead my party at a time when Indian politics witnessed three other important developments. Firstly, in spite of the menacingly huge majority that the Congress government enjoyed in Parliament, it meekly surrendered, in 1986, to the politics of minority appeasement in the Shah Bano controversy. The case, in which Rajiv Gandhi's government legislatively annulled the Supreme Court's ruling in favour of a sixty-two-year-old widow's right to alimony from her former husband, became a milestone in the Muslim women's search for gender justice. Secondly, the leadership of the government disgraced itself, and was defeated in the 1989 parliamentary elections, due to its involvement in the Bofors deal, India's biggest defence corruption scandal. Lastly, a legitimate demand from the Hindus for the construction of a befitting temple for Lord Ram at his birthplace in Ayodhya was opposed by a set of pseudo-secular political parties, many of whose leaders privately saw merit in the demand but were afraid of saying so publicly for vote-bank considerations.

My party's active participation in the movement for the reconstruction of the Ram temple soon snowballed into the largest mass movement in the history of independent India. The spectacular public response to my Ram Rath Yatra from Somnath to Ayodhya in September-October 1990 far exceeded my own expectations. Just as the struggle against the Emergency opened my eyes to the Indian people's unflinching faith in democracy, the Ayodhya movement opened my eyes to the deep-rooted influence of religion in the lives of Hindus of all castes and sects across the country. Recalling what Swami Vivekananda had said about the place of religion in India's national life, I realised that if this religiosity were to be channelled in a positive direction, it could unleash tremendous energy for national reconstruction. The Ayodhya movement also brought to the fore people's revulsion for pseudo-secularism, as practised by the Congress party, communists and some other parties, and projected my party, the BJP, as a spirited champion of genuine secularism.

This clash between pseudo-secularism and genuine secularism manifests in different ways even today, and forms one of the main themes of this book. I dare say that the future of India depends much on the outcome of this struggle.

Having said this, I also realise, with much pain in my heart, that the Ayodhya movement followed a course that I had not envisaged. In particular, the demolition of the Babri structure on 6 December 1992 was most regrettable. As I said on that very day, it was the saddest day of my life. Had the demolition not taken place, the Ayodhya movement, I am confident, would have progressed on healthier lines and reached a positive denouement, both fulfilling the Hindu demand and promoting communal harmony.

The Ayodhya movement catalysed a process of nationwide ideological churning that witnessed my party's spectacular rise in India's political history—and possibly in the history of any democratic country in the world. The BJP's rise culminated in the formation, in March 1998, of the first truly non-Congress coalition government at the Centre—that of the NDA—under Atalji's leadership. With a renewed mandate in 1999, that government served the nation with great dedication and distinction for six years. My own role as Atalji's deputy in this government, with the specific charge of the Home Ministry, was highly gratifying to me. I feel proud of the NDA government's various achievements especially in the fields of national security and national development. Some of them, such as the bold decision to make India a nuclear power and our sincere efforts to normalise relations with Pakistan in spite of the latter's betrayal, will have a permanent place in our country's history. History will record that India became a stronger, and a more self-confident nation, under Atalji's visionary leadership. Understandably, a good part of this book is devoted to the triumphs and tribulations of our party's six years in governance.

※

The unexpected defeat of the BJP-led NDA in the May 2004 parliamentary elections has brought a new challenge before my party. I have acknowledged in this book, my own share of responsibility for the setback. In retrospect, I feel that many things could have been done differently. These lapses made the vital difference between victory for the Congress and defeat for the BJP. And, numerically, what a narrow difference it really was!

Nevertheless, the BJP's defeat cannot mask the truth about one of its most enduring achievements—namely, my party's success in transforming India's polity from being dominated by a single party to one that is now essentially bipolar. We do not claim that we have made it into a two-party system, but none can deny that it is now bipolar, with the BJP and the Congress as two principal poles around which India's political constellations will configure and re-configure themselves. This book attempts to recount the story of how this was achieved and what its implications are for India's democracy and development.

As I write this, my party has gone through a prolonged exercise of introspection since May 2004. Many lessons need to be learnt, and they are still being learnt. Many correctives need to be applied, and they are indeed being applied. Hopefully, readers will appreciate that I am not lacking in candour in reflecting on this crucial development in my party's, and my own political life. With honest introspection also comes self-confidence. For, I have not the slightest doubt that, as it has done in the past, the BJP will bounce back again.

This optimism is based on several factors. Firstly, notwithstanding the current fragmentation of the polity in India, our democracy will always need two stable national parties to act as two distinct poles around which, other, smaller parties can coalesce. The BJP fulfils this need—as a national and nationalist party, as the torchbearer of India's integral development and as a champion of good governance.

But there is another reason for my hope. Since 1951, when the Jana Sangh was born, our party has consciously evolved a culture of working together and towards a common goal. I am reminded here of a deeply gratifying incident that took place in 2003. Both Bhairon Singh Shekhawat, Vice President of India at the time, and I, who was the Deputy Prime Minister, had gone to Prime Minister Vajpayee's residence to greet him on his birthday on 25 December. We were photographed, with me standing behind the two of them seated. The following day, *Dainik Jagaran*, a widely circulated Hindi daily, carried not only that photograph, in colour, but, adjacent to it, another almost identical-looking photograph, in black-and-white, showing the three of us in our youth. The latter photograph was, in fact, taken in Kota in Rajasthan in 1952, where those associated with the fledgling Jana Sangh had congregated for a meeting. The common caption for the two photographs in *Dainik Jagaran* was: 'Working Together, For Over A Half-Century'. This long comradeship with Atalji and other colleagues in the party, as this book will describe, is a source of great pride and an invaluable treasure of my political life.

I fervently hope that leaders of my party at various levels—leaders of today as well as those of the future—will internalise this culture of camaraderie and safeguard the spirit of unity.

*

When I look back at India's political journey over the past six decades, I feel deeply saddened by the heap of unrealised aspirations and unfulfilled dreams of 1947. My moment of greatest agony, each year, is when I see two reports: Transparency International's annual report which ranks countries on the basis of corruption index, in which India is always ranked high; and the United Nations' annual report on the Human Development Index (HDI), which ranks India low amongst the most unsatisfactory performers. In spite of all the visible successes of our economy, our HDI position remains below that of over a hundred countries in the world, placing us, in respect of some developmental parameters, in the category of sub-Saharan countries in Africa. We have been unable to provide clean drinking water to hundreds of millions of our citizens; more than half of our population, both in urban as well as rural areas, is deprived of something as basic as a clean toilet; hunger still stalks the bodies of many of our brethren in rural and remote areas; and, as a consequence of all these deprivations, we have condemned our poor, most of whom also do not have good housing, to become vulnerable to eminently avoidable but often fatal diseases. What can be more shaming than to read that many infants in our tribal areas die of malnutrition? And what can be more shocking than the fact that several thousand of our distressed farmers have committed suicide in recent years? Social injustice and atrocities committed on women agitate my mind. The lost childhood of millions of our children, who are forced to toil when they ought to be playing and studying, saddens my heart. The squalor of our urban slums and the desolate look of many of our villages convince me, as they are sure to convince any thinking person, that something has gone seriously wrong with our development process.

True, our economy, in respect of some macro parameters, is booming like never before. Today's high GDP growth rates are a far cry from the tardy economic progress in the era of the licence-permit-quota raj, which had stifled the entrepreneurial spirit of our people. But growth has to be much more than statistics that conceal more than they reveal. While it is technically true that the growth rate is nine per cent, this growth is *far* from being evenly distributed across geographical and demographic segments. The entire country is not growing at nine per cent. While a small section of urban India might be growing at twenty per cent or even more; the majority of India is still stuck at low digits, if it is even growing at all. The 'trickle down' theory is an iniquitous response to this dilemma, and unsustainable in a democracy, since the 'have-nots' who are waiting for the 'trickle' are seeing, plainly, that there is a waterfall among the 'haves'. This is generating serious levels of conflict across the country. Clearly, the time has come to take a hard relook at our economic policy. We must, in all honesty, ask ourselves: Why has it not delivered to India's poor what it has delivered to India's rich?

We are failing on other fronts as well. The Indian State still remains soft on the menace that terrorism, sponsored by anti-India forces abroad, poses to social peace and internal security. Many of our democratic institutions, including Parliament and the judiciary, are not living up to the expectations of our people. True, we have always had smooth and peaceful transfer of power after periodic elections. However, the electoral system itself has been debilitated by growing money and muscle power. Diversity is indeed our strength, but sometimes it is emphasised so one-sidedly that it harms national unity and social harmony.

I have mentioned these contradictions and concerns because our desire to build a better India can only be fulfilled if we develop the ability to address them. In this book, I have tried to present my thoughts on the formidable tasks ahead.

✵

It will perhaps be obvious to the readers that my memoirs are not only about India's past, but also about India's future. While writing this book, I have often felt the compelling need to communicate to India's youth—the young of the present and future generations. As I look ahead in the sixtieth year of our independence, the greatest reason to be optimistic about India's future is our young population. Over sixty per cent of Indians—now 1.03 billion—are in the age group of below twenty-five years. It is not just their numerical strength, but the power of their rising ambitions and enhanced abilities that make me feel confident that India will shine brighter in the coming decades of the twenty-first century. For, it is they who will build what we failed to build, it is they who will complete many of the tasks that we were unable to complete, and it is they who will add new chapters of accomplishment to the saga of India's evolving history.

A LIFE IN FIVE PHASES

A few words about the structure of this book. I have categorised my life so far in five broad phases. The first phase of two decades spans the period from 1927 to 1947, which I spent in Sindh, mainly in Karachi. The second phase lasted one decade, from 1947 to 1957, when I worked in Rajasthan as a RSS *pracharak* and as an activist of the Bharatiya Jana Sangh. This phase grounded me in public life and politics. It also steeled my resolve to live a spartan and disciplined life that is dedicated to the ideology and idealism of my organisation. The third phase lasted two decades, from 1957 to 1977. It began with my being asked, by Pandit Deendayal Upadhyaya, the main ideologue, guide and organiser of the Jana Sangh, to shift my base to Delhi and work as a political aide to Atalji, who had just been elected to the Lok Sabha for the first time. It is during these two decades that I gained advanced experience in political organisation, political strategy and leadership.

I see the fourth phase, from 1977 to 1997, as a continuation of the previous one, in so far as these two decades placed greater political and organisational responsibilities on me in the national capital. It was also the phase that saw many dramatic developments in Indian politics. The fifth phase traces the decade from 1997 to 2007. This was the time when I had to shoulder a major responsibility in governance. This experience helped me gain a better understanding of the challenges and opportunities before an India in rapid transition. I also narrate here my memorable visit to Pakistan in 2005 and reflect upon its unexpected political fallout.

The fifth phase brings this book to a close, but my active involvement in India's political journey will continue. As a disciplined soldier of my party, I shall dutifully carry out whatever responsibilities are entrusted to me. Duty, Dedication and Discipline—these are the three principles that I learnt before I started my life as a political activist, and I shall continue to be guided by them.

*

An autobiography is as much a communication with oneself as it is with the reader. I am, therefore, all too aware of my limitations and weaknesses. I am aware also of the mistakes I have committed in life. This book will make no attempt to gloss over them. Readers may agree or disagree with my perception and analyses of events and issues. It is their inalienable right. However, they will find a writer who is honest with them and with himself.

I have known from my own long association with books that, once written and published, a book belongs as much to the reader as to its author. Hence, if this work succeeds in communicating something meaningful to the reader, I will have the satisfaction that publishing it was indeed a worthwhile exercise.

New Delhi: 1 March 2008

Sindh & India
An Unbreakable Bond
1927-47

'Partition was a double-tragedy for the Sindhi Hindus. Unlike Punjab and Bengal, which were divided on 14/15 August 1947, Sindh was not. As a consequence, we had no land of our own or, rather, the whole of divided India became our land. When I look back, I find it amazing that the Sindhi Hindu community has survived, and survived well. Like the Phoenix from the ashes, it has risen from being down and out, to a people who have accomplished a lot in a lot many fields.'

Phase One

❖

1

TRIUMPH OF FREEDOM, TRAGEDY OF PARTITION

India is a single geographic unit. Her unity is as ancient as Nature. Within this geographic unit, and covering the whole of it, there has been a cultural unity from time immemorial. This cultural unity has defied political and racial divisions. In any discussion on Pakistan, the fact cannot be lost sight of, namely, that the starting point, if not the governing factor, is the fundamental unity of India.

—Dr B.R. Ambedkar in *Pakistan* or *The Partition of India*[1]

'We won't eat these sweets,' said the Hindu children in Karachi schools on that fateful day. When children refuse sweets en masse, one knows that something has gone terribly wrong. Childhood, it is said, is the sleep of reason and the celebration of innocence. In the case of these children, the age of innocence had rudely come to an end.

There was sullenness, fear, anxiety, anger and above all, uncertainty, writ large upon their faces, which hardly surprised me as I moved from one Hindu colony to another on my motorcycle that day. The same heart-rending emotions combined with the question 'What to do next?', had also welled up in the minds of their teachers and parents. For, it was not an ordinary day. News of a bloodbath in the neighbouring province of Punjab, and the resultant mass-migration of Hindus and Muslims in reverse directions had been doing the rounds. In the months that followed, all, yes all, those children in Karachi, along with their parents, teachers and friends, would be leaving their schools and homes and playgrounds behind forever. Panic-stricken Hindu families fled in hordes to seek refuge in new towns, located across a newly drawn-up border. Along the way, thousands would be killed and tens of thousands separated from their near and dear ones. In no time, Karachi, and the rest of the Sindh province, would be cleansed of almost its entire Hindu population.

'In this cyclonic holocaust,' Sadhu T.L. Vaswani, a widely revered Sindhi spiritual leader, would later gravely reminisce, 'no one knew where one would find even a humble abode to rest their tired limbs and to have a simple meal. No one knew whether they would ever again be united with their friends and dear ones. In this terrific uprooting of humanity, my two sisters and I had been mercilessly separated from our parents who continued to be in Sindh while we were forced to seek safety in Hindustan. In this worst of tragedies that had befallen our young lives, we had felt totally benumbed.'

All those who migrated from Sindh were Indians until that tragic day, and would continue to remain proud Indians in the refugee colonies that became their new homes in Bombay (now Mumbai), Kalyan, Delhi, Indore, Jaipur, Calcutta (now Kolkata), Kandla…. But their own homeland had, overnight, become a foreign nation and their beloved Karachi had become its capital.

It was the 14th of August 1947.

It was the day Pakistan was carved out of united India as a separate Muslim nation. For some years, I had been hearing an ominous phrase—'Two Nation' theory. My young mind had rejected it instinctively. 'How can Hindus and Muslims belong to two separate nations, just because they belong to two different faiths?' It made no sense to me, especially when

I looked at the social fabric and cultural milieu of Sindh, in which the Hindu could not be separated from the Muslim, and vice versa. Similarly, Sindh could not be separated from India. 'No, Pakistan cannot happen,' I had believed, and so had most of the Hindus in Sindh. 'We have been part of India for thousands of years and will always remain so. India can never be partitioned on the basis of religion.'

And yet, it was.

Partition, which had seemed a fantasy until a few years ago, had become a reality. I recall that there was no jubilation in a large part of Karachi, although there were fireworks and nightlong revelry in some areas. The following day, India became independent. Again, there was no jubilation, in our part of the city. Instead, a pall of gloom had descended. The Union Jack was lowered forever in both India and Pakistan. But, two separate flags had been hoisted in its place—the tricolour in Delhi and the green flag with a crescent and a star in Karachi. 'What an accursed fate mine is,' I remember thinking in the days that followed. 'I did not even celebrate India's freedom on 15 August,' even though for the past five years, ever since I became a *swayamsevak* of the Rashtriya Swayam Sevak Sangh (RSS), I had been dreaming of nothing else but the arrival of this day. That sad and bitter thought would hurt me for years to come.

WHY SINDH GOT DISENCHANTED WITH THE CONGRESS

The Sangh's mission, to achieve independence for a united India, had become my personal mission, ever since I joined it in June 1942. I was attracted to its ideology of nationalism and inspired by its emphasis on idealism.

That life-transforming event had taken place in Hyderabad, the second largest city in Sindh. After two years of college there, I had returned to Karachi and become a *pracharak* of the RSS, one of the seventy-five such full-time organisers and propagators working in the ten districts of Sindh. Indeed, our province at the time had the highest number of *pracharaks* per district in all of India. The RSS started its activities in Sindh only in 1939. Nevertheless, in a very short span of time, it had become highly popular and powerful in all the urban centres of the province. Those days, Hindus formed a majority in the population of almost every city in Sindh, Karachi and Hyderabad included. They were also more prosperous, educated and dominant in professions such as law, medicine and government service.

My responsibilities in the RSS grew quickly and, in January 1947, I was made its City Secretary. My tasks involved monitoring the functioning of *shakhas* (daily assembly of Sangh volunteers), which had suddenly begun to attract thousands of youth, and interacting with eminent members of the Hindu community. Although my family lived in Karachi, I had moved into the RSS headquarters in the company of fellow-activists. I had a motorcycle at my disposal, to move around in the city for my organisational work. It was one of the ten vehicles provided by the Sangh to its *pracharaks*.

It would surprise many people today to know that there was no antagonism between the RSS and the Congress in Sindh those days. Hindus believed that both were wedded to the cause of India's independence from British rule. Of course, young *swayamsevaks* like me were told by our seniors that the Congress' method of peaceful struggle would neither force the mighty British to leave India nor ensure its unity. I believed them. However, that difference of opinion with regard to strategy did not make me think of the Congress as an adversary, much less as an enemy. The entire Hindu population in Sindh was a staunch supporter of the Congress. Moreover, I knew many Congress families that encouraged their young boys to join the RSS. The best example was that of the late K.R. Malkani*, who became my close friend and colleague for over six decades. The advice he had received from Prof. N.R. Malkani, his elder brother and a widely respected Congress leader was: 'Join the RSS. It's a good organisation which teaches patriotism and discipline to young men.'

---

* Kewal Ratanmal Malkani (1921-2003) was my fellow *swayamsevak* of the RSS in Karachi. After Partition, he migrated to Delhi and worked for many years as the widely acclaimed Editor of the *Organiser,* where I was his deputy. Author of many books, he was the Vice President of the BJP and, during the NDA government, Lieutenant Governor of Pondicherry (now Puducherry).

Within a few months of my joining the RSS, Mahatma Gandhi gave the clarion call of 'Quit India', and I remember how enthusiastically all the Hindus and nationalist Muslims in Sindh had welcomed it. They were angered, and inspired, by the martyrdom of Hemu Kalani, a nineteen-year-old patriot who was hanged by the British in 1943. He was one of the tens of thousands in Sindh who had heeded Gandhiji's call of 'Do or Die'. While marching to the gallows, he saw his mother sobbing. 'Mother,' he said to her, 'hadn't you taught me from the *Bhagavad Gita* that the soul is indestructibile? I promise you that, if I am born again, I shall sacrifice my next life also to the cause of India's Freedom.'

My own maternal uncle, Ramchand, was a committed Congressman, who courted imprisonment during the 1942 movement. Ramchand's son Moti, who passed away in 2007, married Tara, an outstanding Sindhi writer. Tara has recently written a serialised biography of Ramchand detailing his contribution to India's freedom movement.

The first signs of a strain in the relationship between the Sindhi Hindus and the Congress appeared when the dark clouds of Partition started to hover in the skies. Congress leaders had earlier pledged that they would, under no circumstance, allow India to be partitioned. As time passed, they affirmed that Sindh would not become a part of Pakistan. Still later, they held out the assurance that Hindus would be safe and secure even after Partition. These hopes were somewhat reinforced by the call given by Mahatma Gandhi that Hindus and Sikhs in West Punjab, Sindh, Baluchistan and NWFP should not leave their homes to come to India and, similarly, Muslims in East Punjab, UP and Bihar should not migrate to Pakistan. Alas, even the Mahatma's assurances could not control the evil winds of hatred and violence that the call for Partition generated.

As the scheduled date of departure of the British drew closer, the Hindus felt, with great dismay, betrayed by the Congress. They now had only one organisation to turn to with hope: the RSS. The organised strength of the RSS reassured the Hindus that they would be able to safely stay in their own province even after the creation of Pakistan.

Sadly, the RSS in 1947 was not strong enough nationally to prevent the tragedy of Partition.

IN KARACHI, THREE LEADERS ARRIVE IN ONE WEEK

The first week of August 1947 witnessed the arrival of three important leaders in Karachi. The first was Acharya Kripalani (1888-1982), who happened to be the President of the All India Congress Committee (AICC). He was the best-known freedom fighter from Sindh and one of Gandhiji's trusted followers. In the past, every Congress leader visiting Sindh would receive a rousing welcome. Therefore, a Congress President, that too a Sindhi, visiting his own home province and in the same month that India was going to attain freedom, ought to have been a spectacular event. But, it was not to be. Acharya Kripalani was shocked to see the thin crowd that came to greet him at the airport. Angry and disenchanted, Hindus in Karachi had finally deserted the Congress. The meeting that he addressed, on the tennis court of the Amil Institute, was barely attended by four to five hundred people.

The following day—either the 2 or 3 August, I do not quite remember—came M.S. Golwalkar* the *Sarsanghchalak* or Chief of the RSS, who was reverentially known as Shri Guruji. His annual visit to Sindh since 1943 had greatly contributed to the process of Hindu unity. Every year he travelled extensively within the province, visiting Karachi, Hyderabad, Sukkur, Shikarpur, and Mirpur Khas. During these visits he met religious leaders like Sadhu T.L. Vaswani and Swami Ranganathananda; Dr Choithram Gidwani, Prof. N.R. Malkani and other Congress leaders; Shivrattan Mohatta, Lalji Mehrotra, Bhai Pratap and others from the business world; Nihchaldas Vazirani, Dr Hemandas Wadhvani and Mukhi Gobindram, who were Ministers in the Sindh government; and, of course, many academics,

---

* Shri Madhav Sadashiv Golwalkar (1906-73) became the second *Sarsanghchalak* (chief) of the RSS after the demise of its founder, Dr Keshav Baliram Hedgewar (1887-1940). Dr Hedgewar founded the RSS as a nationalist organisation of Hindus committed to India's independence and subsequent Hindu renaissance. Shri Guruji was essentially an ascetic, influenced by the mission of Ramakrishna Paramahamsa and Swami Vivekananda. He chose service to the nation through building the RSS as his path to spiritual attainment. I had the good fortune of interacting with him closely both before and for long after Partition.

lawyers and other professionals. The broadbased nature of these meetings was proof of the fact that the RSS had succeeded in winning the hearts and the minds of most of the Hindu community in Sindh.

Thanks to the influence of the RSS, the Hindus overcame the divide between Amils and Bhaibands, Hyderabadis and non-Hyderabadis, urbanites and ruralites, Sanatanis and those who followed the Arya Samaj or the Brahmo Samaj. More importantly, boys from both Congress and Hindu Mahasabha families could be seen playing together at the RSS *shakhas* and saluting the same *Bhagwa Dhwaj* (saffron flag).

But Shri Guruji's visit in 1947, unlike the previous years, was taking place in an extraordinary context. Partition, and the separation of Sindh from India, had become imminent. And the Sindhi Hindus were feeling shipwrecked in the midst of a tempestuous sea with no hope of being rescued. I had gone to receive Shri Guruji at the railway station. I mentioned to him that Acharya Kripalani had also arrived in Karachi the previous day. He looked at me for a while, his saintly face showing a hint of suppressed anger, and then responded with a sharp comment: '*Sindh ganvaake ab Sindh aaye hain?*' (After losing Sindh, he has now come to Sindh?)

On 5 August—just ten days before Partition—Shri Guruji addressed what turned out to be the last, but also the largest ever, gathering of Hindus in the history of Karachi. I was in charge of the pre-rally march of *swayamsevaks* through the streets of the city. It turned out to be the largest march in the history of the RSS in Sindh. The sight of as many as 10,000 *swayamsevaks* marching in unison and uniform—khaki shorts, white shirts and black caps—to the tunes of patriotic songs being played by a semi-military band, conveyed a message partly of defiance, aimed at the would-be government of Pakistan, and partly self-assurance, aimed at the Hindu population in Sindh. When the marchers finally arrived at the venue of the rally, there was an assembly of over one lakh people to greet them. Sadhu Vaswani, who presided over the function, said that history would record the Sindhi Hindu community's eternal gratitude to the RSS for standing by it in its hour of misery and trial.

In his speech, Shri Guruji said, 'A calamity has befallen our Motherland. The Partition of India is a sin and those responsible for it will not be forgiven by posterity. It is unnatural and will have to go. What has happened is the culmination of the British policy of divide-and-rule. The Muslim League has secured Pakistan through coercion and violence, before which the Congress leadership has surrendered. Muslims have been misled into thinking that they are a separate nation only because they profess Islam. They should know that they belong to the same race as the Hindus. Their forefathers were Hindus. Their culture and civilisation is Indian, and not Arabic. Unfortunately, they have been made to believe that what existed before the advent of Islam is not theirs. It is unthinkable that Sindh, through which flows the sacred Sindhu River, is being severed from India.... However, every ordeal is a test of the human spirit. The Hindus must defend themselves. But self-defence requires strength, and strength comes from unity. Our *swayamsevaks* will do their utmost for the security of the Hindus in Sindh. They will be the first to sacrifice their lives and the last to think of their own comfort and safety. Let us pray to God Almighty that He will give us the power to overcome this misfortune.'

In a situation marked by maddening uncertainty, fear and tension, these words of Shri Guruji instilled much-needed confidence among the Hindus in Sindh.

The third leader to arrive in Karachi was Mohammed Ali Jinnah, supremo of the Muslim League and the principal architect of Pakistan. He flew in from Delhi on 7 August to a tumultuous welcome by his followers. Although the Hindu areas greeted him with angry silence, the rest of the city reverberated with slogans of 'Pakistan Zindabad'. The streets everywhere were decorated with green flags and festoons. The newspapers were full of photographs of Jinnah, a thin, tall man wearing a long coat and a boat-shaped fez cap. The images seemed peculiar, since, until very recently, when he was engaged in Partition talks with the Congress leaders and British authorities in Delhi, I had seen photographs that showed him in clothes that were impeccably English.

I must say that Jinnah was an enigma to me, and to most of the Hindus in Sindh. I had not heard of him until 1943-44. I learnt from my seniors in the RSS that, although a staunch Indian nationalist in the early phase of his political career, he went on to skilfully exploit the separatist sentiments amongst a section of the Indian Muslim population to divide India on the basis of the Two Nation theory. He was born in Karachi on 25 December 1876, but he was not a Sindhi. His parents, Mithibai and Jinnahbhai Poonja, were Khoja Muslims from Kathiawad in Gujarat, the same region that, incidentally, produced Mahatma Gandhi. They had migrated to Karachi only a few years before his birth, in search of better business prospects. Jinnah's bond with Karachi was at best tenuous, because he had spent almost all his educational, professional and political life in Bombay and London. He was neither a popular figure in Sindh, nor very familiar. Most people in Sindh came to know of him only when the Muslim League, under his leadership, adopted the Pakistan Resolution* in Lahore in 1940, demanding a separate nation for Indian Muslims.

The Jinnah who arrived in Karachi in August 1947 was, thus, a hero who had turned the resolution into a reality almost single-handedly. Now known as Quaid-e-Azam (The Great Leader), he would in a week's time become the first Governor General of Pakistan.

PARTITION—A DOUBLE-EDGED TRAGEDY FOR HINDUS FROM SINDH

Sindh was more or less peaceful almost until the creation of Pakistan. However, communal violence of a horrific kind broke out in neighbouring Punjab in the latter half of 1947. This was followed by similar violence in UP, Bihar, Rajasthan and elsewhere in the East. News about ghastly massacres—the exodus of Hindus from Punjab to the East, and the trains that reached the Indian side laden with corpses—created widespread fear and panic in Sindh as well. Migration of affluent families had started a few months prior to the date fixed for Partition. July and August were extremely tense months in Sindh. September, however, saw this phased migration turn into a deluge. By this time, the number of Muslim *muhajirs* coming to Karachi from UP, Bihar and other parts of India had also swelled.

---

* To commemorate the adoption of the Pakistan Resolution in Lahore on 22-24 March 1940, *Minar-e-Pakistan*, a monument in the shape of a minaret has been built at the site where the Resolution was passed.

All of us in the RSS had been tirelessly working to dissuade the people in Sindh from leaving their homeland. Our efforts bore some fruit, yet the happenings in other parts of the newly-formed Pakistan had resulted in a bloodbath, conveying a more dire message to the Hindus: 'Leave Sindh, without any delay.' One day in early September, as I was travelling on my motorcycle on a road near Karachi's main railway station, I saw the body of a man who had been stabbed to death. A small distance ahead, I saw another corpse, and then a third… This was unusual and disturbing for me as it was the first time in my life that I had seen corpses lying on streets.

I later learnt that in December 1947, after I had left Karachi for good, Hindus in Hyderabad were targeted by grisly communal violence. This created panic in Karachi too. Hindu houses and businesses would be marked at night, and in the mornings mobs would loot them and forcibly occupy them, with official connivance. The 6th of January 1948 would go down as the blackest day in the history of Sindh as it witnessed the worst manifestation of violence and religious cleansing in Karachi. A particularly horrifying incident took place at the Aryapath Sindhi Sabha, which had a temple and a school. The Sindhis coming from outside Karachi used to be accommodated there for the night in order to enable them to board a ship leaving for Bombay the next day. It was attacked one night, in which nearly three hundred Hindus and Sikhs were massacred. There is no record of the number of Hindus killed in the Partition riots in Sindh, but the number, as widely believed, ran into thousands.

Thereafter, the Hindus, a peaceful and non-aggressive community, became fully convinced that staying back in Sindh was no longer an option for them. In barely three months, approximately 1.25 million, constituting more than ninety per cent of the total Sindhi Hindu population, left their beloved native land. Suddenly, the cruel hand of history tore them away from the protective shelter of Sindh, which had been their home for thousands of years; which was the cradle of Indian civilisation; where Hindus and Muslims had lived like brothers and evolved a uniquely syncretic culture; where tyrant Muslim rulers were jointly resisted by Hindu and Muslim saints as well as lay people of both religions. Suddenly, our ancestral homeland became part of an alien country for us.

Most of the migrants settled on the outskirts of Bombay, bringing with them virtually nothing but their unwavering determination to rebuild their lives and to contribute to India's nation-building. That Partition was a double-edged tragedy for Sindhi Hindus has been painstakingly chronicled by my wife's sister-in-law, Lata Jagtiani, in her book *Sindhi Reflections*.[2] This is a heart-rending and, at the same time, inspiring story of the lives of various Hindu refugees who served India with devotion and distinction.

On 12 September when I left Karachi for Delhi, I had not yet turned twenty. But before I come to the journey that brought my life in Sindh to an end, I should first describe how it began. Further, I should anchor that story in a brief history of the city and land of my birth.

2

SINDH AND INDIA: AN UNBREAKABLE BOND

Gange cha Yamune chaiva Godavari Saraswati,
Narmade Sindhu Kaveri Jalesmin Sannidhim Kuru
Pushkaraadyaanii tiirthaani Gangaadyaah saritas tathaa
Aagacchantu pavitraani Snaanakaale sadaa mama

(Bless with thy presence, O holy rivers Ganga, Yamuna, Godavari, Saraswati, Narmada, Sindhu and Kaveri. May Pushkara, and all the other holy waters and rivers always come at the time of my bath.)

—A MORNING PRAYER THAT INVOKES THE IDEA
OF INDIA'S NATIONAL INTEGRATION

Some changes in history are natural and inevitable, such as India gaining freedom from British rule. For, no people can live in perpetual slavery. As Lokamanya Bal Gangadhar Tilak, the foremost nationalist leader in the pre-Gandhi era, uttered the prophetic words: 'Freedom is the birthright of every nation.' However, some changes in history are unnatural and an aberration, such as the Partition of India. The division of India on communal lines is the single biggest tragedy to have befallen our ancient nation. It was neither inevitable nor, certainly, necessary. This belief of mine is rooted in the history of Karachi and Sindh, which I shall briefly narrate.

KARACHI: 'THE GLORY OF THE EAST'

Although Karachi, located on the coast of the Arabian Sea, is now a megapolis with a population of fourteen million, it is not a city with a hoary history. Until the early decades of the eighteenth century, it was just a swampy fishermen's settlement called Kalachi-Jo-Goth (Village of Kalachi), named after a fisherwoman known as Mai Kolachee. It was surrounded on all sides, except the southern coast which lies on the Arabian Sea, by a bleak and expansive desert. Since trading is in the very genes of the Sindhi community, a trader by the name of Bhojumal made the village the seat of his commercial activities in 1729. However, it was only after the arrival of a ship belonging to the British East India Company (EIC), a hundred years later, that the fortunes of this village by the mouth of the Sindhu (Indus) river changed and, within four years, the capital of Sindh was shifted to Karachi from Hyderabad, a town about 110 miles away.

Sindh was annexed to the rapidly expanding base of the EIC by Sir Charles James Napier (1782-1853), the British Commander-in-Chief in India, in 1843. The main objective of the bloody military conquest was the famed wealth of the Amirs of Sindh. It is said that Napier literally waded through blood to reach the treasures of Sindh. He found, in the tower of Hyderabad Fort alone, twenty million sterling—thirteen million in coins and the remaining in jewels. He was handsomely rewarded for this by the Directors of the Company. Nevertheless, he despised his employers and was rather candid in describing the mercenary nature of their operations: 'The English were the aggressors in India, and, although our sovereign (Queen Victoria) can do no wrong, her ministers can; and no one can lay a heavier charge upon Napoleon than rests upon the English ministers who conquered India and Australia, and who protected those who committed atrocities.... Our object in conquering India, the object of all our cruelties was money...a thousand million sterling are said to have been squeezed out of India in the last ninety years. Every shilling of this has been picked out of blood, wiped and put in the murderers' pockets; but, wipe and wipe the money as you will, the "damned spot" will not come "out".'

My second language in school was Latin and so it helped me understand a famous pun associated with Napier. There is a story that after he defeated the Amirs, he sent a telegram to his bosses in London with just one word *Peccavī*. It is a Latin word which means 'I have sinned'; what he actually meant was: 'I have *Sind*'.

After its annexation to the British India Empire, Karachi, along with the rest of the province, was brought under the jurisdiction of the Bombay Presidency. It was only in which only in 1936, Sindh who separated. As Napier left the shores of Karachi, which he had transformed into one of the best port cities this side of the Suez Canal, he exclaimed: 'Thou shalt be the Glory of the East. Would that I could come again to see you, Kurrachee, in your grandeur.'

Apart from Napier, Karachi owed much of its subsequent development to Sir Bartle Frere (1815–84), who was the Chief Commissioner of Sindh and later became the Governor of the Bombay Presidency. He was one of the first British administrators who, after India's First War of Independence in 1857, was convinced that the religions and cultural heritage of India should be preserved and not Christianised. Some of the magnificent buildings and public places in both Karachi and Bombay were his creations.

The planning of the city by the British had ensured wide avenues, a magnificent harbour named Keamari, with enchanting seaside promenades, and some splendid architectural landmarks such as Frere Hall, Empress Market and St. Patrick's Church. While these had a distinct European character, Mohatta Palace, built in the early 1930s in Rajput style, by Shivratan Mohatta, a rich businessman proudly exhibited the grandeur of Indian architecture. Whenever I passed by Mohatta Palace*, I used to stand

---

* During my visit to Pakistan in May-June 2005, I felt both delighted, and nostalgic, to see a magnificent exhibition at Mohatta Palace, the theme of which was 'Karachi

Contd...

in awe of its beauty and also the beauty of the large garden surrounding it. During my childhood, we regularly went on family outings to Clifton Beach and Manora Island, where the distant horizon that separated—or, rather, joined—the sea and the sky would always spark my boyish imagination. My pre-Partition memories of Karachi have always been that of a tidy, neat city. Indeed, in undivided India, Karachi shared with Bangalore the reputation of being one of the two cleanest and most beautiful cities in the country.

I also remember the strong Sindhi character of Karachi, despite its all-too-evident cosmopolitanism. Britishness was its exterior appearance, but Sindhiyat was its soul. By the end of the nineteenth century, Karachi prided itself on being home to a diverse society comprising Hindus, Muslims, Parsis, Goan Christians, European traders, Iranians and Lebanese, all living amicably together. One of the earliest estimates of Karachi's population was 13,000 in 1813. When the British conducted the first nationwide census in India in 1891, Karachi had a population of 96,000. Even at the time of India's Partition in 1947, its population was just over 400,000 people. However, within three years, as shown by the census of 1951, it had more than trebled, as Muslim *muhajirs* from India made their way to the city. Since almost all the Hindus fled Karachi and other parts of Sindh in the wake of Partition, there was a mad rush to grab the lands and properties they had left behind.

Contd...

under the Raj 1843-1947'. I was invited to see it by Hameed Haroon of the renowned *Dawn* group of newspapers, who has not only beautifully restored the palace but also curated the Raj exhibition. It showed the immense contribution of the Sindhi Hindus to the growth and glory of Karachi, and of Sindhiyat in general, something which neither the present-day residents of the city nor young Sindhis in India know much about. I wish the exhibition, and similar efforts in the fields of arts, music, literature, spirituality and scholarship in Sindh, could travel to India so that the new generation of Indians become aware of how a hiatus of sixty years, since 1947, is nothing but an unnatural aberration in the millennia-old bond between Sindh and the rest of India. After Partition, Mohatta Palace was used as the residence of Fatima Jinnah, sister of Mohammed Ali Jinnah, the founder of Pakistan, until her death in 1967.

SINDHU: THE SOURCE OF INDIA'S CIVILISATIONAL IDENTITY

The immediate pain and suffering of migration after Partition may have now become a distant memory, but Sindhi Hindus, especially of my generation, still cannot accept the absurdity of Sindh's separation from India. As many Sanskrit hymns prove, the Hindus consider the Sindhu river sacred, not only in Sindh but all over India. Many Muslims in Sindh used to believe that the water of the Indus was no less holy than that of Zam Zam, the sacred well in Mecca. The very name and identity of the Indus Valley Civilisation, the cradle of the subcontinent's civilisational heritage, is derived from the river 'Sindhu'. Pandit Jawaharlal Nehru wrote in *The Discovery of India*: 'The word Hindu is clearly derived from Sindhu, the old, as well as the present, Indian name for the Indus. From this Sindhu came the words Hindu and Hindustan, as well as Indus and India.'[1]

Sindh is home to one of the world's earliest settled civilisations, the physical evidence of which was found in the excavations at Harappa and Mohenjo-Daro during the British rule. Located about twenty kilometres from Larkana, these ruins show a magnificent and highly urban settlement. Its inhabitants worshipped the mother-goddess and fertility deities, like most people in India do even today. Larkana, incidentally, is the hometown of the late Zulfikar Ali Bhutto, and his late daughter Benazir Bhutto, both of whom became Pakistan's Prime Ministers. India's legal luminary, Ram Jethmalani, also hails from the same town.

Like other ancient human settlements across the world, Sindh too was nurtured by a river—in this case, the mighty Sindhu, nearly 3,000-kilometres-long, which originates in Tibet, passes through the upper reaches of Ladakh and empties itself into the Arabian Sea, known as Sindhu Sagar in the Vedic period. Kanhayalal Talreja, my colleague in the BJP and a fellow migrant from Sindh, has written rather ecstatically about the Vedic roots of the Indus Civilisation in his scholarly book *Pearls of Vedas*. 'When the ancient holy *rishis* recited the sweet *mantras* of Vedas melodiously on the banks of River Sindhu, the waves of Sindhu vibrated and the sky above the soil of Sindh echoed the sweetness and symphony of Vedic hymns.'[2]

Many scholars believe that what is known as the Indus civilisation was actually the seat of the Sindhu-Saraswati civilisation. River Saraswati*, which has now disappeared, is among the Sapta Sindhu, the seven holy rivers mentioned in the *Rig Veda*. It has been ingrained in the cultural memory of Hindus all over India that what is known as Triveni Sangam at Prayag (Allahabad) is a holy confluence of not only the Ganga and Yamuna, but also Saraswati, which is *gupt* (hidden). The Maha Kumbh Mela at Prayag, which is attended by tens of millions of people every twelve years, is the largest gathering of pilgrims anywhere in the world.

The invasion and subsequent conquest of Sindh by Mohammad Bin Qasim, an Arab marauder who came from present-day Iraq in AD 711-13, was a defining moment in the history of not only Sindh but all of India. It was unsuccessfully defended by the local Hindu ruler Raja Dahir, who died on the battlefield. Post-Partition historians of Pakistan describe it as an event that liberated Sindh from 'Brahminical tyranny' and facilitated the introduction of Islam. However, many—both Hindus and Muslims—even today view the invasion as an assault on the honour and distinctive identity of Sindh, and adore Raja Dahir as a valiant hero. For example, the widely respected Sindhi leader G.M. Syed, who was jailed for founding the 'Jiye Sindh Movement'†, argues that Sindh, before Qasim's invasion, was a land

---

* Unfortunately, some Western and Indian Marxist scholars deny the very existence of the river Saraswati. The Indian government should encourage archeological and other areas of research to affirm the evidence of Saraswati, which, because of its Vedic roots, also symbolises learning.

† 'Jiye Sindh' (Long Live Sindh) is the name of the movement founded in 1973 by Ghulam Murtaza Shah Syed (1904-95) that aimed at establishing an independent Sindhi state ('Sindhu Desh'). Syed, a renowned Sufi philosopher and revolutionary political activist, is considered to be the founder of Sindhi nationalism. He was formerly with the Muslim League and, ironically, under his leadership the Sindh assembly was the first Indian legislature to pass a resolution in favour of Pakistan. However, after Partition, many Sindhi Muslims and he felt alarmed that the distinctive Sindhi culture and identity would be lost, firstly, due to the huge influx of settlers from Uttar Pradesh and Bihar and, secondly, because of the domination of Punjab in the army and governance of Pakistan. Convinced that the Sindhis had been deceived, he started advocating their right of self determination, for which he became the first political prisoner of Pakistan.

Contd...

of religious tolerance and liberal mindedness. People of various religions coexisted peacefully—Hindus had their temples; Parsis (Zoroastrians) had their fire temples; Buddhists had their stupas; and Arab Muslims who had settled along the coast, as in Kerala, had their mosques.

Mass conversion of defeated populations was the hallmark of the succession of fanatic Muslim rulers in later centuries. During this dark period, Hindu scriptures were burnt, our temples destroyed, and it was forbidden to talk about the pre-Islamic culture of Sindh. In spite of this, Sindh never lost its ethos of religious harmony, pluralism, mutual tolerance and peaceful coexistence. This was primarily due to two factors: the Sindhi language and the propagation of religious forbearance by both Hindu spiritual leaders and Muslim Sufi saints. The Sindhi language is the repository of the rich heritage of Sindhi art, music, literature, culture and spiritualism. All the great Hindu and Muslim poets and saints communicated their inspiring ideals through the beauty of Sindhi. Their compositions, and the songs in their honour, are sung even today in the social gatherings of Sindhis, both Hindu and Muslim. Jhule Lal, a revered spiritual figure for Sindhi Hindus frequently figures in Muslim songs, just as Shahbaz Qalandar, an equally revered Sufi saint, is honoured in Hindu bhajans. The song *Dama Dam Mast Kalandar*, popularised by Bangladeshi singer Runa Laila, has made Jhule Lal and Shahbaz Qalandar household names in the entire Indian subcontinent.

Religious fanaticism was foreign to both Muslims and Hindus in Sindh. This is best illustrated by the teachings of Shah Abdul Latif 'Bhitai', who was born in the late seventeenth century and is universally regarded as the greatest Sindhi poet of all times. A yogi himself, he writes in *Sur Ramkali*,[3] a book of poems about renunciates: 'Yogis carry nothing with themselves, certainly not their own self (ego).... They have sewed up their hearts to Rama.... For them joy is the same as sorrow; they offer *aarati* with

---

Contd...

He spent thirty years either in jail or in solitary confinement. I was delighted to meet Syed when he came to Delhi in July 1987. Two days later, I took a group of MPs from different political parties met him. While in Delhi, he also met the late Prime Minister Rajiv Gandhi.

their tears of blood.... If you want to be a yogi, follow the guru, forget all desires and proceed to Hinglaj. Yogis respond to an ancient, timeless call—a call given well before Islam. They have given up everything, to be one with Gorakhnath.'

Sachal Sarmast, a Muslim previously named Abdul Wahab (1739-1829), was another great Sindhi poet who sang: 'I am neither a mulla nor a Brahmin; I am neither east nor west, neither earth nor sky. I am a Jogi.' He advocated brotherhood among Hindus and Muslims under one single benevolent God. Hindus going to Muslim *dargahs* was a common sight in Sindh. Indeed, Sindh before Partition had more shrines than mosques dedicated to Sufi pirs. Similarly, Muslim spiritual seekers accompanied Hindu yogis on pilgrimages to Hindu *dhams* (sacred places).

Muslims joined Hindus in dancing, in great ecstasy, to the music of songs composed by Bhagat Kanwar Ram (1885-1938), considered the 'Tansen of Sindh'. In one of his songs, he asks God what would please Him: 'Shall I be a Muslim, say my prayers? Or shall I be a Hindu and go to a temple? Or shall I be a dancer, expressing my devotion through the pulsating rhythms?' When he was shot dead in 1938 by a religious fanatic, all of Sindh was plunged into gloom. After Partition, Sindhi philanthropists named many institutions after this martyr to the cause of communal harmony.

The Sufi tradition is deeply ingrained, even today, in my wife Kamla's family. Her mother, Gangadevi Jagtiani, was a devoted follower of the famous Sufi saint, Sain Qutab Shah, whose dargah in Hyderabad she regularly visited. She used to sing Sufi *kalaams*, *gurbani* and songs about Ram and Krishna with equal piety, and also teach youngsters. Kamla and her elder sister Sarla recently published a collection of their mother's own compositions of Sufi songs, in simple Sindhi, in a book titled *Gaibi Aawaz* (Mystical Voice). Sarla and her husband Hiroo Advani, who became a successful businessman in Bombay, visit Pakistan almost every year to pay obeisance at the dargah of Sain Nasir Faqir, another widely respected Sufi saint, near Khairpur.

Sain Qutab Shah's disciple, Dr Rochaldas Mansharamani, was a highly revered saint himself. After Partition, he settled in Kalyan, near Bombay, where he became a source of solace for tens of thousands of Sindhi refugees. Kamla's mother used to take her children to him frequently, seeing in him the continuation of the guru tradition of Sufism in Sindh. Kamla would never miss having *darshan* of Sain Noor Husain Shah, the post-Partition custodian of Sain Qutab Shah's dargah, whenever he visited India. Indeed, when I went to Pakistan in 2005, along with Kamla, our son Jayant, daughter Pratibha and daughter-in-law Geetika, Sain Noor Husain Shah, who was in Dubai at the time, specially flew down to Karachi to bless my family.

It would be appropriate here to recall the words of Bhagwan S. Gidwani, one of the greatest Sindhi historians who now lives in Montreal. He belonged to a distinguished family in Karachi. His father, Shamdas Gidwani, was the President of the Hindu Mahasabha in Sindh, and his uncle Dr Choithram Gidwani was President of the Sindh provincial unit of the Congress. Both lived and worked under the same roof. In 1994, Gidwani published the widely acclaimed book *The Return of the Aryans*, a fictionalised recreation of the birth, 8,000 years ago, of the Aryan civilisation in the land of the Sindhu basin, and its evolution across the length and breadth of India. In 1995, he met me in Delhi and presented his book to me with the inscription: 'From one Hindu to another'.

'Remember', Gidwani[4] writes, 'Sindh is the land where our ancestors resided, where the ancient Sanatana Dharma was formed in 8,000 BCE leading to the formation of the roots of Hinduism. It was on the banks of our rivers of Sindh—Sindhu and Saraswati—where the Vedas were composed, where the 'Om' mantra was first uttered. Sindh it was under whose guidance Bharat Varsha, and later Arya Varsha, was formed. Nor do I forget the inspiration of Latif Shah Bhitai, Sachal "Sarmast", Sami and other Sufi saints. We are the survivors and inheritors of that glorious heritage. And to contemplate its extinction for us is not only to rob ourselves alone, but more so, our children and their children to whom this legacy left to us by our ancestors, rightfully belongs. I would not like Sindhiyat to disappear from the land of Sindh for then it would be a barren desert—lifeless and soulless, just as Pakistan would like it to be.'

Gidwani adds: 'In my student days, at Sadhbela (a famous Hindu temple) at Sukkur in Sind, I saw Zulfiqar Ali Bhutto*—he was known as Zulfie then. He was at a Langar, the community meal of Sadhbela, and I also saw him taking away a little *halwa*, which was served with the meal. He could not have been there just for the free meal, for he was always flush with money. Maybe he was there to render thanks for a wish fulfilled, or to seek blessings for a wish for the future. I don't know. I sat with him and exchanged greetings, for like many of us, I had enjoyed the hospitality of his household at Larkana, but certainly did not ask him why he was at Sadhbela. Recently, a South Indian friend questioned me: How come, no one asked Bhutto, why he was there? Only a non-Sindhi would ask such a question. For us, it was not too uncommon in Sindh to see Hindus in dargahs and Muslims at Hindu holy places.... Sindhi Muslims accepted our ancient heritage of Mohenjo-Daro as their own. When Muslims from India poured into Sindh, bent on loot and massacre, it was Sindhi Muslims who protected Hindus.'[5]

This great tradition of tolerance and religious syncretism has been carried forward by many post-Partition Sindhi poets and writers. One of the greatest among them, Shaikh Ayaz (1923-1997) wrote: 'I belong to the religion of all men, all women and all children. I am the "madan-mast" plant which grew up wherever there fell the drops of blood shed by Ladi, wife of Dahir, fighting the ruthless Arabs. I am the cave of Goddess Kali's thousand idols which I wrought in stone and which I have been worshipping all my life.'

Sadly, this tolerant, harmonious and pluralist tradition of Sindh has been under severe attack since Partition. It is sought to be destroyed by Wahabism†, the extremist sect from Saudi Arabia, which has invaded Muslim societies around the world, including India. The spiritual and cultural

---

* Zulfikar Ali Bhutto's (1928-1979) mother was a Hindu.
† Wahabism is an ultra-conservative sect of Sunni Islam founded in the eighteenth century by Muhammad ibn Abd-al-Wahhab. It is the creed upon which the kingdom of Saudi Arabia was founded. It is known to preach intolerance towards not only non-Muslim faiths but also Sufism and other moderate schools of Muslim thought.

aspects of Sindhiyat are being virulently castigated in the burgeoning number of madarasas and mosques built with Saudi money and Saudi-trained preachers. The loser in this assault is not merely Sindh, but the future of humanity itself which depends upon a tolerant and inclusive global culture in order to survive.

SINDH'S GLORIOUS ROLE IN INDIA'S FREEDOM STRUGGLE

The above narration suffices to show how inseparable the bond was between the Hindus and Muslims in Sindh, on one hand, and between Sindh and the rest of India, on the other. This can also be seen in Sindh's contribution to India's freedom struggle, about which I cannot write without a sense of pride in my heart. Sindh never lagged behind in expressing its nationalist sentiment at any stage of the struggle. For example, this is what the *Sindh Times* wrote on 20 May 1884: 'Nadir Shah looted the country only once. But the British loot us every day. Every year wealth to the tune of 4.5 million dollars is being drained out, sucking our very blood. Britain should immediately quit India.' The important thing to note here is that this was a year before the Indian National Congress (INC) was born and long before Gandhiji gave the call 'Quit India'.

When Bal Gangadhar Tilak was sentenced to six years' imprisonment in Mandalay in Burma (now Myanmar) in 1908, many Sindhi young men began to sleep on the floor. When he visited Sindh in 1920, for the first time women came out of their seclusion and offered *aarati* (devotional offering) to him. A young patriot who impressed him most was Dr Choithram Gidwani (1889-1957), about whom Tilak wrote in his paper *Kesari*: 'If every province had men like Dr Choithram, we could break the chains of bondage in no time'. Gandhiji's tribute to him, in *Young India* in 1924, was equally affectionate: 'Dr Choithram has sacrificed everything and turned into a faqir, all for the cause of his country.' After Partition, it was he who convinced a reluctant Jawaharlal Nehru to compensate the Hindu refugees for their property losses.

When the Prince of Wales visited Karachi in March 1922, not a single man from the public went to receive him. Gandhiji's Satyagraha movement in 1930 was a huge success in Sindh. During a peaceful protest action, two satyagrahis were killed in police firing and a prominent Congress leader, Jairamdas Daulatram Alimchandani, was shot in the thigh. The entire country was shocked. Gandhiji sent a telegraphic message that said: 'I have not known anyone more pure-hearted than Jairamdas. It is with the blood of such Indians that the temple of Swaraj will be built.' Jairamdas (1891-1978)*, a great Gandhian, later became General Secretary of the Congress. After Independence, he served as the Editor of the *Complete Works of Mahatma Gandhi*.

Karachi was the venue of the annual session of the AICC in 1931, which was presided over by Sardar Vallabhbhai Patel. It was here that a resolution was adopted for the first time promising universal adult franchise in free India.

The best known freedom fighter from Sindh, and one of the trusted followers of Gandhiji, was, of course, Acharya Kripalani (1888-1982). I must mention here another great Congress leader from Sindh, N.R. Malkani (1860-1974), who, under Gandhiji's influence, renounced his professorship in a college and joined the freedom movement. He later helped Gandhiji build the Harijan Colony in Delhi and influenced a powerful Sindhi politician, Allah Bux Soomro (1900-43), to wear khadi. Soomro, who was a widely respected premier of Sindh, championed the cause of Hindu-Muslim unity and strongly contested the Muslim League's claim of being the only party to represent the Muslims of India. He paid for this with his life; he was murdered in 1943.

One of the most inspiring and informative accounts of the Sindhis' contribution to the freedom movement is given in *The Sindh Story* by K.R. Malkani. Malkani narrates an interesting incident to highlight the special affection that Sindhis had for Netaji Subhas Chandra Bose: 'Once when Subhas Bose was leaving Hyderabad by train, someone humorously suggested that he should marry a Sindhi girl; he could then donate the

---

* I later became a relative of Jairamdas Daulatram. My sister Sheela married Santu Bhavnani, a railway engineer in Bombay. Santu's sister Susheela, who studied with me in college in Hyderabad, wedded Jairamdas's son.

handsome dowry to the national cause. Subhas Bose said he was willing to marry if Dr Choithram led the way. Inquiries revealed that most of those present were unmarried. Thereupon Subhas Bose said: "Let us form a party of the bachelors of India, with Choithram as president and myself as secretary. We'll call it 'Jai Hind Party'. Our object will be to sacrifice married bliss for the joy of serving the country." Obviously he had "Jai Hind" in his mind long before he founded the Indian National Army (INA) in 1942.'

Of all the leaders of the freedom movement, Sindhis have the greatest respect for Gandhiji, who visited Sindh seven times—in 1916, 1917, 1920, 1921, 1929, 1931, and 1934. 'Everything in India attracts me', he wrote in 1929. 'But when I first visited Sindh in 1916, it attracted me in a special way and a bond was established between the Sindhis and me that has proved capable of bearing severe strains.'

When the Sindhis were subjected to the untold travails of Partition, it was Gandhiji, who, more than any other national leader stood by them. As the Sindhi Hindus started to flee in 1947, Gandhiji wrote: 'If even a single Sindhi leaves Sindh, it will be a matter of shame to Mr Jinnah as Governor-General.' He told his prayer gathering on 27 May 1947: 'The people of Sindh want me to go to them. I have not been to Sindh for many years but I have maintained such close relations with the people of Sindh that at one time I used to call myself a Sindhi.' He repeatedly urged both the Nehru government and the British authorities to do everything for the refugees. He spoke to the Maharao of Kutch and got land in Kandla (Kutch, Gujarat) for the Sindhu Resettlement Corporation. Incidentally, my father settled in Kandla and worked in this corporation.

On the last day of his life, 30 January 1948, Gandhiji received a Sindhi delegation, led by Dr Choithram. After listening to the tales of killing and looting of the refugees, he said, 'If there can be war for Kashmir, there can also be war for the rights of Sindhi Hindus in Pakistan.' Malkani tells us in his book that his brother met the Mahatma only an hour before he was shot dead. 'He had been just appointed by the Indian government as Additional Deputy High Commissioner in Karachi to organise orderly migration from Sindh. Gandhiji gave him his blessings and advice: "Take

out everybody. See that you are the last to come out. And tell Khuhro*
I want to visit Sindh to re-establish peace. Let him consult Jinnah and
inform me telegraphically." When Malkani told him how the Hindus in
Sindh had to wear "Jinnah Cap" and carry around an Urdu paper or *Dawn*
to pass off as Muslims, for security reasons, he said he would mention
it in his prayer meeting that evening. Alas, he died before he could visit
Sindh—or expose the excesses there!'

Sindh is now a part of Pakistan, an independent and sovereign nation,
a fact that has to be accepted. But from a civilisational perspective, neither
can Sindh be separated from India nor can India forget Sindh.

---

* Mohammad Ayub Khuhro, of the Muslim League, was the Chief Minister of Sindh at the time of Partition.

Life in Sindh

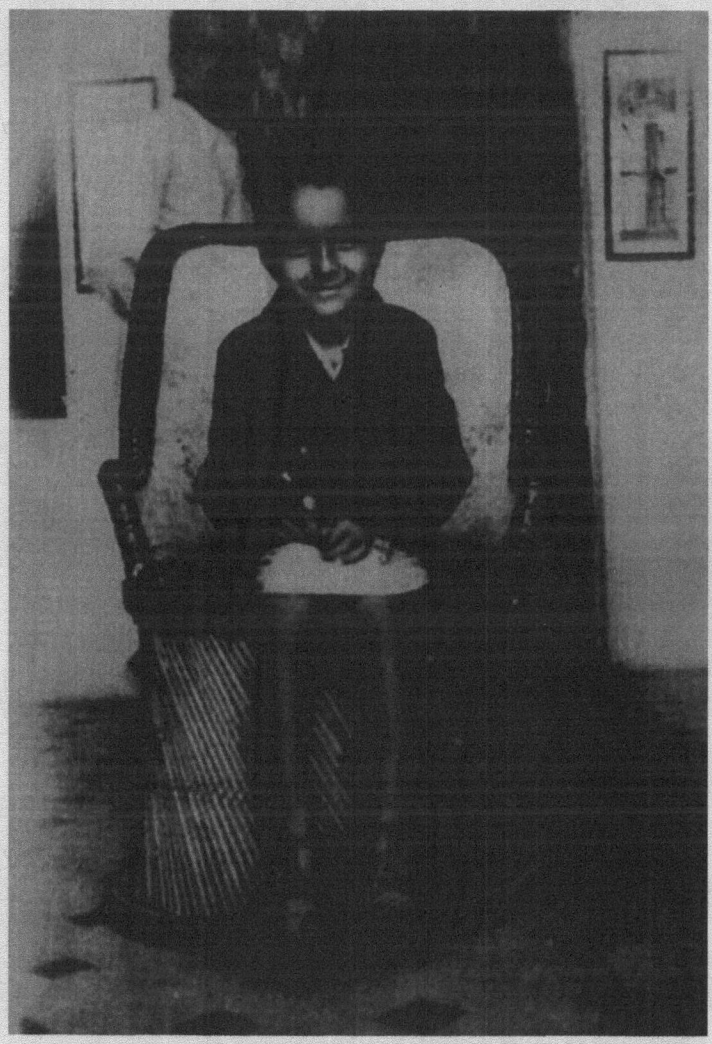

'Lal', as L.K. Advani was fondly called, at age five in Lal Cottage in Karachi.

An adoring and protective brother with younger sister Sheela.

Above right: *Stepping into the threshold of youth as a RSS pracharak in Karachi; Kamla Advani's mother, Gangadevi; father, Premchand Jagtiani.*

A family portrait: *Lal with his parents Gyanidevi and Kishinchand and younger sister Sheela.*

(Above) *With parents; and* (right) *Lal as a schoolboy with sister Sheela.*

(Left) *Sister Sheela with father Kishinchand.*

(Below) *The family now, on a visit to Karachi in 2005. Sitting on Advani's bed from his childhood spent in Lal Cottage, are* (left to right) *wife, Kamla, daughter, Pratibha, L.K. Advani, son, Jayant and daughter-in-law, Geetika.*

St. Patrick's School, (original building) in Karachi.

The school's register of students in Class III with L.K. Advani's name highlighted

The school cricket team. Lal is sitting front row, extreme left.

With his principal Father Modestine (centre) and other teachers during a visit to his school in Karachi in 1978 as Minister of Information & Broadcasting.

Advani with his family during his visit to St Patrick's School in 2005.

The Indus Valley Civilisation seal
Asaanjo Abaano Varso *(The Proud Heritage of our Forefathers).*

The revered 'Guru' of Sindhis, Jhule Lal.

Raja Dahir, the last Hindu king of Sindh.

Symbols of the syncretic Hindu-Muslim spirituality in Sindh: Shrine of Shah Abdul Latif; and (below) Entrance to Sehwan and Lal Shahbaz's tomb.

The Ramakrishna Mission in Karachi, where a young Advani used to attend Swami Ranganathananda's discourses from the Bhagvad Gita every Sunday.

(Right) Dr S. Radhakrishnan, former President of India, with Swami Ranganathananda, head of the Ramakrishna Mission in Karachi.

Dr. K.B. Hedgewar, who founded the RSS in 1925.

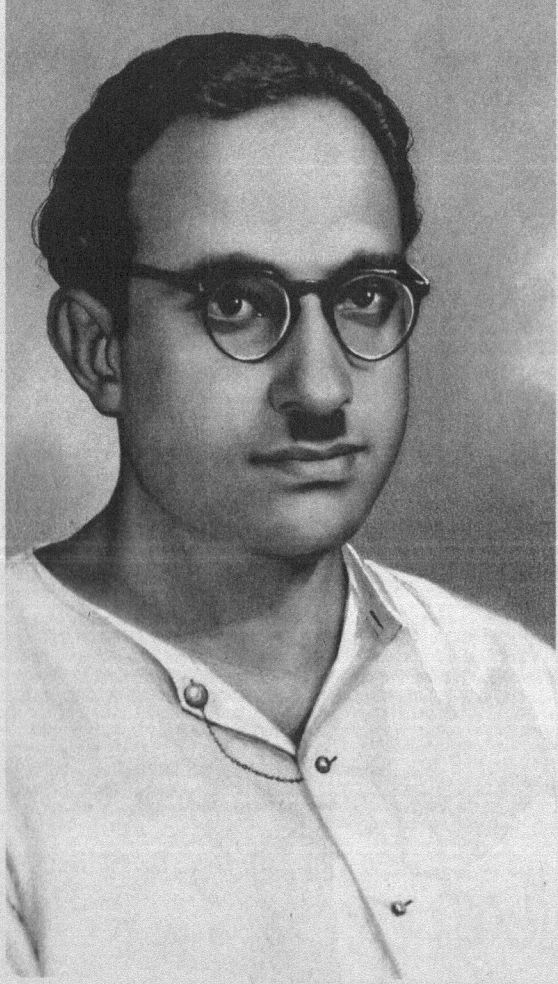
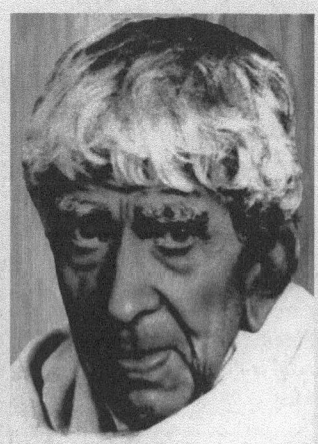

(Clockwise from above left) *Bhagat Kanwar Ram, known as the 'Tansen' of Sindh. He was assassinated by fanatics in 1938; Shaheed Hemu Kalani, who was martyred in the 1942 Quit India Movement in Sindh; Sadhu T.L. Vaswani, a revered spiritual leader; Rajpal Puri, the provincial head of the RSS in Sindh. Rajpalji had a profound influence on Advani in his youth.*

In Indepedent India

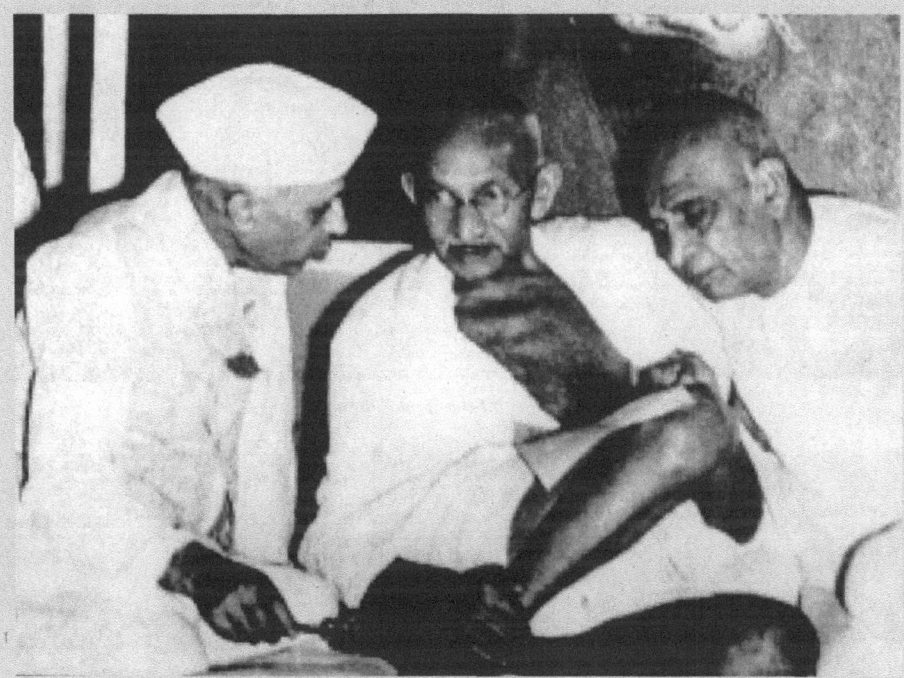

The triumverate of Pandit Nehru, Mahatma Gandhi and Sardar Patel.

Dr B.R. Ambedkar, the principal architect of the Constitution of India. His 1946 book on Pakistan was incisive.

The flag of the Jana Sangh

(Above) *Madhav Sadashiv Golwalkar, or 'Shri Guruji' as he was known, was Chief of the RSS between 1940-73.*

(Right) *Dr Syama Prasad Mookerjee, freedom fighter and founder of the Bharatiya Jana Sangh.*

Advani (sitting extreme right in centre row) as a young RSS pracharak in Rajasthan.

Pandit Deendayal Upadhyaya, whose treatise 'Integral Humanism', became the basic ideological guide for the BJP.

(Centre right) Balraj Madhok, former President of the Jana Sangh.

(Right) K.R. Malkani, Editor of the Organiser *and a fellow RSS activist in Sindh.*

Prem Nath Dogra, a leader of the Kashmir integration movement being felicitated by the Jana Sangh workers led by Pandit Upadhyaya in the early 1950s.

(Left) Two stalwarts of the Jana Sangh — Pandit Deendayal Upadhyaya and Atal Bihari Vajpayee in 1967.

With Atalji at a party conference and (below) with Kushabhau Thakre on his left, who later became President of the BJP.

'Sindh is now a part of Pakistan, an independent and sovereign nation, a fact that has to be accepted. But from a civilisational perspective, neither can Sindh be separated from India nor can India forget Sindh.'

3

My First Twenty Years In Sindh

Let positive, strong, helpful thoughts enter into your brains from very childhood. Lay yourselves open to these thoughts, and not to weakening and paralysing ones.

—Swami Vivekananda

I was born in Karachi on 8 November 1927. My family comprised my parents Kishinchand and Gyanidevi and my younger sister, Sheela. Our house, in a locality called Jamshed Quarters, was built soon after my birth; and so was named 'Lal Cottage'. It was a fairly spacious, beautifully designed, single-storied bungalow. We had a horse-driven Victoria at home. To outsiders, it may have seemed a status symbol; to me it was a source of curiosity during my early childhood. But curiosity, as they say, 'kills the cat', and one day I found myself under one wheel of the Victoria. The wound on my thigh took several days to heal.

There were many Parsi families in a part of Jamshed Quarters known as Parsi Colony and most of them lived in mansions, they being a prosperous community. The old-world charm of these mansions, which is sadly at odds with the rapidly shrinking population of the Parsis, can still be seen in Karachi—and also in Bombay, a city with which Karachi shares close historical ties and many common characteristics.

The Advani family belonged to the Amil branch of Sindhi Hindus. Traditionally, the Amil was a revenue official who assisted *munshis* in the administrative set-up of Muslim kings. It was one of the two main divisions of the Lohano clan which was linked to the Vaishya (business) community. In time, Amils came to dominate government jobs and professions in Sindh. Generally speaking, Hindus in Sindh had a strong tradition of revering the Guru Granth Sahib, the sacred scripture of the Sikhs, Guru Nanak and other Sikh gurus. There is an interesting story behind this strong Sikh influence.

It is believed that the city of Hyderabad was destroyed by a fire in the mid-eighteenth century. The Muslim ruler of Sindh was looking for someone who could rebuild the city. His officers mentioned a person named Adiomal (founder of the Advani clan) living near Multan (now in Pakistan). Satisfied with his credentials, the king offered him an attractive remuneration for rebuilding the city on a new site. Adiomal was a devout follower of the Guru Granth Sahib. Therefore, he told the king: 'I shall rebuild this city only if you first allow me to build a gurdwara where I can read the Granth Sahib without any Muslims harassing me.' The king agreed. For completing the task, Adiomal sought the cooperation of his fellow Amils—a civil engineer named Gidumal (of Gidwani clan) and a financial expert named Wadhumal (of Wadhwani clan). Soon Hyderabad had a large Amil population settled along Advani, Gidwani and Wadhwani streets.

My paternal grandfather, Dharamdas Khubchand Advani, was a Sanskrit scholar well settled in life as the principal of a government high school. He passed away before I was born. My father, had four brothers, three elder to him and one younger. The elder three—Gobindram, Parasram and Ramchand—were in Hyderabad, while my father and his younger brother Gopaldas lived in Karachi. Gobindram, a civil servant, retired as Deputy Collector of Hyderabad. Parasram was a lawyer. Ramchand and my father were businessmen, and Gopaldas was a professor of chemistry in

D.J. Sindh College, Karachi. As I have mentioned, three of my uncles have the names Gobindram, Ramchand and Gopaldas. By a curious coincidence three of my *mamas* (maternal uncles) also had those very names!

Karachi and Hyderabad together had a population of approximately six lakhs, mainly Hindus. But with the Amil community confined mainly to these two places, families were quite closely knit. During those days nuclear families were unheard of; large, extended families were the norm. So, when I look back and identify the numerous first cousins I grew up with, I can count as many as thirty-four!

THE ATMOSPHERE OF *PAVITRATA* AT HOME

The most vivid memory of my early childhood is the affection I received from everyone in the family, including my grandparents and my three *mausis* (mother's sisters). We received a lot of intense love and care as our mother had passed away when I was just thirteen, and Sheela only seven. Indeed, Sheela, who now lives in Mumbai, was brought up almost entirely by our Jamni Mausi and Mausa Chandiram Wadhwani.

I have very fond memories of my childhood. Even the trauma of Partition, which forced our family, like lakhs of other Hindu and Sikh families in Sindh, to migrate to this part of undivided India, has not erased those memories. On the contrary, these memories have become all the more precious because of my family's forced separation from our homeland, in which I spent the first twenty years of my life.

The one person who had the greatest influence on my personality in my childhood years was my father. He was a gentle human being who embodied simplicity, and without any overt preaching, he quietly shaped my mind with his impeccable conduct. I was extremely attached to my mother as well, but after she passed away it was from my father that I received both love and guidance.

Prior to 1936, Sindh was part of the Bombay Presidency which comprised, besides Sindh, Gujarat, Maharashtra, northern Karnataka and parts of Nizam's Hyderabad. In most of these areas, the general practice is to use the father's name as a middle name. In Mahatma Gandhi's case, for instance, his father's name was Karamchand, Mohandas was his own given name and Gandhi his surname. Similarly, in my case, the letter 'K' in L.K. Advani stands for my father's name, that is 'Kishinchand'. My first name is just Lal. In course of time, my father's name started being written as Krishenchand. Later still, the first part of this became appended to my own name, and I started being addressed as Lal Krishna Advani.

As I look back, what strikes me most about the atmosphere in our household was the pervasive air of *pavitrata* (piousness and purity). Most Hindus in those days were Nanakpanthis—followers of Guru Nanak, the founder of Sikhism. Indeed, the main 'deity' in our home was the Granth Sahib. We would not only pray to it, but my grandmother also used to read from it everyday, in the presence of all the family members. The largest gurdwara in Karachi used to be in Amil Colony, not very far from our own residence in Jamshed Quarters. Popularly known as Guru Mandir, this place became a bustling hub of religious activity and festivals for both Sikhs as well as Hindus, mainly because of the devout dedication of Dada Chellaram (1904-64), a renowned Sahajdhari Sikh saint. He travelled widely singing and preaching *gurbani*, Guru Nanak's inspired word. After Partition, Dada Chellaram and his family moved to Delhi where he founded 'Nij Thanw' (Pure Vessel), which today runs a chain of gurdwaras in several cities and towns.

Sikh ritualism was part of the family's tradition, and the Granth Sahib was duly venerated and recited regularly not just by my grandmother, but also by my mother and elders. No wonder, even as a child, my awareness about my own birthday was not simply that I was born on 8 November 1927, but that it was just a day after Guru Nanak Jayanti, which falls on Kartik Poornima (the night of the full moon as per the Hindu calendar in the month of Kartik). I also recall that on my birthday there used to be an *akhand paath* (full and continuous reading from the Granth Sahib), followed by *bhog* (consecrated meal).

In 2004, a party colleague suggested to me that an *akhand paath* and *langar* (community meal) be organised at my residence where some of the best *raagis* (singers of Sikh *shabad*) of Punjab would be happy to come. I welcomed the idea and asked Kamla, my wife, whether we could have the function on her birthday which was on 27 November. She readily agreed. When I glanced at the list of holidays for the year, I discovered that 26 November was Kartik Poornima, so Guru Nanak Jayanti that year fell on the same day. Thus, Kamla's birthday according to the Gregorian calendar and my own birthday according to the Hindu calendar coincided that year!

The function was memorable for the entire family. I invited Prime Minister Dr Manmohan Singh, who graciously accepted. So did Baba Gurinder Singh Dhillon, the revered head of the Radhasoami* sect of Beas.

A few days prior to the function, Pratibha asked her mother what gift she wanted on her birthday. Kamla replied: 'I would like you to sing a *shabad** (a Sikh hymn) at the *akhand paath* being organised.' So for the next few days, Pratibha skipped office, found an excellent music teacher and prepared herself in right earnest for a melodious rendering of 'Satnam Waheguru'. Her performance took the entire audience, including the Beas Guruji, completely by surprise. In fact, all of us in the family were also unaware that Pratibha could sing so well.

On that day, I vividly recalled the precious tradition of religious harmony in Sindh. Temples and gurdwaras were both accepted as abodes of God and all Hindus went there to offer prayers. Hindus would join the celebrations of Nanak Jayanti and Guru Gobind Singh Jayanti at gurdwaras, where Diwali and Dusshera festivities were also held. I was completely unaware that those who wore beards and those who did not, belonged to different faiths. In fact, as far as Hindus and Sikhs are concerned, it is only after migrating to this part of India after Partition that, for the first time, I began to hear and understand that the two are different communities. It was also common for Hindus to pay homage at the shrines of Sufi saints and for Muslims to celebrate Hindu festivals.

---

* Radhasoami Satsang was founded by Soami Shiv Dayal Singh in 1861 on the bank of River Beas in Punjab. He preached that human beings could reach God realisation only through listening to the *shabad* (sound) and *naam* (name) of the Lord. The community is guided by 'Sant Mat', the teachings of the saints.

These are the pluralist *samskaras* (traditions) which were passed on to me as a child and have shaped my personal ethics since.

HAPPY YEARS AT ST. PATRICK'S HIGH SCHOOL

My schooling in Karachi was at St. Patrick's High School for Boys, which was the biggest, and also the most highly rated school in the city. I studied there for six years from 1936-42. It was founded in 1845 by Catholic missionaries from Ireland, initially to cater to the Goan Christian community in the city. To the right of our school was the magnificent St. Patrick's Church (now Cathedral), which had a commanding view from across the length and breadth of Clarke Street. To its left was St. Joseph's Convent School for Girls. My school's reputation, the loving and nurturing by its teachers, its architectural beauty and its quiet environs—all these made me feel proud to belong to St. Patrick's.

There was a marked difference between the educational levels of Hindus and Muslims those days. Literacy among Hindus was almost hundred per cent, although opportunities for higher education were quite limited. Only three cities had colleges—Karachi, Hyderabad and Shikarpur—and only Karachi boasted of more than one college. Even big towns like Larkana, Sukkur, Jacobabad and Mirpur Khas had no colleges. The enrollment of Muslim boys in schools was quite low, and it was lower still in colleges. Even at St. Patrick's there were very few Muslim students. As far as education for Muslim girls was concerned, it was virtually non-existent.

As far as I can remember, I stood first in every class till my matriculation. Thus, all the teachers knew me. I also happened to be the youngest in my class. When I completed my matriculation, I had just turned fourteen. In later years, when my teachers learnt about my political achievements, they were both happy and immensely proud. A particularly memorable moment for me was when I was able to visit my school during my brief trip to Karachi in 1978 as India's Information & Broadcasting Minister. All those teachers who had taught me attended a special reception that was organised for me in the school's auditorium. Father Modestine, the school's highly respected principal from my time, was also present. It was after a gap of thirty-six years that I was stepping onto the premises of my school, every nook and corner of which was so fondly familiar to me.

When I went to Karachi in 2005, I visited my school again. At the reception held there, I met a few people who had studied with me and had grown up to become priests and teachers at the same school. But this time around, none of the teachers who had taught me were present. Understandably so. After all, I was going there after an interlude of nearly three decades since my last visit in 1978. And over six decades had elapsed since I had stepped out of the school in 1942. Time had inevitably taken its toll, leaving me to muse, sadly, about the transience of human life.

My pleasant memories of the school were revived, most unexpectedly, when Pakistan's President, General Pervez Musharraf, who is also an alumnus of St. Patrick's, visited India in early 2005 and gave me a unique present. It was an album of documents and photographs from my school years and contained, besides my school admission certificate of 1936, photographs of my teachers and principal. As he presented the album to me, we exchanged memories about the school, and Musharraf asked me, 'Were you ever punished in school, Advani sahib?' I said, 'No, never.' Punishment, in our days for coming late to school or for any pranks, was the class monitor taking the student out of the class and smacking his hand four times with a cane. Musharraf said, 'As for me, I got the taste of the cane several times.'

In school, we had an option to learn a second language. Many students opted for French, some took Persian, but I chose Latin. I remember scoring very high marks in the board exam in Latin. My one big regret in life, however, has been that I did not learn Sanskrit in school. It was not commonly taught in schools and, being a Catholic institution, St. Patrick's did not offer Sanskrit at all.

It may surprise many readers to know that I was not very eloquent in Hindi while I was in Karachi. I used to understand it somewhat because of the Hindi movies I watched and could even manage some broken conversation. I started reading, writing and conversing in Hindi only after migrating to India in 1947, when I was already twenty years old. Here is an interesting example of the extent of my unfamiliarity with a language that, in the later years of my life, became the principal medium of communication both in my political and my family life.

On one occasion, during my student days, I saw my grandmother writing a postcard. I asked her why she was writing the letter in Hindi? She replied: '*Beta*, this is not Hindi. It is Sindhi, but the script is Gurmukhi. I have never been to school. I know Sindhi because that is our mother tongue. And I learnt Gurmukhi because that is the language in which Granth Sahib is written.' When she read out the letter to me, I was surprised that the language was Sindhi although the script was Gurmukhi. This hybrid bilingualism was quite common among Hindu women of my grandmother's age in Sindh.

I was introduced to another linguistic surprise—this time by the collection of books belonging to my grandfather, who was a great Sanskrit scholar. One day I found an old bulky book in his cupboard titled *English to Sindhi Dictionary*. When I opened it, I found that there was no Sindhi in it. I asked my father if that was an English-to-Sindhi dictionary, why was there only Sanskrit in it. Why was it so? My father told me that it was not Sanskrit but Sindhi. 'You could not recognise it because Sindhi is written in Arabic script these days. But in earlier times, when my father gave this book to me, Sindhi used to be written in Devnagari and not in Arabic,' he explained.

In post-Partition decades, there have been heated debates in the Sindhi community on whether those who have migrated to this part of India should continue to use the Arabic script or revert to the Devnagari script. I have always been of the view, primarily for practical reasons, that we should revert to Devnagari. This is because the younger generation of Sindhis can speak their mother tongue but, being totally unfamiliar with the Arabic script, cannot read or write in it.

MY LOVE FOR CINEMA, CRICKET AND BOOKS

Of my four maternal uncles, Sundar Mama, the youngest, became a good companion even though he was much older to me. We used to frequently watch films together and he was one of the main reasons for my early interest in them, both Hindi and English. I saw many horror films in my childhood along with him, and the one I still remember is *Frankenstein*.

Then came a time, from 1942 to 1956, when I did not watch a single movie. It was, again, a horror film that ended this long abstinence from cinema. In 1956, I had gone to Bombay and was staying at Sundar Mama's place. He said, 'Come, let's go watch a film.' Saying 'No,' I added that I hadn't seen a film in fifteen years. He was indeed very surprised! It so happened that the next morning's newspaper carried a news item about the death, due to a heart attack, of a man while he was watching a three-dimensional horror film at Strand Cinema. The film was *The House of Wax*, a 1953 classic remake of a 1933 film. But being the first 3D film by Warner Brothers, and that too shot in colour, it had become hugely popular all over the world. The news item mentioned that movie-goers were provided with a special pair of spectacles to experience the film's 'realistic' 3D effect. This made me curious and I told Sundar Mama, 'Let's go to see this film.' I never again allowed such long gaps in my enjoyment of watching movies.

In school, many meritorious students earn good marks in science and mathematics and hence they tend to think that their aptitude lies in these 'scoring' subjects. But this is far from the truth. As one grows older, one begins to have a better appreciation of one's true interests. In my case, I discovered during my college years that I was more inclined towards English literature. By the time I joined Dayaram Gidumal National College in Hyderabad in 1942, the Quit India Movement had begun in right earnest. Due to the disturbed conditions in the city, the college rarely functioned smoothly and most students would just wander around. I spent most of my time in the college library, voraciously reading every book that caught my fancy.

It is here that my lifelong love for books began. I read all the novels of Jules Verne, the famous nineteenth century French science fiction writer, including *Journey to the Centre of the Earth, Twenty Thousand Leagues Under the Sea, Around the World in Eighty Days,* and others. These novels were quite prescient and accurate in describing technological inventions that materialised many decades later. For example, *Paris in the 20th*

Century talked about air conditioning, television, etc., which were non-existent in Verne's time. Similarly, the description in the novel *From the Earth to the Moon*—three astronauts launching into space from Florida and returning to the earth by landing on the ocean—now seems almost like a preview of the voyage of Apollo 11 in 1969. It was also in my college library that I read all the novels of Charles Dickens and Alexander Dumas and some other classics by European and American writers. I was particularly impressed by Dickens' *A Tale of Two Cities* and Dumas' *The Three Musketeers*. Quite a few of the novels that I had read then were subsequently made into films, and I would never miss an opportunity to watch them in my later years.

My other love in school was cricket. I was not an extraordinary player, but I was an avid listener of A.F.S. Taleyarkhan's radio commentary of Test cricket, Ranji Trophy and the highly popular Bombay Pentangular matches, played among the five teams of Hindus, Muslims, Parsis, Europeans and the rest. Each year the final match in the Pentangular Tournament was invariably between the Hindu and Muslim teams. It was fought with the same excitement and passion that we witness these days, when India plays Pakistan. Taleyarkhan's was a legendary voice on radio, and, like many cricket fans, I too was as interested in his style of commentary as in the match. I used to frequently entertain my friends by mimicking his description and analysis of the game. I remember that the only time I bunked school was when, instead of only listening to the radio commentary, I was able to watch the five-day Ranji Trophy final in Karachi between the teams of Sindh and Maharashtra. The Maharashtra team was led by D.B. Deodhar, who lived to the ripe age of one hundred years. In the same match I also watched other great cricketers like Vijay Merchant, Vinoo Mankad and Naoomal and M.J. Mobed from the Sindh team play.

I don't remember being mischievous in school, but I did play a prank on my grandmother once, when we were in Hyderabad in 1943. The mercury would rise very high in the summer months in that part of Sindh, and women generally used to sleep on traditional *jhoolas* (large-sized cradles) in their houses. I remember that the temperature once touched 119 fahrenheit. In the afternoons, my grandmother would comfort herself with a bamboo fan and doze off to sleep on the *jhoola*. One day, as she was about to fall asleep, I quietly took the fan out of her hand and replaced it with a *datoon* (a thin neem stick used to brush teeth). Her hand continued to move, but without producing any cooling effect. She suddenly woke up to discover my mischievous deed and was very angry with me that day. I felt quite bad and never repeated such pranks on anybody.

I looked forward to school and was not one to exult in unexpected holidays. Nevertheless, there was one reason, and season, every year for the school's closure when I could not help suppress my boyish instinct for rejoicing. It used to rain very little in Karachi—at the most, about five inches in a year. The sky would be overcast during the monsoon but the clouds would rarely ever send showers down. Therefore, even when it simply drizzled a bit, we used to indulge in great merriment, more so because the school would declare an official holiday on that day just to let the students have fun. I used to cycle to school, covering the distance of about two miles in fifteen to twenty minutes. On days when the city was blessed with a rare drizzle, despite knowing that the school would be closed, I would still cycle down to the school just to experience the innocent thrill of seeing the announcement, in big letters, on the board at the front gate: 'The school is closed today on account of the rains.'

AT FOURTEEN, A SWAYAMSEVAK OF THE RSS

There is always one moment in childhood, it is said, 'when the door opens and lets the future in'. In my case, that moment of stepping into the future came, unexpectedly at a playful moment, when I joined the RSS. I was only fourteen years and a few months old then. After I completed my matriculation, my father shifted base from Karachi to Hyderabad in Sindh. During my vacation and before joining college, I started playing tennis. One of my regular partners on the tennis court was a friend, Murli Mukhi. One day, right in the middle of the game, he said, 'I am going.' Utterly surprised, I asked him, 'How can you go like this, without even completing the set?' He replied, 'I have joined the RSS a few days ago. I cannot be late for the *shakha* because punctuality is very important in that organisation.'

This was my introduction to the term 'RSS'. I probed him a bit further and he said I could go along with him. I declined, saying that I wanted to continue with the game and would go some other day. That moment came soon enough. After a couple of days, I accompanied him to a *shakha*. In those days, as martial law had been imposed in Sindh, public drills were banned. So my first visit to a *shakha* was conducted on the terrace of a large bungalow belonging to Ram Kripalani*, a prominent member of the *shakha* ended with *swayamsevaks* standing at attention to sing the Sangh prayer for our Motherland—'*Namaste Sada Vatsale Matrubhoome...*' From that day till now, for sixty-five long years, I have remained a devoted, committed and proud *swayamsevak* of the Sangh.

Soon after joining the RSS, I came in contact with Shri Rajpal Puri, who was *prant pracharak* (full-time provincial organiser and motivator) from Sialkot in Punjab (now in Pakistan). His affectionate, intelligent and inspiring personality left a deep impact on me. In a quiet way, he shaped my value system and kindled the fire of patriotism in me. If anyone were to ask me about the greatest influences in my life, I would unhesitatingly name, besides my parents, two persons—Rajpal Puri and, after I migrated to this part of India, Pandit Deendayal Upadhyaya, the philosopher, guide and leader of the Bharatiya Jana Sangh which later became the Bharatiya Janata Party.

I should explain here what motivated me to join the RSS. As long as I was in school, my universe was limited to my home and studies. In school, I absorbed all the knowledge that I received from my teachers and

---

* After Partition, I lost contact with Ram Kripalani since he had settled in Trinidad and Tobago, which has a large population of people of Indian origin. In 2007, the High Commissioner of Trinidad and Tobago in New Delhi invited me to participate in the annual Diwali celebration where one of his country's illustrious sons, Nobel Laureate writer Sir V.S. Naipaul, was also going to be present. The High Commissioner asked me, 'Have you ever visited Trinidad and Tobago?' I said, 'No. But someone I knew during my Karachi years, Ram Kripalani, settled in your country.' At this, my host said, 'Ram Kripalani? He became a leading businessman and philanthropist of our country.'

books, while at home the love, affection and *samskaras* that I received from my family also shaped my personality. This was the capital I accumulated in my childhood. However, I knew little about the goings-on in the world, beyond the walls of my home and school. My introduction to the momentous political developments taking place in India and the world, at that time, was only after I started attending the RSS *shakha*. One day, as I, along with the other volunteers, sat listening to the *bauddhik* (intellectual talk) by one Shyam Das*, he posed us a question: 'You receive so much from society, but what are you giving back? Isn't it your duty to do so? India is now under foreign rule. Isn't it our responsibility to liberate our Motherland?' His words gently opened a new door within my inner self and set me on a path of self-enquiry.

Rajpalji and other seniors at the *shakha* explained to us the evolution of the freedom movement in India, how the Congress under the leadership of Mahatma Gandhi had adopted the path of non-violence, and how revolutionaries like Netaji Subhas Chandra Bose had charted their own independent course. There was no disrespect in their attitude towards the Congress, but I noticed a degree of disapproval over the strategy adopted by it. 'Congress leaders believe that India would get her independence by sending memorandums and petitions to the British,' RSS seniors would tell us. 'We don't think that the *angrez* (British) are going to go away so cheaply.'

I should point out that, just as the RSS seniors used to criticise the Congress strategy for gaining freedom, they also disapproved of the path chosen by great revolutionaries like Bhagat Singh saying that the *angrez* are not going to go away if some patriotic individuals confront them with guns in their hands. Of course, even while criticising both these approaches, the RSS seniors used to speak deferentially about both Mahatma Gandhi and Shaheed Bhagat Singh.

The question that troubled me was: 'How can the *angrez* be made to leave India?' There was no direct answer forthcoming from RSS seniors. 'Our first task right now is to organise *shakhas* like this one all over the

---

* Shyam Das settled in Jaipur after Partition, where he actively worked for the RSS and the Bharatiya Jana Sangh.

country, so that we can create a large voluntary force of patriotic, idealistic, disciplined and selfless Indians willing to sacrifice everything for the liberation of Bharat Mata. What this force will exactly do, and when, to achieve India's freedom are not questions to be answered now. We will know the answers in due course of time. Right now, we must remember that, without a well-organised population, and without a voluntary force at its core consisting of individuals strong in character and imbued with the spirit of sacrifice, nothing tangible can be achieved.' To my young mind, this explanation was convincing enough.

I also learnt, from RSS seniors, about the Muslim League and its plan to divide India in order to carve out a separate Muslim nation called Pakistan. When the phrase 'Two Nation Theory' first fell on my ears, it felt as if I had touched a live wire! The idea instantly seemed abhorrent to me. I simply could not bring myself to accept a scenario where my country would one day be vivisected and that my homeland would become a part of Pakistan. I said to myself: 'True, the British rule in India must be ended. But is Partition the price to be paid for gaining freedom?' I have no qualms in admitting that my commitment to the RSS became deeper when I learnt about the Muslim League's diabolical demand.

I must mention here three of my fellow *swayamsevaks* from my Karachi days who did yeomen's service to society throughout their lives. Jhamatmal T. Wadhwani became the President of the Bharatiya Sindhu Sabha and also served as the National Treasurer of the Bharatiya Jana Sangh. Hashu Advani, who founded the Vivekananda Education Society in Mumbai, was one of the pillars of the Jana Sangh in Maharashtra and served as the state's Finance Minister. Manhar Mehta served as President of the Bharatiya Mazdoor Sangh, the largest trade union in India.

MY EARLY PATRIOTIC INFLUENCES

Attending the *shakha* and discussing national and international issues with my seniors had another immediate effect on me: it imparted a new edge, urgency and purpose to my love of books. I started reading all the available literature on Indian history, especially the history of great patriotic warriors like Shivaji, Rana Pratap and Guru Gobind Singh. Once I read five books, at a stretch, on Shivaji, including *The Grand Rebel*[1] by Dennis Kincaid, a renowned British historian. What impressed me about this book, apart from Shivaji's bravery and patriotism, was something that Kincaid wrote: 'In spite of the character of a Crusade which Saint Ramdas's blessings gave to Shivaji's long struggle against the Moghul rule, it is remarkable how little religious animosity or intolerance Shivaji displayed. His kindness to Catholic priests is an agreeable contrast to the proscriptions of the Hindu priesthood in the (largely Marathi-speaking) Indian territories of the Portuguese. Even his enemies remarked on his extreme respect for Mussulman priests, for mosques and for the Koran. Whenever a Koran came into his possession, he treated it with the same respect as if it had been one of the sacred works of his own faith. Whenever his men captured Mussulman ladies, they were brought to Shivaji, who looked after them as they were his wards till he could return them to their relations. It is perhaps remarkable that this century in Europe was noteworthy for the activities of Tilly in Germany and Cromwell in Ireland.'

I also read *Aurangzeb* and *Shivaji* by Jadunath Sarkar, a great historian from Bengal, whose books traced the fall of the Mughal Empire and the resurgence of national consciousness under the Maratha ruler.

In 1943, a year after I joined the RSS, I came to Indore to do my first year Officers' Training Camp (OTC). On my way back, I took a detour to spend a few days travelling in Rajasthan. Ever since I had read Colonel James Tod's two-volume classic *Annals and Antiquities of Rajasthan*, written in the early nineteenth century, I had developed a fascination for this land of heroes and martyrs. I travelled to see the fort of Chittorgarh and the city of Udaipur. I also visited Haldighati, where Maharana Pratap confronted the Mughal Emperor Akbar in an epic battle. On the walls of Chittorgarh Fort, I was pained to see thousands of idols of Hindu deities broken and defaced by intolerant Muslim invaders. Not one was left intact.

All these experiences were bringing about a strange transformation within me. The question of why and how India lost its freedom started to agitate my young mind. Simultaneously, as a teenager exposed to patriotic ideals I started to dream about India as a free nation in the future. When dreams acquire the wings of idealism and are propelled by ideas about a history-transforming mission, they begin to soar far and high. I began to believe that no mountain was impossible to scale and no task was impossible to achieve. India's freedom began to look easily attainable—and imminent, too.

Of course, there was, about these notions, a certain boyish naïveté that made every task look simpler than it really was. But naïveté frequently provides courage to take up otherwise insurmountable challenges. In my case, it won me the trust and confidence of my seniors in the organisation who started to involve me in important activities.

For a RSS *swayamsevak* to be given any responsible position in the organisation, he has to undergo training for the OTC. The training is complete when the *swayamsevak* undergoes the third year OTC in Nagpur, the RSS headquarters, which I underwent in 1946. In between I had done my second year OTC in Ahmedabad. Thus began my association with Gujarat, which continues even today. The *prant pracharak* of the RSS in Gujarat those days was the late Madhukarrao Bhagwat, father of Shri Mohanrao Bhagwat, presently *Sar Karyawah* (General Secretary) of the RSS.

When I was seventeen, I took up the first professional 'job' of my life—as a teacher at the Model High School in Karachi. I taught English, history, maths and science to class five and six students. In those days, it was not necessary to have a diploma or bachelor's degree in education to become a teacher. Since I was quite young, many of my students were nearly my age. My association with the RSS motivated me to become a teacher. The Sangh had taught me that students should internalise the ideals of patriotism, develop good character, enrich their knowledge base and acquire a natural readiness to serve society. As a *swayamsevak*, I desired that more and more youngsters should join the *shakha* and receive the *samskaras* of the Sangh. I thought that a teacher's profession was best suited to achieve both ends. I was greatly encouraged in this endeavour by the guidance I received from Rajpalji. And thus, I became a teacher.

'HOW TO WIN FRIENDS & INFLUENCE PEOPLE'

What I greatly admired about Rajpalji was the special care he took to expose me to new ideas and inculcate new qualities for the development of my personality. One day he asked me if I was interested in reading books. I replied, 'Of course.' He placed a book in my hand and said, 'Read this.' It was Dale Carnegie's *How to Win Friends & Influence People*. I would clearly rate it as one of the five or six life-transforming books I have read so far. Of course, if I were to read it now, my opinion about it would be very different and I would probably say it is quite an ordinary book. But at that time, when I was only fourteen-and-a-half, the book influenced me deeply. Learn to listen more and talk less; express your opinion in clear and concise terms; but don't challenge others in an argument beyond a point even if you know that the other person is in the wrong—these and other such pieces of advice were highly useful and I began moulding my behaviour accordingly.

I remember, in particular, the example Carnegie gives of a conversation between two friends, in which one of them cites a quotation and says it is Shakespeare's. His friend disagrees with him and says it's from the Bible. The argument becomes heated with neither of them yielding ground. Carnegie writes: 'Nine times out of ten, an argument ends with each of the contestants more firmly convinced than ever that he is absolutely right.' His advice, therefore, is: 'Once you have made your point and your friend doesn't agree, what's the point in stretching the argument? It will only create a rift in your friendship because he will resent your triumph. If you cannot convince him, simply keep quiet. If your friend creates a doubt in your mind about your information, go back to the source and check it out for yourself. But don't argue unnecessarily.' Here is a limerick from that book which I remember even now:

> *A man convinced against his will*
> *Is of the same opinion still.*[2]

Another example from the book was that of a dreaded gangster called the 'Two-Gun Crowley' in New York City. He had committed several murders and routinely terrorised people. When he was sentenced to death and was being taken for execution, he angrily complained, 'This is what I get for defending myself.' Pointing out that even a gangster like him thought that society was doing him an injustice, Carnegie argues that human nature is not predisposed to admitting one's own mistakes. Therefore, it is futile to point out others' flaws, and far better to try and rectify our own. 'Instead of condemning people, let's try to understand them. Let's try to figure out why they do what they do. That's a lot more profitable than criticism; and it breeds sympathy, tolerance and kindness. "To know all is to forgive all." God himself does not propose to judge man until the end of his days. Why should you and I?'

This advice was to have a lasting effect on my conduct with people in my political and organisational work in later years. My close colleagues would often ask me, not without a tinge of frustration: 'Advaniji, even when you know that a person in the party has a flaw in his character, you do not go beyond a point in reprimanding him and insisting that he correct himself. Why?' My reply, always, has been, 'Human beings do not change the way they live simply by listening to others' advice. They have to realise the need for change themselves.'

Another book that left a deep imprint on me was Paul Brunton's celebrated travelogue *A Search in Secret India*. Brunton (1898-1981), a British writer, was one of twentieth century's greatest explorers of the spiritual traditions of the East. The book tells the captivating story of his journey around India, living among yogis, mystics and gurus, and how he finally found the answer to his question 'Who am I?' at the feet of the great sage, Sri Ramana Maharishi (1879-1950), at Arunachala in Tamil Nadu. What amazed me then was Brunton's description of Sri Ramana's extraordinary power of silence; his devotees felt elevated merely being in his holy presence. Even though I did not understand many of the mystical experiences narrated in the book, it nevertheless introduced my young mind to a fascinating new dimension of India's heritage.

Rajpalji introduced me to another book those days which inspired me immensely. It was Vinayak Damodar ('Swatantryaveer') Savarkar's book *1857–The War of Independence*. It was banned by the British and hence unavailable. However, I was told that I could get it from a person selling underground literature. I purchased it from my accumulated pocket money—for rupees twenty-eight, which was a handsome amount in those days.

The book* gives a stirring account of India's first national uprising against the British rule, and contributed largely to my desire to devote my life to the cause of the nation. Savarkar writes that those were the days when 'Hindus and Mahomedans proclaimed that India was their country and that they were all brethren, the days when Hindus and Mahomedans unanimously raised the flag of national freedom at Delhi. Be those grand days ever memorable in the history of Hindustan!' If he showers praise

---

* I wrote an article in the *Indian Express* on 10 May 2007, when India commemorated the 150th anniversary of the First War of Independence. Recalling my own introduction to 1857 through Savarkar's book, I wrote: 'The story of the journey of the book's manuscript from India to England, France, Germany, Holland and back, and the role it played in inspiring revolutionaries after its clandestine publication, is as thrilling as any of the battles fought in 1857. Savarkar wrote it in London, where he had gone to study law but soon got involved in revolutionary activities, when he was only twenty-five. The original text in Marathi was completed in 1907, to mark the fiftieth anniversary of 1857, and was secretly sent to India. But it could not be printed in India because the British authorities, who had come to know of it, raided the printing press. Miraculously, the manuscript was saved and sent back to Savarkar in Paris. His fellow-revolutionaries translated it into English but no printer in England or France was willing to print it. Finally it was printed in Holland in 1909 and copies of it were smuggled into India. But the author was arrested in London in 1910 on charges of sedition, brought to India, convicted for two life imprisonments, and transported to 'Kala Pani', the dreaded Cellular Jail in Andaman and Nicobar Islands. It was the same place where the British had deported thousands of patriots who had participated in the uprising of 1857. Savarkar spent eleven years in near-solitary confinement in a dark, dingy cell that overlooked the gallows where prisoners were routinely executed. Though banned, the book went into several reprints. Madame Cama brought out the second edition in Europe. Lala Hardayal, a leader of the revolutionary Ghadar Party, brought out an edition in USA. It was printed for the first time in India in 1928 by Bhagat Singh and his comrades. Netaji Subhas Chandra Bose and Ras Behari Bose got it published in Japan in 1944, and the book became almost a textbook for the soldiers of the Indian National Army. Hence, this was not a book written by an ordinary historian enjoying his comfort, safety and academic support structure, all of which he takes for granted. Rather, it was penned by a revolutionary who suffered unimaginable hardships for his activities and which in turn motivated countless other revolutionaries in their common goal of liberating India.'

on the bravery of Rani Laxmibai, Nanasaheb Peshwa and Tatya Tope, he is no less fulsome in eulogising the contribution of Maulvi Ahmed Shah and Azimullah Khan. It is, indeed, shocking that a great revolutionary figure like Savarkar from India's freedom movement has become the target of a vilification campaign by our ideological adversaries in the Congress and communist parties.

I met Savarkar (1883-1966) only once, in November 1947, soon after migrating from Karachi. I had gone to Bombay for two days, on what was my first visit to the city. The person I was staying with asked me which places I wished to see. I asked him to take me to Veer Savarkar's house. As I sat in awe of his magnetic presence at his Shivaji Park residence, he asked me about the situation in Sindh and the condition of Hindus after Partition. Remembering the question that Savarkar had asked me prompts me to recall the sad memory of one of my close friends in Karachi. One of them, Hira Singh, a Sikh, was my classmate and used to live close to my house in Karachi. He was one of the most dedicated *swayamsevaks* of our *shakha*. When communal violence broke out in the city in the run-up to Partition, his family faced grave hardships and had to flee. The only way he could save his own life was by trimming his hair and shaving off his beard. This experience had traumatised him so much that he became mentally disturbed for a long time. I often met him in Bombay, where he had settled, but he still carried the scars of that ordeal.

AT THE FEET OF SWAMI RANGANATHANANDA

During the last three years of my life in Karachi, I was exposed to another life-transforming influence. Every Sunday evening, I started going to the Ramakrishna Mission Ashram to listen to the discourses on the Bhagavad Gita by Swami Ranganathananda. I was as fascinated by Swamiji's personality as I was by his elucidation, in clear, direct and profound manner, of Lord Krishna's mesmerising philosophical dialogue with warrior Arjuna on the battlefield of Kurukshetra in the Mahabharata war.

Swamiji was, at that time, the President of the Ramakrishna Mission in Karachi, where he lived for six years propagating the teachings of

Ramakrishna Paramahansa and his disciple Swami Vivekananda. He had come to Karachi after having served for several years in the Ramakrishna Mission in distant Burma. And he hailed from Kerala! Swamiji, who had taken to the path of spirituality and humanitarian service at a very young age, was a disarmingly simple and amiable person. He soon developed a great fondness for me. In no time, his dedicated, mission-oriented and intellectually towering personality began to hold great attraction for me. 'I should develop these qualities,' I told myself.

Initially the audience for the Gita discourses was small—about fifty to hundred. But the number increased week after week and soon reached a thousand! As the Ashram was located in a Muslim locality, some Muslims also began to attend the lectures, as did Christians and Parsis, including Jamshed Nasarvanji Mehta, the former Mayor of Karachi. The Ashram also became a beehive of voluntary social service, in which I too contributed my bit. I recall the Bengal famine of 1943, in which millions died due to British war time policy. Swamiji issued an appeal to mobilise food and other relief material for the famine-stricken people. It evoked a generous response and nearly five lakh rupees were collected in no time. Swamiji used the funds to purchase rice and requested the Sindh government for an export permit to send it to Bengal in a steamer via Sri Lanka. An officer told him, 'You have to wait for your turn. The Muslim League also wants export permit for the same purpose. We'll give you the quota after they have used theirs.' After some weeks, the same officer told Swamiji, 'The Muslim League sent only sixty tons. The rest of the quota is all yours.' The Ashram sent 1240 tons.

Swamiji used to invite many distinguished personalities to visit the Ashram. I recall a memorable visit by Dr S. Radhakrishnan*, the great philosopher who was then the Vice Chancellor of the Banaras Hindu University (BHU), in October 1945. He delivered two talks, one at the Ashram and the other at D.J. Sindh College, both of which drew large crowds. Dr Radhakrishnan had requested Swamiji to collect some donations

---

* Dr Sarvepalli Radhakrishnan (1888-1975) was one of the most internationally renowned Indian philosophers and educationists of the twentieth century. He was the first Vice President of India (1952-62), and the second President of India (1962-67).

for BHU. The residents of Karachi gave him a purse of Rs 50,000, which was quite a significant amount those days.

I left Karachi in September 1947, whereas Swamiji continued living there until it became impossible to carry on the activities of the Ramakrishna Mission in the city. With a heavy heart, he closed down the Mission and left Karachi in August 1948. My association with him continued almost till the time he passed away in February 2005, at the age of ninety-eight. I would meet him regularly when he was the head of the Ramakrishna Mission in Delhi in the 1960s, and also when he headed the mission in Hyderabad for a long time thereafter. My last meeting with him was in 2003, when I had gone to Kolkata for a function, and Swamiji, after having become the all-India President of the Ramakrishna Mission, was living at Belur Math, the mission's headquarters in the city.

Our conversation at this last meeting centred on our days in Karachi, the tragic developments triggered by Partition and the role of Mohammed Ali Jinnah. Swamiji, in particular, lauded Jinnah's historic speech in the Constituent Assembly of Pakistan on 11 August 1947 and said, 'The true exposition of the meaning of secularism can be found in this speech.' In a subconscious way, this last conversation with Swamiji was to play a decisive contributory role in my own remarks about Jinnah when I went to Pakistan in May-June 2005.

Swami Ranganathananda was one of the brightest spiritual lights that shone upon Indian society in our times. He was an evolved soul, a seeker who began his life by working as a cook and dishwasher in the Ramakrishna Math, and rising to become one of the most revered propagators, both in India and abroad, of the teachings of Ramakrishna and Vivekananda. He was not a conventional spiritual preacher concerned predominantly with an individual's quest for self-realisation. His inspiringly crafted motto was: 'Godward passion transmuted into manward love.' His was a lifelong mission to tell the world that the myriad problems and challenges confronting it can be addressed only through a radical spiritual reorientation to human affairs.

Swamiji was prolific with both the spoken and the written word. A wandering monk, he gave thousands of lectures in cities across India and the world. For a spiritual leader who was completely detached from the material world, his lectures and writings covered a wide range of topics, including the role of teachers, administrators, scientists and businessmen in nation-building. He also interacted with political and social leaders from diverse backgrounds, leaving a positive impression on all of them. His four-volume work *Eternal Values for a Changing Society* pays respectful tribute to the teachings of all religions.

I recently came across a concise edition of Swamiji's four-volume writings on the *Bhagavad Gita*. Titled *The Charm and Power of the Gita*, Swamiji in the book gives an example to illustrate the difference between the traditional orientation towards the *Gita* and the new **man-making** and **nation-building** orientation towards the *Gita*, which was imparted by Swami Vivekananda. 'In the past', Swamiji writes, 'people mostly read the *Gita* as a pious act, and for a little peace of mind. We never realized that this is a book of intense practicality. We never understood the practical application of the *Gita*'s teachings. If we had done so, we would not have had the thousand years of foreign invasions, internal caste conflicts, feudal oppression and mass poverty. We never took the *Gita* seriously; but now we have to. We need a philosophy that can help us build a new welfare society, based on human dignity, freedom and equality. This new orientation, this practical orientation was given to the *Gita* for the first time in the modern age by Swami Vivekananda.'

In September 2007, I was invited to release a biography of Swami Ranganathananda at Ramakrishna Math in Paranattukara in Trichur district in Kerala, not far from his birthplace. In that biography, I came across an essay by Dr T.I. Radhakrishnan, a longtime associate of Swamiji, who records an interesting incident. Once when Swamiji was delivering a lecture on Islam and Prophet Mohammed in Karachi, one person entered the hall and sat in the last row. It was Mohammed Ali Jinnah. After the lecture, Jinnah reportedly rushed to the dais and said, 'Swamiji, so far I had believed that I am a real Muslim. After listening to your speech, I understand that I am not. But with your blessings, I will try to become a real Muslim.' The author of this essay says that Swamiji had similar experiences with Christians when he lectured on 'The Christ We Adore'.

BIDDING ADIEU TO SINDH

I do not know how good a Muslim Jinnah was in his faith and practice. But history is witness to the fact that, next to the British, he was the principal architect of the Partition of India on communal lines. It was he who declared, in 1940, that 'Hindus and Muslims are two different nations who can never live together.'[4] At the same time, there is also considerable evidence to show that, once Pakistan was created, he was not in full control of his own creation. According to Dr Ajeet Jawed, who has written a well-researched and widely acclaimed book on Jinnah, 'He was a sad and sick man. He cried in agony, "I have committed the biggest blunder in creating Pakistan and would like to go to Delhi and tell Nehru to forget the follies of the past and become friends again." He had even begun to hate Liaqat Ali, on whose request and persuasion he had come back to India from England in 1937 and has assumed the leadership of the Muslim League.'[5]

M.S.M. Sharma, who was the Editor of the *Daily Gazette* of Karachi at the time of Partition, and was quite close to Jinnah, records many revealing incidents from the last year of Jinnah's life in Pakistan. These portray a frustrated man suffering from inner conflict, apart from failing health. 'He was anxious to revert to his old and familiar role of Ambassador of Hindu-Muslim unity. He proposed that he should continue as the champion of minorities in Pakistan as he had been, for several years now, the champion of the minorities in India.' He even told Sharma: 'Now, my dear friend, I am going to constitute myself as the Protector-General of the Hindu minority in Pakistan.'[6] According to several authors, Jinnah even had tears in his eyes when he visited a Hindu refugee camp in Karachi.[7]

*

Sadly, as I have described in the first chapter, the situation on the ground in Pakistan was totally different. Nothing that Jinnah said or did was able to allay the fear and panic that increasingly gripped the lives of Hindus in Karachi and other parts of Sindh after the formation of Pakistan. Hence, my last days in Sindh were full of turmoil and turbulence. The mammoth rally of Hindus in Karachi on 5 August, organised by the RSS and addressed by Shri Guruji, was no doubt a morale booster. But it could not stop the tempest of communal hatred and violence wrought by Partition.

Around this time, an unexpected incident occurred which precipitated the end of my own days in Sindh. On 9 September, a bomb explosion took place in the elitist Shikarpuri Colony of Karachi. In the wake of this blast, the RSS *Sanghchalak* Khanchand Gopaldas and nineteen other prominent *swayamsewaks* of the RSS were arrested. Rajpalji had gone to Delhi to attend a national meeting of RSS *prant pracharaks*.

I had known nothing about the blasts. Nevertheless, since the local press started to level wild charges against the RSS, my colleagues advised me to leave Karachi. Accordingly, I left for Delhi by air on 12 September. Accompanied by Murlidhar, a fellow RSS *swayamsevak*, I boarded a BOAC propeller aircraft. This was my first ever journey by plane, made more memorable by the fact that I was travelling as a refugee from Pakistan, like millions of others, seeking shelter and a new beginning in truncated India.

4

PARTITION: WHO WAS RESPONSIBLE?

Woh waqt gaya woh daur gaya jab do qaumon ka naara tha
Woh log gaye is dharti se jinka maqsad batwaara tha

(That time, and that era, are gone when the slogan of 'Two Nations'
rent the air. And gone from this world are those people whose
purpose was to partition our Motherland.)

—Sahir Ludhianvi, a renowned film lyricist

The BOAC aircraft, carrying me from Karachi to Delhi, was so unlike the planes we fly in today that it would be considered primitive by modern standards. But it was state-of-the-art in aviation those days. A twenty-year-old youth like myself would, in normal circumstances, have been completely enthralled by the pleasure of maiden air travel. But I had to forego that pleasure, on that morning of 12 September 1947, due to the extraordinary and tragic situation of my departure from Karachi to Delhi.

While on the flight, I never realised when I left Pakistan's air space behind and entered into India's. On the ground, however, the boundary, invisible from the sky, was being drawn in blood, literally. Instead of the joy of freedom from the British rule, there were shrieks of communal killings and frantic migration of panicked families, hundreds of thousands of them, in both directions. Delhi was by no means free from this tension and turbulence. Most of the Punjabi refugees, Hindu as well as Sikh, were pouring into the national capital.

My in-flight reflections too were focused on my own immediate concerns—Who would I meet in Delhi? How could we ensure the safety of people migrating from Sindh and where could they be rehabilitated? What would we do to secure the release of the *swayamsevaks* arrested in Karachi? It was not possible for me at the time to think of the larger tragedy, of which I too was a victim. However, with the passage of time, I have repeatedly reflected upon the one question that millions of people on both sides of the border have asked themselves: *Could this tragedy have been averted?*

It was no ordinary tragedy. Partition riots resulted in the slaughter of nearly one million Hindus, Sikhs and Muslims on both sides of the hurriedly drawn borders. The haste and indiscriminateness that marked the British action of drawing the borders also caused the largest ever cross-migration of population in human history. More than ten million people became refugees within a time span of merely six months. Irrespective of whether they were Hindu, Muslim or Sikh, their suffering was the same. Partition was bad enough. But it was made immeasurably worse, with its painful memories lasting for a long time, by the callous manner in which it was carried out.

Most of the migrants were wondering why the exit of the British resulted in their own exit from their ancestral homes and villages, where their families had lived for centuries. In the copious literature on Partition that I have read in subsequent years, I was deeply touched by the comments from two ordinary refugees. 'This country has seen many changes of rulers,' an old Muslim villager in Punjab said. 'Rulers have come and gone. But this is the first time that with a change of rulers the subjects are also being forced to change.' Similarly, an elderly Hindu woman posed this question to Pandit Nehru, 'Partitions take place in all families. Property changes hands, but it is all arranged peacefully. Why this butchery, loot and abductions? Could you not do it the sensible way families divide?'

Who was responsible for the division of the great Indian Family, and the butchery that accompanied it? I hold the Muslim League primarily guilty. The Two Nation Theory propounded by it to rationalise its demand for the creation of Pakistan as a separate 'Muslim homeland' was deeply flawed. As I have explained earlier, it had no basis in truth—social, cultural or spiritual. To argue that Hindus and Muslims constituted two separate nations was an affront to their shared history of over a thousand years. The flaw in the Muslim League's demand was further aggravated by its aggression and obstinacy in attaining this demand. The Direct Action* call given by the League on 16 August 1946 resulted in the killing of thousands of innocent persons, mostly Hindus, in Calcutta in what came to be known as 'The Week of Long Knives'. The panic created by the massacre in Calcutta could be felt even in distant Karachi. Although few could foresee it then, the bloodshed was a precursor to what was to happen in the months immediately before and after Partition.

But was the Muslim League alone responsible for the tragedy of Partition? I do not believe so. We cannot forget the culpability of the British, which was evident not only in the 'Divide and Rule' policy adopted by them, especially vigorously, after the 1857 War of Independence, but also in the manner in which they finally divided India. I have found the most persuasive account of Britain's guilt in imparting a bloody denouement to Partition in Stanley Wolpert's book *Shameful Flight: The Last Years of the British Empire in India*. Wolpert, an eminent American historian, who has authored many acclaimed books on India and Pakistan, became a good acquaintance of mine after he met me in New Delhi in 1998. He had brought his latest book *India*, which begins with a profound description

---

* 'Direct Action' was the campaign launched by the Muslim League to demand immediate acceptance of its demand for Pakistan. It started on 16 August 1946, when massive riots were instigated by the League in Calcutta and the surrounding regions of Bengal and Bihar. Within 72 hours, more than 6,000 people lost their lives, at least 20,000 were seriously injured and 100,000 residents of Calcutta were left homeless.

of our country: 'India is the world's most ancient civilization, yet one of its youngest nations. Much of the paradox found everywhere in India is the product of her inextricable antiquity and youth.'*

In *Shameful Flight* (2007) Wolpert holds Lord Louis Mountbatten, the last Viceroy of India, primarily guilty for the horrendous human tragedy that accompanied his ill-conceived time-table for partitioning Punjab and Bengal. British Prime Minister Clement Atlee had announced on 20 February 1947 that His Majesty's Government (HMG) intended to transfer power to Indians, in a united or partitioned India, by June 1948. Mountbatten arrived in India in March 1947. In a maddeningly short span of five months, he completed the task of dividing India in August 1947, with little regard for the horrific consequences of such rushed action.

Wolpert shows that Mountbatten was well aware of the likely violence and the lack of an effective plan to deal with it. The maps of India and Pakistan drawn by Cyril Radcliffe were guarded with utmost secrecy, and the people residing in areas that were to fall along the boundary lines were deliberately kept in the dark. This naturally created tremendous uncertainty in their minds. And uncertainty often results in suspicion, which turns neighbour against neighbour, more so in a communally charged atmosphere. Coupled with the sudden collapse of the British law and order machinery, it aggravated fratricidal violence. The bitterness and prejudice that this 'Shameful Flight' generated has continued to blight relations between India and Pakistan even sixty years after that tragic event.

It is, of course, equally true that there are countless accounts of neighbour protecting neighbour; these inspiring acts kept the flame of hope and brotherhood from being completely extinguished by the typhoon of bestiality. Nevertheless, these isolated incidents of benevolence cannot lessen the human loss, grief and pain caused by the Partition riots. Whether Partition itself could have been avoided or not is a question that has beguiled historians. I am, however, convinced that Partition riots were, to a large extent, avoidable.

---

* Stanley Wolpert wrote the following inscription in a copy he presented to me: 'To one whose leadership has brought the Party of Bharat to central power.'

My reflections on the tragedy of Partition would remain incomplete if I did not express my views on the role of the Congress leadership. I share the highest regard and a deep sense of gratitude that every patriotic Indian has towards the stalwarts of India's freedom movement. Nevertheless, in the face of a colossal catastrophe in the life of a nation, it is natural for an inquisitive mind to ask the question: 'Should our leaders have conducted themselves differently to avert the blood-soaked division of India?' In answering this question, I tend to agree with the analysis of the eminent socialist leader Dr Ram Manohar Lohia, with whom I would interact closely in later years. In his book *The Guilty Men of Partition*, Dr Lohia contends that, with the exception of Mahatma Gandhi, most Congress leaders were 'tired' after long years of struggle and wanted to see India become independent in their own lifetime. They agreed to Partition, much against the advice of Gandhiji, because they were led to believe by Mountbatten that it was the best and the quickest solution to the Hindu-Muslim dispute. Clearly, it was an error of judgement, though not one of intent.

Pandit Nehru himself later admitted the blunder in these words: 'When we decided on Partition I do not think any of us ever thought that there would be this terror of mutual killing after Partition. It was in a sense to avoid that that we decided on Partition. So we paid a double price for it, first, you might say politically, ideologically; second, the actual thing happened what we tried to avoid.' Sardar Patel also later stated that he should never have consented to Partition. 'You cannot divide the sea or the waters of the river,' he said.

Only the Mahatma remained unreconciled to Partition until the very end. Above all else, he believed India's division on communal lines to be an ungodly act. Although he too ultimately gave his consent, he did so in the desperate hope that Partition could bring the ongoing communal bloodbath to an end. He harnessed his entire moral force to spread the message of peace and harmony in the midst of flames of hatred and violence. He did succeed, but only partially and locally, such as in Noakhali where he undertook a heroic *padyatra*. Elsewhere, he too was powerless to stop the killings and the two-way movement of refugees. Clearly, Partition and its cruel aftermath, once set in motion, had attained a force of inevitability beyond any human control.

As we reminisce, we cannot but be struck by the collective inability of the leaders of our freedom movement to anticipate the likely negative course of events and, hence, to try to prevent its inevitability. One way of looking at their failure is to recognise that they too were, after all, human. And to err is human. More often than not, it is not human beings who control their own history but history that controls them. Having said this, I also feel that a nation is better served if its people and leaders acquire a better understanding history and forge stronger unity and, thereby, a greater ability to shape its destiny. For this, we—and by 'we' I mean both the people and their leaders—need not only a truer knowledge of India's past but also a sounder vision of India's future. We should know where we as a nation have come from, and where we ought to go. We should know, too, the fundamental basis of India's unity so that we appreciate the basic absurdity of India's Partition. This, according to me, is the main lesson that we should learn from the epochal development that took place in India's history in August 1947.

FARSIGHTED AND OPTIMISTIC THOUGHTS OF TWO SEERS

In the preceding pages, I have described the seminal influence that Swami Ranganathananda, the head of the Ramakrishna Mission in Karachi, had on me in my formative years in Sindh. Like me, he and his institution in Karachi too were victims of Partition. The Ramakrishna Math was vandalised by communal mobs and, with great reluctance and utter helplessness, Swamiji left Karachi for good in August 1948.

While still in Karachi, Swami Ranganathananda wrote a lengthy essay on 15 August 1947 reflecting upon the past, present and future of India. I consider this, along with Maharshi Aurobindo's radio address to the nation on the previous day, as the two most profoundly philosophical articulations of Indian nationalism. Reading these two, I feel as if it is the Soul of India that is speaking. Both belong to India's long and hoary *rishi parampara* (tradition of seers) and both have prophesied that the division of India is not the final and irreversible development in the history of our ancient nation.

Swami Ranganathananda writes: 'When the abnormalities of the present situation with its gushing passions and blinding hates will pass away, leaving the Indian sky clear, the country will recognise the correctness and cogency of the above faith and vision; the faith of a steady few will then become the enthusiasm of the many, leading to a reconciliation and reunion of the sundered parts, and the unsettling of a settled fact through popular will.'

Similarly, Maharshi Aurobindo, too, says: 'The old communal division into Hindus and Muslims seems now to have hardened into a permanent political division of the country. It is to be hoped that this settled fact will not be accepted as settled for ever or as anything more than a temporary expedient.… This must not be; the partition must go. Let us hope that that may come about naturally, by an increasing recognition of the necessity not only of peace and concord but of common action, by the practice of common action and the creation of means for that purpose. In this way unity may finally come about under whatever form—the exact form may have a pragmatic but not a fundamental importance. But by whatever means, in whatever way, the division must go; unity must and will be achieved, for it is necessary for the greatness of India's future.'

I seek the indulgence of the readers to reproduce the two texts as appendices. Suffice it to say here that the hope of Mahayogi Aurobindo (Appendix I) and Swami Ranganathananda (Appendix II) remains my hope too. It is a hope that Pandit Deendayal Upadhyaya and Dr Rammanohar Lohia, the great socialist leader, had articulated in the form of a confederation between India and Pakistan in their historic joint statement in 1964. It is the same hope that I have often expressed by endorsing the concept of the confederation, which should also include Bangladesh.

*

All that I have written above on the calamity of Partition, those responsible for it, and how we might possibly undo its worst effects in the future is, obviously, a perspective I have gained in hindsight in later decades. It is the outcome of study and contemplation during my life as a political activist in India, throughout which, with the passing of each year, my departure from Sindh has become a distant memory. However, as I have mentioned earlier, the thoughts that preoccupied me as I departed from Karachi on the BOAC flight were anchored in my own immediate concerns: How will I meet Rajpalji? How will I find the RSS office in Delhi?

I should, therefore, take this narrative to the point where my air journey from Karachi to Delhi brings the formative phase of my life in Sindh to an abrupt end, and also inaugurates the next phase of my life—as a RSS *pracharak* in Rajasthan.

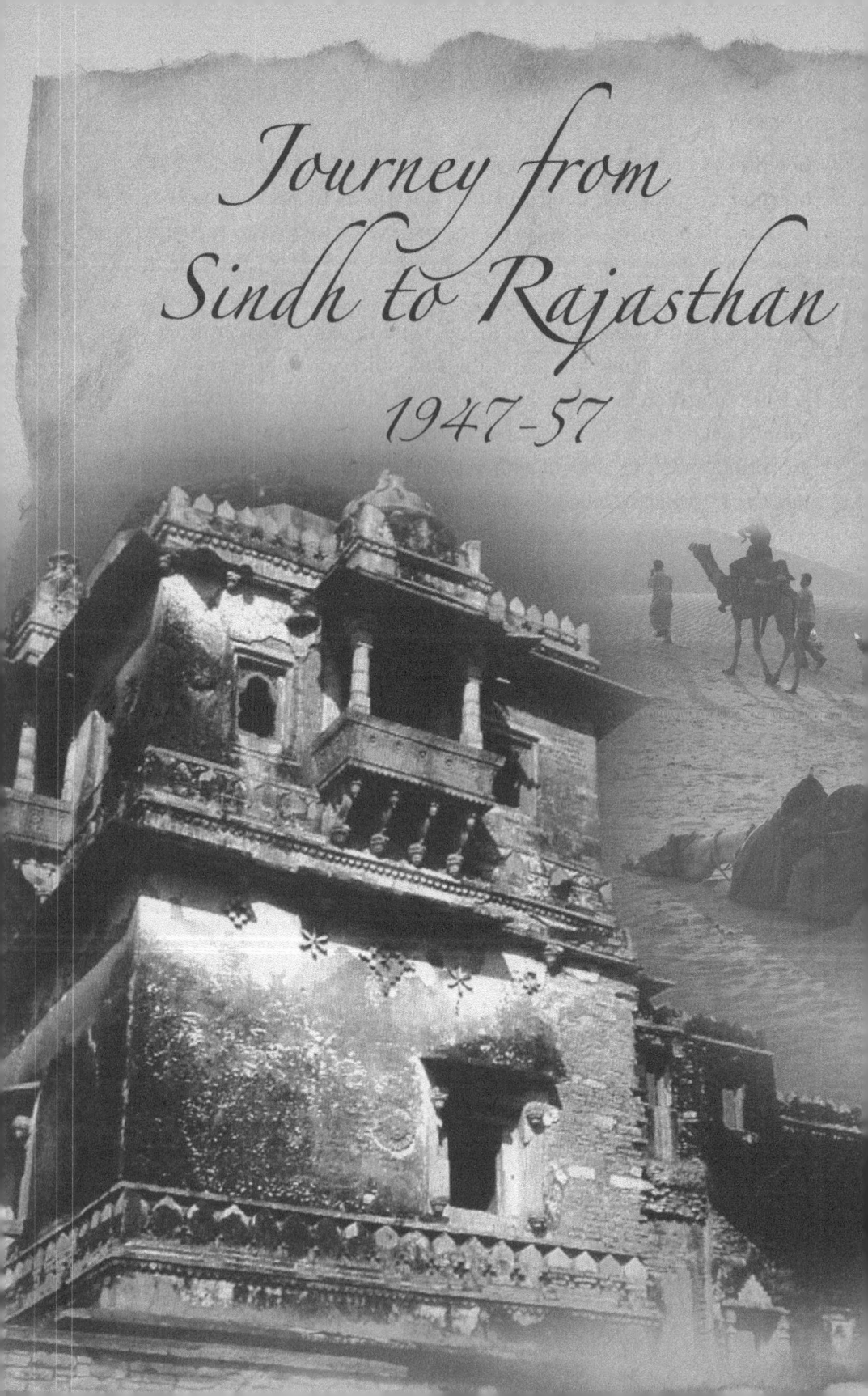

Journey from Sindh to Rajasthan
1947-57

'My experiences as a RSS pracharak toughened me during the ten years I spent in Rajasthan. They made me aware of the harsh realities of life under which millions of my countrymen were condemned to live. Life was hard in terms of physical comfort, but extremely rewarding by way of psychological and spiritual satisfaction. One day, in 1952, while on a tour of Rajasthan, Pandit Deendayal Upadhyaya asked me to take up organisational responsibility for the Jana Sangh in the state. Thus began my journey as a political activist.'

Phase Two

1

MIGRATION FROM SINDH TO RAJASTHAN

Ladeenda vanjan tha pakhi, desh pehnjo chadeenda vanjan tha

(Birds are migrating, birds are leaving their own lands)

—From a song by Sindhi poet Master Chander

The BOAC flight landed at Delhi's Palam airport around noon. The journey from Karachi to Delhi, which now takes about ninety minutes, lasted nearly six hours.

Delhi was an unfamiliar city for both my colleague and fellow-traveller, Murlidhar, and me. Our first and foremost task was to meet Rajpalji, our *prant pracharak* in Sindh who had come to Delhi for an important meeting of the RSS. But we had no idea where to find him. I had only heard of two names in Delhi: Vasantrao Oak, who was the *prant pracharak*, and Lala Harichand, Delhi's *sanghchalak* who lived somewhere in Sitaram Bazaar. The purpose of our visit was two-fold: firstly, to hold consultations with Rajpalji as to what should be done in the wake of the sudden turn of events; and secondly, to request him not to return to Sindh, because he was likely to be arrested.

When we entered the nearby Delhi Cantonment area, we asked someone, 'Do you know any RSS worker here?' The man said, 'Go to the shop out there. He is an RSS man.' Walking up to the shopkeeper, I said, 'We want to go to the RSS office at Sitaram Bazaar.' He looked at us with bemused eyes, and said, 'That's very far. It is in the city. Besides, you cannot go there; it is under curfew on account of riots.' We then asked him if he knew any RSS leader in a non-curfew area. He looked at us intently again and said, 'Relax. You seem to be tired after a long journey. Come to my house, have a bath, eat something, and I'll take you to the right person.'

Through his contact, we were finally able to meet Vasantrao Oak, who informed us that Rajpalji had left for Jodhpur *en route* to Karachi. The news unnerved me. I had to somehow contact Rajpalji and stop him from going back to Sindh. The same night, Murlidhar and I boarded a train to Jodhpur to meet him.

Upon reaching Jodhpur, I was told that a message had come from Sindh that I should not return. Besides, I learnt that all *pracharaks* and senior leaders of the RSS from Sindh had been asked to assemble in Jodhpur where, in due course, we would receive instructions regarding the tasks to be carried out in the coming days. Meanwhile, Rajpalji had already left Jodhpur for Karachi by train, totally unaware of the developments that had taken place in Karachi during his absence. It was at the railway station in Mirpur Khas, about 220 kilometres from Karachi, that he learnt about the developments. He immediately broke journey, contacted local *swayamsewaks* and proceeded to Karachi by car. Ensuring the safety of the Hindu community in Sindh, he felt, was his predominant responsibility. It was later that I came to know of the harrowing time trying to avoid the police he had during his stay at Karachi.

The RSS leaders instructed the *swayamsewaks* who had come from Pakistan that their main task to help channelise the migration of refugees in a smooth and systematic manner. We were also required to assist in the relief and rehabilitation of the immigrants. The latter half of 1947 saw us plunging ourselves in this work wholeheartedly.

Those days there was an informal understanding between the Governments of India and Pakistan on the exchange of prisoners. Hindu prisoners in Pakistani jails, who wished to migrate to India were exchanged for Muslim prisoners in Indian jails, who were desirous of going to Pakistan. The agreement also stipulated that political prisoners would be set free after the exchange. However, those convicted for criminal activities were required to serve the remaining period of their jail term after migration. There was also an understanding on the exchange of persons mentally disturbed by the trauma of the riots. Sadat Hasan Manto, the well-known Urdu writer, later wrote a deeply moving story titled 'Toba Tek Singh' on this theme.

I was asked by Rajpalji to go to Ferozepur to receive the prisoners who were being exchanged—all the twenty RSS workers who had been arrested in the Shikarpuri Colony Bomb Case on 9 September 1947. When the train arrived, I could only see their leader Khanchand Gopaldas. 'Where are the others?' I asked him, in a worried voice. He was equally surprised and concerned. 'I don't know. They made me board the train at Karachi, and said that the others were travelling in a different compartment.' The Pakistani authorities were obviously up to some mischief.

We met Shri Guruji in Delhi and informed him about the missing nineteen RSS prisoners from Karachi. He immediately tried to contact Home Minister Sardar Patel, but he was unavailable. He then got in touch with N.V. Gadgil, Minister in Charge of Refugee Affairs. Gadgil assured him, 'Don't worry. It is my responsibility to ensure the release of every RSS worker arrested in Pakistan.' Within a month, much to our relief, the remaining nineteen *swayamsevaks* arrived safely from Karachi.

One of them, Dhanraj Ojha, continued his political activities in Delhi and went on to become the General Secretary of the city unit of the Jana Sangh. Most of the others settled in Bombay. Prominent among them were Nand Badlani and Dr Ram Hingorani.

RSS *SWAYAMSEVAKS'* COMMENDABLE RESCUE AND REHABILITATION WORK

The first and most urgent task for the RSS at that time was to provide protection to Hindus and Sikhs in riot-torn areas and to mobilise relief work for the deluge of refugees from Punjab and other parts of newly created Pakistan. I should explain here why the responsibility fell squarely on the shoulders of the RSS. The Hindus and Sikhs had pinned high hopes on the Congress leaders to foil the Muslim League's mission to divide India on communal lines, but save for the Mahatma, most of the other Congress leaders had acquiesced in the fatal decision.

This came as an unprecedented shock for the Hindus and Sikhs in Pakistan. The refugees who fled from Pakistan were totally vulnerable in the wake of the communal conflagration. They, as well as the native Hindu and Sikh residents on the Indian side, needed—and expected from the Indian government—protection when Partition became a *fait accompli*. The scale and severity of communal violence was such that Sardar Patel, India's Home Minister, declared that the government was not in a position to protect the life and honour of every individual. In such a desperate scenario, the RSS had to step in to protect the people.

Later, Sardar Patel appreciated the rescue and relief operations carried out by the RSS. This is what the *Hindu* of 7 January 1948 reported: 'Sardar Patel realised that they (RSS) were not actuated by selfish motives. The situation demanded they should strengthen the hands of the Government and assist in maintaining peace…. He also had a word of warning for some of his own partymen. He said, "In the Congress those who are in power feel that by virtue of their authority they will be able to crush the RSS. You cannot crush an organisation by using the *danda* (stick). The *danda* is meant for thieves and dacoits. After all the RSS men are not thieves and, dacoits. They are patriots who love their country."'

2

My work as a RSS Pracharak

Namaste Sadaa Vatsale Matrubhoome

(My salutation to you, ever loving Motherland)

—The patriotic prayer recited in the rss SHAKHA

After the Jodhpur camp was over, all of us from Sindh were sent to different parts of Rajasthan to continue the activities of the RSS. For the next decade, Rajasthan, beautiful yet forbidding, was to be my *karmabhoomi* (place of work), first only as a *pracharak* of the RSS but, mid way through, also as a whole-time party activist of the Bharatiya Jana Sangh.

I had a fascination for Rajasthan even before I set foot on its soil, rendered sacred by the martyrdom of hundreds of its patriotic people. This land of brave Rajputs, Jats, Bhils, Ahirs, Gujars, Meenas and other tribes had borne the brunt of recurring Muslim invasions. The numerous forts of Rajasthan and their unsurpassed majesty is a testament to the valour of the kings who had built them. They have been a mute witness to the highs and lows of Rajasthan's history. It was here that Mewar's King Rana Sanga fought Babur in the Battle of Khanua (1527). This great figure of medieval India, who lost an eye, a leg and an arm in the battlefield and had eighty wound marks on his body, was nevertheless a threat to the Mughal army. It was here that Maharana Pratap had an epic encounter with Akbar in Haldighati (1576). I was especially mesmerised by the saga of Chittorgarh Fort, which had been sacked thrice by Allauddin Khilji, the Sultan of Delhi (1296-1316), and whose evil designs to lay hands on the beautiful Queen Padmini were thwarted by her ritual self-sacrifice, *jauhar*.

I had read these inspiring tales during my years in Hyderabad and Karachi. And now that destiny had brought me to Rajasthan, I felt that the work of the RSS was, in many ways, a continuation of the state's glorious tradition of patriotism and selfless service.

At the outset, I looked after the Sangh's activities in Alwar city. Thereafter, my responsibility extended to the entire district. Later still, it was extended further to the neighbouring Bharatpur district. The process of integration of all the nineteen princely states into a single entity called Rajasthan was a cumbersome process, involving seven stages, over a period of eight years (1948-56). In the first stage in 1948, a provincial entity described as *Matsya Raj* was formed. This comprised the princely states of Alwar, Bharatpur, Karauli and Dholpur. Informally, as a *pracharak* in the region, I was responsible for these four states.

My organisational work entailed two tasks: strengthening and expanding the activities in the existing *shakhas* and, also, opening new ones. It also necessitated constant travelling. Many places were accessible by bus, although the roads then were a far cry from what they are now. However, there were other places to where the only mode of transport was either a bicycle or a camel. I remember travelling often to a village called Narayanpur in the Alwar district. The bus from Alwar would go only up to Thana Gazi, from where Narayanpur was twelve miles away. The final destination could only be reached only on camel.

I was to recall and relive this experience after more than a half century. Once in 2001, when I was the Union Home Minister, I went to Jaisalmer in Rajasthan to inspect the forward deployment of the Border Security Force (BSF). Jaisalmer, which is located in the desert area of the state, borders

Pakistan. For vast stretches of the territory, all one sees is undulating sand dunes that lend a delicate, almost unearthly touch of beauty to the landscape. Here BSF jawans are trained in camel riding, which in many parts of the state is the only means of transportation. In fact, during the Republic Day Parade held in New Delhi every year, a special attraction for the viewers is the spectacular Camel Contingent of the BSF, and also its band, the only contingent of its kind in the world. During my visit, a BSF officer asked me if I was keen on a camel ride. I readily agreed and as I mounted this gentle animal, I remembered my *pracharak* days in the Alwar district, and my long camel rides to Narayanpur.

Travelling in Rajasthan was always an adventure. I remember an incident while returning from Bharatpur, which is home to India's best-known bird sanctuary. One day I had to go to a small town called Sikri for a RSS programme. The journey required taking a bus from Bharatpur to Kama, and then another bus from Kama to Sikri. After reaching Kama, I was told that the bus to Sikri had been cancelled because of heavy rains. But since it was an important function which I could not skip, I decided to undertake the journey on foot, walking forty-five kilometres to reach Sikri in time for the function. It took me ten hours or so, and was the longest of many such walkathons I undertook as a RSS *pracharak*.

Apart from organising routine activities at RSS *shakhas*, I used to take special interest in teaching young volunteers, thus continuing the pedagogic hobby that I had cultivated in Karachi. Most of the volunteers were keen on learning English, and other subjects taught in English. Even now, I sometimes receive visitors from Alwar, telling me that I had taught them a particular subject.

THE LESSONS IN HARDINESS AND DISCIPLINE

A RSS *pracharak* lives very simply. He is austere and hardworking. I regularly used to wash my own clothes besides cooking. If I returned late from work or was too tired to cook, I would just have a glass of hot milk, sometimes with a local sweet called *gajak*. I was never deterred by hardships on account of food, money, travel or the harsh climate of

Rajasthan. However—and this may surprise readers—I was scared of one thing: tapeworm. After the ban on the RSS was lifted in July 1949, I was assigned work in the Hadoti region of the state, which comprised the three districts of Kota, Bundi and Jhalawar. Here I was intrigued by the daily sight of somebody or the other in the *shakha* sporting a bandage on his leg. I was told that they were victims of *nerwa*, a water-borne tapeworm disease.

In the entire area, only Kota had tap water supply. Everywhere else, people depended on ponds and wells for drinking and all other purposes. Since these were not well maintained and only infrequently purified, they had become sources of a peculiar disease with which I was completely unfamiliar. When the worm broke through the skin on the victim's leg, the victim would dip his leg in water to ease the pain and itching. This immersion in water caused the worm to further protrude from the victim's body. The victim then had to take a small wooden stick, spool the worm around, and slowly and patiently pull it out. However, if the worm broke in the process, it would quickly retreat and pop out from some other place on the leg. This was an extremely painful experience. Hence, for all the years I was working in this area, whenever I saw a *swayamsevak* with a bandage on his leg I would fearfully wonder—'What if I too get *nerwa*?'

I had a different, fearful experience when I was once in a village in the Chittor district. I had stayed overnight at a *swayamsevak*'s house. When I got up in the morning, he asked me, '*Bhai sahab*, would you like to have a bath at the well or shall I fetch some water for you here?' I replied that I would prefer going to the well. When we went there, I discovered that it was hardly a well, just a small *bawdi* (water hole). When my companion saw the look of surprise on my face, he said, 'Don't worry. Just jump and you'll enjoy it.' I did so, flapping my hands and legs as much as I could in the water, and after a while came back to the top. As I glanced back at the well, I was shocked by what I saw. On the surface there were literally hundreds of snakes, which must have been resting against the walls, but had obviously been disturbed by my swimming. As I rushed back, my bemused host said to me, 'Nothing to be scared of. These are harmless water snakes!'

I remember another tormenting experience from my days in Rajasthan. I had to unexpectedly go to Delhi for some urgent work. It was already evening and I had to be there the following morning. Unfortunately, there was no bus or passenger train available at that time. There was, however, a slow-moving goods train that was scheduled to arrive soon. The only option for me was to somehow find a place on this freight train, with the permission of the guard. He was a kind person who said, half-jokingly, 'Make yourself comfortable on one of these salt-beds.' It happened to be a train carrying salt in uncovered carriages. It was December, one of the coldest months in North India. To make things even more 'comfortable' for me, the winter mist had spread a wet blanket over the heap of salt. With wet salt as my bed and the winter air as my blanket, I shivered the entire night.

It is experiences like these which toughened me during my ten years in Rajasthan. They made me aware of the harsh realities of life faced everyday by millions of my countrymen and also imparted a welcome discipline to my daily habits. I learnt to live frugally. Of course, I was, by no means, an exception in this regard. I had no personal expenses as such. The life of all RSS *pracharaks* was tough in terms of physical comfort, but extremely rewarding by way of psychological and spiritual satisfaction.

3

Mahatma Gandhi's tragic assassination

*Generations to come will scarce believe that such
a one as this walked the earth in flesh and blood.*

— Tribute to Mahatma Gandhi by Albert Einstein,
the great physicist

Very early in my life in Rajasthan, the RSS had to face, what was undoubtedly the greatest ordeal in its history. I was in Alwar when, on the evening of 30 January 1948 came the tragic news that Mahatma Gandhi had been assassinated in Delhi while he was proceeding to his customary all-faith prayer meeting. To say that I was shell-shocked is an understatement.

The RSS had some differences with Gandhiji regarding his approach to securing India's freedom. But these were minor, which never detracted from the high regard the Sangh had for the Mahatma. Speaking for myself, I had developed, even at that early stage in my public life, a deep respect for him—and a reverence that would only grow stronger with the passage of time. What had impressed me most about Gandhiji was his absolute honesty and the purity of his personality.

The person who had committed this sinful crime was Nathuram Vinayak Godse, an activist of the Hindu Mahasabha from Maharashtra. He had once been a *swayamsevak* of the RSS, but had left the organisation nearly fifteen years ago due to his strong ideological differences with the Sangh. He had in fact become a bitter critic of the RSS, charging that 'the RSS has made the Hindus impotent'. His main grouse was that the RSS had sublimated the 'militant spirit' among the Hindus, making them incapable of aggressive action. He ridiculed the Sangh's focus on character-building. His articles in the Marathi magazine *Agrani* (which means 'Pioneer') from 1933 onwards show how bitter he was toward the RSS.

The RSS Chief, Shri Guruji, was in Madras when he heard the news of Gandhiji's assassination. He immediately sent a telegram to Prime Minister Jawaharlal Nehru, Deputy Prime Minister Sardar Patel and Mahatma's son, Devdas Gandhi, expressing his shock and sorrow at the 'cruel and fatal attack on a great personality.' On the same day, he also sent a telegram instructing all units of the Sangh to observe a thirteen-day mourning, as per the Hindu custom, at the 'sad death of revered Mahatmaji'. We were ordered to suspend all activities of the organisation during this mourning period.

In a letter which Shri Guruji sent to Prime Minister Nehru from Nagpur the following day, he condemned Godse's crime in even more anguished and unambiguous terms. 'This reprehensible deed by an unthinking and corrupt-hearted person has smeared our society in the eyes of the world. Even if a person from an enemy country had committed this black deed, it would have been unpardonable because Poojya Mahatmaji's life had transcended the boundaries of a specific society and was dedicated to the welfare of the entire humanity. But since the perpetrator of this sinful act belongs to our own country, it is not surprising that the heart of every nationalist is today filled with unbearable pain. From the time I heard this news, a void has filled my inner being. Such attack on an adept leader who could bring together people of different tendencies and set them on a righteous path is indeed treacherous—not only towards the victim but the entire nation.' He went on to exhort the Prime Minister to deal with the Mahatma's assassin in an 'appropriate manner'. 'Howsoever harsh the treatment meted out to him may be it would necessarily seem mild in comparison to the bereavement we have suffered.'

GANDHIJI AND RSS—A MUTUTALLY RESPECTFUL RELATIONSHIP

I have quoted from Shri Guruji's letter because it exposes the lie, still being spread by our detractors today, that the RSS was filled with hatred for Gandhiji and had a hand in his assassination. The letter clearly underscores the RSS's respect and admiration for Gandhiji and its abhorrence toward his assassin. It is necessary to dwell a little more here on the mutually respectful relationship between the two. In its *Ekatmataa Stotra*, a set of Sanskrit prayers as an ode to India's national integration, the RSS regards the Mahatma as one of the *pratah smaraneeya* personalities (persons worthy of being reverentially remembered every morning). Addressing the Sangh Shiksha Varg (the annual training session for would-be organisers of the RSS) of 1946—when Gandhiji was still alive—Shri Guruji had described him as *Vishwa vandaneeya* (deserving of being revered across the world).

Gandhiji first visited a RSS camp on 25 December 1934 at Wardha in Maharashtra, where he had established one of his ashrams. Gandhiji had come to Wardha and learning that about 1,500 *swayamsevaks* of the RSS had assembled in the town, he expressed his desire to visit the camp. He was accompanied by Mira Behn and his secretary Mahadev Desai. He was garlanded with flowers and given a guard of honour. 'I am tremendously impressed,' said Gandhiji speaking of his visit, referring, in particular, to the fact that there was no caste distinction among the volunteers and no untouchability towards those belonging to so-called 'low' castes.

Soon after Independence, when the atmosphere in the country was marred by communal violence and lack of trust between Hindus and Muslims, Gandhiji sent out a message that he wanted to talk to Shri Guruji. Shri Guruji immediately went to Birla House to see him on 12 September 1947. Gandhiji mentioned to him the various complaints about the Sangh that he had received in Calcutta and Delhi. Shri Guruji assured him that, although he could not vouch for the behaviour of each *swayamsevak*, the Sangh's policy was purely service of Hindus and Hinduism. It did not threaten any other community, he clarified. The Sangh might not believe in *ahimsa* (non-violence), but neither did it advocate aggression. The *swayamsevaks* were only taught the art of self-defence.

In this meeting between Gandhiji and Shri Guruji, both agreed that every effort should be made to control the communal frenzy immediately. During his evening prayer meeting that day, Gandhiji referred to his talk with Shri Guruji and told the audience that the RSS leader was anguished over the gruesome violence all around and that he would make an appeal for peace and normalcy. The appeal was duly published in the press and also broadcast by AIR.

In the same meeting, Gandhiji told Shri Guruji that he wished to address a gathering of RSS workers. Accordingly, on 16 September 1947, he came to meet some five hundred RSS *swayamsevaks* assembled at Delhi's Bhangi Colony. Here he recalled his visit, thirteen years earlier, to the RSS camp in Wardha. 'Some years back, when the founder of the Sangh was alive, I had visited your camp. I was highly impressed to see the spirit of discipline, complete absence of untouchability and simple, rigorous style of living. Any organisation inspired with the high ideal of service and self-sacrifice will never fail to grow in strength all the time.'

It should be evident from the above that, despite its differences with Gandhiji on certain issues, the RSS held him in high esteem. It is also evident that Gandhiji reciprocated this positive attitude. Therefore, the thought of assassinating him would have seemed heinous and sinful to the Sangh. But, sadly, falsehood often triumphs over truth in a nation. Thus, in spite of the RSS having had no role whatsoever in Mahatma's murder—a fact that would later be established by a government-appointed commission of enquiry—there was a shrill demand from some quarters for a ban on the RSS.

Even those in the Congress who were suspected to be sympathetic towards the RSS were not spared from this malicious campaign, launched primarily by the communists. They publicly demanded Sardar Patel's resignation 'for his failure to protect' the Mahatma and also called for the removal of Dr Syama Prasad Mookerjee from the Union Cabinet for his association with a 'communal organisation', meaning, thereby, the Hindu Mahasabha. Ironically, they disregarded the fact that it was at Gandhiji's insistence that Pandit Nehru had included Dr B.R. Ambedkar and Dr Mookerjee, both of whom did not belong to the Congress, in his first Cabinet formed after August 1947. Gandhiji had made this suggestion to the Prime Minister because he wanted India's first government to be truly broad-based in its representation and national in its character.

IN ALWAR JAIL, FOR THREE MONTHS

With the leftist demand for a ban on the RSS intensifying, the government yielded to it on 4 February 1948. Three days before that, in a countrywide swoop, tens of thousands of RSS *swayamsewaks*, including most *pracharaks*, were put behind bars. I was incarcerated in Alwar Central Jail. Along with many other Sangh activists, I spent the next three months there in the company of ordinary criminals.

I later learnt why the government had specially targeted RSS volunteers in Rajasthan. There were rumours—baseless and malevolent—that since many RSS functionaries migrating from Sindh in Pakistan had been working in Rajasthan, they were part of the conspiracy behind the Mahatma's murder. Unfortunately, these rumours had gained currency on account of a letter written by Prime Minister Nehru to Sardar Patel on 5 February 1948: 'It appears that considerable numbers of prominent RSS people have gone to some of the states, notably Bharatpur and Alwar. They have also taken a good deal of material with them of various kinds. It is possible that they might organise bases there for the purpose of carrying on secret activities elsewhere.'[1]

Prison life was hard. The greatest source of our discomfort was the food, which consisted of only three thick *rotis* and tasteless *dal*, served twice a day. Our discomfort with prison food led to an amusing incident one day. The jailor called me and said, 'The other inmates of the prison are going to observe a fast until tomorrow evening on account of

Maha Shivaratri*. Would you and your colleagues like to join them in the fast?' I said I would consult my colleagues and let him know. When I did so, all of them said, 'No way. As it is, with the kind of food we get here, we observe a fast practically everyday. We do not want to observe any more.' I communicated our decision to the jailor. He said, 'Fine, you'll get your normal lunch tomorrow morning.'

The bell, indicating lunch time, rang at 11 am, and we ate our normal bland meal. But when it rang again at around 5 pm, we were surprised. 'It is not dinner time yet. So why have they rung the bell?' We soon learnt that the other inmates were breaking their Shivaratri fast at the time and prison authorities had arranged special *halwa*, a sweet dish, for them. We were indeed envious of them!

After a consultation among ourselves, we trooped in to the jailor's office the next morning and said, 'We are fasting today. So please make the necessary arrangements.' He asked in bemusement: 'But Shivaratri fast was yesterday. Why are you fasting today?' A quick-witted inmate amongst us came up with an instant response. 'Yesterday was Shivaratri for the Shaivas. For Vaishnavas, it is today.' The jailor gave us a knowing smile and said, 'If you want *halwa* in the evening, I'll arrange for that. You don't have to fast for it.' And in the evening we savoured the sweet dish, the only time it was served during our stay in the prison.

After my release in August 1948, I spent the next four to five months underground, along with a fellow *swayamsevak* named Devendra Swarup. This was under instructions from my seniors who apprehended re-arrest and persecution of key RSS activists. Underground existence was one of the most harrowing experiences of my life. The biggest trial was finding a safe roof over our heads. Within a few days of staying in anyone's house, we would hear the same story: 'Sorry, we cannot let you stay here any longer. There

---

* Maha Shivaratri, which means 'The Grand Night of Shiva', is a Hindu festival that marks the day Lord Shiva was married to Parvati. The festivities, which are preceded by fasting, usually take place at night. Shiva, the aspect of the Supreme Being which destroys, is one of the Divine Trinity, the other two being Lord Brahma, the Creator, and Lord Vishnu, the Preserver.

are fights in our household over your presence here.' Householders were understandably afraid of imminent raids by the police, who used to scour the neighbourhoods searching for RSS activists in hiding. I soon lost count of the number of houses we changed while moving incognito in Alwar and Bharatpur districts. Adding to our woes was the harsh climate of Rajasthan. Alwar is quite simply the hottest of all the places I have lived in. Those days, there was no tap water in Bharatpur. As a result, every morning, we had to go to a pond outside the town for our bath.

RSS EMERGES FROM THE *AGNI PAREEKSHA* WITH ITS HEAD HELD HIGH

The ban against the RSS was lifted on 12 July 1949. Under Shri Guruji's leadership, the organisation had emerged from this *agni pareeksha* (trial by fire) with fortitude and undiminished conviction in its goals and ideals. The lack of justification for the ban was evident from a telltale fact: not a single RSS *swayamsevak* was chargesheeted, let alone convicted, in the Mahatma's assassination case. This proved that the ban, as well as the imprisonment of the RSS activists, was based entirely on unfounded, politically motivated accusations.

The above fact was also evident from the correspondence between Patel and Nehru. Replying to the Prime Minister's letter urging him to ascertain the RSS connection in the case, Patel sent a categorical reply on 27 February 1948, less than a month after Gandhiji's assassination: 'I have kept myself almost in daily touch with the progress of the investigations regarding Bapu's assassination case. All the main accused have given long and detailed statements of their activities. It also clearly emerges from the statements that the RSS was not involved in it at all.'

In spite of this, Shri Guruji was arrested again on the night of 13 November 1948 under the notorious Bengal State Prisoner's Act. It was the very Act which Nehru had condemned before Independence as a 'black law'. Soon after his arrest, Shri Guruji wrote a letter to all the *swayamsevaks*: 'This state of affairs is humiliating. To continue to submit meekly to this atrocious tyranny is an insult to the honour of citizens of free Bharat and a blow to the prestige of our civilised free State. I therefore request you to stand up for our great cause.' He gave a call for nationwide satyagraha on 9 December 1948. The main slogan of the satyagrahis was a blatant challenge to the Nehru government: 'Prove the charges against the RSS or lift the ban.'

The satyagraha was a huge success all over the country.

The government soon realised that public opinion was going against Shri Guruji's illegal arrest. So in order to break the stalemate, Patel communicated a request to Shri Guruji to prepare a written constitution for the RSS and to send it to the Government of India for its perusal. Until then, the RSS had been functioning without a constitution. Shri Guruji readily agreed to this suggestion and the text of the Sangh's constitution was sent to the government in June 1949. This paved the way for removal of the ban on the RSS on 12 July 1949, followed by Shri Guruji's release the following day. Sardar Patel's letter to Shri Guruji on this occasion made a telling remark: 'Only the people near me know as to how happy I was when the ban on Sangh was lifted. I wish you all the best.'

After the ban was lifted, Shri Guruji embarked on an all-India tour in August 1949, touring the country extensively for six months. Wherever he went, he received a tumultuous welcome. The massive ovation he got in Delhi on 23 August 1949 attracted international attention. BBC radio reported: 'Golwalkar is a shining star that has arisen on the Indian firmament. The only other Indian who can draw such huge crowds is Prime Minister Nehru.' In his speeches, Shri Guruji endeared himself to many people outside the Sangh ranks with his magnanimity and moderation. 'Let us close this chapter of the ban on the Sangh,' he told *swayamsevaks* and RSS sympathisers. 'Do not let your minds be overcome with bitterness for those who, you feel, have done injustice to you. If the teeth were to bite the tongue do we pull out the teeth? Even those who have done injustice to us are our own people. So we must forget and forgive.'

KAPUR COMMISSION ABSOLVES RSS IN MAHATMA'S MURDER CASE

The Nehru government's communiqué of 4 February 1948 had given several reasons for banning the RSS, the foremost of which was the charge of complicity in Gandhiji's murder. It said: 'It has been found that in several parts of the country individual members of Rashtriya Swayamsevak Sangh have indulged in acts of violence involving arson, robbery, dacoity, murder and have collected illicit arms and ammunitions. They have been found circulating leaflets exhorting people to resort to terrorist methods, to collect fire arms, to create disaffection against the Government and suborn the Police and the Military. These activities have been carried on under a cloak of secrecy.... The objectionable and harmful activities of the Sangh have, however, continued unabated and the cult of violence sponsored and inspired by the activities of the Sangh has claimed many victims. The latest and the most precious to fall was Gandhiji himself.'

Ironically, when the same government lifted the ban, its communiqué made no mention of any of these charges, including the gravest of them all—inspiration for Gandhiji's murder. Instead, it claimed that since the RSS had consented to have a written constitution, the organisation would now be allowed to function.

Even this did not put a full stop to the campaign of calumny against the RSS. After a lapse of nearly two decades, the government, headed this time by Indira Gandhi, set up a new judicial commission in 1966 to thoroughly enquire into the plot to murder the Mahatma. It was headed by Justice J.L. Kapur, a retired judge of the Supreme Court. It examined over a hundred witnesses and submitted its report in 1969. According to the Kapur Commission, 'they (the accused) have not been proved to have been members of the RSS, nor has that organization been shown to have had a hand in the murder.' (vol. I, p. 186) 'It (RSS) had a slant against Gandhism, but its anti-Gandhism did not seem to go to the extent of personally harming Mahatma Gandhi.' (vol. II, p. 75) Further, the Commission observed: 'In Delhi also there is no evidence that the RSS as such was indulging in violent activities against Mahatma Gandhi or the top Congress leaders.' (vol. I. p. 66)

What pains me is that even after a government-appointed judicial commission was established, categorically and conclusively, the innocence of the RSS in the Mahatma's murder case, some of our adversaries, especially leftists, have continued to malign the Sangh. They seem to believe in Goebbels' doctrine that a lie repeated a hundred times becomes a truth.

It may not be out of place here to mention that a significant section of the Congress Party, which believed in the patriotic credentials of the RSS and was convinced about its innocence in the Mahatma's murder case, was keen that the Congress and the Sangh should work together. The CWC, on 7 October 1949, even went to the extent of asking RSS members to join the Congress Party. This immediately triggered off a controversy.

A.G. Kher, who was a Minister in Uttar Pradesh and a known follower of Sardar Patel, countered the critics by asking why certain Congressmen opposed the entry of RSS members when members of the Arya Samaj or Jamat-ul-Ulema were eligible. 'It cannot be that they were involved in Gandhi's murder, for they were exonerated of that charge in Court of Law.' Kher also said, 'Calling them fascists, abusing and insulting them, and again and again repeating old charges does not serve any purpose, nor is it a Gandhian method.'

Unfortunately, Pandit Nehru could never overcome his personal prejudice against the RSS. And after Sardar Patel passed away on 15 December 1950, there was no one left in the Congress Party to counterbalance Nehru's negative views on various important issues.

MY FIRST LESSON IN SECULARISM

I was following these debates and developments concerning the RSS as closely as I could from Rajasthan where I was working as a *pracharak*. Once I was in Delhi for some Sangh-related work. Shri Guruji was also in town. I went to meet him at Lala Hansraj's residence on Barakhamba Road, where he was staying. I asked him for his guidance on a question that had been plaguing me: 'Even though the RSS is not involved in Gandhiji's murder, newspapers say that the ban on our organisation will not be lifted for two reasons. Firstly, the RSS is a secret organisation which does not even have a written constitution. Secondly, it does not believe in secularism. After all, the Constitution of independent India which currently is being framed is going to be a secular Constitution. How do we counter this criticism?'

Shri Guruji responded to my questions by saying, 'How can we be described as a secret body just because we do not have a written constitution? Even a country like the United Kingdom does not have a written constitution. That does not make its government a secret organisation, does it? In any case, not having a constitution is not a major issue. The RSS is ready to have a formal constitution, if that is the only problem that the government has with our organisation.'

'So far as the second part of your question is concerned,' he continued, 'it is ironic that the government is talking about secularism after having chosen the symbol of a theocratic state—Ashoka Chakra—as India's national emblem. According to the Hindu tradition, the state always has to be secular. It has never accepted theocracy. It grants total freedom to every individual to follow a mode of worship of his or her choice. It does not permit discrimination on the basis of one's faith, either in society or in the State's relationship with its citizens. It has never identified the State with any single form of worship, whereas Ashoka did describe his as a Buddhist State. If we object to the conduct of some Muslims in our society, it is not because they follow Islam but rather because of their lack of loyalty to India. The Partition of India has proven us right. Therefore, to call the RSS anti-secular is to show one's ignorance of what secularism stands for and what the RSS stands for.'

This was my first lesson in secularism. I was twenty-one then.

I would like to mention here that I had a small role to play in the preparation of the RSS's constitution, thanks to two leaders who had the most inspiring influence on my political life—Rajpalji and Pandit Deendayal Upadhyaya. I had first met Deendayalji in Delhi in 1947, albeit briefly. It was 1948 onwards that he became the most important source of ideological, political and moral influence on my life.

The ban on the RSS was yet to be lifted then. Shri Guruji had accepted Sardar Patel's suggestion that the Sangh should adopt a written constitution, and he had assigned the task of framing the constitution to a four-member committee comprising Deendayalji, Rajpal Puri, S.S. Apte and Eknath Ranade. Rajpalji knew me closely from my Sindh days. When he met me in Delhi, he immediately said to me, 'You come along and participate in our work.'

Once the RSS leaders showed its written constitution to the government, they had no difficulty in securing approval for the same. The whole exercise seemed to be merely a technical formality. If this was all that the government wanted from the RSS, what was the need and justification for the ban?

4

Dr Mookerjee and formation of the Bharatiya Jana Sangh

We must be able to show that India is not only in theory, but also in fact, a country where Hindus, Muslims, Christians and everyone will be able to live without fear and with equality of rights. That is the Constitution that we have framed and which we propose to apply rigorously and scrupulously.

— Dr Syama Prasad Mookerjee, in a speech in Parliament on the Kashmir issue in August 1952

It was during my years in Rajasthan that a momentous political event took place which would impact my life fundamentally in the years that followed. Two independent but simultaneously unfolding developments converged to cause the birth of a new party, which in course of time would decisively reshape the content and course of Indian politics.

The first of these developments concerned Dr Syama Prasad Mookerjee (1901-53), a great nationalist leader from Bengal. He was the son of

Sir Ashutosh Mookerjee, an eminent educationist and fervent patriot, who was widely respected for his unique role as the Vice Chancellor of Calcutta University and a judge of the Calcutta High Court. What enhanced his uniqueness in Bengali society was that his son, Syama Prasad, too became the Vice Chancellor of Calcutta University when he was only thirty-three, making him the youngest VC in the history of Indian universities.

Soon thereafter, Dr Mookerjee plunged into the nationalist politics of Bengal, deeply concerned by the communal politics of the Muslim League which was clearly pointing to the possibility of a re-division of Bengal. He had a completely non-communal approach to issues, as is evident from his active association with Fazal-ul-Haq of the Krishak Praja Party and his close friendship with Qazi Nazarul-Islam, one of the greatest poets of Bengal. But Dr Mookerjee was worried about the imminent threat to the unity and integrity of India, and the growing marginalisation of Hindus in the eastern part of the country. This concern brought him close to the Hindu Mahasabha, which was then led by Veer Savarkar. In 1939, Dr Mookerjee became its acting President. He declared complete and immediate independence of united India as the goal of his party. It is worth mentioning here that his joining the Hindu Mahasabha was welcomed by Mahatma Gandhi, who felt that 'somebody needed to lead the Hindus after Madan Mohan Malaviyaji'. Gandhiji had full faith in the nationalist outlook of Dr Mookerjee and, while blessing his joining the Hindu Mahasabha, said to him: 'Patel is a Congressman with a Hindu mind. You be a Hindu Sabhaite with a Congress mind.'

As mentioned earlier, it was again Gandhiji who insisted on Dr Mookerjee's inclusion in Pandit Nehru's first post-Independence Cabinet. As India's first Minister of Industries, he laid the foundation of many large public sector undertakings such as the Hindustan Aeronautics in Bangalore, the Chittaranjan Locomotive Factory and the Sindhri fertilizer plant. His vision and administrative acumen were evident in his outstanding achievements during his short stint.

Working together with Nehru in the government did not, however, minimise Dr Mookerjee's political differences with the Prime Minister. He was unhappy with Nehru's handling of the Kashmir issue and especially critical of the pact that Nehru signed with his Pakistani counterpart Liaqat Ali Khan in 1950,* which he thought was a betrayal of the interests of Hindus in East Pakistan. Dr Mookerjee wanted Pakistan to be held directly responsible for the influx of millions of Hindu refugees from East Pakistan. Their migration, he argued, was the result of religious persecution and government-supported violence. Having failed to prevent the signing of the pact, Dr Mookerjee chose to resign from the Cabinet and made his views known to the country through a compelling and scintillating speech in the Lok Sabha on 19 April 1950. Regarded as one of the greatest political speeches in the annals of independent India, it confirmed his reputation as the 'Lion of Parliament'. Dr Mookerjee said:

> When the partition of our country became inevitable, I played a very large part in creating public opinion in favour of the partition of Bengal, for I felt that if that was not done, the whole of Bengal and also perhaps Assam would fall to Pakistan. At that time, little knowing that I would join the first Central Cabinet, along with others, I gave assurances to the Hindus of East Bengal stating that if they suffered at the hands of the future Pakistan Government, if they were denied elementary rights of citizenship, if their lives or

---

* Makkhan Lal's book *Secular Politics Communal Agenda* has a revealing piece of information about Nehru-Liaqat talks in 1950 (pp. 207-208). Quoting from the autobiography of N.V. Gadgil, the Minister of Public Works and Refugee Rehabilitation in the Central Government, he states that the draft Indo-Pak agreement, which Nehru placed before the Cabinet for its approval, contained provisions for 'reservation for Muslims in proportion to their population in the government services and representative bodies in the constituent states of India'. Since most ministers kept their mouths shut, Gadgil said, 'These (provisions) nullify the whole philosophy of the Congress. The country had to pay the price of division as a result of acceptance of separate electorates. You are asking it to drink the same poison again.' After a detailed discussion in the Cabinet the next day, the entire provision of reservation was dropped. When Pakistan's Prime Minister met Sardar Patel and brought up the issue of reserved jobs and seats in legislature for Muslims, the latter told him bluntly: '(My) party will not accept it and the country will not swallow this bitter pill. We have conceded one Pakistan; that is more than enough.' All this shows why Dr Mookerjee was upset over Nehru's bungling over Pakistan and decided to resign from his Cabinet.

honour were jeopardised or attacked, Free India would not remain an idle spectator and that their just cause would be boldly taken up by the Government and people of India.... I have never felt happy about our attitude towards Pakistan.... It has been weak, halting and inconsistent. Our goodness or inaction has been interpreted as weakness by Pakistan. It has made Pakistan more and more intransigent.[1]

After his voluntary exit from Nehru's Cabinet, Dr Mookerjee keenly felt the dire need for a suitable nationalist political platform to challenge the wrong policies of the Congress government. By this time, he was also disillusioned with the Hindu Mahasabha. He, therefore, decided to organise a new political party that would unite all Indians, irrespective of their caste, creed and linguistic affiliations, on a common nationalist and democratic platform. He named it the Bharatiya Jana Sangh.

In an independent but concurrent development, many people in the RSS had begun to articulate the need for establishing a nationalist political platform. This was felt necessary in the wake of the politically motivated ban on the organisation after Mahatma Gandhi's assassination and the absence of any effective support from within the political establishment. In the course of an intense debate within the top echelons of the RSS, those in favour of a new political party argued: 'We should have a like-minded political party that safeguards national interests and reflects the nationalist ideology of the RSS in the political field. The Bharatiya Jana Sangh is the creation of a renowned leader with impeccable nationalist credentials. The RSS should therefore work actively to expand and strengthen this new party.'

Shri Guruji initially was not in favour of the RSS associating itself with political parties, and certainly not with any particular party. His aloofness from politics often bordered on aversion. He believed that the primary objective of the RSS was to contribute to India's national renaissance based on social unity, individual character-building, and revival of its glorious cultural and spiritual heritage. This endeavour, he felt, would be adversely affected by the competitive and often divisive nature of politics.

He also contended that power politics exerted a corrupting influence on its practitioners who, unless they were men and women of great integrity, would lose sight of the lofty ideals of nation-building in pursuit of their own selfish interests.

Shri Guruji was a person of firm beliefs and it was not easy for the proponents of a new political party to persuade him to change his stance. If, in the end, he did agree to the RSS lending support to the Bharatiya Jana Sangh, it was principally because of his high regard for the towering personality of Dr Mookerjee. Soon an understanding was reached between Dr Mookerjee and Shri Guruji. The former was a national leader, but without an organisational base of his own. The RSS was in search of a like-minded political platform. Thus, the synergy between Dr Mookerjee and the RSS was perfect. Shri Guruji agreed to Dr Mookerjee's request to depute some capable activists of the Sangh to work for the Jana Sangh. He assigned his most trusted colleague, Pandit Deendayal Upadhyaya, and some other *pracharaks* the task of assisting Dr Mookerjee in building the Jana Sangh.

The founding session of the Bharatiya Jana Sangh took place in New Delhi on 21 October 1951. Concluding his Presidential address, Dr Mookerjee said:

> Let all our *karyakartas* (party workers) always remember: people's trust and support can be won only through sacrifice and ceaseless service. We are wedded to the mission of India's renaissance and reconstruction. Mother India is calling upon her children. Let us set aside the differences of class, caste and religion, and get down to the task of serving her. Howsoever dark may be the present, our future is bright. And India has many big things to do in the world. Our party's symbol is *Deep* (lamp); it emits the light of hope and unity, commitment and courage. May we carry this light in our hands and dispel the darkness and gloom that has pervaded our nation after its partition. This is only the beginning of our long yatra. May God Almighty give us the strength and courage so that we always walk along the path of righteousness; so that fear may

not deter us and attractions may not lure us; so that we can make our fullest contribution to re-building India as a great and mighty power, spiritually as well as materially; and so that India reborn can become a reliable and sacred instrument for the protection of world peace and promotion of global progress.

How many times in independent India have such eternally inspiring words been spoken from a political platform?

The formation of the Jana Sangh was a turning point in my life. One day, while on a tour of Rajasthan, Deendayalji asked me to take up the organisational responsibility for the party in the state. I did so in early 1952, along with my senior colleague Sundar Singh Bhandari, who later became one of the main pillars of the Bharatiya Jana Sangh and the BJP at the national level. As my organisational tasks grew, I shifted my base from Kota to Jaipur, the state capital.

Thus began my journey as a political activist, a journey that has continued uninterrupted for the past fifty-six years.

The first plenary conference of the Bhartiya Jana Sangh was held at Kanpur in February 1953. I had gone there with the Rajasthan contingent of delegates to attend the session. It was here that I came into close contact with Dr Mookerjee, Atal Bihari Vajpayee, Nanaji Deshmukh and several other leaders of the party. In no time, Dr Mookerjee discovered what an outstanding thinker and organiser Deendayalji was.

The Kanpur session of the Bharatiya Jana Sangh will always be remembered for its historic decision to launch an all-India agitation, aimed at fully integrating Jammu & Kashmir into the Indian Union. By this time, the process of integration of the princely states initiated by Sardar Patel had been successfully accomplished all over the country. Jammu & Kashmir, however, was the sole exception. This posed a grave danger to the unity, integrity and security of India. The problem was further complicated by its unnecessary internationalisation by Prime Minister Nehru, who agreed to Lord Mountbatten's suggestion to refer the issue to the United Nations. Sardar Patel had strongly advised against it. Naturally, there was great resentment, concern and anger among the people.

The Bharatiya Jana Sangh articulated its patriotic sentiment in a slogan which in no time became very popular: '*Ek desh mein do vidhan, do pradhan aur do nishaan, nahin chalenge, nahin chalenge.*' (We shall not accept in one nation two constitutions, two presidents and two flags.) This is still remembered as one of the most inspiring slogans in the political history of independent India. Not many people now may be aware that this was a time when the tricolour could not be hoisted in any part of Jammu & Kashmir. Equally worrisome was the fact that no Indian outside Jammu & Kashmir could enter the state without a special permit. Neither the Supreme Court, nor the Election Commission (EC), nor the Comptroller and Auditor General (CAG), nor even the Rashtrapati had any authority over the state. In August 1952, while addressing a mammoth rally in Jammu, Dr Mookerjee had thundered: 'I will get you the Indian Constitution or lay down my life for it.'

A man of action, Dr Mookerjee led a massive nationwide satyagraha the following year against the non-applicability of the Indian Constitution in Jammu & Kashmir. When in 2005, the Bharatiya Janata Party celebrated its *Rajat Jayanti* (silver jubilee) and re-enacted some of the major events since the days of the Jana Sangh, I was invited to address a massive rally organised just across the Pathankot bridge. For it was here that Dr Mookerjee was arrested on 11 May 1953; the Jammu & Kashmir police had taken him into custody on the pretext that he had entered the state without a permit. Along with their party President, thousands of Jana Sangh activists from all over the country also entered the state without a permit. All of them courted arrest, faced police brutalities and made sacrifices for the cause of India's unity and integrity. At the rally in 2005, I had the privilege of honouring an old lady whose husband was killed by police bullets while hoisting the tricolour just after crossing the bridge.

But the biggest sacrifice in the Kashmir Satyagraha was that by Dr Mookerjee himself. After his arrest, he had been detained in a house on the outskirts of Srinagar. There he fell seriously ill and died on 23 May 1953 under mysterious circumstances. His death in custody raised well-warranted widespread suspicion. Demands were made for an independent enquiry. His mother Jogmaya Devi even wrote a letter to Prime Minister

Nehru. However, no enquiry commission was set up. Not long after Dr Mookerjee's martyrdom, the government revoked the hated 'permit system'. It also abolished many of the restrictions over the jurisdiction of the institutions of the Indian Republic in Jammu & Kashmir. Thus, the authority of the EC and the CAG was extended to the state. The title of 'Prime Minister' of Jammu & Kashmir was abolished. Nevertheless, our concern over '*Do Vidhan*'—two Constitutions—especially with regard to Article 370, still remains unaddressed more than half a century later.

My personal interaction with Dr Mookerjee was rather limited, although I had met him three or four times. This is because he was based in Delhi and I was working from Rajasthan. Nevertheless, whenever I met him, or listened to his speeches in Parliament during my visits to Delhi, or read his writings, especially pertaining to education and democracy, I was deeply impressed by his thoughts and the greatness of his personality. When I look back and ask myself what I learnt from various inspiring sources, the answer I get is this: from the RSS, I received my grounding in nationalism and disciplined service to society; Pandit Deendayal Upadhyaya inculcated within me great idealism and a realisation of the need for purity and probity in public life; and from Dr Mookerjee, I learnt the indispensability of value-based democracy as a vehicle for nation-building.

5

THE THRILL OF PARTICIPATING IN THE FIRST GENERAL ELECTIONS

India was the motherland of our race, and Sanskrit the mother of Europe's languages: she was the mother of our philosophy; mother, through the Arabs, of much of our mathematics; mother, through the Buddha, of the ideals embodied in Christianity; mother, through the village community, of self-government and democracy. Mother India is in many ways the mother of us all.

— WILL DURANT, AMERICAN HISTORIAN AND AUTHOR OF
THE STORY OF PHILOSOPHY

During my initial years in Rajasthan, the Constituent Assembly, which had been formed in 1946, was busy debating the contents of the future Constitution of India. I was deeply interested in these debates, and tried to follow them as much as I could from the rather scanty reports in the available newspapers in mofussil towns. The adoption of the Constitution and proclamation of India as a Republic on 26 January 1950 was a historic day in the life of our ancient nation, almost as momentous as 15 August 1947. I was in Alwar on that day. The festive mood in Rajasthan was palpable. The common *praja* (people) had finally become rulers in a land of rajas and maharajas.

The adoption of the Constitution was soon followed by the announcement of the first general elections to be held in March 1952. This gave a big fillip to political activity in the country. It also gave me an opportunity to participate in the greatest festival of democracy: elections. I worked in Bharatpur in the first general elections and, in 1957, looked after the poll battle in the Kota, Bundi and Jhalawar areas. Since then, I have participated in every single general election in India, including the latest one in 2004, which elected the 14th Lok Sabha.

How things have changed with the passage of time! Most people today cannot even imagine the kind of difficulties involved in conducting elections in 1952. Since there was no precedent, even the EC was inexperienced. Nowadays it is quite common to see assembly elections in an entire state completed in one or two days. In contrast, I remember that in the first general elections, it took three weeks to complete the polling exercise in a single assembly constituency! Polling would be conducted in five polling stations on a day and, after a day's gap, would be held in five more stations, and so on. So, if an assembly constituency had sixty to sixty-five polling stations, which was the average size, the whole exercise took twenty to twenty-five days. After completing the polling in five stations, the administrative staff would physically carry all the boxes and other paraphernalia to the next five polling stations. As activists, we would pack up our things, get into a truck and follow the officials to their next destination.

Not only was electronic voting unheard of in those days, but even the balloting process was completely different. The ballot paper had no names of candidates, nor symbols of the contesting parties. There was not even stamping of the ballot paper. Instead, there were separate boxes for each candidate in the polling booth, bearing his or her name and the party symbol. The voters were required to put the ballot—a piece of shiny paper no bigger than a one-rupee note (now extinct)—in the box of the candidate of their choice.

The 'science' of rigging was also born in the first general elections itself, and it quickly exploited the chinks in the balloting system. Agents of some candidates would stand outside the polling booth and tell the voters: 'Don't put the ballot inside the box. Put it in your pocket and bring it with you. We'll give you a one-rupee note if you give us your ballot paper.' One rupee was a lot of money in those times. After collecting twenty-five to thirty such ballots, one of the agent's men would go in and drop them off in his candidate's box.

There was another loophole, since symbols were allotted constituency-wise, it was possible for the same symbol to be granted to candidates of the different parties in different constituencies. It was only in 1962, during the third general elections, that multiple ballot boxes were replaced with a single box and the secret 'marking system' was introduced. All said, 1952 was a major learning experience for one and all in India's fledgling democracy—for parties, leaders, candidates, the administration, the EC and, of course, the voters themselves.

For the first general elections, the Commission recognised fourteen 'national parties' and sixty 'state parties' on the basis of the claims presented by various political groups. No objective criterion such as performance in the last election was available. Each national party had a symbol reserved exclusively for its candidates throughout India, while each state party had a symbol reserved for its candidates in the state. All other candidates were supposed to choose a symbol from the list of 'free' symbols.

After the elections the four parties that received more than three per cent of the nationwide Lok Sabha votes were recognised as 'national parties'; twelve parties won over three per cent of the vote in the state Vidhan Sabha elections and these were recognised as 'state parties' in their respective states.

Sukumar Sen, India's first Chief Election Commissioner (CEC) during the first general elections was an upright and brilliant official. To him goes the credit for all the elaborate groundwork of this massive exercise, made even more challenging in our vast and populous country. In a country with widespread illiteracy, having people vote only on the basis of names was a serious problem. It was Sen who conceived the idea of having symbols allotted to candidates in order to enable even illiterate voters to identify the party of his or her choice.

MY FIRST BRUSH WITH TWO BASIC REALITIES OF ELECTIONS

Shortly after the elections, an assembly by-election took place in the Kotputli constituency. Kotputli is a small town in Rajasthan situated about forty-five kilometres from Jaipur on the main road to Delhi. In this by-election I had an interesting experience which provided my initial insight into two principal factors that influence a voter's choice in Indian elections.

My party had entrusted me with the responsibility of managing the campaign in Kotputli. After studying the problems of the region, I prepared some literature explaining how the Jana Sangh would try to solve these problems if the people elected our candidate. I had also brought copies of the party's manifesto for Rajasthan.

I reached the constituency about a month before the polling and resolved to remain there until the elections were over. As I began unloading the poll literature that I had brought from Jaipur, I saw our candidate, Ram Karan Singh, standing at a distance and watching me bemusedly. I was half his age at the time, but he addressed me very respectfully and said, 'Advaniji, would you like me and my workers to distribute this literature in the constituency? But where is the need for it? This manifesto and these pamphlets are totally useless in our election strategy. We would have to spend a lot of time and energy in distributing them. If you insist, we will do it. But that will not fetch us even a single additional vote.'

He then added: 'Let me tell you one thing, Advaniji. No one can defeat me in this election. This is a predominantly Gujar constituency. And I am the only Gujar in the contest.' His next statement opened my eyes even further regarding the reality of elections in India. 'Firstly, every single Gujar who goes to the polling booth is going to vote for me simply because I am a Gujar. Secondly, a majority of non-Gujars will also cast their votes for me because they know that in this constituency I am the most likely winner. They would not like to waste their vote by giving it to a losing candidate!'

The first factor, namely of caste, is peculiar to India. Every individual is conscious of several simultaneous identities: his nation, his birthplace, his religion, his language, his family. But in India, especially among Hindus, one of the most defining identities is that of caste. This was not so in Sindh. After my migration from Sindh to Rajasthan in 1947, I recall that whenever I used to introduce myself by my name, and added that I was from Sindh, almost always the follow-up question would be: '*What* are you?' which in a more straightforward way meant: 'What is your *caste*?'

So far as the second factor mentioned by Ram Karan Singh is concerned, western political scientists call it the 'Bandwagon Phenomenon'. Many voters would like to cast their votes in a manner as to hoist them atop the Victory Bandwagon! It is because of this that in some democracies statutory restrictions have been imposed on opinion polls.

The classic case of how opinion polls influence actual poll outcomes is that of the United States' 1948 Presidential election. It was a battle between Democrat Harry Truman and Republican Thomas Dewey. All of the major polls predicted that Dewey would win hands down, by close to fifteen percentage points. However, the actual election results shocked the Republicans. Truman won by over four percentage points. The principal pollster George Gallup Jr. later explained: 'We stopped polling a few weeks too soon. We had been lulled into thinking that nothing much changes in the last few weeks of the campaign.'

This episode showed how opinion polls can influence voter behaviour. After the 1948 fiasco, pollsters adopted several reforms. First, they continue polling right up to election day. Second, they improved their ability to predict winners from non-winners.

PRINCIPLED STAND ON ABOLITION OF THE JAGIRDARI SYSTEM

Our party secured eight seats in the first legislative assembly of Rajasthan, which then had 160 members. Predictably, the Congress had won the majority and thus formed the government. Soon a politically significant revolt took place in the legislative wing of the Jana Sangh, and the leadership had to expel as many as six out of the eight MLAs from the party. Rajasthan before Independence, was a land of nineteen princely states. These, along with all the other princely states in the rest of the country, had merged into the Indian Union before 1950.

Nevertheless, the jagirdari system of land ownership, which enabled aristocratic families to own hundreds or thousands of acres of agricultural land, had continued. At the insistence of Dr Mookerjee and Pandit Deendayal Upadhyaya, the party in its manifesto had promised to abolish the jagirdari system as a step towards egalitarianism. It so happened that all eight MLAs who had won on the Jana Sangh's ticket were themselves jagirdars. Six of them protested when, after the elections, the party decided to press for the implementation of its commitment in the manifesto. Only Bhairon Singh Shekhawat and one other MLA, Jagat Singh Jhala, supported the abolition of jagirdari. When the 'rebellion' of the six MLAs was communicated to the party's central leadership, both Dr Mookerjee and Deendayalji came to Jaipur and discussed the matter with each of them. When the MLAs did not relent, our leaders said, 'Expel them from the party. We cannot compromise on a matter of principle.'

Shekhawat soon emerged as a charismatic leader of the party in Rajasthan and went on to become the state's Chief Minister thrice. In 2002, he also became the Vice President of India. I would say that the bold and principled stand he took on the jagirdari abolition issue way back in 1952 made a vital and foundational contribution to his subsequent political ascent.

On the eve of the first general elections, the EC gave ad hoc recognition as All India Parties to nearly two dozen different political parties. It also announced that a final decision about recognition of All India Parties would be taken only after the elections were over. Only those parties that secured at least three per cent of the total votes would be recognised.

On the basis of this touchstone, only four parties emerged from the 1952 Lok Sabha polls as All India Parties. These were: Indian National Congress—45.0 per cent; Praja Socialist Party—5.8 per cent; Communist Party of India—3.3 per cent; and Bharatiya Jana Sangh—3.1 per cent. In these elections, the Congress secured 364 out of 479 seats in the Lok Sabha. Compared to this, the Jana Sangh barely managed to acquire the

EC's prescribed minimum and got only three seats. One of the three winners was Dr Mookerjee from West Bengal.

It was the outcome of the second general elections that brought my decade-long work in Rajasthan to a close and brought me to Delhi.

Entry into National Politics
1957-77

DEMOCRACY IN SHACKLES

'Independent India has zealously guarded its status as the world's largest democracy. However, this achievement was temporarily eclipsed when, in June 1975, Prime Minister Indira Gandhi brought India under the draconian Emergency Rule. Nineteen months later, the eclipse disappeared as the result of a glorious struggle launched by the people against the Congress party's authoritarianism. If the Emergency was the darkest period in India's post-1947 history, the righteous struggle for the restoration of democracy was undoubtedly the brightest.'

Phase Three

❖

1

MOVING FROM RAJASTHAN TO DELHI

Let the narrow spirit of partisanship, of class and communal warfare,
of sectional domination disappear from our minds. What matters is My
Beloved Motherland. Everything that is said or done has to be tested from
this supreme standpoint: does it or does it not constitute an offering that
can worthily be placed at the altar of My Sacred Motherland. Dauntless
must be our determination, unflinching our faith for carrying India's
struggle to its glorious end.

—Dr Syama Prasad Mookerjee

Life is an ever-changing, ever-flowing current of events. The Creator, who governs the journey of every living being, constantly juggles the pattern of life, changing the fate of individuals and families. Sometimes the change is so dramatic, and linked to such a larger change, that it constitutes an abrupt discontinuity, almost rupturing the solid foundation of one's life.

The Partition of India in 1947, and the forced migration of my family from Karachi, was one such drastic upheaval. Until 1957, Rajasthan was my *karmabhoomi*, but as the decade drew to a close, destiny effected yet another change in my life. My area of work shifted to Delhi. This change was not as drastic as the previous one; indeed, it was a logical progression of my life as a political activist.

In the first Lok Sabha, we had a stalwart like Dr Syama Prasad Mookerjee representing the Bharatiya Jana Sangh in Parliament. His untimely demise in 1953, while in detention in Kashmir, left a sadly conspicuous vacuum in the party on the parliamentary front. For this reason, Pandit Deendayal Upadhyaya, the organisational General Secretary of the party, decided that Atal Bihari Vajpayee should contest the 1957 Lok Sabha polls. He made Atalji contest from three constituencies—Lucknow, Balrampur and Mathura—all in UP, a move that reflected his keen desire that Atalji should represent the party in Parliament by winning from at least one of the three seats. As Atalji would jocularly say in later years, 'Of the three places that I contested from, I forfeited my deposit in one (Mathura), lost by a thin margin in another (Lucknow), and won handsomely in the third (Balrampur).'

The party also won three additional seats—another in UP and two in Maharashtra. Although the Jana Sangh won only one seat more in 1957 than its total tally of three in 1952, its popular vote of 5.9 per cent, had nearly doubled in five years. In UP, the most populous state in the country, it had more than doubled its share, winning nearly fifteen per cent of the total votes polled. A notable aspect of the 1957 elections was that even the Hindu Mahasabha and the Rama Rajya Parishad had opposed us, which prompted many political pundits to pen obituaries for the Jana Sangh. Deendayalji gave them a befitting reply: 'After the death of Dr Syama Prasad Mookerjee, it was presumed in the political circles that the Jana Sangh would now be finished. We have fought against this presumption for the last five years. Now the results of the second general elections have proved that the Jana Sangh is not only alive but is also progressing.'

LEARNING THE ROPES OF PARLIAMENTARY WORK

It was in early 1957 that Deendayalji asked me to shift base from Rajasthan to Delhi to assist Atalji and the other newly elected Jana Sangh MPs in their parliamentary work. Thereafter, Delhi became the centre of my political activity. My new responsibility gave me an opportunity to learn about the functioning of Parliament and the government, besides enabling me to develop my skills in drafting statements, formulating questions, and preparing points for the party's political propaganda. When Parliament was in session, I used to regularly observe the proceedings. The debates in both the Lok Sabha and the Rajya Sabha then were far more diverse, purposeful and substantive than now. And seeing stalwarts from both the ruling, and Opposition benches in action, was indeed a learning experience, especially since I was still a novice in the art of public speaking. Particularly thrilling for me were the moments when Atalji made his mark as an outstanding orator in Parliament.

In the first Lok Sabha, which was elected in 1952, the two best speakers were both Mukherjees—Dr Syama Prasad Mookerjee from the Jana Sangh and Hiren Mukherjee from the CPI. In the second Lok Sabha, elected five years later in 1957, the two best orators were Atalji from the Jana Sangh and Dr Prakash Veer Shastri, an independent MP who belonged to the Arya Samaj. The first pair of speakers had an extremely good command over the English language, while the latter were master orators in Hindi.

The Presiding Officers in both Houses of Parliament during the 1950s were highly meticulous in matters of time allotment. As the Jana Sangh had only four members in the Lok Sabha, the time share of our MPs used to be insignificant. Very often, even after thorough preparation for a debate, Atalji would be denied an opportunity to speak. Once he was debating on foreign policy while Prime Minister Nehru was present in the House, and his eloquence attracted everyone's attention. The Presiding Officer saw that even Pandit Nehru was highly impressed by Atalji's oratorical skills. As the Leader of the House, Nehru told the Presiding Officer that he would like to see the young Jana Sangh MP contribute more to parliamentary debates.

One of my most satisfying contributions was when I assisted Atalji in his parliamentary work in the unhappy aftermath of the Chinese aggression in 1962. I had learnt from my study of the functioning of the House of Commons in Britain that a member could demand, from the government, a White Paper containing specific information on an important topical issue. I suggested to Atalji that he should seek a White Paper on the Chinese aggression, with specific reference to India's foreign policy and defence preparedness prior to the war. Atalji and I did a fair amount of research on the subject. In the history of Parliament, he became the first MP to demand a White Paper from the government. Prime Minister Nehru accepted the demand, and Atalji's speech was widely hailed as one of the best ever. It enhanced the Jana Sangh's reputation among the common people all over the country.

The then Speaker of the Lok Sabha, M. Ananthasayanam Ayyangar, had filled the void created by the sudden demise of G.V. Mavalankar, the first Presiding Officer of the Lower House of Parliament. I had heard much about Mavalankar, whose ten years as Speaker (1946-56) made so great an impact on our parliamentary institutions that he came to be known as the 'Father of the Lok Sabha'. Besides conducting the House with remarkable decorum, dexterity and impartiality, both he and Ayyangar, who was his deputy, established the rules, procedures, conventions and customs that I came to greatly admire when I started my own parliamentary career. The Jana Sangh had no members in the Rajya Sabha at that time. Nevertheless, I would frequently watch its proceedings from the visitors' gallery, and admire, especially, the sage-like dignity with which Dr S. Radhakrishnan, India's first Vice President and Chairman of the Upper House of Parliament, would guide its deliberations. It was in those early years of internship that I learnt about the question hour, adjournment motions, bills, resolutions, standing committees, calling attention notices, privileges of members, etc., which are now an integral part of the functioning of Indian Parliament. It was a time when the stalwarts sitting on the Opposition benches fully matched the stature and competence of those in the treasury benches. And the Speaker functioned as a 'genuine custodian of the rights of the Opposition'. It is these fine traditions, set jointly by the Presiding Officers and MPs, which imparted vibrancy to India's fledgling democracy and bolstered its international reputation.

FIRST FORAY INTO ALLIANCE POLITICS—WITH COMMUNISTS

My first entry into alliance politics was in the municipal affairs of Delhi. The city, which was a union territory then, saw the formation of the Delhi Municipal Corporation in 1958. It was constituted out of several smaller municipal bodies that managed civic affairs in different parts of the city. Since the Jana Sangh had a good support base in all of them, the establishment of the corporation provided it with an opportunity to play a dominant role in the municipal governance of the capital city. This, we reckoned, would yield positive benefits for the Jana Sangh's growth in other parts of the country.

So in addition to my work in the party's parliamentary wing, Deendayalji asked me to look after the Delhi unit of the Jana Sangh as its General Secretary. My first challenge was to prepare the party to face the maiden corporation elections in 1958. We were pitted against the Congress, which at that time had a predominant presence in Indian politics. The Jana Sangh's electoral strength was being tested for the first time in Delhi, and it passed this trial with remarkable success. In a house of eighty, we won twenty-five seats, only two less than the Congress. The CPI had eight members. It may come as a surprise to many today but the Jana Sangh's first foray into alliance politics was with the communists, who had just enough seats in the corporation to tip the balance in favour of either the Congress or the Jana Sangh. But this alliance did not happen without some riveting drama.

Soon after the elections, the CPI, in order to keep the Jana Sangh out, offered to enter into an alliance with the Congress, provided the latter agreed to make one of its members, Aruna Asaf Ali, a prominent freedom fighter and star of the Quit India movement, the first Mayor of Delhi. The Congress agreed. However, the alliance broke up within a year due to constant internal squabbles, not dissimilar to the ones witnessed under the present-day United Progressive Alliance (UPA)-Left alliance. These were exacerbated by the Nehru Cabinet's decision to dismiss the first-ever communist government in Kerala, led by E.M.S. Namboodiripad, in 1959.

Here was an opportunity, and also a challenge, for our party to devise a strategic alliance with the communists to take on the reins of the corporation. We did succeed in this endeavour, thanks to Deendayalji's support for the alliance. We also received support from a lone member of the Hindu Mahasabha and some independents. The Jana Sangh and the CPI entered into a written agreement, whereby the offices of Mayor and Deputy Mayor would be shared by the two parties on a rotational basis. In keeping with that, Aruna Asaf Ali would be Mayor for the first year, and Kedarnath Sahni, who later became a prominent leader of the Jana Sangh and the BJP, the Deputy Mayor. For the second year, Sahni was to be the Mayor, and a CPI nominee the Deputy Mayor.

It was for me a useful initiation in the art of political leadership and strategy-making. I can confidently say that this is where I had my initial grounding in alliance politics, something that held me in good stead on many occasions in subsequent years and decades. To the leaders of the CPI and the CPI (Marxist) who now consider the BJP as untouchables, I would like to pose a question: Why did they join hands with the Jana Sangh in the Delhi Municipal Corporation elections in 1958? I shall discuss later, another instance of a Jana Sangh-CPI alliance for the formation of the Samyukta Vidhayak Dal (SVD) government in Bihar after the 1967 assembly elections.

While mobilising party workers for the Delhi Municipal Corporation elections, I also received my first lesson in what I would call 'social diversity management'. During those days, Delhi had a large population of Hindu and Sikh refugees from Pakistan who were staunch supporters of the RSS and the Jana Sangh. Another important section of our support base was the local trading and business community. However, some differences arose between the migrant and local populations, which threatened to turn serious on the eve of elections. I successfully averted a serious problem by patiently talking to both sides, listening to their points of view and helping them recognise the larger interests of the organisation. This experience taught me that, if a political leader wants to succeed in conflict prevention and resolution, he or she should develop six basic qualities: keeping one's ears to the ground through constant interaction with the masses, impartiality, sincerity, patience, fairness, and firmness.

LIFE WITH ATALJI AND DEENDAYALJI

The first house I lived in after moving from Rajasthan to Delhi was Atalji's official residence at 30 Rajendra Prasad Road. He had to share it with a fellow Jana Sangh MP, Premjibhai Ashar from Chiplun in Maharashtra. A distinguishing characteristic of the Jana Sangh was that the entire party functioned like an extended family, with close interpersonal ties. Ashar's wife used to cook for all of us, and we helped with the household chores. Atalji was also a good cook and, every once in a while, he used to treat us to his delicious preparations.

An interesting outcome of staying at 30 Rajendra Prasad Road was that, in addition to my other responsibilities, I also became an in-house interpreter! Ashar's wife knew neither Hindi nor English; she spoke only Kutchi or Marathi. This was because, Ashar, though originally from Kutch, had settled in the Ratnagiri district of Maharashtra. One day, I heard her speak to her husband in Kutchi, a language which seemed strangely familiar. Kutchi and my mother tongue Sindhi are similar, a natural consequence of the geographical proximity between Kutch and Sindh. So, whenever the need arose, I acted as an interpreter between the lady and others at home.

I stayed with Atalji for over a year. After I started to oversee the party's organisational work in the city. I then shifted to the Jana Sangh's central office at Ajmeri Gate in Old Delhi. It was quite small, more of a party 'commune', where I lived with Deendayalji, Kedarnath Sahni and Jagdish Prasad Mathur, another committed activist who served both the Jana Sangh and the BJP with great devotion all his life, right from 1951 until his demise in 2007. Life here was very simple, but had its own charm.

In spite of the change in my residence and functional responsibilities, my close personal and political interaction with Atalji continued. I was now in the thick of the party's political activities in Delhi. However, destiny was about to deal me with another significant change in my professional life—and, later, also in my personal life. After working as an Organising Secretary of the party in Delhi for over three years, it was now time for me to begin a new chapter in my life as a journalist by joining *Organiser*, a weekly journal inspired by the RSS ideology.

It was also time when there would be a change in my personal life.

2

THE ORGANISER YEARS

Free press can, of course, be good or bad, but, most certainly without freedom, the press will never be anything but bad.

—Albert Camus, French novelist and Nobel laureate

It is seldom easy for a political activist to balance his commitment to public life with his family obligations. I know many leaders and workers who are agonised, especially towards the end of their political life, over their neglect of family responsibilities. Apart from the pain and the sense of guilt that it results in, it also adversely affects the person's professional life. I have learnt from my own experience, and from the experience of many other political activists, that the quality of our performance in the public sphere depends vitally on the stability, depth and 'happiness quotient' in our family relationships. And happiness in family life, as also in public life, depends not so much on what you get from others but on what you give to others.

An essential difference between the Indian and western approach to life is that, in India, the pursuit of happiness is linked not to one's rights but to one's duties. The first duty that is enjoined on an adult individual is to take care of one's parents. And this is what was weighing on my mind with the passage of time after my family's migration from Sindh in 1947.

I had lost my mother early in life. My father had brought me up with redoubled love and care, which was enhanced by the attention I received from my grandmother and other close relatives. Thus, the family atmosphere I grew up in, in Karachi, not only gave me immense happiness, but also a strong foundation in Hindu traditions. True, Partition had uprooted our lives but nobody in my family had allowed bitterness or despondency to creep in. We continued to be a close-knit family typified by caring for each other. Nevertheless, I had a growing concern: after I had chosen to live the life of a *pracharak*-cum-political activist, first in Rajasthan and later in Delhi, I rarely saw my father, who had settled in Kutch after Partition. I regularly wrote to him and to my other relatives, but meetings had become infrequent.

After migrating to Kutch in Gujarat, my father worked in the Sindhu Resettlement Corporation at Adipur near Kandla. He was now close to retirement, and I had to take care of him. Additionally, I had to think of Radhi, my elder cousin, who also lived in Adipur. One day I shared my worry of how to fulfil my filial duties with Deendayalji. He was a leader whose heart was always brimming with empathy for fellow party workers. He advised me to take up a job in *Organiser*. 'It is our own journal,' he said to me. 'And you'll like the work there because you have always loved writing. The journal also needs a person like you. Besides, it gives you the freedom to continue your political work for the party.' Thus, in 1960, I joined *Organiser* as an Assistant Editor.

A COLUMNIST WITH MULTIPLE PSEUDONYMS

Founded in 1947, *Organiser* had a relatively small circulation but its visibility and influence in intellectual and political circles was considerable. Its Editor, K.R. Malkani, was a fine writer who, like me, was a RSS activist in Sindh prior to Partition. We had done our OTC together in Nagpur in 1946. Under Malkani's able editorship, *Organiser* began to be read avidly by friends and foes alike of the RSS and the Jana Sangh. He had known me not only as a *swayamsevak* from my days in Karachi, but also as an *Organiser* correspondent from Rajasthan. I used to regularly send reports to the weekly on the political activities in the state and proceedings in the legislative assembly. Now that I was on the journal's staff, Malkani gave me full creative freedom to express myself on a wide variety of issues. Soon, I started writing three columns under different pen names! This was partly due to my own enthusiasm and also because there were very few writers in those days.

My salary was quite modest—Rs 350 per month. This was because *Organiser* was not a commercial venture. Besides, for a long time after Independence, salaries, even in mainstream media, were quite low. Unlike now, journalism in the 1960s was not a financially lucrative career. It was chosen, generally, by two categories of people: those who had a strong personal aptitude and a natural flair for writing; or those who were idealistic and ideologically driven, and needed a platform from which to express themselves.

Since my needs were simple, what I earned was sufficient for me. The real benefit of the job was that, after I became an accredited journalist, I was allotted a house in Ramakrishna Puram, in 1962, from the government's annual quota for four journalists. I was far down on the waiting list and, hence, not eligible for a house that year. However, R.K. Puram was a newly established colony, and those who were eligible refused to go, saying that it was too far away. The comment would sound ludicrous today because Delhi has spread so widely on all four sides that a government flat in R.K. Puram would be envied by many.

My work in *Organiser* necessitated a change in my sartorial appearance. Ever since I started working as an RSS *pracharak* in Rajasthan, I had stopped wearing trousers and shirt and, instead, switched over to the Indian-style dhoti and kurta. However, when I joined *Organiser*, my colleagues said to me, 'A dhoti-kurta is the dress of a *neta* (political leader). It doesn't suit journalists.' I have never believed that western attire is a sign of modernity. I have always felt more comfortable, in body and in mind, wearing a dhoti-kurta. At the same time, I was never dogmatic about these matters. I saw some merit in the advice given by my colleagues and started wearing trousers once again.

One day in our editorial review meeting, we discussed the common perception that 'our journal was too dry and only wrote about political issues'. Malkani responded, 'That's true. We should also cover other interesting facets of life, such as films. But who will write on films?' I volunteered and began writing a regular cinema column under the pen name 'Netra' (eye).

As a cinema critic, I had an opportunity to attend international film festivals and other film related functions in New Delhi. Many years later, when I became the Minister of Information & Broadcasting in Morarji Desai's government in 1977, and started interacting with renowned filmmakers, at least two of them, Khwaja Ahmed Abbas and Prithviraj Kapoor, said to me, 'I have seen you before somewhere but I can't figure out where?' I had to remind them that, as film critic of the *Organiser*, I had attended their press conferences at their film releases. And both of them, separately, remarked: 'I am pleasantly surprised that we have a Minister who has earlier been a film critic.'

During my *Organiser* years, Deendayalji began to write, on my persuasion, a weekly column called 'Political Diary'. He chose a topical event or issue of the week and commented upon it with insightful analysis. Very soon the column became popular among our readers. (A collection of the columns was later published in the form of a book with the same title.) One day I said to him, 'Deendayalji, why don't you write the column as a proper diary, recording your personal travels, observations, interactions with people, etc.?' He said, 'No, I cannot do it. For there will be too much of "I" in it, which I dislike.' When I persisted, saying the readers would like a first-person account by him, he reluctantly agreed.

After writing two columns, Deendayalji came to me and said, 'Lal, I cannot continue. It's not in my nature to write like this. I'll write about issues, not about myself.' I have cited this episode on many later occasions, while speaking about Deendayalji's humble and self-effacing personality. His utter inability and unwillingness to think about himself was of a kind that is unimaginable today.

THE CHINESE AGGRESSION OF 1962

In October 1961, Malkani secured a fellowship at Harvard University and left for the US for two years. In his absence, I took over as Acting Editor of *Organiser*. During this period, one of the big issues we covered, week after week with intense passion, was the Chinese aggression of 1962. The Jana Sangh favoured peaceful ties between India and all its neighbours. However, right from the early 1950s, our party was apprehensive about the rather sentimental manner in which Prime Minister Nehru was trying to befriend China as part of his grandiose vision of internationalism. After the abrupt occupation of Tibet by China, in October 1950, we were quite concerned about India's security along our long mountainous border with China. These concerns were fully shared by Deputy Prime Minister Sardar Patel. In fact, in a prescient letter to Prime Minister Nehru on 7 November 1950, just five weeks before his death, Patel had written*:

> The Chinese government has tried to delude us by professions of peaceful intention.... Even though we regard ourselves as the friends of China, the Chinese do not regard us as their friends. With the Communist mentality of 'whoever is not with them being against them', this is a significant pointer, of which we have to take due note.

Referring to the Chinese occupation of Tibet, Patel writes:

> We have to consider what new situation now faces us as a result of the disappearance of Tibet as we knew it and the expansion of China almost up to our gates. Throughout history, we have seldom been worried about our north-east frontier. Thus, for the first time, India's defense has to concentrate itself on two fronts simultaneously. Our defense measures have so far been based on the calculations of superiority over Pakistan. In our calculations, we shall now have to reckon with Communist China which has

---

* The full text of Patel's letter to Nehru has been reproduced in Jaswant Singh's book *A Call to Honour*, Rupa & Co., 2006, pp. 394-400.

definite ambitions and aims and which does not, in any way, seem friendly disposed towards us.... In my judgment the situation is one which we cannot afford either to be complacent or to be vacillating.'

These concerns were powerfully, and repeatedly, articulated both in the editorials and reports of *Organiser*, as well as in the Jana Sangh's resolutions and statements. Indeed, one of Atalji's most memorable speeches in Parliament was on the issue of Tibet. Sadly, Defence Minister V.K. Krishna Menon was not in favour of expanding India's military strength. Nehru trusted him. Nehru also trusted the Chinese, believing that China would never attack India. Those were the days when the slogan '*Hindi Chini Bhai Bhai*' was very much in vogue, thanks to a vigorous propaganda by the government media, which projected it as a great triumph of Nehru's foreign policy. But, when China suddenly attacked India in October 1962, Nehru was heartbroken. He saw it as an act of betrayal by a friend. However, because of his wrong approach, India was unprepared militarily and paid a heavy price in the war. The bitter memory of defeat in 1962 has still not been completely erased from the collective memory of Indians, even after the passage of nearly half a century.

Soon after the end of the war, on 25 December 1962, I went to Ladakh, as part of a twelve-member journalists' team, on a visit arranged by the government. Six members of the team were foreign correspondents while the remaining were Indians. Our four-day tour of Leh and surrounding places opened my eyes to the extremely harsh geographical and climatic conditions in which our Army was called upon to defend India's borders. We visited many places including Chushul, the highest point, located at an altitude of about 15,000 feet. Due to such forbidding heights, air pressure was low, which made breathing difficult. The winter temperature dipped to sub-freezing levels. However, in spite of the harsh conditions, Defence Ministry officials had made excellent arrangements for our team. Each of us was provided with sufficient tinned food, special shoes and headgear, and thick woollens to beat the cold. But, to my utter dismay, I found that our jawans did not even have proper winter clothes and shoes to wear. I was overcome by a huge sense of guilt.

It was after the Chinese aggression that the Indian government created the Indo-Tibetan Border Police (ITBP), for the security of the frontiers along the Himalayan border, covering 2,115 kilometres from Karakoram Pass to Lipulekh Pass at the tri-junction of India, Nepal and China. Many years later, as India's Home Minister, I had the opportunity of frequently interacting with our paramilitary forces, including the ITBP. During all my visits to this beautiful part of Jammu & Kashmir, I made it a point to stay with the ITBP contingent.

As in the case of Kashmir in 1947-48, the Chinese aggression of 1962 exposed dangerous flaws in India's foreign and defence policies. It also uncovered the extra-territorial loyalty of Indian communists. They supported China both during the war and after India's defeat. As a result, the government was compelled to put many top communist leaders behind bars. On the other hand, the nationalist approach of the Jana Sangh and the RSS was widely appreciated both in governmental circles and, even more so, among the people at large. RSS *swayamsevaks* and Jana Sangh workers organised a nationwide blood donation and fund collection drive, and worked tirelessly to rouse patriotic sentiments among the masses through a range of activities.

END OF THE NEHRU ERA

The Chinese aggression of 1962 was, in many ways, a major turning point in the history of post-Independence India. The outcome of the war had shattered the spirit of Pandit Nehru, from which he never fully recovered. When he passed away on 27 May 1964, the curtains came down on a significant era in Indian politics. I had mixed feelings about him when he was alive, and my appreciation of his personality and his legacy has not changed much in all these years.

Nehru was undoubtedly a great patriot. He struggled and sacrificed a great deal for India's freedom. After becoming India's first Prime Minister in 1947—courtesy Mahatma Gandhi's preference of him over Sardar Patel, who, it is worth recalling, was the choice of a majority of Congress leaders across the country—he laid a firm foundation for India's self-reliant economic development. In the initial years of Independence, the public sector perforce had to play a dominant role in India's industrialisation process. However, Nehru was also responsible, under the influence of the Soviet Union, for laying the foundation of a doctrinaire license-quota-permit raj, which constrained the growth of India's private entrepreneurship. His daughter, Indira Gandhi, further tightened the grip of the flawed Soviet model on India's economic development—and she did so for reasons of brazen political expediency.

I have, on many occasions, praised Nehru's contribution to the establishment and strengthening of the system of parliamentary democracy in India. Nevertheless, there was also a strong imperious streak in him. His personal animosity towards colleagues he disliked, occasionally manifested in small-mindedness. For example, he did not show Dr Rajendra Prasad, India's first President, the respect he deserved both on account of the high Constitutional office he held and his significant contribution to the freedom movement.

Nehru's personal prejudice towards Dr Syama Prasad Mookerjee, who had quit his Cabinet to establish the Bharatiya Jana Sangh, was well known. The latter was unanimously considered a far better orator in Parliament than Nehru. One day, Nehru threatened in Parliament: 'I will crush the Jana Sangh.' To which, Dr Mookerjee retorted: 'And we will crush this crushing mentality of the Prime Minister.'

History, however, will locate Nehru's greatest failures in his flawed handling of the war with Pakistan in 1948 and the war with China in 1962. Had he remained firm and uncompromising when Pakistan made its first audacious attempt to capture Kashmir, the issue could have been settled once and for all, and India would have been spared the enormous pain and loss that it has suffered in subsequent decades. Similarly, had Nehru been less 'starry-eyed' in his policy towards China, India could have evolved its relations with Beijing, on a more realistic basis. Perhaps, even the border dispute could have been settled peacefully.

THE INDIA-PAKISTAN WAR OF 1965

The question, 'Who after Nehru?', had become a topic of debate in his final years. The answer lay in Lal Bahadur Shastri, a dedicated Congressman known for his simplicity, modesty and incorruptibility. His personal qualities soon won him the goodwill of the nation. Unlike Nehru, he did not harbour any ideological hostility towards the Jana Sangh and the RSS. He used to often invite Shri Guruji for consultation on national issues. As a representative of *Organiser*, I met him several times in his South Block office or at his Janpath residence, each time carrying a positive impression of this remarkably short-statured but large-hearted Prime Minister.

Within a year of Shastri's premiership, the Jana Sangh was compelled to launch a major countrywide satyagraha against the Kutch Agreement in 1965. When India was partitioned, Sindh became a part of Pakistan, but the whole of the princely state of Kutch acceded to India. However, Pakistan persisted with its obdurate claim that the border between the two countries ran through the middle of the Rann of Kutch. The dispute involved some 3,500 square miles of territory. In April 1965, Pakistan's army made unexpected and lightning incursions into Kutch and occupied a part of our territory. The border skirmish that followed ended with a ceasefire brokered by the British government. The agreement between the two sides entailed a reference of the issue to a neutral international body for final settlement. The Jana Sangh opposed it because it provided legitimacy to Pakistan's armed violation of India's territorial integrity. Our party was also concerned that by referring the issue to international arbitration, India would accept Kutch as a disputed territory and this would set the wrong precedent for settling the larger issue of Kashmir. The culmination of the nationwide Kutch Satyagraha was to be in the form of a rally, in Delhi, on 16 August 1965.

As Secretary of the Delhi unit of the Jana Sangh, I was responsible for organising a large army of volunteers for the protest action. On the appointed day, more than five lakh volunteers marched in front of Parliament and congregated for a rally at the Boat Club lawns. The *Statesman* newspaper described it as 'the biggest ever witnessed in the capital so far'. BBC and other western media called it 'gigantic', 'breathtaking' and 'unprecedented'.

What won everyone's praise was the protestors' orderly and disciplined conduct. The Jana Sangh's prestige rose enormously all across the country on account of this rally.

The armed incursions into Kutch were only a prelude to Pakistan's full-scale invasion of Kashmir in September 1965. The military rulers in Islamabad had deluded themselves into believing that the Indian Army would be unable to defend itself, following a loss to China in 1962. Shastri faced the crisis with iron will. 'Force will be met with force,' he assured the nation. 'Go forward and strike,' was his command to the armed forces. He lit the fire of patriotic fervour in the country by coining the immortal slogan '*Jai Jawan Jai Kisan*' (Hail the Soldier, Hail the Farmer) and calling upon the people to skip one meal a week to tide over the food shortage facing the country. There was unprecedented response to this call. Once again, RSS and Jana Sangh workers were in the forefront of mobilising support to the Indian Army, which almost reached the outskirts of Lahore.

At the end of three weeks of warfare, when Pakistan was on the verge of facing a humiliating defeat, international pressure forced a ceasefire. This was followed by summit-level talks between Prime Minister Shastri and Pakistan's President, General Muhammad Ayub Khan, at Tashkent in the erstwhile USSR in January 1966. Alexei Kosygin, Premier of the Soviet Union, was the intermediary. The Jana Sangh opposed the Tashkent talks. A delegation of our party, led by Atal Bihari Vajpayee, called on Shastri and urged him not to go for the summit meeting. We were apprehensive that international pressure might force the Indian side to return Haji Pir and Tithwa, the two important posts captured by the Indian Army in Pakistan-occupied Kashmir (POK).

A few weeks before Shastri was scheduled to leave for Tashkent, I met him in his office to interview him for *Organiser*. I expressed the widespread fear that India might be pressured into relinquishing Haji Pir and Tithwa posts to Pakistan. The Prime Minister's response was categorical. 'Rest assured,' he said, 'that will not happen.'

Sadly, this is exactly what happened when Shastri signed the Tashkent Declaration on 10 January 1966 along with General Ayub Khan. Indians expected him to talk to Pakistan from a position of strength because India's military had already demonstrated its superiority on the battlefield.

He had resisted, till the very end, any compromise deal. At one point, when Kosygin said to him, 'You will have to give up Haji Pir and Tithwa,' Shastri had even retorted, 'In that case, you will have to talk to some other Prime Minister.'

Mysteriously, at the end of the prolonged negotiations, Shastri agreed to withdraw Indian forces from these two posts in return for a vague Pakistani assurance not to resort to arms to settle bilateral issues. The outcome of the summit was not to his liking, and he probably carried a heavy burden of guilt on his conscience. He died of a massive heart attack in Tashkent on 11 January, within hours of signing the joint declaration.

The news stunned and shocked the nation. In a very short period, Shastri had risen to great heights in people's esteem. His sudden and untimely demise had a major effect on the subsequent power struggle within the Congress party.

*

My life in Delhi after I joined *Organiser* was very satisfying and fulfilling. As a journalist, I got the opportunity to interact with many renowned national leaders such as Jayaprakash Narayan, Dr Ram Manohar Lohia* and Morarji Desai. The journal gave me both space and freedom to indulge, my love for writing. At the same time, I could continue my work as a political activist in the Jana Sangh. Above all, I enjoyed the trust and affection of my colleagues, both in *Organiser* and in the party.

At this happy juncture came a new turn in my life, bringing greater happiness.

---

* Ram Manohar Lohia (1910-67) was a firebrand freedom fighter and a towering socialist intellectual and leader. An ardent follower of Mahatma Gandhi, he was a close friend of Nehru in his younger years but later turned a bitter critic of India's first Prime Minister, resolving to end the one-party domination of the Congress in Indian politics. This brought him closer to the Jana Sangh. He also became an admirer of the RSS, but felt that it did not know how best to use its vast organisational strength. Lohia once told me: 'If I had the army of dedicated and disciplined volunteers like what the RSS has, I would have by now brought about a political revolution in India ending the monopoly of the Congress.'

3

THE BLISS OF FAMILY LIFE

To put the world right in order, we must first put the nation in order; to put the nation in order, we must first put the family in order; to put the family in order, we must first cultivate our personal life; we must first set our hearts right.

—CONFUCIUS, 551-479 BC

The *pracharak* system in the RSS is unique in many ways. For example, a *pracharak* cannot take up a job or do a business. He has to live on the modest honorarium given by the Sangh and follow strict rectitude in financial matters. Secondly, the Sangh generally requires its *pracharaks* to remain unmarried. The idea behind this obligation is that a *swayamsevak* who voluntarily chooses to become a *pracharak* devotes his entire life to serve the cause of the nation with undivided attention. In other words, he becomes 'wedded' to the goals and ideals of the nation.

One of the inspiring mottos of the RSS is: *Rashtraya swaha. Rashtraya idam na mama.* In free rendering, it means—'I offer my all to the nation. This, my all, belongs to the nation, not to me.'

I had accepted this motto when I joined the RSS in Karachi at the age of fourteen. My conviction grew stronger with the passage of time, and especially after my migration from Sindh. Hence the idea of marriage had never seriously crossed my mind when I was working in Rajasthan or even after moving to Delhi. And since I was living and working with other full-time members of the Jana Sangh, many of whom were also *pracharaks* of the RSS, I was rarely conscious of being the odd man out. However, things changed after I joined *Organiser*; I became financially independent and started living in my own house. I had thus ceased to be a *pracharak*.

In 1957 my younger sister Sheela married Santo Bhavnani and settled in Bombay. It was she who began to insist that I too get married and start a family. She kept reminding me of the fact that I had already crossed thirty. I was slowly warming up to her idea. However, since I had never befriended any lady in my life, I consented to her suggestion that she would find a suitable life-partner for me.

In early 1965, I had gone to Vijayawada in Andhra Pradesh to attend a conference of the Jana Sangh. I was then a member of the National Executive of the party. Incidentally, it was here that Pandit Deendayal Upadhyaya presented, for the first time before the party's executive, his philosophical treatise on 'Integral Humanism'. On my way back, I spent a few days in Bombay. Sheela had arranged for me to meet Kamla Jagtiani, whose family, like ours, hailed from Karachi. I readily agreed. The brief meeting with Kamla on that day was the beginning of a lifelong companionship with her.

Kamla's side of the family knew very little about the nature of my work, except that I was a journalist and also a political activist. At a get-together of the two families, someone brought that day's issue of the *Times of India* and asked me, 'Is this your name in the newspaper?' The paper had mentioned, in a news report from Vijayawada, my name as a member of the four-man committee set up by the Jana Sangh to revise the party constitution. When I answered in the affirmative, I could see that they were both surprised and impressed by the answer.

Kamla and I were married in Bombay on 25 February 1965. It was a simple ceremony according to Vedic rites. The reception was held on the terrace of K.C. College near Churchgate, which was established by two great Sindhi philanthropists, Principal K.M. Kundnani and Barrister Hotchand Advani. Kamla belonged to a rich and renowned family in Karachi. Unlike mine, hers was a large family—she had four brothers and a sister. In the aftermath of Partition, her family had to flee in extremely trying circumstances, reaching India in a dispossessed condition. Kamla's father, Premchand Jagtiani, a noble soul who did not take any compensation from the government for his lost property, passed away in 1952. Thereafter, she took upon herself the task of looking after her family. She worked in the General Post Office first at Gol Dak Khana in Delhi for eight years and, later, near V.T. Station in Bombay for nine years.

Thus, like me, Kamla too, was used to living a hard life. This made it possible for us to live happily with modest means in Delhi. In the initial months of our marriage, Kamla was astonished to see me washing my own clothes. She did not like it. 'Why do you do this?' she asked me.

I said, 'I have been doing this ever since I started working as a *pracharak* in Rajasthan.'

'No, I won't let you do this anymore. I'll wash them,' she said, and forced me to give up this practice.

Life is full of gifts from God. One of the most precious of these is the bliss of family life. Kamla and I had our first child, Jayant, on 18 February 1966. Our happiness was redoubled when Pratibha was born on 6 September 1967. Both were born in Bombay. In fact, Pratibha stayed with her *nani* (grandmother) for a couple of years in Bombay, and received her early *samskaras* from this saintly lady.

Seeing our children grow up was a source of immense joy and amazement for me. I remember, as a child, Jayant insisting every evening that I take him to show '*paani mein batti*' (lamps in water), his imaginative description of the illuminated fountains at India Gate in Delhi. Soon both Jayant and Pratibha joined Raghubir Singh Junior Modern School at Humayun Road, and I would drop them at school in my green newly purchased Fiat. I assisted them in their homework and rarely missed their sports and cultural events—generally, Jayant's cricket matches and Pratibha's ballets and elocution performances.

There is one speech that Pratibha gave in the morning assembly in her school, some time in February 1977, which I recall with much pride. The Emergency had been lifted in January and most of the political prisoners had been set free. I had returned to Delhi after spending nineteen months in Bangalore's Central Jail. Prime Minister Indira Gandhi was compelled to hold stalled parliamentary elections. Jayaprakash Narayan, under whose angelic leadership many Opposition parties had agreed to form a single platform called the Janata Party, had emerged as the hero of India's 'Second Freedom Struggle'. Pratibha was only ten years old, and this is what she said in her speech:

> In March, our country is going to elect its new Lok Sabha. The principal contest is going to be between the Congress and the Janata Party. The short form of the Janata Party is JP. It was formed largely due to the efforts of Jayaprakash Narayan, also known as JP. If I may be allowed to mention, my brother's name is Jayant and mine is Pratibha, and we also add up to JP!

In bringing up our children, I never imposed my views on them in any matter. I let them develop freely according to their own innate potential. The atmosphere in our family was such that the basic values of patriotism and good character were embedded in Jayant and Pratibha at a young age. Children are better learners than grown-ups can imagine. They learn much more from the conduct of parents and others in the social surrounding than from the spoken word. There is a beautiful poem titled 'Children' by Khalil Gibran, the celebrated Lebanese poet, which I recommend to all parents:

> *Your children are not your children.*
> *They are the sons and daughters of Life's longing for itself.*
> *They come through you but not from you,*
> *And though they are with you yet they belong not to you.*
> *You may give them your love but not your thoughts,*
> *For they have their own thoughts.*

You may house their bodies but not their souls,
For their souls dwell in the house of tomorrow,
which you cannot visit, not even in your dreams.
You may strive to be like them,
but seek not to make them like you.
For life goes not backward nor tarries with yesterday.

You are the bows from which your children
as living arrows are sent forth.
The archer sees the mark upon the path of the infinite,
and He bends you with His might
that His arrows may go swift and far.
Let our bending in the archer's hand be for gladness;
For even as He loves the arrow that flies,
so He loves also the bow that is stable.

❋

It is said that women hold up half the sky. I think in Kamla's case, this is a gross understatement since the full credit for supporting, sustaining, and raising our family goes to her. Because of my mounting political responsibilities and frequent travels across the country, I could not devote enough time to my family. I was also totally unfamiliar with money-related matters, partly because of my temperament and partly on account of my *pracharak* background. This increased the burden on Kamla's shoulders. Indeed, throughout my stay in jail during the Emergency, my family had no income. Yet, she managed the household and children's education on our meager savings and some help from her sister Sarla in Bombay. With the passage of years and decades, I have been repeatedly surprised by her quietly courageous personality, her almost limitless capacity for hard work, her meticulous handling of family finances, and, above all, her boundless love and care for me and our children. Indisputably, she has been the mainstay of our family.

A political activist's house is rarely a quiet place; there is always a steady stream of visitors. Here again, Kamla was an enthusiastic hostess.* Often senior leaders of the RSS and the Jana Sangh would come to our modest house, informally or on specific work. Besides Deendayalji and Atalji, these included Dattopant Thengdi, who founded the Bharatiya Mazdoor Sangh (BMS) and developed it into India's largest trade union; Rajendra Sharma, who managed the party's parliamentary office for many years; Sundar Singh Bhandari, my party colleague from Rajasthan days; and N.M. (Appa) Ghatate†, a young lawyer and party activist and his wife Sheila. All of them were almost members of my family. I especially developed a very close personal rapport with Thengdiji, even though I did not agree with his rather cynical approach to politics and political parties. All of them, unfailingly, found the atmosphere warm and hospitable.

I would like to describe here, at some length, my association with one such person who spearheaded a remarkable project of national renaissance.

EKNATH RANADE, A TRUE KARMAYOGI

One of the outstanding leaders of the RSS with whom I worked closely during my *Organiser* years, and whose personality left an indelible impression on me, was Eknath Ranade. He was not only a man of vision but also a man of action, a rare combination indeed. Once he resolved to do something, he would never rest till the task was accomplished.

A towering testimony to such perseverance was a project, which Eknathji had himself envisioned—to construct the Vivekananda Rock Memorial at Kanyakumari, at the point where, in Gandhiji's words, the three seas meet to wash the feet of Bharatmata, our Motherland. This is the rock on

---

* Pratibha and I call Kamla *annapurna* (bestower of food), since one of her greatest sources of happiness is to make guests happy with meals cooked by herself.
† Appa Ghatate served as Vice Chairman of the 17th Law Commission. His family in Nagpur has rendered distinguished service in the RSS. Sheila assisted me in my parliamentary work for some years.

which Swami Vivekananda meditated for three days in December 1892, during his extensive travels in South India. He would say later that he meditated about the past, present and future of India. The following year, on 11 September 1893, the meditation found its most eloquent expression in Swamiji's historic speech on universal brotherhood and inter-faith harmony at the World Parliament of Religions in Chicago.

It was Eknathji's dream that India honour this peerless patriot-monk—'a lion among men', as Maharshi Aurobindo described him—with a suitable memorial at Kanyakumari. The idea evoked a prompt and positive response from Shri Guruji and others with whom he discussed it. Eknathji's took charge as the Organising Secretary of the Vivekananda Rock Memorial Committee in 1963. Branches of the committee were set up in many cities across the country. I was appointed Organising Secretary of the Delhi committee. This gave me an opportunity to work closely with Eknathji and absorb some of his indefatigable energy.

The project encountered many roadblocks along the way, including one at the very beginning. Eknathji had written a letter to Prime Minister Indira Gandhi seeking permission from the Government of India for the construction of the Vivekananda Rock Memorial. The matter was referred to Humayun Kabir, who was the Minister of Education and Culture. Kabir rejected the proposal, expressing his views on record that any construction at the mid-water rock in Kanyakumari would ruin the unique aesthetic beauty of the place where the three oceans meet.

Eknathji was disappointed, but not deterred. He asked me, 'What should we do now?' I suggested that he should write letters to all MPs describing the concept of the project and its national importance, and seek their support for the same. 'How many signatures do you think we can obtain?' he asked me. I told him I couldn't say but it was worth making the effort. We pursued the task vigorously and met leaders of various political parties. To our amazement, we received the signatures of over 300 MPs, most of them from the Congress party, and several even from the CPI and CPI(M). Backed with the endorsement of a large cross-section of MPs, we made a fresh request to Prime Minister Indira Gandhi. She gave permission for the project.

There were a few other obstacles to the project, but these were minor and were easily overcome. For example, Christians in Tamil Nadu said that it was not Vivekananda Rock but St. Francis Xavier's Rock, and hence demanded a memorial to be constructed in honour of the sixteenth century missionary from Spain. The government of Tamil Nadu turned down this demand.

From the very beginning, Eknathji wanted to garner support for this project from all parties and all sections of society. Notwithstanding his RSS background, he had good personal relations with Indira Gandhi and others with divergent political and ideological leanings. The fact that he had worked for many years in Bengal and could speak fluent Bengali endeared him to many communist leaders too. Almost everyone he met was impressed by the sincerity and conviction with which he spoke, and how he embodied Swami Vivekananda's ideals of *tyaga* and *seva*—renunciation and service. Consequently, he also received full support and cooperation for his endeavour from all the spiritual leaders of the country. Two such revered personalities who blessed and guided the project at every stage were Swami Ranganathananda and His Holiness Shri Chandrasekhara Saraswati Swamiji of Kanchi. It was a tribute to Eknathji's exceptional leadership qualities and organisational skills that the Rock Memorial mission was never entangled in any controversy.

Eknathji was determined to collect most of the estimated amount of Rs 1.25 crore, needed for the project, not from the rich but from ordinary people in the form of small donations of one or two rupees each. This gave an opportunity to tens of thousands of volunteers all over the country to reach out to the common people and spread the message of Swami Vivekananda. Since it was to be a national memorial, Eknathji also sought contributions from the central and state governments. The Government of India donated rupees ten lakhs. Donations also came from all the state governments, except one. Eknathji gives a vivid description of this exception: 'Leaders of every political party, whether in power or in the Opposition, became willing partners of the Vivekananda Rock Memorial at Kanyakumari. The only Chief Minister who sent me back empty-handed without contributing any amount to the Rock Memorial fund was the then Kerala Chief Minister Comrade E.M.S. Namboodiripad. I can say this much about my abortive interview with him. It was like conversing with a sphinx. It was monologue all the way on my part. Only an empty stare from the other side.'

Eknathji was a hard taskmaster. During the six years (1964–70) it took to build the memorial, he would often stay at my small flat at R.K. Puram. Sometimes he would even come at 2 o'clock in the morning and say, 'Lal, we have to draft this appeal.' The magnificent memorial was finally inaugurated on 2 September 1970, and dedicated to the nation by V.V. Giri, who was, at that time, the President of India. How this grand monument, a tribute to one of the greatest saints of modern India, came to be built is truly an inspiring saga. I feel privileged and humbled that I could play a small role in this national effort.

After this mammoth but immensely satisfying task, Eknathji set out to establish a 'Thought Memorial' to implement his ideals in India's national life. Thus was born the Vivekananda Kendra in Kanyakumari in 1972. This spiritually oriented service mission trains men and women, especially youth, to do *nishkama karma* (selfless service) in various areas of nation-building. Eknathji travelled extensively, especially in the far-flung tribal-populated areas of the North-East and Andaman and Nicobar Islands, to establish the branches of the Vivekananda Kendra there. He was a true *karmayogi* who worked tirelessly almost till the end of his life—even after he recovered from a stroke that severely incapacitated him. To those who advised him rest, he would say, 'I was dead for a few months, I had closed my eyes; but now that I am back, it means God still wants me to work. I do not want to rest and rust. I must work now harder to complete my tasks during the time granted to me. Life without work is like death to me. God will keep me as long as He wishes; let me work.'

Eknathji breathed his last on 22 August 1982.

4

My Entry into the Delhi Metropolitan Council

Let every man make known what kind of government would command his respect, and that will be one step toward obtaining it.

—Henry David Thoreau

My seven-year stint with *Organiser* came to an end in 1967. An important responsibility paved my return to Delhi's politics. Delhi was a full-fledged state from 1952 to 1955. However, its statehood was annulled by the Central Government on the recommendation of the States' Reorganisation Commission in 1955. It was declared a Union Territory, with two municipal bodies: New Delhi Municipal Corporation (NDMC), to look after the civic needs of New Delhi, which was then almost entirely confined to offices and residential quarters of the Central Government; and Municipal Corporation of Delhi (MCD), to run the civic services in Old Delhi and other new areas of the city, most of which came into being in the past two or three decades.

The decision to revoke the statehood of Delhi had not gone down well with its citizens. Jana Sangh articulated their aspirations and became the first party to demand full statehood for the national capital. The party also led a mass agitation on this issue. As a compromise, the Central Government consented to constitute the Delhi Municipal Council, which had the status of a deemed State Legislative Assembly. It also announced that the new Council would be elected along with the fourth general elections scheduled in March 1967. This did not satisfy people's aspirations and, hence, the government was forced to establish an interim Council in October 1966. Its members were nominated by parties on the basis of their respective strengths in the MCD. The Jana Sangh nominated me to the Council and I became the leader of the Opposition in it.

Within five months, Delhi witnessed three elections, almost simultaneously—to the Lok Sabha, Metropolitan Council and the Municipal Corporation. The Jana Sangh triumphed in all three elections. Our party secured six out of seven Lok Sabha seats; fifty-two out of hundred seats in MCD; and thirty-three out of fifty-six seats in the Council. This staggering triple-victory in the national capital, along with the substantial increase in our tally in the Lok Sabha from fourteen in 1962 to thirty-five in 1967, catapulted the Jana Sangh as a potentially powerful force in Indian politics.

I had not contested the Council elections since I was entrusted with the responsibility of organising my party's city unit for the three polls. Under the Delhi Metropolitan Council Act, the Union Home Ministry could nominate five members to the Council. Making use of this provision, Atalji persuaded the Union Home Minister Y.B. Chavan to nominate me to the Council. The party then decided to field me as a candidate for the election of the Council's Chairman. I won the election and became the Presiding Officer. Vijay Kumar Malhotra, my colleague in the Jana Sangh, became the Chief Executive in the Council. He is now my colleague in the Lok Sabha too, serving as the Deputy Leader of the BJP.

The Chairman's role was primarily to preside over the affairs of the legislature, more like that of the Speaker of a legislature. In order to maintain the neutrality of the new office I was occupying, I voluntarily resigned from all party positions, retaining only its primary membership. I also quit my job as the Assistant Editor of *Organiser*. K.R. Malkani was among the many people who felicitated me on becoming the Chairman of the Council. In an embarrassingly euphoric praise for me in the journal, he wrote: 'Lal…has no enemies, not even any critics. He should go far in public life. *Organiser* is happy to wish him the best of luck in the service of the motherland.'

Neelam Sanjiva Reddy, who later became the President of India (1977-82), was the Speaker of the Lok Sabha during those days. My new responsibility as the Presiding Officer of the Council enabled me to come in close contact with him. I attended all the conferences convened by him for the Speakers of state legislatures, which were highly educative for me in terms of learning about the intricacies of India's democratic parliamentary system. I had to be scrupulously non-partisan in conducting the proceedings of the Council, giving full opportunity to members of all parties to express their views. I tried my best to steer the discussions in a constructive and meaningful direction, conscious of my duty to set healthy precedents in the newly constituted body. Sometimes, my rulings were not liked by my own partymen in the government. Once, some of them insisted on removing a Congress member from the Council for his continued absence from the House. The manner in which the duration of absence was being computed was very arbitrary. I intervened saying, 'No, it's not proper to do so. I shall not allow it.' When I relinquished my office on 17 March 1970, I was touched by the warm send-off given to me by the entire Council.

My nearly three-year-long stint as the Council's Chairman was relatively free of hectic activity. I had neither any executive responsibility in the Council nor any organisational duty in the party. This gave me ample time to study several issues related to the functioning of the parliamentary system as well as the role and responsibilities of the speaker. It was during this period that, at Deendayalji's suggestion, I started a serious study of the history of electoral reforms in various democracies, especially in the UK. After many years, I could once again indulge myself in my love for books. To this, I added a new love—that of theatre and music concerts.

Above all, I had the satisfaction of spending more time with Kamla and our two young children.

The Lieutenant Governor of Delhi during those three years was Adityanath Jha, perhaps the last surviving Indian Civil Service (ICS) officer. When Indira Gandhi first joined the government in 1964, as Minister of Information & Broadcasting in Shastri's Cabinet, Jha was a Secretary in the Ministry. Due to his long experience as a senior bureaucrat, interacting with him informally was always a pleasure. Once when Jha and I were discussing the question of minister-bureaucrat relations, Jha recounted to me an interesting fable. This was about a centipede which became afflicted with arthritis. Naturally, for the centipede, the ailment was extremely agonising. Her family, unable to see their mother suffer such excruciating pain, advised her to consult the Wise Owl living on a nearby tree. The centipede went to the Wise Owl who, after listening to her woes, gravely pronounced: 'Your problem is that you have too many feet. The remedy is simple. Convert yourself into a crow, and the pain will be considerably mitigated.'

Mother centipede returned home very happy, and shared the Wise Owl's prescription with her children. One of the little ones asked: 'Mother, but how will you convert yourself into a crow?' The centipede felt stumped. 'I forgot to ask him that,' she said, and forthwith proceeded to the Wise Owl again to get his guidance.

Jha completed his narrative thus: 'The Wise Owl's response was that of a typical minister: *My* function is to lay down policy; how to execute it is *your* job!'

By this time, I had shifted to a new house on Pandara Road. As the chairman of the DMC, I was entitled to a big bungalow. But I did not take it, preferring a flat which is allotted to accredited journalists. Apart from not having any desire for a bungalow, I also had a lurking apprehension. 'I cannot be sure of the longevity of my stint in the Council,' I said to myself, 'and may well have to go back to *Organiser* after some time. It's better therefore to live in a flat that journalists are accredited to.'

As the sun set on the decade of the 1960s, my stint at the Council also drew to a close. With this began a phase in my life—the beginning of my parliamentary career. Jana Sangh wanted me to enter the Rajya Sabha, to which I was elected in April 1970.

THE DIVISIVE DEBATE ON HINDI

Before I gallop to the 1970s, I would like to recall that the decade of the 1960s witnessed a deeply divisive debate on the status of Hindi in our national life. The Constitution of India, which came into existence on 26 January 1950, had enshrined Hindi and English as the 'Official Languages' of the Central Government for a period of fifteen years, after which Hindi was expected to be the sole 'national and official' language of India. Initially, there was no resistance to this policy. However, as 1965 drew closer, it invited strong opposition in Tamil Nadu (then called the state of Madras). Rigid positions were taken by some people in both South and North India, which raised the spectre of a threat to national unity and integrity. Eventually, the anti-Hindi agitation subsided with the government declaring that both Hindi and English would be the 'Official Languages' of the Central Government.

This debate posed a peculiar challenge before the Jana Sangh. Most of our supporters were in the northern states and hence their solidarity with Hindi was understandable. It was also undeniable that Hindi deserved to be recognised as the national language, in view of its preeminent role in unifying people across the states. However, our party was also sensitive to the concerns of non-Hindi speaking people and, even more, to the imperative of preserving national cohesion. In this delicate situation, Deendayalji guided the party along a principled path that simultaneously showed our commitment to the promotion of Hindi, our respect for all other Indian languages, and our appreciation of the importance of English. Atalji, who had developed a good personal relationship with C.N. Annadurai (1909–69), Tamil Nadu's charismatic and first non-Congress Chief Minister, also contributed to the evolution of a balanced language policy by the Jana Sangh.

In the context of the correct language policy for India, one cannot overlook the conscious strategy of the British to make Indians feel inferior about their own native language and culture. I recall here Lord Macaulay's revealing remarks in his address to the British Parliament on 2 February 1835:

> I have traveled across the length and breadth of India and I have not seen one person who is a beggar, who is a thief. Such wealth I have seen in this country, such high moral values, people of such caliber, that I do not think that we would ever conquer this country, unless we break the very backbone of this nation, which is her cultural and spiritual heritage, and, therefore, I propose that we replace her old and ancient education system, her culture, for if the Indians think that all that is foreign and English is good and greater than their own, they will lose their self esteem, their native culture and they will become what we want them—a truly dominated nation.

Macaulay's colonising strategy was engrained in the education system introduced by the British in India.* Somehow, its effect has survived even after Independence. Those who speak only Hindi or other Indian languages, and are not very conversant in English, are generally looked down upon in our country. I have often given a personal example to illustrate this point. I knew very little Hindi during the first twenty years of my life that I spent in Sindh. However, I studied it diligently after I came to Rajasthan. But it was only when I shifted to Delhi in 1957 that I realised how English enjoys a higher social status in India. For example, whenever the telephone rang and I happened to pick it up, my first expression would be—it still is—'*Haan ji*' (Hindi for 'yes, please'). To which, many times the response from the other side used to be: '*Sahab ghar mein hain?*' (Is sahib at home?). And I would tell them, '*Aap ko Advani se baat karni hai, to main bol raha hoon.*' (If you wish to speak to Advani, you are talking to the right person.)

In the context of the language debate in India, I have always maintained that our opposition is not to *Angrezi* (English) per se, but to *Angreziyat*

---

* Dr Ram Manohar Lohia was a particularly strong proponent of Hindi. He said that the British ruled India with bullet and language—'*bandook ki goli aur angrezi ki boli*'.

(Englishness), which makes people harbour a sense of an inferiority complex about their own roots and culture. Having said this, I must hasten to add that the importance of English as a global language in India's development is undeniable. Unfortunately, some mistakes were committed in this regard in the past, especially when we had Samyukta Vidhayak Dal (SVD) governments in several north Indian states in the late 1960s. The Jana Sangh was a part of the SVD those days, and so was the Socialist Party. Under the latter's influence, the governments decided to make English an optional subject in the school curriculum. It was a mistake as it discouraged the people in Hindi-speaking states from learning English which proved to be a disadvantage in later decades.

Another peculiar aspect of the language debate in the 1960s was on the kind of Hindi used for official purposes and in government-run media. For example, Pandit Nehru used to frequently take exception to the Hindi used by Akashvani (All India Radio). He would complain that the Hindi was too complicated and could not be understood by the common people. 'We should use only simple Hindi,' he would insist. By this he generally meant that there should be more Urdu words in it because, according to him, Urdu was more widely understood in North India.

Prime Minister Nehru's views on this matter invited a lot of criticism. As a journalist, this subject interested me deeply. Once I went to meet N.G. Ranga, a veteran Congress leader, on this matter. He said, 'When Pandit Nehru talks of "simple Hindi", he is generally influenced by his Lucknow concepts. For me, it is easier to understand Vajpayee and Prakashveer Shastri rather than Pandit Nehru.' When I asked him why, Ranga, whose mother tongue was Telugu, explained that, in most languages in northern, western and eastern India, as also in at least three of the four South Indian languages—Telugu, Kannada and Malayalam—there are many Sanskrit words that are common to Hindi. He was, thus, really projecting an all-India perspective of Hindi.

It was during those days that I came in contact with Dr Raghuveera. He was a renowned orientalist, linguist and a strong critic of de-Sanskritisation of Hindi. I discussed this matter with him once, and I was greatly impressed by the example he gave. He said, 'We call our law minister "Vidhi Mantri".

Some people say, why not call him "qanoon mantri"? Their justification is that "qanoon" can be understood by more people, at least in northern India, than "vidhi". But let us realise that when we are developing a language for a specific purpose in governance, where several related terms with precise meanings are required to be derived from a root word, we must use such root words that give us ample scope to do so. Now, "law" is not the only word that we have to translate, where people may be more familiar with "qanoon" than "vidhi". We have to also think of the right translations for compounds like "legal", "lawful", and "legitimate", where "vidhi" leads you to "vidhivat", "vaidhanik" and "vaidh", which are commonly used and understood. In contrast, the derivatives of "qanoon" sound quite strange and unfamiliar.'

One of the frequent criticisms was regarding Akashvani using 'difficult'—meaning Sanskritised—Hindi words, rather than words that are commonly understood. Dr Raghuveera's comment on this was equally persuasive. He said, 'Surely, people expect the expressions used by the Hindi newsreader to be as precise as those used by the English newsreader. Now, take an example where the English bulletin says, "The President today issued an ordinance on such and such subject." The Hindi newsreader would broadcast the same news by saying, "*Aaj Rashtrapati ne ek adhyaadesh jaari kiya jiske anusaar...*" Some people would ask, "Why did the Hindi bulletin use a difficult word like *adhyaadesh*? Why not '*aadesh*'? Why not '*hukum*'?" Now, if an English newsreader were to use "order" instead of "ordinance", on the plea that "order" is more commonly understood, he would be taken to task.'

These were simple examples, but to me they brought home an important insight into the language debate. I realised how we were, and still are, ignoring the immense richness and adaptability of Sanskrit. I also understood why it was necessary to safeguard the sanctity and specific identity of every Indian language.

Dr Raghuveera, though a prominent Congressman, had profound admiration for the ideology and organisational ethos of the Jana Sangh. Soon a time came when he decided to join the Jana Sangh. The Chinese aggression and his differences with Pandit Nehru on various national issues contributed to this decision. Even when he was in the Congress, everyone in our party respected him. In 1963, the party elected him as the national President. However, it was a great misfortune that, within a few months, he passed away in a car accident while campaigning for the party in a by-election in UP.

5

Pandit Deendayal Upadhyaya
Thinker, Organiser, Leader Par Excellence

*In life, we shall find many men
that are great, and some men
that are good, but very few men
that are both great and good.*

— Charles Celeb Cotton, eighteenth century English writer

I realised early on in my political life that politics in India is an occupation in which the fame, power, honour and recognition associated with its practitioners often have no relation to their inherent qualities. If a person enters politics, he is automatically seen as a *neta* (leader). Before long, he starts receiving the kind of media publicity that would be the envy of persons in other professions who are far more talented and have a markedly superior record of service to society. In addition, if the person has the capacity to be a rabble-rouser or a troublemaker, he can be sure of becoming more widely popular simply because notoriety, unfortunately, has its assured benefits in politics. While I readily admit that such persons do not constitute a majority among politicians, the negative image of the political class that they create often makes people wonder if there ever can be ideal persons in politics.

This chapter is about one such ideal political leader. It is about a leader who detested fame, and actually felt embarrassed talking about himself. He practiced what he preached. His leadership was rooted in a holistic philosophical outlook that embraced Nature, Humanity, Nation and the Individual. He was a politician who was least fascinated by power, but still wielded enormous moral authority over tens of thousands of his followers. Together with them, he built the solid foundation of a party which, in its new avatar in a few decades, would emerge as a worthy alternative to the Congress.

This chapter is my tribute to my political guru, Pandit Deendayal Upadhyaya.

HOW DEENDAYALJI INFLUENCED ME

As I have expressed earlier, two people—Rajpal Puri and Pandit Deendayal Upadhyaya—exerted the deepest influence on my public life. Rajpalji moulded my character in my teens, an impressionable age when ideas and ideals, once engraved on the mind, are not easily erasable. He was the one who taught me patriotism and showed me the path of selfless service to the nation. The fact that I worked with him in Karachi in the tumultuous years preceding India's Partition added to the emotional content of his influence on me. The land where I played, studied and roamed about was on the verge of having a new and unfamiliar name: Pakistan. It was at this cataclysmic juncture that Rajpalji came into my life, giving it the proper orientation of patriotism and idealism, and intensifying my passion to serve my Motherland. In many ways, Pandit Deendayal Upadhyaya's influence on me was, both intellectually and emotionally, a continuation of what I had received from Rajpalji. It provided the right foundation to my life as a political activist.

Politics is the life-breath of a democracy. It is an important and necessary medium of serving the nation. However, politics can also be a pollutant. Unprincipled quest for power can be murky and confrontational, degrading both its practitioners and the society in which they operate.

It frequently becomes the arena where political parties jettison the larger national interests for narrow and myopic considerations; ideals are sacrificed for the pursuit of individual ambitions; camaraderie is killed by conspiracies against one's own colleagues; and high-sounding words about public good become a camouflage for fulfillment of private greed. True, these negative attributes of Indian politics were not as marked in the 1950s and '60s as they are now.

The Jana Sangh had been formed to strengthen India's democratic system by presenting itself before the people as a superior alternative to the Congress Party. However, both Dr Syama Prasad Mookerjee, its founder, and Deendayalji, who was its chief ideologue and organiser, were very clear that the pursuit of power by *any means* was not to be our objective. The new party had to be a party with a difference. And the difference had to manifest itself not only in its ideology and policies, but also in the *conduct* of its activists and leaders. Deendayalji was well aware of the possibility of the Jana Sangh falling prey to the emerging political culture in India. Therefore, with an audacity and determination rarely seen in the post-Independence era, he set about building the new party on a completely new footing of discipline and dedication, ideology and idealism. I deem it my good fortune that I began my own political life at the feet of this ideal leader.

ORDINARY BACKGROUND, EXTRAORDINARY ACHIEVEMENT

Deendayalji was born on 25 September 1916 in a modest family in a village near Mathura. Fate brought many tragedies, bereavements and hardships to him, both in his early and later years. Braving the odds, he passed the intermediate board examination with distinction from Birla College in Pilani, BA from Kanpur, and MA from Agra. But he was not inclined to take up a job and raise a family. Having come under the spell of the RSS, which he joined in 1937, he decided to devote his entire life to the Sangh as a *pracharak*. In a remarkable letter to his uncle in 1942, he wrote:

> God has blessed our family with some means. Can we not offer at least one of our members for the service of the nation? Having

provided me with education, moral instruction and all sorts of qualifications, can you not turn me over to the Samaj (society), to which we owe so much? This will hardly be any kind of sacrifice, it will rather be an investment. It is like providing the farm of the Samaj with manure. We are nowadays interested only in reaping the harvest and have forgotten to provide the field with manure. There is thus the danger of our land becoming barren and unproductive. Can we not forgo a few worthless ambitions for the protection and benefit of a Samaj and a faith, for which Rama suffered exile, Krishna bore innumerable hardships, Rana Pratap wandered about from forest to forest, Shivaji staked his all, and Guru Govind Singh allowed his little sons to be buried alive?

If this letter gives a glimpse of his early resolve to devote his life to the service of the Motherland, the quintessentially moral nature of his personality is borne out by an incident narrated by Nanaji Deshmukh, who was his roommate during his MA years in Agra and later became an important leader of the Jana Sangh.

One morning we both went to the market and bought vegetables worth two paise. We returned and had almost reached home when Deendayalji suddenly stopped. His hand was in his pocket and he said, 'Nana, there has been a mistake.' When I asked him, he replied, 'I had four paise in my pocket, and one of them was a bad coin. I have given that bad coin to the old woman selling vegetables. What would she say? Come, let us go back and give her a good coin.' A sense of guilt could be seen on his face. We returned to the vegetable-seller and told her what happened. She said to him, 'Who will find out your bad coin? Go along, whatever you have given is ok.' But Deendayalji would not listen. He searched in the old woman's heap of coins and found out the bad paisa. Only after he had given her a good one did a look of relief and satisfaction light up his face. The old woman's eyes became moist and she said, 'Son, you are a good boy. May God bless you.'

'IF I COULD GET THREE MORE DEENDAYALS...'

When the Jana Sangh was formed in October 1951, Deendayalji was one of the first batch of *pracharaks* that Shri Guruji deputed to assist Dr Mookerjee in building the new party. At the party's first national conference in Kanpur in January 1953, Dr Mookerjee made him the party's all-India General Secretary. Indeed, he was so impressed with this thirty-seven-year-old trusted lieutenant that he remarked, 'If I could get two or three more Deendayals, I will change the entire political map of India.'

Tragically, destiny snatched away Dr Mookerjee within a few months and the party was robbed of a towering leader. All its other office-bearers were young and inexperienced. This prompted quite a few political pundits to write-off the Jana Sangh. In that hour of gloom and despair, Deendayalji assumed the reins of leadership and, after fifteen years of untiring efforts, brought the party to a level where a new set of political pundits began to see it as a distinct alternative to the Congress. Although the Jana Sangh had a succession of Presidents between 1953 and 1967, as its constitution stipulated that the President's tenure could be of only one year, everybody knew that Deendayalji, its General Secretary in charge of the organisation, was the mind, heart and soul of the party. As a matter of fact, he was more than the organisational head of the party. He was its philosopher, guide and motivator all rolled into one.

It was Deendayalji's conscious choice not to become the party President and, instead, remain in relative anonymity to build the party, patiently and meticulously. He travelled across the country, training thousands of young men and women with his motivational lectures, encouraging them to live a life of struggle and sacrifice in service of the nation, grooming new leaders, and giving the right guidance to the fledgling party on a wide variety of political, economic and social issues that dominated the national scene. Deendayalji loved to interact with people of all categories and of diverse ideological inclinations, giving them a patient hearing and also communicating his own thoughts to them. Thus, he soon had admirers all across the political spectrum.

In view of Deendayalji's track record of service to the party and his growing stature in national politics, his colleagues at the Central level as well as the state units of the party would, almost every year, urge him to become the party chief. But he would politely decline each time. Such was the level of his natural inclination for self-effacement that he was uncomfortable carrying the designation of presidentship of the party; attachment to any symbol of power was out of sync with his personality.

THE JANA SANGH'S HISTORIC CALICUT SESSION

It is only towards the end of 1967, when Balraj Madhok's presidency the previous year had created serious destabilising problems for the party, that Deendayalji could no longer resist accepting the call from colleagues all over the country. Accordingly, he was elected the party President at its plenary session in Calicut in Kerala in December 1967. About this, Shri Guruji later wrote: 'He really never wanted this high honour, nor did I wish to burden him with it. But circumstances so contrived that I had to ask him to accept the presidentship. He obeyed like a true *swayamsevak* that he was.'

The Calicut session was an unforgettable landmark in the history of the Jana Sangh, generating a new wave of self-confidence and hope among members and sympathisers of the party, and heralding a new possibility of change in the Congress-dominated politics in India. I regard his Presidential speech in Calicut as one of the most significant documents in Independent India's political history.

The decade of the 1960s saw a major upsurge in mass protests in various parts of the country. This was due to the Congress governments' failure to fulfil people's legitimate expectations. There was a minority view within the Jana Sangh that the party should not get associated with agitational politics. Deendayalji refuted this view in his Presidential speech by saying, 'People's agitations are natural and necessary in a rapidly changing social system. As a matter of fact, they are a manifestation of a new awareness in society.... Hence, we have to go along with them and provide leadership to them. Those who want to perpetuate the status quo in the political, economic and social fields, are fearful of people's agitations. I am afraid we cannot cooperate with them. They want to stop the wheel of time, they want to halt India's pre-destined march, which is not possible.'

In his inspirational address, Deendayalji gave another proof of his forward-looking vision. 'We are energised by the glory of India's past, but we do not regard it as the pinnacle of our national life. We have a realistic understanding of the present, but we are not tied to the present. Our eyes are entranced by the golden dreams about India's future, but we are not given to sleep and sloth; we are *karmayogis* who are determined to translate those dreams into reality. We are worshippers of India's timeless past, dynamic present and eternal future. Confident of victory, let us pledge to endeavour in this direction.'[1]

MURDER MOST FOUL AT MUGHAL SARAI

Inscrutable are the ways of the Almighty. Just when the Jana Sangh had ascended one peak of glory, and was all set to scale further summits of success in the years to come, tragedy struck. The cruel hand of destiny took away Deendayalji's life within two months of his becoming the party President. He was murdered by unknown assailants while travelling in a night-train from Lucknow to Patna on 11 February 1968. His body was found near the tracks at Mughal Sarai railway station.

I went numb with shock hearing the tragic news. Rarely in my life have I been shaken so completely as I was on that day. Indeed, the entire nation was shell-shocked. Till date, his murder has remained an unsolved mystery, although outwardly it appeared to have been a case of ordinary crime. The government accepted the demand of a group of MPs belonging to different political parties for a judicial enquiry, which was headed by Justice Y.V. Chandrachud. (He later became the Chief Justice of India.) The report he submitted, in which he said that he found no political angle to the murder and that it was a case of ordinary crime, satisfied no one. All of us in the Bharatiya Jana Sangh found ourselves suddenly pushed under a pall of gloom. It was the second calamity to have struck our young party in less than fifteen years. The first was the death of Dr Mookerjee, founder of the Jana Sangh, in 1953, under equally mysterious circumstances while he was under arrest in Srinagar.

Rail journey was almost an inseparable part of Deendayalji's political life. A leader who led the life of an ascetic, he mostly travelled by passenger train, and rarely by air. 'This gives me two advantages,' he would say. 'Firstly, it gives me an opportunity to meet common people. Secondly, it gives me time to read and write.' He travelled light, carrying with him a small suitcase with a couple of sets of clothes, bedding and a bag full of books, notebooks and letters. The last was always the heaviest item in his luggage!

Years later, at the founding session of the Bharatiya Janata Party in Mumbai in 1980, Atalji would recall the loss of Dr Mookerjee and Deendayalji in his own inimitable style. Reminding workers of the newly born party of the Herculean task that lay in front of them, he said, 'Dr Mookerjee and Pandit Deendayalji have been our tallest leaders. One died in prison, and the other breathed his last on a train. Our entire political journey has been so full of hardships and sacrifices that it can be summed up as—*Ek pair rail mein, ek pair jail mein* (one foot in the train and the other in prison). But we remain undeterred. We have decided that we shall rebuild the party on the basis of three points of action: *sangathan* (organisation), *sangharsh* (struggle) and *samrachana* (constructive social service).'

Who could have any motive in killing an *ajatashatru* (a person without enemies) like Deendayalji? I asked myself, after recovering from the initial shock. I haven't found an answer to the question yet. My only surmise is that: It was a crime not so much against an individual as against the nation, since Deendayalji embodied the best of the Indian tradition in politics and was by far the most promising political leader towards the end of the 1960s. And at the time of his death, he was not even fifty-two years old!

IDEOLOGICAL FLEXIBILITY IN THE NATIONAL INTEREST

Deendayalji's personality was a rare combination of commitment, clarity and pragmatism. I recall an incident that took place at the Calicut session of the Jana Sangh. An issue that caused a heated debate was whether the Jana Sangh should have joined hands with the CPI to form the SVD governments in Bihar and Punjab in 1967. Several delegates argued that it was wrong on the part of the Jana Sangh to have allied with the CPI. In particular, Vishwanathan, a Tamilian whose family had settled in Punjab, delivered a powerful speech criticising Deendayalji's line. He was a compelling public speaker of those days. He said, 'Let not the Jana Sangh delude itself that by cohabiting with the communists, we will be able to change them.' He then tried to drive home his point with a vivid metaphor: '*Kharbooja chakkoo par gire ya chakkoo kharbooje par, katega to kharbooja hi.*' (Whether the melon falls on the knife or the knife falls on the melon, it is the melon that gets cut.)

Deendayalji's speech that day at the end of the debate was full of practical wisdom, and has served as a beacon of light for the party till today. He said, 'It is an irony of the country's political situation that while untouchability in the social field is considered to be evil, it is sometimes extolled as a virtue in the political field. If a party does not wish to practise untouchability towards its rivals in the political establishment, it is supposed to be doing something wrong. We, in the Jana Sangh, certainly do not agree with the communists' strategy, tactics and their political culture. But that does not justify an attitude of untouchability towards them. If they are willing to work with us on the basis of issues, or as part of a government committed to an agreed programme, I see nothing wrong in it…. These (SVD) governments are a step towards ending political untouchability. The spirit of accommodation shown by all parties, despite their sharp differences, is a good omen for democracy.'

This sage advice by Deendayalji would later guide our party both in our fight against the Emergency rule (1975–77) and also in the post-Emergency period. It was on this basis that the BJP decided, in 1989, to lend outside support to V.P. Singh's government, which also received support from the communists. In fact, it has been the guiding principle in the various strategic alliances adopted by the Jana Sangh and the BJP in later years.

INDO-PAK CONFEDERATION CONCEPT MOOTED

Another example of Deendayalji's creative and non-doctrinaire approach is the following important joint statement for the Indo-Pak confederation that he signed, on 12 April 1964, with Dr Lohia. They were both good friends despite differences on certain ideological issues. Their friendship became stronger after the Chinese aggression of 1962, when Dr Lohia endorsed the Jana Sangh's demand for India to produce its own nuclear weapon. Their joint statement said:

> Large-scale riots in East Pakistan have compelled over two lakh Hindus and other minorities to come over to India. Indians naturally feel incensed by the happenings in East Bengal. To bring the situation under control and to prescribe the right remedy for the situation it is essential that the malady be properly diagnosed. And even in this state of mental agony, the basic values of our national life must never be forgotten. It is our firm conviction that guaranteeing the protection of the life and property of Hindus and other minorities in Pakistan is the responsibility of the Government of India. To take a nice legalistic view about the matter that Hindus in Pakistan are Pakistani nationals would be dangerous and can only result in killings and reprisals in the two countries, in greater or lesser measure. When the Government of India fails to fulfill this obligation towards the minorities in Pakistan, the people understandably become indignant. Our appeal to the people is that this indignation should be directed against the Government and should in no case be given vent to against the Indian Muslims. If the latter thing happens, it only provides the Government with a cloak to cover its own inertia and failure, and an opportunity to malign the people and repress them.
>
> So far as the Indian Muslims are concerned, it is our definite view that, like all other citizens, their life and property must be protected in all circumstances. No incident and no logic can justify any compromise with truth in this regard. A state, which cannot guarantee the right of living to its citizens, and citizens who cannot assure safety of their neighbours, would belong to the barbaric age. Freedom and security to every citizen irrespective of his faith has indeed been India's sacred tradition. We would like to reassure every Indian Muslim in this regard and would wish this message to reach every Hindu home that it is their civic and national duty to ensure the fulfillment of this assurance.
>
> We hold that the existence of India and Pakistan as two separate entities is an artificial situation. The estrangement of relations

between the two Governments is the result of lop-sided attitudes and the tendency to indulge in piecemeal talks. Let the dialogue carried on by the two Governments be candid and not just piecemeal. It is out of such frank talk that solutions of various problems can emerge, goodwill created and a beginning made towards the formation of some sort of Indo-Pak Confederation.[2]

The idea of an Indo-Pak Confederation was born out of an intensive discussion between Deendayalji and Dr Lohia. It had its origin in the latter's concern that the Jana Sangh's and RSS's belief in the concept of 'Akhand Bharat' (India Undivided) put Muslims in Pakistan at unease and posed a hurdle in the progress of Indo-Pak relations. Dr Lohia told Deendayalji: 'Many Pakistanis believe that if the Jana Sangh came to power in New Delhi, it would forcibly reunify Pakistan with India.' Deendayalji replied: 'We have no such intentions. And we are willing to put to rest Pakistani people's concerns on this score.'

This dialogue, and its outcome, is one of the finest examples in India's political history of cooperation and consensus-building between two leaders with divergent ideologies, but common commitment to national interest. In later years, I have often approvingly reiterated the concept of an Indo-Pak Confederation by referring to the joint statement of these two great leaders.

When the Arab-Israel war broke out and almost everybody in the Jana Sangh was pro-Israeli, Deendayalji issued a word of caution: 'We should not become blindly pro-Israeli just because the Congress is blindly pro-Arab. We should not view the world as if it were peopled by angels and devils. We must judge every issue on its own merit.'

The same principled flexibility, the same readiness to revise one's previous views on a subject in the larger interests of the nation was also evident in his approach to the issue of language. Deendayalji, like most leaders of the Jana Sangh those days, was a strong proponent of Hindi. But when the anti-Hindi agitation in Tamil Nadu in the mid-1960s took a virulent turn, and some of its influential leaders started to threaten the state's secession from the Indian Union, he agreed to the continuation of according official language status to English. He was criticised for doing so, by several North

Indian colleagues in the party, but he stood his ground. Also, in a clear departure from the Jana Sangh's tradition, he got his Presidential speech at Calicut printed in both Hindi and English, on facing pages, in the same booklet. Earlier, the official version of the presidential speeches would invariably be printed first in Hindi, and only later in English.

Around the same time, another issue that was being hotly discussed in the media was whether the Civil Services examination should be conducted only in Hindi besides English, or in other Indian languages too. The debate had assumed a confrontational form of Hindi versus regional languages. When Deendayalji's opinion was sought on this issue, he said, 'Leave the question to be decided by the candidates themselves. Those who opt for service in any state of India, outside their own, will naturally choose Hindi. Others will choose their own regional language.'

The only time Deendayalji entered the electoral fray was in 1963, when he contested and lost a by-election to the Lok Sabha from Jaunpur in UP. In spite of the defeat, he proved to be a leader of unshakeable principles. An election in Jaunpur, and in many other constituencies in eastern UP, invariably used to be fought on caste lines, mainly between Rajputs and Brahmins. Since Deendayalji was born into a Brahmin family, the Congress fielded a Rajput candidate and conducted an aggressive campaign to woo Rajput votes. When some local Jana Sangh leaders wanted to play the Brahmin card, Deendayalji warned them: 'If you try to win the election on caste lines, I shall immediately withdraw from the contest.'

SOME PERSONAL REMINISCENCES

I first met Deendayalji in Delhi sometime in late 1947. It was a very brief meeting. I came in closer contact with him only after 1948. My early interaction with him was during extremely difficult times of the ban on the RSS after Gandhiji's assassination on 30 January 1948. I was a *pracharak* in Rajasthan at the time. After my release from prison, I had come to Delhi. Shri Guruji, the RSS Chief, was also in town. I went to meet him at the residence of Lala Hansraj on Barakhamba Road, where he was staying. It was here that I met Deendayalji, bespectacled, soft-spoken, and completely unassuming in his dhoti and kurta.

When I started interacting with him more closely in later years, what struck me was that Deendayalji was very creative in his thinking. The notion that conventional wisdom was necessarily right was alien to him, just as the rebuke of juniors for questioning the beliefs of seniors was abhorrent to him. He once asked me: 'There is a quotation that says, "The younger generation these days has no respect for elders. They are not carrying forward the traditions of the past. They are getting corrupted. Things were so good when we were young." Tell me whose quotation is it?' I said it was Socrates. To which Deendayalji said, 'So now you see that this complaint against the younger generation has been going on since the past 2,000 years. And it will continue in the future too.'

Deendayalji would regularly come to our house at Pandara Road and spend hours together in the balcony reading or writing. He was fluent in English but Hindi was his natural language of communication. I used to translate his speeches and statements in Hindi, into English. A powerful writer, Deendayalji had a flair for conveying motivational thoughts by invoking familiar idioms. For instance, he once wrote an article in a special issue of a Hindi magazine on the occasion of Navaratri festival, when it is common in many families to play the traditional Indian game of stakes. (Pandavas and Kauravas played it in the *Mahabharata*). It is especially popular among Vaishyas (the business community), who have to take risks and gamble in order to succeed in their profession. Titled '*Dao lagaao zindagi pe*' (put a stake on your life), Deendayalji's article, after giving a fascinating history of the dice game, exhorted the readers: 'A monotonous life, lived without any purpose or direction, is not worth much. To achieve anything big in life, you should be prepared to risk your all and take a leap of faith for whatever they believed in.' I always remember this advice of Deendayalji whenever there is risk involved in taking an important but necessary decision in politics.

'INTEGRAL HUMANISM'

No tribute to Deendayalji would be complete without introducing the philosophical dimension of his life to contemporary readers. He will be remembered not only as the principal architect of the Jana Sangh, but also as the author of a profoundly original political treatise, which has come to be known as 'Integral Humanism'. India after Independence has produced few leaders who were also political philosophers. Deendayalji was one of the few, and the finest.

After the formation of the Jana Sangh in 1951, there was an intense urge to anchor it in a distinctive and comprehensive ideology of its own. Dr Mookerjee's life at the helm of the party was too short, and too eventful, for him to undertake this exercise. After his demise, the need for a guiding ideology continued to hover in Deendayalji's mind. It was a time when the world was witnessing a conflict between two rival ideologies—Capitalism and Communism. The debate had also dominated the political thinking in India after Independence, with various parties subscribing to either of the two theories with different degrees of rigidity.

Deendayalji felt that both Capitalism and Communism were flawed philosophies, which view the human being and society essentially from a partial, materialistic perspective. One considers man a mere selfish being hankering after money, having only one law, the law of fierce competition, in essence the law of the jungle; whereas the other views him as a feeble lifeless cog in the whole scheme of things, regulated by rigid rules, and incapable of any good, unless directed. The centralisation of power, economic and political, is implied in both. They pit one section of society against the other, the individual against the collective, man against nature, etc. This is one of the root causes of all the poverty, injustice, strife and violence in the world. Both, therefore, result in dehumanisation of man.

In contrast, according to Deendayalji, the Indian perspective of viewing human aspirations in a four-fold manner*—*dharma, artha, kama* and

---

* Indian philosophy takes cognisance of all aspects and needs of life, both individual and social. The four *purusharthas* set down the four purposes of man's life: *Dharma* (righteousness), *artha* (wealth), *kama* (sensual pleasure) and *moksha* (emancipation through communion with God or the Infinite). Similarly, the four stages of life, called *Ashramas*, each of which has its responsibilities and obligations, are: *Brahmacharya* (observing celibacy in student life, first twenty-five years), *grihastha* (householder,

Contd...

moksha, and its well-conceived four-stage progression of individual's life through *brahmacharya*, *grihastha*, *vanaprastha* and *sanyasa*—promised the balanced development of both the individual and society. 'The keynote of Bharatiya *sanskriti* (Indian ethos),' Deendayalji noted, 'is its integral approach to life.... Man, the highest creation of God, is losing his own identity. We must re-establish him in his rightful position, bring him the realisation of his greatness, reawaken his abilities and encourage him to exert for attaining divine heights of his latent personality.'

Deendayalji presented his thoughts for the first time at a four-day *Chintan Shibir* (camp for collective thinking) at Gwalior in 1964, in which some five hundred Jana Sangh activists participated. A fuller version of the same philosophy was presented at the party's plenary meeting in Vijayawada in 1965. Shortly thereafter, he presented it in its final form in a series of four lectures in Bombay. The title 'Integral Humanism' was deliberately chosen by him to contrast it with the thesis of 'Radical Humanism' put forward by M.N. Roy, a renowned one-time communist leader. I was present both at Gwalior and Vijayawada, and was witness to a new persona of Deendayalji.

The great merit of 'Integral Humanism' lies in its successful attempt to deal with a problem that has defied so many political philosophers of our age: how to conceptualise a practical approach to achieve peace and harmony within man and society. Hence, rejecting the theory of class conflict (as in communism), it posits inter-dependence between various sections of society and working together for common welfare. Similarly, rejecting notions of any inherent contradiction between the individual and society (as in capitalism), it emphasises the essential concord between the two. 'A flower is what it is because of its petals, and the worth of the petals lies in remaining with the flower and adding to its beauty.'[3]

Deendayalji was anything but doctrinaire in his approach. Though a strong critic of imitating the western way of life, he accepts that 'western

---

Contd...

twenty-five to fifty years), *vanaprastha* (scriptural studies and meditation, fifty to seventy-five years) and *sanyasa* (cultivation of God-consciousness through monastic way of life, seventy-five to hundred years).

principles are a product of a revolution in human thought and it is not proper to ignore them'. His critique of the western political and economic thought does not call for its total rejection; it only highlights its inadequacy. Referring to 'nationalism, democracy, socialism, world peace and world unity', which were the hotly debated 'Big Ideas' in India and elsewhere in the sixties, he says, 'All these are good ideals. They reflect the higher aspirations of mankind.' But the manner in which the West has voiced them shows that 'each stands opposed to the rest in practice.'

To those who criticised Hinduism as an oppressive, change-resisting belief-system, Deendayalji gave a reply befitting a social revolutionary. For 'Integral Humanism' calls for rejection of all those customs ('untouchability, caste discrimination, dowry, neglect of women') that are symptoms of 'ill-heath and degeneration' of our society. It affirms the self-regenerative impulse of Indian society by saying: 'We have taken due note of our ancient culture. But we are no archaeologists. We have no intention to become the custodians of a vast archaeological museum.' Deendayalji's espousal of Dharma Rajya (which does not connote theocracy but only a law-governed state and a duty-oriented citizenry) echoes Gandhiji's concept of Ram Rajya. 'Dharma sustains the nation. If dharma is destroyed, the nation perishes.'

Does Dharma Rajya negate democracy? Not at all. Deendayalji creatively expands the meaning of Lincoln's famous words: 'In the definition of democracy as "government of the people, by the people and for the people", *of* stands for independence, *by* stands for people's rule, and *for* indicates dharma. Dharma Rajya encompasses all these concepts.'

A unique conceptual contribution of 'Integral Humanism' is that it resurrects, from the works of ancient Indian rishis (sages), two definitional traits of nationhood—called *chiti*, the nation's soul, and *virat*, the power that energises the nation. 'The ideals of the nation constitute its *chiti*, which is analogous to the soul of an individual. *Chiti* determines the direction in which the nation is to advance culturally. Whatever is in accordance with *chiti* is included in the national culture. On the strength of this *chiti*, a nation arises, strong and virile. It is this *chiti* that is demonstrated in the actions of every great man of a nation.'

'Integral Humanism' likens *virat* in the life of a nation to that of *prana* (life force) in the human body. 'Just as *prana* infuses strength in various organs of the body, refreshes the intellect and keeps body and soul together; so also in a nation. With a strong *virat* alone can democracy succeed and the government be effective. Then the diversity of our nation does not prove an obstacle to our national unity. When the *virat* is awake, diversity does not lead to conflicts and people co-operate with each other like the various limbs of the human body or like the members of a family. We have to undertake the task of awakening our nation's *virat*. Let us go forward in this task with a sense of pride for our heritage, with a realistic assessment of the present and a great ambition for the future. We wish neither to make this country a shadow of some distant past nor an imitation of Russia or America.'

Deendayalji concludes his treatise on a note of supreme self-confidence and unshakeable resolve. 'With the support of Universal knowledge and our heritage, we shall create a Bharat which will excel all its past glories, and will enable every citizen in its fold to steadily progress in the development of his manifold latent possibilities and to achieve through a sense of unity with the entire creation, a state even higher than that of a complete human being; to become Narayan from *nar* (man). This is the external divine form of our culture. This is our message to humanity at a cross roads. May God give us strength to succeed in this mission.'

The Jana Sangh adopted 'Integral Humanism' as its guiding ideology at the party's Vijayawada session in 1965. Similarly, the BJP, in its constitution, has enshrined it as the 'basic philosophy of the Party'. Deendayalji's basic impulse in developing his discourse was humanistic, and not political in the narrow sense of aiding a particular party. No wonder, its appeal transcends its political affiliation and resonates in the mind of every right-thinking person in the world.

*

The reasons for devoting so many pages to the life of a person that ended four decades ago are two-fold. Firstly, Deendayalji was, and still remains, a central figure in my political life. Secondly, I firmly believe that the

India of today—and tomorrow—has as much of a need to know him and his philosophy as it did during his lifetime. 'Integral Humanism' may not have received the kind of attention that has been showered on various shades of Marxism and other western political theories in India. However, I have no doubt that serious and unbiased seekers of truth will find it illuminating and inspiring, and worthy of being placed alongside the works of Mahatma Gandhi and Dr Ram Manohar Lohia, with both of whom Deendayalji had so much in common.

6

THE BEGINNING OF MY PARLIAMENTARY CAREER

Democracy has a habit of making itself generally disagreeable by asking the powers-that-be at the most inconvenient moment whether they are the powers-that-ought-to-be.

—JAMES RUSSELL LOWELL (1819-1891), A FAMOUS AMERICAN POET, ESSAYIST, DIPLOMAT

In the fairly long life that I have lived, there is one truth that I have encountered repeatedly—change is the only constant, both in nature and in the life of human beings. In my childhood in Karachi, the change of seasons was a source of limitless amazement for me. Often I used to wonder how the same ocean that retreated into its silent ebb in one part of the day would be roaring with wild waves in another. It was also a source of awe to me. As I grew up, I realised that ups and downs, victory and defeat, loss and renewal, are all a way of life in politics. One should be prepared to take everything in one's stride. This taught me the virtue of equanimity. When difficulties mount or when tragedy strikes—and it can befall any time and in the most unimaginable of forms—I learnt that it helps not to give in to despair. For, as the wheel of change rotates, it can bring in its wake, better days. The important thing is to develop patience, courage and self-belief, and continue doing one's work. I have experienced in my own life how a situation of utter gloom inevitably comes to an end, and with time ushers in light and hope. This is true for individuals as well as organisations.

✱

ATAL BIHARI VAJPAYEE AT THE HELM OF THE JANA SANGH

The sudden and tragic demise of Deendayalji in February 1968 had plunged our party into darkness and despondency. Our loss was all the greater because the veil of mystery that covered his murder would not lift even though months had passed. Who did it? Who could have been behind it? And why? Each one in the party was asking themselves these questions, with no answers forthcoming. Often the inability to comprehend why we have lost someone dear to us causes more pain than the loss itself.

It was in this dark hour of adversity that the party turned to Atal Bihari Vajpayee for leadership. He was elected the party President when he was all of forty-three years old. Already renowned as an outstanding orator and parliamentarian, he was now called upon to lead the party. And he answered the call splendidly. According to Thomas Carlyle (1795–1881), the great historian of the Victorian era, 'Adversity is the diamond dust that Heaven polishes its jewels with.' Atalji was the jewel that shone on the national scene 1968 onwards.

As party President, Atalji faced two immediate challenges: firstly, to enable the party to get over the mood of dejection caused by Deendayalji's murder and, secondly, to resolve the problems caused by internal bickerings in the SVD governments in various states in which the Jana Sangh was an alliance partner. A resolution adopted by the party's Working Committee on 14 June 1968 advised all our alliance partners to 'scrupulously confine themselves to the agreed minimum programme, refrain from trying to cast the entire government in their respective party moulds and avoid playing to the gallery'.

The early days of Atalji's presidency were far from smooth. The SVD governments in Bihar, Uttar Pradesh and Punjab were tottering on account of constant bickering among allies. Although the Jana Sangh tried its best to bring cohesion into the coalition, the efforts were not bearing fruit. As a result, we too became a victim of people's dissatisfaction. When midterm elections were held in early 1969 to elect new assemblies in these states, the party fared badly.

Atalji faced another major problem from within the party. Balraj Madhok, a former President of the Jana Sangh, continued to oppose him almost at every turn.

Madhok disagreed with Deendayalji and Atalji on their economic policies, which he thought had a 'leftward' tilt. He had questioned Deendayalji's support, endorsed by the party's Working Committee, to the demand for effective implementation of the law on agricultural land ceilings as part of our commitment to the principle of 'land to the tiller'. The party in those days was quite cautious in responding to Indira Gandhi's populist measures such as bank nationalisation. We did not voice outright opposition to them. This had angered Madhok. He favoured an alliance with the Swatantra Party, both on political and economic issues. Later, he even called for a merger between the Jana Sangh and the Swatantra Party, which advocated a free market model for India's development. An overwhelming majority of the leaders and workers of the Jana Sangh did not agree with Madhok's line. Atalji was quite clear that the Jana Sangh should be considered as a 'common man's party', and not as a party of the rich and the powerful. At the same time, he clearly articulated the Jana Sangh's opposition to the Soviet or Chinese model of development as championed by the two communist parties. On this as well as all other points raised by Madhok, the party stood solidly behind Atalji's leadership.

Atalji began re-energising the Jana Sangh by constantly touring the country, interacting with party workers and sympathisers, and addressing hugely attended public meetings. He had a dedicated band of colleagues assisting him—Nanaji Deshmukh, Sundar Singh Bhandari, Kailashpati

Mishra, Kushabhau Thakre, Jagannathrao Joshi, to name a few—and they worked as tirelessly as him. Atalji's personal rapport with me enabled me to contribute to the deliberations during these trying times. Atalji's new thrust was to expand the party's base among the Scheduled Castes, Scheduled Tribes and Other Backward Classes. He also continued Deendayalji's focus on strengthening the party in Maharashtra, Gujarat and other states, such as in southern and eastern India, where it was weak. State units were asked to take up issues of the common people, especially *kisans* (farmers), specific to their regions and launch peaceful agitations. Party leaders, both at the Central and state levels, were seen to be constantly on the move.

THE YEAR 1969—INDIRA GANDHI PRECIPITATES CONGRESS SPLIT

Around the same time, the Congress was going through its worst crisis in its post-Independence history. After Shastri's death in January 1966, top leaders of the Congress Party had chosen Indira Gandhi, Jawaharlal Nehru's daughter, to be India's new Prime Minister. This, however, was not a natural choice, nor was it enthusiastic. There were many leaders senior to her in the party—Morarji Desai, K. Kamaraj and Jagjivan Ram—being the most prominent. Since they could not agree upon a consensus candidate amongst themselves, they reluctantly placed the crown on Indira Gandhi's head, believing erroneously—and what a costly error it would later prove to be—that they could keep her under their control. Morarji Desai, the Finance Minister, was made Deputy Prime Minister to offset her position in the government.

The Congress managed to retain power at the Centre in the 1967 general elections, winning 283 out of 515 seats in the Lok Sabha, a big plunge from its tally of 361 in 1962. In most states in North India, the party was voted out of power. This set the stage for a serious power struggle within the Congress, one in which Indira Gandhi would ultimately triumph with her combativeness, ruthlessness, shrewdness and, above all, populist demagoguery. She unleashed a blitzkrieg of seemingly anti-rich decisions—abolition of privy purses to former rajas and maharajas;

nationalisation of banks, insurance companies and several enterprises in the core sector; state control over import and export trade; stricter controls over private-sector businesses; more sweeping land-ceiling laws; and public distribution system for essential food items. Each of these lent credence to her slogan of *'Garibi Hatao'* (Banish Poverty), which captured the imagination of the common people. Subsequently, she also dismissed Morarji Desai from the Cabinet and retained the Finance Ministry.

Indira Gandhi took this infighting within her own party to a higher political plane at the time of the presidential election in August 1969, which was necessitated after the demise of Dr Zakir Hussain, the incumbent President of India. The 'Syndicate' faction put forth Neelam Sanjiva Reddy as its candidate and also managed to get this decision approved by the CWC. As a result, Reddy became the official candidate of the ruling party. He could have easily got elected since the Congress commanded an overwhelming majority in the electoral college. But Indira Gandhi opposed his candidature, and fielded V.V. Giri, who was then the Vice President of India, as an independent candidate. When she herself filed Giri's nomination papers, and appealed to her party's MPs and state legislators to exercise their 'conscience vote' in his favour, it became clear that the Congress was headed for a vertical split.

I remember penning an article on the ruling party in the thick of these political convulsions. In the British parliamentary system, I wrote, there was no whip on legislators to follow their party's line in voting on such matters and that they were permitted to vote according to their conscience. However, quoting a British jurist, I opined: 'Conscience in the singular is a virtue, whereas, in the plural, it is a conspiracy. It is tantamount to indulging in collective indiscipline.' Here was a case of the Prime Minister indulging in indiscipline, and also goading her partymen to follow suit. However, concepts like discipline, self-restraint and party unity meant little to Indira Gandhi, who at the time was on a warpath, going all-out to win it.

I recall here a humorous incident, involving Jagannathrao Joshi, one of the main pillars of the Jana Sangh. His personality was a rare combination of two outstanding traits: selflessness and a sparkling sense of humour.

The Jana Sangh and other non-communist opposition parties were in the process of selecting their common candidate for the Presidential race. (Eventually, it was Dr C.D. Deshmukh, the first Indian Governor of the RBI and Finance Minister in Nehru's Cabinet.) One day, Joshi, a member of the Rajya Sabha, was sitting with some fellow MPs in the Central Hall of Parliament, which is a place for informal meetings and light-hearted banter among parliamentarians and journalists. A colleague asked him, 'Why don't you become Rashtrapati, Jagannathraoji?' Pat came the answer from Joshi, a *pracharak* of the RSS who had chosen to remain a bachelor: 'Who will make me Rashtrapati, when nobody is willing to accept me even as an ordinary *pati* (husband)?'

In this tug-of-war within the Congress, Giri won the Presidential election by a narrow margin. After four months of bitter infighting, the Congress formally split up at the AICC session held in Bangalore in December 1969. Ironically, it was the year of the birth centenary of Mahatma Gandhi, which was observed by the two factions of the Congress Party by sparring and splitting for power. Indira Gandhi's rivals constituted themselves into Congress (O), 'O' standing for Organisation. To the public, however, 'O' symbolised the 'Old' leadership of the Congress since the younger generation of Congressmen backed Indira Gandhi's Congress (I). The Congress (O) managed to command the allegiance of only about a quarter of the MPs. The spilt in the Congress, however, reduced Indira Gandhi's government to a minority in Parliament but she managed to continue in office for about a year with the support of the communists and the Dravida Munnetra Kazagham (DMK). However, mid-term elections were inevitable, and they took place in February 1971.

In the campaign, Indira Gandhi used her carefully crafted pro-poor image to the hilt. She castigated her rivals as protectors of 'capitalism' and projected herself as the sole champion of 'socialism'. Sensing her growing popularity with the masses, the non-communist opposition parties forged a grand alliance comprising the Jana Sangh, the Congress (O), Swatantra Party and the Samyukta Socialist Party (SSP). This, however, found no favour with the voters, who gave Indira Gandhi a two-thirds majority (352 out of 518 seats) in the Lok Sabha. Under the impact of the '*Garibi*

Hatao' wave in favour of the Prime Minister, the Jana Sangh could win only 22 seats, 13 less than in 1967.

WHAT INDIRA GANDHI'S VICTORY PORTENDED

I will offer here some of my own reflections on what the split in the Congress Party, and the manner in which it came about, implied for India's economy, polity and society. After remaining in power at the Centre uninterruptedly for more than two decades, and with no single strong opposition party to challenge its monopoly, the Congress towards the end of the 1960s was certainly in a state of stagnation and internal tension. Its poor performance in the 1967 general elections had provided enough warning signals that the people of India were dissatisfied with its rule and were looking for an alternative party to take the lead. The Congress leadership's response to this challenge was neither based on strong adherence to democratic principles, nor guided by the long-term interests of the nation. Both factions were guilty of this.

The culpability of the Syndicate leaders lay in the fact that, after having chosen Indira Gandhi as India's Prime Minister, they went about undercutting her authority. They also failed to recognise that the organisation of the Congress had become obsolescent in terms of its social base, ignoring the common people in the country's development. The slow rate of economic growth was not producing either prosperity or employment. Radical sections in the communist movement, having worldwide appeal then, were accusing the Congress Party of being the guardian of big landlords and wealthy capitalists.

Indira Gandhi, who was smarter than all her opponents in the party, was well aware of this. She had a better appreciation of the situation both in India and the world. She played the 'socialist' card, on the one hand, to neutralise the mass appeal of the leftists and ultra-leftists and, on the other hand, maligned her own opponents in the Congress Party by calling them 'rightist reactionaries'. A retrospective assessment of her '*Garibi Hatao*' measures, however, clearly shows that they were not the outcome of any deep ideological conviction. Rather, they were policy 'weapons' used by Indira Gandhi to eliminate her rivals within the party, and establish her own supremacy over both the Congress organisation and the government. Some of the decisions, like the tightening of the licence-permit-quota raj, had deeply deleterious effects on the economy. Far from boosting economic growth and reducing poverty, they actually had the opposite impact: they stifled growth, debilitated employment generation in the economy, bred corruption, lengthened the red-tape, and throttled the entrepreneurial energy of the Indian people. It needed the economic reforms of the Narasimha Rao and Vajpayee governments in the post-1990s era to undo the damage done by Indira Gandhi's politically motivated pseudo-socialist economic policies.

Indira Gandhi's greater guilt, however, lay in what she did to undermine dissent within the Congress Party, a precursor to what she did to suppress democracy in the country in 1975. Instead of guiding the Congress organisation to overcome the new challenges before the party and the country, and to address them unitedly, she consciously placed her own personal interests above those of the organisation. The process of undermining democratic consultation and decision-making within the Congress had begun with Nehru himself. He often defied the party's decisions and once, in 1951, even resigned from the CWC to protest against Purushottamdas Tandon's election as Congress President. It was also Nehru who had planted the seeds of dynasticism in the party by consciously grooming his daughter as his successor.

The self-image of being born to rule is an attribute of monarchy, and not democracy. And it was the driving impulse behind all that Indira Gandhi did before and after the Congress split. She triumphed in her battle against her adversaries, but, in the process, she wrote the epitaph of democracy inside the Congress Party. Thereafter, dissent within the party, which is the spirit of democracy, was not welcome. And the position and authority of the party's supreme leader could not be challenged by anybody. Sycophancy and the cult of personality, generally seen in dictatorial regimes, had infected the Congress organisation.

The Congress (I)'s decisive victory in the 1971 parliamentary elections also revealed other symptoms of the rot that was setting in the ruling party.

While its popularity was never in doubt, its high margin was clearly due to rampant electoral malpractices, including rigging in many places. Never before had the governmental machinery and resources been so blatantly misused to help the ruling party's candidates. The Jana Sangh was deeply apprehensive of what the two-thirds parliamentary majority for Indira Gandhi would entail for the country and its democratic institutions. In a resolution adopted by the party's national Working Committee in March 1971, soon after the elections, the country was forewarned: 'There is a danger that the absolute power now given to Smt. Gandhi's party may make the Congress even more disdainful of democratic procedures and norms than it already is. The Prime Minister's first reference after the elections about the Supreme Court has confirmed the people's worst fears about the ruling party wanting to denigrate and devalue the independent status of the Judiciary. All democrats inside and outside Parliament must keep vigilant watch over these trends, and firmly resist all such attempts.'

This warning would soon prove to be prophetic!

MY ENTRY INTO THE RAJYA SABHA

Even as these momentous developments were taking place in the life of the nation, I reached an important milestone in my own life. In April 1970, I moved from the office of the Chairman of the Delhi Metropolitan Council to India's Parliament. There was a vacancy created in the Rajya Sabha after the term of Inder Kumar Gujral who was a member from the Union Territory of Delhi. The party fielded me and I was elected on the strength of the Jana Sangh's majority in the Council.

In my early speeches in the Rajya Sabha, I articulated my thoughts on some issues that I have subsequently raised in Parliament in one way or the other during the past decades. These were: how to strengthen the unity and integrity of the country; how to safeguard our democratic institutions and make them more effective; why the ruling party must learn to respect the voice of the Opposition; and how to make Centre-state relations smooth and harmonious.

One of the specific demands I made was that the President of India set up an Inter-State Council to resolve disputes among the states, and also between the states and the Centre. Article 263 of the Constitution empowers the President to establish an Inter-State Council for carrying out specific tasks spelt out in the Article, besides contributing to federal coordination and cohesion. Our party had always been in favour of getting Article 263 implemented. The Sarkaria Commission on Centre-state relations also strongly recommended it, reinforcing our views. The Council was ultimately set up in 1990. Sadly, the Inter-State Council became nearly defunct soon thereafter. Till 1996, it did not hold a single meeting. I am happy that, as the Union Home Minister in Atalji's government, I was able to revive it and convene annual meetings. Consequently, the Council took several decisions of far-reaching significance.

CAMPAIGN FOR ELECTORAL REFORMS

Electoral reforms had been my favourite subject of study since the mid-sixties. Like many other democracy-loving political activists in the country, I was concerned over two major ills plaguing India's electoral system: defection and the growing influence of money power. In my very first speech in the Metropolitan Council after becoming its Chairman in 1967, I had observed: 'Defections are polluting the political life of India. Therefore, there should be a ban on defections.' The phrase *'Aya Ram, Gaya Ram'* (Here Today, Gone Tomorrow) was widely prevalent in political discourse those days because of the ruling party's propensity to flagrantly engineer defections whenever it suited the Congress. After entering Parliament, I helped Atalji raise the issue of defections in a big way in the Lok Sabha in 1970.

Apart from defections, Atalji and I identified the corrosive and corrupting effect of misuse of money in elections as a problem plaguing India's electoral system. The cost of contesting a parliamentary or legislative assembly election, and also the gap between the prescribed limit and the actual expenditure, had grown considerably since the first general elections in 1952—of course, it has risen by leaps and bounds since then. Atalji drew the nation's attention not only to the financial corruption that costly elections entailed, but also to the immoral act of submitting false declarations by elected representatives. He further demanded setting up a Joint Parliamentary Committee (JPC) to comprehensively look into electoral reforms, which also received the support of other Opposition parties, forcing a reluctant government to constitute the first ever JPC on Electoral Reform in 1970. Atalji from the Lok Sabha and I from the Rajya Sabha were nominated to serve on this Committee. Unfortunately, due to the dissolution of the Lok Sabha in 1971, the Committee too got dissolved.

After the 1971 general elections, we again raised the demand and a new JPC was constituted. Both of us were on this committee too. During the deliberations, several of our recommendations like reducing the voting age from twenty-one to eighteen years were accepted although the Legislation for it came much later. We also demanded that the election expenses of political parties be publicly funded. The ruling party, however, had strong reservations regarding our demand. Due to our forceful advocacy, the JPC made the following recommendation in its final report:

> It is generally conceded that the statutory ceilings on election expenses are seldom observed in practice and the actual expenditure incurred by a candidate does not bear any relation to the maximum limits laid down. More or less open admissions have been made of substantial sums of money being spent by a candidate. The law in this regard is clearly inadequate to counter the ingenuity of a candidate in circumventing its provisions successfully and with impunity. The Committee, however, considers that basically the problem of election expenses, which has not only agitated the minds of the candidates and the thinking of political parties but also of the general public, can be solved only if it is accepted in principle that all election expenses ought to be a legitimate charge on the public funds and efforts should be made to achieve that end.

> The Committee feels that a process should be initiated whereby the burden of legitimate election expenses at present borne by the candidate or the political party would be progressively shifted to the State.

Atalji and I were dissatisfied with this rather weak and non-specific recommendation. We therefore appended to this report a dissent note which said:

> As the situation stands today, the law of ceilings is a farce. An overwhelming majority of legislators embark on their parliamentary careers today with a gross lie—the false election returns which they submit. About this sordid fact the Committee was broadly agreed. But it feared that abolition of ceilings altogether "would aggravate the evil of overspending and the corrupt influence of money in politics". This fear is not unjustified. But failure to recommend any radical measures for curbing election expenses means reconciling with the status quo which is certainly undesirable. The Committee has done well to accept in principle that "all election expenses should be a legitimate charge on public funds" and that "the burden of legitimate election expenses at present borne by the candidate or the political party would be progressively shifted to the State". But the measures recommended for the implementation of this radical principle are feeble and halting. The corroding influence of money power in elections is tremendous. The malady calls for drastic remedies. Half-heartedness will not do. In this context, we think the proposal of giving election grants to recognised political parties partly in advance on the basis of their performance in the preceding election and partly after the elections on the basis of their actual poll performance needs to be seriously considered.

Outside Parliament too, I actively participated in the efforts of the Jana Sangh to make electoral reforms an important issue of national debate. In 1972, Jana Sangh became the first political party to pass a resolution on election expenses of recognised political parties to be borne by the State. The resolution also raised another important issue. 'Indeed, there is need to review the utility of the prevailing electoral system itself. Under this system, the number of seats secured by a party in the legislature has often no relation to the mass support it enjoys. Therefore, all democrats, irrespective of party affiliation, should ponder seriously over the question and devise ways and means to make the present electoral apparatus reflect the people's will faithfully.'

It is one of the abiding disappointments of my political life that our political establishment has been unable to introduce comprehensive electoral reforms to cleanse our democratic system of its ills. Apart from the JPC that I have mentioned, several other committees have gone into this question subsequently and made valuable suggestions. Notable among these are the Tarkunde Committee (1974), Dinesh Goswami Committee (1990), V.R. Krishna Iyer Committee (1994) and Indrajit Gupta Committee (1998). The 15th Law Commission also conducted an extensive study of the Representation of People Act, 1951 and made vital recommendations. The NDA government did push forward the agenda of poll reforms with some positive initiatives but I cannot claim that we could make a significant difference.*

THE YEAR 1971—WAR WITH PAKISTAN AND THE GENESIS OF BANGLADESH

The decade of the 1970s heralded a momentous event in the history of South Asia. What began as an electoral dispute in neighbouring Pakistan ended up redefining the geopolitics of South Asia. For the second time, within a quarter of a century, the map of the Indian subcontinent was

---

* As President of the BJP, I launched in 1997 an initiative called *Aajivan Sahyogi Yojana*, a scheme to collect small but regular (annual) contributions from all those who wish to be lifelong associates of the party. It is meant to strengthen the concept of self-financing for the party's day-to-day activities.

redrawn with the birth of Bangladesh, the delivery being mid-wifed by India.

I must confess that, as a victim of history when the map of the subcontinent was first redrawn in 1947, I took special interest in the developments leading up to the third war between India and Pakistan, in December 1971, culminating in the division of Pakistan and the creation of Bangladesh as a separate nation on 16 December 1971. When the dust had settled, I was reminded of an oft-quoted saying by Karl Marx—'History repeats itself, first as a tragedy and second time as a farce.' However, the genesis of Bangladesh could by no means be called a farce. I felt that Marx's saying needed to be modified thus: 'History repeats itself, first as a tragedy and second time as a punishment'.

The creation of Pakistan in 1947 was the outcome of an aggressive, hate-charged movement inspired by a historical falsehood—namely, that the Hindus and Muslims of undivided India constituted two distinct nations and hence Muslims needed a separate homeland. But, apart from carrying the burden of this historical misrepresentation, Pakistan was also an embarrassing advertisement of geographical absurdity. West and East Pakistan were physically separated by a distance of over 1,200 miles, with India sandwiched in between. World history presented no such example of an artificial nation except if it was the colony of some imperial power. As the Jana Sangh noted in a resolution adopted at its national session in Udaipur in July 1971: 'An ideology that assumed that Dacca could feel itself closer to Islamabad, and that a citizen of East Bengal could find greater affinity with a citizen of West Punjab than with his next-door non-Muslim Bengali neighbour is as preposterous as it is illogical, unscientific and unrealistic.'

If the very creation of Pakistan was an affront to both history and geography, the callous manner in which the successive governments in West Pakistan both ignored and suppressed the legitimate aspirations of the people of East Pakistan was an assault on the notion of a common nationhood. The final breaking point came inevitably, when the military dictatorship of General Yahya Khan refused East Pakistan's Sheikh Mujibur Rehman to form the government, even though the latter's Awami League had won more seats in the National Assembly elections, held in December 1970, than Zulfikar Ali Bhutto's Pakistan People's Party (PPP) in West Pakistan. Worse still, the military junta imprisoned Mujibur Rehman and began a violent crackdown of the democratic protests in East Bengal, its savagery confirming that it actually behaved like a colonial power towards its distant eastern half. Houses were burnt, wells were poisoned and crops were indiscriminately destroyed. A shockingly large number of women were raped as part of wartime crimes.

According to well-researched books, General Yahya Khan told his top military brass: 'Kill three million of them and the rest will eat out of our hands.' The commandment was followed; close to three million people were killed in the genocide. What its perpetrators did not realise then was that, by so doing, they had also killed the 'Two Nation' theory, which was the basis of the existence of Pakistan. The genesis of Bangladesh was thus a just retribution to the arrogance and inhumanity of Pakistan's rulers.

Another important dimension of the atrocities of the Pakistani military in East Bengal was a huge influx of refugees into India, their number touching almost 1.5 crores by November 1971. The 'Mukti Bahini', a guerrilla force of about 100,000 mostly civilian fighters, was waging a heroic resistance against the Pakistani army. Though grossly lacking in military expertise, it possessed moral power and the solidarity of the freedom-loving people around the world, especially in India. Prime Minister Indira Gandhi made commendable efforts to make rulers in major world capitals understand, in the right perspective, the grave humanitarian crisis developing in India's neighbourhood, which began having a direct impact on our country. Sadly, the Nixon administration in Washington chose to view the situation through the prejudiced Cold War mindset and continued to support Pakistan, both politically and militarily. President Richard Nixon ordered the dispatch of the US aircraft carrier task force from the Seventh Fleet in the Indian Ocean to enter the Bay of Bengal, with a view to terrorising India.

Around this time, I once led an angry demonstration of Jana Sangh workers in front of the US Embassy in Chanakyapuri, New Delhi, to protest the American arms aid to Pakistan. At this crucial juncture, the Jana Sangh was in the forefront of Indian people's solidarity with the struggle of the Bangladeshis for national liberation. Atalji delivered, during this period, some of the most electrifying and thought-provoking speeches ever heard in Indian Parliament.

The harsh reality of the developments of 1971 was such that it only needed a trigger for Pakistan to wage a new war against India. And the inner logic of the war, which began on 3 December, was such that it culminated in the defeat of Pakistan and the liberation of Bangladesh. In a magnificent display of top-level military planning and ground-level execution, the Indian Army surrounded Dhaka in just ten days and held as many as 93,000 Pakistani soldiers as Prisoners of War (POWs). It was the largest surrender since the Second World War. On 16 December, Pakistan finally accepted defeat and surrendered unconditionally.

India's victory in the 1971 war was quite simply the grandest hour in the annals of our Armed Forces. The entire nation was ecstatic. Undoubtedly, the two big heroes of the war were General Sam Maneckshaw (who later went onto become India's first ever Field Marshall) and Lt. Gen. J.S. Aurora, with whom Pakistan's Lt. Gen. A.A.K. Niazi signed the Instrument of Surrender. But there was also a third hero: Lt. Gen. Aurora's Chief of Staff, Maj. Gen. J.F.R. Jacob, who later joined the BJP and also served as the Governor of Goa, and later, Punjab, with great distinction.

After the war was over, Prime Minister Indira Gandhi received well-deserved praise for her firm and courageous leadership. Since we in the Jana Sangh were trained never to see national issues, especially issues concerning national security, from a narrow political perspective, we had wholeheartedly supported the government through all the developments of 1971. Now, in the hour of national glory, the party did not lag behind in complimenting the Prime Minister. At a special session of Parliament, held in the Central Hall, the most lavish words of praise for Indira Gandhi came from Atalji.

It is widely believed, even today, that Atalji described Indira Gandhi as 'Durga' after her triumphant leadership of the 1971 war. However, to the best of my recollection, he never used that word. What actually happened

New Beginnings

Advani with Kamla at their wedding reception in Bombay in February 1965.

With Kamla, Jayant and Pratibha at their home in Pandara Park, New Delhi in 1973.

Helping the children with their studies.

Nurturing his life-long passion for books in his library at Pandara Park.

(Above) *A caricature by daughter Pratibha when she was ten.*

(Left) *A treasured personal moment with wife Kamla.*

The world-renowned Vivekananda Rock Memorial, Kanyakumari; (Inset) Its founder Eknath Ranade, a respected RSS leader. Advani served as Secretary of the Delhi Committee to mobilise public support for the erection of the memorial.

(Below from left to right) Socialist leader Dr Ram Manohar Lohia, and the Jana Sangh leaders Pitambar Das, Pandit Deendayal Upadhyaya and Nanaji Deshmukh.

(Above) *With former Prime Minister Indira Gandhi and former Chief Executive Councillor and party colleague Vijay Kumar Malhotra in 1967.*

(Right) *With former Lok Sabha Speaker Dr. Neelam Sanjiva Reddy, addressing a National Conference of Presiding Officers.*

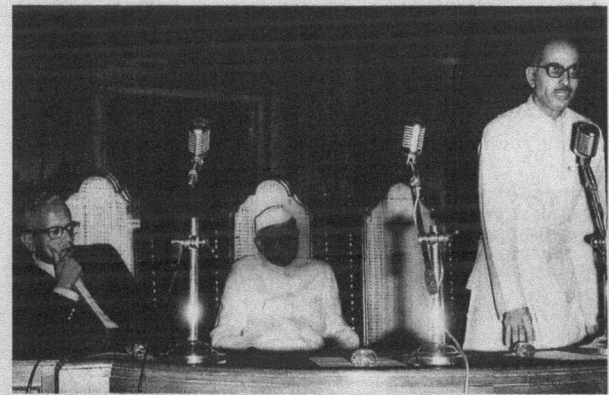

With colleagues from the Delhi Metropolitan Council. Advani became Chairman of the Council in 1967.

Presiding over the Jana Sangh convention in Kanpur, 1973.

Jana Sangh workers felicitating Advani after his election as party President in Kanpur.

(Above) Serving food to party delegates during a Jana Sangh adhiveshan after being elected party President in 1973.

(Right) With wife Kamla while being welcomed by Atalji and other party colleagues in Kanpur.

Presiding over a party meeting. To Advani's right is Jagannathrao Joshi, a longtime colleague.

(Above) *At a Boat Club rally in New Delhi. Also seen are Madanlal Khurana on the right and Kedarnath Sahni on the left.*

(Right) *Exchanging notes with Atalji during a party meeting.*

(Below) *Participating in a party demonstration along with Kanwarlal Gupta and other Delhi Jana Sangh leaders. To the extreme right is Jagdish Prasad Mathur, a founding member of the party.*

Challenging Indira Gandhi's authoritarian regime just prior to Emergency, with Rajmata Vijayaraje Scindia and Atalji in 1974.

(Left) *Addressing a Jana Sangh conclave flanked by senior colleagues Atalji and Bhai Mahavir.*

(Below) *Former RSS Sarsanghchalak, Shri Balasaheb Deoras, addressing* swayamsevaks *at the annual Vijayadashami congregation in Nagpur.*

Battle for Democracy

Jayaprakash Narayan addressing a Jana Sangh meeting in New Delhi in 1975 during which he affirmed, 'If Jana Sangh is fascist, then I am also fascist.'

Jayaprakash Narayan, in 1974, addressed numerous rallies all over the country to mobilise public opinion against the looming dictatorship.

To mark the 25th anniversary of the Emergency (2000) Advani revisiting the Bangalore Central Jail where he had spent nineteen months during the Emergency.

Justice H.R. Khanna of the Supreme Court was victimised for giving a dissenting judgment during the Emergency.

Senior RSS functionary Dattopant Thengdi was a prominant leader of the underground movement against the Emergency.

George Fernandes, another leader of the underground movement, being taken to court hand-cuffed.

Two heroes of the Emergency: Madhu Dandavate and S.N. Mishra. Both were Advani's prisonmates in Bangalore.

Advani in front of Bangalore Central Jail with two former Karnataka Chief Ministers Rama Krishna Hegde and J.H. Patel, both of whom were his co-prisoners during the Emergency.

(Right) *The famous cartoon by Abu Abraham showing the former President of India, Fakhruddin Ali Ahmed, signing the proclamation of Emergency from his bathtub.*

After the Emergency was revoked, in 1977, the Janata Party became the rallying point for various non-Congress parties. Seen in the photo with Advani are Morarji Desai, Acharya Kripalani, Madhu Dandavate, Raj Narain and other prominent leaders.

At a Boat Club rally with Mulayam Singh Yadav, H.N. Bahuguna, Ram Dhan, N.T. Rama Rao, and others.

Jayaprakash Narayan with his trusted colleague and Jana Sangh leader Nanaji Deshmukh; (Centre) with Morarji Desai, who became the Prime Minister after the Janata Party's spectacular victory in 1977.

(Bottom) Advani visiting Desai at his residence in Bombay.

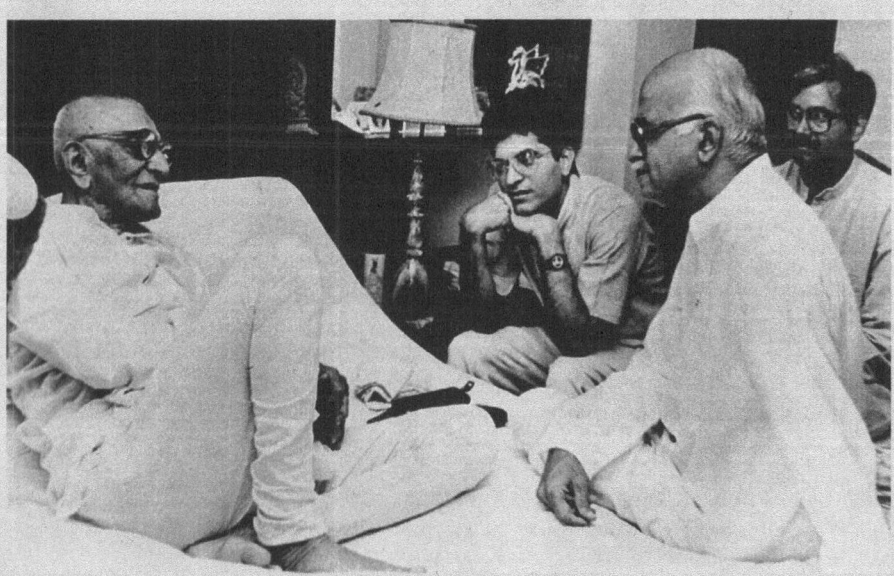

With J.P. Mathur and Rajmata Scindia.

Arun Jaitley (left) and M. Venkaiah Naidu, both senior BJP leaders now, were active in the ABVP's struggle against the Emergency.

With stalwarts of the non-Left Opposition in 1988. Seen are Biju Patnaik, V.P. Singh, N.T. Rama Rao, Ramakrishna Hegde, Atal Bihari Vajpayee, Chandrashekhar, H.N. Bahuguna and Devi Lal.

'Long-lasting and fulfilling relationships in politics are possible only on the basis of mutual trust, respect and commitment to certain shared lofty goals. Politics driven by power play is competitive and conflict-ridden. But politics driven by a common ideology and nurtured by common ideals is a different matter altogether.'

was that at the national session of the Jana Sangh, held in Ghaziabad in 1971, V.G. Deshpande, a member of the Working Committee and a great admirer of Indira Gandhi, remarked in his speech: 'Indiraji, lead the nation with courage. We are all with you. If you help Bangladesh to become free, posterity will remember you as Durga.'

THE SHIMLA AGREEMENT AND LESSONS OF THE 1971 WAR

In both the previous wars that India fought against Pakistan, in 1948 and 1965, an unfortunate precedent had been set: what our jawans had won on the battlefield, our political rulers had surrendered by way of feeble diplomacy. In 1948, when it seemed certain that the Indian Army was in a position to completely foil the attack by Pakistan-backed tribal invaders and free the entire territory of Jammu & Kashmir from Pakistani occupation, Nehru inexplicably agreed to refer the Kashmir issue to the United Nations. His blunder resulted in India losing two-fifths of the territory to Pakistan. Similarly, after the 1965 war, as I have mentioned in the previous section, the Tashkent Declaration undid the gains made by the Indian Army in capturing Haji Pir and Tithwa in POK. Sadly, the same pattern continued even after India's decisive triumph in the war for the liberation of Bangladesh.

In July 1972, Indira Gandhi and Zulfikar Ali Bhutto (who had by now become Pakistan's Prime Minister after the exit of Gen. Yahya Khan) met in Shimla for a summit meeting. Learning from the experience of the Tashkent Declaration, the Jana Sangh took the pains of reminding the government not to yield ground at Shimla. A resolution passed in March 1972 by the party's Working Committee said:

> Ever since the end of the 14-day war with Pakistan, pressure is being mounted to force India to repatriate Pak prisoners of war (PoWs) and to withdraw Indian troops from Pakistani territory, *irrespective of whether or not there is an overall peace settlement between India and Pakistan*. [emphasis added] The Communist Party of India's resolution calling for withdrawal of Indian troops to

> the 1948 ceasefire line can well be regarded as reflecting Moscow's mind.... Any piecemeal settlement of issues that suits Pakistan would be wrong, impolitic and against the best interests of India. There should be no question of withdrawing Indian troops unless all pending issues are thrashed out and a package deal has been arrived at in the interest of a durable peace between India and Pakistan.

As party President, Atalji met Prime Minister Indira Gandhi in Shimla and urged her not to agree to the release of the PoWs and withdrawal of Indian troops without securing a permanent settlement with Pakistan on the Kashmir issue. Sadly, the Shimla Agreement turned out to be another betrayal. The Indian government consented to send back all the PoWs, return the entire 9,000 square kilometres territory under the possession of the Indian Army, and pardon all war criminals (whose trial was demanded by Bangladesh). In return, Pakistan's commitments under the agreement were minor and intangible, and it could violate them, as it indeed did, without incurring a heavy cost.

In his book *Surrender at Dacca: Birth of a Nation*,[1] Gen. Jacob praises Indira Gandhi's role during the war but bemoans that she was badly advised on the Shimla Pact. 'We had won a decisive victory in the marshes and rice paddies of Bangladesh. The advantages gained on the battlefield were frittered away at the Shimla Conference.' Jacob mentions that Bhutto had agreed verbally to convert the LoC into a permanent border between India and Pakistan. But the Indian side failed to get an official commitment from him on this important point.

As I had said at a public meeting in New Delhi at the time, Indira Gandhi 'wasted a golden opportunity for a mass of verbiage'.

India's 1971 war with Pakistan taught us many valuable lessons. The first and foremost lesson was to be fully prepared and capable of reliably defending our nation in case of any eventuality. I say this because, as war became imminent, India found itself in a situation when, internationally, no major power was *fully* supportive of India's search for a permanent settlement with Pakistan. Indeed, the US decision to dispatch nuclear-armed Seventh Fleet vindicated the demand made by the Jana Sangh, as far back as in 1966, that India should develop her own nuclear deterrent. The demand was scoffed at by leaders of the ruling party then. However, after this bitter experience, Indira Gandhi took the bold step of conducting in 1974, a nuclear test at Pokharan, in the desert region of Rajasthan. It was an action which the Jana Sangh wholeheartedly endorsed. The two communist parties, predictably, opposed it just as they would go on to oppose Pokharan II by the Vajpayee government in May 1998.

I must here record with gratitude the timely support, both diplomatic and military, that India received from the erstwhile Soviet Union during the 1971 war. The twenty-year Indo-Soviet Treaty for Cooperation was a direct outcome of the American support to Pakistan. The treaty was welcome. However, it could never be a substitute to India becoming self-reliant in national defence. In addition, as events in succeeding years showed, the communist rulers in Moscow used the treaty to interfere in the internal affairs of India, the most brazen being their support to Indira Gandhi's Emergency Rule in 1975 and castigation of Jayaprakash Narayan and his movement for democracy as 'fascist' and 'reactionary'.

The second lesson of the 1971 war relates to the safety and security of Hindus in Bangladesh. It is today largely forgotten that Hindus were specifically targetted by the Pakistan Army during the war. A majority of the Bengali refugees who had fled to India were Hindus. A disproportionately large number of the victims of rape and genocide were Hindus. It is necessary to understand the reasons for this. The rulers in Pakistan clearly wanted to implement a policy of 'religious and cultural cleansing' as they identified the Bengali culture in East Pakistan with Hindu culture. For example, they could never stomach the fact that Rabindranath Tagore, the national poet of India, was not only popular but highly venerated in East Bengal. After its liberation, Bangladesh was to declare *'Amar Shonar Bangla...'*, a song written by Tagore, as its national anthem. Similarly, it infuriated the Islamist rulers of Pakistan that Kazi Nazrul Islam, who would later be honoured as Bangladesh's national poet, had penned many poems in praise of Hindu deities such as Durga, Rama and Krishna, and also the Ganga, Sindhu and Saraswati rivers, which are regarded as holy by the

Hindus. They were determined to remove all traces of Indian influence from the life of Muslims in East Pakistan, just as they had done, with far greater success, in West Pakistan.

*

Soon after the end of the war, elections were held for state assemblies in March 1972. This was the first time, after the first general elections in 1952, that assembly polls were not being conducted simultaneously with the Lok Sabha polls. Riding the wave of war victory, the Congress scored big victories in most of the states. The Jana Sangh's performance was poor. Atalji as party President owned moral responsibility for the defeat and, in a rare display of gracefulness, asked Senior Vice President, Bhai Mahavir, to preside over the national session held in May 1972 in Bhagalpur. 'I am doing so, because there should be a frank discussion and delegates should feel free to criticise the leadership,' he said. However, there was, in Atalji's mind, the desire to find a new leader for the party. He had already served as President for nearly five years after Deendayalji's demise. And this search for the President, after a prolonged and circuitous route, ended by Atalji urging me to take the baton from his hand.

With this, once again, came a turning point in my life.

7

THE JOURNEY FROM KANPUR TO KANPUR

Today politics has ceased to be a means. It has become an end in itself. We have today people who are engaged in power politics rather than aim at political power with a view to achieving certain lofty social and national objectives.

— PANDIT DEENDAYAL UPADHYAYA

Kanpur holds a special place in the history of the Bharatiya Jana Sangh, as also in my own political life. The Kanpur session of the party in December 1952, presided over by Dr Syama Prasad Mookerjee, will always be remembered for the decision to launch a nationwide satyagraha for the complete integration of Jammu & Kashmir into the Indian Union. It forms one of the proudest chapters in the history of the Jana Sangh and the BJP. It is also one of the saddest moments in our party's history, since Dr Mookerjee became a martyr in this struggle.

I had attended the 1952 session in Kanpur as a young twenty-five-year-old delegate from Rajasthan. I still vividly remember Dr Mookerjee and his magnetic personality, which radiated self-confidence and lofty idealism. His oratory, particularly in English, was inspiring. This made young activists like me feel highly optimistic about the party's future. Little did I imagine then that, twenty years later in February 1973, the Bharatiya Jana Sangh would hold its plenary session in Kanpur to elect me as the party President. Both for the party and for me, this journey from Kanpur to Kanpur was a highly exhilarating and challenging one.

BECOMING PARTY PRESIDENT FOR THE FIRST TIME

I was a most reluctant party President. How the mantle of presidentship fell on me merits a mention. Atalji, who had become the party President in February 1968, was seriously considering stepping down after the 1971 general elections. Around the beginning of 1972, Atalji told me, 'You become the party President now.' When I asked him why, he replied, 'I have already completed four years in this office. It's time for a new person to take over.'

I said, 'Atalji, I cannot even speak at a public meeting. How can I head the party?' In those days, I was apprehensive of speaking publicly, believing that I was a poor orator. I must confess that I had developed this complex largely on account of my close association with Atalji, who used to captivate the audience with his magical speeches.

'But you have now begun speaking in Parliament. So why this diffidence?' Atalji persisted.

I said, 'Speaking in Parliament is one thing, and giving a speech in front of thousands of people is another. Besides, there are many senior leaders in the party. Let one of them be made party President.'

'Even Deendayalji was not an orator,' Atalji continued. 'But people listened to him with rapt attention because of the profound thoughts that his words contained. So, it's not necessary to be a great speaker to lead the party.'

I remained unconvinced and said, 'No, I can't be the party President. Please find another person.'

'Who can it be, then?' he asked.

I said, 'Why not Rajmata?'

Vijayaraje Scindia, known as the Rajmata of Gwalior*, was married to the Maharaja of one of the largest and richest princely states in India. After her husband's death, she became a MP on a Congress ticket in 1962. Five years later, she quit the Congress to join the Jana Sangh, guided by her ideological conviction. Though hailing from a princely family, she endeared herself to one and all in the party with her honesty, simplicity and commitment, soon emerging as one of the pillars of strength of the Jana Sangh. She was later jailed during the Emergency in 1975.

Atalji agreed to my suggestion and we both went to Gwalior to persuade her to accept the post. After a lot of persuasion, she finally said 'Yes'. Relieved and happy, we thanked her for her assent. Just then, she said, 'But please wait. You have to give me another day to give my final consent. As you know, I do not take any important decision in my life without seeking the approval and blessings of my Guruji at Datia.' The same day, she went to Datia, a small district town in Madhya Pradesh, and returned the next day with the bad news. 'My Guruji has said "No".'

'What do we do now?' Atalji asked.

I said, 'Why don't we persuade Mahavirji?' Dr Bhai Mahavir, son of the noted freedom fighter Bhai Parmanand†, was a Senior Vice President of the Jana Sangh and a member of the Rajya Sabha then.

---

* Rajmata's only son, late Madhavrao Scindia, began his political career with the Jana Sangh but later joined the Congress. Her daughter, Vasundhara Raje, one of the younger-generation leaders in the BJP, is currently the Chief Minister of Rajasthan. Another daughter, Yashodhara, is a BJP MP in the Lok Sabha from Madhya Pradesh.

† Bhai Parmanand was one of the most fascinating personalities in the Indian freedom movement. In my early years in the RSS, I had read his book *Hindu Sangathan*. A Vedic missionary who belonged to the Arya Samaj movement, Bhai Parmanand was also a member of the revolutionary Ghadar Party. He travelled around the world in the early years of the twentieth century and, along with Lala Hardayal, a fellow revolutionary, propagated the cause of India's Independence. He visited South Africa to meet Mahatma Gandhi and stayed in his ashram. He was arrested by the British in the first Lahore Conspiracy Case and was imprisoned in the Andaman Islands. He died of a heart attack in 1947 when India was partitioned. His son, Dr Bhai Mahavir, who was in Lahore before Independence, has been a veteran RSS leader and was General Secretary of the Jana Sangh when the party was founded. He later became Governor of Madhya Pradesh, from 1998-2003.

Atalji agreed with me and both of us, accompanied by Jagannathrao Joshi, went to meet Mahavirji at his residence at Pant Marg in New Delhi. He agreed, after some persuasion. Just as we were feeling relieved at the success of our mission, he said, 'Please wait a minute. I would like to consult my wife.' He went inside, and returned after some time with the bad news. 'My wife is not agreeable.'

When we left, Atalji said to me, 'No more of this fruitless search now. You have no option but to say yes to what I say.' Thus, I was formally elected President of the Bharatiya Jana Sangh in December 1972. Soon thereafter, I presided over the eighteenth annual session of the party in Kanpur.

As I look back, I am struck by the workings of fate that made me, a young and relatively inexperienced entrant in national politics, the party President. First of all, I was touched by Atalji's trust in me. Secondly, I was humbled by the fact that other leaders in the party such as Nanaji Deshmukh, Sundar Singh Bhandari, Kushabhau Thakre and Jagannathrao Joshi, who were senior to me in both age and experience, readily agreed to my candidature. All of them being *pracharaks* of the RSS were never motivated by considerations of office or designation. Sadly, as I recall this, I am also troubled by the fact that this spirit of camaraderie and mutual trust, idealistic and goal-oriented approach to party work, is something that has got diluted over the years.

'NEITHER RIGHT, NOR LEFT: JUST FORWARD!'

I would like to recall here two points from my maiden Presidential speech at Kanpur, believing that both hold significant contemporary relevance for the BJP. It was a time when there was a lot of debate in the media about the Jana Sangh being a 'rightist' or a 'leftist' party. Referring to this debate, I said:

> Our party is not wedded to any economic 'ism' and that terms such as 'left' and 'right' are just not relevant in the Indian context. Having said this, I think there is a need to analyse the comments

that are being made to identify precisely where we stand in relation to this analysis. In Western democratic politics the term 'left' has come to mean, broadly, propensity in favour of State control. Two other important criteria on which the left-right distinction has been based in the West are: attitude to equality and attitude to change. Judged by the first criterion, the Jana Sangh can be called a 'rightist' party. However, tested on the touchstone of the two other attributes, the Jana Sangh would be classed as a 'leftist' party. Truth is that, it is neither rightist nor leftist, it is forward-looking.

The second point concerned the two basic commitments of the Jana Sangh, and now the BJP—nationalism and development-oriented democracy. I said:

> The journey from Kanpur to Kanpur has been a memorable one.... During these twenty years, the Bharatiya Jana Sangh has made a place for itself in the hearts of the people as a patriotic party comprising disciplined cadres, fired by a sense of devotion to the Motherland. The party's Bharatiya character has been indisputably established.... Apart from nationalism, the second central plank of the Jana Sangh's philosophy is democracy, political as well as economic. Our Sangh is not only a Bharatiya Sangh, it is also a Jana Sangh—a party of the *demos*, of the people. It is this Jana character of our party that needs to be brought home to the country even more forcefully during the coming years.

One of the first tasks I had to attend to after becoming party President was indeed troublesome. As per the decision taken by the party's Working Committee, I had to expel Balraj Madhok, a former President of the Jana Sangh, with whom I had worked quite closely, for indiscipline. He complained that I had not consulted Shri Guruji in this matter. As a matter of fact, Shri Guruji had concurred with the party's decision. Just before the Kanpur session, he happened to be in Delhi on a short visit and I went to meet him at the airport. It was my first meeting with him after being elected the party President. He asked me about Balrajji. I said that things were going from bad to worse, and conveyed to him that the party was contemplating his expulsion. Guruji then said to me, 'In matters of violation of discipline, you should take all such steps as are required to safeguard the health of the organisation. Nobody, not even a former President of the party, should have immunity in this regard.'

The action against Madhok had a salutary effect, greatly enhancing the Jana Sangh's reputation as a party that attached utmost importance to discipline. I must, however, note here with some degree of pain and concern that, in subsequent decades, the BJP has not been able to maintain the same reputation.

SHRI GURUJI, A SANYASI IN CEASELESS ACTION, PASSES AWAY

Within a few months of the party's Kanpur session, on 5 June, Shri Guruji passed away in Nagpur after a prolonged and courageous battle against cancer. When I heard the news, I was in Indore where I had gone as part of an extensive tour of Madhya Pradesh and Rajasthan. I immediately rushed to Nagpur by car to join thousands of *swayamsevaks* of the RSS and Guruji's admirers to pay my personal homage to this great soul.

Shri Guruji is a much-misunderstood personality in India's post-Independence history. I would even say that the misunderstanding and deliberate misrepresentation that he was a victim of, are in direct proportion to his innate greatness. The essential *pinda* (core) of Shri Guruji's personality was that of a *sanyasi* (hermit). The fact that he had decided, in his youth, to become a monk in the Ramakrishna Mission and had even received his *diksha* (spiritual initiation) from Swami Akhandananda, a direct disciple of Ramakrishna Paramahansa, had imparted a distinct spiritual dimension to his life. Had his guru not passed away within a month of that event in early 1937, Shri Guruji would most likely have lived the rest of his life as a *sanyasi*. Three years later, at the age of only thirty-four, he became the *sarsanghchalak* of the RSS after the death of Dr Keshav Baliram Hedgewar, its founder.

The thirty-three years that he was at the helm of the RSS were marked by severe trials and tribulations. During this period, the Sangh grew from a sapling into a mighty banyan tree. Indeed, I would dare say that there is no other example of a leader in the history of independent India who, despite facing so many ordeals, succeeded in building an organisation as large, as widespread, and as committed to the ideology of nationalism as Shri Guruji. The severest challenge in the life of the RSS came after Mahatma Gandhi's assassination and it emerged unscathed thanks to the courageous, calm and strong-willed personality of its leader. In spite of all that, he and his organisation had to suffer on account of the ban and imprisonment on the one hand, and unrestrained vilification on the other, there was not a trace of personal bitterness in Shri Guruji's mind towards the Congress leadership. He did have his differences with Gandhiji, however, contrary to the systematic anti-RSS propaganda, these never came in the way of his sincere and respectful attitude towards the Mahatma, either before or after his assassination.

Whenever there was a crisis before the nation, Guruji's commandment to all the *swayamsevaks* of the RSS was: 'Follow the noble ideal of Dharmaraj (Yudhishthira) in the *Mahabharata*.' When the Kauravas came with the avowed intention of humiliating the Pandavas, but were themselves captured by Gandharvas, Yudhishthira commanded Arjuna to go to the rescue of the Kauravas, saying, 'Between ourselves we are five and they are hundred. But before the enemy, we are hundred plus five—*Vayam panchaadhikam shatam*.' When the accession of Jammu & Kashmir was creating problems for the Indian Union, Guruji urged Maharaja Hari Singh to join the Indian Union without any further delay, explaining to him the mischief Pakistan was up to and emphasising, too, the futility of making Jammu & Kashmir an independent nation. The magnificent show of patriotic service by the RSS during the Chinese war in 1962 had an effect even on Nehru, who invited 3,000 uniformed *swayamsevaks* to participate in the Republic Day Parade, on 26 January 1963, in Delhi. When Pakistan attacked India in 1965, Prime Minister Lal Bahadur Shastri invited Shri Guruji to attend the All-Leaders Conference, and the latter extended full cooperation to the government on behalf of the Sangh. We thus see that the Congress leaders of those days were not as petty and prejudiced towards the RSS as many of their present-day successors.

During Shri Guruji's stewardship of the RSS, he inspired the creation of many affiliate organisations such as the Vishwa Hindu Parishad (VHP), Akhil Bharatiya Vidyarthi Parishad (ABVP), Bharatiya Mazdoor Sangh (BMS), Vanavasi Kalyan Ashram, Vidya Bharati and Shishu Mandir educational institutions. Each of these institutions has rendered valuable and selfless service to the nation in their respective areas of activity. When the nationalist beliefs of a leader have their basis in the spiritual and cultural traditions of his society, and when the leader himself is a man of high character, he is naturally able to elevate the character of the entire movement that he leads.

Bearded and bespectacled, and proficient in about a dozen Indian languages, Shri Guruji was the very embodiment of austerity with an aura of dynamism around him. In his presence, I always had the feeling that here was a person who wanted to banish sloth and pettiness from the world, and preferred only that which accords with his notion of Karma Yoga. I attended many of his *bauddhiks* (lectures) for *swayamsevaks*. He was no doubt an impressive speaker, erudite and forceful. But he was one of those rare personalities in public life who impress others not on account of their oratory or any other outward attribute, but because of their purity and spiritual stature. On meeting him in person, many people outside the RSS circle were startled at the schism between the reality of his personality and the image, created by a section of the political class, of a menacing leader heading a demonic organisation. One of them was the renowned journalist Khushwant Singh, who was then the Editor of the *Illustrated Weekly of India*. He did an interview with the RSS Chief in November 1972, beginning it with the following words: 'There are some individuals whom we start to hate without even bothering to know them. Guru Golwalkar comes first on my list of such persons.'

When Khushwant Singh asked: 'What are your thoughts on Muslims' issues?' Shri Guruji's answer was revealing: 'I have not the slightest doubt that historical factors alone are responsible for the divided loyalty that Muslims have towards India and Pakistan. Moreover, both Muslims and Hindus are equally to blame for this. Nevertheless, it is not right to hold the entire community responsible for the guilt of some people. We have to win over the loyalty of Muslims with love. I am optimistic and I believe that Hindutva and Islam will learn to co-exist with one another.' Those who consider him 'anti-secular' and 'communal' would do well to read his following views on Indian Muslims, as expressed in another interview given to Dr Saifuddin Jeelani, an Arabic scholar:

> According to our religious belief and philosophy, *a Muslim is as good as a Hindu*. It is not the Hindu alone who will reach the ultimate Godhead. Everyone has the *right* to follow his path according to his own persuasion.... Follow your own religion. The God of Islam, Christianity and Hinduism is the same and we are all His devotees.... Give people true knowledge of Islam. Give people true knowledge of Hinduism. Educate them to know that *all religions* teach men to be selfless, holy and pious.... Indianisation does *not mean making all people Hindus*.'*

Shri Guruji was no doubt critical of what he considered as the 'separatist mentality' in the conduct of a section of Indian Muslims. He also did not mince words while questioning their tendency to glorify Muslim invaders and intolerant Muslim rulers. He strongly advocated the 'Indianisation' of Indian Muslims, especially after the creation of Pakistan on the communal basis of the Two Nation Theory. Nevertheless, those who deduce that he was anti-Muslim and nursed a hatred for Islam are clearly barking up the wrong tree.

Whenever a critical issue of a divisive nature arose before the nation, Shri Guruji's approach was invariably pragmatic, farsighted and nationalistic. This can be seen from his direction to the Sangh when an intense Punjabi versus Hindi row broke out in Punjab in the early 1960s. Some Hindus were opposed to Punjabi being declared the state language of Punjab. And even though their own mother tongue was Punjabi, they insisted on declaring Hindi as their mother tongue. This naturally created resentment among Sikhs. Shri Guruji foresaw that this could undermine Hindu-Sikh unity and weaken national integration. Under his guidance, the RSS dissuaded

---

* *Bunch of Thoughts* by Madhav Sadashiv Golwalkar.

Hindus in Punjab against declaring Hindi as their mother tongue and, instead, accept Punjabi.*

Some might find it hard to believe today that Shri Guruji was, by nature, completely aloof from politics, especially power politics. In fact, he had a distinct dislike for politics conducted for personal gain. Although he accepted politics to be an important and essential part of national life, he kept the RSS detached from it, leaving its conduct almost entirely to the *pracharaks* and *swayamsevaks* working in the Jana Sangh. For him, the responsibility of the RSS lay in a different, wider and more basic area of national life—namely, creating a large number, generation after generation, of selfless individuals with high character dedicated to nation-building in diverse spheres of activity and serving as role models for the rest of society. In the twenty-two years (1951–73) that he interacted with the Jana Sangh, he never interfered in the functioning of the party or questioned its policies and programmes. He had implicit faith in the leadership of Dr Mookerjee and Deendayalji.

Perhaps the best tribute to Shri Guruji came from R.K. Karanjia, the renowned Editor of *Blitz* weekly: 'He had no axe to grind, and in the pursuit of his ideals rancour was not in his heart, weakness was not in his word, weariness was not on his brow. It would be good if other political leaders emulate his example of dedicated life and win the respect and confidence of his followers.' I might mention here that Karanjia, whose weekly had a pronounced pro-communist and pro-Congress tilt, and called the Jana Sangh and BJP 'communal', changed his views later. He became a big supporter of the Ayodhya movement and came to my house in 1990 to compliment me. He even attended a national session of the BJP in Bangalore in 1994.

*

---

* A funny aside is worthy of mention here. Two major newspapers of Punjab those days, *Pratap* and *Milap*, had large circulations. In the tussle over the official language of the state, *Pratap* was backing Hindi and *Milap* was campaigning for Punjabi. Interestingly, both were being published in Urdu!

I have dwelt at some length on the personality of Shri Guruji as I feel it is necessary to remove the misconceptions and prejudices that have grown over the years around the RSS in particular, and the Sangh Parivar, in general. It is therefore necessary for a fair and well-informed debate about Shri Guruji and his worldview. It has not happened so far principally because of a deliberately distorted projection of the RSS and its most respected ideologue in strong-pitched communist propaganda. He was truly a *tapasvi* (sage), whose penance was conducted not in a forest or on a mountain but in towns and villages, and whose aim, in the hallowed tradition of the Ramakrishna Mission that he did not join, was to bring about a new renascent awakening in the Indian nation.

JAYAPRAKASH NARAYAN: AN OLD MAN WHO IGNITED YOUNG MINDS

When I look back at my years as the President of the Bharatiya Jana Sangh in the first half of the 1970s, I recall that the one person who influenced me the most and with whom I had the privilege of working together on a common national cause was the legendary socialist leader Jayaprakash Narayan (1902–79). JP, to his countless followers and admirers, he animated the decade of the Seventies with a revival of Gandhian idealism like no other person has done either before or after Independence. Indeed, in the post-1947 political history, there is quite simply no other prominent personality who travelled across as wide an ideological spectrum, yet remained as true to his convictions at every stage of his life. Also, with the exception of Gandhiji, there is no other leader who influenced the nation's polity without ever occupying any position of power.

One of the radical young leaders in the 1930s and '40s, Jayaprakashji, who had spent over five years in jail for India's freedom, became the chief motivator and organiser of India's second freedom movement in the 1970s—freedom from dictatorship in the form of the Emergency Rule. He was well past seventy then. Yet, he inspired hundreds of thousands of students and youth in their twenties and thirties all across the country to join the struggle for the restoration of democracy.

A confirmed Marxist in his younger days, Jayaprakashji had been a bitter critic of the RSS and the Jana Sangh right up to the late 1960s. He was convinced that the RSS had a hand in Gandhiji's assassination, even going to the extent of staging a demonstration against the RSS in front of the *Organiser* office in Delhi in 1948. Therefore, it was not easy for a person like him to start building bridges with the Jana Sangh. I consider it to be one of the most satisfying achievements of my political life that I could play a certain role, along with my other colleagues like Atalji and Nanaji Deshmukh, in bringing him closer to our party and our movement.

The transformation in Jayaprakashji's outlook took place for two important reasons. He was convinced that bringing together all anti-Congress forces on a common platform was necessary in the national interest for the protection of democracy. Since he was a man of great intellectual honesty and abhorred opportunism in politics, he first wanted to have his doubts about the RSS and the Jana Sangh cleared through candid dialogue. And we succeeded in fully satisfying him on this score.

I had known Jayaprakashji from my *Organiser* days. In fact, once after reading an article I had written on democracy and electoral reforms, he expressed the desire to meet me. I readily agreed. Thereafter, I met him on several occasions. When he constituted a committee for the study of electoral reforms under the chairmanship of Justice V.M. Tarkunde, he asked me to contribute to its deliberations, which I did by preparing a discussion paper. My earlier acquaintance helped me build a closer and stronger political association with him after I became the President of the Jana Sangh.

One day in early 1973, he called me to his home and asked: 'I hear persistent questions about the RSS' alleged role in Gandhiji's assassination. I want to study this matter in detail and would like you to furnish me all the information.' I answered all his queries, and subsequently sent him full information, with documentary evidence, about every aspect of the matter—how Nathuram Godse, Gandhiji's killer, had severed links with the RSS in 1933, how he had begun to bitterly criticise the RSS, the Nehru government's decision to lift the ban on the RSS, the correspondence between Sardar Patel and Guruji, the hearings before the Justice Kapur Commission, and the latter's final judgment. Jayaprakashji called me after some days and said, 'I have studied this matter thoroughly. I am now finally convinced that the RSS had no hand in the assassination of Mahatma Gandhi.'

What brought Jayaprakashji closer to the Jana Sangh was another factor: his belief that idealism was more important than ideology in politics. Even when he felt that the Jana Sangh's ideology was not compatible with his beliefs, he was an admirer of the idealism of its activists. He genuinely believed that the leaders and cadres of the Jana Sangh were patriotic, honest and incorruptible.

The two-thirds majority that Indira Gandhi had secured in the Lok Sabha in the 1971 elections had made Jayaprakashji highly concerned about the rise of corruption and authoritarian tendencies within the Congress party. After his disillusionment with Marxism, Jayaprakashji had turned increasingly towards Gandhiji's ideals of probity in politics and governance. Through most of the 1950s and '60s, he had devoted himself to non-political social service of various Gandhian organisations, occasionally making vital contribution to the efforts to resolve national issues such as in Kashmir and Nagaland. He was disillusioned with Nehruvian socialism. He was deeply suspicious of Indira Gandhi's '*Garibi Hatao*' slogan, believing it to be a politically motivated gimmick lacking any real conviction.

Above all, he could not tolerate the growing stench of corruption in the Congress governments at the Centre as well as in the states. The public curiosity about the irregularities in the Maruti car project was proving to be uncomfortable for the Prime Minister. The Reserve Bank of India (RBI), several other banks, and the then Congress government in Haryana had bent many rules to favour this questionable project. Later it was revealed that the officers collecting information on the Maruti project were being watched by the police to ascertain whether it was they who were providing information to the Opposition leaders. Once a reporter asked Jayaprakashji: 'The Prime Minister has said that she also wants to fight corruption. What is the difference between your method of combating corruption and hers?' His answer was pithy: 'She is probably concerned about corruption at the bottom. I want to fight it at the top.'

Two significant developments around this time convinced Jayaprakashji that corruption in high places could not be fought by pleading and petitioning a callous and collusive government. The first was the Nav Nirman agitation of various student organisations in Gujarat in 1973–74, which demanded the dismissal of the corrupt Congress government headed by Chimanbhai Patel. The students sought Jayaprakashji's support for their agitation, which he gave readily. As protests paralysed the state, the Congress high command had to finally yield to the agitationists' demand. Soon thereafter, in a second development, a coalition of student and youth organisations, called the Bihar Chhatra Sangharsh Samiti, started a movement to seek redressal for a set of issues, including unemployment and corruption. Here too student leaders turned to Jayaprakashji for guidance.

In both these agitations, the ABVP, a student organisation inspired by the RSS, played a pivotal role. As a matter of fact, it was during the Bihar students' agitation that I first met K.N. Govindacharya, a prominent ABVP leader. I was impressed by his dynamism and, a decade later, inducted him into the BJP as one of its general secretaries.

'IF JANA SANGH IS FASCIST, I AM ALSO A FASCIST!'

As in Gujarat, the Congress government in Bihar too tried to suppress the peaceful agitation with brute force, forcing the agitationists to demand the resignation of Chief Minister Abdul Gaffoor and dissolution of the legislative assembly. While Jayaprakashji was leading one of the many protest marches in Patna, on 4 November 1974, the police started an indiscriminate assault on the participants and their leaders, in which he received lathi blows and collapsed to the ground. He was saved from a more serious injury by Nanaji Deshmukh, who immediately provided a protective cover for him and took subsequent lathis on himself. 'I have never been manhandled like this before,' said Jayaprakashji later. 'I do not know if Mahatma Gandhi was ever tear-gassed. But I had the experience of both for the first time.'

This barbaric treatment of one of the heroes of the freedom movement shocked the nation's conscience. Atalji and I went to Patna to meet him and, upon our return raised this issue in Parliament. On 18 November, a protest rally was organised under Jayaprakashji's leadership at Patna's Gandhi Maidan, in which nearly a million people participated. I attended it on behalf of the Jana Sangh. The rally was a clear indicator that the JP movement was no longer confined to Bihar but had the potential to change the political agenda of the nation. This was also clear from the new goal of *Sampoorna Kranti* (Total Revolution), which Jayaprakashji placed before India.

During the course of his movement, Jayaprakashji became convinced that neither non-political student-youth organisations nor any single non-Congress party could fight the menace of corruption and authoritarianism. This realisation prompted him to start a dialogue with all the Opposition parties to create a common pro-democracy and anti-corruption front. He was well aware of the deep aversion that several non-Congress parties, especially the communists, had towards the Jana Sangh. However, he had by now decided that the Jana Sangh should be invited to become a part of the broad-based struggle against Congress rule. One day, he called Atalji and me and said, 'I need your cooperation. You should join me in my movement.' I convened a special meeting of senior leaders of the party in Hyderabad to consider Jayaprakashji's proposal. In fact, I saw an opportunity in the JP movement to significantly expand the Jana Sangh's mass appeal and support base across the country. In my opening remarks at the meeting I said, 'The country must get rid of the misrule of the Congress party. However, no single party can achieve this. We in the Jana Sangh have reached a point where further growth can be achieved and the dominance of the Congress ended only by joining hands with others who share this objective. Therefore, if we want to move ahead politically and to serve the nation at this important juncture, we should accept Jayaprakashji's proposal.'

The Hyderabad conclave gave its approval. As a result, the Jana Sangh was able, for the first time at the national level, to forge close working relationships with a number of non-Congress and non-communist parties.

During this period, I was personally able to closely interact with a number of stalwarts belonging to these parties—George Fernandes, Madhu Limaye, Madhu Dandavate, Charan Singh, Ramakrishna Hegde, Deve Gowda, Karpoori Thakur and several others.

Jayaprakashji's invitation to the Jana Sangh to join his movement, and our acceptance of it, drew a sharp reaction from both the CPI and the CPI(M). The CPI's fulminations were understandable, since it was a non-Congress party only in name. Under instructions from Moscow, it was behaving more loyal than the king and endorsing every policy and action of the Indira Gandhi government. In a throwback to how the undivided communist party had branded Gandhiji, Nehru and other nationalist leaders as 'lackeys of the British', the CPI had begun to call the JP movement a handiwork of 'American imperialism'.

In contrast, the CPI(M) had some differences with the ruling party, as it was pitted against the Congress in both West Bengal and Kerala*.

---

* One of the prominent leaders of the CPI(M), who was a staunch critic of the Emergency, was A.K. Gopalan (1904–77). A man of great integrity and idealism, he made a powerful speech in Parliament against imposition of the Emergency. According to my late colleague Jana Krishnamurthy (he later became the President of the BJP in 2001), who as an underground activist used to meet Gopalan frequently in hospital in the last phase of the latter's life, the communist leader had developed much admiration for the Jana Sangh's spirited resistance to the Emergency. According to Krishnamurthy, he said: 'I wish we communists opposed Indira Gandhi's authoritarianism as strongly as your party is doing. There is some lofty idea which is capable of inspiring such deeds of bravery and stamina for sacrifice.' The Sangh Parivar accounted for nearly eighty per cent of all the detenus and satyagrahis during the Emergency.

Another communist leader for whom I had great admiration was Prof Hiren Mukherjee (1907–2004). An outstanding parliamentarian and scholar, this veteran CPI leader's was the most moving speech at an all-party meeting at Delhi's Ramlila Maidan to pay homage to Pandit Deendayal Upadhyaya, after the assassination of the Jana Sangh President on 11 February 1968. His name was proposed as the candidate of the combined opposition, against the Congress party's Giani Zail Singh, in the Presidential election in 1982. When the BJP's view was sought on his candidature, I said, 'We have no objection since we respect Prof Mukherjee.' My positive reply surprised those in communist circles. However, his candidature could not materialise since his name was

Contd...

But when it, too, criticised Jayaprakashji for including the Jana Sangh in his broad front for political renewal in India, it became obvious that the CPI(M) was more concerned about the Jana Sangh than about the Congress. Suddenly, posters and wall-writings could be seen all over Calcutta, saying, 'JP Jana Sangh ek aashe.' (JP and Jana Sangh are one and the same.) E.M.S. Namboodiripad, who was then the General Secretary of the CPI(M), went to meet Jayaprakashji and said, 'How can you invite a rightist and communal party like the Jana Sangh to join your movement? We least expected this from you. After all, don't you remember that you were in the forefront of the campaign in 1948, soon after Gandhiji's assassination, to demand a ban on the RSS? You had even led a demonstration against the RSS in front of the *Organiser* office! This is a betrayal.'

On 6 March, JP gave a call for a protest march to Parliament, to mark the completion of one year of the Bihar movement. It was a resounding success. Jayaprakashji had insisted that all the participating political parties come under one banner, without carrying their individual flags. His speech was stern: 'The conditions such as those in India would have easily sparked off a violent revolution in any other country. But here, even after persistent betrayal of the trust of the people by the Congress rulers, only peaceful mass action is being staged. This is good for the future of Indian democracy. However, I hope that the Prime Minister cares to read the message of this march to Parliament. I say to her, "Mend your ways in time, otherwise the already impatient people will throw you out."'

Contd...
missing in the voters' list. We then chose Justice H.R. Khanna, one of the heroes of the Emergency, as our common candidate.

I should also mention here that Tridib Chaudhary, a widely respected leader of the Revolutionary Socialist Party (RSP), was fielded as the common Opposition candidate, against Fakhruddin Ali Ahmed of the Congress, in the Presidential election in 1974. As the President of the Jana Sangh, I accompanied Chaudhary on his tour of state capitals to mobilise non-Congress MLAs' support for him. One day he told me, 'I have special affection for the Jana Sangh because in my younger days I had an occasion to meet the founder of the RSS, Dr. K.B. Hedgewar, who was a member of Anushilan Samiti (a revolutionary group fighting for India's Independence) in Bengal. I was highly impressed by his patriotism.'

By including the Jana Sangh in the march to Parliament, Jayaprakashji had already demonstrated that he disregarded the Marxist protests. But the following day, he did something more audacious in his show of confidence in the Jana Sangh, which startled both friends and foes of our party. On 7 March, our party had convened a national session in Delhi, so that all its delegates from different states, about 40,000 of them, could participate in the protest action on the previous day. Preceding this session, on 23 February, I had been re-elected as the President of the Jana Sangh for the second time. I suggested to my senior colleagues that we invite Jayaprakashji to attend the session as a special guest of honour. 'But will he come?' they asked, to which I said, 'Why don't we try?'

Atalji and I went to meet Jayaprakashji and conveyed our request. He readily agreed.

The news electrified the political atmosphere in the country. Many people tried to dissuade him from doing so, saying, 'Jayaprakashji, you are getting too close to a fascist party like the Jana Sangh.' He answered his critics in his speech at the Jana Sangh meeting by defiantly stating, 'I have come to this session to tell the country that the Jana Sangh is neither fascist nor reactionary. This I want to declare from the Jana Sangh platform itself. *If the BJP is fascist, then Jayaprakash Narayan is also a fascist.*' [emphasis added]

What he said next was truly prescient: 'The sun of fascism is rising somewhere else.'

It was indeed rising, in the unscrupulous machinations of the ruling party.

8

Two Events that Changed History

Autocratic power everywhere entrenches itself and tends to perpetuate itself in the name of public good. History records that abuse of constitutional despotism inevitably leads to absolute despotism.

— K. Subba Rao (Former Chief Justice of India, speaking at a seminar in New Delhi on 15 March 1975)

In August 1974, election to the office of the President of India took place following the completion of V.V. Giri's five-year term. Given the Congress Party's domination in both Parliament and state legislatures, the victory of its candidate, Fakhruddin Ali Ahmed, was a foregone conclusion.

Prior to the election, I had an occasion to argue on behalf of my party in the Supreme Court on the issue of the composition of the electoral college for this poll. Giri, the outgoing President, had referred to the Supreme Court under Article 143 of the Constitution seeking its view on whether the Presidential election could be held while the electoral college was still incomplete. The problem had arisen because the Gujarat legislative assembly had been dissolved following an indefinite fast, in March 1974, by Morarji Desai, leader of the Congress (O) in support of the demand of the Nav Nirman Samiti.

The Supreme Court called upon various political parties to present their case. This posed a minor problem before the Jana Sangh regarding which lawyer to engage to argue our case. Several colleagues said to me, 'Why don't you do it yourself? After all, you have studied law and know this subject better than anyone else.' True, I had graduated in law from the Government Law College, Bombay. But I had never practiced it as a profession, nor had I argued any case in a court until then. Nevertheless, I agreed to the suggestion.

Thus, for the first time in my life, I presented my arguments before a distinguished seven-judge Bench. When I concluded, a judge asked me if I was a lawyer as he thought that the case had been well argued. I said, 'No, My Lord, but I am qualified in law. I am a political activist and I am appearing for the first time in a court of law.' The Chief Justice of India A.N. Ray, and Justices H.R. Khanna and Y.V. Chandrachud were all present. Fali Nariman, a distinguished advocate in the Supreme Court, told me later, 'Mr Advani, I was very impressed. If you ever decide to quit politics, you have an alternative profession.'

Even though the Jana Sangh lost the case, as the Supreme Court ruled that the dissolution of a state legislative assembly was not a hurdle in the election of the President, this episode gave me the confidence that I could argue on legal issues as well.

MORARJI DESAI AND THE BEGINNING OF UNITED POLITICAL ACTION AGAINST CONGRESS MONOPOLY

In life you often meet someone without realising that destiny will bring you closer to that person, unexpectedly, at a later point in time, in an altogether different context, but for some common purpose. In a book by the famous Swiss psychologist Carl Jung, who was greatly influenced by Indian philosophy, I read that this is called 'synchronicity'. Jung calls it the 'acausal connecting principle', an underlying pattern in meaningful relationships which is not evident initially and cannot be explained in terms of direct causality. Such significant, often life-changing, connections happen in everyone's life.

I consider my first meeting with Jayaprakash Narayan as one example of 'synchronicity'. The other is my first meeting with Morarji Desai in the 1960s as a journalist working for *Organiser*. I had least expected then that, about a decade later, I would work closely with him to build bridges between my party, Jana Sangh, and his party, Congress (O), under the common inspiration of Jayaprakashji and, for a few eventful years, actually serve as a Minister under his Prime Ministership. An avowed Gandhian, he too had misgivings about the Jana Sangh in the 1950s and '60s. Here again I happened to play a significant role in changing his misconceptions both about the RSS and the Jana Sangh.

Morarjibhai, as he was commonly known, caught the imagination of the people, in April 1975, by going on a fast unto death to press for early elections to the Gujarat legislative assembly, which had been dissolved a year earlier. His two other demands were also highly significant: revocation of the external Emergency promulgated during the Bangladesh war in 1971, and an assurance from Indira Gandhi's government that the draconian provisions of the Maintenance of the Internal Security Act (MISA) would not be used against political opponents. He was already eighty when he undertook the fast. Prime Minister Indira Gandhi yielded on the seventh day, and Gujarat elections were announced for 9 June.

Under Jayaprakashji's guidance, all four parties—Congress (O), Jana Sangh, Socialist Party and Lok Dal—decided to fight the elections in Gujarat under the common banner of Janata Morcha. Congress (O) was the main party in the state. Naturally, we decided to contest the elections under Morarjibhai's leadership. As President of the Jana Sangh, I had to negotiate with Morarjibhai in matters of allocation of seats and other poll-related matters. I found him remarkably fair and easy to work with. The close proximity I acquired with him during this period, and the mutual trust we developed, was of great help when the Janata Party's government was formed two years later.

During those days, both Jayaprakashji and some of his close colleagues felt that all the non-communist parties in the Opposition should merge into a single political entity. The Jana Sangh's stand on this issue was that an instant merger was neither feasible nor desirable. However, we were willing for progressive and definite steps towards pursuing the ultimate merger. The party's National Executive meeting in Jammu in November 1974 had suggested that all parties participating in the JP movement should regard elections as an extension of agitational politics and, hence, should work out a concerted electoral strategy. They should put up a common candidate in all by-elections hereafter. The candidate may have the symbol of the party to which he or she belonged, but the person should be projected to the electorate as a 'Janata candidate'.

This strategy was put into operation by the Jana Sangh in the assembly by-election in Bhopal. Babulal Gaur, the Jana Sangh candidate, who later served as the Chief Minister of Madhya Pradesh, became the common candidate of the non-communist Opposition and recorded a resounding victory. Next was the Lok Sabha by-election in Jabalpur. Here, a socialist nominee, Sharad Yadav, who is today the President of the Janata Dal (United), was put up as an agreed Janata candidate. He too won. Shortly thereafter, two by-elections were held in Haryana, where the Opposition won by adopting the same strategy.

In the plenary session of the Jana Sangh in New Delhi in March 1975, I explained the Jana Sangh's stand on this issue in my Presidential address:

> The Indian political scene today is in a state of flux. The JP movement has had a very powerful catalytic effect in bringing Opposition parties together. This is so because the key issues of the movement have nothing to do with ideology. But all political parties participating in the movement are conscious that unless the movement throws up a stable, institutionalised arrangement to which the people can look up to as an alternative instrument for the country's governance, the aims of the movement may not be fully realised. One view espoused is that all the parties in the campaign should renounce their separate identities, merge themselves into one party here and now, and then concentrate all

attention on the ouster of the Congress party. This view fails to take into account the fact that anti-Congressism by itself is too frail a bond to keep a party together. Programmatic unity, we think, is a must. But for a party to become an instrument of purposeful change, an attribute even more vital than programmatic unity is the prevalence of a spirit of camaraderie and mutual trust at all levels, from the grassroots to the top. This trust and confidence can be achieved only by working together, and by struggling together for common causes. The agitation in Bihar, and its extensions outside, have given us an excellent opportunity to achieve this. Let us, therefore, widen and intensify the movement.... Thus, working together in the movement, formation of a joint block in Parliament, and a concerted election strategy based upon a common minimum programme, common Janata candidates, and a common symbol are the measures which we think can lead up to an institutionalised alternative to the Congress.

The results of the Gujarat elections were announced on 12 June. The Janata Morcha had trounced the Congress. Right from Independence, Gujarat had been an impregnable fortress for the Congress. But it tasted defeat at the hands of the Janata Morcha, under Desai's bold leadership. Babubhai Patel, a veteran leader of the Congress (O), was elected the new Chief Minister.

If this was important news of the day, 12 June would be remembered for an even more important—indeed, politically earth-shaking—news. What was it?

Strangely, the answer was foretold by the stars!

'PANDITJI, AAP KE NAKSHATRA KYA KEHTE HAIN?' (WHAT DO YOUR STARS PREDICT, PANDITJI?)

In public life, many political leaders believe strongly in astrology. I too have come across many astrologers, genuine or otherwise, who keep knocking at the doors of political leaders. When infighting began in the Janata government, I saw many astrologers putting ideas in the minds of various ambitious leaders and making them quarrel with one another! Therefore, I have generally kept my distance from soothsayers. However, there was one incident that shook my deep disbelief. One of our own party activists, Dr Vasant Kumar Pandit, was a renowned professional astrologer from Bombay, with a Ph.D. in the subject. He was a member of the Maharashtra Legislative Council for eighteen years and, thereafter, a member of the Lok Sabha from 1977 to 1984.

On 12 June 1975 two incidents took place, which were to change the direction of politics in the country. As I mentioned earlier, results of the elections to the Gujarat legislative assembly were declared and they dealt a big blow to the Congress. The second was truly historic. The Allahabad High Court delivered its judgment in a petition filed by socialist leader Raj Narain, in which Justice Jagmohan Lal Sinha declared Prime Minister Indira Gandhi guilty of electoral malpractices. She was found culpable on three counts: dishonest election practices, excessive election expenditure, and misusing government machinery and officials for party purposes. The judge not only disqualified her election to the Lok Sabha from Rae Bareli, but also barred her from contesting any election for six years.

These two developments, especially the second one, sent shock waves through the Congress party, while simultaneously producing euphoria in non-Congress circles. Immediately, a meeting of the National Executive of the Jana Sangh was called in Mount Abu. While relaxing after lunch, I casually asked Dr Pandit, who was a member of the executive from Maharashtra. *'Panditji, aap ke nakshatra kya kehte hain?'* (What do your stars predict, Panditji?) His reply banished all the casualness from my query. He said, 'Advaniji, frankly I don't understand. I feel intrigued by my own assessment.'

Puzzled by his statement, I asked, 'What do you mean?'

His answer was categorical. 'What I can read from the stars tells me that we are headed for a two-year exile.'

I was even more perplexed. 'Exile *kahan se aa gaya*, Panditji?' (Where has this exile come from?) Everything is going against the Congress. The Prime Minister has lost her membership of Parliament. Her party has lost the election in Gujarat. I cannot understand what you are saying.'

'Nor do I understand, Advaniji,' he responded, 'but this is what the stars predict.'

Before the month of June ended, our exile, in the form of nineteen months of imprisonment, had actually begun!

MARCH 1975—A PRESCIENT 'REVOKE EMERGENCY' SEMINAR

I cannot, in all honesty, say that anyone amongst us knew that the exile would come in the form of the Emergency. Rather, many of us were at the time worried about the 'External Emergency', which was already in existence. Three months before 'Internal Emergency' was declared, in March 1975, the Deendayal Research Institute held a seminar in New Delhi. Its theme 'Revoke Emergency' was eerily prescient. The seminar had been organised to mobilise public opinion against external Emergency, which was still in force, even though the circumstance which necessitated it, the 1971 war, was long over. Little did we realise then that instead of revoking the external Emergency, Indira Gandhi's government would unleash a far more draconian rule in India.

The continuation of the extraordinary powers that the government had arrogated to itself, during the war period, had alarmed many in India's political, judicial and intellectual circles. With the Congress leadership's extreme belligerence towards the JP movement and other struggles, such as the historic Railway Strike of 1974, they felt that the provisions of external Emergency would be used to restrict democracy in India. Not surprisingly, the seminar evoked a good response. It was inaugurated by K. Subba Rao, a former Chief Justice of India. Among the other luminaries who participated included JP, Nanaji Deshmukh, Justice Grover, Justice K.S. Hegde and Rabi Ray.

In my speech at the seminar I said that lifting the external Emergency needed, primarily, parliamentary and presidential activism, rather than judicial initiatives. I held that the constitutional position could be modified by making the proclamation of the Emergency subject to the same limitation of periodic review as the declaration of President's Rule in a state. The proclamation should be issued for one year in the first instance and extended on a six-monthly basis subject to Parliament's approval. As subsequent developments would prove, I was then somewhat underestimating the crucial role that the judiciary and constitutional experts could play in the imminent fight against authoritarianism.

In my analysis of the political situation of the country, I said, 'The ruling party is face to face with the situation that, if an election were held today, it would be defeated. Therefore, the Congress party may evoke Article 83(2), which deals with the term of the Lok Sabha, to extend the life of the present Lok Sabha beyond 1976, if that appears to the government the only way to avert electoral ouster. The one-party experiment in Bangladesh could be tried in India too. The continuation of the Emergency cannot be viewed in isolation. It should be seen in conjunction with the systematic subversion of democratic institutions that is going on for the past several years.'

I emphasised that the JP movement had gained remarkable legitimacy owing to the fact that democratic norms had been eroded a great deal in the country. 'Therefore, it is the duty of every citizen to strengthen the movement of JP and all that it stands for to fight authoritarianism. Public opinion, however, feeble or anemic, is the best remedy against dictatorial tendencies on the part of the ruling party.'

Those dictatorial tendencies would bare their fangs on the midnight of 25 June 1975.

9

Emergency: Democracy Imprisoned

Freedom became one of the beacon lights of my life and it has remained so ever since. Freedom with the passing of years transcended the mere freedom of my country and embraced freedom of man everywhere and from every sort of trammel—above all, it meant freedom of the human personality, freedom of the mind, freedom of the spirit. This freedom has become the passion of my life and I shall not see it compromised for bread, for security, for prosperity, for the glory of the state or for anything else.

—Jayaprakash Narayan

Every age in history is characterised by one 'Big Idea' that shapes the destiny of nations by influencing what many scientists and political thinkers have termed as the 'Collective Mind' of the people. When that idea grips the minds and hearts of a large number of people, it becomes a motive force of history. Viewed from this perspective, it can be clearly seen that much of the movement of world history in the twentieth century was influenced by two inter-related big ideas: Freedom and Democracy.

Nation after subjugated nation struggled against colonial rule in search of freedom. Although most of these struggles for national liberation began in the eighteenth and nineteenth centuries, they fructified mainly in the twentieth century. Along with national Independence came another powerful aspiration: People's Rule, as against the rule of a monarchy, a military dictator, a totalitarian communist party, or another kind of authoritarian regime. In some countries, this struggle for democracy was nearly as difficult, and as violently suppressed, as the campaign for national liberation. Future historians will record that, if the two World Wars were a blot on the twentieth century, the triumph of freedom and democracy was the glorious achievement of this age.

We, in India were fortunate that, unlike many of our neighbouring countries and elsewhere, we did not have to wage a separate battle for democracy after India gained Independence from British rule in 1947. Democracy came to independent India as naturally as secularism did, and the natural adoption of both these ideals, as shall be discussed later, was principally on account of India's Hindu philosophy. Nevertheless, human history is replete with examples that no ideal, however exalted and deep-rooted in a country's cultural-spiritual being, is permanently immune to attack from individuals driven by egotism and blinded by lust for power. When such attacks are mounted, the targeted ideal does suffer a momentary eclipse. But in its very suffering, it inspires large masses of people to struggle for the eradication of resultant darkness. It is almost as if history deliberately creates the ordeal as an opportunity for the nation to learn the right lessons and thereby reinforce its commitment to that ideal.

This is precisely what happened in India, in June 1975, when Prime Minister Indira Gandhi brought democracy under an eclipse by bringing India under Emergency Rule. Nineteen months later, the eclipse disappeared as the result of a glorious struggle launched by the people of India against the Congress party's authoritarianism. If the Emergency was the darkest period in India's post-Independence history, the righteous struggle for the restoration of democracy was undoubtedly the brightest. It so happened that I, along with tens of thousands of my countrymen, was both a victim of Emergency and a soldier in the Army of Democracy that won the battle against it.

TWO FATEFUL EVENTS IN JUNE 1975

In the six decades of India's independence, there are two dates, both in June 1975, which can never be forgotten. The first was 12 June. To the surprise of all political analysts, the Indira Congress was roundly trounced in the Gujarat Assembly elections. Secondly, on the same day the Allahabad High Court declared Prime Minister Indira Gandhi's election to the Lok Sabha from Rae Bareilly as void, and furthermore, disqualified her for a period of six years on grounds of electoral corruption.

The second date was 25 June. For those who cherish democracy, that date will always remain one of the darkest days in the history of free India. This fateful date triggered off a chain of events that converted the world's largest democracy into the world's second largest dictatorship.

June is pretty much the hottest month in Delhi. Therefore, I was quite pleased when the Joint Parliamentary Committee (JPC) dealing with a proposed law against defection scheduled its meeting on 26-27 June in the garden city of Bangalore, known for its pleasant weather. Both Atalji and I were members of this committee, which also included Congress (O) leader Shyam Nandan Mishra. However, when, on 25th morning, I boarded a flight from Delhi's Palam airport for Bangalore, I had no idea that this journey would be the beginning of the nearly two-year-long 'exile' that Dr Vasant Kumar Pandit, our party's MP, had predicted during the Mount Abu meeting.

At the Bangalore airport, Mishra, who was on the same flight, and I were received by the Lok Sabha officials. We were taken to the Legislators' Home, located near the imposing building of the state legislative assembly. Atalji had arrived the previous day. The chairman of this JPC was Darbara Singh of the Congress Party, who later became the Chief Minister of Punjab. Around 7.30 am on the 26th, I received a phone call from the local Jana Sangh office. There was an urgent message for me, from Delhi, from Rambhau Godbole, one of the Secretaries of the Jana Sangh, saying that soon after midnight, Jayaprakash Narayan, Morarji Desai and several other important leaders of the Opposition had been arrested. 'The arrests are continuing. The police may shortly be coming to arrest Atalji and you.' I shared the information with Shyambabu, and then together went to Atalji's room. After a brief discussion, we decided that we would not evade arrest.

At 8 o'clock that morning, as I tuned in to the news bulletin on AIR, I found myself listening to Indira Gandhi's somber voice. It was her unscheduled broadcast to the nation. While stating that the President had proclaimed a state of Emergency under Article 352 of the Constitution, she went on to say why it had become necessary to meet the threat of internal disturbances. I could not believe my ears when she said that the country needed to be saved from a massive conspiracy by the Opposition. Even more fantastic was her charge that some elements, under the *garb* of democracy, were intent on destroying India's democracy, which needed to be prevented.

Atalji and I quickly prepared a joint press statement condemning the arrest of Jayaprakashji* and other leaders, denouncing Emergency and affirming that 26 June 1975 would have the same historic significance in the history of Independent India as 9 August 1942 had in the pre-Independence era, when Mahatma Gandhi asked the British rulers to 'Quit India'. However, the statement was an exercise in futility. There was no way for its contents to reach the people, since the government, in the proven tradition of dictatorship, had taken care to clamp press censorship along with the proclamation of Emergency. This was the first time, post-Independence, that press censorship† had been imposed.

The police came to arrest us at around 10 am. Madhu Dandavate, an eminent Socialist Party leader who was in the city to attend a meeting of another parliamentary committee, was also arrested. The four of us

---

* The most searing comment on Indira Gandhi's decision to impose the Emergency and arrest opposition leaders came from Jayaprakash Narayan, who said: '*Vinaash kaale vipareet buddhi*' (When the time of destruction comes, the mind loses its capacity to think right.)

† I later learnt that a gutsy and imaginative democracy-lover had inserted the following item in the 'Obituaries' section of the Bombay edition of the *Times of India*, in its edition on 27 June 1975:

> D'Ocracy—D.E.M., beloved husband of T. Ruth, loving father of L.I. Bertie, brother of Faith, Hope, Justice, expired on 26th June

were taken to Bangalore Central Jail. The entry in my diary* on that day reads: 'June 26, 1975 may well prove to be the last day in the history of Indian democracy as we have understood it. Hope this fear will be proved unfounded.'

HOW THE POLITICAL EARTHQUAKE SHOOK DELHI

Since prison was to be my home for the next nineteen months, I had no immediate knowledge of how exactly the political earthquake had upset the national capital on the fateful day. Even without any sanction from, or discussion within the Union Cabinet, Indira Gandhi had secured the signature of President Fakhruddin Ali Ahmed for a notification declaring Emergency. Simultaneously, the President issued an order under Article 359 suspending the right to move any court for the enforcement of Fundamental Rights conferred by Article 14 (Right to equality before law), Article 21 (Right to life and personal liberty), Article 22 (Protection against arrest and detention in certain cases). Thus, the decision to throttle democracy proved how contemptuous of constitutional provisions the Prime Minister and her coterie of advisors were.

Perhaps the best account of the events of 25-26 June can be found in Bishan N. Tandon's *PMO Diary*, which was published twenty-five years after Emergency was lifted. Tandon, an outstanding IAS officer, was then a Joint Secretary in the PMO. He was my neighbour in Pandara Park. His brother, Gopal Tandon, later became my Special Assistant in the Information & Broadcasting ministry. Incidentally, Bishan Tandon was appointed Principal Secretary to Prime Minister Vajpayee during the latter's thirteen-day government in 1996. Tandon's foreboding daily jottings about the goings-on in the PMO shed light on a political culture where fear

---

* During my nineteen-month stay in jail, I maintained a diary about my daily observations, reflections and conversations with fellow-prisoners. These diary jottings were published in the form of a book titled *A Prisoner's Scrapbook* in 1977 after the Emergency was lifted. The book carried a 'Foreword' by Prime Minister Morarji Desai. In this chapter, I have made several references to my diary.

and cowardice gripped not only the lower rungs of the Congress Party but also, shockingly, the Union Cabinet and the President's august office. He writes*:

> As I was leaving for the office, Sharada Prasad (the Prime Minister's Principal Information Officer) phoned to say, 'You must have heard. It is all over.' He sounded very dejected. On reaching office I went straight to Sharada's room. He told me in detail whatever he knew. Last night the PM had summoned him and Prof. (D.P.) Dhar to her house at 10 p.m. (Devkant) Barooah and (Siddharth Shankar) Ray were already there. When Prof. Dhar and Sharada reached there, the PM told them, 'I have decided to declare an Emergency. The President has agreed. I will *inform* the Cabinet tomorrow.' Saying this, she handed over the draft of the Emergency proclamation to Prof. Dhar. He and Sharada were stunned. They had only been summoned in order to be informed and for their advice on the propaganda to follow. She also told them to prepare a draft of her address to the nation. They were at the PM's house till about 1 a.m. The Cabinet was to meet at 6 a.m.
>
> Not a single minister opposed the Emergency during the cabinet meeting. This is a very serious matter. According to the rules framed under Article 77 of the Constitution, a meeting of the Cabinet was necessary before the President could issue a proclamation of Emergency. But these rules also contain a provision that if the Prime Minister deems it necessary, he or she can take a decision without referring it to Cabinet. But the question here is whether a Cabinet meeting could not have been held to discuss the Emergency. The decision was taken by the PM alone. Why? The other question is: Why did the President accept the PM's 'advice' under these circumstances? He would not have acted unconstitutionally if he had told the PM that he wanted the

---

* B.N. Tandon, *PMO Diary—I: Prelude to the Emergency*, Konark Publishers, 2003, pp. 414-416.

advice and opinion of the entire cabinet on this matter. This is the first time in my knowledge that the President has taken such an important decision on the advice of the Prime Minister alone.

The well-known journalist, D.R. Mankekar, was someone I had known closely and respected deeply. His book *Decline and Fall of Indira Gandhi*, written soon after the Emergency was lifted and after the Congress tasted bitter defeat in the Lok Sabha polls that followed, provides some additional information complementing Tandon's account. He notes that even Home Minister Brahmananda Reddy was kept in the dark about the Prime Minister's decision. 'As darkness fell (on June 25)', Mankekar writes: 'at about 8.30 pm Mrs Gandhi accompanied by Siddharth Shankar Ray (who was not even a member of her Cabinet but the Chief Minister of West Bengal) motored to Rashtrapati Bhavan informally to intimate to the President her momentous decision to proclaim an internal emergency. At 11 pm, Reddy was summoned to the Prime Minister's residence and told about her decision.... With the exception of Om Mehta (Reddy's Deputy in the Home Ministry), a 'Palace' confidante, none of the other Cabinet ministers knew about it on that night. It was not until 6 o'clock the next morning that the Cabinet was convened to be informed about the proclamation of Emergency in the country.

'The Cabinet meeting lasted just 15 minutes. The assembled ministers were shocked out of their wits. After a couple of minutes, Swaran Singh regained balance and tried to seek some clarifications. The external emergency was already on the statute book, he said. The Prime Minister tersely drew his attention to Jayaprakash Narayan's speech overnight, in the course of which he had reportedly threatened to gherao her house (to seek her resignation following the Supreme Court's refusal to grant unconditional stay over the Allahabad High Court's judgment disqualifying her from membership of Parliament).'

THE EVENTS OF 1975—TRACED BACK TO 1973

Every crime inevitably leaves a trail. And the trail begins at the point where the motive for the eventual crime is first implanted in the perpetrator's mind. Thus, looking back it does seem that Emergency rule was an exercise in self-preservation, the threat to which was first perceived when Indira Gandhi's election to the Lok Sabha in 1971 was challenged in the Allahabad High Court. Tandon's book gives clinching evidence that Indira Gandhi's efforts to undermine the judiciary's independence began two years before Emergency was declared and had its origin in her desperation to get a favourable verdict in the electoral malpractices case.

The most crucial, among several dubious steps that Indira Gandhi took in this direction was in 1973, when her government appointed A.N. Ray as the Chief Justice of the Supreme Court, superseding three senior judges—J.M. Shelat, K.S. Hegde, and A.N. Grover. Ray, incidentally, was a close relative of Siddharth Shankar Ray, the then Chief Minister of Bengal who would, two years later, become the Prime Minister's most trusted legal advisor on the suppression of democracy. The unprecedented decision of superseding the three judges was taken in line with the theme of 'committed judiciary', which was zealously advocated by Congress and leftist leaders those days. It was also done in spite of President V.V. Giri's objections. 'She ignored him (Giri),' records Tandon. 'Gokhale (law minister) said the PM was adamant. In the end, he said that everyone had agreed that no risk should be taken in the PM's election case and that Hegde could not be "trusted".'

According to Tandon, Gokhale had met Indira Gandhi on 3 June 1975 (nine days before the Allahabad High Court judgment) and afterwards, discussed her case with A.N. Ray. The Chief Justice of India told him that 'if the Allahabad High Court gave an adverse ruling, there should be no difficulty in getting an absolute stay'. Tandon observes: 'I keep thinking: had Hegde or one of those three been the Chief Justice, would Gokhale have had the temerity to speak to him?'

I have earlier referred to the Jana Sangh's prophetic resolution, as far back as in March 1971, expressing apprehensions that the two-thirds majority in Parliament secured by Indira Gandhi may 'make the Congress party even more disdainful of democratic procedures and norms than it already is'. In the run-up to the Emergency, the Prime Minister started to show her disdain for one democratic institution after another. And she had her own ignoble reasons for doing so. Apart from the Allahabad High Court hearings on the petition about her corrupt electoral practices, she had to protect her government from mushrooming corruption scandals.

One of these scandals, involving Railway Minister L.N. Mishra*, had rocked Parliament, with the Prime Minister refusing to accept the Opposition's demand for an impartial parliamentary inquiry. G.S. Dhillon, then Speaker of the Lok Sabha, was a fair-minded person. Tandon writes in his book that, on 9 December 1974, K.V. Raghuramiah, the Minister for Parliamentary Affairs, acting on the Prime Minister's instructions, met the Speaker to request him not to give the ruling in favour of an enquiry. 'The Speaker was furious. He upbraided Raghuramiah. He told Raghuramiah that he would not change his ruling. When Raghuramiah reported the outcome, Indira Gandhi became very angry. She told Dhar (Principal Secretary to PM) that she was going to resign and that he should prepare a draft immediately. She said she was going to see the President right away, and added in a raised voice: 'Now there would either be a new PM or a new Speaker. The Speaker is refusing to appreciate the situation. How dare he refuse to listen to me?' Ultimately, the Speaker had to yield.

This clearly elucidates how Indira Gandhi's instinct for self-preservation, coupled with the systematic destruction of inner-party democracy after the Congress split in 1969, led her inexorably to impose Emergency in June 1975.

LIFE INSIDE, AND OUTSIDE, PRISON

During our period of detention, we found that the entire legal fraternity, with virtually no exception, was sympathetic towards us. Everyone felt outraged over the government's action. That tens of thousands of political activists belonging to the Opposition, including eminent patriots like Jayaprakash Narayan, Morarji Desai, Atal Bihari Vajpayee and Chandrashekhar should

---

* Lalit Narayan Mishra, an influential Congress leader from Bihar, was Railway Minister in Indira Gandhi's government from 1973–75. His death, in a bomb blast in January 1975, still remains a mystery.

be dubbed as threats to national security, and put behind bars under MISA was, to say the least, shocking beyond belief. The Shah Commission, appointed later by Morarji Desai's government to investigate the excesses and atrocities committed during the Emergency, records that 34,988 persons were detained under MISA, and that another 75,818 persons were arrested under the Defence of India Rules (DIR).

Even during the British Raj, the Indian press had not been subjected to such censorship as was done during the Emergency. It was a crime even to publish how many, and who all, had been detained or to write where they had been kept under detention. The only source of information for people was the fully-controlled government media. The entire network of mass media, including the all-pervasive AIR, was harnessed for the purpose of brainwashing the people into believing that liberty, civil rights, press freedom, judicial independence, etc., were all elitist concepts, which had nothing to do with the common man's welfare and that the nation should feel grateful to the Congress government for bringing India under the Emergency rule.

Let me cite here the example of the eminent journalist Kuldip Nayar, who was detained under MISA in July 1975. The government was angry that he had organised a meeting of pressmen to protest against the censorship. More than that, even after the Emergency had been imposed, he had continued to write articles strongly criticising authoritarian trends, be it in the context of Pakistan or America or other countries. The hint was too obvious to be missed. Nayar's wife filed a *habeas corpus* petition in the Delhi High Court. At the hearing it was discovered that the official who had signed Nayyar's detention order and who was supposed to have personally satisfied himself that his detention was imperative for the country's security, was ignorant even of the fact that he was a journalist. Nayar's detention was declared illegal. The government had sensed the court's mood during the hearing itself. So it tried to retrieve its position by releasing Nayyar four days before the verdict was due to be delivered and then pleaded with the court not to pronounce it as the detenu had already been set free. The High Court refused to oblige, and formally quashed the detention order.

It is now fairly well documented that Indira Gandhi actively explored the possibility of installing a presidential system of government, with one-party dominance, in place of a multi-party parliamentary system of democracy. An editorial in *National Herald*, the Congress Party's own daily newspaper, made this abundantly clear by arguing that a multi-party system resulted in weakening of the Centre—and hence of the nation—and also by eulogising the one-party system in African countries like Tanzania. The paper wrote: 'The Westminster model need not be the best model, and some African states have demonstrated how the people's voice will prevail whatever the outward structure of democracy.... By stressing the need for a strong Centre the Prime Minister has pointed out the strength of Indian democracy. A weak Centre threatens the country's unity, integrity and very survival of freedom. She has posed the most important question. If the country's freedom does not survive, how can democracy survive?'

Like other dictators, Indira Gandhi too tried to project her own personal interests as being coterminous with the nation's interests. In justification of her decision to impose the Emergency, she once said, 'The nation is more important than democracy.'

In order to shore up support for her own hunger for uncontrolled power, Indira Gandhi used to frequently invoke the non-existent threat to India from a 'foreign hand'. In an interview to the *Times of India*, she said, 'The aim of the Opposition parties was obvious. It was to paralyse the government and indeed all national activity and thus walk to power over the "body" of the nation.... A few more steps would have led to disintegration, which would have exposed us to foreign danger.'

How unapologetic Indira Gandhi was for having imposed Emergency can be gauged from her broadcast to the nation on 11 November 1975. She took this harsh decision, she explained, because, 'we felt that the country has developed a disease and if is to be cured soon it has to be given a dose of medicine, even if it is a bitter dose. However dear a child may be, if the doctor has prescribed bitter pills for him, they have to be administered for his cure. The child may sometimes cry and we may have to say, "Take the medicine, otherwise you will not get cured". So, we gave this bitter medicine to the nation.... Now when a child suffers, the mother suffers too. Thus, we were not very pleased to take this step. We were also sad. We were also concerned. But we saw that it worked just as the doctor's dose works.'

Ironically, the only reliable sources of information those days were the BBC, Voice of America, Voice of Germany and Radio Australia. These were the four foreign stations that my small transistor could catch, besides, of course, Radio Moscow which worked more like the overseas propaganda organ of Indira Gandhi's government. In the division of labour among the political prisoners, it was my self-assigned duty to listen to the news bulletins on radio and transmit the information to my colleagues.

One day BBC reported that the Indian government had banned some twenty-five organisations, including the RSS, Jamaat-e-Islami (JeI) and Ananda Marg. Many *swayamsewaks* of the RSS and members of JeI and other banned organisations were brought to the jail and detained under MISA. The jail authorities put the Ananda Marg members along with RSS *swayamsevaks*, but accommodated the Jamaat people with Muslim prisoners arrested under COFEPOSA* on charges of smuggling. The Jamaat detenus resented the classification on grounds of religious homogeneity and requested that they be housed with the RSS men.

In my diary noting on 5 July 1975, I wrote: 'It is interesting that a Government which claimed to promote secularism perpetuated religious and other denominations by everyone of its acts. Here is a graphic example. Instead of putting all political detenus together, they were sought to be segregated on the basis of religion which led to lumping political prisoners with those suspected of criminal activity. It was by its policy of dividing Muslims and Hindus that the so-called secularism was promoted.'

We were housed in two large-sized rooms facing each other. Shyambabu and Dandavate occupied one of the rooms and Ataljl and I shared the other. We settled in quite quickly. The jail authorities gave us utensils, crockery, foodstuff—cereals and vegetables—in accordance with the specifications laid

---

* The Conservation of Foreign Exchange and Prevention Of Smuggling Activities Act, 1974.

down in the prison manual. Atalji volunteered to supervise the cooking. The *Lok Sabha Who's Who* had listed 'cooking' among his hobbies. The food he cooked was simple but wholesome.

With the exception of good crime novels, jail is the only place where one gets to know that lesser-known reality of life—the life of criminals, including their human side. I met many of them, but the one who impressed me and my fellow political prisoners, while in prison in Rohtak, the most was a ten-year-old boy, a professional pick-pocket who had been jailed after he was caught in the act. Ever cheerful and talkative, he was a source of entertainment for all of us. He would vividly narrate his exploits of how, with only a tiny, almost invisible, blade attached to a finger-nail, he would pick the pockets of unsuspecting persons at bus stands, railway stations and other crowded places. 'If I get caught, my *seth* (employer) knows how to get me released from the police or the courts.' One day I asked him, 'You are such a smart boy, why do you pickpocket? Haven't you thought of going to school or doing some work?' He replied: 'Which other work will give me as much as I earn by doing this? Even after giving my *seth* his share, I get enough to send home to my poor parents and keep some for myself.'

All prisoners viewed the detenues and satyagrahis who had come because of their battle against the Emergency with great respect. So much so that, anyone from among other prisoners, whose sentence had ended and was being released, would invariably come to our block in the prison and ask, 'Do you have anything to send to anyone outside?' In this way, we managed to maintain a link with the outside world, especially with party colleagues working underground.

Some of the Opposition leaders, even after they were put behind bars, did not believe that the Emergency could last long. One of them was Shyambabu. 'This madness cannot last long,' he said with a great amount of assertion. 'We will all be out within two-three weeks.' I told him what Dr Vasant Pandit had predicted. 'Bunkum,' said Mishraji.

OUR LEGAL BATTLE FROM INSIDE THE PRISON: A FARCICAL THREE-ACT PLAY

Soon after our detention under MISA, the four of us decided to challenge the order in the Karnataka High Court. Assisted by three eminent counsels whom we knew quite well—N. Santosh Hegde and M. Rama Jois from Bangalore (both of them later became High Court Chief Justices) and N.M. Ghatate from Delhi—we filed writ petitions before the Karnataka High Court, in which, after setting out the necessary facts, a petition was made before the court:

(1) to declare that continuance of external emergency declared in December 1971 even after the cessation of war between India and Pakistan and signing of the Simla Pact is unconstitutional and therefore void;

(2) to declare that the proclamation of internal Emergency on 25 June 1975 is unconstitutional and therefore void;

(3) to quash the detention orders.

On 14 July, the writ petitions were posted for preliminary hearing. The court was packed to capacity with advocates and other members of the public. Just a day before, Atalji had become extremely unwell, and had to be taken to the Victoria Hospital where he was operated upon for appendicitis. Only after the operation was over was it discovered that the appendix was quite healthy and the intense pain he had experienced was for another ailment. Later he was taken to the All India Institute of Medical Sciences (AIIMS) in New Delhi, where he was diagnosed as suffering from a slipped disc. For this he had to undergo a major operation.

So, it was only Mishra, Dandavate and myself who were brought to the high court that day. There was a huge crowd keen to get a glimpse of us, and to greet us. For me, personally, a very pleasant surprise was in store. Awaiting my arrival in court that day were my wife Kamla, my ten-year-old son Jayant and my eight-year-old daughter Pratibha. They had gathered that the high court had fixed 14 July for the hearing of our *habeas corpus* petitions, and so had travelled from Delhi to Bangalore just to meet me.

We three argued our own case. We pointed out to the court that even while we were in prison we had learnt that the next session of Parliament had been convened on 21 July 1975. We requested Chief Justice Shankara Bhatt and Justice B. Venkataswamy, who were hearing our case, that our petitions be disposed off before the date so as to enable us to attend Parliament. After hearing our plea, the court decided to issue a notice to the respondents. The Advocate General, appearing for the state and the Senior Standing Counsel appearing for the Government of India requested for two weeks' time to file objections. The Chief Justice observed that in England *habeas corpus* petitions are required to be taken up for hearing within forty-eight hours. In a *habeas corpus* writ petition in which the liberty of an individual is involved, the state must file its objections forthwith. The court further observed that as the Parliament session was scheduled to commence from 21 July, the cases had to be necessarily disposed of before the said date. The court then fixed 17 July as the date for the next hearing.

On that date, however, we were to witness dramatic developments of a totally different kind.

It must have been around 6.00 am when we were all woken up by the Deputy Superintendent of jail, Desai, who asked us to get ready to leave. 'You have all been released,' he told us. 'The Superintendent will soon be coming to give you the details.' Desai did not try to conceal the cheerfulness in his voice. Soon Jail Superintendent H.L. Chablani, arrived, all smiles. He had been woken up very early and intimated that all four of us—including Atalji who was still in the hospital after his operation—were to be released.

The news, more than surprising, puzzled us. We could visualise three possibilities: firstly, that all MPs were being released in view of the impending Parliament session; secondly, we were being released only to be rearrested, for there were some very obvious flaws in the first detention order; and thirdly, the Government of India was upset by the attitude of the Karnataka High Court during the preliminary hearing of the *habeas corpus* petitions, and so perhaps wanted to detain us in Delhi or some other place outside the jurisdiction of this high court. It was the third possibility that eventually turned out to be the right one.

We took our own time packing and had a leisurely breakfast. By the time Shyambabu completed his routine including doing *yoga*, it was past 9 o'clock. Our co-prisoners Krishnappa, Venkata Rao and Shanker Lal, who had been assigned duties in our ward as help-mates and who became close to all of us, and expressed their joy that our jail term was ending.

'Who knows, we may be back soon!' I remarked casually. At that time, I did not know how prophetic indeed those words would turn out to be!

Desai got us a taxi. But just as the taxi emerged from the jail compound and turned left on the main road, we found a posse of police blocking the way. A fleet of police vehicles lined the road. We later learnt that they had been waiting there since 6.30 am. A senior police official, Naik, who was to give us company several times later, stepped forward to tell us: 'I am very sorry. It is my unpleasant duty to arrest you again.' He then requested us to get into a police car, and directed the taxi to follow his car to the police station.

At the police station, Naik served us fresh detention orders, under MISA, issued by the Government of India and signed by A.G. Sen, Deputy Secretary, Union Home Ministry. An additional paper delivered to us declared that our detention was necessary 'for effectively dealing with the Emergency'. Both the orders, as also the order revoking the earlier detention, given to us by the Superintendent were dated 16 July. Thus the new detention order was issued at a time when we were *already under detention*. Under Section 16A of MISA, this declaration dispensed with the need to provide us with the grounds of detention.

Within fifteen or twenty minutes all the formalities were completed and we were driven back to jail. After our luggage had been off-loaded we were reminded that at 10.30 am we were to be produced in the high court for the hearing of our *habeas corpus* petitions. Scene One of the day's farcical drama was over but there was much more left.

✸

The court-room of the Chief Justice of Karnataka was packed. The spectators spilled over into the corridors and the staircase leading to the road. The gathering waved enthusiastically when we arrived. But neither they, nor even our counsel, were aware that the detenus arrested on 26 June by the Karnataka government had been released, and that we were now guests of the Government of India, albeit in Bangalore.

The information about the change in our status was officially conveyed to the court by Attorney-General Niren De, who had arrived in Bangalore the previous night. Presumably, he had personally brought the fresh detention orders from New Delhi. As soon as the hearing began, De rose to submit that he had a statement to make. He told the court that the detention orders of 26 June 1975, which had been challenged in the writ petitions, had been revoked by the Government of India; fresh detention orders had been made out and executed. Therefore, the pending writ petitions had become infructuous and should be dismissed.

Rama Jois, followed by the three of us, protested against what the government had done and urged that we be permitted to amend our petitions in the light of the new developments. Jois pointed out that the relief sought by the petitioners was not confined to having their detention orders quashed but also to having the two Emergency proclamations declared invalid and to get the ordinance amending MISA struck down. Revocation of the original detention order met, if at all, only the prayer in respect of the impugned detention. The other issues still remained.

The Chief Justice maintained that filing a fresh petition would be the proper course in the situation. When it was pointed out to him that the detenus were facing difficulty in obtaining legal assistance, he said that necessary orders could be issued in that regard. Turning to the Attorney General, he said: 'I suppose there would be no objection to providing them necessary legal aid', who said he had none.

The Chief Justice thereafter dismissed the earlier writ petitions and issued a direction to the Superintendent of the Bangalore Central Jail that the four detenus be given due facilities for consultations with their counsel in order to enable them to file fresh petitions.

*

In the Jail Superintendent's office, where we were having a cup of coffee with the jail authorities immediately on our return from the court, Mallayya, the Inspector-General of prisons, remarked that he had a hunch that we would be transferred from Bangalore. 'I am not sure,' he said, 'but I was asked by the authorities whether Atalji was in a position to move—and this makes me feel that a transfer is in the offing.'

Actually, it seems, the Attorney General had also brought with him a transfer order and while assuring the court that he had no objection to it issuing directions to the Jail Superintendent, with regard to legal assistance for the detenus, he was committing a constructive contempt of the court by misleading it. This fact agitated the high court the very next day when an application filed on behalf of Atalji whose transfer order could not be enforced because the doctors would not permit his shifting. When the application came up before the high court, the court took a very serious view of the development and issued orders forthwith restraining the government from transferring Atalji.

By lunch time, the transfer order arrived. It stated that we were to be 'transferred to Rohtak by air'.

A special Air Force plane took the three of us to Delhi. We were accompanied by the Jail Superintendent, Chablani, District Surgeon, Sadasiva Reddy, and Assistant Commissioner of Police, Naik. The Dakota took off from the Air Force landing ground at Yelahanka at about 4.30 pm. The flight was quite bumpy as the weather was far from fair. It was around 11.30 pm when the aircraft landed at Delhi's Palam technical area.

The central government's reception to us at Delhi was in sharp contrast to the Karnataka government's sendoff. The three state officials accompanying us must have found it very conspicuous. A police inspector of the Delhi administration was sent to the airport with instructions that the 'three prisoners' be transported from Palam to Rohtak, a town in Haryana about 120 kilometres away. The inspector, Inder Jeet Singh, told us later that he did not have even the vaguest of idea who the prisoners were, or even as to the category they belonged. He had the impression that three alleged smugglers were being transferred.

As we alighted from the aircraft, the officer stepped up to inquire joyfully, '*Kaun kaun aaye hein?*' (Who all have come?) As we came closer, he saw me and said a little more deferentially, 'Advani *Sahab ko jaanta hoon; aur kaun sahab hein?*' (I know Advani; who are the others?). I introduced Shyambabu and Dandavate to him. He then asked us to board a ramshackle truck that he had brought. 'Are we to go to Rohtak tonight or tomorrow?' we asked him. He said he wasn't aware and added, 'We shall be going to the Palam police station first, and there we shall get further instructions. Board the truck.'

In contrast with the courteous treatment we received in Karnataka, the attitude of officialdom in New Delhi was cavalier and even boorish. We all felt it, including the Karnataka officials. Shyambabu was particularly annoyed. He gave uninhibited expression to his annoyance by lashing out at the police inspector. 'I cannot go tonight; my health does not permit it', he curtly told the officer. 'And you must arrange some other vehicle. We shall not go in this; we are not prisoners, we are political detenus.' (This last remark by him was often cited by Dandavate in a lighter vein later.)

Inder Jeet Singh was evidently in no mood for a tiff either with us or with his bosses. But his way of avoiding trouble was not quite straightforward. If he really had any intention of taking us to the Palam police station, he abandoned it after sensing Shyambabu's mood. Without informing us, he quietly told the driver of the van to head straight to Rohtak. Later, he was later apologetic about it but tried to explain it by saying that if we had gone to the police station, and tried alternative arrangements it would only have meant a futile, sleepless night for all of us.

Neither the officer nor any of the three constables accompanying him was familiar with Rohtak. So they had to inquire at a number of places about the location of the jail. It was drizzling all through. Understandably, the streets were deserted at that unearthly hour. It was about 2 o'clock in the morning when we finally reached the jail.

Our first encounter with the jail authorities in Rohtak was far from happy. The Deputy Superintendent of the jail, one Saini, who was to complete the formalities regarding our entry, asked a convict warder to search our luggage. And what a search it was! Not satisfied with rummaging through our clothes and books, the warder began to examine the soles of our slippers in the hope of finding hidden papers! Shyambabu, seething with pent-up anger over the jerky journey and the sleepless night, exploded at Saini. Madhu Dandavate flung a good-humoured barb at him remarking: 'Mrs. Gandhi has no doubt called for soul-searching; but that is s-o-u-l, and not s-o-l-e searching.'

It was nearly 3.00 am when we finally reached the barracks where Biju Patnaik and others were lodged and where we were to stay for the next ten weeks. Friends there had information that three or four detenus were expected, but they had no idea who they were or from which jail they were being transferred or whether they were fresh arrivals!

While I was in Rohtak jail, Kamla approached the Home Ministry for a pass to enable her and our two children to meet me. The Home Ministry issued a pass which read: 'For two persons only'. Jagannathrao Joshi, MP, who had not been arrested till then, personally intervened to plead that the pass should be for three. However, the curt reply was: 'The rule has to be followed.' Ghatate, our lawyer, told Kamla, 'Take both the children, and let's go.' At Rohtak, the Jail Superintendent saw the pass, but said: 'All of you may go inside.'

Later, whenever it was argued by Congressmen that excesses were not committed by people at the top but by the employees at lower levels, I used to give this example to debunk the theory.

'FOR A CASE OF THIS KIND, I WOULD HAVE COME EVEN IF I HAD BEEN ON MY DEATHBED!'

In August 1975, we again prepared our writ-petitions, this time making them much more elaborate than earlier. As our arrest the second time had also taken place in Bangalore, we decided to send our petitions once again to the Karnataka High Court. We were soon informed by Rama Jois that hearing of our petitions had been fixed for 29 September 1975. On 8 September, we sent a telegram to the Chief Justice expressing our desire to be present at the hearing. Our request came up for orders before the court on 10 September. The court directed that the three detenus be brought from Rohtak to Bangalore before 26 September.

Meanwhile, all editors of newspapers and news agencies in Karnataka received a significant letter from the Department of Information & Publicity, Karnataka, on 29 September, which read:

Dear Editor,

The message received from the Chief Censor is reproduced below for information and necessary action:

'Please ensure that news relating to the hearing of the writ petitions in the High Court of Karnataka against the detention of Sriyuths Atal Behari Vajpayee, Madhu Dandavate, L.K. Advani and Shyamnandan Mishra, is not published in any of the newspapers.'

Yours sincerely,
(sd/- R.M. Purandhare)
for Director.

The hearing of this historic case came up before Justices D.M. Chandrasekhar and B. Venkataswamy on 29 September. The news of Mohammedali C. Chagla, one of the country's most distinguished lawyers, appearing for the detenus spread to all the members of the bar and some members of the public. His very appearance in court, in our defence was a stinging indictment of the Emergency. After all, he was a man of sterling credentials. A former Chief Justice of the Bombay High Court, and a former ambassador to the US and High Commissioner to the UK, Chagla had also been Minister of Education in Nehru's Cabinet and Minister of External Affairs in Indira Gandhi's Cabinet. Naturally, the court was packed to capacity on 29 September to hear this courageous champion of civil liberties and democratic rights.

Chagla opened the case and stated that though he had given up his practice and stopped appearing in courts, he had specially come from Bombay to Bangalore as he felt that this was national duty. He said that he was not there to argue just any case. He argued that the continuance of external Emergency declared on 3 December 1971, after the war with Pakistan had come to an end, was a clear fraud on the Constitution.

He added that the declaration of Emergency on 25 June was not for the purpose for which the power was conferred on the President under Article 352 of the Constitution but for a collateral purpose—namely, for ensuring the continuance of Indira Gandhi as Prime Minister. At this stage he complimented Justice Jagmohanlal Sinha of the Allahabad High Court as a symbol of independence and fearlessness of the Indian judiciary. He said that on 12 June, the day he delivered the judgment setting aside Indira Gandhi's election, was a memorable day in the history of post-Independence India.

In his argument Chagla added that irrespective of the legal controversy whether, after the conditional stay order granted by the Supreme Court, Indira Gandhi could have continued as Prime Minister until her appeal was decided by the apex court or not, respecting the democratic norms and precedents, and as a model to all the citizens in obeying the decision of judiciary, Indira Gandhi ought to have resigned forthwith. On an earlier occasion, she herself had insisted that Channa Reddy quit the Union Cabinet after his election to the Lok Sabha was set aside. Her stand was the same as in the case of D.P. Mishra under similar circumstances. Both of them had resigned, but when it came to her own case she disregarded those healthy democratic norms, and refused to quit. Instead, she decided to misuse the state machinery and constitutional powers for perpetuating her stay in office.

Commenting on the detention of Jayaprakash Narayan and prominent leaders of the Opposition, including the petitioners in these cases, Chagla said that their patriotism and their devotion to the service of the nation was unquestionable. 'They are eminent parliamentarians, and their arrest under the draconian provisions of the Maintenance of Internal Security Act, is something beyond my comprehension,' he observed. 'Under the provisions of the MISA only such persons who are guilty of violent activities in an attempt to overthrow a constitutionally formed government by violent methods can be arrested. In a democratic system, it is not only the right but it is also the duty of the Opposition leaders to demand the resignation of any person, including the Prime Minister, under such circumstances. If these Opposition leaders had failed to demand the resignation of Indira Gandhi from the office of Prime Minister after her election to the Lok Sabha was set aside, they would not have been worthy of being Opposition leaders.'

Chagla continued his arguments the next day as well. We later gathered that 30 September was his birthday, and that his family members were extremely upset at his being in Bangalore. They tried hard to hold him back but his firm response was: 'What better way can there be of celebrating one's birthday than fighting for the people's freedom and civil liberties?' Indeed, while arguing our case Chagla became very emotional. His arguments were, very ably, reinforced by Shanti Bhushan and Venugopal.

When we expressed our deep appreciation to Chagla for his presence despite his ill health, he said, 'For a matter of this kind, I would have come even if I had been on my deathbed.' He lamented about the stifling conditions prevailing in the country. As an example, he said that some of his friends in Bombay had applied for permission to celebrate Gandhi Jayanti, but the government denied it. At this, Dandavate quipped: 'If it had been Indira Gandhi *Jayanti*, it would have been permitted.' We later learnt that in Delhi and many other places, people were arrested under DIR for celebrating Gandhi Jayanti. At the Gandhi Samadhi at Rajghat, no less a Gandhian than Acharya Kripalani, found himself in the hands of the police when he tried to hold a prayer meeting. Among those physically restrained along with J.B. Kripalani were Rajmohan Gandhi, Gandhiji's grandson, and socialist leader H.V. Kamath.

In this main *habeas corpus* battle, the Karnataka High Court turned down the preliminary objections raised by Attorney General Niren De, on behalf of the Government of India, that our writ petition should be rejected at the threshold. Thus, at the high court level, as in Bangalore, MISA detenus in other parts of the country also won this preliminary battle. But when the matter went to the Supreme Court, the highest judiciary of the country headed by Chief Justice A.N. Ray, rejected the unanimous view of the high courts and held that during the Emergency the 'fundamental right to life and liberty' was suspended and so no court could even entertain a *habeas corpus* plea. In the Supreme Court, the Attorney General argued that once the President in exercise of his powers under Article 359 suspends the enforcement of the fundamental right to life and liberty conferred by Article 21, a citizen has no right to approach the court of law and challenge his arrest. He went on to affirm that even if an order of detention is in direct contravention of mandatory provisions of the law and even if it is malafide, a *habeas corpus* petition had to be disallowed by the court at the threshold.

I later learnt that Justice H.R. Khanna, who was on this five-judge Bench of the Supreme Court, put a pointed question to the Attorney General: 'Article 21 confers on citizens a right not only to "liberty" but even to "life". If a person jailed during the Emergency is shot down by those in authority for personal reasons, do you mean to suggest that his associates have no judicial remedy?' The Attorney General is said to have replied, 'I do not feel happy saying this, but legally, Lordship, that is precisely the position.'

Justice Khanna* gave a dissenting judgment in this case, which made the *New York Times* hail him as a judge whose name will go down in letters of gold. He said that a writ petition against an order of detention, on the ground that it is contrary to mandatory requirements of law under which it was passed or on the ground that it was *malafide*, is outside the scope of Article 359, which authorises the President to suspend Fundamental Rights. He held that the President had no authority to suspend 'rule of law' which requires every executive authority to act *bona fide* and in accordance with law.

---

* Justice Hans Raj Khanna, who later became a dear friend of mine, passed away on 25 February 2008 at age ninety-five. In giving the dissenting judgment that the right to life is an inviolable Fundamental Right, he knew fully well that he would incur the wrath of Indira Gandhi. Her government superseded him for the Chief Justice's post in January 1977 and, instead, appointed Justice Mirza Hamidullah Beg. This is what Justice Beg had said about those imprisoned during the Emergency: 'We understand that the care and concern bestowed by the state authorities upon the welfare of detenus who are well-fed and well-treated, is almost maternal. Even parents have to take appropriate preventive action against those children who may threaten to burn down the house they live in.' About Justice Khanna, *New York Times* wrote in its 30 April 1976 editorial: 'If India ever finds its way back to the freedom and democracy that were proud hallmarks of its first 18 years as an independent nation, someone will surely erect a monument to Justice H.R. Khanna of the Supreme Court.'

I have earlier mentioned the name of Rama Jois, a young lawyer from Bangalore who was looking after our legal problems right from the start. When the *habeas corpus* petition was being heard in the Supreme Court, out of natural interest in the matter, he had gone to Delhi to follow the proceedings. He was in the Supreme Court from 15-19 December 1975. When on 22 December, the Jail Superintendent in Bangalore sent us a message that Rama Jois had come, I thought that he was there to inform us about the developments in New Delhi. When I went to the Jail Superintendent's office, I was shocked to see that Jois was there not as our lawyer but as a prisoner! He had been brought by the police as a MISA detenu. A man of courage, conviction and competence, Jois rose to become the Chief Justice of Punjab & Haryana High Court. Post retirement, he was appointed Governor of Bihar and Jharkhand. But as I look back, I am unable to find a parallel case even during British days where a person was vindictively punished in this manner only because he was acting as a counsel for the government's political opponents. This shows that the government was keeping an eye out for conspiracies and conspirators everywhere.

In his widely acclaimed autobiography *Roses in December*, Chagla writes about his speech* at the All-India Civil Liberties Conference in Ahmedabad in October 1975. 'I pointed out that the conspiracy Indira was talking about was not a conspiracy by the Opposition, but a conspiracy by her to overthrow democracy and establish an authoritarian regime. I ended up by saying that "when the night is darkest, the dawn is not far", and that for thousands of years we had survived invasions and all sorts of troubles and we would survive both Indira and her dictatorship.' The speech was published in a Gujarati periodical *Bhoomi Putra*, edited by Narayan Desai, son of Mahadev Desai, who was Gandhiji's Secretary. The Central Government initiated proceedings for the forfeiture of Desai's press under the Emergency laws.

That any government could turn hostile to men like Chagla and Desai was in itself a testimony on the debased character of the Emergency.

---

* A civil liberties conference could be held in Ahmedabad those days only because Gujarat at the time had a non-Congress government headed by Babubhai Patel.

Every dictatorship gets intoxicated on its own sense of power, and in that inebriated state its actions become irrational; sometimes even bordering on paranoia. One day the papers reported Indira Gandhi as saying that in the absence of the steps she had taken, a Bangladesh* would have been enacted in India as well. It was unbecoming of the Prime Minister of India to mouth such an outrageous and outlandish lie. All the four top leaders of the Janata movement—Jayaprakashji, Morarji, Charan Singh and Atalji—literally abhorred violence. Therefore, even to insinuate that they had been scheming a bloody coup was a slander, vile and contemptible.

MY UNDERGROUND PRO-DEMOCRACY LITERATURE

One of the rare boons of my life in Bangalore jail was solitude, and the means to put it to good use. Apart from a well-stocked library and a quiet reading room, the jail premises had a badminton court and table tennis hall, where I played regularly. In fact, Jayant, who is now a regular and top-class table tennis player, first picked up a liking for this game when he, along with Kamla and Pratibha, came to visit me in the Bangalore jail. Since many of the fellow-prisoners were from Karnataka, I started learning Kannada and made considerable progress both in reading newspaper headlines and speaking basic sentences.† My favourite pastime, of course, was burying myself in books in the library.

I recall reading, amongst many other books, William Shirer's *The Rise and Fall of the Third Reich*, a definitive and widely acclaimed account of

---

* On 15 August 1975, Bangladesh witnessed a military coup in which a group of junior army officers invaded the presidential residence with tanks and killed Sheikh Mujibur Rehman, his entire family and the personal staff. Only his daughters Sheikh Hasina Wajed and Sheikh Rehana survived as they were abroad. Sheikh Hasina Wajed later became the Prime Minister of Bangladesh.

† In June 2000, I had gone to Bangalore to participate in a function to mark the twenty-fifth anniversary of the imposition of the Emergency. I visited the Bangalore Central Jail along with, among others, two of my fellow-prisoners—Ramakrishna Hegde and J.H. Patel, both of whom later became Chief Ministers of Karnataka. In my speech on the occasion, I said, 'If Indira Gandhi had kept me in jail here for some more time, I would have learnt Kannada so well as to be able to speak to you in your own mother tongue today.'

Nazi Germany under Adolf Hitler. It was this book that provided me with valuable inputs for a booklet I wrote, titled *A Tale of Two Emergencies*, as my contribution to the underground literature for use by pro-democracy activists through the Lok Sangharsh Samiti formed by JP. I had compared what Hitler had done in Germany to what the Congress government was doing in India.

When the Weimer Constitution was adopted in 1919, it was hailed as the 'most liberal and democratic document of its kind the 20th century had seen'. Shirer described it as 'mechanically well-nigh perfect, full of ingenious and admirable devices which seemed to guarantee the working of an almost flawless democracy.' But the Weimer Constitution, like our own, had its Emergency provisions, incorporated into it in good faith by the founding fathers with the confidence they would be used only in the times of grave crises, such as war. In the essay, I wrote:

> Every other day, Indira Gandhi and her cohorts keep asserting that whatever they have been doing these past months is 'within the four corners of the Constitution'. The charge being leveled against them by the opposition and by the Western press that they have subverted democracy is therefore untenable, it is argued. The history of Nazi Germany conclusively shows that doing anything constitutionally is not necessarily the same thing as doing it in a democratic manner. Hitler always used to boast that he had done nothing illegal or unconstitutional. Indeed, he made a democratic constitution an instrument of dictatorship.

Shirer has noted: 'Though the Weimer Republic was destroyed, the Weimer Constitution was never formally abrogated by Hitler. Indeed, and ironically, Hitler based the legality of his rule on the despised republican Constitution.' A vigorous Opposition, a free press and an independent judiciary are the three essential features of democracy. These are the institutional checks which a democratic polity possesses to restrain the executive from going the authoritarian way, but also the legislature from becoming the handmaid of an arbitrary tyrannical majority.… Hitler had no use for the opposition: nor has Indira Gandhi, who never tires of referring to opposition parties as 'a minority seeking to subvert the wishes of the majority'.

Workers carrying on a campaign against the Emergency outside chose to distribute this pamphlet at a Commonwealth conference which was being held in New Delhi. The government was naturally upset about it. Some officials were actually sent to Bangalore to inquire from the state government and prison authorities whether this had emanated from our jail. It so happened that only a few days earlier, I, with a desire to learn typing, had requested the Jail Superintendent whether I could be permitted to get a typewriter from outside. He declined to do so. Therefore, when the officials from Delhi asked him about the pamphlet, he was able to tell them with a straight face that there was no way anyone from his jail could have written it.

But later the same Jail Superintendent and some other officers came to me and said, 'As far as the inquiry from Delhi is concerned, we have said what we had to say and it has been wound up. But if the pamphlet has really been written here, can we have a copy of it? We would like to read it.' I smiled, and gave them a copy. In fact, I wrote five pamphlets while in prison and all of them were published during the Emergency as underground literature. They were later included in my book *A Prisoner's Scrapbook*.

It would infuriate me to read, in the newspapers and magazines that we got in prison, glowing accounts by the apologists of the Emergency about how the trains in India, infamous for running late, were now running on time, how agitations had come to an end and how there was 'discipline' all around. Refutation of this kind of rationalisation of authoritarianism was the subject matter of another of my underground pamphlet titled *Anatomy of Fascism*. 'Indira Gandhi,' I wrote, 'never tires of branding her opponents as "fascists". Apparently she thinks that by sheer repetition, people will come to believe her. But "fascism" has a precise meaning and connotation. Besides, there is historical experience of how "fascists" behave and what the purpose of "fascism" is. This should serve to show who are the real "fascists" in India—Indira Gandhi or her opponents.'

In this essay, I quoted from the famous educationist Maria Montessori: 'Discipline must come through liberty. We do not consider an individual disciplined only when he has been rendered artificially silent as a mute, and as immovable as a paralytic. He is an individual *annihilated*, not *disciplined*.' Indira Gandhi's talk of discipline was a smokescreen for suppression of democratic rights—shackling the judiciary and emasculating the Constitution.

CONSTITUTION MANGLED, JUDICIARY MAIMED

When the Constituent Assembly adopted, after intensive and prolonged deliberations, the Constitution of India in January 1950, it had scarcely imagined that a day would come when the statute would be mutilated and democracy endangered by the government itself. Nevertheless, the astute and farsighted makers of the Constitution had built in many defences to ensure it served as a reliable shield against assaults by despotic rulers in the future. The Prime Minister and her coterie of sycophantic advisors knew this too well. Hence, soon after the imposition of the Emergency, they set in motion systematic measures to dismantle, one by one, the democratic defences laid out in the Constitution.

In the very first farcical session of Parliament in the monsoon of 1975, the government got the 39th Constitution Amendment Bill passed. After enactment, it became the 38th Amendment. It made the proclamation of the Emergency non-justiciable and protected the provision of the President's 'satisfaction' from judicial scrutiny not only in the matter of Article 352 (Proclamation of Emergency), but also with regard to Article 123 (Proclamation of Ordinances) and Article 356 (Imposition of President's Rule in States). The Governor's power to issue ordinances under Article 213 was similarly protected. Protection was also accorded to the power of the President to suspend citizens' Fundamental Rights under Article 359. Clearly, the government was laying the foundation for an authoritarian state, in which the political executive (the Prime Minister) first turned the incumbent of the Rashtrapati Bhavan into a rubber-stamp, and made the rubber-stamp, and itself, unaccountable to the judiciary.

MISA was amended to make it more draconian. The constitutional obligation on the government to furnish a detenu with the grounds of his or her detention was done away with. No person arrested under the amended Act could be released on bail or bond. The DIR, 1971, was an outcome of the external Emergency imposed at the time of the war for the liberation of Bangladesh. This too was amended to make its stringent provisions applicable in the internal Emergency of 1975. The Criminal Procedure Code (CrPC) was amended to abolish the distinction between cognisable and non-cognisable offences.

But there was something more preposterous to follow. On 4 August, the government introduced the Election Laws (Amendment) Bill to change certain provisions of the Representation of People's Act and the Indian Penal Code (IPC). I was listening to the afternoon Punjabi news bulletin on AIR, which reported that Law Minister Gokhale had introduced a Bill in the Lok Sabha to redefine, *with retrospective effect*: (a) When a person becomes a candidate in an election; (b) What assistance given by a government official to a candidate would be deemed corrupt; and (c) When a Government servant's resignation would become effective.

I quickly sensed that some major mischief was afoot. Just to reconfirm what I had heard, I listened, shortly thereafter, to AIR's Urdu bulletin, which repeated the news. Soon there was a wave of anger and alarm in the entire community of political prisoners in the barracks. In my diary on that day I wrote: 'Anyone could see what the Bill was intended to achieve. It was a shameless attempt to undo the Allahabad verdict on Indira Gandhi's electoral corruption. It was like amending the rules of a game and applying the new rules to a match already played with a view to declaring the loser the winner. All the loudmouthed protests that the Emergency has nothing to do with, the Allahabad case or with Indira Gandhi's person are now dramatically repudiated by the Government itself with this Bill.'

Within a few days, the Bill was passed, with hardly any debate, in both Houses of Parliament.

On 7 August, the government introduced the 40th Constitution Amendment Bill, the strangest-ever legislation of its kind to be considered by Parliament. It aimed at preventing the courts from hearing petitions challenging the election of the President, Vice President and MPs holding the office of Prime Minister and the Speaker of the Lok Sabha. These elections, the amendment provided, could be challenged only before a special forum to be created by Parliament. The most obnoxious feature of the Bill was its fourth clause, which declared that all decisions taken by a high court with regard to the election of any of these four dignitaries would be deemed null and void! Under the cloak of exercising its amending power, Parliament had thus usurped the powers of the judiciary.

As the following sequence of events shows, this was also the fastest Constitutional amendment in India's history.

- 7 August 1975   Introduced in the Lok Sabha
- 7 August 1975   Passed by Lok Sabha after a two hour 'debate'
- 8 August 1975   Introduced in the Rajya Sabha
- 8 August 1975   Passed by Rajya Sabha
- 9 August 1975   Passed by State Legislatures on a single day!
- 10 August 1975 President gives his assent

Only a fascist state could have vandalised the Constitution in this manner. Ironically, those who were committing this crime were accusing the Jana Sangh and other followers of Jayaprakashji of being 'fascists'!

Why was the Congress party in such crude haste to amend the Constitution? Because, the Supreme Court was to hear Indira Gandhi's election petition on 11 August 1975! On 7 November, the Supreme Court validated Indira Gandhi's election. It also retrospectively validated the Constitutional amendment.

But there was another interesting question: Having already amended the Election Law and made sure that the Supreme Court would have no option but to set aside the Allahabad High Court judgment in Indira Gandhi's election case, why did the government have to resort to this additional device? When we prison-mates were discussing these Constitutional amendments, Dr Bhai Mahavir recounted an interesting story. In Western society, the mother-in-law is a common object of ridicule. A person received a telegram saying that his mother-in-law had suddenly died. She had been living with his family but had gone visiting some friends. The wire added: 'Should she be buried or cremated? Awaiting instructions.' Without a moment's hesitation, the bereaved son-in-law wired back: 'Take no chances, do both.' Mahavir commented that Gokhale was evidently taking no chances with the law!

On 8 August, I wrote in my diary: 'In theory, the Indian Constitution was still republican. For all practical purposes, however, the law was being so distorted as to make Indira Gandhi like the Queen of England, legally unassailable for any wrong she committed. What else should be done to put the constitutional imprimatur to such an Indira-can-do-no-wrong concept?'

The next day, which was to be the last day of the Rajya Sabha session, Gokhale produced the most outrageous of monstrosities, the Constitution (41st Amendment) Bill. By amending Article 361, it sought, in the main, to confer upon the Prime Minister immunity against criminal proceedings in just about every conceivable case. I expressed my complete outrage in my diary:

> That such a measure should have been conceived is itself shocking. It destroys the republican character of our Constitution. On the pretext of protecting the Prime Minister from unnecessary litigation, it seeks to legalize crimes committed by her or him. The same protection is conferred upon the President and the State Governors. At present, Article 361 of the Constitution confers immunity on the President and the Governors in respect of criminal or civil proceedings, but only during their term of office. No such immunity is provided to the Prime Minister or the Chief Ministers who are essentially political officers as answerable to law as other citizens. Equality before the law is an essential ingredient of republicanism.
>
> The rationale for the protection given to the President and the Governors is that they are only constitutional heads of State who do not perform Executive functions. Even so, the immunity is only for the duration of their tenure. The new amendment, however, seeks to absolve the President and the Governors of responsibility for any crime they may have committed before assuming the office and after laying it down. The person holding the office of Prime Minister is put on par with them, for purposes of the immunity.

Looking at the 40th and 41st Amendments, one is reminded of Procrustes, the fabled Greek robber who used to stretch or cut his captives' limbs to make them fit his bed. The Constitution is being twisted and tailored, mangled and mutilated to subserve the interests of a single individual.

As I look back on the day's entry, I am reminded of how livid I was.

In 1976, the government introduced in Parliament the Constitution (44th Amendment) Bill which, after adoption, would become the 42nd Amendment. Apart from providing for a six-year term for the Lok Sabha and the state assemblies, it sought to drastically curtail the Fundamental Rights of citizens and make the most rapacious encroachments into the independence of the judiciary. Almost all laws and government actions were made unchallengeable in court. It also had two particularly pernicious provisions: (1) It authorised the President to amend the Constitution through an executive order for two years! (2) It abolished the need for quorum in Parliament, which meant that just two or four could make laws for the country! When the government introduced this Bill in Parliament, veteran Socialist Party leader H.V. Kamath sharply remarked: 'This is not to amend the Constitution, but to end the Constitution.'

This atrocious mutilation of the statute provoked me to pen another angry underground pamphlet titled 'Not An Amendment, It's a New Constitution'. I wrote: 'The Emergency itself is phoney, and the proclamation *mala fide*. That apart, a Lok Sabha which has given itself an extended tenure for avowedly emergency reasons is essentially a caretaker Parliament, politically competent to undertake only routine legislation. A major constitutional metamorphosis such as this one is certainly outside its ken. The second objection is that at the moment, more than thirty senior members of Parliament* are in jail, detained without trial. They do

---

* Apart from the names I have already mentioned, some of the other prominent MPs who were behind bars were Ram Dhan, who was expelled from the ruling party; veteran Socialist Party leaders Samar Guha and Madhu Limaye; Rabi Ray and Raj Narain, who belonged to the Bharatiya Lok Dal; rebel Congress leader Mohan Dharia; DMK leader Murasoli Maran; and CPI(M)'s firebrand MP Jyotirmoy Basu.

not know why they have been jailed. They cannot even go to Court. The only reason they can guess is that the gigantic fraud that is this Emergency can be palmed off on the people only when all the three main sources of popular enlightenment—the Parliament, the Press, the Judiciary—are blacked out. Some time back, questioned about the number of MPs in detention, Indira Gandhi glibly said that the number was not large; "perhaps not even twenty", she added. It is rather surprising that Indira Gandhi should be ignorant of this. Or was she?'

'The 44th Amendment Bill,' I warned, 'is an undisguised bid to destroy all checks and balances built into the Constitution. Depradations are to be made into the realm of all institutions except the Executive. The upshot of this would be that the Prime Minister would become a constitutional dictator. If Parliament does pass this Bill, the Constitution which they, the people of India, gave unto themselves on January 26, 1950, would have been buried fathoms deep. A new Constitution will usurp its place.'

The hallmark of every dictatorial regime is that it is never honest and transparent with its own people. To illustrate this, let me cite here another underground essay, titled 'Not Property, but Democracy is her Bugbear', which sought to expose how the Congress government was trying to 'project the Constitution as a scapegoat for its own failure on the economic front', and thereby making out a case for dismantling its basic structure. At its session in Chandigarh in December 1975, the AICC had called for a 'second look' at the Constitution. Umashankar Dikshit, a senior Minister in the government, had declared that if the present limitations on Parliament's power of amendments were not removed, a new Constituent Assembly would have to be convened to frame a new Constitution. Another key player in the ruling set-up, Siddhartha Shankar Ray (who had accompanied Indira Gandhi to Rashtrapati Bhawan on the evening of 25 June to get the President's consent to declare the Emergency) had publicly stated that the power of judicial review of Parliament's decisions was 'preventing the emergence of a new economic order'.

Strange though it may sound to those belonging to the post-Emergency generation, the Congress Party at the time, under the influence of communists within the country and its supporters in the Soviet Union, was carrying on a propaganda that the main reason for India's poverty was the constitutionally guaranteed right to property. For years, the Supreme Court's judgment in the Golak Nath case was being flaunted as a major roadblock on the path of economic progress. This judgment, delivered in 1967, held that Parliament had no right to abrogate or abridge any of the Fundamental Rights through the constitutional amending procedure set out in Article 368. It said that the Fundamental Rights occupied a 'transcendental' position in the Constitution, so that no authority functioning under the Constitution, including Parliament was empowered to amend them. As the judicial constraint on Parliament's amending power protected the Right to Property also, the Government went hammer and tongs at the judgment, and maintained that all its pro-poor schemes had been hamstrung because of it.

Then came the 24th Amendment, seeking to undo the Golak Nath judgment. The amendment conferred on Parliament the right to amend any provision of the Constitution including those related to Fundamental Rights. During the debate, we in the Opposition objected to the sweeping powers sought to be acquired by Parliament through this amendment. We suggested that while Parliament may be empowered to abrogate or abridge Article 31 pertaining to property, the other Fundamental Rights, such as, freedom of expression, freedom of religion, etc., should remain inviolable. The validity of this amendment was challenged. The case that ensued, the Keshavananda Bharati case, in which the verdict was delivered in April 1973, has now become a landmark in Indian Constitutional history. Drawing up a *Lakshman rekha*—a thus-far-and-no-further limit—the court held that 'the amending power of Parliament is wide, but limited. Parliament has no power to abrogate or emasculate the basic elements or the fundamental features of the Constitution'. Since then, this has come be known as the doctrine of the Basic Structure of the Constitution.

If the government had honestly believed that the Right to Property was obstructing any of its welfare measures, it could have gone ahead and abrogated it without much ado. The highest judicial tribunal in the country had given it the necessary clearance. The government did nothing of the kind. All that it did was to unleash a fresh campaign projecting the Keshavananda Bharati judgment as the newest hobgoblin, holding back the economic bounties Indira Gandhi's government was yearning to shower on the people.

During the Keshavananda Bharati hearing, government counsel were put searching questions from the Bench as to what exactly they meant when they claimed an unfettered amending power for Parliament. Government counsel were brutally frank and forthright in their replies. According to them, it included the power to: (1) destroy the sovereignty of this country and make this country the satellite of any other country; (2) substitute the democratic form of government by an authoritarian form of government; (3) extend the life of the two Houses of Parliament, indefinitely; and (4) amend the amending power in such a way as to make the Constitution legally, or at any rate practically, unamendable.

The Supreme Court very rightly refused to accept this contention. It felt that this was like empowering government even to scrap the Constitution, if it could somehow manage the requisite majority in Parliament. Justices Hegde and Mukherjee during the case noted: 'At one stage, counsel for the Union and the States had grudgingly conceded that the power conferred under Art. 368 cannot be used to abrogate the Constitution, but later under pressure of questioning by some of us they changed their position and said that by 'abrogation' they meant repeal of the Constitution as a whole. When they were asked as to what they meant by saying that the power conferred under Art. 368 cannot be used to repeal the Constitution, all they said was that while amending the Constitution, at least one clause in the Constitution must be retained; though every other clause or part of the Constitution including the Preamble can be deleted and some other provisions substituted. Their submission, in short, was that so long as the expression Constitution of India is retained, every other Article or part of it can be replaced.'

On this aspect of the question, Justice Khanna, whose judgment became decisive in this case, made this very crisp observation: 'Art. 368 (Article relating to the amending procedure) cannot be so construed as to embody the death-wish of the Constitution or provide sanction for what might perhaps be called its lawful *harakiri*.'

The government was deeply unhappy, indeed exasperated, with this judgment. The government's annoyance with the verdict was officially proclaimed when in October 1975, A.N. Ray, the government's hand-picked Chief Justice of India, announced that, in deference to a request made by the Attorney General of India, he had decided to constitute a full Bench of the Court to review the Keshavananda Bharati judgment. The announcement surprised everyone. To members of the Bar it appeared odd, to say the least, that a review bench was being created only because the government wanted it. But if the Constitution of the Bench was a surprise, its abrupt winding up just two days after the hearing commenced was an even greater surprise.

It was at this juncture that the legal fraternity in India recorded one of its greatest ever triumphs in defence of the 'Basic Structure' of the Constitution. The hero of this battle was another illustrious lawyer from Bombay: Nani Palkhivala. Before the Emergency, he had consented to be Indira Gandhi's lawyer to argue her review petition in the Supreme Court seeking annulment of the Allahabad High Court's verdict against her. However, once the Emergency was imposed, he courageously returned her brief and became an outspoken critic of the authoritarian regime. His legal genius and his deep commitment to democracy shone forth when Chief Justice Ray hastily assembled a Bench of thirteen judges, presiding over it himself, to determine how to assist the government violate the basic structure of the Constitution.

Palkhivala argued brilliantly against the government's application for reconsideration of the Keshavananda decision. So powerful and persuasive were his submissions that some of the judges accepted his argument on the very first day, the others did so the next day. By the end of the second day, Chief Justice Ray was reduced to a minority of one! The following day, he simply dissolved the Bench, ending a shameful attempt to alter the basic structure of our Constitution.

Justice H.R. Khanna, whose daring role in defence of democracy I have earlier mentioned, said this about Nani Palkhivala's performance in that episode. 'The height of eloquence to which Palkhivala had risen during the hearing has seldom been equaled and has never been surpassed in the history of the Supreme Court.'

In my essay, I recalled what Dr B.R. Ambedkar, the chief architect of the Indian Constitution, had said about Article 32, the provision comprising writ jurisdiction of courts. Speaking in the Constituent Assembly on 9 December 1948, Ambedkar commended Article 32 in these words: 'If I was asked to name any particular article in this Constitution as the most important, an article without which this Constitution would be a nullity—I would not refer to any other article except this one. It is the very soul of the Constitution and the very heart of it.' It is this heart and soul of the Indian Constitution which the Congress government was itching to destroy.

*

Many of the letters I wrote from my prison cell in Bangalore were addressed to Appa Ghatate, my lawyer, and also Atalji, in New Delhi. The letters written to him, and received from him, used to be opened and routinely, often arbitrarily, censored—with ugly strikethroughs—by jail authorities. In a letter on 15 December 1975, I congratulated both him and Rama Jois, my lawyer in Bangalore, on conducting our case in the Supreme Court brilliantly. 'No one expects the case to yield any tangible result in terms of the detentions. Nevertheless, it has been serving as an instrument of exposing illegalities. Every move of ours has led to another desperate bid to cover up one more illegality.'

Since writing was the only avenue of self-expression for me while in prison, I also used it to comment on the newspapers and books I happened to read. In the same letter to Appa, I wrote: 'The newspapers these days read dull and drab. They are full of conformist crap. Amidst this, Abu Abraham's cartoons stand out as an oasis as it were. Please look up his phone number and convey to him my sincerest appreciation and compliments. Tell him that all of us here have been enjoying every single piece of his—from his 'Barefoot Humour' to his 'Bathtub Humour'*! Only

---

* The 'Bathtub Humour' refers to a cartoon by Abu Abraham, which was one of the most stinging indictments of President Fakhruddin Ali Ahmed's craven consent to Indira Gandhi's proposal to impose the Emergency. It showed Ahmed signing the Emergency proclamation from his bathtub in the Rashtrapati Bhavan. It is reproduced in this book.

yesterday, *Sunday Standard* carried that one about a parrot's prattle; it was delightful.'

I also wrote: 'I have just completed reading this much-talked about book *Freedom at Midnight* by Dominique Lapierre and Collins. For sheer readability, it's real good. As racy as fiction. The pity is that in parts it *is* fiction, and still it wears the pretensions of being history.'

While in prison, some of my happiest moments would be when I either received letters from Kamla and our children, or on those few occasions when they came down to Bangalore to see me. I learnt that class teachers would often ask Jayant and Pratibha, *'Papa vaapis aaye?'* (Has Papa come back?). My children used to feel a stab of pain in saying, 'No, not yet.' I never regretted my imprisonment since it was the inevitable price to be paid for the defence of democracy. Nevertheless, the thought of anything causing pain to my children would fill me with agony.

MY DRAMATIC ENCOUNTER WITH A STRANGER

No account of the struggle against the Emergency would be complete without a reference to the underground movement conducted by several people, most notably George Fernandes. The government charged him and others (noted industrialist Viren Shah, who later became the Vice President of the BJP and, later still, the Governor of West Bengal was one of them) with smuggling dynamite to blow up government establishments and railway tracks in what came to be known as the Baroda dynamite case. This made George Fernandes, who was arrested in June 1976, a hero of the anti-Emergency battle. Indeed, he fought the 1977 Lok Sabha election from Bihar while in jail as an undertrial, and yet won with a huge margin. His supporters campaigned with his photo in handcuffs being led to the prison by cops. The Janata Party government, in which he became Industries Minister, withdrew the case against him and others.

Many political prisoners during the Emergency were victims of physical torture. The case of Lawrence Fernandes, brother of George Fernandes, was heart-rending. An even more tragic case was that of Snehalata Reddy, the lead actress in the award-winning Kannada film, *Samskara,* an associate

MEMBER OF PARLIAMENT
(Rajya Sabha)

Bangalore,
Dated 19. 11. 76.

My dear Appa,

Thanks for your letter of the 16th. It has reached me this morning. I hasten to reply to it — first of all, to reiterate that in my case, we need not contest.

— Our petition in the High Court was based on two grounds:

(a) I have been elected to the Rajya Sabha. Article 99 obligates me to take my oath. I must be enabled to fulfil this constitutional obligation even while under detention.

(b) Under the Salaries and Allowances Act, a member, as well as his family, becomes entitled to several facilities — relating to housing, telephone, medical, travelling etc. — apart from salary, only after he takes oath and takes his seat in the House.

The High Court decided in my favour but on the basis of (b) above. It directed GOI to take me

Examples of personal letters being censored during the days of the Emergency

to Parliament on April 3 — the first day on which new members took their oath — and enable me to take my oath and take my seat.

This order was stayed by the Supreme Court. After April 3, that order, I presume, automatically becomes infructuous. Besides the Salaries and Allowances Act has been amended to entitle members to various facilities from the date on which their election is gazetted. The Amendment Bill was signed by the President on Sep. 9. So, in my case, the facilities will begin from Sep. 9, 1976. Anyway, the basis on which the High Court decided in my favour no longer obtains.

Therefore, I see no point in contesting the case.

Affectionate regards for Sheila, Bhalchandra, Vinayak. Do be writing.

Lal.

Bangalore,
23rd October, 1975

My dear Appa,

So happy to hear from you after such a long time. Your letter of the 20th has reached me just now. Thanks for all the news. I had learnt about Atalji from the Parliamentary Bulletin. Friends outside had the impression that he had been released, and they conveyed this to us. It was the Lok Sabha Bulletin which clarified the position. Your letter provides the explanation also. Hope his health is all right. An earlier letter had indicated that he had had to be admitted to the hospital again. That had given all anxiety.

I was happy to know that Shri Servai is to lead the arguments in the Supreme Court on behalf of the detenues. I know about one — Ohmiah's case. Whatever the other cases like. So far as my own case is concerned, I doubt

(2.

if it is worthwhile... in arguing, after the amendment made in the Salaries and Allowances Act. I have had no ~~route~~ official communication in this regard from the Rajya Sabha Secretariat. But my understanding is that the amendment made, entitles a member to all his facilities etc, and is no longer related to his oath taking, in the date his election is gazetted. If that is so, the basis on which the High Court had given me relief is knocked out. ~~letter~~ I have written to the Rajya Sabha today asking them to clarify the position. And if the position is ~~that~~ I understand it to be, we need not contest at all.

How is Shri Shyam Babu? and how is is mother? We haven't heard from him ~~on~~ his departure from here.

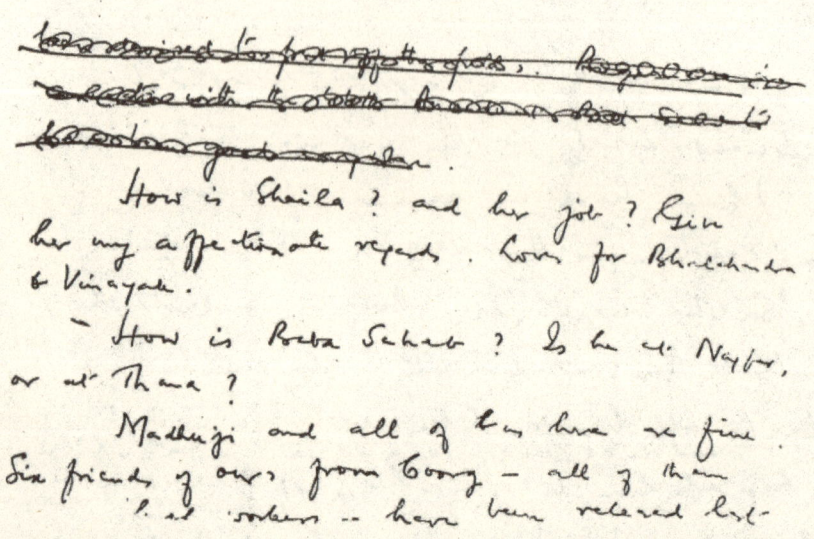

of socialist party leader George Fernandes, who had gone underground during the Emergency. She was arrested for not revealing information about Fernandes and interrogated for eight months in our jail, where she fell seriously ill. She died within five days of her release in January 1977.

Excesses like these were not few and far between. Even though they were not reported in the media, the people began to learn about them as months passed by. And this knowledge brought in its trail frustration, anger and hatred for the government.

Tyranny brings out the worst in the oppressor. But sometimes it also brings out the undesirable in the oppressed. I realised this through a dramatic encounter with a stranger while in jail. The Emergency was a year old and it seemed as if it would continue endlessly. Even though we were in prison, we could gather from reports filtering in from outside that despondency and anger were both equally on the rise among the politically conscious sections of the populace. It was in these circumstances that, one day in June 1976, an old man walked into Bangalore jail and told the prison authorities that he wanted to meet the President of the Bharatiya Jana Sangh. I went to see him. Tall, slim and moustached, he wore a visage of perfect calmness. But I soon realised that his quiet exterior was misleading.

After the exchange of pleasantries, he came straight to the point. 'I am sixty-five,' the man said. 'I cannot tolerate what she is doing. I've done whatever I wanted to in life. I have nothing more to live for. Tell me what to do. Peaceful methods won't do. I am prepared to die. Before Parliament meets for its next session, I can go and…I have a licensed revolver, but, unfamiliar as I am with New Delhi, I do not know where to find *her*.'

The person speaking to me was an educated, mature, old man. The intensity with which he argued was moving. He was not a fanatic. But he was honestly convinced that what he was suggesting was the only way to save Indian democracy. I could see his wife anxiously watching us from a distance.

'No,' I quickly interrupted him. 'You shouldn't do that. This line of thinking is totally perverse and the course of action you have in mind will irreparably damage the cause which you want to serve. Whatever else may emerge out of such a plan, it certainly will not be democracy.'

He said that those inside the jail were not adequately aware of the intensity of the popular anger against the Emergency. There was a growing feeling, he added, that the leadership of political parties that was behind the bars had become complacent with no clear plans for mounting a struggle against Indira Gandhi's dictatorship. I told the visitor that no authoritarian regime had been overthrown by violence. 'The outcome of individual acts of violence is often worse than the regime against which violence is used. There is no alternative but to wait for the common people to rise and restore democracy through democratic means.'

A little later, his wife came and said to me that she was relieved at the advice I had given to him.

I do not know what the old man thought about my response. I never saw, or heard from him again.

My diary entry on that day reads: 'Today's episode fully corroborates the thesis propounded by Ashis Nandy in the course of an article he wrote for *Quest* (November-December 1975) some time back. I wonder if the censor had seen that article. Perhaps not. If they had seen it, the journal would have been banned and the publisher and the author of the article put behind bars. The article is real dynamite. It warns Indira Gandhi almost in so many words that if you persist in what you are doing you will be assassinated!' This issue of *Quest* was among the books and journals sent by friends outside for our reading. It would be worthwhile reproducing at some length excerpts from the article. Unambiguously titled "Invitation to a beheading: A psychologist's guide to assassinations in the third world", the article says:

> The relationship between an assassin and his victim is deep and enduring. Death only openly and finally brings them together. Of course, there are tyrants who turn virtually everyone in a country into a prospective assassin and leaders who build bastions against their assassination in the minds of men, thereby reducing the circle of prospective assassins to the microscopic group of hired psycho-paths and the mentally ill.

Emperor Nero belonged to the first category and Martin Luther King to the second.

> There is also the special case of rulers who by the consent of the majority are tyrannical within the country and, to the extent they get the chance, in the world outside. Their pathology leads to collective suicides rather than individual assassinations. Adolf Hitler is the hackneyed but glaring example of the species.
>
> But such leaders are hardly typical. There is a much broader range of situations where the ruler is popular and charismatic but propelled by his inner drives, prepares the ground for his assassination. In such cases there is a close fit among the motivational imperatives of such a man, his attempts to remould the polity after his own psychological needs, and the type of invitation he extends to his potential assassins.
>
> The first characteristic of such a ruler is an inability to trust deeply and wholly. Though his flamboyant style may hide it for a long time, he lives in an inner world peopled by untrustworthy men. Even when he trusts some, it is transient. A chain of lieutenants

comes in and goes out of his favour in a fashion reminiscent of people getting in and out of a railway compartment.

The ruler suspends this suspiciousness only in the case of his family members, men recruited from outside politics to act as 'commissars', and politicians who have no independent bases and are fully dependent on him....

Power, thus, continues to be concentrated in the ruler's hand. Worse, he is seen as all powerful. As a result, all grievances gradually begin to be directed at him. After a while there remain no intermediate shock-absorbers whom he can fob off as subverters or reactionaries within the ruling circle....

The regime which Richard Nixon built must have nurtured many political assassins and those who hooted him out might have, for all we know, saved his life. Sheikh Mujib's Bangladesh, too, was an instance of such a polity.

Not merely may the ruler become too deeply identified with the regime, the regime may seem closed to internal competition to large numbers of people.

Yet no regime is psychologically closed. It could be so only normatively. Even the most rigidly closed regime is open to one whose values permit him to include in the available means of political competition—revolution, rebellion, coup and assassination.

Of these, revolutions require immense planning, massive organisation, first-rate mobilizational skills, and a developed ability to feel the pulse of a large section of the population....

To some extent, the pre-conditions of revolutions apply to rebellions and coups, too.

On the other hand, an assassination is the cheapest of the four means mentioned, requires the least planning and organisation, and does not need the assent of any section of the population. Understandably, it is AT a premium in the Third World. In some part of it, such killings have, in fact, become a standard means of deciding political succession. In Latin America, for instance the popularity of political assassinations is exceeded at the moment only by bull fights....

The tragedy of the assassinated ruler is that though he can avoid the fate towards which he often moves blindly and inexorably, he is in effect a driven man. Like his killer, he rebels against a part of himself which seeks self-preservation, rationality and contact with the real world of people.

INDIRA GANDHI: A VICTIM OF HER OWN INSECURITY

This incident has also been described in Uma Vasudev's book *Two Faces of Indira Gandhi*, which gives an objective, vivid and frequently terrifying account of the dark happenings during the Emergency. An enterprising journalist, she came to interview me soon after the Emergency was lifted. Uma asked me: 'There was so much anger against Indira Gandhi at the time. Do you think she might possibly have been assassinated then, or if she had managed to scrape back to power later?'

I said, 'Considering the extent to which she had gone, she might have, perhaps—had this been another country. But not in India. It's not in the temperament of the people. Besides, the leadership of the political forces opposed to her is positively opposed to this kind of thing also. They disapprove of these measures. There is too strong a commitment to peace.'

The Opposition parties were, of course, quite unhappy at Indira Gandhi's periodic insinuations, even before the declaration of the Emergency that her life was in danger. Once, she accused the Bharatiya Jana Sangh directly. 'The Jana Sangh is planning to murder me,' she said. We felt that a person occupying the high office of Prime Minister of India should not have made such strong insinuations against a responsible political party like ours, and so we decided to meet her. In our meeting, she neither substantiated her charge nor withdrew it. She didn't even say that she was misquoted. Actually, she didn't say anything!

The meeting left me flabbergasted. It nevertheless reinforced my assessment that Indira Gandhi had two streaks in her authoritarian personality: insecurity and haughtiness. Both were evident in varying measures at different times in her political career.

Insecurity was one of the prime reasons behind her decision to establish her supremacy by effecting a split in the Congress party in 1969. That sense of insecurity and mistrust would sometimes take the form of paranoia. All that I could make out of our fruitless and frustrating meeting with Indira Gandhi, in response to her charge, was that here was a power-hungry person who perched herself above the normal standards of accountability and even rationality. All dictators in history have shown this trait.

Many observers of modern Indian history, including some who knew Indira Gandhi closely, have referred to the basic insecurity in her personality, which coloured her approach to politics soon after her father's demise. Noted journalist and writer Khushwant Singh, who was a strong supporter of Indira Gandhi during the Emergency, later had this to say about her: 'In her insecurity, she destroyed the institutions of democracy. She packed Parliament with her supporters with loyalty being more important than ability; she superseded judges; she corrupted the civil service. Favouritism became a great sport with her. She also knew how to use people against each other and was quite a master of that. She would patronise somebody and when she thought he was getting too big, instead of appointing him to a senior post, she would appoint his close associate, knowing this would create a rift between them. In the long run it was not good for the country to play such games as she did.'

Khushwant Singh became a good acquaintance of mine after the Emergency. I admired his writing and his substantial scholarship on many subjects. He, in turn, admired our party for its role in fighting the Emergency and, later, in helping the Sikh community during the anti-Sikh carnage in Delhi in 1984, in the aftermath of Indira Gandhi's assassination. However, our relationship soured after the Ayodhya movement when he became quite critical of me.

ANIMAL FARM AND NINETEEN EIGHTY-FOUR REVISITED

For all those who became actively involved in politics in the late forties or early fifties, the principal fault line in political thinking used to be the one that divided the communists and the non-communists. My RSS values of proud, uncompromising patriotism created within me a bias against an organisation which unashamedly flaunted its extra-territorial loyalty towards a foreign power.

It is in those years that I read George Orwell's *Animal Farm*, a satirical fable against Communism and *Nineteen Eighty-four*, which alerted the world to the catastrophic consequences of an all powerful authoritarian state on human values.

India had a brief bitter taste of this traumatic catastrophe during the Emergency. The electoral debacle Indira Gandhi and her party suffered in 1977, no doubt, had a salutary impact on the country's politics and politicians. But some of the habits acquired by the system have persisted.

Orwell's *Nineteen Eighty-four* was about a totalitarian empire in which the Big Brother at the helm of affairs, through a technologically advanced telescreen, was able to keep watch over all the goings-on in his realm. The developments in Information Technology have now belied some of Orwell's predictions. This has happened because of the collapse of Communist totalitarian empires, the amazing advances made in the field of personal computers, e-mails, internet, etc. But, as I said earlier, in India the Emergency era left behind some ugly remnants, which need to be consciously erased. One of them is phone-tapping.

A decade after the imposition of the Emergency, in 1985, I had an interesting encounter. One morning a stranger arrived at my house with a briefcase full of papers. This briefcase, he told me, contained 'dynamite' which could blow up this government. He opened his briefcase and out poured some two hundred sheets of closely-typed transcripts of telephone conversations of a host of VIPs.

I scanned these papers. They were not as 'explosive' as the gentleman who had brought them presumed but they were certainly startling and extremely interesting. I went through portions of my own telephonic conversations with Atalji. It only confirmed our suspicion that Big Brother was watching us! But what really shocked me was the fact that these transcripts included tape-recorded conversations not only of Opposition leaders but also of eminent journalists and some extremely distinguished VVIPs.

The 25th of June 1985 happened to be the tenth anniversary of the Emergency. Addressing a press conference on the occasion, Atalji said: 'I have known for long, that my phone as well as that of my party colleague Advani have been under surveillance. But lately I have gathered that the telephones of many other senior leaders like Chaudhary Charan Singh, Jagjivan Ram and Chandra Shekhar and journalists like G.K. Reddy, Arun Shourie, Kuldip Nayar and G.S. Chawla also are being regularly tapped. But what has really left me flabbergasted is that the Intelligence Bureau (IB) has had the temerity to tap the telephones of the President and the Chief Justice also. All this is not only politically immoral but also unconstitutional and illegal.'

In democracies the world over, the legitimacy and limits of phone tapping has been a matter of continuing debate. In the US, this issue became the subject matter of bitter acrimony during the Watergate days. Angry public opinion and the threat of impeachment led to Richard Nixon's ouster from office. His successor Gerald Ford granted him full pardon. But three years later in a television interview with David Frost (19 May 1977), Nixon made a sensational statement. He affirmed that burglaries and other crimes are not illegal if ordered by the President!

In 1977, President Jimmy Carter asked Congress to approve a plan which would make it impossible for the executive to intrude upon a citizen's privacy without judicial authorisation. This plan, Carter contended, would successfully resolve the 'inherent conflict' between national security and a citizen's basic right to privacy. Subsequently, legislation has been enacted wherein all security authorities, including the FBI, have been obligated to seek prior judicial approval for any wire-taps.

In Britain, there is no law governing wire-tapping but several parliamentary committees have gone into the question in depth. In 1957, a three-man committee of Privy Councillors headed by Norman Birkett was set up to inquire into the 'interception of communications'. The Birkett committee described wire-tapping, or for that matter, all forms of intercepting private communications as 'inherently objectionable', but felt that the practice may be permitted within certain clearly defined parameters, and with appropriate safe guards. It laid down that wire-tapping may be permitted for the police and security agencies only for the purpose of crime investigation or to check subversive or espionage activity. Even for this, the committee laid down rigorous guidelines. Till date, no one in Britain has ever accused their government of abusing these powers.

What is really required in India to deal with this issue is to set up a parliamentary committee on the lines of the Birkett committee to examine all aspects of the problem, scrap the outdated Indian Telephone Act of 1885 and replace it with a new legislation, which formally would provide statutory safeguards to make it impossible for governments to abuse its powers against political activists, pressmen and the citizens in general.

SHAH COMMISSION'S INDICTMENT OF THE EMERGENCY

Before concluding this chapter on the Emergency, it is apposite to mention here the findings of a government-appointed commission of inquiry about this dark period in India's history. In 1977, the Government of India appointed a one-man commission, headed by Justice J.C. Shah, a retired judge of the Supreme Court, to inquire into all the excesses committed by the Indira Gandhi government during the Emergency. Calling the Emergency a 'fraud on the President, a fraud on the council of ministers and a fraud on the people', the Shah Commission observed at the end of its report.

> As borne out by the records of the Government and the depositions of several responsible Government servants, dishonesty and falsehood became almost a way of official life during the Emergency. As Robert Frost said, 'Most of the change we think we seek in life is due to truth being in or out of our favour.' If the administrative machinery in our country is to be rendered safe for our children, the Services must give a better account of themselves by standing up for the basic values of an honest and efficient administration. That alone can resurrect the people's lost faith once again in our Services. If a democratic heritage is to be left for future generations, we should want the truth again to be enshrined in its legislative

place in the social, political and economic scheme of things in our country. There is nothing unattainable or profound in this. It is a simple human message.'

It is not surprising then that the report of the Shah Commission was virtually banned when Indira Gandhi returned to power in 1980.

BJP's Spectacular Rise 1977-97

Somnath Temple

Proposed Ram Temple at Ayodhya

'The Ayodhya movement, the biggest mass movement in the history of independent India, was the most decisive transformational event in my political journey. Sadly, the issue of construction of Ram Temple, which could have been resolved peacefully and amicably, was converted into a divisive Hindu vs. Muslim dispute. I fervently hope that the Ayodhya mission will be completed through the joint effort of Hindus and Muslims, thereby making a lasting contribution to mutual reconciliation and national integration.'

Phase Four

1

THE END OF THE DARKEST PERIOD IN INDIA'S HISTORY

A dictator must fool all the people all the time and there's only one way to do that, he must also fool himself.

—WILLIAM SOMERSET MAUGHAM, ENGLISH NOVELIST AND PLAYWRIGHT

With 1976 fading away, there were growing indications that the sun would set on the Emergency rule too. Indira Gandhi's unpopularity at home was increasing by the day and, internationally, the only supporters that she had were the Soviet Union and its puppet regimes in the communist bloc. In spite of strict press censorship, information about the excesses and atrocities committed by her government was spreading across the country and abroad at a speed that unnerved the Prime Minister. I am always amazed by the power of word-of-mouth publicity, which dictators fear more than the printed word but are utterly powerless to censor. This primitive mode of communication became the most effective carrier of the truth about the Emergency.

As a result, nothing damaged the reputation of both Indira Gandhi and her son Sanjay, more especially in North India, than stories of forcible sterilisations. As part of the government's family planning programme, government employees were given 'targets' to fulfil, and they, in many places, started targeting poor and illiterate people in rural areas for mass vasectomy and hysterectomy operations. Population control was no doubt a laudable objective in a country like India, but here was a classic case of a good idea going out of control, and consequently earning a bad name due to its coercive implementation.

If *nasbandi* (the forcible sterilisation programme) earned the wrath of the common masses, the class of educated Indians was aghast at the brazen sycophancy of the Prime Minister and her son in Congress circles. The slogan 'Indira is India and India is Indira', coined by the then Congress President Devkant Barooah, repelled people's patriotic sensibilities. Barooah had once declared during the Emergency: 'The country can do without the Opposition. They are irrelevant to the history of India.'

To make matters worse for Indira Gandhi, cracks were developing in the cozy alliance between the Congress and the CPI. In November 1975, *Mainstream*, a pro-CPI Delhi-based weekly carried, with critical observations by its widely respected Editor Nikhil Chakravartty, the text of a paper on drastic changes proposed in the Constitution, including a Presidential system of government. The paper, which was described as having the blessings of 'important Congressmen', evoked a sharp reaction in the country, especially from the legal fraternity. So powerful and spontaneous was the reaction that the government beat a hasty retreat, disowning any official connection with the draft paper. 'The uproar that followed the document's circulation', Chakravartty wrote in an editorial, 'led Congressmen to repudiate their own brainchild'. However, in the fall-out he had to suspend the publication of *Mainstream*.

Sanjay Gandhi's outspoken criticism of the communists in the latter half of 1976 surprised many within the country. In a candid and lengthy interview given to journalist Uma Vasudev in July 1978, he criticised the left-inspired economic policy of his mother's government, saying, 'I think a public sector should function only in competition with the private sector, and where it cannot function in competition with the private sector, it should be allowed to die a natural death.' The views he had expressed on many issues were so iconoclastic that, soon after the transmission of excerpts of the interview by Press Trust of India (PTI) and United News of India (UNI), the Prime Minister instructed her staff to ask the news agencies to withdraw the interview. Nevertheless, some newspapers had already carried it.

Sanjay Gandhi's criticism of his mother's economic policy did have some merit, as evidenced by the wide-ranging reforms that had to be introduced in the early 1990s to liberate the Indian economy from the shackles of the growth-impairing Soviet model. However, here again a good intention was marred by political authoritarianism. Democracy—which is the touchstone of all good ideas, and is itself both an ideal means and a noble end—was anathema to both the mother and the son.

Towards the end of 1976, Indira Gandhi began to realise that she was getting increasingly isolated. The Emergency rule, she knew, could not be sustained indefinitely. The term of the 5th Lok Sabha had already ended in mid 1976. Through a Constitutional amendment, the Prime Minister had the life of the Lok Sabha extended by one year, allowing herself to rule by decree till the end of 1977. She had three options before her: (a) to further prolong the Emergency rule and also the term of Parliament beyond 1977; (b) to hold fresh parliamentary elections in conditions of the Emergency; and (c) relax some of the harsh provisions of the Emergency, release political opponents from jail, hold parliamentary elections quickly, get re-elected and continue the authoritarian rule in a new form.

Indira Gandhi understood that the first two options were simply out of the question. Either of them would have intensified violent revolts at home against the Emergency regime and also exposed her government to harsher condemnation from the world community. After all, she could not have completely ignored her father's widely acclaimed legacy of nurturing parliamentary democracy in newly independent India. But she reposed her confidence in the last option, reckoning that, since the Opposition parties were out of action since mid-1975, she would easily romp home if she held elections in early 1977. Like all dictators, she allowed herself to be swayed by the relentless propaganda being carried out by her own government-controlled media about the success of her 'Twenty-Point Programme', to which Sanjay had added his own 'Five-Point Programme'. Her sense of invincibility was further boosted by the coterie of 'yes-men' she had surrounded herself with.

I had no doubt that the new year would be the harbinger of positive developments. The entry in my prison diary on 31 December read: 'The closing day of the year brings particularly happy tidings for our jail. Madhu Dandavate's detention is revoked. He is given a warm and affectionate send-off.'

While in Bangalore, I was in regular communication with political prisoners in more than forty jails across the country, often receiving letters from them in coded language. On 7 January, I received a telegram with the following message:

> Met prominent members of joint family about the new house to be set up. Proceeding to see grandfather today.
>
> —Madhu Bala Advani

I knew that the telegram was from Madhu Dandavate and decoded its contents. I was happy that after his release he had been able to contact colleagues from different Opposition parties, discuss with them the idea of forming a single new political party, and was now proceeding to Patna to seek the guidance of Jayaprakash Narayan in this matter.

My diary entry on 16 January was: 'The *Indian Express* carries a lead story saying that the Lok Sabha polls are likely by March-end or April beginning and that a formal announcement to this effect may be made on the opening day of Parliament's next session'. Sure enough, two days later, on 18 January 1976, Prime Minister Indira Gandhi announced the dissolution of the Lok Sabha.

'THEY STOLE THE FREEDOM OF 600 MILLIONS, BUT THEY JUST COULD NOT DESTROY THEIR HOPE!'

Something interesting happened on the morning of 18 January, which I learnt of later. Having no idea of the impending political developments, Kamla, my wife, had come to Bangalore in early January, along with our children. She was anxious about when my prison sentence would end and I would be back at home. On 17 January, a relative of hers, at whose place she was staying, asked her, 'You seem to be very restless. Why don't you go to Whitefield and have *darshan* of Sathya Sai Baba*, who is staying there these days? You will get some peace of mind.'

Kamla, who had never met Baba, agreed to go the very next day. An early morning car journey brought her and our two children to Whitefield, a suburb of Bangalore, where Baba's ashram is located. As usual, there was a large gathering of devotees waiting to see Baba, who was seated on a chair at one end of a large hall. Kamla, along with her relative and our children, was standing at a distance, indistinguishable in the assembly. To her utter surprise, someone came up to her and said, 'Baba is calling you.' She went to Baba, and did *namaskar*, at which Baba placed his hand on her head and said, 'Your husband will be released from prison soon.'

For Kamla, this came as a complete surprise. She had not been introduced to Baba, nor had she told him anything about me. With her heart palpitating wildly, she returned to her relative's house, only to be greeted by a waiting police officer who said, 'Advaniji is going to be released from the Central Jail shortly. Would you like to come there to receive him?'

As I stepped out of prison, I was greeted by Kamla, Jayant and Pratibha. It remains one of the most unforgettable moments of my life. I was happy to be a free man once again after spending nineteen months as a political prisoner in free India. Nevertheless, I was rather reluctant to

---

* Sathya Sai Baba is one of the most revered Indian spiritual personalities. His main ashram is in Puttaparthi in Andhra Pradesh. There are over 1,200 Sathya Sai Baba Centres in 114 countries worldwide with millions of followers engaged in a wide range of devotional and humanitarian activities. Baba's motto is: 'Love All Serve All'.

come out of jail, since many of the other hundred-odd political activists held under MISA at the Bangalore Central Jail were not yet freed. Kamla, however, reassured me saying, 'If they have released you, they will surely release the others, too.'

My last diary entry, just before my release on 18 January, read:

> It is around 1.30 in the afternoon when the jail superintendent, Chablani, comes to my room and says that a wireless message has arrived from New Delhi revoking my detention order.... I spent two or three hours in the other wards. There is the usual send-off function as well. Somehow the release news has not made me happy. The bulk of those still inside the jail are Jana Sangh activists. They are releasing only the leaders or legislators to gain publicity. In fact, as the head of the organization, I feel oppressed by a sense of guilt that while I am being released, junior colleagues of mine are still held back.... When at 5.30 or so I returned to my room I found a heap of letters lying on my table. They are more than 600, all of them from abroad, sent by members or associates of Amnesty International. Most of them are Christmas or New Year greeting cards, but there is a line or two inscribed on each, which gave strength, confidence and hope to all of us engaged in the struggle. Here is a sample—a Christmas greeting from one Laurie Hendricks from Amsterdam. She wrote:
>
> *Freedom and hope don't go hand in hand. They can steal your freedom, but can't take away your hope.*
>
> Yes, they stole the freedom of 600 millions, but they just could not destroy their hope!

THE POLLS ARE ANNOUNCED; AND THE BIRTH OF THE JANATA PARTY

After spending a day in Bangalore, I left for Madras (now Chennai) the next day, from where I flew to Delhi on 20 January. Kamla and the children returned home by train. By this time, Atalji too had been freed; He had earlier been shifted to AIIMS in New Delhi, where he was convalescing after a slipped-disc operation. Morarjibhai was released from detention at Tawdu in Haryana. Three days later, on 23 January, Indira Gandhi announced fresh elections to be held in March. The announcement was followed by the release of many more political prisoners.

Political developments in the country moved at such lightning speed that on the day of the announcement of fresh elections, Jayaprakashji declared the formation of the Janata Party and named a twenty-eight member national executive committee, with Morarji Desai as its Chairman and Charan Singh as Vice Chairman. Its members were drawn from the four constituent parties—Jana Sangh, Congress (O), Socialist Party and Lok Dal—which had merged to give birth to the new party. Along with Madhu Limaye, Ram Dhan and Surendra Mohan, I was made one of its four General Secretaries.

The birth of the Janata Party electrified the political situation in the country. It was as if a colossal and benign force was releasing India from nineteen months of tyranny. Even though elections were still several weeks away, and the people were yet to give their verdict on the Emergency, there was a sense of the spirit of victory of democracy over dictatorship in the air. I felt as if India was standing at the cusp of a dramatic transformation, denoting the end of an era and the beginning of a new one, something that could be compared only to the epochal transition that India experienced three decades earlier in 1947. Surely, a second Freedom Struggle had been won in India!

I should explain here that the Jana Sangh, which had given conditional assent, before the declaration of the Emergency, to Jayaprakashji's proposal for the formation of a single non-communist political party as a credible alternative to the Congress, now readily and enthusiastically backed the idea. The trial and trauma of the Emergency made all of us in the Jana Sangh realise that the Congress could not be defeated without the broadest possible Opposition unity. A major factor that additionally weighed on our minds was the trust that Jayaprakashji had reposed in the Jana Sangh, as well as in the RSS, both before, and during the Emergency. In fact, he had declared that, in the event of his arrest, Nanaji Deshmukh, a Jana Sangh stalwart and his trusted comrade, would take over full responsibility of the Lok Sangharsh Samiti, which JP had formed in 1974 as a broadbased platform to fight authoritarianism. I have already mentioned how he consented to attend a National Council session of the Jana Sangh in Delhi in March 1975 and declared, 'If the Jana Sangh is fascist, then Jayaprakash Narayan is also a fascist.' He had to face virulent criticism from the communists because of this, but he stuck to his stand.

As for us, the respect that we had developed for JP before the Emergency had grown manifold on account of the unbending, inspiring and sagacious leadership he provided to the democratic movement even when he was himself under detention and his health was steadily failing. I recall what Balasaheb Deoras, the third *Sarsanghchalak* of the RSS, said about JP at a rally in Delhi on 1 December 1974: 'Jayaprakash Narayan is a saint who has come to rescue our society in dark and critical times.' Therefore, when JP himself took the initiative of forming the Janata Party in January 1977, Atalji, I and others in the Jana Sangh had no hesitation whatsoever in deciding to dissolve our party and merge it into the new organisation. The same enthusiasm was also shown by our friends in other like-minded parties who agreed to merge into the Janata Party.

The formation of the Janata Party greatly encouraged several ministers in Indira Gandhi's government who were unhappy with the Emergency and the Prime Minister's style of functioning, but could not express their dissent earlier. On 2 February, the Prime Minister received a major setback when Jagjivan Ram, a senior member of her Cabinet and a towering Scheduled Caste leader of the Congress, resigned. He had been a Minister in every government in New Delhi after Independence, and also in Pandit Nehru's interim government in 1946. After revolting against Indira Gandhi, he formed a new party called the Congress for Democracy (CFD), along with other one-time Indira loyalists such as Hemvati Nandan Bahuguna and Nandini Satpathy. The CFD soon merged with the Janata Party, further boosting the morale of the anti-Emergency forces across the country.

There was very little time left to prepare for the Lok Sabha polls, which had been scheduled for 16 March. Once the decision was taken to form a single and cohesive new political platform, there was an interesting discussion on the Janata Party's flag. About a dozen leaders of the constituent parties met at Morarjibhai's house in late January. Atalji and I were present as representatives of the Jana Sangh. Piloo Modi, the ever voluble leader of the Swatantra Party, was the first to give his opinion and said that the flag should be blue. To that Charan Singh said, 'I agree that it should have a single colour, but that colour should be green and not blue. Green represents agriculture and shows our commitment to *kisans*, who are the backbone of our society.' This drew an angry reaction from Sikandar Bakht, who was in the Congress (O) those days; he later joined the BJP. 'How can you have a green flag? It is the colour of the flag of Pakistan.' I suggested that the flag should be saffron in colour, and gave the example of how even the Congress Flag Committee had proposed in 1931 a plain saffron flag with a blue *charkha* (spinning wheel).

Finally, Morarjibhai said, 'Neither green only nor saffron only. Let's have both.' It was then decided that the flag be two-thirds saffron and one-thirds green in two vertical sections, with the image of a *haldhari kisan* (plough-carrying farmer) in the saffron section. The symbol of the farmer also became our election symbol.

A SILENT AND PEACEFUL BALLOT-BOX REVOLUTION

Although I have participated, either as a campaigner or as a contestant, in every single parliamentary election held so far—from the first in 1952 to the fourteenth in 2004—I would unhesitatingly say that it was the one held in 1977 that is the most memorable one for me. On no other occasion, did the survival of Indian democracy depend so critically on the outcome of the elections. Similarly, no other election became a greater testimony to the innate democratic wisdom of the Indian electorate as this one. The 1977 Lok Sabha poll was nothing short of a silent and peaceful ballot-box revolution, carried out by India's humble voters.

The Janata Party faced many daunting difficulties right from the onset of the poll campaign. Our flag and election symbol were new, and hence little known to the voters. In contrast, the people were quite familiar with the Congress party's poll symbol of the *charkha*. Our party was starved of resources, whereas the Congress was flush with funds. The latter also had the entire government-controlled media at its disposal. Since the Emergency was formally still in force, people were generally fearful and suspicious. They were unwilling to openly express their views on who they would vote for. True, the Janata Party's election meetings attracted huge crowds, but, at least in the initial days, there were no signs whatsoever of an impending anti-Congress wave. In fact, Congress flags far outnumbered the Janata Party's, both in villages and towns.

And, yet, there was a whiff of change in the air. An electoral earthquake was in the offing.

I distinctly remember one election meeting that I addressed in Amethi in Uttar Pradesh during the election campaign. As I was passing through the main market, I could see only Congress flags fluttering outside every shop. I went into a small shop and started talking to its owner. He was initially reluctant to be dragged into any discussion about the elections. Once he developed enough confidence in me, I asked him, 'Who will win from this constituency?' I was taken aback by his reply, 'Of course, the Janata candidate will win hands down. No doubt about it.' I said, 'How can you be so sure? I don't see any signs here that the Congress is going to be defeated. Even your own shop has displayed a *jhanda* (flag) of the Congress party.'

'*Bhai sahab*, you only see the *jhanda*. Don't forget that there is also a *danda* there, on which it is hoisted. We fear the *danda*, which is why we have put up the Congress *jhanda*.'

In a flash, I learnt one of the greatest lessons in democracy: never underestimate the common people's political understanding or their commitment to democracy. India's voters may be illiterate or semi-literate; sometimes they may even be swayed by caste and religious considerations. But when it is time to defend big ideals like democracy or freedom, the multitudes rise like a mighty, united force.

This was resoundingly proved when the results were declared on 20 March. The Congress was defeated for the first time since Independence. The Janata Party won a clear majority by securing 295 seats in a House of

542 seats. The Congress tally was abysmal: only 154 seats. In terms of vote-share, too, the Janata Party's performance was spectacular—41.32 per cent as against 34.52 per cent for the Congress, a difference of nearly seven per cent. For the ruling party, the defeat became more humiliating when news spread that Indira Gandhi was defeated in Rae Bareli and her son Sanjay was trounced in Amethi, both being their own constituencies.

The official media tried to suppress the news of the Congress debacle and, especially the defeat of the Prime Minister and her son as long as they could. This gave rise to many wild rumours and speculations. I later came across an account of what happened on that fateful day in the memoirs of K.P. Krishnanunny, a PTI correspondent.[1] Once the results of the counting in most constituencies showed that the Janata Party was heading towards a great victory, Krishnanunny typed out the story whose lead line was: 'The 30-year Congress rule in India has ended and a non-Congress Ministry will assume office soon....' To his surprise, his Editor asked him to hold on to the story, and according to Krishnanunny, told him that Indira Gandhi was meeting the three chiefs of staff 'apparently to know their mind whether they would extend support to her if she continued in power despite adverse election results'. Only after ascertaining that the 'service chiefs had turned down Mrs Gandhi's attempt to remain in power' did the Editor release the story.

Emergency was officially lifted on 23 March 1976. With that ended the darkest period in the history of the Indian Republic.

2

My Stint in the Information & Broadcasting Ministry

Eternal vigilance is the price of freedom.
—Thomas Jefferson, the third president of
the United States of America

The popular response to the Janata Party's triumph in the 1977 Lok Sabha elections was unprecedented in its enthusiasm and spontaneity. There were victory rallies all over the country, including in South India, where the Congress had managed to protect its fortress. People belonging to all classes, castes and communities participated in the celebrations. Never after Independence had India witnessed such unity, transcending all diversities, on a democratic platform. And, truly, never has it been seen in any other election since then.

Paradoxically, it was the unity within the Janata Party that had begun to show the first signs of tension at the time of countrywide celebrations over its victory. As soon as it became clear that the Janata Party would form the next government in New Delhi, a thorny question cropped up: Who would be the Prime Minister? The largest number of the newly elected members of Parliament belonged to the erstwhile Jana Sangh: ninety-three, followed by the Lok Dal led by Charan Singh (seventy-one) and the Congress (O) led by Morarji Desai (forty-four). The Socialists accounted for twenty-eight MPs, and an equal number belonged to the CFD, the breakaway group from the Congress, led by Jagjivan Ram. But the choice of Prime Minister was not going to be decided by the numerical strength of the constituent units of the Janata Party. After all, they had dissolved their individual identities in the new party. We, from the Jana Sangh background, made it very clear that the choice of Prime Minister should be based solely on merit and the long-term interests of the nation—and, more importantly, the decision should be based on consensus.

The greatest responsibility of ensuring unity, cohesion and consensus in the Janata Party rested, naturally, on the frail shoulders of Jayaprakashji. Detention during the Emergency had taken its toll on his health. His kidneys had failed and he was saved by a timely operation at Jaslok Hospital, Bombay, in November 1976. However, he would be on dialysis for the rest of his life. Even in this critical condition, he had put his moral weight behind the Janata Party's election campaign. He was convalescing in Bombay when the election results were announced. Although he was the principal architect of the Janata Party's triumph, he was never in the race for power. Like Mahatma Gandhi, whose ardent follower he was, JP had renounced power politics. This had further enhanced his moral stature in the country.

Not surprisingly, all eyes were now focused on this seventy-five-year-old saintly figure, as his was going to be the decisive voice in the selection of the new Prime Minister. JP returned to Delhi on 23 March and the very next day did something extraordinary. He summoned all the leaders and newly elected MPs of the Janata Party to Raj Ghat, on the banks of the Yamuna River, the site of Mahatma Gandhi's samadhi. There, from his wheelchair, he administered to all of us an oath of unity and service to the nation. The photograph of that event ranks among the most historic images of independent India. Conspicuous by his absence at the event was Charan Singh. His absence was not deliberate; he was, indeed, indisposed on that day. Nevertheless, it was deemed as a bad omen for the new party.

HOW MORARJI DESAI BECAME PRIME MINISTER

Soon after the Janata Party's victory, Atalji, I and some Jana Sangh friends met together to deliberate on the issue of the Prime Minister. Three names were under consideration: Morarji Desai, Jagjivan Ram and Charan Singh. However, the first two were the main contenders. The opinion in favour of one or the other was evenly divided. Both had their widely acknowledged strengths. Both belonged to the generation of freedom fighters. Both were also highly experienced in politics and governance. Morarjibhai had been consistently fighting against Indira Gandhi's leadership even before the Congress split in 1969. He was also amongst the first political leaders to protest actively against her authoritarianism, as was evident from his leadership of the pro-democracy movement in Gujarat, which resulted in a highly demoralising defeat for the Congress in the state in June 1975. Jagjivan Ram, on the other hand, had quit the Congress only after the dissolution of Parliament in January 1977 and announcement of elections thereafter. However, all of us agreed that his quitting the Congress was a major blow to the ruling party, especially in North India. We also had a high opinion of him as a good administrator who abhorred delays in decision-making.

Although I was personally for Morarjibhai, most others favoured Jagjivan Ram. They were guided by one overriding consideration: having a scheduled caste Prime Minister, and one with political eminence and proven administrative acumen, would send a powerful message of social reform and justice. Former Socialist leaders like George Fernandes and Madhu Dandavate were also of the same opinion. Furthermore, we reckoned that since Charan Singh had bitter relations with Morarjibhai, he would accept Jagjivan Ram. How mistaken we were!

All the MPs were to assemble in the Central Hall of Parliament post lunch on 24 March to decide the leadership issue. The moment Charan

Singh learnt that internal opinion in the newly formed party was veering round towards Jagjivan Ram, he shot off a letter to Jayaprakashji, from a local hospital where he was recouping, saying that he strongly favoured Morarjibhai for the post. JP and Acharya Kripalani,* who had been authorised to decide the leadership issue after consulting the leaders and newly elected MPs of the Janata Party, ultimately announced Desai's name. Later, Charan Singh would frequently cite his letter to JP as evidence to claim that it was he who put Morarjibhai in the prime ministerial chair.

Jagjivan Ram was understandably upset, but his sense of disappointment was further exacerbated when Charan Singh was made deputy Prime Minister and given the crucial Home portfolio. Consequently, Jagjivan Ram refused to join the Cabinet. It required much persuasion on our part to make him change his mind. The effects of these inauspicious developments, at the very infancy of the new government, were strongly felt as months passed by.

LIFE AS A MINISTER, IN A PORTFOLIO CLOSE TO MY HEART

Morarji Desai was sworn in as India's fifth Prime Minister on 24 March 1976. Two days later, a nineteen-member Cabinet was sworn in. I was one of the three persons from the erstwhile Jana Sangh who joined the new government. Atal Bihari Vajpayee was made the External Affairs Minister while Brijlal Verma was given the Industries portfolio. The Prime Minister

---

* Acharya (Jivatram Bhagwandas) Kripalani (1888-1982) was a widely respected Gandhian socialist, who was President of the INC for the crucial years around India's Independence in 1947. Born in Sindh, he plunged into the freedom movement during his student years. A critic of Nehru's policies, he moved the first ever no-confidence motion in the Indian Parliament in 1963 after India's failure to counter the Chinese aggression in the previous year. In the early 1970s, he joined Jayaprakash Narayan in voicing strong criticism of Indira Gandhi's authoritarianism. He paid a price for it—at the age of eighty-nine, he was put behind bars soon after the Emergency was declared in June 1975. His wife Sucheta Kripalani was also a prominent Congress leader who served in several Central ministries and became the first lady Chief Minister of Uttar Pradesh.

asked me which portfolio I wanted. Without a moment's hesitation I said, 'Information & Broadcasting'. When he asked me why, I explained to Morarjibhai that, having worked as a journalist in the 1960s, I had developed a deep interest in media-related matters. I had frequently written about the partisan use of the government-run media by Indira Gandhi and her party. In the Rajya Sabha, I had raised the demand for granting autonomy to AIR and Doordarshan. 'But above all,' I said, 'the Emergency period was used by the Congress government mainly to undermine press freedom. There is an urgent need now to dismantle the legal and administrative infrastructure of censorship that was erected during the Emergency regime. So, even in terms of the challenges that the new government faces, I&B seems to me to be an important portfolio.' Morarjibhai said, 'I agree with you. I need you in this crucial ministry.'

Soon after being sworn in, I went to my office in the Ministry of Information & Broadcasting on the first floor of Shastri Bhavan. A newly constructed office complex, situated not far from Parliament, Shastri Bhavan housed many ministries of the Government of India. It lacked the grandeur and aesthetics of South Block and North Block, the two majestic British-era buildings near Rashtrapati Bhawan on Raisina Hill, in which the PMO and the Ministries of Home, Finance, Defence and External Affairs are located. I attributed the architectural mediocrity of Shastri Bhavan, built during the sixties, to the overall deterioration of standards in public life witnessed lately.

My first task as I&B minister was to present in Parliament a White Paper on the misuse of the mass media during the Emergency. Having given a resounding verdict against the Emergency rule, the people of India had a right to know all the atrocities committed under the garb of press censorship, how it was justified, and how it was resisted. The people knew, somewhat, about the ill-treatment of the media and harassment of journalists who refused to be cowed down. Nevertheless, they were unaware of the full extent and intensity of the attack on the media, which, indeed, was an attack on the citizens' right to information. This could be made public only through a comprehensive, well-researched and authoritative report. Therefore, I quickly appointed a special committee, headed by a former Secretary in my ministry, to prepare it. The committee completed its job in record time and I could table the White Paper in Parliament in August 1977. The facts and figures that it revealed were shocking.

As many as 253 journalists were arrested during the Emergency. Of these, 110 were arrested under MISA, 110 under DIR and thirty-three under other laws. Entry into India was banned for twenty-nine foreign journalists, which included Mark Tully, the highly popular BBC correspondent. The government disaccredited fifty-one foreign journalists, and expelled seven of them.

Every newspaper and news agency had a censor, a government officer, sitting in its premises. With a red pencil in hand, he would go through every report, editorial and special articles. Sometimes, even advertisements were scrutinised for any hidden message. Most censors were incompetent to do the job at hand and hence, used the red pencil indiscriminately. Their inflated sense of authority and inborn insecurity made them despise the editors. Scared of allowing anything that might incur the wrath of their bosses, they played safe by simply cutting and slashing whatever seemed 'politically incorrect' and insidious to them.

Soon after imposing the Emergency and clamping press censorship, Indira Gandhi had effected a crucial replacement in the I&B Ministry. Inder Kumar Gujral, the incumbent Minister (who was later to become India's Prime Minister in 1997) was, according to her, too mild-mannered and diplomatic for a job that required ruthlessness in the new circumstances. Hence, she brought in her trusted lieutenant Vidya Charan Shukla. He started a systematic campaign to emasculate India's famously independent press. Even after the imposition of the Emergency, the press continued to have access to a small window of freedom in reporting debates in Parliament. This was, paradoxically, due to a law that had been passed at the initiative of Feroze Gandhi*, Indira Gandhi's deceased husband

---

* Feroze Gandhi (1912–60), a Parsi who was married to Indira Gandhi in 1942, was a Congress Lok Sabha MP, having been elected in 1952 and 1957. In Parliament, he often criticised his father-in-law's government. He is best remembered for having started a campaign against corruption involving, most prominently, the then Finance Minister, T.T. Krishnamachari, who was forced to resign.

and a well-known Congress MP. The law gave reporters of parliamentary proceedings immunity from any action for defamation. Shukla, at the behest of the then Prime Minister, had it repealed towards the end of 1975.

With the help of pro-government owners and editors of newspapers—and there was no dearth of such people—Shukla had a new 'code of conduct' prepared and foisted upon the press. This evoked a caustic response from V.K. Narasimhan, Chief Editor of the *Indian Express*, one of the most courageous journalistic voices against the Emergency. 'Is it an accident,' wrote Narasimhan in his weekly column, 'that nowhere in the code of conduct does the word "freedom" appear?' The *Indian Express*, owned by the irrepressible Ramnath Goenka, stood its ground firmly during the Emergency. Its open anti-government stance from pre-Emergency days continued unabated, the government resorting to every form of harassment to make Goenka fall in line. Using a pro-Congress industrialist who owned a rival newspaper, it even tried to oust him from the ownership of the *Indian Express*. All this had no effect on the doughty Goenka, who remained steadfast in his support of Jayaprakash Narayan and his pro-democracy movement.

Among others who held aloft the torch of press freedom during the Emergency were some eminent personalities: B.G. Verghese, whose sacking from the editorship of the *Hindustan Times* in February 1975 I had raised in the Rajya Sabha; C.R. Irani, Editor of the *Statesman*; Chunibhai Vaidya, Editor of *Bhumi Putra*, a Sarvodaya journal in Gujarati; my friend and colleague K.R. Malkani, Editor of the *Organiser* and *Motherland*; and editors of several non-English publications inspired by the RSS. I especially recall a witty article in *Mainstream* written by C.L.R. Shastri. Titled 'On Saying No', it bemoaned the proliferation of yes-men in the country and put in a powerful plea for no-men. 'One does not come across many articles of this kind nowadays', Shastri wrote. 'Both the author and the publisher have to have the guts for such writings. Freedom of expression is the first of the celebrated four freedoms, and one ought in my considered opinion to be appreciated as much for saying "no" as for saying "yes". I should like to go further and affirm that one ought to be appreciated more for saying "no" than for saying "yes". To me, "no" is as musical as Apollo's lute.'

And how can I forget *Shankar's Weekly*, founded by late Kesava Shankara Pillai, the high priest of political caricatures and cartoons? The hugely popular journal parodied all, but none complained since Shankar pursued his art in good taste and without malice. Pandit Nehru once said to him at a public function, 'Don't spare me, Shankar. Hit, hit me hard.' But Shankar was not spared by the Emergency's censors. I wrote in my prison diary on 31 August 1975: 'Today is a sad day for Indian journalism. *Shankar's Weekly*, the only cartoon weekly in the country, has decided to wind up. The last issue carries an editorial captioned 'Farewell'. The word Emergency does not even find a place in the editorial. But there can scarcely be a more devastating indictment of the Emergency than this piece. Shankar writes: "In our first editorial we had made the point that our function was to make our readers laugh—at the world, at pompous leaders, at humbug, at foibles, at ourselves. But only those people have a developed sense of humour who have certain civilized norms of behaviour, where there is tolerance and a dash of compassion. Dictatorships cannot afford laughter because people may laugh at the dictator, and that wouldn't do. In all the years of Hitler, there never was a good comedy, not a good cartoon, not a parody not a spoof".'

As a subscriber to *Seminar*, a reputed monthly journal devoted to serious intellectual debate, I received a letter, while in jail, on 23 July 1976. Its editor Romesh Thapar had written: 'It is not going to be possible to print any more issues of *Seminar*. On the morning of 16 July a precensorship order was imposed on our journal. This means that the censors claim the right to alter by deletion the analysis and opinion of the intellectuals and academicians who have been contributing to the pages of *Seminar* for the past 17 years. Obviously, a responsible journal like ours devoted to thoughtful debate cannot surrender the right of free expression in this way.'

It is intrepid journalists and intellectuals like these who tried, at great risk to themselves, to keep the torch of press freedom burning during the Emergency. But, alas, their number—especially the number of courageous media proprietors—was quite small in an atmosphere of ubiquitous acquiescence.

'ASKED TO BEND, MANY OF YOU SHOWED A WILLINGNESS TO CRAWL.'

In my early days as I&B Minister, I convened a meeting of Editors, Bureau Chiefs and Senior Correspondents belonging to various media organisations at the Indian & Eastern Newspapers Society (IENS) building in New Delhi. I asked them to freely share their experiences during the Emergency. There was a flood of grievances and complaints about how they were harassed and pressurised into toeing the government line. After listening to them, I observed—and it's an observation that I would subsequently repeat several times elsewhere:

> Three sections of society were directly affected by the Emergency. These were—political activists, journalists and the legal fraternity. My greatest expectations were from the political activists belonging to opposition parties. Although I am satisfied with the resistance put up by my own ideological Parivar, on the whole the record of the opposition was disappointing. We ought to have put up a more spirited and combative resistance. As far as pressmen are concerned, you are professionals. For political activists, politics is a mission. However, this cannot be applied to journalists. What was expected of you was professional integrity. But I am saddened by the fact that, whereas the government wanted you only to bend, many of you showed a willingness to crawl.

I also said that, of the three categories affected by the Emergency, the third category, of legal professionals, acquitted itself the best. More than the lawyers, it was a courageous section of the judiciary that emerged from the trauma in a manner that the country felt proud. At the same meeting I said that even during the British Raj, no lawyer had been incarcerated because he was defending someone waging a struggle against the government. This did not happen even in the case of a revolutionary like Sardar Bhagat Singh, who was given a death sentence. But during the Emergency, Rama Jois, our counsel in Bangalore, was arrested under MISA. His crime? He was fighting our case. 'The press in India,' I said, 'should be a watchdog, an educator and a social reformer, all rolled into one.' I later elaborated on it in the 'Declaration of the Press Freedom in India', a report I formally released in November 1977.

DISMANTLING THE EMERGENCY'S LEGAL EDIFICE

I was determined to make a clean break from the Emergency's unsavoury legacy as far as its effects on the Indian media were concerned. Morarji Desai supported me fully on this. In his maiden press conference as Prime Minister, he told the press to be fearless—without even waiting for the formal lifting of censorship. As I&B Minister, my principal mandate was to ensure that all the restrictions and controls on press freedom imposed during the Emergency were removed. For this, I took three important initiatives. Firstly, all the directives issued for press censorship were immediately withdrawn. There was, for instance, some ludicrous injunction against publishing the names and number of people in prison. All such prohibitions were lifted. At the same time, several laws also had to be amended. Within a fortnight of the formation of the new government, I tabled two bills in the Lok Sabha. One sought to repeal the Prevention of Publication of Objectionable Matter Act. The other was aimed at restoring the Parliamentary Proceedings (Protection of Publication) Act, popularly known as the Feroze Gandhi Act. The two bills were passed with great enthusiasm.

Getting the draconian laws of the Emergency period repealed was not difficult in the Lok Sabha, where the Janata Party and its allies had a massive majority—364 seats. But in the Rajya Sabha, the Janata Party had a strength of only twenty-six. Even with our allies, we had only thirty-six MPs. When Morarjibhai made me the Leader of the House in the Rajya Sabha, there was a fair amount of trepidation in my mind as to how I would have the necessary bills passed to annul the anti-democratic provisions. However, to my own surprise, I faced little resistance in my task. Whether it was because of the total demoralisation in the Congress camp after the debacle in the election or whether, barring the party leadership, the entire Congress rank and file felt a sense of guilt and repentance, we never had any problems in undoing all the legislative excesses committed during the Emergency period, including the highly objectionable 42nd Constitutional Amendment.

PROTECTING THE CONSTITUTION BY UNDOING THE 42ND AMENDMENT

The 42nd Amendment, 1976, was the most controversial of all the Constitutional amendments introduced during the Emergency. In its scope and importance, it was almost like changing the basic structure of the Constitution. Almost all parts of the Constitution, including the Preamble, saw changes through this amendment. One of the major achievements of the Janata government was the restoration of the sanctity and supremacy of the Constitution through the enactment of the 44th Amendment Bill, 1978, moved by Law Minister Shanti Bhushan, a legal luminary who had boldly opposed the Emergency. The most significant change that this amendment brought about was to take away the power of the Executive to impose Emergency by citing internal disturbances. In its statement of objects and reasons, the Bill affirmed: 'A Proclamation of Emergency under article 352 has virtually the effect of amending the Constitution by converting it for the duration into that of a Unitary State and enabling the rights of the citizen to move the courts for the enforcement of fundamental rights—including the right to life and liberty—to be suspended. Adequate safeguards are, therefore, necessary to ensure that this power is properly exercised and is not abused. It is, therefore, proposed that a Proclamation of Emergency can be issued only when the security of India or any part of its territory is threatened by war or external aggression or by armed rebellion. Internal disturbance not amounting to armed rebellion would not be a ground for the issue of a Proclamation.'

In order to prevent repetition of the arbitrary and acquiescent manner in which President Fakhruddin Ali Ahmed had obliged Prime Minister Indira Gandhi by signing the Emergency Proclamation without even asking for a formal resolution of the Cabinet, the Bill also stated: '... an Emergency can be proclaimed only on the basis of written advice tendered to the President by the Cabinet. In addition, as a Proclamation of Emergency virtually has the effect of amending the Constitution, it is being provided that the Proclamation would have to be approved by the two Houses of Parliament by the same majority which is necessary to amend the Constitution and such approval would have to be given within a period of one month. Any such Proclamation would be in force only for a period of six months and can be continued only by further resolutions passed by the same majority. The Proclamation would also cease to be in operation if a resolution disapproving the continuance of the Proclamation is passed by the Lok Sabha. Ten per cent or more of the Members of the Lok Sabha can requisition a special meeting for considering a resolution for disapproving the Proclamation.'

By any reckoning, these were the most effective Constitutional safeguards for the protection of democracy.

In the case of ordinary legislation, a failure to have it passed in the Rajya Sabha can be overcome by getting it passed in a joint session of both Houses of Parliament. However, in the case of a Constitution Amendment, the two Houses have to pass the bills separately proposed by the government—and that too by a special majority. In spite of our meager presence in the Rajya Sabha, we managed to dismantle the entire authoritarian legal edifice erected during the Emergency period. This was truly a great achievement of the Janata Party government.

At that time, the Leader of the Opposition in the Lok Sabha was Yashwantrao Chavan and his counterpart in the Rajya Sabha was Kamalapati Tripathi, a veteran Congress leader. Whenever I used to go to Kamalapatiji with an anti-Emergency legislative proposal, he would simply wave his hand and say, '*Arre bhai, aap ko jo karna hai karo. Humein koyi aapatti nahin hai.*' (Do what you want. We have no problem).

I also wanted to demonstrate that AIR and Doordarshan were no longer the instruments of propaganda for the government or the ruling party. Thus, a day after the new Prime Minister's customary address to the nation, I invited the Leader of the Opposition in the Lok Sabha to broadcast his views to the nation on AIR and Doordarshan. To establish the credibility of these organisations, I sent out a directive that their editors and producers were free to function without any interference from the government, the only condition being that their programmes should be unbiased, unprejudiced and balanced. For the first time, all national and state-level political parties were allowed to broadcast their appeals as part of their election campaigns, with equal time given to all of them. I may mention here, that I specifically asked AIR and Doordarshan not to project me, as the Minister, in their news bulletins and programmes.

I also initiated a serious debate, both within and outside Parliament, on the need for institutional autonomy to AIR and Doordarshan. A working group under the chairmanship of B.G. Verghese was set up for this purpose. The concept of Prasar Bharati, an autonomous corporation to run the two media organisations, was a recommendation of this committee. I introduced the Prasar Bharati (Broadcasting Corporation of India) Bill in Parliament in 1977. It could not be passed in the Rajya Sabha, since the Congress, which had a majority in the House, was not in favour of it.

During my tenure, I reversed all the draconian decisions of the previous government that were meant to harass the press. Thus, justice was done to all those newspapers whose newsprint quota and government advertisements had been reduced and to journalists whose accreditation had been cancelled. Housing facilities to accredited journalists were restored. Many dailies, weeklies and monthlies had ceased publication during the Emergency. I instructed officials in the ministry to look into each case and set things right. In my interactions with media professionals, I emphasised that freedom of press did not mean freedom of the proprietor but that of the editor and other journalists.

One of the arbitrary steps of the previous government was the amalgamation of four autonomous news agencies—PTI, UNI, Hindusthan Samachar and Samachar Bharati—into a single entity called 'Samachar'. This had created a certain amount of resentment both among journalists working in these agencies and also in the newspapers that subscribed to it. I had appointed a committee, under the chairmanship of Kuldip Nayar, to examine the future of 'Samachar'. Following its recommendation, I announced the revival of the four independent news agencies. The entire process was transparent, with minimal government intervention and full participation of the media fraternity. Naturally, the final decision was widely welcomed by all.

As a part of this corrective exercise, my ministry reconstituted the Press Council of India, which had been scrapped during the Emergency. Far from filling it with cronies of the ruling party, I nominated to the Press Council, members who were known for their professional eminence and independence. I should mention here that some people belonging to my own party questioned my choice of Nikhil Chakravartty. 'How can you nominate him on the Press Council. Isn't he a leftist?' I said, 'His being a leftist is neither a point of qualification nor disqualification as far as I am concerned. I respect him as a journalist, and especially because he showed the courage to raise his voice against the Emergency.'

An interesting incident took place when I took charge of the I&B Ministry. Soon after Morarji Desai became the Prime Minister, he carried out a thorough reshuffle of almost all Secretaries in the Central Government after speaking to the Ministers concerned. This was done on the well-grounded appraisal that many of the bureaucrats had, wittingly or unwittingly, allowed themselves to be misused by the Emergency regime. The Secretary in the Ministry of I&B happened to be a Muslim officer named Burney. One day, Nirmal Mukherjee, an upright civil servant who was appointed as the new Cabinet Secretary, said to me, 'The Prime Minister has asked me to know from you if you would like the Secretary in your ministry replaced.' I said, 'Why?'

He said, 'The Prime Minister thinks that you are hesitant only because he is a Muslim!' Mukherjee replied.

It is true that Burney happened to be the only Muslim Secretary in the Government of India at that point of time. However, I told Mukherjee, 'Why should I want him out of my ministry just because he is a Muslim? I have no knowledge that he acted in a partisan manner during the Emergency. Of course, it would be a different matter if some concrete information came to me showing his professional bias in the past two years.' The matter rested at that.

A few weeks later, K.K. Das, whom I had appointed as head of the committee to prepare a White Paper on the misuse of the mass media during the Emergency, came to me with a thick file. 'Sir, this contains information about how the Secretary in your ministry conducted himself in the recent past.' I was startled to find how the Secretary had written poem after poem in praise of Indira Gandhi and how he gave instructions to people in the ministry to fully cooperate with the government's propaganda campaign during the Emergency. I immediately contacted the Cabinet Secretary and asked him to suggest a replacement for Burney.

MY ASSOCIATION WITH THE FILM WORLD

Although the film industry in India has always been independent, the I&B Ministry does have a significant interface with it as the Censor Board, which gives approvals for the public screening of all movies, works under the ministry. The Emergency regime had tried to run roughshod with this industry, too. There was the infamous case about the Hindi film *Kissa Kursi Ka* (Tale of the Throne), about a corrupt and evil politician, which was banned by the previous government. All its prints were confiscated. Being a connoisseur of films, and also having been a movie critic during my *Organiser* years in the 1960s, I took keen interest in knowing about the problems, needs and aspirations of the film fraternity.

In August 1977, I placed before representatives of the film industry, a liberal policy framework to reduce the government's legal powers to hear appeal or revision against the decisions of the Censor Board. I emphasised the need for greater self-regulation by the industry, as against regulation by any external body, to curb violence and obscenity in films. Responding to the demand of the industry, I lifted the blanket ban on shooting abroad that had been imposed during the Emergency. The rule regarding re-certification of ten-year-old films was also abolished.

During one of my visits to Bombay, I convened a meeting of prominent film directors, producers and artistes. Among other things, I appealed to them to make movies based on our great epics *Ramayana* and *Mahabharata*. 'I have been an avid film-goer since my childhood,' I said to them. 'I have observed that the best Hollywood films on biblical themes were made by the most outstanding directors such as Cecil B. DeMille, who directed the hugely successful movie *The Ten Commandments*. The cast of these films included top-notch Hollywood stars.' I also told them that we have an inexhaustible reservoir of themes from our epics and other ancient works with contemporary relevance. 'Nevertheless, the films made on these have been quite ordinary so far. We don't seem to realise how great an appeal these stories have on the Indian mind. Therefore, good films made on these themes will not only be artistically rewarding, but also commercially successful.'

The truth of what I said then was vindicated with the arrival of cable TV in India in the early 1990s. Ramanand Sagar's TV serial *Ramayana* was a trailblazer, a cultural phenomenon unprecedented in modern times. The entire country would virtually come to a standstill every Sunday morning when the serial was telecast on Doordarshan. The only objection came from some leftist intellectuals who questioned the government as to why the *Ramayana*, a 'Hindu religious text', was being serialised on national television.

I had an amusing encounter with the mass popularity of this serial once when I was travelling by a night train from Bhopal to Delhi. The train, which was scheduled to arrive at 7 am, was running one hour late. I asked an attendant, '*Aur der hogi?*' (Will there any further delay?). The attendant's reply was: '*Chinta mat keejiye. Driver ko bhi Ramayana dekhana hai. Is liye zaroor jaldi pahunchaayega.*' (Don't worry. The driver also wants to watch *Ramayana*. Therefore, he'll certainly take the train to Delhi soon.)

I cherish the acquaintances I made during this period with many distinguished film personalities. Amongst them were Raj Kapoor, Dev Anand, Manoj Kumar, Mala Sinha, music composer Jaidev and singer Penaz Masani. I especially treasure my meeting with the legendary moviemaker Satyajit Ray, whose realistic and deeply sensitive Bengali films, had already earned international renown. I had seen nearly all his films and admired his work greatly. My first introduction to his cinema is an interesting anecdote in itself. In 1956 or 1957, I had gone to Calcutta to participate in a meeting of the Bharatiya Jana Sangh, in which all the senior leaders of the party were also present. On the last day of the meeting, the local organisers offered to take the leaders to watch a Bengali film, *Pather Panchali*, Ray's debut film, which had been just been released. Most of my colleagues said, 'Arre bhai, hum to Bengali nahin samajhenge.' (We won't understand Bengali). Nevertheless, they were persuaded to come. I too didn't know any Bengali then, but when we came out of the movie theatre after the movie screening, I exclaimed, moved by the film's universal humanist appeal, 'This is going to be rated as one of the greatest movies ever made.' I was pleased when it went on to win numerous national and international awards. (In 2005, it was included in *Time* magazine's All-Time 100 Movies list).

I later thought to myself that I did, after all, understand a little bit about good cinema. This was one of the reasons why I had volunteered to work as a cinema critic with *Organiser*. I recounted this incident to Ray when, as the I&B Minister, I organised a special screening of *Pather Panchali* in Delhi.

MEMORABLE VISITS ABROAD

My first visit abroad as the I&B Minister was to Moscow in 1977 to attend the Moscow Film Festival. At that time, I.K. Gujral was our Ambassador in the Soviet Union. Both during the Emergency and in the years preceding it, the communist rulers in Moscow had been strong supporters of the Congress party and bitter critics of Jayaprakash Narayan and all those who were backing him. Indeed, Moscow, in what was a blatant interference in India's internal affairs, had even dubbed JP's movement as 'fascist'. During the briefing prior to my official meetings, Gujral told me that the victory of the Janata Party and the trouncing of the Congress had come as a great shock to the rulers in USSR. He was right. In all my meetings with the officials in Moscow, I could sense that they were apologetic and highly eager to make up.

In 1978, I visited communist-ruled East Germany.* It was then known as the German Democratic Republic. After travelling to several parts of the

---

* I should recount here an interesting episode from my earlier visit, as a member of a parliamentary delegation in 1970, to another communist-ruled country which was a part of the Soviet bloc—Czechoslovakia. In 1968, the Soviet Union had invaded it

Contd...

country, I came to my last halt—Berlin. I remember watching a Sanskrit play that was going on in the city. An interesting episode occurred just before my departure. I asked our Ambassador in Berlin whether he could arrange a visit to Frankfurt and thereon to Delhi by an Air India flight.

The Ambassador said, 'I can do that, but your hosts will not like it. Instead, I suggest that you go from here to London or Amsterdam and catch the Air India flight from there.' Thus, I returned from Berlin to India via Holland.

I have recounted this episode many times in later years just to illustrate how countries that are very bitter towards each other can still overcome their past and usher in a new chapter in their history, as in the case of the two Germanys. I visited re-unified Germany in 2000, as Home Minister in the NDA government. The Berlin Wall had already become history. And this time, I visited both Berlin and Frankfurt—and several other places—at the same time.

My first trip to Karachi after Partition was when I visited Pakistan in November 1978. I was on my way back from Paris, where I had gone to attend a UNESCO conference. It was a short trip, just two days, because

---

Contd...

to halt democratic reforms ('Prague Spring') initiated by reformist leader Alexander Dubcek. In spite of heavy propaganda that everything was hunky dory after the Soviet invasion, I could feel that the people were angry and sullen. One of the interpreters assigned to assist our delegation, who spoke good Hindi, approached me when I was alone and said, 'Are you from the Jana Sangh?' I said yes. 'I want to talk to you, but cannot do so in the hotel. You please tell my boss that you want to do some shopping and need a Hindi-speaking interpreter. He will naturally ask me to accompany you.' I did as he had told me. Once we reached the market, he said, 'I wanted to speak to you because yours is the only party in India that condemned the Soviet invasion of our country. I am proud of India because it is a democracy. I would like you to know, and make the people of India aware, that the situation is far from normal in Czechoslovakia. There is intense resentment, but there is also fear because of the presence of Soviet tanks.' I asked him, 'Why didn't the mass resistance to foreign occupation continue?' His reply was insightful. 'Czechoslovakia is the only country in the Soviet bloc which has attained a level of prosperity somewhat comparable to what is seen in Western Europe. With prosperity has come comfort, which has weakened the revolutionary spirit of our people.'

the Parliament session was about to commence and I had to return to Delhi soon. Oddly, it was cricket that took me to Karachi. For the first time, Doordarshan was covering an Indo-Pak Test match and I was invited in my capacity as India's I&B Minister. I was naturally overjoyed. I wanted only two things from the visit: an opportunity to visit my house and my school. It was really a delightful surprise to find Father Modestine, who was the principal of St. Patrick's High School when I used to study there, and who had long since retired, personally present at the school gate to receive me. Incidentally, it was in Karachi in 1978 that I first met M.J. Akbar, an erudite Editor and author, whose friendship I have cherished since then. He was working for *Sunday* magazine those days and I recall that he covered my 'homecoming' in his report on the cricket match.

It was also in Karachi that I met General Zia-ul-Haq, the military ruler of Pakistan who, just two months earlier, had deposed Prime Minister Zulfikar Ali Bhutto and sent him to prison. Within a few months, Bhutto was hanged. General Zia was present at the cricket match the entire day. As we were sitting next to each other, he exchanged pleasantries with me. He was effusive in his welcome, but I could feel that there was something artificial in his cordiality.

My maiden ministerial experience was rather brief, slightly over two years. But the satisfaction I derived from it was immense.

3

THE PEOPLE BETRAYED
The Fall of The Janata Government;
Return of Indira Gandhi

God defend me from my friends; from my enemies I can defend myself.

—A PROVERB

The Janata Party, when it was formed in January 1977 at the insistence of Jayaprakash Narayan, was the embodiment of the hopes and aspirations of all the democracy-loving people in India. JP was perceived by many in the country as the 'Second Mahatma' leading India's 'Second Freedom Struggle'. The coming together of four major Opposition parties gave people the confidence that they could use the parliamentary elections to defeat the Emergency regime. The victory of the Janata Party proved to the entire world that dictatorship can indeed be brought to an end through democratic and peaceful means.

Sadly, the Janata government's glory was shortlived. Internecine squabbles within the party soon brought about its early demise, before it could complete even half its term. Morarji Desai resigned as Prime

Minister on 15 July 1979. Charan Singh, his Deputy, was sworn in as Prime Minister with the support of Indira Gandhi, the very person against whom the people had delivered a decisive verdict in March 1977. Indira Gandhi, however, was no friend of Charan Singh. She used him to wreck the Janata Party and then quickly wrecked his government by withdrawing support to it in less than six months. Thus, one betrayal followed another in quick succession.

The country then witnessed another unfortunate development. After Charan Singh's resignation, the Janata Party decided to lay claim to forming the next government under the leadership of Jagjivan Ram. However, Neelam Sanjiva Reddy, the then President of India, overlooked Jagjivan Ram's legitimate right of being invited to form the government and dissolved the Lok Sabha on 22 August 1979. Mid-term elections were thus forced upon the country in January 1980. The electorate, disillusioned by the power struggle and the split in the Janata Party, voted Indira Gandhi back to power.

Rarely in history does a government get the kind of opportunity, and enjoy the amount of goodwill, which the Janata government did. Equally rare is the instance in history when such a government squanders the opportunity and betrays people's hopes in as reckless a manner. Thus, if the birth of the Janata government was a lesson in defending democracy, its demise was a harsh reminder about the propensity of power-hungry leaders to undo the gains of a popular democratic movement.

My book *The People Betrayed* (Vision Books, 1980) describes in considerable detail the ecstasy and agony associated with the rise and fall of the Janata government. Since it was written immediately after the destabilisation of Morarjibhai's government, and before the 1980 parliamentary elections, the book analysed the events almost as they happened. When I look back at the same events in hindsight, I find that the main conclusions I had drawn then are relevant even today. Therefore, what follows is a recapitulation of that climactic period with additional analytical observations necessitated by the passage of time.

Dangerous Corner: A British play that mirrored Indian politics

All of us wonder, at some time or the other in our lives, as to what might have happened if things had been done differently, especially when events take a turn quite contrary to one's expectations. The formation and subsequent fall of the Janata Party government was one such uncanny development that prompted many of us to ask ourselves that question.

As this question agitated my mind, I recalled a remarkable play titled *Dangerous Corner*, which I had seen some years ago at the Fine Arts Theater in New Delhi. It was written by Britain's celebrated playwright J.B. Priestley (1894-1984). Since his plays always speak for the right in its struggle against the wrong, they sustained the morale of the British people through the worst months of the Second World War. *Dangerous Corner* has an ingenious suspense story. It opens with a lively dinner party attended by friends and colleagues, where all is well until a can of worms is suddenly jerked open by an innocuous remark. In the very first act of the play, one of the characters identifies a cigarette case in possession of another as belonging to a third person. The second person refutes the first's assertion. The argument becomes acrimonious, one lie leads to another, one scandalous exposure to another, and the story moves on at a frenetic pace to a nerve-shattering climax. In the end, all the characters in the play lie exposed as a bunch of mean, scheming and selfish individuals.

Having achieved this exposure, Priestley takes us back to the party in Act 1. The play starts all over again, but with a twist. The first character recognises the cigarette box as belonging to the third, but when the second questions the first's assertion, the latter quietly accepts the statement. The party moves on smoothly, with no repetition of the rumpus witnessed earlier and the respectable exterior of all the characters is primly preserved. Priestley describes the first character's earlier decision to join argument with the second as that 'dangerous corner' which affected the lives of all the characters in the play.

I have always wondered as to what exactly was the 'dangerous corner' where the Janata government took a wrong turning. What, for example, would have happened if in June-July 1978, when Charan Singh and Raj Narain were dropped from Morarji Desai's government, Atalji and I had unreservedly backed the decision, instead of trying—successfully as it turned out—to get Charan Singh back into the Cabinet? Whatever else may or may not have happened, the respectable exterior of many of our colleagues would surely have been preserved.

The pulling down of the Janata Party's government had all the ingredients of a suspense thriller. On 29 June 1978, Prime Minister Desai summoned an emergency meeting of the Cabinet at his residence. On agenda was a crucial question: the disciplinary action to be taken against Home Minister Chaudhary Charan Singh, who had issued an unusual press statement the previous evening, criticising the government for what he described as its 'failure to put the former Prime Minister (Indira Gandhi) behind the bars by now'. This 'failure', according to him, had made people conclude that 'we in the government are a pack of impotent people who cannot govern the country'. The press release stated:

> Many Emergency victims have come to me repeatedly and implored me that not only should Mrs. Gandhi be arrested immediately but that she should be kept in Chandigarh in the same circumstances in which Loknayak Jayaprakash Narayan was kept...I have no doubt that if we in the Government could only persuade ourselves to accept and implement this suggestion, there would be hundreds of mothers of Emergency victims who would celebrate the occasion as befittingly as another Diwali. Of course, in another country, she would have by now been facing a trial on the lines of the historic Nuremberg trial.

Not long after this outburst, Charan Singh colluded with Indira Gandhi to cause the downfall of the Desai government. On 28 July 1979, he fulfilled his life's ambition of becoming the Prime Minister with the help of the very same person for whose non-arrest he had publicly upbraided Morarji Desai. The supreme irony was that the failure for which Charan Singh had indicted Morarjibhai's government was, indeed, his own. As the Home Minister in that government, he had never brought any proposal before the

Cabinet about Indira Gandhi's arrest for her government's excesses during the Emergency. It is another matter that, the Cabinet, in my opinion, would not have given its consent to this proposal. Not only Jayaprakashji but also most of us in the government were clear in our minds that political revenge was not the path that we should follow. For her wrongdoings, Indira Gandhi had already been salutarily punished by the people.

Indeed, Charan Singh had invited ridicule upon himself and the government by trying to arrest her in October 1977 on a charge of receiving some jeeps from an industrial house for use in the parliamentary elections held earlier that year. This had seemed an act of personal vendetta. Charan Singh's ill-advised and unilateral action was just the kind of faux pas that Indira Gandhi needed to begin her own political resurrection.

Charan Singh had few to support him within his own Lak Dal faction of the Janata Party after he badmouthed Prime Minister Desai and his own other colleagues in the Cabinet as 'a pack of impotent people'. When Morarjibhai called a Cabinet meeting to gauge the reaction to the Home Minister's outburst, all of us were unanimous in expressing our shock and outrage. We authorised the Prime Minister to take whatever action he deemed fit against his deputy. The other Minister, a follower of Charan Singh, against whom action was recommended was Raj Narain. Desai asked the two errant Ministers to submit their resignations. The matter ought to have been left at that. But that was the point, the 'dangerous corner', when Atalji and I took a wrong turning. Our emotional attachment to the fledgling party's unity got the better of our political judgement. We decided to bring about a rapprochement between Charan Singh and the Prime Minister by ensuring the former's re-induction into the government. The re-induction wrecked the party.

THE KANTI DESAI CONTROVERSY PROVES COSTLY

There was a visible difference between the commitment and style of functioning of the Prime Minister and his deputy. Morarjibhai was totally focused on the issues of governance and, despite his age—he was eighty-three when he became the Prime Minister—he spent long hours paying keen attention to important aspects of every ministry. Charan Singh, on the other hand, was busy stoking disaffection against Morarjibhai. One could see that he was sniffing around for issues to embarrass the Prime Minister and create trouble for the government. He would often issue press statements criticising the government or write letters to the Prime Minister and leak them to the media. Once, in April 1978, he had suffered a heart attack and was admitted to AIIMS. Morarjibhai was to leave on an official tour of the United States that day. He called on his colleague at the hospital and spent some time with him. That very evening Charan Singh issued a press statement criticising the government's economic policies. He complained that, like the Congress regime earlier, the new government too had neglected agriculture and 'surrendered' itself to the 'heavy industry first' policy.

The attack was aimed as much at the Prime Minister as it was at Industries Minister George Fernandes and Finance Minister H.M. Patel. There was no doubt that Charan Singh cared deeply for the growth of the agriculture sector. In this, the Jana Sangh members were with him. However, we were all upset at his public criticism of his own government as it was not only against the principle of collective responsibility of the Cabinet, but was also tailor-made to boost the morale of the discredited Congress party.

However, the issue that brought much disrepute to our government was the controversy surrounding the alleged charges of corruption against Kanti Desai, the only son of Prime Minister Desai. Here too, Charan Singh played a negative role. He demanded the setting up of a commission of inquiry to probe the allegations. According to me, the charges were not of a very serious nature, and certainly not deserving a commission of inquiry. The truth was that Kanti Desai, who had been staying with his father at the Prime Ministerial residence, was the proxy target of his father's political opponents. Unfortunately, he made things difficult for his father by not showing the circumspection and political aloofness that his position demanded.

The demand for a probe created a furore in political circles, with Charan Singh launching an epistolary battle against the Prime Minister.

Between 11 and 29 March 1978, the Prime Minister and he exchanged six letters on the matter. Morarjibhai duly replied to all the points raised by the Home Minister, but the fact that the top leaders of the government were thus engaged in a war of letters did grave damage to its credibility, as also to the prestige of the Prime Minister.

As the controversy over Kanti Desai was raging, circumstances dragged me into it in a manner that pained me deeply. Since a senior Minister himself was lending credence to the allegations against the Prime Minister's son, the Congress party started to fish in troubled waters to disturb the steady waters of the popularly elected government. The platform which the Congress used for this purpose was the Rajya Sabha, where the party had a majority. The Congress subsequently paralysed the functioning of the House by raising the Kanti Desai issue in a high-pitched manner. I was leader of the House in the Rajya Sabha, and, in that capacity, had to defend the government during the debate on the issue. The Congress party demanded that the letters exchanged between the Prime Minister and his deputy in the Kanti Desai issue be laid on the Table of the House. I felt that the government's response to this should be credible and political, and not just technical.

Morarjibhai was technically right that it would be improper, and against precedent, to lay on the Table of the House confidential letters exchanged between two Ministers. However, I felt that since Charan Singh's letters were politically motivated and had not been written in confidence—after all, they had been leaked to the press—laying them in Parliament, along with the replies given by the Prime Minister would take the wind out of the Opposition's sails. After considerable persuasion, the Prime Minister offered to refer to the Chief Justice of India any written complaint made by a MP in the Kanti Desai matter. This, however, did not satisfy the Congress and other opposition members, who continued to stall the proceedings of the Rajya Sabha.

In order to break the deadlock, I discussed the issue with all the Opposition parties in the House. I found that, although the Congress was bent on keeping the issue alive, others, including the communists, were willing to dissociate themselves from the Congress stand if, instead of insisting on a written complaint from any MP, the government could agree to *suo motu* refer the debate in the House to the Chief Justice of India. A representative group of the Janata Party members from the Rajya Sabha met the Prime Minister and tried to convince him that this would provide a reasonable solution to the tangle. Morarjibhai, however, remained unmoved. This disappointed me. As the Leader of the House, I was unable to persuade the Prime Minister to agree to what many members regarded as reasonable. It is in this context that I thought it proper and necessary to resign from the government. However, the Cabinet intervened and set up a sub-committee to recommend a course of action. This sub-committee endorsed the very step that I had earlier suggested. Accordingly, I withdrew my resignation.

'YOU ARE FROM SINDH, YOU JUST CANNOT UNDERSTAND CASTE.'

It was through my interactions with Charan Singh that I understood the important role caste identity plays in Indian politics. One day, shortly after his expulsion from the Cabinet over his diatribe against his own ministerial colleagues, I paid him a courtesy visit. He went into a long discourse about the political conspiracy against him because he was a Jat. 'You are from Sindh, you just cannot understand the caste motivations in this part of the country,' he told me. He was right, insofar as caste was an unimportant aspect of the Hindu society in Sindh. But what he said next made me realise the level of his bitterness. 'Chaudhary Charan Singh can be thrown out of the government, not Atal Bihari Vajpayee—only because he is a Brahmin and I am a Jat!' I tried telling him that his ouster had nothing to do with his caste, but he kept reminding me about my Sindhi background.

It is true that, because of my Sindhi background and the strong influence of the RSS ideologies, I have a natural disinclination towards the caste factor while thinking about political issues. However, over the years I have become increasingly aware of the criticality of caste and its role in promoting 'identity-based politics' in India.

In spite of his politically motivated machinations, I was always fascinated by Charan Singh's immense popularity in North India, especially among the farmers. In him they saw a leader who was their own, who voiced their concerns and aspirations, and who gave them a sense of empowerment. Looking back, I feel that he could have, if he had so wished, used this strength to impart enduring stability to the Janata Party.

During the Janata rule, even those who admired Charan Singh for his passionate espousal of farmers' interests felt that his image was being sullied by Raj Narain. His main lieutenant had unleashed a virulent tirade against Chandrashekhar, questioning his legitimacy to continue as the President of the Janata Party after one year of the formation of the party. He would also often attack Jagjivan Ram. These internal quarrels caused a deepening disillusionment among the workers and supporters of the Janata Party. Raj Narain was a model of what public behaviour should not be. The *Times of India* once called him 'The Indian Mephistopheles' (one of the seven devils in Greek mythology). Describing him editorially as the 'Vandal at Large', the *Indian Express* wrote: 'The damage that Raj Narain has done to the Lok Dal is not for us to worry about. What must worry all is that abuse of norms of political morality is allowed to go on unchallenged.'

As a rule, I had refrained from commenting publicly on these unhappy developments. However, once while addressing the media in Trivandrum in April 1978, I summed up my analysis of these squabbles as the continuing battle for Prime Ministership. After returning to Delhi, I once went to call on Charan Singh at his residence, as he was unwell. He referred to my Trivandrum statement and said, with an air of injured innocence, '*Aap to bahut sanjida hain, aap bhi aisa kehte hain?*' (You are extremely sober; you too are saying this?) And he went on, 'I do not want to become Prime Minister. Let Morarjibhai remain Prime Minister for his entire life.' This conversation took place towards the end of May 1979. In less than six weeks, he was to ascend the Prime Ministerial *gaddi* with Indira Gandhi's support.

PRESIDENT SANJIVA REDDY'S QUESTIONABLE ROLE

When Charan Singh was sworn in as India's sixth Prime Minister by President Neelam Sanjiva Reddy on 28 July, he had only sixty-four MPs with him—all defectors from the Janata Party—in the Lok Sabha. How unconditional was the outside support extended by the Congress party and its allies became clear when they, under instructions from Indira Gandhi, withdrew support a day before the Lok Sabha was due to meet for the first time after the formation of the new government. Charan Singh resigned and fresh elections were held in January 1980. In other words, during his six-month tenure as Prime Minister, he never faced the Lok Sabha even once!

The collapse of Morarji Desai's government, followed quickly by that of Charan Singh's, contributed immensely to the quick political resurrection of Indira Gandhi. Her victory in 1978 in a by-election to the Lok Sabha from Chikmagalur constituency in Karnataka had already put some life back into her despondent party. After the harakiri committed by the Janata Party, more and more people started believing that Indira Gandhi was on a comeback trail.

President Sanjiva Reddy played a highly controversial role in Indira Gandhi's return to power. After Charan Singh tendered his resignation on 20 August 1979, all Constitutional pundits were unanimous in their view that the President should have given another chance to the Janata Party to form a government. Notwithstanding the defections, it was still the single largest party in the Lok Sabha. Indeed, within a couple of hours of Charan Singh's resignation, Jagjivan Ram went to Rashtrapati Bhavan to inform Reddy that he was in a position to form a government and prove his majority in the House. However, Reddy shocked the entire nation by dissolving the Lok Sabha on 22 August. There were several questionable aspects to his decision. Firstly, the communiqué of the Rashtrapati Bhavan gave no reasons for the dissolution of the House. Secondly, after Morarji Desai's resignation on 15 July, Reddy had given Charan Singh thirteen days to explore the possibility of forming a government, which he did with the help of Indira Gandhi, whereas while examining Jagjivan Ram's claim, he did not even wait for two days before rejecting it and ordering the dissolution of the House. This, in spite of the fact that Jagjivan Ram already had the support of as many as 202 MPs of the Janata Party. Moreover, due to Atalji's initiative, M.G. Ramachandran of the All India

Anna Dravida Munnetra Kazagham (AIADMK) in Tamil Nadu, who had eighteen MPs in the Lok Sabha, had pledged support to Jagjivan Ram. There were also indications that the breakaway Congress, led by Yashwantrao Chavan, was willing to support a government led by Jagjivan Ram. Against this backdrop, Reddy's decision to dissolve the House gave rise to widespread suspicion that he had already made up his mind not to invite Jagjivan Ram to form a government.

I should recall here a significant conversation that took place between Reddy and Chandrashekhar, the Janata Party President. On 21 August, Chandrashekhar went to Rashtrapati Bhavan and conveyed that the Janata Party was in a position to form the government. Reddy's said sarcastically: 'How will you do it? By encouraging defections?' To which, Chandrashekhar retorted forthrightly: 'Having nominated a defector as Prime Minister, why should you object to defections?'

Reddy's conduct during this period lacked neutrality, transparency and honesty. One example should suffice to prove this. On 22 August, at around 10.15 am, Chandrashekhar came to my residence to discuss matters relating to government formation. He received a phone call from Jagjivan Ram that President Reddy had invited the two of them to meet him at 11 am. We presumed that it was in connection with our claim to form the government. The President received Jagjivan Ram and Chandrashekhar with unusual cordiality. He even made enquiries about the support that Jagjivan Ram had been able to mobilise to form a government. Chandrashekhar informed him that the Janata Party and its new allies would prove their majority in any way the President wanted—either on the floor of the House or by submitting a signed list of MPs. To this, the President replied that he was in no hurry.

From Rashtrapati Bhavan, Jagjivan Ram and Chandrashekhar headed for the Janata Party office in Parliament and apprised us of the discussion with President Reddy. All of us got busy finalising the list of MPs supporting our claim. We were confident that, by evening, we would comfortably garner the support of a clear majority of MPs, with a tally of 275-280, supporting Jagjivan Ram in the Lok Sabha.

However, shortly after noon, news arrived that the President had dissolved the House!

Clearly, Reddy had acted in a preemptive and malafide manner. In doing so, he had betrayed the faith installed in a person holding the country's highest Constitutional office. Worse still, he had violated a principle that he had himself articulated while he was the Speaker of the Lok Sabha (1967-69). In 1968, as Chairman of the Delhi Metropolitan Council, I had the privilege of participating in the All India Conference of Presiding Officers, convened by Reddy. One of the topics under discussion was the power of Governors to dissolve state legislatures wherein Reddy had said: 'In no circumstances should it be left to the Governor to determine whether a Chief Minister continues to enjoy the support of the majority of the members or not, even if the members make their opinion known to the Governor in writing. It is the prerogative of the Assembly to decide this issue.' However, as the President of India (1977-82), he would flout the same code when it came to determining whether or not Jagjivan Ram commanded majority support in the Lok Sabha. Reddy's partisan conduct angered us so much that Chandrashekhar even called for his impeachment.[1]

MORARJI DESAI—AN APPRAISAL

Of the three top leaders of the Janata Party that I worked closely with, Morarji Desai was head and shoulders above Charan Singh and Jagjivan Ram. He surpassed them in national stature and experience in governance. Although those who did not know him closely viewed him as a rather rigid and inflexible person, my experience with him was far from negative. I enjoyed a very cordial working relationship with Morarjibhai. On matters where his principles were not in conflict, he was open to reason and willing to listen to his colleagues' points of view. Of course, he would be uncompromising in what he believed was right. For instance, he was totally opposed to the Jana Sangh's demand for making India a nuclear weapons state. However, that did not prevent him from admiring the Jana Sangh for its patriotism, idealism and discipline. He fully supported

Atalji, who held the External Affairs portfolio, in his efforts to normalise relations with Pakistan and China.

I enjoyed a very cordial working relationship with Morarjibhai. I admired him for the strong core of conviction in his personality. I have always held that men of principles, even if one does not share all of them, are more worthy of admiration and respect than weathercocks. My respect for Morarjibhai stemmed primarily from his honesty, unimpeachable integrity and the courage with which he fought for democracy both before and during the Emergency. His three-volume memoirs, titled *The Story of My Life*, are an inspiring account of his long service to the nation. I would like to present to the readers the following two excerpts from the book:

> She (Indira Gandhi) laid down several conditions for lifting the Emergency. They included giving up the right of satyagraha. Whatever may be the view of others, I would prefer death to giving up these precious and inalienable human rights and duties. I would prefer life-long detention to becoming the Prime Minister in conditions such as the Emergency. I believe there will be hope for the nation's and society's future only so long as there are a few people still prepared to pay the extreme penalty to keep the torch of freedom burning. There is no future for a nation which suffers from fear. Material and physical comfort without human freedom is sufficient only for the well-fed domestic animals and birds. It is not so for men.*

Morarjibhai was a man of unshakable faith in God. What he wrote in his memoirs on this subject is indeed a useful guidance for one and all.

> My detention helped me to reinforce my faith in God. It is this faith which enables me to be at peace with myself in the midst of worldly storms... I lived introspectively. How could I improve myself? I asked myself that question constantly...I realized that

---

* Morarji Desai, *The Story of My Life*, Volume III, S. Chand & Company Ltd., 1979, pp. 130-131.

> worry does not help at all. On the contrary, it clouds judgement. It prevents one from helping others and therefore retards progress. By surrendering myself completely to God's will I transcended all mental anguish. I believe that everything happens according to God's law. His will is benevolent, not malevolent. One must accept all that happens as part of that. Whatever comes to one's life according to that law must be taken as His will; only then can one be at peace under all conditions.*

The only baggage that Morarjibhai carried was that he had a blind spot for his son. I once asked him why he continued to defend Kanti so untenably? The question brought tears to his eyes. I had heard distressing stories about the suicides that had earlier taken place in his family. I got a feeling during this interaction that he feared that firmness with his son might lead to yet another tragic consequence.

I continued to keep in regular touch with Morarjibhai even after the fall of the Janata government. He led a quiet, austere and dignified life at his sea-facing flat at Nariman Point in Mumbai, where he breathed his last on 10 April 1995. He was mentally alert right till the ripe age of ninety-nine, which was a testimony to the simple, disciplined and dedicated life he lived.

*

As the Janata Party was going through this self-created turmoil, many of us sorely missed the guiding presence of Jayaprakash Narayan. He was the greatest among the tens of thousands of pro-democracy activists who were arrested when the flame of democracy was extinguished by Indira Gandhi. In detention, his health suffered badly, but, inspite of his weak body and failing kidneys, he had continued his crusade and succeeded in giving the Emergency regime a befitting burial. Finally, this conscience-keeper of the nation breathed his last on 8 October 1979. Perhaps the most moving

---

* Morarji Desai, *The Story of My Life*, Volume III, S. Chand & Company Ltd., 1979, pp. 136-137.

tribute to him was paid by Atalji: 'JP was not merely the name of one person; it symbolized humanity. When one remembered him, two pictures came to one's mind. One was reminded of Bhishma Pitamaha lying on a bed of arrows. There was only one difference between Bhishma Pitamaha and JP; while the former fought for the Kauravas in the Mahabharata battle, the latter fought for justice. The second picture was one of Christ on the Cross and JP's life reminded one of Christ's sacrifices.'[2]

THE SUICIDAL 'DUAL MEMBERSHIP' CONTROVERSY

While the Janata Party's defeat in the 1980 parliamentary elections was predictable, the drubbing it received was severe. It showed that the angry electorate wanted to punish the party for its betrayal of the mandate of 1977. The party secured only 31 seats, compared to the 298 that it had won in 1977. In this, the Jana Sangh's own tally was a mere sixteen, compared to ninety-three in 1977. On the other hand, the Congress (I) led by Indira Gandhi made a spectacular comeback by more than doubling its strength from 153 MPs in 1977 to 351 MPs in 1980, which was almost a two-thirds majority in a house of 542 members.

With the benefit of hindsight, some may ask if an alliance, instead of a merger of all the constituent parties could have worked. I doubt it. The mood during the Emergency was such that almost everyone felt that only a common organisational platform of all democratic forces could defeat the Congress party. Jayaprakashji also wanted a more cohesive single-party structure.

The decision about the merger was, in itself, not incorrect. But two factors proved to be the undoing of the Janata Party. The first was the self-centred and undisciplined conduct of certain excessively ambitious leaders, who put their self interest above the interest of consolidating the gains of a hard-won battle against authoritarianism. The second was the fear on the part of some leaders that people from the erstwhile Jana Sangh constituent would soon dominate the Janata Party. Which is why, when the issue of starting a membership drive and holding organisational elections came up, they raised the bogey of 'dual membership'.

Essentially, a brainchild of Madhu Limaye, the 'dual membership' issue was aimed at disempowering those members of the Janata party who had earlier been a part of the Jana Sangh, and continued to be associated with the RSS. Even before the Janata Party was a year old, Limaye, one of the party's General Secretaries began insisting that no member of the Janata Party could simulataneously be a member of the RSS. Although Limaye possessed a sharp and scholarly mind, his deep prejudice against the Jana Sangh coloured his political perception. He had indeed confided in many of his close friends that breaking the Janata Party had become a 'historical necessity' and that he had made it his 'personal mission'.

Limaye's demand was a crude attempt to embarrass, weaken and marginalise the MPs from the erstwhile Jana Sangh who formed the largest section of the Janata Party, accounting for one-third of its MPs in the Lok Sabha. Nevertheless, when Morarji Desai offered only three portfolios to us in his nineteen-member Cabinet, we never once made an issue of it. Nobody could question our loyalty to the newly formed party or our commitment to preserving its unity and cohesion. Ironically, our only 'fault' was that the Jana Sangh, of all the five constituents of the Janata Party—others being the Congress (O), Lok Dal, Socialist Party and Jagjivan Ram's CFD—was the most organised at the grassroots level. The newly formed Janata Party did not have any organisational network of its own. All constituents of the newly formed party had quite a few leaders with national stature, but only the Jana Sangh had built a huge mass of party activists. Its disciplined cadre base, spread across many parts of the country, was something that ought to have been considered an asset and a source of strength by all those who had agreed to merge their previous identities into the new identity of the Janata Party.

Sadly, Limaye and some others saw this as a threat. They reckoned that, in the event of a membership drive and organisational elections at district, state and national levels, we would wrest effective control of the party. This baseless fear was the root cause of the 'dual-membership' controversy. In order to whip up this fear among others in the party, Limaye and his friends also began a whispering campaign that the Janata

Party would alienate Muslim voters* if the former Jana Sanghites were allowed to keep their association with the RSS.

Atalji, Nanaji Deshmukh and I naturally took strong exception to the demand that we dissociate ourselves from the RSS. After all, we had made the Jana Sangh's relationship with the RSS very clear to Jayaprakash Narayan and all the other leaders of the 'Save Democracy' movement, prior to the formation of the Janata Party. Therefore, we countered Limaye and others by asking them: 'How can you raise the question of "dual membership" after the formation of the Janata Party? How can we, who have spent almost our entire lives as *swayamsevaks* of the RSS, suddenly sever all relations with the Sangh, and that too for an organisation to which we have belonged only for a few months?'

We argued that the RSS was a non-political organisation, dedicated to the cause of India's national renaissance based on our ancient culture and values. We pointed out that it was also a reformist organisation wedded to removing ills, such as untouchability, afflicting the Hindu society. 'If some of us are associated with the RSS, there are also others in the Janata Party who are linked to some other non-political organisations. Charan Singh,

---

* A significant incident took place at Vithalbhai Patel House in New Delhi towards the end of 1974. JP had convened a meeting of representatives of various Opposition parties and prominent pro-democracy intellectuals to discuss how the movement against Indira Gandhi's authoritarianism could be strengthened. Addressing the participants, Shamim Ahmed Shamim, a Lok Sabha member from J&K, observed that Muslims were not being attracted to JP's movement because of the presence of the Jana Sangh. This immediately provoked a response from Atalji. 'The Jana Sangh,' he said, 'would very much like all sections of society to be involved in JP's movement. However, if the Jana Sangh's presence is causing hurdles, we are willing to stay out.' Atalji's intervention was not meant to be a threat, nor did it sound like one. Nevertheless, almost all those present in the hall retorted, 'No, Jana Sangh's exit is out of the question. We want you and your colleagues in the movement.'

The canard that the Jana Sangh's presence in the JP movement would 'communalise' it and alienate Muslims had been thoroughly exposed by the results of the 1977 Lok Sabha elections. In spite of a vicious propaganda by the Congress that 'a vote for the Janata Party is a vote for the Jana Sangh', Muslims and Hindus had together voted overwhelmingly in favour of the Janata candidates.

for example, is a staunch Arya Samajist. One of the cardinal planks of the Arya Samaj is *shuddhi* or religious reconversion. Would it be right on that account to bar him from membership of the Janata Party, to some of whose members *shuddhi* may be absolute anathema?'[3]

At a meeting of the Janata Party's national executive held on 2 September 1979, I referred to my association with the RSS since my childhood and said, 'I have had my training in patriotism and public conduct from the RSS. There is no other voluntary organisation in the country with such a large band of dedicated, selfless cadres and with enormous capacity for constructive work. The RSS is like my *alma mater* and I am proud of my continued association with it. No amount of calumny is going to make me disown my links with the RSS.'

I also warned that keeping the RSS bogey alive in any form would only mean betraying a 'suicidal streak' and 'playing into the hands of the Congress party'. 'Limaye and his supporters would accomplish in months what Indira Gandhi had failed to do in years,' I said. I was indeed proved right. The 'dual membership' controversy, more than anything else, destroyed the unity of the Janata Party and led to its rapid disintegration.

During the heated debate on the 'dual membership' issue, timely advice came from Achyut Patwardhan, a renowned Gandhian and freedom fighter. In an article titled 'Janata, RSS and the Nation', in the *Indian Express* of 9 June 1979, he wrote: 'It is on the strength of the weighty contribution to the mass struggle against the Emergency that the Bharatiya Jana Sangh was inducted into the Janata Party as one of its major constituents. What has the Jana Sangh and/or the RSS said or done from the time the Emergency was lifted to date which has provoked Mr. Madhu Limaye, Mr Raj Narain and their supporters to launch a rabid campaign of denigration?'

I must mention here that one prominent socialist leader who disagreed with Limaye on the 'dual membership' issue was George Fernandes. Sadly, Patwardhan's sane advice as well as the persuasive counsel of colleagues like Fernandes fell on deaf ears. By this time, Charan Singh, who had backed Limaye's stand on the 'dual membership' issue, had already shown his eagerness to defect from the Janata Party, and cause the downfall of Morarji Desai's government.

One day, Chandrashekhar came to my office in Parliament saying that he wanted to discuss something 'important' with Atalji and me. He told us that H.N. Bahuguna, then a camp follower of Charan Singh, and some others were willing to stay back in the Janata Party if the Jana Sangh was no longer in Morarjibhai's government. Bahuguna had also indicated this directly to us. After Chandrashekhar left, we discussed the matter amongst ourselves. After consulting Brijlal Verma, the third Jana Sangh member in the Cabinet, we reached a unanimous decision. The three of us went to the Prime Minister's room in Parliament and conveyed to him our readiness to quit the government in the interest of ensuring its survival and stability.

Morarjibhai did not even weigh the offer. He rejected it outright saying, 'Why should you resign? What wrong have you committed? Even if your offer is going to help my government, it would be immoral on my part to accept your resignations. I would rather quit myself, instead of making you quit.' On 15 July, when Morarjibhai lost his parliamentary majority due to defections, he tendered his resignation. He preferred to sacrifice his office instead of accepting an unprincipled compromise.

Bitter at all that had happened, I reflected for many months on the root cause of this suicidal tendency displayed by some of our colleagues in the Janata Party. I could only compare this tendency to what I had read about the behaviour of lemmings, the only species, among all those created by God, which was believed to commit mass suicide. Those who were out to wreck the party knew that their conduct would certainly cause the downfall of the Janata government and pave the way for the political resurrection of Indira Gandhi. But they were simply beyond caring.

In the entire debate on the 'dual membership' issue, two constructive interventions happened—one from Atalji and another from Balasaheb Deoras, the then RSS chief. In a candid article in the *Indian Express* of 2 August 1979, titled 'We are all to blame', Atalji made four important points: (a) Janata Party's problems arose mainly out of Charan Singh's 'inability to reconcile himself to being No. 2 in the Central Cabinet'; (b) The RSS issue is 'a bogey assiduously built up by some followers of Charan Singh as retaliation for the firm refusal of erstwhile Jana Sangh members to destabilise the Centre'; (c) The RSS has nothing to do with communal violence in the country; (d) Apprehensions about the RSS 'aiming at capturing political power are without foundation'. Atalji concluded his article by making three specific suggestions to the RSS. These were: (a) Journals connected with the RSS should not take sides in the power game going on in the political world; (b) RSS should not be involved in youth bodies that interact with political parties, or with trade unions. (c) RSS should formally enunciate its accepted stand that by 'Hindu Rashtra' it meant 'Bharatiya Rashtra'.[4]

The first two suggestions were aimed at allaying misgivings that the RSS had any political ambitions. The third, which was also reiterated by Morarji Desai and Jagjivan Ram, was intended to underscore the RSS's commitment to secularism.

In his annual address at the Vijayadashami rally in Nagpur in October 1979, Balasaheb Deoras made a remarkable observation whose relevance remains intact even today.

'It is said by some that the Sangh is changing and that it has to change further. All living beings do change in their natural course. It is a sign of their evolution. That which does not change is not living, it is dead. But this change should not take place by cutting itself from the arteries of life-sap. The Sangh too has changed in keeping with the necessities of the times, and will keep changing in future too.'[5]

*

Nearly three decades have passed since the 'dual membership' debate first surfaced to wreck the unity of the Janata Party. In retrospect, I ask myself: What did its votaries achieve? Clearly, they could not succeed in marginalising the political stream that the Jana Sangh represented. Instead, they ended up getting marginalised themselves. I can only say that, by finally expelling us from the Janata Party, they did us a great service. For it enabled us to revive ourselves in the form of the Bharatiya Janata Party in April 1980 and thus write, in the years to come, a proud new chapter in Indian politics.

4

THE LOTUS BLOOMS
The Birth of the Bharatiya Janata Party

There will be no end to the troubles of states, or of humanity itself, till philosophers become kings in this world, or till those we now call kings and rulers really and truly become philosophers, and political power and philosophy thus come into the same hands.

—PLATO

A subject that has fascinated me throughout my political life is how Indian voters determine their preference in elections. At times, the pattern is predictable; most often, it is not. Given the vast diversity of the Indian electorate, it is usually impossible to predict the outcome of a poll. However, there are times when the voters, collectively, behave almost as if they are guided by a single emotion, and give advance indication of their behaviour. 'Collective Consciousness' and 'Group Mind' are concepts that are increasingly engaging the attention of psychologists and behavioural scientists. However, even without a formal training in these concepts, an experienced political activist can, at most times, predict which way the electoral wind is blowing.

I had done so before the 1977 general elections, which were held in the aftermath of the Emergency. And I did so again when mid-term elections were held in early 1980 after the dissolution of the 6th Lok Sabha. I knew that the Janata Party was heading for a rout and Indira Gandhi would return to power. The reason was simple. If 'anger' against the Emergency was the emotion that had swept the Janata Party to power in early 1977, another emotion—disillusionment with the Janata government's collapse under the weight of its own internal power struggles—was going to influence the behaviour of the voters this time around.

The gigantic scale of the Janata Party's defeat made me aware of a new aspect of electoral behaviour. When voters want to teach an errant political party a lesson, it is mostly anger that prompts them to do so. However, in 1980, we learnt that even intense disillusionment can provoke them to punish a party that does not live up to their expectations.

Indira Gandhi's winning slogan in the 1980 elections was: 'Vote for a Government that Works'. It had its effect on the voters since they were repelled by the constant infighting in the Janata Party. Even the various achievements of Morarjibhai's government—such as restoration of democracy and civil liberties; bringing prices under control; agricultural and industrial growth; sincere efforts to normalise relations with Pakistan and China; success in strengthening relations with the United States without jeopardising the traditional cooperative ties with the Soviet Union, etc.—were eclipsed by the self-destructive political conduct of some Janata leaders. This gave credence to Indira Gandhi's pejorative description of the Janata government as '*khichdi* sarkar*'.

Jana Sangh members expelled from the Janata Party

The electoral debacle intensified the debate within the Janata Party over the 'dual membership' issue, which had remained dormant till the

---

* *Khichdi* is a traditional Indian rice and *dal* dish in which many items are mixed. In a non-culinary context, it refers to a mishmash of unrelated things.

parliamentary elections. On 25 February 1980, Jagjivan Ram wrote a letter to party President Chandrashekhar demanding a discussion on the issue. An attempt was made to blame the defeat entirely on the 'obduracy' of those who had earlier belonged to the Jana Sangh and had refused to sever their association with the RSS. Atalji and I took strong exception to this.

In one of the party meetings, I said that we were being shunned like Harijans—political untouchables—within the party. 'The Janata Party,' I observed, 'had five constituents—Congress (O), Bharatiya Lok Dal, Socialist Party, CFD and the Jana Sangh. Of these, politically speaking, the first four were 'dvijas'*, the twice-born members of the party, whereas the Jana Sangh was kind of a Harijan adopted into the family. On the occasion of the 'adoption' in 1977, there was a lot of rejoicing. But as time passed, the presence of a 'Harijan' in the family began to pose problems for it. Enemies of the family began ostracising it on the grounds that it had a 'Harijan' in its fold. You throw out the Jana Sangh, only then can we have communion with you: this became the attitude of many in the political world towards the Janata Party. Not that they have anything to complain about the conduct of the 'Harijan' boy. In fact, they often praise him. But they cannot forget his caste. It is his parentage that is the obstacle.'

I was not alone in my thinking; my observation echoed the feelings of lakhs of activists and supporters of the erstwhile Jana Sangh across the country. In February-March 1980, Sundar Singh Bhandari, a senior office-

---

* According to the varna-based system in Hindu society, 'dvija' refers to one who is twice born. Brahmins, Kshatriyas and Vaishyas are included in dvija. A person born in these varnas is assumed to be born another time at the time of Upanayanam, a Vedic ceremony of initiation. Shudras, who belong to the fourth varna, do not have the obligations that are associated with the initiation. Varnas are categories of social division of labour. Initially, the division was based not on birth but on a person's karma and innate qualities. In course of time, varnas gave rise to many castes, with notions of 'high' and 'low'. Harijans, or those belonging to what the Indian Constitution describes as the 'Scheduled Castes', were considered the 'lowest' castes and treated as untouchables. The term 'Harijan', which means 'people who are dear to God', was coined by Mahatma Gandhi. In his campaign for reform of the Hindu society, he declared that 'untouchability is a crime against humanity'. In recent decades, the term 'dalit', which means the downtrodden, has largely replaced 'Harijan' in political parlance.

bearer of the Jana Sangh and I, travelled throughout the country to gauge the opinion at the grassroots of the Janata Party. Everywhere we went, we discovered deep resentment among former Jana Sangh activists over what they considered was the 'second-class' treatment they were receiving within the party. The persistent anti-RSS campaign within the Janata Party had dampened their enthusiasm in the 1980 Lok Sabha elections. This had clearly benefited the Congress and contributed to the dismal performance of the Janata Party in the polls.

Buoyed by her victory, Indira Gandhi decided to hold early elections to legislative assemblies in many states in early 1980. This imparted an added urgency and sharpness to the debate on the 'dual membership' issue within the Janata Party. The voice of those who wanted to expel erstwhile Jana Sangh members from the party was getting more and more shrill. In this context, two important developments took place in the first week of April. On 4 April, the National Executive of the Janata Party was scheduled to hold a crucial meeting in Delhi to take a final decision on the 'dual membership' issue. In anticipation of the outcome of this meeting, we, the former members of the Jana Sangh, decided to hold a national convention in Delhi the following day. Morarji Desai and some others made a last-ditch effort to retain us within the Janata Party on the basis of a mutually acceptable compromise. But the die had been cast. The Janata Party's national executive rejected, by a vote of seventeen to fourteen, the compromise formula and resolved to expel all former Jana Sangh members from the organisation.

Strangely, the very next day, Jagjivan Ram quit the Janata Party to join the Congress (U) then headed by Y.B. Chavan. Charan Singh had already left the party to resurrect his own Bharatiya Lok Dal, which had performed quite well by securing forty-one seats in the Lok Sabha elections. Thus, what was left of the original Janata Party was a mere rump, presided over by Chandrashekhar. In due course of time, even the rump would disintegrate into many new parties, making it a butt of many jokes. Some critics poked fun at it by introducing a pun in a famous film song: '*Is dil ke tukde hazaar huye. Koyi yahan gira, koyi wahan gira*'. (This heart shattered into a thousand pieces; some fell here, some fell there.) Changing the word '*dil*' (heart) into '*dal*' (political party), the satirists said: '*Is dal ke tukde hazaar huye. Koyi yahan gira, koyi wahan gira*'. (This party shattered into a thousand pieces; some fell here, some fell there.)

THE 6TH OF APRIL 1980: A NEW POLITICAL JOURNEY BEGINS

Our expulsion from the Janata Party came as a big relief to all of us from the Jana Sangh. But at the same time, we were deeply saddened by it. After all, our merger in the Janata Party in 1977, responding to the call of venerable Jayaprakash Narayan, was total and unconditional. Both psychologically and politically, we had identified ourselves completely with the new party. Those of us from the Jana Sangh never indulged in groupism, nor tried to gain partisan advantage for our own 'faction' while in power. On the contrary, we made sacrifices for the sake of preserving unity and cohesion in the Janata Party. Therefore, our moment of final parting from the Janata Party evoked mixed emotions in my heart, and in the hearts of all my colleagues: loss, sadness, good-riddance and finally, liberation!

The two-day national convention on 5-6 April 1980 added another invigorating emotion—that of determination. Over 3,500 delegates assembled at Delhi's Ferozeshah Kotla ground and resolved, on 6 April, to form a new political organisation called the Bharatiya Janata Party. Atal Bihari Vajpayee was elected its first President and I, along with Sikandar Bakht and Suraj Bhan, was given the responsibility of General Secretary. There was considerable speculation in political circles about whether the new party would mark the revival of the Jana Sangh. Atalji dispelled these speculations with a categorical assertion in his presidential speech. 'No,' he said, 'we shall not go back. We do not want to project that we want to revive the Jana Sangh in any way. We will make use of our experience in the Janata Party. We are proud to have been associated with it. And although we are out of it now, we do not want in any way to disown this past. We look to the future, and not to the past, as we begin our endeavour to rebuild our party. We shall move ahead on the strength of our original thinking and principles.'

Thus, our stress right from the beginning was not on harking back to our Jana Sangh past, but on making a new beginning. This was also evident in the vigorous debate that took place among senior colleagues on the name of the new party. Some felt that it should again be called the Bharatiya Jana Sangh. But an overwhelming majority endorsed Atalji's proposal that it be named 'Bharatiya Janata Party', which, while affirming our proud link with both the Bharatiya Jana Sangh and the Janata Party, connoted that we were now a new party with a new identity. We were determined to chart a new course, while, at the same time, retaining the old. By including the word 'Janata', we made it clear to the people of India that we considered ourselves to be the true inheritors of the legacy of the Janata Party.

Our association with Jayaprakash Narayan had a significant influence on our new thinking. We were inspired by his personality and his core beliefs. The effect was greater since he too had, jettisoning his earlier misconceptions about us, built a bond of respect and mutual trust. Our new thinking was also evident in the symbolism of the new party. The backdrop on the dais at the BJP's inaugural convention at the Kotla ground displayed the portraits of Dr Syama Prasad Mookerjee, founder of the Jana Sangh; Pandit Deendayal Upadhyaya, the ideological guide of both the Jana Sangh and the BJP; and, notably, Jayaprakash Narayan.

The new party also decided on a new symbol and flag. The '*diya*' (lamp) of the Jana Sangh gave way to the 'lotus'. The new flag bore some resemblance to that of the Janata Party: it had one-third green and two-thirds saffron with a lotus placed in the latter section of the flag. Subsequently, the lotus also became the election symbol of the BJP. There is an interesting story about this. Having come out of the Janata Party, we had already constituted ourselves as a separate entity; it was therefore necessary for us to go to the voters with an election symbol different from the Janata Party's 'plough-bearing kisan'. However, we did not have sufficient time to register ourselves with the Election Commission (EC) as a separate party and contest the elections on our own party symbol, which was not yet allotted to us.

On behalf of the party, I was asked to head a delegation to discuss the matter with S.L. Shakdhar, who was then the Chief Election

Commissioner (CEC). He told us: 'It is difficult for me to add a new symbol at this stage since the election process is now under way and your party is not yet registered. However, you are free to choose one of the many symbols that are available to independent candidates. I will allow all your candidates to have the same symbol, so that they will have a uniform organisational identity.'

We looked at the available set of symbols. Pleased to see that the lotus was one of them, I asked the CEC if he could give us the lotus symbol. Shakdhar, who knew that we had chosen the lotus to be in the BJP's flag at the party's founding conference in Delhi, smiled at us and said, 'Alright, request granted.' But I saw that the rose was also among the available symbols in the independents' quota. The appearance of the two flower-symbols was such that they looked somewhat identical. I then requested Shakdhar if he could remove the 'rose' from the list since voters would be confused if they saw the two flowers on the same ballot paper. He smiled again and said, 'Ok, request granted.'

There was another important aspect wherein the BJP differed from the Jana Sangh. A large number of non-RSS activists had got attracted to our party during the 1974-1980 period owing to our work during and after the tumultuous period of Emergency. As such, it was deemed necessary for us to have a somewhat different organisational set-up and growth strategy. Unlike the rigidly cadre-based structure of the Jana Sangh, we decided to combine it with a mass-based composition.

There was also a subtle but significant ideological re-projection of the new party. Although Pandit Deendayal Upadhyaya's 'Integral Humanism' continued to be the guiding philosophy of the BJP, the party also affirmed its commitment to 'Gandhian Socialism'. This evoked considerable interest and debate both outside and inside party circles. It continues to interest students of Indian politics even today. Several factors contributed to our decision.

Firstly, the BJP was formed after we had been forced to part ways with the Janata Party. Secondly, the new party had begun to attract the attention of many well-meaning people from various backgrounds. They were not with us in the Jana Sangh, but they had admired our courageous fight against the Emergency, our faith in democracy, our idealism, and our commitment to probity in public life. Shanti Bhushan, who was the Law Minister in the Janata government, joined us. And so did Ram Jethmalani, the illustrious lawyer who rose to national fame because of his bold stand against the Emergency. J.D. Sethi, an eminent Gandhian economist, started interacting with us. Ashok Mehta, the veteran Congress (O) leader, was also keen to join the BJP.

Thirdly, 'Gandhian Socialism' seemed to us fully compatible with 'Integral Humanism', and also radically different from the Marxist concept of socialism. Deendayalji's economic thinking laid a strong emphasis on egalitarianism, *swadeshi*, economic decentralisation, revitalisation of agriculture and small-scale industries, and the primacy of labour over capital. However, his philosophical framework ruled out the flawed communist principle of class struggle. Rather, it emphasised the mutual inter-dependence of different classes in society, all working together for the common well-being of all citizens. Also, unlike the Marxist preference for 'violence as the midwife of revolution', Gandhian Socialism was rooted in an uncompromising acceptance of peaceful and democratic methods for socio-economic transformation.

Lastly, we wanted to counter the communists' claim to be the sole champions of the poor. We wanted to demonstrate that the concept of 'socialism', like the concept of 'secularism', has Indian roots, and that only the Indian way of achieving economic and social justice would ultimately succeed. We wanted to reaffirm that all the great thinkers and social reformers in the Hindu tradition, including Swami Vivekananda and Mahatma Gandhi in the modern era, had been votaries of what can be termed as 'Spiritual Socialism'. Our ancient seers did not regard man only as an economic being with purely material and physical needs. Rather, they had an integrated approach to life which urged the fulfilment of both material and spiritual needs of all human beings. The neglect and negation of the spiritual dimension of man had rendered the communist experiment, in country after country in Europe and Asia, utterly dehumanising. Therefore, the BJP adopted Gandhian Socialism as a positive Indian alternative to communism.

Of course, not everyone in the party was happy with this decision. One senior leader who was upset over this was the late Rajmata Vijayaraje Scindia, who circulated a note in the party's Working Committee contending that adoption of 'Gandhian Socialism' would make the BJP look like a 'photocopy' of the Congress. She later withdrew the note after an elaborate inner-party discussion re-emphasised the 'Indian content' of our economic philosophy.

'WHO SAYS THERE IS NO ALTERNATIVE TO THE CONGRESS? I AM SEEING ONE IN FRONT OF ME.'

As we embarked upon a new phase in our political journey, an unforgettable milestone came in the form of the BJP's first plenary session in Bombay on 28-30 December 1980. Nearly 50,000 delegates congregated under a specially erected tent at a sprawling open ground near Bandra Reclamation adjoining the Arabian Sea. The venue was appropriately called 'Samata Nagar' to underscore the BJP's commitment to social and economic equality.

The plenary session of the party's National Council was marked by a display of overflowing enthusiasm, confidence and determination on the part of both the leaders and the delegates. In a short period since the formation of the BJP in April, as many as twenty-five lakh new members had been enrolled and party units had been set up in practically every state in India. Even the Jana Sangh at its peak had only sixteen lakh members. As per the BJP's constitution, Atalji was formally elected President by the National Council. His presidential address on that occasion must rank as one of the important speeches in the political history of independent India.

Explaining the context that made the formation of the BJP a necessity, Atalji said, 'It was not with any happiness that we parted company with the Janata Party. From beginning to end, we kept exerting in order to preserve the unity of the party. We were conscious of the pledge we had taken at Raj Ghat in the presence of Loknayak Jayaprakash Narayan to maintain the unity of the party. But by converting the non-issue of dual-membership into an issue, a situation was created in which it became impossible for us to continue in the Janata Party with any honour and self-respect.... The

Janata Party, formed because of the inspiration of Loknayak Jayaprakash, has disintegrated. But his vision of a glorious India is still with us. We shall not allow it to be obliterated. His dreams, his labours, his struggles and his unflinching commitment to certain basic values are part of an invaluable legacy that we have inherited. The Bharatiya Janata Party is pledged to pursuing his unfinished task.'

Declaring that the BJP would be a 'party with a difference', Atalji said, 'We can organise the party only if we are able to establish credibility in people's minds. The people must feel convinced that here is a party different from the crowd of self-seekers who swamp the political stage, and that its aim is not somehow to sneak into office and that its politics is based on certain values and principles.... Manipulative politics has no future. There is no place in the BJP for people madly in pursuit of post, position and pelf. Those who lack courage or self-respect may go and prostrate themselves at the Delhi Durbar. So far as we are concerned, we are determined to wage a relentless struggle for democracy and social justice. With the Constitution of India in one hand and the Banner of Equality in the other, let us get set for the struggle.'

Atalji's concluding words, spoken in poetic Hindi and with the oratorial flourish that was uniquely his, were full of hope and inspiration. 'Standing on the shores of this ocean beneath the Western Ghats, I can say with confidence about the future: "*Andhera chhatega, sooraj nikalega aur kamal khilega!*"' (Darkness will be dispelled, the sun will rise and the lotus shall bloom!)

The Bombay session will also be remembered for the special appearance of Mohammed Currim Chagla, a former minister in several Congress governments at the Centre and a hero of the struggle against the Emergency. In his address, Chagla, who had by then long retired from politics, remarked, 'Who says there is no alternative to the Congress in the country? I see the alternative right in front of me in the form of the Bharatiya Janata Party. And in Atal Bihari Vajpayee, I see the alternative to Indira Gandhi.'

Chagla pointedly refuted the charge that the BJP was a communal party. 'Indira keeps repeating,' he said, 'in the newspapers and on radio every other day that this party is dominated by the RSS, that it is communal, and that every communal riot that takes place is caused by the RSS. This is a charge that I would like to refute. The BJP is not a communal party.'

Advising the BJP to project itself as a national alternative to the Congress, he said, 'I admire your discipline, your honesty and your dedication. Let me now suggest that you project your future as a national party.... Look at other parties, like the Lok Dal or the Congress (U). These parties have leaders without followers. The communists may have a following, but they are not national parties. They look to Moscow or Peking to get their orders. So their credentials for consideration as replacements for Indira Gandhi are immediately ruled out. Therefore, this is the only party left.'

All the newspapers in the country took note of the historic significance of the Bombay session of the BJP. I must make a special mention here of what Janardan Thakur, who was then the Editor of *Onlooker* weekly, wrote: 'I have just returned from the BJP session in Bombay with one certainty: Atal Bihari Vajpayee will, sooner or later, become the country's Prime Minister. I am not saying he *may*, I am saying he *will*. Mine is not a prediction based on stars, for I am not an astrologer. It's a prediction based on a close hard look at the man and his party. Vajpayee leads the party of the future. Both have blossomed.'

BIRTH-PANGS OF THE NEW PARTY

The formation of the BJP did not result in immediate electoral gains for the party, nor was it expected to by the leadership. The Congress, because of the euphoria created by Indira Gandhi's comeback in the 1980 parliamentary elections, continued to do well in the polls to the state assemblies. The BJP was able to make its presence felt in South India by winning 18 seats (out of 224) in the Karnataka Assembly in 1983. In the previous year, the party had won slightly less than half the seats in Himachal Pradesh. Overall, our electoral performance did not show signs of an early take-off for the party. A particularly demoralising setback was in the 1983 assembly elections in Jammu & Kashmir. The Jammu region, with its majority Hindu population, has traditionally been a stronghold of the Jana Sangh and, later, the BJP. In 1983, a large section of our voters deserted the BJP to vote for the Congress, since Indira Gandhi in her campaign had taken a strong stand against Sheikh Abdullah, the one-time separatist leader from Kashmir. The defeat in Jammu made many people apprehensive about whether the BJP would face similar setbacks in other parts of the country too, if it neglected its traditional support base among the Hindus.

There was considerable debate within the party at the time on which political line to pursue for electoral success. There were two options: go-alone or form alliances with non-Congress and non-Communist parties. Because of our bitter experience in the Janata Party, many in the BJP were wary of going along with other Opposition parties. At the same time, the Janata experiment itself had also taught us the advantages of joining forces with others to counter a then-powerful adversary like the Congress. Atalji, as party President, was in favour of pursuing a strategy of bringing together all the nationalist and democratic forces in the form of a National Democratic Front (NDF). While I supported this idea, I emphasised the need to steadily increase the BJP's own strength, both organisationally and politically, in different states. Out of extensive inner-party deliberations, we evolved a three-pronged strategy: (1) The BJP will do nothing to compromise on its separate identity; (2) We will act in concert with other Opposition parties on issues of national importance; and (3) We will build our own mass movements around issues concerning the people and the nation, with a view to strengthening and expanding our support base.

The early 1980s was a period when, independent of the BJP, other parties were also eagerly exploring the possibility of greater opposition unity. Two persons making sincere efforts in this direction were Biju Patnaik, a charismatic leader from Orissa, who served as the state's Chief Minister for two terms; and N.T. Rama Rao, a superstar of Telugu cinema who launched his own political party called the 'Telugu Desam' in March 1982 and, in the very next year, trounced the Congress to become the Chief Minister of Andhra Pradesh. Several opposition conclaves were held, the most notable among these being the one held in Srinagar in 1983, which passed a resolution for transforming Centre-State relations, with devolution of greater powers to the states in the true spirit of federalism.

The beginning of the 1980s witnessed another important development in Indian politics. On 23 June 1980, Sanjay Gandhi, the younger of the two sons of Prime Minister Indira Gandhi, died in an airplane crash in New Delhi. After this, a systematic campaign was orchestrated inside the ruling party to induct Sanjay's elder brother Rajiv, who was then a pilot with Indian Airlines, into the leadership position. In less than two years, Rajiv was made the General Secretary of the Congress party, a move that sent clear signals that Indira Gandhi had made up her mind to ensure dynastic succession.

The biggest electoral setback to our party came in 1984 from a factor that was as unexpected as it was tragic. On 31 October, Prime Minister Indira Gandhi was gunned down inside her official residence by two of her own bodyguards—Satwant Singh and Beant Singh. The assassination was in line with a prolonged campaign of Pakistan-supported terrorist acts in Punjab by those who wanted to create a separate Sikh nation called 'Khalistan'. If Indira Gandhi's assassination was a national tragedy, an equally shocking and shaming tragedy was the large-scale massacre of innocent Sikhs in Delhi and other places in North India in the ensuing days. Over 3,000 Sikhs lost their lives in targeted killings in the national capital itself with the connivance of the government machinery. Many local Congress leaders were blamed for orchestrating the violence.

Even as Indira Gandhi's body was lying in state, Rajiv was administered the vote of office as Prime Minister by President Giani Zail Singh in the evening of 31 October. At forty, he became India's youngest Prime Minister, with no prior ministerial experience. In a cynical move to exploit the sympathy wave, the government dissolved the Lok Sabha and called for fresh elections to be held within forty-five days. More shockingly, the Congress party carried out a thinly veiled anti-Sikh propaganda during the elections to garner votes. Commenting on the carnage in Delhi, Rajiv Gandhi sought to rationalise it by saying at a Boat Club rally, 'When a giant tree falls, the earth below is bound to shake.'

In the 1984 Lok Sabha elections, the BJP became the worst victim of the 'sympathy wave'. Our party could win from only two constituencies in a House of 542 MPs—one in Gujarat and the other in Andhra Pradesh. Unbelievably, even Atalji lost his seat from Gwalior in Madhya Pradesh. The Congress won as many as 401 seats, better than its best performances during the premiership of Nehru or Indira Gandhi.

Naturally, the pall of defeat hung over the party as its national executive met in Calcutta in March 1985. 'As the President of the party,' Atalji said, 'I take full moral responsibility for the failure of the BJP in the Lok Sabha elections, and I shall be gladly willing to undergo any punishment that the party decides.' The party, however, promptly turned down his offer to resign. For, everyone in the BJP knew that our tally of two seats in the Lok Sabha was by no means a true reflection of our party's real presence in Indian politics.

Nevertheless, Atalji insisted on me taking over the presidentship of the party, saying he had had a long innings since its inception. At that time there was no provision in the party's constitution that a person may remain President only for two consecutive terms of two years each. This limit was incorporated later. However, Atalji was insistent: 'Let there be no permanent fixtures for any post.' Thus, I was elected President of the BJP at the plenary session of its national council, held at Indraprastha Stadium in New Delhi, in May 1986.

With this began a new phase in both my party's and my own political journey.

5

THE 1980s: THE BJP'S PHOENIX-LIKE RISE

Being defeated is often a temporary condition.
Giving up is what makes it permanent.

—MARLYN VOS SAVANT, AN AMERICAN COLUMNIST

My taking over as BJP President in May 1986 was preceded by an intense debate within the party on several basic ideological and organisational issues. The BJP's poor performance in the 1984 parliamentary elections, quite naturally, had produced widespread disillusionment among its members and supporters. When the party was formed in 1980, it had set for itself, the ambitious goal of emerging as the 'alternative' to the Congress. Five years later, far from moving towards that goal, the party's strength in the Lok Sabha—of merely two MPs—had fallen steeply to a level lower than that of the Jana Sangh after the first general elections in 1952. Clearly, soul-searching was in order.

While introspecting about the party's journey since its birth in 1980, Atalji, speaking at the meeting of the national executive in Calcutta in March 1985, posed two pertinent questions: (1) Was the party's defeat because of our decision to merge the Jana Sangh with the Janata Party in 1977 and the subsequent withdrawal from the Janata Party in 1980? (2) Should the BJP go back to revive the Bharatiya Jana Sangh? The National Executive constituted a twelve-member working group to examine these two questions. Krishan Lal Sharma, Vice President, was made the Convener of this group, from which senior leaders like Atalji and I were consciously left out to facilitate free and open discussion.

The report submitted by this working group, in my opinion, is the most in-depth and useful of all the review documents in the party's history. It reaffirmed that neither the Jana Sangh's decision to merge into the Janata Party in 1977, nor our decision to leave it three years later, was wrong. As such, it ruled out the question of reviving the Jana Sangh.

The study deduced: 'The notion that there has been very serious erosion in our electoral base is not quite correct.' This was based on a meticulous examination of our electoral performance, especially of the percentage of votes polled by us during the three stages of our political journey—by the Jana Sangh from 1952 to 1971, by the Janata Party between 1977 and 1980, and by the BJP in 1984. The Jana Sangh had secured 3.1 per cent of the total votes polled in 1952, 4.9 per cent in 1957, 6.44 per cent in 1962, 9.4 per cent in 1967 and 7.4 per cent in 1971. Benefiting from the anti-Emergency wave, the Janata Party had secured 42.1 per cent of the votes polled and 298 seats in 1977. Since the Jana Sangh constituent's share in this tally was 93 seats, the working group deduced that our vote share was about one-third of 42.1 per cent—that is, 14 per cent. In 1980, the Janata Party's vote share had come down to 18.93 per cent and its seats reduced to 31. Of these, the share of the Jana Sangh constituent was sixteen. This translated into a vote share of 8.6 per cent for the Jana Sangh.

In 1984, the BJP contested the parliamentary elections for the first time independently and secured 7.66 per cent of the votes polled. In other words, our share had dropped by only one per cent even in an extremely adverse situation following Indira Gandhi's assassination, arguably an aberration. Moreover, some important truths were concealed behind our performance in 1984. Firstly, although the BJP won only two seats, it had come second in as many as 101 seats. Secondly, its vote share was the highest among all the opposition parties. Thirdly, in the absence of a sympathy wave in favour of the Congress, the BJP's projected vote share, the working group reported, 'would have gone up anywhere between ten to fifteen per cent, keeping in mind the enlarging circle of sympathisers and supporters and our success in many by-elections'.

The conclusion of this analysis was clear: there was no need for the BJP to feel despondent about its future.

GANDHIAN SOCIALISM AND INTEGRAL HUMANISM

Another significant recommendation made by the working group was in the sphere of ideology. In 1980, the BJP had adopted 'Gandhian Socialism' as its guiding philosophy. I have mentioned earlier that, even at that time, a section of the party's leadership, most notably Rajmata Vijayaraje Scindia, had resisted this decision. The working group opined that the decision had blurred the ideological distinctiveness of the BJP. People who had come from the Jana Sangh background had not been able to identify themselves with 'Gandhian Socialism' as their political philosophy. The report said: 'The statement that the BJP is a party with a difference means that the party, amongst other things, possesses an ideology *which is not fully shared by others*. In ultimate analysis, the strength and spread of a political party will also depend on its ideological appeal'. (emphasis added)

Accordingly, the group recommended that 'Integral Humanism', propounded by Pandit Deendayal Upadhyaya, be enshrined as the basic philosophy of the BJP. At the same time, it took care to emphasise that it did not reject 'Gandhian Socialism'. 'Socialism all over the world has acquired different connotations', it said. 'In India it is understood as a synonym for social justice. Socialism enshrined in the Indian Constitution is thus a creed for the upliftment of the poor and downtrodden. In this sense, it is quite in line with Integral Humanism.' The group recommended adoption of the following 'Five Basic Commitments' of the BJP. (1) Nationalism and National Integration; (2) Democracy; (3) Gandhian approach to socio-economic system—that is, a society based on equality and freedom from exploitation (*samata-yukt* and *shoshan-mukt*); (4) Positive Secularism—

that is, Sarva Pantha Samabhaav; and (5) Value-based Politics. These recommendations of the working group were accepted, and incorporated into the BJP's constitution at a meeting of the party's National Council at Gandhinagar in October 1985.

THE BJP AS A CADRE-BASED MASS PARTY

The working group's report imparted clarity on another issue that had been agitating the minds of some people in the party. They were concerned that, after the formation of the BJP, the cadre-based character of the Jana Sangh had been eroded. My view was that there was no contradiction between continuing to widen the base of the BJP on the one hand and, on the other, making the party's organisation stronger, more disciplined and dynamic by preserving its cadre base. Echoing this view, the report stated: 'We have succeeded in building a cadre-based party. But a cadre-based organisation by itself will not enable us to reach our goal. It will indeed limit our base to our cadre. If we are to have a wide base, then it can be only with the help of this cadre. We should become a cadre-based mass party. Cadre base and mass base seem to be contradictory in terms. However, there can be a happy marriage between the two'.

I would like to mention here that my views on the organisational character of the BJP were influenced by a book by Hampton Thomson Davey Jr., an American scholar at the University of California, Los Angeles. His Ph.D. thesis, on 'The Transformation of an Ideological Movement into an Aggregative Party: A case study of the Bharatiya Jana Sangh', was a comparative study of two types of political parties in India: 'Ideological Parties' and 'Aggregative Parties'. He felt that in a diverse society like India, a purely ideological party did not have much scope for expansion whereas aggregative parties have the ability to expand their support base among newer sections of society. 'During its formative years, the Jana Sangh was little more than a political wing of the RSS. But the party organization has become more open during the past decade. This is partly reflected in changing patterns of leadership recruitment. The party has tended increasingly to recruit leaders without RSS ties. Relations between the Jana

Sangh and other political parties have changed significantly since 1967. The leaders of other national opposition parties seem to have adopted a more flexible approach to cooperation with the Jana Sangh. Changes in Jana Sangh's programmes reflect both the socialising effects of interaction within the system and the development of aggregative tendencies. Party programmes have tended increasingly to stress secular domestic issues. Its foreign policy stands have become more similar to those of other national parties.'[1]

This thesis convinced me that the Jana Sangh needed to further transform itself and become more of an aggregative party with a strong ideological identity. The belief was further reinforced after the experience of the broadbased anti-Emergency struggle and the formation of the Janata Party under Jayaprakashji's influence.

TAKING THE BATON OF PRESIDENTSHIP FROM ATALJI

It is against this backdrop that I took the baton of party presidentship from Atalji. I delivered my presidential speech at the plenary session of the BJP's National Council in New Delhi, in May 1986, by expressing my feelings of gratitude towards Atalji. 'Since its launching in 1980,' I said, 'the Bharatiya Janata Party has been singularly fortunate in having a leader like Shri Atal Bihari Vajpayee to guide the party. He combines in himself a statesman's liberal vision with a pragmatist's hard-headed realism. A deep and abiding concern for the underdog, sharply characterises all his thinking and actions. In his personality, the people find a rare blend of capability and charisma. According to a public opinion survey conducted last month, it is in him that people see a clear alternative to the present Congress leadership.' I also expressed the hope that Atalji's example of stepping down from office after two terms 'may well have a healthy catalytic effect on other parties also, some of whom have come to have permanent life-time presidents'.

My speech covered a broad range of issues related to the policies and actions of the eighteen-month-old government of Rajiv Gandhi, which had already begun to belie the expectations created by his massive electoral success. However, the concluding part of the speech summed up the kernel of my effort, ever since I became the President of the Jana Sangh in 1973 and of the BJP in 1986, which was to build my party not only as a political alternative to the Congress but also as one that can offer an alternative political culture.

'For nearly two decades now, Indian politics has been oscillating between hope and despair. This kind of recurring ebb and tide of popular expectations is creating cynicism about all politicians and political parties—nay, about the system itself. Let the BJP exert to dispel this cynicism and by dint of conduct and performance, service and sacrifice, prove to the people that this party inspired by Gandhi and Jayaprakash, by Mookerjee and Upadhyaya, is really a party with a difference. It may not yet have a nationwide political set-up to offer as an alternative to the ruling party, but it certainly has an alternative political culture to offer.'

In the two decades that have elapsed since, my party has certainly become bigger and stronger politically, even succeeding in forming the first stable non-Congress coalition government at the Centre. But I must admit that our quantitative gain has been at the cost of a considerable qualitative loss. I am acutely aware that my party cannot today claim, as confidently as we could in 1986, that we offer 'an alternative political culture'. The BJP still has many fine attributes of which I am proud of but I would like each member of my party to introspect not only on the loss and the gains but also on how to fully recover our proud tradition of cultivating a superior political culture.

As party President, I gave top priority to bring in fresh and young blood into my team of office bearers. Thus, Pramod Mahajan was made one of the four General Secretaries, along with Kedarnath Sahni, Krishanlal Sharma and Dr Murli Manohar Joshi. Although Pramod was only thirty-seven years old then, he had attracted the attention of all the seniors in the party as a young leader of exceptional organisational and oratorical abilities. Other young activists whom I inducted into the team, and who later went on to become prominent leaders in their own right were Sushma Swaraj, M. Venkaiah Naidu, Arun Jaitley, Narendra Modi, Rajnath Singh and K.N. Govindacharya. An important new entrant into the BJP, who did not come from the RSS background but, nevertheless, emerged as a prominent leader soon, was Jaswant Singh.

RAJIV GANDHI RAISES HOPES WITH HIS MR CLEAN IMAGE

When I became the BJP President, the domestic political climate was extremely challenging. Rajiv Gandhi, who was in the second year of his premiership, was at the peak of his popularity. In contrast, my party, at least in terms of numerical representation in Parliament, had only a peripheral presence in national politics. I recall a particularly awkward situation, soon after taking over as party President, when a foreign dignitary called on me at the party office. He asked me many questions about my party's history, its ideology and its policies on various national and international issues, and seemed quite impressed with my replies. He then posed a question, which put me in a spot: 'Yours certainly seems to be a very important national party in India. How many members do you have in the Indian Parliament?'

I was too embarrassed to answer his question. Hence, in order to divert his attention, I pretended as if I had not heard this query and, instead, asked him, 'O, I forgot to inquire. Would you like to have some tea or coffee? Or do you prefer a cold drink?'

I must admit here that Rajiv Gandhi had endeared himself phenomenally to the people of India in the first year of his premiership. His charismatic appeal transcended the barriers of caste, creed, class, region, age and gender. This can be attributed to several reasons. Firstly, the sympathy wave that brought him to power was still operative. Secondly, since he was India's youngest ever Prime Minister, the youth were naturally drawn towards him. But the most important reason for his mass appeal was what was captured in a new term coined by the media: 'Mr Clean'. Rajiv was seen as incorruptible and idealistic, qualities which were not generally associated with Congress politicians.

His presidential speech at the AICC session in Bombay in December 1985 to mark the Congress party's centenary celebrations became a subject of considerable debate in political and media circles. Striking a rare and refreshing note of candour and self-criticism, he observed: 'Millions of ordinary Congress workers throughout the country are full of enthusiasm for the Congress policies and programmes. But they are handicapped, for on their backs ride the brokers of power and influence, who dispense patronage to convert a mass movement into a feudal oligarchy. They are self-perpetuating cliques who thrive…by enmeshing the living body of the Congress in their net of avarice. For such persons, the masses do not count. Their lifestyle, their thinking—or lack of it—their self-aggrandisement, their corrupt ways, their linkages with the vested interests in society, and their sanctimonious posturing are wholly incompatible with work among the people. They are reducing the Congress organisation to a shell from which the spirit of service and sacrifice has been emptied. How have we come to this pass?'

On the cancer of corruption, Rajiv did not mince his words: 'We talk of the high principles and lofty ideals needed to build a strong and prosperous India. But we obey no discipline, no rule, follow no principle of public weal. Corruption is not only tolerated but even regarded as the hallmark of leadership. Flagrant contradiction between what we say and what we do has become our way of life. At every step, our aims and actions conflict. At every stage, our private self crushes our social commitment.' After this forthright diagnosis of the disease, he held out the promise: 'The war on corruption will go on without let or hindrance. The country needs a clean social and political environment; the Congress is determined to give it.'

India had not heard such strong words of resolve to fight corruption even during the Prime Ministership of Pandit Nehru. Although Rajiv's speech contained fulsome praise of his mother, it was evident to anyone who could read between the lines that his remarks were a severe indictment of the culture of venality and sleaze that had become the hallmark of the Congress party under Indira Gandhi's leadership.

In fact, during my speech at one of the party conferences, I recognised the change in the style of functioning of both mother and son. 'Mrs Gandhi was aloof and abrasive. The new Prime Minister, on the other hand, is soft-spoken and amiable. Smt. Gandhi's relations with the Opposition were extremely strained. With the arrival of Rajiv Gandhi there has been a perceptible thaw. Perhaps, never before have there been so many formal government-opposition get-togethers as during these last nineteen months.' Personally speaking, Rajiv showed great courtesy in his interactions with me. I felt, initially at least, that it was out of his genuine respect for age and experience.

THE BOFORS SCAM AND ITS COVER-UP

Sadly, I discovered just after a year or so that the change was more in style than in substance. Rajiv's 'Mr Clean' image received a huge jolt when the Bofors corruption scandal broke out. Our party's National Executive was meeting at Rohtak in Haryana on 17 April 1987. The previous day, the Swedish State Radio had broadcast a startling report about an under–cover operation carried out by Bofors, Sweden's biggest arms manufacturer, whereby sixteen million dollars (equivalent to rupees twenty crores at the time) were allegedly paid to 'members of Prime Minister Rajiv Gandhi's Congress' in connection with the purchase of 155 mm Howitzer guns by the Government of India. Four installments of the payoff totalling five million dollars had already been paid in 1986 into secret accounts in Swiss banks. In my presidential speech, I said, 'If the allegation is false, then the Swedish government itself is guilty of slander, and this calls for a vigorous, forthright response. But, if there is even an iota of truth in what has been said, the Prime Minister must immediately order a suitable probe whose impartiality is accepted by all, and while the probe is on, Mr Gandhi should step down from office and let his party elect a new leader.'

The Swedish radio's report hit India as a thunderbolt. It was, expectedly, dismissed by the government as 'false, baseless and mischievous'. However, the murky details of the payoffs in the Bofors deal soon came to light thanks to a meticulous and sustained journalistic investigation carried out by N. Ram and Chitra Subramaniam and published in the *Hindu*, a respected national daily headquartered in Chennai. In a stiff competition for the purchase of artillery guns between Bofors and a French company, the Army had settled for the latter. In spite of this, the order went to

Bofors because someone had swung the deal in its favour by getting the government to work at breakneck speed, under instructions from none other than the Prime Minister himself. Who could it be? The capital was abuzz with talk about a certain 'Italian connection' in the Bofors deal. In what must certainly rank among the finest examples of investigative reporting anywhere in the world, Ram and his colleague presented voluminous documentary evidence to show that the middleman was indeed an Italian named Ottavio Quattrocchi.

Close observers of Rajiv Gandhi's government had already known that Quattrocchi, who was working as the Delhi-based agent of an Italian multinational, had developed extremely close ties with the Prime Minister's family due to his links with Rajiv's Italian wife, Sonia Maino Gandhi. Because of his reputation as a wheeler-dealer with direct access to the Prime Minister's residence, many ministers in the government were known to entertain, and be entertained by, Quattrocchi. When his name cropped up in media reports in the context of the Bofors scandal, people naturally recalled Rajiv Gandhi's historic speech about 'power-brokers' in the Congress party and started wondering as to how Mr Clean had allowed a power-broker to operate from his own residence?

What had sullied the Prime Minister's credibility, especially, was the fact that the payoffs—which were later revealed to be close to fifty million dollars—were in flagrant violation of assurances repeatedly given by Bofors to the Indian government that it had no agents or representatives in India for the gun deal. Rajiv, himself, had assured the nation that middlemen would not be allowed 'for the purpose of winning the contract'.

As Ram wrote: 'The documented facts have bribery written all over them. A massive order of illegitimate and unacknowledged payments, termed "commissions" and calculated on a percentage basis, was made by the Swedish arms manufacturing company into secret Swiss bank accounts after the Indian howitzer contract was won on March 24, 1986.... The documents in the CBI's possession establish Quattrocchi's deep-end involvement in the Bofors corruption scandal'.[2]

Had Rajiv Gandhi responded to the media exposures in a transparent and honest manner, I have no doubt that his political stock in the country, which was already very high, would have gone up enormously. Sadly, quite the opposite happened. Almost from day one of the Bofors revelations, even his admirers started to feel that a cover-up was afoot. One of the most convincing accounts of this sordid saga is discussed in the book written by B.M. Oza, India's Ambassador to Sweden.[3] As soon as the Swedish media broadcast allegations about the Bofors payoffs to Indians, Oza, as is the duty of any conscientious diplomat, started to press the Swedish government for a serious probe into the matter. To his utter disbelief, he soon learnt that the Indian Prime Minister did not want the truth to be revealed. Indeed, Rajiv Gandhi spoke to his Swedish counterpart, Ingvar Carlsson, and told him that, since Bofors had already denied any payoffs, there was no need for any further investigation. Shockingly, Ambassador Oza was kept in the dark about this conversation.

There was similar lack of transparency in the Prime Minister's interactions with his Minister of State in Defence, Arun Singh, who was directly dealing with the purchase of the gun system. This prompted Singh, who until then was considered one of Rajiv's closest friends, to resign in July 1987. Bowing to sustained pressure from the Opposition, the government appointed a Joint Parliamentary Committee (JPC) to look into the allegations of the Bofors payoffs. However, both the choice of the person to chair it, B. Shankaranand, a particularly servile minister in the Congress government, and the opaque working of the committee soon confirmed the Opposition's apprehensions that the JPC was actually being used to bury, rather than unearth, the truth. There are many more well-documented instances of how Rajiv Gandhi personally intervened to suppress the truth about the Bofors payoffs.

Rajiv's credibility received a severe blow when V.P. Singh, a senior minister in his government, raised a banner of revolt. Singh's portfolio had been shifted from Finance to Defence in January 1987 amid speculation that the Prime Minister was not too happy with his crusade against certain corporate wrong-doers. In his new ministry, Singh immediately ordered an investigation into an alleged scandal involving the acquisition of German submarines. This was criticised by the Prime Minister, who said he had not been consulted. Singh resigned from the government, alleging a cover-up.

Shortly thereafter, he was expelled from the Congress party. Two more close lieutenants of Rajiv Gandhi, Arun Nehru and Arif Mohammed Khan, also abandoned him to join Singh. In October 1987, they formed the Jan Morcha, which metamorphosed into a full-fledged political party called the Janata Dal a year later. Singh made the Bofors cover-up the main plank of his political campaign, which gained phenomenal popularity in a short span of time and earned him the epithet 'Mr Cleaner', one who promised to reveal the truth about 'Mr Clean'.

The campaign against the cover-up in the Bofors deal caught the attention of the common people because it was about corruption in a defence deal. It demonstrated how deep the common Indian's concern was for national security. In the case of Rajiv Gandhi, people's disillusionment was greater since they had given him a massive mandate in 1984 precisely out of concern for national security arising out of Indira Gandhi's assassination. Thus, within three years of Rajiv's stint, his government was in doldrums. The shameful saga of the cover-up of the Bofors scam continued long after his government was voted out in the parliamentary 1989 elections, and, indeed, has persisted even in the present government of Dr Manmohan Singh. This is evident from the brazen manner in which the Congress-led UPA government misused the institutions to defreeze the overseas bank accounts of Quattrocchi and virtually allowed him to go scot-free in the Bofors case.

SURRENDER TO MINORITYISM IN THE SHAH BANO MATTER

If over the Bofors controversy Rajiv Gandhi's integrity reached its nadir, his capitulation in the Shah Bano case, once again placed a question mark over his maturity as a leader. In modern Indian history, there is no other example of a government enjoying unassailable majority in Parliament and, nevertheless, surrendering before religious fanaticism. The government's action was sheer misuse of its majority to overturn a progressive verdict of the Supreme Court in favour of gender justice.

Shah Bano, a sixty-two-year-old Muslim woman from Indore, Madhya Pradesh, was divorced from her husband in 1978. Since she had no means to support herself and her five children, she approached the courts for securing maintenance from her fairly wealthy husband. However, he refused to pay even the paltry amount of Rs 500 per month that the lower courts had asked him to pay. He appealed in the Supreme Court, which ruled in favour of Shah Bano, invoking Section 125 of the Code of Criminal Procedure, which is applicable to everyone regardless of caste or creed. The apex court's ruling enraged the orthodox leaders of the Muslim community, who argued that it was an encroachment of the *Sharia'h*, the Islamic religious law. These leaders came together under a common platform called the All India Muslim Personal Law Board (AIMPLB) and threatened nationwide agitation if the verdict was not nullified by the government through suitable legislative action. There were angry rallies in several cities. Some leaders of the AIMPLB even called for a boycott of the Republic Day celebrations on 26 January 1986!

Rajiv Gandhi's initial reaction to the demand for nullifying the Shah Bano judgment was quite praiseworthy. Like most people in the country, including the progressive sections of the Muslim community, he believed that the Supreme Court had done the right thing by upholding the maintenance rights of a divorced and needy woman. This was evident from the fact that he personally encouraged Arif Mohammad Khan, then a junior minister in his government, to speak in favour of the judgment during a debate in Parliament over a private member's bill introduced by G.M. Banatwala, a Muslim League MP. Khan earned the encomiums of most members of the House, both on ruling and Opposition benches, with a scintillating speech which was characterised, in equal measure, by scholarship, courage and oratorical flourish.

Within two months, however, the Prime Minister started to vacillate. One day, in early 1986, he came to see me at my Pandara Park residence to offer his condolences over the passing away of my father, in December of the previous year, in Adipur in Kutch, Gujarat. After he had inquired about my family, Rajiv said, 'Advaniji, what do you think should be done in the case of the Supreme Court's judgment in the Shah Bano matter?' I was taken aback by the question and quickly realised that he had made up his mind to backtrack on the issue and was probably seeking my party's support for his move. I replied, 'What do you mean by asking what should be done? Is there anything to be done apart from sticking to the right stand that your government has taken?'

'No, but I think something needs to be done.'

'But, Rajivji, you have yourself fielded Arif Mohammed Khan to defend the Supreme Court's verdict in Parliament. And, by all accounts, he has done a wonderful job. All the women's organisations are supporting your government's stand. Even many Muslim intellectuals have hailed it.'

'That's true,' he remarked, 'but the opposition is building up fast. There could be a serious situation if something is not done quickly.'

At this, I said firmly, 'You are the Prime Minister. You have the requisite majority in Parliament to do what you want. But you would be doing a disservice to the nation if you conceded the demand to legislatively nullify the Supreme Court's judgment.'

I must say that Rajiv Gandhi went down several notches in my esteem that day. Soon, the government employed its absolute majority in Parliament to pass the Muslim Women (Protection of Rights on Divorce) Act, 1986 to overturn the judgment of the Supreme Court. The Act restricted the liability of the husband to pay maintenance to his divorced wife only during *iddat*, the mandatory period of togetherness before the divorce becomes operational. This time around, Rajiv Gandhi fielded another Muslim minister in his Cabinet, Z.R. Ansari, whose speech was the exact antithesis of the one delivered earlier by Arif Mohammed Khan. Ansari even lambasted the learned judges of the Supreme Court who had delivered the judgment. When the press severely admonished the minister, Rajiv Gandhi publicly rushed to his defence. Justifying this regressive legislation, he cited it as an example of 'secularism'!

It was obvious, however, that far from strengthening India's secular fabric, the government's appeasement of the Muslim vote bank against genuine demands of gender justice had greatly weakened secularism and national integration.

In my first presidential speech at the meeting of the BJP's National Council in Delhi in May 1986, I dealt extensively with the Shah Bano controversy. 'The government's somersault on the Shah Bano verdict,' I said, 'has been even more distressing. It is an unforgivable assault on the Constitution. Today in the field of criminal law there is a uniform code. Article 44 of the Constitution enjoins upon the state to endeavour towards uniformity in the field of civil law as well. The Muslim Women Bill runs counter to this Directive Principle, violates Articles 14 and 15 of the Constitution, and, besides, disrupts the existing uniformity in the field of criminal law. History will never forgive this government for the fact that when a debate ensued within the Indian Muslim community in regard to the rights of women, and a sizable—and very enlightened—section of the community risked opprobrium at the hands of the obscurantists in the community to espouse the cause of social reform and a fair deal for women, this government sided with the fanatics! How ironic that between an Arif and an Ansari, the "twenty-first century" Prime Minister has chosen to lock arms with the Ansari who is still in the Middle Ages! A wholesome by-product of this year's long debate on the Shah Bano judgement has been the acute awareness it has created in the country about Article 44 of the Constitution and among enlightened sections of the Muslim community about the urgent need of reform in the Muslim personal law.'

I strongly argued for the introduction of a Uniform Civil Code in India. 'Our Constitution charges the State with the duty to move towards such a code. It is unfortunate that until now there has not even been a proper debate on what this code should be like. I suggest that the Law Commission undertake a special exercise in this regard. Part of the civil law—laws relating to contracts, transfer of property, etc.—is already uniform. The diversity that exists is in respect of marriage, divorce, maintenance, adoption, etc. The Law Commission should examine the various personal laws in vogue in the country—Hindu law, Muslim law, Christian law, Parsi law, civil law, etc.—identify the fair and equitable ingredients in these laws, prepare a draft uniform code on the basis, and throw it open for national debate.'

It should be clear from this that, contrary to the false and motivated propaganda of our adversaries, the BJP was not—and, even now, is not—conspiring to impose the Hindu law on Muslims.

THE INDIAN PEACE KEEPING FORCE FIASCO IN SRI LANKA

Rajiv Gandhi's next big blunder was in sending the Indian Peace Keeping Force (IPKF) to Sri Lanka in 1987. This was done under the peace accord signed between the Indian Prime Minister and the President of Sri Lanka, J.R. Jayewardene, to end the conflict between Liberation Tigers of Tamil Eelam (LTTE) and Sri Lankan armed forces.

Sri Lanka had been rocked by a violent ethnic strife since the early 1980s. Successive governments in Colombo had been insensitive to the social, cultural, economic and ethnic-identity aspirations of the Tamil-speaking population in northern and eastern parts of Sri Lanka. Indeed, some of the laws passed by the Sri Lankan government had led Tamils to believe that they were being reduced to second-class citizens. Since there have been historical and blood ties between the people of Tamil Nadu and the Tamils of Sri Lanka, India has a special interest in ensuring justice for the latter within the framework of a united Sri Lanka.

However, the Indo-Lankan accord was flawed in many ways. Firstly, it excluded the LTTE or the other Tamil groups from the talks. Secondly, although the IPKF was meant to be only a peacekeeping force, it soon got actively involved in combat operations. More fatally, through a sequence of unfortunate but avoidable incidents, it locked horns with the LTTE. Ironically, both under Indira Gandhi and later under Rajiv Gandhi, Indian governments had earlier provided support to the LTTE, even providing them sanctuary in India. The Indian troops got increasingly dragged into the ethnic conflict of another country, and at their peak the Indian soldiers in Sri Lanka numbered nearly 100,000. However, even after India had lost over 1,100 soldiers, the political and military stalemate in the island country could not be diffused. Consequently, the IPKF came to be viewed as an invading force by the Sinhalese and an oppressing force by the Tamils. Rajiv Gandhi's Sri Lanka policy had ended up as a failure both diplomatically and militarily.

Commenting on the situation, the BJP National Executive stated in a resolution adopted at its meeting in Ernakulam in January 1988: 'The government's misadventure and mishandling of the Sri Lankan situation is costing us blood and finances that is going to shock the country. At the same time, it has cost us the goodwill of the Sinhalese and the Tamils alike…. As a result, we have a potential Lebanon on our hands in Sri Lanka.'

Rajiv Gandhi made another ill-advised move when his government introduced the notorious Anti-Defamation Bill in 1988, which sought to curtail press freedom and rekindled the dark memories of the Emergency. This was in response to frequent reports in Indian newspapers and magazines of corruption and misuse of power by those close to the Prime Minister. The intention of the bill was clearly to intimidate the press by broadening the definition of defamation. Unlike in 1975-77, the media fraternity, led by the intrepid owner of the *Indian Express*, Ramnath Goenka, organised protests on a far bigger scale and forced Rajiv Gandhi to withdraw the bill. My party—indeed, almost all non-Congress parties—also stoutly opposed the bill.

I should mention here an important episode from this period. President Giani Zail Singh's five-year term was coming to an end in 1987. Although once a close confidante of Indira Gandhi, Zail Singh's relations with Prime Minister Rajiv Gandhi had greatly soured since 1986. This was no longer a secret in the political circles. There were even rumours that the President was contemplating dismissal of the Prime Minister. I, who was President of the BJP at the time, felt that doing so would not only be patently illegal but would also precipitate a grave and unprecedented Constitutional crisis. This view was fully shared by Atalji and other colleagues in the party. I, therefore, called on Zail Singh in Rashtrapati Bhavan and conveyed my views on the matter in no uncertain terms. Fortunately, the simmering tension between the Head of State and Head of Government did not reach a boiling point and, in 1987, R. Venkataraman, who was then Vice President, succeeded Zail Singh.

CONGRESS DEFEATED, BJP SURGES AHEAD

The multiple blunders of Rajiv Gandhi's government made the Opposition feel increasingly confident, after 1988, that the Congress could be defeated in the parliamentary elections scheduled for the following year. The BJP launched a nationwide satyagraha in January 1988 demanding Rajiv Gandhi's resignation and holding of mid-term elections. On 18 January, Atalji led the satyagraha in Delhi. Two days later, I did the same in Lucknow.

I was re-elected as party President on 3 March 1988. At the plenary session of the party's national council in Agra a month later, I lamented that a great country like India was being ruled by small men. In August 1988, seven Opposition parties, excluding the BJP and the Left parties, came together on a common platform called the National Front (NF). N.T. Rama Rao became its President and V.P. Singh its Convenor. In October of the same year, another significant political development took place. Taking the process of political aggregation forward, the Janata Dal was formed with the merger of V.P. Singh's Jan Morcha, Chandrashekhar's Janata Party and two factions of the Lok Dal, one led by Devi Lal and the other by Ajit Singh.

A major milestone in BJP's history during this period was the meeting of its National Executive in Bombay on 25 September 1989. At its previous meeting, held in Palampur in Himachal Pradesh in June 1986, the national executive had decided to enter into an alliance with the Shiv Sena. The Mumbai meeting, therefore, provided the right setting for Balasaheb Thackeray, the Shiv Sena's Founder-President, to come as a special guest and address the BJP's top decision-making forum. The atmosphere in Shanmukhananda Hall, the city's largest auditorium where the meeting took place, was upbeat because the party was then bubbling with self-confidence against the backdrop of the impending parliamentary elections. In my presidential address, I said, 'For our ideological school of thought, the Seventh General Elections in 1984 marked the lowest point in our progress graph. Let the deliberations and decisions of this Bombay session of ours fire us with a determination to make the Eighth General Elections the peak point in our onward journey.'

Around this time, many common well-wishers of the BJP and the Janata Dal were making efforts for an alliance between the two parties in the 1989 elections. The BJP would have gladly agreed to this alliance. After all, our common objective was to defeat the Congress and, going by the strong anti-Rajiv wave then, a combined effort of the two main non-Congress and non-Left parties would have certainly fulfilled it. Sadly, what came in the way was V.P. Singh's negative attitude. He was totally opposed to an alliance with the BJP, which he called a 'communal party'. As a result, some leaders in the Janata Dal, who were earlier rooting for the alliance, started dithering.

In my speech at Shanmukhananda Hall, I took note of this confusion in the Janata Dal. Quoting Veer Savarkar, I said, ' "If they come, *with* them; if they don't, *without* them; and if they oppose us, *in spite of* them." Irrespective of what the Janata Dal decides, we in the BJP are determined to throw out this corrupt and incompetent government of Rajiv Gandhi.'

Soon after the Bombay session, and before the elections were held, some leaders of the Janata Dal went to meet Bhaurao Deoras, a senior RSS leader. He was a highly experienced and thoughtful person, known for giving sound and balanced advice to the BJP on all important issues. Moreover, he had amiable personal relations with leaders in many other political parties, including the Congress, and was well-respected by all of them. His friends from the Janata Dal said to him, 'Only a broad agreement between the Janata Dal and the BJP can oust the Congress. Ours will be the largest party in the Lok Sabha. But we will need the support of the BJP to form an alliance government. We have come to seek your guidance and assistance in this matter.' They showed a sense of urgency to receive our assent because the Political Affairs Committee of the Janata Dal was to meet soon to deliberate on this matter.

A pre-poll alliance between the BJP and the Janata Dal was out of the question because of V.P. Singh's unfriendly attitude, but seat-sharing and joint campaigning was possible. Singh, however, was against seat adjustments between our two parties in Uttar Pradesh and Bihar, the two northern states that together accounted for as many as 125 seats in the Lok Sabha. All the BJP leaders were naturally upset with the hypocrisy of a leader who wanted to benefit from seat-sharing and joint campaigning with our party in states where we were strong—such as Madhya Pradesh, Rajasthan, Gujarat and Maharashtra—but did not want to join hands with us in the two big Hindi-speaking states for fear of losing Muslim votes. I, therefore, conveyed to the Janata Dal leadership, through common friends, that the BJP would have a seat-sharing and joint campaigning arrangement either in *all* the states or in *none at all*. This firm stand had the desired impact and benefited both parties.

When the results of the 1989 parliamentary elections were announced, the Rajiv Gandhi government was expectedly thrown out. The Congress managed to secure only 193 seats—a precipitous comedown from the 401 seats it had won in 1984. By bagging 141 seats, the Janata Dal emerged as the single largest opposition entity and was invited by the President, R. Venkataraman, to form the government. Although the Janata Dal would lead the coalition government, it was the BJP's spectacular performance that caught everyone's attention. Our tally went up from two MPs in 1984 to eighty-six MPs in 1989.

Analysing the outcome of the elections, I said in my presidential address at the party's National Executive meeting in New Delhi on 1 December, 'This 1989 Lok Sabha result is no doubt a verdict against the Rajiv Gandhi government's corruption and incompetence. All Opposition parties, including the BJP, have been the beneficiaries of the negative vote generated. But in the case of the BJP, its victory has a substantial positive content as well.'

What was the positive content in my party's spectacular performance? 'Over the years,' I said, 'the BJP has succeeded in projecting itself as a distinct political personality, committed to certain principles and policies which it was not willing to sacrifice at the altar of electoral expediency. At our Bombay session, I had referred to the national debate on secularism and communalism, and said that the *BJP believes in positive secularism, the Congress and most other parties subscribe only to 'vote secularism'. Positive secularism means—Justice for All, but Appeasement of None. In the ensuing elections, let this become the BJP's distinctive message to the nation.* This approach, I hold, has made no mean contribution to our success.' (emphasis added.)

The latter half of the 1980s witnessed an important turning point in my political life. I had been a member of the Rajya Sabha for nearly two decades, having been elected for the first time in 1970. My third term as a member of the Upper House had ended in 1988, and I was elected for a fourth term that year. I could have continued in the Rajya Sabha for another six years. However, I had, by now, made up my mind to become a people's elected representative in the true sense of the term—by entering the Lok Sabha, where a member is directly elected by the general electorate*. I contested my first Lok Sabha election from New Delhi constituency and won by a comfortable margin against Mohini Giri of the Congress.

---

* Rajya Sabha (Council of States) is the Upper House of the Parliament of India. Its membership is limited to 250 members, 12 of whom are nominated by the President. Unlike the Lok Sabha (House of the People), which has 543 members, it cannot be dissolved. Whereas the Lok Sabha is ordinarily elected every five years, the term of office of a Rajya Sabha member is for six years, with one-third of its members facing re-election every two years.

6

THE AYODHYA MOVEMENT
When India's Soul Spoke

I am proud of our inheritance and our ancestors who gave intellectual and cultural preeminence to India. How do you feel about this past? Do you feel you are also sharers in it and inheritors of it and, therefore, proud of something that belongs to you as much as to me? Or do you feel alien to it and pass it by without understanding it or feeling that strange thrill that comes from the realisation that we are the trustees and inheritors of this vast treasure?

—JAWAHARLAL NEHRU, IN HIS CONVOCATION ADDRESS
AT ALIGARH MUSLIM UNIVERSITY, 24 JANUARY 1948

I regard the Ayodhya movement as the most decisive transformational event of my political journey. As every student of India's contemporary history will attest to, its impact on our society and polity—indeed, on our sense of national identity—has been tremendous. Destiny made me perform a certain pivotal duty in this movement, in the form of the Ram Rath Yatra from Somnath to Ayodhya in 1990. I performed the duty with conviction, sincerity and to the best of my abilities and, in doing so, discovered India anew while rediscovering myself. The Ayodhya mission for me was thus both a time of intense action and intense inner reflection.

Why did the demand for the construction—rather, reconstruction—of a temple at Ramjanmabhoomi in Ayodhya gain such unprecedented support from the Hindu society? Why did it give rise to the biggest mass movement, with pan-national appeal, in the history of independent India? Why were hopes belied for the peaceful, lawful and amicable resolution of an issue that had needlessly been converted into a divisive Hindu vs Muslim dispute? Did not the Congress party play a duplicitous role in the events that led to the demolition of the Babri structure on 6 December 1992—and also to the construction of a proto-temple of Lord Ram in Ayodhya? What is now the way forward to reach a lasting solution to this dispute?

RECONSTRUCTION OF THE SOMNATH TEMPLE
What it meant for India's renaissance

To understand the Ayodhya movement in its right perspective, it is necessary first to know the history of another landmark temple reconstruction endeavour in independent India—the Somnath Temple at Prabhas Patan on the coast of Saurashtra in Gujarat. Those unfamiliar with our country's mythological and historical past will find it difficult to appreciate how this single ocean-front temple reveals so much about India's travails and triumphs, its national self-assertion as well as its cosmic quest.

One of the books I had read in my youth was Dr K.M. Munshi's historical novel *Jai Somnath*. Originally written in Gujarati, I had read its Hindi translation, which left a deep impact on me. Munshi, who is better remembered as the Founder-Chancellor of the Bharatiya Vidya Bhavan, an institution renowned for the propagation of Indian culture and philosophy worldwide, was a great scholar, dedicated Gandhian and a respected freedom fighter from Gujarat. His novel provides a riveting description of the glory of the ancient temple of Somnath, the first of the twelve revered *jyotirlingas* across the country.

The concept of *jyotirlingam* is one of the many fascinating facets of Hinduism. In Sanskrit *jyoti* means light and *linga* is the cosmic phallus. *Jyotirlingam* is thus a pillar of light, infinite and omnipresent, with neither a beginning nor an end. Shiva is the male principle that represents the inert cosmic consciousness, the unchanging substratum behind all change in the universe. In contrast, Shakti, the female principle of power, is the cause of all change in the universe. The *Shivalinga* is a symbol of Shiva-Shakti union, which is the source and sustainer of the rhythm of life.

The twelve *jyotirlinga* shrines are located in different parts of India, from Kedarnath on the snowy heights of the Himalayas to Rameshwaram in Tamil Nadu where Ram is believed to have worshipped Shiva before building a bridge across the sea to rescue Sita from her abductor Ravana, the king of Lanka. These and other abodes of God are closely linked with legends, myths and people's beliefs since the dawn of the Indian civilisation. Indeed, the millennia-old tradition of pilgrimage, cutting across linguistic, geographical and caste identities, to these shrines, has created a unique sense of national identity. Our rich and diverse cultural heritage would be incomprehensible without an understanding of our people's deeply entrenched faith in these shrines.

In his widely acclaimed recent book *Siva: Siva Purana Retold*, Ramesh Menon, a fine writer who has specialised in edifying the English-reading population about India's ancient wisdom, says: 'The length and breadth of India is strewn with temples that have a startling commonality of themes. I do not believe the Puranas, the books that describe these themes, are merely fictions of men of old. Rather, they seem to describe a human history more primal than the one of a few thousand years to which we habitually think of ourselves as belonging. In the Puranas, we see reflections of a cosmic history, when this earth was open to the universe. The characters in the Purana are "cosmic" in dimension, even the lesser ones; as is the sweep of time, space and spirit we encounter here. We can easily dismiss it all as the exaggerated fantasies of nameless writers of the dim past. Or else, we begin to suspect there is more to learn here than we dreamt: that human history is fundamentally different from what we have been taught.'[1]

Perhaps no other pilgrimage in India combines the eternal with the historical as vividly as that to the Somnath temple. Its very location and architecture leave a spellbinding effect on the visitor. A shrine at the top of a mountain—and many Hindu shrines are indeed located at the summit of mountains, necessitating an arduous climb to get a *darshan* of the deity—makes the devotees think of the heaven above, and of the life beyond our transitory earthly existence. In contrast, an ocean-front temple makes them think of both the geography and history of their Motherland. Whenever I have visited Prabhas Patan and watched the waves of the sea lapping up the feet of the Somnath temple, I have wondered how much of India's timeless history has been witnessed by this imposing and lonely-looking shrine.

Munshi's novel provides a poignant account of how Somnath was both a witness to, and a target of, foreign invasions during the medieval period. Mahmood Ghazni, a Turkish sultan of the province of Ghazni in Afghanistan, attacked India seventeen times in a span of twenty-five years between the years AD 1001-26. Somnath was a particularly coveted target for him. Muslim chronicles indicate that 50,000 Hindus died in the battle for Somnath in AD 1024. The Shiva lingam was destroyed by the sultan himself. After the battle, Mahmood and his troops are believed to have carried away vast amounts of gold and other riches stored in the temple. They are also said to have taken Hindu statues and buried them at the entrance of a mosque in Ghazni so that the faithful could trample on them. Munshi's novel describes not only the destruction and pillage of the Somnath temple, and the betrayal by some Hindus on account of petty caste considerations, but also the heroic defence by its devotees, who would reconstruct it after each successive attack.

There are various accounts of why and how Mahmood Ghazni attacked Somnath. In his book *Pakistan or The Partition of India*, Dr B.R. Ambedkar refers to the raids on Somnath and quotes the description given by Al'Utbi, the historian of Mahmood Ghazni: 'He demolished idol temples and established Islam. He captured…cities, and destroyed the idolaters, gratifying Muslims. He then returned home and promulgated accounts of the victories obtained for Islam...and vowed that every year he would undertake a holy war against Hind.'[2]

We now know that Mahmood Ghazni was not the only bigoted king to have targeted the Somnath temple. The last of such assaults took place in 1706 when Prince Mohammed Azam, a Viceroy of the Mughal kingdom in Gujarat, implemented the orders of Aurangzeb 'to destroy the Temple of Somnath beyond possibility of repair'. Thus, if the Somnath temple is testimony to the religious hatred and violence perpetuated by some Muslim invaders and rulers, it is at the same time an inspiring symbol of the people's courageous resistance to the alien marauders.

I should at this point clarify what I mean by 'alien' because it goes to the heart of the truth that the post-Independence resolve of many of our nationalist leaders for the restoration of the Somnath temple was not guided by Hindu versus Muslim considerations; rather, it was meant to affirm the unwillingness of our tolerant, secular, inclusive and self-respecting national self to quietly accept the intolerant and vindictive acts of the un-Indian forces in history. The deeds of Mahmood Ghazni and Aurangzeb are alien to our ethos not because they were Muslims. After all, over ninety per cent of the Muslims in India have an Indian ancestry as they were actually Hindus who converted to Islam. The actions of these bigoted rulers were alien because they violated India's national tradition of tolerance and respect for all faiths. They were meant to humiliate Hindus, remind them of their status as a conquered people, and to establish the dominance of Islam as the victors interpreted it.

It is appropriate for me to quote here what Swami Vivekananda said about the lesson of medieval iconoclasm in India's history. 'Temple after temple was broken down by the foreign conqueror, but no sooner had the wave passed than the spire of the temple rose up again. Some of these old temples of South India, and those like Somnath in Gujarat, will teach you volumes of wisdom, which will give you a keener insight into the history of the race than any amount of books. Mark how these temples bear the marks of a hundred attacks and a hundred regenerations, continually destroyed and continually springing up out of the ruins, rejuvenated and strong as ever! That is the national mind, that is the national life-current. Follow it and it leads to glory.'³

HOW SOMNATH WAS REBUILT
Sardar Patel's resolve, Mahatma Gandhi's blessings, K.M. Munshi's battle and Rajendra Babu's Presidential stamp.

It is therefore only natural that, when India became independent, many Hindus felt that 1947 should signify not only freedom from British rule but also a clean break from those aspects of the pre-British history that were identified with subjugation, assaults on Hindu temples, vandalising idols and erosion of our noble cultural traditions. Further, since India's independence was accompanied by blood-soaked Partition on the basis of a communal demand by the Muslim League, it was only natural that the cultural reaffirmation of India's nationalist spirit would, to some extent, to seek appropriate Hindu idioms and symbols to articulate itself.

One such occasion presented itself in the princely state of Junagadh in Gujarat's Saurashtra region where the Somnath temple is located. Over eighty per cent of Junagadh's population was Hindu, but its Nawab was a Muslim. On the eve of Independence, the nawab announced the accession of his state to Pakistan. This enraged Junagadh's Hindus whose revolt against the nawab culminated in their setting up a parallel government under the leadership of Samaldas Gandhi, a local Congress leader. The Nawab, an uncaring and decadent ruler, who was highly unpopular with his people, sought the support of Pakistan. All his tricks were of no avail, so one night he finally fled to Pakistan. Samaldas Gandhi and the Dewan of Junagadh, Sir Shah Nawaz Bhutto, who, incidentally, was Zulfikar Ali Bhutto's father, conveyed to India that Junagadh was acceding to India. Munshi recalls in his book *Pilgrimage to Freedom* that Sardar Vallabhbhai Patel, India's first Home Minister and the chief architect of the integration of the princely states into the Indian Union, handed over the telegram of accession to him with the words: 'Jai Somnath'.⁴

Four days after the take-over of Junagadh on 9 November 1947 by the Government of India, Patel visited Saurashtra. He was accompanied by

N.V. Gadgil, the Minister of Public Works and Rehabilitation of Refugees in Nehru's Cabinet. They received a rousing welcome from the people of Junagadh. At a public meeting in his honour, Patel made an important announcement: the government of independent India would reconstruct the historic temple of Somnath at the same spot where it stood in ancient times, and re-install the *jyotirlingam*. Maulana Abul Kalam Azad, who was the Minister of Education in Nehru's Cabinet, suggested that the site should be handed over to the Archaeological Survey of India (ASI) to be preserved as a historical monument. Patel's response to this was firm and unyielding. He said: 'The Hindu sentiment in regard to this temple is both strong and widespread. In the present conditions, it is unlikely that this sentiment will be satisfied by mere restoration of the temple or by prolonging its life. The restoration of the idol would be a point of honour and sentiments with the Hindu public.'[5]

With Sardar Patel assuming an uncompromising stand on the matter, the proposal received the approval of Nehru's Cabinet. It is notable that this decision was fully supported and blessed by Mahatma Gandhi. His only caveat was that the funds for the temple's reconstruction should be collected from the public and should not come from the government's exchequer.

This is where Munshi reappeared in the story of the Somnath temple, not as a narrator of history this time, but as a creator of history. As Minister of Food and Agriculture in Nehru's Cabinet, he headed the official committee set up to supervise the reconstruction of the temple. But Munshi's was not an easy job. It was rendered enormously harder by Sardar Patel's untimely demise on 15 December 1950. Subsequently, Munshi faced opposition not only from leftist intellectuals and politicians outside the government, but also from the Prime Minister himself. Nehru had now come to believe that the Government of India's official involvement in the Somnath project was violative of its commitment to secularism. After the death of Patel, who was the initiator and the chief votary of this project, the Prime Minister felt emboldened to voice his disagreement openly. Now Munshi was practically isolated in his mission. Although many of his ministerial colleagues privately supported the cause, they were not prepared to express their views openly, thereby risking the Prime Minister's censure. Once, after a Cabinet meeting, Nehru called Munshi and said, 'I do not like your trying to restore Somnath. It is Hindu revivalism.'[6]

A leader's character is tested when his convictions are challenged. Faced with these roadblocks, Munshi wrote a letter to Nehru on 24 April 1951.[7] It is undoubtedly one of the best examples of a letter written by a courageous Minister to a Prime Minister. Munshi said:

> Yesterday you referred to Hindu revivalism. You pointedly referred to me in the Cabinet as connected with Somnath. I am glad you did so; for I do not want to keep back any part of my views or activities.... I can assure you that the 'Collective Subconscious' of India today is happier with the scheme of reconstruction of Somnath sponsored by the Government of India than with many other things that we have done and are doing.

Emphasising the social reform aspect of Somnath's reconstruction, Munshi added:

> The intention to throw open the temple to Harijans has evoked some criticism from the orthodox section of the Hindu community. However, the objects of the Trust Deed make it clear that the temple is not only to be open to all classes of the Hindu community, but, according to the tradition of the old temple of Somnath, also to non-Hindu visitors. Many have been the customs which I have defied in personal life from boyhood. I have laboured in my humble way through literary and social work to share or reintegrate some aspects of Hinduism, in the conviction that that alone will make India an advanced and vigorous nation under modern conditions.

Munshi concluded his letter with words that deserve to be preserved in perpetuity:

> It is my faith in our past which has given me the strength to work in the present and to look forward to our future. I cannot

value India's freedom if it deprives us of the *Bhagavad Gita* or uproots our millions from the faith with which they look upon our temples and thereby destroys the texture of our lives. I have been given the privilege of seeing my incessant dream of Somnath reconstruction come true. That makes me feel—makes me almost sure—that this shrine once restored to a place of importance in our life will give to our people a purer conception of religion and a more vivid consciousness of our strength, so vital in these days of freedom and its trials.'

On reading this letter, V.P. Menon, the legendary civil servant who assisted Sardar Patel in the gigantic task of the integration of the princely states, wrote a missive to Munshi. 'I have seen your masterpiece. I for one would be prepared to live and, if necessary, die by the views you have expressed in your letter.'

How Munshi faced these odds and finally succeeded in his endeavour is an inspiring account, penned in his highly readable book *Somnath: The Shrine Eternal*. His other book *Pilgrimage to Freedom* also contains several chapters on the Somnath issue. In it he lamented that, after the demise of Mahatma Gandhi and Sardar Patel, 'secularism' had come to mean allergy to Hinduism. 'In its name, again, politicians in power adopt a strange attitude which, while it condones the susceptibilities, religious and social, of the minority communities, is too ready to brand similar susceptibilities in the majority community as communalistic and reactionary. How secularism sometimes becomes allergic to Hinduism will be apparent from certain episodes relating to the reconstruction of Somnath temple.

'These unfortunate postures have been creating a sense of frustration in the majority community. If, however, the misuse of this word "secularism" continues, if Sanskrit, the bond of unity is not given a place in our language formula, if every time there is an inter-communal conflict, the majority is blamed regardless of the merits of the question, if our holy places of pilgrimage like Banaras, Mathura and Rishikesh continue to be converted into industrial slums by establishing huge industries, the springs of traditional tolerance will dry up. While the majority exercises patience and tolerance, the minorities should learn to adjust themselves to the majority. Otherwise the future is uncertain and *an explosion cannot be avoided*.'[8] (emphasis added.)

As Patel had passed away, Munshi approached Dr Rajendra Prasad, the first President of independent India, to inaugurate the newly reconstructed temple and ceremonially install the *jyotirlingam*. He was, however, apprehensive that Rajendrababu might not accept the invitation. The Prime Minister, he thought, might object to the President's inaugurating a Hindu temple. Alternatively, the President himself might say no, since he was aware of Munshi's correspondence with the Prime Minister. To his delight, Rajendrababu readily agreed. 'I would do the same with a mosque or a church if I were invited,' he added. 'This is the core of Indian secularism. Our state is neither irreligious nor anti-religious.'

Munshi's foreboding proved correct. Nehru vehemently protested the President's decision. To his credit, Rajendrababu disregarded Nehru's objection and kept his promise. The speech he delivered on the occasion is one of the most important statements on secularism delivered by a President of India. 'Even as the Creator of the Universe, Brahma, resides in the navel of Lord Vishnu, similarly in the heart of man reside the creative urge and faith, and these surpass in power all the armaments, all the armies and all the emperors of the world. In the ancient era, India had been a treasure-house of gold and silver…. Centuries ago, the major portion of the gold of the world was in the temples of India. It is my view that the reconstruction of the Somnath temple will be complete on that day when not only a magnificent edifice will arise on this foundation, but the mansion of India's prosperity will be really that prosperity of which the ancient Temple of Somnath was a symbol.'

Describing Somnath temple as a symbol of national faith, the President elaborated: 'By rising from its ashes again, this temple of Somnath is to say proclaiming to the world that no man and no power in the world can destroy that for which people have boundless faith and love in their hearts… Today, our attempt is not to rectify history. Our only aim is to proclaim anew our attachment to the faith, convictions and to the values on which our religion has rested since immemorial ages.'

It is not out of place here to mention that the news of the reconstruction of the Somnath temple met with angry condemnation in Pakistan. A public meeting was held in Karachi to denounce the Indian government's action.

The Somnath temple today stands as a sobering reminder that a weak nation that cannot defend itself against external attacks stands to lose much more than its political freedom; it risks losing its cultural heritage, which is the heart and soul of India. By reconstructing the Somnath temple, as one of the early acts of the Government of India, Sardar Patel and Munshi, with the blessings of Mahatma Gandhi and Rajendra Prasad, made it a proud testimony of India's determination to erase the history of bigoted alien attacks and regain its lost cultural treasure. In this sense, Somnath is truly unique among the tens of thousands of temples that dot the landscape of India.

PART I

SOMNATH'S ECHO IN AYODHYA
Expressions of national identity

I have given this historical background of the destruction and restoration of the Somnath temple as I deem it necessary to understand the context and causes that led me to spearhead my party's mass campaign for the reconstruction of the Ram temple in Ayodhya. Everything that Mahatma Gandhi, Sardar Patel, Rajendra Prasad and K.M. Munshi said and did in transforming the dream of reconstruction of the Somnath temple into reality echoed loudly in my mind when the Ayodhya issue rose to the centre-stage of national politics in the mid-1980s. Indeed, in many ways, the Ayodhya movement was the continuation of the spirit of Somnath.

When the BJP decided in 1990 that I, as its President, should lead the Ram Rath Yatra to mobilise people's support for the Ayodhya movement, it took no time for me to choose Somnath as the starting venue of this historic journey. Somnath became my point of reference in the debate on Ayodhya, which polarised India's political and intellectual classes on lines not quite dissimilar to what was evident in the early 1950s, but on a much larger scale.

Munshi was indeed prophetic on two counts. Firstly, 'secularism' had yet again come to mean allergy to Hinduism. Secondly, precisely because of this allergy and utter disregard for the patience and tolerance of the majority community, an 'explosion' could not be avoided. The explosion, in the form of the demolition of the disputed structure (where a mosque, known as the Babri Masjid, was built after destroying a temple that marked the birthplace of Lord Ram) at Ayodhya on 6 December 1992 was highly unfortunate. But anyone who follows, with an unprejudiced mind, the sequence of events leading up to that fateful day will scarcely be surprised by it. Equally, they will not be surprised that the 'explosion' led not only to the demolition of the disputed structure, but also to the construction of a small, makeshift temple, with idols of Ram Lalla duly installed inside it.

It is both ironic and highly significant that the latter development took place when the Congress government at the Centre, led by P.V. Narasimha Rao, was effectively in control of Ayodhya and the rest of Uttar Pradesh. (The Chief Minister of Uttar Pradesh, Kalyan Singh, had already resigned in the afternoon of 6 December and the state had been brought under President's Rule.) Ironic because the Congress party and government had maintained, both before and after the events of 6 December, that the disputed structure was a mosque and a temple would not be allowed to be built on its site. Significant because, by design or due to helplessness, the Central Government not only allowed the makeshift temple to be built but also made arrangements for daily *puja* (prayers) to be performed there and for devotees to pay obeisance to the idol of Lord Ram at his *janmasthan* (birthplace). I do not know whether to attribute this to the 'shrewdness' of the then Prime Minister or to an act of divine intervention.

RAM: AN INSPIRING SYMBOL OF INDIAN CULTURE

Every mass movement has a dynamic of its own insofar as it gathers within itself the aspirations, energies and passions of millions of its participants.

But rare are the moments when the articulation of a collective aspiration of the masses echoes with the assertion of the soul of a nation. When the two come together, they produce a force that truly moves history. Only a phenomenon of this kind is worthy of being described by that profound but often loosely used word 'movement'.

Why did the Ram Janmabhoomi movement acquire the kind of sweep and strength that it did? The search for an answer has to begin by understanding the significance of Ram and the *Ramayana* in the national life of India. The *Ramayana*, along with the other great Indian epic, the *Mahabharata*, has influenced the cultural personality and ethical value-system of Indians over centuries. Ram was an ideal king; hence the concept of 'Ram Rajya', the epitome of good governance, was extolled as the ideal for India by no less a person than Mahatma Gandhi. Ram was also an ideal human being; hence the title 'Maryada Purushottam' (an exemplar among good human beings) was accorded to him.

The entire story of the *Ramayana* is a confluence of deeply experienced human emotions and moral dilemmas, which are as eternal as they are universal. Each and every character in the epic—Ram and his consort Sita; his brothers Laxman, Bharat and Shatrughna; his devoted servant Hanuman, the highly revered monkey-god; his father Dashrath, his mother Kausalya and step-mother Kaikeyi; sons Luv and Kush; the demon king Ravana; and scores of others—is etched in the hearts and minds of all Indians. Even apparently minor characters in it animate widely popular moral lessons. Shabari, the poor tribal woman pining for a *darshan* of Ram, who could not believe her good fortune when he gladly accepted her hospitality during his fourteen-year exile in forest, is a good example. There is also the adorable character of Shravana Kumar, who epitomises the virtue of a son's duty towards his old parents. How the *Ramayana* came to be written by Valmiki, a tribal hunter transformed into a venerable *rishi*-poet by the inspiration of a tragic experience, is itself a fascinating story.

There is scarcely a language in India into which the *Ramayana* has not been translated—or written with its own creative flavour. There is hardly a folk tradition, which does not immortalise the life and legend of Ram. There is no caste or region in India which does not have names without Ram in some form or the other. All the saintly personalities in Indian history—from Tulsidas to Surdas, from Kabir to Tukaram, and from Sankaradev in Assam to Kamba in Tamil Nadu—have sung the praises of Ram in their mission for social reform. Sikhs, Jains, Buddhists and Arya Samajis (who do not believe in idol worship) have their own version of Ram and the *Ramayana*. The *Guru Granth Sahib*, the sacred scripture of the Sikhs, invokes the name of Ram about two thousand four hundred times.

Many Indian Muslims, too, have seen in Ram an ideal ruler and an embodiment of great human qualities. Allama Iqbal*, the renowned Urdu and Persian poet, described him as India's 'Imam-e-Hind' (the spiritual leader of India) and wrote the following eulogy[10]:

> The cup of India has always overflowed
> With the heady wine of truth.
> Even the philosophers from the West
> Are her ardent devotees.
> There is something so sublime in her mysticism
> That her star soars high above constellations
> There have been thousands of rulers in this land
> But none can compare with Ram;
> The discerning ones proclaim him
> The spiritual leader of India.
> His lamp gave the light of wisdom
> Which outshone the radiance
> Of the whole of humankind
> Ram was valiant, Ram was bold, yielded deftly his sword,
> He cared for the poorest of poor
> He was unmatched in love and compassion.

---

* In his later years, Iqbal (1877–1938) became a strong votary of the Muslim League's demand for Pakistan and even went to the extent of disowning his poem on Ram. After the creation of Pakistan, he was declared as its national poet. He is best known in India as the poet who penned the highly popular patriotic song '*Saare jahan se achcha, Hindustan hamara…*'

Gandhiji's lifelong devotion to Ram *naam*, the pious utterance of the name of Ram, formed the spiritual soil in which the tree of his social and political thought received nourishment. 'Ram *naam*,' he said, 'purifies while it cures, and, therefore, it elevates.' He did not perceive Ram purely as a Hindu deity, but rather as a divine force of universal brotherhood and, in the context of India, of national integration. For instance, his daily all-faith prayer meetings were never complete without the collective singing of the Ramdhun *'Raghupati Raghava Rajaram, patita pavana Sitaram; Ishwar Allah tero naam, sab ko sanmati de Bhagwan'*. This song affirms that Ishwar and Allah are both names of the same Divine Power, to which the devotees should pray to grant them a virtuous mind. It is worth recalling that the Muslim League criticised Gandhiji's prayer meetings because his socio-political sermons were invariably accompanied by the chanting of the Ramdhun. Some Marxists and Muslims even today hold the view that Gandhiji gave a 'Hindu communal' orientation to India's freedom movement by positing Ram Rajya as its goal. This criticism stems from ignorance and prejudice. As Gandhiji himself clarified, 'By Ram Rajya I do not mean Hindu Raj. I mean Divine Raj, the Kingdom of God.' The last words that Gandhiji uttered as life ebbed out of him were 'Hey Ram!'

Ram, therefore, is a unique symbol of India's national identity, unity and integration. In many ways, he is an ideal for Indians' aspiration to live a life of higher values. Thus, it is hardly surprising that the place of Ram's birth in Ayodhya, which was the capital of his kingdom, has been the focal point of deepest devotion for the Hindus through the millennia.

THE BABRI MOSQUE
Evidence of the destruction of a pre-existing Hindu temple

Sadly, as in the case of Somnath, the temple at the birthplace of Ram in Ayodhya also became a target of attack by an invader, Babar, who founded the Mughal Empire. In 1528, Babar ordered his commander Mir Baqi to erect a mosque at Ayodhya to make the spot a 'place of descent of angels'—hence, the name Babri Masjid. Hindus widely believe that

Mir Baqi established the mosque after demolishing a temple located at Ramjanmabhoomi.

It is rightly said that the conquered rarely write the history of their defeat, whereas the victors always keep a record of their conquest. Thus, Mughal sources contain enough evidence about Ayodhya. Abul Fazal's *Ain-i-Akbari*, written in the late sixteenth century, says that Awadh (the region where Ayodhya is located) was the abode of Shri Ram Chandra of Treta Yug and that Ram Navmi was celebrated with great festivity here. *Safiha Chahal Nasaih Bahadur Shahi*, written by Bahadur Shah Ibn Alamgir's daughter during the seventeenth or eighteenth century states: 'The place of the birth of Kanhaiya (Krishna), the place of Rasoi Sita, the place of Hanuman....were all demolished on the strength of Islam, and at all these places mosques have been constructed'. Similarly, *Hadiqa-i-Shahada* by Mirza Jan (1856) says: '...the temple of Janmasthan was the original birth place of Ram, adjacent to which is Sita Ki Rasoi, Sita being the name of his wife. Hence, at this site, a lofty mosque has been built by Babar Badshah under the guidance of Mir Ashikan...'

The archaeological evidence of a pre-existing temple at Ayodhya is compelling. Indeed, all those who visited the three-dome structure before its demolition on 6 December 1992 were struck by two anachronisms. Firstly, a mosque right in the middle of a holy Hindu town, surrounded by temples, ashrams and other Hindu religious establishments on all sides, looked unnatural and out of place. Secondly, the interior of the Babri Mosque was replete with Hindu motifs and architectural elements. For example, the mosque structure contained fourteen pillars of black stone on which tell-tale Hindu symbols were carved. Such motifs can be found in several mosques from medieval times. In the 1970s, a team of the ASI, led by Prof B.B. Lal, conducted some excavations outside the mosque structure. The team found rows of pillar-bases, suggestive of a larger building that may have existed earlier. All this evidentiary material was presented by the VHP to the Special Cell on Ayodhya created by the Narasimha Rao government, which was headed by Naresh Chandra, an experienced and widely regarded civil servant who later served as India's Ambassador to the United States.

Further archaeological, sculptural and epigraphic evidence in support of a pre-existing temple at the disputed site came in the post-demolition period. This was the result of new antiquities found in the rubble as well as in a special scanning survey of the site's underground ordered by the Allahabad High Court. Among the finds were a statue of Vishnu, one of whose ten avatars is Ram; an ancient stone inscription in Devnagari script; and two black basalt columns bearing fine decorative carvings with two cross-legged figures on a lotus in bloom. There was also a sculpture of Ganesh. Perhaps the most important of the discoveries were three Sanskrit inscriptions written in Nagari script of eleventh-twelfth century AD. One inscription speaks of Janmabhoomi and of a grand temple of Vishnu-Hari built with stones like a high mountain. The same antiquity also says that it was built in Ayodhya, 'which is full with high and lofty temples, situated in the *mandala* (district) of Saketa'. It is unfortunate that no systematic and scholarly study of these findings has so far been conducted in order to put an end to the dispute once and for all.

As Dr Koenraad Elst, a Belgian scholar born into a Flemish Catholic family, writing extensively on the Ayodhya issue says: 'There was testimony after testimony of Hindus bewailing and Muslims boasting of the replacement of the temple with a mosque; and of Hindus under Muslim rule coming as close as possible to the site in order to celebrate Ram's birthday every year, in continuation of the practice at the time when the temple stood.'

HISTORICAL ROOTS OF THE AYODHYA DISPUTE
From 1936 to 1949, the structure was a de facto temple

Historical records show that Hindus had been waging an unremitting struggle for over four hundred years to reclaim this holy place. This was only natural, given the deep religious significance that Ramjanmabhoomi had for them. For Muslims, however, the place had no special significance, religious or cultural. Hindus continued to go on pilgrimage to Ayodhya throughout the long history of the Muslim rule. For Muslims, its significance lay, if at all, only in it being a symbol of conquest by a Muslim invader in medieval times. This added a new element to the Hindu disquiet: the location of the Babri Masjid was seen not only as an unacceptable religious affront, but also as a deliberate statement of national subjugation.

Ayodhya was not the only holy Hindu place that bore evidence of destruction and desecration by Muslim kings who subscribed to an intolerant and supremacist view of Islam. The two other shrines, which shared a similar fate and are at par with Ayodhya, in terms of religious importance to Hindus, are the Krishna Janmabhoomi in Mathura and the Vishwanath temple in Kashi, the holiest place for all Hindus.

As far as Ayodhya is concerned, the point to note is that the Hindu attempt to reacquire the place where the Babri Masjid stood dates back to several centuries. It is necessary to highlight this fact in order to counter the propaganda that the movement is nothing but an artificial creation of the RSS-VHP-BJP combined to promote a 'Hindu political agenda'.

At least two major Hindu-Muslim clashes over Ramjanmabhoomi have been recorded in the nineteenth and twentieth centuries. About the first incident in 1855, the *Gazetteer* of Faizabad District in Uttar Pradesh states: 'When the Muslims mounted an attack in 1855, they took possession of the Ramjanmabhoomi and attacked the Hanuman Garhi, but were repulsed. The king's army (Nawab Wajid Ali Shah's army) stood by. The Hindus retook the Ramjanmabhoomi and the structure there.' The armed communal encounter in 1934 resulted in many deaths and a serious damage to the contentious structure. After this incident, the doors of the disputed structure were locked and the situation remained so until 1950. Nevertheless, Hindus continued to offer prayers outside the locked doors and in other shrines dedicated to Hindu deities within the temple complex.

For a long time before and after Independence, the Hindu effort to reclaim the Ramjanmabhoomi site mainly followed a legal course. After the 1885 incident Mahant Raghubardas, a local Hindu leader, appealed to the Faizabad District Court that an order be given for the construction of a temple on Janmabhoomi. On 18 March 1886, the judge of the court, a Britisher named Col F.E.A. Chamier, passed the following order: 'I visited the land in dispute yesterday in the presence of all parties. I found that the Masjid built by Emperor Babar stands on the border of Ayodhya, that is to say, to the west and south. It is clear of habitants. It is most unfortunate that a Masjid should have been built on land specially held sacred by the Hindus, but as that event occurred 356 years ago, it is too late now to agree with the grievances. All that can be done is to maintain the party in status quo. In such a case as the present one any innovation may cause more harm and derangement of order than any benefit.'

After India's independence, Hindus in and around Ayodhya resumed their legal battle with renewed vigour, in the hope that the Nehru government's precedent of Somnath would be followed in the case of Janmabhoomi too. On the night of 22-23 December 1949, some people installed the idols of Ram, Sita and Lakshman inside the disputed structure, which had remained locked since 1934. K.K. Nayar, the District Magistrate of Faizabad at the time when the province of UP was ruled by a Congress government, allowed *puja* of the idols to be performed daily in the sanctum sanctorum. In the judicial proceedings that followed, the Faizabad City Civil Court granted an injunction against removing the idols and upheld the Hindus' right to offer worship before the deity. While confirming the injunction, the Civil Judge of Faizabad recorded: '…at least from 1936 onwards the Muslims have neither used the site as a mosque nor offered prayers there and… the Hindus have been performing their pooja etc. on the disputed site'.

On a writ filed by some Muslims, the Allahabad High Court, in its judgment of April 1955, upheld the Hindus' unrestricted right of worship. On the dispute concerning the title of the property, the high court stated: 'It is very desirable that a suit of this kind is decided as soon as possible and it is regretted that it remained undecided after four years.'

How ironical—and regrettable—that the case has remained undecided even today!

It is significant that from 1936 to 1949, the disputed structure was a *de facto* temple; post 1955, it became a *de jure* temple as well. This is something that the courts themselves have decided. Further, the courts have held that the status quo cannot be changed.

THE NEHRU GOVERNMENT'S VIEW ON THE AYODHYA DISPUTE
Sardar Patel's sound advice ignored

How Pandit Nehru's government at the Centre viewed the 1949 development is quite instructive. Concerned perhaps by the fact that India had just suffered the trauma of Partition and the accompanying communal bloodbath, the Prime Minister sent a telegram to the then Chief Minister of Uttar Pradesh, Pandit Govind Ballabh Pant, on 26 December 1949, just three days after the incident. It read: 'I am disturbed at developments at Ayodhya. Earnestly hope you will personally interest yourself in this matter. Dangerous example is being set there which will have bad consequences.'

Pandit Nehru showed the telegram to his Home Minister Sardar Patel, who, on 9 January 1950, wrote a letter to Pant. The letter outlined an approach to the resolution of the Ayodhya dispute which was flawless. Had it been adopted, the problem could have been solved long ago—and that too, amicably and expeditiously. In view of its importance, I would like to reproduce it in full.

My dear Pantji,

The Prime Minister had already sent to you a telegram expressing his concern over the developments in Ayodhya. I spoke to you about it in Lucknow. I feel that the controversy has been raised at a most inopportune time both from the point of view of the country at large and of your own province in particular. The wider communal issues have only been recently resolved to the mutual satisfaction of the various communities. So far as Muslims are concerned, they are just settling down to their new loyalties. We can reasonably say that the first shock of Partition and the resultant uncertainties are just beginning to be over and that it is unlikely that there would be any transfer of loyalties on a mass scale. In your own province, the communal problem has always been a difficult one. I think it has been one of the outstanding achievements of your administration that despite many upsetting factors, communal relations have generally improved very considerably since 1946. We have our own difficulties in U.P. organisationally and administratively as a result of group formations. It would be most unfortunate if we allowed any group advantage to be made on this issue. On all these grounds, therefore, I feel that the issue is one which should be resolved amicably in a spirit of mutual toleration and goodwill between the two communities.

I realise there is a great deal of sentiment behind the move which has taken place. At the same time, such matters can only be resolved peacefully, if we take the willing consent of the Muslim community with us. There can be no question of resolving such disputes by force. In that case, the forces of law and order will have to maintain peace at all costs. If, therefore, peaceful and persuasive methods are to be followed, any unilateral action based on an attitude of aggression or coercion cannot be countenanced. I am therefore quite convinced that the matter should not be made such a live issue and that the present inopportune controversies should be resolved by peaceful and persuasive means. To that extent, any accomplished facts should not be allowed to stand in the way of an amicable settlement. I hope your efforts in this direction will meet with success.

In my deposition before the Justice Liberhan Commission in April 2001, I was asked for my opinion on this letter. My unequivocal reply was: 'I would endorse every word of what he has said. There is not one word with which I, when I participated in the Ayodhya movement, would disagree. Sardar Patel has emphasised, on the one hand, that "I feel there is a great deal of sentiment behind the move which has taken place" and, on the other, that, "At the same time, such matters can only be resolved peacefully, if we take the willing consent of the Muslim community with us." This is precisely the approach that I have tried to emphasise whenever I have spoken about the Ayodhya issue. And the second aspect that I have emphasised is that nothing should be sought to be changed by force. It is, therefore, that even though I have been praising the Ayodhya movement as such, I felt extremely distressed when the structure was demolished on 6 December 1992, because that was an illegal, forceful action.'

The Commission also asked me what I thought of Prime Minister Nehru's telegram to the UP Chief Minister. I answered: 'I am sure that the then Prime Minister's telegram to Pant and the then Home Minister's letter to him must have weighed with the UP government when it presented its case to the Civil Judge of Faizabad in 1949 and again later in 1986. The court's order must have taken all these factors into account.'

HOW THE AYODHYA ISSUE RESURFACED IN THE 1980S
Rajiv Gandhi's government opened the lock to the shrine's gate

I have described in some detail the history of the Hindu claim on the disputed structure just to puncture the propaganda that there never was any serious dispute and that it is just a concoction of the RSS-VHP-BJP combined to gain political mileage. Equally, it is no less instructive to recall how the Hindu efforts gained momentum in the 1980s, nearly five years *before* the BJP formally decided to support the Ayodhya movement in 1989.

How the Ayodhya issue resurfaced in the early 1980s, who contributed to its appearance on the national political scene for the first time, and why, are questions that shed much light on the evolution of the dispute. From 1951 till 1986, when the gates of the disputed structure were unlocked under the patronage of the Congress governments in Lucknow and New Delhi, the Ayodhya issue had remained a purely local issue. In fact, until then I had never had an occasion to speak on this matter, even though I had been a politician activist since 1952.

Three factors led to a dramatic change in the profile of the dispute. Firstly, disquiet was building up among Hindu religious leaders in Ayodhya over the fact that their long wait for a judicial verdict on the title of the disputed structure was proving to be both futile and frustrating. Secondly, the presence of a mosque structure at the birthplace of Ram continued to irk Hindu pilgrims from Uttar Pradesh as well as from other parts of the country. This annoyance was further accentuated by the fact that only a priest could enter the locked gates of the shrine to perform prayers.

Out of this disquiet arose the idea of a mass movement in 1983. Significantly, this happened in a completely non-political setting—at a public meeting at Muzaffarnagar in Uttar Pradesh, which was attended, among others, by Gulzarilal Nanda*, a veteran Gandhian and a highly respected Minister in the governments of Jawaharlal Nehru, Lal Bahadur Shastri and Indira Gandhi. Others present at this meeting were: Prof Rajendra Singh (Rajju Bhaiyya), a senior leader of the RSS who later became its Chief in 1993, Daudayal Khanna, a former Congress Minister in Uttar Pradesh, and Paramahans Ramachandradas, a widely respected saint from Ayodhya who had been championing the temple cause since 1949. Later, in April 1984, the first *Dharma Sansad* (parliament of Hindu religious leaders from all parts of the country) in Delhi unanimously resolved to 'liberate' the birthplace of Ram through a peaceful mass movement. For this purpose, a broadbased front called the Ramjanmabhoomi Muktiyajna Samiti (Ramjanmabhoomi Liberation Committee) was formed in July 1984. It goes to the credit of the VHP that it brought all the leading figures belonging to diverse Hindu religious establishments on a common platform dedicated towards a common goal.

Between September and October 1984, a mass awareness yatra was undertaken from Sitamarhi in Bihar to Ayodhya, demanding the opening of the temple's locks. It evoked enthusiastic response all along the route. The timing of this part of the campaign is significant because it took place when Indira Gandhi was still Prime Minister. The Ramjanmabhoomi movement steadily gained momentum in 1985, the first year of Rajiv Gandhi's Prime Ministership. Uttar Pradesh had a Congress government, headed by Vir Bahadur Singh. The BJP was yet to recover from the shock of the rout suffered in the 1984 Lok Sabha polls. Significantly, it was the Congress governments at the Centre and in UP which made the most

---

* Gulzarilal Nanda (1898-1998) was India's interim Prime Minister on two occasions, in 1964 and 1966. He passionately strove for the protection of India's spiritual heritage. He was the chief inspiration behind the Kurukshetra Development Board in Haryana, which renovated and beautified scores of pilgrimage places at the battle-site in the Mahabharata, where Lord Krishna narrated the Bhagavad Gita to warrior Arjuna.

crucial decisions in the Ayodhya dispute. On 19 January 1986, a conference of Hindu religious leaders resolved in Lucknow to break open the locks on *Maha Shivaratri* day (8 March) if the government did not do so by that date. The swiftness with which the Congress governments and the judiciary then acted, amazed one and all.

The state government filed an application in the Faizabad District Court to open the locks within two days. It was rejected on 28 January. Thereafter, an appeal was filed and an order for unlocking the doors of the disputed structure was passed within three days, on 1 February. The judge passed this order only after the Congress government in Lucknow testified before the court that the unlocking would not lead to any law and order problem. The order was enforced within hours. Furthermore, Doordarshan, which was at that time completely a handmaiden of the Congress government and directly controlled by the PMO, gave full-blast publicity to the event and to devotees thronging to watch the prayers to the Ram Lalla idol.

There is another instance when Rajiv Gandhi's government supported the temple movement, albeit in a vacillating manner and without any conviction. In September 1989, the VHP announced its plan to carry consecrated bricks (Ram *shilas*) from all over the country to Ayodhya and perform *shilanyas* (laying the foundation) of the temple on 10 November. The Congress governments, both at the Centre and in UP, permitted the *shilanyas* ceremony by declaring, on 8 November, that the site of foundation-laying adjacent to the disputed structure was undisputed, although the Allahabad High Court, only a day earlier, had ruled otherwise. Significantly, it was a Harijan from Bihar, Kameshwar Chopal, who laid the first brick for the foundation of the Ram temple. However, the very next day, the same government ordered the construction to stop. The government's decisions, with regard to Ayodhya, had nothing to do with the merits of the issue. Rather, they were determined by the set of people able to influence the Prime Minister's mind at a given point of time.

The Congress party's fluctuating attitude towards the Ayodhya issue is not unrelated to Rajiv Gandhi's decision to start the election campaign for the 1989 parliamentary elections from Ayodhya, with a promise to establish 'Ram Rajya'. I am not saying this just to criticise the Congress party on this count but because it exposes the blatant inconsistency and rank opportunism of the then government. After all, its decision to facilitate the unlocking of the disputed structure allowed for only one interpretation: that is, Rajiv Gandhi supported the Hindu claim on the site. Yet, neither he nor his party, after his tragic death, showed the courage of conviction to remain steadfast on his commitment. Therefore, in retrospect, it appears to me that Rajiv chose the course of supporting the Ayodhya cause only in order to counter-balance his government's handling of the Shah Bano case, which was widely perceived as surrender under Muslim pressure.

The enactment of the Muslim Women's (Protection of Rights on Divorce) Bill in 1986, which annulled the judgement of the Supreme Court, was a blatant act to appease the minority vote-bank. It created a strong wave of resentment among Hindus (and also among moderate Muslims) and contributed immensely to making Ayodhya an all-India issue. National focus on it was further enlarged when certain Muslim organisations and personalities started to oppose the unlocking of the gates of the disputed structure at Ayodhya. Until 1986, no Muslim organisation in independent India, least of all a national-level organisation, had thought of resorting to agitation for a change in the court orders of 1951. However, the situation had changed after the Shah Bano issue. They now felt that they would face no difficulty in having the judicial order of 1951 and the administrative order of 1986 changed if requisite Muslim pressure on the government was built up. This was the understanding that led to the formation of the All India Babri Masjid Action Committee (AIBMAC).

WHY THE BJP JOINED THE TEMPLE MOVEMENT
Rajiv Gandhi's surrender in the Shah Bano case was the trigger

I would like to categorically state here that had the Congress party remained consistent in its support of the Ramjanmabhoomi cause, the BJP would not have joined the Ayodhya movement in the manner in which it later did. For us, it was not a question of who got the credit for ensuring construction of the temple. We would have been sufficiently pleased if the Congress had achieved the fulfilment of what Atal Bihari Vajpayee appropriately later called, when he became the Prime Minister, the 'national aspiration'. However, to our deep disappointment, we found the Congress party and Rajiv Gandhi wavering, and even backtracking at crucial moments. We were also increasingly alarmed by the virulently negative response of some Muslim organisations to the Hindu community's legitimate demand in Ayodhya. At this point, what surprised and shocked me the most was the deliberate attempt to project defence of the 'Babri Masjid' as a life-and-death issue affecting Muslims of India. This, I believe, was adding communal colour to a legitimate demand of the majority of Indian people. The comparison between the Ram Temple and the Babri Masjid, and hence, between Ram and Babur, was outrageous. The leaders of these Muslim organisations did not pause to consider that the birthplace of Ram has a sacred connotation in the hearts of crores of Hindus, in the same way as Kaaba in Mecca has for Muslims worldwide. In contrast, the Babri Masjid had no religious significance whatsoever for Indian Muslims. If Muslims are entitled to an Islamic atmosphere in Mecca, and if Christians are entitled to a Christian atmosphere in the Vatican, why is it wrong for Hindus to expect a Hindu atmosphere in Ayodhya?

Disregarding this basic question, the AIBMAC was trying to mobilise Muslims all over the country on the apocalyptic slogan of *'Islam khatare mein hai'* (Islam is in danger). It observed a black day throughout the country, going to the extent of calling for Muslim boycott of Republic Day in 1987, revealing the relative importance of religion and nation for AIBMAC. The call was later withdrawn only because of a nationwide outcry, including from moderate Muslims.

The Congress party, in spite of having a mammoth majority in Parliament, was both unable and unwilling to put the Ayodhya issue in the right perspective before the Muslim community. The opposition to the Ayodhya movement reached a feverish pitch when, on 1 February 1989, over one lakh saints and sadhus assembled at Prayag on the occasion of the Kumbha Mela and declared that the foundation stone for construction of the Ram Temple would be laid on 10 November. It was also decided that Ram *shilas*, would be collected and carried by karsevaks (those doing voluntary service at religious places) from lakhs of villages. This had an electrifying effect on the Hindu community all over the country. However, the situation presented a paradox. On the one hand, there was a groundswell of popular support for the Ayodhya movement. On the other hand, the movement was sans political support in the country. Most of the mainstream political parties refused to publicly support the Hindu demand, although their leaders would privately express their solidarity with it. The reason was clear: they feared losing Muslim votes. The fragmented votes of Hindus and the consolidated votes of Muslims have created a pernicious dynamic in Indian politics. Sadly, many political parties succumbed to the lure of this vote-bank politics, and justified it in the name of secularism.

Thus, the Ayodhya issue no longer remained limited to construction of the Ramjanmabhoomi temple. Rather, it became the symbol of a struggle between genuine secularism and pseudo-secularism. It also provided the context for a sharply polarised debate between two opposite conceptions about the source of India's nationhood and national identity: the unifying concept of cultural nationalism and the dividing concept of anti-Hindu nationalism. It was in this context that the BJP decided to support the Ramjanmabhoomi movement. Until then, our colleagues like Rajmata Vijayaraje Scindia and Vinay Katiyar had participated in the movement in their individual capacity, but the BJP as a party had kept itself out of it. The time had come for it to formally endorse the Ayodhya campaign and join the battle to safeguard genuine secularism and cultural nationalism. The party's National Executive, meeting at Palampur in Himachal Pradesh in June 1989, passed a resolution to this effect. I drafted this resolution, which, in its operative part, said:

> The BJP believes that theocracy is alien to our history and tradition. It is, therefore, that in 1947 even though India was partitioned on religious grounds and even though Pakistan declared itself an Islamic state, India opted for the present Constitution, and guaranteed equality to all citizens irrespective of their religion.

Secularism, according to our Constitution-makers, meant *Sarva Pantha Sama Bhava*. It did not connote an irreligious state. It certainly did not mean rejection of our history and cultural heritage.

The National Executive records its appreciation of the attempts made by some Shia leaders to persuade the community that it was contrary to the tenets of Islam to have a mosque built upon a place of worship of another religion, and that, therefore, the site in dispute should be handed over to the Hindus and a mosque built at some other suitable place. The BJP calls upon the Rajiv Government to adopt the same positive approach in respect of Ayodhya that the Nehru Government did with regard to Somnath. The sentiments of the people must be respected, and Janmasthan must be handed over to the Hindus—if possible through a negotiated settlement, or else, by legislation. Litigation certainly is no answer.*

The BJP also made it clear right at the outset that, while it supported the cause of construction of the Ram temple, it would like to see this done without hurting the sentiments of the Muslim fraternity. Hence, we were in favour of respectfully relocating the disputed structure, so that a mosque could be constructed, through Hindu-Muslim cooperation, at another location outside Ayodhya.

It should be thus clear from the above narrative that it was *not* my party which created the Ayodhya issue to gain political mileage.

PART II

THE RAM RATH YATRA
From Somnath to Ayodhya

Elections to the 9th Lok Sabha were held in November 1989, the results of which administered a shock treatment to the Congress party. After having

---

* The full text of this historic resolution of the BJP is reproduced as Appendix IV.

secured four-fifths majority in 1984, Rajiv Gandhi was *ousted* from power five years later chiefly due to the Bofors scam, his surrender in the Shah Bano case and his vacillating positions on the Ramjanmabhoomi issue.

The elections yielded a hung Parliament, with the Janata Dal emerging as the largest single party. V.P. Singh became the Prime Minister in December 1989 at the head of a National Front coalition, which was supported from outside by the BJP and the left parties. The very fact that V.P. Singh sought the BJP's support to form the government placed upon him a moral and political obligation to be sensitive to the issue of Ram Mandir in Ayodhya, which was one of the chief planks in our election manifesto. We expected him to be fair, honest and transparent in his handling of this issue. Sadly, he belied our expectations.

Before the elections, the Ayodhya issue had figured prominently in the several formal and informal talks on seat-adjustments between the BJP and Janata Dal. These talks were facilitated by some common well-wishers, who were keen to ensure that India was freed from the corrupt rule of the Congress. During one of these talks, Singh made a startling statement. It has been mentioned in the BJP White Paper on Ayodhya and the Ram Temple Movement (1993). 'To break the deadlock', the White Paper states: 'An important meeting was arranged at the Express Towers in Bombay. The participants in the meeting included Ramnath Goenka, Chairman of the *Indian Express* newspaper group; Bhaurao Deoras, Prof Rajendra Singh and Nanaji Deshmukh, senior leaders of the RSS; Prabhash Joshi, a renowned Hindi journalist; and S. Gurumurthy, who was a close advisor of Goenka. It was in that meeting that Singh said: "*Arre Bhai, masjid hai kahan? Yeh to abhi mandir hai.*" (Where is the mosque in Ayodhya? it is already a temple). Pooja is going on. It is so dilapidated that if you give a push, it will fall. Why does one have to demolish it?' This was the meeting to which Arun Shourie referred in an article which was published in October 1990.

Singh's statement is indeed symptomatic of the bane of Indian politics. He was by no means alone in making such a statement in private conversations. Many prominent leaders of other political parties, who were familiar with the ground reality in Ayodhya, have said similar things behind closed doors.

I must admit that, due to this background of mistrust between the BJP and V.P. Singh, I had my own doubts about how well the National Front government would function and how long it would last. Soon after the formation of the new government, the saints associated with the Ramjanmabhoomi movement decided to resume the *kar seva* in February 1990. On 8 February, the Prime Minister invited them for a meeting in Delhi and sought more time, while expressing confidence that the problem would be solved within four months. Since nothing happened in the stipulated period, the leaders of the movement, who met in June, set 30 October as the date for the *kar seva*.

In the last week of June, I had gone to London as a member of a parliamentary delegation led by Rabi Ray, who was then Speaker of the Lok Sabha. Just before my departure, Tarun Vijay, Editor of *Panchajanya*, a weekly Hindi journal inspired by the RSS, interviewed me. One of the questions he asked me was: 'V.P. Singh's government, which the BJP is supporting, had promised to sort out the Ayodhya tangle within four months. Although four months have elapsed, nothing has happened. And now the VHP has announced *kar seva* at Ayodhya on 30 October. What do you think is going to happen now?' My reply comprised four points. One: between June and October, the government still had four more months. Hence, I expressed the hope that the government would find an amicable solution. Two: I committed my party's full support to the decision to start the *kar seva* at Ayodhya on 30 October. Three, I said that the BJP would participate in any campaign for the purpose of temple construction. Lastly, I cautioned Singh's government that any attempt to scuttle the *kar seva* would lead to 'the greatest mass movement' independent India had ever witnessed.

Frankly, I had forgotten about this interview once I left for London. Indeed, in all my interactions and meetings there, I was the principal member of the delegation defending the V.P. Singh government on all issues. When I was about to depart from London, my wife called me up and said, 'What have you said? The papers here have reported with blaring headlines: "On Ayodhya, Advani threatens the biggest mass movement in the history of independent India".'

The die had been cast. Relations between leaders of the *kar seva* and the government were souring. However, I wanted to avert a confrontation by exploring every possibility of an amicable solution while ensuring survival of the National Front government. After all, the Congress party's defeat in the 1989 parliamentary elections was a major triumph for India's democratic forces. The gains of this victory needed to be consolidated. Towards this end, I took an important initiative at a function in New Delhi on 13 August, while releasing Koenraad Elst's book *Ram Janmabhoomi vs Babri Masjid: A case study in Hindu Muslim conflict.* I offered to the Muslim leaders that I would personally request leaders of the VHP to relinquish their demand on the Hindu shrines in Mathura and Varanasi if the Muslim claim over Ramjanmabhoomi was voluntarily withdrawn, paving the way for the construction of the Ram Temple.

I was deeply disappointed when Muslim leaders rejected this offer. I had proposed this compromise after much reflection. After all, anyone who is even cursorily familiar with the sites of the Hindu temples at Kashi and Mathura would aver that the presence of mosques inside these shrines can only be the result of a deliberate religious assault. Therefore, not to press the demand for shifting the mosques out of the precincts of these holy shrines was a major goodwill gesture towards Muslims. By refusing to compromise, the AIBMAC leaders once again showed their obstinacy, insensitiveness and fanaticism.

I considered my proposal important for another reason: it also addressed a deep-seated Muslim concern. After Ayodhya became a national issue, the fear of common Muslims was: 'Will this be the beginning of a long process of Hindu claims on other Muslim places of worship?' The unarticulated corollary of this fear was that, if the Hindu organisations gave a credible assurance on this count, the average Muslim, who in any case had no emotional attachment to the Babri Masjid, would not mind relocation of this mosque to some other site to pave the way for construction of the Ram Temple in its place. I was really annoyed that the AIBMAC leaders did not reflect the widespread desire for reconciliation among common Muslims.

While articulating my views on the Ayodhya issue during those days, I would often give the example of Poland. In the course of the first Russian occupation of the Polish city of Warsaw (1614-1915), the Russians built an Eastern Orthodox Christian Cathedral in the principal square in what had been the capital of the once independent Roman Catholic Christian country. After Poland gained independence in 1918, its people pulled down the cathedral. They did so because they felt that the purpose for which the Russians had built it had not been religious but political. 'Our approach will be different,' I would say. 'We would like to respectfully relocate the Babri structure.'

The example of Poland was, indeed, one of the major points in the speech that Arnold Toynbee, one of the greatest historians of the twentieth century, had delivered in his Azad Memorial Lecture in New Delhi in 1960. Interestingly, Toynbee had cited the Polish experience in the context of the history of idol breaking and temple demolition in India during the reign of some Muslim kings. 'I do not greatly blame the Polish government for having pulled down that Russian church,' he said. 'On the other hand, I do greatly praise the Indian government for not having pulled down Aurangzeb's mosques: I am thinking particularly of two that overlook the ghats at Benares, and of one that crowns Krishna's hill at Mathura. Aurangzeb's purpose in building those three mosques was the same intentionally offensive political purpose that moved the Russians to build their Orthodox Cathedral in the city centre at Warsaw. Those three mosques were intended to signify that an Islamic government was reigning supreme, even over Hinduism's holiest of holy places.'

THE GENESIS OF THE RATH YATRA
A voice inside me said, 'Do it.'

Events moved swiftly thereafter. With VHP taking the lead, Kar Seva Samitis were constituted all over the country. There was a tremendous response to the endeavour to mobilise devotees of Lord Ram for the big event on 30 October. People from all across the country were eager to converge at Ayodhya—from villages, far-off hamlets and urban slums. I had an intuition that history was about to be made. My mind, however, was preoccupied with the role of the BJP in this movement and what I, as Party President, could do to promote the cause.

By now I was fully convinced that this movement was not only about building a temple in Ayodhya. It was not even merely about reclaiming a holy Hindu site from the onslaught of a bigoted foreign invader in the past. It was equally about reclaiming the true meaning of secularism from the onslaught of pseudo-secularism. It was about reasserting our cultural heritage as the defining source of India's national identity.

In early September, when Kamla and I were spending a quiet evening in our Pandara Park home, Pramod Mahajan, one of the four General Secretaries of the BJP, dropped in. Although it was a casual visit, it was obvious that Ayodhya was uppermost on his mind, too. He began telling me how the proposed *kar seva* in Ayodhya was creating a buzz all over the country. Pramod had a very sharp mind which picked up socio-political trends well before they manifested on surface.

'I am thinking of undertaking a pad yatra (journey on foot) from Somnath to reach Ayodhya on 30 October,' I told Pramod and Kamla. 'I can start it either on 2 October, which is Gandhi Jayanti, or on 25 September, which is Deendayal Jayanti.' I added that it would give me an opportunity to meet people, including villagers and explain to them the significance of the Ayodhya movement.

Pramod, a meticulous organiser of political campaigns, quickly began a mental exercise of how much distance I would be able to cover in a day and, hence, what would be the right route to choose from Somnath to Ayodhya. After a pause, he remarked, 'A pad yatra is a good idea, but not very useful for the purpose you have in mind. You'll at the most be able to cover a small part of Gujarat, Rajasthan, Madhya Pradesh, Delhi and half of UP.'

I asked him for an alternative saying, 'Travelling in a car does not appeal to me because I'll not be able to interact with the people. Maybe, a jeep yatra would be better.'

'Why don't we plan this as a Rath Yatra? After all, it is for a Ram temple,' Pramod suggested. 'We can take a mini-bus or a mini-truck, redesign it in the form of a rath and you can travel in it. Since it is for the purpose of creating mass support for the construction of the Ram Temple in Ayodhya, we'll call it the Ram Rath Yatra.' He added that the rath could travel across at least a dozen states covering a large part of western, southern, central, northern and eastern India. 'Advaniji, you leave the route planning and logistics to me. You just tell me when you want to start.'

'We are already in the first week of September. Do we have enough time to prepare and plan everything, if we decide to commence the *yatra* on Deendayalji's birthday?' Although the novelty of a Rath Yatra had appealed to me and I was also convinced of its effectiveness as a mode of mass campaign, I still had lingering doubts about some organisational aspects. Also, my initial reaction to the idea was that it was too theatrical as I felt it did not suit my temperament.

In spite of this, something within me said, 'Do it.'

I asked Pramod to immediately call a meeting of General Secretaries and all the other important party colleagues. The proposal met with instant and enthusiastic approval. On 12 September, I called a press conference at the party office at 11 Ashoka Road and announced my decision to undertake a 10,000-kilometre-long Rath Yatra, starting from Somnath on 25 September and reaching Ayodhya on 30 October to join the *kar seva*.

THE RAM RATH ROLLS ON
The chariot becomes an object of worship

The last week of September in Saurashtra in Gujarat is a time when the monsoon has bid goodbye but the winter is yet to set in. This imminent but uncertain climatic transition was an apt metaphor for the way I was feeling about my own political life when I arrived in Somnath to herald my Ram Rath Yatra. I had never undertaken such an extensive mass-contact programme and that too in such a novel fashion. Although I could sense that this was a significant milestone in my political life, I hadn't the slightest idea about what the future held in store for me. The only thing I knew was that I had to perform my duty, and not bother about the outcome of my karma.

On the morning of 25 September, I offered prayers at the *jyotirlingam* in Somnath temple. I was accompanied by Pramod Mahajan, Narendra Modi (another promising young leader of the party who has now become Gujarat's dynamic Chief Minister), other senior functionaries of the party in Gujarat, and members of my family. Rajmata Vijayaraje Scindia and Sikandar Bakht, both Party Vice Presidents, had come to flag off the Rath. Before leaving we all paid floral tribute to the imposing statue of Sardar Patel just outside the temple. In my mind, I thanked and drew inspiration from all the great men who had toiled for the reconstruction of the temple.

Amidst a large crowd that had gathered to greet and bless us, we climbed the Ram Rath which had been decorated with marigold flowers. Then, to the accompaniment of the sound of the ceremonial conches and full-throated slogans of 'Jai Shri Ram' and '*Saugandh Ram ki khate hain mandir wahin banayenge*' (In the name of Ram, we resolve: We shall build the temple there—at Ramjanmabhoomi—itself), the Rath rolled on. In subsequent days, these slogans, along with a theme song sung by Lata Mangeshkar*, India's Nightingale, would become the signature tune of the Rath Yatra wherever it went.

I was truly overwhelmed by the response to the yatra within the first few days of our journey in Gujarat. The Rath was received by tumultuous crowds everywhere—in villages, towns and even along roads where people from nearby hamlets would gather under trees eagerly waiting for the Rath to arrive. The response reached a crescendo in bigger towns and cities, where it would take hours for us to reach the venue of our meetings. However, from the very first day, our schedule started to go awry. Our last meeting would last well beyond midnight. The pattern continued for the next four days that we travelled through Gujarat.

---

* One day before the start of my campaign, I received a cassette from Manoj Kumar, the popular film star and maker of several patriotic movies. It contained a song by Lata Mangeshkar, which became the title song of my Ram Rath Yatra.
Ram Naam jaadu aisa, Ram Naam man bhaye
Man ki Ayodhya tab tak sooni, Jab tak Ram na aaye re
(The name of Ram is so magical that it brings peace and happiness to one's mind; The Ayodhya in my mind remains empty and silent until Ram enters it.)

Frankly, I did not expect such an overwhelming response. Looking at my gestures of amazement, Pramod, who was chosen by the party to be my companion throughout the yatra, quipped, 'Advaniji, the response is so big because this is Gujarat. The people here are traditional and religious. Don't think that it would be like this when we enter Maharashtra from Gujarat.'

Pramod was wrong, totally wrong. The response was as big, even bigger, in Maharashtra as well as in all the subsequent states that we travelled through. People everywhere greeted the Rath by erecting ceremonial arches and showering flowers. The most astonishing sight for me was the manner in which people, especially women, would come forward and perform *aarti*. What I soon realised was that for many people, I was secondary and incidental to the campaign. I was only a *sarathi* or a charioteer; the principal messenger of the Rath Yatra was the Rath itself. And it was worthy of worship as it was headed for Ayodhya for the sacred mission of construction of the Ram Temple at his birthplace. Whatever I said at meetings was only an elaboration of the context.

This was perhaps the most striking case of *saguna* puja in the Hindu tradition (worship of the Creator in His infinite forms, as against *nirguna* puja, which is worship of the formless Him). In this more popular form of worship, common people see manifestation of the Divine in any idol or object—a tree, a mountain, a river or a lake, etc—that they believe is sanctified. The Rath had thus come to acquire divinity.

The most touching moments of the yatra were witnessed in villages and remote hamlets populated by the scheduled castes and tribes. The piety on the faces of the village folk was of a purer and deeper kind than what I saw in cities. As Gandhiji describes in his book *Hind Swaraj*, the village folk were devoid of the influences of city life, commercialism and competitive instincts. Many of them were either illiterate or nominally educated. They had not learnt about Ram by reading; it was as if the knowledge flowed through them, passed on from one generation to the other, or through tales heard in congregations and plays organised at village fairs or on annual festivals like Ram Navami. At many places, I found an odd villager who would come quietly, without shouting any slogans, perform a *puja* before the Rath, greet me and walk away. I was truly humbled by experiences like these.

I had never realised that religiosity was so deep-rooted in the lives of Indian people. I had read about the phenomenon, and even seen glimpses of it. But never had I witnessed such a spontaneous manifestation in each village, town, and state I passed through. It was during the Ram Rath Yatra that I first understood the truth of Swami Vivekananda's statement that 'religion is the soul of India and if you want to teach any subject to Indians, they understand it better if it is taught in the language of religion.' It was the Rath Yatra that made me realise that, if I were to communicate the message of nationalism through the religious idiom, I would be able to transmit it more effectively and to a wider audience.

In my speeches, delivered mostly from the specially designed raised platform on the vehicle, I would explain the purpose of the yatra and the circumstances that compelled the BJP to actively participate in the Ayodhya movement. Although the people's response to the Rath Yatra was mainly religious, the focus of my speeches was on nationalism. I dwelt on how a perverse understanding of secularism was being used by certain political parties as a cover to deny the cultural and civilisational roots of Indian nationhood. I underscored how this perversion stemmed not from any real conviction but from the considerations of wooing the minority vote-bank.

A recurrent theme in my speeches was that the power of a positive approach to religious faith can contribute greatly to social transformation and nation-building. I would say: *'Ram Bhakti se Lok Shakti jagrut ho sakti hai.'* (The power of devotion towards Ram can unleash people's power.) I especially commended the people for transcending the barriers of caste and sub-caste and coming together for a common national purpose, welcoming the presence of large numbers of Harijans in the gatherings and reminding the audience how Mahatma Gandhi used the power of religion to educate the people about the evil of untouchability.

In my addresses, I stressed on the equal status that our Muslim brethren enjoyed in independent India. I emphasised that, even though Pakistan, and later Bangladesh too, declared themselves as Islamic states, India chose to remain non-theocratic and secular. This, I added, was principally due to the age-old secular ethos of Hinduism. I appealed to leaders of the Muslim community to respect the Hindu sentiments over Ayodhya.

The common message of all these diverse points in my speeches invariably hit home. It was received with thunderous applause. My speeches from atop the Rath were just about five minutes long, because I had to address nearly twenty to twenty-five such roadside receptions each day. In most towns and cities, I had to get down and address public meetings attended by tens of thousands of people. The media had already started reporting about the huge response to the Rath Yatra in Gujarat and Maharashtra. As a result, the turnout in subsequent states became even larger. In many places, the last meeting would not begin before 2 o'clock in the morning. Once, in Andhra Pradesh, the Rath arrived at the last destination of the day at five in the morning! However late the programme might have ended the previous day, the Rath would invariably commence its next day's journey at ten in the morning.

CALUMNY AGAINST THE RATH YATRA
'Not an iota of communal bigotry in my speeches'

Was my campaign anti-Muslim? Not in the least. However, unnerved by the massive response to the Rath Yatra, our political adversaries intensified this calumny against me. Their propaganda was baseless and motivated. I challenged them to point out a single utterance in my speeches that could be construed as directed against Muslims or Islam. There wasn't any, throughout the yatra. On the contrary, whenever I heard someone raise an inappropriate slogan in my meetings, I promptly expressed disapproval. For example, at some places people shouted: *'Jo Hindu hit ki baat karega, vahi desh pe raj karega'.* (They alone shall rule India, who speak of Hindu interests.) I immediately stood up to affirm that the BJP represents every citizen of India irrespective of whether he is a Hindu or a Muslim or a Christian or a Parsi or any other faith. I said that the policies we promote seek to benefit hundred per cent of the Indian people, not just Hindus who constitute eighty-two per cent. Of course, we strongly disagree with pseudo-secularists for whom eighty-two per cent just do not matter and who are concerned only about the eighteen per cent! Therefore, I said that if a slogan had to be raised, let it be: '*Jo Rashtra hit ki baat karega vahi desh pe raj karega*' (They alone shall rule India, who speak of the nation's interests).

Another lie in the propaganda by our adversaries was that the Ram Rath Yatra left a bloody trail of communal clashes. As records show, there was not a single instance of communal violence along the route of my yatra. There were indeed riots in several parts of the country, but none at all along the Rath Yatra trail. I was, therefore, pained to see a section of the media carry reports that had sensational titles like 'Advani's blood yatra'.

Dr Koenraad Elst, in his two-volume book titled *The Saffron Swastika*, marshals an incontrovertible array of facts to debunk slanderous attacks on the BJP by a section of the media. About the Rath Yatra, he writes: 'But what about Advani's bloody Rath Yatra (car procession) from Somnath to Ayodhya in October 1990? Very simple: it is not at all that the Rath Yatra was a bloody affair. While in the same period, there was a lot of rioting in several parts of the country (particularly Hyderabad, Karnataka and Uttar Pradesh), killing about 600 people in total, there were no riots at all along the Rath Yatra trail. Well, there was one: upper-caste students pelted stones at Advani because he had disappointed them by not supporting their agitation against the caste-based reservations which V.P. Singh was promoting. Even then, no one was killed or seriously wounded. It is a measure of the quality of the Indian English-language media that they have managed to turn an entirely peaceful procession, an island of orderliness in a riot-torn country, into a proverbial bloody event ("Advani's blood yatra"). And it was quite a sight how the pressmen in their editorials blamed Advani for communal riots of which the actual, non-Advani-related causes were given on a different page of the same paper. Whether Advani with his Rath Yatra was at 500 miles distance from a riot (as with the riot in Gonda in UP), or under arrest, or back home after the high tide of the Ayodhya agitation, every riot in India in the second half of 1990 was blamed on him'.

My yatra was scheduled to enter Deoria in Uttar Pradesh on 24 October. However, as I had anticipated, it was stopped at Samastipur in Bihar on 23 October and I was arrested by the Janata Dal government in the state then headed by Laloo Prasad Yadav. I was taken to an inspection bungalow of the irrigation department at a place called Massanjore near Dumka on the Bihar-Bengal border. This action invited angry and spontaneous protests all over the country. I spent five weeks in detention in Massanjore before being released.

Thus ended my Rath Yatra, which was indeed an exhilarating episode in my political life.

THE STORY OF A STILLBORN ORDINANCE
The V.P. Singh government's sordid flip-flop

Many attempts were made by several people, including V.P. Singh and his colleagues in the National Front government, to untie the Ayodhya tangle. When the Ayodhya issue became the focal point of nationwide debate, there was a line of thought, both among Hindus and Muslims that the issue should be resolved through a common effort of the religious leaders of the two communities without the involvement of political parties. I was not averse to this idea. In early 1990, V.P. Singh's government attempted a new non-political initiative, which centred on a compromise formula: the disputed structure and the site would be handed over to a new Hindu trust on the condition that it would build the Ram temple without disturbing the existing structure and a wall would be constructed between the temple and the disputed structure.

The Prime Minister engaged the services of the late Krishna Kant, the then Governor of Andhra Pradesh who later became the Vice President of India (1997-2002), to mobilise support for this formula. Krishna Kant suggested that Swami Jayendra Saraswati of Kanchi Kamakoti Math could head the new trust. Accordingly, he arranged a meeting between the Swamiji and Ali Mian, the revered Muslim theologian from Nadwa in Uttar Pradesh at Kanchipuram in Tamil Nadu. The meeting was partially fruitful. Addressing a press conference after the dialogue, Swamiji stated that political elements should be kept out of the Ayodhya issue, and the government should call a meeting of religious leaders of both sides to find a durable and peaceful solution.

Later, Krishna Kant travelled to Udupi and confirmed the contents of this compromise formula in his talks with Vishwesha Teertha Swamiji of Pejawar Math. Swamiji, one of the founding leaders of the VHP, said that he would consult others and convey their collective response to the government. After some days, Krishna Kant took Swamiji by a special aircraft to meet the Prime Minister.

Singh cannot be faulted for not making any efforts to amicably resolve the Ayodhya issue. But he certainly must bear the blame for not displaying the courage to follow through on some of the constructive initiatives of his own government, which he personally seemed to be convinced were just and fair. If the abortive initiative involving the swamijis of Kanchi and Udupi was one example, another came in the form of the Singh government's bizarre withdrawal, within forty-eight hours, of an ordinance that it had itself promulgated.

On 15 October 1990, Singh invited S. Gurumurthy, who was acting as an important interlocutor between leaders of the temple movement and the government, for a meeting. This was subsequent to the announcement of 30 October as the date for the commencement of the *kar seva*. Moreover, it was when my Rath Yatra was already underway. The Prime Minister was obviously getting reports about the surging popular support for the temple movement from all across the country. He was also aware that some of his own partymen, especially the Chief Ministers of UP and Bihar, were trying to outdo each other in their rhetoric against the Rath Yatra. It was in this context that he called Gurumurthy with a view to diffuse the situation.

Gurumurthy suggested a three-point solution: (1) The total land of the proposed temple complex is around seventy acres, of which only two and a half acres are disputed. The remaining sixty-seven acres, on which *shilanyas* was performed in 1989 with the approval of Rajiv Gandhi's government, was undisputed. The proposal was that the central government should acquire the entire disputed and undisputed area, and hand over sixty-seven acres of undisputed land to the Ramjanambhoomi Nyas so that *kar seva* could be performed there; (2) The disputed structure would be retained by the central government in an 'as is' condition with a thirty feet area around it under its title and possession; and (3) In respect of the disputed site, the central government would make a single-point reference to the Supreme Court, under Article 143 of the Constitution, to give its opinion on whether there was at any time in the past a temple at the site which was destroyed and a mosque built in its place. Whether or not Ram was born there was not to be a part of the proposed reference. After all, no court could determine that issue.

Singh readily accepted the suggestion. Gurumurthy communicated this to the leaders of the temple movement and relayed back their acceptance to the Prime Minister. Three days later, two senior members of Singh's Cabinet—Railway Minister George Fernandes and Information & Broadcasting Minister P. Upendra—met Ashok Singhal and other leaders of the temple movement at the RSS headquarters in New Delhi. They said that the government proposed to promulgate an ordinance on the Ayodhya issue on the lines indicated by the Prime Minister.

The same evening, the Prime Minister invited K.N. Govindacharya, General Secretary of the BJP, and Arun Jaitley, who was then Additional Solicitor General to discuss the Ayodhya issue. There was agreement on the three-point solution. After the discussion, a senior official in the PMO was called around midnight and asked to initiate steps to implement the proposal. Accordingly, the proverbial mid-night oil was burnt to prepare a draft ordinance, which was finalised at the Cabinet Secretary's residence at 5 am. At 10 am, the Cabinet met at the Prime Minister's residence and approved the ordinance and the three-point solution.

Gurumurthy, who was in Chennai on that day, was called by the Prime Minister for another important meeting. I happened to be in Delhi for a short Diwali break in the Rath Yatra. While planning the Rath Yatra, we had taken cognisance of the fact that Diwali was falling in the middle of our programme and it would not be appropriate to disturb the festivities. So the schedule of the yatra was drawn up in such a manner as to enable the Rath to reach Delhi on 14 October, a couple of days before Diwali.

I was scheduled to leave for Calcutta on 18 October in order to resume my yatra from Dhanbad in Bihar. On the 18th evening, the Prime Minister called me to know what I thought about the proposed solution. My reply was that I viewed the proposal positively. He then added: 'You are proceeding to Kolkata tomorrow, but I understand that your Rath Yatra is to start from Dhanbad only the day after. This is to request that you stay on here tomorrow. Some ray of light has become visible today. Why can't we convert it into full light? Thereafter, you and I together can go to perform *kar seva*.'

Shortly thereafter, I received a similar call from Jyoti Basu, the communist Chief Minister of West Bengal. Like the BJP, his party, the CPI(M), was also supporting Singh's government from outside. Basu also made the same request. I decided then to cancel my Kolkata trip and proceed directly to Dhanbad on 19 October.

During my stay in Delhi, emissaries kept the dialogue going between the government and leaders of the temple movement. As part of these talks, on the morning of 19 October, I went to the Sundar Nagar Guest House of the *Indian Express* for a meeting with Ramnath Goenka, the legendary owner of the newspaper. A fighter of many battles against Congress governments' corruption scandals, he was a close confidante of V.P. Singh. Gurumurthy and some other common friends of Goenka and the Prime Minister were also present. Some of them expressed the apprehension that my Rath Yatra, which I was scheduled to resume on the following day, might bring about the fall of the National Front government, which enjoyed the support of the BJP. I made it abundantly clear that it was not my intention to bring down the government. I also unambiguously stated that I welcomed the ordinance and the three-point solution, whether or not the VHP was made a receiver of the disputed structure. I reiterated my position when Gurumurthy and Arun Jaitley came to my residence even as I was preparing to go to the railway station on my way to Dhanbad to resume the Rath Yatra.

The same afternoon, Gurumurthy spoke to the Prime Minister to convey the outcome of the morning's meeting. But he was unpleasantly surprised to notice that a major change had come about in V.P. Singh's stance. For the Prime Minister said that not just the disputed structure, but all the 'disputed' land around it would also be in the possession of the government, and would not be handed over to the temple trust. When Gurumurthy pointed out that this was not the basis of the ordinance or the three-point solution agreed to earlier, the Prime Minister told Gurumurthy that I should defer my Rath Yatra by a day, so that a solution could be hammered out. Significantly, he also added, 'Once we arrive at a mutually satisfactory solution, I will go along with Shri Advani to Ayodhya for the *kar seva*.'

Gurumurthy conveyed this to me. I told him to let the Prime Minister know that my presence was not required, and that if the ordinance and the proposed solution as discussed earlier in the day were given effect to, that would be agreeable to me. I could sense that the Prime Minister was either insincere or lacked the courage to withstand the pressures that he was obviously subjected to from those who did not want an amicable solution to the dispute.

I later learnt from Gurumurthy and Jaitley that they were called for a marathon meeting the same evening at the Prime Minister's residence. Singh was assisted by four senior ministers—George Fernandes, Arun Nehru, Ajit Singh and Dinesh Goswami. Goswami, who was the Law Minister, argued that it was not possible to issue the Ordinance because of the multiplicity of lawsuits and 'hundreds of contentious issues' involved. Once again, it required Gurumurthy and Jaitley to rescue the kernel from the welter of inessential information. The 'hundreds of contentious issues', they explained, fell under just three heads: one, whether Ram was born at the disputed site; two, whether there was a pre-existing Hindu structure at the disputed site; and three, whom did the different lands adjacent to the disputed site belong to. The first question, they added, was not capable of judicial or even legislative determination. The second question lent itself to judicial opinion or verdict, based on an examination of the evidence and records available. The third aspect was capable of legislative action under the government's undisputed power of compulsory acquisition.

This explanation was so logical and irrefutable that the Prime Minister and his colleagues had no arguments against it. Accordingly, the government informed the nation of its decision to issue the ordinance through a late night press release. Comically, the government reversed its own decision the very same night. Apparently, the Prime Minister faced a threat from Mulayam Singh Yadav that he would not allow the ordinance to be implemented. The ordinance was withdrawn on 21 October. The news came as a big disappointment and betrayal to the leaders and followers of the temple movement.

THE FALL OF V.P. SINGH'S GOVERNMENT
Chandrashekhar made earnest efforts to find a solution

The BJP-supported V.P. Singh government sealed its own fate on the day that a Chief Minister belonging to the Prime Minister's own party stopped my Rath Yatra and ordered my arrest in Bihar. The BJP's National Executive, at its meeting in New Delhi on 17 October, had passed the following unambiguous resolution: 'The BJP calls upon the Union government to honour the sentiment of the people and allow a temple to be built at the Janmasthan. The Executive warns the government that if it fails to do so, or, if it disrupts the Rath Yatra which has come to symbolise this sentiment, the BJP would be constrained to withdraw support to this government.' Therefore, soon after my arrest on 23 October, a BJP delegation led by Atalji met President R. Venkatraman and presented a letter withdrawing support to the V.P. Singh government.

Although it was now certain that the government had lost support of the majority in Parliament, and had hence lost its political and moral authority to rule the country, V.P. Singh continued to behave as if he was the hero of the hour. He insisted on seeking a vote of confidence in the Lok Sabha and even boasted that he would prove his majority. Simultaneously, he and some of his party colleagues now dropped all moderation and vowed to prevent the *kar seva* on 30 October at any cost. Unfortunately, there was a contest of sorts between the two Janata Dal Chief Ministers of UP and Bihar—Mulayam Singh Yadav and Laloo Prasad Yadav—each trying to project himself as more 'secular' than the other. The Chief Minister of Bihar had taken the credit for stopping my yatra. Now it was the turn of the UP Chief Minister to try to outdo him in competitive bravado. He declared that his government would make the security arrangements so tight that 'not even a bird will be allowed to fly into Ayodhya' on 30 October, leave alone a karsevak.

In spite of his threat, tens of thousands of devotees from all over the country started to arrive in Ayodhya for the scheduled *kar seva*. Ashok Singhal, President of the VHP, managed to reach on 28 September. *Kar seva* was performed on the appointed day. Viewing this as a defeat for the government, the police and paramilitary forces were ordered to drive the devotees away from the narrow lanes and by-lanes of Ayodhya by firing bullets and tear-gas shells at them. While it outraged Hindus all over the country, in Ayodhya it led to a defiant reaction from angry *kar sevaks* which portended the events of 6 December 1992—some of them climbed the domes of the Babri structure and hoisted saffron flags. The 2nd of November turned out to be one of the bloodiest days in the long history of the movement. On that day, a contingent of unarmed *kar sevaks*, who were approaching the Ramjanmabhoomi, were fired upon by the state police. Over fifty of them died while hundreds more were injured.

President Venkataraman had asked V.P. Singh to seek a vote of confidence on 7 November. By this time, the Janata Dal had split—Chandrashekhar had walked out of it with fifty-eight MPs to form a separate party called the Janata Dal (Secular). Singh lost the confidence vote by a long margin: 151 for and 356 against. His resignation evoked mixed feelings in me. I was certainly not unhappy that his government had fallen. Nevertheless, I was sad that yet another non-Congress alternative had foundered, giving an opportunity to the Congress to bounce back. Not surprisingly, Rajiv Gandhi took a leaf out of his mother's political manual and announced, as she had done in the case of Charan Singh in 1979, that the Congress would lend outside support for Chandrashekhar to form the next government.

With the formation of the new government at the Centre, I took the first opportunity to visit Ayodhya. The journey from Faizabad to Ayodhya on 19 November remains etched in my mind. Tens of thousands of people had lined up on both sides of the road; their full-throated slogans rending the sky. My vehicle, an impromptu rath, was moving at a snail's pace. In my speech on that day, I thanked the people of Ayodhya for sheltering *kar sevaks* when Mulayam Singh Yadav's forces had resorted to brutish confrontation on 30 October. I also warned: 'No government in India can survive if it adopted an anti-Hindu posture and showed disrespect to Lord Ram.'

Although Chandrashekhar's government lasted only seven months, I must admit the fact that of the four Prime Ministers who dealt with the Ayodhya issue before 1992, he made the most sincere and consistent efforts to find a negotiated solution to the problem. His government arranged the first official meetings between the VHP and the AIBMAC, to evolve an agreed solution to the problem. The Hindu side made it clear that the birth of Ram at Janmabhoomi is a matter of faith held by crores of Hindus, which cannot be challenged, proved or adjudicated. This, of course, is true about many core beliefs in all religions. Hence, the central question in the dialogue got focused on: Was the disputed structure built by demolishing a Hindu temple?

At the start of the negotiations, the AIBMAC had taken the position that the disputed structure could be relocated if it was proved that the Babri Masjid had been built after demolishing a temple. Subsequently, however, this stand was significantly modified: they would agree for the structure's relocation only if evidence showed that a Ram Temple had been destroyed.

The government, as the intermediary and facilitator of the dialogue process, requested both sides to exchange documents in support of their respective positions. After studying each other's documents, they were also expected to file rejoinders. The VHP submitted, besides art-historical and archaeological evidence, voluminous documentary evidence based on Hindu literary sources, Muslim history books, archival materials, European accounts, government gazetteers, and revenue records.

The crux of the AIBMAC case was: the story of the *Ramayana* is mythological and not historical. The Ayodhya of today is not the Ayodhya described in the *Ramayana*; the Babri Masjid was never built by destroying any temple or other construction; there is no evidence of a Ram Temple having existed at that site; and the Muslims have been in continuous possession of the Babri Masjid right until 1949 when the idols were placed.

Arun Shourie, renowned journalist and prolific author, was one of the few who analysed the relative merits of the evidence tendered by the VHP and the AIBMAC. About the documents submitted by the AIBMAC, he said[11]: 'I was appalled when I saw what the AIBMAC had furnished. It was just a pile of papers. ...It wasn't just that so much of it was the stuff of cranks: pages from the book of some chap to the effect that Ram was actually a Pharaoh of Egypt; an article by someone based he says on what he had learnt from one dancer in Sri Lanka, and setting out a folk story, knowledge of which he himself says is confined to a small part of a small district in that country, to the effect that Sita was Ram's sister whom he married, etc.

'It was that document after document in this lot buttressed the case not of the All India Babri Masjid Committee but of the VHP! They show that the mosque had not been in use since 1936. They show different groups or sects of Muslims fighting each other for acquiring the property. They show the Hindus waging an unremitting struggle to regain this place held, the documents say, "most sacred" by them; they show them continuing to worship the ground in spite of the mosque having been super-imposed on it; they show them constructing structures and temples on the peripheral spots when they are debarred from the main one. Most importantly, AIBMAC's papers showed that the disputed structure was "not even listed in the lists of either the Shia or Sunni Waqf Boards, as the law required all waqf properties to be".'

About the evidence submitted by the VHP, Shourie said: 'In complete contrast the VHP documents are pertinent to the point. They contain the unambiguous statements of Islamic historians, of Muslim narrators—from Aurangzeb's grand-daughter—to the effect that the mosque was built by demolishing the Ram temple. They contain accounts of European travellers as well as official publications of the British period—gazetteers of 1854, of 1877, of 1881, of 1892, of 1905; the Settlement Report of 1880; the Surveyor's Report of 1838; the Archaeological Survey Reports of 1891, of 1934—all of them reaffirming what the Muslim historians had stated;

that the mosque was built by destroying the temple, that portions of the temple—e.g., the pillars—are in the mosque still, that the Hindus continue to revere the spot and struggle unremittingly to reacquire it.

'They contain revenue records of a hundred years and more which list the site as "Janmasthan" and specify it to be the property of the mahants....Most important of all, they contain accounts of the archaeological excavations which were conducted at the site from 1975 to 1980. These are conclusive: the pillar-bases, the pillars, the door jamb, the periods of the different layers, the alignment of the bases and the pillars, the stone of which the pillars are made.... Everything coheres. And everything answers the issue the government and the two sides had specified in the affirmative, and unambiguously so.'

There have also been instances of suppression or deletion of 'inconvenient' Muslim literary sources on Ayodhya. For instance, Shourie refers to a book about India in Arabic, by Maulana Hakim Sayyid Abdul Hai (d. 1923), rector of the famed Islamic academy *Nadwatul-Ulama* in Lucknow. It was translated and published by the academy in Urdu in 1973 and in English in 1977. The foreword was by the author's son, Maulana Abul-Hasan Ali Nadwi, better known as Ali Mian. He was a renowned rector of the same institute from 1961 to 1999 and later became the Chairman of the Muslim Personal Law Board.

Shourie writes: 'The Urdu version, contains a 17-page chapter on *Hindustan ki Masjidein*, the mosques of Hindustan. Of seven mosques, the author relates how they had replaced Hindu temples, either by redesigning or by demolition and reconstruction (largely using the same stones). One of these is the Babri Masjid at Ayodhya. 'Translated into English, it reads like this: 'This mosque was constructed by Babar at Ayodhya which Hindus call the birthplace of Ramchandraji. There is a famous story about his wife Sita. It is said that Sita had a temple here in which she lived and cooked for her husband. On that very site Babar constructed his mosque in H. 963...'

Thus, if the dispute was to be settled on the basis of evidence and counter-evidence, the Hindu case was unimpeachable.

PART III

ECSTASY AND AGONY
Journey towards the fateful day

A significant milestone in the history of the Ayodhya struggle was the victory of the BJP in the state assembly elections in July 1991. Support for the Ram Janmabhoomi issue was already on the upswing before the polls, cutting across caste and class lines. And then came the police firing on *kar sevaks* by Mulayam Singh Yadav's government, which created a wave of anger among the Hindus in UP as well as the rest of the country. Kalyan Singh, a dedicated and popular mass leader of the party, became the state's new Chief Minister. His government began earnest efforts to resolve the Ayodhya issue, which had been thwarted by judicial proceedings, with a new initiative.

At the crux of this initiative was the decision to delink the decision on the disputed structure from the commencement of the construction of the temple in the adjoining area. Consequently, the UP government acquired 2.77 acres of land adjacent to the disputed structure by a notification under the Land Acquisition Act in October 1991. It is worth emphasising that, out of the 2.77 acres, 2.04 acres was acquired from the VHP itself. The VHP had earlier acquired it by purchase or as a gift from the previous owners. Thus, there was no dispute whatsoever about the ownership of eighty percent of the acquired land. Most importantly, this plot of 2.77 acres was the same site where Rajiv Gandhi's government at the Centre had allowed *shilanyas* to be performed in 1989, after declaring that there was no dispute over this land.

Sadly, even this reasonable approach of Kalyan Singh's government was thwarted by the AIBMAC. The acquisition was challenged in the High Court, which passed an order allowing the government to take possession of the notified land, and directing that no structure of any permanent nature be put up.

Meanwhile, Chandrashekhar's government at the Centre had fallen in March 1991. The Congress, which had supported his government from outside, withdrew its support on the flimsy ground that a few policemen were seen 'spying' around Rajiv Gandhi's residence. In the ensuing parliamentary elections, the Congress failed to win a majority. Significantly, analysis of the results showed that even the modest tally of 232 seats (as compared to 415 in 1984) that it reached was largely on account of the sympathy wave generated after Rajiv Gandhi's assassination in the midst of the electoral process.

The BJP further improved its strength in Parliament from 86 to 119 seats. Nevertheless, since the Congress was the largest single party, it formed a minority government under the leadership of P.V. Narasimha Rao. I should add here that I had high expectations from the new Prime Minister. He was an erudite and soft spoken politician who had risen to the top from the grassroots. As a result, he possessed enviable political and administrative experience. He did begin on a positive note, giving indications that he believed in the path of consensus-building. This necessarily required the government to reach out to the Opposition in a process of dialogue based on mutual trust and respect.

I must confess that I was much impressed by Rao's deliberate abandoning of haughtiness that so characterised previous Congress governments at the Centre. This was perhaps because he did not belong to the 'dynasty'. In my admiration, I went to the extent of stating, publicly, that 'Narasimha Rao is the best Prime Minister India has got after Lal Bahadur Shastri.' It was a remark that did not withstand scrutiny in the light of Rao's subsequent conduct.

The leaders of the Ramjanmabhoomi movement also had high expectations from Rao. Their hopes stemmed from two factors. Firstly, he had an intimate knowledge of India's history. Well versed in many Indian and foreign languages, he was, after Nehru, the most scholarly Prime Minister India had ever had. Also, as someone who joined India's freedom movement by plunging into the anti-Nizam struggle in Hyderabad under the inspiration of Swami Ramanand, he had a good understanding of the trials and tribulations of Hindus under fanatical Muslim rulers. Secondly, in the specific context of Ramjanmabhoomi, he had the advantage of being aware of the complete background of the Hindu community's struggle, having been appointed by Prime Minister Rajiv Gandhi in 1987 as the head of the special group of Ministers to advise the government on the Ayodhya issue.

In his private meetings with Hindu religious leaders, Rao had assured that he would continue governmental efforts on finding a solution to the Ayodhya issue from where Chandrashekhar had left it. In other words, the government-mediated dialogue between leaders of the temple movement and the AIBMAC would be resumed. However, Rao took no steps in that direction. In order to shake up the government's inertia, a Vishal Hindu Sammelan was organised on 4 April 1991 at the Boat Club in Delhi. It was perhaps the biggest rally ever held in the nation's capital. *Kar seva* indeed started on 9 July. It went on for seventeen days, with nothing untoward happening either in Ayodhya or elsewhere.

This prompted the Prime Minister to invite the Sants to Delhi for a discussion. He assured them that he expected the problem to be solved within four months and requested them to discontinue the *kar seva*. The Prime Minister also spoke to both Vajpayee and me to prevail upon the leaders of the temple movement to give him some time. The Sants responded positively to his assurance and stopped the *kar seva*.

Again, there was no initiative from the government. During this period, Bhairon Singh Shekhawat and Sharad Pawar (both of them were known to cultivate good contacts in different social and political organisations) mediated to restart the dialogue between the VHP and AIBMAC. One such meeting did take place, but it was fruitless. Leaders of the temple movement now decided to resume the *kar seva* in November.

Events moved swiftly hereafter. On 28 November, the Supreme Court permitted *kar seva*, on the assurance given by the UP government that it would be symbolic. The Dharma Sansad, the highest platform of Hindu religious leaders, decided to carry out the *kar seva* from 6-10 December. Since the Lucknow bench of the Allahabad High Court was expected to deliver its judgment on the validity of the UP government's acquisition of 2.77 acres adjacent to the disputed structure, the Dharma Sansad also decided to commence construction immediately thereafter.

Here we need to know why the Allahabad High Court's judgment was crucial and eagerly awaited. Its significance lay in the fact that irrespective of whether it upheld or struck down the UP government's decision, it would have paved the way for the construction to continue. If the acquisition was ruled valid, the state government would be entitled to hand over the entire 2.77 acres of the acquired land to the Ram Janmabhoomi Nyas. If, on the other hand, the high court found it to be invalid, the state government would be well within its rights to give back the portion of 2.04 acres out of the acquired land, which was rightfully owned by the Nyas itself. Thereafter, the Nyas would be legally free to continue the temple construction on its own land.

BARREN TALKS WITH RAO'S MINISTERS
The role of Kamal Nath and P.R. Kumaramangalam

During those days, two ministers from Narasimha Rao's government used to meet me regularly to discuss the Ayodhya issue. They were Kamal Nath and P.R. Kumaramangalam. Kamal Nath is an important leader of the Congress party from Madhya Pradesh and has held ministerial positions in several Congress governments. He is now the Union Minister of Commerce in Dr Manmohan Singh's government. Kumaramangalam, son of the distinguished communist leader Mohan Kumaramangalam (who joined Indira Gandhi's government during her 'leftist' phase in the early 1970s) was a close confidante of Rajiv Gandhi. He later joined the BJP and served as a Minister in Vajpayee's government until his untimely death in 1999.

Kamal Nath's meetings with me began in July 1992 and ended in the second week of October. Some time in September, I told Kamal Nath that the central government should expedite the acquisition case in Allahabad. I explained to him how, irrespective of whether the judgment was in favour or against the UP government's acquisition of 2.77 acres, work on the temple construction could begin without, in any way, prejudicing the status quo of the main disputed structure.

Kamal Nath said that my understanding of the case was not correct. The next day, he told me that it was not possible for the central government to request the court to expedite its judgment. Interestingly, just two or three days later, in the second week of October, he came back to me and asked: 'Suppose the Central Government acquires the land for building a temple and gives it to the Ramjanmabhoomi Nyas on the condition that the structure was not touched till there was a judicial verdict. Would it be acceptable?' He further suggested that the dispute about the main structure could be settled subsequently either through judicial verdict or mutual agreement between leaders of the Hindu and Muslim communities.

I did not hesitate even for minute to state that the proposal would be acceptable. My only suggestion was that, instead of 'judicial verdict', we could use the phrase 'due process of law' to describe the mode of eventual resolution of the main dispute. 'Due process of law', I explained, also opened the door for a legislative solution to the dispute. Kamal Nath found my suggestion acceptable.

Within a day or two, Rao invited senior RSS leader Nanaji Deshmukh to meet him. When Nanaji mentioned Kamal Nath's proposal to him, Rao's reply was: 'There is no such proposal.' When I confronted Kamal Nath about the Prime Minister's rejection of the proposal, Kamal Nath said, 'The PM had perhaps thought of the proposal as his trump card and its premature revelation has possibly upset him.'

As a matter of fact, I was totally upset with the Prime Minister's conduct. A few days later, Kumaramangalam told me that Rao had not authorised Kamal Nath to mediate on Ayodhya. This was quite contrary to Kamal Nath's affirmation that he was coming to me on behalf of the Prime Minister. Indeed, after every discussion, he would go back to the Prime Minister and in his next meeting, mention to me how the Prime Minister had reacted. Therefore, I had, at no point of time, the slightest reason to believe, or even to suspect, that he was an unauthorised emissary. Curiously, even as Kamal Nath was negotiating with me, Kumaramangalam had mentioned the same formula to Shekhawat, who felt that it was a workable solution.

All these facts just go to prove that the Prime Minister was not his own master when it came to formulating his government's approach to the Ayodhya issue. There were wheels within wheels in his government and his party; games were being played to scuttle a peaceful resolution. Evidence was mounting that each time the Prime Minister initiated a constructive move, he would be checkmated by his ministerial colleagues who reportedly accused him of 'promoting the saffron agenda'.

JUSTICE DELAYED IS JUSTICE DENIED
How 6 December could have been averted

If the adage 'justice delayed is justice denied' needed any illustration, it was provided by the manner in which the Allahabad High Court kept on postponing its judgment on the UP government's acquisition of 2.77 acres of land near the disputed structure. I have earlier described that the Kalyan Singh government's decision to delink the status of the disputed structure from commencement of the temple construction in the adjacent area was constructive, practical and non-controversial. Its acquisition of 2.77 acres near the disputed structure was meant to give effect to this delinking. But some Muslim individuals challenged this acquisition in the Allahabad High Court, which was expected to give its judgment by December 1991. Whatever its verdict, temple construction could have started—either on the entire plot of 2.77 acres or the smaller area of 2.04 acres that originally belonged to the temple trust.

Even the Supreme Court had stated that it expected the High Court to take up the acquisition writ petitions for final disposal by December 1991. Sadly, the Allahabad High Court did not even begin hearings on the writs until May 1992. In August, the Supreme Court again said: 'It is also appropriate that the High Court should decide the case most expeditiously'. In spite of the fact that a special Bench was exclusively set-up, the hearings were prolonged mysteriously and unnecessarily.

Fortunately, by the time the Dharma Sansad announced, on 30 October 1992, its decision to commence the *kar seva* on 6 December, the hearings on the acquisition writs had virtually come to an end. Actually, they concluded on 4 November and the court reserved its judgment on that day. On 25 November, the Supreme Court again mentioned the 'need for a most expeditious decision of the matter'.

As such the leaders of the temple movement were entirely justified in expecting the verdict to be pronounced in November, or in the first week of December. Why were they, and the BJP, so eagerly awaiting the Allahabad High Court's verdict? I can mention two reasons. Firstly, once the judgment was delivered, the earlier judicial orders staying construction activity would automatically get annulled. Hence, both the *kar seva* and the subsequent normal building activity could take place legally, without any ambiguity or doubt.

Secondly, once the *kar sevaks* got involved in their work, conserving and protecting the disputed structure would offer no problem whatsoever. This was because leaders of the temple movement had completely endorsed the UP government's plan to delink the *kar seva* and construction on the adjoining plot of land (2.77 acres or 2.04 acres, depending on the judgment of the High Court) from the status of the disputed structure. They had categorically accepted that efforts to settle the status of the disputed structure could move on a parallel track by pursuing one of the three options—judicial verdict, legislative action, or mutual settlement on the basis of a Hindu-Muslim rapprochement. It was the sincere hope of my party, and also of all the leaders of the temple movement that, the smooth commencement of the *kar seva* on 6 December would be in consonance with Kalyan Singh government's commitment to the Supreme Court and Narasimha Rao government's commitment to Parliament and the National Integration Council.

Sadly, the judgment that was reserved on 4 November did not come even on the day of the *kar seva*. It came finally on 11 December, five days after the tragic happenings of 6 December. If this was the fate of a writ petition that involved a very narrow issue, the case of the title suits filed in 1959 and 1961 has been far worse. They continue to remain in limbo until today.

I should mention here that no effort was spared by the leaders of the BJP and the temple movement to impress upon the central government to initiate steps to prevent the looming imbroglio. On 2 November, senior RSS leaders Rajju Bhaiyya and Moropant Pingle, accompanied by Bhairon

Singh Shekhawat, who was then the Chief Minister of Rajasthan, met Sharad Pawar and Kumaramangalam in Mumbai. On 8 November, Swami Chinmayananda, a revered Hindu leader, called on the Prime Minister. Rajju Bhaiyya had two meetings with the Prime Minister, the last one on 3 December. On 25 November, Swami Paramahans Ramachandradas, the most venerable Ayodhya-based leader of the temple movement, called on Rao. Vajpayee and Nanaji Deshmukh met Rao on 30 November. Nanaji had another meeting with Rao as late as on 5 December. I too met the Prime Minister twice in November.

In all these meetings, we made just one plea—let the central and UP governments jointly approach the Supreme Court or the high court for expediting the judgment. We further pleaded that the Prime Minister should take steps to ensure that, if not the whole judgment, at least its operative part was pronounced before 6 December. In fact, Rajju Bhaiyya told Rao, 'Lakhs of people will be assembling at Ayodhya. We have made elaborate arrangements to see that they conduct the *kar seva* within the parameters of the court order. But what if the court order does not come and something untoward happens? I hope it does not happen. It is, therefore that I am impressing upon the government the need to secure a verdict before 6 December.' The Prime Minister's reply was: 'I am confident that with you all in control, nothing untoward would happen.' But he gave no assurance of his government requesting the court to give an expeditious verdict.

A last-ditch effort was made on the morning of 5 December by B.P. Singhal, a former bureaucrat who had joined the BJP. He spoke to Naresh Chandra, the distinguished civil servant who had been appointed by the Prime Minister to head the Special Ayodhya Cell in the PMO. Both of them agreed on a plan of action: on the same afternoon, the UP government would plead before the Allahabad High Court that it deliver, at least the operative part of the judgment, and the counsel for the central government would support the plea. Accordingly, the UP government did move the application as agreed. However, the counsel for central government failed to turn up in court. As a result, the state government's application was summarily dismissed.

To say the least, in the eyes of the leaders of the temple movement all this cast grave doubts about the sincerity and motives of the Prime Minister and his government. In a way, by frustrating all initiatives of the leaders of the Ayodhya movement, they were just compelling a mass upsurge.

In his appearance before the Liberhan Commission, Narasimha Rao was asked why the Centre did not request the court for an early verdict on the UP government's land acquisition matter. His reply was: 'How could the Central Government make any such request even if it wanted to, when it was not a party to the proceedings before the Allahabad High Court?' I was quite surprised when I learnt this. For at no point of time during his numerous meetings with representatives of the temple movement did he tell us what he later told the Liberhan Commission. Had he done so, we would have followed a different course.

KAR SEVA FOR TEMPLE CONSTRUCTION
Unprecedented manifestation of Hindu unity

When the BJP felt that the Narasimha Rao government had become totally insensitive to the aspirations of the Hindus and stood against construction even when it was delinked from the structure, it decided to send Dr Murli Manohar Joshi, who was President of the BJP at the time, and me on a yatra in Uttar Pradesh. The purpose of the yatra was to explain to the people the hostile attitude of the Congress government at the Centre and also to mobilise them for the *kar seva* in Ayodhya. Accordingly, I commenced my yatra from Varanasi and Joshi did so from Mathura on 3 December.

The response to our yatras was beyond our expectations. In fact, on the third day, we had to appeal to the people to defer their departure to Ayodhya because, by that time, over one lakh Ram Bhakts (devotees of Lord Ram) had already arrived in Ayodhya. I must mention here that the anger generated by the uncooperative attitude of the central government had made the people even more determined to come to Ayodhya. The inexplicable delay in the pronouncement of the Allahabad High Court's judgment had further contributed to this mass resentment. As a result, the *kar seva* had become, in the eyes of the people, as much an act of defiance as of piety.

Another aspect of the movement deserves special mention here. People from every imaginable section of the richly diverse Hindu community were rushing to Ayodhya from all corners of the country. In fact, the representation of the scheduled castes, scheduled tribes and so-called backward castes far outnumbered that of the Brahmins and other 'upper castes'. And they came from places as far off as Kerala in the south and Assam in the North-East. There was also large and spirited participation by Sikhs from Punjab and other parts of the country. Also, all these were people coming on their own, quite unlike the way crowds are mobilised for many political rallies today. There was an unmistakable air of spontaneity, religiosity, voluntariness and high-spiritedness.

Moreover, every village and town that the *kar sevaks* came from, they received a ceremonial send-off. All along the route of their travel, they were greeted by common people with *aarati*, given food and most touchingly, also their support and blessings. For obvious reasons, there were more men than women among *kar sevaks*. But it must be noted that women outnumbered men in ceremonial preparations for the send-off or in their welcome en route to Ayodhya. In this way, every karsevak who came to Ayodhya carried the prayers of tens of thousands of people back home and all across the country. India had never seen a spectacle of this kind. The scene infused joy in the hearts of those who always despaired over the disunity in the Hindu society. It also surprised and stunned those who always believed that the unity of the Hindus was a myth, that the demand of the Ram Temple in Ayodhya appealed only to 'upper-caste' Hindus, and that the entire Ayodhya movement was an artificial construct of the 'Sangh Parivar'.

PART IV

6 DECEMBER 1992
What happened—and why

The progress of human history rarely follows a linear path. And mass movements, which are often the engines of historical changes, seldom unfold entirely according to a predetermined script. Events sometimes take an unexpected turn. Untoward incidents take place. Setbacks happen. Often, in the setback, one finds that the movement has accomplished something that is irreversible, something that was not desired by the leaders and not even anticipated by the followers.

What happened in Ayodhya on 6 December belongs to this extraordinary category of history-changing events. A disputed mosque structure that stood for over four hundred years in the heart of one of the holiest Hindu towns, a structure that Hindus believed was built on the birthplace of Lord Ram, a structure that was seen as a symbol of national subjugation and religious bigotry, and for reclaiming whose site Hindus had waged a long and protracted battle, finally suffered extinction as the outcome of a mass frenzy.

I arrived in Ayodhya after addressing my last public meeting in Lucknow on 5 December. It was around midnight. I spent the night at Janaki Mahal, where I normally stayed whenever I visited Ayodhya. The following morning, I was first taken to the place where the symbolic *kar seva* was intended to be performed with a fistful of sand from the banks of the Saryu river. From there, along with other leaders of the temple movement, I was taken to the dais, which had been put up on the terrace of the Ram Katha Kunj. Around 10 am, even before speeches by the leaders on the dais could start, someone came and told us that a small group of *kar sevaks* had mounted one of the domes of the disputed structure. It was visible from the roof-top of the Ram Katha Kunj. I thus got visual confirmation of the message just received.

The leaders on the dais immediately started pleading—through the public announcement system—with the *kar sevaks* on top of the domes to come down. This was, however, to no avail. In fact, more and more people appeared to be climbing the dome. Soon, I could see them carrying some implements and hammering away at the dome. I was upset, and so were other leaders on the dais. We felt that something was amiss. All the leaders made vehement appeals to the errant persons to immediately climb down and follow the discipline laid down by the organisers. I spoke with great distress in my heart. Senior RSS leader H.V. Seshadri, who knew several languages, spoke in all of them since it was unclear who had broken the ranks and taken law into their own hands. Rajmata Scindia, a highly respected leader of the movement, made a passionate plea: 'I am appealing to you as your mother not to do what you are doing.' It was clear from all these appeals that what was happening on the dome was against the goals and principles of our movement.

All this, however, seemed to have no effect. I then asked Uma Bharati, who would be identifiable as a *sanyasin,* to go to the spot and appeal to those who had mounted the dome to come down. She did go there and returned about forty-five minutes later to convey to me that some of the *kar sevaks* had heeded her advice, while many did not. She incidentally mentioned that those who were still on the dome seemed to be talking in Marathi. I therefore requested Pramod Mahajan, who had come with me from Lucknow, to go and stop what was happening. He went there and came back after sometime with a similar experience as that of Uma Bharati. Thereafter, I asked the lady police official, who was in charge of my security, to accompany me to the place of vandalism. Her reply surprised me. 'Since I am in charge of *your* security, I will not agree to your going there,' she said. Around this time, Ashok Singhal tried to go to the spot to persuade these *kar sevaks* to desist from attacking the domes. I was told that he had been manhandled while making these attempts.

I then told the lady police official that I would like to speak to Kalyan Singh, the Chief Minister of UP, who was in Lucknow. We alighted from the dais and went in search of a telephone. We found one, but I could not contact Lucknow. It was there that I heard the first thud and was told by someone that one dome had fallen. I went rushing back to the roof-top of the Ram Katha Kunj. What I saw from there is etched in my mind. While the leaders on the dais were shocked at the unforeseen turn of events, the mood among the milling crowds below was quite the opposite. All of them seemed filled with a sense of relief and many among them were even elated. After some time, another dome fell. The third dome met with the same fate soon thereafter. By now, the mood of elation had begun to have its influence on some leaders on the dais too.

Someone came and started distributing sweets. I said, 'No, I will not have sweets today.'

Meanwhile, I got the message that I could speak with the Chief Minister in Lucknow. He had learnt about the demolition. The essence of my conversation with him was that, in view of his government's failure to abide by the assurance he had given to the Supreme Court, he ought to tender his resignation. He agreed.

I was feeling both distraught and helpless. Sensing my mood, Pramod Mahajan said, 'Advaniji, you will feel more depressed if you continued to stay here. Let us go back to Lucknow.' So we left Ayodhya at around 6 pm. I had made up my mind that I too would tender my resignation from the only official position that I occupied at that time—namely, the Leader of Opposition in the Lok Sabha. As soon as I reached Lucknow, I sent my letter of resignation by fax to the Speaker of the Lok Sabha.

I recall vividly an experience en route from Ayodhya to Lucknow. In spite of strict security all along the 135-kilometre journey, I could see people engaged in celebrations everywhere. Within half an hour of our departure from Ayodhya, our car was stopped by the police. On seeing that the car carried Pramod Mahajan and me, a senior officer of the UP government walked up to us said, '*Advaniji, kuch bacha to nahin na? Bilkul saaf kar diya na?*' (I hope nothing of the structure is surviving and that it has been totally razed to the ground.) I am recounting this incident only to highlight the general mood of the populace, including employees and officials of the state government, after the tragic development in Ayodhya—that of jubilation.

AFTERMATH: THE CONGRESS GOVERNMENT'S DOUBLE-SPEAK
The Official White Paper was a whitewash job

After the demolition, Prime Minister Rao charged the leaders of the temple movement with conspiracy, criminal intent, and perfidy. But was the demolition of the disputed structure pre-planned? No. Was it part of a conspiracy known to, or having the approval of, the leaders of the temple movement? No. Indeed, the charge of conspiracy and pre-planning was denied by no less a person than S.B. Chavan, who was the Home Minister in Rao's government. The *Pioneer* reported on 3 January 1993: 'Union Home Minister S. B. Chavan sprang a surprise on Friday when he stated that the demolition of the Babri Masjid was not pre-planned. He said that the intelligence agencies, too, had not given any inkling of what was to happen on that fateful day. 'In fact, we have been consistently saying that if we had any prior information, we would definitely have taken preventive steps,' he pointed out.

My role in the events of 6 December became the subject of unbridled vilification. I was accused of inciting the crowds to demolish the disputed structure. This, indeed, has been the crux of the chargesheet against me. Nothing can be further from the truth. All the impartial eye-witnesses of the fateful developments in Ayodhya on 6 December know that I was among those leaders who were making impassioned appeals to the unruly kar sevaks to stop the demolition. Many Indian and foreign journalists witnessed me and my mood on that day. One of them, Jeff Penberthy, who was then the New Delhi bureau chief of *Time* magazine, said this in an article 'What I witnessed on December 6' in *The Asian Age* of 17 September 2004.

> At the time, I was the recently-arrived New Delhi bureau chief for *Time*. Anita Pratap was then our Delhi correspondent. Anita had travelled south to observe Mr L.K. Advani's rathyatra as it progressed towards Ayodhya, and I drove there from Lucknow. On December 6, we got to see the destruction of the Babri Masjid because we had started early. Anita and I took up our positions on the roof of the Manas Bhavan facing the Masjid at 10 am. There

were roughly 300,000 people at Ayodhya. Finally, Mr Advani arrived, and began to speak at noon as the vast crowd gathered. In my memory, the BJP leader looked distressed, and as the first young men with iron bars broke through the fence and were sprinting towards the mosque, he was pleading into his microphone 'Please don't do this,' before he was hustled away.

The proponents of the conspiracy theory have alluded to the fact that the idols of Ram Lalla, which were under the central dome since 1949, were brought to the VHP's camp office around 3 pm and later reinstalled in the makeshift temple that came into being at the demolished structure. How is it that amidst all the chaos the idols were taken out intact and put back again? Doesn't this, ask the critics, suggest a certain degree of planning and prior arrangement? My answer is 'No'. The critics' view is presumptuous and betrays a lack of understanding of the *kar sevaks'* sentiments for the idol of Ram Lalla. Once the first dome was demolished, it was obvious to all those present in the vicinity of the structure that the two remaining domes too would come down. It was also clear that *kar sevaks* on the ground were concerned about the safety of the idols inside the shrine located under the central dome. In those circumstances, any one of them could have carried the idols from the crumbling structure and take them to a safer place.

In February 1993, Narasimha Rao's government released a White Paper, giving an official version of the Ayodhya events. It accused the UP government of 'criminal inaction' and 'abdication of responsibility'. It held Chief Minister Kalyan Singh responsible for it because of his instructions to the police 'not to use force'. As a matter of fact, this charge also holds true for the Congress government at the Centre. For, the last dome had fallen at 4.50 pm on 6 December. Kalyan Singh tendered his resignation at 5.30 pm. Shortly thereafter, the Centre dismissed his government and imposed President's Rule in UP. As the chronology of events on that day clearly show, after the demolition of the domes, *kar sevaks* continued to dismantle the rest of the disputed structure and started to remove the rubble from the site. All this happened when Ayodhya had already come under the administrative control of the Central Government.

More importantly, all through the night, the *kar sevaks* busied themselves in erecting a makeshift temple at the site. After completing the task, they ceremonially installed the idols of Ram Lalla, Sita, Lakshman and Hanuman inside the temple. The Prime Minister, Home Minister and all the other important officials of the central government in Delhi knew exactly what was happening in Ayodhya *after* UP had been brought under the President's Rule. Still, not only did the Central Government remain a mute spectator, but actually *permitted* the *kar sevaks* to construct the makeshift Ram temple at the disputed site.

Thus, paradoxically, a government that did not allow *kar seva* to be performed on the undisputed land in the vicinity of the disputed structure ended up permitting *kar seva* at the disputed site itself! This was by no means a symbolic *kar seva*. It resulted in the construction of the Ram temple, albeit a small and provisional one, at Ramjanmabhoomi. It is in a way a blessing in disguise that the construction of the makeshift temple and the installation of the idols took place when Ayodhya had already come under President's Rule. For it contributed to the legitimacy of the temple. The Allahabad High Court further reinforced its legitimacy by permitting, in an order in 1993, pilgrims to have *darshan* of Ram Lalla at the makeshift temple. It is worth mentioning here that even the government's own White Paper admits, on the very first page of the document, that 'In effect, from December 1949 till December 6, 1992 the structure had not been used as a mosque'.

In the immediate aftermath of 6 December, some political leaders demanded that the 'Babri Masjid' should be rebuilt. Prime Minister Rao himself made this promise on 7 December. Ironically, he was promising to rebuild 'the mosque' after he had already allowed the *kar sevaks* to build the makeshift Ram temple! As a result, his party and he lost the trust of both Hindus and Muslims.

WHY I SAID, 'IT'S THE SADDEST DAY IN MY LIFE.'

After 6 December, Rao's government went on a political offensive against the BJP and leaders of the Ayodhya movement to obtain maximum political mileage. I was arrested on 8 December along with Dr Murli Manohar Joshi, Ashok Singhal, Vishnu Hari Dalmia, Vinay Katiyar and Sadhvi Uma Bharati. I was detained at Mata Tila near Jhansi, where I remained until the court ordered our release on 10 January 1993. On 10 December, the government imposed a ban on the RSS, VHP and Bajrang Dal, along with Jamait-e-Islami Hind and the Islamic Sevak Sangh. On 15 January, the Centre dismissed the BJP governments in Rajasthan, Madhya Pradesh and Himachal Pradesh. This was a purely vindictive action, since these democratically elected governments had nothing to do with the developments in Ayodhya. It was done perhaps to counter the simmering dissent against the Prime Minister within the Congress party in the aftermath of Ayodhya.

My detention at Mata Tila was my fourth experience as a political prisoner in independent India. I first courted arrest in 1948 when the government banned the RSS following Mahatma Gandhi's assassination. It lasted about three months. The second time was during the Emergency (1975-77), which was my longest stay in prison. The third time was when my Rath Yatra was stopped at Samastipur in Bihar and I was made to spend a month or so in detention at Massanjore. Long or short, life as a political prisoner is a highly enlightening experience.

One of the first lessons a political activist learns, while under arrest, is that struggle and sacrifice are inseparable parts of politics. If you strongly believe in something, then you must be prepared to pay the price for your beliefs. Those who dream of politics as a bed of roses, or are loath to suffer the dust and din of mass campaigns, are not fit for this calling. Of course, we in India ought to consider ourselves fortunate since being a democracy the struggles and sacrifices are not as severe as they would be under tyrannical regimes.

After several tension-filled months, the tranquility at Mata Tila 'jail' was overpowering. The detention gave me an opportunity for quiet reflection on the stormy events that had culminated in the upheaval of 6 December. I poured out my thoughts in an article published in the *Indian Express*, in two parts, on 27 and 28 December 1992. In this, I described the genesis and evolution of the Ayodhya movement. I also analysed the causes that led to the unfortunate denouement on 6 December. I strongly defended the movement and my party's involvement in it. At the same time, I expressed my feelings on the ill-fated culmination of the movement. I mentioned that I could not share the sense of elation that some leaders of the movement exhibited. 'It was the saddest day in my life,' I wrote. 'I have seldom felt as dejected and downcast as I felt that day.'

This expression of sadness prompted media persons to later ask me if I was apologetic about my association with the Ayodhya movement. I emphatically denied that! The two statements—one about feeling remorse and the other about not feeling apologetic—may sound contradictory. I have sometimes been criticised for the first statement by my colleagues in the temple movement. As for my critics, they have doubted the sincerity of my first statement and reproached me for the second. I must, therefore, put forth my honest observations and reflections on the developments of 6 December, and on the larger socio-political context in which they took place.

As I explained in my article in the *Indian Express:* 'My sadness did not stem from any disenchantment with the Ayodhya movement or with the path the party had chosen for itself. In fact, the post-demolition developments have fully vindicated our misgivings about the opponents of this movement. I felt sad that a meticulously drawn up plan of action, whereunder the UP government was steadily marching forward towards discharging its mandate regarding temple construction without violating any law or disregarding any court order has gone awry. If the exercise contemplated has now been short-circuited in a totally unforeseen manner the organisations involved in the movement can be faulted for not being able to judge the impatience of the people participating in the movement, but they were certainly not responsible for what happened on that day'.

In one of my media interactions during those days, Manini Chatterjee, a prominent journalist then with the *Telegraph*, asked me an unusual question. 'What is the one word that appeals most to you in your life?' I said, 'Credibility.' Whatever I am, and whatever I have been able to do for my country and my party is because of the credibility I have earned in my life. It is not only my personal credibility, but also my party's. Even the critics of the Jana Sangh and the BJP used to admit that 'here is a party that practices what it preaches, and preaches what it practices'. The reason why the demolition of the disputed structure pained me was because it severely dented our credibility in the eyes of the people.

We in the BJP had all along declared that our goal was to construct the Ram temple at Ramjanmabhoomi after respectfully relocating the mosque structure, and that we would like to achieve this either by a due process of law or through an amicable settlement between the Hindu and Muslim communities. However, as it turned out, we could not live by our word. The exhortations of the leaders of the temple movement were disregarded by some of the assembled *kar sevaks*. As a result, the credibility of the entire movement was undermined by those who took the law in their own hands on 6 December. It is in this sense that I felt, and I continue to feel so, that our entire movement suffered a setback on that day.

At the same time, I was appalled when some well-meaning and otherwise respectable personalities resorted to hyperboles, condemning it as 'national shame' or a 'crime comparable to Mahatma Gandhi's assassination.

I cannot in all honesty deny that 6 December represented an epoch-making day in the life of India and also of Hindus. It was the clearest signal in modern India's history that the Hindu community would not forever tolerate denial of and disrespect towards its legitimate sentiments. Those who took Hindu concerns and aspirations for granted, and tried to thwart them through an endless process of political machinations and judicial delays, got an answer which they will hopefully not forget.

As I have said earlier, mass movements sometimes acquire an inner dynamic of their own which even its leaders cannot always comprehend or fully control. Thus, through an action that neither the leaders of the temple movement nor the leaders of the central government could control or prevent, a group of *kar sevaks* delivered their own verdict on some of the seminal questions of Indian history, both medieval and modern. Ram or Babar? Genuine secularism or pseudo-secularism? Justice for all or always appeasement of some? Are Hindus to perpetually remain divided on caste, regional and linguistic lines or should they unite when fundamental challenges confront faith and nationalism?

It is not my claim that 6 December answered all these questions in the most satisfactory manner. But it did mark a day of Hindu awakening of truly historic import.

V.S. NAIPAUL, NIRAD C. CHAUDHURI AND GIRILAL JAIN
Three insightful observers of the Ayodhya movement

Whenever an epochal development takes place in a country, it is bound to provoke diverse and often diametrically opposite reactions. The criticism of the Ayodhya movement in a section of India's intellectual community is well-known. I never disregard critical viewpoints, for they make you introspect and re-evaluate your own beliefs and actions. I was, however, disappointed to find that some critics were only obsessed with the outward manifestations of the Ayodhya developments and did not care to dispassionately examine its significance and impact from a historical perspective.

In this context, I was most heartened by the comments and analyses of three distinguished intellectuals—a novelist, a writer, a journalist—neither of whom was previously known to be a believer in the Hindu worldview. One is Nobel laureate Sir V.S. Naipaul, the Trinidad-born Britain-based writer of Indian origin. The second was late Nirad C. Chaudhuri, Oxford-based author of the famous book *Autobiography of an Unknown Indian* (1951); and the third was late Girilal Jain, the Editor of the *Times of India* (1978-89) who traversed an interesting intellectual journey from being a follower of M.N. Roy (one of the founders of the international communist movement who was later disillusioned with communism), admirer of Nehru, defender of Indira Gandhi and supporter of Hindu revival. His book *The Hindu Phenomenon* (1994) was a summation of his lifelong reflections. It described the Ayodhya movement as an integral part of the historical process of Hindu self-renewal and self-affirmation, and brought the civilisational underpinnings of Indian nationalism to the centre-stage of the political discourse in India.

I present these three viewpoints here in order to explain to readers why I am proud of my association with the Ayodhya movement.

On 18 July 1993, Dilip Padgaonkar, then Editor of the *Times of India* carried a widely debated interview with Naipaul under the heading: 'An Area of Awakening'—an apt take-off on Naipaul's highly critical non-fiction book on India called *An Area of Darkness* (1964). Here are a few excerpts from that interview.

Padgaonkar: The collapse of the Soviet Union and the subsequent rise of Islamic nations in Central Asia, the Salman Rushdie affair, similar harassment by fundamentalists of liberal Muslim intellectuals in India: all these factors taken together persuaded some forces to argue that a divided Hindu society cannot counteract Islamic fundamentalism.

Naipaul: I don't see it quite in that way. The things you mentioned are quite superficial. What is happening in India is a new, historical awakening. Gandhi used religion in a way as to marshal people for the independence cause. People who entered the independence movement did it because they felt they would earn individual merit.

Today, it seems to me that Indians are becoming alive to their history. Romila Thapar's book on Indian history is a Marxist attitude to history, which in substance says: there is a higher truth behind the invasions—feudalism and all that. The correct truth is the way the invaders looked at their actions. They were conquering, they were subjugating. And they were in a country where people never understood this.

Only now are the people beginning to understand that there has been a great vandalising of India. Because of the nature of the conquest and the nature of Hindu society such understanding had eluded Indians before. What is happening in India is a mighty creative process. Indian intellectuals, who want to be secure in their liberal beliefs, may not understand what is going on, especially if these intellectuals happen to be in the United States. But every other Indian knows precisely what is happening: deep down he knows that a larger response is emerging even if at times this response appears in his eyes to be threatening.

Padgaonkar: How did you react to the Ayodhya incident?

Naipaul: Not as badly, as the others did, I am afraid. The people who say that there was no temple there are missing the point. Babar, you must understand, had contempt for the country (that) he had conquered. And his building of that mosque was an act of contempt for the country. In Turkey, they turned the Church of Santa Sophia into a mosque. In Nicosia churches were converted into mosques too. The Spaniards spent many centuries re-conquering their land from Muslim invaders. So these things have happened before and elsewhere. In Ayodhya the construction of a mosque on a spot regarded as sacred by the conquered population was meant as an insult. It was meant as an insult to an ancient idea, the idea of Ram, which was two or three thousand years old.

*

Nirad C. Chaudhuri, who died in 1999 at the age of 101, was one of the first few Indian English writers to have earned international fame. Though born in Bengal, he remained, to his last day, a proud Victorian gentleman who never hid his sympathies for what he considered the positive aspects of the British Raj. Indeed, he dedicated his autobiography to '*the memory of the British Empire in India.*' In 1993, he startled many observers by describing the events of 6 December as a turning point in Indian history. 'Indians are finally learning how to create history,' he remarked. He articulated his views on the Ayodhya issue with characteristic candour in an interview with Padgaonkar.

There must be a complete recognition of the historical responsibility on both (Hindu and Muslim) sides. They must not try to avoid it. All Hindu historians are liars. From 1907 onwards we became aware of the Hindu-Muslim problem as regards the nationalist movement. From that day till 1946 every fellow Bengali I have asked and every other Indian too had only one standard argument: The Hindu-Muslim problem does not exist. It has been created by the British. "My point is that it is the very nature of things. That what happened in Ayodhya should not have happened is another matter. But I say that the Muslims do not have the slightest right to complain about the desecration of one mosque. From 1000 AD. every Hindu temple from Kathiawar to Bihar, from the Himalayas to the Vindhyas has been sacked and ruined. Not one temple was left standing all over northern India. Temples escaped destruction only where Muslim Power did not gain access to them for reasons such as dense forests. Otherwise it was a continuous spell of vandalism. No nation with any self-respect will forgive this.

The Muslims were the first to invent the theory of permanent revolution. The communists took over from them. No Muslims can live under the political domination of non-Muslims. Secondly, Muslims divide the world into two: regions of peace and regions of conflict. It is the duty of every Muslim to bring the latter within the fold of Islam. The Arab equivalent of the caliph is 'Commander of the Faithful'. And his obligation is jihad (holy war). Why, I ask the English people, do you call them fundamentalists in Kabul and nowhere in England? The reason is that the English people have become completely ignorant. What is more, like us, they cannot face reality.

*

Following are two excerpts from an article that Girilal Jain wrote in which he described the Ayodhya movement as 'A Historical Watershed'. In the first excerpt, Jain emphasises Pandit Nehru's belief in the Hindu spirit of India.

1992 will doubtless go down in Indian history as the year of Ayodhya. The meaning of Ayodhya is that India has regained, to a larger extent than hitherto, the capacity to behave and act as a normal living organism. She has taken another big step towards self-affirmation. All truth, as Lenin said, is partisan. So is mine. I do not pretend to be above the battle, or, to rephrase Pandit Nehru, I am not neutral against myself. But partisan truth is not demagogy and patently false propaganda, which is what advocates of 'composite culture' have engaged in. Pandit Nehru also wrote and spoke of the spirit of India asserting itself again and again. Surely, that spirit could not be a composite affair.

For Nehru, secularism, both as a personal philosophy and state policy, was an expression of India's cultural-civilization personality and not its negation and repudiation. Secularism suited India's requirements as he saw them. Sheikh Abdullah was not too wide off the mark when he wrote in *Aatish-e-Chinar* that Nehru was 'a great admirer of the past heritage and the Hindu spirit of India. He considered himself as an instrument of rebuilding India with its ancient spirit.'

In the second excerpt, Jain views the Ayodhya movement as the outcome of a 200-year-old endeavour for self-affirmation by Hindus.

Only on a superficial view, resulting from a lack of appreciation of the history of modern India, beginning with Raja Rammohan Roy in the early 19th century, can the rise of Ramjanmabhoomi issue to its present prominence be said to be the result of a series of 'accidents': the sudden appearance of the Ramlalla idol in the structure in 1949 and the opening of the gate under the Faizabad magistrate's orders in 1986 being the most important. As in all such cases, these developments have helped bring out and reinforce something that was already growing—the 200-year-old movement for self-renewal and self-affirmation by Hindus.

If this were not so, the 'accidents' in question would have petered out. Similarly, while it cannot be denied that the RSS, the VHP, and the BJP have played a major role in mobilizing support for the cause of the temple, it should also be noted that they could not have achieved the success they have if the general atmosphere was not propitious and the time not ripe. At the conscious level, the BJP, among political formations, has chosen to be an instrument of India's cultural and civilization recovery and reaffirmation. As such, it is natural that it will figure prominently in the reshaping of India in the coming years and decades. But others too will play their parts in the gigantic enterprise.

When a historic change of this magnitude takes place, intellectual confusion is generally unavoidable. The human mind, as a rule, trails behind events; it is not capable of anticipating them. But it should be possible to cut through the mass of confusion and get to the heart of the matter. The heart of the matter is that if India's vast spiritual (psychic in modern parlance) energies, largely dormant for centuries, had to be tapped, Hindus had to be aroused; they could be aroused only by the use of a powerful symbol; that symbol could only be Ram, as was evident in the twenties when the Mahatma moved millions by his talk of Ram Rajya; once the symbol takes hold of the popular mind, as Ram did in the twenties and as it has done now, opposition to it generally adds to its appeal.

Historians can continue to debate whether a temple, in fact, existed at the site of Babri Masjid in Ayodhya; whether it was, in fact, a Ram temple; whether it was destroyed; or whether it had collapsed on its own. Similarly, moralists and secularists can go on arguing that it is not right to replace one place of worship by another, especially as long as the foregoing issues have not been resolved. But this is not how history moves and civilization issues are settled. Pertinent is the fact that for no other site have Hindus fought so bitterly for so long with such steadfastness as over Ramjanmabhoomi in Ayodhya.

*

During my visit to the UK in 1989, I met Niradbabu, known and respected for long as a great writer. Jain and Naipaul became good friends of mine because of the Ayodhya movement. I may add here that Jain presided over the meeting in New Delhi in which I released the book on Ayodhya by Koenraad Elst. In his speech, he complimented me on my role in the Ayodhya movement and said, 'You have made history.'

PART V

MISSION INCOMPLETE
Hindu-Muslim reconciliation is the ideal way forward on Ayodhya

Nearly nineteen years have elapsed since my exhilarating Ram Rath Yatra. Over two decades have passed since Rajiv Gandhi's government allowed opening of the locks at the Ramjanmabhoomi shrine. *Shilanyas* for the construction of a grand Ram Temple was performed, again with the approval of Rajiv's government, eighteen years ago. And 6 December 2007 marked the fifteenth anniversary of a day that was, in the assessment of supporters as well as opponents of the Ayodhya movement, a watershed in the social and political life of modern India. All these milestones are a part of a much longer historical struggle, dating back to nearly five hundred years, for reclaiming the place that crores of Hindus believe is the holy birthplace of Lord Ram.

I am quite aware that some vocal Hindus will question my agitation over a piece of land and the need to build another temple. As individuals, many of them are good human beings and as patriotic as any others. The very fact that they are so vocal is a tribute to the ethos of tolerance in Hinduism as also to the freedom of thought and expression that it affords. I accept their freedom of thought and expression. However, my question to them is: Do they respect the thoughts, beliefs and sentiments of the majority among the majority community in India? I am afraid not.

Hindus by nature are accommodative, broad-minded and magnanimous. Their approach to life and history is basically one of reconciliation and integration, and not that of doctrinaire rigidity and confrontation. I, for one, deeply cherish these attributes of Hinduism and would be horrified if these were to disappear from the individual and collective life of Hindus. But I would be equally dismayed if these traits were taken as a sign of weakness and meekness, under the belief that Hindus do not have—or need not have—any fundamental beliefs at all. Since I belong to the political class, I am appalled when many of my colleagues in other parties behave as if Hindus have no religious sentiments and only the sentiments of non-Hindus need to be given importance; as if what is holy for Hindus does not matter at all whereas one must be sensitive to what is sometimes not even holy for non-Hindus. And all this is justified in the name of secularism!

Need I point out that non-Muslims are not even allowed to enter Mecca and Medina, the two holiest places for Muslims? Indeed, in the entire territory of Saudi Arabia, non-Muslims cannot even practise, much less preach their faith, publicly? Of course, India cannot, and must not, follow the Saudi example of intolerance. However, was it too much for Hindus to expect that, at least one of their three holy places should be free of the symbol of foreign, religious and national conquest?

THE AYODHYA ISSUE IN THE NDA RULE

When the BJP was voted as the single largest party in the 1998 parliamentary elections, and was able to form a government of the National Democratic Alliance, our party faced a peculiar situation. On the one hand, the BJP's steady rise to power, from 1989 onwards, owed considerably to its spirited espousal of the Ayodhya cause. Construction of the Ram Temple in Ayodhya was an important commitment in the party's election manifesto in 1998. On the other hand, the BJP did not have the requisite majority on its own in Parliament to fulfill this commitment. We were bound by the NDA's common minimum programme, which did not include the BJP's commitment on Ayodhya. This was a compulsion of coalition politics, which most supporters of the BJP well understood.

The challenge posed by this situation was two-fold. Firstly, there was, quite understandably, a keen expectation and desire amongst the supporters of the temple movement that, with a BJP-led government in New Delhi, there would be some forward movement towards the realisation of their dream. We had to reassure them that the BJP's commitment to the Ayodhya issue remained unshaken. Secondly, as the leader of the ruling coalition, the BJP also had to reassure its alliance partners that it remained committed to the NDA's common agenda.

I am proud of the fact that my party handled both challenges with conviction and honesty. This was reflected in an imaginative slogan coined by my colleague M. Venkaiah Naidu, who served as the President of the BJP between 2002 and 2004. The slogan—'*Ek haath mein BJP ka jhanda, Doosre haath mein NDA ka agenda*' (the BJP's flag in one hand and the NDA's agenda in the other)—educated the BJP's cadres about the imperative need of strengthening our twin constituencies.

Both Atalji and I, along with our senior colleagues, used to have regular meetings with leaders of the RSS and VHP, and also with the representatives of various religious organisations, on the Ayodhya issue. Our effort in these deliberations was to impress upon them both our conviction and our compulsion. Speaking in Parliament on 6 December 2000, Prime Minister Vajpayee remarked: '*Ayodhya mein Ram Mandir ka nirman rashtriya bhavana ke prakatikaran ka karan tha, jo abhi tak poora nahin hua*' (Construction of the Ram temple at Ayodhya was an expression of national aspiration which is yet to be realised).

Another occasion for reaffirming our stand on this issue came when, on 1 August 2000, both Atalji and I visited Ayodhya to pay homage to Mahant Ramchandradas Paramhans, who had passed away the previous day. The highly revered ninety-year-old Chairman of the Ramjanmabhumi Nyas had been striving for the cause of the Ram Temple since the 1940s. Addressing thousands of mourners at the Tulsi Ghat on the bank of River Saryu, the Prime Minister said it was the mahant's dream to build a temple at Ram Janmabhoomi. 'We will fulfill his wish. We are confident that all impediments in the way of the construction of Ram temple would be removed, I believe that good sense will prevail upon those who are opposing the construction of the temple in Ayodhya.' Speaking on the same occasion, I said the greatest tribute to the mahant would be to transform the existing make-shift temple at the sanctum sanctorum into a magnificent shrine for Lord Ram. 'A temple is destined to be built there,' I declared.

VHP President Ashok Singhal welcomed our statements, saying, 'We are elated at the direct commitment of the Prime Minister and the Deputy Prime Minister towards the construction of the temple at Ayodhya.' 'We believe that they are bound by the NDA agenda and coalition dharma. But we wanted to hear their personal views.'

I should record here a painful episode that took place during my tenure in the Home Ministry. Leaders of the temple movement had felt that they could legally begin construction activity in the area outside the disputed structure, which had rightfully belonged to the Ramjanmabhoomi Nyas. The *Dharam Sansad* (religious leaders' congregation) at the *Maha Kumbh* held at Prayag in January 2001 adopted a resolution urging removal of 'all hurdles' in the way by 12 March 2002, the day of Mahashivaratri. There was, clearly, a dichotomy between the impatience of certain leaders of the temple movement and the compulsions faced by our government in clearing all the legal hurdles. Our parleys failed to find a satisfactory way forward. Meanwhile, on 24 February 2002, leaders of the temple movement began a hundred-day *purnahuti yagna* in Ayodhya as a prelude to the temple construction. The situation in the country was getting tense and, as Home Minister, I was worried.

Three days later, on 27 February, a train was stopped, attacked and torched in Godhra, a small town in Gujarat, in which fifty-eight passengers, most of them *kar sevaks* returning from Ayodhya, were burned to death. In early March, the government received a letter from leaders of the temple movement seeking permission to perform a symbolic *puja* on 15 March on the undisputed acquired land. The Supreme Court prohibited 'religious activity of any kind by anyone either symbolic or actual' and also forbade the Government of India from handing over any 'part' of the acquired land to 'anyone'.

Sadly, an unfortunate incident happened in Ayodhya on 17 October 2003, when the VHP had organised a large congregation to reaffirm its commitment to construct the temple. The programme led to a confrontation

I & B Ministry

Jayaprakash Narayan administering a pledge to Ministers in the Janata Party government from his wheelchair at Mahatma Gandhi's samadhi in New Delhi in March 1977.

Vice President B.D. Jatti administering oath of office to L.K. Advani as a Minister in Morarji Desai's government in 1977.

With Pakistan's military ruler Gen. Zia-ul-Haq in Karachi in November 1978, watching the first India-Pakistan cricket Test match televised live by Doordarshan.

With Dev Anand, the Hindi film industry's evergreen hero and (right) with noted film personalities Raj Kapoor, Shashi Kapoor and Ramanand Sagar.

With film maker Shyam Benegal.

Seen here with Satyajit Ray, whose films L.K. Advani is a fan of. Young Pratibha is also seen.

Dawn of the BJP

Legal luminary M.C. Chagla, chief guest at the BJP's inaugural conference in Bombay in 1980, had predicted that the BJP would emerge as an alternative to the Congress. Also seen are Dr M.M. Joshi, Ram Jethmalani and Atalji. L.K. Advani is to the extreme left.

Leading, along with Atalji and Dr Joshi, a march of BJP MPs to Rashtrapati Bhavan. Also seen is Sikandar Bakht (extreme right).

The BJP was in the forefront of mass protests against Pakistan-supported Khalistani terrorism in Punjab in the 1980s and early '90s. Seen in the picture with Advani is Dr Baldev Prakash, President of the BJP in Punjab.

Ayodhya Movement

'Ram is a unique symbol of India's national identity, unity and integration. In many ways, He is an ideal for Indians' aspiration to live a life of higher values. Thus, it is hardly surprising that the place of Ram's birth in Ayodhya has been the focal point of deepest devotion for the Hindus through the millennia.'

(Above) *On the shore of the Somnath Temple in Gujarat, whose reconstruction after Independence provided inspiration for the Ayodhya movement;* (Right) *Performing yagya — with Kamla, Jayant and party activists — associated with start of the Ram Rath Yatra.*

Advani's Ram Rath Yatra from Somnath to Ayodhya in 1990 was a high point of his political life.

Advani's 10,000-kilometre Rath Yatra was stopped in Bihar before it could reach its destination, Ayodhya, on 30 October 1990. He was arrested and kept under detention for five weeks in Massanjore in Bihar. The photograph shows him returning to New Delhi after being released.

Sundar Singh Bhandari, one of the pillars of the BJP.

(Left) *An eloquent portrayal of partnership.*

(Below) *With Rajju Bhaiyya, former Sarsanghchalak of the RSS. Also seen (left) are Pramod Mahajan, the BJP leader who accompanied L.K. Advani on his Somnath-Ayodhya Yatra and Gopinath Munde (extreme right).*

Marching Ahead

A happy Atalji celebrating with sweets after the Delhi High Court quashed the charge of corruption against L.K Advani in the 'Hawala' case in April 1997.

With former Prime Minister P.V. Narasimha Rao.

Advani and Atalji share a happy moment with former Prime Minister V.P. Singh (extreme left) and CPI(M) leader Harkishan Singh Surjeet in 1909.

On a visit to Mumbai after serial bomb blasts killed over 250 persons on 12 March 1993.

At the BJP's Maha Adhiveshan *in Mumbai in 1995, Advani, as party President, declared Atalji (second from left) as its Prime Ministerial candidate in the 1996 parliamentary elections. Also seen are Dr Murli Manohar Joshi (extreme left), Manohar Joshi, Gopinath Munde, Bhairon Singh Shekhawat and Madanlal Khurana.*

BBC's celebrated India correspondent Sir Mark Tully readying Advani for an interview.

(From left) with Krishanlal Sharma, Bhairon Singh Shekhawat, Jaswant Singh, Sushma Swaraj and Deepak Chopra.

Addressing a political rally in UP.

Yatras

With Gujarat Chief Minister Narendra Modi at the start of the Bharat Suraksha Yatra in Rajkot in April 2005.

In Mumbai at the start of the Swarna Jayanti Rath Yatra in May 1997. Also seen on the dais are George Fernandes (fourth from left) and Atalji.

The Swarna Jayanti Rath Yatra travelling through Bengal.

Visiting earthquake-hit Jabalpur during the Swarna Jayanti Rath Yatra.

At the start of the Bharat Uday Yatra in Kanyakumari in 2004.

The BJP President, L.K. Advani followed a conscious strategy of building alliances with various political parties. Seen here with Shiv Sena chief Balasaheb Thackeray, Dr Murli Manohar Joshi, Shiv Sena leader and former Maharashtra Chief Minister, Manohar Joshi and Atalji in Mumbai in 1989.

With Kanshi Ram, founder of the Bahujan Samaj Party, Mayawati and BJP leader Kalyan Singh in 1995. The BJP-BSP alliance formed a government in Uttar Pradesh twice, headed by Mayawati on both occasions.

PAINTING BY KRISHN KANHAI

'I have performed every responsibility, minor or major, that has been entrusted to me from time to time in the course of my long political journey with honesty, devotion and commitment. This accounts for the credibility I have earned in public life.'

between the VHP and the Uttar Pradesh government. Over 30,000 *kar sevaks* were arrested all over the state. There was a lathi charge by the police on those who had managed to enter the temple town. Singhalji was pushed around by the police and, along with other leaders of the VHP, arrested amid the bursting of teargas shells. This, to me, was a deeply agonising experience. Personally, I had felt that there was no need for the VHP to organise this programme. At the same time, since I myself have been associated with the Ayodhya movement, it pained me to see that those with whom I had worked closely were ill-treated by the police.

THE WAY TO END THE AYODHYA DISPUTE
A solution was imminent during Vajpayee's rule

As one of the principal participants in the Ayodhya movement, it had been my endeavour throughout the six years of the NDA rule to see how the dispute could be resolved speedily and peacefully. The three options for dispute-resolution were obvious: 1) Legislation; 2) Judicial verdict; and 3) Amicable settlement between representatives of the Hindu and Muslim communities. After a thorough review of both the political and judicial aspects of the Ayodhya issue, I came to the conclusion that the best path to follow was the last option—and I articulated it on several occasions, both inside and outside Parliament.

In a nutshell, my view was: 'The potential for a legislative solution cannot be ruled out, but its chances are slim. The judiciary may give its verdict, but it is likely to upset one side or the other. The third option offers the prospect of a solution of mutual acceptability and durability. Of course, even a mutually acceptable settlement has to be sanctified by the judiciary, which has to extinguish all the pending cases before it. In this sense, the ultimate solution will be a combination of options 2 and 3.'

I am happy that Atalji and I succeeded in convincing our allies in the NDA to endorse this constructive approach. Accordingly, the alliance's election manifesto for the 2004 parliamentary elections stated: 'The NDA believes that an early and amicable resolution of the Ayodhya issue will strengthen national integration. We continue to hold that the judiciary's verdict in this matter should be accepted by all. At the same time, efforts should be intensified for dialogue and a negotiated settlement in an atmosphere of mutual trust and goodwill.'

I am gratified to record here that, as Home Minister, I had made considerable progress in bringing influential representatives of the Hindu and Muslim communities on a common negotiating platform. This endeavour was facilitated by some sincere and well-meaning mediators on both sides. Several rounds of talks, beyond the glare of publicity, took place. A mutually acceptable solution was clearly in sight, which would have paved the way for construction of the temple. The principles and contours of a workable agreement had emerged in the beginning of 2004, and it was decided by the two sides that an announcement to this effect could be made immediately after the elections to the 14th Lok Sabha in May. Of course, this was done on the expectation, on both the Hindu and Muslim sides, that the Vajpayee government would win a renewed mandate in the election and take the responsibility of implementing the mutually agreed formula. Sadly, that was not to happen.

Nevertheless, my faith in the third option for resolving the Ayodhya dispute—amicable settlement between representatives of the Hindu and Muslim communities in an atmosphere of mutual trust and goodwill—remains as strong today as it was in the NDA rule. Indeed, it is bolstered by an important positive development that has taken place in the national mood fifteen years since 6 December 1992. No political party of any consequence today talks of rebuilding the 'Babri Masjid' at the disputed place. In heat of the moment, several non-BJP parties had voiced their support to this demand. With the passage of time, almost all of them have stepped back from that position, knowing fully well that no power on earth can now ensure its reconstruction at the same place in Ayodhya. None of them is even demanding removal of the makeshift temple at the disputed site, or stopping the daily prayers. Of course, this does not mean that they have begun to support the Hindu claim on the disputed site. All of them are unanimous in saying: 'Let the courts decide'.

Neither my party nor I have any objection to the judiciary deciding the matter. But the obvious question that most of our adversaries are silent on is: Why has the judiciary not been able to settle this matter for over a half century? And is it proper on the part of the judiciary to keep a sensitive and contentious issue alive like this for decades together?

I am, however, a firm believer in destiny. I am convinced that the rise of a befitting temple at Ramjanmabhoomi in Ayodhya is pre-destined. How and when it will happen is a matter of secondary importance to be determined by the forces of history. But the fact that it will happen is as certain as the certainty that brought the oft-demolished and oft-reconstructed Somnath temple into existence yet again.

I am humbled by the awareness that destiny granted me an opportunity to play a role in this collective national effort that is waiting for the fulfilment of a centuries-old Hindu resolve. My only wish and appeal is that our Muslim brethren come forward with a gesture of magnanimity and goodwill that matches that of the Hindus. After all, Ram may be a holy religious figure worthy of worship for the Hindus, but he is also a preeminent symbol of India's cultural heritage which belongs to the Hindus and Muslims alike. I, therefore, fervently hope that the Ayodhya mission will be completed through the joint effort of Hindus and Muslims, thereby writing a new chapter in mutual reconciliation and national integration.

7

THE TRAUMA AND TRIUMPH OF PUNJAB

Dehi Shiva Bar Mohe Ihe
Shubh Karman Se Kabhun Na Taron
Na Daron Ari Son Jab Jai Laron
Nischey Kar Apni Jeet Karon

(O God, give me these boons
Never shall I shirk from doing good deeds
Never shall I fear when I go to fight the enemy
And with surety I shall attain victory)

—GURU GOBIND SINGH (1666-1708), THE TENTH GURU OF THE SIKHS

No history of independent India is complete without an account of the traumatic episode of terrorism in Punjab that lasted nearly a decade and a half. It was nothing short of a proxy war waged by our hostile neighbour, which not only tested the power of the Indian State to protect its unity and integrity, like no other crisis until then but also put to test the depth of Hindu-Sikh unity. As time would tell, the episode ended much to the chagrin of the external sponsors of terrorism and separatism, and reinforced the unifying force of the Indian people and state.

I can claim with all humility that my party played a substantial role in this struggle. Scores of our leaders and workers in Punjab became martyrs. Their sacrifices, I hope, will keep us vigilant against all such evil designs hatched by India's enemies, now and in the future.

Punjab has been peaceful for over a decade now. But the heavy price India had to pay before the back of terrorism was finally broken should not be erased from our memories. Between 1981 and 2001, a total of 21,608 people, including 11,776 civilians and 1,748 security personnel, were killed in the fight against militancy in the state.[1] I remember that, at the peak of terrorism in Punjab, there was hardly a month when I did not travel to the state to visit the site of a massacre or to participate in a gathering to pay homage to a party colleague or someone else killed by militants.

In 1988, I visited Bulgaria as member of a parliamentary delegation. But within hours of reaching Sophia, its beautiful capital, I got a shocking piece of news from Chandigarh that Hitabhilashi, President of the Punjab unit of the BJP, had been killed in a terrorist attack. I immediately rushed back to India.

The effects of terrorism in Punjab transcended far beyond the boundaries of the state, with tragic and long-ranging consequences for India's polity and society. Prime Minister Indira Gandhi was assassinated by her two Sikh bodyguards inside her official residence in Delhi on 30 October 1984. In the anti-Sikh carnage that followed her assassination, over 3,000 innocent people were killed in the national capital and some other north Indian cities within five days, with the government machinery being a mute witness to the bizarre spectacle.

Why did Punjab—and India as a whole—have to suffer this trial by fire? Could it have been avoided, or mitigated? What mistakes were committed? And what can we learn from those mistakes?

HISTORICAL ROOTS OF THE PROBLEM

Punjab—the land of Shaheed Bhagat Singh, an immortal hero of India's freedom struggle, is also home to Ghadar revolutionaries like Lala Lajpat Rai, Bhai Parmanand and countless other patriots. No other land has made more sacrifices for India both before and after 1947 than Punjab. Punjab is also the land of saints, the greatest of them being Guru Nanak Dev, the founder of Sikhism and the first of the ten Sikh gurus. No other community has fought more bravely for the protection of Hindus and Hinduism than Sikhs. The Khalsa Panth was created three hundred years ago by Guru Gobind Singh, the last of the ten gurus, to defend the Hindus and protect Hinduism from the bigoted Muslim rulers of the time. The social, cultural and spiritual bonds between Sikhs and Hindus are so strong and multifaceted that there exists a unique brotherhood between them in the religious history of the world.

In my own family, in Sindh, reading of the holy *Granth Sahib* was the most important religious rite. In Punjab, there has been a tradition in Hindu families to make their own contribution to the strengthening of the Sikh faith by ordaining the eldest male child to be a turban-wearing Sikh. The two communities also share many festivals. Inter-community marriages are common, and so is the sight of Hindus praying at gurdwaras and Sikhs praying at Hindu temples. And yet, in flagrant defiance of this historical and contemporary reality, a nefarious conspiracy was hatched to instigate the Sikh community to demand a separate homeland.

The root of the problem was the 'divide and rule' policy of the British rulers. At their goading, a section of Muslims had claimed separate representation for their community under the Minto-Morley reforms* of 1909. This prompted a section of Sikhs to raise a similar demand. Later, when the Muslim League raised the demand for the creation of Pakistan for Muslims to be liberated from the clutches of 'Hindu India', a similar

---

* The Government of India Act of 1909 passed by the British parliament, also known as the Morley-Minto Reforms, gave Indians limited roles in the central and provincial legislatures, known as legislative councils. The initial electorate was a minuscule minority of upper-class Indians enfranchised by property ownership and education.

demand for a separate homeland for Sikhs was raised by a tiny minority in the community, which asked provocatively: 'Muslims got Pakistan. Hindus got Hindustan. What did Sikhs get?' However, this did not find favour with the vast majority of Sikhs, who considered themselves part and parcel of the larger Indian family and who were proud of their community's struggles and sacrifices for India's freedom.

Given the strategic location of Punjab and the distinctive character of Sikh history and ethos, the Congress party and its government at the Centre needed to exercise greater care and sensitivity in dealing with issues relating to the state. Unfortunately, this was not always the case after India gained independence. In the 1950s, Pandit Nehru's rigid and undemocratic stance towards the demand for linguistic reorganisation of states created unrest in several parts of the country. Although many new states were created in 1956 with language as the main criterion, the Congress government at the Centre remained insensitive to the Akali Dal's demand, raised under the leadership of Master Tara Singh, for the creation of a Punjabi Suba or a Punjabi-speaking state.

Two factors added to the complexity of the situation. Firstly, Punjabi-speaking people did not form a majority in the undivided Punjab at the time. Secondly, Sikhs were not in a majority in the undivided Punjab. Guided by its myopic vision, the Congress party tried to take electoral advantage of the situation. It misrepresented the Akali Dal's demand for Punjabi Suba as a demand, actually, for a Sikh-majority state. This made many Punjabi-speaking Hindus to declare Hindi as their mother tongue in the censuses of 1951 and 1961.* This, in turn, gave a pretext to certain divisive elements in the state to allege that the Centre had hatched a 'conspiracy to destroy the religion, language and culture of Sikhs'. Massive, albeit peaceful, demonstrations were held during this period to press for the Akali demand. The situation had the potential to create a serious rift between Hindus and Sikhs of Punjab. An especially ominous aspect of

---

* I have described earlier how, guided by the goal of safeguarding Hindu-Sikh unity, the then RSS chief Shri Guruji urged Hindus of Punjab to declare Punjabi as their mother tongue.

the situation was that Pakistan was showing a keen interest in the issue of the Punjabi Suba and, through daily radio and television broadcasts, even assured 'full Pakistani support' for the agitation.

Finally, in September 1966, the Indira Gandhi government accepted the demand for a separate Punjabi Suba by trifurcating the original province into Haryana in the south and Himachal Pradesh in the north. Nevertheless, her party remained unreconciled to the domination of the Akali Dal, which had always enjoyed the support of a majority of Sikhs, in the politics of Punjab. Being habituated to 'one-party' rule both at the Centre and in states, it tried to undercut the Akali influence in Punjab, often by resorting to undemocratic and potentially dangerous means.

A single example should suffice to drive home this point. During the elections to the state legislative assembly in 1967, the Akali Dal emerged as the single largest party on the strength of its successful agitation for the establishment of a Punjabi-speaking state. Subsequently, it formed the government in alliance with smaller parties, including the Jana Sangh, with Justice Gurnam Singh, a former Chief Justice of the Punjab High Court, as Chief Minister. The Congress, however, was unwilling to accept the people's verdict. It plotted the downfall of Gurnam Singh's government by engineering defections from the Akali Dal and propped up Lachhman Singh Gill, a rebel Akali leader, to form the government with Congress support. Significantly, the Finance Minister in this unethically installed government was Dr Jagjit Singh Chauhan, who later became the self-styled 'President of Khalistan'.

The situation in Punjab worsened due to Indira Gandhi's authoritarian tendencies. A large number of Akali Dal leaders, including Prakash Singh Badal, whose government had been wrongfully dismissed in 1971, were imprisoned during the Emergency. In indepependent India, no political person has suffered incarceration for as long a period as Sardar Prakash Singh Badal who has remained behind bars for nearly thirteen years. With the government's attention focused almost entirely on saving itself and suppressing democracy, it ignored a dangerous conspiracy being hatched across the border.

PAKISTAN'S HOSTILE HAND BEHIND THE MILITANCY IN PUNJAB

After the defeat of Pakistan at the hands of India in 1971, and its subsequent dismemberment with the creation of Bangladesh, the anti-India elements in Islamabad had come to an important conclusion. Since India could not be defeated in an open war, a proxy war by spreading terror, instigating communal violence and plotting sabotage was the only other viable option. General Zia-ul-Haq, who wrested power in 1977, adopted a new strategy whose three objectives were: (a) to disintegrate India; (b) to deploy the Inter-Services Intelligence agency (ISI) to build a network of local recruits, sleeper cells and support infrastructure within India to carry out its plans of subversion and terrorism; and (c) to exploit India's porous borders with Nepal and Bangladesh to set up bases and conduct militant operations.

I shall later describe how the same strategy was put into effect in Jammu & Kashmir to foment militancy and secessionism there. It needs to be stressed here that, in this strategy, there was both a logical and logistical link between Punjab and Jammu & Kashmir. As the late Satya Pal Dang, an Amritsar-based communist leader whom I admired for his courageous campaign against Khalistan, has said in his book *Terrorism in Punjab*[2]: 'By supporting the Sikh militants, Pakistan had ambitions to cut Kashmir off from India and grab it.' 'It was not surprising,' Dang points out, 'that the secessionist movement was specially concentrated in the two border districts of Amritsar and Gurdaspur; if these could be destabilised and dismembered, India would lose control over the crucial connectivity from Punjab to Kashmir'.

Therefore, support for the Khalistan movement—and, by extension, for terrorism—became an integral part of Pakistan's state policy. The support came in many forms: arms and ammunition, training, safe haven, finance, propaganda through radio, television and newspapers, and mobilisation of diplomatic resources in support of the Sikh cause against the Indian state. Helping the young supporters of Jarnail Singh Bhindranwale* to

---

* Jarnail Singh Bhindranwale (1947–84) was a little-known religious preacher in rural Punjab before he emerged as the principal face of the terrorist and separatist movement

Contd...

cross over to Pakistan and brainwashing them against Hindus through distortion of Sikh history was a crucial part of the training at the camps set up across the border. ISI agents resorted to incitement of members of Sikh *jathas* (groups of pilgrims) from India who visited various Sikh shrines in Pakistan. They also worked in close concert with several self-styled spokesmen of 'Khalistan', such as Ganga Singh Dhillon, Jagjit Singh Chauhan and Gurmit Singh Aulakh, who lived in Canada, the United Kingdom and the United States respectively.

Zia-ul-Haq routinely denied Pakistani involvement in terrorism in Punjab. But the evidence to the contrary was overwhelming. In 1985, the National Council of Khalistan wrote a letter to the Pakistan President stating: 'Hindu Government is crushing the Sikhs, but Sikh fighters are facing this boldly. Sikhs in general are helping in this fight, but we are thankful to you for the help given to us in the shape of weapons, ammunition, training and shelter.'[3]

The United States was fully aware of what Pakistan, its favourite 'frontline state' was doing. In an interview to CBC television in February 1994, Robert Gates, who was the Deputy National Security Adviser to President George Bush, Sr., and is now the Defence Secretary under George Bush, Jr., said: 'When President Bush sent me to Pakistan and India in May 1990, one of the specific requests that I made of the President of Pakistan was that they close the training camps that were providing people to carry out operations in Kashmir as well as in Indian Punjab.'[4]

THE CONGRESS' ROLE IN APPEASING MILITANCY

The instability caused by the fall of the Janata Party government in July 1979 was used by Pakistan to foment militancy in Punjab. After Indira Gandhi's return to power in early 1980, the country witnessed a worrisome policy of appeasement of militancy and, worse still, of using the militants

---

Contd...

in Punjab. Along with his heavily armed followers, he challenged the Indian state from his refuge in the Golden Temple in Amritsar. All of them were killed during 'Operation Blue Star' carried out by the Indian Army in the first week of June 1984.

both in the factional fight within the Congress as well as in its political battle against the Akali Dal. In the late 1970s, a *hukamnama* or religious edict was issued by the Akal Takht to excommunicate the Nirankari sect*. This was followed by several violent clashes between Bhindranwale's followers and Nirankaris. In April 1980, Baba Gurbachan Singh, leader of the Nirankaris, was shot dead in an incident in which Bhindranwale was one of the twenty accused. All of them were later set free, with the then Union Home Minister, Giani Zail Singh, stating that Bhindranwale was not involved in the murder.

Another landmark in the rise of militancy in Punjab was the murder, on 9 September 1981, of Lala Jagat Narain, founder of the Hind Samachar group of newspapers† and a highly respected journalist. The *Punjab Kesari*, a widely circulated Hindi newspaper that he edited, was a fearless critic of Bhindranwale. Once again, Zail Singh announced in Parliament that there was no evidence about the involvement of Bhindranwale, who was released after a brief stay in jail.

The situation in Punjab progressively deteriorated after Indira Gandhi's return to power in 1980. There are many well-documented instances of the Congress party seeking Bhindranwale's support for the success of its candidates in elections. There are also instances of the Congress supporting such rivals of the Akali Dal who were known for their sympathies for the extremist cause. Sometimes, even intra-party rivalries in the Congress saw one faction seeking the help of extremists to isolate the rival faction. A sinister aspect of militancy in Punjab was the misuse of religious places to preach bigotry, store arms and harbour miscreants. In doing so, they were cleverly exploiting the religious sentiments of ordinary Sikhs. Although

---

* Sant Nirankari Mission was launched in Punjab in 1929 as a spiritual movement with the objective of establishing universal brotherhood.
† I should make an appreciative mention here of the 'Shaheed Parivar Fund' established by the Hind Samachar group of newspapers in Punjab to help families of martyrs who laid down their lives to maintain unity and integrity of India. I have participated in several programmes organised by the group to honour the martyrs in the struggle against terrorism. I commend this patriotic initiative by Vijay Chopra, the Editor-in-Chief of *Punjab Kesari* and other publications of the group.

the Sikh masses never supported the demand for 'Khalistan', they were, in the initial phase of the militancy, helpless since it had a religious connotation. In our speeches and statements on Punjab, both Atalji and I used to repeatedly appeal to religious leaders to safeguard religious places from being used for criminal activities.

One of the major mass agitations in the history of the BJP was launched in the first week of May 2004, when we undertook a ten-day satyagraha against what we termed as the government's 'virtual surrender' before Bhindranwale and his private army who had made the Golden Temple in Amritsar, the most sacred shrine of the Sikh community, their operational headquarters. On 3 May, Atalji, along with Choudhary Charan Singh (with whose party we had entered into an alliance), led a contingent of 15,000 protestors to court arrest, following it with another large contingent of demonstrators the next day. I raised the issue in the Parliament, charging the government with abdication of its responsibility in the face of an unprecedented challenge to national unity and the rule of law.

Indira Gandhi's wavering policy, lack of firm action, and the tendency to seek partisan political advantage aggravated the problem in Punjab. With her credibility, both at home and abroad, at stake, the Prime Minister was ultimately forced to use the military to liberate the Golden Temple from its anti-national occupants. In what was termed as 'Operation Blue Star', the Indian Army entered the temple complex on 5 June 1984. What surprised everyone was the fierce resistance offered by the militants, who possessed highly sophisticated weaponry and had converted all the main buildings in the temple complex, each with its own religious history and significance, into fortifications. This made the task of the Indian Army extremely difficult, since it had to exercise considerable caution in order to protect the sanctity of the shrine.

By the time the operation ended, and Bhindranwale's challenge had been overcome, nearly 500 civilians had lost their lives inside the Golden Temple. The Army suffered as many as eighty-three casualties. Several structures were destroyed and Akal Takht (The Seat of the Timeless One), the headquarters of the Sikh clergy inside the Golden Temple complex, bore witness to the exchange of bullets and shells.

It was one of the most painful moments in the history of our Republic. The tragedy, however, did not end with the success of Operation Bluestar. Its consequences were equally catastrophic—the assassination of Prime Minister Indira Gandhi on 31 October, followed by the anti-Sikh pogrom in the national capital and other major cities in North India. Two years later, General Arun S. Vaidya, the Chief of the Army Staff at the time of Operation Blue Star, was gunned down in Pune.

MILITANCY TAKES A SERIOUS TURN POST OPERATION BLUESTAR

The situation within Punjab showed no signs of abating. A plethora of militant groups, such as the Khalistan Commando Force, Khalistan Armed Force, Babbar Khalsa International, Bhindranwale Tiger Force of Khalistan, and Khalistan Liberation Force, were established to wage an armed struggle against the Indian state and to form 'Khalistan', an independent Sikh state. In early 1986, these formed an apex body known as the 'Panthic Committee'. In April, the Panthic Committee declared the formation of 'Khalistan' from the Golden Temple complex. This necessitated another action by security forces.

Meanwhile, with Pakistan's full support, terrorist activities continued, to create a communal divide between Hindus and Sikhs. Guided by this nefarious objective, innocent Hindus were targeted systematically. There were many instances of Hindu passengers in buses being forced to alight at gunpoint, lined up and shot dead. But Sikhs were not spared either; those who refused to toe the militants' line or dared to protect their Hindu brethren fell prey to their bullets.

The BJP organised numeorus Hindu-Sikh unity rallies during this period where a memorable slogan used to be: *Hindu-Sikh nu lad nahin dena; San santalis hon nahin dena.* (We shall not let clashes to take place between Hindus and Sikhs; We shall not allow 1947 to be repeated.) On 6 June 1985, along with Dr Baldev Prakash, President of the Punjab unit of the BJP, I led a Punjab Bachao Satyagraha, in which over 30,000 people courted arrest.

I remember one particularly horrendous act of terrorism that took place in Moga. In the early morning hours of on 25 June 1989, when RSS *swayamsevaks* were conducting their daily *shakha* in Nehru Park, some Khalistani terrorists came on motorcycles, raised provocative slogans and started firing indiscriminately. By the time they fled, twenty-seven *swayamsevaks* had been killed. The terrorist attack was designed to trigger Hindu-Sikh clashes in Moga and other towns in the state. Significantly, the RSS and the BJP took the lead in ensuring that nothing untoward happened. I visited Moga and congratulated the town's Sikh and Hindu residents for their mature and exemplary response in the face of a grave provocation.

To illustrate the proud role of the BJP and RSS in defending Hindu-Sikh unity during those years of trials and tribulations, I can do no better than quote this excerpt from *A History of the Sikhs* by Khushwant Singh, an eminent writer and journalist. 'It was the Congress leaders who instigated mobs in 1984 and got more than 3000 people killed. I must give due credit to RSS and the BJP for showing courage and protecting helpless Sikhs during those difficult days. No less a person than Atal Bihari Vajpayee himself intervened at a couple of places to help poor taxi drivers.'[5]

CYNICAL EXPLOITATION OF A NATIONAL TRAGEDY

An unfortunate fallout of the terrorism in Punjab, for considerable time after Indira Gandhi's assassination, was that Sikhs continued to be viewed with suspicion by the government machinery in many states in India. The Congress party did little to curb it. I recall an incident that occurred in 1987. State assembly elections were being held in Kerala. In the course of my campaigning, I ran into three Sikh youths who told me that they were dealers in automobile spare parts and had come that very morning from Delhi to Ernakulam in connection with their business, but had decided to go back immediately. On enquiring as to why they were rushing back so abruptly, they told me a distressing tale.

Prime Minister Rajiv Gandhi was scheduled to visit the city the next day. The three young men had checked into a medium-sized hotel. Shortly thereafter, a possé of policemen arrived, whisked them away to a nearby police station and directed them not to stir out of their hotel rooms until after the Prime Minister's departure the following evening. They were told that all Sikhs in town had been put under similar constraints. When they protested, they were threatened with incarceration. Ultimately, the police let them go only after they agreed to return to Delhi that very day!

This was not an isolated incident. The Congress party launched a sinister and systematic campaign following Indira Gandhi's assassination to defame the entire community as terrorists, and to make Sikhs feel as second class citizens. In 1982, Sikhs from Punjab on way to Delhi to witness the Asiad went through many harrowing and humiliating experiences. Demonisation of Sikhs by the ruling party did not end even after the pogrom in Delhi following Indira Gandhi's assassination. As if to justify the pogrom, Prime Minister Rajiv Gandhi, addressing a large public rally in Delhi that had been organised to pay homage to his slain mother, remarked: 'When a big tree falls, the earth beneath is bound to shake.' To add insult to injury, the Congress party's advertisement campaign for the 1984 Lok Sabha elections included inserts which sharply underlined this Sikh-is-a-terrorist slander. One of these inserts pointedly posed the sly question as to why a citizen felt a sense of fear if the driver of the taxi he had boarded happened to belong to a certain community!

Indeed, the Congress party's cynical exploitation of a national tragedy for its narrow electoral gains had begun within hours of Indira Gandhi's assassination. The government made the most brazenly partisan use of Doordarshan, the government-owned national television broadcaster, which was at the time the only TV channel in the country. Even as Delhi had been taken over by goons indulging in targeted killing of innocent Sikhs, Doordarshan was showing Congress workers raising provocative slogans near the Prime Minister's residence. The DD cameras focused almost exclusively on Rajiv Gandhi sitting beside his mother's bullet-ridden body. Homage offered by Opposition leaders was completely blacked out. Indeed, many Opposition leaders were prevented from entering the place where her body was kept. Even at the funeral on 2 November, DD consciously chose not to show the presence of Opposition leaders, even though many of us—such as Atalji, Chandrashekhar, Madhu Dandavate and myself—were present. Later, Atalji and I received many calls and letters from people across the country asking us whether the Opposition had boycotted Indira Gandhi's funeral!

With the passage of time, these images and events have certainly dimmed in the collective memory of India. In a way, it is good that evil recedes from the centre-stage of our mental space so that wounds are healed and a new beginning can be made. However, whenever I recall the grim and grisly happenings of those days, I wonder: What kind of political culture did the Congress nurture to allow such contemptuous disregard for basic democratic norms and basic human values? Was all this necessary to gain electoral victory? Would all means, fair or foul, be resorted to for achieving dynastic transition?

As a protest against the massacre of Sikhs in the national capital, the Akali Dal had decided to boycott the 1984 Lok Sabha polls. It was obvious, therefore, that the Congress would win all the seats in Punjab. In such circumstances, a mature leader would have conducted his party's campaign in a restrained and responsible manner. But not Rajiv Gandhi. He continued his attacks on the Akali Dal in his campaign speeches. He made the Anandpur Sahib Resolution* the principal plank of his attack, saying that the Akali stand on the matter was a threat to national unity, alleging, further, that the BJP was supporting it. This was a white lie. As far as our party was concerned, we had consistently opposed the Anandpur Sahib Resolution. As early as 1981, Atalji had described it as a 'Charter of Disintegration' of India. Paradoxically, after winning the election, Rajiv Gandhi had no hesitation in giving legitimacy to the same resolution by incorporating it in the Punjab accord† that he signed with the Akali leader Sant Longowal.

---

* The Anandpur Sahib Resolution was adopted by the Shiromani Akali Dal (SAD) in 1973. It demanded autonomy to Punjab, with the Union government devolving all powers to the state except in the four areas of defence, foreign relations, currency and communications.

† After its victory in the 1984 parliamentary elections, the Congress government at the Centre tried to find a political solution to the problem in Punjab through an accord

Contd...

THE BJP-AKALI DAL ALLIANCE IN PUNJAB

I feel a sense of pride at my party's principled stand throughout the period of militancy in Punjab and thereafter. In the 1984 polls, however, we had to pay a heavy price for this. Nevertheless, we earned the goodwill of the Sikh community on account of our forthright condemnation of the 1984 massacre and our brave efforts to protect innocent Sikhs. This goodwill was, indeed, further reinforced when the BJP formed a government in Delhi after the 1989 assembly elections. For a full decade the perpetrators of the 1984 carnage had remained immune to the law. Only a BJP government headed by Madan Lal Khurana was able to shake up the law-enforcement machinery from its slumber and put in motion a process for punishing the wrong-doers.

Looking back, the achievement in Punjab today is in no small measure due to the BJP's impeccable and uncompromising stand, guided as it was by national unity, on one hand and Hindu-Sikh amity, on the other. When I speak of achievement, I do not refer merely to my party's electoral gains. No doubt, the alliance between the BJP and the Akali Dal in Punjab, now forty years old, has benefited both parties. The Akali Dal has been one of the first and most unwavering allies of the BJP. It was a valued partner in the NDA government at the Centre. Our parties currently run a coalition government in Punjab under the leadership of Prakash Singh Badal, who has served as the state's Chief Minister four times.

At the same time, I do not regard these political achievements as the most important gains of my party's consistent stand on the Punjab problem. It is the preservation of the Hindu-Sikh unity, and the strengthening of harmony and mutual trust between the two communities, which has been our most valuable success. I would like to recall here my presidential speech at the BJP's national council session in Vijayawada in January

---

Contd...

signed in 1986 between Prime Minister Rajiv Gandhi and Harchand Singh Longowal, the then President of the Akali Dal. Longowal, a widely respected moderate leader, was assassinated by militants a few months later. The BJP welcomed some aspects of the accord. However, we opposed legitimacy being given to the separatist Anandpur Sahib Resolution and to the proposal for an all-India Gurdwara Act.

1987 when militancy in Punjab was at its peak: 'There is a silver lining to the situation. While elsewhere, in situations of strain, a minor altercation between citizens belonging to different communities easily sparks off a communal conflagration, in Punjab despite all the murder and mayhem that has been going on, there have been no communal riots, no group clashes. The BJP in Punjab has been assiduously exerting to maintain communal harmony. But the real credit for this happy aspect of the situation goes to our centuries-long history that just cannot accept Sikhs being separated from Hindus. Tradition and culture and families and even religion all are interlinked and intertwined inextricably.'

Many Congressmen even today accuse the BJP and Akali Dal of 'opportunism'. It is an alliance purely for electoral ends, they say. When in 1967, the Akali Dal led by Justice Gurnam Singh and the Jana Sangh led by Dr Baldev Prakash came together, that was essentially a poll alliance to defeat the Congress. But in these last forty years, many momentous events have taken place in the history of Punjab and the country. Our common approach and joint participation in these developments have cemented the bonds of friendship in such a manner that it can be said that the Akali Dal and BJP are parties just 'made for each other'! Speaking for myself, I can say that I have had the best working relationship with all the three main Akali leaders—Prakash Singh Badal, Surjeet Singh Barnala (a former Chief Minister of Punjab and presently Governor of Tamil Nadu) and the late Gurcharan Singh Tohra, who was the president of the Shiromani Gurdwara Prabhandak Committee (SGPC).

I have many enduring memories of my travels and experiences in Punjab. Once, during an election campaign, I had an opportunity to visit Fatehgarh, the site where Fateh Singh and Zorawar Singh, sons of Guru Gobind Singh, the tenth Guru of the Sikhs, were interred in a wall by the order of Wazir Khan, Governor of Sirhind. A gurdwara has been constructed at the spot while the wall in which the two brave boys were martyred has been preserved just below the shrine. A visit to such a place is at once inspiring and sanctifying. It was, indeed, a pilgrimage for me.

LESSONS TO BE LEARNT

The harrowing experience in Punjab taught some important lessons which must not be forgotten by governments, political parties and the people at large.

First and foremost, a problem should be nipped in the bud rather than being allowed to assume grave and threatening proportions. In the nearly two-decade-long history of militancy in Punjab, there were many occasions when timely and decisive action by Indira Gandhi's government could have averted the need for 'Operation Bluestar' in June 1984. Most of its tragic consequences, too, could probably have been avoided.

Secondly, those in power, or those who desire to retain power, must desist from appeasing extremism and terrorism. The history of militancy in Punjab clearly shows that Bhindranwale became a 'Bhasmasur'* precisely because of the Congress party's policy of using him and his followers for its narrow political ends. In other states, too, the Congress has followed the same counter-productive policy. In Assam, it has often supported, and sought the support of, United Liberation Front of Assam (ULFA) to defeat its main rival, the Asom Gana Parishad (AGP). In Andhra Pradesh, Jharkhand and Chhattisgarh, it has similarly encouraged naxalites for short-term electoral gains.

Thirdly, whenever extremists and terrorists seek the cover of religion to justify their nefarious activities, it is the primary responsibility of the followers of that religion to denounce and isolate such elements. In the specific context of Punjab, nobody has articulated this thought more forcefully and convincingly than K.P.S. Gill, a person whose contribution I regard as the bravest in combating terrorism in the state. It was under

---

* Bhasmasur is a demon in Hindu mythology. His prolonged worship of Lord Shiva pleased the latter, who asked him what he wished for. Bhasmasur said, 'Give me the power to destroy anybody by putting my hand on the person's head.' Shiva fulfilled his wish. Intoxicated by the extraordinary power that he had gained, Bhasmasur planned to destroy Shiva himself in order to become more powerful than his benefactor. The story goes that Shiva was saved by Lord Vishnu, who disguised himself as a beautiful woman, seduced Bhasmasur into dancing with her, and, in the course of the dance, making him put his hand over his own head.

his competent and clear-headed leadership of the Punjab police that the terrorist campaign for 'Khalistan' was finally and comprehensively defeated. I have often consulted him on matters of internal security during my tenure as India's Home Minister in the NDA government. In his book *Knights of Falsehood*,[6] Gill writes:

> The virulent campaign for 'Khalistan' was fought in the name of religion—specifically, my religion, Sikhism. The Sikhs have been involved in warfare almost throughout their history, but no campaign has ever brought odium and disgrace upon them and upon their Faith as this despicable movement did. And yet the Faith, and a majority of the community, in whose name the most unforgivable atrocities were committed—against every explicit tenet of that very Faith—had nothing whatsoever to do with this lunatic and savage adventure. Indeed, it was this very community that most vigorously resisted, and eventually helped defeat, the scourge of terror in Punjab.

These words hold profound significance for terrorism and extremism elements that hide behind the cloak of Islam.

Lastly, we must pay far greater attention to states bordering other countries than what we have been doing in the past sixty years. It is not accidental that the terrorism-backed demand for 'Khalistan' was raised in a state that is contiguous to the country that was created on the basis of the 'Two Nation' theory. Pakistan's rulers have followed the same strategy in Jammu & Kashmir. As we look to the future of West Bengal and some North-eastern states which have undergone dramatic change in their demography due to infiltration from Bangladesh, it is only appropriate that we recall the lessons learnt in Punjab.

8

THE ENTRY AND EXIT OF TWO PRIME MINISTERS IN TWO YEARS

There is great danger of things going wrong. Times are fast changing. People are getting tired of government by the people. They are prepared to have government for the people and are indifferent whether it is Government of the people or by the people. If we wish to preserve the Constitution in which we have sought to enshrine the principle of Government of the people, for the people and by the people, let us resolve not to be tardy in the recognition of the evils that lie across our path and which induce people to prefer Government for the people to Government by the people, nor to be weak in our initiative to remove them. That is the only way to serve the country. I know of no other.

—DR B.R. AMBEDKAR, DELIVERING THE CLOSING SPEECH OF THE FIRST CONSTITUENT ASSEMBLY OF INDIA, 25 NOVEMBER 1949

It may be a mere coincidence, but I am struck by the fact that the end of every decade since the 1960s has brought forth political turmoil and instability in India. The year 1969 witnessed a split in the Congress party, which had a deep and long-term impact on the country's politics. In 1979, the Janata Party disintegrated, leading to the formation of Charan Singh's government, which was doomed to collapse. In 1999, the Congress destabilised the government of Atal Bihari Vajpayee and precipitated unnecessary mid-term elections. What happened towards the end of 1980s? It was a similar story, albeit with a bit of a twist. Not one but two minority governments collapsed within a span of eighteen months.

I have already described how the Bofors scam and its subsequent cover-up heralded the downfall of Rajiv Gandhi's government in the 1989 elections. Subsequently, the Janata Dal emerged as the largest Opposition party and, hence, its leader V.P. Singh was entitled to be invited by the President to form the next government. But its tally of 141 seats was far from the halfway mark of 272. Together with some smaller parties, the Janata Dal had formed an alliance called the National Front, with N.T. Rama Rao, chief of the Telugu Desam party in Andhra Pradesh, as its Chairman. However, it too did not have the required numbers to add up to a majority in the Lok Sabha. The composition of the Lok Sabha was such that V.P. Singh could form a government only with the support of the BJP, on the one hand, and the Left parties, on the other.

It is in this context that, on 28 November 1989, I received a letter, jointly signed by Rama Rao and Singh, seeking the BJP's support for the formation of a National Front government. I made my party's view known to them in a formal reply. It merits quoting in full.

> Dear Shri N.T. Rama Raoji and Shri V.P. Singhji,
>
> I am in receipt of your letter. I agree that the people have given a clear verdict against the Rajiv Government. But simultaneously this is also true that there has been no positive verdict in favour of any one party, or in favour of the five-party National Front.
>
> Your letter amounts to seeking unconditional support from the BJP for forming a minority government. The BJP has some reservations in extending such support to your government. Our two principal reservations are:

(1) The National Front and the BJP fought these elections on two separate manifestos, not on a common manifesto. A manifesto is a party's solemn commitment to the people. Our manifestos have several common features, such as grant of autonomy to Akashvani and Doordarshan, enactment of a Right to Information Act, incorporation of Right to Work as a fundamental right in the Constitution, elimination of corruption by the creation of an institutional watchdog like the Lokpal, taking steps to give debt relief and ensure remunerative prices to the farmer, etc. But there are aspects on which our two manifestos differ. We would like the NF Government to confine its governmental programmes to issues on which we agree.

(2) The main constituent of the National Front is the Janata Dal. Ever since its launching, the Janata Dal leadership, with its utterances and actions, has been consciously trying to convey to the people an impression that it regards the BJP as a communal party, and that it would rather sit in the opposition than ever share power with the BJP. The JD's public postures have thwarted the building up of any abiding relationship of trust and friendship between our two parties. If it is acknowledged by the Janata Dal that it does not regard the BJP as communal, although the JD and BJP differ on issues like Article 370, Uniform Civil Code, the Human Rights Commission, Ram Janmabhoomi, etc, that would go a long way in removing the misgivings in our rank and file.

I hope that the National Front will take note of these reservations and exert to obviate them.

The BJP is keen to see that the Ninth General Election marks the end of the Congress rule in New Delhi. It is, therefore, that even while expressing these reservations, we have not made our support to you conditional to your agreeing to remove them. In response to your letter, the BJP wishes to convey to you its readiness to give general but critical support to the National Front Government.

With kind regards,
Yours sincerely,
L.K. Advani

V.P. SINGH BECOMES PRIME MINISTER

Within the BJP, our cadres were a bit unhappy with the idea of supporting a government led by the Janata Dal. The primary reason for this was Singh's abrasive conduct towards our party. While calling the Left parties his 'natural allies', he left no opportunity unexplored to antagonise the BJP's rank and file during the election campaign. The most distasteful incident took place in Mathura where an election rally was being held in support of a Janata Dal candidate. As per prior agreement, the BJP and Janata Dal had arrived at seat adjustment in UP and many other states, supporting each other's candidates in the election campaign. Accordingly, the BJP had announced its support to the Janata Dal candidate in Mathura and was openly campaigning for him. But when Singh came to address the election rally in this temple town, he was furious at seeing BJP flags, alongside those of the Janata Dal, on the dais. 'I am not going to address the rally unless the BJP flags are removed,' he thundered.

Naturally, our party workers were flabbergasted and angry. After all, it was the Janata Dal that had sought seat sharing and a joint election campaign with the BJP. Even after the election, when it was time for government formation, V.P. Singh had no compunction in seeking, and accepting, the support of the BJP. Simultaneously, he had this tendency of projecting himself as an 'uncompromising secularist' who would have nothing to do with the BJP. This was certainly a blatant display of double standards. V.P. Singh's hypocrisy was not hidden from any unbiased observer of the Indian political scene. In spite of this, we decided to lend outside support to the National Front government. The Left parties, led by the CPI(M), also followed suit. It was not the most cohesive arrangement for a minority government but since the mandate of the electorate had to be respected, we in the BJP made sincere efforts in helping the new government find its feet. Thus, the National Front government came into being on 2 December 1989, with V.P. Singh as the Prime Minister.

Although our decision was guided by national interest, a few secondary factors also influenced our decision. There were several other leaders in the Janata Dal with whom Atalji and I had had long and friendly association in the common struggle for democracy. These included George Fernandes, Madhu Dandavate, Ramakrishna Hegde, Devi Lal, Dinesh Goswami, Nitish Kumar and Sharad Yadav. However, there was also another prominent person in the National Front, whose relationship with us, though of a more recent vintage, had left a deep impression on us. He was none other than N.T. Rama Rao.

A cine superstar from Andhra Pradesh before he joined politics by founding the Telugu Desam in 1982, NTR, as he was popularly known, had single-handedly demolished the Congress fortress in the southern state. His appeal for the protection of 'Telugu pride' had a huge impact on the people as opposed to the servility of Congress leaders in Andhra Pradesh before their party's imperious 'high command' in New Delhi. Though a votary of Telugu *atma gauravam* (regional self-pride), NTR was a patriot to the core. Indeed, he set a fine example of harmonising legitimate regional aspirations with strong and unshakeable nationalist commitment. What I especially liked about NTR was his genuine concern for forming a democratic and stable alternative to the Congress at the Centre. In pursuit of this objective, he tirelessly strove to mobilise Opposition parties on a common platform and was the binding spirit behind many 'Opposition conclaves' organised in the early 1980s. A genuine leader with a strong conviction, NTR never exhibited the prejudice and hypocrisy towards the BJP that several other Opposition leaders did.

COMMUNIST HYPOCRISY

Since V.P. Singh headed a minority government, dependent on support from parties holding two opposite ends of the ideological spectrum, proper coordination was a day-to-day necessity. The government's survival and success demanded sincerity of approach and commitment to common goals. I was happy that a semi-institutionalised framework for three-way coordination between the National Front, BJP and Left parties came into being soon. Every Tuesday, leaders of the three constituents used to meet for dinner at the Prime Minister's official residence to discuss important issues before the government. Apart from Prime Minister V.P. Singh, those who regularly attended the weekly dinner meetings included CPI(M) leader Harkishan Singh Surjeet, CPI leader Indrajit Gupta, and Atalji and myself from the BJP. Jyoti Basu, West Bengal Chief Minister and a veteran leader of the CPI(M), used to join us whenever he was in Delhi.

These meetings were cordial and fairly useful. For me, it was the first opportunity to interact closely and regularly with communist leaders and MPs. Of them, the person who impressed me the most was Indrajit Gupta. He was a man of impeccable integrity and great simplicity, besides being an outstanding parliamentarian. There was a perceivable naturalness in the way he interacted with Atalji and me. In contrast, leaders of the CPI(M) were always conscious of being 'politically correct' in their dealings with us.

I should recount an interesting incident that transpired six months after the formation of V.P. Singh's government. One day, Jyoti Basu sent a message to us from Calcutta through a common friend: 'This government is not functioning properly. I feel that the three of us—Atalji, you and I—should meet to discuss the situation. Why don't we meet for dinner at Viren Shah's residence in Delhi?'

The message had come from Viren Shah, a well-known Mumbai-based industrialist who, though an office-bearer of the BJP for some time, was also a good acquaintance of Basu. The NDA government later appointed him Governor of West Bengal, after, of course, consulting with and getting enthusiastic concurrence from Chief Minister Jyoti Basu.

Atalji and I welcomed the idea of an informal dinner meeting. Nonetheless, we were a little puzzled. We conveyed our response to the intermediary: 'We thank Jyotibabu for his suggestion. If he is interested in meeting us, we are prepared to go to Calcutta to meet him there.

Otherwise, if he wants the meeting to take place in Delhi, he is most welcome to come to either Atalji's house or my house for dinner. But we don't understand why we should meet at some other place.' Basu sent us a prompt response. 'No one should know about our meeting. Especially, people in my party would not like it.'

Ultimately, we met at Shah's residence but to me, this was yet another instance of the hypocritical outlook and conduct of the communists, especially those belonging to the CPI(M). The same was also evident in the way they behaved during mutual interactions in Parliament. On several occasions, the BJP and the Left parties adopted floor-coordination when Congress governments were in office. Their MPs would tell us: 'We should try to isolate the Congress on this matter.' To which, we would say, 'Fine, let's meet. Either we'll come to your office or you come to the BJP's parliamentary office.' Their response would invariably be in the negative. 'No, no, we can't come to your office, nor can you come to our office. Let's meet in the Parliament lobby!' Their logic was that a confabulation in the lobby would be judged by passersby as a chance encounter between MPs of the Left and the BJP that necessitated an exchange of pleasantries, and nothing more. Such is the politics practiced by the communist parties, especially the CPI(M)!

V.P. SINGH PLAYS THE MANDAL CARD FOR SURVIVAL

The performance card of V.P. Singh's government was a mixed bag of achievements, blunders and politically-motivated initiatives. The first big bungle took place within days of his assuming office. Militants in Srinagar kidnapped the daughter of the Union Home Minister Mufti Mohammad Sayeed, demanding release of their jailed colleagues in exchange of Sayeed's daughter. Much against the advice of the BJP, and the outraged sentiments of the people all over the country, Singh and his Home Minister surrendered to the militants' demand. This single symbolic act of governmental weakness laid the foundation of Pak-sponsored terrorism in the state.

On the positive side, Singh's visit to the Golden Temple and his seeking forgiveness for Operation Bluestar contributed a good deal towards the normalisation of the situation in Punjab. Similarly, it was Singh who withdrew the IPKF from Sri Lanka in March 1990, thus bringing to an end an eminently forgettable chapter in India's military history.

However, V.P. Singh is best remembered for a decision that was, indeed, the outcome of an internal rivalry within the National Front and political one-upmanship between him and Deputy Prime Minister Devi Lal. Singh dropped his deputy from the Cabinet on 1 August 1990. Six days later, he announced acceptance of the recommendations of the Mandal Commission, extending reservation in government jobs to Other Backward Classes (OBCs). This was clearly a preemptive strike by the Prime Minister against the erstwhile Deputy Prime Minister, who had planned a massive rally of farmers in the national capital.

I had requested the Prime Minister not to announce implementation of the Mandal Commission's report before we had an opportunity of discussing its implications in the informal coordination committee comprising the leaders of the National Front, BJP and the Left parties. I specifically mentioned that both Somnath Chatterjee, the CPI(M) leader, and I wanted to discuss the issue with him. 'In any case,' I told him, 'our regular Tuesday dinner meeting is only two days away'. V.P. Singh's reply was, 'No, I cannot wait. I have to announce it tomorrow'. Singh did not specifically refer to the scheduled *kisan* rally by Devi Lal but it was obvious to me that he was using the Mandal issue for sheer political survival.

The Constitution of India had already provided 15 per cent reservation of educational and civil service seats for the Scheduled Castes and 7.5 per cent for the Scheduled Tribes. The Mandal Commission was set up in December 1979 by Prime Minister Morarji Desai with a mandate to identify other backward sections of society for the purpose of reservations for them in government employment and educational institutions. The five-member panel was headed by Bindheshwari Prasad Mandal, a former parliamentarian and socialist leader from Bihar. The Commission submitted its report in December 1980, when Indira Gandhi was the Prime Minister. Adopting various social, educational and economic criteria, the commission identified 3,743 castes and communities as OBCs. It recommended reserving 27 per cent of all jobs in government services and public sector undertakings and 27 per cent of all admissions to institutions of higher education for OBCs, over and above the existing 22.5 per cent reservation for SCs and STs.

It is worth noting that neither Indira Gandhi nor Rajiv Gandhi took any initiative to implement the Mandal Commission's recommendations. Its report remained idle for nearly a decade after its submission. In fact, not once did Prime Minister Singh bring it up for discussion during our Tuesday dinner meetings nor was it ever discussed in Parliament. Therefore, when he announced reservations for OBCs, the entire nation was taken aback. It also evoked strong and widespread protests, the agitation taking a violent turn in several places. Here, sadly, was a classic case of a socially progressive measure earning a bad name because of its blatant politicisation.

My party was, therefore, constrained to say the following in a resolution adopted by its National Executive, meeting in New Delhi on 17 October 1990. 'The BJP has been in favour of reservations for socially and educationally backward classes. However, the manner in which the government announced its decision about the Mandal Commission report without any consultation with the supporting parties and without qualifying it with any economic criteria, was utterly wrong. The decision was prompted not for any concern for the backward classes but considerations of political expediency. The government's decision can only lead to dividing and subdividing society. The result has been not only serious disturbance of peace and enormous loss of life and property but the immolation of some of the flowers of our youth.'

Some of my adversaries claim that I did not support the recommendations of the Mandal Commission. This allegation, however, is baseless. I have never opposed reservations for the backward classes or, for that matter, for the scheduled castes and tribes. If I have expressed reservations about reservations, it is limited only to the insincere, narrow-minded and short-term political considerations that have often guided the decisions of certain parties. For example, I recall the debate in Parliament on the Mandal Commission recommendations, which was opened by Hukum

Dev Narain, a backward class leader from Bihar who was in V.P. Singh's party but later joined the BJP. I consider his speech as one of the best I have heard on the subject. In fact, immediately after the debate, I went up to him and complimented him warmly saying that his speech was eloquent, logical and sincere. I also added that I just could not give this certificate of sincerity to his government!

An important speech that the Lok Sabha heard, during the debate on the Mandal Commission's recommendations, was that by Rajiv Gandhi on 6 September. It was one of the longest speeches ever delivered in Indian Parliament; it lasted two-and-a-half hours. Rajiv, who was then the Leader of the Opposition in the House, accused Prime Minister V.P. Singh of threatening the unity and integrity of India. 'You have ignited caste violence all over the country,' he charged. Rajiv questioned the propriety of providing the benefit of reservations for the privileged sections among the OBCs. Citing the example of a judge belonging to a backward caste who had been in that job for fifteen years, Rajiv said, 'He (the judge) then joins politics and becomes a minister. Should he be given the benefit of reservations? Should his children be given such assistance? That assistance should go to someone else who needs it. Do we want the benefits of reservations to be cornered by the ministers, their sons and their families? Do we want these benefits to go to landlords who have big properties?'

Those who remember the Mandal Commission debate know that on the question of excluding the 'creamy layer' from the beneficiaries of reservations, there was unanimity among the BJP, Communist parties and the Congress. Significantly, the Supreme Court in its judgment in 1992 on the implementation of Mandal Commission recommendations upheld the exclusion of the 'creamy layer' from reservations.

TWO MEMORABLE VOTE-OF-CONFIDENCE DEBATES IN PARLIAMENT

The National Front government did not last long; it could not even complete one year in office. The circumstances that led to its collapse on 10 November 1990 were related to the Ayodhya movement, which I have described in the previous chapter. After the BJP withdrew support to the

National Front government, following the stoppage of my Somnath-to-Ayodhya Rath Yatra and my arrest in Bihar on 23 October 1990, the Prime Minister ought to have tendered his resignation immediately. It was clear to one and all that V.P. Singh's government no longer commanded a majority in the Lok Sabha. Nevertheless, he insisted on proving his majority in the House. Accordingly, the President asked him to seek a vote of confidence on 7 November. I, who was under arrest at Massanjore in Bihar at the time, was brought to Delhi to enable me to participate in the crucial debate. I regard my speech during the debate on the confidence vote as one of the most important, and also most satisfying, of my parliamentary career.

In the course of the debate, several non-BJP MPs accused my party of 'opportunism' since we withdrew support to Singh's government only because my Rath Yatra had been stopped by his party's government in Bihar. I refuted the charge and referred to the BJP National Executive's categorical resolution of 17 October. However, I made it clear that my party's disenchantment with V.P. Singh's government was not limited to its insincere and shifty stand on Ayodhya. 'It was related to several factors. This government's attitude to Ayodhya was the last straw. Mr Speaker Sir, I do not want to recount the unpleasant episode of the Mahabharata, but it seems my friends in other parties are insisting upon that example being given. Shishupal started hurling abuse after abuse at Shri Krishna, and everyone felt surprised as to why Krishna was tolerating all that. Krishna had made up his mind already to tolerate Shishupal's abuses but he had also fixed a limit of hundred, and the moment that hundreth abuse came, Krishna struck at him.'

Much of my speech was devoted to countering the allegation that the Ayodhya movement was communal in nature. 'Mr Speaker Sir,' I said, 'in this entire debate the focus has been on what is secularism, what is communalism and what is nationalism. Let this debate not be confined to the four walls of this House. Let us take it to the people. Let us seek people's opinion on these issues, and let an election be held on the basis of this debate.'

Since the exit of V.P. Singh's government was a foregone conclusion, I used the debate as an opportunity to draw the attention both of the

Parliament and the nation to the Congress's plans to prop up another rickety government in its place. In order to drive home my point, I referred to a witty example from British Parliament that I had come across in a book titled *Speechmaker* by Greville Janner, a widely respected Jewish MP belonging to the Labour Party. I had met Janner during my visit to London in June 1989 as part of a parliamentary delegation. The friendship that we struck then has continued even today. I said:

> Recently, I came across an anecdote about Herold Wilson, former Prime Minister of Britain. When Wilson handed over prime ministership to James Callaghan, he gave him three envelopes to be opened, one by one, when his government faced any crisis. When the first crisis came, Callaghan opened the first envelope to find a chit which read: 'Blame the preceding government.' He did precisely that. Then came the second crisis. Callaghan fished out the second envelope, opened it and read the advice: 'Sack your second in command.' The day the BJP adopted its resolution of 17th October, this anecdote came to my mind and I felt that Prime Minister V.P. Singh has already availed the first two envelopes and now was the time for it to open the third one. The third one, when opened, yielded the advice: 'Please prepare three envelopes!'

Dinesh Goswami, who was Law Minister in V.P. Singh's government, interjected: 'Are you suggesting this for the new captain?'

I said, 'I am suggesting it for everyone. Mr Speaker Sir, as I can visualise the post-7 November scenario, I am sure the country is going to witness a replay of 1979.' My allusion was to how Indira Gandhi propped up Charan Singh, who had defected from the Janata Party, to set up a government and caused its collapse soon thereafter by pulling away the prop.

India did witness a replay of 1979. Chandrashekhar defected from the Janata Dal with fifty-four MPs to form a separate party called the Janata Dal (Secular). Rajiv Gandhi pledged the Congress party's outside support to Chandrashekhar to form the next government. The President of India swore him in as Prime Minister on 10 November and asked him to seek a vote of confidence six days later. In my speech during the debate, I called it 'a government without political legitimacy'.

I said, 'A mandate is a contractual obligation that every Member of Parliament and every government has with the electorate. Now, suddenly I find that the party which is in office today, instead of a contract with the people has a contract with the Congress party.... The Prime Minister himself has described it as a government of exigency. I would like to think that it is a government of expediency, nothing more.'

It was obvious that Chandrashekhar had to give certain assurances to the Congress party in order to ensure its support, the most important being scuttling the investigation into the Bofors scandal. Therefore, in my speech in Parliament I said, 'The first unhappy remark that Chandrashekhar made was that follow-up on the Bofors investigation was a matter to be dealt with not by the Prime Minister but by a sub-inspector of police. In the last forty years, very often the issue of political corruption has been raised in various elections and so many rackets have been talked about. But I do not know of a single scandal which has become so incorporated in the vocabulary of the common man as the word "Bofors"'... I would like to appeal to the Prime Minister not to view it as yet another scandal. He must view it in this manner that if at the highest levels of public life, there are people indulging in malfeasance and getting away with it, and the entire penal machinery of the state is engaged only in catching petty thieves here and there, the authority of the state would be undermined.'

I had high regard for Chandrashekhar as a self-respecting political leader. His principled revolt against Indira Gandhi's authoritarianism, his courageous campaign against the Emergency and his role as the President of the Janata Party during Morarji Desai's rule were praiseworthy aspects of his personality. Nevertheless, I deemed it necessary to forewarn the new Prime Minister. 'I am not accusing Chandrashekhar of being a puppet,' I noted in my speech. 'No, not at the moment. But I am saying that the temptation to act the puppeteer is very strong. And so, for Chandrashekhar it will be a persistent dilemma. If he agrees to act as the puppet, the consequences would be extremely harmful both for the government as well as for the country. But if he refuses to act as the puppet, his government might come to an end.'

Here again, I was proved right. Chandrashekhar's earnest efforts to solve the Ayodhya issue, combined with the remarkable progress that he was making in this direction, rang alarm bells in the Congress party. Hence, it withdrew support to his government barely four months after he was sworn in as Prime Minister. The ludicrousness of the reason given—the presence of two policemen from Haryana on a 'surveillance duty' outside Rajiv Gandhi's residence—is matchless in the history of political insincerity.

Chandrashekhar was asked to continue as the caretaker Prime Minister till the mid-term polls in May 1991. The forthcoming elections would prove to be another landmark in the history of Indian democracy as also in the onward journey of the BJP. However, in between the polls, a tragedy struck the nation in the form of the assassination of Rajiv Gandhi.

9

FIVE YEARS OF P.V. NARASIMHA RAO'S GOVERNMENT

When there is rain, the world enjoys prosperity; when the king rules with justice, his subjects prosper

—THIRUVALLUVAR, AUTHOR OF *THIRUKKURAL*,
THE TAMIL BOOK OF SACRED VERSES

The 21st of May 1991. It was well past 10 pm. I was addressing an election rally in Gandhinagar, from where I was contesting for the Lok Sabha. Mid-term parliamentary polls, necessitated by the fall of Chandrashekhar's government, were underway. The Election Commission had scheduled them to be held in three phases—on 20, 23 and 26 May. This was to be my last election rally in my constituency.

There was a huge crowd at the election meeting. In the midst of my speech, I was handed a slip that read: 'Rajiv Gandhi assassinated in a bomb blast in Tamil Nadu a short while ago.' The message was shocking, but I felt it was necessary to have it confirmed. I cut short my speech almost mid-sentence, and said, 'Friends, I have just received some very tragic news, because of which I have to bring this meeting to a close now.'

I rushed to the Circuit House in Ahmedabad and was informed that the news from Tamil Nadu was indeed true. But there was no information available yet as to who was behind the assassination. At the Circuit House, I found a group of flag-carrying Congress workers angrily shouting slogans: 'BJP *Murdabad*' (Down with the BJP) and '*Rajiv Gandhi amar rahe*' (Long live Rajiv Gandhi). They had already concluded that my party had a hand in the assassination.

At the Circuit House, I met Chaudhary Devi Lal, who was Deputy Prime Minister in Chandrashekhar's caretaker government. He asked me, 'I am rushing back to Delhi. Would you like to join me in my plane?' I readily agreed. It was long past midnight when I reached home. I was numb with sadness over the sudden death of a young and warm-hearted leader. Also, I was feeling greatly troubled over the immediate uncertainty as well as the long-term consequences of the tragedy.

As details of the tragedy and early findings of the investigation started pouring in, the entire nation was outraged by the diabolical nature of the crime. For the first time common people were made aware of a new killer weapon called the 'human bomb'. For, it was a woman activist of the LTTE named Dhanu who had, beneath her loose-fitting dress, strapped explosives around her waist; managed to mingle among the crowds greeting Rajiv Gandhi as he arrived at the venue of an election meeting in Sriperumbadur in Tamil Nadu; and, while pretending to garland him, detonated herself. The resultant blast extinguished the life of the Congress President and India's former Prime Minister instantly. About a dozen more persons lost their lives, including Dhanu.

As the investigation progressed, more chilling facts came to light. They revealed the involvement of the LTTE at the highest level in the conspiracy. People in India, cutting across political affiliations, were aghast that a separatist outfit in a neighbouring country had managed to kill a prominent national leader. Inevitably, there was also some discussion in the ensuing months about Rajiv Gandhi government's disastrous IPKF policy but it was subdued under the weight of shock and grief experienced by the entire nation.

On the constitution of the 10th Lok Sabha, I, as the Leader of the Opposition, paid fulsome tribute to the departed leader: 'I remember one incident in 1985 when Shri Rajiv Gandhi became the Prime Minister after winning the elections with a huge majority. He invited prominent leaders of all political parties and held separate meetings with them for an hour. I returned with an indelible mark of his personality on my mind that though that young man had entered politics only a few days back and did not have enough knowledge of politics, yet, as a person he was very polite, very cordial and very gentle. I can say that though my party was critical of his politics, yet the impression he left on my mind at the personal level in the first meeting will continue to remain in my mind forever. We had been very close to each other and, as such, I can imagine and realise the loss his family members and the country have suffered due to his sad demise.'

NARASIMHA RAO BECOMES PRIME MINISTER

In the aftermath of Rajiv Gandhi's assassination, polling of the second and third phases was postponed to mid June. Once again, the Congress party tried to capitalise on the 'sympathy factor' over what it termed as the 'martyrdom' of the former Prime Minister. Although we in the BJP were as aggrieved and outraged as anyone else over the terrorist act that had claimed Rajiv Gandhi's life, we failed to understand how his demise could be termed 'martyrdom'.

The results of the elections highlighted two startling facts. Firstly, because of the postponement of the second and third legs of polling, the 'sympathy' factor did help the Congress—but only in averting a defeat and not in securing a big victory. The number of seats it won in constituencies where polling took place in the post-assassination period was considerably more than it did in the first phase on 20 May. However, even the 'sympathy factor' was not strong enough for the Congress to win a majority. Its total tally of 232 seats was well below the halfway mark of 273. Therefore, political pundits concluded that the Congress would have won much less seats if Rajiv Gandhi had not been assassinated; in fact, it could have probably suffered a second straight defeat in parliamentary polls under his leadership.

The second and the most important aspect of the poll results was the BJP's eye-catching performance. Our tally went up from 86 seats in 1989 to 121 in 1991. We emerged as the second largest party, and as the largest Opposition party, in the Lok Sabha. Commenting on the BJP's major stride forward, the *Economist* gave a telling caption to its article on India's poll verdict saying: 'Winner comes second'. My party elected me the Leader of the Opposition in the Lok Sabha. I felt that Atalji should rightfully perform that role, but he too insisted that I assume the responsibility.

My party's profile in national politics was further enhanced by its victory in the assembly polls in UP. The BJP won 221 out of 415 seats and, for the first time, formed a government in India's most populous and politically important state. Kalyan Singh became the state's Chief Minister.

Even though the Congress had not secured a majority in the Lok Sabha, it was clear that it alone was in a position to form a government at the Centre. However, when it came to selecting the person to head the government, the party showed how completely it had surrendered before the principle of dynastic leadership. The CWC requested Sonia Gandhi, widow of the slain leader, to become Prime Minister. She had no political, paramilitary or adminstrative experience whatsoever at the time. When she declined the offer, P.V. Narasimha Rao, the senior most leader of the party who had previously held many important portfolios in the governments of both Indira Gandhi and her son became the natural choice to lead the government.

In my speech during the vote of confidence debate in Parliament on 12 July 1991, I pointed out three oddities that marked Rao's government. Firstly, this was the fifth minority government in India's political history and the third in the previous twenty months. The first instance was in 1969 when the Congress party split, reducing Indira Gandhi's government to a minority status; it survived only because of the support it received from the CPI and the DMK. The second minority government came in 1979 when Chowdhary Charan Singh was sworn in as Prime Minister, supported by the Congress party from outside. The third was in 1989, as a result of the electoral verdict, when V.P. Singh formed his minority government with the BJP as well as the Left parties supporting it from outside. The fourth minority government came into force in 1990 and it had no relation to the peoples' verdict. It was in fact in violation of the peoples' mandate. The Congress party supported the Chandrashekhar government, which had a total strength of only 54 in a House of 545—indeed, less than the number stipulated for a quorum of 55 for the House to conduct its business.

'Now, this is the fifth minority government,' I observed, 'but in many respects it is the oddest of all'. Firstly, it was not just a minority government but also a minority government in a truncated House. This is because the Election Commission had deferred the elections in as many as thirty-six seats. Two states—Punjab and Jammu & Kashmir—were totally unrepresented in the Lok Sabha. The decision in respect of Punjab, which had been taken almost at the last minute, had raised many an eyebrow, with even the Governor of the state, General O.P. Malhotra, saying, 'I have been through three Wars, I have been a general in the Wars, but I have never felt as defeated as I feel today after this announcement by the Election Commission that the elections have been postponed.'

Secondly, in the case of the earlier four minority governments, although the parties running the government were in a minority, they nevertheless had a majority in the Lok Sabha because of adequate external backing from the supporting parties. In contrast, Rao's was the first government that could not claim majority support in the House.

The third oddity of Rao's government was that, at the time of its formation, three senior Ministers, including the Prime Minister, were not MPs. The other two were Finance Minister Dr Manmohan Singh and Defence Minister Sharad Pawar. In fact, Rao had declined to contest the Lok Sabha polls, citing his failing health as the reason. Article 75(5) of the Constitution provides that even though a person is not a MP, he can be a minister for a period of six months. But he or she has to become an MP within this period. Rao did get elected to the Lok Sabha in a by-election from Nandyal in November 1991, but the huge margin of his victory evoked widespread allegations about electoral malpractices.

Dr Manmohan Singh chose to get elected to the Rajya Sabha from Assam. Strangely enough, the only election to the Lok Sabha that he has ever contested was in 1996, from South Delhi, when he lost to BJP's V.K. Malhotra. And he has not deemed it necessary to become a member of the Lok Sabha even after becoming Prime Minister in 2004. This, as I shall deal with later, is one of the many oddities of Dr Singh's government.

'BEST PRIME MINISTER AFTER SHASTRI'

My personal and political relations with Prime Minister Rao underwent a dramatic change—from friendly to frosty—during his five years at the helm of the government. People have often asked me, 'Why did you initially praise Narasimha Rao as the best Prime Minister India has had after Lal Bahadur Shastri?' Coming from the Leader of the Opposition, this remark did create a flutter both within the BJP as well as the Congress circles. Some Congressmen, especially those who were not happy with Rao, even wondered: 'Is there any devious intent behind this?' As a matter of fact, there was none. My praise was genuine, and was prompted by several reasons.

Firstly, I admired Rao's erudition. He combined a scholarly understanding of national and international affairs with rich political and administrative experience. Secondly, in my initial meetings with him, I found that his views on several critical policy issues to be congruent to those of the BJP. For example, in economic policy, Rao brought about a radical shift by introducing a series of delicensing and decontrol measures to herald a new era of reforms. The BJP and, previously, the Jana Sangh had always demanded the dismantling of the licence-permit-quota raj since it was both corruption-breeding and growth-hindering. The Congress governments of the past had erected an elaborate edifice of licences, quotas and controls in the name of 'socialism' but which, in effect, had kept India poor and backward by stifling the entrepreneurial energies of our people. Under the garb of giving the public sector 'the commanding heights of the economy', the Congress governments had taken political patronage, red-tapism, inefficiency and low productivity to new heights.

In his own quiet way, Rao started to send out signals that, in spite of heading a minority government, he was keen to give a radically different direction to India's crisis-ridden economy. A glaring manifestation of the crisis was the decision of the previous government, headed by Chandrashekhar, to mortgage India's gold reserves, to tide over a grave Balance of Payments (BoP) situation. The country's foreign exchange level had dipped so low that it was barely enough to cover the country's import bill for about eight weeks. India was in danger of becoming a defaulter, and had that happened, the nation's prestige in the international community would have been badly affected. In the mindset of an average Indian, pledging family gold to repay debts or to meet household expenses is the surest sign of economic ruin. The Chandrashekhar government's gold-pledging decision had thus made even common people aware that something was seriously wrong in the management of the national economy.

It is necessary to emphasise here that Chandrashekhar's regime alone was not responsible for this precarious situation. After all, it had lasted only three months; the additional four months it was in office was in caretaker capacity. Wrong policies of the previous Congress governments, combined with long years of economic mismanagement, were at the root of the crisis that necessitated mortgaging of national gold.

In such a scenario, it was courageous of Rao to try and effect a paradigm shift in the country's economic policy. Equally audacious was his decision to appoint Dr Manmohan Singh, a widely respected economist but someone totally outside of the political system, as Finance Minister in his Cabinet. This decision made me feel that he meant business. As Prime Minister, he provided the much-needed political backing to Dr Singh to embark on a bold agenda of economic reforms that slowly but steadily started demolishing the 'pseudo-socialist' edifice erected by the earlier Congress governments. I remember that once, during a debate in Parliament, Chandrashekhar had bitterly criticised the Finance Minister, even insinuating that he was an agent of the World Bank and the International

Monetary Fund (IMF). I openly defended Dr Singh in Parliament. Some people in my own party questioned me over this, but I said that we should not counter the government on every issue just for the sake of opposing. In a recent television interview, I recalled this incident and said that, never before were the relations between the government and the Opposition as constructive as during the initial phase of the Rao government. (Times Now TV, 18 September 2007)

My cordial relations with Dr Manmohan Singh were established during those days. At a personal level, these relations are marked by warmth and mutual cordiality even now. However, my main grievance against Dr Singh after he became Prime Minister is that he has allowed devaluation of his high office by surrendering to the authority of the Congress President. I said in the television interview that, in the case of every other Prime Minister of India, the most important political address in New Delhi was invariably the incumbent Prime Minister's residence. It is only during Dr Singh's tenure that that distinction has shifted to 10 Janpath, the residence of Sonia Gandhi.

In fact, even Narasimha Rao had faced the difficult task of managing his relations with 10 Janpath, which many in his Cabinet regarded as the only legitimate centre of power both in the Congress party and in a Congress government. But Rao, a shrewd politician, handled this task deftly, never ceding political authority to an extra-constitutional centre of power. Therefore, I began admiring him when, like Lal Bahadur Shastri, he too soon acquired Prime Ministerial stature on his own, without belonging to the Nehru-Gandhi dynasty.

India's new policy towards Israel under Rao's premiership was another issue on which I found him in alignment with the BJP. In early January 1992, I had gone to the United States for the founding conference of the 'Overseas Friends of the BJP'. The visit took me to about nine to ten places across the US. Invariably, Jewish groups would meet me and ask me: 'We are friends of India. We want India to become a strong power and play a major role in world affairs. But why has your country not yet established full diplomatic relations with Israel?' My reply to them was:

'My party is fully in favour of full normalisation of relations with Israel. But we are not in power. The Congress party, which has been in power for the longest period since Independence, is opposed to it, and so are the communist parties.'

After returning from the US, I went to meet the Prime Minister and I learnt that he was himself leaving for the States in a couple of weeks. After briefing him about my meetings with the American Jewish groups, I said, 'Narasimha Raoji, before you go, take a bold decision on establishing full diplomatic relations with Israel.' He replied, 'I am all for it, but my party is not ready.' The second part of his reply was well known, but I was heartened to hear the first. 'I do not understand,' I remarked, 'why our policy towards Israel is still trapped in this imaginary apprehension over the reaction of some Muslims in India. After all, several Muslim countries are planning to open diplomatic relations with Israel. Egypt and Turkey have already done so. Even Palestinians want to co-exist with Israel. Therefore, if something is in our national interest, we should explain it to people who may be opposed to it. In any case, our foreign policy should be immune to such false considerations of domestic pressure.' Rao responded by saying, 'I agree. I'll do it. But I'll do it by forming a group of ministers to make the recommendation so that the decision will have wider ownership.' He kept his word. What I liked about the decision was the care the Prime Minister took to inform Yasser Arafat, the leader of the Palestinian Liberation Organisation (PLO), about the decision before it was made public. To his credit, Arafat's response to Rao was: 'Very good, at least we now have a common friend.'

There was another reason for my appreciation of Rao in the initial phase of his premiership. The fall of two minority governments in quick succession, Rajiv's assassination and the economic crisis looming before India, had made many of us in the BJP think that the Opposition and the government should sincerely try to evolve consensus on crucial national issues. Both Atalji and I had identical views on this matter. Another influential person who strove for establishing mutual trust and constructive cooperation between the Congress government and the BJP during those days was Bhaurao Deoras, a senior leader of the RSS. Rao and he had known each other for a fairly long time. Bhauraoji had played a pivotal role in trying to resolve the Ayodhya issue amicably during the tenures of the two previous governments through his interactions with V.P. Singh, Chandrashekhar, and those close to them. The initial communication between Rao and him suggested that the new Prime Minister was genuinely interested in picking up the threads of the fruitful Ayodhya negotiations from where Chandrashekhar had left them. I shared this hope with several others in the BJP.

I should mention here that Atalji too felt warmly towards Rao, who fully reciprocated. Two instances are worth mentioning in this context. In 1993, Rao appointed Atalji as the leader of the Indian delegation to the conference of the United Nations Human Rights Commission (UNHRC) in Geneva. The conference had assumed great importance in view of Pakistan's sustained propaganda about 'human rights abuses' by the Indian government in Jammu & Kashmir. The real motive behind the propaganda was, of course, to hide Pakistan's own role in aiding and abetting terrorism in J&K and also in other parts of India, as the serial bomb blasts in Mumbai in March 1993 had clearly shown. Rao's decision to send the leader of an Opposition party as the head of the Indian delegation for such a crucial international conference was widely praised, both at home and abroad. And so was Atalji's performance at the Geneva meet.

Another example of the bonhomie between Atalji and the Prime Minister was when the latter came as the chief guest in 1994 to release *Meri Ikyavan Kavitaayen* (*My Fifty-One Poems*) penned by Atalji. The function witnessed a rare spectacle of light-hearted banter between two mutually admiring leaders of rival parties. The disappearance of such cordial relationship in recent years is something which I regard as a sign of the degradation of the political culture in India.

'WHAT WOULD HAPPEN IF SINDH DEMANDED SELF-DETERMINATION?'

In September 1991, Prime Minister Rao deputed Mani Shankar Aiyer, a Congress MP who was earlier a close aide of Rajiv Gandhi, and me to represent India at an international conference in Strasbourg, Austria, organised by the European Parliament. The theme of this conference, which is held every four years, was 'Challenges before Emerging Democracies'. Since our Parliament was in session, the government was not keen on sending a delegation. However, when our ambassador informed that Pakistan was going to send a large and high-powered delegation and was likely to raise the issue of Kashmir from this global forum, the Prime Minister asked Aiyar and me to attend the conference.

We told the conference organisers that they should not allow Pakistan to raise bilateral issues on this forum. We were assured on this score. Nevertheless, the ten-member Pakistani delegation, led by the Speaker of its National Assembly, raised the Kashmir issue in an indirect manner, saying, 'Newly emerging democracies face a big problem, which can be seen in some older democracies, too.... People's desire to exercise self-determination over their land is sought to be suppressed through brute force.'

While speaking next, I did not mince any words in responding to this propaganda. 'The Pakistani delegate,' I said, 'has not explicitly mentioned Kashmir, but the participants here are left in doubt that this is Pakistan's charge against India. Let me tell him and all others here that since gaining independence in 1947, we have succeeded in building a single nation-state and a strong, vibrant and vigorous democracy, in which elections are held in a free and peaceful manner both at the Centre and in states, including in Jammu & Kashmir. However, all large countries that have emerged from colonial rule have encountered a problem of strengthening their national unity and integrity. Very often, those who are opposed to unity and integration raise the banner of self-determination. But what is "self" after all? India is a multi-religious and multi-lingual country, in which non-discrimination on the grounds of faith is guaranteed by the Constitution and our own age-old culture. So the whole of India is a single united "self". We cannot even think of each linguistic or religious group seeking self-determination, because that is the surest way to disintegration and undoing all that we have strenuously achieved since 1947.'

I further added: 'Before raising the issue of self-determination for Kashmir, let my friends from Pakistan ponder over a question. What if the people of Sindh demanded self-determination? What will be the consequences? Do you think Pakistan, which has already suffered division once with the liberation of Bangladesh, stands any chance of remaining united?'

After the session was over, two members of the Pakistani delegation, who were from Sindh, met me separately and said in Sindhi, 'Advani sahab, you did the right thing by paying them back in their own coin. These people from Punjab raise the issue of Kashmir day in and day out. We are fed up with them.'

DISILLUSIONMENT WITH RAO

My disillusionment with Rao started with the sensational disclosures relating to a stock market scandal in the middle of 1992. The central character in this episode was Harshad Mehta, who manipulated the Indian banking system to misappropriate funds for engineering an artificial bull run in a select group of scrips on the Bombay Stock Exchange (BSE). When the scam broke out and Mehta was arrested, the stock market crashed causing huge losses to tens of thousands of ordinary investors. The scandal came to symbolise the 'get-rich-quick' culture that was the unfortunate by-product of economic reforms. But what brought Rao under a cloud was when Mehta publicly announced that he had paid rupees one crore to the Prime Minister as donation to the Congress party for getting him out of the trouble.

The blot of sleaze started growing bigger when it came to light that the Congress party had bribed four erstwhile MPs belonging to the Jharkhand Mukti Morcha (JMM), including its leader Shibu Soren, in order to secure their votes against a no-confidence motion in July 1993. This issue became murkier when Soren's private secretary, who allegedly knew about the bribery, was abducted in May 1994 in Delhi and later murdered in Ranchi.

Around the same time that the stock market scam broke out, there were media revelations about the Prime Minister's sons and daughters suddenly turning into business tycoons, handling projects worth hundreds of crores of rupees. But what dishonoured Rao's reputation the most was his proximity with the controversial godman, Chandraswamy. In spite of facing many criminal allegations, he enjoyed total immunity from investigation during the five years of Rao's rule. He even had unhindered and any-time access to the Prime Minister's residence at 7 Race Course Road. In one of my meetings with Rao, I asked him, 'Why are you so close to Chandraswamy? I am constrained to ask this question because your personal reputation and the office of the Prime Minister of India are being sullied because of this association.' Taken aback by my question, he said, 'No, there is no association as such. I don't do anything for him.'

The operation to cover up the truth about the Bofors scandal, which had begun during Rajiv Gandhi's premiership, continued unabated during Rao's rule. There was a sensational disclosure in the media in February 1992 that Madhavsinh Solanki, India's former Foreign Minister, carried a letter to his Swiss counterpart asking him to suspend the Bofors investigations. Solanki had said that the letter, which was unsigned and undated, had come from the Prime Minister of India. He was forced to resign when the details of the letter leaked. Why did Rao use his ministerial colleague for such a blatantly malfeasant operation? And at whose behest did he do it? The country still awaits answers to these and many other related questions.

The second audacious action of the Rao government to derail the Bofors investigation was in 1995, when Ottavio Quattrocchi, the Italian middleman who allegedly pocketed most of the kickbacks in the arms deal because of his proximity to Rajiv Gandhi's family, was allowed to flee the country. Who tipped him off, especially when the Supreme Court was on the verge of directing him to appear before it? Why was his passport not impounded? At whose behest did the government permit him to fly out of India? Again, the Congress party continues to evade these questions.

The most important cause of my disillusionment with Rao, however, was his lack of firmness, made worse by his cunningness, in dealing with the Ayodhya issue. I have reason to believe that, in his heart he was convinced about the genuineness of the Hindu demand and that the opposition to it, including from within his own party, was motivated by considerations for Muslim votes. I shall buttress my point to drawing the readers' attention to the first and the last paragraphs of his book *Ayodhya: 6 December 1992*,[1] which was published posthumously in 2006. 'Conquerors throughout history have treated the conquered humiliatingly, and with varying degrees of barbarity. Women, slaves and property of all kinds were captured as of right and the conqueror became their lord and master by virtue of the conquest. Religious bigotry, where it manifested itself, led to forcible conversions, desecration of religious monuments or the conversion of the conquered into the conqueror's religion. In his arrogance of power, man sought to change the shape of God by force of arms'.

And this is how he ends his book, in an attempt to explain how he was not guilty for the events of 6 December: 'I tried to explain all these things to my colleagues, but on their side also political and vote-earning considerations definitely prevailed and they had already made up their minds that one person was to be made historically responsible for the tragedy, in case the issue ended up in tragedy. If there had been success (as there definitely seemed to be, in the initial months) they would of course have readily shared the credit or appropriated it to themselves. So they were either playing for success, or an alibi through a scapegoat in the case of failure! It was a perfect strategy. They could loudly proclaim later that the Muslim vote did not come to the Congress after the demolition of the Babri Masjid solely because of me.'[2] Coming from a person who was both the Prime Minister of India and Congress President, this is the clearest proof of my party's charge that the Congress has been opposing the Hindu demand for construction of the Ram Janmabhoomi temple not on the basis of the merits of the issue, but solely because of the fear of losing Muslim votes.

Ironically, Rao himself was not above playing the minority card on the Ayodhya issue. In his statement in Parliament on 7 December 1992, he said: 'The demolition of the mosque was a most barbarous act. *The Government will see to it that it is rebuilt.*' (emphasis added.) Here was a Prime Minister whose government had allowed, barely a few hours earlier, the construction of a small, makeshift temple at the site of the demolished structure in Ayodhya. And the same person was now assuring Parliament by saying that 'the mosque would be rebuilt'! It is because of such blatant lack of conviction that Rao lost credibility both among Hindus and Muslims.

It is worth noting here that no Prime Minister since then has reiterated the promise to 'rebuild the Babri Masjid'. If nothing else, the reluctance to do so suggests growing recognition that the only solution to the Ayodhya issue is to facilitate, amicably and lawfully, construction of the Ram temple or, rather transformation of the present makeshift structure into a magnificent mandir.

THE HAWALA FRAME-UP: TOUGH TIMES DON'T LAST; TOUGH MEN DO

One of the most challenging periods of my life was the early 1996 when the Narasimha Rao government framed a false and motivated case against me charging involvement in a 'hawala' transaction. I was in the party office on the morning of 16 January when my colleague Sushma Swaraj came into my room saying that she had learnt from her lawyer-husband, Swaraj Kaushal, that the Central Bureau of Investigation (CBI) had filed a case against me and several other political leaders under the Prevention of Corruption Act. This came as a rude shock to me.

The hawala scandal, as it came to be known, implicated many politicians belonging to different parties, including some ministers in Rao's cabinet, who were alleged to have received sleaze money through hawala brokers. As evidence, the CBI produced diaries maintained by two Bhopal-based businessmen—S.K. Jain and J.K. Jain. The same hawala route, it was alleged, was used to channel funds to militants in Jammu & Kashmir. The charge against me was that I was not only guilty of ordinary corruption 'demanding and accepting' illegal gratification—rupees twenty-five lakhs when I was an MP and an additional rupees thirty-five lakhs when I was not an MP—but also of 'criminal conspiracy' in league with the Jains and others.

As a political activist who had participated in numerous agitations, there was hardly anything extraordinary in having to face a criminal charge. Very often it used to be violation of Section 144, sometimes for apprehension of breach of peace and, in the case of the Ayodhya movement, even harsh charges. But to be accused of corruption was an unsettling new experience. Never in my entire political life had even my adversaries made allegations of bribery or financial fraud against me.

I checked on the information from a couple of sources, and they confirmed that the CBI had actually instituted the case. I took two immediate decisions. Firstly, I would tender my resignation from membership of the Lok Sabha. Secondly, I would announce that I would not contest the Lok Sabha elections until I was exonerated by the courts of this false accusation. I conveyed this over the phone to Atalji. Soon he and other colleagues gathered at the party office. Some of them said that it was too drastic a step for me to take, as the parliamentary elections were not far away. I replied in the negative saying, 'This alone is the appropriate response for people to realise that I have nothing to hide and am ready to face trial.'

Within a couple of hours I convened a press conference in the party office, where I made both the above announcements.

Here I would like to recall another maliciously instituted and inordinately prolonged case against me. In 1982, I had enrolled myself as a voter in Gwalior, where my cousin sister used to live. Some opponents of my party questioned this before the EC who examined the matter and upheld the validity of my status as a voter from Gwalior. Nevertheless, a criminal case was filed against me in a local court in the same matter. And this false case had been going on and on, with no end in sight.

Thus, even after my decision to resign from the Lok Sabha, the unsettled fate of the Gwalior case loomed large in my mind. If a minor case relating to an entry in the electoral rolls could drag on for fourteen long years, I was well aware that my announcement could virtually mean the end of my parliamentary career.

The 'hawala' case went on for sixteen months in the Delhi High Court. Finally, on 8 April 1997, Justice Mohammad Shamim delivered the verdict quashing the charge of corruption against me. As it turned out, my name did not appear in any of the meticulously maintained daily *khatas*, the monthly diaries, the periodic ledgers, and not even in the 'mother diary', which the CBI had confiscated from the Jains in May 1991 but on a loose and apparently interpolated sheet of paper. I will let Sudheendra Kulkarni's article in the *Pioneer* speak for itself:

> A conspiratorially placed taint on the life of a clean and honest political leader has been judicially rubbed out. A plot to finish off, or at any rate severely disable, the political career of the BJP President, and thereby halt the seemingly unstoppable progress of his party has come to naught. Justice Shamim's 70-page judgement, a work of high legal discipline and exceptional fidelity to facts, has not only quashed the charges against Mr Advani but held that the case is not even worth consideration for trial. He found no evidence with the prosecution to establish that industrialist, Mr SK Jain, paid out and Mr Advani received the alleged Hawala cash.
>
> Not that this was not known to the CBI or its mentors in the South Block when Mr Advani was chargesheeted on January 16, 1996. The legally untenable nature of the case was known to anyone who had even an elementary understanding of the Evidence Act and other relevant aspects of the law. But what was known even more widely was that it was also politically untenable. Mr Advani's life-long record of personal probity and integrity had never been questioned even by his bitterest ideological and political opponents. Yet, a pliant CBI sought to make out a case against him. It was, therefore, a frame up, clear and simple. In discharging the case against Mr Advani, Justice Shamim has understandably stuck to the purely legal dimensions of the matter. But those who can jog their memory and their political mind will come to the inescapable conclusion that the CBI's chargesheet was a cunning attempt by the then Government.... A beleaguered Prime Minister wanted to diffuse and deflect the charge of corruption against himself. And what better way to achieve it, Mr Narasimha Rao must have thought, than to 'fix' his political opponent in a corruption scandal in which many of his own ministers and partymen were also going to be named. That is why, when judicial pressure mounted on the Rao Government in the latter half of 1995 to begin probing the

sensational Hawala scandal, an ever-obedient CBI included Mr Advani's name among those politicians mentioned in the Jain diaries to show that, if the Congress president was merely facing *allegations* of corruption, the BJP chief actually carried *charges* of corruption.

For 16 months Mr Advani suffered the fate of being categorised with the knaves and crooks in the system at a time when the common people were being conditioned to believe the worst about their politicians. That Mr Advani's honour has been restored is his personal gain. That the case against the BJP chief has been summarily discharged is the party's gain. But there is a bigger gain in Justice Shamim's verdict, and it is the gain for India's political class and its democracy. One does not have to be a sympathiser of the BJP to appreciate this broader point.[3]

The CBI challenged the Delhi High Court's verdict in a petition filed in the Supreme Court. A three-judge bench of the apex court dismissed it on 2 March 1998 saying: 'So far as Shri Advani is concerned, we find that no one has ever spoken about him in their statements…. We have found that no primafacie case has been made out against him of committing any offence under section 7 of the Prevention of Corruption Act.' The court also held that even the first requirement of Section 10 of the Evidence Act which pertains to 'things said or done by the conspirator in reference to common design' was not fulfilled.

Looking back, I feel very satisfied about my decision. It was not only the right moral response to an accusation of corruption against me, but it also raised the stature of the BJP in the eyes of the people. My family has been my greatest source of strength in all such trials and tribulations I have faced in life. I recall an unforgettable incident. The morning after my resignation, I was sitting alone in my office room at my residence. Finding that I was in a somber mood, my daughter Pratibha came to me and said, 'Dadu, why are you sad? Please read this poem I have found for you.' On a beautiful wooden wall-plate was the poem, titled *Footprints*:

※

*One night a man had a dream.
He dreamed he was walking along the
beach with the Lord.
Across the sky flashed scenes from his life.
For each scene, he noticed two sets of
footprints in the sand; one belonging to
him, and the other to the Lord.
When the last scene of his life flashed
before him, he looked back at the
footprints in the sand.
He noticed that many times along the
path of his life there was only one set
of footprints.
He also noticed that it happened at the
very lowest and saddest times in his life.
This really bothered him and he questioned
the Lord about it.
'Lord, you said that once I decided to follow
you, you'd walk with me all the way.
But I have noticed that during the most
troublesome times in my life there is only
one set of footprints.
I don't understand why when I needed
you the most you would leave me.'
The Lord replied, 'My precious, precious child,
I love you and I would never leave you.
During your times of trial and suffering, when
you see only one set of footprints in the sand
it was then that I carried you'.*

*

I put it up on the wall of my office room, where it still remains. Around the same time, Father Bento Rodrigues of Father Agnel's High School in Delhi met me and presented me the book, *Tough Times Don't Last. Tough Men do.*

ANNOUNCING ATALJI'S NAME AS CANDIDATE FOR PRIME MINISTER

Just two months prior to CBI's false case against me, I had made an important announcement in my address at the BJP's 'Maha Adhiveshan' (mega conference) held in Mumbai on 11-13 November 1995. In what is still the largest ever congregation in the annals of the party, nearly 100,000 delegates from all over the country had come to attend the three-day plenary session of its National Council. It was held on the sprawling Mahalaxmi Race Course ground overlooking the sea, aptly renamed Yashobhoomi (Victory Ground). In the evening of the second day, all the delegates, joined by the party's supporters from all over Maharashtra, marched to Shivaji Park in Dadar, a venue which, like the Ramlila Maidan in Delhi and the Brigade Parade Ground in Kolkata, has witnessed many a historic political rally. The timing of the meet was significant. It was the penultimate year of Narasimha Rao's increasingly unpopular government, and the people of India were beginning to pin their hopes on the BJP as the viable alternative to the Congress. The mammoth political conference served as a platform to project the BJP as a serious contender for power in the 1996 parliamentary elections.

In my presidential address, I traced the party's highs and lows from its evolution to the founding conference in Mumbai in 1980—how our strength in Parliament had gone up from two in 1984 to eighty-six in 1989 and to 121 in 1991. Expressing the hope and confidence that the BJP would win the people's mandate to form the Central Government in the 1996 Lok Sabha elections, I declared, 'We will fight the next elections under the leadership of Shri Atal Bihari Vajpayee and he will be our candidate for Prime Minister. For many years, not only our party workers but also the common people have been chanting the slogan *"Agli baari, Atal Bihari"*. (It is Vajpayee's turn to be the next Prime Minister.) I am confident that the BJP will form the next government under Atalji's premiership.' What transpired on the dais after this announcement is best described in a column by Kanchan Gupta in the *Pioneer*:

> ...For a moment there was stunned silence. Then followed thunderous applause. The declaration came at the fag end of Advani's

speech. It was not a matter-of-fact statement, but an emotional announcement. He later told some of us it was a 'historic moment' for both him and the party, something that he had been waiting for years to declare.... Before Advani, his voice by then choking with emotion, could return to his place on the dais, Vajpayee got up, took the microphone and, giving a pass to his long pauses, said, 'The BJP will win the election, we will form the Government and Advaniji will be Prime Minister.' Advani said, '*Ghoshana ho chuki hai.* (Announcement has already been made).' A smiling Vajpayee retorted, '*To phir main bhi ghoshana karta hoon ki pradhan mantri...* (Then I too shall announce that ...).' Advani chipped in, '*Atalji hi banengey* (Atalji will become the Prime Minister.).' Vajpayee said: '*Yeh to Lakhnawi andaaz me pahley aap, nahi pahley aap ho raha hai,* (What the people are witnessing here is Lucknow's famed custom of courteousness—'You be the first...' 'No, you have to be the first'). For a while, both of them looked at each other, two old colleagues and close friends who had nursed the Bharatiya Jana Sangh since its formation and later the BJP, both of them clearly moved to tears.... In the summer of 1996, Advani's public declaration came true. The BJP emerged as the single largest party and was invited by President Shankar Dayal Sharma to form the Government. Vajpayee was sworn in as Prime Minister....

The rest is history'.[4]

My announcement took everybody by surprise. Until then, neither the BJP nor other non-Congress political parties had declared a Prime Ministerial candidate ahead of any parliamentary election. (The Congress party in this respect is in a class of its own because its Prime Ministerial candidate invariably belongs to the 'dynasty' or is nominated by it.) Moreover, I had not discussed Atalji's candidature with him. He later said to me, '*Kya ghoshana kar di aapne? Kum se kum mujh se to baat karte.*' (What kind of announcement did you make? You should have told me at least.) To which, I replied: '*Kya aap maante agar hum ne aap se poocha hota?*' (Would you have agreed if I had asked you?)

The announcement, which I made in Mumbai in my capacity as President of the BJP, produced a surge of enthusiasm among the rank and file of the party, besides being warmly welcomed by the general public. It was not only my own personal conviction that the country deserved a government under the leadership of Atalji, but also the sentiment of millions of Indians.

After the announcement, there were some murmurings suggesting that although I had announced Atalji candidature for Prime Ministership, I was not sincere about it. Frankly, I was saddened and hurt by these insinuations.

Therefore, when, in the wake of the hawala episode in January 1996, I pledged not to enter the Lok Sabha until my exoneration—I did so despite being fully well aware that the judicial verdict might take decades—that declaration lent credence to my earlier announcement made in Mumbai. Several political commentators took note of the fact that my pledge not to contest elections was not an after-thought. Vir Sanghvi, a prominent media personality, wrote: 'It is often unfairly claimed that Advani only stepped aside *after* he was framed in the hawala scandal. In fact, he had proposed Vajpayee's name much before hawala.'[5]

REINS OF PARTY PRESIDENTSHIP AGAIN

One of the important milestones in the evolution of the BJP during the early 1990s was the Ekta Yatra undertaken by Dr Murli Manohar Joshi. Soon after becoming the President of the party, he embarked on a forty-seven-day journey from Kanyakumari to Kashmir to spread the message of national unity and integration. The highlight of the yatra, which was flagged off on 11 December 1991, was the hoisting of the national flag at Lal Chowk in Srinagar on Republic Day, 1992. Ever since Pakistan-backed militants started their separatist campaign in the Kashmir Valley, they had been preventing the hoisting of the Indian tricolour at the capital's main square. Therefore, the success of the Ekta Yatra was indeed a landmark in India's battle against cross-border terrorism.

At the end of Dr Joshi's two-year term, the party once again asked me to assume the reins of presidentship, which I did in June 1993. I was re-elected to the office in October 1995. On both occasions, I insisted that a younger person be entrusted with this responsibility but I was overruled.

The BJP suffered a major electoral setback in 1993 when assembly elections were held in Uttar Pradesh, Madhya Pradesh, Rajasthan and Himachal Pradesh. These were the four states in which the incumbent BJP governments had been dismissed and President's Rule was imposed by the Centre after the demolition of the disputed structure in Ayodhya on 6 December 1992. My party failed to retain power in UP, MP and HP. In Rajasthan, however, Bhairon Singh Shekhawat formed the government on the strength of the 95 seats that the party had won in a house of 200. Another happy outcome of the 1993 assembly elections was the BJP's victory in Delhi, bringing Madanlal Khurana to the post of Chief Minister.

My party was able to form governments in two more states for the first time—Gujarat and Maharashtra, where assembly elections were held in 1995. Keshubhai Patel became the Chief Minister of Gujarat, where the BJP won 121 seats in a house of 182. In Maharashtra, the Shiv Sena-BJP alliance emerged as the winner with Manohar Joshi of the Shiv Sena becoming the Chief Minister and Gopinath Munde of the BJP the Deputy Chief Minister.

On the whole, the first half of the 1990s was a period when the BJP made remarkable strides in many new states, while rapidly emerging as the only real alternative to the Congress at the Centre. By the time of the elections to the 11th Lok Sabha in April-May 1996, two powerful and synergistic forces had emerged in Indian politics. Both the Indian people and the party's rank-and-file had developed an intense desire to bring the BJP to power. The combined effect of these two forces was evident in the election results—BJP 161 seats; Congress 136 seats; Janata Dal 46 seats; CPI(M) 32 seats; and CPI 9 seats.

The 1996 parliamentary elections were, thus, a watershed in Indian democracy. For the first time since Independence, the Congress was dethroned from its preeminent position and the BJP became the single largest party in the Lok Sabha.

10

Three Prime Ministers in Two Years

> The Seven Social Sins
> 1. *Politics without principles*
> 2. *Commerce without morality*
> 3. *Wealth without work*
> 4. *Education without character*
> 5. *Science without humanity*
> 6. *Pleasure without conscience*
> 7. *Worship without sacrifice*
>
> —Mahatma Gandhi

The mid-1990s was a period of great instability in Indian politics. The country saw as many as three Prime Ministers within a span of less than two years—to be precise, between May 1996 and March 1998. The sheer absurdity of the manner in which the Congress and some other parties used 'secularism' as the fig-leaf to prevent the BJP's ascent reflected their hunger for power.

A party that had the highest number of MPs, 161, in the Lok Sabha could not last in government beyond thirteen days, whereas a party with only 46 MPs got an opportunity to form the government headed by a person who was neither one of its front-ranking leaders nor known outside his state. He was followed by another fortuitous Prime Minister belonging to the same party, with no mass base of his own. Both these governments were supported by the Congress from outside, which pledged 'unconditional support for five years'. But ironically both were pulled down by the Congress party on grounds so untenable that they cannot stand scrutiny on any test of political morality.

The reader will see how India was subjected to this debilitating bout of destabilisation and, also, how the destabilisers ultimately got a drubbing from the people. All this set the stage for India's first-ever BJP-led government in 1998.

*

The 11th Lok Sabha was the third hung House in a row. Nevertheless, it will be remembered as the year when the Indian polity got bi-polarised. Even in 1977, when the Congress had lost power for the first time, it was the single largest party. In 1996, however, it managed to win only 136 seats, twenty-five less than the BJP, which emerged as the single largest party in the House. The Janata Dal won forty-six seats, CPI(M) thirty-two seats and CPI nine seats.

No less significantly, the Congress party's popular vote, despite its contesting from the largest number of constituencies in the country, went down in the third consecutive election: from 39.53 per cent in 1989 to 37.57 per cent in 1991 and, this time, to 28.2 per cent in 1996. In contrast, in spite of the BJP contesting far less number of seats than the Congress, its vote share in the three elections had consistently gone up: from 11.36 per cent in 1989 to 20.11 per cent in 1991 to 20.29 per cent in 1996. This was a clear manifestation of the people's choice of the BJP over the Congress.

ATAL BIHARI VAJPAYEE'S THIRTEEN-DAY GOVERNMENT

The meaning of the verdict was clear: The people had given a mandate in favour of the BJP under the leadership of Atal Bihari Vajpayee and against the Congress, which was then led by P.V. Narasimha Rao. As far as the other parties were concerned, they were nowhere in the reckoning. Naturally, Dr Shankar Dayal Sharma, who was the President of India, invited Atalji to form the government, swore him in as Prime Minister on 16 May, and asked him to seek a vote of confidence in the House within fourteen days.

Dr Sharma's decision of inviting Atalji to form the government was severely criticised by some Opposition leaders and Left-leaning commentators. They contended that the President adopted a purely 'arithmethic' approach towards government formation. This was nothing but an ideologically prejudiced criticism, since the 'arithmetic' approach was nothing but the only constitutionally valid approach before the President. In a hung Parliament, the President is duty-bound to invite the leader of the party, or the pre-poll alliance, that has the largest number of seats to form the government. Only upon the failure of that leader to demonstrate majority support in the House can he extend the invitation to the next largest party or pre-poll alliance. Dr Sharma's decision was unimpeachable on four grounds that should always guide presidential decision-making: constitutional propriety, impartiality, transparency and national interest.

Prime Minister Vajpayee answered his detractors in his address to the nation on 19 May:

> Rashtrapatiji invited me to form the government since the Bharatiya Janata Party and its allies won the largest number of seats. This decision of Rashtrapatiji is entirely in tune with established democratic norms; in fact, it strengthens them. I have accepted this responsibility in all humility. It is the essence of the electoral mandate of 1996. I am dismayed, and I am sure that most of you share this sentiment, that this decision has been unfairly criticised by some groups. Those that have undergone many splits, have come together only to fragment, who have formed conflicting combinations but failed to win more seats than the BJP, are now prepared to join hands, without any hesitation, even with those whom they opposed in the polls with great vigour. This can only

be termed as politics without principles, motivated by the sole aim of coming to power by any means.

During the last one week, we have not heard them say even a word about what they would do for you or for the country. They seem to have a single-point agenda: Stop the Bharatiya Janata Party at any cost. To achieve this, a determined campaign has been launched to paint us in adverse colours. Instead of entering into a debate on 'communalism', or the true meaning of 'secularism', a resolute effort is being made to obscure issues, to avoid an honest and meaningful debate. This has only one purpose: to defeat the mandate given by the people.

Atalji's broadcast to the nation evoked an extremely positive response from the general public. The *Indian Express*, in its editorial said: 'If the yardstick of success in politics is measured purely in terms of survival, it is possible that the BJP-led government of Atal Bihari Vajpayee may yet be found wanting on the day the Lok Sabha votes on the motion of confidence. However, if popular endorsement is a consideration, the new Prime Minister appears to have surged ahead of his challengers.... Vajpayee appears to have successfully diluted the BJP's untouchability among the people, even if he has not been able to translate that mood for the political classes.... In spelling out a liberal, conciliatory and federalist agenda, the Prime Minister has made it that much more difficult for the anti-BJP forces to claim the moral high ground. Using his agreeable image to full advantage, he has shown that whereas he has a vision, they have a target. *Even if he loses the battle, he may end up winning the war.*' (emphasis added.)

The attempt of the Congress, National Front and Left Front parties to cobble together an anti-BJP coalition drew an even sharper reaction—quite uncharacteristically—from the *Hindustan Times*. Its Editor V.N. Narayanan wrote a front-page editorial titled 'Respect the Voter': 'If the untouchability law is still in force in this country, leaders of an assortment of political parties which want to be part of the government in Delhi should be chargesheeted under it.'

Atalji's government lasted only thirteen days since the BJP could not muster enough support to prove majority in the Lok Sabha. That he would have to resign was a foregone conclusion. Nevertheless, he used the debate on the vote of confidence to counter the bogey of 'threat to secularism', raised by the Congress, National Front and the Left Front parties to isolate the BJP. His speech on the occasion was one of the finest in his parliamentary career. Since the debate was being telecast live by Doordarshan for the first time, the entire country was glued to their television sets. The verdict of those who watched the debate was clear: the loser was, indeed, the real winner. Before announcing that he was going to Rashtrapati Bhavan to submit his resignation, Atalji defiantly proclaimed: 'We are going to come back. We know how to get into the *chakravyuha**, but we also know how to get out of it.'

His words certainly turned out to be prophetic!

An editorial titled 'Stealing the Show', which appeared in the *Indian Express*, reflected the general mood of the people: 'If the live television coverage transformed the two-day debate on the vote of confidence into a happening in which every Indian was an active participant, the credit has to go to Atal Bihari Vajpayee. To say that the veteran BJP leader stole the show is an understatement. Using his formidable oratorical skills to the hilt, Vajpayee successfully transformed the dubious reputation of presiding over India's most short-lived government into a political achievement.

---

* *Chakravyuha,* a wheel-shaped battle formation, symbolises a situation in which a person or an organisation finds itself isolated and cornered by the adversaries, with little chance of surmounting the situation. It appears in an engaging description in the Mahabharata. On the thirteenth day of the battle, the Kauravas challenged the Pandavas to break the formation. Only Arjuna and Krishna knew how to penetrate it, but Dronacharya, the commander of the Kaurava army, created a ploy to distract them into another part of the battlefield. When the Pandava troops were despondent at their inability to face the challenge, Arjuna's young son Abhimanyu offered to successfully penetrate the formation. He fought the Kaurava ranks with great courage and valour, leaving Dronacharya both amazed and alarmed. However, Abhimanyu's attempt to get out of the *Chakravyuha* was thwarted by the Kauravas, who, in violation of all the rules of war, killed him. Arjuna avenged his son's death by defeating the Kuru's army with Krishna's help in the battle on the following day.

As he wound up the debate with the dramatic announcement of his resignation, he was not merely achieving political martyrdom. He was elevating himself to the role of a folk hero.'

I should mention here that there was some discussion within the BJP about whether or not Atalji should accept the President's invitation to form the government since the tally of the BJP, along with that of our pre-poll allies (Akali Dal and the Shiv Sena) was only 181 seats. Some colleagues were of the view that the BJP should let go of the opportunity and, instead, try to come back with a bigger strength in the next elections. They were also of the view that Atalji should not have left out of his broadcast to the nation any reference to the three important issues in the BJP's 1996 election manifesto—construction of the Ram Temple at Ayodhya, abrogation of Article 370 of the Constitution relating to Jammu & Kashmir, and enactment of a uniform civil code. I did not support this view. The mere fact of Atalji being sworn in as India's Prime Minister, I argued, would greatly enhance the BJP's popularity and prestige among the people. And that is, precisely, what happened.

I was not a member of the Cabinet in Atalji's thirteen-day government since I had not contested the 1996 Lok Sabha elections. This was owing to my own self-imposed constraint not to enter Parliament until I was cleared of the false charges in the hawala case. I should record here with much gratitude and appreciation that, as an act of solidarity, Atalji chose to contest from two Lok Sabha constituencies—Lucknow, which is his own traditional constituency, and Gandhinagar, which is mine. He won from both. He later resigned from Gandhinagar and kept his membership from Lucknow. In another sign of solidarity, he insisted on coming to my Pandara Park residence for all party-related meetings even after being sworn in as Prime Minister, since I was then the BJP President.

DEVE GOWDA BECOMES PRIME MINISTER

Anticipating the fall of Atalji's government, the Congress party decided to support a new alliance called the United Front, an updated version of the National Front, led again by the Janata Dal. The farcical nature of this government was evident even before it was born, from the manner in which it went about selecting its Prime Minister. There was no consensus over any name from amongst the national leaders of the Janata Dal or its allies in the United Front. This was because they were guided, not only by the mission of 'Stop-the-BJP-at-any-cost', but also 'Stop-the-other-person-from-becoming-PM'. There was bitter politics underway to grab the Prime Minister's chair. V.P. Singh ruled himself out, more out of compulsion than choice, since there was no way the Congress would have supported a government under his leadership, given his rebellion against Rajiv Gandhi on the Bofors issue.

This made leaders of the new front turn to Jyoti Basu, the veteran leader of the CPI(M) and Chief Minister of West Bengal. He was willing, but his own party's Central Committee vetoed the proposal; it was a decision that Basu was to later famously describe as a 'historical blunder'. Without going into the merits of the CPI(M)'s decision, I must confess that I was impressed by it on two counts—firstly, the party displayed the courage to stick to its own principles even when Prime Ministership was offered to it on a platter; and, secondly, the discipline that marked the inner-working of its highest decision-making body.

The process of elimination finally led the United Front leaders to choose H.D. Deve Gowda, the Chief Minister of Karnataka, who had never played any role in national politics until then. Thus, on 1 June, he was sworn in as India's eleventh Prime Minister. Around the same time, the country witnessed another dramatic development. P.V. Narasimha Rao was summarily removed from the presidentship of the Congress party, which blamed him summarily as the villain for the debacle in the 1996 parliamentary elections. He was replaced by Sitaram Kesri, who had been the treasurer of the party for many years. It is not for me to comment on why he was chosen to become the Congress President. However, I must say that my party and I were aghast at a highly irresponsible statement made by Kesri in February 1998. During the campaign for the parliamentary elections that year, I had gone to address a rally at Coimbatore in Tamil Nadu. Just before my arrival, a series of bomb blasts took place at the venue of the election meeting and elsewhere in the city, killing fifty-eight persons.* After the blasts, Kesri made an outrageous statement that the bomb blasts were the handiwork of the RSS and, moreover, that he had the proof of the RSS involvement in the terrorist act.

Kesri will be remembered for yet another malicious political manoeuvre. In April 1997, he suddenly announced withdrawal of the Congress party's support to Deve Gowda's government. People were astounded by the reason he gave for his decision: 'The Prime Minister is not giving due respect or recognition to the Congress, although his government's survival depends on us.'

How Deve Gowda's government ran for eleven months can be gauged from what one of its own senior, and widely respected, minister said about it long after it had become a footnote in modern Indian history. According to Indrajit Gupta, the CPI leader who was the Home Minister in Deve Gowda's Cabinet, 'The replacement of Deve Gowda was not entirely Sitaram Kesri's doing; within the United Front also there was a desire to replace him. Gowda was seen as autocratic. I mean, I was his Home Minister; He refused to speak to me. He never spoke to me, never consulted me. I can't say these things publicly, I couldn't say it then also, I had to keep quiet.'[1]

Clearly, the United Front government was anything but united. Within the Union Cabinet itself, discord and disorder were the order of the day. Collective responsibility as a fundamental principle of sound Cabinet functioning had been conspicuous by its absence, for which the Lok Sabha Speaker, P.A. Sangma, himself had to admonish the government. In the previous government headed by P.V. Narasimha Rao, Home Minister S.B. Chavan and his deputy, Rajesh Pilot, were not on talking terms. The United Front government surpassed this—even the Prime Minister and his Home Minister did not speak with each other on such important issues as appointment of Governors or dealing with the problem of terrorism and secessionism in Kashmir and the North-East. Perhaps the most graphic description of the state of affairs in the ruling coalition came from one

---

* I have described this incident in greater detail on page 531.

of its own veteran leaders, Biju Patnaik, who called the United Front 'a cluster of lobsters clawing at one another'.

I.K. GUJRAL BECOMES PRIME MINISTER

Deve Gowda was replaced by I.K. Gujral, who was the External Affairs Minister in his Cabinet, on 21 April 1997. Commenting on this development, I said that it was a miraculous feat of 'head surgery' performed on the United Front government, in which the ruling coalition had meekly submitted to its own decapitation by the Congress. Others called it 'Operation Ganesh' where the body of the government remained the same, only the head was replaced by that of another person. But, what was the reason and the urgency for this swift operation? The answer came in the form of an egregious decision taken by Gujral soon after becoming Prime Minister. He removed Joginder Singh from the directorship of the CBI, since he was proving problematic for the Congress party in the investigation of the Bofors scandal and for Laloo Prasad Yadav in the investigation of the fodder scam*.

I must confess that, although I had known Gujral for many years and shared a good personal rapport with him, I was highly disappointed by his premiership. Consequently, my remarks about him in my presidential speech at the BJP's national executive in New Delhi in July 1997 were quite candid. 'In the beginning, Shri Gujral's sympathisers and well-meaning critics might have given him the benefit of doubt by attributing

---

* Laloo Prasad Yadav, President of the Rashtriya Janata Dal (RJD) and, currently, Railway Minister in Dr Manmohan Singh government, has been charged with several corruption cases, the most famous being the multi-crore 'Fodder scam'. It refers to siphoning off of the funds meant for cattle fodder from the animal husbandry department, when he was the Chief Minister of Bihar. He refused to resign even after being chargesheeted in the scandal. He used his political influence over former Prime Minister I.K. Gujral to get the CBI off his back. Finally, judicial and political pressure combined to compel him to step down in 1997. While doing so, he made his wife Rabri Devi the Chief Minister. The fifteen years (1990-2005) during which he and his wife ruled Bihar caused the state's steep decline in socio-economic development and saw corruption, criminalisation and casteism rise to frightening levels.

his pathetic condition to his helplessness. But as days passed, and as he unprotestingly took one insult after another from his own partymen and Front partners as well as from a scheming Congress party, it was clear that the Prime Minister was a victim not so much of helplessness as of a personal craving for power.'

Predictably, the Congress pulled the carpet from under the feet of the second United Front government even sooner than it had done in the case of the first. This time, the pretext was the Jain Commission's interim report on Rajiv Gandhi's assassination. Justice Milap Chand Jain Commission was appointed by the government in August 1991, three months after the assassination, to probe the larger conspiracy behind the crime. In its seventeen-volume interim report, submitted on 28 August 1997, it indicted the DMK for having allowed the LTTE to find sanctuaries in Tamil Nadu, where the party was in power in 1991. Parts of the interim report were leaked to a national fortnightly, reportedly by a senior leader of the Congress party who did not have good relations with Kesri. Since the DMK was a member of the ruling United Front coalition, the Congress party demanded that Gujral sack three DMK ministers from his government. When the United Front refused to budge on this demand, the Congress withdrew support to Gujral's government on 28 November. It was widely believed that the Congress simply needed an excuse, any excuse, to destabilise the United Front government. I should once again refer here to what Indrajit Gupta said about this development in his interview to *Frontline*: 'The whole idea about the DMK was that they were alleged to be hobnobbing with the LTTE. The Congress said, the LTTE are the people who have killed our leader, so how can we go on supporting a government in which these fellows are there? That was the excuse given. But they had not read the final report. So we refused to get rid of the DMK. How can you count on these chaps?'

CONGRESS POLITICKING BEHIND PROBE INTO RAJIV GANDHI'S ASSASSINATION

I have mentioned that the Congress party has often used flippant excuses for destabilising governments to which it lent outside support. However, the ploy that it resorted to pull down Gujral's government was not only flippant and irresponsible but also downright dishonest. Consider this irony: the very party that pulled down Gujral's government in 1997 on the ground that its demand for the sacking of DMK ministers was not met, has no qualms about including DMK ministers in Dr Manmohan Singh's government!

In February 2004, Congress President Sonia Gandhi personally visited the DMK headquarters in Chennai and sought an electoral alliance between the two parties for the impending Lok Sabha elections. When journalists reminded her about the Congress party's withdrawal of support to Gujral's government on the issue of the DMK's presence in the Cabinet, she replied that, 'There were no negative comments in the final report. Since the final Jain report had exonerated him (Karunanidhi), how could the interim report stand?'

It is true that the final report of the Jain Commission did not name any individual or organisation in India, including the DMK, as having a hand in the conspiracy to murder Rajiv Gandhi. But neither Sonia Gandhi nor any of her colleagues has till date given a satisfactory explanation for her party's decision to withdraw support to Gujral's government on the basis of what they knew was only an interim report.

The Congress leadership clearly has much more explaining to do to the Indian people. To elaborate on this, I will fast-forward the narrative to the time when I was Home Minister in the NDA government. One of my first decisions was to table the Commission's final report in Parliament on 31 July 1998, along with an Action Taken Report (ATR) on its findings. Replying to the debate on the subject in the Lok Sabha, I said that the assassination of the former Prime Minister was a national tragedy and gave a categorical assurance that our government was determined to 'go into the depth of it to unravel the whole truth', including domestic and foreign dimensions of the 'wider conspiracy' behind it.

When P. Shiv Shanker, the Deputy Leader of the Congress in the House, said that the ATR was not acceptable to his party, I said that setting up another judicial commission at this stage would not serve any purpose. I suggested, instead, that an executive body with statutory powers be entrusted to follow up the report of the Jain Commission. This suggestion found acceptance from the Congress party and, accordingly, our government constituted a Multi-Disciplinary Monitoring Agency (MDMA) under the CBI to bring those accused in the case, including the absconders, to trial.

What surprised me was that, in a veiled criticism of former Prime Minister P.V. Narasimha Rao, Shiv Shanker said that the governments at the Centre after 1991 did not want the Jain Commission to find out the truth. Certain forces within the Congress, as well as outside it were against Rajiv Gandhi since the day he became Prime Minister and they wanted to replace him, he alleged. He insisted that the role of certain bureaucrats, politicians, the alleged links of godman Chandraswamy with the Central Intelligence Agency (CIA) and Mossad, the national intelligence agency of Israel, and efforts by some people to wind up the Jain Commission, should be probed further.

Then, on 19 August 1998, a delegation of Congress leaders, including Dr Manmohan Singh, Arjun Singh, Pranab Mukherjee, Mani Shankar Aiyar, Suresh Pachauri and others, met me in my North Block office. They said they were not happy with the ATR on the Jain Commission's report, especially as regards the probe into the role of Dr Karunanidhi and others who had been exonerated by the Commission. They submitted to me a seven-page letter which detailed several areas of concern, and one emphatic demand: 'The Congress insists that the agency be directed by the government to investigate all matters relating to Mr M. Karunanidhi as adverted by the Commission and proceed against him in a court of law, if warranted by the evidence which will be uncovered.' The delegation certainly could not have put forward this demand without the concurrence of Sonia Gandhi, just as the decision to pull down Gujral's government on the DMK issue could not have been taken without her approval.

I did not fail to notice that, until then, the Congress had avoided naming -Even during the debate in Parliament, they had refrained from targeting any political leader. Although they did not say it in so many words, by demanding that these matters be subjected to detailed investigation by the MDMA to ascertain if there was 'any mala fide intention' behind the obstructions, it was clear that they were targeting Narasimha Rao.

The most intriguing aspect of the letter given to me by the high-powered Congress delegation was that it had been written *after* the Jain Commission had already submitted its final report to the government. In other words, the Congress leadership continued to suspect the DMK's hand in the conspiracy behind Rajiv Gandhi's assassination even after the final report of the Jain panel had exonerated Dr Karunanidhi and his party. Therefore, it was rather disingenuous on the part of Sonia Gandhi to say before the media in Chennai in February 2004, while defending the Congress-DMK alliance: 'Since the final Jain report had exonerated Karunanidhi, how could the interim report stand?'

My friend S. Gurumurthy, one of the most trenchant commentators on social and political developments in India, was far harsher in judging Sonia Gandhi's conduct in this matter. 'She vindicates him (Karunanidhi), but indicts herself, by lies,' he wrote in an article in the *New Indian Express* (8 May 2004). 'She clinched the (Congress-DMK) alliance by burying the Rajiv assassination issue.'

Another pointer to how the Jain Commission was being used by rival factions of the Congress party to snipe at each other was revealed when S.B. Chavan, Home Minister in Narasimha Rao's government, told in his deposition before the commission on 11 December 1997: 'What was uppermost in our mind was to save the name of the Gandhi family.' After all, it was well-known that the governments of Indira Gandhi and Rajiv Gandhi had been providing aid and training to the LTTE in the early 1980s.

*

It is now sixteen years since Rajiv Gandhi's assassination. The Jain Commission submitted its final report nine years ago. The MDMA, which was instituted to unravel the external as well as internal angles of the 'wider conspiracy' behind the assassination, has also been in existence for nine years. Its work has not yielded any tangible result so far. However, I would like to pose two questions before the country's political class and intelligentsia: Firstly, who were the persons responsible for the disastrous policy of sending the IPKF to fight Tamils in Sri Lanka, a policy that led to the deaths of hundreds of Indian soldiers, besides the tragedy of Rajiv Gandhi's assassination by a terrorist organisation based on foreign soil? Secondly, unearthing the complete truth behind Rajiv Gandhi's assassination is an important matter not only for the Congress but for the entire country. But has not the Congress leadership given primacy to political expediency over political morality in respect of investigation of this case? These two questions deserve to be debated seriously, both within as well as outside the Congress party.

11

THE SWARNA JAYANTI RATH YATRA
A PATRIOTIC PILGRIMAGE

THE INDIA OF MY DREAMS

Lord Macaulay once cynically remarked that an acre in Middlesex is better than a principality in Utopia. Hard-boiled politicians may be inclined to agree with this dictum, and scoff at dreamers. But independent India is acutely conscious of the fact that it is the dreams of visionaries like Vivekananda, Aurobindo, Tagore and Gandhi that have inspired the nation during the freedom struggle and finally helped liberate it. These great seers, each in his own inimitable way, described the India of their dreams—a great and glorious India, commanding the respect of the entire world. I hold that India's Constitution-makers very ably encapsulated these dreams of theirs in the Preamble to the Constitution, which beckons to the day when all Indian citizens would secure:
'Justice, social, economic and political;
Liberty of thought, expression, belief, faith and worship;
Equality of status and of opportunity; and to promote among them all;
Fraternity assuring the dignity of the individual and the unity of the Nation'.
As a political activist, I identify myself completely with this sublime, yet eminently attainable, vision of future India. I longingly look forward to its realisation.
(From my article in the *Illustrated Weekly of India*, Independence Day special, 1987)

Ten years after I wrote this, in 1997, an event occurred that gave me an opportunity to propagate my vision through a unique political campaign—the golden jubilee of India's Independence, which ushered in a mood of patriotism all over the country.

Sometime in February, I called a meeting of my colleagues in the party office to discuss how the BJP should commemorate 1997. After considering several suggestions, we decided to pay homage to all the heroes and martyrs of the freedom movement by visiting places associated with them across the country. My young team of office-bearers and other colleagues soon translated the idea into a concrete plan in the form of a nationwide road journey called the Swarna Jayanti Rath Yatra: *Rashtrabhakti Ki Teerth Yatra* (A Patriotic Pilgrimage). Travelling to places sanctified by the struggles and sacrifices of the heroes of the freedom movement was akin to undertaking a pilgrimage. I felt this would help me strengthen my own as well as my party's, nationalist and idealist moorings.

Three factors, however, seemed problematic: timing, climate and the sheer number of places we would need to visit. The yatra had to be undertaken before 15 August, but only after the schools and colleges had completed their examinations. It also had to be concluded before the onset of the rains, which arrive sooner in the south than in the north. Since all the states needed to be covered, the yatra would take not less than two months. In other words, I needed to be on the road in the peak of the forbidding Indian summer—and the condition of roads then was not half as good as it is today. This concerned some of my colleagues who were doubtful of subjecting me to this strain and also because I was to soon turn seventy. I was, however, firm and decided to go ahead with the yatra.

THE YATRA'S RAISON D'ETRE

There were a couple of reasons why I agreed to undertake this campaign. The first was personal: the golden jubilee of India's Independence was a highly emotional occasion for me. However, it was as much a time for introspection as celebration. Therefore, it was also necessary to take stock of the successes, shortcomings and failures of the first fifty years of free India, and, simultaneously, to catalyse a serious debate on the content and direction of India's future development.

The second reason was political: I wanted to project the BJP as a party committed to good governance. Although India had attained swaraj or self-governance in 1947, it had not been transformed, even after fifty years, into *su-raj* or good governance. Consequently, people had started perceiving all politicians as unprincipled, unscrupulous, self-seeking and power-hungry. It was necessary, therefore, for the BJP to rededicate itself to a loftier goal for being in politics, an ideal that went far beyond the immediate goal of pursuit of political power and linked itself to the task of freeing India from the yoke of hunger, fear and corruption.

The government of I.K. Gujral, like that of H.D. Deve Gowda, was showing clear signs of early mortality. The prospect of another mid-term parliamentary poll was looming large, and the Congress party, which had lost power, was getting discredited as a destabiliser. On the other hand, the fact that Atal Bihari Vajpayee's government could not last beyond thirteen days, in spite of the BJP having emerged as the single largest party in the 1996 parliamentary elections, had greatly disappointed the people. They were craving for stability and better governance. The situation was, thus, rapidly turning in BJP's favour. I reckoned that a nationwide yatra at this time would serve both my purposes.

My young party colleagues—Pramod Mahajan, M. Venkaiah Naidu, Sushma Swaraj, K.N. Govindacharya, Narendra Modi and Sadhvi Uma Bharati—began preparations for the yatra, which was to take place in four continuous phases in fifty-nine days, from 18 May to 15 July, covering a distance of over 15,000 kilometres through as many as twenty-one states and union territories, making it by far the longest and widest mass contact programme undertaken by any political party since Independence. (The seven North-Eastern states, where the rains arrive much earlier than elsewhere, had to be covered separately after Independence Day.) I addressed 750 scheduled public meetings, besides speaking to people at several thousand unscheduled wayside receptions in villages and hamlets. My colleagues later estimated that the yatra established direct contact with as many as two crore Indians from the time of its beginning in Mumbai to its conclusion in Delhi.

I had been cautioned by some people against undertaking this second yatra, since comparisons with my Ram Rath Yatra of 1990, from Somnath to Ayodhya, would be inevitable. Also, unlike the Ram Janmabhoomi issue, which was religious and hence emotive in nature, a yatra for the golden jubilee celebrations would fail to draw the crowds, they said. In reality, however, the Swarna Jayanti Rath Yatra evoked a stupendously positive response, giving me deep and enduring satisfaction. It also helped me learn a lot about the proud history of India's freedom movement, which in many places in the country began well before the First War of Independence in 1857. But for this countrywide journey, I would not have known about so many less renowned heroes and martyrs, whose names are a part of the local folklore in every state and whose exploits can inspire the young and the old for generations to come

But the Swarna Jayanti Rath Yatra was not only about India's past. It was equally about India's present and future. The campaign enabled me to talk about a wide range of issues of contemporary and future importance—corruption, criminalisation, casteism, communalism, terrorism, poverty, women's empowerment, education, environment, work culture and economic development guided by the swadeshi principle with a focus on agriculture and employment. Above all, it reinforced my conviction, first formed during the Ayodhya movement, that there is no greater method than a yatra to reach out to the common people in a vast country like ours, and no better way to galvanise the large army of one's own party workers and sympathisers.

What follows is a recapitulation of my campaign.*

---

* A fuller account of this campaign is given in a book *Swarna Jayanti Rath Yatra: A Patriotic Pilgrimage* by my colleague Sudheendra Kulkarni, who accompanied me throughout the journey. It was published by the Bharatiya Janata Party in August 1997.

FLAG-OFF, MUMBAI

August Kranti Maidan in Mumbai was an ideal place for the commencement of the journey for it was here that Mahatma Gandhi gave the clarion call of 'Quit India', on 8 August 1942 which marked the beginning of the end of the British rule in India.

In my speech at the inaugural function on the morning of 18 May, I paid tribute to the great patriots of Maharashtra—Shivaji to Tilak, Dadabhai Naoroji to Madame Cama, Veer Savarkar to Babu Genu*, and Jyotiba Phule to Dr Babasaheb Ambedkar—whose sheer devotion to the cause was like the oil to the undying lamp that guided the freedom struggle. While presenting the theme of the yatra, I said, 'Mahatma Gandhi had given the call "Britishers, Quit India". The time has come for us to raise a similar battle-cry: '*Bhookh, Bharat Chhodo, Bhay, Bharat Chhodo, Bhrashtachar, Bharat Chhodo.*' (Hunger, Fear and Corruption, Quit India). Why have these maladies continued to afflict India even after fifty years of freedom? The root cause for this is the erosion of national identity and national values in politics.'

At the end of the function, Atalji flagged off the creatively redesigned rath—a Tata 709E truck which bore a large picture of Bharat Mata and portraits of Mahatma Gandhi, Lokamanya Tilak, Sardar Vallabhbhai Patel, Dr B.R. Ambedkar, Rani Jhansi Laxmibai, Veerapandya Kattabomman, Shaheed Bhagat Singh, Chandrashekhar Azad, Ashfaqullah Khan, Swatantryaveer Savarkar, Netaji Subas Chandra Bose and Dr Keshav Baliram Hedgewar.

MAHARASHTRA

The yatra received a tumultuous welcome when it reached Pune the first night. At the entrance of the city, I garlanded the memorial built for the Chaphekar brothers, who were martyred in 1898 for their role in the armed resistance against the British rule. I then went to the residence of

---

* Babu Genu was an ordinary textile mill worker in Bombay who was gunned down by the British in 1930 for his participation in the Swadeshi movement.

Lokamanya Tilak (1856-1920), whose defiant words '*Swaraj* is my birth right, and I shall have it' had shaken the colonial masters. Here I was received by Jayantrao Tilak, Lokamanya's grandson and a respected Congressman. He presented me with a copy of *Gita Rahasya*, a book of seminal scholarship which Tilak wrote during his six-year-long incarceration in Mandalay jail in Burma (now Myanmar). Speaking later at a rally at Shaniwarwada, I recalled what Mahatma wrote about this foremost leader of the freedom movement in the pre-Gandhi era: 'Tilak knew no other religion but love for the country. With his fearlessness and burning love for the country, he challenged both the westernised social reformer as well as the spirit of orthodoxy.'

In Satara, a historic city associated with the glory of the Maratha empire, I had the first experience of how educative the journey was going to be for me. As I was preparing to leave after a night-halt, some local party colleagues asked me if I wanted to see a banyan tree nearby. On asking about its significance I was taken to *Phanshicha Vad*, a memorial tree on which five local patriotic fighters were hanged by British rulers in 1857. Addressing a meeting later in the day, I said: 'Usually people go on a religious pilgrimage for self-purifying spiritual experience. For me, however, a visit to Lokamanya Tilak's birthplace in Pune last night or to *Phanshicha Vad* this morning has provided the same experience.'

A few weeks later in UP, I had two similar experiences: in a village called Chhavani in the eastern part of the state, I visited a banyan tree on which over 150 patriots were given *kacchi phansi*, a particularly savage form of 'slow-motion' hanging, on a single day. The very next day, in Bareili, I went to another banyan tree, on which 257 freedom fighters were condemned to *kacchi phansi* on a single day.

In Nashik in Maharashtra, the birthplace of Tatya Tope, a legendary hero of 1857, it felt as if the entire city, on the banks of the Godavari, was present to welcome the rath. Patriotic songs of Veer Savarkar, many of which he had penned during his eleven-year-long solitary confinement in Cellular Jail in Andaman Islands were echoing around. I went to Bhagoor village, his birthplace, to pay homage to this childhood hero of mine.

In Kolhapur, I paid tributes to Shahu Maharaj, a progressive ruler of the princely state, who was one of the earliest supporters of Dr Ambedkar in his crusade for social reform. Speaking at a 1921 conference of untouchables organised by Dr Ambedkar, the king had prophetically observed: 'You have found your saviour in Ambedkar. I am confident that he will break your shackles. Not only that, a time will come when, so whispers my conscience, Ambedkar will shine as a front-rank leader of all-India fame and appeal.' Dr Ambedkar's life-mission, I said, continues to remind us that all our dreams for India's future would remain unrealised so long as the socially marginalised and economically excluded sections of our society do not enjoy the fruits of equality.

I dealt with the theme of India's future from a different perspective in my speech at a mammoth rally in Aurangabad. 'We are barely two and a half years away from the beginning of a new century and a new millennium, what will be the picture of the world in the next century? And what will be the place of India in that picture? Futurologists have prophesied that, if the twentieth century belonged to Europe and America, the twenty-first century will be an Asian century. But should we Indians be satisfied if it remains only Japan's century or China's century, keeping India out of the reckoning? No. We must strive collectively to make it Bharat's century. But this cannot happen only through a change in leadership. There is also a need for a change in the mindset of the people. Political transformation alone is not sufficient. We also need social transformation. If we are able to achieve this, the day is not far off when India will be propelled into the front ranks of the international community.'

GOA

In neighbouring Goa, the yatra recalled the struggle waged for its liberation from Portuguese rule in 1961. More than a hundred patriots became martyrs in this struggle, in which a large number of people from other states also participated. I spoke about the contributions made by the great heroes of that movement—Dr Ram Manohar Lohia, Jagannathrao Joshi, S.M. Joshi, Vasantrao Oak, Madhu Limaye, Nath Pai and others. Later, a delegation of the Goa Freedom Fighters' Association met me, seeking my support to their demand that the central and state governments drop the scandalous idea of commemorating the 500th anniversary of the arrival of Vasco da Gama—and that too in collaboration with the government of Portugal! I fully supported their demand and said it was akin to celebrating, in collaboration with the government in Beijing, the anniversary of India's defeat in the 1962 war against China. Consequently, the idea was soon shelved.

KARNATAKA

When the rath reached the border town of Belgaum in Karnataka, which has for many years been a bone of contention between Karnataka and Maharashtra, I urged the people to eschew linguistic chauvinism and preserve the age-old fraternal bonds between Kannadigas and Marathi-speaking people. I reminded them that both had jointly organised the historic AICC session in Belgaum in 1924, the only time when Mahatma Gandhi became President of the Congress party.

I went to the nearby town of Kittur to pay homage to Rani Chennamma, the gallant queen of a small principality, who fought against British rule in 1824—much before the start of the First War of Independence in North India. The British, always in search of a pretext to annex Indian kingdoms, had raised objection to Chennamma, who was a widow of Kittur's king, administering the affairs of the state on behalf of a minor boy she had adopted. Her only 'guilt' was that she had not taken the permission of the local British collector before adopting the boy! Her defiance led to a war. The British had played a similar ploy with Rani Laxmibai of Jhansi. Like Rani Laxmibai, a Chennamma led her forces from the front and inflicted three humiliating defeats on the superior army of the British. When she was finally captured, Chennamma took her own life in prison.

Many places that I visited during the yatra had not only historical but also contemporary significance. Thus, in Hubli, I recalled the BJP's patriotic struggle in 1993 to hoist the flag on Independence Day and Republic Day at a municipal-owned ground called the Idgah Maidan. A section of the Muslim community had opposed this on religious grounds. All the pseudo-secular parties and intellectuals had opposed the BJP on this issue, creating an unnecessary nationwide controversy. In the agitation that the BJP launched, five pro-flag hoisting fighters were shot dead by the police. Undaunted, my party continued the struggle, which ultimately ended in victory.

In my speeches, I tried to combine the patriotic appeal with the theme of India's accelerated development. For instance, in Mangalore in coastal Karnataka, I called upon the people to build a new India which would, in every developmental parameter, rank among the best in the world. 'Take the case of your own city. Mangalore is already emerging as an important port city on the west coast. Now it should aspire to become as big, modern and efficient as Amsterdam, which handles more cargo than all Indian ports put together.'

KERALA

It would surprise many to know that the yatra evoked an enthusiastic response in Kerala and West Bengal, the two states where the BJP is admittedly weak and the communists, our ideological adversaries, are quite strong. As my rath entered Kasargod, a border town near Karnataka, I was amazed to see that there was an almost endless human chain on both sides of the road, formed by thousands of youth shouting patriotic slogans, *Bharat Mata ki jai* and *Vande Mataram*. The scene repeated itself in town after town. Wherever the rath stopped, it was greeted by women performing *aarti*, a traditional welcome ritual.

In my speeches, I sought to emphasise Kerala's contribution to Indian nationalism as the land of Adi Shankaracharya, who travelled on foot all over India and spread the message of spiritual unity more than a thousand years ago; and Narayan Guru, the great social reformer who campaigned against caste discrimination by invoking the basic Vedic principle of oneness of all creation. I also referred to the patriotic warrior-king, Palasi Raja, who organised tribals for a guerrilla battle against the British rule well before 1857. I said that both the communists and the Muslim League, another important force in the state's politics, were playing a divisive role since they neither accepted nor respected the cultural basis of India's nationalism.

I flayed the spate of violent attacks by Marxist cadres on the activists of the BJP, RSS and ABVP* and also expressed concern over the fact that Kerala was becoming a fertile ground in recent years for anti-national forces working in close coordination with the ISI of Pakistan. At Malappuram, I also administered 'Rashtra Raksha Pratigya' (A Pledge to Defend the Nation) to the people.

TAMIL NADU

Tamil Nadu's contribution to India's freedom struggle has been colossal. Sadly, there is insufficient awareness about this in the north. I went to the port town of Tuticorin, the birth place of V.O. Chidambaram Pillai, one of the most versatile personalities of the freedom struggle. V.O.C., as he was called, was both a successful entrepreneur and a militant patriot. He angered the colonial rulers by starting the Swadeshi Steam Navigation Company to compete against British ships. An ardent devotee of Tilak, he attended the historic Surat conference of the Congress Party in 1906 and came back surcharged with the speeches of Lal, Bal and Pal†. The British government stopped his shipping service and sentenced him for life on the charge of sedition. So widespread was his fame that no less a person than Rajendra Prasad, India's first President who was then a young lawyer in Patna, went all the way to Ottapidaram, V.O.C.'s village, volunteering to fight his case. When my rath reached Ottapidaram, I was told that I was the only national leader to have visited the village during the golden jubilee year.

---

* Akhil Bharatiya Vidyarthi Parishad (ABVP) is a nationalist student's organisation inspired and guided by the RSS. However, unlike other major students' organisations that are affiliated to some or the other political party, ABVP is independent of the BJP.
† In the early decades of the last century, 'Lal-Bal-Pal' was a popular description of the three great leaders of India's freedom struggle—Lala Lajpat Rai, Bal Gangadhar Tilak and Bipin Chandra Pal.

In Sengottai, I garlanded the statue of the town's proudest son: Veer Vanchi. This little-known martyr of the freedom struggle was a member of the Bharat Mata Sangham, a revolutionary outfit. On hearing that the British sub-collector of the district had pronounced a life sentence on V.O.C, Vanchi, who had got married just a few weeks earlier, avenged the injustice by gunning down the officer in 1911. Unable to escape, he shot himself dead right there. In my speech, I recalled this brave episode as described by Veer Savarkar in his famous book *Kala Pani*.

Yet another destination was Ettayapuram, the birthplace of Rashtrakavi Subramania Bharati (1882-1921), who is regarded as the greatest Tamil poet of modern times. *Vande Mataram*, one of his most famous poems, became the mantra of nationalism. His works are an emphatic refutation of the artificial Dravidian-Aryan divide and, at the same time, an embodiment of the highest ideals of Hindu culture. In a popular poem *En Thai* (My Mother), Bharati wrote: 'My Mother has thirty crores faces, but their body and soul is one. She speaks in eighteen languages, but the thought she expresses is one.' I reminded the audience in my speech that Prime Minister Atal Bihari Vajpayee had recited this poem—in Tamil first and then in Hindi translation—during his celebrated confidence-motion speech in Parliament in May 1996.

Bharati's house, which has now been converted into a memorial museum has an impressive collection of photographs and artifacts. One of the exhibits was a letter he wrote in 1908 to Tilak, whom he addressed as 'Dear Guruji', urging him to start Hindi classes in the south! Another exhibit showed a letter Gandhiji wrote to Bharati in June 1945—and this one was in Tamil, in the Mahatma's own handwriting. I cited this in my speeches saying that we had a lot to learn from the leaders of our freedom struggle on how to unite the people across the barriers of language, region, religion and caste.

A particularly exhilarating experience for me was the visit to Veer Pandya Kattabomman's fort at Panchalamkurichi in the Tuticorin district. Kattabomman, one of the earliest martyrs in the struggle against British colonialism, was the ruler of a small principality. The officers of the EIC, in a bid to expand their hegemony, attacked his dominion. Kattabomman prayed to goddess Jagammal (Jagadamba in the north) and launched a fierce guerilla battle against the company. He was captured and hanged in 1799.

I mentioned in my speech on that day that the first Tamil film I had seen in my life was *Veerapandia Kattabomman*, which starred the legendary actor Sivaji Ganesan. Although I was unable to follow the language, the film had made a lasting impression on me. I personally complimented Sivaji Ganesan for his role in the film, when I met him in Parliament after his nomination to the Rajya Sabha in 1982.

At the time of my yatra, the southern districts of Tamil Nadu had been rocked by caste clashes between thevars and dalits. In my appeal to end caste strife, I gave the example of Kattabomman, who promoted social unity by consciously involving people of all castes in the rebellion against the British. His two most trusted lieutenants were Vellaiyaiah Thevar, who belonged to the 'lower' thevar caste, and Sundaraligam, who was a dalit. I should mention here that the yatra's theme song gave a pride of place to Kattabomman, thus popularising the memory of this little-known Tamil martyr of the freedom struggle all over the country.

My next stop was Virudunagar, the birthplace of K. Kamaraj, one of the most respected figures in Congress history. He was the personification of honesty, self-respect and dedicated service to the nation. The gesture of the BJP President honouring an eminent Congress leader was widely appreciated by the media in Tamil Nadu. There was also appreciation for a press statement that I issued in Chennai on 27 May, the death anniversary of Pandit Jawaharlal Nehru. I paid him rich tributes for his contribution to the freedom movement and also to the subsequent development of parliamentary democracy in India.

CELLULAR JAIL IN ANDAMAN ISLANDS

From Chennai, the yatra took an aerial route to visit the Cellular Jail in Port Blair, capital of the Andaman & Nicobar Islands. This was the dreaded 'Kala Pani' of yesteryears, which was used by the British as a concentration camp to incarcerate thousands of patriots after 1857. Two important leaders of the revolt who were known for their high moral character and scholarship—Allama Fazlul Haq Khairabadi and Maulana Liaqat Ali—lived and died here as prisoners.

We reached there on 28 May, the 114th birth anniversary of a famous inmate, Swatantryaveer Savarkar. Here, in Cell No 123, one of the 698 tiny ill-lit rooms, the best-known chronicler of 1857 spent nearly eleven years of his life (1911-21). The inmates were so isolated from one another that, even though Savarkar's elder brother and fellow revolutionary, Ganesh Damodar Savarkar, was also imprisoned there, the two brothers learnt of it after a full two years! It was in these horrific conditions that Savarkar wrote, first on the bare walls of his cell and later, after his release, on paper, many immortal patriotic poems. In one of them titled 'Liberation', he sang: *Tuja sathi marana he janana/tuja vina janana he marana* (Dying for your cause, O Motherland, is itself life/And death is nothing but living without serving you).

Besides the Savarkar brothers, some of the other noted freedom fighters who were incarcerated here were Barindrakumar Ghosh (younger brother of Maharshi Aurobindo Ghosh), Ullaskar Dutt, Indubhushan Roy, Trailokyanath Chakravarty, Pulin Das, Baba Prithvi Singh Azad, Gurmukh Singh, Bhai Paramanand, Motilal Verma and Ladha Ram. The portraits of these and many others are displayed in a museum here. The guide who took me around the memorial was a local school teacher named Rashida Bibi, whose own father, Anaulla Khan from Peshawar, was an inmate of the jail for many years in the 1930s.

After planting a neem sapling at the Savarkar Park outside the memorial, I addressed a small crowd of party activists and visitors. Striking a reminiscent note, I described how I was influenced by my childhood hero: 'I learnt my first lesson in patriotism after reading Savarkar's banned book on 1857, a torn copy of which I had stealthily bought at a princely sum of rupees twenty-eight in 1942. Today, on the occasion of the fiftieth anniversary of India's Independence, all of us should recall the struggles and sacrifices of our great patriotic heroes and pledge to create India of their dreams.'

ANDHRA PRADESH

The yatra faced two challenges in Andhra Pradesh. In all the five days that we traversed through the state, the mercury hovered above forty-five degrees celsius. Secondly, the BJP's local organisers had to brave threats issued by the People's War Group, a naxalite organisation. Despite these adversities, the yatra turned out to be highly successful.

One of the largest public meetings was in Nellore, which occupies a proud place in the state's history. It is the birthplace of Potti Shriramulu, whose fifty-two-day fast, culminating in his self-immolation in December 1952, forced Pandit Nehru to accede to the demand for the reorganisation of states on linguistic lines in 1956. After felicitating a large number of freedom fighters from the district, I said in my speech: 'Why have their dreams of a New India remained unfulfilled even after fifty years of freedom? What would all the patriots and martyrs of the freedom struggle think if they were to see India of today, her polity steeped in corruption and her society reeling under poverty and social disharmony? The freedom fighters discharged their duty in their time. Now we have to do our duty.'

Exactly at the stroke of midnight, we reached Vijayawada, the third largest city in Andhra Pradesh where a massive crowd was awaiting our arrival. Here I paid tributes to Alluri Sitarama Raju (1897-1924), a legendary freedom fighter who mobilised tribals in the struggle against the British. Baba Prithvisingh Azad, the great Ghadar revolutionary from Punjab, had been imprisoned by the British in a jail in distant Rajahmundry town in eastern Andhra Pradesh. When Raju learnt of this, he vowed to free Azad. In the process, he was caught by a British officer, tied to a tree and shot dead. The youth wing of the BJP presented me a torch, called Alluri Sitarama Raju Jyothi, which they had brought from Rajahmundry. Similarly, another group of party workers had brought a *kalash* bearing the sacred soil from Alluri's birthplace, Krishnadevipet. These gestures truly overwhelmed me.

At Ongole, I garlanded the statue of Tanguturi Prakasam Pantulu (1872-1957), the first Chief Minister of Andhra Pradesh. Popularly known as the 'Lion of Andhra', this freedom fighter had bared his chest and dared the British police to shoot him during the mass protest against the Simon Commission in 1928—much like what the 'Lion of Punjab', Lala Lajpat Rai, had done. At Ponnooru, I garlanded the statue of N.G. Ranga, yet another illustrious Congress leader who was a dedicated peasant leader, able parliamentarian (he was indeed the longest-serving MP) and crusader against untouchability.

I had a touching experience at Chebrolu, a small village in the Prakasam district. As I was getting ready to board the rath after addressing a meeting, the villagers requested me to visit the house of a ninety-year old freedom fighter, Varinder Chandrashekhar Rao. He had mobilised forty-two men from his village to take part with him in the Quit India movement in 1942. I was told by the villagers that he was almost on his deathbed. His face lit up as he welcomed me and I took his blessings. The very next day he breathed his last.

My speeches in all my meetings in the Telangana area of Andhra Pradesh, where a strong movement for a separate state has been going on since the mid-1960s, carried two messages. Firstly, I said that the BJP supported the demand for a separate Telangana, which, in terms of size, is larger than as many as eleven Indian states. Secondly, that the BJP is against the politics of Left-wing extremism, which is quite strongly rooted in the region. Addressing a huge public meeting at Warangal, a hotbed of naxal activities, I said, 'There is, of course, a lot of injustice in our society and it is experienced by the people of Telangana, too. But the history of the entire world has repeated proved the truth that the politics of violence and terror never succeeds in removing injustice. Ballot, not bullet, is the only means of bringing about changes in a free and democratic nation.'

Once, two police officers came to me at a night-halt to caution me against a naxalite threat to attack the yatra. They said, 'The PWG does not issue empty threats. We, therefore, request you to use a bullet-proof car.' I refused so they asked me to use a bullet-proof vest. I refused that too and added firmly that there was no question of my abandoning the rath, threat or no threat.

GUJARAT

After Maharashtra for the second leg of journey, the yatra came to Gujarat, where it took me to the birthplaces of Mahatma Gandhi, Swami Dayanand Saraswati and Sardar Vallabhbhai Patel. First on the itinerary was a visit, for the first time in my life, to Tankara, near Rajkot, the birthplace of Swami Dayanand Saraswati (1824-83). Founder of the Arya Samaj, he belongs to that unique category of towering personalities who contributed to India's freedom movement without entering politics. Addressing a huge gathering at the village, I said, 'Swamiji catalysed India's national renaissance with his powerful message to his countrymen to shed their slavish mentality and rekindle the flame of *swadesh, swabhiman* and *swabhasha* (nation, national pride and national language) through a re-discovery of Vedic knowledge. He taught India that caste discrimination was not a part of the Vedic tradition, and also that the true source of happiness is not money but honest service of society.'

I have visited Keerti Mandir, Mahatma Gandhi's ancestral house in Porbandar several times and each time I experience the presence of something pure and sacred. This is where, on 2 October 1869, one of the greatest men in human history was born. After offering prayers, I wrote in the visitors' book: 'After Partition, I came to Delhi from Sindh. That is when I once had a *darshan* of Mahatmaji. After that I kept on "seeing" him only by reading his literature. Today, upon coming to Porbandar and seeing his place of birth, I gained an altogether new inspiration.'

Karamsad, a ninety-minute drive from Baroda, is where Sardar Patel, the 'Iron Man' of India, was born in 1875. His ancestral house is modest by any standards, with none of the regality that surrounds 'Anand Bhavan' in Allahabad, where Nehru was born. But Karamsad gives an inkling of why Patel was more down-to-earth than Nehru. His greatest achievement is the firm and tactful manner in which he, as the country's first Home Minister, secured the merger of 562 princely states to the Indian Union, applying all the methods of *sama* (make friends), *bheda* (divide your enemies) and *danda* (show the stick to the recalcitrant). Many Indians, including me, believe even today that the Kashmir problem would have been solved in 1947-48, had Nehru entrusted the task to Patel.

I remember a heartening visit to Janjharaka, a small village on the way from Bhavnagar to Ahmedabad, where the *yatris* had lunch at a beautiful 'dalit temple' which, interestingly, belongs to the Nath sampradaya (Lord Krishna's tradition). Founded by a dalit social reformer, Sant Savnath, from Punjab 250 years ago, it has been endeavouring to end caste discrimination. When I saw the portraits of Dr Babasaheb Ambedkar, Gandhiji and Hindu deities displayed in the same row, I felt reassured that it is indeed possible to fight the ills in Hindu society with the help of the progressive resources within the Hindu tradition.

That was the time when Gujarat was rocked by the 'Waghela episode': an agonising chapter of the BJP's history when Shankarsinh Waghela, a senior leader of the party, had defected and joined hands with the Congress to fulfil his desire of becoming Chief Minister. In my speeches, I dwelt on the evils plaguing politics in contemporary India: factionalism, lust for power, placing one's ambitions above the interests of the organisation.

RAJASTHAN

The journey through Rajasthan was made memorable by visits to two of the inspiring symbols of Rajput pride, self-respect and valour: the forts of Chittorgarh and Kumbhalgadh. I had visited Chittorgarh before Partition when I was still a student in Karachi. It was gratifying for me to recall this in my speech before a packed crowd of over 50,000 people at Chittorgarh's Gora Badal Stadium. At Kumbhalgarh, the birthplace of Maharana Pratap (1540-97), the greatest Rajput warrior who fought against the mighty Mughal Emperor Akbar, I said, 'Maharana Pratap and his followers battled for self-pride. Today, self-pride consists in banishing hunger, fear and corruption, and making India a fully developed nation in the twenty-first century.'

We received an ecstatic reception in Kota. Tens of thousands people had lined up on both sides of the road—and those who couldn't manage a place on the streets chose rooftops for a vantage view. There was not a single street corner which did not proudly sport big portraits or tableaus of martyrs and heroes of the freedom struggle. For two hours, there was a continuous shower of rose petals and marigold flowers as the rath passed through the various streets of the city. In my thanksgiving speech, I said that Kota was the place where I worked for several years in the early 1950s as a young functionary of the Bharatiya Jana Sangh. The huge growth of the party, especially in the 1990s, had filled me with a sense of satisfaction, I added.

A particularly touching moment in Rajasthan was when, in Bhilwada, I unveiled a bust of Hemu Kalani, a young patriot who was hanged by the British in Sindh for responding to Gandhiji's call of 'Do or Die' in 1942.

A happy feature at all the public meetings and roadside receptions in Rajasthan, a state known for its social conservatism, was the large and enthusiastic presence of women. During my stint as an RSS *pracharak* and Jana Sangh activist in the late 1940s and early '50s, I had rarely seen women in public life. This silent social revolution was, to a large extent, due to the implementation of thirty-three per cent reservation for women in Panchayati Raj institutions. At several roadside receptions during the yatra, I was welcomed by women *sarpanchs*, who garlanded me and put *tilak* on my forehead. I declared here my party's support for the demand of thirty-three per cent reservation for women in Parliament and Vidhan Sabha, which elicited an enthusiastic response.

MADHYA PRADESH

The drive through the forest areas of Madhya Pradesh was not a very pleasant experience. Also, we could see the forest cover nearly stripped bare by large-scale tree-felling by corrupt politicians and contractors. Another depressing experience was the visit to Jabalpur, which had been rocked by a major earthquake a couple of weeks earlier. Over sixty persons had died and as many as 60,000 houses had been either razed to the ground or badly damaged. When I reached there, after a gruelling nineteen-hour drive, the slow and inefficient relief and rehabilitation efforts forced me to observe in anguish: 'It is as if the earthquake has rocked this place just yesterday or day before.' The only silver lining in the dark scenario was the tireless rehabilitation effort undertaken by the RSS, Bharat Seva Sangh and a few other NGOs.

Much of this depression vanished when we reached a small town called Kawardha in Rajnandgaon district for a night halt. It was 2 am but even at this unearthly hour, the entire 30,000 population of the town was out on the streets to accord an unforgettable reception to the yatra. I said to the gathered people, 'I have no words to express my feelings of gratitude. Your affection and enthusiasm have overwhelmed me. The only reason I can think of to explain this unimaginable response is that the people of India are looking at the BJP as the only ray of hope in the country's dark political scenario.' Incidentally, Dr Raman Singh was the BJP's MLA from Kawardha. He is now the Chief Minister of Chhattisgarh, a state carved out of Madhya Pradesh in 2000.

In Bhopal, I remember the rousing reception we received at the colony of Bharat Heavy Electricals Ltd. Recalling that Prime Minister Nehru had described BHEL and other pioneering developmental projects as 'Temples of Modern India', I said: 'People sometimes ask me why the BJP is so insistent on the construction of the Ram Temple in Ayodhya. I tell them that our movement for Ram Mandir is an integral part of our vision to build a magnificent resurgent Indian nation in which will be enshrined all the highest ideals of our ancient culture and civilisation. To build this New India, we must create a new work culture in our country. Each one of us must work with devotion to move the wheel of the nation's progress. If we have to work for eight hours a day, let us work for nine hours; but let us not work for seven, thereby "stealing" one hour's contribution to the nation's development.'

ORISSA

Adversaries of the BJP claim that ours is an urban-based and upper-caste party with no base among the poor and tribals. A fitting reply to them has been given by the people of Orissa and other tribal-populated regions in central and eastern India, where the BJP has, in recent years, performed exceedingly well in both parliamentary and assembly elections.

What struck me in Orissa was the deeply religious, and spontaneous way in which tribal men and women welcomed us. They would run out of their hamlets at the sight of the chariot, with their hands folded in *namaskar* and their faces lit with devotion. At every place where the rath halted, women would welcome me with *aarati* and *ulook dhwani* (a conch-like sound, produced by the mouth, which is meant to blow evil spirits away).

The term 'rath' has a deep psychological and sociological connotation for the people of Orissa because of the centrality of the annual Rath Yatra in Jagannath Puri in the collective life of the people. Hence, one of the recurring messages in my speeches was that of social harmony (*samajik samarasata*) between tribals and non-tribals of different castes, for which I invoked a popular aphorism: '*Na jaat na paat/Jagannath ka bhaat/jag pasare haath.*' (The blessings of Lord Jagannath are available to the entire humanity, irrespective of caste or creed distinctions.)

Reaching the last destination of the day around midnight had become almost a pattern. I used to worry that the long delay might affect the turnout at the concluding meeting, but that was never the case. I remember that it was well past midnight when the rath reached Sambhalpur. A massive crowd was still waiting, and greeted me with rhythmic shouts of '*Swagatam Swagatam Advaniji Swagatam*'. Here I paid tributes to Veer Surendra Sai, a proud local hero and one of the earliest freedom fighters of Orissa who was martyred in a British jail in 1884.

I should mention here that, of all the states in India that we traversed through, by far we encountered the best roads in the 200-kilometre-long stretch from Sambhalpur to Rourkela. Built and maintained by Larsen & Tourbo, it was one of the first experiments of private sector participation in road construction. Referring to this in my speech in Rourkela, I said: 'Why shouldn't we build world-class highways in our country? Why is the condition of roads in most parts of India so appalling? Why do common people have to pay bribes even to get a telephone connection or a gas connection? Why do we have such shortages in the provision of basic necessities of life in our country? I assure you that we will change this state of affairs when the BJP comes to power at the Centre.' I mention this here because, when the Vajpayee government took the reins of governance in 1998, it indeed started to build a world-class highway infrastructure, ushered in a telecom revolution, and banished shortages in the supply of LPG connections.

Travelling with me in Orissa was my colleague Sushma Swaraj. A brilliant speaker, what she said in her speeches about the BJP's prospects in Orissa is worth recalling: 'I have no words to thank you for your affectionate welcome. Before entering Orissa, a state where the BJP is not yet a dominant force, we were a little apprehensive about the kind of response the yatra would get. But the first three days have been an eye-opener. Political analysts debate whether the BJP's support base has increased in the state. Well, they do not have to go far to look for the proof. The proof has itself descended on the roads.'

WEST BENGAL

The response in West Bengal was as animated as in Kerala. Young and old, rich and poor, tribal and non-tribal, all lined up along the route to greet the chariot. I was especially struck by the piety of Bengali women who, like their counterparts in Orissa, accorded a highly religious welcome to the rath, performing *aarti* in a plate bearing rice, sandalwood paste, fruit and coconuts. I received a similar welcome in other states, too, but there was something deeply devotional in the way women in West Bengal and Orissa related to the Swarna Jayanti Rath Yatra. It was a sight reminiscent of my experience all over the country at the time of the Ram Rath Yatra.

At a village near Gopiballabhpur, I saw a young woman, standing alone and carrying a huge garland. I asked the rath to stop in order to enable her to come and greet me. She was a tribal (Santhal) woman, appropriately named Kusum (which means flower), who had brought a garland of 108 lotuses. I asked her why she had done that and her reply in Bengali was, 'It is for the Ayodhya Baba.'

I travelled through West Bengal for five days, covering 1,340 kilometres. It was apparent that a good part of the reason behind the enthusiastic reception to the yatra was the people's hunger for change. They wanted to get rid of the twenty-year-old communist rule, which had pushed Bengal, once reputed for its pioneering role in India's industrialisation, into the category of backward states.

Subsequently, I also visited Shantiniketan and paid tribute to Rabindranath Tagore. On 23 June, I participated in a special meeting in Calcutta to mark the martyrdom day of Dr Syama Prasad Mookerjee, the founder of the Bharatiya Jana Sangh. Referring to the fact that Dr Mookerjee was a great educationist who had become, at the age of thirty-three, the youngest Vice Chancellor of Calcutta University, I said, 'Expansion and improvement of education, both at primary and higher levels, should become our priority for transforming India from a developing nation into a developed nation.' In all my speeches, I invoked Bengal's incomparable contribution to India's freedom movement—the enduring message of social reformers and philosophers like Ramakrishna Paramahamsa, Swami Vivekananda and Maharshi Aurobindo, the eternal appeal of *Vande Mataram* by Bankim Chandra Chatterjee, the soaring patriotism of Netaji Subas Chandra Bose, and the inspiring martyrdom of Khudiram Bose.

I contrasted this nationalist tradition with the Communists' continuous saga of betrayals before and after Independence: the betrayal of national freedom in 1942 when the Communists opposed the Quit India movement; betrayal of national unity in 1947, when they supported the Muslim League's demand of Pakistan under the pretext of 'self determination' by Muslims; betrayal of national security in 1962 when they supported the Chinese aggression on India; betrayal of democracy in 1975, when the CPI actively supported Indira Gandhi's Emergency Rule and the CPI(M) resisted it weakly; and betrayal of the people's mandate in 1996-97, when they had been actively helping the Congress to come back to power through the backdoor, in spite of it being rejected by the electorate in the elections to the 11th Lok Sabha.

Pointing to the collapse of communist regimes worldwide, I said that the Indian Marxists' refusal to introspect had prompted them to forever search for a demonology for self-sustenance. 'The Communists have now invented a new demon: BJP. Indeed, both the communists and the

Congress have become allies in the politics of anti-BJPism. I am confident that the people of Bengal will see through this game. India's march to becoming a great nation will not gain momentum unless Bengal returns to its nationalistic roots.'

BIHAR

Bihar had become a by-word for *kushasan* or malgovernance during the fifteen-year rule (1990-2005) of Laloo Prasad Yadav's RJD. Naturally, the yatra's message of good governance struck a chord with the people. The rallies and road side receptions along the 1,300-kilometre-long route, stretching from Purnea on the Bengal border to Buxar on the UP border, were attended by tens of thousands of people. Their slogan '*Bhrashtachari, Gaddi Chhodo*' (The corrupt must quit the Government) was an eloquent statement on the state of affairs in Bihar.

Two things were notable about my journey in Bihar: the abysmal quality of roads (which was matched only by the roads in communist-ruled West Bengal) and virtually no power at night in most parts of the state. Only the stage, from where I addressed the meetings, would be lit up with the help of a generator, but I could hardly see the people. Their presence was felt only through their full-throated slogan shouting!

I was fortunate to visit Jagdishpur, the birthplace of Veer Kunwar Singh, the state's leading light in India's First War of Independence. What shocked me was that Kunwar Singh's ancestral house was in a state of utter neglect. Part of it had been converted into a cattleshed. No less distressing was my experience when, on the outskirts of Sasaram, I went to pay homage to Shaheed Nishan Singh Vaddi, an associate of Veer Kunwar Singh. The British had captured Nishan Singh, placed him at the mouth of a canon and blown him up. In his memory, a library called Nishan Niketan Vachanalaya was set up. But when I went there, I could not see a single cupboard in the library! And its three employees had not been paid their salaries for several months.

I remember my visit to a small town called Obara, on the outskirts of Aurangabad, where thousands of people had gathered, despite rains, to watch me pay a floral tribute at a martyr's memorial. It was erected in the memory of Jagpati Kumar, a local youth who, along with six of his fellow-patriots, was gunned down by the British police on 11 August 1942 while trying to hoist the national flag at the Legislative Assembly in Patna. In my speech on the occasion, I urged the audience to ponder over this question: 'Did all our sung and unsung heroes of the freedom struggle want the British rule to go only to see the misrule of the kind we see in your state? Why has Bihar, which was one of the better administered states in the country until the early 1960s, become the poorest and the worst-ruled state today? I see three reasons for this degeneration: Corruption, Criminalisation and Casteism. What is especially tragic is that Bihar is being ruled by those who were the products of the JP Movement, which was the most powerful anti-corruption movement that India has seen since 1947. Let us rid Bihar of these three chronic diseases, and make it healthy and prosperous, worthy of its glorious past.'

Travelling through the tribal-populated areas of the state I praised the inspiring role of Birsa Munda, a legendary tribal revolutionary, in the anti-colonial struggle. While in Bihar, I also paid tributes to the two other great sons of the state in the modern era: Rajendra Prasad and Jayaprakash Narayan.

As in Andhra Pradesh, naxal groups had threatened to attack the yatra in Bihar. But my message in the naxalite-dominated areas of Bihar was the same: 'Ballot, and not bullet, is the answer to the ills of our society. Nowhere in the world has the politics of bullet solved any problem. Therefore, let us strengthen the democratic system in our country and together solve the problems before us.'

UTTAR PRADESH

On the night of 1 July, the yatra entered UP from Bihar in the border district of Ballia, home to Mangal Pandey, the first martyr of 1857. A sepoy in the Bengal Native Infantry of the East India Company, he had called upon his fellow soldiers, both Hindus and Muslims, to rebel against the *angrez*, who came to India as traders but became its rulers. I felt ennobled by setting foot on a land that was the main battlefield in 1857, a land made sacred by the sacrifices of Mangal Pandey, Rani Laxmi of Jhansi, Chandrashekhar Azad and countless others.

I said in my speeches that the freedom movement in UP, as in other states of India, saw people belonging to different ideological backgrounds working together for a common goal. This diversity was also evident in the Congress party itself. It brought Pandit Nehru, Maulana Abul Kalam Azad, Pandit Madan Mohan Malaviya, Purushottamdas Tandon and Dr Ram Manohar Lohia on a common platform. A true way of remembering them during the Swarna Jayanti year, I said, was for all political parties to dedicate themselves to certain common national goals.

One of the biggest meetings in my yatra took place in Shahjahanpur. This town in central UP is associated with the everlasting memory of three martyrs of the freedom struggle—Ramprasad 'Bismil', Ashfaqulla Khan and Thakur Roshan Singh. They were convicted by the British in the Kakori Conspiracy Case.* As I garlanded the busts of these three young revolutionaries in a small street corner park, the sky reverberated with the slogan '*Amar Shaheedon ka balidan, Yaad rakhega Hindustan*'.

The trio truly set an unforgettable example in patriotic valour. Ramprasad 'Bismil' was both a poet and a revolutionary activist. On 19 August 1927, when he was only thirty, he was hanged in Gorakhpur jail. His body perished, but his poetry continues to inspire millions of people even today: *Sarfaroshi ki tamanna ab hamare dil mein hai; Dekhana hai zor kitna bazu-e-kaatil mein hai.* (There is one supreme longing in our hearts – the longing to sacrifice ourselves. We wish to see how mighty the hands of the executioner are.) Four months later, his poet-friend and fellow-revolutionary, Ashfaqulla Khan was hanged in Faizabad jail. His last act was to kiss the noose and proclaim: 'For many years my mother was after me to get married. I was refusing, saying I hadn't found the right bride. Today, mother, you should be happy that I have found the bride of my choice!' He then took the noose around his neck, and uttering the

---

* The Kakori Conspiracy Case, one of the several cases instituted by the British government against Indian revolutionaries, was used to incriminate twenty-nine patriots in a false case of train robbery at Kakori (near Lucknow) on 9 August 1925.

name of God breathed his last. On the same day that Ashfaqulla Khan climbed the gallows, the third son of Shahjahanpur, Roshan Singh, was hanged in Naini jail. Holding a copy of the *Gita* in his hands, he uttered his last words: 'Vande Mataram'!

When the rath reached Ayodhya on 3 July, I exclaimed that it was the most important day during my yatra! I saw an intrinsic link between my two journeys, which I expounded in my speech at a public meeting held on the recently beautified embankment of Saryu river: 'My yatra in 1990 was aimed at the construction of a magnificent Ram Mandir. This yatra in 1997 aims at mobilising the people for the construction of an equally magnificent Rashtra Mandir. To make this happen, we have to channelise our *Ram Bhakti* (power of devotion) into *Rashtra Shakti* (power of the nation).'

After the public meeting, I went to offer prayers at the make-shift Ram Temple at Janmabhoomi, accompanied by Kalyan Singh, a hero of the Ayodhya movement, other party colleagues and members of my family, which evoked mixed feelings. On the one hand, I was happy that the makeshift temple stood at the birthplace of Lord Ram as a testimony to the partial success of the Ayodhya movement. On the other hand, I was distressed to see that the entire temple complex, now under the control of the Central Government, was heavily barricaded with security forces. I could not help voicing my anguish: 'The construction of the planned magnificent temple for Shri Ram will, of course, take time. But what is the rationale for keeping the make-shift temple under such barricaded conditions?' I added, 'The mandir already exists at Janmabhoomi and devotees go there to take *darshan* of Ram Lalla. No power on earth can reverse this situation now. But they will not be happy until the barricades are removed and a suitable temple is erected there.'

The second memorable moment was on the night of 3 July, when Atalji welcomed the yatra as it entered Lucknow, his parliamentary constituency. It was an emotional moment for me as I embraced my longtime colleague and leader. We travelled together on the rath to reach Begum Hazrat Mahal Park, where we addressed a large rally. Lucknow had recently been rocked by a violent Shia-Sunni conflict; several parts of the city were still under curfew. Both Atalji and I appealed to the people belonging to the two Muslim sects to resolve the dispute amicably through mutual negotiations. After the meeting was over, UP's Chief Minister Mayawati, who then headed a BJP-BSP coalition, came to the state guest house, where I had a night-halt, to extend a welcome to me.

My six days of travel in the state gave me an unprecedented opportunity for mass contact. I was especially gratified by the stupendous response to my first such campaign in Uttar Pradesh, since the Ram Rath Yatra had been stopped in Bihar before it reached Ayodhya. A major achievement of the 1997 yatra in UP was that, with the Congress party having lost both its base and relevance in the state's politics, the BJP emerged as the true inheritor of UP's proud nationalist legacy.

HIMACHAL PRADESH

Travelling by the winding roads of Himachal Pradesh, the beautiful state in the lower reaches of the Himalayas, is a feast for the eyes. We received a heartening welcome at every town and hamlet along the road from Parwanoo to Shimla. At most of these places, local party workers arranged for me to felicitate surviving freedom fighters, war heroes and even war widows. Along the way, Dr Shanta Kumar, the former Chief Minister of Himachal Pradesh who was travelling with me, suggested that I pay homage to Yashpal, the great Hindi novelist and a comrade-in-arms of Shaheed Bhagat Singh, at his native village Bhoompal in Hamirpur district. Shanta Kumar, himself a reputed Hindi writer, knew Yashpal well and has erected a fitting memorial to him in his ancestral village.

JAMMU & KASHMIR

As the rath crossed the Punjab border to enter Jammu & Kashmir at the Ravi river near Lakhanpur, emotions surged within me as it was here in 1953 that Dr Syama Prasad Mookerjee was arrested by the government of Sheikh Abdullah for entering J&K without a prior permit. In 1997, the Gujral government was making conciliatory gestures to militant groups in the Kashmir Valley. There was even talk of restoring the pre-1953 status to J&K. Addressing a large meeting at Lakhanpur, I flayed this move and said, 'This would mean reversing the clock of history. It would mean dishonouring Dr Mookerjee's martyrdom in Srinagar. What the nation needs is complete integration of J&K with India by abolishing Article 370 of the Constitution.'

Before proceeding to Jammu, the yatra halted at Hiranagar where I paid homage to two martyrs of the Jana Sangh's 1953 Kashmir satyagraha: Vihari Lal and Bhikham Singh, who were shot dead while trying to hoist the Indian flag on Indian soil!

PUNJAB

Every state in India has made its own contribution to the glorious struggle for India's freedom. But when my yatra reached Punjab, I could sense that it was now in a land that is synonymous with sacrifice. An overwhelming majority of the martyrs of the freedom struggle came from Punjab. Of the 2,646 patriots of 1857 who were banished to Kala Pani, 2,147 were from Punjab. In recent times, Punjab is where both Sikhs and Hindus showed exemplary unity, against the gravest of provocations, to break the back of Pak-sponsored Khalistani separatist movement.

As we crossed the Ravi river and entered Madhopur from Jammu on 11 July, we were received by a large contingent of BJP and Akali leaders. The two slogans raised on the occasion—*Jo bole so nihaal, Sat Shri Akal* and *Jai Shri Ram*—were an eloquent testimony to the deeper social significance of the BJP-Akali alliance in the state. Prakash Singh Badal, the state's popular Chief Minister, travelled with me as a *saha-yatri* almost for the entire stretch of the journey in Punjab. In every town along the way, the rath was greeted by a long human chain of Sikhs and Hindus waving cheerily and shouting, *Hindu Sikh ekta zindabad* and *Punjabi bhaichara amar rahe*.

'I feel a sense of *pavitrata* upon reaching the land of Punjab.... If anyone wishes to see a concrete manifestation of Hindu-Sikh unity, it is available here in the form of the joint commemoration of the Swarna

Jayanti year by the BJP and Akali Dal,' I said in one of my speeches. On his part, Badal said, 'I have no words to express my feelings of gratitude towards Shri Advaniji. By taking out the Swarna Jayanti Rath Yatra to commemorate the fiftieth anniversary of our Independence, he has truly awakened the soul of the nation.'

Khalistani terrorism had not fully disappeared from Punjab at the time. Only a week earlier, a bomb blast in a train near Bhatinda had killed thirty passengers. In another incident, a powerful bomb had been found in a Hindu temple. Referring to these incidents, Badal said, 'I want to speak something openly today. Who's behind these conspiracies? Such acts cannot be committed by ordinary criminals. Only those who are enemies of the nation, and who are supported by enemies of our nation across the border, can indulge in them.' In Amritsar I visited two centres of pilgrimage—one spiritual and the other patriotic, and both in close vicinity of each other. I went to the Golden Temple to offer prayers at Harmandir Sahib and then to Jallianwala Bagh to pay homage to the nearly 1,500 persons martyred on 13 April 1919, the worst instance of colonial carnage during the British rule in India. What gave me special satisfaction was the fact that, during my yatra, I was able to visit three of the holiest Sikh shrines—at Nanded in Maharashtra, Patna in Bihar and now Amritsar.

I visited village Dhudike in Moga district, where Lala Lajpat Rai (1865–1928), the 'Lion of Punjab', was born. He became a martyr in Lahore, where he received fatal lathi blows while leading a protest march against the Simon Commission. Before breathing his last, he said, 'Every blow aimed at me is a nail in the coffin of British imperialism.' In the visitors' book kept at the memorial, I wrote: 'The twentieth century is drawing to a close. The first two decades of this century were, insofar as India is concerned, dominated by the popular Trio of Lal-Bal-Pal. The first amongst them was the fearless patriot Lala Lajpat Rai who fell a martyr to British lathis, but who in the process touched off the doom of the British empire. I feel privileged to visit this hallowed birthplace of this great soul.'

On the same day, my yatra visited Huseiniwala in Firozepur district, which is only a few dozen yards away from the Indo-Pak border. Located here are the shrines of the three immortal martyrs of the freedom movement—Bhagat Singh, Sukhdev and Rajguru, who were convicted by the British in the Lahore Conspiracy Case. After being hanged in Lahore Central Jail on 21 March 1931, their bodies were brought to the nearby Huseiniwala village and cremated there in the dead of night. As I stood in silence there, I thought to myself that we should never forget the supreme sacrifice of these young revolutionaries who embraced death so willingly!

HARYANA

Haryana was the penultimate destination of the yatra before it culminated in Delhi. The visit to two places in the state are etched in my mind. The first was Kurukshetra, the battlefield of the Mahabharata. After visiting several sacred sites in this temple town, I said in my speech before a large gathering: 'The very utterance of the name "Kurukshetra" creates an experience of the sacred. This is where Lord Krishna gave Arjuna the eternal message about the victory of *dharma* (truth) over *adharma* (falsehood). Today, on the occasion of the golden jubilee of India's independence, all of us—the political class as well as the people—should internalise this message of the Mahabharata.'

The second place was Bahadurgadh, where thousands of farmers had gathered to bid farewell to the yatra. It is named after Bahadur Shah Zafar, the last king of the Mughal empire and the first ruler of 'free India', during the brief period in 1857 when Delhi was liberated from the British rule. A famous slogan of the patriotic warriors in 1857, as they marched towards the city to liberate it, was: '*Dilli ab door nahin!*' I referred to it in my speech and remarked that, as far as the BJP's march towards power at the Centre was concerned: '*Nayi Dilli ab door nahin!*' Our party has already established its government in Delhi. Whenever the parliamentary elections are held, the BJP will complete its journey from Delhi to New Delhi.

DELHI

The Swarna Jayanti Rath Yatra entered Delhi on 15 July, exactly a month before India celebrated the golden jubilee of its Independence. As my journey came to a close at the historic Red Fort, after being joyously greeted at every street along the way, I had the satisfaction of having made my own small but meaningful contribution to its commemoration. The grand finale of the campaign was marked by a rally at Chandni Chowk, where all that was left for me to say was a sincere 'Thank You' to all those who had contributed to making it successful and unforgettable.

'AIR-CONDITIONED COMFORT'?

A few days before the start of the yatra, one of the national English dailies carried a news report with a headline that read: 'Advani's fiery rhetoric from air-conditioned comfort'. A few days after the journey had commenced, journalists who accompanied me even on short stretches of the journey started asking me how I suffered such a torture day after day. The cabin inside the vehicle had a bed to lie down, but it was anything but comfortable to take a nap on because of the bumpy ride. In any case, for most parts of the journey, I was present in the front enclosure of the rath so that people could see me. The yatra rarely concluded its final meeting of the day before midnight. In fact, on 23 June, I reached Calcutta so late that I addressed a meeting at 3.30 am. In spite of the delay the previous night, the following day's schedule almost never changed: press conference at 8.30 am and departure at 9 or 9.30 am. In Kerala, where the road from north to south has a continuous stretch of human habitation on both sides, and where there was an endless series of road side receptions, I had to remain standing for three days in row. At the end of it, I developed a swelling on my feet, which the doctors described as 'standing oedema'!

To the frequently asked question by journalists as to how I didn't feel tired travelling on the road for so many days and addressing so many meetings from morning till midnight I said: 'By God's grace, I happen to suffer from good health even at the age of seventy. Yes, I do sometimes feel tired when I read in some newspapers the next morning that the Yatra has received "lukewarm' response"!'

I would relate to journalists travelling with me a saying by the great poet Kalidas, whose truth I repeatedly experienced during my yatra—*Kleshah phalena hi punarnavatana vidhatte* (Whatever be the afflictions of the body, they disappear and the body renews itself when the task it has undertaken bears the desired fruit). This was told to me by my colleague Prof Vishnukant Shastri*, a man of great learning, who travelled with me for a good part of the yatra.

This yatra, as also my other yatras and election-time campaigns, convinced me yet again about the importance of good health and stamina for political activists. The life of physical hardship that I had endured during my ten years as a RSS *pracharak* in Rajasthan, soon after I had turned twenty, has stood me in good stead. Therefore, my advice to youngsters in politics is: 'Take good care of your health.'

THE YATRA'S NON-PARTISAN MESSAGE

I can quite easily submit that the Swarna Jayanti Rath Yatra has been one of the few political campaigns since 1947 to present the legacy of the freedom movement in a non-partisan and *undivided* manner. I repeatedly stressed in my speeches that India's freedom struggle was a confluence of diverse ideologies and strategies. There were men and women who followed Gandhiji's path of non-violent satyagraha, and this indeed was the dominant stream in the movement. But there were also others, like Bhagat Singh and Netaji Bose, who took the path of armed resistance and military mobilisation. There were sages like Maharshi Aurobindo, who left the path of revolutionary activity altogether and followed the path of national reawakening through spiritualism. And then there were persons like Dr Keshav Baliram Hedgewar who, after having worked in leadership positions in the Congress party, decided to channelise the

---

* Prof Vishnukant Shastri (1929-2005) was Vice President of the BJP and Governor of Uttar Pradesh. He was widely respected for his scholarship in both Hindi and Bengali.

patriotic energies of young people by forming a non-political organisation called the Rashtriya Swayamsevak Sangh.

In spite of the differences in their ideologies and strategies, I said, they were all united by their common commitment to the cause of India's liberation and subsequent nation-building. I urged the people to salute the memory of all the great leaders of the freedom movement, without exception and irrespective of their divergent backgrounds. In my speeches and statements during the yatra, I paid fulsome tributes even to leaders of the Congress and the Communist parties for their contribution to the national cause. These included Pandit Nehru, Kamaraj, Gopabhandhu Das, T. Prakasam, Y.B. Chavan, Vasantdada Patil, S. Nijalingappa, Veerendra Patil, A.K. Gopalan, and Pramode Das Gupta. Inspite of the BJP's ideological differences with some of them, I have always held that, what truly matters is their idealism and their service to the nation. The yatra helped revive memories of a large number of little-known and rarely-honoured local-level martyrs and heroes. At 279 places, activists of the Bharatiya Janata Yuva Morcha, the youth wing of the party, brought urns carrying sacred soil from the birthplaces of martyrs of the freedom struggle. Activists of the BJP Mahila Morcha planted 50,000 saplings at different places. Equally importantly, it provided an opportunity to felicitate over 800 surviving freedom fighters in different parts of the country.

NEED TO CHANGE THE IMAGE OF THE 'UGLY INDIAN POLITICIAN':

I have always believed that the popular perception that all politicians are corrupt is not only untrue, but, if unchecked, it can pose a grave threat to our democratic system. There are upright politicians in all political parties, more in some and less in others. As a political activist myself, I have deeply felt the need to change the image of the ugly Indian politician. The yatra, therefore, was an occasion for me to articulate my thoughts on the subject. I emphasised that self-correction must begin in every political party. 'Corruption flows from top to bottom, not from bottom to top,' I would say in my meetings. 'In this regard, the blame must rest on the entire political system, and, to some extent, I do not exclude my own party from it. Politics during the freedom movement was a mission.

In many advanced democracies, politics is a profession, like many other professions, and it requires a professional grounding. Sadly, for many people in India today, politics has become pure commerce. This situation must be changed. If we want Good Governance, we must ensure that honest and competent people dominate the country's politics.'

THE ROLE OF CITIZENS AND THEIR RESPONSIBILITIES

As I have stated before, the yatra was a campaign to boost the BJP's political appeal among the people. In all my meetings, I called for a political transformation in the country in the form of a clear mandate for Atal Bihari Vajpayee as India's next Prime Minister. At the same time, I underscored the need for social transformation. 'I do not wish to create any illusion among the people that a mere change in leadership—necessary though it is—will make India a great nation. During the past five decades, and especially after the mid-sixties, corruption has spread to each and every sphere of our social life.... I can give [sic.] many examples—of government servants who don't work for eight honest hours, doctors who fleece their patients through unnecessary tests and medication, teachers who don't teach in schools but ask their students to join private tuition classes, and policemen who intimidate the poor and the helpless to make money on the side.'

Bemoaning the alarming degradation in the ethical values of our society, I said, 'Steadily, both the rulers and the ruled came to believe that patriotism and discipline, which may have had their use during the freedom movement, are not needed anymore. In the absence of these uplifting values, the vacuum has been filled by selfishness, dishonesty, and corruption in the daily lives of all of us. This decay cannot be cured by either legislation or governmental action. We cannot build India of the dreams of our martyrs and freedom fighters unless this degradation is arrested. And in this, each one of us has a duty to perform.'

In order to further drive home the role and responsibility of citizens themselves, I administered a 3-Point Swarna Jayanti Pledge to millions of people during the yatra:

On the occasion of the Swarna Jayanti of India's Independence, I resolve that:

1. I shall neither take nor give bribes.
2. In whatever profession I am engaged in, I shall work with honesty, dedication and discipline. In the spirit of a New Work Culture, I shall always give priority to my patriotic duty over my narrow self-interest.
3. In whatever decisions I take in my life, I shall not discriminate on the basis of caste or creed but, instead, be guided solely by rational considerations and interests of my Motherland.

APPEAL TO INDIAN MUSLIMS

Predictably, adversaries of the BJP tried to paint the yatra as yet another campaign to 'spread communal venom' and disturb peace in the country. In doing so, they repeated their old lies about the Ram Rath Yatra of 1990. Their attempt, clearly, was to alienate Muslims from the event. In reality, the yatra left a positive impact on our Muslim brethren. All those who attended my meetings could see that there was nothing 'communal' or 'anti-Muslim' in the yatra's message. I would tell them to beware of our adversaries' propaganda against the BJP. 'Before 1947, the Muslim League used to call the Congress a Hindu party that suppressed Muslim interests. Today the Congress is saying the same thing about the BJP.'

In Bhopal, I issued an appeal titled 'The BJP urges Indian Muslims to understand Cultural Nationalism and forge heart-unity with their Hindu brethren'. It stated:

> One of the important factors which influenced the course of the freedom movement, and also the complexion of the polity after independence, was the divisive role played by the dominant religio-political leadership of the Muslim community. Before independence, the fanatical and uncompromising espousal of the two-nation theory by the Muslim League, which sought to keep the Muslim community away from the mainstream national movement, resulted in the tragic Partition of India. After independence,

influential sections of the Muslim leadership, encouraged by the pseudo-secular practices of the Congress and other parties, have continued to obstruct the community's all-sided integration with the national life. This has created multifarious problems impeding the progress and well-being of both the Muslim community and the nation at large.

Our adversaries' vote-bank propaganda about the BJP has often affected my party in the electoral arena. But the Muslim community itself has been the real loser in every sense of the term—politically, economically, socially, educationally and, most important, in terms of earning the goodwill of the majority community.... The BJP believes in genuine secularism, which means justice and security for all, but appeasement of none. We are interested in, and will sincerely strive for, a qualitative change in the relationship that now obtains between our Party and Indian Muslims. The very thought of excluding such a large section of Indian population from our universe of concerns is repugnant to us.

The statement carried a four-point appeal to Indian Muslims:
(1) Let there be no remnant of the Two-Nation theory in the mindset of any section of Indian Muslims. ('I appeal to Muslim theologians and intellectuals to proclaim that they have stopped considering Hindus as *kafirs*.') (2) Bury vote-bank politics to make democracy healthier. (3) Understand Cultural Nationalism. ('This does not in any way erase the identity of Islam. For my Party not only respects but celebrates the multi-religious, multi-lingual and multi-ethnic diversity of Indian society, which is united at its core by Hindutva.') (4) Let us concentrate on educational development and economic elevation of poor Muslims.

❋

As I look back at the two months that I was on the road, traversing the length and breadth of India, and honouring the sacred memory of hundreds of martyrs and heroes of our freedom struggle, I feel gratified that the yatra truly lived up to its description: A Patriotic Pilgrimage.

'India has limitless potential for progress, and is blessed with rich resources, both human and natural, to realise that potential. Above all, we have an invaluable spiritual and civilisational heritage to guide us. Using our resources properly, employing the power of modern science and technology, and being guided by our heritage, we can indeed create a Strong, Prosperous and Enlightened India. May India become more united and emerge taller, with its Tomorrow far better and brighter than its Today for all my billion-plus compatriots.'

Phase Five

1

THE BEGINNING OF A NEW ERA

The spiritual genius of our race has always recognised the fundamental Unity that underlies all forms and classes of diversities and differences.

—BIPIN CHANDRA PAL

The BJP's Swarna Jayanti Rath Yatra in May-July 1997 was, in many ways, a prelude to the mid-term parliamentary elections, looming large on the political horizon. A month before the yatra, I had told my colleagues in my presidential remarks at a meeting of the BJP National Executive in New Delhi: 'Let us begin in right earnest, our internal preparations as well as our work among the people for the mid-term polls to the Lok Sabha which may take place any time hereafter. I say this because the recent political developments (resulting in the fall of Deve Gowda's government and installation of I.K. Gujral's) are not of an ordinary or routine nature. Suddenly, a falsehood has come crashing down. Suddenly, a monumental lie is lying exposed in the precincts of power, frantically and desperately trying to cover itself up in tatters that cannot hide the shame, no matter which expert clothier takes upon himself to stitch together a new ruling coalition.'

The claim of unity of the self-styled 'anti-communal' forces was a myth. Even though the Congress had been squarely defeated in the 1996 Lok Sabha elections, and the BJP had emerged as the single largest party in the 11th Lok Sabha, our adversaries had justified keeping our party out of power on the grounds that India had to be saved from the threat of 'fascism and national disintegration'. And upon this foundation of trickery was hurriedly built the shaky superstructure of the United Front (UF) government, propped up in power by the very party, Congress, which had been rejected by the people at the hustings. Barren anti-BJPism and a desperate desire to cling to ministerial chairs were the only ingredients of the glue that held the United Front, as also the UF and the Congress together. But such formations with no real grounding in principles have to, sooner or later, give way. And it did, when the Congress played spoilsport to two Prime Ministers in quick succession. This made it clear beyond a shadow of doubt that the real concern of our adversaries was not secularism, but lust for power. They wanted power even when they had been blatantly rejected by the people.

The chaos and stasis in the governing setup at the national level opened unprecedented frontiers for the BJP. For the first time since the founding of the party seventeen years ago, I felt hopeful, indeed confident, that we would be able to form a stable government at the Centre. There was a basis to my optimism. In a democracy, a political party that aspires to come to power must first establish its rule in the hearts and minds of the majority of the people. The BJP definitely measured up to this yardstick. Therefore, my message to the party's National Executive was clear and action-oriented: 'Let us get ready for governance. The famous French writer Victor Hugo once said, "Greater than the tread of mighty armies is an idea whose time has come." Similarly, BJP as the party of governance at the Centre is an idea whose time has indeed come!'

THE YEAR 1998: A WATERSHED PARLIAMENTARY ELECTION

With the Congress party withdrawing support from the Gujral government in November 1997, President K.R. Narayanan had only one option before him: dissolve the Lok Sabha and call for fresh elections, which were subsequently announced for February-March 1998. The BJP sought a mandate from the people with a simple slogan, which stood out for its positive content and direct appeal: Vote for a 'stable government' under an 'able Prime Minister'. Our manifesto for the 1998 Lok Sabha elections stated: 'In Shri Atal Bihari Vajpayee, the people see a leader who combines ability with integrity, charisma with character and experience with universal acceptability. He is not a person who claims leadership by birth in, or relationship with, any dynasty. He is a leader by virtue of his long and dedicated service to the nation and its people in and out of Parliament.'

As soon as I hit the campaign trail, I realised that this election would be a watershed in the history of the Indian Republic. I could see tremendous enthusiasm for the BJP in almost all parts of the country, including states such as Tamil Nadu and West Bengal, where we had never won a Lok Sabha seat. Atalji's charisma was palpable among all sections of society. The people were eager to elect, for the first time ever, a completely non-Congress government under a non-Congress leader. It did not take much to predict which party would emerge as the frontrunner to form the government. The pollsters' task, therefore, was limited to projecting the BJP's tally.

The actual results, when they started pouring in, showed that the BJP had literally redrawn the political map of India, having significantly improved its 1996 performance (161 seats) by winning 182 out of the 384 seats that it contested. In contrast, the Congress, contesting from a much greater number of seats, 462, managed to win only 141—as against 140 that it had won in 1996. The strength of the United Front too came down from 183 to 86. A closer look at the results revealed many notable advances for the BJP, and sharp reverses for the Congress. Firstly, this was an election in which Sonia Gandhi campaigned extensively for her party. Secondly, the Congress' vote share came down to 25.72 per cent—a fall of 14 per cent since 1989, the last time it formed the government at the Centre. The BJP's vote share, 25.38 per cent, almost equalled that of the Congress but, no less important, it had risen by 14 per cent since 1989. Thirdly, the BJP could boast of representatives in the Lok Sabha from more states and union territories than the Congress.

Both Atalji and I won comfortably from our traditional constituencies of Lucknow and Gandhinagar respectively. What was particularly gratifying to me was that the BJP had succeeded in expanding its social and geographical base. For the first time since 1952, the BJP had representation from Tamil Nadu, West Bengal and Assam. In UP, our success was staggering: we won fifty-seven out of eighty-five seats. Another interesting feature was that in the new Parliament, the BJP had the highest number of women MPs, (sixteen, as against ten belonging to the Congress), as well as the largest number of MPs belonging to the Scheduled Castes (twenty-four) and Scheduled Tribes (fourteen). In short, the goal of becoming an alternative to the Congress, which we had set for ourselves at the founding conference of the BJP in 1980, had finally been realised in 1998.

THE COIMBATORE BOMB BLASTS: HOW A TV INTERVIEW SAVED ME!

In the second week of February 1998, I was in South India to campaign for my party's candidates. After a whirlwind tour, I reached Chennai on 13 February. After a night-halt, I was scheduled to leave the next morning for Coimbatore, renowned for its textile and engineering industries, to address an election rally in support of C.P. Radhakrishnan, a popular local leader and the BJP's candidate from the constituency.

I was to leave for the airport at 8.30 am, where my party colleagues had arranged a small chartered plane to take me to Coimbatore since there was no commercial flight available for me to return to Chennai immediately after the rally and proceed to my next destination. Just then, Deepak Chopra, my longtime Private Secretary, came to me and said, 'There is a request for a television interview.' I said it would be difficult as time was short. But he said that he had rescheduled my departure from Chennai and ensured that the day's programme would remain unaffected, adding that the request came from ETV who wanted to air a comprehensive interview on the eve of the elections. He said it would be useful if I gave the interview since ETV, promoted by *Eenadu*, Andhra Pradesh's preeminent newspaper, had in a very short time become the most popular Telugu channel. I agreed. The delay in our departure from Chennai by a couple of hours due to the interview turned out to be providential.

When our plane landed in Coimbatore, after a forty-minute flight, I found something amiss in the atmosphere at the airport. Usually, at small airports, the first thing I see is a large posse of flag-carrying and slogan-shouting party workers. This time there was an eerie silence. A police officer, accompanied by a few local party leaders, met me at the tarmac and said, 'Advaniji, I am sorry to inform you that bomb blasts have rocked the city, including near the podium at the venue of your election meeting. Many people have been killed.'

I was stunned by the news. I spoke to my party colleagues to get more information about the unfortunate incident. They said that they had come straight from the venue and had seen many people dead or injured. 'It happened at the time scheduled for your arrival at the meeting place. It is very lucky that your flight got delayed.' The police officer added, 'Sir, there is panic and tension in the city. I regretfully have to request you to return to Chennai from the airport itself.' I told him that I would not do so as many of those killed had come to attend my election rally. It was my duty to offer condolences to the dead and help the injured. Coimbatore, which was under curfew by then, wore a funereal look with as many as fifty-eight dead. The scene at the government hospital was heart-rending. I told journalists that those behind this worst act of terrorism in South India were enemies of the nation and must be brought to justice as soon as possible.

The wheels of justice took nine years to pronounce that the blasts, whose aim, as stated by the Tamil Nadu's Special Investigation Team, was 'to eliminate Mr L.K. Advani', were the handiwork of an Islamist outfit called Al Ummah. In August 2007, a special court in Coimbatore convicted A. Basha, the founder of the organisation, and thirty-five of his colleagues for their involvement in the terrorist act, which was codenamed 'Operation Allahu-Akbar'. However, it acquitted the prime accused in the case, Abdul Nasser Mahdani, President of the People's Democratic Party in neighbouring Kerala, since the investigating agency failed to substantiate any charge against him. In 1991, he founded the Islamic Swayamsevak

Sangh (ISS) and was consequently implicated in many cases because of his incendiary speeches against the Hindus, in general and the RSS-BJP combine, in particular.

During the eight years that Mahdani spent in jail for his suspected role in the terrorist incident in Coimbatore, both the Congress and the communist parties in Kerala vied with each other to seek his release. His pronouncements after he was freed lacked the fiery rhetoric of the past. 'If there is anything I have learnt from all those years in jail, it is that humanity is more important than everything,' he said in a recent newspaper interview, while adding, 'I never meant to attack the Hindus, their customs or their gods, only the RSS and the likes of L.K. Advani'.[1]

Whether full justice has been done to the victims of the terrorist act in Coimbatore is for the moral conscience of the rulers in Tamil Nadu to answer. As far as I am concerned, whenever I have referred to the Coimbatore blasts in my subsequent speeches, I have said, 'I am standing in front of you because of that ETV journalist. Had he not delayed my departure from Chennai on the morning of 14 February 1998, I do not know what would have happened to me.'

THE NDA IS FORMED, ATALJI IS SWORN IN AS PRIME MINISTER

Since a BJP-led government at the Centre seemed a certainty, a large number of parties expressed their willingness to extend their support. At this stage, my party took a major strategic decision. We decided to form a post-poll alliance based on a common minimum programme acceptable to all the constituent parties. The process of alliance formation was smoothened once we made it known that the CMP, which came to be known as the National Agenda for Governance (NAG), would not include three commitments that were a part of the BJP's election manifesto for the 1998 elections—construction of a temple at Ramjanmabhoomi in Ayodhya; enactment of a uniform civil code; and repeal of Article 370 of the Constitution which gave a special status to Jammu & Kashmir. While all other allies agreed to join the government, one of them, the TDP in Andhra Pradesh, headed by its Chief Minister N. Chandrababu Naidu, declared that it would support the Vajpayee government from outside.

There was much bonhomie when leaders of all the alliance parties assembled at Atalji's residence on Safdarjung Road in mid-March to formally elect him as their leader. We also had to settle a small matter—the name of our common platform. Several suggestions were made. Ultimately, my suggestion—National Democratic Alliance (NDA)*—was readily accepted. For us in the BJP, it had an emotional resonance. The name of the conglomeration of Opposition parties, headed by Dr Syama Prasad Mookerjee in the 1st Lok Sabha, was National Democratic Front. I suggested the slight change because 'Front' implied ad hocism, whereas 'Alliance' carries a sense of durability.

Another matter of immense satisfaction for all of us in the BJP was that we could persuade our allies to include in the NDA's Common Minimum Programme an important commitment we had made in our 1998 election manifesto: 'The BJP rejects the notion of nuclear apartheid and will actively oppose attempts to impose a hegemonistic nuclear regime. (We shall) re-evaluate the country's nuclear policy and exercise the option to induct nuclear weapons. We will not be dictated to by anybody in matters of security requirements and in the exercise of the nuclear option.'

Even though it was evident that the BJP-led alliance on its own had the mandate to form the government, this did not deter some of our adversaries from trying to stitch together an alternative minus the BJP. 'We

---

* During the six years of the Vajpayee government, the NDA had the following members: Shiv Sena in Maharashtra led by Balasaheb Thackeray; Shiromani Akali Dal (SAD) in Punjab led by Prakash Singh Badal; Janata Dal (United) in Bihar led by George Fernandes and Nitish Kumar; Biju Janata Dal in Orissa led by Naveen Patnaik; Trinamool Congress in West Bengal led by Mamata Banerjee; Indian National Lok Dal in Haryana led by Om Prakash Chautala; All India Anna Dravida Munnetra Kazhagam (AIADMK) led by Dr J. Jayalalithaa; Dravida Munnetra Kazhagam (DMK) in Tamil Nadu led by Dr M. Karunanidhi; Marumalarchi Dravida Munnetra Kazhagam (MDMK) in Tamil Nadu led by Vaiko; Pattali Makkal Katchi in Tamil Nadu led by Dr Ramadoss; Indian Federal Democratic Party in Kerala led by P.C. Thomas; Nagaland People's Front in Nagaland; Mizo National Front in Mizoram; Lok Jan Shakti Party in Bihar led by Ram Vilas Paswan; and Jammu & Kashmir National Conference led by Dr Farooq Abdullah. Some of these parties left the NDA during the incumbency of the government to join the Congress.

will not allow the BJP and its allies to form the government at the Centre. There will be a coalition government of the United Front and Congress,' said departing Prime Minister I.K. Gujral. A Congress spokesman said, 'Although the BJP is the single largest party, we don't expect the President to call them first because the Congress and the United Front will reach an understanding…and send him a communiqué.'

Ultimately, the logic of elementary mathematics prevailed over the lust for power. 'We have no numbers to form a government, so we are not staking a claim,' conceded Sonia Gandhi* after meeting President Narayanan. It was clear from her statement that what prevented her from staking claim was the failure to rustle up the necessary numbers, not the realisation that the Congress had been denied a mandate by the people. I am saying this here because her words hid an intent, indeed the seeds of a conspiracy to destabilise the Vajpayee government, which would become manifest in a big lie spoken in the premises of Rashtrapati Bhavan in May 1999.

The ten-day delay by President Narayanan in inviting Atalji to form the government raised many eyebrows. He had set a new precedent concerning the appointment of Prime Minister—namely, if an election to the Lok Sabha produced a hung House with no party or pre-election coalition having a majority, then only that person would be appointed Prime Minister who succeeds in convincing the President, through letters of support from allied parties, of his ability to secure the majority. In doing so, he diverged from the actions of his two illustrious predecessors, R. Venkataraman and Shankar Dayal Sharma, who had invited the leader of the single largest party or pre-election coalition to form the government without ascertaining their ability to secure the confidence of the House. Both the Supreme Court's directive in the famous Bommai judgment of 1994 as well as the Sarkaria Commission's report on Centre-State relations, have clearly laid down that the Governor is duty-bound to invite the leader

---

* Within days of the party's electoral defeat, Sonia Gandhi was elected Congress President by unceremoniously ousting Sitaram Kesri, who was manhandled by his own party workers at the AICC headquarters.

of the single largest party or pre-poll alliance to form the government and whether or not he enjoys the confidence of the House should be decided on the floor of the legislative assembly, and not in Raj Bhavan (Governor's House).

This being the spirit of the Constitution, the President of India could not possibly legitimise a different procedure in appointing a Prime Minister. Narayanan, who came to be known as an 'activist President', asked Atalji to furnish letters of support to demonstrate the NDA's ability to secure a majority. This gave time and opportunity to the Congress party to indulge, vainly, in some unholy politicking to wean away some of our potential allies. No doubt, it failed in its attempt, but the indirect encouragement it received from the President in 1998 whetted its deep-rooted destabilisation instincts in 1999.

Atalji was able to meet the President's demand and was sworn in as Prime Minister on 19 March, on the condition that he would prove his majority in the Lok Sabha within ten days. I remember the proud occasion on that bright Thursday morning. The forecourt of the majestic Rashtrapati Bhavan was aglow in the warm sunshine of early summer. After Atalji, it was my turn to be sworn in. After a gap of almost twenty-one years, I was back as a Minister in the Government of India. There were, however, two differences. In 1977, the swearing-in ceremony was an indoor affair: it had taken place in the Ashoka Hall of the Rashtrapati Bhavan. More importantly, Atalji, who had then been sworn in as a Minister in Morarji Desai's government, had now become the Prime Minister. I became the Home Minister in his Cabinet.

MY FIRST OFFICIAL DUTY: PAYING HOMAGE
TO COMRADE E.M.S. NAMBOODIRIPAD

It may surprise readers to know that the first official duty I performed as Home Minister in the Vajpayee government was to pay homage to a veteran communist leader. Soon after being sworn in on 19 March, I had gone to North Block, where the Home Ministry is located, to take charge of my responsibility. I had called all the senior officers in the ministry for an introductory session. The same evening, I received a call from Atalji on RAX, a special high-security phone system for internal communication. 'Have you heard the news from Kerala?' he asked me. 'Comrade E.M.S. Namboodiripad has passed away.' The news saddened me. For although EMS (1909-98), who served the CPI(M) as its General Secretary for many years, was my political and ideological adversary of long standing, I respected him for his firm commitment to his own principles. The Prime Minister told me that the funeral was to take place the following morning and that an all-party meeting had been organised in Thiruvananthapuram. He asked me if we should send someone on behalf of our government to pay homage to EMS. I said, 'Certainly, we should. And if you agree, I can go.' He replied in the affirmative and I took a special Air Force plane to reach Thiruvananthapuram at night. Thus, attending the funeral of the veteran communist leader became my first official assignment in the NDA government.

The all-party meeting was attended by Harkishan Singh Surjeet, A.K. Antony, E.K. Nayanar, who was then the Chief Minister of Kerala, and several other leaders. In my speech, I referred to the fact that E.M.S. Namboodiripad was an ideologue of the CPI(M) and a person who inspired all who were in the communist movement. I added that since my childhood I drew inspiration from Dr Keshav Baliram Hedgewar, who founded the RSS. 'It strikes me as significant that at the same time that Dr Hedgewar was the General Secretary of the Vidarbha Congress, EMS was General Secretary of the Malabar Congress. Both had different ideologies. Yet, both were office-bearers of different regional units of the Congress party and under its banner both were fighting for India's independence from colonial rule. In spite of the differences in ideology, what was common to both of them was idealism. And I pay homage to Comrade EMS for his idealism.'

Most of the people present were surprised that a BJP Prime Minister would send, on the very day of his being sworn in, the highest-ranking Minister in his government to attend the funeral of the leader of a party which considered the BJP its 'number one enemy'. What surprised some even more was my rich tribute to EMS. 'Advaniji, we are really touched by your government's gesture,' quite a few of them said to me. I replied saying what I have often felt about the communists' attitude towards the BJP. 'If untouchability is wrong and unjustifiable in social relationships, how can it be right and justifiable in political relationships?'

STEPPING DOWN AS PARTY PRESIDENT, CALL FOR A 'NEW BJP'

After I became a Minister in Atalji's government, I felt it was time for me to relinquish my responsibilities as the President of the BJP, an office I had been serving since 1993. Kushabhau Thakre, a veteran of the Bharatiya Jana Sangh and the BJP who was widely respected for his selflessness, simplicity and organisational capabilities, was unanimously elected as my successor at the meeting of the BJP National Executive in April 1998.

The political resolution adopted by the National Executive stated: 'The BJP whole-heartedly thanks the voters for bestowing upon it the privilege of serving the people of this great nation. This is both the end of an era and the dawn of a new one. The Vajpayee government heralds a new chapter of optimism in India's post-Independence history, having set itself to the task of renewing hope, regenerating resources and reviving nationalist fervour so that India is fully prepared to meet the challenges of the twenty-first century.'

I used my presidential speech* to articulate my thoughts on the challenges before the party as it stood on the threshold of a new and historic transition in its history. I also felt it necessary to place before the party's cadres and supporters the compulsions, as well as the opportunities, inherent in leading a coalition on the basis of a CMP. And since this matter has come up for discussion again and again within the ideological fraternity—the 'Sangh Parivar'—to which the BJP owes its allegiance, what follows in the next couple of pages has contemporary relevance.

It is necessary to recall here that a lot of heat and dust had been created by our adversaries over the so-called 'hidden agenda' of the BJP, after we

---

* As things turned out, it was not to be my last speech as the President of the BJP. In October 2004, I was again called upon to take the reins of presidentship of the party.

decided to keep the three issues in our election manifesto—Ayodhya, Article 370 of the Constitution and Uniform Civil Code—out of the National Agenda of Governance adopted by the BJP-led alliance. 'The Prime Minister,' I said in my speech, 'has already effectively refuted this specious charge on the floor of the House, by stating that the government was committed only to NAG and not to any "hidden agenda". But since the National Executive is a party forum, and also since the three issues that have been left out of NAG have been particularly significant in shaping the BJP's ideological identity, I am duty-bound to explain how this is in conformity with our basic ideology of nationalism.'

Firstly, I affirmed that, 'Everything we hold dear and everything we have espoused in our political journey since 1951, finds its expression in the broad rubric of nationalism. Thus democracy, secularism, good governance, distributive justice, social justice, gender justice, greater power to the states and panchayat bodies, all this and others carry meaning for us not as separate principles, but as canons which are harmonised in all-embracing commitment to nationalism.' Secondly, 'Individual principles do not carry any abstract meaning in themselves; rather their significance and their relative importance in overall scheme of things are determined by the higher imperatives of nationalism. The imperative of nationalism in today's specific situation is to arm India with a stable, strong and honest government.'

I explained that in the ruling alliance that had emerged after the 1998 parliamentary elections, in which the BJP did not secure a majority on its own, it was natural for the constituent parties to agree to keep only consensual issues in the NAG. 'But where does this leave the three above-mentioned issues that have been a part of our ideological identity? Have we acted in an opportunistic and unprincipled manner?' After posing the questions so sharply, and reaffirming that the BJP's ideology is indeed the source of its idealism, I set out to answer them by making two points. 'One, a large area of governance does not have much to do with ideology—any ideology—except the overriding principle of national interests. Indeed, good governance in most spheres of national life becomes possible only when it is de-politicised. Thus, if any issue, in spite of its inherent validity, acquires a strongly ideological character—in fact, so strong an ideological character as to make coalition governance, and hence stable governance, difficult—it is only proper to leave it out. This is precisely what we have done in the National Agenda.'

Secondly, while reiterating my own, as well as the party's, commitment to the three 'core' issues, I submitted 'a bold new approach for the consideration of the National Executive'. As far as the government was concerned, I said, it would be guided by NAG. However, as for the party and the nation, 'I feel the only right approach is to continue a peaceful, constructive and assertive debate and dialogue on all the three issues.'

On Ayodhya, in particular, I articulated my approach succinctly—and I wish to state that this approach not only guided me in my efforts to find a solution to the Ayodhya issue during my six years in government, but continues to do so even now. 'Let this issue be taken out of both the judicial and legislative spheres and confined only to exploring a peaceful and amicable solution through concerted dialogue. Let us use the coming decade exclusively for nation-building—in other words, for building a magnificent *Rashtra Mandir* in which all the children of Bharat Mata can live in peace, prosperity and security, irrespective of their caste, religious or regional affiliations.'

Since the BJP had come to power at the Centre for the first time, I deemed it necessary to make the party realise fully the magnitude, and the historic nature, of the responsibility to leaders and workers at all levels. The BJP had to most urgently transform its organisational mindset from that of a party in the Opposition to that of a party of governance—moreover, a party wedded to the ideal of good governance. The BJP had to deliver on its promise of good and stable governance, if it was to consolidate its electoral gains and seize the space that was fast being abdicated by a 'discredited, dissipated and dynastic Congress'. I warned that, arrogance of power and temptation to use the state machinery for personal ends must be resisted since these, precisely, were the vices which brought so much disgrace to the Congress party. Drawing the attention of my party to the imperatives of 'coalition dharma', I said, 'As the largest party in the ruling alliance—nay, the very mind and heart and soul of the coalition—the

BJP must act with the highest sense of responsibility, foresight and sense of mission. I would like all our colleagues to realise the attitudinal and operational imperatives that follow from this. The interests of the coalition at the Centre are paramount. The party's strategies in states must be subordinate to its national strategy.'

On the organisational front, I said: 'What this means in specific terms is that the BJP must consciously and systematically transform itself as a party embracing all sections of society and all regions of India. Every Indian, irrespective of their caste, religion, region, race and language must find the same place in our individual and collective mindscape.' I concluded my speech, which I regard as one of the most important speeches of my political career, with a future-focused appeal to my colleagues: 'The BJP must now become a "New BJP". Only a New BJP can shoulder the responsibilities of the new era that is opening up for both India and for our own party. The BJP will be guided not by the issues of yesterday but by the agenda of tomorrow. The New BJP will be fully alive to the changing world scenario and enable India to face the challenges...of the twenty-first century.'

POKHARAN II: INDIA GOES NUCLEAR

The Vajpayee government got down to the task of governance in right earnest. The first and foremost task was to make India a nuclear weapons power—a vital commitment in every election manifesto of the BJP since 1967. That our government implemented this promise within two months of assuming office showed that we had the courage, as they say in contemporary parlance, to walk our talk.

As I look back, I find that the people of India have noted many contributions of the Vajpayee government towards the development of India's infrastructure—highways, rural roads, telecom, IT, power sector reforms, etc. But our government's greatest achievement was instilling a sense of pride, confidence and hope in Indians, both within and outside India. A major contributor to this national resurgence was, of course, a historic event that took place on 11 May 1998, confirming our resolve to make India '*shaktishali* (strong), *samruddha* (prosperous) and *swabhimani* (self-confident)'.

It was on the auspicious occasion of Buddha Purnima, the day of Gautam Buddha's birth, when this long-standing commitment of the BJP was translated into reality. On that very morning, Atalji had shifted his residence from 7 Safdarjung Road to the Prime Minister's official address: 7 Race Course Road. The mandatory puja had been completed but the day was destined to become memorable for him, and for the nation, for another reason.

Sitting in the Prime Minister's living room were seven of us—Atalji, Defence Minister George Fernandes, Deputy Chairman of the Planning Commission Jaswant Singh, Finance Minister Yashwant Sinha, the Prime Minister's Political Advisor Pramod Mahajan, his Principal Secretary Brajesh Mishra, and myself. We were eagerly awaiting a message from the deserts of Rajasthan—to be precise, from Pokharan. The message came, slightly before 4 pm, on a specially installed top-security telephone line: 'Tests successful'. India's nuclear scientists had succeeded in conducting three simultaneous nuclear explosions, heralding India's emergence as a nuclear weapons state. None of us in the room could control our emotions. I, perhaps the weakest in this regard, had tears in my eyes. Atalji thanked the scientists who made it happen—in particular, Dr A.P.J. Abdul Kalam, Head of the Defence Research and Development Organisation (DRDO); R. Chidambaram, head of the Department of Atomic Energy (DAE); Dr Anil Kakodkar (who is now the head of DAE); and Dr K. Santhanam, Chief Advisor to DRDO.

Shortly thereafter, he went to the sprawling lawns of his residence to make the following announcement before the media: 'Today, at 1545 hours, India conducted three underground nuclear tests in the Pokharan range. The tests conducted today were with a fission device, a low yield device and a thermonuclear device. The measured yields are in line with expected values. Measurements have also confirmed that there was no release of radioactivity into the atmosphere. These were contained explosions like the experiment conducted in May 1974. I warmly congratulate the scientists and engineers who have carried out these successful tests.'

Two more nuclear tests were conducted at Pokharan on 13 May, thus completing the planned series of underground tests. What stunned the rulers in western capitals was the complete failure of their intelligence agencies to penetrate the cover of secrecy surrounding the tests. Speaking about the two series of tests in Parliament on 27 May, Prime Minister Vajpayee said, 'India is now a nuclear weapons state.... It is not conferment we seek, nor is it a status for others to grant.... It is India's due, the right of one-sixth of humankind.' He clarified that India would neither use nuclear weapons 'for aggression' nor 'for mounting threats against any country'. India needed nuclear weapons only for self-defence, 'to ensure that India is not subjected to nuclear threats or coercion'.

The Prime Minister's announcement sent waves of joy and pride among Indians. To understand the sentiment fully, it is necessary to know what the codename of the tests, 'Operation Shakti', conveys to the Indian mind. For over a thousand years, India had been a victim of foreign rule due to the superior military power of the invaders. Therefore, when India won freedom from British rule in 1947, national defence became the highest priority for nationalists so that the shame of defeat and enslavement was never repeated. Hence, self-reliance in developing weaponry capable of defending the nation, in the face of gravest of threats, became an unshakeable principle for them.

Sadly, after Independence, the Congress party and its government under Nehru did not share this popular sentiment. His gross neglect of national defence often bordered on sanctimonious disdain. As a result, India had to pay a heavy price during the Chinese aggression in 1962. Its unpreparedness was compounded by its shoddy diplomacy. In our national memory post-Independence, no other event evokes so much pain as the experience of military defeat and loss of territory during the 1962 war.

INDIA'S NUCLEAR DETERRENT: OUR CONSISTENT STAND SINCE 1964

For us in the BJP, Pokharan II, as the tests came to be known, was a matter of special pride because we were the first ones to demand, way back in 1964, that India develop nuclear weapons as a deterrent. Apart from the experience of 1962, what had prompted us to do so was that, in June 1964, China had declared itself a nuclear weapons state after conducting a nuclear test at Lap Nor. I recall the Central Working Committee (CWC) of the Bharatiya Jana Sangh, meeting in Patna in December 1964, and adopting the following resolution:

> The Bharatiya Jana Sangh deeply regrets the government's failure to realise the seriousness of the threat posed to India's security by China's entry into the nuclear club. The lackadaisical manner in which the government has been dealing with this matter is evidenced by the fact that an issue of so vital importance has not even been referred to the central cabinet for its considered opinion. The Bharatiya Jana Sangh has always been of the view that the nation's determination to build up military strength adequately enough to frustrate the gravest challenge to its independence and integrity should not be limited by any pseudo-pacifist inhibitions.

The resolution criticised the Nehru government not only for its 'smug ostrich-like complacency' in refusing to consider the implications of China's bomb with respect to India's security, but also for 'confusing and misinforming public opinion by raising an economic bogey'. India's economy, it was then contended, could not bear the cost of producing an atom bomb. 'The Jana Sangh disagrees basically with this approach. No price can be considered too high where the country's defence is involved. But in the matter of this particular debate, recent statements made by the Chairman of the Atomic Energy Commission (AEC), Dr Homi Bhabha*, have made it clear that the question of cost at least cannot be pleaded to justify a policy of nuclear self-denial.'

---

* Dr Homi Bhabha, the architect of India's nuclear programme, was well aware that the Chinese were planning a nuclear test and had been secretly agitating with the government for a vigorous effort to match China's plans. On 4 October 1964, on a visit to London, Dr Bhabha announced that India could detonate a nuclear bomb within eighteen months if such a decision were taken; however, he asserted: 'I do not think such a decision will be taken.' Quoted from *India's Nuclear Bomb: The Impact on Global Proliferation*, University of California Press, 1999, p. 65.

The Jana Sangh's resolution pointed out another gaping flaw in Nehru's approach saying:

> It is jejune in the extreme to argue that China's nuclear threat can be faced by mobilising world opinion against it. India's recent experience at the Cairo conference and the fact that not a single Asian country has joined India in condemning China's nuclear explosion should have been an eye-opener for us. But it seems that the capacity of the Congress leaders at indulging in self-deception is unlimited. The nation's concern is that in this particular matter, the government's airs of superior international morality have jeopardised India's security and freedom…. The Bharatiya Jana Sangh, therefore, considers it imperative that an all-out effort be made by India to build up an independent nuclear deterrent of its own.

I have quoted *in extenso* from the 1964 resolution of the Bharatiya Jana Sangh only to show how our party's stand on the nuclear issue has always been guided by the supreme interests of national security and also how, international developments since then have fully vindicated the validity of our government's action in 1998. I may mention here that both Indian and foreign commentators criticised our acquisition of nuclear weapons calling India a land of peace and tolerance. My reply to them was simple and straightforward: A weak person cannot pretend to be tolerant. Here I would like to quote from a famous Hindi poem by Rashtra Kavi Ramdhari Singh 'Dinkar'—*Kshama shobhati us bhujanga ko jiske paas garal ho*. (Forgiveness befits only the mighty serpent that has venom.)

It has been my consistent belief since 1964 that equipping India with a nuclear weapons deterrent was a key pre-requisite for making India strong. Every nation has an inalienable right to defend itself and take reasonable measures, consistent with the nature of the regional and global security scenario. India's security, I argued, would always be in peril in an uncertain world where certain big powers possessed nuclear weapons, practised 'nuclear apartheid' towards other countries and put pressure on them to sign discriminatory treaties. At the same time, I would underscore the fact that the BJP, and also the Jana Sangh previously, always backed

India's longstanding demand for complete, universal and non-discriminatory nuclear disarmament. Thus, there never was any contradiction between my party's commitment to world peace and our unapologetic advocacy for a nuclear deterrent purely for national self-defence.

On the nuclear issue, as on any matter concerning national security, we had no hesitation in supporting the Congress party whenever its governments took a right decision. Thus, when Indira Gandhi's government carried out a nuclear test on 18 May 1974 my party complimented the government unhesitatingly. This, despite the fact that our political relations with the Congress party and the Prime Minister at the time were extremely adversarial. In a resolution adopted on 2 June 1974, the Jana Sangh's CWC described 18 May as 'a red letter day in Indian history'. and said, 'The party salutes the Indian scientists who have placed India on the nuclear map of the world.' In an article in *The Motherland* journal, I wrote: 'Only twice in recent years has one witnessed such a mood of national elation. First, when the Indian Army entered Dacca to liberate Bangladesh, and now when India has entered the nuclear club.' It is another matter that Indira Gandhi's government called it a 'peaceful nuclear explosion' and denied India's intention to become a nuclear weapons power.

It was, by now, well known that the proposal to conduct fresh nuclear tests were under the consideration of many Congress and Congress-backed governments since 1974. But none had shown the courage to implement it. Some had even backed down, almost at the eleventh hour under external pressure. This fact has been publicly confirmed by no less a person than former President, R. Venkataraman, who has cited an instance when he was India's Defence Minister. In a letter[2] to the Prime Minister on 27 May 1998, congratulating Atalji for showing the courage that previous Congress governments had lacked, he claimed that all preparations for an underground nuclear test at Pokharan had been completed in 1983, when he was Defence Minister. 'I went down the shaft to see things for myself. It was shelved because of international pressure. The same thing happened in 1995.'

This was also indirectly corroborated by a cover story in *India Today*. 'Earlier regimes attempted to deal with the pressure by skirting the problem and postponing a final decision. Vajpayee has taken the bull by the horns in a dramatic show of defiance. In the process, he has taken Indian foreign policy to nationalist heights, something most of his predecessors secretly preferred, but lacked the political will to pursue.'[3]

Within a fortnight of Pokharan II, and quite predictably, Pakistan followed suit by conducting underground nuclear explosions at its Chagai testing range in Baluchistan. However, there were significant differences between the nuclear security policies of India and Pakistan. Unlike Pakistan's nuclear weapons programme which is entirely India-centric, India's is not Pakistan-centric; it takes into account the present and future challenges, both regional and global, to our national security. Unlike Pakistan which does not abide by a no-first-use doctrine, India does. Pakistan's nuclear infrastructure has been built largely with Chinese assistance, with considerable contribution from clandestine methods, whereas India's is based on self-reliance, with an impeccable record in its dealings with international partners. The most important difference, however, is that whereas the international community recognises India as a responsible nuclear power state, it has serious concerns about Pakistan because of its proven hand in illicit nuclear proliferation. Indeed, Dr Abdul Qadeer Khan, founder of Pakistan's nuclear programme, confessed in January 2004 to his involvement in nuclear weapons technology transfers from Pakistan to Libya, Iran and North Korea.

Courageous and principled decisions invariably carry a risk, which for India came in the form of sanctions imposed by the United States and other big powers. But these sanctions, which failed to browbeat or hurt India, were met with firmness and sophistication. Indeed, some of the very quarters that had imposed sanctions later praised India as a 'responsible nuclear power' and in the course of time, most of the sanctions were withdrawn. The swiftness with which India's critics in the international community came forward to re-establish normal relations was an accomplishment that has perhaps few parallels in global diplomacy. All this boosted India's profile and prestige in the eyes of the international community. I have heard innumerable Indians, both in India and abroad, say that the Indian government's action in Pokharan, along with its deft post-Pokharan diplomacy, not only made them feel prouder than before, but also that it made foreigners look at India and Indians with greater respect.

CRITICISM FROM THE CONGRESS AND COMMUNISTS

However, what surprised those of us in the government was the criticism from the Congress and communist leaders at home. The Congress party's criticism was articulated by none other than the present Prime Minister, Dr Manmohan Singh, who was then the Leader of the Opposition in the Rajya Sabha. Participating in a debate in the 1998 monsoon session of Parliament, Dr Singh warned of the consequences of the tests and a costly arms race, which would send defence expenditure skyrocketing—to a point where 'there would be nothing left to defend'.

Congress President Sonia Gandhi's reaction was ambiguous, to say the least; at best, it was a grudging endorsement of the public mood and, at worst, denunciatory. 'On her part, Congress President Sonia Gandhi was pressed by Congressmen like Salman Khurshid and Mani Shankar Aiyer to unambiguously denounce the N tests as being the harbinger of an arms race in the region. She hesitated and ultimately yielded before the strength of public opinion'.[4] According to another source: 'Congress party was divided. Party President Sonia Gandhi had on 11 May drafted a statement criticising the tests, but this was pre-empted by senior Congress leader Sharad Pawar's premature congratulation of India's nuclear scientists for their "achievement".'[5]

The CPI(M) accused the government of unilaterally reversing India's nuclear policy. In an article titled 'Pokharan II: BJP's Harmful Legacy' published in *Ganashakti* in 1999, Prakash Karat, who later became the party's General Secretary, wrote: 'The one year since the Pokharan tests have amply shown the fallacy of this decision. India has not emerged stronger, but is weakened by this adventurist policy. India found itself isolated internationally from its friends and the Non-Aligned community of nations.' It is for unbiased observers to decide whether, nearly a decade after Pokharan II, India is weaker than in pre-1998 times or isolated internationally from its friends—within or outside the Non-Aligned Movement (NAM).

I would like to pose the following questions to the communists: Have you ever dared to criticise the nuclear weapons policy of China and the erstwhile communist-ruled Soviet Union as a 'harmful legacy' and demanded that it be undone? Or, is it your understanding that our national security is *weakened* if India becomes a nuclear weapons power, whereas it is *strengthened* when a communist-ruled foreign country does so?

Of course, the debate about India's nuclear deterrent did not end in 1998. It resurfaced in a far more politically explosive manner in 2007 in the context of the Congress-led United Progressive Alliance (UPA) government's decision to enter into a Nuclear Cooperation Agreement with the United States. It is an unequal deal, promising the illusion of energy security but, in reality, seeking to undermine India's national security. It undoes India's proud achievements in Pokharan I and II and compromises India's sovereignty in matters of strategic nuclear policies.

I presented my views on this issue in a comprehensive speech while participating in a debate in the Lok Sabha on 28 November 2007. I said that whereas Indira Gandhi did India proud with Pokharan I in 1974 and Atal Bihari Vajpayee brought greater strength and pride with Pokharan II in 1998, the Indo-US nuclear deal ensures that no future Indian Prime Minister would be able to conduct Pokharan III even if considerations of national defence necessitated such a step. This is because the Hyde Act* passed by the American legislature, which would govern the Indo-US nuclear cooperation agreement, has in-built provisions for punitive measures against India if India conducted fresh nuclear tests. 'Which self-respecting country can agree to embed a likely punitive action against itself in a bilateral agreement signed by it?' I asked. I also argued how the

---

* The Henry J. Hyde United States-India Peaceful Atomic Energy Cooperation Act of 2006 is the legal framework for a bilateral agreement between India and the United States under which the US, which had earlier barred India from having access to civilian nuclear technology and access to nuclear fuel, would do so in exchange for International Atomic Energy Agency (IAEA)-safeguards on civilian Indian reactors. However, the Act clearly stipulates that, in the event of India conducting nuclear tests in the future, the cooperation would be terminated and the US would take back its reactors and other material supplied by it.

Indo-US nuclear deal would bring India, through the backdoor as it were, within the ambit of the Nuclear Non-Proliferation Treaty (NPT), which every previous Indian Prime Minister, from Indira Gandhi to Vajpayee, had rejected as discriminatory. In the same speech, I also described as unfortunate Sonia Gandhi's remark, made in a rally in Haryana in October that 'those who are opposed to the deal are not only enemies of the Congress but also of India's development'.

Under the Indian Constitution, the Central Government is not obliged to get the approval of Parliament for signing bilateral treaties with other countries. Such parliamentary approval may not be necessary in the case of ordinary treaties. However, the case of the Indo-US nuclear deal, in which the UPA government did not enjoy the support of either the BJP-led opposition or its own supporters in the Left Front, was different. The Prime Minister and his Cabinet simply did not have the support of parliamentary majority to go ahead with the deal. Therefore, in my speech, I also proposed that there should be an amendment to the Indian Constitution making it mandatory for the government of the day to seek parliamentary ratification for all bilateral treaties that have a bearing on India's unity, national security, and territorial integrity. I am happy that my proposal has been backed by several non-Congress parties.

ATALJI'S HISTORIC BUS YATRA TO LAHORE

Pokharan II raised both the stature of Prime Minister Vajpayee, as also the popularity of his government, immensely. After demonstrating that he was a worshipper of *shakti* (power), he now set out to prove that he was, equally, a votary of *shanti* (peace). Establishment of enduring peace and amiable relations between India and Pakistan was a goal dear to Atalji. As Foreign Minister in Morarji Desai's government, he had left a deep imprint with his advocacy of friendly ties between our two countries. Now, with both India and Pakistan having become nuclear weapon states, it was all the more necessary to find lasting solutions to the contentious issues that consistently generated tension and strife.

Out of this deep commitment to peace came the novel idea of Atalji's historic bus yatra to Lahore on 20 February 1999. The ostensible purpose of the journey was to inaugurate a cross-border bus service between Delhi and Lahore. However, by choosing to travel in the inaugural bus (he actually travelled from Amritsar to Lahore, a distance of sixty kilometres), the Prime Minister captured the imagination of the common people both in India and Pakistan. It was the first visit by an Indian Prime Minister to Pakistan in ten years.

Atalji's bus journey to restart the peace process with Pakistan was blessed by Prof Rajendra Singh (Rajju Bhaiyya), who was then the Chief of the RSS. I suggested to the BJP President, Kushabhau Thakre, to go to the Wagah Border to personally convey the party's best wishes to Atalji on his bold initiative. Thus, the entire party and the larger Sangh Parivar was solidly behind what was, until then, the NDA government's most important diplomatic move.

The then Prime Minister of Pakistan, Nawaz Sharif, welcomed the Indian Prime Minister at the Wagah border. Speaking at a banquet in Atalji's honour, he said:

> The bus service between Lahore and Delhi is not a means only to ease travel from one country to another. The running of the bus between the two countries symbolises the desire of the people to improve relations and come together. Indeed, if this was only a bus made of metal, it would not have caused such excitement and expectations, not only in our two nations but all over the world. I have brought but one message from India. There can be no greater legacy that we can leave behind than to do away with mistrust, to abjure and eliminate conflict, to erect an edifice of durable peace amity, harmony and co-operation.

On the following day, the two Prime Ministers signed the 'Lahore Declaration', containing three salient points. Firstly, it reiterated the determination of both countries to 'implementing the Shimla Agreement in letter and spirit'. Secondly, it recognised that 'the nuclear dimension of the security environment of the two countries add to their responsibility for avoidance of conflict'. The third point was of special significance for India. Pakistan had agreed to join India in condemning 'terrorism in all its forms and manifestations' and affirming its 'determination to combat this menace'.

Atalji's visit to Minar-e-Pakistan, a monument built to commemorate the Muslim League's resolution, on 23 March 1940, calling for the creation of a country for Muslims in the Indian subcontinent, had considerable symbolic significance—not dissimilar to that of my own visit to Jinnah's mausoleum in Karachi in June 2005. In the visitor's book at the monument, Atalji affirmed: 'A stable, secure and prosperous Pakistan is in India's interest. Let no one in Pakistan be in doubt. India sincerely wishes Pakistan well.' His visit to Minar-e-Pakistan and his inscription there went a long way in dispelling the scepticism in a section of the Pakistani society that the BJP was not reconciled to the creation of Pakistan.

All in all, the Lahore bus journey was a big success. It raised the hopes across both sides of the border for a peaceful solution to all the complicated problems between India and Pakistan. Not all hopes, however, end in desired results. Setbacks and betrayals are a part of life, as much in politics and governance as in non-political endeavours. In this particular instance, the Peace Bus was hijacked and taken to Kargil, but that was entirely due to the peculiar power dynamics in Pakistan. In the next chapter, I shall deal with the Kargil betrayal and the heroic war that India fought, and won, on the world's highest battlefield.

CONGRESS' DESTABILISATION PLOT WORKS;
VAJPAYEE GOVERNMENT LOSES BY ONE VOTE

Like Pokharan II, the Lahore peace initiative also greatly enhanced the Prime Minister's popularity and the NDA government's standing in the eyes of the people. In February 1999, Finance Minister Yashwant Sinha presented his first full-fledged budget which was widely appreciated. Thus, the three 'Bs'—bomb, bus and the budget—together signalled a process of consolidation and stabilisation of the NDA government even before it had completed one year in office. Alarmed by these positive developments, the Congress party returned to its old game of destabilising non-Congress governments. It raised a demand for the dismissal of the DMK government, a demand which the Vajpayee government could not have acceded to. Had we done so, it might have helped our government to survive, but only at the cost of its credibility. Both Atalji and I were firm on not committing the sin that the Congress, while in power at the Centre, had repeatedly committed by invoking Article 356 of the Constitution to dismiss state governments run by rival political parties.

On 14 April 1999, the AIADMK withdrew support to the NDA government. Once again, President Narayanan played a key role in the heated political developments. He asked Prime Minister Vajpayee to seek a vote of confidence in the Lok Sabha within three days. In spite of the short time available, the NDA was able to garner the support of several smaller parties. The debate that ensued was bizarre in many ways. There really was no issue that warranted bringing down of the government. What wrong had our government committed to invite the prospect of ouster? None. Was there a valid reason for the country to be pushed to the brink of another mid-term election? No. The Congress party was really at a loss to explain why it wanted our government to go, except by raising the old bogey of the BJP being a 'communal party'. As the Prime Minister pointed out in an eloquent and impassioned speech, his government was working well. It had taken steps such as Pokharan II to make India strong, steps from which earlier governments had shied away for years. Even as the worst ever crisis struck the South-East Asian economies, the NDA government had taken effective steps to insulate and save the Indian economy. The country was at peace. Communal tension and violence had substantially come down. 'I sometimes wonder,' Atalji said, 'as there was no issue, was the fact that we were doing everything possible to make India strong and prosperous the reason the government was sought to be brought down?'

What lent a tragi-comic air to the debate was the utter inability of the Congress and its allies to tell the nation about their own plans, in case the Vajpayee government fell. 'What is the alternative you have in mind?' the Prime Minister asked them. 'Who is going to be your Prime Minister? Which parties will the new government consist of? What is going to be the crux of your common minimum programme?' Speakers from the Opposition simply scoffed at these questions and said, 'We will provide the alternative in *five* minutes.'

Finally, when the motion was put to vote, the Vajpayee government lost by the smallest conceivable margin—one vote. The motion was defeated by 269 to 270. And even that one decisive vote was morally and politically fraudulent, albeit technically valid. It was that of Giridhar Gomango, a Congress MP from Orissa, who had already been sworn in as the Chief Minister of his state. But since he had not yet resigned from the Lok Sabha, he was specially called from Bhubaneshwar by Congress managers to cast his vote against the confidence motion.

All of us—Atalji, I and other leaders of the NDA—were crestfallen when the outcome of the secret ballot was announced. We came out of the House to assemble in Room No 10, the Prime Minister's chamber in Parliament. Atalji, who was unable to control his emotions, said, 'We lost by one vote—only one vote!' But we told him in unison: 'Atalji, we might have lost the government by one vote. But when fresh elections are held and we go back to the people, we will ask each and every voter to bring you back as the Prime Minister with their single vote.'

SONIA GANDHI'S 'OUTER VOICE': 'I'VE THE SUPPORT OF 272 MPS'

The leaders of the Congress and other Opposition parties had boasted on 17 April that they would form the alternative government in 'five minutes'. Ironically, they could not do so even after five days. As soon as the Vajpayee government was voted out, two contradictory aspects of the destabilisation plot came to the fore. Firstly, the Congress party, which had only 140 members in the Lok Sabha and no formal alliance with any other party, made it known that it alone would lead the next government. Such was its arrogance, and so derisive was its attitude towards most parties in the Opposition, that it did not even bother to consult their leaders, except, of course, CPI(M)'s General Secretary Harkishan Singh Surjeet, who was a part of the inner circle of conspirators. It simply reckoned that they would have no option but to support a Congress-led government.

President Narayanan started to play an 'activist' role again. On 20 April, he wrote to Sonia Gandhi inviting her to hold discussions with him the following day. After her meeting, she made a startling claim before TV and print media journalists in the forecourt of Rashtrapati Bhavan—that she had the support of 272 MPs and intended to form a government. The Congress would form the government on its own with outside support.

All of us in the NDA were taken aback by Sonia Gandhi's audacious announcement, which not only indicated that she wanted to become the Prime Minister of India but also that she had the requisite support in the Lok Sabha. But we were not the only ones to be so stunned. Many among the non-Congress parties also wondered how the Congress President could utter such a white lie, in front of Rashtrapati Bhavan, when the arithmetic on the Opposition completely refuted her claim. True, the leaders of CPI(M) and CPI conveyed to the President their unconditional support to the government led by the Congress. But they, too, had no control over some other powerful groups that had colluded in the plot to destabilise Atalji's government.

Late in the night of 21 or 22 April, George Fernandes, Defence Minister and NDA Convenor, called me to say, 'Lalji, I have some good news for you. Sonia Gandhi cannot form the government,' he replied. 'On what basis are you saying this?' I asked him. 'You will know it very soon. An important person from the other side wishes to meet you. But we cannot have the meeting in either your house or mine. We will meet at Jaya's* house in Sujan Singh Park. Do not come in your car, since your security convoy will also accompany you. Jaya will come to pick you up and you come in her car.'

When I reached Jaya Jaitley's house, I found Mulayam Singh Yadav, President of the Samajwadi Party, and Fernandes there. The two share a socialist background, having been loyal followers of Dr Ram Manohar Lohia. They also have a long-standing personal relationship, which has survived the divergent political paths they chose after the fall of V.P. Singh's government in the late 1990s. Fernandes, whose aversion to the Congress is boundless, said, 'Lalji, I have firm commitment from my friend that his

---

* Jaya Jaitley, a noted social and political activist, was President of the Samata Party, founded by George Fernandes.

twenty MPs will not, under any circumstances, support Sonia Gandhi's bid to become Prime Minister. And I have brought him to meet with you so that you can be sure of this.'

Yadav reiterated the commitment to me. But he also said, 'Advaniji, I have one condition. Once I announce that I am not going to support Sonia Gandhi's claim to form the government, I want you to commit that the NDA will not again lay claim to form the government. I want fresh elections to take place.' I said, 'Mulayamji, I thank you for your bold decision. As regards the other thing you have mentioned, let me tell you that many of us in the NDA are ourselves of the view that we should not lay claim to form the government again and, instead, face mid-term elections.' Yadav stood by his word. On 23 April, he gave a letter to the President stating that his party would not support a Congress-led government. Representatives of the All India Forward Bloc and the Revolutionary Socialist Party (RSP), both of whom are partners in the CPI(M)-led Left Front, also communicated the same to the President.

When Sonia Gandhi called on the President again on 23 April, she could produce a list of only 233 MPs, far less than the 272 that she had claimed only two days earlier. Significantly, when she asked for more time, the President granted her two more days! As my colleague Arun Shourie said, 'The President was straining to see one combination out and a particular one in.' The official statement issued on that day by Rashtrapati Bhavan was quite revealing: 'Smt Sonia Gandhi gave to the President a list of 233 MPs who would extend support for the formation of a Congress government. When it was put to her that the numbers did not add up to the requisite strength, she conveyed to the President that she would continue her discussions with parties and individuals who voted against the Motion of Confidence on April 17, 1999 and *advise the President on her efforts, as early as possible*.' (emphasis added.) For all of us in the NDA, it was unbelievable to read that Sonia Gandhi told the President that she would 'advise' him of the results of her efforts! Who was advising whom?

On 25 April, Sonia Gandhi met the President, informing him of her inability to get the support of any more MPs. She also informed him that her party would not support a Third Front government. What followed thereafter is even more instructive for those who wish to study sound practices by the incumbents of Rashtrapati Bhavan. When Prime Minister Vajpayee met the President at 8.40 pm on 25 April, Narayanan conveyed to him—and I quote from a communiqué issued by the President's Office on 26 April—that '(a) the non-BJP parties had not succeeded in coming up with an alternative; and (b) no accretion in the number supporting the BJP-led alliance had been brought to his notice either. The President gave the Prime Minister his assessment that the Twelfth Lok Sabha was not capable of yielding a Government with a reasonable prospect of stability...and informed him that, in his perception, the dissolution of the Twelfth Lok Sabha had therefore become necessary. The Prime Minister responded by saying that he would discuss the position in the Cabinet the following day'.

The next morning, Atalji called George Fernandes, Jaswant Singh, Pramod Mahajan, Murasoli Maran (a leader of the DMK who had played a very positive role in strengthening the NDA) and me to his residence. Although we were not keen to approach the President to explore the possibility of forming the government again, we did find it odd that he should have thought of dissolving the Lok Sabha, when it had barely completed the first year in its five-year tenure, by precluding the option of inviting Atalji to form a minority government. As a matter of fact, if Gomango's questionable vote was excluded—in any case, he would have had to resign his membership of the Lok Sabha after having become the Chief Minister of Orissa—Vajpayee would have had the support of exactly the same number of MPs as those opposed to him. Above all, there was the sound precedent set by President R. Venkataraman who, after the 10th Lok Sabha elections in June 1991, allowed P.V. Narasimha Rao to form a minority government. Indeed, its minority status continued for two years and it was required to prove its majority only when the Opposition brought a no-confidence motion against his government. In other words, it was the President Narayanan's subjective conclusion that a government having the proven support of 269 MPs had no right to continue in office and that the Lok Sabha had to be dissolved.

At the Cabinet meeting held shortly thereafter, we passed a carefully worded minute, which clearly put the onus for the dissolution of the Lok Sabha on the President: 'In deference to the President's assessment of the situation, as conveyed by him to the Prime Minister on April 25, the Cabinet decides to recommend to him that he may dissolve the House.' What surprised us later was how Rashtrapati Bhavan's press communiqué on 27 April distorted the meaning of the Cabinet's minute. It said: 'The Cabinet met at 12 noon on April 26, 1999 and recorded a Minute recommending to the President that he may dissolve the Twelfth Lok Sabha so that a fresh mandate could be obtained from the people as early as possible. *The Minute converged with the President's own analysis of the situation*'. (emphasis added.) This was certainly not true. There was wide *divergence* in the President's perception of the situation and that of Atalji's government.

Consequently, the Lok Sabha was dissolved on 26 April. It was an a peculiar decision on the part of President Narayanan, all the more so since it defeated what the Rashtrapati Bhavan's own communiqué had stated: 'In commencing these consultations, the President had two major objectives: (1) the need to avoid ordering a mid-term election: and (2) the importance of seeing whether a party, or a combination of parties, can provide a workable, viable alternative government with the prospect of stability for a substantial period of time if not for the remaining term of the Twelfth Lok Sabha'. Had Narayanan allowed Atalji to form the government again in the Twelfth Lok Sabha—on the legitimate ground that he enjoyed the support of 269 MPs as against 233 MPs supporting Sonia Gandhi—both these objectives would have been served.

I have recounted at some length this episode from the summer of 1999 as its lessons for the nation is relevant even today. Firstly, the myth of 'unity of secular forces' was blown to pieces. The Congress and other parties came together to pull down Atalji's government in the name of 'saving secularism' but their unity simply evaporated when they were called upon to form an alternative government. Secondly, I was filled with anguish to see how parties, especially smaller ones, were sought to split, individual MPs were poached, and money used in this entire sordid drama. These were a blot on the integrity, vitality and prestige of India's democracy.

At the same time, I was happy at the manner in which almost all the parties in the NDA stuck together in this hour of crisis. Besides Fernandes and Maran, whose names I have already mentioned, I must record here my appreciation for the solidarity shown by Prakash Singh Badal, Bal Thackeray, Naveen Patnaik, Vaiko, Mamata Banerjee and smaller parties in the North-East. All of them showed genuine empathy and respect for Atalji, who, of course, conducted himself in an extremely dignified manner.

*

While the memory of all other events will fade away with the passage of time, one date, and the television image associated with it, cannot be forgotten by those who treasure democracy. It is Sonia Gandhi's claim. This claim, which turned out to be false, put a big question mark on her truthfulness her 'inner voice' that persuaded her to make the much-trumpeted 'sacrifice' of Prime Ministership in 2004. Her 'inner voice' in 2004 was in stark contrast to her 'outer voice' in 1999, for nobody who has closely followed the political conspiracy to destabilise Atalji's government in 1999 would be left in doubt that its sole aim was to install a Congress government under her leadership.

The credit for foiling this game must necessarily go to Mulayam Singh Yadav. But why did he do it? The answer that Yadav himself gave at a press conference in Lucknow about a week later goes to the heart of another issue of great significance in Indian polity. Training his guns at the Congress, he said that the Samajwadi Party had saved the country from foreign power by refusing to extend unconditional support for the installation of the minority Congress government led by Sonia Gandhi. When asked if he was opposed to Ms Gandhi's candidature only because she was a foreigner, Mr Yadav said his party opined that crucial posts like that of the President, Vice President, Prime Minister and Lok Sabha Speaker should not be held by a foreigner.[6]

In the wake of the political uncertainty, Atalji was asked by the President to continue to head the caretaker government. The attention of all the parties—indeed, of the entire nation—was fixed on the elections to the 13th Lok Sabha. But, alas, a major national crisis erupted soon in the form of the Kargil War. From the electoral battle, the focus got immediately shifted to the conflict between India and Pakistan.

2

THE KARGIL WAR: A DECISIVE VICTORY FOR INDIA

Chah Nahin Main Sur Bala Ke/Gehnon Mein Guntha Jaaon
Chah Nahin Devon Ke Sar Par/Chadhoon, Bhagya Par Itraoon
Mujhey Tod Lena Banmali,/Us Path Par Tum Dena Phaink
Matru Bhoomi Per Sheesh Chadhaney,/Jis Path Jaayen Veer Anek

(A humble flower tells the gardener: 'I desire not to adorn the head of a beautiful girl. I desire not to be offered to any deity. I only wish that you throw me on that path which is traversed by heroes marching to sacrifice their lives in defence of their motherland.)

—FROM MAKHANLAL CHATURVEDI'S PATRIOTIC
HINDI POEM *PUSHP KI ABHILASHA*

History has never followed the straight and narrow path. Rare are human endeavours that produce predictable results. Individuals and nations should be judged on the basis of not only the outcome, but also the intention and earnestness of their actions. If the intention is honest, and the cause is just, the ultimate outcome will definitely be positive.

When Prime Minister Vajpayee courageously took the peace initiative by travelling to Lahore, Pakistan in a bus on 20 February 1999, little did he or any of us in the NDA government realise that a sinister conspiracy to wreck the peace process was already underway. Even as Pakistan's Prime Minister Nawaz Sharif was welcoming his guest with a hug at the Wagah border, his own army, under the guidance of its newly appointed chief, General Pervez Musharraf, was planning an audacious cross-border incursion into the Indian territory. And barely had the ink dried on the Lahore Declaration, signed with much optimism by the two Prime Ministers, when Pakistan violated it flagrantly, precipitating, in the process, a fourth war with India since 1947. As in the previous three wars, it suffered a humiliating defeat.

VIOLATED: NOT JUST THE LINE OF CONTROL, BUT ALSO THE LINE OF TRUST

In the second week of May 1999, the Prime Minister called me and a few other senior Ministers for an informal meeting to discuss 'some urgent matter'. The Army had informed him about some strange movement of unidentified people crossing the LoC in Kargil district in the Ladakh region of Jammu & Kashmir. It being a high-altitude and rugged region with sparse population, the intrusions were first detected, quite accidentally, by local shepherds on 3 May, who were occasional informers of the Army in the Batalik sector. The Army sent out patrols in the area and found that the intrusions extended not only to the Batalik sector but also to Dras, Mushkok and Kaksar sectors. The infiltrators were heavily armed and had entrenched themselves in at heights of 16,000-18,000 feet along a 150-kilometre stretch on the Indian side of the LoC, and threatened the strategic Srinagar-Leh highway that lay below. Consequently, Defence Minister George Fernandes visited the area on 12-14 May. Upon his return, he and senior Army officers gave the Prime Minister a detailed briefing on a situation whose gravity had certainly not been fully understood earlier.

The Cabinet Committee on Security (CCS) concluded that adequate troops, along with artillery and other equipment, should be moved to attack locations along the LoC. Finally, on 26 May, the Indian Army launched the counter-offensive, which was code named 'Operation Vijay'.

There is no doubt that the Army was caught unawares by the large-scale infiltration. However, it should not be forgotten that, extreme cold weather conditions and the hazardous terrain in that part of Jammu & Kashmir, had led both armies, since long, to abandon their forward posts along the LoC and reoccupy them in spring. Patrols and aerial reconnaissance along the LoC, though undertaken even in winter, did not guarantee detection of intrusions, particularly as severe snowstorms often led to their having to be abandoned midway. The difference in 1999 was that the Pakistan Army occupied the forward posts long before the scheduled time, as part of a hostile plan to intrude into, and capture, Indian territory.

All of us in the government were shocked by the turn of events that proved Pakistan, once again, to be unreliable and devious. As for Prime Minister Vajpayee, the feeling of hurt and outrage was especially deep. He felt that he had been personally betrayed by his Pakistani counterpart. As he would say on many occasions later, Pakistan had violated not only the Line of Control, but also the Line of Trust. He phoned Nawaz Sharif, who, almost five years later, disclosed the contents of that conversation: 'I got a call from Vajpayee saab, saying "*Nawaz saab, yeh kya ho raha hai* (Mr Nawaz, what is happening)? Your army is attacking our army".[1] Surprisingly, Sharif claimed to have no knowledge of it. 'I said there was no Pakistan army fighting against his army.... I suppose I should have known about all this. But frankly, I hadn't been briefed. I hold Mr Musharraf responsible for this. I did not know that I was being stabbed in the back by my own General.'

Pakistan's objectives for the Kargil incursion, code-named 'Operation Badr', were five-fold: (1) To choke the Srinagar-Leh highway, since it was the main supply line for Indian troops in Ladakh; (2) To force Indian troops to withdraw from the Siachen Glacier; (3) To use the crisis to strengthen its own bargaining position so that India could be compelled to negotiate a settlement of the Kashmir dispute on favourable terms; (4) To use the

Kargil war to further incite militancy in Jammu & Kashmir; and (5) To internationalise the Kashmir issue, projecting Kargil as a potential trigger for nuclear showdown.

OPERATION VIJAY

As Pakistan made swift initial advances, inflicting many casualties on the Indian side, there was discussion going on in the CCS on the deployment of the Indian Air Force (IAF). One view was that the use of offensive air power close to the LoC could result in escalation. There was a danger of our fighters crossing the LoC. After some deliberation, the CCS, at its meeting on 25 May, authorised the engagement of the IAF. It also gave clear directions to the armed forces to take whatever steps needed to vacate the intrusion but with one condition: 'Do not cross the LoC'. In operational terms, the self-imposed restriction of not crossing the LoC made the Air Force's mandate extremely difficult. Nevertheless, the IAF acquitted itself with flying colours. With the combined and concerted affect of the infantry and air attacks, India quickly neutralised Pakistan's initial gains. With the tables turned on them, it was now the turn of the Pakistani troops' to be totally surprised.

The LoC, it must be emphasised, is not an international border. It merely delineates PoK, which, in any case, is claimed by India as its own territory. Therefore, crossing the LoC would not have amounted to violation of any international rule. Moreover, Pakistan was an aggressor in this case. Why then did India impose this restriction on itself? The answer, as I shall soon explain, was that our government wanted to achieve a larger agenda—and achieve it did, with spectacular effect.

Victory in the Kargil War was one of the finest hours in the annals of India's armed forces. Defending India on what was arguably the highest battlefield in the world, with temperatures dipping to even below −15°C, which was accentuated further by the wind chill factor and forbidding terrain, was extremely challenging. Initially, Pakistani attackers had a relative locational advantage since they had occupied the heights, from where they could observe Indian soldiers in their line of sight. As such, our Army had to mount many frontal assaults, which often resulted in a hand-to-hand combat with the enemy. In spite of all these odds, our armed forces, displaying indomitable fighting spirit, grit and determination, evicted every single enemy soldier from our territory and regained every inch of land from Pakistani occupation. Finally, after seventy-four days, 'Operation Vijay' became *vijayi* (triumphant) on 26 July 1999, which is celebrated each year as Kargil Victory Day.

Kargil was also India's first war with television accessible to Indian homes. This enabled much of what was happening on the battlefield to be watched by people across the country. The mood of national unity, solidarity and self-confidence witnessed was truly unprecedented. There was no Hindu-Muslim tension anywhere in India during the Kargil War. The martyrs belonged to all castes, creeds and regions of the country, and were a source of inspiration to one and all.

No less inspiring was the fortitude of the near and dear ones of the martyrs. 'I will not hesitate to send all my three sons to the front,' said Santosh Kanwar, widow of Kargil hero Mangej Singh. 'Why should I cry? Everyone dying there is my son,' said Malti, mother of Major R. Adhikari, who died in the war. A brave lady from Andhra Pradesh who, after losing her husband in the war, told the state's Governor and Chief Minister who had visited her residence to console her, 'I want you to share my sense of pride and not grief.'

Atalji's leadership during the Kargil episode was outstanding. Never once did he seem ruffled by the unexpected turn of events. His calm and confident words inspired the nation. On 7 June, in an address to the nation, he said, 'I do want to make it plain: if the stratagem now is that the intrusion should be used to alter the Line of Control through talks, the proposed talks will end before they have begun.' He also urged the people, 'Have confidence in the ability of our armed forces. The armed forces shall accomplish this task and ensure that no one dares to indulge in this kind of misadventure in future.' However, his greatest triumph was that in the Kargil War, in contrast to the four previous wars fought under the leadership of Congress prime ministers—1948, 1962, 1965 and 1971—not one inch of Indian territory was either lost in the battlefield or 'negotiated away' in the diplomatic field.

Two days after the war ended, I visited Ladakh to convey the nation's gratitude and appreciation to its brave people. It is the most sparsely populated region in the country; only 2.5 lakh people live in an area of 45,000 square kilometres. Yet, their contribution towards India's victory in the war was immense. As many as twenty-five soldiers from this region laid down their lives. I had gone to Shey, about ten kilometres from Leh, the capital of Ladakh, to participate in the two-day annual Sindhu Darshan festival. Accompanying me were Defence Minister George Fernandes and Jammu & Kashmir's Chief Minister Dr Farooq Abdullah. Addressing a large gathering of devotees who had assembled there, I said, 'Though India has won all the previous wars against Pakistan, it had never successfully convinced the world community about the intentions of the aggressor. For the first time in 1999, we have defeated Pakistan both politically and diplomatically. Today the international community has appreciated India's point of view and charged Pakistan with being the aggressor.' I appropriately dedicated the festival to the great martyrs of Kargil.

PAKISTAN'S DEFEAT IN DIPLOMATIC ARENA

Diplomacy, it is said, is a continuation of war by other means. This may or may not be true in every situation, but it certainly was in the case of the Kargil War. If India's jawans were at their heroic best on the battlefield, our Foreign Service professionals were at their best in the diplomatic arena. Similarly, if Pakistan's army tasted a mortifying rout on the heights of Kargil, its defeat at the high table of diplomacy in world capitals was no less humiliating.

I have earlier stated that the Vajpayee government had a larger agenda in imposing upon itself the no-crossing-the-LoC restraint. It was designed to win international support for the Indian position and to show Pakistan as the aggressor that violated the Shimla Agreement and the Lahore Declaration. It helped allay fears of the international community, especially its influential constituents in the West that the conflict could spiral out of control and result in nuclear confrontation. Although the irresponsible language of 'nuclear blackmail' was indeed heard during the conflict, it was entirely from the Pakistani side. It just contributed to the increasing global isolation of the ruling establishment in Islamabad.

Nothing caused greater insult and embarrassment to Pakistan than its false claim that the intruders were not its soldiers but mujahideen fighting for the cause of Kashmir's 'liberation' from 'Indian occupation'. The evidence of its full-fledged involvement was so overwhelming that its perfidy stood exposed to the full glare of the international community. A particularly damning piece of evidence was revealed to the world by my redoubtable colleague, Jaswant Singh, who was India's External Affairs Minister then, at a press conference in New Delhi on 11 June. It was held on the eve of an important visit by Pakistan's Foreign Minister, Sartaj Aziz, who was coming to propose ways 'to defuse tension'. The context as well as the content of what Singh disclosed on that day is best captured by reproducing here the statement[2] that he issued to the media:

> Foreign Minister Sartaj Aziz will be visiting Delhi tomorrow. His visit is taking place in the context of Pakistan's armed intrusion and aggression in the Kargil sector of Ladakh, in Jammu & Kashmir. I wish to share with you, ladies and gentlemen of the media, and through you, with all the citizens of our country, as also the international community, some, and I repeat that this is only some, of the incontrovertible evidence that we have obtained about many aspects of this intrusion and aggression. This establishes beyond any doubt the involvement and complicity of the Pakistani establishment in this misadventure. It raised serious doubts about the professed aim of 'defusing tension' as averred by Foreign Minister Sartaj Aziz. The evidence will also establish that the management of this enterprise is in the hands of those who put it in place in the first instance. It raises serious doubts about the brief that Minister Aziz carries and at whose dictates he is actually working.
>
> The making public of this evidence at this juncture, is to expose the Pakistani game plan to the entire world, to preempt any designs that Pakistan may be nurturing about obscuring the central issue of their involvement, complicity and continued support

to an armed intrusion and aggression in which Pakistani regular troops are participating; to defeat in advance the Pakistani aim of dangerously attempting to reopen the sensitive and settled issue of the Line of Control; and, above all, to reemphasise and reassert the Indian position. There is only one aspect of this misadventure that can be discussed: earliest restoration of the *status quo ante* and reaffirmation of the inviolability of the Line of Control. This is the very minimum imperative for the maintenance of peace and security in the region.

Ladies and gentlemen, I will now ask that two recorded conversations between the Chief of Army Staff of the Pakistani Army (General Pervez Musharraf) and his Chief of the General Staff (Lt. Gen. Mohammed Aziz) be played. The transcripts of these conversations will be distributed simultaneously.

The intercepts pertained to conversations on 26 May and 29 May 1999, between General Musharraf in Beijing and his Chief of General Staff Lt. General Mohammed Aziz in Rawalpindi. The first conversation made it clear that Pakistan's Foreign Secretary Shamshad Ahmed had been briefed about the Kargil conflict, along with the Corps Commanders. In the second conversation, Musharraf explicitly stated Pakistan's war objectives, preceding any diplomatic engagement with India. Aziz told Musharraf that he would ensure Foreign Minister Sartaj Aziz would give 'no understanding or no commitment on [the] ground situation' during talks with New Delhi. Musharraf instructed Aziz to tell the Foreign Minister that 'we have been sitting here for long. Emphasise that for years, we are here only.' Frankly, I was surprised that the General could be so foolhardy.

In his meeting with Sartaj Aziz on 12 June, Singh, partly because of his own Army background and partly owing to his political beliefs, was as scathingly blunt as he could be without sounding undiplomatic. India's demands that he placed before his Pakistani counterpart were categorical: (1) Immediate vacation of the aggression; (2) Reaffirmation of the validity of the Line of Control; (3) Abandoning cross-border terrorism; (4) Dismantling the infrastructure of terrorism in Pakistan-occupied Kashmir; (5) Reaffirmation of the Shimla Agreement and the Lahore Declaration.

India's missions abroad did a splendid job of presenting before foreign governments a convincing case of Pakistan's aggression in Kargil and, in the process, also of its baseless claim on Jammu & Kashmir, which it had been pursuing by resorting to cross-border terrorism. The climax on the diplomatic front arrived when, faced with imminent defeat on the battlefield and total isolation from the world community, Pakistan's Prime Minister desperately sought an appointment with the US President Bill Clinton to negotiate a settlement of the conflict. Clinton agreed to the request, but only after cautioning Sharif that he ought to fly to Washington DC, for a meeting on 4 July*, only if he recognised 'what great mistakes Pakistan had made and moved in for immediate rectification'.[3]

Pakistani establishment's 'rectification' or rather capitulation was complete, as evidenced by the joint statement issued after Sharif's meeting with President Clinton. Pakistan swallowed the bitter pill by agreeing to 'respect the Line of Control in Kashmir, in accordance with the 1972 Shimla Accord' and to take 'concrete steps' for the restoration of the 'sanctity of the LoC'. It also agreed that the 'bilateral dialogue begun in Lahore in February provides the best forum for resolving all issues dividing India and Pakistan, including Kashmir'. It is important to mention here that, soon after he received Sharif's request for a meeting with him, President Clinton phoned Prime Minister Vajpayee and invited him to join the talks. Atalji politely but firmly rejected the invitation. The contrast between the conduct of the two Prime Ministers could not have been starker. One beseeched for a meeting, in order to seek a face-saving formula from a superpower while the other turned down a superpower's invitation for the same meeting, saying there was nothing to discuss since what was expected from the aggressor was crystal-clear.

The difference between India and Pakistan was also stark from the manner in which each treated its fallen soldiers. In India, the heroes of the

---

* On the day that the Pakistani Prime Minister was in talks with President Clinton to find an honourable exit route, the Indian troops effected a major turning point in the Kargil War by capturing Tiger Hill.

Kargil War became household names. For the first time after Independence, our government allowed the mortal remains of martyrs to be carried to their native town or village for a ceremonial funeral with full military honours. This decision was widely appreciated as it helped create a strong patriotic mood across the country. Pakistan, however, refused to take back its own dead soldiers or acknowledge the grief of those who lost their loved ones. On numerous occasions, Indian soldiers performed final rites for them according to the Islamic tradition.

India's voluntary decision of not crossing the LoC was applauded—and, by extension, India's stand on resolution of the Kashmir issue was supported—by the US, European Union (EU), Group of 8 (G8) nations, and the Association of South-East Asian Nations (ASEAN) Regional Forum. Even China refused to come to Pakistan's rescue during the Kargil war.

What would India's stance have been if Pakistan had not agreed to 'rectify' its misadventure? Suffice it to say that the Indian leadership had made up its mind, and made it known to key international interlocutors, that our armed forces would be authorised to chase the enemy across the LoC to achieve the desired results.

KARGIL AND PAKISTAN'S INTERNAL CRISIS

When an evil mind tries to inflict harm on others, it ends up inviting trouble upon itself. This is the immutable law of nature. The effects of the Kargil fiasco were predictably negative for Pakistan.

Benazir Bhutto, the late Prime Minister and President of the PPP described Kargil as 'Pakistan's biggest blunder'.[4] Sharif put the blame squarely on his Army Chief, saying, 'It was Musharraf who behaved irresponsibly and it was he who planned the whole affair.' In his official biography, *Gaddaar Kaun? Nawaz Sharif Ki Kahani, Unki Zubani* (Who is the traitor? Nawaz Sharif's story in his own words), written by Suhail Warraich, he even levelled the startling charge that 'Musharraf moved nuclear weapons in Kargil war'. Sharif is reported to have said: 'During my post-Kargil misadventure meeting with the American President (Bill) Clinton, I was told by the American leader that the nuclear warheads had been shifted from one station to the other during the Kargil War. I was taken aback by this revelation because I knew nothing about it. The American President further told me during the meeting that the nuclear warheads have been moved so that these could be used against India. I was asked by Clinton as to why I was unaware of these developments despite being the elected Chief Executive and the Prime Minister of the country. It was a very irresponsible thing to do on part of General Musharraf.'

Ayaz Amir, one of the best-known columnists in Pakistan who never fails to interest me with his incisive and well-written articles in *Dawn*, called the Kargil misadventure 'The Great Climbdown'. He wrote: 'That the Kargil adventure was ill-conceived, if not downright foolish, was becoming clear, albeit slowly, even to the congenitally blind and benighted. That consequently Pakistan, swallowing its pride and not a few of its brave and gallant words, would sooner or later have to mount a retreat was also becoming clear.'

Since the outcome of the Kargil War for Pakistan was not only defeat but also a bitter blame-game, it was perhaps inevitable that the animosity between its Prime Minister and Army Chief should come to a head sooner rather than later. When it did, in the form of a *coup d'état* in Islamabad on 12 October 1999, its denouement was truly dramatic. General Musharraf ousted Sharif from power, jailed him, and then sent him to Saudi Arabia to seek asylum.

After the Kargil War, there has been much debate about whether, and how much, Prime Minister Sharif knew of the clandestine operation that his army was planning when he was signing the Lahore Declaration with Prime Minister Vajpayee. Whatever the truth of the matter, the misadventure proved one grim truth about the country: The world realised that the army in Pakistan was a rogue army. Pakistan was—and even now is—not a democracy like India where the elected representatives have the last word. There are autonomous centres of power in Islamabad that act on their own*.

---

* My good friend R.V. Pandit, a well-known journalist, publisher and a crusader of many worthy national causes, brought out a full-page advertisement titled '*A State within a Contd...*

KARGIL REVIEW COMMITTEE

Another difference in the conduct of India and Pakistan during the war deserves mention. The latter's defeat prompted many people in Pakistan to demand the setting up of a public commission of inquiry to investigate the people responsible for initiating the conflict. However, none was instituted either by the Sharif government or the one that replaced it. Nearly seven years later, Sharif's party, the Pakistan Muslim League (N) issued a White Paper, which claimed that his government had set up an inquiry committee that recommended a court martial for General Musharraf.

In contrast, on 29 July 1999—that is, within three days of the conclusion of the war—the NDA government constituted what came to be known as the Kargil Review Committee to (i) 'review the events leading up to the Pakistani aggression'; and (ii) 'recommend such measures as are considered necessary to safeguard national security against such armed intrusions'. Defence Minister George Fernandes tabled the committee's report in Parliament on 23 February 2000. The alacrity with which our government acted in this matter has no parallel in the history of independent India.

The four-member Kargil Review Committee, which was chaired by noted Defence Analyst K. Subrahmanyam, sought to analyse the situation that led to the nation being caught by surprise by the Pakistani aggression. Specifically, it tried to analyse the shortcomings and failures in the functioning of our intelligence agencies. It met former President R. Venkataraman, Prime Minister Vajpayee, and ex-Prime Ministers V.P. Singh, P.V. Narasimha Rao, I.K. Gujral, my colleagues George Fernandes, Jaswant Singh and me. The committee held over a hundred meetings, having full

---

Contd...

State: A modern Rogue Army with its Finger on the Nuclear Button!' in the *Washington Post* (30 June 1999), the *New York Times* (1 July 1999), the *Times*, London (6 July 1999) and several other newspapers during the Kargil War. The following year, he conducted a similar advertisement campaign, titled *'Jihad for Pakistan, Agony for India'*, to draw the global community's attention to Pakistan-sponsored cross-border terrorism in India. Independent initiatives by patriotic citizens like him effectively complemented governmental efforts to highlight the danger that the situation in Pakistan posed not only to India but to the whole world.

access to highly classified information. Right from the beginning, the Prime Minister's stand, fully shared by his Cabinet, was that the government had nothing to hide and, hence, the greater the transparency in the systemic shortcomings in the Kargil War, the greater would be the usefulness of the committee's report.

The conclusion of the report was certainly unambiguous and upbeat. It concluded that:

> The outcome of the Kargil operation was both a military and diplomatic triumph for India. The Pakistani intruders were evicted with heavier casualties than those suffered by India. The sanctity of the LoC received international recognition and Pakistan was isolated in the comity of nations. While attending to such shortcomings as have been brought to light, the nation can be proud of the manner in which the Armed Forces and the people as a whole acquitted themselves.

To me, it is not the words of congratulation but the words of criticism, concern and caution that hold greater value. It said:

> There was inadequate coordination at the ground level among Army intelligence and other agencies.... The heavy involvement of the Army in counter-insurgency operations cannot but affect its preparedness for its primary role, which is to defend the country against external aggression. Such a situation has arisen because successive Governments have not developed a long-term strategy to deal with the insurgency.... The Army's prolonged deployment in a counter-insurgency role adversely affects its training programme, leads to fatigue and the development of a mindset that detracts from its primary role.... The paramilitary and Central Police Forces are not trained, raised and equipped to deal with trans-border terrorism by well-trained mercenaries armed with sophisticated equipment who are continuously infiltrating across the border/LoC. Over the years, the quality of these forces has not been appropriately upgraded to effectively deal with the challenge

of the times and this has led to the increased dependence on the Army to fight insurgency.... The net result has been to reduce the role of the Indian Army to the level of a paramilitary force and the paramilitary forces, in turn, to the level of an ordinary police force. Pakistan has ruthlessly employed terrorism in Punjab, J&K and the North-East to involve the Indian Army in counter-insurgency operations and neutralise its conventional superiority. Having partially achieved this objective, it has also persuaded itself that nuclear blackmail against India has succeeded on three occasions. A coherent counter-strategy to deal with Pakistan's terrorist-nuclear blackmail and the conventional threat has to be thought through.

The committee made some harsh comments on the successive governments at the Centre, holding them responsible for the 'many grave deficiencies in India's security management system'. It said: 'A framework recommended by Lord Mountbatten was accepted by a national leadership unfamiliar with the intricacies of national security management. There has been very little change over the past 52 years despite the 1962 debacle, the 1965 stalemate and the 1971 victory, the growing nuclear threat, end of the Cold War, continuance of proxy war in Kashmir for over a decade and the revolution in military affairs. It would seem that the political and bureaucratic class of independent India had not drawn any lessons even from the three battles of Panipat, let alone the recent wars of 1948, 1965 and 1971. The political, bureaucratic, military and intelligence establishments appear to have developed a vested interest in the status quo. National security management recedes into the background in time of peace and is considered too delicate to be tampered with in time of war and proxy war.'

The committee made several important recommendations, most of which were duly implemented. Its major recommendation was the call for 'a thorough review of the national security system in its entirety', not 'by an over-burdened bureaucracy', but by an 'independent body of credible experts, whether a national commission or one or more task forces or otherwise as expedient'. It was implemented expeditiously.

One of the few recommendations not accepted was regarding the National Security Council, which had been set up by the Vajpayee government in April 1999. 'Whatever its merits, having a National Security Advisor who also happens to be Principal Secretary to the Prime Minister, can only be an interim arrangement. The Committee believes that there must be a full time National Security Advisor and it would suggest that a second line of personnel be inducted into the system as early as possible and groomed for higher responsibility.'

Many senior ministers in the government and I felt that there was much merit in this suggestion. We repeatedly urged the Prime Minister to bifurcate the two posts held by Brajesh Mishra. Atalji, however, had a different view and did not implement this recommendation. It was, of course, the Prime Minister's prerogative to do so. In my view, the clubbing together of two critical responsibilities, each requiring focused attention, did not contribute to harmony at the highest levels of governance.

KARGIL VICTORY AND CONGRESS CRITICISM

My party had consistently maintained that India's victory in the Kargil War was a national accomplishment that transcended political barriers. After India's triumph in the 1971 war with Pakistan, which led to the liberation of Bangladesh, the Jana Sangh had demonstrated its readiness to rise above political considerations by profusely congratulating the government of the day, led by Indira Gandhi. Unfortunately, the Congress reaction, both during and in the immediate aftermath of the Kargil War, was diametrically different. It did not have the magnanimity to appreciate a national success achieved during the rule of a BJP-led government.

What pains me is to note that its attitude has not changed even with the passage of time. Thus, even as late as in October 2007, Prime Minister Dr Manmohan Singh launched a tirade against the Vajpayee government, saying, 'We know why the Kargil War took place. When the infiltrators were coming in, the government in Delhi was sleeping.'[5] In fact, what Dr Singh has said is no different from what the Congress party's spokesman, Kapil Sibal, had said in 1999: 'Vajpayee and his government are responsible for the total fiasco in Kargil for they went to sleep after the bus ride to Lahore and turned a blind eye while intruders were occupying Indian territory.' He said he would 'prove that the Prime Minister, the Home Minister and the Defence Minister were aware of the intrusion'.[6] This allegation has been conclusively disproved by the Kargil Review Committee, which stated in its report: 'The Committee has not come across any assessment at operational levels that would justify the conclusion that the Lahore summit had caused the Indian decision-makers to lower their guard.'

I was in Chennai to address a gathering of party workers, when the Congress party levelled this outlandish charge. It provoked me to say, 'Is anyone advising them (Congress leaders) to do this? Nothing but suicidal tendencies could make them choose such an agenda for the elections. Indian troops have won against the enemy on the Kargil heights and the government has secured a signal diplomatic triumph. Every country in the world, except Pakistan, is now praising Prime Minister Vajpayee and his government. Every party in our own country is praising Vajpayee, except the Congress.'

I would like to ask leaders of the Congress party, who continue to rubbish the outcome of the Kargil War as a fiasco for India, the following questions:

- Have they done any introspection over Prime Minister Nehru's handling of the Kashmir issue during the first Indo-Pak war in 1947-48? He unilaterally declared ceasefire on 1 January 1949, when our armed forces were chasing the invaders to a point where India could have recovered the entire occupied territory of Jammu & Kashmir. Did Nehru take Parliament or our countrymen into confidence before 'gifting' away 83,100 square kilometres of our territory to Pakistan? Did he evolve a national consensus—or even a consensus within his own Cabinet—before needlessly referring the Kashmir issue to the United Nations?
- After India's debacle in the Chinese aggression in 1962, the Congress party issued a circular that termed anyone as traitors who 'are not being respectful enough, helpful enough and prayerful enough towards

Prime Minister Jawaharlal Nehru. It is wrong to permit Opposition parties to take advantage of the emergency for throwing mud against the Congress'. Veteran Swatantra Party MP, Prof N.G. Ranga, cited this circular during the Lok Sabha debate on the Defence of India Bill in 1962. Can they deny this?

- Will they explain why the Henderson Brooks report, which did an operations review of India's defeat in the 1962 war, has not been declassified even after the passage of forty-five years? Is it because the authors of this official report, two officers of the Indian armed forces: Lieutenant-General Henderson Brooks and Brigadier P.S. Bhagat, commandant of the Indian Military Academy, were believed to be highly critical of the leadership of Prime Minister Nehru and Defence Minister V.K. Krishna Menon?
- Will they explain to the nation why the Congress government timidly returned Haji Pir, which had been recovered by the Indian Army in the 1965 war, to the aggressor Pakistan at the negotiating table in Tashkent in January 1966?
- Will they tell the nation why Indira Gandhi did not try for a full and final settlement of the Kashmir issue after India's decisive victory over Pakistan in the 1971 war, especially when we had as many as 93,000 Pakistani PoWs in our custody?
- Above all, can they recall whether the international community supported India's stand on the Kashmir issue as widely and strongly at any time before the Kargil War?

Did the people of India believe in the Congress propaganda that the Vajpayee government's handling of the Kargil War was a fiasco? The answer to this question, as the next chapter will describe, was delivered by them with the declaration of the results of the mid-term elections to the 13th Lok Sabha held in September-October 1999.

3

THE NDA RETURNS TO POWER

The NDA is a representative of both national interests and regional aspirations. The NDA is the mirror-image of our nation's unity in multifaceted diversity, rich pluralism, and federalism.

—FROM THE MANIFESTO OF THE NDA FOR THE ELECTIONS TO THE 12TH LOK SABHA IN 1999

As the summer of 1999 drew to a close, the guns that had boomed for seventy-four days along the LoC at Kargil fell silent. The war ended in a resounding victory for India and an unforgettable rout for Pakistan. The aggressor's misadventure had ended in a boomerang effect.

Back at home, too, the same boomerang effect hit the Congress party's misadventure of destabilising the Vajpayee government, when elections to the 13th Lok Sabha were held in September-October 1999. It was not the best time for holding parliamentary polls, as parties had to conduct their campaign during the monsoon. But since the Lok Sabha had been dissolved in the last week of April, a new House had to be elected within six months, as stipulated by the Constitution.

Unlike in 1998, when the NDA had become a post-poll alliance, it contested the 1999 elections jointly and on a common manifesto. The size of the alliance, too, had expanded; it now had twenty-four parties. The three main issues on which we sought a renewed mandate from the people were: security, stability and development. The Vajpayee government's bold decision to make India a nuclear weapons power had made Indians proud. This feeling of national pride had become more intense after the victory in the Kargil War. If this had endeared the NDA to the people, they were also influenced by our call for stability. Leaders of the NDA reminded them how the Congress and its allies had pulled down the government without offering an alternative, thus pushing the country into needless mid-term elections. We also emphasised the direct link between governmental stability, the nation's development, people's welfare and national security. It was a message the voters quickly grasped since India had had four governments within a span of three years. In my long experience of interacting with Indian voters, I have understood one thing very clearly: they consider mid-term elections, unless caused by natural or unavoidable factors, a costly and avoidable burden imposed on the country.

Our appeal to the voters was simple: 'They brought our government down *by one vote*, a fraudulent one at that. Now, each of you has the power to teach them a lesson by re-electing us with your *one valuable vote*. But let your mandate not be fractured as before. Atalji's first government of 1996 lasted only thirteen days. His second government of 1998 lasted only thirteen months. Now give him a decisive mandate to govern the country for full five years. And we promise you that the success that India has achieved in the arena of national security will be repeated in the arena of national development.'

The electorate responded splendidly to this appeal. The NDA won a comfortable majority with 306 seats, in a house of 545. The BJP secured 182 seats, one more than in 1998. In contrast, the Congress tally hit rock-bottom: only 114 seats, 26 fewer than its 1998 total of 140. The BJP's vote share was 23.75 per cent, less than the 1998 figure of 25.59 per cent, but this was because the party contested far less number of seats: 339 in 1999 as against 388 in 1998. The rest of the seats were left for our allies in the NDA. On the morning of 13 October, the forecourt of Rashtrapati Bhavan witnessed Atal Bihari Vajpayee being sworn in as India's Prime Minister for the third time. I, too, took the oath of office and headed straight to my office in the Home Ministry in North Block. In view of the smooth continuity in governance, the mid-term elections seemed utterly superfluous.

But there was another thought, too, that starkly highlighted the contrast between the triumph of democracy in India and the crisis of democracy in Pakistan. Television viewers in India, and around the world, had seen the Indian Prime Minister being sworn in on 13 October. Just the previous day, they had also seen Pakistan's Prime Minister Nawaz Sharif being toppled in a military coup. Soldiers loyal to General Pervez Musharraf, who captured power, had stormed Sharif's official residence, arrested him and put him in jail. The contrast between the two images was also the contrast between the failed idea of Pakistan and the vibrant idea of India.

SONIA GANDHI'S 'FOREIGN-ORIGIN' ISSUE

Before proceeding further, I should dwell on an important issue that figured prominently in the 1999 election campaign—the foreign origin of Congress President Sonia Gandhi. The NDA, in its common manifesto, had promised to introduce a legislation to ensure that 'important offices of the Indian State can be occupied only by those who are India's natural citizens by their Indian origin'. The BJP and its allies were not the only ones to hold this view. The TDP, led by Andhra Pradesh Chief Minister Chandrababu Naidu, also favoured a change in the Statute to bar persons of foreign origin from holding high constitutional posts of President, Vice President and Prime Minister. As mentioned by me earlier, this issue was the principal reason behind the decision of the Samajwadi Party leader, Mulayam Singh Yadav, not to support Sonia Gandhi's claim to become the Prime Minister in April 1999. He even publicly justified 'shattering Sonia's dreams to be the Prime Minister'.[1]

Interestingly, the most dramatic articulation of concern over Sonia Gandhi's foreign origin was seen within the Congress party itself. On

16 May 1999, three senior Congress leaders, all of them members of the CWC, addressed a letter to party President Sonia Gandhi. They were: Sharad Pawar, former Chief Minister of Maharashtra and Defence Minister in P.V. Narasimha Rao's government; P.A. Sangma, former Speaker of the Lok Sabha; and Tariq Anwar, a Congress leader from Bihar. In view of its importance in India's political history, I reproduce here a longish extract from it.

Respected Congress President,

It is with a deep sense of responsibility, and an overwhelming sense of concern that we write to you. The founders and the leaders of the Congress party like your eminent grandfather-in-law had always encouraged a tradition of free and uninhibited exchange of views amongst Congressmen. They have built the foundation of Indian democracy on the four pillars of liberty of opinion, freedom of expression, responsibility of action and, above all, nation before self. We believe we are being true to these ideals in placing our views before you.... Madam President, India is a country with a history and tradition going back to thousands of years. It is a confident culture and a proud nation. Above all, it is a country which is self sufficient in every sense of the word. India always lived in the spirit of the Mahatma's words 'Let the winds from all over sweep into my room', but again he said: 'I will not be swept off my feet.' We accept with interest and humility the best which we can gather from the North, South, East or West and we absorb them into our soil. But our inspiration, our soul, our honour, our pride, our dignity, is rooted in our soil, it has to be of this earth.

Soniaji, you have become a part of us because you have all along respected this. We, therefore, find it strange that you should allow yourself to forget it at this crucial juncture. It is not possible that a country of 980 million, with a wealth of education, competence and ability, can have anyone other than an Indian born of Indian soil, to head its government. Some of us have tried to initiate and open broader discussions on this issue within the party. It is an issue which affects not just the security, the economic interest and the international image of India, but hits at the core pride of every Indian. Unfortunately, this initiative has been thwarted at every stage.

At the risk of repetition we would like to emphasise that as Congressmen, we look up to you as a leader who kept the party together and is a source of strength to all of us. But, as a responsible political party, we also have to understand the genuine concern of the average Indian who may or may not be a Congressman. That India is concerned about the person who will guide the course of his destiny for at least five years. India's prime ministership is probably the single most difficult job in the world today. A country the size of a subcontinent, with a population of 980 million; a vibrant, vocal democracy, a struggling economy, fissiparous forces tearing the social fabric and; insurgency and terrorism which cuts at national unity. No government anywhere in the world faces the type of complex problems and multidimensional issues that need attention in India. A person who is to take the reins of this country needs a large measure of experience and understanding of public life. That is why the founders of the party insisted that people who aspired for higher positions should first spend time working their way up. This way, the party worker got acquainted with the complexity of issues in the country.

The average Indian is not unreasonable in demanding that his prime minister have some track record in public life. The Congress party needs to respect this very justifiable expectation.... We believe, Madam President, that even now it is not too late. We have discussed this matter today in the CWC at great length. We stand by the views we have expressed there.... We believe that it is our responsibility as Congressmen and political leaders to formally place on record our view and request the CWC and you to consider the following suggestion which we feel would set at rest the controversy currently being debated across the country.

The Congress manifesto should suggest an amendment to the Constitution of India, to the effect that the offices of President, Vice-President and Prime Minister can only be held by natural-born Indian citizens. We would also request that you, as Congress president, propose this amendment. This will be in line with your own consistent stand that your sole concern in entering public life was to revive and rejuvenate the party.

*

All the three rebel leaders, who raised the 'foreign origin' issue, were quickly expelled from the Congress. They later formed their own political outfit called the Nationalist Congress Party (NCP). It is another matter that the NCP is now in alliance with the Congress, both in Maharashtra and at the Centre.

Why did the Italy-born Sonia Gandhi's foreign origin become an election issue in India? Why did so many political parties—and not the BJP alone—take a common stand on the matter independently, without any mutual consultation? As far as the BJP is concerned, there were no personal considerations that guided our stand. I strongly disapproved of certain personalised comments on Sonia Gandhi during the campaign. Such personal criticism of a woman, and a widow at that, is clearly barred in India's cultural tradition, and nor can it have a place in democratic discourse. But, fundamentally, it was a matter of principle for us. I have good reasons to believe that other political parties, too, had similar principled and basic concerns. Why? To know this, a few facts have to be borne in mind.

- Sonia Gandhi, whose earlier name was Sonia Antonia Maino, came to India after her marriage to Rajiv Gandhi in 1968. But she did not apply for Indian citizenship even after she entered Prime Minister Indira Gandhi's household. Instead, she filed an application for permission to stay as a *foreigner* in India, which is granted for five years. After the expiry of the first five-year period, she re-applied twice, in 1973 and 1978, for permission to stay in India while keeping her status as a foreigner. Only on 27 April 1983, just three days before her third five-year permit expired, she renounced her Italian citizenship and opted to become an Indian citizen. The timing of her decision was revealing. It was influenced by the fact that her husband was then being groomed as the successor to Indira Gandhi. Therefore, the question that weighed on the minds of many Indians, and it continues to do so even now, was: Why did Sonia Gandhi not take Indian citizenship for fifteen long years after coming to India, and even after giving birth to her two children here? Till date, she has not answered this question satisfactorily. In an interview telecast on Doordarshan on 6 September 1999, she claimed that she became an Indian citizen the day she became Indira Gandhi's daughter-in-law and that any other view is merely 'technical'. It was a peculiar explanation, to say the least.

- Question marks have been placed on some of Sonia Gandhi's actions during the period that she was not an Indian citizen. These have been well-documented in the investigative articles by A. Surya Prakash compiled in the book *Issue of Foreign Origin: Sonia Under Scrutiny*. It was published in 2004 by the New Delhi-based India First Foundation, which has been established by my colleague Dinanath Mishra. For instance, Sonia Gandhi had cast her vote in the 1980 parliamentary elections even though she was not a citizen of India then. How did she get her name registered in the voters' list?

- In many democratic countries, including USA and Italy, the law prohibits a person from holding the highest public office unless he or she is native born. Similar laws exist in Indonesia, Philippines, Finland, Bulgaria, Congo, Algeria, Brazil and Iran. In India there is no such law, principally because the makers of our Constitution did not visualise a situation when the issue of foreign-origin of a political personality would dominate national debate in a manner that it did in the late 1990s. I would like to mention here that even Henry Kissinger, the legendary former Secretary of State of the United States, cannot run for presidential election in his country because he is foreign-born. Article II, Section 1 of the US Constitution allows only natural-born citizens to serve as the President. The same limitation applies to Madeleine Albright, another former Secretary of State, and Arnold Schwarzenegger, the incumbent Governor of California.

Speaking for myself, what influenced my thinking on this issue was not so much the legal aspects of citizenship, important though they are in themselves. India is an open society and our culture is exceedingly accommodative and assimilative, especially when it comes to a person who enters one's family as a daughter-in-law. The mere fact of a person being foreign-born has never come in the way of Indians accepting such a person as their own. Two outstanding women from the pre-Independence era, who were foreigners but became an integral part of India's mind and soul, were Sister Nivedita* and Dr Annie Besant†. Indian people recall their names with reverence even today.

Like every other Indian, I have my sympathies for Sonia Gandhi for the tragedies that she has experienced in her life. I also admire the courage that she has displayed in overcoming them. Nevertheless, if there is one thing that has disappointed me the most, it is her active and irrefutable collusion in covering up the role of fellow Italian, Ottavio Quattrocchi,

---

* Sister Nivedita (1867-1911), who was born in Ireland as Margaret Elizabeth Noble, met Swami Vivekananda in 1895 in London and dedicated the rest of her life to the service of India. A devoted spiritual seeker, great intellectual and tireless social worker, she made an important contribution to national awakening in India in the first decade of the twentieth century. Impressed by her intellect and spirit of service, Rabindranath Tagore praised her as *Lokmata* (Mother of the People), Aurobindo called her *Agnishikha* (Flame of Fire) and her own teacher Swami Vivekanand described her as 'a real lioness'. Her writings have continued to inspire generations of Indians.

† Annie Besant (1847-1933) was a prominent British socialist who became an ardent spiritualist after being influenced by the Hindu view of life. She was elected President of the Theosophical Society, a worldwide body promoting Universal Brotherhood based on the wisdom underlying all religions. After her first visit to India in 1893, she became progressively involved in India's freedom movement, established the Indian Home Rule League that attracted many nationalist leaders, and was even elected President of the Indian National Congress in 1917. Her voluminous writings on theosophy, politics, culture, education, women's emancipation and social reform have an enduring message for India and the world.

in the infamous Bofors scandal. It is devoid of any political morality and unbecoming of a person aspiring to hold the highest executive office in India. For achieving this cover-up, almost every institution of the Indian Republic—Prime Minister's Office, Law Ministry, Foreign Ministry, Defence Ministry, judiciary, CBI, JPC, government-run media—has been misused. Congressmen will never be able to explain away this stigma on their leader and their party.

The issue of her foreign origin resurfaced again in May 2004, after the elections to the 14th Lok Sabha, and is still far from settled.

4

Review of the Working of the Indian Constitution

> JUSTICE, *social, economic and political;*
>
> LIBERTY *of thought, expression, belief, faith and worship;*
>
> EQUALITY *of status and of opportunity;*
> *and to promote among them all*
>
> FRATERNITY, *assuring the dignity of the individual*
> *and the unity and integrity of the Nation.*
>
> —From the Preamble to the Constitution of India

Within a fortnight of being sworn in, the Vajpayee government put into action a key commitment made in the election manifesto of the ruling alliance: setting up the National Commission to Review the Working of the Constitution (NCRWC). It was intended to study a half-century's experience of the Constitution and make suitable recommendations to meet the challenges of the future. It was also mandated to examine replacing the present system of the no-confidence motion by a system of 'Constructive Vote of Confidence' and a fixed term for the Lok Sabha and the Vidhan Sabhas, in order to prevent political instability both at the Centre and in the states.

The idea of setting up a constitutional review panel was essentially mine. Since the Constitution had come into force, successive governments—mainly the Congress or Congress-supported government—had amended it, out of administrative or political necessity, more than eighty times! My party had, however, felt the need for a comprehensive review of the Constitution, principally for three reasons. Firstly, with the passage of nearly fifty years since its adoption in 1950, it was evident that a schism had developed between the original ideals and goals of the Constitution and the actual performance of the Republic. This gap needed to be bridged. Secondly, the working of, and coordination between, the institutional tripod of parliamentary democracy—legislature, executive, judiciary—left a lot to be desired. Also, growing demands for the devolution of powers from the Centre to states, and from state governments to the Panchayati Raj institutions and municipal bodies had not been addressed. The third and the most pressing reason was the problem of political instability. The manner in which the Congress party had destabilised the Vajpayee government in April 1999, without providing an alternative, and thus precipitating mid-term elections within thirteen months of the five-year term of the Lok Sabha, had convinced us that the country needed to look for viable democratic measures to ensure stable governance.

Accordingly, the government set up the NCRWC in February 2000. Its independent and non-partisan nature could be easily gauged by its broadbased composition*. It was chaired by Justice M.N. Venkatachaliah,

---

* Other members of the commission included Justice R.S. Sarkaria, a former Judge of the Supreme Court who headed the Sarkaria Commission on Centre-State Relations; Justice B.P. Jeevan Reddy, a former Judge of the Supreme Court of India; P.A. Sangma, former Speaker of the Lok Sabha and a Minister in Rajiv Gandhi's government; Dr Subhash C. Kashyap, former Secretary General of the Lok Sabha and an eminent Constitutional expert; Justice K. Punnayya, a former Judge of the Andhra Pradesh High Court; K. Parasaran, former Attorney General of India; Soli J. Sorabjee, incumbent Attorney General of India; Dr Abid Hussain, former Ambassador to the United States of America; C.R. Irani, Chief Editor of the *Statesman*; and Sumitra G. Kulkarni, a former MP.

the widely respected former Chief Justice of India and a former chairman of the National Human Rights Commission (NHRC). The terms of reference of the Commission left no scope for controversy. It was explicitly stated that its recommendations would be '*within the framework of parliamentary democracy*', and '*without interfering with the basic structure or feature of the Constitution*'. The Commission went a step further to allay any misgivings in the minds of the people about its work by stating that its function '*is to review the working of the Constitution* and not to *rewrite* the Constitution.' (emphasis added.)

Unfortunately, right from the onset, Congress and communist parties mounted a vitriolic attack on this initiative. Their criticism was based on gross misrepresentation of the intent and purpose behind it. They charged the government with having a 'hidden agenda', saying that the comprehensive review of the Constitution was designed to help the BJP 'to selectively tamper with the Constitution and ensure that they continued to remain in power if the NDA coalition broke up in the future'. They also rejected the idea of having a fixed term for the Lok Sabha on the grounds that it would render the elected representatives unaccountable to citizens for the entire period of five years. On 14 April 2000, the Congress party observed the birth anniversary of Dr B.R. Ambedkar as 'Save the Constitution Day', and unleashed a propaganda campaign to paint the BJP as 'anti-Ambedkar' and 'anti-dalit'.

A CRITICISM WITH MORE HEAT THAN LIGHT

Criticism from our political opponents, though unwarranted and unmerited, was understandable but what disappointed us the most was the baseless censure of the initiative by President Narayanan. Using the occasion of a function held in the Central Hall of Parliament on 27 January 2000 to mark the fiftieth anniversary of the enforcement of the Constitution, he made certain comments that grossly misrepresented the government's stated perspective. He said: 'Today when there is so much talk about revising the Constitution or even writing a new Constitution, we have to consider whether it is the Constitution that has failed us or whether it is we who have failed the Constitution.... The form of government, the parliamentary democratic form, was chosen by the founding fathers after deep thought and debate. In the Constituent Assembly, Dr Ambedkar explained that the Drafting Committee in choosing the parliamentary system for India, preferred more responsibility to stability, which could slip into authoritarian exercise of power.... Our recent experience of instability in government is perhaps not sufficient reason to discard the parliamentary system in favour of the presidential or any other system.... We should ensure that the basic philosophy behind the Constitution and fundamental socio-economic soul of the Constitution remain sacrosanct. We should not throw out the baby with the bath water.'*

His remarks were misleading because the government had formed the commission neither with a mandate to 'write a new Constitution', nor to discard the parliamentary system. His berating of the people's concern for stability was unfortunate and seemed politically motivated. Speaking on the same occasion, Prime Minister Vajpayee convincingly allayed the unfounded apprehensions raised by the President by assuring the nation, once again, that 'the basic structure and the core ideals of the Constitution' would not be violated.

There was another point that our opponents had conveniently overlooked. Constitutional amendments can be enacted only by a majority of members of both the Lok Sabha and the Rajya Sabha, with a minimum of two-thirds of MPs present. Certain constitutional amendments also need to be ratified by at least half of the Vidhan Sabhas. The composition of the two Houses then was such that, although the NDA had a majority in the Lower House, it lacked one in the Upper House. Therefore, no Constitutional amendment bill could possibly have been passed by the NDA without the cooperation of the Opposition. As such, the allegation that we had some 'hidden agenda' to rewrite the Constitution was pure hogwash.

---

* The President's address to Parliament is a formal statement of government policy, the text of which is prepared and finalised by the Cabinet and read out by him in accordance with a well-established convention. The President may, however, express his personal views in his speeches on other occasions.

Readers will perhaps better appreciate my views on this important subject by going through excerpts from a comprehensive speech I had delivered at a function in Patna on 26 April 1998. The occasion was a memorial lecture in honour of Thakur Prasad*, a former party colleague in Bihar.

Disinformation is being spread in some quarters that the Vajpayee government wishes to scrap the Ambedkar Constitution and adopt an entirely different Constitution by throwing secularism overboard and scrapping the policy of reservations for the SCs, STs and OBCs. These allegations are utterly baseless and politically motivated. Both secularism as well as reservations are essential features of the Constitution, which cannot be, and will not be, tampered with in any way. Article 368 of the Constitution lays down how the Indian Constitution can be amended. Its history is really fascinating. Commending this provision to the Constituent Assembly, Dr B.R. Ambedkar, Chairman of the Drafting Committee, quoted at some length Thomas Jefferson, the great American statesman who had played a key role in the framing of the American Constitution: 'We may consider each generation as a distinct nation, with a right, by the will of the majority, to bind themselves, but none to bind the succeeding generation, more than the inhabitants of another country.' Dr Ambedkar went on to add: 'What Jefferson has said is not merely true, but is absolutely true…. The (Constituent) Assembly has not only refrained from putting a seal of finality and infallibility upon this Constitution, but has provided a most facile procedure for amending it.' Those who try to propagate these days that the present government is seeking to undo the good work done by Dr Ambedkar would do well to study Dr Ambedkar's own views in this regard.

We in the BJP-led alliance believe that the problems which this country faces today—poverty, unemployment, illiteracy, poor health,

---

* His son, Ravi Shankar Prasad, is a young leader of the BJP. He was a Minister in the Vajpayee government.

underdevelopment—cannot be attributed to the Constitution. Dr Rajendra Prasad as Chairman of the Constituent Assembly had rightly observed: 'If the people who are elected are capable, and men of character and integrity, they would be able to make the best even of a defective Constitution. If they are lacking in these, the Constitution cannot help the country. After all, the Constitution, like a machine, is a lifeless thing. It acquires life because of the men who control it and operate it and India needs today nothing more than a set of honest men who will have the interest of the country before them.' Clearly, the debate on the review of the Constitution demands more light than heat.

RECOMMENDATIONS OF THE CONSITUTION REVIEW PANEL

The Commission submitted its report to the Prime Minister on 31 March 2002, having done a competent job in a remarkably short time. Let me summarise, along with my own comments, a few progressive and path-breaking recommendations made by the Commission.

Political Stability: The panel proposed that, in a situation where no single political party or pre-poll alliance secures a clear majority in the Lok Sabha after elections, rules may be changed 'to provide for the election of the Leader of the House' by all members of the Lok Sabha along with the election of the Speaker and in the like manner. 'The Leader may then be appointed as the Prime Minister. The same procedure may be followed for the office of the Chief Minister in the state concerned'. It also recommended the adoption of a system of constructive vote of no-confidence. 'For a motion of no-confidence to be brought out against a government, at least 20% of the total number of members of the House should give notice. Also, the motion should be accompanied by a proposal of an alternative Leader to be voted simultaneously.'

Electoral Reforms: The panel made several recommendations for reforming the electoral system. (a) Electoral rolls should be prepared by issuing a foolproof voter ID card, which may also serve as a multi-purpose citizenship card. (b) The Chief Election Commissioner and the other Election

Commissioners should be appointed on the recommendation of a body consisting of the Prime Minister, Leader of the Opposition in the Lok Sabha, Leader of the Opposition in the Rajya Sabha, the Speaker of the Lok Sabha and the Deputy Chairman of the Rajya Sabha. Similar procedure should be adopted in the case of appointment of State Election Commissioners. (c) The provisions of the Tenth Schedule of the Constitution should be amended to provide that all persons defecting—whether individually or in groups—from the party or the alliance of parties, on whose ticket they had been elected, must resign from their parliamentary or assembly seats and must contest fresh elections. (d) The existing ceiling on election expenses should be raised to a reasonable level reflecting the increasing costs. (e) The threshold criterion of eligibility for recognition of political parties should be raised to discourage the proliferation of smaller parties. (f) The practice of having oversized ministries should be prevented.

The NDA government implemented some of these reforms through an appropriate law in 2003. In a step to curb bulk political defections, defectors were barred from holding any public posts. The size of ministries was limited to fifteen per cent of the strength of the legislature with a minimum figure of twelve. While most of the Commission's ideas on electoral reforms were welcome, I was, however, disappointed by its failure to recommend state-funding of elections on the plea that 'regulatory mechanisms' were absent. I was even more disappointed by its escapist posture on the 'foreign-origin' issue, on which it said that it 'should be examined in-depth through a political process after a national dialogue'. The panel's reluctance to take a stand on this issue forced P.A. Sangma, one of its distinguished members, to resign.

Fundamental Duties: I was pleased to see that the Commission had recommended addition of the following in the list of 'Fundamental Duties' of citizens in Article 51A of the Constitution: Vote in elections; actively participate in the democratic process of governance; pay taxes; and foster a spirit of family values and responsible parenthood in the matter of education, physical and moral well-being of children.

MP's Local Area Development Scheme (MPLADS): The panel was right in recommending 'immediate discontinuation' of the MPLADS, since it was 'inconsistent with the spirit of the Constitution'. I have always considered it to be ironical that in India, an MP acquires maximum visibility in the eyes of the people on account of his work under the MPLADS, although it is not his primary duty as a legislator. Given the nature of our multi-party democracy, the level of socio-economic development, and poor governance in local areas, I can understand why people expect their MP to do 'something' about bad or non-existent roads, ill-equipped schools, much-needed healthcare facilities, etc. But I believe that such issues of development are better addressed by MPs spending more time and energy on formulation of better laws, closer scrutiny of policies, and rigorous evaluation of governmental programmes.

Executive and Public Administration: The panel made two important recommendations to improve efficiency in civil service. 'All posts in the Government of India, above the Joint Secretary level, should be open for recruitment from a wide variety of sources. Government should specialize some of the generalists and generalise some of the specialists through proper career management which has to be freed from day to day political manipulation and influence peddling. There should be social audit of officials for developing accountability and answerability.' It also mooted a law to guarantee the citizens' right to information 'for ensuring speedy disposal of cases, minimising manipulative and dilatory tactics of the babudom, and putting check on graft and corruption'. I am happy that the UPA government accepted this recommendation and legislated the Right to Information Act in 2005.

Judicial Reforms: For the appointment of judges of the Supreme Court, the panel recommended the setting up of a National Judicial Commission comprising the Chief Justice of India (Chairman), two senior most Judges of the Supreme Court, Union Minister for Law and Justice, and one eminent person nominated by the President of India. It made many suggestions for de-clogging the Indian judicial system, which has over two crore cases pending before various courts, many of them for years together. It also said that 'judgments of the Supreme Court and High Courts should ordinarily be delivered not later than ninety days from the conclusion of the case'.

Speedy Socio-economic Development: The Commission recommended numerous measures for accelerated and equitable socio-economic development, with a strong focus on the welfare and empowerment of the Scheduled Castes (SCs), Scheduled Tribes (STs) and OBCs. It said: 'There must be a body of high status which reviews the state of the level of implementation of the Directive Principles and Economic, Social and Cultural Rights and in particular (i) the Right to Work, (ii) the Right to Health, (iii) the Right to Food, Clothing and Shelter, (iv) Right to Education up to and beyond the 14th year, and (v) the Right to Culture.' It entrusted the duty on the Planning Commission to ensure that the Directive Principles of State Policy (DPSP) were realised more effectively. 'Every Ministry/Department of the Government of India should make a special annual report indicating the extent of effectuation/realization of the Directive Principles of State Policy, the shortfall in the targets, the reasons for the shortfall, if any, and the remedial measures taken to ensure their full realisation, during the year under report. Parliament should discuss the report within a period of three months and pass a resolution about the action required to be taken by the Ministry/Department concerned. A similar mechanism as mentioned above may be adopted by the States.'

Decentralisation: Echoing a demand long espoused by Gandhians and many others in our country, including the BJP, the Commission rightly observed that 'the system can deliver the goods only through devolution, decentralisation and democratisation thereby narrowing the gap between the base of the polity and the super structure'. The 73rd and 74th amendments of the Constitution, introduced by Rajiv Gandhi's government, were meant to empower institutions of the Panchayati Raj as feasible bodies of self-governance. However, few steps had been taken to transfer the three F's—funds, functions and functionaries—to Panchayati Raj bodies to ensure their financial and administrative empowerment. Therefore, the panel suggested that the Eleventh and Twelfth Schedules to the Constitution be restructured in order to create 'a separate fiscal domain' for panchayats and municipalities. 'An enabling provision should be made in Part IX of the Constitution permitting the State Legislature to make, by law, provisions that would confer on the Panchayats full power of administrative and functional control over such staff as are transferred following devolution of functions, notwithstanding any right they may have acquired from State Act/Rules. They should also have the power to recruit certain categories of staff required for service in their jurisdiction.'

Another far-reaching recommendation in this regard was to consider a district as a basic unit of planning and implementation of development schemes. 'This would, to a substantial degree, correct the existing distortions and make officials directly answerable to the people to ensure proper implementation of development programmes under the direct scrutiny of people.' Here, in my view, the commission could have been bolder. I personally believe that the time has come to consider the concept of a 'district government', by further empowering zila parishads, as a third tier of governance below the Union and state governments. The population of many of our districts is higher than the population of provinces or states in several countries around the world. Also, some of our states are larger in size, and more populous than many countries in the world. Therefore, to achieve the goal of good governance, we will have to think of decentralising governance and administration through appropriate institutions in the future. Another concept worth considering in this context is that of 'city government' in some of our mega-cities*, with suitably empowered mayors and corporators, for realising the objectives of urban renewal and better municipal governance.

Centre-State Relations: Reiterating the view expressed by the Sarkaria Commission, the panel urged for more effective use of the Inter-State Council for expeditious decision-making, the lack of which is slowing the implementation of many developmental and administrative measures. It underscored the need for stronger institutional cooperation between the Centre and the state for the management of disasters and emergencies. Responding to the demand of state governments for a higher share in the tax on services, which now account for the biggest share in India's Gross Domestic Product (GDP), it called for 'an appropriate amendment to the Constitution to include certain taxes, now levied and collected by the Union, to be levied and collected by the states'. It also suggested

---

* Needless to say, these metropolises should continue to be a part of their respective states.

ways for speedy settlement of river water disputes, keeping the 'national interest paramount'.

The panel favoured setting a time-limit of six months for the Governor of a state to take a decision on whether to grant assent for a bill passed by the legislature or to reserve it for consideration of the President. 'If the bill is reserved for consideration of the President, there should be a time-limit, say of three months, within which the President should take a decision whether to accord his assent or to direct the Governor to return it to the State Legislature or to seek the opinion of the Supreme Court regarding the constitutionality of the Act under article 143.'

Appointment of Governors: The Commission observed that 'the powers of the President in the matter of selection and appointment of Governors should not be diluted'. However, it recommended that 'the Governor of a State should be appointed by the President only after consultation with the Chief Minister of that State'. Since the Home Ministry is directly responsible for interacting with Governors, it is a matter of considerable joy that the NDA government followed this sound principle long before it was proposed by the Constitution Review Panel. During the six years of the NDA government, not a single Governor was appointed without consulting—indeed, without taking prior approval of—the Chief Minister of the respective state. We scrupulously followed this principle even in respect of Congress and communist Chief Ministers. Indeed, both Jyoti Basu, the previous Chief Minister of West Bengal, and his successor, Buddhadeb Bhattacharya, were pleasantly surprised at this, since their experience with the Congress governments in the past had been quite different.

I leave it to the judgement of readers to decide whether the above recommendations of the Venkatachaliah Commission prove the allegations levelled by our opponents that our government had a 'hidden agenda' to alter the basic structure of the Indian Constitution. I would just like to remind the people of India that many of those levelling this charge were silent when the basic structure of the Constitution was, in reality, sought to be destroyed during the Emergency.

*

Indeed, some Governors who had been appointed by the Congress or Congress-supported governments before the NDA came to power in 1998, were equally surprised when we re-appointed them for a second term, solely on the basis of their good performance. I may mention here the names of Dr P.C. Alexander, the Governor of Maharashtra, who was known for his proximity to two former Prime Ministers, Indira Gandhi and Rajiv Gandhi, having served as Principal Secretary to both of them; and M.M. Jacob, the Governor of Meghalaya, who had been a minister in Rajiv Gandhi's government. Similarly, Ved Marwah, a distinguished former Police Commissioner of Delhi who had no connection with the BJP whatsoever, was surprised when I asked him if he would go to Jharkhand as the Governor.

Dr Alexander's re-appointment led to unexpected and unfortunate consequences. He was never known to be close to the BJP. In fact, my own interaction with him before the NDA government assumed office was very limited. I had met him at the Raj Bhavan in Mumbai when he was the Governor of Maharashtra at the time of the formation of the BJP-Shiv Sena government in 1995. I was impressed with his fair, non-partisan and meticulous approach in dealing with various political parties. Frankly, that was the only reason for our decision to offer him a second term. However, this did not find favour with many people in the Congress establishment, including Sonia Gandhi. As Dr Alexander records in his memoirs: 'She (Sonia) was frank enough to admit that she had indeed felt unhappy when she heard about my acceptance of a second term as Governor[1].'

Of course, my frequent interactions with him after 1998 helped me realise Alexander's outstanding qualities as an individual, his rich experience in public service and his profound scholarship on a wide range of issues. Hence, when Dr K.R. Narayanan's term as the President of India ended in 2002, and the NDA had to choose its candidate for the Presidential election, both Atalji and I agreed that Alexander was best-suited to occupy the country's highest constitutional office. Almost everybody in the NDA approved his candidature, and only the formal announcement was left to be made. At the last minute, however, this was thwarted by what Alexander calls in his book the 'dirty tricks' campaign launched against him by a 'clique'. The Congress party's leadership communicated to us that we could not bank on its support if he was our candidate.

Alexander writes: 'Deeply anguished at the reports I received about the insidiousness of some Congressmen, I wrote to the Prime Minister and the Home Minister exposing the utter hollowness and maliciousness of these stories. Fortunately, the two top leaders were in no way influenced by the antics of these men. In fact, Advani was pained at this campaign of vilification against me. In his letter of 2 June 2002, he wrote: "The campaign unleashed against you is really distressing. It only reveals the depths to which some political elements can descend to subserve their narrow objectives".[2]

Given the composition of the electoral college for the presidential election at the time, the NDA needed the support of the Congress and other Opposition parties to ensure the victory of its candidate. We achieved this by fielding Dr A.P.J. Abdul Kalam, a renowned scientist and one of the heroes of Pokharan II, as the NDA's candidate. Dr Kalam went on to become one of the finest and most popular Presidents ever. Not only did he uphold the dignity of the high constitutional office, but also inspired Indians of all generations, especially children and the youth, with his vision of India as a developed nation. He communicated with great conviction his faith in India's spiritual and cultural heritage, even as he exhorted the people to embrace the best of what modern science and technology had to offer. The NDA was willing to support Dr Kalam's re-election in the presidential election in July 2007, but the Congress was opposed to the idea.

I am glad that Alexander has presented in his memoirs a no-holds barred, and yet objective account of that unfortunate episode in 2002. His book shows the contrast between two opposite political cultures—that of the Congress leadership, which is habituated to looking at persons in public life through the prism of 'our man vs their man', and of the BJP, whose decisions are guided by national interest and preserving the integrity of our democratic institutions.

5

AT THE HELM OF THE HOME MINISTRY

God, give us Men! A time like this demands
Strong minds, great hearts, true faith and ready hands;
Men whom the lust of office does not kill;
Men whom the spoils of office cannot buy;
Men who possess opinions and a will;
Men who have honor; men who will not lie;
Men who can stand before a demagogue
And damn his treacherous flatteries without winking!
Tall men, sun-crowned, who live above the fog
In public duty and in private thinking.

—JOSIAH GILBERT HOLLAND (1819-81), AN AMERICAN POET

When the results of the March 1998 parliamentary elections showed a clear mandate in favour of a BJP-led government headed by Atal Bihari Vajpayee, some of my colleagues suggested that I should not join the Council of Ministers but instead, continue to look after strengthening the party. My own initial impulse was similar. However, the overwhelming majority of the people within the party wanted me to join the government. They argued that this was necessary to lend solidity to the new governing set-up and also to avoid any baseless speculation about dual centres of power. Atalji himself was keen that I assist him in running the affairs of the government.

The Prime Minister asked me to choose whichever ministry I wished to look after. My choice, Home Ministry, was premeditated. Both in my election campaign for the 1998 parliamentary polls, as well as during my two-month long Swarna Jayanti Rath Yatra, I had highlighted security as one of the main planks of the BJP's agenda of good governance. I had pointed out that throughout world history, the primary responsibility of any State has been to guarantee security to the common man. Sadly, even fifty years after Independence, the Indian State seemed to be failing in this basic duty. We were generally perceived, both within and outside the country, as a 'Soft State', one that could not protect its legitimate security interests vis-à-vis powerful nations as well as smaller and much weaker neighbours. India was seen as lacking in strong-willed political leadership whose shortcomings were compounded by an ineffective, unfocused, meagerly supported, excessively bureaucratic and endemically corrupt security apparatus.

The BJP in its election manifesto in 1998 had said: 'The security of the nation is our paramount duty. In fulfilment of this sacred duty we will ensure that the neglect of defence preparedness by the previous governments during the last decade shall be corrected.... We are committed to ensuring the safety and security of all citizens in all parts of the country. For reaching this goal we will take effective steps to create a riot-free order and a terrorism-free India.'

My choice of the Home Ministry thus sprang from a keen desire to make a personal contribution, however modest, to the fulfilment of this promise. It was also influenced by a second serious problem that the NDA government had identified when it assumed office. A mapping of the various long-term and immediate-term threats to India's national security clearly indicated a sharp rise in the relative importance of internal vis-à-vis external security. True, the threats from inter-state wars had significantly declined but the threats to internal security had considerably increased.

And, as shown by many studies, this trend was most likely to continue both in the short and medium terms.

Pakistan's proxy war against India had begun in the early 1980s, as a direct outcome of the strategy adopted by its then military ruler Zia-ul-Haq. After its debacle in the 1971 war, for the liberation of Bangladesh, Pakistan had realised that it could not defeat India in conventional warfare. Therefore, it adopted a new strategy of waging a 'war through other means'—the means employed was terrorism; the manpower deployed a combination of mercenaries, religious zealots who had become 'unemployed' after the end of the Soviet occupation of Afghanistan, and misguided youth who were trained in Pakistan by the ISI; and the weapons used was the huge cache of leftovers from the Afghan war.

By its very nature, it was a war without boundaries, one in which the invisible enemy could strike anywhere. Soon, cross-border terrorism was no longer limited to the two border states of Punjab and Jammu & Kashmir. On 12 March 1993, serial bomb blasts in Mumbai by ISI-trained operatives left 257 innocent people dead. It was an audacious attack, carried out at ten different places in the city within a span of a few hours. Among the targets were the imposing building of the BSE and sea-facing headquarters, which clearly proved that the attackers' intent was to cripple the country's financial capital. Investigations soon revealed that the mastermind was Dawood Ibrahim, a Mumbai-born Dubai-based underworld don who was subsequently given refuge in Pakistan. Most of the key operatives who executed the gruesome terror attack also found a safe haven in the country where the conspiracy was hatched.

I too had been the target of a terrorist act in Coimbatore in February 1998, in which fifty-seven persons died. I mention the terrorist attacks in Mumbai and Coimbatore because, together with all that had been happening in Punjab and Jammu & Kashmir, they provided evidence, when the NDA government assumed office, of Pakistan's strategy of 'bleeding India by inflicting a thousand cuts'.

As Home Minister, I felt it was my duty to ensure that India wins this war on terror.

A TROUBLED VIEW FROM THE NORTH BLOCK

When I took charge of the Home portfolio, I was appalled by the mismatch between the majesty of the building that houses the ministry and the sloth and stagnation that marked its functioning. North Block (in which the Home Ministry, along with the Ministry of Finance, is located) and South Block (which houses the PMO, Ministry of External Affairs [MEA] and the Ministry of Defence [MoD]) form two identically designed buildings on New Delhi's Raisina Hill. They are separated by Raj Path, a long avenue, at one end of which stands the splendid Rashtrapati Bhavan. At the other end is Delhi's famous landmark—India Gate. The eye-catching beauty and symmetry of this ensemble of structures that form the seat of power of the Indian state are such as to evoke immense national pride. Located at a walking distance from North Block is the magnificent circular-shaped Indian Parliament building, whose most striking feature is the colonnade on the first floor resting on 144 massive sandstone columns. This architectural manifestation of the Indian State no doubt makes New Delhi one of the most impressive capital cities in the world*. Nevertheless, the very colonial origins of this place seemed to have still left an archaic influence on the functioning of India's security apparatus.

When India became independent, it inherited a security system which was essentially designed to meet the requirements of a colonial rule and protect the political, economic and military interests of the British empire. The administration maintained a distance from the public and expected the people to view it with awe and servitude. The deficiencies in this system, and its inability to serve the nation's needs, became starkly evident as India entered the last two decades of the century. Its internal security situation became highly vitiated by many threats. Besides cross-border terrorism, which was supported by Pakistan as a key element of its state policy, our country faced the rise of various militant and separatist

---

* New Delhi and all its majestic symbols of state power were designed by Edwin Lutyens, an English architect, after British India decided to shift its capital from Calcutta to Delhi in 1911. I must add, however, that it is unfortunate that independent India has been unable to construct similar indigenous symbols to reflect the majesty of our Republic.

outfits in the North-Eastern states; the growing attacks of left-wing extremist groups along a large tract called the 'Red Corridor' extending from Nepal to the southern Indian state of Andhra Pradesh and beyond; and the sprouting of foreign-controlled modules of sabotage, subversion, espionage, fake-currency operation and drug-trafficking in different parts of the country.

India had an insecure and porous border with both Pakistan and Bangladesh, an unsettled border with China, and a totally unguarded border with Nepal. Illegal immigration from Bangladesh had assumed the dimension of a demographic invasion, posing a grave threat to India's unity, integrity and security. Successive governments in the past had paid little attention to India's geographical and historical vulnerabilities in the North-East, which is home to as many as eight out of twenty-eight states (Arunachal Pradesh, Assam, Manipur, Meghalaya, Mizoram, Nagaland, Tripura and Sikkim). Yet, as much as ninety-eight per cent of the nearly 2,000-kilometre-long border of our North-eastern states is shared with foreign countries and only two per cent is with India alone. The region's only land connection with the rest of India is a narrow twenty-two kilometre-wide corridor above north Bengal, called, quite ominously, the Chicken's Neck.* Practically every state in the region has witnessed insurgency, and the proliferation of separatist outfits. The largest stretch of this highly porous border is with Bangladesh, a country where some politicians have openly advocated the policy of Lebensraum (a German word that conveys its claim for more 'living space' on Indian territory for its teeming millions). Sadly, many political parties in our country, most notably the Congress, have knowingly turned a blind eye to this problem.

And then there was the prolonged neglect of India's coastal border, where poaching and large-scale smuggling through high seas was a regular phenomenon. Our Exclusive Economic Zone (EEZ) of over two million

---

* In contrast, the North-East has a 1,272-kilometre-long border with Bangladesh, out of the 4,095-kilometre Indo-Bangladesh border. Sixty per cent of this border in the North-East is porous and unfenced.

square kilometres, in the waters of the Indian Ocean, Arabian Sea and the Bay of Bengal, was insufficiently guarded and marginally utilised. A major chunk of the Indian Army had been diverted from its conventional role of national defence to helping civil administration in maintenance of internal security. This adversely impacted on its combat preparedness, training, and morale. Despite having paramilitary forces at its disposal, the Centre was finding it difficult to cope up with the ever-increasing requirement of different state governments in the wake of a law and order crises. This took a huge toll on the security forces in terrorist-infested areas. Alarmingly, the average casualty figure for policemen alone was over 1,000 a year.

Successive governments in the past had failed to formulate the nation's long-term security policy objectives based on a futuristic assessment of threats, and to lay down appropriate action plans for achieving them. National security engaged the government's attention mostly in times of wars or serious crises. The attention span of those in the government coincided with the time span of the problem; thereafter it was business as usual. As a result, the initiative of confrontation or negotiation remained mostly in the hands of our adversaries.

Although it did not directly concern my ministry, I was appalled that since the late 1980s, the combat preparedness of the nation's defence forces had come down due to steady decline in defence budgets in real terms. The process of defence modernisation had remained in deep freeze for over a decade due to injudicious budget cuts. Inordinate delays plagued not only routine procurement programmes, but even ambitious indigenisation projects like the Light Combat Aircraft (LCA) project, which had been launched in 1983, and the 'Arjun' Main Battle Tank project, sanctioned in 1974. Many programmes of the DRDO had also suffered a setback. I heard from many experts that there was a sense of unease in India's defense establishment due to the lowering of operational preparedness, training, maintenance of equipment and logistic support to our fighting forces. 'Political bosses often take decisions on considerations other than the best national interests,' I was told by experts.

There were also problems linked to the organisational structure and working of our national security system. Bureaucratism and compartmentalism ruled the roost, leading to avoidable turf wars. Our security apparatus though huge was inadequately trained. Over the years, it had not only rusted, but had become highly susceptible to pressures, corruption and machinations of vested interests. All this only helped the adversaries. Transforming this system was difficult but indisputable.

Foreign policy is an instrument to protect and effectively promote core national interests, especially the nation's security interests. Unfortunately, internal security remained an issue of low priority in our diplomatic initiatives. As a result, we could not persuade the international community to adequately support us in respect of Pakistan's proxy war against India. For quite some time, Pakistan was successfully able to project militancy in Punjab and Jammu & Kashmir as indigenous freedom struggles. Islamabad also sought to portray, in important capitals around the world, the counter-offensive by our security forces as a violation of human rights.

What distressed me in particular were the conceptual, legal and systemic obstacles in the country's security management. The makers of India's Constitution in the early years of Independence could not have visualised the paradigm shift in the threats to its national security in the decades ahead. Our system had been built on the premise that national security was the responsibility of the Centre, whereas law and order, as laid down in the Constitution, was within the functional domain of state governments. This premise was sound in an era where a war manifested only in the nature of a conventional military attack. But it is untenable in the new scenario of a 'proxy war', in which the enemy can inflict much damage at a low cost to itself. How could one view terrorism, secessionist movements, left-wing extremism, sabotage, and espionage—all of which endangered national sovereignty, unity, integrity and stability—purely from a 'law and order' perspective? Here goal-definition, planning, resources and training for the crime were all external; only the occurrence of the crime was internal. The state in which the crime took place could not be expected to nab, investigate and prosecute its perpetrators, who had a nationwide network, and, much less, its conspirators, who often masterminded it from across the borders.

Yet another legacy from the past bedevilled India's response to the perpetrators of mass murder and mayhem. Our criminal justice system, also of the colonial vintage, had proved unsuitable to meet the present challenges. Our courts were—and continue to be—very slow and biased in favour of the accused or the suspects. The courts do not try to find the truth; rather, they only try to weigh evidence. The long delays, coupled with the very low rate—less than ten per cent—of conviction even in cases involving crimes of grave nature, frustrated the investigative agencies and emboldened the anti-national elements. As the Malimath Committee* on reforms in the criminal justice system later noted in its excellent report:

> The success or failure of a case depends entirely on the work of the police officer investigating the offence. Unfortunately, our system does not trust the police. The courts view the police with suspicion and are not willing to repose confidence in them. Any confession made by the accused before the police officer is not admissible and cannot be made use of during the trial of the case. The valuable material collected by the investigating officer during investigation cannot be used by the prosecution. The victim, whose rights are invaded by the accused, is not accorded any right to participate except as a witness. The system is thus utterly insensitive to the rights of the victim. Witnesses come to the court, take oath and quite often give false evidence with impunity. Witnesses turning hostile is a common feature. There is no law to protect honest witnesses. Cases are adjourned again and again making the witnesses to come to court several times leaving aside all their work. Witnesses who are treated in this manner become an easy prey to the machinations of the accused. These are some of the major problems that have contributed to the failure of the Criminal Justice System.

In addition to all these problems of national security, there was yet another difficulty that resided in our country's collective mindset. Centuries of

---

* The Committee on Reforms of Criminal Justice System, chaired by Justice V.S. Malimath, former Chief Justice of Karnataka and Kerala High Courts, which was appointed by my ministry in November 2000, submitted its landmark report in March 2003.

foreign invasions and subjugation had generated a deeply ingrained defeatist and escapist element in the Indian psyche. National cohesion was frequently weakened by religious, caste and linguistic divisions. Centuries of persecution and domination had drained the people of their will and capacity to arrest the degradation of their collective cultural and civilisational heritage. The strong sense of nationalism which had been generated during India's freedom movement could not sustain and channelise in succeeding decades to the task of nation-building and ensuring its security.

The vote-bank politics, coupled with the wrong policies of successive governments, had created fissures in India's civil society whose religious, caste, ethnic and linguistic diversity often turned into a source of discord. The nexus between crime and politics had assumed painful proportions. Corruption had permeated every area of governmental functioning and consequently, even when good policies were formulated, the delivery system of the administration failed to provide succour to the common man. Bad governance caused disaffection, alienation and anger amongst people, particularly in tribal and backward areas, which in turn were exploited by anti-national forces bent upon creating instability and spreading violence and lawlessness.

*

Therefore, when I occupied the far-corner room on the first floor of North Block on 19 March 1998, I had the uneasy realisation that India was entering the new millennium with heavy historical baggage, which was retarding its march towards becoming a strong, secure and integrally developed nation. Once again there was a need to emphasise our united national identity, based on common pride in our civilisational and cultural heritage, which could subsume religious, caste, linguistic, and ethnic identities. There was the need, equally, to scrupulously follow the principles of good governance in the management of India's national security, especially the internal security of the country.

Two things in the room caught my attention. One was the large map of India. It became a constant reminder of the tasks ahead of me.

A huge landmass with a coastline of nearly 7,500 kilometres, with land borders that were double in length; home to nearly a billion people; the second most populous and seventh largest country of the world; an emerging economic power in the world and poised to play a major role in regional and global affairs. And yet, hobbled by serious threats to its internal security. The second was a portrait of Sardar Vallabhbhai Patel, India's first Home Minister and the source of my inspiration*; a man of iron will, clear vision and indomitable courage. I wanted to be worthy of the chair that had once been occupied by this great man.

UNPRECEDENTED REVIEW AND REFORM OF THE NATIONAL SECURITY SYSTEM

The shortcomings in the prevailing security systems, as detailed above, influenced the BJP to envisage in its election manifesto the establishment of the National Security Council. However, before the NSC could properly take off, India had to fight the Kargil War, which gave the government another compelling reason to address its security-related problems comprehensively. True, India had won a famous victory over Pakistan but the episode had also brought to light several unflattering aspects of the state of affairs in our national security apparatus. Here I would like to stress that the BJP-led government had not created this apparatus. We were only the inheritors. After all, Kargil happened just thirteen months after we had assumed office, and that too when we had been functioning as a caretaker government following a successfully hatched conspiracy of destabilisation by the Congress. It is a tribute to the government that it was responsive to the legitimate criticism that began to be voiced, post-Kargil, by the security community.

As I have explained in an earlier chapter, the Kargil Review Committee, headed by K. Subrahmanyam, urged 'a thorough and expeditious review of the national security system in its entirety'. Accordingly, the Vajpayee

---

* In one of my first decisions in the Home Ministry, I asked the officials to install a large portrait of Sardar Patel in the reception area of the ministry's office in North Block.

government set up, for the first time since Independence, a Group of Ministers (GoM), chaired by me, to examine the national security system in its entirety and to prepare a comprehensive set of recommendations to strengthen both internal and external security. Members of the GoM were George Fernandes, Defence Minister; Jaswant Singh, Minister of External Affairs; and Yashwant Sinha, Finance Minister. Brajesh Mishra, National Security Advisor, who was also the Principal Secretary to the Prime Minister, was a special invitee to the GoM's meetings.

In the very first meeting of this group, I observed, 'Security of the country is indivisible and cannot be dealt in watertight ministerial or departmental compartments. The traditional structures and processes for the management of national security are under considerable stress. We need to cope with the new and emerging challenges facing us in the areas of intelligence, internal security, border management and defence management, so as to help develop a more efficient and cost-effective national security system for the twenty-first century.'

In order to facilitate its work, the GoM constituted four Task Forces, each of them headed by, and comprising, experts of impeccable credentials, mostly from outside the government. G.C. Saxena, former Chief of the Research & Analysis Wing (RAW) and incumbent Governor of Jammu & Kashmir, chaired the Task Force on Intelligence. N.N. Vohra, formerly a Secretary in the Ministries of Home and Defence, chaired the Task Force on Internal Security. Dr Madhav Godbole, another former Secretary in the Home Ministry, headed the Task Force on Border Management. The fourth Task Force on Management of Defence was headed by Arun Singh, who was Minister of State of Defence in Rajiv Gandhi's government. Satish Chandra, a highly competent officer who was Secretary, National Security Council Secretariat (NSCS), served as Secretary to the GoM. The reports submitted by the four Task Forces, each of them meticulously researched and marked by a spirit of constructive criticism, are truly a milestone in the study of India's security system.

The GoM held as many as twenty-seven meetings and completed its work in ten months. Without sounding immodest, I would say that the GoM's analysis and recommendations, based essentially on those contained in the reports of the four Task Forces, constitute the most comprehensive blueprint ever prepared for the overhaul of India's national security system. The overarching philosophy which guided my approach to the deliberations of the GoM was as follows: To be strong and secure, India should look beyond military power, and strengthen all the other ingredients of state power like technology, infrastructure, human capital, financial resources, enterprise, culture, etc. National security must be factored into all major decisions, including in seemingly non-security areas like energy, water resources, environment, and communications. National security and national development are interdependent. Therefore, all national policies should be so architected that security and developmental policies fully complement each other.

I also held that national will is not only an intangible component of national power, but by far the most vital. All the other determinable ingredients of power fail to achieve desired results in the absence of this crucial element. India should build the collective will of its billion-strong population and counter all efforts to erode and weaken it. India's perceived image as a soft state, a fragmented and corrupt society, a country which can be bled with impunity by its external and internal adversaries, must be corrected. This requires not only concerted actions and effective power projection, but also perception management. In particular, terrorism, armed insurgency and activities of foreign mercenaries should be crushed with an iron hand.

On 11 May 2001, the government accepted almost all the 340 recommendations of the Group. Indeed, before it demitted office in May 2004, our government had initiated action on more than two-thirds of them.

- In the area of defence, the centrepiece of the GoM recommendations was the creation of the Chief of Defence Staff (CDS), who would act as the permanent chairman of the Chiefs of Staff Committee (COSC). The GoM felt that a CDS was necessary (a) to provide single-point advice to government; (b) to administer the strategic forces and to oversee the triservice Andaman and Nicobar Command; (c) to enhance the efficiency and planning process through intra and inter service prioritisation; (d) to ensure jointness in the armed forces. Regrettably, a decision on the set of recommendations pertaining to the CDS was deferred by the government partly due to lack of support from the Opposition. With a CDS not appointed, the chairman of COSC was expected to perform this role.

- With a view to ensure the smoother and speedier induction of equipment in the services with a long-term perspective planning, a number of new structures were created. These mainly include: the Defence Acquisition Council and the Defence Technology Council under the Defence Minister. These in turn are assisted by a Defence Procurement Board, Defence Production Board and the Defence R&D Board. These steps were helpful in addressing the problem of long delays, resulting in huge cost-overruns, which plagued procurement as well as indigenous production of weapon systems and equipment for the armed forces.
- An Intelligence Coordination Group (ICG) was constituted under the National Security Advisor (NSA) as an apex body to synergise and coordinate the work of the various intelligence agencies.
- A National Information Board was established under the NSA for national level policy formulation on information warfare and information security.
- The complete responsibility for internal security operations was delegated to the IB. Its Director was given wide and autonomous powers. A Multi-Agency Centre (MAC), acting under the IB, with representatives from defence forces, paramilitary organisations, enforcement agencies under the Ministry of Finance, and central intelligence agencies was constituted. MAC was chartered to pool up intelligence from all available sources, covert and overt, and coordinate real-time response on issues like terrorism, sabotage, subversion, espionage, etc. Police powers under the Indian Constitution are vested with the states. In order to combat national-level security threats effectively, active involvement of state governments is essential. Therefore, a Joint Task Force on Intelligence (JTFI), with representatives from states, was created under the IB for bringing about seamless integration between the security agencies of the Central and state governments.

- The mandates of the Economic Intelligence Council and the Central Economic Intelligence Bureau were duly widened in view of the growing impact of the global economy and finance on our national security.
- A landmark initiative in improved management of India's borders was the introduction of the 'one border one force' concept. Earlier, all our borders were being jointly managed by several paramilitary forces. As a result, none of them could develop area-specific specialisation and control, and none could be held fully accountable when problems arose. Thus, Assam Rifles was shifted from the Defence Ministry to the Home Ministry and entrusted with the overall responsibility of manning the Indo-Myanmar border. The Special Service Bureau (SSB), which had been raised in the backdrop of the Chinese aggression of 1962, was transferred to the Home Ministry in 2001 and assigned the new role of guarding the Indo-Nepal Border. (Its name was changed to Sashastra Seema Bal in March 2004.) The Border Security Force had the full responsibility for guarding the Bangladesh border. The Indo-Tibetan Border Police was given the charge of our border with Tibet.
- Similarly, the security of all the forty-five airports in the country was handed over to a single agency—the Central Industrial Security Force. The bureau of immigration was totally overhauled and immigration control work at all the international check posts was entrusted to it. Strict measures were taken to check illegal infiltration and overstay of foreigners. For the first time since Independence, a state-wise list of Pakistani nationals over-staying in India was prepared and steps taken for their detection and deportation.
- The Coast Guard was strengthened and provided new vessels and equipment for effective patrolling, quick operational response and greater coordination with the Indian Navy and governments of coastal states. The water wing of the BSF was strengthened, particularly in Gujarat and West Bengal. In Gujarat, it was given special responsibility in Sir Creek area, which is of vital economic and strategic importance for us on the Indo-Pak border.

The significance of the IB in the enhanced role deserves a special mention. Congress governments in the past had routinely misused the IB for partisan political purposes. For the first time in the history of this apex intelligence service, its functions were made specific and focused on its core responsibility for national security. The IB was made the nodal organisation for counter-terrorist and counter-intelligence work. The bureau was also tasked to create India's first dedicated police computer network and terrorism database.

With its role for gathering political intelligence de-emphasised, a paradigm shift occurred in IB's functioning and it was able to focus its attention on combating terrorism and other forms of covert threats. It now had greater responsibility, coupled with accountability, in gathering operational intelligence. This is highly essential in tracking the 'invisible enemy' operating in the form of 'sleeping cells' that remain dormant for many years before becoming suddenly and briefly active at critical moments of the 'strike'. This is how the terrorist modules established by the ISI operate in India.

I should mention here that I was aghast when I was told about the ease with which the ISI created 'sleeping cells' in various parts of India. One day, early in my stint in the Home Ministry, Ajit Doval, a senior IB officer who had a great reputation as an 'operations man' (he later became the Director of IB), came to me and said, 'Sir, we have been able to bust an ISI module in Orissa's Balasore district.' The details he mentioned to me were frightening. The module had been targeting at India's integrated missile testing range at Chandipur-on-Sea. The local kingpin was an innocuous Bengali-speaking tea-stall owner, who, over the years, had been gathering information from persons working on our missile programme and discretely passing it on to his contacts in Kolkata, from where it travelled to Bangladesh before reaching its destination in Pakistan. The tea-stall owner, who belonged to a family of infiltrators from Bangladesh, had been picked up by an ISI operative when he was a ten-year-old boy in Delhi. He was sent to study in a madarasa in Pakistan for about ten years. After indoctrination and training, he was sent to Bangladesh with instructions to enter India through the Bengal border, contact the ISI's cell in Kolkata, and open a tea-stall near the missile testing range, posing as a Bengali-speaking Hindu.

Then there was the case of a blind madarasa teacher in a village in the Muzaffarnagar district in western UP, who later worked in a madarasa in the Kupwara district in Jammu & Kashmir. In 1997, he entered Bangladesh through its border with Assam, and from there flew to Pakistan, along with a Hizb-ul-Mujahideen (HuM) activist. After returning from Pakistan, he began setting up HuM cells in UP, J&K and in the border districts of Assam by recruiting a large number of local Muslim youths who underwent arms and explosive training in Pakistan. Since he was blind, the local police did not suspect his involvement in any subversive activities. But it was the coordinated efforts of the IB and other intelligence agencies that succeeded in laying a trap for him in 1999 as he was trying to smuggle a large quantity of RDX explosives, timer devices, etc., into Assam from an ISI operative in Bangladesh.

In the years ahead, I would hear scores of such accounts of the ISI penetration in India. An innocent-looking poultry farmer in Hyderabad turned out to be a long-standing ISI agent. A suave businessman dealing in leather products in Agra was found to be involved in an elaborate anti-national operation. I was filled with anger to know that it was through such local support that the ISI was able to set off bomb explosions with frightening regularity, foment anti-India feelings among local populations, recruit local youths for training in terror camps in Pakistan, and smuggle in deadly weapons—all with the design of sowing the seeds for India's eventual disintegration. I told Doval, 'I want the busting of these modules to become the IB's topmost priority. The agency will get whatever support or resources it needs for this purpose.' It is a matter of gratification for me that between 1998-2004 our intelligence and security agencies were able to bust 272 ISI-linked modules, which included ninety-seven espionage networks, and 113 modules of sabotage and subversion. In the preceding five years, from 1994 to 1998, only twenty-eight such modules had been busted. Sadly, since the UPA government assumed office in 2004, the average has once again dipped to previous levels.[1] My experience in this regard convinced me that it is important for the political leadership not to interfere with the working of intelligence agencies in busting the cells of terrorist and extremist organisations, and keeping a close eye on their support structures among local populations. Our country has paid, and is continuing to pay, a heavy price because of the wrong signals that intelligence agencies often get from their political bosses.

POLICE REFORMS AND MODERNISATION

An important decision that the NDA government took in view of the GoM's recommendations was about modernisation of India's police forces. Most policemen in our country still work, and live, in conditions that are not ideal for professionals who have been entrusted with the responsibility of law enforcement. Since the police are employees of state governments, those in power at the Centre previously felt no obligation to improve their working and living conditions. For their part, most state governments faced a resource crunch and thus neglected the needs of their police forces. For the first time since Independence, the NDA government initiated an ambitious scheme of police modernisation with an outlay of Rs 10,000 crores spread over ten years. This amount was to be given by the Centre to state governments for training, acquisition of better equipment, weapons, state-of-the-art communication systems, etc. In addition, a modernisation plan costing more than Rs 4,000 crores for the central police organisations was also approved.

In India, less than half the police personnel have access to departmental housing. Even in big cities like Delhi, Mumbai and Kolkata, many policemen are forced to live in slums and this naturally affects their morale. In my interactions with state police chiefs, I said that it should be our endeavour to ensure that no Indian policeman is deprived of decent departmental accommodation. For this purpose, we made a special allocation for police housing in the modernisation fund.

I must mention here that even my best efforts met with failure in one key area of police reforms: VIP security. This, in my opinion, is a major drain on police resources. I ordered a thorough review of the need and provisions of security to all the VIPs, and was startled to find that only twenty-five per cent of them genuinely needed protection. For the rest, having gun-totting policemen accompanying them everywhere was a mere status symbol. I tried to scale down or altogether remove the security of many VIPs, but had to face howls of protests. Paradoxically, some highly placed dignitaries, who had publicly declared their opposition to VIP security, were the first ones to urge me to restore their security to its previous level after the ministry decided to downscale it. In this context, I can do no better than to quote from an article written by R.K. Raghavan, a distinguished former Director of the CBI. 'I remember a valiant L.K. Advani trying his best to trim numbers. The howl of protests that his attempt evoked was not merely ugly but vulgar as well. Unless there is a change of culture in the ruling class, I see no way we can bring down the numbers frittered away in dignitary protection.... The first thing that a Minister or his pompous Personal Assistant looks for is whether the local Sub-Inspector is present at a meeting to be addressed by him. If the latter is not present by any chance, all hell is let loose. Dominated by this tribal quest for paraphernalia, the ambience is one in which you can hardly save on police manpower.'[2]

Of course, modernisation of weaponry, equipment and other essentials is only a part of police reforms. No less important, from the point of view of the common citizen who has to deal with the police constable and officer, is the modernisation of their mindset. Here, I must confess that the progress is far from satisfactory. As India's Home Minister, it worried me deeply to know that the public image of our police force continued to be far from people-friendly. An ordinary citizen, if he can help it, will never venture into a police station to seek help. Paradoxically, the poor and the vulnerable have the least faith in the police, although they need the most protection. Fear of the police, the perception that they are corrupt and ill-mannered, and the belief that they enforce the law differently for the rich and the poor, are rampant. Of course, this is a perception and not always true. There have always been honest, conscientious and upright policemen, ready to help the needy and unbending before the lure of money or pressure of power. Unfortunately, they have not been able to change the overall image of the police force in India.

In my speeches and interactions at the annual conferences of the chiefs of state police organisations, I unfailingly dealt with this subject. My experience in the Home Ministry has led me to the conclusion that the situation can improve only through the combined effort of three factors: police leadership, political leadership, and the media. Firstly, the leadership of the Indian Police Service (IPS) must play a proactive role in bringing about positive behavioural and attitudinal changes in police professionals at all levels. It does not require money or governmental policy to reform the mindset of the police force. Secondly, political leaders must stop misusing the police, or interfering in law enforcement, for their own ends. Once a police constable or officer knows that he is expected only to do his duty, and not to please the authority, he will surely start to deal with citizens differently. Similarly, when there are no scandals in recruitments and promotions, the level of professionalism among police personnel is bound to go up. Most important of all, if the police feel that they have a free hand in dealing with criminals and law-breakers, and that the latter enjoy no protection from politicians, it will bring about a sea-change in their functioning.

The third agent of change is the mass media, which should shun the temptation of always highlighting negative tales about the police. Our men—and, increasingly, women—in khaki should be rewarded or acknowledged for performing under trying conditions. Media and societal recognition for good and upright police officers, and consistent exposure of those who seek to misuse the law-enforcement system, will enhance the self-image of the police as well as their public image

My other regret about an unfulfilled task is about a new federal law to empower the Central Government in dealing with major threats like terrorism and naxalite violence. This was an important recommendation of the GoM on national security, further reiterated by the Malimath Committee on reforms in the criminal justice system. At all meetings of the Inter-State Council, the two special Chief Ministers' conferences on internal security that I convened, or the annual meetings of the heads of state police forces, my speeches used to have a common theme: 'In dealing with threats to internal security, we must liberate ourselves from the "law and order" mindset. We must evolve greater Centre-state and inter-state cooperation and coordination. For this, let us enact a new federal law, through a necessary Constitutional amendment, to empower the Centre, concurrently with the states to deal with federal crimes.' My appeal met with a rather strange response. Almost every Chief Minister agreed with me privately. However, in their public utterances, they maintained that any law that gives the Union a role in policing would encroach upon the states' Constitutional rights. I fervently hope that state governments change their view, and political parties evolve a consensus in this regard so that some day soon India is able to have an effective federal law to strengthen our internal security.

6

Cross-Border Terrorism
A Pak-Jihadi Challenge and Our Response

Victory at all costs, victory in spite of all terror, victory however long and hard the road may be; for without victory there is no survival.

—Winston Churchill

It was 24 December 1999. I was in my North Block office on that rather cold Friday afternoon. As it always happens at this time, the country was eagerly awaiting the arrival of the new year. But there was a keener edge to this expectancy now. In a week it would be not just the new year, but also a new century and a new millennium. The following day was Christmas and also Prime Minister Atal Bihari Vajpayee's seventy-fifth birthday.

The turbulent year was at its fag end. Atalji's bus yatra to Lahore, our government's fall by a solitary vote, a war in Kargil due to Pakistan's betrayal, mid-term elections and a renewed mandate—this was more than enough to make the year eventful, and all of us in the government looked forward to a period of quietude.

THE HIJACKING OF INDIAN AIRLINES FLIGHT IC 814

The news that actually terrified the nation, and added further turbulence to the outgoing year, was the one I received as I was leafing through some official papers on Christmas Eve. Slightly before 5 pm, Shyamal Dutta, Director, IB, phoned me to say, 'Sir, an Indian Airlines plane coming from Nepal has been hijacked.' I was stunned by what I heard. 'How many passengers are there on the flight?' I asked. 'More than 160,' he said. The Delhi-bound IC 814, which had taken off from Kathmandu, was hijacked by five armed men who ordered the pilot to fly to Lahore. When the airport authorities in Lahore refused landing permission, the aircraft landed in Amritsar where the hijackers demanded that it be refuelled.

In the wake of the sudden developments, the Prime Minister called an emergency meeting at his residence. It was decided that our first priority would be to immobilise the plane at Amritsar and make it impossible for it to take off to any other destination outside the country. The Crisis Management Group (CMG), chaired by Cabinet Secretary Prabhat Kumar, was immediately activated to dispatch the message to the police authorities in Punjab. The CMG decided to send a fuel bowser to the aircraft, carrying commandos who would deflate its tyres. Unfortunately, minutes before it could reach the plane, the hijackers ordered the captain to take off. Its next stop, with just enough fuel for the trip, was Lahore, where Pakistani authorities not only refuelled the aircraft but also refused our request to prevent it from taking off. The hijackers then commandeered IC 814 to a military airbase near Dubai. There, they dumped the body of one of the passengers they had killed, Rupin Katyal, and released twenty-eight others. They asked the pilot to fly the aircraft, with 161 hostages on board, to Kandahar* in southern Afghanistan, which was then under Taliban rule.

---

* Kandahar was the capital of an ancient Hindu kingdom. Its princess Gandhari was married to Dhritarashtra, uncle of the Pandava brothers in the epic *Mahabharata*. Under Kanishka, the legendary Kushana emperor, Buddhism flourished in Afghanistan. Bamiyan Buddha, the tallest single-rock carving of Lord Buddha in the world, were created in the Kushana period. They were destroyed in 2001 by the Taliban government, which also allowed the ransacking of the famous Kabul museum, which housed priceless exhibits showing Afghanistan's deep civilisational links with India. Until some decades ago, Kandahar had a significant Hindu and Sikh population.

I spent the entire night at the CMG's office at Rajiv Gandhi Bhavan, where Brajesh Mishra, the National Security Advisor, and other officials were also present, closely monitoring the developments and revising the strategy to secure the release of the hostages in the fast-changing scenario. When the aircraft landed in Dubai, I spoke to Robert Blackwill*, the US Ambassador in India, seeking urgent American assistance. We had received information that the American Ambassador in the United Arab Emirates (UAE) had reached the airport. Curiously, the UAE authorities had not allowed the Indian Ambassador in Dubai to enter the airport. I felt that the Americans, with their considerable military presence and diplomatic influence in the Gulf region, could have taken some effective proactive steps to put the hijacked plane out of action, so that Indian commandos could be sent there to rescue the hostages. I was deeply disappointed that they did not even try. A few days after the crisis had ended, when Blackwill called on me, I expressed my displeasure to him. 'This is not what we understand by Indo-US cooperation in fighting terrorism,' I told him. That experience reinforced my belief that India has to fight its war on terror essentially on its own. I was to express this thought on several occasions later.[1]

We soon learnt that the hijackers had been demanding the release of thirty-six terrorists from Indian jails, besides a ransom of US $200 million. But their main demand was for the release of Mohammad Masood Azhar, leader of one of the most dreaded terrorist organisations in Jammu & Kashmir, who had been arrested in 1994. The CCS decided to send a team of three officials—Ajit Doval, a senior officer in the IB known for handling tough operations, Vivek Katju, a Joint Secretary in the Ministry of External Affairs, and C.D. Sahay from the RAW—to Kandahar to negotiate with the hijackers as well as the Taliban authorities.

I was initially not in favour of exchanging the terrorists with the hostages. However, the situation that our government was faced with was

---

* Blackwill was one of the US officials who was generally sympathetic to India's concerns. When he first came to New Delhi, he had a different idea of the situation in the Indian subcontinent. I would like to believe that I was able to bring about some change in his outlook.

truly extraordinary. The fact that the hijackers had taken the plane to Kandahar had rendered the situation much more complex and difficult. Usually, in such a situation, the captors are at least as much under pressure as the government of the country whose plane has been held captive, to conclude the negotiations quickly and strike a bargain. In this case, however, the hijackers were under no pressure at all and were prepared to prolong the period of captivity since they had three advantages. Firstly, they were in a hospitable territory—Taliban-ruled Afghanistan, with which India had no diplomatic relations*, and they showed no signs of putting any pressure on them to end the hijack or leave the country.

Secondly, we had credible information that every move of the hostage-takers was being masterminded by the ISI in Pakistan. Since the Taliban was a creation of the ISI, Pakistan had control over not only the plane, but also the airport. The Indian government had the option of sending its airborne commandos and troops to Kandahar in an attempt to rescue the hostages, but we received information that the Taliban authorities, under instruction from Islamabad, had ringed the airport area with tanks. Our commanders could have disarmed the hijackers inside the plane. However, outside the plane, an armed conflict with Taliban forces would have endangered the very lives that needed rescue.

There was another risk. Even the rescue planes would have had to fly over Pakistan's airspace, the permission for which would have certainly been denied. We also had credible information, which was corroborated by the subsequent findings on the hijacked aircraft, that the hijackers were

---

* Afghanistan under the Taliban rule (1996-2001) was recognised by only two countries in the world—Pakistan and Saudi Arabia. The functionaries and followers of the Taliban government, professing an extremist version of Islam, were indoctrinated in the madarasas in Pakistan. They were trained and equipped to wage 'jihad' by the ISI. One of its chief financiers and patrons was Osama bin Laden, the Saudi-born chief of the global terror network Al Qaeda, who, in turn, got a safe haven in Afghanistan. Both the Taliban and Osama bin Laden were initially backed by the US-Pak alliance in Afghanistan's war against Soviet occupation (1980–89). All these developments not only caused massive devastation in Afghanistan, but pushed this traditional friend of India, much against its will, to accept the domination of anti-India forces.

carrying grenades and explosives and were ready to blow up the plane. One of them had been heard saying that this ammunition was going to be used as a 'millennium present for the government of India', a spectacular terrorist act on New Year's Day.[2]

Thirdly, and the most unfortunate part of the entire episode, pressure was being mounted on the Indian government to 'somehow' save the lives of the hostages. As the crisis entered its third day, hysterical demonstrations by the relatives of some of the hostages were staged in front of the Prime Minister's residence, and I regret to say that these were at least partly instigated by the BJP's political adversaries. Some television channels chose to hype up these protests with round-the-clock publicity, creating an impression that the government was doing 'nothing' when the lives of so many Indians were at stake. All this made me wonder: 'It used to be said that the Indian State is *a soft state,* but has Indian society also become *a soft society*?' However, it was somewhat reassuring to see that these televised protests led the relatives of Kargil martyrs to urge the families of the hostages to be patient.

With mounting pressure from relatives on one hand, and the possibility of hijackers taking recourse to some desperate action on the other, the government most reluctantly took the option of minimising the losses. Three jailed terrorists, including Masood Azhar, were released on 31 December and handed over to the Taliban authorities in Kandahar. Our negotiating team in Kandahar bargained hard and was able to bring down the demand of release of thirty-six persons in jail to just three. All the passengers and crew members of IC 814 were released and returned to Delhi the same night. Thus ended a crisis, which presented to the world, a new face of warfare; a small group of ready-to-die terrorists challenging a country with a large standing army.

Throughout the hijack episode, my colleague Jaswant Singh, and his colleagues in the MEA, worked tirelessly to bring the crisis to a satisfactory end. As for the hijackers, escorted by their ISI mentors, they headed back to the country that had sponsored their heinous act. Indeed, a few days after his release, this is what Masood Azhar had to say to a cheering crowd in a mosque in Karachi: 'I have come here because it is my duty to tell you that Muslims should not rest in peace until we have destroyed America and India.'³

Pakistan's CEO, General Pervez Musharraf, said in an interview to an international television network that the hijack incident was planned by India to discredit Pakistan.⁴ However, the elaborate statement I made in Parliament on 6 January 2000 showed Pakistan's neck-deep involvement in the episode.⁵

> The security forces pursuing the trail of Pakistan's Operation Hijack have made a significant breakthrough. Working in tandem with central intelligence agencies, the Mumbai Police have nabbed four ISI operatives, who comprised the support cell for the five hijackers of the Indian Airlines plane. All these four are activists of the Harkat-ul-Ansar (HuA), a fundamentalist tanzeem based in Rawalpindi (Pakistan), which in 1997 was declared by USA as a terrorist organisation. After this declaration, the tanzeem has rechristened itself as Harkat-ul-Mujahideen (HuM). Interrogation of these four operatives has confirmed that the hijack was an ISI operation executed with the assistance of Harkat-ul-Ansar, and further, that all the five hijackers are Pakistanis.

As if to endorse the information I had given in Parliament, Pakistani media reported on the same day that the released terrorists had surfaced in Karachi. Thus, it was obvious that the hijack crisis was part of Pakistan's continuing proxy war against India. Credible evidence has subsequently surfaced to suggest that the terrorists and their patrons linked to the hijack of IC 814 were also associated with the conspiracy that resulted in 9/11.⁶

BILL CLINTON'S LANDMARK VISIT TO INDIA

The hijacking episode was one of the most agonising periods during my stint as India's Home Minister. So was it for the Prime Minister and my colleagues in the government. But the experience helped us reach one important conclusion: 'We have to step up our diplomatic and political initiatives to sensitise the world community, especially the western countries, about what Pakistan is up to.'

Bill Clinton got some idea of it when he came to visit India in March 2000, the first by an American President after a gap of more than two decades. On the eve of his arrival in New Delhi, thirty-six Sikhs in Chattisinghpora village in Kashmir were gunned down by terrorists belonging to Pakistan-based Lashkar-e-Taiba (LeT). Prime Minister Vajpayee described it as an 'act of ethnic cleansing'. Echoing his views, I said: 'Till now the militants had targeted the Hindu community in the Kashmir Valley. Now the objective is to see to it that Sikhs also begin a process of migration.'[7]

In his much-applauded address to the Indian Parliament, Clinton said, 'Americans understood the pain and agony you went through during the Indian Airlines hijacking. And I saw that pain firsthand when I met with the parents and the widow of the young man who was killed on that airplane. We grieve with you for the Sikhs who were killed in Kashmir—and our heart goes out to their families.' Clinton's visit, during which he was accompanied by his wife Hillary and daughter Chelsea, was a huge diplomatic success. It heralded what he himself called a new 'dynamic and lasting partnership' with India. The Clintons endeared themselves to Indians, and vice-versa, with a naturalness and spontaneity that marks the bilateral relationship of only those countries that cherish freedom, democracy, pluralism and openness. True, India and the United States could not agree on certain issues, most notably on our nuclear weapons programme, but it was obvious to any perceptive observer that America's new-found respect for India had itself much to do with our nuclear programme.

Above all, Clinton's mere six-hour stop in Pakistan, that too in an atmosphere completely devoid of the bonhomie and public contact that hallmarked his five-day sojourn in India, showed the basic flaw in America's hitherto hyphenated India-Pakistan approach to subcontinental diplomacy. In Islamabad, he spoke about the twin evils plaguing Pakistan: 'violence and extremism'. He was also candid in reminding his hosts, in a clear allusion to Pakistan's terrorist campaign to capture Kashmir, that the new era did not support those who sought to 'redraw borders in blood'.

9/11 VINDICATED ATALJI'S PROPHETIC WORDS

India had been a victim of Pak-sponsored terrorism since the beginning of the 1980s. But it is only the determined and concerted efforts of the NDA government that made western democracies accept that Pakistan was, indeed, the sponsor of cross-border terrorism against India. As a matter of fact, our diplomatic offensive succeeded in another related objective: in making them realise that Pakistan's abetment of terrorism was a threat not only to India but to the entire world. In the past, our friends in the West used to pretend, in spite of knowing the facts on the ground, that terrorism in India was due to local factors which the governments in New Delhi had failed to address. Some of them would even blame India for human rights violations in its fight against terrorism. It goes to the credit of the Vajpayee government that it not only put across the case against Pakistan with facts, figures and arguments, but did not hesitate to warn the US and other countries that their equivocation would prove costly to them.

No leader of the world spoke more prophetic words than Prime Minister Vajpayee in his address to the joint session of the US Congress in Washington DC on 14 September 2000. 'No region is a greater source of terrorism than our neighbourhood. Indeed, in our neighbourhood—in this, the twenty-first century—religious war has not just been fashioned into, it has been proclaimed to be, an instrument of state policy. *Distance and geography provide no nation immunity against international terrorism.* You know, and I know: such evil cannot succeed. But even in failing it could inflict untold suffering.' (emphasis added.)

Almost exactly a year later, on 11 September 2001, the United States—indeed, the entire world—realised the truth of these words. I was sitting in my office late on that Tuesday evening, when my Private Secretary Deepak Chopra came rushing in and said, 'Sir, there has been a major terrorist attack in the United States.' He switched on the TV, and what I saw would have been unbelievable had it not been for those stark visuals being telecast live from the US. First one, and later the second of the twin towers of the World Trade Centre, which were as much a landmark of New York as the nearby Statue of Liberty, were razed to the ground by aircraft that had been turned into missiles by hijackers on a suicide and mass-homicide mission. Another set of hijackers crashed a third passenger aircraft into the Pentagon, while yet another plane, headed for the White House, crashed into a field in rural Pennsylvania. Nearly 3,000 people were killed in this most audacious attack in the history of global terrorism. Among them were as many as 117 Indians, or persons of Indian origin. What stunned the world was the revelation that all the nineteen hijackers, though of Arab origin, had been indoctrinated and trained in the epicentre of global terrorism—Talibanised Afghanistan and its patron Pakistan.

12/13: TERRORIST ATTACK ON THE INDIAN PARLIAMENT

In less than a month after 9/11, on 1 October 2001, Pakistan-based terrorists carried out a suicide attack on the Jammu & Kashmir state legislative assembly in Srinagar. A car bomb exploded near the assembly killing thirty-eight people. The bombing was followed by an armed assault into the assembly premises by three armed terrorists. An even more sinister attack took place on 13 December 2001 in New Delhi. The target this time was the Indian Parliament.

At the time of the attack, Parliament was undergoing its winter session. However, both Houses had been adjourned following the Opposition's protest demanding Defence Minister George Fernandes' resignation over the 'coffin scandal'*. I was sitting in my chamber in the Parliament building,

---

* The Congress party made a vile allegation against the Vajpayee government in general and George Fernandes in particular, in what was billed as the 'coffin gate scam'. It raised a demand for the Defence Minister's resignation on the charge that he had indulged in corruption in the procurement of imported aluminum caskets for the Army. Congress MPs disrupted Parliament's proceedings for several days by shouting slogans such as *'Kafan Chor, Gaddi Chhod' (Coffin robber, resign)* and *'Sena khoon bahati hai, sarkar dalali khati hai.'* (Soldiers shed blood, government takes commission in the purchase of coffins meant for the martyrs of the Kargil War). Sonia Gandhi made this accusation even in her campaign speeches in the Lok Sabha elections in 2004. Fernandes, when he was Minister, had shown this to be a false, malicious and defamatory charge, using pertinent documentary information. Revealingly, in the nearly four years that the UPA government has been in office, it has not bothered to order a probe and establish the truth about its own allegation against Fernandes.

when at around 11.40 am, I heard some loud sound, ominously similar to bullet-shots. I rushed out of my office to see what was happening, but within a few yards into the circular corridor I was stopped by security forces who said, '*Sahab, aage mat jaayiye. Aatankvaadiyon ne hamla kiya hai.*' (Sir, don't go further. There has been a terrorist attack.')

With lightning reflexes, security personnel belonging to the Central Reserve Police Force (CRPF), ITBP and Delhi police took up positions and started returning fire. Simultaneously, the watch and ward staff closed all the doors of the Parliament House and ensured that no MP or anybody else remained in the corridor. I immediately phoned the Prime Minister, who had chosen to work at his home office at 7 Race Course Road after hearing that Parliament had been adjourned, and apprised him of the development. A pitched battle continued between the terrorists and security forces outside which lasted for about thirty minutes. Then there was complete silence. Besides Vice President Krishan Kant, Lok Sabha Speaker G.M.C. Balayogi and Deputy Chairperson of the Rajya Sabha Najma Heptullah, there were over 200 MPs inside the Parliament at the time. Several MPs, including Congress President Sonia Gandhi, had left the premises after the House was adjourned. There were also a large number of journalists and TV cameramen inside the complex, and their presence helped the whole world witness the attack on the Indian Parliament.

It was later revealed that five terrorists entered the Parliament complex in a white Ambassador car with a Home Ministry label and a forged Parliament entry pass from the main entrance on Parliament Street. All of them were killed. One of them shouted before collapsing: '*Hamara mission poora hua, Pakistan zindabad.*' (Our mission has been accomplished. Long live Pakistan.)[8] Nine brave security personnel sacrificed their lives in preventing the terrorists from entering the main Parliament building.*

---

* Following are the names of the brave and diligent security personnel and others who were martyred while combating the terrorist attack on Indian Parliament: (1) J.P. Yadav (2) Matbar Singh (3) Kamlesh Kumari (4) Nanak Chand (5) Rampal (6) Om Prakash (7) Ghanshyam (8) Bijender Singh (9) Desh Raj. A TV cameraman working for ANI, Vikram Singh Bisht, also lost his life.

The Prime Minister addressed the nation at 3 pm. 'Now the battle against terrorism has reached a decisive moment. This is going to be a fight to the finish,' he declared. It was followed by a meeting of the CCS and, later, the full Cabinet. Addressing a press conference after the meeting, I read out the resolution adopted by the Cabinet. 'It has been an attack not just on a building but on what is the very heart of our system of governance, on what is the symbol and the keystone of the largest democracy in the world. By the attack, the terrorists have yet again flung a challenge at the country. The nation accepts the challenge. We will liquidate the terrorists and their sponsors wherever they are, whoever they are—as our valiant security forces have done in this particular instance.'

Pakistan's first reaction after the attack on Parliament was shocking, to say the least. General Musharraf's spokesman, Major General Rashid Qureshi, claimed that the attack 'is a drama staged by Indian intelligence agencies to defame the freedom struggle in occupied Kashmir. Lashkar and other Jihadi organisations are not involved in the attack'.9 I had to place facts before the world, which I did five days later, on 18 December, in a comprehensive statement that I made in Parliament. I said, 'The terrorist assault on the very bastion of our democracy was clearly aimed at wiping out the country's top political leadership. It is a tribute to our security personnel that they rose to the occasion and succeeded in averting what could have been a national catastrophe. In doing so, they made the supreme sacrifice for which the country would always remain indebted to them.' Based on the investigation until then, I was informed that the terrorist assault was executed jointly by two Pak-based terrorist outfits, LeT and Jaish-e-Mohammad (JeM), which received patronage from Pakistan's ISI. Subsequent revelations fully corroborated these early findings. Indeed, all the five terrorists who formed the suicide squad were Pakistani nationals.

The breakthrough in the investigation was achieved with the arrest of Syed Abdul Rehman Geelani, a lecturer in a Delhi college, whose interrogation led to the identification of two other accomplices, Mohammed Afzal and Shaukat Hussain Guru. Navjot Sandhu alias Afsan Guru, wife of Shaukat Hussain, disclosed that her husband and Afzal had, on the afternoon of

13 December left for Srinagar. This information was immediately conveyed to the Jammu & Kashmir Police who apprehended both of them. They were later brought to Delhi. Interrogation revealed that Afzal was the main coordinator of the attack, who was assigned this task by a Pakistani national, Gazi Baba of JeM. Afzal had earlier been trained in a camp run by the ISI at Muzaffarabad in Pak-occupied Kashmir. The hideouts for the five terrorists were arranged by Shaukat Hussain Guru, two in Mukherjee Nagar and one in the Timarpur area in North Delhi. During the subsequent raids, the police recovered a lot of incriminating material from two of these hideouts.

Pointing out that the hijacking of the Indian Airlines flight IC 814 to Kandahar, the terrorist intrusion into the Red Fort, and attack on the Jammu & Kashmir legislative assembly complex in Srinagar were all masterminded and executed by ISI-supported militant outfits, I said, 'Last week's attack on Parliament is undoubtedly the most audacious, and also the most alarming, act of terrorism in the nearly two-decades-long history of Pakistan-sponsored terrorism in India. Naturally, it is time for all of us in this august House, and all of us in the country, to ponder why the terrorists and their backers tried to raise the stakes so high, particularly at a time when Pakistan is claiming to be a part of the international coalition against terrorism. The only answer that satisfactorily addresses this query is that Pakistan—itself a product of the indefensible 'Two Nation' theory, itself a theocratic state with an extremely tenuous tradition of democracy—is unable to reconcile itself with the reality of a secular, democratic, self-confident and steadily progressing India, whose standing in the international community is getting inexorably higher with the passage of time.'

*

Mohammed Afzal was convicted of conspiracy in the attack on Parliament and awarded the death sentence by the trial court in 2002. The Delhi High Court and the Supreme Court later upheld it. The apex court, which said there was clinching evidence against Afzal of his nexus with the terrorists killed in the attack, rejected his review petition. Of the three others accused in the case, the trial court had awarded death for Afzal, Shaukat Hussain and Geelani, and five-year imprisonment to Navjot Sandhu alias Afsan Guru, wife of Shaukat Hussain. The Supreme Court reduced Shaukat Hussain's death sentence to ten-year imprisonment and acquitted Geelani and Afsan Guru.

The death sentence against Afzal was scheduled to be carried out on 20 October 2006. However, it has been stayed because the Home Ministry in the UPA government has refused to convey to the President of India, its opposition to the clemency sought by Afzal. It is shocking indeed, that the Congress and several other political parties have communalised this issue and, for purely vote-bank considerations, chosen to support a concerted campaign by some NGOs for granting pardon to Afzal. My party and I have stoutly opposed this demand. I said, 'The Supreme Court said it was an act of war, because the target was the Indian Parliament. Therefore, this crime should not be viewed at par with a terrorist attack at some other place.'[10] What can be a more shaming indictment of the Congress party's politics of minority appeasement than the fact that the relatives of the valiant security personnel who became martyrs in the 13 December terrorist attack returned the President's gallantry medals in protest against the UPA government's refusal to give a go-ahead for Afzal's execution.

✻

The attack on the Indian Parliament was actually the apogee of a long series of murderous activities by Pakistan-sponsored terrorist groups in 2002 and 2003. In January 2002, they attacked the American Cultural Centre in Kolkata, killing four policemen. In March, a fidayeen attack on Jammu's famous Raghunath temple killed seven persons. The same temple became the target of a second fidayeen attack in November, when thirteen devotees were killed. In May, terrorists massacred thirty persons, most of them members of the families of Army personnel, at Kaluchak Cantonment near Jammu. In the same month, they gunned down Abdul Ghani Lone, a senior and moderate, leader of the Hurriyat Conference in Srinagar. He was killed during a rally taken out to mark the twelfth death anniversary of former Mirwaiz of Kashmir Maulvi Mohammad Farooq, who too had been gunned down by militants. It showed how the elimination of influential pro-peace voices in Kashmir was an integral part of Pakistan's terrorist campaign in India. In July, twenty villagers were killed in Kasim Nagar near Jammu. In August, they mounted an attack on pilgrims to the annual yatra to Amarnath, a sacred cave temple of Lord Shiva in Kashmir, in Pahalgam killing eight of them. A year earlier, Pahalgam had witnessed the massacre of thirty-three Amarnath yatris, on a day when terrorists gunned down nearly a hundred persons at different places in Jammu & Kashmir. In September, they stormed the Akshardham Temple in Gandhinagar in Gujarat, killing twenty-nine devotees, most of them women and children.

In March 2003, terrorists in police uniforms attacked Nadimarg village near Srinagar, killing twenty-four men, women and children. In the same month, a bomb exploded inside a local train in Mumbai killing ten passengers. In August, two powerful car-bomb explosions in south Mumbai killed forty-six persons.

The above is not by any means an exhaustive list of the terrorist activities in India in those two years but nevertheless it gives a snapshot of the agony and outrage that Indians have been experiencing year after year since terrorism raised its ugly head in the early 1980s. It also provides, unmistakably, an idea of what Pakistani authorities, using terrorists as their tools, wanted to achieve through this campaign. Apart from the physical elimination of voices of peace and moderation in Jammu & Kashmir, they wanted to accomplish 'religious cleansing' by driving away Hindus from most parts of the state. Elsewhere in the country, they conspired to foment communal tension and violence between Hindus and Muslims. Our security forces also busted some cases of conspiracy to kidnap or assassinate political leaders.[11]

*

ISLAMIC EXTREMISM AND ITS IDEOLOGICAL SUPPORT TO TERROR

Why was India targeted—and is still being targeted—by this vicious and religiously inspired campaign of terrorism? What are the ideological roots of terrorism in India? Unless these questions are squarely put and honestly answered, we can neither understand the phenomenon of terrorism nor succeed in combating it. I agree with all right-minded people that no religion should be denigrated, and no religious community should be typecast, by pasting the label of terrorism on them. All religions at their core, preach peace and brotherhood, and urge its adherents to follow the path of righteousness. No faith condones the killing of innocent persons and, therefore, terrorists have no religion. Nevertheless, it is also an irrefutable fact that one of the most virulent forms of terrorism in our times seeks the cover of Islam. It calls its murderous campaign 'jihad', thereby trying to justify itself in the eyes of pious God-fearing Muslims. Terrorists, inspired by the distorted and self-serving interpretation of jihad, actually pursue a definite objective: to establish worldwide domination of political Islam, which is also called 'Islamism'. Naturally, India's multi-faith society, the constitutional principle of secularism that has anchored the Indian state, and the cultural-spiritual ethos of Hinduism that have defined the character of both the Indian society and state, are anathema to Islamism.

Hence, the ideological basis of terrorism in India has been unmistakably anti-national in its intent and pan-Islamic in its appeal. It is the manifestation of a deeper malaise of the spread of extremism in most parts of the Muslim world, funded as it is by fundamentalist groups based mainly in Saudi Arabia and the Gulf countries. As in Pakistan and other Islamic countries, these groups are targeting madarasas for indoctrination of young impressionable minds. There has been large-scale mushrooming of madarasas, particularly, but not exclusively, in India's border areas in the past two decades. Quite a few of them have been extensively misused for subversive and terrorist activities. They preach intolerance and bigotry. Saudi-funded organisations owing allegiance to ideologies like that of Ahle Hadis are known to propagate Wahabism (see footnote on page 22), an extreme form of Islam practiced in Saudi Arabia, which does not even tolerate the Sufi and native influences on Islam in India. For example, the kind of syncretic Islam that I have seen in my childhood in Sindh, would be maligned as anti-Islamic by the Wahabis and sought to be violently weeded out.

Before 1998, I had a general idea about the activities of various radical Muslim organisations in India that were guided by an extremist agenda. But even I was shocked by what I learnt about them, and their links with extremist groups internationally, during my six years in the Home Ministry. For example, the footprints of the Students Islamic Movement of India (SIMI) could be seen in the terrorist activities and communal riots in many parts of India. Intelligence agencies brought to me, year after year, incontrovertible information about SIMI's links with pan-Islamic extremist groups abroad. Safdar Nagouri, its General Secretary asserted that 'Osama bin Laden is not a terrorist and neither is Jammu and Kashmir an integral part of India.'[12] Its official publication *Islamic Movement* in July 2001 insisted: 'The ideologies of democracy, secularism and nationalism have replaced the objects of worship of the past. It is our duty to demolish these ideologies and establish the Caliphate as enjoined upon us by Allah.'

Fazlur Rehman Khalil, General Secretary of HuM, exhorted his cadres in September 2000: 'We are fighting not only for Kashmir but to hoist our flag in New Delhi. Our war will continue till restoration of the Muslim rule in India.'[13] Organisations like LeT have never hidden their conviction that the 'jihad' in Jammu & Kashmir is 'not a battle over territory, but a part of an irreducible conflict between Islam and kafirs'. Supported by Pakistan's ISI and inspired by Osama bin Laden, it proclaims its ultimate aim to be 'creation of a Caliphate to rule over all the world's Muslims', and asserts that a 'jihad-without-end must continue until Islam, as a way of life, dominates the whole world and until Allah's law is enforced everywhere in the world'. It views Indian rule in Jammu & Kashmir as necessarily evil and oppressive. According to LeT's founder Hafeez Mohammad Saeed, 'The Hindu is a mean enemy and the proper way to deal with him is the one adopted by our forefathers, who crushed them by force.'[14]

Pakistan's support to these organisations was central to the growth, sustenance and survival of terrorist outfits operating in India. A large number of training camps and transit-cum-office camps were located in POK and Pakistan. Leaders of Islamic fundamentalist groups and other Islamic scholars engaged by the ISI were frequently used for recruitment and motivation of the youth. Most of the top leaders of Hizbul Mujahideen, United Jihad Council, Al Umar Mujahideen, Markaz-Daawa-wal-Irshad, LeT, Al Badr and JeM, etc., had been trained and weaponised, provided shelters, operational bases and all facilities for organising terrorist acts in India. If some organisation had to be banned under international pressure, it merely reared its head in some other name.

Simply put, the challenge that was hurled at the Indian Republic was dire. Mass-killing of innocent citizens and security personnel, infiltration across the borders, driving away Hindus and Sikhs from Kashmir and parts of Jammu as an integral element in the secessionist movement, systematic propagation of anti-India sentiments in the garb of foreign-funded religious preaching, fomenting communal tension and violence, hijacking, arms smuggling, infusion of counterfeit currency…and the attack on Parliament. Which self-respecting nation would tolerate all this meekly? Which democratic government, worth its salt, could keep quiet?

POTA: HOW THE CONGRESS COMMUNALISED AN ANTI-TERROR LAW

The Vajpayee government decided to respond to this challenge through a multi-pronged strategy that incorporated three components: legal, administrative and diplomatic. The legal response was in the form of a historic legislation: the Prevention of Terrorism Act (POTA), passed in March 2002, within four months of the terrorist attack on Parliament. It covered a wide spectrum of activities including recruitment, enticement, harbouring or participating in meetings of the terrorists besides possession, procurement and transportation of arms, explosives and other items of terrorist use. It incorporated stringent provisions for dealing with the financing of terrorism, distribution and use of funds, and made it possible under the law to freeze, seize or forfeit such funds/property. It provided various strict provisions for preventive detention without bail of suspected terrorists. The Act brought about some major procedural changes to deal with the terrorist cases like admissibility of certain types of evidence, which considerably strengthened the hands of police.

Sadly, our government faced considerable difficulty in getting POTA on to the statute book. This was principally because of the opposition from the Congress party, which ensured the defeat of the bill in the Rajya Sabha, where the NDA was in minority. This forced us to convene a joint session of both Houses of Parliament; it was only the third time in fifty years of its existence, that this rare constitutional provision had been invoked to pass an important bill. The ten-hour debate turned out to be one of the most acrimonious that I have witnessed in my long parliamentary career. Congress President Sonia Gandhi denounced POTA as violative of 'the basic human rights of individuals', and declared that the Congress-ruled states would not implement the law. She argued that existing laws were sufficient to deal with terrorism. If this was so, she did not explain why Maharashtra, which was then ruled by a Congress-led government, had enacted a special law (Maharashtra Control of Organised Crime Act or MCOCA*) in 1999 to handle terrorism-related cases. Shockingly, she had conveniently disregarded the fact that POTA was, qualitatively, no different from the Terrorist and Disruptive Activities (Prevention) Act (TADA), which had been introduced by the Rajiv Gandhi government in 1987.

In my reply to the debate, I reminded Sonia Gandhi and others in the Opposition, how TADA was formulated in the backdrop of the growing terrorist violence in Punjab, and also how the BJP had supported the Congress government on this much-needed measure. Indeed, it was the first legislative effort by the Central Government to define and counter terrorist activities. After all, the terrorists involved in the 1993 serial bomb blasts in Bombay were being tried by a special TADA court—they were subsequently convicted in 2007.

---

* Here is another instance of the Congress party's double standards. The BJP government in Gujarat got the state legislative assembly to pass the Gujarat Control of Organised Crime Bill, 2003, which was patterned exactly after the Maharashtra Control of Organised Crime Act, 1999. Because of the obstructionist stand of the Congress-led UPA government at the Centre, the Gujarat legislation has not received Presidential assent even after four years.

After the lapse of TADA in 1995, members of the security community had been forcefully urging successive governments at the Centre to enact a similar legislation, since they were finding themselves legally handicapped in the battle against terrorism. Also, the threat of terrorism had vastly increased, both in its gravity and geographical spread since 1995. Indeed, several Chief Ministers belonging to the Congress and the CPI(M), including Buddhadeb Bhattacharya of West Bengal, had privately conveyed to me that the country needed to deal firmly with the ISI menace. It is apposite for me to mention here that, in Bhattacharya, I found a rare communist leader whose views on ISI-guided cross-border terrorism and its ideological roots were, to a fair degree, congruent with mine.

Soon after he succeeded Jyoti Basu as the Chief Minister of West Bengal in November 2000, Bhattacharya called on me in my office one day and said, 'Advaniji, I have noticed that when you talk about ISI's anti-India activities in different parts of the country, you mention Maharashtra, Gujarat and other states, but you never mention West Bengal. Why are you silent about the ISI's presence in my state?' Frankly, I was surprised to be asked this question by a communist Chief Minister. I replied, 'I do not want to be silent. After all, the Home Ministry has a lot of information about what the ISI and Muslim extremist groups supported by it have been doing in West Bengal. But I do not mention it publicly because I have generally feared that, if I do, you may deny it.' At this, Bhattacharya said, rather forcefully, 'There is no question of denying it.' He then went to tell me in great detail about the sudden mushrooming of madarasas along West Bengal's border with Bangladesh and how some of them were promoting communal and anti-national elements. He also expressed concern over the huge influx of illegal immigrants from Bangladesh into West Bengal and the North-East, and was supportive of our government's policy in this regard. Indeed, he once even addressed a press conference with me in Kolkata on the issue of infiltration of Bangladeshis.*

---

* The attitude of his predecessor, Jyoti Basu, who was the Chief Minister of West Bengal for twenty-three years, on all these issues was quite different. For example, in 1998 the Government of Maharashtra, which was then ruled by the Shiv Sena-BJP combine,

Contd...

Coming back to the debate on POTA in Parliament, I reminded the Opposition that the law had become necessary after the United Nations passed several resolutions on terrorism, calling on member states to enact effective laws in consonance with those resolutions. India was not only a signatory to these, but had actually played a major role in urging the UN to take stiff anti-terrorism initiatives. I asked the Congress and other Opposition leaders: 'How can India ask the world community to act tough on terrorism, if it is unwilling to do the same at home?'

Although the bill was passed with a comfortable majority in the joint session of Parliament, the Opposition parties' attack on the government continued unabated. They would frequently, and rather tauntingly, ask me: 'Has your POTA prevented terrorist acts in India?' It was an absurd question, indeed. No law in the world guarantees total prevention of a crime. But the recurrence of that crime cannot be an argument against the law itself. There have been laws against murder and rape; nevertheless, murder and rape have continued. Does this mean that we should do away with these laws? The basic intent and utility of any criminal law, I emphasised, is three-fold: (a) to act as a deterrent for potential perpetrators of a crime; (b) to make it easier for the law enforcement agencies to detect a crime, nab the criminals and prosecute them; (c) to ensure that convicted persons receive exemplary punishment. Since cross-border terrorism is no ordinary crime and threatens the very security and unity of the nation, it necessitates provisions that are naturally extraordinary. The enemy who aids and abets such crimes tries to measure the tolerance threshold. Hence,

---

Contd...

decided to deport around eighty illegal immigrants from Bangladesh, out of tens of thousands living in the state, through the international border at West Bengal. Its action was fully in consonance with the Foreigner's Act. However, Basu's government protested this move strongly. It claimed that some of the immigrants were bonafide Indians, and demanded that it be given advance notice since the deportations were to take place on its soil. It insisted on being given thirty days to ascertain if any potential deportee was actually from West Bengal. It also said that the deportation be carried out only after the mode of sending back the infiltrators was discussed. All in all, the Basu government's obstructionist attitude was an eye-opener for me on how difficult, almost impossible, it is for India to deport Bangladeshi infiltrators.

the enactment of a strong anti-terrorist law sends out a signal about our seriousness and commitment not to tolerate terrorist crimes.

No government scraps a criminal law just because it cannot completely stop occurrence of the crime it is intended to fight. Similarly, no army is disarmed on the spurious argument that all weapons can be potentially misused. Therefore, no nation can shy away from making laws which are necessary for the safety and security of the state and its citizens. True, no law is completely immune to misuse. Indeed, there had been many cases of state governments misusing TADA against their political opponents. Therefore, we had introduced several safeguards in POTA. I had instructed my officials to carefully study the Supreme Court's observations and directives on the misuse of TADA and incorporate all those safeguards into POTA, which they did. As a result, India's anti-terror law turned out to be far milder than the ones that USA and the UK passed after 9/11. Nevertheless, when instances of misuse of POTA were reported, our government amended it in December of 2003 with an ordinance designed to expand the scope of judicial review.

Sadly, even this did not stop the Congress and other Opposition parties' tirade against POTA. Instead of discussing how to reduce the scope of abuse, our friends in the Opposition were hell-bent to reduce the efficacy of India's battle against terrorism. What a tragedy, indeed.

I was deeply disappointed over the Congress party's proclivity to view POTA through the prism of vote-bank politics. Together with its allies, it had conducted a contemptible campaign to project POTA as 'anti-Muslim'. But what filled me with agony was that when the Congress-led UPA government repealed POTA in September 2004, and even advertised this blatant legislative disarming of India's battle against terrorism to be one of its proud achievements. I would like all patriotic Indians to think about the grave security implications of such short-sighted and expedient policies, which have made India 'a soft state'.

With the repeal of POTA, India today has no law that can, among other things, effectively track those involved in financing and facilitating terrorist activities. If USA and other western democracies have been able to snap the money trail of terrorists and terrorism-supporting individuals in their countries, it is because their new anti-terror laws empower their governments to monitor the movement of every dollar going out of, or coming into, their banking systems. India, on the contrary, has become a safe haven for anti-national elements, a land where benami* asset creation, hawala transactions, illegal immigration, fake passport procurement, corruption of security agencies, endless judicial delays, and worse, have become rampant. This surely is not the way to make India secure for future generations.

HARNESSING ADMINISTRATIVE MIGHT AGAINST TERRORISM

In the administrative offensive against terrorism, the Vajpayee government took a number of strong measures. Around thirty major terrorist groups operating in India and abroad like Al Qaeda, LeT, JeM, HuM, Harkat-ul-Ansar (HuA), Babbar Khalsa International, Khalistan Commando Force (KCF), International Sikh Youth Federation, SIMI, etc., were banned under POTA. This step made it possible for India to prevail upon USA, UK, EU, etc., to declare these as terrorist organisations. During the NDA rule, nearly 9,000 terrorists were killed and nearly 1,000 of them were arrested, which remains an unmatched achievement.

My direction to officials involved in these operations was simple: 'Do your job without fear or favour.' While urging them to be mindful about excesses and human rights violations, I nevertheless assured—and I lived by the assurance—that I would stand by any bold measures they might have to take in the conscientious discharge of their duty. It helped in raising their morale and strengthening their motivation, so important for men who risk their lives for the sake of the country. There were also other problems that plagued the functioning of these agencies: how considerations of caste, creed, region, contacts, and bribery influenced postings and transfers. Sadly, these problems were, and still are, endemic to the working of almost all the limbs of governance in India. I am proud of the fact that every single case of appointment or promotion in my ministry, which came to my table, was done on the criterion of merit alone.

---

* Benami refers to false declaration of ownership.

The Indian Army was used essentially to contain trans-border infiltration, disruption of communication and logistic supply networks and undertaking surgical operations against terrorist targets requiring higher firepower. As a result of all these measures, in Jammu & Kashmir alone, over 7,100 terrorists, over forty-five per cent of them foreign terrorists, were killed between 1999 and 2003. Over 2,100 terrorists were killed in the year 2001 alone, marking it the highest level of terrorist neutralisation since the inception of terrorism in the state. It was an unparalleled record in the fight against terrorism anywhere in the world. More importantly, it broke the will, disrupted the infrastructure and denuded the terrorist groups of their senior leadership. Infiltration of Pak-trained militants reduced substantially: in 1997 the Jammu & Kashmir government had reported 2,600 infiltrators. In 2003-04, the last completed year in office by the NDA government, the figure stood at 383.

My efforts to sensitise foreign governments about India's battle against cross-border terrorism were integral to the Vajpayee government's overall policy of assertive and coercive diplomacy to isolate Pakistan and the jihadi groups that it patronised.

7

Pakistan's Proxy War
How India engaged USA and the World

All States shall:

Refrain from providing any form of support, active or passive, to entities or persons involved in terrorist acts;

Deny safe haven to those who finance, plan, support, or commit terrorist acts, or provide safe havens;

Prevent those who finance, plan, facilitate or commit terrorist acts from using their respective territories for those purposes against other States or their citizens.

—UN Security Council Resolution 1373 (2001)

An important lesson I learnt during my years as India's Home Minister was that the war against terror is indeed very different from 'war' as is normally understood. It has to be fought on many levels, on several fronts, with diverse tools. People should be educated about the fact that the fulfilment of its objective—for every war has to have a clear objective—necessarily requires a prolonged and protracted effort. It is natural for popular sentiments to be agitated after a terrible terrorist attack, and the attack on Parliament was certainly the most warlike act of terror that India has witnessed. Many people in the country, including in my own party, were in a mood 'to teach Pakistan a lesson'.

But it is not given to mature nations to react to provocations on the basis of the anger and outrage they generate. It is the responsibility of the leadership to weigh the situation carefully and in its entirety, and then decide on a course of action that is both firm and proper. And this is what Prime Minister Vajpayee did after the terrorist attack on Parliament on 13 December 2001. Both in the formal meetings of the CCS, and in the informal discussions with senior colleagues and service chiefs, he sought the views of one and all, which were offered freely and frankly. Any decision involving the military had to meticulously calibrate the timing, political objectives, operational goals, combat readiness and other factors, the most important among them being the likelihood of the conflict climbing up the 'ladder of escalation'. He also gave due consideration to the non-military tools available to India. The Prime Minister took the right decision that India's response to the attack on Parliament would be a combination of military mobilisation; political initiatives in Jammu & Kashmir to isolate Pakistan-supported militancy; and coercive-plus-assertive diplomacy in important capitals around the world.

The military component of this strategy was 'Operation Parakram', which was mobilisation of troops on the Indo-Pak border. It was indeed the largest peace-time deployment of troops in the country's history. Its aim was to warn Pakistan, and also to demonstrate to the international community, that India was prepared to exercise the military option if the rulers in Islamabad continued to retain terrorism against India as their state policy. Its message was simple: just as Islamabad's misadventure in violating the LoC at Kargil did not succeed, cross-border terrorism would not work either.

MY FIRST VISIT TO USA IN 2002

The government undertook a number of diplomatic initiatives to reinforce this message. One of them was my visit to the United States in January 2002. My visit had three purposes: to express solidarity with the government and the people of the United States in their ongoing struggle against terrorism; to thank them for their understanding and support for India's struggle against the same menace emanating from the same source; and to discuss, in the aftermath of 9/11 and 13 December, ways of giving effect to our common resolve to defeat terrorism decisively and speedily.

I visited 'Ground Zero' in New York commemorating 9/11, and paid tribute to the unflinching determination of the Americans to defend their nation in the face of the worst ever terrorist attack in human history. Addressing a press conference at the Indian embassy in Washington DC on 9 January, I described India and USA as the 'Twin Towers of Democracy'. Pointing out that both were victims of terrorism, I said, 'The common threat that we face has underscored the need for a strong and longer-term partnership between us. After all, it is instructive to know why international terrorism has made India and the United States its principal targets. I think that this is because our two countries cherish and celebrate all that the terrorists abhor and consider impediments to the realisation of their own strategic objective. We both believe in pluralism and secularism, which is rooted in respect for all faiths. We are both open societies, in which freedom of the press, judiciary and enterprise are constitutionally guaranteed. The terrorists may have destroyed the steel and concrete structures of the WTC, but they can never harm the structures and the spirit of our two democracies.'

The high point of this visit was my thirty-minute meeting with the US President, George W. Bush, in Washington DC the next day. He shook my hand vigorously and remarked: 'I hear that you are the strong man in the Indian government. Your reputation has preceded your arrival in Washington DC.' I conveyed to him, more forcefully than I have done in my talks with any other foreign leader, the menace that religiously inspired terrorism, emanating from Pakistan, posed to India, the United States, and the rest of the world. 9/11 had demonstrated this with chilling effect. I described to him the horrendous consequences of 13/12, if the conspiracy behind had succeeded. I emphasised that the US should not employ 'double standards' in its approach to fighting terrorism, and pointed out that sufficient proof of Pakistan's involvement in cross-border terrorism had been furnished by the Indian side in my meeting with senior US officials.

President Bush assured that his administration expected Pakistan to 'abandon terror as an instrument of state policy'. He conveyed to me that he expected General Musharraf 'to take all necessary steps' in fighting terror. 'He (Musharraf) has done it in the case of the Taliban, and I expect him to do it in the case of India also. I have urged him to take appropriate steps against extremists operating in and from Pakistan.' He also stressed the importance of solving the Indo-Pakistan 'differences' through diplomatic and political means. I could sense that Washington had taken due note of 'Operation Parakram'.

I had raised the same issues in my meeting with the Secretary of State, Colin Powell, the previous day. He too stressed that the situation between India and Pakistan needed to be dealt with through 'political and diplomatic means'. I said I agreed with him, but added that the US, too, needed to exert itself more in condemning Pakistan's terrorist campaign against India. Powell understood my point of emphasis, and replied, 'The United States is engaged in a campaign against all forms of terrorism and will work with all of our friends to remove this scourge from the face of the earth and as a threat to civilisation. Because it is no longer acceptable in the twenty-first century for nations to live under this kind of threat.'

In my meetings with all the US officials—among them was Attorney General John Ashcroft—I focused on Pakistan's fundamental and continuing role in sustaining international terrorism. The Taliban, I pointed out, was created and propped up by Pakistan's ruling establishment as a 'force multiplier' in its proxy war against India. Over the past two decades, terrorism, sponsored and directed by ISI has claimed nearly 60,000 of our innocent civilians and security personnel—in Punjab, Jammu & Kashmir, and other parts of India. Therefore, I said, Indians were bemused when Pakistan effected a sudden U-turn in its policy towards the Taliban and decided to join the US-led coalition against terror in Afghanistan. 'We cannot understand how Pakistan can now claim to be opposed to terrorism on its west and continue to rationalise, justify and patronise it on its east.'

Just a week before my visit to the US, the Pakistani President had yet again claimed, at the (SAARC) summit in Kathmandu, that the terrorist acts in Jammu & Kashmir were part of a legitimate 'freedom struggle', to which he had reaffirmed his government's continued support. I referred to this in my press conference saying, 'I would like our friends in USA and elsewhere in the world to ponder: "What type of freedom fighters are these who set off serial bomb blasts in Mumbai, hijack a civilian airliner and take it, unsurprisingly, to Taliban-controlled Kandahar, routinely conduct mass killings of innocent civilians, carry out a terrorist attack on the Jammu & Kashmir Legislative Assembly and strike at India's Parliament, the heart of the world's largest democracy?" We fully agree with President Bush's exhortation that "there cannot be good terrorists and bad terrorists". Obviously, President Musharraf seems to think otherwise. He would like the world to believe that there are "good terrorists" at work in furtherance of Pakistan's stand on Kashmir.'

Aware of the concerns of Americans and others in the world over the build-up of Indian troops along our border with Pakistan, I observed, 'India has never been wanting in self-restraint. We have shown immense restraint during the prolonged proxy war waged by Pakistan, in which we faced many grave provocations. India made several sincere and bold efforts in the past three years to seek peace with Pakistan. Each time, Pakistan responded with betrayal. As far as India is concerned, 13 December has been the gravest of provocations so far. Prime Minister Vajpayee has spoken for one billion Indians when he said that it has "breached the limit of our endurance". We shall not take another betrayal this time around. Pakistan must act—sincerely, decisively, demonstrably and speedily.'

I said the touchstone of Pakistan's sincerity would be its positive response to the following demands by India, which I had conveyed in my official talks during the visit:

1. Handing over to India twenty terrorists, whose names, along with evidence of their criminal acts against India, have been given by us to the government of Pakistan. Many of these terrorists are Indian nationals and have been sheltered in Pakistan.*
2. Closure of facilities, training camps, arms supply, funding and all other manner of direct and indirect assistance for terrorists on Pakistani soil, including on areas controlled by it.
3. Stoppage of infiltration of arms and men from Pakistan into Jammu & Kashmir and elsewhere in India.
4. A categorical and unambiguous renunciation of terrorism in all its manifestations and wherever it exists, irrespective of the cause it seeks to further.

MY DISMAY OVER DAWOOD IBRAHIM'S NON-DEPORTATION

The account that now follows describes one of the deep disappointments I experienced during my stint in the Home Ministry when India was

---

* Some of the names in this list of twenty most-wanted terrorists, whose extradition was demanded by India, were: (1) Dawood Ibrahim, a mafia don who was the brain behind the serial bomb blasts in Mumbai in March 1993 in which 257 people died. He lives in Karachi. (2) Maulana Azhar Masood, leader of JeM, named as 'principal accused' in the attack on India's Parliament. He is also wanted for an attack on J&K legislature on 1 October 2001, in which thirty-seven people were killed. (3) Hafiz Mohammad Saeed, co-founder of LeT, also blamed for the attack on Parliament in New Delhi. (4) Chhota Shakeel, a key associate of Dawood Ibrahim. Wanted for murder, extortion, kidnapping, blackmail of businessmen and film stars. He also lives in Karachi. (5) 'Tiger' Ibrahim Memon, convicted for masterminding the 1993 serial blasts in Mumbai. He smuggled in over 300 kg of RDX from Pakistan. Another key associate of Dawood Ibrahim, he also lives in Karachi. (6) Ibrahim Athar, an associate of Maulana Azhar Masood and one of the hijackers of Indian Airlines flight IC 814 from Kathmandu to Delhi in 1999. He is a member of Jaish-e-Mohammad and lives in Bahawalpur. (7) Wadhawan Singh Babbar, chief of Babbar Khalsa International, is wanted in over a dozen cases of sedition and murder, including the assassination of Punjab's former Chief Minister Beant Singh. He lives in Lahore. (8) Paramjit Singh Panjwar, leader of the KCF, is wanted in more than a dozen cases of murder, including the assassination of General A.S. Vaidya in 1986. He lives in Lahore.

denied a major success in its war against Pakistan-supported terrorism by way of bureaucratic non-cooperation that I have not been able to fully fathom.

The officials travelling with me to USA had handed over the list of twenty most wanted Pak-based terrorists, along with copious and compelling evidence, to their American counterparts. Topping the list was Dawood Ibrahim, an underworld don who had planned and financed thirteen serial explosions in Mumbai on 12 March 1993 in which 257 people died. Head of an organised crime syndicate in Mumbai called 'D-Company', he had shifted base to Dubai to evade arrest in the many cases of murder, arms supply, smuggling, counterfeiting and drugs trade. After plotting the 1993 blasts in Mumbai, he was given shelter in Karachi, where Pakistani authorities also provided safe haven to many others who were involved in that horrendous terrorist act. Many investigative reports, including those published in Pakistan,[1] have demolished claims by Musharraf* and others in the Pakistani establishment that Dawood does not live in Karachi.

In fact, in October 2003, the United States designated Dawood Ibrahim as a 'global terrorist' having links with Al Qaeda and financing activities of LeT and other terrorist organisations.[2] All his assets within the US were frozen. A statement issued by the US Treasury Department said: 'We are calling on the international community to stop the flow of dirty money that kills. For the Ibrahim syndicate, the business of terrorism forms part of their larger criminal enterprise, which must be dismantled'. It not only said that Dawood was in Karachi, but affirmed that he possessed a Pakistani passport whose number was 0869537 under the individual category. A 'Fact Sheet' issued by the Treasury Department said that, in the 1990s, he travelled to Afghanistan under the protection of the Taliban, adding, significantly, that his 'syndicate has consistently aimed to destabilise the Indian government through inciting riots, acts of terrorism, and civil disobedience. (He) has been helping finance increasing attacks in Gujarat by LeT.' No wonder, he was called 'Karachi's Osama', who was kept in a safe

---

* See page 699 for Musharraf's lie on Dawood Ibrahim, during my conversation with the Pakistan President.

house by the ISI. This should explain why I was so insistent on securing the deportation of Dawood and other Pak-based terrorists and ensuring that they stand trial in India.

When news came that the US government had declared Dawood as a 'global terrorist', I was naturally elated. I described it as 'a major development', adding that 'India stands vindicated'.[3] Coincidentally, the news came within hours of my raising the issue of Pakistan giving shelter to India's most wanted terrorists in my inaugural address at an Interpol-organised international conference on fugitives, then being held in New Delhi. The *Hindu* newspaper reported: 'The Deputy Prime Minister, L.K. Advani, has reasons to be a somewhat satisfied man, after the United States decided to designate Dawood Ibrahim a "designated global terrorist". Officials associated with the intelligence community were all praise for Mr Advani's "doggedness" on the question of pursuing the "most wanted 20".'[4]

At the conference on fugitives, I called upon the international community to take steps to isolate nations that practise terrorism as an instrument of state policy. 'There are nations that profess to be members of the global coalition against terrorism. Yet, they take no steps to curb the export of terror from their soil. The perpetrators of some of the dastardly criminal acts on the Indian soil, including acts of terrorism, have found safe havens in our neighbourhood and elsewhere.' I said half the battle against terrorism, organised crime, global economic frauds and international fugitives would be won if countries took concrete steps to prevent its spread from their soil instead of offering only lip sympathy.

*

During my visit to the US, I said to both Secretary of State Colin Powell and National Security Advisor Condoleezza Rice that if the Bush administration could force Musharraf to deport many of those linked to 9/11 and other terrorist acts aimed against the United States, India expected it to exert similar pressure on Pakistan to hand over Dawood Ibrahim and others for trial in India. This, I said, would convince the people of India that the US truly practices what it preaches—namely, that it is against terrorism in whatever form and everywhere in the world. While interacting with the media after my meeting with Powell, journalists put, *inter alia,* two questions to the Secretary of State.

Q: Mr Secretary, I understand that Mr Minister is carrying a list of twenty terrorists that India is wanting from Pakistan, or they are based in Pakistan. What do you have to say about those terrorists, whether you are going to ask General Musharraf to hand over those terrorists based in Pakistan to India?

Powell: With respect to the list of twenty, I have seen that list, and I know that President Musharraf has the list. *We have discussed the list with him.* I know he is examining it. And I hope he will take *appropriate action* on the list. (emphasis added)

Q: The United States has consistently said that it does see President Musharraf taking credible steps against terrorism, but the Indians have not exactly seen it that way and say that they have yet to see credible steps. Was there a large gap between the two sides in your meetings today with the Indians? Are they giving Musharraf any credit at all?

Powell: I think President Musharraf has taken some steps. He has arrested the leaders of the JeM and the LeT. He has closed down offices. He has spoken out against terrorism. He has also arrested other individuals. But I think there is room for *additional work on his part.* We're looking forward to the speech he will be giving later this week, which I think will be a powerful signal to his nation and to India and the rest of the world. *But it's not just the speech; we will be looking to see what additional action he has taken.* I believe he has taken quite a bit of action in recent months. But as you well know, *the Indians believe more action is required. And we will see what happens in the days and weeks ahead.* (emphasis added)

I have given Powell's replies verbatim because they conveyed a certain readiness on the part of Americans to act on the Indian demand, especially with regard to the list of 'Top Twenty'. This is how the *Times of India* reported my meeting with Powell. (*Excerpts*)

*Advani convinces Powell
Pak should act, not talk*

By Chidanand Rajghatta

10 Jan 2002, Washington: The United States has agreed with India that Pakistan and its military ruler Pervez Musharraf need to do more than just talk against terrorism. They have to take 'additional action' on top of some of the measures announced. Pakistan also needs to take 'appropriate action' on the list of 20 terrorists New Delhi has handed over to Islamabad. In a perceptible departure from the earlier US stance that pressed India to respond to Pakistan's verbal assurances, secretary of state Colin Powell switched to the 'we-need-action-from-Pakistan' mode after a forceful presentation from Home Minister L.K. Advani questioning Pakistan's sincerity in combating terrorism.... The comments suggested that Washington substantially agreed with India's argument that Pakistan has not done enough to address its concerns on terrorism. And they came after the American establishment, including Powell, a few law-makers, and some of the US media drummed up Musharraf's forthcoming address as if it had already been delivered and indicated the onus was now on India to respond to Pakistan's climb-down. Not so, Advani told his US interlocutors. Pakistan continues to be duplicitous about terrorism and had done very little about it. India was not the belligerent part, and on the contrary, had acted with great restraint in the face of a decade of proxy war initiated by Pakistan.

In what was described by officials as a lawyerly and clinical presentation to Powell, the Home minister questioned the premise that Pakistan was taking any significant action against terrorism. On the contrary, it had issued cavalier statements and had trivialised the attack on the Indian Parliament. Specifically, Advani drew Powell's attention to the statement by Musharraf's spokesman Rashid Qureshi soon after the attack on Parliament that Indian agencies had themselves perpetuated the strike.... In a separate press conference following day-long talks with US officials, Advani, who was clearly in an uncompromising mood, said he was satisfied with the exchanges and was optimistic that Washington would recognise India's situation. Judging by Powell's remarks, the Home minister appeared to have achieved considerable success in putting across India's position.

Within ten days of my meeting with Powell in Washington, he came on a whirlwind tour of India and Pakistan in a bid to lower tension between our two countries following 12/13 and 'Operation Parakram'. He gave even clearer indication that the Bush administration had decided to ask Musharraf to combat terrorism, especially by taking concrete action on the list of twenty most-wanted terrorists. He told his Indian interlocutors that Pakistan would hand over underworld don Dawood Ibrahim to India 'with some strings attached', and also that Musharraf needed '15 to 20 days more' for doing so. 'He is under tremendous pressure from the international community to rein in terrorism directed against India,' Powell said, 'and has been told that this time India is not likely to go for de-escalation until it got something tangible from Islamabad[5].'

About the 'strings attached' to Dawood's deportation, we learnt that: (a) Dawood's testimony would be used only for the Bombay blasts case and no other case; and (b) Dawood would not be used by the Indian government to sully Pakistan's image in the international community. This was further corroborated when Robert Mueller, chief of USA's Federal Bureau of Investigation (FBI) came to India in the following week and held talks with Home Secretary Kamal Pande, Director, IB K.P. Singh, and CBI Chief P.C. Sharma.

In spite of this persistent and single-minded pursuit of getting Dawood Ibrahim back, I started facing hurdles. Recalling this now is not a very happy experience. When Powell came to India, I was unpleasantly surprised to know that I was not among the Indian officials meeting him. The PMO's explanation, from what I gathered, was that since I had met the US Secretary of State only ten days earlier in Washington, there was no need for me to meet him again. It bewildered me. My interest in meeting Powell was, specifically, to find out about the Bush administration's follow-up on the Indian demand for the extradition of Dawood Ibrahim and others in the list submitted to Pakistan.

In the months that followed, there was no Pakistani action on the Indian demand on Dawood Ibrahim; there was only fibbing and foot-dragging. In my interactions with visiting Americans, I began to see, strangely, a certain lack of enthusiasm. 'We do not have the clout to compel Pakistan to act on this issue,' they started saying. Contesting this explanation, I once told US Deputy Secretary of State, Richard Armitage, 'There is no way Pakistan will not accept US diktats. After all, Musharraf yielded to your pressure in the case of fighting the Taliban in Afghanistan. Your clout was evident in the handing over of over 500 Al Qaeda men to the US. Pakistan cannot disregard what you say*, as they are so dependent on you.'

I suspected, not without basis, that somebody in the bureaucratic system was trying, in India's dialogue with Americans, to de-emphasise or derail the issue of getting Dawood Ibrahim and other Indian terrorists back from Pakistan. I was deeply upset by this. Success on this score would have not only hugely embarrassed the rulers in Pakistan, but would also have meant a major psychological victory for India in its prolonged campaign against cross-border terrorism. Secondly, it would have brought tremendous political dividends to the BJP and the Vajpayee government. My disappointment and frustration on this score was greater since our government had made considerable progress, through unrelenting and resolute efforts, in our bid to get another of India's most wanted terrorists,

---

* There is stark admission about American clout over Pakistan in General Pervez Musharraf's memoirs. The morning after 9/11, Colin Powell phoned Musharraf. '(He) was quite candid: "You are either with us or against us." I took this as a blatant ultimatum.... When I was back in Islamabad the next day, our Director General of Inter Services Intelligence, who happened to be in Washington, told me on the phone about his meeting with the US Deputy Secretary of State, Richard Armitage. In what has to be the most undiplomatic statement ever made, Armitage added to what Colin Powell had said to me and told the Director General not only that we had to decide whether we were with America or with the terrorists, but that if we chose the terrorists, then we should be prepared to be bombed back to the Stone Age"'. (*In the Line of Fire*, Free Press, 2006, p. 201)

Abu Salem, deported from Portugal. Salem, once a close aide of Dawood Ibrahim, was wanted in various criminal cases, including the 1993 serial blasts in Mumbai. Although India had no extradition treaty with Portugal, I was determined to see that Salem was brought back to India and made to stand trial for the various crimes he had committed. I wrote to the Portuguese authorities and Interpol requesting his deportation. Our talks with them progressed satisfactorily. However, there was one hitch: capital punishment is banned by European Union countries. After getting due legal advice, I assured the Portuguese government that Salem would not face the death penalty in India. Our persistence paid off and, finally, he was deported to India in November 2005. It was a significant victory for India in its fight against terrorism, and a tribute to the combined efforts of the CBI, officials of the Ministries of Home, Law and External Affairs, and our embassy in Lisbon.

MY SECOND VISIT TO USA IN 2003

My second visit to the United States was in June 2003, this time as India's Deputy Prime Minister. My agenda this time was more comprehensive than in 2002, covering several other issues in our bilateral relations, such as civilian space cooperation, cooperation in nuclear energy and promotion of high-technology trade. Nevertheless, I was keen on further deepening America's understanding of, and support for, India's position on terrorism in general and the Kashmir issue in particular.

Once again, the highlight of this visit was my meeting with President Bush, and he dropped in at my scheduled meeting with Condoleezza Rice*.

---

* 'Bush virtually hijacks Advani-Rice meeting', by Aziz Hanifa in Washington, Rediff.com, 10 June 2003. This is how Hanifa reported the meeting. 'President George W. Bush didn't just drop in on the meeting between Deputy Prime Minister Lal Kishenchand Advani and National Security Advisor Condoleezza Rice. With him being there for 30 of the 38 minutes Advani spent with Rice, it was virtually a Bush-Advani summit during which he assured the Indian leader of doing some blunt talking with Pakistan President Pervez Musharraf on cross-border terrorism. Administration and diplomatic sources said that Bush, who walked into the meeting between Advani and

Contd...

He affirmed his 'strong desire' to continue the process of transforming India-US relations. He expressed warm admiration for the leadership of Prime Minister Vajpayee, who, during his visit to Kashmir a couple of months earlier, had made a bold overture to restart dialogue with Pakistan. 'He has gambled for peace and provided political space for resolving differences, without foregoing the concern for security. I have already conveyed this to your Prime Minister and I would be speaking to President Musharraf about creating a climate in which this initiative could succeed.' Bush also told me that he saw India as one of the leading drivers of the high-tech world and had contributed significantly to the increase in US productivity by providing Indian manpower, know-how and entrepreneurship.

On my part, I assured him that we in India did not view our relations with the United States as a matter of convenience, but as a partnership of trust and confidence, which can stand up to whatever challenges the future brings. As far as Pak-sponsored cross-border terrorism was concerned, I explained to him at length how there was not much difference in the ground situation since my last visit to USA. I said that the officials accompanying me would give his colleagues more documentary evidence to prove that Pakistan was still not sincere in its efforts to contain Islamic fundamentalism, training militants and exporting terrorism. Rice conveyed to me that further steps were being taken to ensure progress on all issues on the bilateral agenda, including the 'trinity' issues (civilian space cooperation, cooperation in civilian nuclear energy and promotion of high-technology trade) in order to provide tangible evidence of the changed relationship.

Earlier in the day, in my luncheon meeting with Attorney General John Ashcroft, we focused on cooperation in combating terrorism and

---

Contd...
Rice a few minutes into their conversation had immediately told Advani how much he admired Prime Minister Atal Bihari Vajpayee's peace initiative and described him as a statesman. Almost on cue, according to the sources, Advani had told Bush that India is committed to peace in the region but that Pakistan continues to foment cross-border terrorism and unless this is halted permanently, New Delhi could not be expected to enter into high level talks with Islamabad or engage in a peace process.'

compared notes on the problems confronting democracies in dealing with this issue. Home secretary N. Gopalaswami* and K.P. Singh, Director IB, who were a part of my delegation, handed over to Ashcroft some vital intelligence information about terrorist organisations in India and their global linkages. My meeting with Secretary, Homeland Security, Tom Ridge, also focused on security issues such as border management, airport and sea-port security and cooperation on both interdiction and consequence management technologies to combat potential threats to internal security.

My visit to USA this time was taking place in the backdrop of the Iraq war. In March 2003, America, joined by the UK and some other countries in a multinational coalition, had invaded Iraq. Thus, in my meeting with President Bush and all his colleagues, they made a strong plea for India to join the coalition by sending at least one division of Indian troops to Iraq. This was conveyed to me most insistently by Secretary of Defence, Donald Rumsfeld, who, instead of a scheduled meeting at the Pentagon, met me in my hotel on the very first day of my visit, and in spite of it being a Sunday. I told them that the matter had been discussed by the CCS, in which certain objections were raised. Prime Minister Vajpayee and his ministerial colleagues, I said, were clear that any decision in this regard had to be based on a broad national consensus, for which the government was keen to have a dialogue with all the Opposition parties.

Right from the beginning of the US invasion of Iraq, Atalji and I were firmly of the view that sending Indian troops to join the American war effort, was out of the question. Neither was the invasion justified, nor was it in India's national interests to support it. Besides, every single political party in India was opposed to the idea. Nevertheless, the Prime Minister's way of handling American pressure on this issue was sagacious. By basing the government's decision on a lack of national consensus, domestically, he took the Opposition parties on his side and, internationally, he let both the US and the rest of the world know that India had a democratic way

---

* An officer of impeccable credentials, N. Gopalaswami later became India's CEC.

of deciding its stand on such issues. The correctness of India's decision not to send its troops to Iraq has been fully vindicated by the tragic consequences of America's folly in 2003.

Keenly aware of how the official view in USA is shaped by its think-tanks and the mass media, I used my visit to America to communicate to a wider audience beyond the governmental establishment in Washington. I was eager to make my modest contribution to India's effort to reach out to the 'American mind', persuading it to realise that the transition of our two countries from being 'estranged democracies' during the Cold War era to becoming 'engaged democracies' at the beginning of the twenty-first century needed to be anchored in the principle of equality and in our shared values. Prime Minister Vajpayee, during his earlier visit to USA, had rightly described India and America as 'natural allies'. It was my endeavour to let our American friends know—and I have persisted in this endeavour both before and after my two official visits to USA—that India was not coming to them to seek their 'help', as a subservient partner, either in our fight against Pak-supported terrorism or in any other matter. No, India was quite capable of fighting its own battles, and winning them, too. I tried to impress upon them that acceptance of a relationship of 'natural alliance' imposes an obligation to be sensitive to each other's legitimate concerns.

I have always believed that the true basis of the relationship between any two nations can be best understood by knowing how each has influenced the great minds of the other. I had an occasion to recall this when I went to address the Chicago Council on Foreign Relations. One of the reasons why India accepts USA to be a natural ally is because of Chicago's unique association with Swami Vivekanand, India's greatest spiritual messenger to the world in the nineteenth century. It was here that, participating in the World Parliament of Religions in 1893, Swamiji made India proud by proclaiming the message of universal brotherhood. But he not only introduced India to America, but also introduced America to India. Here I cited a beautiful poem, 'To the Fourth of July', that Swamiji wrote on the anniversary of the American Declaration of Freedom:

All hail to thee, thou Lord of Light!
A welcome new to thee, today,
O Sun! Today thou Sheddest Liberty!
Move on, O Lord, in thy resistless path
Till thy high noon o'erspreads the world
Till every land reflects thy light,
Till men and women, with their uplifted head,
Behold their shackles broken, and
Know, in springing joy, their life renewed

I said that just as America's struggle for independence influenced the best of Indian minds, India's struggle for independence, led by Mahatma Gandhi, influenced the best of American minds such as Martin Luther King and Albert Einstein. 'Our relationship has been bound by our common commitment to freedom, democracy, tolerance and the rule of law. This commitment to shared values has helped us tide over turbulent times. Today, they form the bedrock of a vastly expanded partnership for the future. Yes, there will always be differences over this or that issue between two sovereign nations. But our convergent interests and views have now acquired such critical mass that they have clearly begun to outweigh our differences.'

My visit to Los Angeles gave me an opportunity to renew my contact with the West Coast,[6] which is a testimony to the immense diversity of USA. From a geo-political point of view, it has a special relation to Asia, a reminder that the United States is not only an Atlantic nation linked to Europe, but also a Pacific nation linked to Asia. I had visited Los Angeles in 1992 to open a chapter of the Overseas Friends of the Bharatiya Janata Party. During an earlier visit in 1990, I had also visited Microsoft's headquarters in Seattle to acquaint myself with the 'buzz' about information technology that was, at the time, most associated with that company and its Founder Bill Gates. Since then, India itself had made huge strides in IT, in terms of both overseas Indians' contribution to the success of 'Silicon Valley' but, more importantly, our software professionals' accomplishments in India itself.

In my address to the World Affairs Council in Los Angeles, I said, 'The India-US strategic partnership is clearly here to stay, and will grow stronger over the years. Of course, differences will remain and we will continue to agree to disagree on certain issues. But as befits two mature and forward-looking democracies, we will move forward on the basis of our shared values and views on a larger set of issues, ever mindful of the fact that cooperation between the world's two largest democracies is essential for the peace, stability and prosperity of the world.'

Earlier in Washington, I also had an interactive session with a group of American scholars from Brookings Institution, Woodrow Wilson Centre, Centre for Strategic and International Studies and the Centre for International Policy at the residence of Ambassador Lalit Mansingh. My overall assessment of my two visits to the United States was a mix of optimism and caution. On the one hand, I could sense that the American government was earnestly endeavouring to recognise India as a major power. On the other hand, the US did not want to offend Pakistan by leaning on it too heavily to stop cross-border terrorism aimed against India. This assessment has not changed much as I write this in 2008. Clearly, India needs to do a lot more talking to the United States on the issue of terrorism and religious extremism, and the latter too needs to take a more honest look, *sans* double standards, at what is happening in Pakistan itself.

*

On my return from the United States, I visited Britain and had candid talks with Prime Minister Tony Blair, Deputy Prime Minister John Prescott, Home Secretary David Blunkett and Foreign Secretary Jack Straw. Here, too, Blair raised the issue of sending Indian troops to join the US-led military operations in Iraq. My response was the same as I had conveyed in Washington. On Kashmir and cross-border terrorism, I found the British authorities, in private conversations, to be far more receptive and appreciative of India's concerns than before.[7] However, their public pronouncements did not fully convey this convergence. Like many of our good American friends, they would say, 'Since we want to have Pakistan as a front-ranking ally in the war on terror, we cannot be saying things about Pakistan that we do believe in.' I would tell them plainly that Indian people are disappointed with the West's double standards, whereby 'you find terrorism hurting you to be more serious, not terrorism that has been hurting us for a much longer period'.

During my talks with Prime Minister Blair, he asked me, 'Tell me candidly what the people in India feel about us.' I said, 'The people of India are unhappy with your attitude. We in (the) government can understand your strategic compulsions to have Pakistan on your side, provided yours is really a war against international terrorism and not merely an operation to avenge 9/11. But, for the common Indian, terrorism is Pak-inspired terrorism. And he is not able to digest how a terrorist state, which has given us trouble for over two decades, has become the front-ranking US and western ally in this war against terrorism. He is not able to digest that.'

I even told the British Prime Minister, 'Mr Blair, people also know that Taliban or Osama bin Laden or ISI, they are all creations in which America has contributed. And they have linkages. All these things are known. Our own conviction has been that those who promote terrorism one day have to bear the consequences. It happened with the Bhindranwale cult, it happened with the LTTE and it has now happened with Taliban and Osama bin Laden.' My plain-speaking perhaps had some effect. At the joint press conference at the British Foreign Office, after my meeting with Secretary Straw, a journalist asked him for his comments on General Musharraf's description of the militants in Jammu & Kashmir as freedom fighters. 'What does Britain call them?' Straw replied, 'Terrorists are terrorists. No matter what name they give their activity. Britain considers them as pure terrorists.'

*

I carried the same message to the other countries—France, Germany, Turkey, Qatar, UAE, Thailand, Singapore and Israel—to which I paid official visits. In Paris, besides a meeting with French Prime Minister Jean-Pierre Raffarin, I held talks with Interior Minister (now President) Nicolas Sarkozy and Defence Minister Michele Alliott-Marie. Sarkozy was quite outspoken on the issues of terrorism, religious extremism and illegal immigration. I signed an Indo-French extradition treaty with Justice Minister Dominique Perben. After Britain and Spain, France became the third major European nation to have an extradition arrangement with India. I told my interlocutors that France, which was then chairperson of G-8, should mobilise other European countries to choke financing of terrorist organisations. On other matters, it was heartening for me to find that the idea of a multi-polar world evoked greater resonance in France. Incidentally, France was one of the very few Western countries that did not criticise India after the Pokharan nuclear test in May 1998.

My visit to Qatar became memorable for a reason absent from the official agenda. Qatar is a small oil-rich country in the Gulf with a population of around six lakhs, nearly one-third of which is accounted for by the ethnic Indian community. Indeed, no other country in the world has such a high percentage of Indians. Islam is the official religion of Qatar, and Shariat is the principal source of legislation. The Amir of Qatar, Sheikh Hamid Bin Khalifa Al-Thani, received me with great warmth. Indians have excellent relations with the Qataris. However, they had one grievance: There was no freedom of religion. As one immigrant pointed out to me, 'If an Indian dies in this country, he is not allowed to be cremated. With great difficulty he is allowed to be buried. But no Hindu likes to be buried.' I took up this point, and also the broader issue of religious freedom for non-Muslims, in my talks with the Amir. He assured me that he would keep this in mind while amendments were being made to the country's constitution.

I also urged Qatar, which at the time was heading the Organisation of Islamic Conference (OIC), a global body of Muslim nations, to address India's concerns on cross-border terrorism. This could be done, I told the Amir, by Qatar and other OIC countries signing an extradition treaty with India, and by putting pressure on Pakistan from within the Islamic world.

As a matter of fact, Turkey was one of the Muslim countries with which I signed an extradition treaty during my memorable visit in 2001. In general, in all my interactions with representatives of Muslim countries, in New Delhi or abroad, I sought to impress upon them that terrorism and religious extremism was threatening peace and stability in the Islamic world as well.

My visits to Thailand and Singapore in February 2003 gave me an opportunity to focus on the threats to India's internal security from 'cross-border terrorism' on our eastern border with Bangladesh. In my talks with Thai Premier Thaksin Shinawatra and Singapore's Prime Minister Goh Chok Tong, I underscored the growing regional and international linkages between terrorist groups active in South-East Asia, and also their links with drug cartels and arms smugglers.

My five-day visit to Israel* in June 2000 renewed my old bond with that country and also proved highly useful in strengthening mutual friendship and bilateral cooperation in the new situation in our respective parts of the world. I had visited Israel as the BJP president in 1995, and feel proud to have played a role in full normalisation of diplomatic relations between our two countries, which have many things in common. I visited Israel's Holocaust museum, Yad Vashem, where I laid a wreath in homage to the six million Jews killed by the Nazis during the Second World War. I met President Ezer Weizman; Prime Minister Ehud Barak; Shimon Peres, who was then the Minister of Regional Development; Mossad Chief Ephraim Halevi and other officials. We formalised an intelligence sharing agreement,

---

* About my visit to Israel, *Ha'aretz* newspaper wrote: 'A clear indication of his ideology and Weltanschauung was audible in an interview with Advani. Unlike other visiting leaders, he did not hesitate to express his views openly and bluntly, even on such a sensitive matter as nuclear cooperation. "Yes," he said, "I am in favor of cooperating with Israel in all areas, especially the nuclear field, and this should be strengthened".' ('India's visiting strongman wants to expand nuclear cooperation with Israel' by Yossi Melman in *Ha'aretz* newspaper, 16 June 2000.) After the visit, Israeli Ambassador in India, Dr Yehoyad Haim, said in an interview to *Outlook* magazine (July 2000): 'Mr Advani is a very unique man. Ideologically and personally he reminds me of some people from an earlier generation of Israelis.'

under which Israeli intelligence agencies would open offices in New Delhi on the lines of the FBI of USA. We discussed further cooperation in internal security management and defence, particularly counter-terrorism measures and technology transfer. I visited Israel's northern border with Lebanon to be briefed on Israel's style of border management.

My visit to Israel was made memorable because of the opportunity to meet the legendary Palestinian leader, Yasser Arafat, at his office in Gaza City. This meeting reinforced India's consistent stand that a durable and just peace between Israelis and Palestinians can be established only through a recognition of the legitimate right of both to exist as sovereign states in a cooperative and non-hostile neighbourhood.

During my six years in the Home ministry, India entered into extradition treaties/arrangements with twenty-four countries; bilateral agreements to combat terrorism and organised crime with eight countries; mutual legal assistance treaties with thirteen countries; and joint working groups against terrorism with seventeen countries. All this was unprecedented. In another major initiative by the Vajpayee government, India piloted the Comprehensive Convention on International Terrorism (CCIT) at the United Nations and supported Security Council Resolutions 1269 and 1378 (which identify terrorism as a threat to international peace and security). It also supported and fully implemented Resolution 1267, 1333 and 1363 relating to the Taliban in Afghanistan. It welcomed and fully supported UN SC Resolution 1373 and took prompt action to submit its national reports to the UN Counter Terrorism Committee.

I can say with some pride that, in its approach to internal security, the NDA government, for all the six years that it was in office, remained consistently proactive, duty-driven and single-minded.

8

DEALING WITH THE KASHMIR ISSUE
How firmness and sincerity yielded progress

Shiv chuy thali thali rozan; Mo zan Hindu La Musalman.
Truk ay chuk pan panun parzanav; Soy chay Sahibas sati zaniy zan.

(Shiva lives everywhere; do not divide Hindu from Muslim. Use your sense to recognise yourself; that is the true way to find God.)

—LAL DED OR LALLESHWARI (1320–92),
KASHMIR'S GREATEST POETESS

Settled borders are one of the sources of—indeed, preconditions for—peace, tranquility, security and progress of a nation in modern times. In the ancient and medieval era, when India was one nation but comprised many kingdoms, there was no concept of exact delineation of borders. There were no national antagonisms between India and her neighbours. Also, in ancient and medieval times, India never sent armies to conquer other lands and establish an 'Indian Empire'. In the eyes of the rest of the world, India existed as a benign culture and civilisation, aloof to the ebb and tide of kingdoms and dynasties. In fact, Hu Shih (1891–1962), a renowned liberal Chinese scholar and China's Ambassador to USA, has paid tribute to civilisational India by saying: 'India conquered and dominated Chuba culturally for twenty centuries without ever having sent a single soldier across her border.'

However, post-colonial and post-Partition India found itself in a totally different scenario. After India became independent, one of the first duties of the first government was to settle our international land boundaries with Pakistan and China. Sadly, Prime Minister Jawaharlal Nehru failed miserably in this duty, leaving a knotty legacy of disputes with our two neighbours that have not been resolved even after nearly six decades. The two disputes were, however, qualitatively different from one another. Although I did not personally deal with the border settlement with China when I was in the NDA government, I shall first present, briefly, some reflections on it in view of its importance to India. Pakistan's hostility with India over Jammu & Kashmir and what I, as Home Minister, did to deal with it will be detailed later.

BORDER DISPUTE WITH CHINA: UNDOING THE LEGACY OF 1962

The issue of the unsettled border with China had its origins in the differences between India and China over the status of Arunachal Pradesh in the East and Aksai Chin in the West. India's claim was that Aksai Chin, a plateau in Ladakh, was a part of Jammu & Kashmir. China, after its liberation in 1949 and communist takeover under the leadership of Mao Zedong, disputed this by claiming the area to be a part of its Xinjiang province. In the East, China refused to recognise the McMahon Line, which stretched from Bhutan to Burma and formed the boundary between Tibet and Assam in British India. It may be noted that Tibet was independent in 1914, when, at the Simla conference, the line finalised by Arthur Henry McMahon, Foreign Secretary to the 'Government of India and chief British negotiator', was accepted as the boundary.

Four factors rendered India's position difficult vis-à-vis its claims in the border dispute with China. Firstly, neither India nor China was truly a master of its own destiny when surveys were carried out by a foreign power in the nineteenth and early twentieth centuries. In conducting these surveys, the British empire was partly guided by its burgeoning rivalry with the Russian empire in what came to be known as 'The Great Game' in Asia. Secondly, during the British rule, Indians had not developed independent cartographic capabilities, nor did India's freedom movement pay adequate attention to potential boundary issues in future. Thirdly, the Chinese invasion of Tibet in 1950, defeat of the Tibetan army, China's affirmation of its sovereignty over Tibet, and India's acquiescence in it created a new post-colonial complication. Indeed, China built a road from Xinjiang into western Tibet through the Indian-claimed territory in Aksai Chin. Further, in 1963, Pakistan illegally ceded parts of PoK to China, adding a new element of complexity in the two border disputes.

The most damaging of all factors, however, was the Nehru government's failure to focus on India's diplomatic efforts, while simultaneously strengthening its military capabilities, to deftly resolve the boundary 'issue' with China. I have deliberately used the word 'issue' and not 'dispute', because in the early 1950s it had not yet become a raging row between the two great Asian neighbours. It could probably have been resolved if the government in New Delhi had based its approach on firmness and realism, rather than on a queer mix of callous neglect of national defence, shoddy preparation of its case, and a starry-eyed diplomacy that did not have its feet on the ground but sought, instead, to secure a leadership role for Nehru in NAM. There would necessarily have been an element of give-and-take—just as there will perforce have to be some mutual compromise whenever the matter is finally resolved. But Nehru, after the demise of Sardar Patel*, showed no alacrity to clinch the issue when the

---

* Sardar Patel forewarned Prime Minister Nehru by giving him prescient advice on Communist China in a detailed and truly historic letter on 7 November 1950. He said: 'The Chinese government has tried to delude us by professions of peaceful intention.... Even though we regard ourselves as the friends of China, the Chinese do not regard us as their friends. With the Communist mentality of "whoever is not with them being against them", this is a significant pointer, of which we have to take due note.' Referring

Contd...

situation was relatively more propitious, choosing instead to believe that his trust in the Chinese leadership, coupled with his advocacy of 'Asian solidarity', would make it resolve itself peacefully. This complacency was rudely shattered by the Chinese invasion in 1962, the outcome of which both shocked and shamed the nation.

My colleague Jaswant Singh, in his book *A Call To Honour*, has given a truly eye-opening account of how Nehru's leadership failed the nation in 1962.[1] Singh, a soldier in the Army in the North-East during the Chinese war, writes with a sense of unconcealed outrage: 'Leaders at the very top, military, diplomatic and political, failed India, criminally and unforgivably. They besmirched the country's honour, yet had no remorse for what they had done. This was independent India's first real test. Those that did not measure up had to accept responsibility. Not one volunteered to do so; an indulgent nation too just looked away, largely in embarrassment, as we do when face to face with an ugly deformity. It wanted to cause no more hurt to Nehru. We are continuing to pay for that act of national generosity.'

He provides shocking information about how, in the wake of the reverses suffered by the Indian Army after China's military invasion in October 1962, Prime Minister Nehru turned to the United States with an SOS. He wrote two letters to US President John F. Kennedy in November 1962—'apparently without consulting any of his cabinet colleagues or officials', according to his authoritative biographer S. Gopal—describing the situation as 'really desperate' and 'seeking immediate dispatch of a minimum of 12 squadrons of supersonic all-weather fighters, to be manned

---

Contd...

to the Chinese occupation of Tibet, Patel writes: 'We have to consider what new situation now faces us as a result of the disappearance of Tibet as we knew it and the expansion of China almost up to our gates. Throughout history, we have seldom been worried about our north-east frontier. Thus, for the first time, India's defense has to concentrate itself on two fronts simultaneously. Our defense measures have so far been based on the calculations of superiority over Pakistan. In our calculations, we shall now have to reckon with Communist China which has definite ambitions and aims and which does not, in any way, seem friendly disposed towards us.' (The full text of Patel's letter to Nehru has been reproduced in Jaswant Singh's book *A Call to Honour*, Rupa & Co, 2006, pp. 394-400.)

by American personnel, to assist the Indian Air Force in any battles with the Chinese in Indian air space. He also asked for two b-47 bomber squadrons to enable India to strike at Chinese bases and air fields, but to learn to fly these planes Indian pilots and technicians would be sent immediately for training in the United States.'

The Kennedy administration's response to Nehru's extraordinarily candid request for military help came in the form of two telegrams from Dean Rusk, Secretary of State, to John K. Galbraith, America's celebrated Ambassador in New Delhi. Here are two extracts:

(1) The United States cannot give maximum military support to India while most of India's forces are engaged against Pakistan *over an issue where American interest in self-determination of the peoples directly concerned has caused us since 1954 to be sympathetic to Pakistan's claims.*

(2) Latest message from PriMin (Prime Minister) in effect proposes not only a military alliance between India and the United States but complete commitment by us to fighting a war. *We recognized this might be immediate reaction of a government in a desperate position but it is a proposal which cannot be reconciled with any further pretence of non-alignment. If this is what Nehru has in mind, he should be entirely clear about it before we even can consider our own decision.* (emphasis added.)

A war tests the true mettle of a leader. Nehru, ill-advised by his Defence Minister V.K. Krishna Menon, failed this test abysmally. As the Indian Army, under-equipped and long-neglected, faced reverses on the battlefront in the NEFA (North East Frontier Agency) region*, the distraught Prime Minister delivered an address to the nation on 19 November 1962. It can no doubt be singled out as one of the darkest episodes in the history of independent India. He said: 'Huge Chinese armies are marching into the

---

* North East Frontier Agency (NEFA) became Arunachal Pradesh in 1972. During the 1962 war, the Chinese army had captured a large part of the NEFA. However, after declaring victory, China voluntarily withdrew back to the McMahon Line.

Northeast of India...yesterday we lost Bomdila, a small town in Kameng division...my heart goes out to the people of Assam!' That last sentence sent shock waves among the people of Assam, who felt that the Government of India had abandoned them to their own fate. It left a deep and long-lasting scar on their psyche, and extremists in the region have since been subtly exploiting this sense of insecurity to fan anti-India sentiments.

My purpose in revisiting this rather sad chapter in the history of independent India is not academic. Rather, it is to caution people about the enormous price, in terms of loss of territory and honour that we have had to pay due to the casual or negligent attitude, of every single Congress government so far, to a greater or lesser extent. It is indeed tragic that a leader like Nehru, whom the entire nation idolised, literally bent on his knees before a foreign power for military assistance to ward off invasion by another foreign power. What did this do to India's proclaimed policy of self-reliance? What did it do to Nehru's own much-trumpeted policy of non-alignment?

Sadly, the Congress has never debated this issue with any degree of honesty and transparency but the present and future generations of Indians must seriously ponder over certain stark questions: Is India secure if our borders are not secure? Can our borders be secure if India continues to be a 'Soft State' that cannot deter foreign powers from laying claim on its territory, cannot stop cross-border terrorism by Pakistan, and actually turns a blind eye to the demographic invasion by infiltrators along our border with Bangladesh?

*

It is indeed heartening to note that relations between India and China have been improving steadily in recent decades. I believe that our two countries should attach great importance and urgency to resolving the border dispute on a fair, reasonable and durable basis, and also in a spirit of accommodation of each other's concerns and recognition of the ground-realities. A great future is beckoning our two ancient civilisations to come together on a path of mutual rediscovery and cooperation in the modern era to promote peace and stability in Asia and all-round enrichment of life in the world. In the present scenario, I believe, our two countries should attach greater importance and urgency to resolving the border dispute on a fair, reasonable and durable basis, and also in a spirit of accommodation of each other's concerns and recognition of the ground-realities.

It is a matter of satisfaction that the resolution of the border dispute with China has, since 2003, been entrusted to an institutionalised mechanism of negotiations by the governments of our two countries. Reassuringly, both New Delhi and Beijing have decided not to allow mutually beneficial cooperation in other fields to become a hostage to the resolution of the border dispute. In other words, cooperation and border-settlement through dialogue have been moving on two parallel tracks, with both sides ruling out the use of force to change the status quo along the Line of Actual Control.

The credit for evolving this sound conceptual framework for normalising and strengthening the bilateral relations between our two great countries goes, principally, to two great leaders: Atal Bihari Vajpayee on the Indian side and Deng Xiaoping on the Chinese side. Atalji became the first Indian leader to travel to China after the 1962 war when he visited the country as Foreign Minister in February 1979. Receiving him warmly in the Great Hall of People in Beijing, Deng Xiaoping said: 'We do have some issues on which we are far apart. We should put those on the side for the moment and do some actual work to improve the climate to go about the problem. Our two countries are the two most populous countries in the world, and we are both Asian countries. How can we not be friends?' Vajpayee and Deng discussed a 'package solution' to the border problem, with both countries making some concessions. I believe that it remains the best way to go forward together.

Of course, I must mention here the contribution made by the historic visit of Prime Minister Rajiv Gandhi to China in December 1988. The famous handshake between Rajiv and Deng, and the warm sentiments they both expressed to restore peace and friendship between our two countries, reinforced the hope that our bilateral relations can, indeed, be unshackled from the unpleasant legacy of 1962. Conversion of this hope into reality was placed on a fast-track mechanism when Vajpayee visited China as Prime Minister in June 2003 and held fruitful talks with President Hu Jintao and Prime Minister Wen Jiabao.

In my own meeting with Hu Jintao in New Delhi, during his visit to India in November 2006, I commended the approach of our two countries to make progress in bilateral relations immune to our efforts to settle the border dispute through dialogue. I added that India would like Pakistan to adopt the same approach to ring-fence resolution of the Kashmir issue through dialogue, while moving ahead on bilateral cooperation in all mutually beneficial areas. I also expressed the hope that the Chinese government would create conditions for His Holiness the Dalai Lama, Tibet's spiritual leader, to visit Tibet before the Beijing Olympics in October 2008.

*

THE KASHMIR PROBLEM: ANOTHER LEGACY FROM THE NEHRUVIAN PAST

India's border dispute with Pakistan, is an issue which has, right since 1947, impacted India's external as well as internal security situation in Jammu & Kashmir. Consequently, the Vajpayee government, and I as India's Home Minister, dealt with it as a high-priority task. Although during the course of time, the wounds of Sindh, Punjab and Bengal have largely healed, those of Jammu & Kashmir have not. On the contrary, the mindset that forced the division of India by demanding the creation of a separate 'Muslim nation' has seen to it that India bleeds daily, even after the passage of six decades.

Like the border dispute with China, the Kashmir problem is also a legacy of the Nehruvian past. It is a product of the weaknesses in India's freedom movement, which were later compounded by the wily designs of the British rulers, on the one hand and mistakes of Nehru's government, on the other. When the India Independence Act, 1947, was passed by the

British Parliament, Jammu & Kashmir was one of more than 560 princely states in India. With the transfer of power to India and Pakistan, the princes were given the choice of acceding to one or the other of the two dominions. There was no provision in the law for taking into consideration the religious complexion of the population of any of the princely states. After some vacillation, Hari Singh, the Maharaja of Kashmir, who had been dreaming of becoming the ruler of an independent state, acceded to India on 27 October 1947. His decision in this regard was forced by an invasion of Kashmir by Pathan tribes, with the collusion of the government of Pakistan. Left with no alternative, Hari Singh sought military help from India on 24 October. Pakistan's plan of forcibly occupying Jammu & Kashmir, and then claiming it as its own since it was a Muslim majority state, was foiled by the Indian Army, which achieved rapid successes in driving the invaders back. What shattered Pakistan's plot further was the lack of support for the tribal invaders from the local populace. Hence, it was only a matter of time before the Indian Army could wrest the entire territory of Jammu & Kashmir back from Pakistani incursion.

It was at this critical stage of the war that Prime Minister Nehru, yielding to pressure from Lord Mountbatten, agreed, quite unnecessarily, to refer the Kashmir issue to the United Nations Security Council on 1 January 1948. This resulted in the constitution of a three-member UN Commission for India and Pakistan (UNCIP) to look into the dispute. The UNSC passed a ceasefire resolution on 13 August 1948, calling for the withdrawal of Pakistani troops and all outsiders, followed by reduction of Indian forces, and determination of the future status of Jammu & Kashmir in accordance with the 'will of the people' through a plebiscite. The plebiscite never took place, because the precondition for it—withdrawal of Pakistani troops from the entire Jammu & Kashmir—never happened. Nevertheless, the very mention of 'plebiscite' and determination of the 'will of the people' in a UN resolution was sufficient for both Pakistan as well as the separatist elements in J&K to carry on a vicious anti-India propaganda worldwide for decades.

India is still paying the price of Nehru's yet another blunder of internationalising the Kashmir issue by refering it to the UN, and that, too, under the pressure of the representative of a departing colonial power. And the price has, indeed, been dear. One-thirds of Jammu & Kashmir was allowed to remain under the occupation of Pakistan. Worse still, tens of thousands of our soldiers, security personnel and civilians have been killed, just because the international boundary between India and Pakistan was not settled once and for all in 1947-48. As far as the Congress is concerned, it has never bothered to provide answers to the following: Why did the Nehru government not carry the war to its logical conclusion by clearing the whole of J&K of Pakistani intruders? Why did the Prime Minister take the Kashmir issue to the United Nations? Why did he accept a ceasefire when India clearly had military superiority?[2]

It is not often that history gives nations a chance to solve large issues, decisively and durably. If the right moment is not seized, the next opportunity may never come at all. Defeating Pakistan comprehensively in the war of 1947-48 was one such opportunity for solving the issue of Jammu & Kashmir's merger with India once and for all. The second occasion came after India's victory over Pakistan in the 1971 war for the liberation of Bangladesh. It was a victory as decisive as one could imagine. Yet, if Nehru frittered away the first golden opportunity, his daughter, Indira, as I have described earlier in the book, did so the second time.

ARTICLE 370: WHY IT SHOULD BE REPEALED

As far as Jammu & Kashmir is concerned, another baneful legacy of the Nehruvian past, which subsequent Congress governments have proudly carried forward till today, is Article 370 of the Constitution. This transitional provision in the Indian Constitution, which was a temporary necessity post-Independence, has been given almost a permanent and unalterable status, thanks mainly to the Congress party's politics of minorityism.

When Hari Singh signed the Instrument of Accession, he surrendered the jurisdiction of only three subjects—defence, external affairs and communications—to the Central Government. Nehru made the mistake of not using effective methods like Sardar Patel did with the Nizam to get the errant maharaja merge his state with India totally, unconditionally and with no residual powers. His next mistake was that, under Lord Mountbatten's pressure, he agreed that the final decision of the accession would be ratified by the Constituent Assembly of Jammu & Kashmir. It was a concession not given to any other princely state. Indeed, no other state in India has a constitution of its own. It is necessary to remember here that although Sardar Patel had the responsibility of securing the merger of all the other princely states into India, Prime Minister Nehru had kept Jammu & Kashmir affairs under his direct charge. I have no doubt that there would have been no Kashmir problem today if only Patel had been given the full responsibility of securing J&K's accession as well.*

For the transitional period, that is, until the ratification of the instrument of accession by the state's Constituent Assembly, some temporary provisions in the form of Article 370 were made in the Indian Constitution. This article specifies that, except for defence, foreign affairs and communications, the Indian Parliament needs the State government's concurrence for applying all other laws. Thus, the executive of the state was given special powers,

---

* I would like to narrate an amusing experience to illustrate the adroitness with which Sardar Patel accomplished the humungous task of integration of the princely states. When I first went to Jodhpur in the early 1950s, during my days as an RSS *pracharak* in Rajasthan, I happened to ask someone on the street, 'What's the time?' His reply, 'Haade haat', made no sense to me, so I asked him again. This time he said, 'Saade saat' (seven-thirty). 'But you said something else earlier,' I remarked. He then recounted an episode from history, showing the allergy that other princes had for the ruling family of Jaipur. The Mughals, who wanted to win over Maharaja Jai Singh of Jaipur to their side, called him and said, 'In our eyes all other rajas are "one", but you are "one and a quarter" (savai). Thereafter, the rulers of Jaipur proudly got 'Savai' affixed to their name. However, this Mughal honour was not liked by the people of other princely states in Rajasthan, who started calling Jaipur's rulers 'havai' and, generally, refusing to utter words beginning with 's'.

When the integration of princely states was taking place, Sardar Patel employed various means to achieve his objective—in most cases, appealing to the innate patriotism of princes, inducing others with titles that carried little real power, and even threatening recalcitrant ones with the use of force. In the case of Jaipur, inducement worked and its ruler was named 'Raj Pramukh', a post equivalent to that of Governor of a state. This upset all other princes in Rajasthan. The Maharana of Udaipur felt particularly offended. Patel offered him a more grandiose title of 'Maharaj Pramukh', assuring him that he too would get the same '21-gun salute' as the ruler of Jaipur. The approach worked and the Maharana of Udaipur fell in line.

which most Chief Ministers in Srinagar have treated as a justification for emphasising Jammu & Kashmir's separate status.

As a matter of fact, the Constituent Assembly of Jammu & Kashmir ratified the state's accession to India in 1954. Subsequently, in the state Constitution adopted in 1956, it framed Section 3 which stated: 'The State of Jammu & Kashmir is and shall be an integral part of the Union of India.' This section was immune from any amendment at any time. Following this, India's Constitution (Seventh Amendment) Act, 1956, included Jammu & Kashmir as one of the States of India under Article I. After all this, there was no justification for retaining Article 370 in the Indian Constitution. Yet, Nehru, disregarding opposition from a large section within the Congress party and not wanting to displease his friend Sheikh Abdullah, disapproved of its repeal.

Although the Union government has extended many of its powers over Jammu & Kashmir since 1953, retention of Article 370 has produced many negative consequences, both for the state as well as for India. Like the earlier demand for plebiscite (which has now receded into the background), it has become a constant source for nurturing the mindset of separatism among a section of Kashmiri politicians, no doubt at the instigation of their patrons across the border. Under Article 19 (1) (e) and (g) of the Indian Constitution, a citizen of India is free to reside and settle permanently in any part of the country, and to practice any profession or carry on any occupation, trade or business. But Article 370 deprives Indians from other parts of the country the right to settle permanently in Jammu & Kashmir. It is even detrimental to the rights of women born and brought up in Jammu & Kashmir itself. If a woman, who is a permanent citizen of the state, gets married to a man from outside the state, she loses her property. She is deprived of even her ancestral property.

My party, first as the Bharatiya Jana Sangh and later as the BJP, has been all along opposed to Article 370. Perhaps no other issue has figured as regularly in our party resolutions, and as many times, as Jammu & Kashmir's full integration into the Indian Union. For example, in a resolution titled 'Abrogate Article 370', passed in Kanpur in January 1966, the Jana Sangh said:

Jammu & Kashmir is an integral part of India. Pakistan has aggressively occupied one-third part of the state since 1947. To get that aggression vacated and secure the liberation of Pak-occupied part of the state is the duty of the government of India.... The question of the constitutional integration of that part of Jammu & Kashmir (which is in our hands) with the rest of India is a purely internal affair of India. The temporary and transitional Article 370 of the Indian Constitution on the basis of which Jammu & Kashmir has a separate constitution of its own is a big hindrance in the way of such integration. It has created a psychological barrier between the people of the state and their counterparts in the rest of India, which has been exploited all these years by anti-national elements and Pak agents to the detriment of India's vital interests. Its abrogation, and application of the Indian Constitution in full to Jammu & Kashmir, is an essential prerequisite for the normalization of the situation within the state.

As I read these lines, I am amazed at their relevance even today, after forty-two years.

Towards the end of his life, and perhaps chastened by the bitter experience of India's defeat in the 1962 Chinese war of aggression, Nehru himself became somewhat more realistic about Article 370. Thus, on 27 November 1963, he said in the Lok Sabha: 'Our view is that Article 370, as is written in the Constitution, is a *transitional*, in other words a *temporary* provision. And it is so...as a matter of fact, as the Home Minister has pointed out, it has been eroded, if I may use the word, and many things have been done in the last few years which have made the relationship of Kashmir with the Union of India very close. There is no doubt that Kashmir is fully integrated.... So we feel that this process of gradual erosion of Article 370 is going on...'

Forty-four years have passed since Nehru's own candid admission about the dispensability of Article 370. And yet, even in 2007, this temporary and transitional provision remains enshrined in the Indian Constitution. How does it reflect on the Congress? The Congress and Communist parties think that its repeal would be an anti-Muslim act. In short, they are more concerned about appeasing one section of the society rather than thinking of national interest. My party, which has been demanding its repeal, is called 'communal' and 'divisive' for doing so. A more pernicious manifestation of pseudo-secularism is, indeed, difficult to imagine.

All this discussion on Article 370 does not have only historical significance; it has a significant bearing on the present and future of the Indian Republic. The nation was shocked on 26 June 2000, during the Vajpayee government's rule in New Delhi, when the Jammu & Kashmir assembly adopted a report of the State Autonomy Committee (SAC) and asked the Centre to immediately implement it. The SAC recommended return of the constitutional situation in J&K to its pre-1953 status, by restoring to the state all subjects for governance except defence, foreign affairs, currency and communication. MLAs belonging to the BJP, Janata Dal (United), Congress and a few other regional parties voted against the motion.

The Union Cabinet, at its meeting on 4 July, rejected the J&K legislative assembly's autonomy resolution. As I told the media[3] on that day, 'its acceptance will set the clock back and reverse the natural process of harmonising the aspirations of the people of the state with the integrity of the nation.' I added: 'If the government were to accept it, it would encourage trends that will not be conducive to national unity.' I emphasised that, although 'there is a clear case for devolution of more financial and administrative powers from the Centre to the states', the NDA government favoured this for all the states, and not for Jammu & Kashmir alone. In any case, devolution of greater powers to states was very different from granting autonomy to states. I also reminded that the issue of restoring the constitutional situation in J&K to its pre-1953 status had been discussed and settled a quarter century ago, in the 1975 accord between Indira Gandhi and Sheikh Abdullah. This agreement had clearly affirmed that 'provisions of the Constitution of India already applied to the state of Jammu and Kashmir without adaptation or modification are unalterable'.

This was one occasion when both Atalji and I had to be very firm with the state's Chief Minister, Dr Farooq Abdullah, whose National Conference was in fact a part of the ruling NDA at the Centre. We advised him not to press for the implementation of the SAC report. Indeed, Atalji told Dr Abdullah to decide whether to continue in the NDA at the Centre following the Union Cabinet's rejection of the state assembly's autonomy resolution. To his credit, Dr Abdullah allowed the issue to lapse.

SARDAR PATEL AND ARTICLE 370: A REVEALING EPISODE

Before I conclude my observations on Article 370, there is another highly significant facet of its history that needs to be taken note of. One day in the early 1990s, I went to the Parliament library to search for archival records about debates on this subject. I found an intriguing remark made by Prime Minister Nehru in which he suggested that this particular provision had Sardar Patel's contribution. In the course of a longish statement on Kashmir made in the Lok Sabha on 24 July 1952, Nehru defended the Article on the ground that, as the issue had been referred to the United Nations, 'the whole matter was in a fluid state'. He went on to add that the matter relating to J&K's position in the Constitution was clinched in November 1949, and that it was Sardar Patel who was 'all this time dealing with it'.

Pursuing the matter further, I discovered that, factually, Pandit Nehru was quite correct inasmuch as, when the Constituent Assembly adopted this particular provision, the Prime Minister had gone abroad, and all affairs of government were being looked after by Sardar Patel, the Deputy Prime Minister. But thereby hangs an interesting tale, recounted in some detail by V. Shankar, Private Secretary to Sardar Patel at that time. In his two-volume book, *My Reminiscences of Sardar Patel*,[4] Shankar says that Sheikh Abdullah 'did not trust the Indian government and while he accepted a constitutional relationship with the Indian Union, he wanted to reserve to the government of Jammu & Kashmir of his choice the final word as to the detailed content of the accession—three subjects of defence, external affairs and communication—and any further accretion to such accession'. Abdullah also wanted full freedom for the state's Constituent Assembly to form its own constitution.

Before going abroad, Nehru finalised the draft provisions relating to Jammu & Kashmir with Sheikh Abdullah and entrusted Defence Minister Gopalaswamy Ayyangar with the task of piloting these provisions through the Constituent Assembly. Obviously, Ayyangar had no idea as to how daunting this task was going to prove. Before formally moving the Article in the Constituent Assembly, Ayyangar spelt out his proposals in the Congress Parliamentary Party. His presentation, Shankar notes, provoked 'a storm of angry protests from all sides, and Ayyangar found himself a lone defender with Maulana Azad an ineffective supporter'. According to Shankar: 'In the party, there was a strong body of opinion which looked askance at any suggestion of discrimination between the Jammu & Kashmir state and other states as members of the future Indian Union and was not prepared to go beyond certain limits in providing for the special position of Jammu & Kashmir. Sardar was himself fully in accord with this opinion, but due to his usual policy of not standing in the way of Pandit Nehru and Gopalaswamy Ayyangar, who sorted out problems in their own light, he had kept his own views in the background. In fact, he had not taken any part in framing the draft proposals with the result that he heard the proposals only when Gopalaswamy Ayyangar announced them to the Congress party.'

Dismayed by the rough reception he had had to face at the meeting of Congress parliamentary party meeting, Ayyangar rushed to Sardar Patel and 'appealed to him to come to his rescue'. What transpired subsequently has been recounted by Shankar thus: 'Sardar heard him (Ayyangar) and lapsed into silence. To my query as to what reply he would like to give, he said he would think it over. Later in the evening, he rang me up and told me that he had sent for Satyanarain Sinha, the Congress chief whip, and had asked him to convene a meeting of the party executive, together with some of the prominent stormy petrels and they would discuss the matter; he wanted me to be present at the meeting. The meeting was held at the appointed hour and Maulana Azad was also present. The meeting was one of the stormiest I have ever witnessed. The opinion in opposition to Gopalaswamy's formula was forcefully and even militantly expressed…even Maulana Azad was shouted down. It was left to Sardar to bring the discussion down to the practical plane and to plead that because of the international complications, a provisional approach alone could be made...'

Reluctantly, it seems, the Congress party fell in line with the Sardar's wishes. Indeed, it is this that explains why in the Constituent Assembly the discussion on this provision was so vapid and sketchy. Apart from Ayyangar's own speech, there was not a single worthwhile intervention, either for, or against. The steam, obviously, had been let off at the party meeting.

Curiously, Sardar's success at persuading Congressmen to reconcile with this 'temporary' provision of Article 370 brought about an estrangement of sorts between Patel and his lieutenant. Shankar writes: 'I was somewhat taken aback at Sardar's acquiescence in the draft formula of Gopalaswamy and strongly felt that Sardar had compromised the position of the Indian Union and other states in accepting that formula as the basis. Frankly speaking, I was resentful of Sardar's attitude and when we returned to his residence during the lunch break, I was silent and sullen and repaired straight to my office room. Maniben (Patel's daughter) came to call me for lunch; I declined to go and told her about the pain and anguish inwardly felt, adding that for the first time I nursed a grievance of betrayal on the part of Sardar. She conveyed my feeling of resentment to Sardar, who sent her back to tell me that I should join the lunch table at least for a talk. I did so, accordingly. As soon as I was seated, Sardar spoke, "So you are annoyed with me for having accepted Gopalaswamy's formula." I queried that if he felt that way, why did he not indicate his mind earlier. He said, "I was deeply concerned at the situation. Gopalaswamy had acted under Panditji's advice. If Jawaharlal were here I could have had it out with him. But how could I do so with Gopalaswamy, who was only acting under orders? If I did, people would have said that I was taking revenge on his confidante when he was away. Gopalaswamy had appealed to me for help. How could I have let him down in the absence of his chief?"'

Shankar continues: 'I then asked why he had let down the country and the other states whose constituent assemblies had been scrapped in accordance with his advice and policy. He conceded the validity of the criticism but pointed out the delicate international position of the state and the issue of its relationship with India. We felt that the present situation had to be tided over without giving up the eventuality and this had been done under the formula. He said that after all, neither Sheikh Abdullah nor Gopalaswamy was permanent. The future would depend on the strength and guts of the Indian government, and if "we cannot have confidence in our own strength we do not deserve to exist as a nation".'

And here is a postscript to this revealing episode. On 24 July 1952, the day on which Pandit Nehru made the Kashmir statement in the Lok Sabha and affirmed that it was Sardar Patel who was dealing with the J&K provision, Shankar, at that time a Joint Secretary in Ayyangar's ministry, ran into his Minister and exchanged notes about the happening. Ayyangar's comment on Panditji's remark was sharp: 'It is an ill-return to Sardar for the magnanimity he had shown in accepting Panditji's point of view against his better judgement.'

I hope that readers of this book, especially young readers, understand the roots of the problem India has been facing in Jammu & Kashmir as sound knowledge of the problem is the first prerequisite to its proper solution.

*

A FOUR-PRONGED STRATEGY: PEACE, DEMOCRACY, DEVELOPMENT, DIALOGUE

By the time the Vajpayee government assumed office in March 1998, several new dimensions had been added to the problem in Jammu & Kashmir—the scourge of Pakistan-supported cross-border terrorism, the systematic campaign to drive away Kashmiri Pandits and Hindu families from their natural homeland, several rigged elections, inter-regional grievances among the people of Jammu, Kashmir and Ladakh, a sharp fall in the number of tourists, domestic or foreign and, of course, stalling of the socio-economic development of the state resulting in widespread unemployment.

Terrorism, partly fed by home-grown militancy wedded to the cause of Kashmir's secession from India, was at its worst when the NDA government assumed office. I knew that surmounting this challenge and bringing peace, normalcy and democratic revival in Jammu & Kashmir would be the main terrain on which history would judge our performance.

It was a matter of considerable satisfaction for us that the National Conference, which was in power in Srinagar at the time, had decided to join the NDA. Its leader and then Chief Minister, Farooq Abdullah, was the son of Sheikh Abdullah, a legendary leader of the Kashmiri people and founder of the National Conference. The Abdullah family's association with the BJP carried a political significance of its own. After all, it was Sheikh Abdullah who had ordered the arrest of Dr Syama Prasad Mookerjee, founder of the Jana Sangh, in 1953 when the latter had entered the state in defiance of the notorious 'permit system'. Dr Mookerjee's martyrdom in Srinagar was for the cause of Jammu & Kashmir's full integration into the Indian Union. The Jana Sangh was a fledgling party in 1953 but by 1998, the BJP, its successor, was a ruling party in New Delhi. Hence, by choosing to ally with the BJP, the Abdullah family had acknowledged the new political reality of India.

In my very first official meeting with him, I said to him: 'Farooq Sahab, let us put history behind us. Destiny has brought you to power in Srinagar and us in New Delhi at the same time. Let us work together to bring about a positive change in the climate in Jammu & Kashmir.' I must say that I established a fairly good working relationship with him. Farooq Abdullah's son, Omar Abdullah, was made a Deputy Minister of Commerce in the NDA government. A young, articulate and well-educated leader, he performed very well during his tenure.

Within a month of my assuming charge of the Home Ministry, a terrible tragedy required Dr Abdullah and me to travel together to Prankote and Dakikote, two hilly villages in the Udhampur district in Jammu, where terrorists had beheaded twenty-six Hindus, including women and children. It was a bloodcurdling sight. Two months later, once again we travelled together to Premnagar village in the Doda district of Jammu, where twenty-five Hindus, participating in a marriage ceremony, had been massacred.

Obviously, the terrorists' aim was to spread terror and force the migration of the minority community from the area. In the condolence meeting in Premnagar, I appealed to the panic-stricken people not to leave their native villages, but my conscience was troubled by merely asking them to stay put, while conveying no credible commitment from the government to ensure their safety and security. Therefore, I told them, 'I have no business to remain the country's Home Minister if I cannot protect you.'

In my meetings with the state Chief Minister, Governor Girish Chandra Saxena and other officials, I said: 'The Central Government will spare no effort or resources to meet the requirements of the state. But we must do all we can to stop these killings. Here we should learn a useful lesson from our success in quelling terrorism in Punjab. Our experience in Punjab taught us that militancy can be defeated primarily with the determined effort of the state police and administration, combined with support from the local population.' In consultation with them, our government evolved a four-pronged strategy to bring peace and normality in Jammu & Kashmir: (a) relentless and ruthless fight against cross-border terrorism; (b) free and fair elections to the state's legislative assembly; (c) acceleration of socio-economic development through good governance measures; and (d) earnest dialogue with representatives of all social and political groups committed to the path of peace.

A major turning point in the political climate in Jammu & Kashmir came when Prime Minister Vajpayee, on a visit to the state in August 2000, declared that the Government of India was willing to talk to any group representing the people of the state. Later in November, he announced a unilateral ceasefire in combat activities on the eve of the Muslim holy month of Ramadan. This had a big emotional impact on Kashmiri people, convincing them about our sincerity and considerably dispelling their apprehensions, created by Pakistani propaganda, about our 'Hindu nationalist party'. Earlier, Atalji's bus yatra to Lahore and Islamabad's betrayal in Kargil had also had the same effect. We were slowly but surely winning the hearts and minds of the Kashmiris.

FREEST ELECTIONS IN THE HISTORY OF J&K

Our biggest test was going to be conducting the assembly elections in J&K in 2002. As mentioned earlier, the state had a long track record of rigged elections during Congress governments at the Centre. This had given rise to a deep-rooted perception among Kashmiris that, irrespective of what the people desired, New Delhi would only install persons of its own choice in power in Srinagar. Pakistan had been adroitly exploiting this grievance to its own advantage. The NDA promised that the elections in J&K would be absolutely free and fair and the people of the state would have the government of their choice. In our judgement, establishment of genuine democracy in Jammu & Kashmir was pivotal not only to the restoration of normalcy in the state but also, indirectly, to India's peace process with Pakistan. For it would knock away an important plank in Pakistan's propaganda that the people of Kashmir had no faith in India and its democracy.

Our assurances, nevertheless, met with much skepticism, especially in the Kashmir Valley because the people felt that the NDA would naturally like to have its own constituent, Farooq Abdullah's National Conference, back in power in the state. Popular opinion, however, was not in favour of a second term for Abdullah's government. The various Pak-supported militant and secessionist outfits were alarmed at the prospect of free and fair elections in the state. Before the polls, nearly 250 people, including political activists, probable candidates and pro-democracy intellectuals who were opposed to the militants' call for boycott of the vote, were killed in terrorist attacks. Prominent among them was Abdul Gani Lone, a leader of the moderate faction of the Hurriyat Conference. The terrorists, and their patrons in Pakistan, were determined to silence all opposition with bullets.

However, in this battle of ballot versus bullet, the former came out on top ultimately. The elections, held in September-October 2002, witnessed a large and enthusiastic voter turnout of about forty-four per cent. What made it different from elections in the past was that nearly all political parties, independent candidates, international observers, NGOs, human rights activists, and the media, both Indian and foreign, acknowledged that it was the freest election in the history of Jammu & Kashmir. After more than two decades in power, the ruling National Conference was voted out. The People's Democratic Party (PDP), led by Mufti Mohammed Syed, emerged as the largest party in the newly elected assembly. It allied with the Congress to form a coalition government in the state.

Around the same time that democracy triumphed in Jammu & Kashmir, it witnessed its mockery in Pakistan. The general elections held in October 2002 were widely believed, both within Pakistan and by the international community, as 'flawed' and 'rigged'.[5] Same goes for the referendum held in April of that year, in which Gen. Pervez Musharraf had himself elected as 'President' with ninety-eight per cent voters casting their ballot in his favour.

One of the best tributes to the Vajpayee government's democratic success in Jammu & Kashmir came from Shekhar Gupta, Editor of the *Indian Express* and a perceptive commentator on national affairs.[6]

> The one common thing between our government's promise of a free and fair election in J&K and Musharraf's first milestone in his own 'roadmap to democracy' was that both chose the instrument of democracy to get out of an impossible-looking situation. Both had a crisis of credibility as well as legitimacy. We were finding it difficult to convince the world, in general, and the people of Kashmir, in particular, that our democracy had given them the best deal possible. Musharraf knew his rule would be morally untenable without an election, no matter how total and how cynically blind his international support. This is where similarities end. It is one thing for a functioning, instinctive and committed democracy to choose the instrument of an election to restore the legitimacy of its national interest even in a situation as complex as Kashmir. It is quite another for a military usurper to use elections to quiet his own people and save his foreign backers embarrassment but with no intention at all to submit to the majesty of his own people's will.

As India savours one of its proudest moments, therefore, we need to wholeheartedly congratulate our government, the vision of its senior-most leaders, the bravery and commitment of our armed forces, the dogged determination of the Election Commission and its staff. We must also congratulate the people of Jammu & Kashmir who defied both terrorist bullet and cynicism born of so many unkept promises and rigged elections of the past.

As I look back, I would rate the restoration of democratic rule and, to a significant but not full extent, normalcy in Jammu & Kashmir as one of the biggest achievements of the NDA government. There is tranquility along the LoC; guns have fallen silent on both the Indian and Pakistani sides. Villagers living in the vicinity of the border have been experiencing an atmosphere of peace which had eluded them for nearly two decades. Tourists are back in Srinagar, Gulmarg, Pahalgam and other parts of Kashmir. The annual pilgrimage at Amarnath attracts tens of thousands of devotees from all over the country. Infiltration of Pak-trained militants from across the border has decreased, though not fully stopped. Most importantly, the indigenous roots of militancy in the Kashmir Valley have considerably withered. People's longing for peace has isolated militants like never before. All this portends well for the future of Jammu & Kashmir.

'LET THE ROAR OF THE GUN BE REPLACED BY THE SOUND OF POLITICS'

My last major initiative as Home Minister towards bringing normalcy in J&K was to hold a dialogue with leaders of the moderate faction of the All Parties Hurriyat Conference (APHC), an umbrella group of religious and political parties and Kashmir's most prominent separatist organisation. Two rounds of talks were held in my office in New Delhi on 22 January and 27 March 2004. The Hurriyat team was led by its Chairman Moulvi Abbas Ansari and its members comprised Mirwaiz Umar Farooq, Bilal Ghani Lone, Abdul Ghani Bhat, and Fazal Haque Qureshi. Why did I decide to hold talks with the Hurriyat Conference, whose pro-Pakistan leanings were well-known, which had boycotted the 2002 assembly elections and some of whose leaders had links with militant organisations? Some in my own party and the Sangh Parivar were surprised at my decision. As a matter of fact, there was an element of surprise and scepticism on the other side, too, since these Hurriyat leaders had insisted on having a dialogue with me, despite my image as a 'Hindu hardliner' and a 'hawk'. This image had gained further currency after Pakistan's President, General Pervez Musharraf, blamed me for the collapse of his summit talks with Prime Minister Vajpayee at Agra in July 2002.

My talks with Hurriyat leaders were, indeed, an integral element, and a logical extension, of the Vajpayee government's overall strategy to establish durable peace and normalcy in the state. Our strategy had two dimensions—external in relation to Pakistan and internal in relation to Jammu & Kashmir—and our government had achieved significant progress on both counts. In January 2004, Prime Minister Vajpayee had accomplished a major diplomatic victory in India's battle against cross-border terrorism. For the first time ever, Pakistan gave a commitment, in black and white in the form of a joint statement issued after a Vajpayee-Musharraf meeting in Islamabad on the sidelines of the SAARC summit that it would not allow any part of its territory, or territory under its control, to be used for terrorist activities against India. Internally, the conduct of free and fair assembly elections in Jammu & Kashmir, and the people's positive response to them, had not only enhanced the Vajpayee government's credibility, both within and outside the state, but also sent a clear message that militancy enjoyed no popular support.

The Hurriyat Conference could not have remained immune to the combined impact of these developments, as was evident from the split it suffered in September 2003. Its moderate leaders, who genuinely desired to see an end to violence and bloodshed in Kashmir, now realised the need for, and usefulness of, participating in the dialogue process, which the Vajpayee government had set in motion in 2001. The Centre's interlocutors—first K.C. Pant, Deputy Chairman of the Planning Commission, then Law Minister Arun Jaitley, and later N.N. Vohra, a high-ranking former bureaucrat with deep knowledge of J&K affairs—had held talks with representatives belonging to the widest socio-political spectrum in the state. One major group that had chosen to remain outside the dialogue process was APHC. The CCS meeting in October 2003, decided that I should hold talks with it, a decision that was immediately welcomed by a majority in the Hurriyat Conference, except Syed Ali Shah Geelani, leader of the breakaway faction of the APHC which continued to support militancy and advocate Kashmir's merger with Pakistan.

I must mention here that there was a significant difference in my approach to the talks with Hurriyat leaders and that of Brajesh Mishra, National Security Advisor and Principal Secretary to the Prime Minister, and A.S. Dulat, a former Chief of RAW, who was serving as an advisor in the PMO on Jammu & Kashmir affairs. I learnt that Dulat, who was in regular contact with the leaders of various groups in Kashmir, had given some Hurriyat leaders the impression that the government was prepared to look at solutions to the Kashmir issue outside the ambit of the Indian Constitution. I was very upset at this and, in my very first meeting with the APHC delegation, I made it clear that there was no question of the government entertaining any proposal outside the Indian Constitution.

The first round of talks*, which lasted nearly two and a half hours, were free and frank and, surprisingly, quite fruitful too. I say 'fruitful' because both the Hurriyat leaders and I agreed, at the conclusion of our meeting, that 'all forms of violence that has plagued Kashmir over five decades should end' and that 'the roar of the gun should be replaced by the sound of politics'. We also agreed to adopt a 'step-by-step approach that would lead to the resolution of all outstanding issues relating to Jammu and Kashmir'.

I began the dialogue by first giving a comprehensive historical overview of the Jammu & Kashmir situation, emphasising three points: our firm commitment to peace, our flexibility on all reasonable issues raised by Hurriyat and other groups, and our uncompromising position on Jammu &

---

* In both rounds of talks, I was ably assisted by a team of officials comprising N.N. Vohra, the government's interlocutor in the dialogue with J&K representatives; Home Secretary N. Gopalaswami; Director IB, K.P Singh; RAW Chief C.D Sinha; Special Secretary (Home) B.B. Mishra; and A.S. Dulat, Officer on Special Duty (OSD) in the PMO.

Kashmir being an integral and inseparable part of India. I made it clear that India would never agree to 'tripartite talks'—between India, Pakistan and Hurriyat Conference—as demanded earlier by both Islamabad and APHC as an option to resolve the Kashmir issue. I also explained to them why the Vajpayee government had rejected granting the pre-1953 status to Jammu & Kashmir. At the same time, I said that the government was willing to consider realistic ideas about certain special powers for the state, which would help the political process to move towards the goal of permanent peace, normalcy, development and integration with the national mainstream.

I said, 'The pain and suffering of Kashmiris is felt by all Indians, because we do not consider you separate.' At the same time, I reminded the APHC delegation about the plight of Kashmiri Pandits living in pathetic conditions in camps outside the Valley for more than a decade. 'I cannot consider any solution honourable and durable which does not result in the return all the Kashmiri Pandits, and also all Muslim residents of Kashmir, who have had to flee their native land because of violence. That is an important touchstone for judging the return of normalcy in the Kashmir valley.'

In presenting their perspective of the situation in the state in the January and March meetings, Hurriyat leaders laid stress on two points: human rights violations by the security forces and political prisoners. 'We do not want Jammu & Kashmir to remain a garrison,' they complained. 'We want to see normal living become possible in Kashmir.' I said, 'We also want to see that people in Jammu & Kashmir begin to lead normal lives, free of fear and bloodshed.' Assuring them that the government would take steps to curb alleged human rights abuses, I told them: 'We have given orders that security forces must have a human face while discharging their duties.' This assurance was swiftly acted upon. Similarly, in the January meeting, I had agreed to look at the release of political prisoners in detention in Kashmir jails on humanitarian grounds, 'except those accused of heinous crimes'. Before the second meeting, the government had released sixty-nine prisoners, and was actively processing more than five hundred other cases.

We agreed to meet again in June, when I told Hurriyat leaders, 'we shall discuss substantive issues'. That meeting did not take place, because the NDA was defeated in the May 2004 parliamentary elections. Significantly, the Hurriyat Conference did not give a call for the boycott of the Lok Sabha elections. Its leaders publicly expressed disappointment that the Vajpayee government lost the elections.

Nevertheless, when I look back at my dialogue with the Hurriyat Conference, I experience considerable satisfaction. Most analysts described my talks with Hurriyat leaders as a 'milestone' on the road to peace. 'We're going forward and not backward and there is a change in thought and attitude at the ground level,' said Abdul Gani Bhatt, spokesman for the APHC delegation.[7]

A major reason for that was I found the Hurriyat leaders to be genuine, earnest and, to some extent, open-minded in their interactions with me. Similarly, on my part, I was able to convince them about my sincerity, and the sincerity of the Vajpayee government, in pursuit of peace in Jammu & Kashmir. This is what, the Washington reporter of the *Daily Times,* a Pakistani newspaper, wrote[8]:

> Mirwaiz Umer Farooq had warm praise for India's hardline deputy Prime Minister L.K. Advani who, he says 'fully' realises the 'sensitivities of the Hurriyat coming to Delhi and talking to him'. In an interview published here this week by *India Abroad,* the Kashmiri leader, who is an important member of the faction that favours talks with India, said, 'We will do our best to strengthen this process which has been initiated by the Government of India.' He said after the meeting, 'My perspective of Advaniji has changed. The manner in which he talked to the Hurriyat Conference showed his sincerity and his realism.'
>
> Mr. Advani told the Hurriyat group that the Kashmir problem would not vanish overnight and it would take time to sort out the 'ticklish' issues. He advocated a step-by-step approach. Mirwaiz Farooq said the delegation was anticipating a 'difference of opinion on many issues', but added that 'whatever issues we mentioned, he

not only listened patiently but agreed with most of the problems we took up'. Mirwaiz Farooq said all credit for opening the talks with Hurriyat should go to Prime Minister Vajpayee whom he called 'a man with a vision' who wants to 'move forward'. He said Mr Vajpayee was fighting the coming election on the issue of peace and would take the credit, with Mr Advani also sharing the 'honour'.

These sentiments were also echoed by Moulvi Abbas Ansari.[9]

> Vajpayee is an apostle of peace. He is a poet at heart and we expect much from him...Advani showed great sincerity during his talks with our delegation. He wants to solve the Kashmir issue and create conditions favourable to carry on a dialogue. It was his sincere attitude that helped in holding good and free discussions.

*

A WISH AND A PRAYER

I hope and pray that Jammu & Kashmir becomes, once again, an abode of peace, joy and harmonious living. This is the land made holy by India's rishis in the ancient era, and by Sufi saints in the medieval period. This is where Shaivism, Buddhism and Islam created a unique mystical confluence. In ancient times, Kashmir was known as *Sharada Peeth*, the seat of Saraswati, the goddess of learning. There is a shrine dedicated to Adi Shankaracharya on a hill that overlooks the scenic Dal Lake in Srinagar. I find so many similarities between my own native province Sindh and Jammu & Kashmir—partly because the mighty river Sindhu originates across the Ladakh region of the state.

Kashmir's greatest poetess, Lal Ded or Lalleshwari, was a messenger of Hindu-Muslim unity. Sheikh Noorudin, the great Sufi mystic, is revered as Nand Rishi by the Hindus of Kashmir. This tradition of harmonious pluralism, which people cherish as *Kashmiriyat*, needs to be preserved. Kashmir's greatest poet in the twentieth century, Ghulam Ahmad Mahjoor (1887-1952) writes[10]:

Bathe in the Sind water, meditate at
Manasbal* and see God on Harmukh†...

As Kashmiris you share the same land, ethos;
Don't alienate one another for naught.

Muslims are milk and Hindus sugar;
Mix milk and sugar in sweet accord.

With Hindus at the helm, Muslims to row;
Thus will our boat float smoothly

Shed ignorance and reckon who are
Friends and foes of our motherland.

Don't invite strangers to mediate in
Internal fueds; resolve them yourself.

Mahjoor has given a lesson in unity;
Remember it and teach it to each other.

This for me says it all!

---

* Manasbal Lake, thirty kilometres from Srinagar, is considered the 'supreme gem among all Kashmir lakes'. There is an eighth century Hindu temple near it.
† Harmukh is a high mountain from whose glaciers flows the Sindhu river.

9

Vajpayee-Musharraf summit in Agra
Why its failure was an eventual success for India

To work alone you have the right, but never claim its results. Let not the result of actions be your motive, nor be attached to inaction.

—Lord Krishna teaching Karma Yoga to Arjuna in the
Bhagavad Gita

In life, not every well-intentioned action is rewarded with success. Failure is as much a part of man's endeavours as success. In politics, I have never shied away from taking a step if it is in the interest of the country, even if it entailed the possibility of failure or carried the risk of bearing the blame for it. However, I have also found that, sometimes, failure transforms itself into success, and what initially comes as a disappointment often ushers in long-term favourable results.

As India's Home Minister, one such episode was the failed summit between Prime Minister Vajpayee and General Pervez Musharraf, in Agra in July 2001. Musharraf held me personally responsible for the letdown—soon after the summit and, later, also in his memoirs. Within

India too, some of the BJP's adversaries in the political and intellectuals spheres, continue to hold that view, attributing it to my 'hawkish' and 'hardline' personality and even imputing some base motives. The record must be put straight.

INVITING MUSHARRAF WAS MY SUGGESTION

Prime Minister Atal Bihari Vajpayee had, at the invitation of Nawaz Sharif, undertaken the bus journey to Lahore in a sincere pursuit of peace in February 1999. His talks with the Pakistani Prime Minister and the Lahore Declaration, which emerged as the outcome of the talks, had raised hopes for a positive move forward in ending the hostility between our two countries. Sadly, the internal dynamics of governance in Pakistan not only hijacked the peace process and precipitated a war with India—the Kargil War in which Pakistan again invited defeat upon itself—but also produced yet another military coup, the fourth in the country's history.

I have narrated earlier how, on the morning of 13 October 1999 when the Vajpayee government was sworn as the consequence of a peaceful, democratic election to the Indian Parliament, the newspapers carried the story of a military coup in Islamabad, with a photograph of soldiers storming the house of a democratically elected Prime Minister to arrest him. The developments that culminated in the ouster of Nawaz Sharif and the capture of power by the Army Chief, General Pervez Musharraf, were truly dramatic. Indians had known Musharraf as the man behind the Kargil aggression. Therefore, both the coup and the coup leader in Pakistan evoked a more-than-normal cold and cynical response in the political and societal circles in India. Nevertheless, we in the government had to formulate an appropriate policy to handle the new situation in Pakistan. We had to be ready to deal with whoever was the ruler, civilian or military, in Islamabad.

Between October 1999 and early 2001, our government adopted a three-pronged approach. We intensified the fight against cross-border terrorism in Jammu & Kashmir and elsewhere in India. In fact, we declared that India would not resume talks with Pakistan unless it stopped aiding and abetting cross-border terrorism. We stepped up our drive to stop infiltration of Pak-trained terrorists into India. And we broadened and strengthened our diplomatic offensive to make the world community understand both the reality of the Kargil War and Pakistan's continued sponsorship of terrorism in India. Pakistan was never as isolated globally on the issue of cross-border terrorism as it was during the Vajpayee government's six-year rule.

As a part of this overall strategy, Prime Minister Vajpayee launched another bold initiative in November 2000. On the eve of Ramzan, he announced a six-month 'ceasefire' in the counter-insurgency operations in Jammu & Kashmir. Although the media used the familiar term 'ceasefire', it was, in reality, a unilateral move of non-initiation of combat operations against the terrorists. Obviously, it meant that the security forces would not sit quiet in the face of provocations. This announcement was received well by the people of the state and helped in weaning away misguided local youth from the path of militancy.

The six-month-long break in combat operations was soon drawing to a close, and Atalji, in informal discussions with Jaswant Singh and me, would ask us: '*Ab aage kya karna chahiye?*' (What should we do next?) I too had been thinking about the issue for quite some time. During those days, I was in close contact with a senior Pakistani diplomat, with Karan Thapar, a noted journalist whom I had known for many years, acting as the intermediary. My discussions with this diplomat, who was not only amiable but also earnest, convinced me that the time was now ripe to restart the dialogue with Pakistan. On the Pakistani side, it seemed that General Musharraf, who had since then assumed the tag of President from CEO, in June 2001, was keen on ending his country's isolation. For that purpose, he too was keen on resuming talks with India. I said to myself that we should test the mind of this military ruler who does not carry political baggage and seems to be his own master in a country where democratically elected leaders have never exercised real power.

Thus, one day in May 2001, when the Prime Minister had called Jaswant Singh and me for lunch at his residence to discuss the next course of action, I suggested to him, 'Atalji, why don't you invite the General to come to India for talks? It does not matter if your Lahore initiative failed. It was highly appreciated both at home and abroad. Similarly, your invitation to him will be welcomed as an act of statesmanship, both within India and internationally.' Jaswant Singh concurred with the suggestion and the Prime Minister accepted it.

Thereafter, there was a flurry of activity. The first question to be settled was about the summit's venue. Initially, we thought of holding the talks in Goa. However, the choice, which was Atalji's own, fell on Agra. It was apt in more than one ways. Agra was the city of Taj Mahal, the famous monument of love, constructed by the Mughal Emperor Shah Jahan for his wife Mumtaz. Nothing could have been a better symbol of the shared history between India and Pakistan.

Predictably, the official announcement of the Agra summit generated much hope and excitement. However, aware of the danger of raising the expectations high, and aware, too, of the complexity of the problems plaguing Indo-Pak relations, the Prime Minister cautioned people against expecting dramatic breakthroughs. I, too, expressed the same sentiment. In an interview to the popular Hindi TV news channel *Aaj Tak* on 24 June 2001, I said: 'This is the second historic opportunity for India and Pakistan, after Vajpayeeji's bold initiative to usher in peace by visiting Lahore in February 1999. I hope that this will help improve relations between India and Pakistan to some extent. However, overnight results should not be expected from the summit, as decades-old issues cannot be resolved in one meeting.'

When the interviewer asked me why Musharraf was being invited in spite of Pakistan having 'back-stabbed' India through the Kargil incursion, I replied: 'There is no question of India compromising its security, which is the topmost priority of our government. Before Kargil, any incident in Jammu & Kashmir would be exploited by Pakistan to internationalise the Kashmir issue. But after Kargil, the international focus has shifted to cross-border terrorism and Islamabad-backed proxy war—much to Pakistan's disadvantage. Therefore, although we had maintained the stand of not talking to Pakistan for one and a half years, now we thought that maintaining the same position may not be helpful. In fact, our invitation to President Musharraf in spite of Kargil proves India's willingness to resolve outstanding issues with Pakistan through dialogue and peaceful means.'

MUSHARRAF'S 'WHITE LIE' ON DAWOOD IBRAHIM

General Musharraf, accompanied by his wife Sehba, arrived in New Delhi on 14 July 2001. Although the bitter memories of the Kargil War were still fresh in the minds of Indians, he was accorded an extraordinarily warm welcome, a testimony to our age-old traditions as well as people's genuine desire for peace. The fact that he was born in India also influenced India's legendary hospitality. Indeed, his visit to Neharwali Haveli in Old Delhi, the ancestral house where he was born in 1943 and lived for four years before his family migrated to Karachi, was one of the high points of the saturated media coverage of his three-day stay in India.

I met Musharraf for the first time at Rashtrapati Bhavan on the morning of 14 July. Our initial banter was centred around the fact that both of us had studied at St. Patrick's High School in Karachi which I have mentioned earlier in this book. After exchanging pleasantries, I said, 'General, although you were born in Delhi, you are visiting your birthplace for the first time after fifty-three years. Similarly, although I was born in Karachi, I have visited my birthplace only once after Partition, and that too for a very brief while. And there are lakhs of families on both sides that are not even as fortunate as we are; they have never visited their native places after migrating to this or that side. Isn't it odd that this should be the case even after the passage of more than a half-century? Shouldn't we find an enduring solution to the issues that are keeping our two countries and two peoples apart?'

'Of course, we must,' Musharraf observed. 'What are your ideas?'

'The most important thing is to build trust in each other.'

He nodded in agreement, and again asked how that could be done.

'Well, I'll give you an example. I have just come back from a fruitful visit to Turkey. I understand that you have a special liking for Turkey, having spent your formative years in that country.'

'Yes, my father was posted there. I can speak fluent Turkish.'

'I had gone there to conclude an extradition treaty between India and Turkey. Now, what great need does India have to have an extradition treaty with Turkey? If an extradition treaty *is* needed, it is between India and Pakistan, so that criminals committing a crime in one country and hiding in another can be sent back to face trial.'

Musharraf's first response, not quite knowing where the conversation was headed, was: 'Yes, why not? We should have an extradition treaty between our two countries.'

'Even before we conclude a formal extradition treaty, you would be making a great contribution to the peace process if you handed over Dawood Ibrahim to India, who is the prime accused in the 1993 Mumbai serial bomb blasts case and who lives in Karachi,' I continued. Musharraf's face suddenly turned red and unfriendly. Hardly able to conceal his discomfort, he said something that I regarded as quite offensive.

'Now, Mr Advani, that is small tactics,' he remarked. I could sense a sudden change in the atmosphere in the room, in which five Indian officials were seated on one side and five from Pakistan on the other.

I said, 'Well, General, you are a military man and you think in terms of strategy and tactics. In Agra, Prime Minister Vajpayee and you are going to discuss the strategy of creating enduring peace between India and Pakistan. The people of both countries will be watching the outcome of the Agra summit with great hope. But let me tell you, as India's Home Minister and as one who has been in public life for over fifty years that, as far as the people of India are concerned, your one act of handing over Dawood Ibrahim to India will generate enormous amount of trust in you and in your country. In any case, there have been instances all over the world where criminals have been extradited by one country to the other without a formal extradition treaty between the two.'

Musharraf, his unease palpable, replied assertively: 'Mr Advani, let me tell you emphatically that Dawood Ibrahim is not in Pakistan.' Several years later, one of the Pakistani officials who was present during the meeting, said to me, 'What our President said about Dawood Ibrahim on that day was a white lie.'

Responding to my suggestion that our two countries need to evolve a broader framework for bringing peace along the border and in the region, Musharraf said that soldiers on the two sides of the border often resort to firing, and that this was nothing unusual. 'Rightly so,' I told him politely, and added: 'But what is not understandable is people getting killed at bus stands and cinema halls for no fault of theirs. Peace should not be held hostage to resolution of any particular issue, irrespective of its importance to either side.'

At this point, he said that the 'core issue is the Kashmir dispute'. I told him that there was a difference of opinion over the issue. 'There is a wide gulf which needs to be bridged. Each issue must be discussed to reduce the gulf, nothing must be left out. But you should not insist that jihad will continue till a particular issue is resolved.' I also reminded him that what Pakistan refers to as disputed territory includes Jammu, Ladakh, PoK as well as the area ceded by Pakistan to China.

I concluded my talk[1] by wishing him and his wife a memorable stay in India and conveying, also, my best wishes for the success of the summit in Agra.

TERRORISM OR FREEDOM STRUGGLE?

Both Indian and Pakistani delegations arrived in Agra on the night of 14 July, after attending a banquet hosted by President K.R. Narayanan at Rashtrapati Bhavan for his Pakistani counterpart. Musharraf and his team stayed at Hotel Amarvilas, where every room has a view of the Taj Mahal. Atalji and the rest of us stayed at Jaypee Palace Hotel, which was also the venue of the talks.

Although it was a summit between the Indian Prime Minister and Pakistani President, Atalji had taken the well-considered decision to have all his ministerial colleagues in the CCS in Agra. It included Defence Minister Jaswant Singh, Finance Minister Yashwant Singh and Commerce Minister Murasoli Maran apart from myself. National Security Advisor Brajesh Mishra, India's High Commissioner in Islamabad Vijay Nambiar, and other officials were also present. Sushma Swaraj, Minister of Information & Broadcasting, had come specially to oversee media arrangements. After all, the Agra Summit was the biggest media event in India's diplomatic history, with journalists from around the world having arrived there to capture an event that combined elements of conflict and peace, betrayal, hope, and enigma.

There was no structured agenda for the summit, as per Musharraf's own preference. To me it seemed okay, since, in their first ever interaction, it was important for the two leaders to get to know each other's minds in an informal atmosphere and then chart a roadmap for future dialogue. At the delegation-level meeting on the morning of 15 July, Atalji presented India's approach to the summit in precise, no-nonsense terms.

> We look forward to a detailed exchange of views on all issues, including that of Jammu & Kashmir. We cannot deny that there are vast differences between us on this. We are willing to address these differences and to move forward. But for this, it is important to create a conducive atmosphere. *The terrorist violence being promoted in the State from across its borders* does not help to create such an atmosphere. We will counter them resolutely. *Let no one think that India does not have the resolve, strength or stamina to continue resisting terrorism and violence.* We firmly believe that a framework to address the differences between us on Jammu & Kashmir *would have to include the issue of cross-border terrorism in its ambit.* (emphasis added.)

No less significantly, the Prime Minister also referred to certain other specific matters, such as the release of fifty-four Indian PoWs in Pakistan, and two more that I had specially discussed with Atalji in advance.

- 'We know that *some terrorists and criminals, guilty of crimes like the bomb blasts in Mumbai in 1993 and the hijacking of the Indian Airlines flight, are living in Pakistan.* We have requested Pakistan that *they should be arrested and handed over to us.* They have to be brought to justice.'
- 'Pilgrims to religious shrines in both countries have to be facilitated and their sentiments respected. *The presence of known terrorists*

who have been allowed to stay in Sikh Gurudwaras in Pakistan is a matter of grave concern to our Sikhs. We have formally requested your authorities that these terrorists be handed over to us to face due process of law in connection with crimes for which they are wanted in India. While on the subject of religious shrines, *the upkeep of Hindu temples and the treatment of Hindu pilgrims is also a matter of concern to us.*' (emphasis added)

I mention these two points in order to allay baseless and mischievous speculation that there were differences between Atalji's and my approach to the issue of cross-border terrorism at Agra. The Prime Minister and President had extensive one-to-one talks, on that day as well as on 16 July, lasting five hours. After their first round of talks, they decided to issue a mutually acceptable joint declaration. The task of drafting it was entrusted to the foreign secretaries of the two countries, under the guidance of their respective ministers.

From India's point of view, two unwelcome things happened at Agra. Firstly, the exercise of drafting a joint statement proved highly unsatisfactory. The inconclusive draft which Jaswant Singh brought from his meeting with Pakistan's Foreign Minister, Abdul Sattar, was discussed at the informal meeting of the CCS that the Prime Minister convened in his suite on the evening of the 15th. I noticed that there was no reference to cross-border terrorism in the draft. 'This cannot be accepted,' I said. My view was unanimously endorsed by all present in the room.

We also noticed the absence of any reference to the Shimla Accord (1972) and the Lahore Declaration (1999) in the text. Musharraf seemed allergic to these pacts, as they were associated with his political rivals. He probably wanted to send a signal to his people back home that he wanted to start Indo-Pak engagement on a clean slate, all on his own terms and bearing his exclusive imprint. On our part, we conveyed that the Shimla and Lahore agreements should continue to remain the cornerstones of Indo-Pak dialogue. Our rejection of the draft was communicated to the Pakistani side, after which efforts continued at the official level to rework it until 4.30 am on 16 July.

Sensing, perhaps, that he would not be able to take home an 'Agra Declaration', Musharraf precipitated the second unhelpful development in the form of his audacious attempt to conduct the remaining part of his summit talks with India through the media. On the morning of 16 July, he turned, what was meant to be an informal breakfast meeting at his hotel with about thirty-five prominent Indian journalists, into a virtual hour-long press-conference. Apart from arranging its telecast on Pakistan's government-run PTV, he also allowed a leading Indian TV channel to telecast it fully. Thus, we in the Indian delegation had the extraordinary spectacle of watching the Pakistani President articulate his rather combative views on Kashmir and cross-border terrorism, even as he was, at that very time, holding closed door talks with the Indian Prime Minister.

In his media interaction,[2] Musharraf insisted that India should accept the centrality of the Kashmir issue in Indo-Pak relations and said, 'We can address all issues, *after* having addressed the main issue. No leader in Pakistan can allow the sidelining of Kashmir for the sake of economy, confidence building, nuclear, everything.' He sought to justify Pakistan's support to the secessionist movement in Kashmir by drawing a parallel with India's support to Bangladesh in its war of liberation. 'See history,' he said. 'There is a tendency to stop at Kargil. I am supposed to be the Kargil man. I can understand how you feel about Kargil. You must understand how Pakistanis feel about 1971 and Siachen. How much hurt was caused when in 1967 the Mukti Bahini (Bangladesh Freedom Army) was being trained, supported by India? How much hurt did it cause to Pakistan when in violation of the Shimla Accord, the Indian army intruded into Siachen?'*

But what shocked Indians watching the televised press interaction the most was Musharraf's assertion about cross-border terrorism. 'We are

---

* Musharraf was disingenuous about Siachen. The Shimla Accord says: 'In Jammu and Kashmir, the Line of Control (LoC) resulting from the cease-fire of 17 December 1971 shall be respected by both sides without prejudice to the recognised position of either side. Neither side shall seek to alter it unilaterally irrespective of mutual differences and legal interpretations. Both sides further undertake to refrain from threat or the use of force in violation of this Line.' The LoC, however, does not extend to the Siachen glaciers.

not encouraging any violence in Kashmir,' he said. 'This is an indigenous freedom struggle going on there. We in Pakistan keep calling it a freedom struggle…. Can someone expect that this violence (in Kashmir) can stop when the dispute itself is not resolved?'

As I watched his media blitzkrieg, I said to myself: 'No wonder the General didn't want any mention of cross-border terrorism in the draft agreement.' After his blatant disregard for the vital concerns of the Indian people, the prospects of an 'Agra Declaration' coming out at the end of the summit simply evaporated. Before returning home, Musharraf and his wife were scheduled to visit Ajmer Sharif to pay obeisance at the dargah of Khwaja Moinuddin Chishti (popularly revered as Garib Nawaz), the renowned thirteenth century Sufi saint. However, he cancelled the visit after his last meeting with Prime Minister Vajpayee and flew back to Islamabad from Agra late on the night of 16 July. At the end-of-the-summit press conference addressed by Jaswant Singh, a journalist asked him if the Indian government had tried to prevent the Musharrafs from going to Ajmer. The reply was both apt and witty. *Meri kya aukaat ki main unhe Garib Nawaaz ke paas jaane se rokun. Kehte hain ki jab tak Garib Nawaaz ka hukum nahin hota, koi vahan nahin jaa sakta.* (Who am I to stop the Musharrafs from visiting the dargah? It is said that nobody can visit the place, without a summon from the saint).³

❋

To be honest, the manner in which the Agra Summit concluded left all of us in the Indian delegation disappointed, none more than the Prime Minister himself. After the unfortunate denouement of his Lahore peace initiative, he was fervently looking forward to a positive outcome in Agra. However, being a seasoned leader with his feet firmly on the ground, he knew why it was unsatisfactory. As he stated in Parliament on 24 July 2001, 'In his presentations, President Musharraf focused almost exclusively on Jammu & Kashmir. Despite the obvious differences in our perspectives, we made progress towards bridging the two approaches in a draft joint document. We sought to incorporate all issues, including Jammu &

Kashmir, in composite dialogue. Eventually, however, we had to abandon the quest for a joint document mainly because of Pakistan's insistence on the settlement of the Jammu & Kashmir issue, as a precondition for the normalisation of relations. Pakistan was also reluctant to acknowledge and address cross-border terrorism. *My Cabinet colleagues and I were unanimously of the view that our basic principles cannot be sacrificed for the sake of a joint document.*' (emphasis added).

One of the many rare qualities in Atalji is his ability to laugh at himself, a trait that has contributed much to his charisma. Thus, replying later to a debate in the Rajya Sabha, he said: '*Atithi bhi apne karmon ke hisab se milta hai, hamare karma hi aise the to hum kya karein?*' (One gets guests depending on one's karma; our karma is such that we got Musharraf).

I, on my part, did a lot of plainspeaking ('*Kaafi khari khari baatein huin.*') I conveyed to Musharraf whatever were my pent-up feelings on Kashmir for the last forty years.... I told him we had already fought three wars and did not want another one.... I also told him that terrorism in the name of jihad would one day spell trouble for his country too.[4]

MUSHARRAF'S ACCUSATION: 'ADVANI SCUTTLED AGRA SUMMIT!'

Who was responsible for the failure of the Agra Summit? Curiously, this question continues to be debated in political, intellectual and media circles in both India and Pakistan. However, even before the Pakistani delegation had departed from Agra, senior members in it, whose proximity to General Musharraf was widely known, had started pointing fingers at me.[5] I was supposed to have been the 'hidden hand' that scuttled the chances of the summit's success. About a month later, Musharraf himself blamed me for the breakdown of talks.[6]

Five years later, in August 2006, Musharraf made this accusation in an even more shocking manner when he published his memoir *In the Line of Fire*. I wasn't named directly, but the inference was obvious enough for everybody including the media. The following excerpts[7] shed much light on the personality of Pakistan's military ruler:

We were approaching the climax of our visit. Instead, it was an anti-climax, when…my Foreign Minister and Foreign Secretary informed me that the Indians had backed out. I could not believe my ears. 'How could that be? Why?' I asked.

'The Cabinet has rejected it, sir,' was the answer.

'Which Cabinet?' I asked. 'There is no Cabinet in Agra.' I became very angry, and my impulse was to leave for Islamabad immediately. The two diplomats cooled me down, asking for some time to try a redraft. I allowed it, and reluctantly canceled my evening visit to Ajmer Sharif.

The redrafting took another two or three hours of intense haggling over words and sentences. But ultimately my team returned, signaling success.[8] They showed me the new draft, which I approved. I thought it still carried the essence of what we wanted, except that now the language was different. They returned to the other hotel to make fair copies of the draft. I assured my wife, saying that the 'Agra declaration' would hit the headlines the next day.

Yet, this was not to be. Just as I was about to leave for the signing ceremony, I received a message that the Indians had backed out again. This was preposterous. I decided to leave immediately, but my Foreign Minister persuaded me to call on Prime Minister Vajpayee before leaving. I consented to fulfill this diplomatic protocol, though much against my wishes…

I met Prime Minister Vajpayee at about eleven o'clock that night in an extremely somber mood. *I told him bluntly that there seemed to be someone above the two of us who had the power to overrule us. I also said that both of us had been humiliated.* He just sat there, speechless. I left abruptly, after thanking him in a brisk manner.

There is the man and there is the moment. When man and moment meet, history is made. Vajpayee failed to grasp the moment and lost his moment in history. (emphasis added)

Musharraf's outrageous claim that 'there seems to be someone above the two of us who had the power to overrule us' and 'both of us had been humiliated' was strongly and unequivocally refuted by Atalji himself. In a press statement he issued on 26 September 2006, he said:

> General Musharraf's reported comments on the failure of our talks at Agra have surprised me. No one insulted the General and certainly no one insulted me. Everyone in our government was acutely alive to the fact that there could be no normalcy in Indo-Pak relations until cross-border terrorism, which had cost thousands of innocent lives, was ended.... But during our talks General Musharraf took a stand that the violence that was taking place in Jammu and Kashmir could not be described as 'terrorism'. He continued to claim that the bloodshed in the State was nothing but the people's battle for freedom. It was this stand of General Musharraf that India just could not accept. And this was responsible for the failure of the Agra summit.[9]

HOW FAILURE IN AGRA BECAME SUCCESS IN ISLAMABAD

Prime Minister Vajpayee achieved the greatest diplomatic triumph of his career in January 2004. He had gone to Islamabad to attend the 12th SAARC summit meeting. The visit provided an opportunity for him to have intensive discussions with President Musharraf. The outcome of these talks, a joint statement they issued on 6 January, was proof of the fact that India's failure in Agra had become its success in Islamabad. For it said:

> Both leaders welcomed the recent steps towards normalisation of relations between the two countries and expressed the hope that the positive trends set by the Confidence Building Measures (CBMs) would be consolidated. Prime Minister Vajpayee said that in order to take forward and sustain the dialogue process, violence, hostility and terrorism must be prevented. *President Musharraf reassured Prime Minister Vajpayee that he will not permit any territory under Pakistan's control to be used to support terrorism in any manner.* (emphasis added.)

For the first time since it had launched the proxy war against India in the early 1980s, Pakistan acknowledged through this joint statement the existence of cross-border terrorism from the territory under its control and committed itself to disallowing it. This is precisely what we had asked Musharraf to do in Agra, which he had refused. Which is why, in his press statement of 26 September 2006, refuting the baseless accusation that Musharraf had made in his memoir, Atalji also said: 'Pakistan came to our view point…in the joint statement of January 2004.… If General Musharraf had been willing to accept our position in 2001, the Agra summit would have become successful, and the three subsequent years may have proved very valuable to take our initiative forward.'

What prompted Musharraf to accept in 2004 what he had rejected in 2001? I will briefly mention three factors. Firstly, after Al Qaeda's terrorist attack on the United States on 11 September 2001, Musharraf was left with no choice but to withdraw support to the Taliban regime in Afghanistan, which had provided safe haven to Osama bin Laden and his fellow warriors. Secondly, as I have explained earlier in the book, Vajpayee government's 'assertive diplomacy' around the world succeeded, to a considerable extent, in getting western powers pressurise Pakistan to curb cross-border terrorism. Lastly, as forewarned by Atalji ('I also told him that terrorism in the name of jihad would one day spell trouble for his country too'), Pakistan itself witnessed a terrifying spurt in terrorist acts between 2001–04, much of it directed against the government, and most strikingly illustrated by the several failed assassination bids on Musharraf's life.

It is, of course, noteworthy that the commitment made by Pakistan in the January 2004 joint statement has not fully translated into concrete and sustained action on the ground. The terrorist infrastructure on Pak-controlled territory is still intact. Infiltration of terrorists into Jammu & Kashmir has not yet fully stopped. The ISI continues to train, arm and network with religious extremists in their murderous and subversive activities in India. It seems that the rulers in Pakistan have not yet completely abjured the temptation of using terrorism as a tool, as a covert policy of their government, to bleed India. Can our country—our people as much as our government—afford to lower its guard in these circumstances? Certainly not.

✳

Partition (1947), three wars (1947-48; 1965; 1971), Shimla Pact (1972), Lahore Declaration (1999), Kargil War (1999), failed summit at Agra (2001), Islamabad Joint Statement (2004), continuing cross-border terrorism.... Can there be no durable peace, no end to enmity and no cooperation between India and Pakistan? Is the future of our bilateral relations going to be more of the seemingly unchanging past? Can we not—indeed, should we not—give our future generations a better future? I believe that we must.

The onus for changing this state of affairs rests with Pakistan since India has not cast its identity, nor does it think of its own destiny, in anti-Pakistan terms. Unfortunately, many in Pakistan continue to view their own country's identity, and its destiny, as inimical to India. This anti-India attitude is deeply ingrained in its military set-up as well as its religious establishment. On this prejudice rests a wholly mistaken notion about India's perceived weaknesses, making some in Pakistan believe that they can wrest Kashmir by bleeding India through a thousand cuts. This will never happen*.

On the contrary, as all right-minded people in Pakistan realise, Pakistan itself will have to pay a heavier price if it persists in this misadventure. For too long, many of its leaders have deluded themselves by claiming that Jammu & Kashmir is the 'unfinished business of Partition' and

---

* A particularly candid criticism of Pakistan's misadventure in Kashmir can be seen in the article 'Kashmir & Power of Illusion' by the well-known Pakistani columnist Ayaz Amir. (*Dawn*, 19 January 2001) He writes: 'The stark truth is that jihad (a term being used loosely here) has no future in Kashmir.... A continuation of the insurgency can bleed India. But it cannot secure the liberation of the state. This much should be clear from the history of the last 53 years. What the Pakistan army has failed to secure in full-fledged battle the jihadis cannot hope to achieve with their hit-and-run tactics. It is also facile to think that jihad in Kashmir will bring India to the negotiating table.'

thereby justifying Pakistan's continued meddling in the affairs of the state. This delusion, which Musharraf exhibited in Agra by describing Pakistan-backed terrorism in Kashmir as indigenous 'freedom struggle', is counter-productive. In this sense, Pakistan today stands at a critical crossroads. It must make the right choice for its own good, and for the larger benefit of South Asia.

I believe that the socio-political constituency in Pakistan for peaceful and friendly relations with India has considerably expanded in recent years. We in India have to work closely with this constituency, by shedding some of the anti-Pakistan prejudices that have got accumulated over the years as a reactive response. But, as I have said earlier, the absolute precondition for any fundamental transformation in India-Pakistan relations is a decisive decimation of terrorism, fuelled by religious extremism on the one hand and state-sponsorship on the other, in Pakistan itself. Once that happens, the two countries can consider an array of creative solutions to the long-standing problems between us, including the issue of Jammu & Kashmir.

10

SECURING ASSAM AND THE NORTH-EAST FOR THE FUTURE

Those who cannot learn from history are doomed to repeat it.
—GEORGE SANTAYANA, AN AMERICAN PHILOSOPHER

Being both a witness and a victim of India's vivisection on communal lines in 1947, I naturally view Assam and the other North-eastern states from the point of view of national unity and national security. During my six-year stint in the Home Ministry this was always my overriding concern in dealing with these states. In the course of discharging my official responsibilities, I became acutely aware of how little we as a nation have learnt from the past mistakes in the North-East.

When I look at the map of India now, and compare it with the one that I was familiar with when I was a student in Karachi, the most obvious difference that strikes me is how much India has shrunk in size. In place of one undivided India, there are now three independent nations occupying the same landmass—Pakistan, a creation of India's Partition in 1947 and Bangladesh, a creation of Pakistan's Partition in 1971. But the map of today's India also reminds me of how those who were in power then failed to pay adequate attention to keeping our country free from future geographical vulnerabilities. I have, earlier in this book, mentioned that India in 1947 could have legitimately laid a claim on the Hindu-majority Tharparkar district in Sindh. It could have given India a geographical presence in Sindh province. I have also mentioned how the failure to settle the Jammu & Kashmir issue once and for all has continued to haunt our country.

But I also see a third area of strategic vulnerability—the North-East being landlocked and poorly connected to the rest of the country. Its pre-1947 rail link with India is now dysfunctional because it passes through Bangladesh. Once blessed with a thriving river transportation system linking its products to international markets, it no longer enjoys access to the sea since its main rivers now flow into Bangladesh. I often wonder why our leaders both in 1947 and 1971 failed to obtain rights to a land route linking the port city of Chittagong, which had a large Hindu population, and the nearest point in Tripura (which is only forty kilometres away). It could have enabled India to reach the North-East from our eastern coast through the Bay of Bengal.

The resultant physical isolation of the North-East was compounded by the failure of successive governments in New Delhi to strengthen the bonds of emotional integration of the diverse communities who inhabit the region. The problem was further worsened by poor governance by state governments and, above all, by anti-India forces operating from the territories of neighbouring countries, primarily Bangladesh. When Pakistan was partitioned and Bangladesh liberated, India believed to have gained a friend in its eastern neighbourhood. Alas, the situation has turned out to be quite contrary.

From the point of view of internal and external security, Assam and the rest of the North-eastern region fill me with a lot of concern. For several decades now, this region has been rocked by separatist insurgencies, ethnic violence, terrorist killings, massacres of poor Hindi-speaking workers from Bihar and Jharkhand*, smuggling of arms and drugs, and massive and unchecked influx of illegal migrants from Bangladesh. The Supreme Court too struck the warning bell by describing the influx of Bangladeshis in Assam as 'external aggression'. I would say that this is a silent, persistent, insistent, constant and continuous demographic invasion of India by Bangladesh, the disastrous outcome of which, if unchecked, will be known in times to come.

Who and what factors are responsible for this situation?

HOW ASSAM BARELY SAVED ITSELF IN 1947

I should first begin with the sordid tale of how the Congress and Communist parties' vote-banks politics has allowed the problem of illegal immigration from Bangladesh to escalate to the level of 'external aggression', threatening the very unity of India. Sadly, my party is the only national-level political organisation, apart from the Asom Gana Parishad (AGP)† at the state level, which has consistently raised its voice of protest against this danger. As early as in 1957, Atal Bihari Vajpayee, then a newly elected MP, had raised this issue in the Lok Sabha. In his inaugural

---

* Hundreds of so-called 'Bihari settlers'—the term is a misnomer, since they have been living and working in Assam for generations—have been killed by extremists belonging to the United Liberation Front of Assam (ULFA). Its main leaders are given shelter in Bangladesh and its cadres are trained in camps situated across the border. ULFA was formed in 1979 as a response to the problem posed by illegal immigration from Bangladesh. However, it turned itself into a secessionist organisation demanding an 'independent' Assam, since it claims that Assam was never a part of India. The Government of India, which has proof of its close links with Pakistan's ISI, has banned it as a terrorist organisation

† The All Assam Students Union (AASU) and the All Assam Gana Sangram Parishad launched a six-year-long agitation in 1979 demanding identification and expulsion of illegal immigrants in the state. Incidentally, the agitation was triggered by the detection of the names of tens of thousands of Bangladeshis in the electoral rolls. It culminated in the signing of the Assam Accord in 1985 when Rajiv Gandhi was the Prime Minister. The accord neither stopped infiltration nor brought peace to the state. More than 20,000 people have been killed in Assam since 1979. Asom Gana Parishad (AGP), a political party, was formed in 1985 as the outcome of the students' agitation.

presidential address at the BJP's founding session in Bombay in 1980, he said: 'I had then warned that the situation would take an explosive turn if no effective remedial steps were taken to prevent such infiltration. But the government failed to realise the seriousness of the problem.... The responsibility for the present situation in Assam rests on those political leaders who, out of selfish motive, not only turned a blind eye to foreign infiltration, but were also guilty of encouraging it. The soul of Assam is already beset with many wounds. The rest of India, by its indifference, and the central leadership, by its shortsightedness, should not commit the sin of its complete destruction.'

In my first presidential address at the BJP's National Council meeting in New Delhi, after taking over the reins of the party from Atalji in May 1986, I had said: 'The problem of foreign nationals in Assam, and of uncurbed infiltration from across the borders, continues. The people of Assam have waged a prolonged struggle to force the central government's hands in regard to the problem of illegal immigrants (which) seriously jeopardises national security.' I had also demanded that 'all citizens of border states be required by law to carry photo-affixed identity cards. In Assam, where no census could be held in 1981 along with the rest of the country, a special census should be ordered. A National Register of Citizens should also be prepared.'

Assam's problem can be traced back primarily to the Muslim League's demand in 1940 for the creation of Pakistan as a separate nation for Indian Muslims. That is when the Assamese started feeling threatened that they would be reduced to a minority in their own land and, therefore, separated from India. After the Partition of Bengal in 1905*, which was

---

* The year 2005 marked the centenary of the Partition of Bengal in 1905 by Lord Curzon. *Vande Mataram*, which later became the battlecry of the nationalist movement, was initially a chant of protest against the Partition of Bengal on communal lines. About 1905, this is what Sri Aurobindo wrote as the fiery young Editor of the journal *Bande Mataram*: 'The (British) Government professedly wanted to create a Muslim province with Dacca as its capital, and the evident object of it was to sow discord between the Hindus and the Muslims in a province that had never known it in the whole history.'
Contd...

a part of the 'divide and rule' policy of the British, and the formation of the Muslim League in 1906 in Dhaka, there was a concerted effort on the part of the latter to enhance the numerical strength of Muslims from East Bengal in Assam through organised migration.

The credit for foreseeing the danger interest in this phenomenon should go to the great Indian nationalist leader and architect of modern Assam, Gopinath Bordoloi, who headed a shortlived Congress-led coalition government in the state in 1937. But for his timely and determined efforts, Assam would have long ceased to be a part of India. He saw through the Muslim League's conspiracy to turn Assam, a non-Muslim majority state, into a Muslim-majority state, so that it could be included in the proposed East Pakistan. Sadly, the central leadership of the Congress party, except Mahatma Gandhi, had virtually made up its mind to give up its claim over Assam. In 1946, when Assam was in danger of being absorbed into East Pakistan, it was Gandhiji who supported Bordoloi and his fellow Congressmen by writing to them: 'If Assam keeps quiet, it is finished.... Assam must not lose its soul*'. He even advised them to come out of the Congress if it was needed to keep alive the demand for Assam remaining a part of India. Ultimately, only Sylhet district, where Muslim migrants from East Bengal had already formed a majority, was merged with East Pakistan on the basis of a referendum.

Contd...

The BJP and other nationalist forces observed the centenary of Bengal's partition by educating the people about its historic significance. Sadly, the Congress and Communist parties, as also the UPA government showed little interest in it.

* The soul of Assam is personified by Sree Shankardev, a fifteenth century Vaishnavite saint who catalysed its all-round socio-cultural renaissance. He was a bright star in the galaxy of poets, saints and social reformers belonging to the Bhakti movement in different parts of India—Chaitanya Dev in Bengal, Jnaneshwar and Namdev in Maharashtra, Ramananda and Kabir in Uttar Pradesh, Vallabhacharya in Madhya Pradesh, Basaveshwar in Karnataka, and others. Shankardev campaigned against untouchability, social inequality, and other corruptions. He sowed the seeds of democracy by introducing village panchayats and encouraging the philosophy of cooperation. Mahatma Gandhi once paid tribute to this great tradition by saying, 'Assam is beyond my dream. My services are not required here.'

ROOTS OF THE ANTI-FOREIGNER MOVEMENT IN ASSAM

In the early sixties, Assam's Congress Chief Minister Bimala Prasad Chaliha launched a campaign to evict illegal immigrants, who had settled in the state after January 1951. However, Prime Minister Nehru advised him against it.[1] When he pressed ahead by passing the Prevention of Infiltration from Pakistan (PIP) Act, 1964, twenty Muslim MLAs threatened to topple his government if he did not stop its enforcement. Chaliha succumbed to pressure and the law was placed in limbo. Something similar happened to another Congress Chief Minister, Hiteswar Saikia. On 10 April 1992, Saikia stated in the state's legislative assembly that there were 'between two and three million' Bangladeshi infiltrators in Assam. This immediately drew an angry reaction from the 'Muslim Forum', headed by Abdul Muhib Mazumdar. Though a Congressman himself, Mazumdar reminded Saikia that it would take 'just five minutes for the Muslims of Assam to throw your government out'. The Chief Minister soon declared that there was not a single illegal migrant in Assam!

Once they understood that the Congress high command was not serious about the problem of infiltrators from Bangladesh, the party's local leaders had no qualms about cultivating them as a vote-bank. Devkant Barooah, a prominent Congress leader from Assam (who, as the party's National President during the Emergency declared that 'Indira is India, India is Indira') used to openly challenge his political opponents: 'Who can defeat the Congress so long as we enjoy the support of *ali* (Assamese Muslims), *kuli* (migrants from Jharkhand and Bihar working in tea-gardens) and *Bengali* (illegal immigrants from Bangladesh)?'

Atalji, Jaswant Singh and I used to visit Assam regularly in the early 1980s to express our solidarity with the students' movement. It was during those visits that I came in close contact with Prafulla Kumar Mahanta and other leaders of the movement. It was also during the Assam agitation that I got to know Arun Shourie more closely. Already a well-known journalist and political commentator, and a staunch supporter and advisor of the movement, Shourie later joined the BJP and became a valued colleague in the party. I was in the Rajya Sabha those days and frequently spoke in the house about Assam's problems. I remember a petition[2] submitted by Golap Barbora, a prominent Janata Party leader from the state. It said: 'No sovereign nation can permit the influx of foreign nationals into its territory. But the North Eastern region of the country in general and Assam in particular have been experiencing the area being utilised as the dumping ground for a large numbers of foreigners from a neighbouring country since a long time. Besides, a large number of such foreigners were appeased with political rights by entering their names in the voters' list of the state for petty political games at the instance of the vested political forces that were at the helm of affairs since Independence.'

I have given this history of Assam's angst only to emphasise that the anti-foreigner movement was not some law and order problem created by some misguided students, as the Congress leaders in New Delhi advertised it to be. It was the inevitable outcome of the failure of the Nehru-Liaqat pact (1950) and Indira-Mujib Accord (1971) to protect Assam from sustained demographic aggression. Unfortunately, even the Assam Accord of 1985, which was trumpeted as one of the greatest achievements of Rajiv Gandhi's premiership, compounded the problem further. Its biggest lacuna was that it failed to set aside a flawed law—called the Illegal Migrants Determination by Tribunal (IMDT) Act—which Indira Gandhi's government had pushed through in Parliament in 1983. Under the IMDT Act, the onus was on prosecution (state government authorities) to prove before the tribunal the foreigner-status of the person to be deported. This criterion ran counter to the provision in the Foreigners Act, under which the onus lay on the suspect to prove his or her Indian citizenship. Shockingly, by fixing 1971 as the cut-off year, the Accord accepted the illegal immigrants infiltrating between 1951 to 1971 as genuine citizens of India.[3]

The fact that the Assamese people were exhausted after six years of intensive struggle was cleverly exploited by the Congress government at the Centre to impose an Accord, which it was clearly not interested in implementing. As a sop to the leaders of the agitation, Clause 5.9 of the Assam Accord said: 'The Government will give due consideration to certain difficulties expressed by the AASU/AAGSP regarding the implementation of the Illegal Migrants (Determination by Tribunals) Act, 1983.' However, even this bland assurance was not fulfilled. As a result, the accord turned to be a case of a cure that was worse than the disease.

Refusal to accept the ominous reality in Assam, even when it is substantiated by official sources, has become the hallmark of the Congress party's central leadership. In 1996, T.V. Rajeshwar, a former Director of the IB and presently Governor of UP, warned that unchecked illegal immigration from Bangladesh into Assam and other border states could some day lead to a third division of India.[4] The Congress party and its governments in New Delhi and Assam kept mum. Similarly, Assam's former Governor, General (Retd.) S.K. Sinha, stated in a report in 2005: 'This (Indo-Bangladesh) border is one of the world's most fluid borders, crossed daily by some 6000 Bangladeshis who come in search of work, often staying to join the estimated 20 million illegal immigrants in the country.' Chief Minister Tarun Gogoi dismissed it as 'totally baseless'.

Prime Minister Dr Manmohan Singh, who is a Rajya Sabha member from Assam, is among those guilty of such motivated denial includes. On 15 July 2004, Sriprakash Jaiswal, Minister of State for Home Affairs, stated in the Rajya Sabha that '1,20,53,950 illegal Bangladeshi migrants were residing in 17 states and Union territories as on 31 December 2001.' He also affirmed that fifty lakh Bangladeshis were residing in Assam. Dr Singh, who happened to visit Guwahati the following day, was confronted by his party colleagues in Assam who expressed concern that his junior Minister's reply in Parliament would hurt the Congress party's prospects in the 2006 assembly elections. Their protest had its effect. The Prime Minister publicly stated that he doubted the authenticity of the information provided by Jaiswal. A week later, Jaiswal himself would tell Parliament that the information provided by his own ministry about Bangladeshi infiltrators 'is unreliable and based on hearsay'. Such are the compulsions of holding on to the chair!

SUPREME COURT'S HISTORIC VERDICT AGAINST IMDT ACT

Ever since its passage in 1983, the BJP had been consistently and unreservedly supporting the Assamese people's demand for repeal of the IMDT Act.

We had organised numerous protest actions on this issue, both within and outside Parliament. This demand figured prominently in all our election manifestos for the parliamentary and state assembly elections. Unfortunately, we could not fulfill this promise during the NDA rule at the Centre for lack of adequate support in the Rajya Sabha.

Meanwhile, judiciary became the main battlefield to fight the Bangladeshi invasion in Assam, and this is where a major victory was won when, on 14 July 2005, the Supreme Court struck down the IMDT Act as unconstitutional. Upholding a petition filed by Sarbanand Sonowal, a young MP belonging to the AGP, a Bench comprising Chief Justice R.C. Lahoti and Justices G.P. Mathur and P.K. Balasubramanyan said that the influx of Bangladeshi nationals who have illegally migrated into Assam posed a threat to the integrity and security of the North-East region. It has given rise to an 'insurgency of alarming proportion making the life of people of Assam wholly insecure and the panic generated thereby has created a fear psychosis'. In the history of independent India, I cannot think of a more stinging censure of the Union government by the Supreme Court in a matter concerning national security. In view of its importance, I deem it necessary to quote the verdict in some detail.

The court took serious note of the report of then Assam Governor Lt. Gen. S.K. Sinha, who was also India's former Deputy Chief of Army Staff, to the Centre on 8 November 1998. The report had warned about the migration causing a 'perceptible change in the demographic pattern of the State' and threatening 'to reduce the Assamese people to a minority in their own State'. It had also cautioned: 'There is a tendency to view illegal migration into Assam as a regional matter affecting only the people of Assam. Its more dangerous dimensions of greatly undermining our national security are ignored. The long cherished design of Greater East Pakistan/Bangladesh, making in-roads into strategic land link of Assam with the rest of the country, can lead to severing the entire landmass of the Northeast, with all its rich resources from the rest of the country. They will have disastrous strategic and economic consequences.'

'The report of the Governor, the affidavits and other material on record show that millions of Bangladeshi nationals have illegally crossed the international border.... This, as stated in the Governor's report, has led to insurgency in Assam.... This being the situation there can be no manner of doubt that the State of Assam is facing "external aggression and internal disturbance" on account of large-scale illegal migration of Bangladeshi nationals. It, therefore, becomes the duty of Union of India to take all measures for protection of the State of Assam from such external aggression and internal disturbance as enjoined in Article 355 of the Constitution. Having regard to this constitutional mandate, the question arises whether the Union of India has taken any measures for that purpose.'

The Supreme Court's observations regarding the ineffectiveness of the IMDT were scathing. 'No elaborate discussion on this aspect is required as the figures disclosed in the affidavits filed by the Union of India and the State of Assam speak for themselves. Though inquiries were initiated in 310759 cases under the IMDT Act, only 10015 persons were declared as illegal migrants and finally only 1481 illegal migrants were physically expelled up to 30th April, 2000. This comes to less than half per cent of the cases initiated. Thus, there cannot be even a slightest doubt that the application of the IMDT Act and the Rules made there under in the State of Assam has created the biggest hurdle and is the main impediment or barrier in identification and deportation of illegal migrants.' The court also held that the provisions of Foreigners Act are more effective in identification and deportation of foreigners residing in India illegally. Thus, on every single count, the Supreme Court's verdict was an endorsement of the stand taken by the BJP and nationalist forces in Assam.

As noted earlier, the Supreme Court had directed the Central Government 'to take all measures for protection of the State of Assam from external aggression and internal disturbance as enjoined in Article 355 of the Constitution'. It is worth mentioning here how the Congress-led UPA government sought to subvert even this unambiguous Constitutional mandate. Instead of taking lessons and making amends for its past mistakes, it amended the Foreigners Act exclusively for Assam and incorporated the worst infirmities of the IMDT Act into the Foreigners (Tribunals for Assam) Order, 2006. This was nothing but contempt of court. Worse still, it was a blatant disregard of the Constitution since the government was consciously ignoring a grave threat to India's unity and integrity.

Once again, it was the Supreme Court which struck down, in its ruling in December 2006, the Foreigners (Tribunals for Assam) Order as unconstitutional. A Bench comprising Justices S.B. Sinha and P.K. Balasubramanyan said: 'It appears that the 2006 order [issued after the Illegal Migrants (Determination by Tribunals) Act was declared unconstitutional] has been issued *just as a cover-up for non-implementation of the directions of this court.*' The Bench further observed: 'The earlier decision (on IMDT) referred to the relevant material showing that such uncontrolled immigration into northeastern States posed a threat to the integrity of the nation. What is therefore called for is a strict implementation of the directions of this court issued (in the earlier judgment), so as to ensure that illegal immigrants are sent out of this country. *We have to once again lament that there is a lack of will in the matter of ensuring that illegal immigrants are sent out.... Instead of obeying the mandamus issued essentially in the interests of national security and to preserve the demographic balance of a part of India, that is Bharat, and implementing the 1964 order in Assam in letter and in spirit, the authorities that be have chosen to make the 1964 order itself inapplicable to Assam.*' Then came the stinging indictment by the Supreme Court: '*Though we would normally desist from commenting, when the security of the nation is the issue, we have to say that the bona fides of the action leave something to be desired.*' (emphasis added)

Therefore, my charge against Congress President Sonia Gandhi and Prime Minister Dr Manmohan Singh is that they have consciously allowed national interests to be sacrificed at the altar of crass vote-bank politics. By enslaving themselves to the politics of minorityism, they are deliberately disarming the legal and administrative organs of the Indian state. My poser to them is: 'If the burden of proving the foreigner status of an illegal migrant is on a tribunal, then why have security forces at all on our border with Bangladesh? Why don't you just allow free and unhindered entry into India for anyone to cross over?'

In private conversations, some Congress and communist leaders concede that large-scale illegal immigration from Bangladesh is a problem. But, publicly, they are afraid of saying so for fear of antagonising their vote-banks. Thus, they have routinely opposed the BJP's 3-D demand—detection and deportation of foreigners and deletion of their names from voters' list—by claiming that the law would be used against local Muslims. This is a lame and self-serving pretext. I have countered this claim by repeatedly affirming that the government's approach in respect of fulfilling its constitutional duty should be: '100 % protection to Assamese Muslims, but 0% protection to Bangladeshi Muslims.'

PERCEIVING THE NORTH-EAST WITH A NEW APPROACH

The challenge in Assam is in some ways symptomatic of the larger problems that India has been facing in the North-East as a whole. For too long, successive governments in New Delhi have viewed them through the narrow law-and-order prism. They have placed far less emphasis on understanding these problems in the context of the specific, and often unique, history and geography of the over three hundred diverse ethnic groups that constitute the region's 3.5 crore population. For instance, the external interface of the region is far more pronounced than any other part of India. The people living on both sides of the international border in Bangladesh, Myanmar, Bhutan and China are bound by age-old linguistic, ethnic, cultural, religious and economic ties. Tribals constitute nearly forty per cent of the region's population who cherish their identities and their traditional systems of self-regulation.

As such, the situation that has emerged in the region after 1947 cannot be viewed purely from the security point of view. National security is, of course, of paramount importance but it is best guaranteed by strengthening people's emotional bonds with India. This requires respect for their individual ethnic or community identities, good governance with people's participation, socio-economic development that assures better living standards, and expanding and deepening the region's multifarious linkages with the rest of India. Thus, dealing with the situation in the North-East requires a combination of security, democracy and development perspectives.

Unfortunately, successive governments in New Delhi and national political parties have not paid enough attention to these tasks in a

In Home Ministry

President Dr K.R. Narayanan administering the oath of office to L.K. Advani as a Minister in Atal Bihari Vajpayee's government on 19 March 1998.

In the forecourt of Rashtrapati Bhavan, with President Dr K.R. Narayanan, Vice President Krishan Kant, Prime Minister Atal Bihari Vajpayee, and other ministerial colleagues.

Sardar Patel, India's first Home Minister who was known as the 'Iron Man', has been a role model for Advani.

At the inauguration of the annual Sindhu Darshan festival near Leh in Ladakh. Also seen are daughter Pratibha, Dr Farooq Abdullah, former Chief Minister of Jammu & Kashmir; Jagmohan, Ananth Kumar, I.D. Swami and Bijoya Chakraborty, who were Advani's ministerial colleagues in the NDA government.

(Above left) *India conducted nuclear tests at Pokharan on 11 May 1998. Seen here are Prime Minister Vajpayee, Defence Minister George Fernandes, and scientists Dr A.P.J. Abdul Kalam and Dr R. Chidambaram.*

Rubbing shoulders with the jawans of paramilitary forces.

Education and healthcare of the girl child has remained Advani's concern for many years. Here he is seen unveiling a Jharkhand government's scheme to distribute bicycles to tribal girl students. Also seen is Jharkhand's former Chief Minister Babulal Marandi.

Advani at a naval fleet review in Mumbai.

(Clockwise from above right) *With jawans and officers of the BSF in Rajasthan.*

With Moulvi Abbas Ansari, Mirwaiz Umar Farooq, Bilal Ghani Lone, Abdul Ghani Bhat and Fazal Haque Qureshi, who represented the Hurriyat Conference at the talks in January 2004.

Indian soldiers celebrate the historic victory in the Kargil war, 1999.

Paying homage to the victims of 9/11 at 'Ground Zero' in New York in 2002.

Leading a march of NDA MPs to Rashtrapati Bhavan against criminalisation of politics in 2005. Seen on Advani's right are Nitish Kumar and Sushil Modi, who are now, respectively, the Chief Minister and Deputy Chief Minister of Bihar.

With Naveen Patnaik, President of the Biju Janata Dal and Chief Minister of Orissa.

(Left) With Sardar Prakash Singh Badal, President of the Shiromani Akali Dal and Chief Minister of Punjab.

At a BJP rally in Ranchi. Seen with Advani are Yashwant Sinha (extreme left), Rajnath Singh (third from left), Narendra Modi, Atal Bihari Vajpayee, Arjun Munda, and Babulal Marandi.

Making a point after an NDA programme in New Delhi: Advani with BJP President Rajnath Singh, NDA Convenor George Fernandes and Sushma Swaraj.

(Above) *Advani and Vasundhara Raje, Chief Minister of Rajasthan.*

(Centre right) *With N. Chandrababu Naidu, President of the Telugu Desam and former Chief Minister of Andhra Pradesh.*

(Right) *Sharing a lighter moment with Dr J. Jayalalithaa, General Secretary of the AIADMK and former Chief Minister of Tamil Nadu.*

Visit to Pakistan

Laying the foundation stone for the restoration of the ancient Hindu temples at Katas Raj near Lahore in June 2005. Also seen are Chaudhry Shujaat Hussain, former Prime Minister of Pakistan Mushahid Hussain, a leader of the Pakistan Muslim League (Q), Pratibha.

At the Army House, Rawalpindi: Advani and Pakistan President Gen. Pervez Musharraf are flanked by Kamla (right) and Pratibha, Shiv Shankar Menon, India's former High Commissioner in Pakistan, and Sudheendra Kulkarni.

At the mausoleum of Mohammed Ali Jinnah, founder of Pakistan, in Karachi on 4 June 2005.

At an engaging dinner-table discussion in Islamabad: (Clockwise) Advani, Pakistan's Foreign Minister Khurshid Mahmood Kasuri, author Aitzaz Ahsan, PPP leader Makhdoom Amin Fahim and Shujaat Hussain.

An animated conversation between Advani and Imran Khan, Pakistan's cricket legend and President of the Tehreek-e-Insaf party.

Enjoying the beauty of Lahore Fort with family and Deepak Chopra (extreme right) with wife Veena.

(Clockwise) *With Benazir Bhutto, former Prime Minister of Pakistan and a family friend, at Advani's New Delhi residence; George Bush, President of USA; Yitzak Rabin, former Prime Minister of Israel; Yasser Arafat, leader of the Palestine Liberation Organisation; Vladimir Putin, former President of Russia; Li Peng, former Prime Minister of China; and Yoshiro Mori, former Prime Minister of Japan.*

(Clockwise) With King Birendra of Nepal; Sheikh Hasina, former Bangladesh Prime Minister; Bill Clinton former President of USA; Tony Blair, former Prime Minister of Britain; and Queen Elizabeth of Britain.

With RSS Sarsanghchalak *Shri K. Sudarshanji* (sitting on left); *and* (Right)*RSS General Secretary Shri Mohanrao Bhagwat.*

Prime Minister Dr Manmohan Singh attended Akhand Paath at Advani's residence on Guru Nanak Jayanti in 2006.

Advani meeting the doyen of Indian industry, J.R.D. Tata. Also seen is Darbari Seth.

Both Advani and son Jayant are ardent cricket fans. Here they are in conversation with the Little Master Sachin Tendulkar. Also seen are cricketers Javagal Srinath and Kirti Azad.

Spiritual Quest

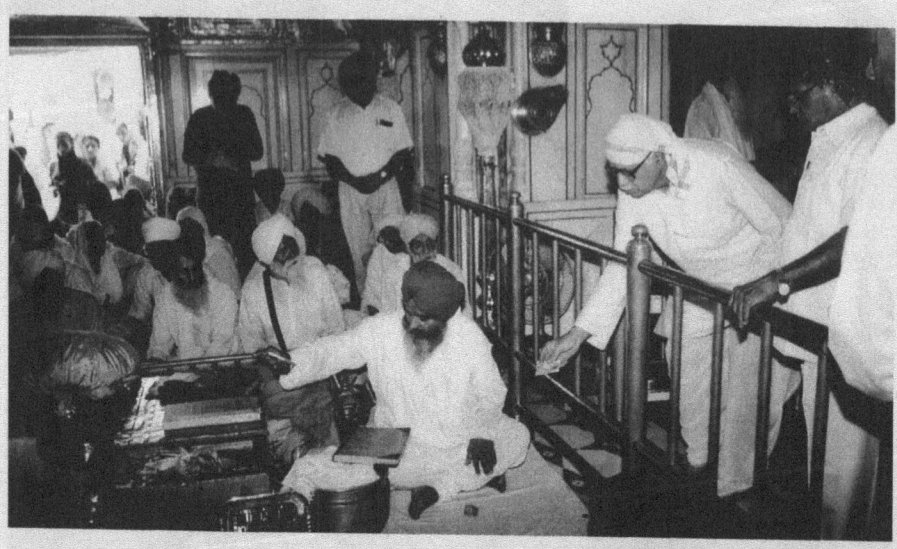

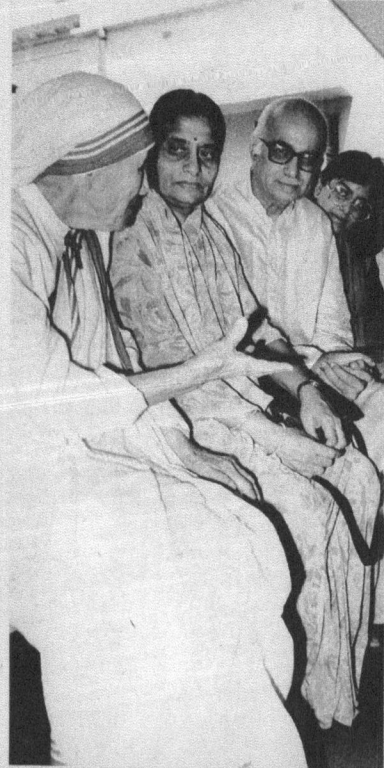

(Clockwise) *Paying obeisance at the Golden Temple, Amritsar, and the dargah of Khwaja Nizamuddin Chishti at Ajmer Sharif; with Mother Teresa in Kolkata.*

(Clockwise) With Pramukh Swami Maharaj of Swami Narayan Sampradaya; Sri Sri Ravi Shankar Maharaj; serving food to 'Rishikumars' at a Gurukul run by Swami Chidanand Saraswatiji of Parmarth Niketan, Rishikesh; participating in an aarti on the banks of the Holy Ganga at Parmarth Niketan; with Dadi Prakashmani of Brahmakumaris.

Family

Forty-three years of blissful togetherness.

With daughter Pratibha: A special bond indeed. A tender moment.

Advani family with the highly revered Dada J.P. Vaswani.

'Nature dangles happiness and meaning before us all, insisting only that we choose between them. I have had the good fortune of experiencing both, and in abundance. Meaning, from a sense of mission in life. And happiness, from my family and friends.'

holistic manner. It is not because sufficient funds were not provided for the development of the region or the welfare of the people. Since Independence, the Centre has channelled enormous amounts of resources to the North-eastern states. But the money has not been well-spent, and the fruits of various well-intentioned schemes have not reached the intended beneficiaries. Regional parties became victims of weak leadership, internal rivalries and tenuous commitment to responsible governance. The political class in the states developed a vested interest in a dependant relationship with the rulers in New Delhi, and the Congress party encouraged it for selfish and short-term motives.

Indeed, there are some cases of local politicians who are hand-in-glove with extremist organisations, and for whom extortion has become a profitable business. Instances of even State funds being diverted to them are quite common. Barring exceptions, officers belonging to the all-India civil services are not motivated enough to serve in the North-eastern states. All these factors have accentuated the people's sense of alienation, which, in turn, is exploited by divisive forces acting at the behest of anti-national forces across the borders.

I shall now briefly describe here some of the salient initiatives of the NDA government in the North-East with regard to internal security. ULFA was, and it still is, the largest and the most menacing extremist organisation in the region. Exploiting geographical proximity and the relatively weak security apparatus of Bhutan, ULFA and other banned extremist groups had established training camps and hideouts for themselves in the Himalayan kingdom. In fact, since the early 1990s, much of ULFA's terrorist activities originated from southern Bhutan. The Government of India had been taking up this issue with the Bhutanese authorities for many years, without success. The NDA government decided to accord high priority to anti-ULFA operations in Bhutan and Prime Minister Vajpayee persuaded the King of Bhutan, Jigme Singye Wangchuck, during the latter's visit to New Delhi in September 2003, to undertake military action to flush out the extremists from Bhutanese territory.

In an operation lasting three weeks in December 2003, the Bhutanese Army, with supportive action by the Indian Army on the Indian side of the border, attacked and eliminated all the thirty training camps of ULFA in the thickly forested areas of South-East Bhutan. More than a hundred militants were killed and over 300 arrested. This combined Bhutan-India operation had a salutary effect on the extremist organisations. It also established a model of bilateral cooperation between two neighbouring countries in fighting the menace of terrorism. Remarkably, our government did not use strong-arm tactics with a tiny neighbour, which is surrounded by India on three sides and is dependent on India in both security and development matters. Instead, we used the power of quiet and sustained diplomacy with a king, with whom India has an excellent rapport. Our government deferred to the King's concerns over his country's sovereignty in not making it an Indian military operation on Bhutanese territory. Therefore, the Indian Army trained its Bhutanese counterpart and limited its role to the Indian side of the border. As the *Hindu*[5] would comment on the Vajpayee government's approach: '(This) must rank as one of India's more exemplary foreign relations exercises. One result of India's restraint is that with time, Bhutan has realised for itself the implications of playing host to dangerous guests…. In the context of ULFA, Bhutan's military moves against the group have only served to highlight Bangladesh's inaction. Despite Dhaka's denials, evidence has built up that the top leadership of ULFA uses Bangladesh as its main base.'

In comparison, our government had a frustrating experience in dealing with Bangladesh both in respect of illegal cross-border migration and action against Indian militant groups operating from its territory. These issues were taken up with Bangladesh authorities at the highest level. I, too, raised them in my meetings with the two former Prime Ministers of Bangladesh, Sheikh Hasina Wajed and Begum Khaleda Zia, as well as with the Bangladesh delegations attending biannual DG-level conferences between India's BSF and Bangladesh Rifles. A particularly low point in Indo-Bangladesh relations was reached when fifteen BSF jawans were tortured and killed by the Bangladesh Rifles on the Assam-Bangladesh border in April 2001. It was a most heinous act, but our government decided not to respond to the provocation, even though our self-restraint did not go down too well with the people in India.

HOW PEACE WAS EFFECTED WITH BODO TIGERS

One of the efforts of the Home Ministry that met with considerable success was when, on 6 December 2003, militants belonging to the Bodo Liberation Tigers (BLT) surrendered their arms to end their decade-old struggle. As a result, the Bodoland Territorial District Area (BTDA) came into existence the following day, fulfilling the aspirations of Bodos, a major tribe in Assam living in the areas north of the river Brahmaputra. BLT leader Hagrama Basumatary handed over an AK-47 rifle to Assam's Chief Minister, Tarun Gogoi, to begin the surrender proceedings. Earlier, he handed over the BLT flag to Swami Chinmayananda, my deputy in the Home Ministry, and also hoisted a white flag to mark the beginning of new era of peace.

This was the culmination of sustained peace negotiations between the Central Government and BLT, after the latter agreed to unilaterally suspend its operation in July 1999. What encouraged me to begin peace negotiations with the BLT, in May 2000, was that, during the Kargil War, it stood by India. I had full sympathy for their concern to protect their language, literature, culture and tradition, which had a strong emotional appeal for the Bodo community and for which Upendra Nath Brahma, regarded as the father of the Bodos, had fought with great commitment. Once BLT leaders agreed to give up the path of violence and accept the framework of the Indian Constitution, our government gave its word to amend the Constitution and widen the scope of the existing Sixth Schedule to facilitate autonomy for Bodos. We also assured them about including the Bodo language into the Eighth Schedule of the Indian Constitution and Bodo Kocharis of Karbi-Anglong in the Scheduled Tribe (Hills) list. The Centre's key negotiator was Dr P.D. Shenoy, a Special Secretary in the Home Ministry, who was successful in infusing the concept of the Bodoland Territorial Council after holding nearly two dozen rounds of talks with their leaders and officials of the Assam government.

My experience of dealing with the representatives of the Bodo community convinced me that, if those in power at the Centre and in the state governments in the North-East, are able to demonstrate their sincerity, sensitivity and ability to fulfil their promises, it is indeed possible to establish peace in the region. It also reinforced my belief that organisations which rely on terrorism as a means to press for their demands, have no faith in the Indian Union and the Constitution, and seek the support of anti-India forces based in foreign countries, must be dealt with an iron hand.

HOW AN INSURGENCY WAS ENDED IN NAGALAND

Nagaland has seen the longest period of insurgency in the entire North-East. I have considerable satisfaction that we succeeded in bringing the menace to an end during the Vajpayee government's regime. In a dramatic development, on 11 January 2003, leaders of the main insurgent group, National Socialist Council of Nagalim (Isak-Muivah), Chairman Isak Chisi Swu and General Secretary Thuingaleng Muivah, declared an end to their campaign against the Indian security forces, after their meetings with Prime Minister Vajpayee and me. We had succeeded in persuading them to end their thirty-five-year-long self-imposed exile and to have peace talks on Indian soil for the first time in five decades. Earlier, the bilateral talks between the government's interlocutor, former Home Secretary K. Padmanabhaiah, and the Naga leaders were held at Bangkok, Kuala Lumpur, Amsterdam and Paris. The last meeting between the Naga leaders and an Indian Prime Minister (Indira Gandhi) in India was in 1967.

The fact that the Naga leaders came to New Delhi on Indian passports and visited Raj Ghat to pay homage to Mahatma Gandhi[6] showed the long road they had travelled towards reconciliation. This journey had been paved by three important decisions of our government—lifting of the ban on NSCN (I-M) in November 2002, extending the ceasefire agreement, reached earlier in 1997, to Naga-inhabited areas in neighbouring states, and our assurance, as in the case of Jammu & Kashmir, to hold free and fair elections in Nagaland. This is how the media reported the meeting between the Naga leaders and Prime Minister Vajpayee, Defence Minister George Fernandes and me: 'Isaac Swu and Muivah said that there would be no more fighting between Indians and Nagas. Comparing the present dialogue with the 1967 talks, they said the earlier talks had made no headway because of the "lack of maturity" and "not-so-realistic" approach of the Indian leadership. "But this time," they said, "the leaders are sincere, mature and are trying to solve it realistically. The government is trying to understand the Nagas' history and the Nagas are understanding that of India.... If the Government of India would respect the reality of Nagaland, the Nagas would respect the reality of India ten times more."'

Our government's decision in 2001 about extending the 'ceasefire' agreement with NSCN (I-M) beyond the areas of Nagaland triggered violent protests in neighbouring Manipur. People in Manipur feared that this would pave the way for the creation of 'Nagalim' (Greater Nagaland), since the Nagas' major demand has been to bring together all Naga-inhabited areas, including certain parts of Manipur and Assam, under a single autonomous administrative unit. The violence subsided after Prime Minister Vajpayee gave a categorical assurance that 'the territorial integrity of Manipur shall be maintained.' This underscored the fundamental challenge before the Central Government, as far as elimination of the source of tension between Nagaland and its neighbouring states are concerned—to find a solution that guarantees lasting peace, is within the Indian Constitution, but is also acceptable to Nagaland, Manipur and Assam. I am confident that this challenge can be overcome through an approach based on sincerity, mutual trust, patience and, above all, by harmonising regional aspirations with a shared sense of Indian nationalism.

I must acknowledge here that Naga Hoho, an apex body of all Naga tribal councils, made a constructive contribution to the peace process by launching a 'reconciliation campaign' to bring about unity among the fifty-two Naga tribes. Our government was instrumental in holding negotiations also with another group of Naga rebels, NSCN (K), led by S.S. Khaplang, who lives across the border in the jungles of Myanmar. After several rounds of meetings at undisclosed places with a team of officers from the Home Ministry, an agreement was reached for the suspension of armed operations, which had been going on for many years. This initiative also contributed to the establishment of lasting peace in Nagaland.

Two Indian leaders for whom Naga people have great respect are Mahatma Gandhi and Jayaprakash Narayan. JP led an important 'Peace

Mission' to strife-torn Nagaland in the 1960s. Both believed that the loyalty of a people to India cannot be secured through use of force, but on the basis of a deep and sincere respect for the distinctive cultural and historical traditions of the diverse communities in the North-East. They not only showed sympathy for the genuine grievances of Nagas and other people in the North-East, but also impressed upon them that these could be addressed within the framework of a united and democratic India. If the Vajpayee government could win the trust of Naga leaders, and also leaders of some other rebel groups, it is because our approach was broadly in alignment with that of these two great Indian leaders.

ARUNACHAL PRADESH: CHINA'S CLAIM REFUTED

Arunachal Pradesh, the largest state in the North-East in terms of area, is also one of the most peaceful. Ever since the 1962 Chinese war, when this was a part of Greater Assam, I have shared a special emotional bond with this state. Arunachal has been able to preserve its religious and cultural identity because of a ban on the entry of foreign missionaries into the state and a law against religious conversions. This state elected BJP MPs from both its parliamentary constituencies in 1999 and 2004. Incidentally, it also became the first state in the North-East to have a BJP government in Itanagar in 2003, with Gegong Apang as the Chief Minister. Sadly, this did not happen through a popular mandate but through mass defection of thirty-seven Congress MLAs. When I addressed a party meeting in Itanagar soon after this event, I mildly rebuked Apang and his supporting legislators by saying that I would be happy when the BJP could get so many MLAs elected in Arunachal Pradesh on its own ticket.

China's territorial claim on the Tawang district in Arunachal Pradesh has always rankled the people of the state. In December 2006, on the eve of President Hu Jintao's visit to India, the Chinese Ambassador to India made a statement that Arunachal Pradesh belonged to China. This prompted me to raise this matter forcefully in the Lok Sabha. I demanded that Parliament pass a resolution denouncing the envoy's remarks. External Affairs Minister Pranab Mukherjee, who was rather agitated by my demand, assured the house that 'This issue is not debatable at all. Arunachal Pradesh is an integral part of India. This continues to remain the position of Parliament and successive governments. There is no change in this position'. In the debate that day, I was truly proud of my party's two MPs from Arunachal Pradesh, Tapir Gao and Kiran Rijiju, who said: 'People of Arunachal have expressed their love and affection towards India. There is not even a separatist movement in our state. We are Indians and we shall always remain Indians.'

AN AGONISING EPISODE IN TRIPURA

My six years in the Home Ministry had their inevitable array of accomplishments, setbacks and disappointments, many tasks fulfilled and quite a few challenges partially addressed. But two failures caused me the greatest anguish. One was the inability to get Dawood Ibrahim, the prime accused in the 1993 Mumbai serial bomb blasts case, extraditated to India. The other was the especially agonising episode of the killing of four RSS *pracharaks* in Tripura in 2001.

In August 1999, I received information that Shyamal Sengupta, Dinen De, Sudhamay Datta and Subhankar Chakraborty, who had been devotedly working for the welfare of the tribal communities in the state, had been abducted from Kanchanpara under Fatikroy police station in North Tripura district. I immediately got in touch with Chief Minister Manik Sarkar, who has been heading a government of the CPI (M) in Agartala since 1998. The state police, he said, knew that it was the handiwork of the National Liberation Front of Tripura (NLFT), a separatist organisation. I called a meeting of Central and state government officials, which was also attended by Sarkar, who told me that his government had evidence of the Baptist Church in Tripura backing NLFT's separatist anti-national activities.[7] We decided at the meeting that the BSF and state police would jointly conduct search operations. Unfortunately, these efforts did not meet with success and, in February 2001, came the shocking information that the four RSS *pracharaks* were executed in Thangnan in the Chittagong Hill Tracts of Bangladesh, following an order by NLFT's top leaders. Tellingly, the information came from a former NLFT commander who had fled from its Chittagong training camp.

I was deeply distressed, and so was the entire RSS community across the country. Some felt that the CPI(M) government in Tripura did not cooperate. This was not true. Sarkar, it seemed to me, was genuinely interested in securing the release of the captives. On more than one occasion, he told me about the threat posed by NLFT and its nexus with the Baptist Church. Some in the Sangh Parivar felt that I did not put enough efforts to save the lives of the four *pracharaks*. As someone who is proud of having been an RSS *pracharak*, I could not have taken this task lightly. Nevertheless, I must say that the government's job became extremely difficult once the kidnapped persons were taken across the border to Bangladesh. In fact, subsequent information revealed that the *pracharaks*, who were initially kept in NLFT's various hideouts in Tripura, were shifted to the Chittagong camp following intensive combing operations by a special BSF commando unit. I raised this issue in my talks with Maj. Gen. A.L.M. Fazlur Rahman, Director General of Bangladesh Rifles, who had come to New Delhi to participate in a biannual meeting between officials of the BSF and BDR. He promised to ascertain the facts, but his response later was sadly in the negative.

The incident highlighted the nefarious activities of some of the foreign-funded church organisations in the North-East, which are engaged in an aggressive drive of religious conversion of local tribal communities. For example, the Baptist Church in Tripura, which was set up by missionaries from New Zealand sixty years ago and has strong financial backing from western Baptist Church groups, particularly the American Baptist Church, has issued edicts prohibiting tribal people from celebrating Durga Puja and other traditional festivals, worshipping their traditional deities, singing Hindu devotional songs, asking their women not to wear bangles or sport bindis, etc., and pressuring them to give up everything associated with the 'heathen Hindu' way of life. NLFT's declared aim is to remove Bengalis from Tripura and to convert the state into a 'Christian nation'. It is involved in the killing of several Hindu priests in the state. On 13 January 2002, on the eve of *Makar Sankranti*, a traditional harvest festival celebrated all over the country, NLFT militants shot dead sixteen persons in Singiche Bazaar in Tripura.

The strongest resistance to the Christian conversion mission in Tripura and in other North-eastern states (as also in tribal areas in other parts of India) comes from the Vanavasi Kalyan Ashram, set up by the RSS. Its dedicated volunteers have been empowering the tribals by setting up schools, dispensaries, employment-generation centres while preserving their cultural-spiritual identity. It is not surprising that the four RSS *pracharaks* in Tripura were kidnapped when they had gone to visit a Shishu Shiksha Mandir run by the Vanavasi Kalyan Ashram*.

*

Recognising the importance of accelerated socio-economic development and employment generation in the North-Eastern region, both the Prime Minister and I felt the need for sustained and focused attention of the central government. Accordingly, a new and separate Ministry of Development of North Eastern Region (DONER) was established in 2001 with Arun Shourie as its first Minister and Dr P.D. Shenoy as its first Secretary. The Prime Minister also directed various developmental ministries to earmark ten per cent of their budgetary allocations for the North-eastern states. Thanks to a close functional relationship between the Home Ministry

---

* The RSS has established a nationwide network of organisations that are engaged in service-oriented and constructive activities. These are Vanavasi Kalyan Ashram, Seva Bharati Vidya Bharati, Sanskar Bharati and Sanskrit Bharati, in which tens of thousands of volunteers have been working. One of its most successful projects is called Ekal Vidyalaya (Single-teacher School), which imparts primary education to underprivileged communities in remote and under-served areas of the country. The Akhil Bhartiya Vidyarthi Parishad (ABVP), an RSS-inspired students' organisation, has been running the Students' Experience in Inter-State Living (SEIL) programme for more than three decades. Under this programme, several thousand students from the North-eastern states are hosted by families in different parts of India. SEIL's slogan is: '*Alag bhasha alag vesh phir bhi apna ek desh*' (Different languages, different attires, but we all belong to one nation). Similarly, hundreds of activists of RSS-affiliated organisations from other states have also lived and worked for prolonged periods in the North-East.

and DONER, our government tried to strengthen the 'development plus security' approach in the region, with emphasis on people's participation in militancy-hit areas. To promote national integration, Doordarshan and AIR were instructed to substantially enhance local programming for nationwide broadcast.

Another important and related dimension of our North-East policy was its synergy with the External Affairs Ministry's 'Look East' policy, which received a tremendous boost during the Vajpayee regime. The Prime Minister visited almost all the countries in South-East Asia, which are rightly described as India's civilisational neighbours. Since 2002, India has been participating in the annual ASEAN summits. India has also been trying to promote sub-regional cooperation as exemplified by two important initiatives—BIMSTEC (Bay of Bengal Initiative for Multi-Sectoral Technical & Economic Cooperation) and the Mekong-Ganga Cooperation. The latter seeks to strengthen linkages between countries (India, Cambodia, Laos, Myanmar, Thailand and Vietnam) through which two of Asia's civilisational rivers flow. One of the biggest beneficiaries of the success of the 'Look East' policy will be our North-eastern region.

*

As I look to the future of this region, I am convinced that everything depends on how thoroughly India learns from the mistakes of the past. Daunting tasks lie ahead of us but we must, as I have stressed earlier, find a satisfactory solution to stop the 'demographic invasion' from Bangladesh. The BJP's campaign against illegal immigrants from Bangladesh in no way detracts from our oft-stated desire to see friendly and cooperative relations between India and Bangladesh, as befit two countries whose shared past far outweighs certain differences created in recent times. Several considerations of geography, history and development compellingly dictate that India and Bangaldesh establish a new mutually beneficial bilateral relationship between two equal and sovereign partners. Bangladesh is landlocked on three sides by India. Its civilisational, cultural and spiritual history has common roots with India. Indeed, Bangladesh's destiny is more closely linked with India's than that of the the Middle-East.

Recurring problems like floods, which wreak havoc both in Bangladesh and in India's North-East, can only be solved through effective regional and sub-regional cooperation. Lastly, the challenge of poverty alleviation and improving the living standards of the teeming millions both in Bangladesh and its surrounding states in India can be effectively met only by integrating the markets, leveraging the natural resources, connecting the infrastructure facilities, and broadening people-to-people contacts. All this, however, should happen in a legal and well-regulated manner, and with due consideration for mutual security.

I do hope that the government of Bangladesh reciprocates India's wish for friendly relations by agreeing to stop infiltration of its nationals and winding up its policy of giving shelter to several ISI-backed anti-India extremist and terrorist groups. This will go a long way in opening up the doors of a bright new future for our two countries, and for the Indian subcontinent in general.

11

NAXALISM, OTHER CHALLENGES AND INITIATIVES

The Communist vision is the vision of man without God.
—WHITTAKER CHAMBERS, AN AMERICAN WRITER

As India's Home Minister, the one challenge that worried me for its sheer geographical spread—and continues to do so—is left-wing extremism, also known as Naxalism. It has engulfed 115 districts in ten states, of which thirty-three districts are highly affected. The activities and influence of various naxal groups are mainly concentrated along a large tract of tribal and other impoverished areas in Bihar, Jharkhand, Chhattisgarh, Orissa, Maharashtra, and Andhra Pradesh, etc., a tract that has come to be known as the 'Red Corridor'. Occasionally, naxal violence is also reported from Uttar Pradesh, Madhya Pradesh, West Bengal, Tamil Nadu, Kerala and, lately, Karnataka. Due to the contiguity of the upper reaches of the 'Red Corridor' with Nepal, and more on account of the ideological affinity between the Maoists in Nepal and Indian naxal groups, this tract is also figuratively described as extending from Pashupati (the famous Shiva temple in Kathmandu) to Tirupati (the town in Andhra

Pradesh where the hill-top temple of Lord Venkateshwara is located).

Using the jungle hideouts in these areas, naxal groups have virtually mounted a proxy war on the Indian State, with targeted attacks on police convoys, looting weaponry from police stations, mass killing of innocent civilians to spread terror, assassination of political leaders belonging to various political parties, threatening the administrative machinery, preventing developmental schemes from being implemented, siphoning of developmental funds through intimidation, extortion of levies on transportation of forest, agricultural and mineral produce, and, in general, running a parallel system of governance in the areas under their control. They undermine the authority of the democratically elected government by holding their own courts, called '*Jan Adalats*', where arbitrary and ruthless punishment is meted out.

Far from being just another manifestation of popular protest against injustice and exploitation, Naxalism is a campaign to destroy India's democracy and establish communist dictatorship. The foreign source of their ideological inspiration is evident from the fact that Naxalism was born as a poisonous offshoot of the communist movement in India, with close links with the international ultra-left movement. Soon after its birth in 1967 in Naxalbari—a village in West Bengal from which the movement derives its name—its leaders coined an incontrovertibly anti-national slogan: 'Chairman Mao is our Chairman'!

Although naxal groups—front-ranking among them being the People's War Group (PWG) and the Maoist Communist Centre (MCC)—have targeted the leaders of many political parties, they have shown a special animosity towards the BJP and other non-Congress parties. In 2004, naxalites blew up former BJP President M. Venkaiah Naidu's helicopter in a village near Gaya in Bihar. Luckily, Naidu escaped unhurt. In the previous year, N. Chandrababu Naidu, the then Chief Minister of Andhra Pradesh, had a providential escape in a powerful bomb blast in Tirupati. Recently, in 2007, the son of Babulal Marandi, a former BJP Vice President and Chief Minister of Jharkhand, was killed by left-wing extremists. I must also make a special mention here of the scores of brave activists of the ABVP, an affiliate of the RSS working among students, who have been gunned down by naxalites because of their spirited opposition to the latter's brutal ideology. As far as the civilians and security personnel killed in naxal violence is concerned, the number runs into thousands*.

In one of my first meetings with officials of the Home Ministry, I made it clear that no nation that values its sovereignty, cherishes its democratic system of governance and upholds the rule of law could ignore the threat posed by left-wing extremism. At the same time, the battle against this menace required to be fought on multiple fronts simultaneously. First of all, it needed close operational coordination between the Centre and the states on the one hand, and also among the affected states themselves. Before the Vajpayee government assumed office, the Centre used to view naxal violence mainly as a problem to be dealt with by the state governments concerned. To accord the problem its due importance, I convened a meeting of the Chief Ministers of the naxal-affected states in Hyderabad in early 1999, where, for the first time, a consensual decision was taken to set up a coordination committee headed by the Home Secretary, with his counterparts from the states and their DGPs.

As decided in the meeting, the committee met every three months to take stock of the situation, and also to take necessary decisions. It urged states to adopt a three-pronged strategy: (a) gain confidence of local people by taking up welfare-related activities in education, healthcare, promotion of sports and cultural traditions, etc; (b) build up infrastructure and implement development programmes with focus on employment generation; and (c) launch intelligence-sharing and joint security operations with neighbouring states. The Home Ministry identified the fifty-three districts most affected by naxal violence and provided them with special assistance, which included reimbursement of up to fifty per cent of all

---

* In the five years between 2002 and 2006, 2,861 civilians and security personnel were killed by naxalites. Five states (Andhra Pradesh, Chhattisgarh, Jharkhand, Bihar and Maharashtra) accounted for all but 171 of these deaths. Source: Annual Report of the Ministry of Home Affairs, 2007. A meticulously researched and highly useful compendium titled *Maoist Insurgency: A Perspective* has been brought out by the Martyrs' Memorial Research Institute, Hyderabad. It was released by me on 25 April 2007. In terms of casualties, the report says: 'The naxal violence is fast catching up with the ongoing mayhem in Jammu & Kashmir.'

security-related expenditure by the Centre. I was shocked to find that, even though a militarised challenge to the Indian state needed to be tackled with a military solution, in many of the naxal-affected police stations in poorer states, the security personnel had little more than batons and rudimentary guns. And they were expected to take Maoist militants, equipped with landmines, AK-47s and self-loading rifles (SLRs), head-on in their hideouts. I directed state governments to give priority to such police stations under the Central Government's Police Modernisation Scheme.

Besides coordinating the security efforts, the committee identified specific initiatives to speed up socio-economic development in areas affected by Left-wing extremism. For example, increased allocations were made, and special guidelines were drawn up, for improving the connectivity of rural roads under the Pradhan Mantri Gram Sadak Yojana (PMGSY)*, which

---

* Pradhan Mantri Gram Sadak Yojana (PMGSY) was launched by Prime Minister Atal Bihari Vajpayee on 25 December 2000, which, incidentally, was his birthday. It is the biggest ever rural infrastructure development undertaken in independent India. When our government took office in 1998, as many as 1,86,000 out of the nearly six lakh villages in the country either had no roads at all or had very poor road connectivity. For PMGSY, the first ever fully Centrally sponsored rural roads scheme with an investment outlay of Rs 60,000 crore, we set an ambitious target: to provide good-quality all-weather roads to all unconnected habitations, with a population of more than 500 persons, by 2007. I am proud to say that our government, with M. Venkaiah Naidu and Shanta Kumar as Ministers of Rural Development, implemented this scheme with great vigour. PMGSY was, indeed, the rural equivalent of the equally ambitious infrastructure programme, the National Highway Development Project (NHDP), also launched by the Vajpayee government, to lay a nationwide network of world-class highways, beginning with the 5,800-km Golden Quadrilateral linking Delhi, Mumbai, Chennai and Kolkata, and a 7,300-km North-South corridor from Kashmir to Kanyakumari and East-West corridor from Saurashtra to Silchar. Not since Sher Shah Suri (1486-1545), who built the Grand Trunk Road from Peshawar to Kolkata, had India seen such a massive highway construction project.

I would like to mention here the inspiration for launching the PMGSY. In January 1999, Prime Minister Vajpayee had come to Bangalore to inaugurate work on the NHDP. At the same time, we had a party meeting in the city. One evening, Atalji and I had gone to the RSS office to meet the late H.V. Seshadri, the organisation's widely respected General Secretary. He complimented the Prime Minister for launching the highway project, but said, 'You should follow it up by starting a similar project to provide good roads to all the villages in India. Our villagers need them more than the city people need highways.'

remains one of the notable achievements of the Vajpayee government.

Since much of the naxal activity is concentrated in areas inhabited by tribals, who form nearly eight per cent of India's population, our government felt the need for focused attention to address their problems. Congress governments in the past used to place problems of the Scheduled Tribes (STs) in the same conceptual category as those of the Scheduled Castes (SCs). This was a wrong approach. Therefore, we created a separate Ministry for Tribal Affairs at the Centre for the first time since Independence. We also created a separate National Commission for Tribal Development. The budget for education, housing, healthcare, children's nutrition, employment and entrepreneurship was significantly raised. The number of ST students getting scholarships for higher education increased several fold.

As I look back, I have to admit in all honesty that what our government achieved in addressing left-wing extremism was insufficient as compared to the magnitude of the problem. The factors that bred naxalism outweighed the systemic efforts to crush it. What disappointed me, however, was that after the exit of our government in May 2004, the UPA regime significantly reduced the pressure on various naxal outfits. There was neither clarity nor consistency in its policy while dealing with the problem. On one hand, Prime Minister Dr Manmohan Singh declared—and rightly so—that naxalism was 'the biggest threat to India's internal security' but on the other, the government run by his own party in Andhra Pradesh lifted the ban on the People's War Group and invited its leaders for a dialogue. There are credible reports that the Congress party has often taken the help of naxal groups in Andhra Pradesh, Jharkhand and Chhattisgarh at the time of elections to browbeat its political opponents. It has similarly used ULFA in Assam for short-term electoral advantage.

I am also disappointed by the UPA government's failure to explicitly mention the well-known link between the Maoist insurgents in Nepal and the naxal outfits in India. The two are twin brothers, both being the offspring of the global monster of communist extremism. Soft corner for the Maoists in Nepal, whose insurgency has caused thousands of lives and greatly destabilised the Himalayan kingdom, is a dangerous policy.

A Maoist takeover must be regarded as deeply antithetical to the interests of both India and Nepal.

India's attitude to developments in a foreign country should be based on the well-established principle of non-interference in the internal affairs of that country, except when they impinge on our national interests. However, in the case of Nepal, with which India shares age-old and unbreakable bonds of culture and spirituality, it has been my party's consistent stand that (a) Nepal should have a vibrant and effective multi-party democracy; (b) the framework of constitutional monarchy should be preserved, since it is a symbol of Nepal's identity and sovereignty, in the same way as is the case in several other countries around the world; and (c) India should assist the fraternal people of Nepal in all possible and necessary ways to realise their aspiration for progressing as a peaceful, stable and developed nation.

In my own way, I have continued to create awareness about the grave threat posed by naxalism even after my stint in the Home Ministry got over. It was a major theme in the thirty-five-day Bharat Suraksha Yatra, which I undertook along with Rajnath Singh, the BJP President, in April-May 2005. In fact, a good part of the journey took place in the naxal-affected areas of Telangana in Andhra Pradesh and Chhattisgarh. I received a good response from the people when I put their own experience of naxal violence in the context of the global history of left-wing extremism. At a press conference in Bilaspur in Chhattisgarh, for example, I exhorted that the naxalites' ultimate aim was to overthrow democracy in India and replace it with communist dictatorship, of the kind that prevailed in erstwhile Soviet Union under Stalin, in China under Mao Zedong and in Cambodia under Pol Pot. 'Our people should be educated about the murderous "bio-data" of Left-wing extremism, which accounts for nearly half of all deaths by atrocity in the twentieth century.

'Under Joseph Stalin, who ruled the Soviet Union with an iron fist from 1924 to 1953, nearly twenty lakh died in gulags, executions and inner-party purges. Nearly twenty lakh people reportedly died due to "unnatural causes" during the so-called Great Proletarian Cultural Revolution (1966–76) in

China, which was unveiled by Mao Zedong himself. Over forty lakh people were detained and investigated. The Cultural Revolution was characterised by political zealotry, purges of intellectuals, and the worst social and economic chaos in modern Chinese history. Another twenty lakh people died earlier in what is probably the worst man-made famine in human history, the result of fanatical policies of China's communist government. In Cambodia, between 1975–80, Pol Pot's Khmer Rouge regime turned the country into a "Killing Field". More than twenty lakh people were killed in this small country, which had a population of only eighty lakh people. The mass murder of nearly one-fourth of the country's population was a human catastrophe rarely paralleled in human history.'*

I am confident that India will never allow naxalism to perpetrate such barbarism in our country. Nevertheless, we cannot afford to be complacent. To save precious human lives, and to protect our proud democratic system, all political parties and all sections of society must join hands to eliminate this cancerous foreign implant from our body politic.

FORMATION OF NEW STATES

Our Constitution, which was adopted in 1950, affirms that India is a Union of States. However, the reorganisation of states on linguistic lines did not happen until 1956. This was preceded by a prolonged agitation by Telugu-speaking people to have their own Andhra state carved out of Madras state. The subsequent formation of many new states was also preceded by people's agitations, as in the case of Maharashtra, Gujarat, Punjab, Haryana and Himachal Pradesh.

When the Vajpayee government assumed office, there were as many as twenty-five states. However, there had been longstanding demands

---

* One book that had profound influence on my thinking about the ideology and practice of communism was *Witness* by Whittaker Chambers (1901–61), an American writer and one-time communist party member who worked as a spy for the Soviet Union but later defected to become an outspoken critic of communism. The book brilliantly describes how communism dehumanises man by impoverishing him spiritually.

for the formation of three more states—Jharkhand to be carved out of Bihar; Chhattisgarh from Madhya Pradesh; and Uttarakhand out of Uttar Pradesh. We in the BJP had consistently backed these demands, in accordance with our long-held view that smaller states facilitate better administration, promote greater people's participation in democratic self-governance, and accelerate socio-economic development. We had also backed the formation of separate Telangana, to be carved out of Andhra Pradesh, and Vidarbha, to be formed by dividing Maharashtra. Indeed, the formation of these five new states was an important commitment in our party's election manifesto in 1998.

As the Union Home Minister, it was my responsibility to convert this promise into reality by piloting a necessary Constitutional Amendment in Parliament. Aware of the divisive passions that this issue had evoked in the past, and aware also of the strong possibility of similar demands arising in the future, I enunciated a sound guiding principle to go ahead in this matter: for Parliament to consider any specific proposal for the formation of a new state, the legislative assembly of the parent state should adopt an enabling resolution to give its consent.

Both Prime Minister Vajpayee and I held a series of informal talks with the leaders of various political parties to evolve maximum consensus on this issue. Our efforts bore fruit when the assemblies of Madhya Pradesh, Uttar Pradesh and Bihar gave their consent. This paved the way for the formation of Chhattisgarh on 1 November 2000; Uttaranchal (later renamed as Uttarakhand) on 9 November 2000; and Jharkhand on 15 November 2000. While replying to the debate in Parliament after the enactment of the legislations for the reorganisation of the three states, I said, 'No one party should claim credit for the creation of the states and I would commend both Houses of Parliament and all political parties, particularly the main opposition party (Congress), and constituents of the ruling alliance (NDA), for the smooth passage of the Bills.'

This was a good example of how consensus-building, rather than confrontation, can yield the desired results.

We could not fulfill our promise in respect of Vidarbha since, apart from the Congress party in Maharashtra, the Shiv Sena, our alliance partner, was not—and is still not—in favour of a division of the state. A peculiar situation has arisen in the case of the demand for a separate Telangana, a demand which is nearly as old as the formation of Andhra Pradesh in 1956. The BJP has consistently backed this demand. However, we could not do anything in this regard since Telugu Desam, which supported the Vajpayee government between 1998-2004, was opposed to it. Since Telugu Desam was in power in Andhra Pradesh at the time, there was no possibility of the AP assembly passing a resolution in favour of Telangana. As soon as the Telugu Desam severed its ties with the BJP, our party has unequivocally reiterated our support to the formation of a separate Telangana.

In stark contrast to this principled stand taken by the BJP, the Congress has shown rank opportunism on the issue of Telangana. It entered into an alliance with the Telangana Rashtra Samithi (TRS) in the Lok Sabha and AP Vidhan Sabha elections in May 2004 by promising a separate state. Sensing that the TRS, which had been formed solely on the issue of Telangana, was gaining popularity in the region, the Congress leadership felt it expedient to support its demand. The Congress-TRS alliance won a thumping majority in the AP assembly. It also bagged the largest number of Lok Sabha seats from the state, on the strength of which the Congress-led UPA government came into being at the Centre, with TRS as a partner in the central government. Since the Congress is now in power both in Hyderabad and New Delhi, there is no hurdle whatsoever for it to fulfill its promise to the people of Telangana. Yet, the promise remains unfulfilled.

The Congress party has been talking about setting up a Second States Reorganisation Commission (SRC II). But I do not think it is a sound idea, since it is bound to set off vociferous demands and agitations for the creation of many new states. Also, it will not be possible to accede to some of the demands on security or practical considerations.

GUJARAT EARTHQUAKE: A TRAGEDY INDIA OVERCAME UNITEDLY

The morning of 26 January every year is a time of pageantry in New Delhi. The long and wide avenue from Rashtrapati Bhavan to India Gate, which is flanked by the lawns of Boat Club, becomes the venue of the spectacular Republic Day Parade graced by the President, Prime Minister, a specially invited foreign head of state, a large number of dignitaries and members of the public. Sadly, not long after the parade had begun on Republic Day 2001, the Prime Minister and I received some news that jolted us. A massive earthquake had devastated Kutch in Gujarat and also hit many other parts of the state.

When full details of the calamity became known, it turned out to be one of the worst natural disasters in India in recent history. The quake measuring 7.7 on the Richter scale killed more than 12,000 people, injured around 55,000 and rendered over a million people homeless. Three-fourths of Kutch was destroyed.

I rushed to Ahmedabad the same afternoon. The quake had taken its toll on many buildings, and many lives had been lost. But this was nothing compared to what I saw in Bhuj, the epicentre of the earthquake. Much of this historic city had been reduced to rubble. In the days, weeks and months that followed, India saw—and also participated in—a rescue, relief, rehabilitation and reconstruction effort that was truly unprecedented. Common people, irrespective of their background, were helping each other in the hour of tragedy. The Army, in particular, played a valiant role. In an inspiring show of solidarity and voluntary service, thousands of NGOs toiled tirelessly to provide succour to the quake-hit people. Corporate houses and the Indian diaspora, especially the large number of non-resident Gujaratis, also rose to the occasion. I must make a special mention of the service rendered by religious organisations of all denominations. I spent several days and nights visiting relief camps in the immediate aftermath of the catastrophe, and calamity-hit places later at regular intervals. About this experience, let me reproduce parts of a report that appeared in the *Pioneer* on 3 Februray 2001.

Advani Sets a Sterling Example

From Deepak Sharma in Gandhidham

He did not utter a word against anybody. But he realised what had gone wrong and what had to be done. Unprecedented destruction needs unprecedented attention. No wonder he rushed to Gujarat for the third time within five days after the quake rocked the State. Spending two days in a tent and eating the same food served to the jawans, 73-year-old Union Home Minister L.K. Advani kept on moving from one site to other, to move the wheels of administration in the quake-hit areas of Kutch.

With communication lines snapped, Mr Advani operated from a mobile phone and kept on calling officials and Ministers one by one. 'Set up more control rooms and rush senior officials to tehsils in the disaster areas,' he instructed a top official. At Kandla port he went inside the ships to see what the naval doctors are doing. 'How many major surgeries have you done in two days? What about seriously injured patients?' he asked Commodore Aspi Bhaskar. At Bhuj, he went inside the Israeli medical camp. 'I am overwhelmed that you all are working round the clock,' he told Dr Ibit, the leader of the 160-member team of Israel Army Medical Services. Within a few minutes he was talking to District Collector Kamal Dayani, 'How long will it take to clear the debris? What more help you need?'

Once in Gandhidham, he mingled with the crowd and spoke to the natives of Kutch in their language. He tried to inspire confidence among the residents who seemed to have lost all hope. He then instructed a state-level BJP leader: *'Aap in sabhi ki baat suniye aur yahin rahen.* (Listen to everyone's grievances and stay put here.) The scene was a bit different in Adipur. The Home Minister appeared to be emotionally charged when he visited the quake-hit (in Adipur) where his father had lived for more than four decades. For a while Advani remained silent, as his distant relatives and erstwhile neighbours flocked to him. The Advanis, after migrating from Karachi had settled in Adipur. In one of the damaged house he simply walked inside a room and hugged a 87-year-old man lying on a bed. He was friend of his father. 'Have faith. We will rebuild Kutch, better than ever,' Mr Advani said, as tears were about to roll from the old man's eyes.

Bolstered by the people's participation, and fully supported by the Centre, the government of Gujarat succeeded, in a remakably short time, in rebuilding battered homes, schools, hospitals, roads, market places and putting the entire state back on its feet. This, indeed, was Gujarati resilence at its best. The state government's efforts won kudos even from the United Nations agencies. Gujarat also became the first state in the country to enact a law on disaster management and set up a state-level body to ensure its adherence.

Natural catastrophes of this kind cannot be predicted, nor prevented. However, the test of good governance is whether the scale and severity of their consequences can be mitigated through better disaster preparedness and management. Therefore, on a parallel track, and in less than a fortnight of the Gujarat earthquake, the Vajpayee government set up a National Committee on Disaster Management to recommend, among other things, 'the necessary institutional and legislative measures needed for an effective and long-term strategy to deal with major natural calamities in the future'. In a conscious effort towards promoting national consensus, the panel comprised leaders of all the major political parties, and the Prime Minister appointed Sharad Pawar, leader of an Opposition party (Nationalist Congress Party [NCP]) to spearhead its activities. This move, which was widely appreciated, was in recognition of the commendable leadership role that Pawar, as the Chief Minister of Maharashtra, had provided in the relief, rehabilitation and reconstruction effort in the wake of a major earthquake in Latur in 1993. The government accepted the recommendations of the Pawar panel. However, before we could implement these, we lost power in the parliamentary elections in May 2004.

When the tsunami struck India (and several other countries in the region) in December 2004, causing massive devastation in Tamil Nadu, Kerala and Andhra Pradesh, I urged the UPA government to implement the recommendations of the Pawar committee and, in particular, set up a specialised disaster response organisation at the national level. I am glad that the National Disaster Management Authority (NDMA) came into being in 2005.

MULTIPURPOSE NATIONAL IDENTITY CARD

A matter of high priority for me in the Home Ministry was the creation of a national register of citizens and the issuance of multipurpose national identity cards to all citizens of fourteen years and above. The card could be used for enrolment in the voters' list, filing income tax returns, getting passports, driving licenses, ration cards, health care, admission in schools and colleges, employment in public/private sectors, and life and general insurance. The government could use it for maintenance of land records, urban property holdings, foreign travel records through emigration bureau, criminal records, etc. Separate coloured cards were proposed to be issued to non-citizens.

This was indeed one of the important recommendations of the GoM on national security. Acknowledging that 'illegal migration has assumed serious proportions' the GoM recommended that 'Multi-Purpose Identity Cards should be introduced initially in the border districts...and then extended to the hinterland progressively.'

The government accepted this recommendation. Its implementation required an amendment to the Citizenship Act, 1955, which was done in December 2003. In consultation with reputed IT companies, the Home Ministry designed highly sophisticated software to run a near-automated system designed to provide a unique national identity number to each Indian citizen, with finger prints and other bio-metric recognition details. The scheme was, indeed, at a take-off stage when our government demitted office in May 2004. Funds had been allocated and a detailed action plan had been prepared. Pilot projects had been launched in some border areas and necessary improvements brought about on the basis of experience gained. It saddens me to note that the Congress-led UPA government has put this important scheme in limbo due to partisan considerations.

CHRISTIAN GRIEVANCES AND DEBATE ON CONVERSIONS

India presents a proud—I may even add, exemplary—example of forging unity in diversity, respect for all modes of worship, and mutually tolerant coexistence among people professing different faiths. Often, in some localised situations, the relationship between different faith-based communities exhibits tension, which occasionally snowballs into violent conflict. This is true even about intra-community relations. But all such incidents, invariably, are aberrations, and not a permanent feature of India's social reality. They are exceptions, rather than the rule.

Even when they are exceptions, no right-thinking person can condone or justify acts of violence in the name of caste, religion or ethnicity. I was, therefore, pained when certain unfortunate and thoroughly condemnable incidents of violence against our Christian brethren were blown out of proportion and projected as a proof of the 'anti-minority' character of the Vajpayee government. A sustained and systematic propaganda campaign was launched to defame the BJP and its government, both within the country and internationally.

The trigger for this campaign was the macabre incident in Manoharpur village in Orissa, where, in the early hours of 22 January 1999, Graham Staines, an Australian evangelist missionary, and his two young sons were burned alive. The barbarity of the crime shook the whole nation, making every Indian hang his head in shame. Our government acted with alacrity. In less than a week, the Home Ministry appointed a commission of inquiry under Justice D.P. Wadhwa, a sitting judge of the Supreme Court. The commission won plaudits from all by submitting a comprehensive report prepared in record time—less than six months. It held one Dara Singh guilty of the crime; his accomplices and he are now serving a life-term in prison.

The fair trial, resulting in prompt conviction of the guilty, was a tribute both to India's secularism and to our independent judiciary. However, when the incident happened, a section of the political class and the intelligentsia quickly proclaimed the RSS and its affiliate organisations guilty of the crime, and used the BJP's association with them to malign our government. I was, therefore, constrained to affirm in Parliament that 'I know these organisations and there are no criminals'. This statement was used by our political adversaries to propagate all over the world that I had defended the killers of Staines. It is worth pointing out that neither the Wadhwa Commission nor the CBI, which probed the crime, found any links between the RSS and those convicted by the court. I appeal to the people to believe facts rather than propaganda.

While the killing of Staines and his sons was no doubt inhuman, the specific social context in which it took place cannot be ignored. The Wadhwa Commission itself noted that 'Tension was brewing between Christian and non-Christian villagers because of the spread of Christianity. (The) tension is caused due to: (i) Christian villagers who were earlier contributing to the village festivals, not giving "chanda" (contribution) after embracing the religion; (ii) their non-participation in local religious festivals and tribal dance etc; (iii) their adoption of anti-tribal customary practice of ploughing land during Raja, Makar Sankranti and other festivals. Such conduct of the Christians was resented by the other villagers.'

The Commission also noted that Staines used to describe 'Sanatan Dharma as an animist sect'. Besides his involvement in leprosy eradication activities amongst the poorest of the poor, 'Staines was also involved in missionary work…driven by a deep commitment to his religion and the belief that he should spread its tenets amongst the people in the area. His missionary activities did lead to conversions of tribals to his faith.'

Although minor incidents involving sporadic attacks on Christian missionaries have been taking place in India for a long time, these received unprecedented and sensationalised publicity, both at home and abroad, during the six years of the Vajpayee government. I have been consistent in condemning them. Speaking in the Lok Sabha on the issue of atrocities against Christians, on 16 December 1998, I said, 'As far as our government is concerned, we firmly believe that no citizen in this country—irrespective of whether he belongs to a minority or a majority community, to this minority or that minority—should feel unsafe.' I also asserted that 'Intolerance has no place in Hinduism. I would go further and say that intolerance has no place in the culture of this country.'

I believe strongly in promoting harmonious relations between Hindus and Christians—indeed, between people following any two different faiths. Christianity came to India nearly 2,000 years ago, well before many Christian nations in the world came in its contact. Christians have enriched our national life with valuable contributions in diverse fields. Having studied in a Catholic school in Karachi, I am well aware of, and highly admire, the exemplary commitment that Christian missionaries bring to bear on their humanitarian work in education, healthcare and care of the destitute. Some of my best personal friends are indeed Christians.

Nevertheless, I have to be candid in stating that I regard the organised foreign-funded conversion campaign by evangelical groups as a threat both to Hindu society and to national integration. I am proud of India's multi-faith character and unequivocally respect the freedom of faith as a fundamental right of every citizen. However, systematic and mass-scale proselytisation of Scheduled Castes, Scheduled Tribes and vulnerable sections belonging to other classes under the garb of social service cannot be justified in the name of freedom of faith. Nor can Hindu organisations be blamed for protesting against this gross abuse of the freedom of faith and demanding legislation against conversion by fraud or inducement.* I would like to invoke here Gandhiji's forthright views on religious conversions:

> I disbelieve in the conversion of one person by another. My effort should never be to undermine another's faith. This implies belief in the truth of all religions and, therefore, respect for them. It implies true humility.... I hold that proselytisation under the cloak of humanitarian work is unhealthy to say the least. It is most resented by people here. Religion after all is a deeply personal thing. It touches the heart.... Why should I change my religion because the doctor who professes Christianity as his religion has cured me of some disease, or why should the doctor expect me to change whilst I am under his influence? (*Young India*, 23 April 1931)

---

* Anti-conversion laws already exist in certain states, such as Arunachal Pradesh, Madhya Pradesh and Orissa, and these were passed by Congress governments. Similar laws exist in many countries around the world.

If I had the power and could legislate, I should stop all proselytizing. In Hindu households the advent of a missionary has meant the disruption of the family coming in the wake of change of dress, manners, language, food and drink. (*Harijan*, 5 November 1935)

It is impossible for me to reconcile myself to the idea of conversion after the style that goes on in India and elsewhere today. It is an error which is perhaps the greatest impediment to the world's progress toward peace. Why should a Christian want to convert a Hindu to Christianity? Why should he not be satisfied if the Hindu is a good or godly man? (*Harijan*, 30 January 1937)

I appeal to well-meaning Christian organisations and their leaders to come forward to allay the fears of Hindus over religious conversions. I would like to remind them about what Archbishop S. Arulappa, a widely respected religious personality in Hyderabad who passed away in February 2005, had once told me: 'I totally endorse your concept of Cultural Nationalism. By birth I am an Indian, by culture a Hindu and by faith, I am a Christian.' This spirit of tolerance, goodness and pride in India's common culture is truly worth emulating by one and all. At the same time, I also appeal to Hindu organisations not to yield to the temptation of bigotry and extremism in dealing with the Christian community. Let us open all doors of dialogue and reconciliation, and close all doors of diatribe and recrimination.

12

COMMUNAL VIOLENCE IN GUJARAT: PROPAGANDA VERSUS REALITY

Why is propaganda so much more successful when it stirs up hatred than when it tries to stir up friendly feeling?

—BERTRAND RUSSELL, BRITISH PHILOSOPHER AND PEACE ACTIVIST

I conclude this account of my six years in the Home Ministry by turning to an event—rather, two inter-related events—that has figured most prominently in the sustained campaign, conducted both nationally and internationally, to malign my party, its ideology and the Vajpayee government's six years in office. I am referring to the communal violence in Gujarat, both in its Godhra and post-Godhra phases, in February-March 2002. I have repeatedly stated that both events were 'indefensible' and 'a blot on my government'. I was all the more distressed by them because they blemished the Vajpayee government's widely appreciated record, until then, of having drastically brought down the number of incidents of communal violence in the country.

After the unfortunate happenings in Gujarat, the Congress and its pseudo-secular supporters took the lead in a sustained campaign against my party by propagating, essentially, three lies, which are still in circulation. The first lie is that the post-Godhra violence was a pre-meditated state-sponsored genocide of Muslims. The second is that the BJP-led government at the Centre did nothing while Gujarat was burning. Thirdly, that the carnage in Godhra, due to the gutting of two compartments of Sabarmati Express, was accidental—or, worse still, self-inflicted. I deem it to be my duty to nail all the three lies.

Speaking in a debate in the Lok Sabha on 30 April 2002, the Congress President described the Gujarat violence as 'genocide' and said, '...but ultimately truth will prevail'. The truth, as contained in official information, and revealed by her own government, was as follows. The religion-wise break-up of those killed was: Muslims 790 and Hindus 254. In addition, 223 people were reported missing.[1] I accept that the unofficial death toll might have been higher. But can a tragic episode of this kind, in which the number of Hindus killed was by no means insignificant, be termed 'genocide' of Muslims? During the debate itself, Prime Minister Vajpayee had cautioned her against such casual usage of a highly loaded term. But since Sonia Gandhi had used it, it gained wide currency and was employed by forces inimical to our country to malign not only our government but also Gujarat and India.

It is also worth emphasising that over 200 rioters were killed in dozens of incidents of police firing in Ahmedabad, Baroda and other places in Gujarat. Nearly 10,000 rounds of bullets were fired by the police. In the initial days, the police made preventive arrests of nearly 18,000 Hindus, as against 3,800 Muslims. Does this speak of a state-managed pogrom of Muslims, with the state's security apparatus remaining inactive?

DID THE CENTRE TURN A BLIND EYE?

Regarding the charge that the Centre turned a blind eye while violence was raging in Gujarat, I let the following facts speak for themselves. Within hours of the massacre in Godhra on 27 February, the Rapid

Action Force (RAF) was deployed both in Godhra and Ahmedabad and a red alert was issued immediately. The very next day, the state government requested the Centre to send the Army. It also requested for armed police reinforcements from neighbouring states. The same night, Prime Minister Vajpayee dispatched Defence Minister George Fernandes to Ahmedabad, where the latter discussed with Chief Minister Narendra Modi details about the deployment of the Army. By the early morning hours of 1 March, plane-loads of Army personnel arrived, and, before noon, their deployment at sensitive points started. The Army staged flag marches in all the violence-hit areas of Ahmedabad, Rajkot and Baroda without any delay. When riots did not abate, the state government gave orders for shoot-at-sight throughout Gujarat.

Within three days of the violence erupting outside Godhra, I visited the state and this is what the media reported.[2]

Advani Reviews Gujarat Situation; Asks Govt to be Tough

Union Home Minister L.K. Advani on Sunday said, 'We will not allow any kind of communal tension.' He added that the mob attack at Godhra and subsequent violence has blotted his party's four-year record of having provided a 'communal tension-free' government. He asserted that the government would give top-most priority to restore communal harmony.... The home minister held meetings with Chief Minister Narendra Modi and senior civil, police and military officials and visited the Civil Hospital and affected areas of Bapunagar, Naroda and Meghaninagar. He said that the government had three primary responsibilities regarding the Godhra mayhem and subsequent spread of violence in the state. 'First, we have to arrest the guilty, second, to prevent recurrence of any kind of violence and third, to ensure peace and security to every citizen and community.' Advani also visited the area where former Congress Member of Parliament Ehsan Jaffrey and 19 members of his family were charred to death. He expressed condolences to the members of the bereaved family.

In New Delhi, the previous evening, I had attended a meeting of prominent Opposition leaders, convened by the Prime Minister to discuss the situation in Gujarat. Concerned over the possibility of violence spreading to other parts of the country, both Atalji and I felt that the meeting should be used to demonstrate the nation's resolve, rising above party lines, to maintain communal peace and harmony. Accordingly, after the Prime Minister's assurance that the Centre would deal with the situation in Gujarat firmly, we requested Opposition leaders to join us in issuing an appeal to countrymen to preserve peace and promote brotherhood and unity at all costs. Among those who signed the appeal, besides Atalji and myself, were former Prime Minister Inder Kumar Gujral, Sonia Gandhi, BJP President Jana Krishnamurthy, CPI(M) General Secretary Harkishan Singh Surjeet and Samajwadi Party leader Mulayam Singh Yadav.

Contrary to our opponents' propaganda, the whole of Gujarat was not engulfed by riots. The combined efforts of the Centre and the state government helped in combating violence to a limited part of the state. No less important is the fact that the Centre took effective steps to ensure that it did not spill over to other states.

On 4 April 2002, Prime Minister Vajpayee visited Gujarat. At the Shah Alam relief camp in Ahmedabad, where nearly 8,000 riot-affected Muslims had been given shelter, he said, 'You are not alone at this time of crisis, we all are with you. The entire country is with you.... *Apne hi desh mein refugee ho jana, yeh dil ko cheerane wali baat hai.* (Becoming refugees in one's own country is heart wrenching.) While what happened in Godhra was condemnable, what followed in other parts of the state must also be deplored.' He lamented that India's standing in the comity of nations had been badly affected by the violence in Gujarat. 'With what face, I do not know, I will go abroad after what all has happened here. *Yeh paagalpan band hona chahiye.* (This madness must stop.)'

Later in April, in the parliamentary debate, I said, 'I am a sad man as I participate in this debate. Our government's clean and proud record of riot-free governance for the past four years has been sullied. When I look at what has happened in Gujarat in its totality, I cannot but say that both Godhra and post-Godhra violence is condemnable and shameful. All the post-Godhra incidents that have been mentioned by honourable members in the House—be it Naroda Patiya and Gulberg Society in Ahmedabad, Best Bakery in Baroda, Sardarpura in Mehsana, or others—are reprehensible. Godhra may explain what happened after that, but Godhra cannot justify either Naroda Patiya or Mehsana or any other killing. I will go so far as to say that in a law-governed society, even revenge of a wrongdoer can have no justification. But revenge against an innocent person? How can it be justified? Whether the victim is a Hindu or a Muslim, there can be no place for revenge in a civilised society. It can only be deemed as barbaric.'

I continued, 'I admit that there must have been some lapses somewhere, in administration, in the functioning of the police, etc. But to charge that the post-Godhra incidents were managed by the government itself, that it was a deliberate carnage, state-engineered mayhem and state-engineered genocide…this, I am afraid, is like providing weapons to the enemies of India to assault our nation.' Thereafter, congratulating Omar Abdullah, a minister in our government and leader of the National Conference (which was then a constituent of the NDA), for his excellent and impassioned speech that he had made earlier in the debate, I strongly endorsed an appeal that he had made: 'We should not only be scoring points but we should give a direction to the country.'

Of the many interventions to save innocent lives that I made during that distressing period of communal bloodletting in Gujarat, I shall recall two here. One day I received a call from Najma Heptulla, Deputy Chairperson of the Rajya Sabha. 'Akbar, my husband, wants to talk to you urgently about an SOS from some Muslim merchants in Ahmedabad,' she said. Akbar told me that the traders of Bohra Bazaar had approached him to urgently contact someone in the government to save them from an imminent attack from armed men in a nearby Hindu basti. I immediately rang up Chief Minister Modi and asked him to take necessary steps to provide protection to the needy. Modi called me back the next day to say that no untoward incident took place and potential miscreants were arrested. After the return of normalcy, a delegation of traders from Bohra Bazaar, along with Akbar, met me in Delhi to express their appreciation and gratitude for the timely steps taken by the Central and state governments.

In another such incident, I received a call one day from Somnath Chatterjee, a veteran parliamentarian of the CPI (M), who later became the Speaker of the Lok Sabha. 'Advaniji, I want to speak to you about an urgent matter,' he said in a tone that immediately conveyed to me his concern and urgency. 'My colleagues in the CPI(M) unit of Bhavnagar phoned me just now to say that a prominent madarasa in that town has been surrounded by a Hindu mob, which is planning to set it on fire. There are a large number of young students and maulvis inside the madarasa. Please do something to stop this.' I immediately spoke to both Modi in Ahmedabad and my own party leaders in Bhavnagar, instructing them to do everything necessary to prevent the attack and defuse the situation. I felt relieved to learn, later, that nothing untoward had happened. In one of my subsequent visits to Bhavnagar, the local CPI(M) activists and maulvis called on me and expressed their thanks. 'We only did our duty,' I told them.

Some months later, Chatterjee himself called me one day and said, 'Advaniji, I am calling from Ahmedabad. My party colleagues from Bhavnagar are here and they are telling me, "We want to thank you profusely. But for your timely intervention, many people in the madarasa would have been burnt to death." I told them, "Why are you thanking me? You should thank Advaniji for this".'

*

I am recalling all this not out of pride, but humility. Whatever I did was out of a sense of duty. I carry the pain that comes with the realisation that, in spite of our government's commitment to the ideal of a riot-free India, hundreds of innocent lives were lost in the fire of communal hatred. It does not matter whether they were Hindus or Muslims. They were all Indians.

Nevertheless, I would like fair-minded people to contrast all that I have narrated above with the anti-Sikh carnage in Delhi and other places in North India in the days following Indira Gandhi's assassination in 1984. During the first three days of mayhem, there was not a single policeman to be seen on Delhi roads. There was not even a single instance of lathi charge. Not only that, even the motorcade of President Zail Singh was stoned when he visited the hospital, where the slain Prime Minister's body was kept. In spite of specific, urgent and personal requests made to the then Home Minister, P.V. Narasimha Rao, on the very first day, the Army was deployed only on the evening of 3 November. On the occasion of his mother's birth anniversary, Prime Minister Rajiv Gandhi said: 'Some riots took place in the country following the murder of Indiraji. We know the people were very angry and for a few days it seemed that India had been shaken. But, when a mighty tree falls, it is only natural that the earth around it does shake a little.'* It took Sonia Gandhi fourteen years to express regrets for the tragic happenings in 1984.

I would also like people with an impartial and unprejudiced approach to contrast the conduct of the Central and state governments in 2002 with that of the Congress governments in New Delhi and Gandhinagar in the numerous previous instances of communal violence in Gujarat. The state has a long history of communal riots. Communal frenzy in the past always took a far longer time to return to normalcy. The 1969 riots in Ahmedabad continued much longer than in 2002, and claimed many more lives. The city remained under curfew for nearly two months. Communal disturbances in many parts of the state in 1985 continued for more than five months, with Godhra reeling under curfew for almost a year.

*

---

* Manoj Mitta and H.S. Phoolka, *When a Tree Shook Delhi: The 1984 Carnage and its Aftermath*, Lotus, 2007. The book mentions my role in the appointment of the Justice G.T. Nanavati Commission in May 2000 to inquire once again into the 1984 carnage. The Commission submitted its report in February 2005, but the Action Taken Report (ATR) prepared by the UPA government drew a howl of protest from all quarters, since it was rightly dubbed as a 'No Action Taken Report'. The book again mentions my role, along with that of the leaders of other non-Congress parties, in forcing the government to review its ATR, ask at least one Central minister implicated in the riots to resign, and get Prime Minister Dr Manmohan Singh to tender an apology to the Sikh community.

In September 2004, the UPA government—to be more precise, the Ministry of Railways headed by Laloo Prasad Yadav—appointed the U.C. Banerjee committee to probe the Godhra train fire. In fact, as subsequently ruled by the Gujarat High Court, its constitution was illegal; it was in violation of the Commissions of Inquiry Act, 1952, which bars the setting up of separate commissions by state and Central governments to probe a matter of public importance. The Shah-Nanavati Commission, appointed by the state government, had already been investigating both Godhra and post-Godhra violence. In October 2005, when Yadav's party (Rashtriya Janata Dal) was looking certain to lose the assembly elections in Bihar, the Banerjee Committee gave its report stating that the inferno in Godhra was 'accidental'. Some critics of the BJP have even insinuated that the kar sevaks, who were charred in the train, were themselves responsible for the fire, so that the incident could be used as a pretext for the post-Godhra violence elsewhere in the state. All I can say about these theories is that they are as fiendish and macabre as the incident itself.

NARENDRA MODI: A VICTIM OF VILIFICATION CAMPAIGN

I have often been criticised for stoutly rejecting the demand for Modi's resignation. This demand was raised within days of the communal violence breaking out in Gujarat, and continued for months and years thereafter. Some of our own allies in the NDA wanted Modi to resign. There was also strong and sustained pressure from certain quarters on Prime Minister Vajpayee, urging him to ask Modi to step down. I resisted this move, including at some very critical junctures.

My reasoning was this, and I expressed it elaborately in the Rajya Sabha on 6 May 2002: 'We should look for a real solution to the situation in the state, and removing Chief Minister Modi is not a solution. There has been a sustained campaign against him, which is not correct. It is also not correct or proper to allege, as Leader of the Opposition Dr. Manmohan Singh has done, that there is gross communalisation of Gujarat police. I plead with everyone not to make such sweeping charges against the police force. There are some shortcomings and I am aware of them, but let us not forget that, in Modi's government, the police force saved a large number of Muslims during the riots.'

I also resisted proposals for Modi's resignation made inside party forums. I am happy that my confidence in him has been fully vindicated by subsequent developments. His Chief Ministership, between 2002–07, was characterised by the fact that there was not a single communal riot in Gujarat, not a single incident of terrorism, and not a single hour of curfew imposed anywhere in the state in those five years. Gujarat made spectacular progress in many areas of social and economic progress during this period, attracting huge amounts of domestic and foreign investment, and emerging as one of the most developed states in the country. But what has given me special satisfaction is that Modi has brought down political and bureaucratic corruption in a way that even his critics have applauded. Needless to add, people of all castes and communities in Gujarat have benefitted from this commitment to security, development and clean administration.

A proof of all this was the renewed mandate, with a resounding majority, that the BJP won in the assembly elections in Gujarat held in December 2007. The Congress and its pseudo-secular supporters had sought to convert these elections into some kind of a national referendum on 'communalism vs secularism'. Needless to say, they failed miserably in their plans. What is worse, they seem to be unwilling to do honest introspection and draw the just conclusions from their defeat.

Modi's re-election has highlighted several lessons which are relevant not only for Gujarat but for the whole country. He has disproved the conventional wisdom that focus on good governance does not make good politics. He has dispelled the notion that elections cannot be won on a development plank. The BJP in Gujarat has also invalidated the belief that elections can be won only by appealing to people's caste and community sentiments. Furthermore, unlike in CPI(M)-ruled West Bengal, the BJP in Gujarat has demonstrated that a renewed mandate can be won without all recourse to electoral malpractices.

I consider the outcome of the Gujarat polls significant for another reason. It showed how a leader with integrity, courage and competence could count on people's support to beat back a personalised campaign of vilification. I cannot think of any other leader in Indian politics in the past sixty years who was as viciously, consistently and persistently maligned, both nationally and internationally, as Modi had been since 2002. Sonia Gandhi even went to the extent of calling him *'maut ka saudagar'* (merchant of death). I am happy that the people of Gujarat have given a fitting reply to the practitioners of this kind of toxic politics.

State assembly elections are quite frequent in our country, but rarely does the people's verdict in a particular state become a 'turning point' in national politics. I have no doubt that my party's spectacular victory in Gujarat would indeed become a turning point because it signals the BJP's resurgence as the frontrunner in the next parliamentary elections.

13

DEFEAT IN POLLS, TURMOIL IN THE PARTY

There is something good in all seeming failures. You are not to see that now. Time will reveal it. Be patient. Do not brood over your past mistakes and failures as this will only fill your mind with grief, regret and depression. Do not repeat them in the future.

—SWAMI SIVANANDA (1887-1963)
FOUNDER OF THE DIVINE LIFE SOCIETY

When, and under what circumstances, does an incumbent government decide to seek a re-election by recommending dissolution of the Lok Sabha? In 1971, Indira Gandhi sought parliamentary elections a year in advance, winning it on the basis of the '*Garibi Hatao*' (Remove Poverty) slogan. In 1984, Rajiv Gandhi advanced the Lok Sabha elections by several months, in a calculated attempt to benefit from the sympathy wave generated in the aftermath of his mother's assassination. In contrast, the mid-term elections held in 1979, 1991, 1998 and 1999 were clearly the result of political instability; they became necessary not because of, but in spite of, the preference of those in power. The government of the day had lost its majority and no alternative government could substitute it.

WHY THE BJP ADVANCED THE LOK SABHA POLLS

Only a party confident of returning to power chooses to go for an early election if the situation, in its judgement, seems favourable. As the Vajpayee government entered the last year of its five-year term in September-October 2003, the BJP certainly found the situation encouraging. The Prime Minister's popularity was at an all-time high. The economy was on the upswing. The steadily swelling foreign reserves had, for the first time, crossed the psychologically significant barrier of $100 billion, a far cry indeed from the time in 1990 when forex reserves were so low that India had been forced to mortgage its gold to tide over a severe balance of payment crisis. Another national accomplishment was when India's GDP growth in the second quarter of 2003 was recorded at 8.4 per cent. It belied Sonia Gandhi's taunting criticism of the NDA government's economic policies in her speech while moving a no-confidence motion during the monsoon session of Parliament, in which she had made fun of the target of an eight per cent GDP growth, likening it to '*Mungeri Lal ke haseen sapne*' (pipe dreams of Mungeri Lal[1]). The fruits of many bold decisions and pioneering initiatives taken earlier, such as construction of a nationwide network of world-class highways, were becoming visible. The telecom revolution had taken off in a big way, thanks to a bold policy reform in 1999. And because of the stunning progress in the information technology sector, India was being hailed as a 'Software Superpower'[2].

Throughout the period between 1999 and 2003, the main Opposition party, Congress, did not appear to be quite vibrant. Indeed, the BJP won impressive victories in the assembly elections held in October 2003 in three big states where the Congress had incumbent governments—Madhya Pradesh, Chhattisgarh and Rajasthan. Our success in these three states gave us the confidence to consider advancing the elections to the 13th Lok Sabha, due in September 2004. Our confidence was further buttressed by media reports and opinion polls which predicted a comfortable win for the BJP-led NDA, if elections were held in the first half of 2004.

An additional factor came into play around this time. The Telugu Desam party in Andhra Pradesh, led by N. Chandrababu Naidu, had lent crucial outside support to the NDA government in 1998. In 1999, sensing a pro-Vajpayee wave all over the country including Andhra Pradesh, Naidu formally entered into an election alliance with the BJP both in the Lok Sabha and Vidhan Sabha polls, which were held simultaneously. The alliance contributed significantly to Naidu's victory in the state and enabled him to become Chief Minister for the second time. However, since his government was becoming unpopular towards the end of his second term, Naidu was keen, once again, on capitalising on Vajpayee's popularity by having early and simultaneous Lok Sabha and Vidhan Sabha polls. Thus, accommodating a key ally's preference also contributed to the NDA's decision to advance the parliamentary polls by about five months from September-October to April-May 2004.

When the idea of having early Lok Sabha elections was broached soon after the BJP's victory in the three northern states, Atalji was among the persons who were initially not too thrilled. I was clearly in favour of the idea, and so was M. Venkaiah Naidu, who was then the party President, and many other senior leaders of the party. There was a broad approval for it even amongst our allies in the NDA. Thus, when the majority view seemed to prefer advancing the Lok Sabha polls, Atalji agreed to it. However, I always had the feeling that he gave his consent rather reluctantly.

A formal decision in this regard was taken at the meeting of the BJP's National Executive in Hyderabad on 11-12 January 2004. On the recommendation of the Prime Minister, President Dr A.P.J. Abdul Kalam dissolved the 13th Lok Sabha on 6 February. Thereafter, the Election Commission announced a four-phase schedule of polling to elect the 14th Lok Sabha between 20 April and 10 May. As far as the BJP and the NDA were concerned, two issues needed to be settled: The plank on which we would seek a renewed mandate; and the nature of our campaign. The first question was easily answered: Atalji's proven stewardship. The people had seen and hailed him as a visionary leader who not only provided stability but had taken India forward on the path of progress and global prestige. Thus, the NDA would seek a mandate for Atalji's continued leadership of India. It was also decided that all the constituents of the NDA would have a common election manifesto. The BJP would, however, prepare a separate Vision Document of its own to present its commitments and ideological perspective on various issues. Arun Jaitley chaired the committee that produced this document. The late Pramod Mahajan was made in charge of the Election Management Committee.

THE BHARAT UDAY YATRA

The answer to the second question, regarding the nature of the campaign, had to take into account an important factor: because of the two knee operations that Atalji had undergone in 2002, his mobility had become somewhat restricted. Therefore, I had to shoulder a major responsibility of the campaign. My colleagues suggested that my campaign should be in the nature of a nationwide road journey. This suggestion, which I readily accepted, was crystallised in the form of the Bharat Uday Yatra, a thirty-three-day-long, 8,500-kilometres drive covering, in two stages, as many as 121 Lok Sabha constituencies in sixteen states. It was flagged off in Kanyakumari on 10 March and reached Amritsar on 25 March. Five days later, it resumed from Rajkot and culminated at Jagannath Puri on 14 April. This was my third major yatra, but the first which was explicitly election-oriented. Once again, it brought me immense satisfaction, reinforcing my conviction from the experience of previous yatras that, for a genuine mass contact programme, there is nothing better for a political leader than a road journey. It enabled me to talk to the people, meet them, and establish that special emotional connection which is the soul of democracy.

The response to the Bharat Uday Yatra was almost uniformly good. I addressed hundreds of meetings in which I expounded my views on the various issues that the election had thrown up. However, all my speeches had a common theme: 'This election is all about who should lead India, and with what vision. The Congress has nothing to offer to the country on both counts. On the contrary, Atal Bihari Vajpayee has shown both leadership and vision. He has also proved that India need not depend only on the Nehru-Gandhi dynasty for stable governance and able leadership. Our government has done much in the past six years, and the results of our performance are there for the people to see. But there is a large unfinished agenda, which can be summed up in one slogan: To make India a Developed Nation by 2020. The realisation of this slogan requires good governance, stability and continuation of Atalji's leadership.'

The media continued to predict a comfortable victory for the NDA, and so did almost every pre-poll opinion survey. Nevertheless, some important political developments were underway the likely consequence of which on the elections we failed to recognise at the time. Firstly, there were some crucial desertions from the NDA. The DMK and a few other smaller parties in Tamil Nadu quit our alliance to join hands with the Congress in January 2004. Earlier, the National Conference in Jammu & Kashmir and Ram Vilas Paswan's Lok Janashakti Party (LJP) also had left the NDA. These gave the impression that the NDA was not as stable as it earlier was. The Congress, on the other hand, showed some quick nimble-footedness by forging potentially rewarding alliances in (apart from Tamil Nadu) various states such as Maharashtra (Nationalist Congress Party), Andhra Pradesh (with the Telangana Rashtra Samithi [TRS]) and Jharkhand (Jharkhand Mukti Morcha [JMM]). Interestingly, this strategy of entering into alliances was, in fact, a negation of the Congress's earlier decision, taken at its conclave in Pachmarhi in September 1998, to strive to regain power on its own without joining hands with other parties.

THE NDA SUFFERS A SHOCK DEFEAT

The counting of votes was to start on 13 May. In the past, the use of paper ballots necessitated manual counting that took hours before the results could be declared. In contrast, the introduction of electronic voting machines all over the country had now made it possible for early trends to be known within a few hours of the commencement of the counting process. I was watching television at home and, by 10 am it became clear that a shock defeat was in the offing.

The people had voted for a hung Parliament, in which no single party or pre-poll alliance secured a majority on its own. However, the Congress emerged as the single largest party with 145 seats (out of the 400 seats from which it contested). The BJP could win only 138 seats (out of the 364 constituencies from where it contested). The difference was, apparently, marginal. But the party's tally had come down from 182 in 1999. The fall in the NDA's strength was even more debilitating: from 304 in 1999 to 186 in 2004. In contrast, the number of MPs belonging to the Congress and its pre-poll allies was 216. In addition, it could safely bank upon the support of sixty-two MPs belonging to the CPI(M) and three other Left parties. Thus, it became certain that the next government would be that of a coalition led by the Congress.

The Prime Minister tendered his resignation around noon. Later in the evening, he addressed the nation and noted that 'my party and alliance may have lost, but India and India's democracy have won'.

Within the next few days, a new ruling coalition called the United Progressive Alliance came into existence. There was, however, some unexpected drama over the choice of the new Prime Minister. President Kalam invited Congress President Sonia Gandhi for a discussion on government formation since she was the leader of the single largest party in the Lok Sabha. Moreover, the Congress had fought the elections under her leadership. No other leader was even remotely projected as a candidate to occupy the top office if the party, together with its allies, won a majority. However, when she emerged from her meeting with the President, she told the media that she needed more time to form a government. Was there a change of mind on her part? If so, why? The answer to these questions came from Sonia Gandhi herself when, addressing a meeting of the Congress Parliamentary Party on 18 May, she sprang a surprise by invoking her 'inner voice' and backing out from the Prime Ministerial race. Instead, she nominated Dr Manmohan Singh for the post.

'I never wanted to be Prime Minister,' Sonia Gandhi claimed in her speech, and this was later trumpeted by her partymen in a well-orchestrated campaign as a 'great sacrifice' on her part*. Of course, the claim was questionable on two counts. Firstly, it was contradicted by her own audacious assertion, made in front of Rashtrapati Bhavan on 21 April 1999, that she was going to form the government and had the support of '272 MPs' for doing so. Secondly, as subsequent developments clearly showed, far from renouncing power, she started to wield more power†

---

* Sycophancy in the Congress party reached new levels following Sonia Gandhi's 'inner voice' speech. This is what the *Hindu* reported on 9 December 2004. 'Sonia Gandhi was saluted today by her partymen on the eve of her birthday tomorrow, which will be observed as "Tyaag Divas" (renunciation day), a celebration of her giving up the Prime Minister's post in May. The occasion was the release of a book, *Sonia Gandhi: Rajniti Ki Pavitra Ganga* (Sonia Gandhi: Holy Ganga of Politics), at Teen Murti Bhavan Auditorium here.' According to the report, Home Minister Shivraj Patil compared her to Lord Rama, Lord Buddha and Mahatma Gandhi, and said: 'All the virtues of these great men are manifest in Ms Sonia Gandhi. She is an asset not just to the Congress party or to India, but to the whole humanity.'

† The halo of sacrificing power became even more suspect when the UPA government appointed Sonia Gandhi to chair a specially created body called the National Advisory Council (NAC). Although she exercised power from this rather unconstitutional platform, she remained outside the pale of accountability to Parliament. Ultimately, she had to resign from chairpersonship of the NAC at the culmination of a wounding controversy over 'office of profit' in 2006. The Congress party had conspired to get Samajwadi Party's Jaya Bachchan, an acclaimed movie actor and wife of the superstar of Indian cinema, Amitabh Bachchan, disqualified from the Rajya Sabha. It had done so on the plea that an innocuous post that she occupied in the UP government was an 'office of profit' under the Members of Parliament (Prevention of Disqualification) Act of 1959. Its politics of vindictiveness boomeranged so badly that the BJP and the rest of the Opposition demanded disqualification of Sonia Gandhi from the Lok Sabha since the post of chairperson of the NAC was also, legally speaking, an 'office of profit'. When the UPA government sought to bring in an ordinance, between two sessions of Parliament, just to save the Congress President, the BJP issued a stern warning that if such an ordinance was indeed introduced, then 'the government will have to go'. Ultimately, Sonia Gandhi was forced to resign her membership of the Lok Sabha and seek re-election. It is worth mentioning here that President Dr A.P.J. Abdul Kalam played a bold and praiseworthy role in this entire episode by returning a bill on the issue to Parliament and forcing the government to set up a Joint Parliamentary Committee to define what constitutes an office of profit. Of course, he had to pay the price later by way of the Congress' stern opposition to his candidature for a second term as President.

than Dr Singh since the effective centre of both political and governmental power shifted from 7 Race Course Road, the Prime Minister's official residence, to 10 Janpath, the residence of the Congress President.

Why did Sonia Gandhi forsake Prime Ministership in May 2004? Frankly, she alone can clear the air by coming out with a factual and more plausible explanation. However, I must respond to the charge that my party mounted a 'racist and 'xenophobic' campaign against her. It is true that some of my party colleagues reacted strongly to the prospect of a person of foreign origin being sworn in as India's Prime Minister. As I have already elaborated earlier in the book, the BJP's stand on this issue was not personality-centric but principle-centric. We were, and we continue to be, opposed to a person of foreign origin occupying high constitutional offices in India. We have neither hidden nor changed our view on this important matter. Nevertheless, I was surprised when a section of the international media commented that 'the campaign to deny her (Sonia Gandhi) the prime ministership was a defeat for Indian democracy'.[3] To describe the BJP's nationalist approach to this matter as racism itself betrays a racist mindset.

WHY THE BJP LOST THE 2004 ELECTION

Why did we lose the parliamentary election in 2004? I must confess that the question haunted my colleagues and me for a long time. The taste of bitter defeat, is by no means unfamiliar to me. Indeed, for most parts of my political life in the early decades, defeat was the norm and victory an exception. This, coupled with my innate nature of reacting to any situation with restraint and moderation, had prompted me to develop a rather philosophical attitude towards the outcomes of elections—neither to get depressed by defeats, nor to let victories breed boastfulness.

Nevertheless, the results of the 2004 polls affected me more deeply than any other setback in the past. Some factors that caused it became apparent to me fairly quickly and I articulated them in my first post-election press conference at the BJP headquarters on 28 May. 'The BJP has accepted the people's verdict with humility,' I noted. 'We have already stated that we will perform the role of a constructive and responsible opposition in Parliament. We wish the new Prime Minister well and assure him of our cooperation in all policies and actions that are in the national and people's interest. At the same time, I would like the Congress-led coalition government not to misread the people's fractured verdict as a decisive mandate for any alliance, much less for any single party, and certainly not for any individual.'

Admitting that the outcome of the elections had 'gone completely against our expectations—indeed, against everyone's expectations, including that of our opponents', I identified four causes for it:

- No single factor of nationwide relevance accounted for the electoral outcome rather, different factors influenced the electorate in different states. Thus, it was not a national verdict, but an aggregate of state verdicts. Our commitment to 'development' and 'good governance' and our appeal to the people to judge our promise on the basis of our performance did not have the kind of sustained nationwide emotional appeal that could transcend the influence of local or episodic factors on the voters. In Karnataka, they worked and the BJP won eighteen out of twenty-eight seats, the highest ever. However, in a crucial state like UP, they did not. We won only eleven out of eighty seats in that state, due mainly to our organisational weaknesses. In Bihar, the influence of caste and communal combination held sway.
- Our failures and shortcomings in alliance management took a rather heavy toll. In some states like Andhra Pradesh and Tamil Nadu, we suffered badly along with our allies. Telugu Desam's tally dropped from thirty-two to five in AP. In Tamil Nadu, the BJP's hastily concluded tie-up with the AIADMK failed to impress the voters; DMK and its allies made a clean sweep by winning all the thirty-nine seats in the state. Jharkhand, Haryana, Jammu & Kashmir and Assam were the other states where we suffered because we did not forge proper alliances. In contrast, the Congress party's electoral success was mainly on account of its alliance strategy.
- Our opponents' negative campaign prevailed over our positive campaign. There is no doubt that India had progressed considerably

in several areas during the six years of the NDA government. However, in retrospect, it was obvious that the fruits of development had not reached all sections of our society. Although equitable development was our unshakable commitment, we failed to effectively communicate to the poor and the deprived that those five years were too short a time to fulfil it. On the other hand, the Congress and the communists carried out a vicious negative campaign, replete with lies, to claim that India had actually suffered ruination under the NDA government. The tone and content of their campaign suggested that poverty and unemployment did not exist during the long Congress rule, but were actually the creation of the NDA government!

- The phraseology of 'Feel Good Factor' and 'India Shining' hurt us. These phrases, though valid in themselves in a particular context, were inappropriate for our election campaign. There was indeed a 'feel good' atmosphere in the country over the past one year, prior to the 2004 elections, on account of a combination of factors: accelerating economic growth; sound macro-economic management; a good monsoon yielding an all-time high food production; praise for India on account of her shining achievements in sectors such as IT; a sharp dip in incidents of cross-border terrorism; the long-hoped for turnaround in the situation in Jammu & Kashmir and the North-East; and anticipation of a new chapter of peace and cooperation with Pakistan. However, by making the 'Feel Good Factor' and 'India Shining' the verbal icons of our election campaign, we gave an opportunity to our political opponents to highlight other aspects of India's contemporary reality—poverty and uneven development, unemployment among the youth, problems faced by farmers, etc., which questioned our claim.

During the same press conference, I also exhorted the workers and supporters of the BJP not to give in to despondency but, rather, undertake honest introspection and corrective action. 'I have no doubt that the future is bright for the BJP,' I said. 'The setback we have received is temporary. In its electoral history, the BJP has seen many ups and downs. The most traumatic setback we suffered was in 1984 when the party could win only two Lok Sabha seats in the whole country. We accepted the 1984 results as a challenge and converted it into an opportunity. We have a large network of dedicated workers all over the country, for whom power for the sake of power has never been the motivation to work in the political sphere. Nor are their labours directed at serving any dynasty's ambitions for power. They have devoted their lives to serve Mother India, undeterred by defeat and ever willing to overcome any challenge. This lofty inspiration and the organised will power of tens of thousands of BJP workers and millions of our supporters is the guarantee that "We Shall Return".

I continued to introspect further on the causes of defeat and presented them at the first post-election meeting of the party's National Executive held in Mumbai in June 2004. One troubling factor was the overconfidence displayed by both leaders and workers of the BJP in the run-up to the elections. It prevented us from keeping our ears to the ground. We became complacent towards popular sentiments on the one hand and about the strategies that our adversaries were hatching on the other.

OUR FAILURE TO NURTURE OUR ELECTORAL, ORGANISATIONAL AND IDEOLOGICAL CONSTITUENCIES

In addition, I identified two other factors for our poor performance. Every political party has three types of constituencies—geographical or electoral, organisational and ideological. All three need to be properly nurtured. Each elected representative has a geographical constituency, and his or her success of getting re-elected from their respective constituencies depends significantly not only on their performance in Parliament but, even more so in the Indian context, on how well they manage their relationship with their voters. I know of MPs, both in my party and in others, who have succeeded in getting re-elected four or five times from the same constituency principally because they have maintained a good emotional rapport with the people. For example, our MP from Jaipur has perfected a unique practice: whenever anyone passes away in his constituency, he or his colleagues carry the ashes to Haridwar for immersion in the Holy Ganga.

A frequent complaint that I encountered against sitting MPs who got defeated was that they did not do any work for their constituency or that they indulged in corrupt practices. While non-performance and corruption are legitimate grievances, what was resented even more by voters and party workers alike was arrogance on the part of their elected representatives. Inaccessibility, insensitivity, rude conduct, and arrogance of power invariably make an MP or a minister unpopular. And if such persons are given a ticket to contest elections again, people and party workers work together to ensure their defeat. The mood in many BJP strongholds was: 'Atalji is anyway going to become Prime Minister again, but let's teach our MP a lesson.'

In recent years, this phenomenon has come to be known as constituency-level anti-incumbency against sitting MPs who are renominated. It cost the BJP dearly in the 2004 elections. Indeed, as many as ninety sitting MPs—which comes to a punishing figure of fifty per cent—failed to get re-elected. In retrospect, I felt that my physical absence from Delhi for a long stretch of time during the Bharat Uday Yatra, and that too at a crucial time when many election-related decisions had to be taken after proper consultation, proved costly for my party. Many faulty and hasty decisions were taken in terms of candidate selection, due to over confidence that the NDA was anyway going to win.

The second constituency which received insufficient attention from us was our own party organisation. Unlike the Congress and some other personality-centric political parties, party *karyakartas* (workers) are the backbone of the BJP. Well-informed, well-organised and enthusiastic political workers often constitute the advance battalion of soldiers going into the propaganda battle in favour of their party's government. At the same time, where party workers remain sullen or insufficiently inspired, they fail to transmit to the public a positive impression about the government. During our six years in office, we ignored our own *karyakartas* to some extent due to persistent shortcomings in party-government coordination. This was certainly not the case all over the country but in many states, party workers at various levels felt that their grievances were not properly addressed and that MPs and ministers became distant from them.

The other reason for the BJP's defeat was our neglect of our core ideological constituency when we were in power. The BJP is not like any other political party; rather, it is part of an ideological movement committed to India's all-round national resurgence, based essentially on a non-sectarian Hindu ethos. We share this goal with many other organisations that belong to what is known as the Sangh Parivar, or the ideological fraternity inspired by the RSS. During the NDA rule, the BJP rightly yielded to the concerns of our allies in the spirit of running a stable and purposeful coalition. Indeed, our success in this regard greatly helped the BJP earn the trust and goodwill of people outside our traditional support base, besides demolishing the Congress party's self-serving claim that it alone can form a stable government at the Centre.

However, while working with our political allies for the goal of running a stable coalition, we failed to pay due attention to the views and concerns of our own ideological allies in the Sangh fraternity. We focused so much on issues of development and governance that we did not remain adequately in contact with those who support us and work for us because of our ideology. In a sense, we took our core constituency for granted, a constituency that has always stood by us in the low and high tide of politics. This happened because of a lack of effective communication between senior BJP leaders in the government on the one hand and our esteemed colleagues in the various Sangh-inspired organisations. It persisted at lower levels, too. In the absence of a structured and sustained dialogue, we could not receive timely and reliable feedback from them on our government's shortcomings. It also prevented us from letting them know of the government's constraints and compulsions behind taking—or not taking—a certain decision.

As a result, even though the Vajpayee government was widely seen as doing good work, our own core supporters did not feel sufficiently involved in its achievements and remained rather indifferent to the victory of our candidates in many constituencies, most notably in UP. Dialogue, I am certain, would have led to a better appreciation of mutual concerns and strengthening of a shared sense of responsibility in consolidating the BJP's hard-earned political dominance at the Centre.

CARRYING THE MANTLE OF PARTY PRESIDENTSHIP AGAIN

The responsibility for the party's shock defeat in the Lok Sabha elections was collective. Hence, there was never any question of pinning the blame on any particular individual. The BJP was, and continues to be, far too deeply steeped in the spirit of collectivism to let electoral defeat become the pretext for finger-pointing. These are totally alien to our organisational ethos, unlike that of the Congress which forced first P.V. Narasimha Rao and then Sitaram Kesri to unceremoniously step down as party President after its electoral defeats in 1998 and 1999 respectively.

Nevertheless, neither expectedly nor inevitably but suddenly, M. Venkaiah Naidu resigned as President of the BJP on 18 October 2004, citing personal reasons for doing so. He also added that, although collective responsibility was the accepted mantra in the BJP, he had taken 'full responsibility as party President' for the BJP's defeat in the Lok Sabha polls. I knew that he had been experiencing considerable inner turmoil, which was exacerbated by the unbecoming conduct of certain party colleagues.

Finding a successor to Naidu became an excruciating task. I was strongly in favour of a colleague from the second rung of leadership to once again take on the reins of the party. There was no dearth of capable leaders from the younger generation—Sushma Swaraj, Arun Jaitley, Pramod Mahajan and Narendra Modi, to name a few. Indeed, it had been my conscious decision since the 1980s to groom a new crop of promising young leaders. But almost all of them felt that the party needed 'a senior leader at the helm at this stage', insisting, further, that I take over as the new party Chief. Frankly, I had no desire to become the BJP President again. I assured them that I was always available to guide the party whenever it was needed. It is only when Atalji, too, urged me to accept the proposal that I gave my consent and was elected President, for the fifth time in BJP's history.

I should be candid in stating that, unlike in the past, the general state of the party morale and organisation worried me. There was some erosion of the team spirit both at the Centre and in several party units. The tendency to voice inner-party differences publicly, and the temptation to use the media to settle scores, was on the rise. Most often these differences had nothing to do with principles or ideology, but were rooted in personal ambitions and animosities. The lure of power had begun to colour the behaviour of certain colleagues, and this in turn promoted groupism and individual loyalties. The ethos of struggle, sacrifice, discipline and idealism—which were the hallmark of the Bharatiya Jana Sangh and, later, the BJP—was weakening. Nothing pained me more than when, in contrast to our own proud projection of the BJP as a 'party with a difference', the media pejoratively started to describe it as a 'party with differences'. I was especially distressed by the instability in Madhya Pradesh, one of the traditional strongholds of the BJP. In spite of winning a massive mandate in the assembly elections in October 2003, we had to change the Chief Minister, not once but twice. I knew that the regression in the party was an aberration, and did not afflict the entire organisation. Nevertheless, it was time to combat the problem.

I used the occasion of the party's National Executive meeting in Ranchi in November 2004 to convey my anguished feelings and thoughts. 'It is my belief,' I said, 'that the Divine Power has cast a responsibility on the BJP and made it His chosen instrument to take our country out of its present problems and to lofty heights of all-round achievements. So long as the awareness of the loftiness of our party's goals lights up our path, we have nothing to worry about. Even if we fail here or there, we will always bounce back, stronger than before. Therefore, we should remind ourselves again and again of the nobility of the mission we have embarked upon. Once we know that what we are doing is noble and lofty—because it is going to make India a stronger nation and a better place for every Indian to live in—that very knowledge will take away so many weaknesses, will wash away so many imperfections within each one of us. When an individual or an organisation is driven by a higher purpose, lower considerations cannot succeed in taking hold of that individual or that organisation.'

I told my colleagues: 'Let us ask ourselves: "What is driving us? What motivates us? Why have we entered politics? In particular, why have we chosen to be in the BJP?" If the answer to these questions is something higher than the ambitions and desires of the individual self, and something that is inspired by our ambitions and desires for our Nation, we'll always be on the right path. Friends, the National Executive represents the cream of the party. The entire party organisation—which means, nearly three crore members of this great party—is looking up to us. They expect to see how we are steering the party through these trying times. If we can ennoble ourselves, we'll be able to show the right path to the entire party. If we can improve ourselves, we'll be able to bring about much improvement in the party down the line. Let the top echelons set high standards. Lower units will certainly follow suit.'

I reiterated this exhortation for organisational self-correction in all my formal and informal interactions with party colleagues. At the same time, I was acutely aware that the party should not remain in an inward-looking mode for too long a time. Both our own supporters and the people at large expected the BJP to become active again in responding to the new situation in the country marked by the Congress-Communist combine occupying the political centre-stage. They expected the BJP to once again exude self-confidence and articulate its vision forcefully.

BJP'S RAJAT JAYANTI CONFERENCE: A MEMORABLE MILESTONE

The year 2005 being the twenty-fifth anniversary of the founding of the BJP, the party's National Council held its special Rajat Jayanti session on 6 April to mark the beginning of the year-long commemoration. If it was Atalji who had presided over the founding conference of the party twenty-five years ago, it was now my proud privilege to preside over its silver jubilee session. In my presidential address, I reminisced: 'This date, this place and this occasion stir up such pleasurable memories in the minds of many old-timers like me that they recreate an experience for us that is as unbelievable as it is unforgettable. Twenty-five years ago, our party was born on this very day and at nearly this very place. The BJP is called a party of yatras. We accept this epithet with pride. But the most memorable and the most rewarding of all our yatras is our yatra of the past twenty-five years. What a journey it has been! And, without sounding immodest or conceited, let me add: how much have we truly accomplished!'

I listed five major accomplishments of the BJP on the occasion. Topping the list was the distinguishing characteristic that made us stand apart from other major Indian political parties, which 'makes us proud but also leaves our critics amazed'—namely, that the BJP has never suffered a split. The Indian National Congress experienced a major split in 1969, within twenty-two years after Independence. The cause of the split was not very complimentary to the party and its original ideals. Whatever came to be known as the real Congress got divided again in 1999. The cause of the split this time was even more unedifying—it was on account of the foreign origin of its President. Similarly, the Communist Party, our main ideological adversary, broke up within nineteen years after Independence. Following closely on the footsteps of its present ally at the Centre, it too suffered another split within a few years of the first break-up.

'In contrast,' I said, 'we have remained a united family. Our unity and our unique ideological identity have been our greatest sources of strength.' I also attributed our unity to the strong foundation laid by Dr Syama Prasad Mookerjee and Pandit Deendayal Upadhyaya. 'They showed us the path. We walked on it, and have come this far. If I look back at the road we have traversed, disappointments there were many, but none deterred us. Successes too have been many, but none has filled us with vanity. At every high and low point in the journey, and at each point in between, we tried to draw the right lessons and continued to march along the *Kartavya Path* (the Path of Duty).'

Secondly, I recalled the jolting experience of 1979 when all those belonging to the erstwhile Bharatiya Jana Sangh were expelled from the Janata Party because of our refusal to sever our links with the RSS. In hindsight, our friends in the Janata Party clearly did us a big favour by removing us from the organisation on the 'dual membership'. We realised that we had to dig our own separate furrow. The quantity of water that initially flowed in that channel was modest. Indeed, after the 1984 parliamentary elections, held in the wake of Indira Gandhi's tragic assassination, it momentarily appeared as if the channel had completely dried up. Some of our adversaries used to joke that by remaining inflexible on the 'dual membership' issue in 1979, we had condemned ourselves to becoming a 'dual-member' party in the Lok Sabha in 1984.

The Congress and the Communists had gleefully written our political obituary. But how dramatically we grew thereafter—from a mere two seats in the Lok Sabha to eighty-six in 1989, to 120 in 1991, to 161 in 1996, to 182 in 1998 and to 182 in 1999. 'It is only in 2004,' I noted, 'that we faced a reversal, when our tally came down to 138 seats in the Lok Sabha. However, nobody can deny that, in a twenty-five-year timeframe, the BJP's overall growth has been nothing short of spectacular.'

Our third major accomplishment, I stated, was that until 1980, anti-Congressism was the main axis around which all the political developments and strategies of our party revolved. In sharp contrast, in 2005 anti-BJPism had become the main axis around which contemporary political events were moving. The Congress no longer dominated the Indian political scene in the same overwhelming manner that it used to in the decades preceding the birth of the BJP. Thus, the BJP had succeeded in demolishing the one-party supremacy of the Congress and transforming Indian polity into a bipolar formation. Moreover, the BJP had also emerged as the stronger of the two poles in terms of ideological distinctiveness, organisational muscle and commitment to the basic values of democracy. 'The unexpected setback that we received in the Lok Sabha elections last year does not in the least negate this truth,' I affirmed. 'We shall learn the right lessons from this experience and forge ahead with even greater resolve to strengthen the pole that the BJP represents.'

Fourthly, the BJP had successfully defeated the strategy of our ideological adversaries to ostracise us as 'political untouchables'. We stood our ground, increased our own strength through dedicated work, turned many of our earlier adversaries into our allies, won new friends, and broke free of the political isolation that the Congress and the Communists had wished on us. All this resulted in the triumphant formation of the NDA in 1998. The NDA defeated the Congress party's destabilisation game and succeeded in winning a renewed mandate in 1999. Indeed, Atalji became the first Prime Minister to lead a stable non-Congress coalition government at the Centre that lasted its full term.

Fifthly, I proudly mentioned how the Ayodhya movement had brought about a paradigm shift in the national discourse on the true meaning of secularism and the roots of our nationhood. Of course, the Congress party continued to malign us by calling us 'communal', for its own narrow vote-bank politics. However, I noted that our principled stand, along with the broadbased support, had forced even the Congress to acknowledge some home truths. In this context, I drew the attention to the resolution of the CWC, passed on 16 January 1999, which stated that 'Hinduism is the most effective guarantor of secularism'. I appreciated this stand and remarked: 'If the Congress is still faithful to this resolution, then all those interested in promoting genuine secularism and protecting India's cultural and civilisational identity can build on this significant point of consensus between the two major political parties in our country.'

Besides pointing to the BJP's major accomplishments since its inception, I also used the occasion of the Rajat Jayanti conference to exhort the entire party organisation to gear up to face future challenges. 'We cannot be content with what we have achieved so far. The long-term task that India's future requires us to fulfil is this: How do we become a stronger party with a durable all-India presence? If the Congress was the main shaper of India's destiny in the first fifty years of our Independence, how can we make the BJP play that role in a qualitatively superior manner in the decades ahead?'

I also listed five major tasks before the party. I encapsulated the first task in two words: consolidation plus expansion. 'In addition to further strengthening our base in states where the BJP remained traditionally strong, and regaining lost ground in states where we have recently slipped, we need to expand our support base in those states where our presence still remains only marginal. Since the aggregate number of parliamentary seats from these states is fairly large, the BJP can ill afford to continue to have only a meager share from this category of states.' If making BJP *'sarva vyapi'* (present all over the country) was one aspect of the expansion strategy, the other was to make it *'sarva sparshi'* (having influence in, and drawing support from, all sections of our diverse society). I said: 'Let us make concerted and sustained efforts to expand our base among the Scheduled Castes, Scheduled Tribes, Backward and Most Backward Classes, and all sections of the poor and the neglected, including those among Muslims and Christians.'

The second challenge before the BJP, I noted, was to make it a party of good governance, capable of bridging the gap between India's potential to become a developed nation free of poverty, unemployment and every vestige of social and regional disparity, and her actual performance. 'If our party has to shoulder this historic responsibility, we must augment our strength in every respect—ideological, organisational, political, and in the idealism and competence of our leading cadres.'

I identified the need to reorient the agenda of economic reforms to benefit *gaon* (village), *garib* (poor), *kisan* (farmer) and *mazdoor* (worker) as another major challenge before the nation as well as the party. 'It bothers me,' I confessed, 'that our party's capacity to give voice to the woes of our *kisans* and other sections of India's rural population, such as artisans, has not kept pace with the speed at which they are mounting. For instance, what can be more worrisome and shameful than to hear that hundreds of our farmers in different parts of the country have been forced to commit suicide to escape their plight? I therefore call upon all patriotic economists, development experts and policy makers and implementers to evolve a progressive re-orientation of the reforms process. No doubt, our economy should utilise every boon of science and technology and seize every opportunity that globalisation offers. But its principal aim should be to unleash the limitless productive potential of one billion Indians, and guarantee a better standard of living for all of them.'

Fourthly, I observed that our party needed to further strengthen its appeal among the youth by promoting young leaders and espousing issues that caught their imagination. 'Let us make BJP the Voice and Choice of Young India. The urgency of this task is self-evident when one considers that sixty-five per cent of India's population today is less than thirty-five years of age.' At the same time, I emphasised that 'our party values both experience and fresh blood, both wisdom that comes with age and dynamism that is the hallmark of the youth. In this sense, the BJP is like a robust ever-growing tree—spreading its roots deep and wide and yet sporting luxuriant new branches with each new season.'

Lastly, I reminded my partymen about a cardinal principle that Atalji had underscored in his presidential speech at the founding conference of the BJP in 1980—making 'constructive activity' an integral part of BJP's politics. 'Vajpayeeji had given our party three mantras: *sangathan* (organisation), *sangharsh* (struggle) and *samrachana* (constructive activity). We have a lot to show for our performance on the first two counts in the past twenty-five years. Many individual members and functionaries of our party have on their own established exemplary models in constructive activity. However, the time has come when the party should put the entire weight of its organisation behind such work.' I presented two reasons for renewing this call. Firstly, in recent decades, the importance of voluntary organisations and NGOs in different walks of our national life has grown immensely. Secondly, wherever our *karyakartas* have founded or patronised NGOs that are seen to be doing good work, they have unfailingly earned people's goodwill both for themselves and for the party. 'This prompts me to make an appeal to you today. On the occasion of the silver jubilee of our party, I call upon every active member of the party to get associated with at least one *seva* (service) or *vikas* (development) project of his or her choice.' I urged our MPs, MLAs and other party workers to get actively associated with activities like the mid-day meal programme for school children, tree plantation for a greener India, mass campaign for a cleaner India and a drive against various social ills such as untouchability, injustice against women, etc.

Although this appeal has not yet had produced a visible effect, I am aware of thousands of commendable constructive projects being run by my partymen across the country. And talking about constructive activities, I cannot but make a mention of the highly inspiring example presented by Nanaji Deshmukh, a veteran RSS leader and one of the founding members of the Bharatiya Jana Sangh. After the collapse of the Janata Party's government in 1979, he took voluntary *sanyas* (retirement) from active politics and devoted himself full-time to various rural development programmes. He was determined to create at least a microcosm where the dream of *antyodaya* (welfare of the last person in society), commonly espoused by Mahatma Gandhi and Pandit Deendayal Upadhyaya, could be realised. He has, indeed, succeeded in his effort by creating such a model in the villages around the holy town of Chitrakoot, on the border of Uttar Pradesh and Madhya Pradesh. Although he is now into his nineties, Nanaji continues to motivate young activists in voluntary social work with his vision and boundless commitment.

※

After the conclusion of the BJP's silver jubilee conference, I was looking forward to a sustained endeavour, in cooperation with all my colleagues, to revive the party. I knew that my task as party President was difficult, but I was full of hope and self-confidence. It was at this stage that an unexpected and most painful episode in my political life took place, following my visit to Pakistan in May-June 2005.

14

My Pakistan Yatra

Bharat-Pakistan padosi, saath-saath rehna hai, / Pyaar karen ya vaar Karen, donon ko hi sehna hai / ...Jo ham par guzari, bachchon ke sang na hone denge / Jang na hone denge!

India and Pakistan are neighbours, we have to live together, / Whether we make friendship or war, we both will face its effects, / What we had to suffer, we shall not let our children suffer, / We shall not let another war take place.

—Atal Bihari Vajpayee

SECTION 1

NOT QUITE MURPHY'S LAW!

I have lived long enough to know that history moves in unpredictable ways. Its movements, twists and turns, defy all human predictions. He is a vain man who thinks he knows exactly what the future consequences of his present actions will be. This element of unpredictability thus imbues the human spirit with the positive qualities of humility and modesty.

Sometimes the consequences of my actions in politics have been on expected lines. At other times, the immediate outcome is so far away from intended lines that I have felt flummoxed. On such occasions, the only reliable guide to judge oneself and one's actions is one's own conscience. 'Have I executed the action with the right motive and right intentions?' If the answer is 'Yes', then my mind is at peace. There is, I tell myself, a higher power who will surely set the consequences right, sooner or later.

My visit to Pakistan in May-June 2005 belongs to that category of human endeavours which remind me of Murphy's Law. Those afflicted by it are inclined to believe that whatever they do would turn out wrong. There is an interesting tale on this told by the renowned Brazilian writer and columnist Paulo Coelho in his book *Like the Flowing River*. The story, which is titled 'The Piece of Bread that Fell Wrong Side Up', runs as follows:

> *A man was quietly eating his breakfast. Suddenly, the piece of bread that he had just spread with butter fell to the ground. Imagine his surprise when he looked down and saw that it had landed buttered side up! The man thought he had witnessed a miracle. Excited, he went to tell his friends what had happened, and they were all amazed; because when a piece of bread falls on the floor, it nearly always lands buttered side down, making a mess of everything.*
>
> *'Perhaps you are a saint,' one friend said. 'And this is a sign from God.'*
>
> *Soon the whole village knew, and they all started animatedly discussing the incident; how was it that against all expectations, the man's slice of bread had fallen on the floor buttered side up? Since no one could come up with a credible answer, they went to see a Teacher, who lived nearby and told him the story. The Teacher requested that he be given one night to pray, reflect and seek divine inspiration. The following day, they all returned, eager for an answer.*
>
> *'It's quite simple really,' said the Teacher. 'The fact is that the piece of bread fell exactly as it should have fallen, but the butter had been spread on the wrong side!'*

I went to Pakistan as a messenger of peace, with an earnest desire to contribute to the normalisation of relations between our two long-estranged nations. I still believe that my visit made a finite contribution to the advancement of this objective. Nevertheless, my visit to Mohammed Ali Jinnah's mausoleum in Karachi and my approbatory references to his speech of 11 August 1947 in Pakistan's Constituent Assembly precipitated quite a controversy back home in India, particularly within BJP's own support base. I was hastily held guilty of committing a grave and unacceptable 'ideological deviation', of having 'betrayed Hindutva', and, in the estimation of some, even of being a '*gaddaar*' (traitor).

The turmoil began while I was still on Pakistani soil and reached a crescendo in the days following my return to Delhi. It culminated in my resignation from the Presidentship of the BJP in December 2005, within about a year of this responsibility having been entrusted to me. The ensuing developments affected the cohesion within the party in an unprecedented manner, and confused the minds of millions of its supporters. They brought me pain, deep and unyielding. This was quite simply the most agonising moment of my political life, more distressing, indeed, than when I faced corruption charges in the 'Hawala' episode in 1996. At that time, my mind was at peace because my party had stood solidly behind me, rejecting the charge with the contempt it deserved. In contrast, in the 2005 controversy over my Pakistan visit, several of my own party colleagues chose not to support me.

But there were many more, both within my own party and outside, who felt that it was a needless controversy: I had only quoted from a largely forgotten speech of Jinnah to remind the people of Pakistan about the vision of a non-theocratic state that its own founder had articulated. Equally significantly, I had done so after formally inaugurating, at the request of the Pakistan government, a project for the restoration of Katas Raj temples (whose antiquity, as I shall soon explain, goes back to the era of the *Mahabharata*), about 100 kilometres from Lahore. It was the first Hindu temple ever to be restored after the creation of Pakistan. I felt sad that some in my own ideological fraternity had failed to appreciate the significance of this event.

When I decided to visit Pakistan, on the invitation of Pakistan's Foreign Minister, Khurshid Mahmood Kasuri, I was confident that I would be able to reinforce the efforts of the Vajpayee government and strengthen Indo-Pak ties further, but I could not have imagined that this visit would enable me to subserve three other valuable, but totally unintended, objectives, namely: (a) by recalling the Pakistan founder's 11 August speech, remind the Pakistan rulers that they owed it to the memory of their own founder to ensure that the Hindus in Pakistan are guaranteed equality before law, and full freedom of faith and worship; (b) prompt the Pakistan government to think seriously in terms of renovating ancient Hindu temples (I should also make a mention here of the Hinglaj temple in Baluchistan); and (c) in just six days of interaction with important personalities in government, political parties, media, intelligentsia and with the common people, I feel I was able to convey very convincingly to everybody in Pakistan, that although my party and I are proud of Hinduism, we are not anti-Pakistan, and certainly not anti-Islam, or anti-Muslim.

I had gone to Pakistan with the best of intentions, but things had gone all awry for me. Had I too become a victim of Murphy's Law? In retrospect, however, I feel that it wasn't Murphy's Law that applied to me, but its very wise interpretation by the Teacher in Coelho's anecdote which did. The man whose slice of bread had fallen buttered side up felt that what had happened was a 'miracle'! In my case also, though the upshot of my trip to Pakistan wasn't anything miraculous, it was a wonderful achievement I could never have dreamt of.

THE PERSONAL AND POLITICAL PURPOSE BEHIND THE JOURNEY

My visit to Pakistan had both personal and political significance. This was going to be only my second visit since my migration from Karachi, the city of my birth, to a divided India fifty-seven years earlier. And it was taking place a full twenty-six years after my first visit in 1979, as India's Minister of Information & Broadcasting. That was a brief, two-day visit, and confined to Karachi only. Moreover, I had gone alone at the time. Although my wife Kamla is also a Sindhi migrant, having been born and brought up in Karachi, she had never gone back to Sindh after Partition. For our two children, Jayant and Pratibha, and Jayant's wife Geetika, it was their maiden visit to Sindh. Hence, the prospect of visiting Pakistan and reconnecting to our Sindhi roots struck a deep emotional chord in my family.

Since I look upon myself and other migrants of the Partition era as 'victims of history', no less emotional for me had been the idea of facilitating, in my own humble way, to change the history of our subcontinent. Only refugee families can feel the pain of forced separation from their places of birth. After the Partition holocaust, millions of Hindu and Sikh refugee families have been unable to visit their native villages and towns in Pakistan even once. Similarly, millions of Muslim *muhajirs* in Pakistan have vainly dreamt of visiting, at least once in their lifetime, their ancestral homes in UP, Bihar, Delhi, Mumbai, Bhopal, Hyderabad and elsewhere in India.

Therefore, as a political activist I had always nursed a deep desire to do whatever I can to change this unfortunate situation, which has persisted even after the passage of six decades. If Berlin Wall could fall, enabling West and East Germany to become one country; if countries of Europe which fought two bitter World Wars against one another could let their citizens travel freely in Europe; and if North and South Vietnam could erase the boundary between them, why shouldn't India and Pakistan at least learn to live like good neighbours in a tension-free atmosphere? This question had been on my personal 'wish list' for a long time.

The desire to work for normalisation of relations between India and Pakistan was also rooted in my conviction that the BJP, among all the Indian parties, was best-positioned to accomplish this goal. This conviction was reinforced by a memorable conversation that I had with a British diplomat in 1990. Soon after the BJP's spectacular performance in the 1989 parliamentary elections, when our tally in the Lok Sabha shot up from mere two seats in 1984 to eighty-six, I received a call from Sir Nicholas Barrington, who was then Britain's High Commissioner in Islamabad. He said, 'Mr Advani, congratulations on your party's superlative performance. Like me, many international observers of India's political scene now believe that it is only a matter of time before the BJP comes to power at the Centre. I am in New Delhi and would like to call on you.'

I thanked him and invited him to see me at the party headquarters. Sir Nicholas said, 'In the British foreign office, I am regarded as an expert on South Asia. For a long time, I have thought about what is needed for establishing peace and good-neighbourly relations between India and Pakistan. And I have come to the conclusion that this is possible only when there is a strong pro-Hindu party in power in New Delhi and a strong military regime in Islamabad.'

Since this argument sounded curious to me, I asked him: 'Why do you say so?' Sir Nicholas Barrington replied: 'Let me draw a parallel between the hostile India-Pakistan relations and similarly hostile relations that earlier obtained between the United States and China. Before 1972, the two countries were sworn enemies of each other. And yet, the Bamboo Wall came crashing down when President Nixon visited China and shook hands with Chairman Mao in that year. This was possible because there was a strong Republican President in Washington DC, and given the Republicans' traditional antipathy towards China, American people did not feel that Nixon was "selling out". Similarly, there was a strong Communist ruler in China, whose strident tirade against American imperialism in the past was well known. If he took the initiative in normalising China's ties with the US, he would not be suspected by his people of betraying their country's interests.'

'Similarly,' the British diplomat added, 'if a BJP government in India and a well-entrenched military ruler in Pakistan decided to resolve all outstanding issues and make peace between the two countries, they would not be under domestic pressure to look over their shoulders to see if they are being accused of a sell-out.'

I was highly impressed by this argument. Therefore, when the BJP did win the people's mandate in 1998 to govern India as the head of the NDA coalition, and won a renewed mandate in 1999, I felt that our government should do all it can to open a qualitatively new chapter in Indo-Pak relations. Prime Minister Vajpayee felt the same, and as strongly as I did. Accordingly, we formulated a two-pronged policy towards Pakistan: firstly, to make earnest, consistent and patient efforts to normalise relations with Pakistan by seeking to resolve all issues, including the issue of Jammu & Kashmir, through dialogue; and secondly, to maintain a firm and uncompromising stand against cross-border terrorism aided and abetted by both state and non-state players in Pakistan.

It is out of this conviction that Vajpayee undertook his historic Bus Yatra to Lahore in February 1999. It was out of this conviction, and in spite of Pakistan's betrayal in Kargil, that, accepting my suggestion, Atalji invited General Musharraf for a summit meeting in Agra in July 2001. The Agra Summit did not yield any result because India refused to accept General Musharraf's stand on terrorism. Again, it was out of this conviction, and in spite of grave provocations like the terrorist attack on Indian Parliament on 13 December 2001, that our government reopened dialogue with Pakistan. The happy result of these endeavours was the historic Joint Statement issued after the Vajpayee-Musharraf talks on the occasion of the SAARC summit in Islamabad in January 2004. Through this joint statement, Pakistan committed itself, for the first time ever, not to allow any part of its territory, or territory under its control, to be used for terrorist acts aimed against India. I consider this to be one of the greatest achievements in India's diplomatic history. And I fully share Atalji's conviction and optimism that, had we won another term in office, we would have achieved a historic breakthrough in Indo-Pak relations.

Sadly, that was not to be. The Congress-led UPA coalition, headed by Dr Manmohan Singh, replaced the Vajpayee government in 2004, which naturally prompted our friends in Pakistan to wonder whether or not the BJP would continue to support the peace process. Both Atalji and I took the first available opportunity to reassure them that there would be no change in our two-pronged policy towards Pakistan. When President Musharraf visited India in April 2005, I called on him and said, 'Mr President, the last time I had a one-to-one talk with you was when you had arrived in New Delhi in July 2001 *en route* to Agra for the summit meeting. I was in government at the time. I am pleased to meet you again, when I am not in government. In fact, our political adversaries are in government now. But in India, foreign policy is always conducted in such a manner that its broad continuity is not affected by changes in domestic politics. We support the peace process with Pakistan because it is a matter of conviction for us. We are proud of the fact that it was started by our government. Therefore, our support to it will continue, provided Pakistan fulfills its commitment in respect of cross-border terrorism by completely and irreversibly dismantling the infrastructure of terrorism on its soil.'

In my conversation with President Musharraf that day, I also recalled the observations Sir Nicholas Barrington had made to me when he met me in 1990. Shortly thereafter, I received a formal invitation from Foreign Minister Kasuri. I had met him a few times earlier and found him to be a polished and amiable person who was genuinely interested in seeing better India-Pakistan ties. The stage was thus set for my long-yearned yatra to Pakistan from 30 May to 6 June. I was to visit three cities—Lahore, Islamabad and Karachi.

In a press statement issued on 29 May, I said that my visit was intended to contribute to the creation of 'an atmosphere of hope that our two countries will be able to leave behind the hostility of the past six decades and create a new future of peaceful, friendly and cooperative relations befitting two sovereign nations that are more than neighbours connected by a border. We are united by the shared ties of history, culture, religion, race, language and a hoary civilisation. Turning the hope of peace into a reality of lasting peace is no doubt a formidable task. Its fruition requires patience, perseverance, sincerity and trust on both sides. As I embark on my second visit to Pakistan, I pray to God Almighty that He show our two countries the path towards enduring peace.'

On the morning of my departure from Delhi*, my colleagues organised a farewell function at the party headquarters. I explained to them the purpose of my visit by showing how it was a continuation of all that the Vajpayee government had sought to achieve through its two-pronged policy towards Pakistan. The response from my party workers was enthusiastically supportive.

---

* Besides my family, I was accompanied by my party colleague Sudheendra Kulkarni, who was at the time National Secretary of the BJP, and my Private Secretary Deepak Chopra.

SECTION 2

INDIA AND PAKISTAN: SO NEAR, YET SO FAR

Greek culture is no more; so has been the fate of
the Egyptian and the Roman
However India has survived the stresses and strains of time.
There is something in her which defies extinction.
Despite the fact that for centuries, the world has been conspiring
against her.

—Allama Iqbal (who later became Pakistan's national poet)

Our Pakistan International Airlines (PIA) flight took off from Delhi's Indira Gandhi International Airport on the evening of 30 May and, in less than an hour, landed at Lahore's Allama Iqbal International Airport. I was surprised that the journey took less time than it takes to fly from Delhi to Mumbai or to Kolkata. If this was geography's pointer to how close the two cities are, history offers many reminders about the kinship between Delhi and Lahore—and, therefore, between India and Pakistan. It is a kinship rooted in our epics, the *Ramayana* and *Mahabharata*, and has continued in every succeeding era.

Delhi's oldest name is Hastinapur, which was the capital of King Bharat, after whom India has acquired its other name, Bharat. Lahore, similarly, is named after Lav, the son of King Ram. Indeed, there is still a small Lav Temple* inside the Lahore Fort. The fort itself is over 3,000

---

* The original proposal from Chaudhry Shujaat Hussain, former Prime Minister of Pakistan and President of the Pakistan Muslim League (Q), who was my host in Lahore, was that I should inaugurate the Lav Temple located inside the Lahore Fort. However, Shiv Shankar Menon, India's High Commissioner in Pakistan (he later became India's Foreign Secretary), advised me that the 'shrine' was too small and could not be made into a living temple where regular puja could be performed. Thereafter, Shujaat Hussain himself suggested that I should inaugurate the project to restore the Katas Raj temple complex near Lahore.

years old and is believed to have been constructed during the time of the *Ramayana*. It was rebuilt by Emperor Akbar. His grandson Shah Jahan built the Red Fort in Delhi when he shifted the capital of the Mughal empire from Lahore to Delhi. But Shah Jahan also built the sprawling Shalimar Gardens in Lahore, besides a mausoleum for Emperor Jahangir, his father. There is a famous Delhi Gate in Lahore, and a Lahori Gate in Delhi, which is the main entrance to the historic Red Fort. If we bring history closer to our times, Lahore is where Bhagat Singh, one of the most beloved figures in India's freedom struggle, was hanged by the British, along with Rajguru and Sukhdev, his two fellow-revolutionaries. His crime: he had hurled a bomb in the Delhi Assembly building in 1929 to protest against the tyranny of the colonial masters. One of the acts of tyranny that had enraged Bhagat Singh was the martyrdom of Lala Lajpat Rai, a great Indian freedom fighter, in an attack by the British police on a procession of patriots in Lahore in 1928.

Here is another amusing pointer to the kinship between Delhi and Lahore. Sir Ganga Ram Hospital is one of the leading hospitals in Delhi, established in 1954. But it was founded initially in 1921 at Lahore by Ganga Ram, a leading philanthropist and town-planner who has left behind many proud landmarks in the city, including the internationally acclaimed Lahore Museum. The grateful citizens of Lahore had actually built a statue in his honour. What happened to this statue is the subject of a famous story by Saadat Hassan Manto, the renowned Urdu writer. In one of his short stories on the communal riots that broke out in both sides of the Punjab in 1947, Manto describes how a frenzied mob in Lahore first unleashed its fury on a Hindu *mohalla*, and then marched to attack the statue of the Hindu philanthropist. They defaced the statue and hit it with stones. Thereafter a man climbed up the statue to complete the act of desecration by putting a garland of old shoes round the neck of Sir Ganga Ram. Just then the police arrived and opened fire. Among the injured was the person carrying the garland of shoes in his hands. As he fell, the mob shouted: 'Quick, quick. Rush him to Sir Ganga Ram Hospital!'

✱

31 May 2005: Islamabad
MEETING WITH PRESIDENT MUSHARRAF

Although we landed in Lahore, we left for Islamabad the same evening where I was scheduled to meet President Musharraf the following morning. Actually, the meeting took place at Army House in Rawalpindi, the twin-city of Islamabad. Musharraf received us warmly and I thanked him for his government's invitation for me and my family to visit Pakistan. I thanked him also for his highly thoughtful gesture of having presented to me, during his earlier visit to India, an album containing the photos of St. Patrick's High School in Karachi (where we both had studied, I being an alumnus before Partition and he after), the teachers who had taught me, and other memorabilia associated with the school.

On his part, he appreciated that the peace process between India and Pakistan was started by the Vajpayee government and that my party had continued to support it even after the formation of a new government in New Delhi. 'Indeed, when I went to India in April, I made it a point to call on Vajpayee Sahab as a special goodwill gesture,' he said. This prompted me to say: 'Before I left for Pakistan, Vajpayeeji phoned me from Manali, where he is presently holidaying, and extended his best wishes for the visit. He also asked me to convey to you his greetings.' With regard to the peace process with Pakistan, I noted that 'all the people in India, the ruling as well as the Opposition parties, are one.' He said, 'The process has now been taken over by the people of the two countries.'

We both agreed that the peace initiative should be made not only irreversible, but also that it should be taken to its fruition. We were unanimous on the point that there was no military solution to the Kashmir issue and that continuation of dialogue was the only way. I said, 'We can no longer say, "Let us give peace an option." The truth is that peace is the *only* option.' He agreed. 'Out of dialogue alone', we both then said almost in unison, '*Solution nikalega, zaroor nikalega.*' (The solution will come, it certainly will come.)

I then mentioned the obstacles to fruitful dialogue. 'General, it is important to ensure that the process of dialogue continues in an atmosphere of mutual trust and free of violence. In this context, let me tell you that the real breakthrough in Indo-Pak relations came when Prime Minister Vajpayee and you issued a joint statement after your meeting in Islamabad in January 2004. What made the joint statement truly historic was the commitment you made on terrorism. It needed a lot of courage to state what was stated in the joint statement. I compliment you for your courage and for taking this risk.'

Musharraf replied, '*Faujiyon ko sirf jang karani hi nahin aati.*' (It's not true that militarymen know only how to wage war.) A lot could be read into this rather self-congratulatory statement.

It so happened that a delegation of representatives of the APHC was scheduled to visit Pak-Occupied Kashmir later in the same week. When Musharraf mentioned this, I informed him that the Vajpayee government had taken the initiative to hold dialogue with all sections of popular opinion in J&K, including leaders of the APHC, and I myself had had two fruitful rounds of talks with the Hurriyat leaders. I underscored that 'Jammu & Kashmir is very diverse and any eventual solution to the issue will have to be acceptable to all the diverse communities in the state and all sections of opinion within the state.'

I brought up the matter of the need to increase people-to-people contacts between our two countries, especially those from the fields of culture, arts, media and intelligentsia. 'Isn't it odd that, in spite of the popularity of Hindi films in Pakistan, they are not shown in theatres here and that so few of our actors, actresses, singers, etc., including Lata Mangeshkar who is very popular here, are able to visit your country? On our part, we in India have no problems in welcoming your artistes and intellectuals. In fact, we would warmly welcome them.' Musharraf didn't respond to this suggestion directly, but expressed optimism that tourism would get a big boost after the normalisation of relations between our two countries. 'A lot of people from India would like to come to Pakistan to discover tourist attractions in Pakistan, and similarly people from Pakistan would like to go as tourists to India in large numbers.'

The Pakistani President said that, following the opening of the Srinagar-Muzaffarabad bus service, the people in the Northern Areas were also demanding the opening of a bus route between Northern Areas and Kargil. He disclosed that he had ordered his railway authorities to complete the broadgauging of the rail link between Khokrapar (in Sindh province) and Munabao (in Rajasthan) by December. He concurred with my suggestion that the sea link between Karachi and Mumbai, via Gujarat, should be restarted. I brought up the issue of frequent harassment and arrests of Indian fishermen by Pakistani authorities. Musharraf asked his officials to look into the matter and ensure that the boats confiscated from Indian fishermen are returned.

Musharraf asked me about the places I would be visiting in Pakistan and, after hearing my response, said, 'Why are you going only to Karachi? You should take your family to other places in Sindh. I can ask my people to make the necessary arrangements.' I thanked him for the offer, but said, 'God willing, we will come to Pakistan again.'

*

Later in the day, I had meetings with Prime Minister Shaukat Aziz and Foreign Minister Kasuri. I was particularly impressed by Kasuri's passionate articulation of a case for peace and normalcy between India and Pakistan. 'We owe this to our forefathers and also to our future generations,' he said and mentioned an emotional autographical detail: his grandfather, father and uncle were all dedicated freedom fighters in undivided India. They were leading figures in the Congress party and made sacrifices for their participation in the movement against the British rule.

What Kasuri told me about his family's association with the anti-British movement prompted me to make a suggestion, in a speech I delivered at a dinner he hosted for me in the evening. It was, in fact, reiteration of a proposal first mooted by Prime Minister Vajpayee when he addressed the twelfth SAARC Summit in Islamabad in 2004. I said that 2007 would mark the 150th anniversary of undivided India's First War of Independence in 1857. It was a proud milestone in the shared history of India, Pakistan and Bangladesh. I mentioned that it was immortalised by Hindu, Luslim and Sikh martyrs and freedom fighters who hailed all the way from Peshwar to

Dhaka, as attested by the names inscribed in the Cellular Jail in Andaman Islands, where political prisoners were kept in confinement in the colonial era. The forefathers of the people in our three countries had fought side by side against the British rulers, transcending religious, regional and linguistic identities. 'Therefore, one way of reminding ourselves of our shared history, and also of the need to overcome our more recent divisions, is to consider a tri-nation commemoration of the war of 1857.'

The year 2007 is now behind us. Sadly, the government of Dr Manmohan Singh took no initiative to translate this idea into reality.

1 June 2005: Islamabad
VISIT TO TAKSHASILA AND OTHER PLACES

The day began with a thirty-five kilometre drive from Islamabad to the famous archaeological site of Takshasila, a name synonymous with the glory of timeless India. Along with Nalanda, it is where one of the world's greatest centres of learning in ancient times was located. The *Ramayana* mentions that it was founded by Ram's younger brother Bharata, who named it after his son Taksha. It also finds a mention in the *Mahabharata* as the place where Emperor Janamejaya, the great-grandson of Arjuna, ruled. It is in the vicinity of Takshasila, on the banks of river Jhelum, that Emperor Alexander's invasion of India was halted by King Porus in 326 BC. I visited several sites of archaeological excavations that display remnants of Hindu, Buddhist and Jain temples and also structures of a highly evolved urban civilisation. All these facts of a shared history, I felt, are as much a source of pride for Pakistanis as they are for Indians.

Although Takshasila lies in ruins, the government of Pakistan has maintained the museum at the site in an excellent condition. Before leaving, I wrote in the visitors' book at the museum: 'I am delighted to have come to see this great place. Takshasila is a name which evokes memories of the immense height to which our civilisation had once reached.'

Later in the day, I visited the Lok Virsa Museum in Islamabad, which displays the artistic and cultural heritage of Pakistan, dating from the earliest history of undivided India and absorbing the influences of Iran and Central Asia. I have visited many museums in different parts of the world but Lok Virsa is truly unique. It is superb both in its content as well as in its display. For me, it instinctively brings to mind the deep civilisational nexus that has subsisted through the ages between India and Pakistan, and made our joint heritage a priceless gift for humanity and the world. In the evening, I visited the famous Shah Faisal Masjid in Islamabad. I was impressed by its massive size, its picturesque location against a mountainous backdrop, and its unusual architecture with sharp, almost geometric, features.

*

I had several important political meetings that day. The first was with Maulana Fazlur Rehman, head of the Jamiat Ulema-e-Islam and Leader of the Opposition in Pakistan's National Assembly. Rahman had paid a highly publicised visit to India in July 2003, during which he had strongly supported the Vajpayee government's peace initiatives. Significantly, he had also met leaders of the RSS and VHP in New Delhi, in an effort to open new channels of communication. We both agreed that the general atmosphere surrounding the relations between India and Pakistan had changed substantially. 'This has given birth to confidence among the people that the path of dialogue is indeed the right path,' I said. 'Compared to the situation that existed earlier, this new-born confidence itself is a big achievement. So many countries in the world have resolved, through a process of dialogue, the contentious issues that once divided them. I believe that there is no issue between India and Pakistan that cannot be resolved through sincere and sustained dialogue. It may take time. *Lekin baat karte karte hal dikhenge.* The solution will present itself before us if we continue talking without losing our patience.'

Rehman's response was positive. 'Your coming to Pakistan has helped the peace process,' he observed. 'The international situation is changing. It compels India and Pakistan to come closer. Therefore, there is a need to enlarge the channels of communication between our two peoples. We are working closely with the Jamiat Ulema-e-Hind in India for this purpose.'

While in Islamabad, I visited Pakistan's National Assembly building and called on its Speaker, Chaudhary Amir Hussain. Chairman of the Senate, Mohammadmian Soomro, graciously invited me to his house and afforded me an opportunity to interact with many members of the two houses of the country's Parliament. Speaking to media persons, I said, 'The time has come for the formation of a Friendship Association of Parliamentarians of India and Pakistan, on the lines of similar associations between the MPs of India and other countries.' Both Soomro and Hussain welcomed the suggestion.

In the evening, High Commissioner Menon hosted a dinner in my honour and invited some select people from the ruling elite in the Pakistani capital. Among the invitees, apart from Foreign Minister Kasuri, were Makhdoom Amin Fahim* a veteran and widely respected leader of the PPP in the National Assembly; Imran Khan, the legendary cricketer and founder of the Tehreek-e-Insaf party; Barrister Aitzaz Ahsan, a distinguished lawyer, pro-democracy activist, and author of *The Indus Saga* and the *Making of Pakistan*; and Abdul Sattar, who was Pakistan's High Commissioner in New Delhi when I first visited Pakistan in 1979, and later rose to become Foreign Secretary, and still later, Foreign Minister. A revealing conversation ensued at the dinner table. One of the Pakistani guests asked me: 'Advani sahab, you are a Sindhi who migrated to India after Partition. Didn't you face any discrimination when you went there? How did you manage to become the President of one of the largest political parties in India and also, later, the country's Deputy Prime Minister? And why do you think the migrants who came here from India—*muhajirs* as they are still called—have not had the same kind of success in Pakistan?'

It was a sensitive question and I had to be a little diplomatic in answering it. 'You will perhaps be surprised to know,' I said, 'that neither I nor any other migrant—Sindhi, Punjabi or Bengali—ever felt like outsiders, whatever professions we chose for ourselves. This is because

---

* Makhdoom Amin Fahim had emerged as the front-runner for the Prime Minister's post after his PPP won the largest number of seats in the elections to the national assembly held in February 2008.

of the essentially tolerant and integrative character of the Indian society. This is true not only with regard to migrants, but also all the diverse religious, caste, linguistic and ethnic groups in India. I would attribute this character basically to our democratic system of governance and India's national ethos rooted in our culture.'

*

BENAZIR BHUTTO: IN REMEMBRANCE

I would like to make a special mention of my truly memorable meeting with four senior leaders of the PPP earlier on that day. The delegation, which was led by Makhdoom Amin Fahim, comprised Raza Rabbani, Sajjat Bukhari and Sherry Rehman. At the outset, Fahim conveyed to me the best wishes of their party's chairperson, Benazir Bhutto, on my visit to Pakistan. 'All of us in the PPP are happy that the process of dialogue with India which our leader, Mohtarma Benazir Bhutto, started when she was the Prime Minister has now picked up momentum,' he said. I requested him to convey my thanks to Bhutto for her greetings. Both Fahim and I agreed on the need to take the peace process between India and Pakistan forward. 'In order to achieve something important and tangible,' I observed, 'we have to first of all have optimism. And in the context of India-Pakistan relations, we must also have the *confidence* that we can make peace happen. In addition, we need one more thing. Since the issues are of a longstanding nature, both sides also require *patience*.'

Fahim and his colleagues said that the PPP had been consistent in wanting peaceful and friendly relations with India. 'We agree that time is needed for the resolution of certain entrenched issues. Until then, our two countries should try to make progress on other issues in an atmosphere free of tension and hostilities.'

What struck me was the tone of earnestness when Fahim praised the BJP for its 'important contribution to the peace process'. He said: 'If Vajpayee Sahab and you had not put the weight of your authority behind this initiative, it would not have come this far.' His observation prompted me to say: 'In public life, both parties and individual leaders sometimes suffer from an image problem. The public image is often contrary to the reality. Such was the case with the BJP for many years with regard to its approach to Pakistan. People were made to believe that the BJP was anti-Pakistan. It was generally felt that, even if the Congress party tried to improve relations with Pakistan, the BJP would oppose it. However, recent history has shown that it was our party and our government, under the leadership of Shri Vajpayee, which took a bold initiative to normalise relations with Pakistan. We not only started the process, but we also carried it forward upto a major landmark point in January 2004, when Prime Minister Vajpayee and President Musharraf issued the historic Joint Statement about cross-border terrorism.' Our talks concluded with the PPP leaders telling me: 'Your visit to Pakistan has indeed changed the earlier perception about you and your party.'

The meeting was made more memorable by a telephone call I received later in the day from Benazir Bhutto in London. As in all our previous and subsequent conversations, she first greeted me and exchanged pleasantries in Sindhi before saying, 'Advani Sahab, I am so happy that you have come to Pakistan with your family. But I am also unhappy that I am not there to receive you. Nevertheless, I have requested my father-in-law, who lives in Karachi, to invite you and your family to have lunch or dinner at our house when you go there. I have also requested him to take you to our ancestral home in Larkana. It would really please me if you went there and to other nearby places in Sindh.' I thanked her for her wonderful gesture and said that I definitely looked forward to meeting her father-in-law in Karachi. 'As for going to Larkana,' I said, 'it has to wait for another occasion because of my inability to extend my stay in Pakistan.'

✳

As I revisit these lines about Benazir Bhutto in early 2008, I am filled with grief and shock at her assassination, in a gun-and-bomb terrorist attack, in Rawalpindi on 27 December 2007. One of the most popular and charismatic political leaders in the history of Pakistan, she became a martyr to the cause of defense of democracy and the global war on jihadi terrorism. She was a friend of our family and, in spite of some ill-advised steps vis-à-vis India that she took during her two stints as Pakistan's Prime Minister (1988-1990 and 1993-1996), she sincerely desired friendly and peaceful relations between our two countries. As soon as I heard the news of her assassination, I spoke to her husband Asif Zardari, who was then in Dubai and ready to leave for Pakistan, and conveyed my heartfelt condolences to him and their three children.

Speaking to the media later in the evening, I strongly condemned the terrorist attack and said, 'The fact that Benazir Bhutto fell to the assassin's bullets in the midst of national elections in Pakistan should leave no one in doubt that Pakistan is not only in the throes of instability but a far more dangerous process of Talibanisation. The enormously sinister implications of this development for India, in our own fight against jihadi terrorism, cannot be overstated.'

I had first met Benazir in May 1990 when she had come to Delhi to attend Rajiv Gandhi's funeral. Her very first sentence to me, spoken with a warm welcoming smile on her face, was: '*Advani Sahab, tawhansaan ta Sindhiya mein gaalhayoon na?*' (Mr Advani, should we not speak in Sindhi?). I replied in Sindhi: '*Haan, zaroor.*' (Of course.) After a few minutes into the conversation, she said: 'I must confess that I am not as fluent in Sindhi as you are.' Since then, whenever she visited India, she had invariably come to my house for lunch or dinner—she would insist on having Sindhi food—and discussed with me Indo-Pak relations and the problem of terrorism. In between, we presented books to each other through common friends.

I remember an interesting episode from 2001 when she had come to our house for lunch. I discovered that she was a jovial type who liked listening to jokes. Those days, the internet had become a major source of jokes and there were many that made fun of both Indian and Pakistani politicians. I told my daughter Pratibha, who never fails to provide mirth to guests at home with her inexhaustible collection of jokes, 'Why don't you tell Benazir that joke about her?' This is how Pratibha narrated it:

Nawaz Sharif comes to Delhi for a meeting with Vajpayee. After dinner, Vajpayee says to Sharif: 'Well, Nawaz Sahab, I don't know what you think of the members of your Cabinet, but mine are all bright and brilliant.'

'How do you know?' asks Sharif

'Oh well, it's simple', says Vajpayee. 'They all have to take special tests before they can be a minister. Wait a second.... He calls Advani over and says to him, 'Tell me, Advaniji, who is the child of your father and of your mother who is not your brother and is not your sister?'

'Ah, that's simple,' says Advani, 'it is me!'

'Well done, Advaniji,' says Vajpayee. Sharif is very impressed. He returns to Islamabad and wonders about the intelligence of the members of his Cabinet. He calls in his Cabinet Secretary, recounts the dinner-table conversation that he had had with the Indian Prime Minister, and asks him to test the IQ of a particular minister.

The Cabinet Secretary calls in the minister and says: 'The Prime Minister has asked me to ask you to answer the following question: 'Who is the child of your father and of your mother who is not your brother and is not your sister?'

The minister thinks and thinks and doesn't know the answer. 'I'll have to think about it a bit further. Please tell Prime Minister sahab that I'll let him know tomorrow?' 'Of course,' says the Cabinet Secretary, 'you've got twenty-four hours.' The minister goes away, thinks as hard as he can, calls in his chief secretaries and joint secretaries, but no one knows the answer. Twenty hours later, the minister is very worried because he still had no answer and only four hours were left.

Eventually, the minister says to himself: 'I'll ask Benazir. She's clever, she'll know the answer.' He calls Benazir. 'Mohtarma,' he says, 'tell me who is the child of your father and of your mother who is not your brother and is not your sister?'

'Very simple,' says Benazir, 'it's me!'

'Of course,' exclaims the minister and rings up the Cabinet Secretary.

'I've got the answer: it's Benazir Bhutto.'

'No, minister sahab,' says the Cabinet Secretary, 'you'll lose your job if you give this wrong answer. The right answer is: 'Advani!'

Benazir could hardly control her laughter after listening to this joke and told Pratibha, 'Will you please give a printout of it? I want to carry it with me.'

*

The last time I spoke to Benazir was on 18 October 2007, the day of her arrival in Pakistan after many years of exile abroad, to resume her battle for her country's democratisation. Her enemies—only a fair and independent investigation can reveal their identities—had made their intention known on that day itself, since her return to Pakistan coincided with a terrorist attack on her cavalcade in which more than 125 persons were killed. In my reaction to the media on that day, I said, 'It is an irony that, at a time when tall claims are being made about Pakistan's democratisation, one former Prime Minister, Mr Nawaz Sharif, was recently prevented from returning to his own country and another former Prime Minister, Ms Benazir Bhutto, has been "greeted" by a terrorist attack on her arrival. I have always been of the view that Pakistan's stability and progress, as also the normalisation of India-Pakistan relations, are best guaranteed by the establishment of genuine democracy in that country, combined with a resolute fight against religious extremism and terrorism. Last night's shocking incident in Karachi leaves no doubt whatsoever that the battle for democracy and the battle against terrorism are inter-related. I join fellow Indians in conveying our solidarity to the people of Pakistan in this arduous two-pronged battle.'

In my telephonic conversation, I said to Benazir, 'I am gratified that you have escaped this bid on your life. The people of India are with you in your struggle against both military rule and terrorism.' Thanking me for my words of solidarity, she had said: 'Advani sahab, I was not in Pakistan when you came here in 2005. Now that I am back, I would like you to come again as our guest.'

Sadly, a cruel fate awaited her when she came back to her Motherland. I send my best wishes to her son Bilawal Bhutto and other members of the Bhutto family.

2 June 2005: Lahore
RESTORATION OF KATAS RAJ TEMPLE COMPLEX

From Islamabad, we flew in a helicopter to Katas Raj in Chakwal district. Chaudhry Shujaat Hussain, his party colleague Mushahid Hussain and others were already there to receive us. The event that followed will remain indelibly etched in my mind forever. A short car drive took us to the base of a hillock. As I climbed it, I had the feeling of trekking up for a sacred pilgrimage to a Hindu shrine that existed in the past but not in the present. The sun was hot and the terrain rugged. From the top of the hillock, I could see relics of many temples which, even in their decrepit state, were suggestive of a glorious bygone era. For this was not an ordinary site. It has a deep significance for Hindus all over the world. With twelve temples and seven large structures (*satgrahas*) for religious learning, this was one of the most important Hindu pilgrimage centres in undivided Punjab. It also had a hallowed association with an important episode in the *Mahabharata*, as attested by the presence of a tranquil pond* at the bottom of the hillock.

At the end of their twelve-year exile, the Pandavas were wandering in the forest near Katas. As they were thirsty, Yudhishthira (also called Dharmaraja), the eldest of the five brothers, asked Nakula to fetch some water. Nakula, with a quiver in his hand, walked a short distance and found a crystal-clear pond, surrounded by trees. As he tried to enjoy a cool drink himself, he heard a voice: 'Don't touch that water before answering my questions. You will face a dire consequence otherwise.' He ignored the warning, and immediately fell dead. When Nakula did not return, Yudhishthira asked Sahadeva to go and see what had happened. Sahadeva

---

* Legend has it that it was created out of a tear-drop from the eye of Lord Shiva. *Kataksha* in Sanskrit means 'flowing eyes'. Hence the name 'Katas Raj'.

came to the pond and thought that Nakula was lying there asleep. Before waking him up, he wanted to quench his own thirst. He heard the same voice; he too ignored the warning, and fell dead. The same fate awaited Arjuna and Bhima. Finally, a worried Yudhishthira himself went in search of his missing brothers. He was perplexed at what he saw. He thought he could awaken his brothers by sprinkling some water on their faces. But he too heard the same voice, which said: 'I warned your brothers. They did not listen to me and are hence lying there dead. You shall be the fifth victim if you do not answer my questions first.'

Thus began the famous question-answer session between Yaksha and Yudhishthira, replete with moral lessons and philosophical insights. Yaksha's last question was: 'What is the greatest wonder in this world?' Yudhishthira answered: 'Day after day countless people die in this world. Yet, those who remain seek to live forever. This verily is the greatest wonder.'

In a brief ceremony, I unveiled the foundation stone for the commencement of restoration of the entire Katas Raj temple complex. I was told that I was the first Indian political personality since 1947 to have been invited to open a project aimed at reviving Hindu temples in Pakistan. What touched me particularly was Shujaat Hussain's unprompted assurance: 'We do not want the restored temples to become mere tourist attractions. We want them to become living temples, where regular *puja* can take place. And in future I would like to see Hindu pilgrims from India come here in large numbers, as used to happen in the past.' As a matter of fact, he had arranged for me and members of my family to perform puja at a small shrine of Shiva by specially inviting a Hindu from a nearby village to conduct the ritual.

After the ceremony was over, we were taken for a lunch-reception at a nearby village. I was truly overwhelmed by the warmth and affection of the people. It was made memorable by two persons who met me there. One was Yousaf Salahuddin, grandson of Allama Iqbal, the greatest Urdu poet. The other was Raja Mohammed Ali from the village of Gah in Chakwal district, which is the birthplace of Prime Minister Dr Manmohan Singh. Ali, who was his classmate in the primary school in Gah, presented to me, to be given to our Prime Minister, a large photograph of the cluster of Katas Raj Temples. On my return to India, I presented it to Dr Singh.

All this was truly a personal honour. More importantly, it was a gesture of immense symbolic value for the people of India. As I boarded the helicopter to go to Lahore, I felt that I owed a debt of gratitude to Shujaat Hussain, a debt I don't think I'll ever be able to repay.

Since the foundation stone laying ceremony, the government of Pakistan has made considerable progress in implementing the project. A team of archaeologists from Pakistan, which visited India in 2006 to learn about temple design, construction and restoration, called on me. I arranged for them to visit the Akshardham Temple on the banks of the Yamuna in New Delhi, which is arguably the finest Hindu temple to have been built in India in modern times. They told me later that they were immensely impressed.

✱

'LET THERE BE NO PLACE FOR ANTI-INDIANISM IN PAKISTAN, AND NO PLACE FOR ANTI-PAKISTANISM IN INDIA'

My first engagement in Lahore on that day was a function organised by the South Asian Free Media Association (SAFMA). The initiative for this was taken by Najam Sethi, an intrepid and renowned Pakistani journalist, who has maintained close contact with me since then. I was buoyed by the Katas Raj experience in the morning, as also the memories of two memorable days spent in Islamabad, and it showed in my talk at the function. 'I must confess,' I said, 'that I am somewhat at a loss to articulate the totality of my feelings and thoughts after this combined experience.'

I congratulated SAFMA for having emerged, in a short period since its inception in 2000, as a credible platform of journalists belonging to SAARC countries, and for promoting the powerful concept of 'South Asian Fraternity'. It has catalysed an invigorating debate on a wide range of current issues and future possibilities such as the South Asian Free Trade Area (SAFTA), South Asian Customs Union, South Asian Common Currency, South Asian Energy Grid, South Asian Development Bank, South Asian Cooperative Security, South Asian Human Security, South Asian Human Rights Code, and South Asian Protocol for Free Movement of

Mediapersons and Media Products. I strongly endorsed SAFMA's call that read: 'Let a South Asian fraternity benefit from the fruits of the new era of peace in which our people could become the master of their destiny while contributing tremendously to the progress of whole humanity regardless of geography, ethnicity, nationhood, gender, creed and colour. This is a historic moment when the people of South Asia have recognised that their security and well being lies not in inter-state conflict but in their peaceful resolution and cooperation. Let the governments hearken to the call of the people.'

Commenting on the most knotty inter-state conflict in South Asia, namely that between India and Pakistan, I put forward five thoughts:

Firstly, 'I would like all the people of Pakistan to know that neither the BJP nor for that matter, any section of India's polity wishes ill towards Pakistan. Let there be no place for anti-Indianism in Pakistan, and no place for anti-Pakistanism in India.'

Secondly, 'both Indians and Pakistanis have to recognise and respect each other's desire for sovereignty, security, prosperity, unity and territorial integrity of their respective countries. No solution to any of the outstanding issues between India and Pakistan, including the issue of Jammu & Kashmir, can work if it erodes the sovereignty, security, unity and territorial integrity of the two countries.'

Thirdly, 'no solution can work if it is sought through non-peaceful means. (It must be recognised) that terrorism is an enemy of the entire humanity, and can have no protection in any civilised country.'

Fourthly, 'for any mutually acceptable solution to emerge, the ruling establishments and the opposition in both India and Pakistan have to work together in a spirit of consensus.'

Lastly, 'we should proceed in tandem on all the outstanding issues, without letting slow progress on any particular issue become a hurdle in the search for faster progress on other issues. There is no substitute for patience, just as there is no substitute for sustained, uninterrupted dialogue in an atmosphere of mutual trust and one that is free of violence.'

I was pleased when the large gathering of journalists and intellectuals responded to my talk, and also to the free-wheeling Q&A that followed, with a prolonged applause.

The day ended with a dinner hosted by Chaudhry Parvez Elahi, the Chief Minister of Punjab. Thereafter, we were taken on a tour of the Lahore Fort, which looked spectacular at night.

3 JUNE 2005: LAHORE
VISIT TO GOVERNOR'S HOUSE, LAHORE MUSEUM AND NANKANA SAHIB

The Governor's House in Lahore has a special place in the history of the Indo-Pak peace process. It was here that Prime Minister Atal Bihari Vajpayee made a memorable speech during his historic Bus Yatra to Pakistan in February 1999, and read out his celebrated poem *'Jang Na Hone Denge'* (We shall not allow a war to break out). Here I called on Lt. Gen. (Retd.) Khalid Maqbool, the Governor of Punjab. Welcoming me, he said: 'Your visit to Pakistan is a courageous step and it has reinforced the ongoing peace process between India and Pakistan. What you have been saying (after coming to Pakistan) sounds like new hope.' I responded by saying, 'Yes, there is hope on both sides. Now it is our joint responsibility to convert this hope into confidence and resolve, so that the peace process reaches its fruition.'

A well maintained museum is indeed a mirror to the history of a nation. From this perspective, I was truly impressed with the Central Museum in Lahore, one of the finest in Asia. To a discerning visitor, it provides a good glimpse into the various phases of the evolution of Indian civilisation and the many layers of the indivisible heritage of what constitutes today's Pakistan: Vedic, Jain, Buddhist, Islamic, Sikh and British. It was fascinating to look at the remarkable collection of coins from ancient, medieval and modern times. I was particularly awestruck to see the museum's most precious possession: a stone sculpture of the Fasting Buddha, from second century AD. I was, however, pained to see the numerous broken icons of Hindu deities.

After paying obeisance at the gurdwara at Lahore Fort (where we also saw the 'Lav Mandir' and Sheesh Mahal), we flew in a helicopter to visit Nankana Sahib, where Guru Nanak Dev, the founder of Sikh faith, was born in 1469. There are many shrines associated with the memory of Guru Nanak Dev's childhood and youth here. I could also see in them a reflection of the glory of the reign of Maharaja Ranjit Singh (1780-1839), who established a large empire with Lahore as the capital. Since the Sikh tradition has been integral to the upbringing of my family, the visit to Nankana Sahib was indeed a pilgrimage for us, a dream come true.

My only regret, while in Lahore, was that I could not visit the place in Central Jail where Bhagat Singh, along with his two comrades Raj Guru and Sukh Dev, was executed by the British in 1931. I had asked High Commissioner Menon if he could arrange my visit, but he told me that the place has been obliterated in the course of Lahore's urban renewal. It saddened me to know that Pakistan has erased the memory of one of the greatest revolutionary martyrs of united India's liberation struggle.

4 & 5 JUNE 2005: KARACHI

When we arrived in Karachi from Lahore, it was past midnight. All of us in my family were thrilled that we were, at last, in Karachi, in Sindh. The drive from the airport to the guest house, where we would stay, didn't quite whet my appetite to see how the city of my birth was looking. But the next two days would not only show me the Karachi of today, a sprawling megapolis almost unrecognizable from what it was when I left it in 1947, but also take me down history's lane, invoking personal memories and reopening some crucial pages from India's—and Pakistan's—past.

For my family and me, the three most important events in Karachi were the visit to the house where I was born and brought up, the school where I studied and, in the case of my wife Kamla, the *darshan* of Sain Noor Husain Shah, the Sufi saint who specially flew down from Dubai to meet her. So much had changed at the address of my family home—Lal Cottage, Jamshed Quarters—that even the local officials in Karachi had been unable to locate it. I had to give them many landmarks and directions before they found the place. When I went there, I could appreciate their difficulty. For, the spacious single-storeyed bungalow with a large compound, which existed even during my last visit to Karachi in 1978, had become extinct. A migrant Muslim family from Gujarat, which had been living there since 1947, had demolished it and constructed in its place a large multi-storeyed apartment complex. The property had been divided among the sons after the demise of their father.

Nevertheless, one of the sons received us warmly and took us inside his home. Everything inside looked alien to me, but, suddenly, I was delighted to see an old ornately-designed wooden bed in one of the rooms. It was my bed in my childhood.

Similar nostalgia marked my visit to St. Patrick's High School, my alma mater. The school had expanded considerably, but without losing its old-world charm. I was received warmly by its present principal, with a band of uniformed school children playing the welcome tune. As in 1979, the school had organised a special reception for me, but this time it was more elaborate than earlier. I was deeply touched by the affection that the teachers and students showered on me. Their affection was also a manifestation of their goodwill for India. In my thanks-giving speech, I reminisced about my student days, paid tribute to the then principal, Father Modestine, and other teachers (some of whom were alive at the time of my 1978 visit), narrated an interesting incident about how I happened to meet a classmate of mine in Israel in 1995, and, of course, my banter with another famous alumnus of the school who was then the President of Pakistan.

Life becomes an age-defying blessing if one is able to keep one's childhood alive. To me, my first twenty years in Karachi are an ever-living present. The fact that I could once again visit my home (or whatever was left of it) and my school, gave me the feeling of being blessed—indeed, doubly blessed since I was able, this time, to show my near and dear ones where I was born and where I studied.

It is an irony of Indo-Pak relations that, notwithstanding the hostility between our two countries, there are many subterranean aquifers of fraternal emotions that gush forth when people-to-people contacts take place. This, according to me, remains the greatest source of hope that, some day, hostility will become history, leading to the establishment of peaceful, good-neighbourly relations. I could sense this in all my other interactions in Karachi. I visited the historic Sindh Assembly building, where I addressed legislators belonging to the Pakistan People's Party. The lunch hosted by Hakim Ali Zardari, father of Asif Zardari and father-in-law of the late Benazir Bhutto, about which I have made a mention earlier, was a very cordial affair. The next day's lunch was hosted by the Chief Minister of Sindh, Dr Arbab Ghulam Rahim, who belongs to the Muttahida Quami Movement (MQM).

I was particularly touched by the civic reception hosted by the MQM, where, in front of a big gathering of enthusiastic followers, a message of greetings from Altaf Hussain, the party's founder and London-based Chairman, was read out. MQM's main support base is the population of post-Partition Muslim migrants from Uttar Pradesh, Bihar and other Indian states. The fact that they hailed me as a 'messenger of peace' carried its own unique significance. I was also pleased to see that a steady process of harmonisation between Sindhis and *muhajirs* is taking place in recent decades.

Another event that I simply cannot forget to mention is a reception organised by the Hindu Panchayat. The number of Hindus in Karachi has no doubt dwindled to a tiny fraction of the city's current population. Nevertheless, they have managed to prosper and succeed, mainly in what they are traditionally good at—business. Against many odds, they have kept their religious traditions alive and patronised the few temples that still exist in the city. (On a drive along the beach at Clifton, I stopped by to see a small shrine of Lord Shiva facing the sea.) The highlight of the reception was a lively concert of Sindhi folk songs and soulful Sufi *kalaams*. Wearing a traditional Sindhi cap, I, along with Kamla, Pratibha, Jayant and Geetika, joined them on the stage to lend our own voices to the familiar Sindhi tunes. Although this was a function organised by the Hindu community, I was happy to see a large number of prominent Muslims gracing the occasion.

To be honest, my two days in Karachi, as also the previous four days that I had spent in Lahore and Islamabad, had caused an emotional upsurge in me. I felt that, in a modest way, I had achieved something for improving the relations between India and Pakistan—and also for projecting a true image of my party before the world.

Sadly, and totally unexpectedly, one event in Karachi turned out to be controversial.

SECTION 3

ANATOMY OF A CONTROVERSY

The ultimate measure of a man is not where he stands in moments of comfort and convenience, but where he stands at times of challenge and controversy.

—MARTIN LUTHER KING, JR.

Criticism is the heart of democracy, and this heart must always remain in a healthy condition for democracy to maintain its vitality. A politician who dislikes criticism is an autocrat. However, for criticism to vitalise democracy, it should go the extra mile to base itself on full and fair information. Failure to do so can lead to unmerited condemnation, unsubstantiated controversy and, sometimes, even unforeseen consequences. It is at such times that the true character and convictions of the target of the controversy is tested. Does he buckle under pressure? Or does he stand firm?

Much of the controversy about my Pakistan Yatra centred around my visit, while I was in Karachi, to the mausoleum of Quaid-e-Azam Mohammed Ali Jinnah, the country's founder and its first Governor General, and some of my positive remarks about him. As I have mentioned earlier, I had arrived in Karachi in the early hours of 4 June, in what was the last leg of my three-city tour. Being a state guest of the government of Pakistan, my first engagement in the city in the morning was the visit to the impressive white-marbled monument, created in memory of a leader who died (on 11 September 1948), just over a year after he had successfully midwifed Pakistan's birth (on 14 August 1947). In India, too, it is customary for visiting dignitaries, especially state guests, to pay a visit to Raj Ghat, the samadhi of Mahatma Gandhi on the banks of the Yamuna in Delhi. After offering my floral tributes at the Jinnah Mausoleum, I inscribed the following message in the Visitors' Book:

> There are many people who leave an inerasable stamp on history. But there are very few who actually create history. Quaid-e-Azam Mohammed Ali Jinnah was one such rare individual. In his early years, Sarojini Naidu, a leading luminary of India's freedom struggle, described Mr Jinnah as an 'Ambassador of Hindu-Muslim Unity'. His address to the Constituent Assembly of Pakistan on August 11, 1947 is a classic, a forceful espousal of a Secular State in which every citizen would be free to practise his own religion but the State shall make no distinction between one citizen and another on the grounds of faith.
>
> My respectful homage to this great man.

As I came out of the mausoleum on that sunny summer morning, I encountered a large possé of journalists, both Indian and Pakistani, representing the electronic as well as the print media. I told them more or less the same thing that I had written in the Visitors' Book a few minutes earlier. In no time, as I came to know later in the day, TV channels in India had begun flashing what was billed as 'BREAKING NEWS'—'Advani calls Jinnah secular'; 'Advani describes Jinnah as "Ambassador of Hindu-Muslim Unity".' Providing visual proof of the news, they were running non-stop telecast of the video footage of my visit to the mausoleum. Shortly thereafter, they also started broadcasting severe criticism of my remarks by some people within the BJP's ideological fraternity who said, 'A person who glorified a traitor is also a traitor. If Jinnah was secular, why then did Advani have to flee Sindh with his family? The BJP President is showing his true colours.' For the next several days, this news, and the negative reactions it triggered, dominated the newspapers and TV news channels in India. I came to know about the nature and intensity of the criticism on the same evening, when I spoke to some of my party colleagues in Delhi on the phone.

Frankly, much of the initial confusion about my remarks was due to inaccurate media reporting. The media, especially TV channels, have a tendency to focus on breaking news and headlines, and reinforcing the initial message through constant 24x7 repetitions. They ignore, wittingly or unwittingly, historical context, nuance, explanatory arguments and the innate complexity of the issues and personalities involved in the news. As a matter of fact, I had *not* called Jinnah 'secular'. I had only referred to a particular speech of his on an important occasion in the history of Pakistan, and stated that it was 'a classic, a forceful espousal of a Secular State'. Similarly, it was not I who called Jinnah an 'Ambassador of Hindu-Muslim Unity'; it was a tribute paid to him by Sarojini Naidu (1879-1949), a widely respected freedom fighter and the first woman President of the Indian National Congress.

If I had done anything as a conscious act, it was to highlight these two little-known facts of history about Jinnah, and that too from the vantage point of Jinnah's Mausoleum, because I wanted people both in India and Pakistan to know about this aspect of our shared history. I also wanted the people of Pakistan to judge the contrast between Jinnah's vision of a secular state" and its subsequent transformation into a theocratic state that marginalised the minorities.

---

* Aitzaz Ahsan, Pakistan's celebrated pro-democracy leader, begins the preface of the 2005 edition of his book *The Indus Saga: From Patliputra to Partition* (Roli Books) with these words: 'On 4 June 2005, Lal Krishna Advani visited the mausoleum of the founder of Pakistan in Karachi. The inscription (he wrote in the Visitors' Book) raised a storm on both sides of the Indo-Pak divide. On the Pakistani side, there was outrage on why the vision of Jinnah, the Quaid-e-Azam, had been described as secular. On the Indian side extremists took umbrage at why Jinnah, the "communalist", had been referred to as a secularist. Both sides objected to the secular credentials attributed to Barrister Mohammed Ali Jinnah. But, oddly, both attributed different meanings to the same word: secular. On the Pakistani side, the word "secular" is a slur. To a large body of Pakistanis a secular state means one that is against religion: a state at war with religion, any religion; a state that prohibits the practice of religion. How could Pakistan, an "Islamic" state, have been conceived as a secular state? On the Indian side, no one who considered the Muslims as a separate "nation" could have been described as secular. Nor could a state conceived by such a one be considered a secular state. To be secular, a state had itself to be neutral among faiths and have none of its own.'

Contd...

Hurt though I was by the negative reaction at home, I felt it to be my duty to further explain my viewpoint on Jinnah, and the context in which I had expressed it, as clearly and unambiguously as possible through a scheduled speech of mine the following day. I did so while speaking to a distinguished gathering of political personalities, diplomats and intellectuals at a function organised by the Karachi Council on Foreign Relations, Economic Affairs & Law. Let me reproduce a pertinent portion from that speech:

> I have many deeply engraved memories of the first twenty years of my life that I lived in Karachi. I shall recall here only one of them, because the person with which that memory is associated, and the philosophy that I learnt from him in Karachi, have a reverential place in my life.
>
> In the last 3-4 years of my life in Karachi, I came in contact with Swami Ranganathananda, who was the head of the Ramakrishna Math here for six years from 1942 until it was closed down in 1948. I used to go to listen to his discourses on the *Bhagavad Gita*. In later years, I maintained regular contact with this great disciple of Swami Vivekananda, who went on to become the head of the Ramakrishna Math and Mission in India.
>
> Swami Ranganathananda passed away in April this year. The last time I met him was in Calcutta last year. He was 97 but still very agile in mind and radiant in spirit. Our talk, among other things, turned to his years and my years in Karachi. He asked me, 'Have you read Mohammed Ali Jinnah's speech in Pakistan's Constituent Assembly on August 11, 1947? It is a classic exposition of a Secular State, one which guarantees every citizen's freedom to practice his or her religion but the State shall not discriminate between one citizen and another on the basis of religion.'

Contd...

'Jinnah was misunderstood on both sides of the border. So, for once, was Advani. But that was only natural because over the last six decades, neither side has really understood, or even truly tried to understand, the other.'

He said he wanted to read Jinnah's speech again and asked me to send him the full text, which I did.

The reason for my recounting Jinnah's historic speech in the Constituent Assembly is two-fold. Firstly, as I said, it is associated with my last conversation with the Swamiji, who was one of the towering spiritual personalities in India. The second reason is that its remembrance was triggered by my visit to the ancient Katas Raj Temples in Chakwal district four days ago. The Government of Pakistan was kind enough to invite me to lay the foundation stone for a project to restore these temples, which are now in ruins but whose legend is rooted in the epic story of the Mahabharata.

I feel it appropriate to read out the relevant portion from Jinnah's speech.

'Now, if we want to make this great State of Pakistan happy and prosperous we should wholly and solely concentrate on the well-being of the people, and specially of the masses and the poor. If you will work in cooperation, forgetting the past, burying the hatchet, you are bound to succeed. If you change your past and work in a spirit that every one of you, no matter to what community he belongs, no matter what relations he had with you in the past, no matter what is his colour, caste or creed, is first, second and last a citizen of this State with equal rights, privileges and obligations, there will be no end to the progress you will make.

I cannot overemphasise it too much. We shall begin to work in that spirit and in course of time all these angularities of the majority and minority communities, the Hindu community and Muslim community...will vanish. Indeed, if you ask me, this has been the biggest hindrance in the way of India to attain its freedom and independence and but for this we would have been free people long ago.

Therefore, we must learn a lesson from this. You are free, you are free to go to your temples. You are free to go to your mosques or to any other places of worship in this State of Pakistan. You may belong to any religion or caste or creed; that has nothing to do with the business of the State.... *You will find that in course of time Hindus will cease to be Hindus and Muslims would cease to be Muslims, not in the religious sense, because that is the personal faith of each individual, but in the political sense as citizens of the State.*'

What has been stated in Jinnah's speech—namely, equality of all citizens in the eyes of the State and freedom of faith for all citizens—is what we in India call a Secular or a Non-Theocratic State. There is no place for bigotry, hatred, intolerance and discrimination in the name of religion in such a State. And there can certainly be no place, much less State protection, for religious extremism and terrorism in such a State.

I believe that this is the ideal that India, Pakistan as well as Bangladesh—the three present-day sovereign and separate constituents of the undivided India of the past, sharing a common civilisational heritage—should follow. I hope that this ideal is implemented in its letter and spirit. The restoration of the Katas Raj Temples is a good beginning.

Esteemed friends from Karachi, people often ask me: 'Does this mean that you want to undo the Partition?' My answer is: 'The Partition cannot be undone.... However, some of the follies of Partition can be undone, and they must be undone.' I dream of the day when divided hearts can be united; when divided families can be reunited; when pilgrims from one country—Hindus, Muslims, Sikhs—can freely go to holy sites located in the other country; and when people can travel and trade freely, while continuing to remain proud and loyal citizens of their respective countries.*

NOT AN EXERCISE IN IMAGE-MAKEOVER

In the weeks and months following my visit to Pakistan, there was heated debate in the Indian media about Jinnah and his role in India's freedom

---

* See Appendix V for the full text of my speech in Karachi.

movement. Suddenly, an important historical figure, who had virtually disappeared from the arena of political debate in India, had come alive. And because of the controversy generated by my Pakistan visit, there was widespread confusion, speculation and misgivings about why I, of all the persons, had chosen to cause this 'resurrection' of Jinnah in the national consciousness. Had I done it for opportunistic reasons? Had I done it for reasons of an 'image makeover'? And what exactly do I think of Jinnah? An impression had been created that, after my return from Pakistan, I had begun to endorse *everything* that Jinnah said or did in his lifetime. This impression was baseless, misleading and false. Like any patriotic Indian, I continue to have serious reservations about the totality of Jinnah's role in India's freedom movement.

Amongst all the leaders involved in India's freedom struggle, Jinnah must bear the largest share of blame for the tragedy of Partition. For it was his fanatical resolve, his tenacious personality, and his skillful and communally-inspired manipulation of the separatist mindset that helped the Muslim League mobilise large-scale mass support for its demand for the division of India and creation of a separate 'Muslim Nation' called Pakistan. At crucial stages in the final phase of the struggle against the British, he showed brinkmanship that unleashed the violent impulse in the Muslim League's demand for Partition. An example of this was the League's call for Direct Action Day (16 August 1946). It heralded what came to be known as 'the Week of the Long Knives', in which over 6,000 innocent people, mostly Hindus, were massacred in Calcutta.

It was Jinnah who lent the cutting edge to the Muslim League's untenable claim that it was the sole spokesman for the Muslim community in India in negotiating its future with the British rulers. For this reason, he doggedly refused to consider the Congress party a national party. Addressing a meeting in Patna in 1938, he said: 'The Congress is nothing but a Hindu body. That is the truth and the Congress leaders know it. The presence of a few Muslims, the few misled and misguided ones, and the few who are there for ulterior motives, does not and cannot make it a national body. I challenge anybody to deny that the Congress is not mainly a Hindu body.' It was Jinnah who lent not only his support but also intellectual rationalisation to the Muslim League's specious Two Nation theory, by stating: 'There is nothing common between Hindus and Muslims. The two are different cultures, different races, different nationalities and they have different histories.'

Nevertheless, Jinnah's negative side as the moving spirit behind the Partition movement should not blind us to a totally different aspect of his personality that was the driving force of his political career until mid-1930s. He joined the Indian National Congress in 1896, and came under the influence of the widely respected moderate leader Gopal Krishna Gokhale (whom, incidentally, Gandhiji had accepted as his political guru). Jinnah regarded Gokhale as his role model, and even expressed his ambition to become the 'Muslim Gokhale'. As a young and promising lawyer in Bombay, he served as defence counsel for Lokmanya Bal Gangadhar Tilak in his sedition trial in 1905.

Jinnah joined the All India Muslim League in 1913 to strengthen the moderate, nationalist opinion within the Muslim community. The 1916 Lucknow Pact that he signed as the President of the Muslim League with Lokmanya Tilak, who represented the Congress party, remains a high point in the Indian people's united struggle against colonial slavery. Speaking in the Legislative Assembly Debates in 1925, he declared: 'I am a nationalist first, a nationalist second, a nationalist last.' Dr K.M. Munshi writes in *I Follow the Mahatma:* 'Jinnah of those days was a thorough-bred nationalist. He captured the Muslim League in the interest of nationalism and worked for the Lucknow Pact. He had not then come to love the community before the nation.'

'Are we Indians first or Hindus and Muslims first?' This question continues to dominate mass-level debates on our nationalism even sixty years after India's independence. It is instructive to see how Jinnah, in the early nationalist phase of his life, dealt with this question. The Raja of Mahmudabad recounts an interesting meeting he had, when he was twelve years old, with Jinnah in Lucknow in 1926. 'I had just returned from school when my father took me to meet him and we sat talking on the terrace.... He called me to his side and asked me about my studies. Then came the question, "What are you, a Muslim first or an Indian first?" Although I had hardly understood the implications of the question at that age, I replied, "I am a Muslim first and then an Indian." To this Jinnah said in a loud voice, "My boy, no, you are an Indian first and then a Muslim".[1]

These days, there is a lot of debate about whether there should be religion-based reservations for Muslims. The Congress party is actively supporting this blatantly divisive demand. It is useful to recall what Jinnah thought about this matter. Speaking at the historic Calcutta session of the AICC in 1905 (in which, incidentally, he condemned the division of Bengal by Lord Curzon, saying that it was aimed at breaking the Hindu-Muslim unity in India), he said: 'I wish to draw your attention to the fact that the Mohammedan community should be treated in the same way as the Hindu community. The foundation upon which the Indian National Congress is based is that there should be no reservation for any community.'

Jinnah's secular approach to political issues led him to oppose the Khilafat movement (1919–24), which was a political campaign launched by Muslims in India to pressure the British government and to protect the Caliphate or the Islamic system of governance in the Ottoman Empire after the First World War. Speaking at the Lahore session of the Muslim League in 1923, Jinnah said, 'I am almost inclined to say that India will get a Dominion Responsible Government the day the Hindus and Muhammadans are united. Swaraj is an almost interchangeable term with Hindu-Muslim unity.'

What turned a staunch nationalist like him into a communalist and a separatist? The most persuasive answer that I have found for this question was given by Mohammed Currim Chagla, eminent jurist, judge, diplomat and a minister in Indira Gandhi's Cabinet, who has figured prominently earlier in this book as the special guest at the BJP's inaugural conference in Bombay in 1980. Chagla as a young lawyer was closely associated with Jinnah as his junior in the Bombay High Court. His fascinating autobiography *Roses in December* sheds much light on the personality of Jinnah and also on Chagla, who was himself in the Muslim League before parting ways with his mentor. He writes[2]:

The Muslim League in those days believed in the cause of Hindu-Muslim unity and was entirely a secular institution, except for the name. People like Jinnah and Mazrul Haq, who belonged to the League, had no truck with the fanatical Muslims whom the Khilafat movement had thrown up. I have always felt that Gandhiji was wrong in trying to bring about Hindu-Muslim unity by supporting the cause of the Khilafat. Such unity was built on shifting sands. So long as the religious cause survived, the unity was there; but once that cause was removed, the unity showed its weakness. All the Khilafatists who had been attracted to the Congress came out in their true colours, that is, as more devoted to their religion than to their country. The Muslim League wanted to fight this element and to make common cause with the secular Congress.

So long as Jinnah remained a nationalist and the Muslim League continued its old policy, I remained with Jinnah and also with the League. But as soon as Jinnah became communal-minded and started his two-nation theory, I parted company with both him and with the League. The evolution of Jinnah from a national to a communal leader remains an enigma. To me, it was inconceivable that Jinnah should ever have come to be the main architect of Pakistan. His nationalism was so genuine, so instinctive, so abiding that to expect that he should swing so violently from one direction to a diametrically opposite direction, seemed to me to be contrary to ordinary expectations about human nature.

Why did Jinnah change? There could be many possible explanations for this. Jinnah's besetting fault was his obsessive egoism. He had to be a leader, and the prime mover in whatever cause he worked. With the emergence of Gandhiji in Indian politics, Jinnah felt that his importance would gradually diminish. Jinnah was the complete anti-thesis of Gandhiji. While Gandhiji believed in religion, in abstract moral values, in non-violence, Jinnah only believed in hard practical politics.... Unfortunately, Jinnah was also antipathetic to Jawaharlal Nehru. These two were never on the same wave length.

One day, a few months after my return from Pakistan, Dr Ajeet Jawed, a political scientist from Delhi University came to present a book to me. The title of her well-researched and meticulously referenced book was *Jinnah: Secular and Nationalist**. 'I have come to convey my appreciation of your observations about Jinnah,' she said. 'In fact, I have mentioned it in my work.' I was amazed to read in this book that Jinnah felt 'homesick' *after* he created Pakistan.

> Jinnah's 'homesickness' in Pakistan was at least partly due to the house he had left behind in Mumbai†. Sri Prakasa, who was India's first High Commissioner to Pakistan, writes, 'Jinnah's heart was not in his Government House in Karachi but in Malabar Hill at Bombay.' When Sri Prakasa told him that the Indian Government was seeking requisition of his house, he was taken aback and almost pleadingly said to him: 'Sri Prakasa, don't break my heart. Tell Jawaharlal Nehru not to break my heart. I have built it brick by brick.... You do not know how much I love Bombay. I still look forward to going back there.'

---

* Dr Ajeet Jawed's widely acclaimed book also informs that 'Maulvis and Maulanas were deadly against Jinnah's concept of Pakistan. When Pakistan had been agreed to, Jinnah was asked at a press conference in New Delhi on 14 July 1947, whether Pakistan would be a theocratic state. Jinnah reacted sharply and replied, "You are asking me a question that is absurd; I do not know what a theocratic state means"'. (Faizbooks.com, 2005, pp. 356-7)

† It is an irony of history that Jinnah's grandson, Nusli Wadia, a prominent Bombay-based Indian businessman, became a staunch supporter of the Bharaitya Jana Sangh and, later, the BJP. Through Nanaji Deshmukh, a veteran leader of the RSS and the Jana Sangh, Nusli came in close contact with Atalji and me, and our relationship has endured over the years. Jinnah had married Rattanbai (Ruttie), the only daughter of Sir Dinsha Petit, one of Bombay's wealthiest Parsi businessmen. Their daughter, and Nusli's mother, Dina wedded Neville Wadia, against the wishes of Jinnah, who disowned her for not marrying a Muslim. 'Jinnah House', the palatial bungalow that Jinnah had built in Malabar Hill in Bombay is now claimed by Nusli Wadia. As an amusing aside, I may mention here that when I launched the Ram Rath Yatra in 1990 to mobilise support for the construction of a Ram Temple in Ayodhya, some of my critics tried to deride me by saying, 'What kind of Ram Bhakt (Ram's devotee) is Mr Advani when one of his close friends happens to be the grandson of the founder of Pakistan?'

Sri Prakasa then asked Jinnah, 'May I tell the Prime Minister that you are wanting to be back there?' The reply given by the creator of Pakistan was: 'Yes, you may.'*

Dr Jawed also writes in her book: 'He (Jinnah) was sad and sick. He cried in agony, "I have committed the biggest blunder in creating Pakistan and would like to go to Delhi and tell Nehru to forget the follies of the past and become friends again".'

*

I have given this rather lengthy description of the two personas of Jinnah just to submit to the readers that we should have a holistic and unprejudiced view of history and historical personalities. As I have indicated above, Jinnah was definitely guilty of having played the lead role in the vivisection of India. And that is how he will be mainly remembered by all those who view the Partition of India to be an unmitigated tragedy.

---

* Sri Prakasa, the Indian High Commissioner to Pakistan, also records that Jinnah intended to make Pakistan a secular state. (*Pakistan : Birth and Early Years*, Meenakshi Prakashan, 1965, pp. 83-84)

15

I Have No Regrets

When you have decided what you believe, what you feel must be done, have the courage to stand alone and be counted.

—Eleanor Roosevelt

When I first learnt, while still in Karachi, about the storm generated by my visit to Jinnah's mausoleum and my remarks about him, I asked my staff to send the complete text of Jinnah's speech in the Constituent Assembly of Pakistan, which projected the vision of a Secular State, to my party colleagues in Delhi. The next day, on 5 June 2005, I also had an advance copy of my own speech at the Karachi Council on Foreign Relations, Economic Affairs & Law, in which I had elaborated on the context and purpose of my reference to Jinnah's speech, sent to the party headquarters.

As a matter of fact, it was not for the first time on a public platform that I had referred to Jinnah's vision of a secular Pakistan. On 28 February 2004, the India First Foundation, established by my colleague Dinanath Mishra, had invited me to release one of its publications, *Dialogue With Pakistan* by Prof. S.G. Kashikar. Mishra, a prominent Hindi journalist, has had a long and close association with the RSS leadership. The function held at my residence was attended by many senior personalities from the party and Sangh Parivar organisations, and well covered by the media. Indeed, I had begun my rather comprehensive speech* on the occasion by mentioning my last meeting with Swami Ranganathananda in Calcutta a few months earlier and our discussion about Jinnah's address to the Constituent Assembly of Pakistan. I had extensively quoted from his speech while presenting my own thoughts on secularism and normalisation of Indo-Pak relations. Therefore, at least to many of my colleagues in my political and ideological fraternity, the specific context in which I had made an appreciative reference to Jinnah could not have been unfamiliar.

I could well understand if some ordinary people had felt surprised, and even upset, at seeing headlines in TV news bulletins or newspapers that said: 'Advani calls Jinnah secular'. But what pained me is that some people thought that I had committed a serious ideological heresy even before acquainting themselves with full facts and background information. Therefore, even before I boarded the Pakistan International Airlines' flight back to Delhi on the morning of 6 June, I had decided, with an anguish-filled heart, to resign from my position as President of the BJP.†

---

* The full text of my speech at the function organised by the India First Foundation on 28 February 2004 is available in a pictorial booklet, published by the BJP in 2005, on the renovation of the Hindu temples in Katasraj in Pakistan.

† I must place on record here that Atal Bihari Vajpayee and Jaswant Singh, among several other party colleagues, stood by me on my Jinnah remarks. The *Tribune* reported on 7 June 2005: 'Making a statement at Bhunter airport, Mr Vajpayee (who was returning to Delhi from his holiday in Manali) backed Mr Advani's statement on Pakistan. The former Prime Minister said that "his remarks on Jinnah are being misinterpreted"'. Similarly, Rediff.com reported on 9 June 2005: 'Advani received a shot in the arm when former External Affairs Minister Jaswant Singh sent him a message from Israel, where he is on tour, saying that he fully agreed with the statement of Advani on Jinnah. "That Jinnah was secular is a historical fact," Singh is supposed to have said in that message.'

Among those who stood by me was also His Holiness Shri Vishvesha Teerth Swamiji of Pejavar Math, Udupi, Karnataka. In a press statement on 16 June 2005, he said, 'I am in New Delhi after attending a two-day meeting (14-15 June) of the Kendriya Margdarshak Mandal of the Vishwa Hindu Parishad, which was held in Haridwar. I

Contd...

I submitted my resignation on 7 June. I told my colleagues that I would not like to head the party if I did not enjoy their full trust and confidence. It would not be an exaggeration to say that I was upset. However, my resignation was not accepted by the BJP's parliamentary board and central office-bearers, who, in a meeting on 8 June, unanimously adopted a resolution urging me to continue leading the party, 'which he has so ably led in the past'. It also stated: 'Shri Advani represents the best values in public life. He has scholarly articulated the debate on nationalism in the past few decades with rationality, logic and with powerful idioms. His contribution to our ideology is unparalleled. The party has benefited enormously from his leadership and needs his leadership in the future also. The party strongly condemns the use of highly objectionable language by some leaders of the VHP about Shri Advani. These statements have lowered the level of public discourse. Such outbursts, indecent protests and abusive language adversely affects the strength of the nationalist movement in the country. These statements also go against the very ethos of Hinduism.'

Meeting again on 10 June, the same body, now also joined by the Chief Ministers of party ruled states, issued the following statement:

> The Bharatiya Janata Party lauds the path-breaking visit to Pakistan by its president, Shri LK Advani. The week-long tour has brought the people of India and Pakistan closer, helped remove a mountain of misunderstandings between them and taken the momentum of better relations to a new level, in continuation of the policy of friendship initiated by successive governments led

---

Contd...

opposed the VHP's resolution on Shri Advaniji's recent visit to Pakistan. The resolution demanded that the BJP President quit his post and take "political sanyas". As one of the founder members of the VHP, I deem it to be my duty to oppose both the content and language of the resolution.... Use of such language to deride a widely admired leader like Shri Advani, who has a long record of service to the Nation and also the Hindu cause, has bewildered the Hindu society. I call upon my colleagues in the VHP to abandon extremist positions, which go against the grain of Hindu culture and ethos, and project a wrong and unflattering image of the Hindu movement in the eyes of the international community.'

by Shri Atal Bihari Vajpayee. The warm and enthusiastic response Shri Advani's visit elicited from both the officials and ordinary people of Pakistan proves the correctness of the NDA's policy of pursuing good neighbourly ties between the two countries.

The party is happy to note that Shri Advani raised the issue of cross-border terrorism with the President of Pakistan and impressed upon him the need to immediately dismantle the infrastructure of terrorism and bring cross-border terrorism to an end. Shri Advani emphasized that lasting peace in South Asia would be possible only when such issues were satisfactorily resolved between India and Pakistan.

The BJP appreciates the Pakistan Government's invitation to Shri Advani to inaugurate a project for the restoration of Katasraj Temples, revered by all Hindus of the Indian subcontinent as a resting place of the Pandavas. The overwhelming response to his Katasraj visit could well go down as a turning point in removing long-held misgivings between the people of the two countries. The BJP hopes that Pakistan will progress further along this path and ensure that the rights of Hindus and other religious minorities are fully protected and that official initiatives to restore and develop other mandirs and gurudwaras continue in the future.

Shri Advani welcomed the event in Katas Raj as a good beginning and in that context without describing Mr. Jinnah as secular, reminded the people of Pakistan of it's founder's address to the country's Constituent Assembly in which he had urged full freedom of faith for all its citizens and no discrimination between its citizens on grounds of religion.

The BJP reiterates that whatever may have been Jinnah's vision of Pakistan, the state he founded is theocratic and nonsecular, the very idea of Hindus and Muslims being two separate nations is repugnant to it. The BJP has always condemned the division of India on communal lines and continues to steadfastly reject the two-nation theory championed by Jinnah and endorsed by British colonialists. There can be no revisiting the reality that Jinnah led a communal agitation to achieve his goal of Pakistan, which devoured thousands of innocent people in its wake and dispossessed millions of their homes and livelihoods.

During the same period, I also received anguished messages from state-level colleagues and *karyakartas* from all over the country, all appealing that I withdraw my resignation. I did so, bowing to the collective wish of my colleagues and also in the best interest of the party.

Many people in Pakistan, who had interacted with me during my visit, were bewildered by the controversy that had broken out in India. Here is a revealing comment by Hamid Mir, a renowned Pakistani journalist, who had interviewed me for GEO TV*.

> L.K. Advani gave two shocks to Pakistan. First was in Islamabad when he claimed in an interview with me that he did not hate Pakistan and he respected Muhammad Ali Jinnah. When his interview was aired by Geo TV many Pakistanis thought that he was lying and he would change his statement after going back to India. Advani repeated his statement about Jinnah again and again in Pakistan. He gave another shock by resigning from the presidentship of the BJP after going back to Delhi and surprised all those who thought that he would change his stance very soon. He is still a hot subject for newspaper columns and editorials in Pakistan. I asked a visiting Indian Cabinet Minister, Mani Shankar Aiyer, for his reaction to Advani's resignation. *Aiyer said, with a smile on his face, 'I am not bothered about him, he is politically dead.'* When Aiyer's reaction was aired on TV, many viewers called me and suggested that I must organise a discussion on the resignation of Advani. I invited Mirwaiz Omer Farooq, the young

---

* One of the questions that Hamid Mir had put to me was: 'What is the difference between yesterday's Advani and today's Advani?' My reply: 'I can claim that what I am today, I was yesterday. I have not changed. I am a misunderstood person in Pakistan. I think that a modern and prosperous Pakistan is in the interest of India. I don't hate Pakistan.' (Rediff.com, 6 June 2005)

separatist Kashmiri leader visiting Pakistan these days, and Sheikh Rashid Ahmed, the federal information minister in 'Capital Talk' on Geo TV. We discussed Advani for 40 minutes. *I was surprised when both of them supported Advani and expressed the hope that he is a man of principles and he will come out of the political crisis very soon.* The young Kashmiri separatist leader said that actually it was Advani who started dialogue with Hurriyat two years ago when he was in the government. *Farooq said that Pakistanis have discovered his soft face recently, but Kashmiris discovered his soft face two years ago.* (emphasis added)

※

'ONE MUST STAND BY ONE'S CONVICTIONS'

Unfortunately, this did not put an end to the turbulence. One day, in the middle of 2005, I was told that I should step down from presidentship of the BJP by the year-end after the conclusion of the party's ongoing silver jubilee commemoration.

All this was profoundly agonising for me. I was in a dilemma. What should I do? How should I respond to this situation? Never in my political life was I enamoured by any post or the power that supposedly came with it. I had not desired to become President of the party once again; on the contrary, I had made it known to all who mattered that another member of the party's younger leadership should take the baton from Venkaiah Naidu when he stepped down in October 2004. I had agreed to assume the organisational responsibility only because of the insistence of my colleagues. My predicament often made me wonder if it wasn't time for me to embrace the peace and comfort of a quiet family life, which had eluded me for so long. My state of mind was not quite unlike that of the unsure Arjuna on the battlefield.

But every time the thought of escapism entered my mind, I was reminded of Lord Krishna's instruction to Arjuna. I gave expression to my thoughts in a speech I delivered while releasing a book *Bhagavad*

Gita: Timelessly Pertinent By Lt. Gen. (Retd.) Surrinder Kochar at a function at my residence on 15 June 2005. 'There is one passage in the book that particularly caught my attention,' I said. 'I must confess that it gave me strength in the situation I find myself in today after returning from my recent visit to Pakistan. 'Is there any need for the study of the *Bhagavad Gita* in our modern times?' the author asks, and also provides the answer: 'The inner shattering of the psychological personality in man is projected out so vividly in the characterisation of Arjun that in the *Bhagavad Gita*, the Pandava Prince represents the confused man of the world—the disillusioned youth of all times. The case-history of Arjun is recorded with scientific precision in the opening chapter of the *Gita*. He is represented as an enthusiastic soldier who had reached this benumbing state of utter dejection. In such a state of dejection, an intelligent man-of-action discovers in himself many a logical argument, each one apparently righteous, to convince himself that he should run away from the field of his duty and positive action. This sense of escapism is detrimental to any great achievement. The exhortation given by Krishna to Arjun, which is also the eternal mantra given by the *Gita* to anyone facing a challenge, is this: One must stand by one's convictions.'[1]

The BJP held a crucial meeting of its National Executive in Chennai on 18-19 September 2005. Before concluding my speech at this session, I made a statement*, which I regard as one of the most important in my political life. I said: 'I deem it a proud privilege that while the first session of the BJP in 1980 was presided over by Shri Atalji, the party's silver jubilee session being held this December at Mumbai is going to be presided over by me. I had accepted this responsibility as party President in October 2004 because Shri Venkaiahji had some personal problems. I have decided, however, that after the Mumbai session, I shall demit office, and the party's stewardship should be taken over by some other colleague.'

The BJP held a special session of the National Council in Mumbai on 28-30 December 2005 to mark the conclusion of the silver jubilee year. It was the last such session that I presided over. I had no regrets and no disappointments. I had the satisfaction of having served my party dutifully

---

* The full text of this statement is given as an appendix.

and conscientiously—and the determination to continue to do so in the future. In Mumbai, I passed on the baton to Rajnath Singh.

INDIA TODAY'S NEWS MAKER OF THE YEAR 2005

For one who is by no means unfamiliar with the ups and downs in one's political life, 2005 saw me remain stoic in the face of adversity. Many BJP-watchers, who probably expected me to retract my statements, noted that I did not do so. Several senior Congress leaders came to me and said, 'Advaniji, we may have had differences with you in the past. We admired you even then. But now we respect you. We cannot even imagine this kind of debate taking place in our party and yet the party remaining united.'

The intense controversy surrounding my Pakistan trip made leading news magazine *India Today* identify me as the NEWS MAKER OF THE YEAR 2005. Its issue dated 16 January 2006 had a cover story on this event. Editor-in-Chief Aroon Purie observed: 'Winston Churchill once defined a fanatic as a person who won't change his mind and can't change the subject. BJP leader L.K. Advani, the creator of the Hindutva movement, has often been labeled as a Hindu fanatic. Well, this fanatic decided to change his mind and change the subject for his party during his Pakistan visit in June last year. Advani declared at Mohammad Ali Jinnah's mausoleum: "His (Jinnah's) address to the Constituent Assembly of August 11, 1947, is really a classic and forceful espousal of a secular state…." It created instant headlines back home and sent shockwaves through the entire political system. It was absolute blasphemy for his party, more so for its mother organization, the RSS. It was almost as if the Pope had converted to Islam. Advani was called a "turncoat" and accused of "fostering a personality cult".'

In the special interview with me taken for this issue Purie and his senior colleague Prabhu Chawla asked me:

Q: 2005 was not a good year for you. Any other regrets?

A: No. If I look at it from a distance, I feel sure it was one of my best years. When I look back, I identify two landmark events in my entire political career: First, the Rath Yatra from Somnath to Ayodhya, Second, the six-day trip to Pakistan. And I can tell you that both, during the Rath Yata and during the six days I was in Pakistan, I had a feeling I was making history. The Rath Yatra yielded immediate dividends for the party. As for the Pakistan trip, a few years down the line there will be people who will think that what Advani did then had strengthened his cause, his party and raised his esteem in the people's eyes.

I continue to hold the view that I had expressed in the *India Today* interview.

*

I thank all those who welcomed my Pakistan visit and also commend all those who converted the controversy into one of the most educative public debates in recent times on a crucial period in the history of India's freedom movement. According to me, this debate is not about the past; it is about the future, in the light of the lessons from the past. For the issue that should be discussed is not so much Jinnah, but the future of Indo-Pak relations in the context of a new vision of peace, inter-religious harmony, and inter-state cooperation in all of South Asia. Let us develop a new mindset for reconciliation, both within and between our countries, without compromising on our principles. Let us not remain prisoners of the past. Rather, let us solve the problems of the present in order to seize the immensely beneficially possibilities of the future for the one-fifth of humanity that resides in South Asia.

16

ATAL BIHARI VAJPAYEE: A STATESMAN WITH A POETIC SOUL
A Tribute to Atal Bihari Vajpayee

Haar nahin manoonga, Raar nayi thanoonga,
Kaal ke kapaal par likhata-mitaata hoon, Geet naya gaata hoon

(I shall never accept defeat; Ever shall I get ready for a new battle; I am he who erases old things and writes new things on the forehead of Time; I sing a new song)

—ATAL BIHARI VAJPAYEE

If I have to single out one person who has been an integral part of my political life almost from its inception till now, one who has remained my close ally in the party for well over fifty years, and whose leadership I have always unhesitatingly accepted, it would be Atal Bihari Vajpayee. Many political observers have noted that it is not only rare but, indeed, unparalleled in independent India's political history for two political personalities to have worked together in the same organisation for so long and with such a strong spirit of partnership. In the *Prologue* to this book, I have referred to a photograph of Atalji, Bhairon Singh Shekhawat and myself, taken in Rajasthan in 1952. It was reproduced by a Hindi daily, along with a similar-looking photograph of the three of us in 2003, with a common caption: 'Working Together, For Over A Half-Century'. I regard this long comradeship with Atalji a proud and invaluable treasure of my political life.

FIRST IMPRESSION, LAST IMPRESSION

I first met Atalji in late 1952. As a young activist of the Bharatiya Jana Sangh, he was passing through Kota in Rajasthan, where I was a *pracharak* of the RSS. He was accompanying Dr Syama Prasad Mookerjee on a train journey to popularise the newly formed party. Atalji was Dr Mookerjee's Political Secretary those days. Looking back, the image I recall most vividly is that of a young and intense-looking political activist, nearly as lean as myself, although I looked leaner because I was taller. I could easily tell that he was imbued with youthful idealism and carried around him the aura of a poet who had drifted into politics. Something was smouldering within him, and the fire in his belly produced an unmistakable glow on his face. He was twenty-seven or twenty-eight years old then. At the end of this first tour, I said to myself that here was an extraordinary young man, and I must get to know him.

Atalji became the Founder-Editor of *Panchajanya*, a nationalist weekly in 1948, and as its regular reader, I was already familiar with his name. Indeed, I had been much influenced by his powerful editorials and some of his poems that the journal published from time to time. The journal was also my introduction to the thoughts of Pandit Deendayal Upadhyaya, who had launched it in Lucknow under the auspices of Rashtradharma Prakashan, a publisher of nationalist literature. I later learnt that, along with Atalji, he used to perform multiple roles in the weekly: a regular contributor who wrote under many pseudonyms, proofreader, compositor, binder and manager. For someone like me, who had recently learnt Hindi, *Panchajanya* was a useful introduction to the innate beauty and purity of the language, as also to its immense capacity to convey patriotic inspiration.

Sometime later, Atalji came alone on a political tour of Rajasthan and I accompanied him throughout his journey. It was during this trip that I got to know him better, my second impression about him reinforcing the first. His remarkable personality, his outstanding oratory whereby he could hold tens of thousands of people literally spellbound, his inimitable command over Hindi, and his ability to effectively articulate even serious political issues with wit and humour—all these traits made a deep impact on me. At the end of this second tour, I felt that he was a man of destiny, a leader who deserved to lead India some day.

FELLOW-TRAVELLERS ON THE LONG POLITICAL JOURNEY

That was a time when, after Dr Mookerjee, the person who mattered the most in the Jana Sangh was Deendayalji. He too thought highly of Atalji and gave him greater responsibility in the party and Parliament after Dr Mookerjee's tragic demise in May 1953. Within a short time, Atalji established himself as the most charismatic leader of the party. Although the Jana Sangh was only a young sapling before a giant tree called the Congress, people thronged to listen to Atalji's speeches, even in places where the party had no roots. Besides his oratory, they were also impressed by the alternative perspective he provided on national issues that distinguished our party from the Congress and the Communists. He thus showed, at a very young age, all signs of emerging as a mass leader with a nationwide appeal.

After Atalji was elected to Parliament in 1957, Deendayalji made another move—one concerning me. Deendayalji asked me to relocate from Rajasthan to Delhi and assist Atalji in his parliamentary work. Ever since then, Atalji and I have worked together in every phase of the evolution of the Jana Sangh and, later, the BJP. Soon after entering the Lok Sabha, he became the voice of the party in Parliament, commanding a reputation far in excess of its numerical presence. A decade later, after the tragic death of Deendayalji in February 1968, he also had to carry the responsibility of party Presidentship. It was an extremely difficult period in the party's history, but Atalji soon emerged as a capable leader, steering the Jana Sangh out of the deep morass. That was when the slogan *Andhere mein ek chingaari Atal Bihari Atal Bihari* (Atal Bihari is the ray of hope in this pervasive darkness) became widely popular with the workers and supporters of our party.

Five years later, in 1973, he entrusted the party's organisational responsibility to me. The camaraderie that I enjoyed with Atalji, Nanaji Deshmukh, Kushabhau Thakre, Sundar Singh Bhandari and others while building the party together, remains a deeply cherished part of my political journey. By the time Indira Gandhi imposed the Emergency in June 1975, the Jana Sangh had already earned the reputation of the strongest and most organised Opposition party. No wonder, it also earned the trust and confidence of Jayaprakash Narayan, and became the most spirited contingent of the phalanx of pro-democracy fighters that he mobilised on a common platform. Once again, Atalji and I fought together, went to prison together and, after the Emergency was lifted, worked together towards the formation of the Janata Party. Indeed, after JP's health started to deteriorate (he passed away on 8 October 1979), no two persons worked harder and with greater conviction than Atalji and I for the cohesion of the Janata Party and the stability of its government.

Paradoxically, the price we paid for our effort to preserve the Janata Party's unity was that we were expelled from the party on the specious 'dual-member issue'. Once again, along with other colleagues, I worked with Atalji in founding the BJP in 1980. True, the party's debut performance in the 1984 Lok Sabha elections was dismal—we won only two seats. Even Atalji was defeated in Gwalior. However, this was entirely due to the extraordinary situation created by the assassination of Indira Gandhi. It wasn't really a Lok Sabha poll; it was rather a 'Shok Sabha'* poll, where the sympathies were bound to be with the bereaved.

The BJP's subsequent trajectory of meteoric growth was due to the Ayodhya movement. It was the time when Atalji chose to remain relatively inactive. However, I have never had any doubt—that the party's journey from the failure to form a stable government at the Centre in 1996 (when

---

* Condolence meeting.

Atalji was Prime Minister for only thirteen days) to the success to do so again in 1998, was mainly due to his personal popularity that transcended the party's support base. Once again, we both worked closely together to forge the NDA, breaking the shackles of political 'untouchability' that the Congress and the Communists had tried to create.

For a long time after I launched the Ram Rath Yatra in 1990, to mobilise support for the Ayodhya movement, a peculiar asymmetry arose in the media's projection of Atalji and me. Whereas Atalji was seen as a liberal, I was labelled as a 'Hindu hardliner'. It hurt me initially, as I knew that the reality was entirely contrary to the image that I had come to acquire. Conveying this feeling to friends in the media was an uphill task and it was then that some colleagues in my party, who were well aware of my sensitivity to my portrayal, advised me not to battle the image problem. They said, 'Advaniji, in fact, it helps the BJP to have one leader who is projected as a liberal and another leader projected as a hardliner'.

In the wake of being falsely charged in the 'hawala case', I had announced that I would not re-enter the Lok Sabha until I was exonerated by the judiciary. Therefore, I had not offered myself as a candidate in the 1996 parliamentary elections. It was Atalji who contested from Gandhinagar in Gujarat, in addition to contesting from his own traditional constituency of Lucknow. I was deeply touched by his public display of trust and solidarity towards me. Expectedly, he won with a huge margin from both constituencies, and although he later resigned from Gandhinagar to keep his membership in Lucknow, his gesture energised the party and gave to the people, at large, an unmistakable message about unity at the top in the BJP. It was the same message that had gone out from the party's Maha Adhiveshan in Mumbai in 1995, when I, as party President, announced his name as the BJP's Prime Ministerial candidate in the parliamentary elections in the following year.

Why did I make that announcement? There was much idle speculation on this point at the time, and some of it, sadly, continues even today. Some people in the party and the Sangh had chided me then for making the announcement. 'In our estimation,' they said, 'you would be a better person to lead the government if the party wins the people's mandate'.

I replied, and did so with all the sincerity and conviction at my command, that I disagreed with their opinion. 'In the perspective of the people, I am more of an ideologue than a mass leader. It is true that the Ayodhya movement has changed my profile in Indian politics. But Atalji is our leader. He has a far higher stature and much greater acceptability among the masses. He has an appeal that transcends the BJP's traditional ideological support base. He would be acceptable not only to the allies of the BJP, but, far more importantly, to the people of India.' Some of them insisted that I had made a big sacrifice by this announcement. However, I was steadfast. 'What I have done is not an act of sacrifice. It is the outcome of a rational assessment of what is right and what is in the best interest of the party and the nation.'

Along with all our other colleagues, the two of us worked together to bring the BJP to power in 1998. I served as his deputy in the government. This relationship was formalised when I was appointed Deputy Prime Minister on 29 June 2002.* I said to the media that day: 'It is a matter of honour for me and I wish to thank the Prime Minister and all our partners in the NDA.' I added, however, that this did not signify any change in my job profile. 'The Prime Minister used to consult me even earlier and I have been doing similar kind of work before. Yes, in the eyes of the public and my cabinet colleagues, my responsibilities have increased.' I also hastened to scotch rumours, which were being spread by some hostile elements in media and political circles, that my formal elevation as Deputy Prime Minister would lead to the creation of a parallel power centre.[1]

THE 2002 PRESIDENTIAL ELECTION

In early 2002, discussions had begun within the BJP and the NDA about who should be our candidate in the election for the new President of India as Dr K.R. Narayanan's term was coming to an end in July. Our

---

* I became the seventh Deputy Prime Minister of India. My predecessors were Sardar Vallabhbhai Patel, Morarji Desai, Charan Singh, Jagjivan Ram, Y.B. Chavan and Devi Lal.

internal deliberations were guided by two overriding criteria. Firstly, the new President should be a person of high stature, and suitable in all respects to occupy the august office. Secondly, we wanted the person to be preferably outside the ranks of the BJP because of our keen desire to convey a message to the nation that our party believed in inclusivity.

Surprisingly, our choice promptly zeroed in on a candidate who had nothing whatsoever to do with our party. Rather, he was closely associated with two former Prime Ministers, Indira Gandhi and Rajiv Gandhi, of the Congress. It was Dr P.C. Alexander, who was then serving as the Governor of Maharashtra. It was I who first proposed Dr Alexander's name to Atalji and to other key leaders in the NDA. I had been highly impressed by his performance as Governor, and so was Atalji, who readily agreed with my suggestion. His name found ready and enthusiastic acceptance from among other leaders of the constituent parties of the NDA. However, due to opposition from the Congress for the candidature of Dr P.C. Alexander, the NDA chose another eminently worthy candidate, Dr A.P.J. Abdul Kalam, to succeed Dr Narayanan.

I would like to mention here a significant development that took place at the time. One day I received a call from Prof Rajju Bhaiyya, who was then *Sarsanghchalak* of the RSS, saying that he wanted to discuss something important with me. I invited him over the following morning and, over breakfast, he narrated to me the details of a meeting he had had with Atalji the previous evening. 'I had gone to the Prime Minister's residence to discuss the issue of the Presidential election. I suggested to him, '*Aap hi kyon nahin Rashtrapati bante?*' (Why don't you become the President?) I gave my reasons for making this suggestion—principally that, in view of his knee trouble*, it would be less taxing for him to shoulder the responsibility of Rashtrapati Bhavan. Besides, the people would consider him to be the ideal choice in view of his stature and experience.'

I asked him what Atalji's response had been. Rajju Bhaiyya said that Atalji had been hesitant. 'He said neither yes nor no. I therefore think that

---

* Prime Minister Atal Bihari Vajpayee underwent two knee-replacement operations in 2000 and 2001 at Breach Candy Hospital, Mumbai.

he has not rejected my suggestion.' I then mentioned to Rajju Bhaiyya that the NDA leaders had formally met only three days earlier to discuss the issue of the Presidential election and unanimously resolved to authorise the Prime Minister to finalise a suitable, nationally acceptable candidate. In the end, everybody unanimously accepted Atalji's decision in the matter.

A RELATIONSHIP MOORED IN MUTUAL TRUST AND RESPECT

Experience has taught me that long-lasting and fulfilling relationships in politics are possible only on the basis of mutual trust, respect and commitment to certain shared lofty goals. Politics driven by power play is, by its very nature, competitive and conflict-ridden. But politics driven by a common ideology and nurtured by common ideals and *samskaras* is a different matter altogether. When a higher purpose brings a set of people together, they learn to overlook and sideline small matters and personality-related issues. Many people have asked me, 'How did your partnership with Atalji endure for over fifty years? Did you never have any differences or problems with him?'

I can well understand the puzzlement in this question. But I can also say, in all honesty that, contrary to what some people have been speculating since decades now, the relationship between Atalji and me was never competitive, much less combative. I do not imply that we never had any difference of opinion. Yes, we have sometimes had divergent views. Our personalities are different and, naturally, our judgements on individuals, events and issues have differed on many occasions. This is natural in any organisation that values internal democracy. However, what lent depth to our relationship were three factors. We both were strongly moored in the ideology, ideals and ethos of the Jana Sangh and the BJP, which commanded all its members to put Nation first, Party next, and Self last. We never allowed differences to undermine mutual trust and respect. But there was also a third and very important factor: I always implicitly and unquestioningly accepted Atalji to be my senior and my leader.

From the very early stages of our association, I always used to submit to whatever Atalji decided with regard to organisational and political matters.

I would put forth my views but once I sensed what Atalji wanted, I would invariably go along with his viewpoint or preference. My responses were so predictable that sometimes my colleagues in the party, or leaders in the RSS, would express their displeasure over what they perceived as my inability or unwillingness to disagree with Atalji's decisions. This, however, made no difference to my conviction that Atalji's must be the last word in all party-related—and, later, in government-related—matters. Dual or collective leadership is a poor substitute to unity in command. I used to tell my colleagues, 'No family can stay together without a *mukhiya* (head), whose authority is unquestionably accepted by all its members. After Deendayalji, Atalji is the *mukhiya* of our family.'

Here I must also add that Atalji had an accommodative approach towards me. If he knew what my thinking was on a certain issue, and if he did not have serious disagreements over it, he would readily say, '*Jo Advaniji kehte hain, voh theek hai.*' (What Advani says is right.) Thereafter, the matter under discussion would be immediately clinched.

Throughout the six years of the NDA government, speculation about the non-existent 'Atal-Advani conflict' was a favourite pastime for few in the media and political circles. Atalji refuted this speculation on numerous occasions, both within Parliament and outside. In an interview given to *India Today*,[2] he was asked: 'How are your relations with Home Minister L.K. Advani? Is the BJP pulling in different directions?' His reply was forthright: 'I talk to Advaniji each day. We consult each other daily. Yet you people speculate. Like a record stuck in a groove. One more time, let me say there is no problem. When there is, I'll let you know.'

SOME DIFFERENCES

Let me cite two examples when significant differences arose between Atalji and me. He had some reservations about the BJP getting directly associated with the Ayodhya movement. But being a thorough democrat by conviction and temperament, and always willing to respect the consensus among colleagues, Atalji accepted the collective decision of the party.

The second instance pertains to the time when communal violence broke out in Gujarat after the mass killing of *kar sevaks* in Godhra in

February 2002. The Gujarat government and, in particular, Chief Minister Narendra Modi attracted severe condemnation on account of the aftermath of the barbaric incident. The demand for Modi's resignation raised by the opposition parties had reached a crescendo. Some people within the BJP and the ruling NDA coalition also had begun to think that Modi should be asked to quit. However, my view on this matter was totally different. I was convinced, after talking to a large number of people belonging to various sections of society in Gujarat, that Modi was being unfairly targeted. He was, in my opinion, more sinned against than sinning.

I therefore felt that it would be unfair to make Modi, who had become the state's Chief Minister less than a year ago, a scapegoat for what was decidedly a complex communal situation. Doing so, I reckoned, could worsen the social fabric in Gujarat in the long term. I knew that Atalji was as profoundly pained as I was due to the happenings in Gujarat. Since the formation of our government in March 1998, we had taken pride in having succeeded in drastically reducing incidents of communal violence in the country. Our performance, prior to 2002, had stood in stark contrast to our opponents' vile allegations that, once the BJP came to power at the Centre, Muslims and Christians would be at the receiving end of Hindu communal frenzy all over the country. Indeed, Atalji's government had started earning the goodwill of not only Muslims in India, but also of Muslim countries around the world. All of a sudden, after the outbreak of communal violence in Gujarat, the image of our party and government at the Centre had been hurt due to the vitriolic propaganda by our ideological adversaries.

This was weighing on Atalji's mind. He felt that something needed to be done, some affirmative action needed to be taken. Meanwhile, pressure was mounting on him to ask Modi to resign. Although Atalji had not expressed his view explicitly on this matter, I knew that he favoured Modi's resignation. And he knew that I disfavoured it.

Shortly thereafter, in the second week of April 2002, the BJP's National Executive was to meet in Goa. The attention of the media and political circles was focused on how the party was going to discuss Gujarat and what it would decide on Modi's fate. Atalji asked me to accompany him on his journey from New Delhi to Goa. Sitting along with us in the special aircraft, in the Prime Minister's separate enclosure, were Jaswant Singh, Minister of External Affairs, and Arun Shourie, Minister of Communications and Information Technology. Early on during the two-hour journey, the discussion veered round to Gujarat. There was a long spell of silence as Atalji went into a contemplative mood, which was broken by Singh asking him, 'What do you think, Atalji?'

Atalji replied, '*Kam se kam isteefe ka offer to karte.*' (Modi should have at least offered to resign.)

I then said, 'If Narendra's quitting is going to improve the situation in Gujarat, I am willing to tell him to offer his resignation. But I do not think that it would help. Also, I am not sure whether the party's National Council or Executive would accept the offer.'

As soon as we arrived in Goa, I called Modi and said that he should offer to resign. He readily agreed. When the deliberations of the national executive began, many members spoke and put across their points of view. After listening to all of them, Modi spoke and recounted in great detail the whole sequence of events, both Godhra-related and post-Godhra. He also gave the background of communal tension in Gujarat and explained how, in the previous decades, it used to erupt in frequent riots, crippling Ahmedabad and other cities for weeks and sometimes months together. He concluded his speech by saying, 'Nevertheless, as head of the government I take responsibility for what has happened in my state. I am ready to tender my resignation.'

The moment Modi said that, the meeting hall reverberated with a thunderous response from the hundred-odd members of the party's top decision-making body and special invitees: '*Isteefa mat do, isteefa mat do.*' (Don't resign, don't resign.) I then separately ascertained the views of senior leaders of the party on this matter. Each one of them, without exception, said, 'No, he must not resign.' Some, like late Pramod Mahajan, were more emphatic: '*Savaal hi nahin uthata.*' (The question of his quitting simply doesn't arise.)

Thus ended the debate inside the party on an issue that had generated deeply divided opinions in Indian society and polity. While the party's decision in Goa did displease many people in the country, it is equally true that it was in line with the wishes of a much larger section of our society. In Gujarat itself, the decision met with the approval of an overwhelming majority of the people.

Politics often entails making difficult choices. The difficulty lies in the very complexity of the issues and situations that one is called upon to deal with. A tough choice is sometimes an unpalatable one. But I believe that, when one is convinced about the merits of one's decision, one must not hesitate to stand by it. History has indeed vindicated the party's decision not to ask Modi to resign.

PHIR SUBAH HOGI

'Memory,' said Oscar Wilde, 'is the diary that we all carry about with us.' When I revisit this 'diary' for all the notings on Atalji, I find that the points of convergence far outnumber the points of divergence, and what we accomplished together gives me far greater satisfaction than where we failed. And even when we did not succeed, we did not let disappointment dishearten us. Life, I believe, is all about cherishing those moments in one's memory when hope triumphed over despair, light dispelled darkness, and a new day of opportunity dawned after each night of adversity. Atalji was the provider of hope and direction at many a difficult turn in our party's long journey, and I am happy to have been his *saha-yatri* (fellow-traveller) all through this journey.

All those who have closely interacted with Atalji know that he is a statesman with rare humility and sensitivity, which are qualities imparted by his poetic soul. His political personality cannot be adequately understood without an appreciation of his poetry. Like all his admirers, I too have been inspired by his poems—especially by his own rendering of them at party conferences and other public events. There is, for example, a poem he wrote during the Emergency, which Dinanath Mishra published in the underground journal *Janavani*. It not only captured the mood of the time, but has continued to motivate democracy-lovers ever since.

Satya ka sangharsh satta se, nyaya ladta hai nirankushata se
Andhere ne di chunauti hai, kiran antim ast hoti hai
Daanv par sab kuch lagaa hai, ruk nahin sakte
Toot sakte hain, magar jhuk nahin sakte

(Truth is battling against power, justice against tyranny / Darkness has thrown a challenge, the last ray of light is vanishing / We have put everything at stake, Stop we now cannot / We might break, but we shall not bend.)

There is another poem that Atalji wrote when he was in the tenth standard, which holds a mirror to his strong nationalist convictions even at a very young age. Till date I have not come across a more powerful poetic expression of patriotism and Hindu pride than in the following lines:

Hokar swatantra main ne kab chaaha hai kar loon jag ko gulaam?
Main ne to sada sikhaya hai karana apne man ko gulaam.
Gopal-Ram ke naamon par kab main ne atyaachar kiye?
Kab duniya ko Hindu karne ghar-ghar mein nara-samhaar kiye?
Koyi batalaaye Kabul mein jaakar kitni masjid maine todi?
Bhoo-bhag nahin, shat-shat maanav ke hriday jeetane ka nishchay
Hindu tan-man, Hindu jeevan, rag-rag Hindu mera parichay

(When have I desired that, after attaining freedom, I should enslave the world? I have all along taught only how to control one's own mind. How many atrocities have I committed in the name of Ram and Krishna? When did I commit carnages in home after home to convert others to Hinduism? Will someone tell me how many mosques did I break in Kabul? My resolve has been to conquer not territories, but the hearts of millions of human beings. My body is Hindu, my mind is Hindu, my life is Hindu, and the identity of my every blood-vessel is Hindu.)

When I look back at the time I have spent with Atalji in innumerable situations, and think of the best way of concluding this tribute to him, the moment I most fondly recall is a film we watched together sometime in 1959 or thereabouts. Watching Hindi movies was our common interest, and, until the mid-1970s, it took us frequently to Regal and other theatres in Delhi. Atalji and I, along with hundreds of workers of the Jana Sangh, had worked hard for some by-election to the Delhi Municipal Corporation. In spite of our best efforts, victory had eluded our party, plunging us into a state of dejection. Atalji then said to me, '*Chalo, koi cinema dekhne chalte hain.*' (Let's go watch a film.) The two of us went to Imperial theatre in Paharganj to watch a film starring Raj Kapoor, the legendary actor and filmmaker.

The film, loosely based on Fyodor Dostoyevsky's acclaimed novel *Crime and Punishment*, was set in the aftermath of India's Independence. It depicted injustice to the poor and people's disillusionment over non-fulfillment of promises of the Nehruvian era. However, it also urged them to be patient and hopeful for the new 'dawn' was yet to come. Its optimistic message, quite appropriate for the downbeat mood that both Atalji and I were in, was captured in its title: *Phir Subah Hogi* (There will be a new dawn again).

On many occasions in later years, especially after a major electoral defeat, I have cited this episode to highlight what has become one of my core beliefs in life: 'This too shall pass.' Our party's unexpected setback in the 2004 Lok Sabha elections was one such occasion. I have no doubt that the darkness of defeat will give way to a new dawn of victory for our party in the next parliamentary elections, a victory that we shall convert into a greater triumph for India's unity, security, democracy and development.

17

REMINISCENCES AND REFLECTIONS

*In religion lies the vitality of India, and so long as the Hindu race do
not forget the great inheritance of their forefathers, there is no power on
earth to destroy them. Nowadays everybody blames those who constantly
look back to their past. It is said that so much looking back to the past
is the cause of all India's woes. To me, on the contrary, it seems that
the opposite is true. So long as they forgot the past, the Hindu nation
remained in a state of stupor; and as soon as they have begun to look into
their past, there is on every side a fresh manifestation of life.
It is out of the past that the future has to be moulded,
this past will become the future.*

—SWAMI VIVEKANANDA

As I pen this penultimate chapter of this book in early 2008, I find it rather difficult to write about the events of the last two years because what is most recent in one's life does not provide either the perspective to evaluate or the distance to reflect, as can be done with regard to the past, or the comfort of speculation, as can be done in the case of the future. William Dixon, a British historian, has put across this sentiment well: 'The facts of present won't sit still for a portrait. They are constantly vibrating, full of clutter and confusion.' There is also another difficulty that a writer faces in this age of information revolution. Thanks to the multiple chroniclers of instant history, namely the media, anything written about recent events runs the risk of falling in the familiar territory.

I shall, therefore, in this chapter deal with certain issues and concerns that are likely to remain at the centre-stage of national debate for quite some time to come and over which I have strongly articulated my views at different points in my life.

WHY I AM OPPOSED TO COMMUNAL RESERVATIONS

The subject of religion-based reservations had figured prominently—and divisively—during India's freedom movement. Mahatma Gandhi had opposed the British government's 'Communal Award' of 1935, under which seats were reserved in the legislature in favour of religious groups. The issue again reared its head in the immediate aftermath of Independence, when the stalwarts of the movement were busy drafting a new republican Constitution for India. The matter had been conclusively settled: An emphatic 'No' to communal reservations. No less a person than Pandit Jawaharlal Nehru had warned: 'This way lies not only folly but disaster.'*

I was, therefore, deeply distressed when the Congress, now headed by Nehru's grand daughter-in-law, started raising, and endorsing, the demand for communal reservations. On 11 July 2004, the newly elected Congress government in Andhra Pradesh announced its decision to introduce five per cent reservation for Muslims in government jobs and educational institutions. I must confess that, although I am accustomed to the Congress party's surrender to the politics of appeasement for the sake of perpetuating its hold over the minority vote bank, the AP government's

---

* I delivered a comprehensive speech on this subject at a convention against religion-based reservations organised by the Rambhau Mhalgi Prabodhini, Mumbai, on 14 August 2004.

decision flummoxed me. The first question that cropped in my mind was: 'Is it the same Congress party that was once led by Mahatma Gandhi and Pandit Jawaharlal Nehru? Does the Congress party know the implications and consequences of what it is doing? Has the party that is principally associated with India's freedom movement become so ideologically bankrupt and so politically perverted that it is willing to mortgage the nation's unity and integrity for its own narrow and short-term political interests?'

Among the few non-BJP political leaders who opposed the AP government's decision was Tamil Nadu Chief Minister Dr J. Jayalalithaa, who said: 'Muslims are not the only minorities in the country. There are Christians and other minorities also. If they also demand religion-based reservations, where will we go?' This is not a baseless concern. Lately, there have been a few voices—marginal, not mainstream—demanding 'minority' status to the Jain community. With the Congress and some other parties announcing religion-based reservations for minorities, some Jains think that securing a 'minority' tag would enable them to enjoy these benefits. If this trend continues, there is a real danger of more and more sections of the Hindu society wanting to be called a 'minority' since belonging to the majority community seems to attract discrimination and handicap. This extraordinary situation, where many segments of the broader Hindu society consider it a burden to be a part of the 'majority', where the majority feels disadvantaged in the constitutional scheme of minority rights, is a perversion of what the Constitution-makers had in mind. I have had several meetings with Acharya Mahapragya, whom I regard as one of the greatest living saints in the world today. He has categorically expressed himself against the idea of the Jains being declared as a 'minority' community and thus being separated from the larger Hindu family.

In 2005, the Congress-led government at the Centre went a step further. It appointed a committee to study 'social, economic and educational status of the Muslim community of India' under the chairmanship of Justice Rajinder Sachar. This committee proposed something unprecedented, unthinkable and egregious: a head-count of Muslims in the Armed Forces. Thus, here was a government casting aspersions on the secular character and impartial conduct of the very guardians of our national defence. The 'inspiration' for carrying out a Muslim head-count in the Army, Navy and Air Force had come from a book *Khaki and Ethnic Violence in India* by Omar Khalidi, an Indian-born American citizen. The very title of the book suggested that its author held an accusing finger at the armed forces, paramilitary forces and state police for what is routinely publicised abroad as violence deliberately targeted against Muslims.

Only a strong outcry from all quarters, not the least from the chiefs of the Armed Forces, forced the government to drop this ill-conceived move. Similarly, the Andhra Pradesh High Court struck down the state government's order on religion-based reservations in response to a public interest litigation. Nevertheless, the mindset of minorityism, which had engendered the above move, was very much active at the highest levels of the Congress party and its government. This became clear when Prime Minister Dr Manmohan Singh, in his address[1] at the National Development Council on 9 December 2006, declared that Muslims should have 'the first claim on the country's resources'.

I have a strong apprehension that the demand for communal reservations, in some form or the other, is again going to be voiced in the years to come. There are even organisations that, every once in a while, call for proportionate reservation in Parliament and state legislatures. It is the duty of all nationalist and genuinely secular-minded people to be vigilant against these ideas which, if not effectively countered and smothered, can threaten the unity and integrity of India in the future. It is for this reason that I consider it to be my duty to recall a highly instructive debate in the Constituent Assembly on how—and why—it rejected communal reservations.

The Constituent Assembly's initial deliberations in August 1947 were so dominated by the issue of minority safeguards that the Assembly had contemplated reservation of seats in Central and Provincial Legislatures for Muslims, Christians and Sikhs on the basis of their population. Later, however, this proposal was considered more thoroughly by the Constituent Assembly's Advisory Committee on Fundamental Rights and Minorities, and Tribal and Excluded Areas headed by Sardar Vallabhbhai Patel. This Advisory Committee consisted of a galaxy of great leaders of the freedom movement including Dr B.R. Ambedkar, Dr S.P. Mookerjee, Maulana Abul Kalam Azad, Dr K.M. Munshi, Purushottamdas Tandon, Pandit Govind Ballabh Pant and Gopinath Bordoloi. Pandit Nehru was a special invitee to the meeting of the committee, which finally expressed that 'the committee are satisfied that the minorities themselves feel that in their own interests, no less than in the interests of the country as a whole, the statutory reservation of seats for religious minorities should be abolished.' Commending his Committee's Report in the Constituent Assembly on 27 February 1947, Sardar Patel said:

> Often you must have heard in various debates in British Parliament that have been held on this question recently and before when it has been claimed on behalf of the British Government that they have a special responsibility—a special obligation—for protection of the minorities. They claim to have more special interest than we have. It is for us to prove that it is a bogus claim, that nobody can be more interested than us in India in the protection of our minorities. Our mission is to satisfy every interest and safeguard the interests of all minorities to their satisfaction within the framework of the overall national interest.... In the long run, it would be in the interest of all to forget that there is anything like a majority or a minority in this country and that in India there is only one community.

In his five-volume monumental study *Framing of the Indian Constitution*, B. Shiva Rao records: 'A lengthy discussion took place on these proposals of the Advisory Committee. The majority of the speakers—and these included members from all communities—Muslims, Christians, Anglo-Indians, Scheduled Castes, as well as Hindus—offered full support to the proposal to abolish reservations on communal grounds. Jawaharlal Nehru described the proposal as a "historic turn in our destiny". Nehru added: "A safeguard of this kind would have some point where there was autocratic or foreign rule; it would enable the monarch to play one community off against the other. But where you are up against a full-blooded democracy, if you seek to give safeguards to a minority, and a relatively small minority, you isolate it. Maybe you protect it to a slight extent, but at what cost? At the cost of isolating it and keeping it away from the main current in which the majority is going—I am talking on the political plane of course—at the cost of forfeiting that inner sympathy and fellow-feeling with the majority".

The only type of reservations, for which there was unanimous support and that found ready acceptance in the Constituent Assembly, was for the Scheduled Castes and Scheduled Tribes. These have accordingly found place in Article 341 of the Constitution. It is instructive to note that in the operationalisation of this provision, the Congress government specifically defined the beneficiaries to be Hindu Scheduled Castes and four Scheduled Castes among the Sikhs (Kabirpanthis, Ramdasias, Sikligars and Mazhbis) only. The Nehru government kept Muslims and Christians outside the purview of reservation for SCs in education and government jobs. This was done through a Presidential Order amending Article 341 of the Constitution, which enables the President of India to notify a particular caste as a Scheduled Caste. According to the amended law, only those Dalits who were Hindus could be considered members of a Scheduled Caste and hence eligible for the benefits under reservations. In 1956, this was extended to include all scheduled castes professing Sikhism. In 1990, dalits who had embraced Buddhism (Neo-Buddhists) were also included among the Scheduled Castes.

For a long time, there have been demands for extending reservations to so-called 'Dalit' Christians and 'Dalit' Muslims. However, successive governments have not paid heed to these demands. Why? This is because the framers of the Indian Constitution were very clear in their minds that caste is a feature of the Hindu society. If some lower caste Hindus converted to Islam or Christianity in the past, it was because of the claim and the promise of these religions that they were casteless and hence offered an equal station to the converts vis-à-vis original Muslims or Christians. It is instructive to refer to an important circular issued by the Ministry of Home Affairs (Govt. of India/No 18/4/58–SCT IV dated 23 July 1959) during Pandit Nehru's rule.

Sub: Status of Scheduled Castes converts to Christianity on their reconversion to Hinduism.

Government of India have recently occasion to consider the question whether a person belonging to a Scheduled Caste, who has renounced Hinduism by converting himself to another religion, will revert to his original Scheduled Caste if he becomes a Hindu again. After careful consideration the Government of India are advised that such reconvert, who originally belonged to a Scheduled Caste, should be deemed to have reverted to his original caste and would be eligible for the privileges and assistance provided for the members of the Scheduled Castes. This decision is brought to the notice of the State Governments/Union Territory Administrations for their information and guidance.

This circular makes the thinking of the Nehru government absolutely clear on the issue of caste as an exclusively Hindu social category. In other words, Congress governments at the Centre—right from Nehru to Narasimha Rao—were never in favour of extending the benefit of reservations even to so-called 'Dalit' Muslims and 'Dalit' Christians, since they could not be considered Scheduled Castes.

It is a moot point to note that religious affiliation does not bar Scheduled Tribes from enjoying the benefits of reservations. Religion is not a criterion for specifying Scheduled Tribes. Scheduled Tribe converts to Islam or Christianity will continue to have the status of STs. This again shows why the Constitution-makers treated caste as a category specific to the Hindu society.

The present leadership of the Congress neither knows nor seems to care for the history of India. However, one would expect it to know at least the history of the Congress party itself and be consistent with its own thinking on the issue of reservation. In other words, today's leaders of the Congress party would do well to recall the views of Pandit Jawaharlal Nehru and Rajiv Gandhi. In a letter addressed to all Chief Ministers on 27 June 1961, Nehru said:

> ...I have referred above to efficiency and to our getting out of our traditional ruts. This necessitates our getting out of the old habit of reservations and particular privileges being given to this caste or that group.... I dislike any kind of reservation, more particularly in services. I react strongly against anything which leads to inefficiency and second-rate standards.... If we go in for reservations on *communal* and caste basis, we swamp the bright and able people and remain second-rate or third-rate. I want my country to be a first class country in everything. The moment we encourage the second-rate, we are lost. I am grieved to learn how far this business of reservation has gone based on *communal* considerations.... This way lies not only folly but disaster.' (emphasis added).

I have not cited Nehru's views to endorse them in their entirety but to bring it to the attention of the present Congress leadership. The BJP, on its part, believes that reservations are indeed needed to help SCs, STs, and OBCs to overcome their social and economic backwardness. The point I wish to make is two-fold: Nehru was aware of the limitation of reservations as the sole instrumentality for the socio-economic uplift of those who are socially and economically backward. Secondly, and more relevant to our present context, he was totally opposed to reservations on *communal considerations*.

I have mentioned in an earlier chapter what Rajiv Gandhi had to say about reservations, when they are introduced primarily for considerations of partisan politics and electoral benefit. In the debate on Mandal Commission recommendations, the then Leader of the Opposition made a marathon speech in September 1990, accusing the then Prime Minister V.P. Singh of threatening the unity and integrity of India. 'You have ignited caste violence all over the country,' Rajiv Gandhi thundered. Specifically, he had questioned the propriety of providing the benefit of reservations for the privileged sections in society—the so-called 'creamy layer'.

Those who remember the Mandal Commission debate know that on the question of excluding the 'creamy layer' from the beneficiaries of reservations, there was unanimity between the BJP, Communist parties and the Congress. Also, the Supreme Court in its judgment on the implementation of Mandal Commission recommendations upheld the exclusion of the 'creamy layer' for the consideration of reservations. My reason for referring to the 'creamy layer' principle in the present context is simply to point out that, in proposing to provide reservations for the Muslim community as a whole, the Congress has disregarded Rajiv Gandhi's own concerns over this principle. In this context, let me quote what the Chairman of the first Backward Classes Commission, Kaka Kalelkar, a respected Gandhian, said in his letter to the government while presenting his report: 'For the purpose of the Backward Classes Commission, we could not accept the view that all Indian Christians and Indian Muslims were backward, without accepting the logical conclusion that all Hindus were also in the same sense equally backward.'

I regard the Congress party's green signal to the policy of communal reservations as the inevitable outcome of its pseudo-secular mindset and its complete surrender to the compromises and compulsions inherent in the politics of minorityism. It just goes to show that the Congress is willing to sacrifice the long-term interest of the nation and abandon its own moorings in the national movement for the sake of re-establishing its hold on the minority vote-bank.

It is apposite for me to quote here a passage from Durga Das Basu's monumental work *Introduction to the Constitution of India*. An acclaimed scholar on Constitutional matters, Basu writes about the 'ominous trends which have been revealed since the General Election of 1980 as regards the ever-aggressive demands of the religious minorities, which run counter to the very foundations of the existing Constitution and which seek to ride roughshod over the pronouncements of the highest tribunal of the land—not on the ground that they are inconsistent with the provisions of the Constitution but because they are not consonant with the separatist ambitions of the religious minorities. The most grievous feature of this post-Independence development is that the minorities have held up their vote as a bait and political leaders of the majority community belonging to different parties have indiscriminately swallowed that bait in their election manifestos and alliances, irrespective of the ideologies that ushered in the Independence of India and which form the bedrock of the existing Constitution. In this background, it is the duty of an impartial academician to point out to a nationalist Indian (every Indian citizen cannot be assumed to have narrow political ambitions) that to accept such anti-nationalist demands of the minorities would be to tear India into pieces.'[2]

I urge all the right-minded people in the country, including silent but concerned Congressmen, to raise their voice against the politics of minorityism. Since India is not a theocratic state, the religious rights and the identities of the various faith-based communities that constitute the Great Indian Family must indeed be protected. But notions of 'majority' and 'minority' should have no place in the politics and statecraft of our nation much less manipulated for vote-bank considerations. This divisive mindset jeopardises India as one united, integral and harmonious nation. The Congress party is trying to the divide the nation by continuously harping on 'minority protection' in the same way that the British rulers did for their own ulterior motives.

Let me make it clear: my party is neither against minorities—Muslims or others—nor against any minority faith in India. We respect all faiths, including Islam. India belongs equally to all Indians, irrespective of their caste or creed. Our ideology of nationalism is inclusive and non-discriminatory. I appeal to the Muslim community to introspect: 'Has your present negative outlook towards my party helped either your own community or the nation at large? Does the Congress party really deserve your support after its irrefutable record of betrayal and its contribution to keeping a large section of your community poor and backward even after nearly sixty years of Independence? The progress, welfare and security of all sections of India's diverse society are inter-related and indivisible. Therefore, come out of the trap of the minority mindset and join the national mainstream with equal rights and responsibilities to build a strong, prosperous and just India.'

PERVERSE INFLUENCE OF PSEUDO-SECULARISM

Closely linked to the politics of minorityism, indeed providing a justification, is the distortion and perversion that has taken place in the concept of secularism. Increasingly, it is being interpreted and practiced in terms that negate the essential cultural and civilisational personality of India. I have dealt with this issue at length in the context of the Ayodhya movement where, in the name of secularism, Lord Ram and Babur were sought to be equated, and the sentiments of crores of Hindus, attached to Ram Janmabhoomi, were disdainfully ignored. 'Can you prove that Ram was born exactly at this site?' asked Communist intellectuals disparagingly, something they would never do in the case of a dispute concerning a non-Hindu community.

In an interview to a Hindi journal *Vama* in 1987, I had said that for any section of Indian Muslims to identify themselves with Babur 'is like the Christians of Delhi picking up a quarrel over the replacement of a statue of George V with that of Mahatma Gandhi on the ground that George V was a Christian. Now, Gandhiji may have been a Hindu by faith, but he belongs to this country and George V does not. Similarly, Ram belongs to this country whether you call him a mythical hero or a historical personage. Even on the issue of history and culture, I would plead with the Muslim leadership of this country that if the Muslims in Indonesia can feel proud about Ram and *Ramayana*, why cannot the Indian Muslims?'

Similar hurt was caused to Hindu sentiments recently, in September 2007, when, in the ongoing dispute over 'Ram Setu'* in the Setusamudram

---

* Hindus believe that Ram Setu is a bridge that Hanuman, the dutiful follower of Lord Ram, and his 'Vanar Sena' (army of monkeys) built to connect Rameshwaram at the southern tip of India with the Sri Lankan island across the Indian Ocean. There is a beautiful story of work ethic associated with the legend of Ram Setu. When Hanuman and his followers were constructing the bridge, a lowly squirrel decided to make its own contribution to the project by depositing sand particles in the crevices between the rocks brought by the monkeys. When asked by them what she was doing, the squirrel replied: 'I am rendering my own little service to Lord Ram, so that he can go to Lanka and liberate Sita from the captivity of Ravana, the cruel king of Lanka.'

Contd...

Ship Canal Project near Tamil Nadu, the UPA government claimed in an affidavit before the Supreme Court that Lord Ram did not exist and that the *Ramayana* had no historical basis. To add insult to injury, a leader of one of the parties in the ruling coalition made certain derogatory remarks about Lord Ram, which were nothing less than libelous. About the government's stand, which drew all-round condemnation, I was constrained to say: 'It is clear that the Congress party's pseudo-secularism has degenerated into sadist-secularism. By filing this shocking affidavit before the country's highest court, the leadership of the Congress party and the UPA government has poured contempt on the religious sentiments of crores of Hindus all over the world. It is blasphemous and arrogant at worst, and insensitivity and recklessness at best, for a government claiming to be "secular" to trash the deepest and noblest sensibilities of the Hindus. In one stroke of its legal pen, the government has sought to negate all that the Hindus consider sacred in their faith.'

'I would like to point out,' I continued, 'that the *Ramayana*, along with the *Mahabharata*, is considered the bedrock of India's national culture and identity by all the great leaders of India's freedom movement—from Mahatma Gandhi to Lokmanya Tilak, and from Jawaharlal Nehru to Sardar Patel. By describing it as a pure myth and a work of fiction, the government has wounded the very Idea of India and sought to rewrite the civilisational identity of our ancient nation.'[3]

Although the government quickly withdrew the slanderous affidavit, it has yet not accepted the demand made by many Hindu organisations and religious leaders for abandonment of the project that would entail destruction of the 'Ram Setu'.

The monkeys mocked her, saying, 'Your contribution is worth nothing.' Seeing this, Lord Ram rebuked them: 'Never boast about your own service and belittle the others, however tiny it may be. This little squirrel is working to the best of her abilities. She is as great as the greatest amongst you, because what really matters is the love and devotion with which one works.' With this, the Lord caressed the squirrel, and legend has it that Ram's finger-marks are still seen on the squirrel's back. This story about 'squirrel's service' is popular all over India and is often invoked to motivate people to contribute their little mite to a big and worthy cause.

I have had many experiences in my political life showing how self-styled defenders of secularism interpret it in an irreligious or anti-religious manner—of course, their secularism is almost always anti-Hindu, and never against any other faith. I recall an instance from 1970, when I was first elected to Parliament as a member of the Rajya Sabha. Every ministry in the Government of India has a consultative committee attached to it, comprising MPs from both Houses. These Committees discuss matters pertaining to the ministry, make recommendations, but do not take any decisions.

A new MP is offered the option of working in a committee of his or her choice. As a journalist by profession, I opted for the Ministry of Information & Broadcasting. At the very first meeting of the committee that I attended, I had to participate in a discussion which I felt was queer. A Congress member had raised a strong objection to the Bhakti Sangeet programme, featuring devotional songs, on AIR every morning. The ambience generated by such programmes is intensely Hindu, he argued, and 'a secular state like ours should not permit this'. The member's arguments did not carry conviction with the committee, and so, in that forum he did not pursue the matter further. I later gathered that some time earlier this MP had taken a delegation to Rashtrapati Bhavan to plead the same issue with our then President Dr S. Radhakrishnan. After listening to their plaint patiently, the Rashtrapati commented: 'Let me tell you, ladies and gentlemen, that I generally do not listen to All India Radio except in the morning hours. The only programme I do like to hear is Bhakti Sangeet!'

In his writings and speeches, Dr Radhakrishnan strongly stressed that a secular state simply means a state which views all religions with equal respect, and treats all citizens equally without any discrimination. However, he underscored that a secular state is not an irreligious state. When Mahatma Gandhi spoke of 'Ram Rajya' or when Gurudev Rabindranath Tagore invoked the prayer for *'Eka Dharmarajya hable a Bharate'* (Let there be one Dharma Rajya, a just and moral order, in India), were they proposing a theocratic or anti-secular state? What both Gandhiji and Tagore meant was that without Dharmic underpinnings—meaning, thereby, spiritual and ethical guidance—the Indian State and society cannot attain their desired goals.

I recall visiting London in 1990 as a member of a parliamentary delegation led by the then Lok Sabha Speaker Rabi Ray. The Speaker of the House of Commons had invited our delegation for dinner at his residence. We all turned up on time. Our host and some select members of the House of Commons were all there. Even after we were seated at the table, the service would not start. 'Are we waiting for someone?', I asked the Labour Party MP sitting beside me. His name was Greville Janner, and he replied: 'Yes, the Chaplain of the House is still to arrive. Dinner will commence only after he comes and conducts the prayers.' I turned to my Indian colleague sitting on the other side, a senior Marxist leader, and asked: 'If something of this kind were to happen in India, what would you do? Walk out?'

Incidentally, when the House Chaplain finally arrived, and prayers were being said, Janner looked at me and, tongue-in-cheek, observed: 'Mr. Advani, you are a Hindu, and I am a Jew; I hope he is including us also in his prayers.' Ever since this dinner meeting, Janner and I have been close friends. He visits India quite frequently, and on no occasion have we failed to meet. I too meet up with him on my trips to London. He has been trying to foster good relations between different religions, both in Britain and abroad.

When Rajiv Gandhi became Prime Minister, he invited me, as President of the BJP, to serve as a member of the National Integration Council. At one of its meetings held in September 1986, there was a heated discussion on what is meant by secularism in India. I had asked fellow members: 'Is it negation of secularism if a new Indian ship is launched by breaking a coconut against its keel? Or should it be done by opening a champagne bottle? How should a VIP formally inaugurate an exhibition—by lighting a lamp or by merely cutting a tape with a pair of scissors?' Many members concurred with me that there was nothing wrong about breaking a coconut or lighting a lamp at functions. However, C. Rajeshwar Rao, an eminent leader of the CPI, reacted sharply to my views, saying: 'No coconuts, no lamps, we are a secular state.' I could not resist joining issue with him. A

Marxist with his conviction that religion is the opium of the masses would understandably be allergic to customs and traditions which have even a remote association to religion. But I felt that the concept of secularism, which India's Constitution makers had in mind, had nothing in common with this Marxist approach. It is not secularism, but pseudo-secularism. In fact, I insisted that, unlike in communism which banished religion even from private life, Indian secularism has its roots in religion—in the Hindu view that all roads lead to God, as enunciated in the Vedic dictum '*Ekam Sat Vipraha Bahudha Vadanti*' (Truth is One; the wise interpret it differently). I reminded Rao and others at the meeting about what Gandhiji had said: 'Politics bereft of religion is absolute dirt, ever to be shunned.'

One of the most comprehensive studies of Indian secularism has been done by Donald Eugene Smith in his book *India: As a Secular State*.[4] It succinctly sums the differences between Gandhiji and Nehru on the issue of secularism, and describes how this divergence sometimes created problems for the government in the early years of Independence. Sardar Patel, Dr Rajendra Prasad, C. Rajgopalachari (Rajaji) and Dr K.M. Munshi belonged to the Gandhian school. I have explained this in detail in narrating the story of the restoration of the Somnath Temple in Gujarat. What is deeply disconcerting, however, is that the Congress, under its present leadership, has become far more insensitive to the proud symbols of our nationalism than was the case at the time of Nehru or Indira Gandhi. The most shocking example of this is how the Congress party indirectly supported a recent vicious campaign against *Vande Mataram* by Muslim fanatics and Marxists, who alleged that India's national song has communal overtones.

The culture of any ancient nation is bound to be composite. But in our country, emphasis on the composite character of Indian culture is generally an attempt to disown its essentially Hindu content. Even though an outsider, Donald Eugene Smith has taken due note of this, and perceptively observed that, despite the composite nature of Indian culture, Hinduism remains by far the most powerful and pervasive element in that culture. Those who lay great stress on the composite nature of

Indian culture frequently minimise this basic fact. Hinduism has indeed provided the essential genius of Indian culture.

The *Ramayana* and *Mahabharata* may evoke feelings of piety and religious reverence in the Hindus. But do they belong only to Hindus? As invaluable treasures of India's cultural heritage, shouldn't every Indian—Hindu, Muslim or Christian—ought to feel proud of them? Breaking a coconut or lighting a lamp may be part of a religious ritual with Hindus but over a period of time these have become distinctive and graceful Indian customs. Only someone who bears a deep-rooted allergy to religion can object to these practices. A secularism that entails hostility to anything that has a Hindu tinge about it would not be acceptable to India. Indeed, so ingrained is the Indian concept of secularism in our national culture that it did not even occur to the architects of our Constitution that they should specially mention it as one of its preambular principles. It is only during the anti-democratic Emergency rule (1975–77) imposed by Indira Gandhi that secularism found a place in the Constitution through the route of amendment without any discussion in Parliament. How could there have been any debate when almost all the main Opposition leaders were imprisoned and the press was gagged?

HINDUTVA: INDIA'S ANSWER TO THE QUESTION 'WHO ARE WE?'

The debate on the two issues, namely, minoritysm and pseudo-secularism, cannot be complete or effective without an elucidation of the concept of *Hindutva*. It is not the ideology of a particular political party simply because the BJP is the only national party to have never shied away from espousing it.

Throughout my political life, I have emphasised that *Hindutva* stands for cultural nationalism, and does not denote religious or theocratic nationalism. The term 'Hindu' in *Hindutva* has a cultural, and not a religious connotation. It does not lend itself to a narrow 'for-Hindus-only' notion of Indian nationhood, which stems essentially from an underlying cultural oneness. Some of us call this sense of nationhood, *Hindutva*; Pandit Deendayal Upadhyaya called it *Bharatiyata*. Some others may call it Indianness. I see no difference between the three terms; they are interchangeable. I, therefore, feel sad when *Hindutva* is misrepresented and maligned, mostly by Marxist Hindus who are ashamed of calling themselves Hindu. A lot of confusion surrounding the term was, however, cleared when the Supreme Court, in a landmark judgment on 11 December 1995, observed:

> ...no precise meaning can be ascribed to the terms Hindu, Hindutva and Hinduism; and no meaning in the abstract can confine it to the narrow limits of religion alone, excluding the content of Indian culture and heritage. It is also indicated that the term Hindutva is related more to the way of life of the people in the subcontinent. It is difficult to appreciate how in the face of these (earlier Supreme Court) decisions the term Hindutva or Hinduism per se, in the abstract, can be assumed to mean and be equated with narrow fundamentalist Hindu religious bigotry.

In 2004, I read Samuel Huntington's new book *Who Are We?*[5] which deals with the important topic of the national identity of the United States of America against the backdrop of large-sale immigration to the US. The central question that he examines is: What distinguishes America in the age of globalisation, in a shrinking world where international frontiers mean less and less? He answers it by saying that it is a strong sense of 'national consciousness', which he believes is critical to America's success or failure—indeed, to its very survival as a single nation in the future. Huntington argues that America's universalism, because of which it accepts immigrants from all over the world, should not become a pretext for denying or debilitating its distinctive national identity. According to him, this distinctiveness is based on 'culture', which he defines as the 'American Creed', an Anglocentric, Protestant-influenced ideology, which safeguards America's core values such as liberty, sense of community, respect for the individual, entrepreneurship, work ethic, and the gospel of success. To expect, therefore, that recent immigrants should 'Americanise' themselves, while cherishing their own identities, is neither unreasonable nor unjust, Huntington argues.

It is not for me to endorse all that the renowned American scholar says about the national identity of the United States. My reason for referring to his book is simply to suggest that all of us in India should ask ourselves the same question: 'Who Are We?' Unlike the United States, ours is an ancient nation with a history that begins with the dawn of human civilisation. Again, unlike in the case of America, an overwhelming majority of our population has been living in India for centuries. Change of the religious identity of a section of the population cannot change their national identity. India has no history of exterminating any native population either. Therefore, if a common, unifying sense of 'Americanness' can be forged in 400 years, certainly there is a case for insisting that a far more robust and intrinsically more humanistic sense of 'Indianness' has unified India's diverse religious, ethnic, linguistic and caste groups for thousands of years. Since the word 'Indian' itself is of recent vintage, this unifying principle is Hindu-ness or *Hindutva*, the name given to a broad-minded, tolerant, pluralistic and inclusive tradition. If India is de-Hinduised, there will be no India left anymore.

I have found a very lucid exposition of what lends unity to India's diversity in Tagore's essay on 'Nationalism'.[6] He writes: 'I draw your attention to the difficulties India has had to encounter and her struggle to overcome them. Her problem was the problem of the world in miniature. India was too vast in its area and too diverse in its races. It is many countries packed into one geographic receptacle. It is just the opposite of what Europe truly is; namely, one country made into many. Thus, Europe in its culture and growth has had the advantage of the strength of the many as well as the strength of the one. India, on the contrary, being naturally many, has all along suffered from the looseness of its diversity and the feebleness of its unity. A true unity is like a round globe; it rolls on, carrying its burden easily. But diversity is a many-cornered thing which has to be dragged and pushed with all force. Be it said to the credit of India that this diversity was not her own creation; she has had to accept it as a fact from the beginning of her history. In America and Australia, Europe has simplified her problem by almost exterminating the original population.... But India has tolerated difference of races from the first, and that spirit of toleration has acted all through her history.... For *India has all along been trying experiments in evolving a social unity within which all the different peoples could be held together, while fully enjoying the freedom of maintaining their own differences. The tie has been as loose as possible, yet as close as the circumstances permitted. This has produced something like a United States of a social federation, whose common name is Hinduism.*' (emphasis added.)

Even Pandit Jawaharlal Nehru, despite his rather prejudiced view of the Jana Sangh, came round to endorsing the essential features of 'cultural nationalism' towards the end of his life. In a remarkable speech he delivered in October 1961 at an AICC session held in Madurai, he identified the main factor that had united India over millennia in these words: 'India has for ages past, been a country of pilgrimages. All over the country you find these ancient places, from Badrinath, Kedarnath and Amarnath, high up in the snowy Himalayas down to Kanyakumari in the south. What has drawn our people from the south to the north and from the north to the south in these great pilgrimages? It is the feeling of one country and one culture and this feeling has bound us together. Our ancient books have said that the land of Bharat is the land stretching from the Himalayas in the north to the southern seas. This conception of Bharat as one great land which the people considered a holy land has come down the ages and has joined us together, even though we have had different political kingdoms and even though we may speak different languages. This silken bond keeps us together in many ways.'[7]

Nehru has not used the word 'Hindu', but his Madurai speech clearly spelt out India's ancient but constantly self-renewing culture as the 'silken bond' that unites our diversities into 'one country' and 'one culture'. Indeed, I am amazed to find that, in spite of professing divergent political ideologies, most of the patriotic-minded thinkers in our country, including some communist leaders, have expressed convergent views on 'cultural nationalism'.

Let me cite another important remark, this one by Dr B.R. Ambedkar, the principal architect of the Indian Constitution, in support of the concept of 'cultural nationalism'. In 1956, he, along with a large number of his followers, embraced Buddhism. He did so as a mark of protest against certain ills, most notably the evil practice of untouchability that had crept into the Hindu society. He was being lured by many to convert to Islam or Christianity. Not only did he refuse to do so, but he gave a revealing explanation about why he chose Buddhism. 'Embracing Islam or Christianity would have meant going away from the cultural soil of India, which I do not wish to do'.[8]

The above quote may give a misleading impression about the place of Islam and Christianity in India. Let me reiterate that I cherish the fact that India is a multi-religious country in which both our Constitution and our age-old culture brook no discrimination on the grounds of faith. Muslims and Christians have the same rights, responsibilities and opportunities as others. I greatly admire the weighty contribution that they have made to enrich many facets of our national life. I hold all faiths to be worthy of respect. Let me cite an example here. When I reached Ajmer in Rajasthan during the course of my Bharat Suraksha Yatra in 2006, my party colleagues suggested that I should visit Pushkar, a sacred Hindu shrine by the side of a lake which is believed to have been created by Lord Brahma himself, I readily agreed. But I said I would also like to offer prayers at the Dargah Sharif of Hazrat Khwaja Moinuddin Chishti, a revered Sufi saint, in Ajmer.* Although a few eyebrows were raised, I nonetheless visited both the holy places.

** Here is a report about my earlier visit to the Ajmer Dargah in 2000. 'Home Minister L.K. Advani on Sunday prayed at Hazrat Khwaja Moinuddin Chishti's dargah here. The local Muslims were ecstatic and thronged the dargah in huge numbers to watch the spectacle. There was a popular request from the crowd: Give a little speech. Advani readily obliged. He said: "India is a multi-religious country and people belonging to all faiths strive to be good people. That is why every community comes to this dargah. Let us be good human beings first. It does not matter if one believes in Ishwar or Allah." He said although the twentieth century was identified with the Western world, "if all communities here worked hard unitedly, then the twenty-first century will certainly belong to Bharat." To this the crowds responded with "Aameen". (So be it).' ('A surprise: Advani prays at Ajmer dargah'; the *Times of India*; 4 December 2000) Later, when a journalist asked me whether my visit to the dargah was part of a larger image changing exercise, I replied, 'My perceptions have always been clear. I am saying the same things now what I said twenty-five years ago.'

The concept of 'cultural nationalism' enjoins upon the adherents of different faiths in India to respect, and take pride in, the common unifying culture of our ancient land while celebrating its many diversities; not to have extra-territorial loyalty; not to denigrate other faiths as false or inferior, but rather to learn from the best that each faith has to offer; not to misuse freedom of religion to expand one's religious population through fraudulent conversions; and not to try to gain political dominance for the purpose of advocating separatism or establishing theocracy. It means nothing more, nothing less.

SOCIAL JUSTICE, EQUALITY AND REFORMS IN HINDU SOCIETY

A subject of utmost importance for India's all-round development and national resurgence is the reform and self-renewal of the Hindu society. Hinduism is the repository of the most exalted teachings about human evolution and realisation of God. Its philosophy is profound and the relevance of its principles is both universal and eternal. Its distinguishing feature is its lack of dogma, its readiness to accept truth in all its manifestations, without putting the seal of finality on any of them, and its emphasis on the need to climb higher on the ladder of human evolution through righteous living. The freedom of thought and expression that it provides in all intellectual, theological and philosophical matters is unmatched. So much so that even Charvaka, who denied the existence of God, was respected as a *rishi* (seer) because of his erudition. Since Hinduism teaches us to see the divine in every animate and inanimate creation of God, the concept of equality of human beings is in-built in its belief system. The *Bhagavad Gita* states emphatically that a man's greatness is determined by his karma and not by his birth.

Nevertheless, due to many historical factors the Hindu society acquired certain negative, regressive and thoroughly indefensible features, which it has still not fully got rid of. The concept of high and low among castes and, in particular, the practice of treating certain castes as 'untouchables' is the most debilitating among these drawbacks. The injustice in many forms that is often meted to women is another. These cannot be tolerated or rationalised on any grounds. They violate the ideals enshrined in the Indian Constitution and run contrary to the spiritual principles that have guided the Hindu way of life for several millennia. Hindu society cannot regain its full vigour or progress to its full potential unless it fights the ills within.

Two points need to be emphasised here. Firstly, time and again the Hindu society has demonstrated both its willingness and capacity to reform itself by rediscovering its own foundational principles as well as by learning from other constituents of humanity. Secondly, considerable progress has indeed been achieved in the modern era, both during the freedom movement and the decades that followed. This is due to the efforts of many modern-day saints and social reformers such as Swami Vivekananda, Swami Dayananda, Raja Ram Mohun Roy, Mahatma Jyotiba Phule and his wife Savitribai Phule, Narayan Guru and, of course, Mahatma Gandhi and Dr B.R. Ambedkar. In this context, I would like to specially commend the work of the RSS and the various organisations inspired by it, all of which emphasise the message of social equality in their mission for Hindu unity and Hindu renaissance. Balasaheb Deoras, the third *Sarsanghchalak* of the RSS, used to say: 'If untouchability is not a sin, then nothing in the world is a sin.'

This progress towards social equality should be further accelerated. The policy of reservations, combined with the scope that electoral politics provides for representation in the power structure at all levels, has considerably enhanced the social, economic and political empowerment of the disadvantaged sections of our society. This is nothing short of a silent social revolution, brought about by our democratic system. This, too, needs to be strengthened. Since quality education has become a key of socio-economic advancement, India's focus in the coming years should be more on educational and economic empowerment of SCs, STs, OBCs and other weaker sections. Castes may still remain as markers of social identity, but casteism must be rooted out of India of the future. In this context, the one slogan that needs to be popularised more and more in times to come is: '*Sab jaati mahaan, Sab jaati samaan*' (All castes are great and all castes are equal).

The all-round empowerment of women is an integral and essential part of building a better and more just society. Of immense and urgent importance is women's political empowerment through a policy of reservations. The BJP was the first party to pass a resolution, in 1994, seeking thirty-three per cent reservation of seats for women in Parliament and state legislatures. Ours is also the first—and, so far, the only—party in the country to have decided to provide thirty-three per cent reservation for women within the organisation at all levels. My colleague Sushma Swaraj, an outstanding speaker and an able parliamentarian, played a key role in persuading the party to pass the two resolutions.

Reservation for women is justified on the simple ground that women face many difficulties in participating actively in public affairs. It is twice as difficult for a woman to play a role in public life as it is for a man—even for such women who are twice as capable and competent as their male counterparts. Women's under-representation in Parliament, state legislatures and ministries is glaring. It is all the more indefensible since women have given an excellent account of themselves after India introduced the 73rd and 74th Constitutional amendments in 1992 guaranteeing the reservation of seats for women in panchayats and municipal bodies. As a result of this revolutionary step, our country has over one million women members in various Panchayati Raj institutions. In addition, women are also elected in cooperative bodies and self-help groups in large numbers. Thus, India today has the proud distinction of having the largest number of women who have been elected in grassroot democratic organisations. Indeed, some of the best-run village panchayats are those that have women as *sarpanch*. It is therefore ironic that, even after many years of debate within and outside Parliament, there is lack of sufficient political will and consensus to pass the law for thirty-three per cent reservation for women in Parliament and state legislatures. It would be a proud and happy day for India when this revolutionary law finally sees the light of the day.

Women's empowerment, however, has many other important dimensions. The handicap they face in education, healthcare and employment must be removed. They must be treated with respect and dignity both at home and in the public sphere. Few things outrage me more than reports of atrocities on women. Hence, my understanding of security envisages a situation in which our sisters and daughters feel safe to travel anywhere and at anytime without any fear or apprehension. The most basic criterion of safety is, of course, the right to live. Therefore, inhuman practices like female infanticide and foeticide, which draw sustenance from indefensible cultural attributes such as preference for sons, can have no place in a civilised society. These social evils, however, cannot be eradicated through laws and governmental regulations alone. We need strong and sustained societal action, supported by proper public education.

LIBERATING INDIA FROM THE CURSE OF POVERTY

As India stands poised for a quantum leap forward in global rankings for economic performance, one of the toughest challenges it faces is the removal of abject poverty and provision of a decent standard of living for all its billion-plus citizens. In recognising this truth, one cannot, of course, overlook the fact that our country has indeed made considerable progress in recent decades in lifting large numbers of people above the poverty line. It will not do to only paint a bleak picture of the socio-economic reality of India in the beginning of the twenty-first century. Economic reforms have, indeed, put India on the path of prosperity through speedier economic growth in certain sectors and certain areas.

At the same time, we must not overlook the other, negative, side of the current Indian reality. Large sections of our population continue to be victims of poverty. Equally distressing is the rapidly growing divide between the rich and the poor, on one hand and between cities and villages, on the other, the latter having caused the largest ever migration of people from rural to urban areas since the onset of economic reforms in the 1990s. The problem is aggravated by regional disparities in development, with the northern and eastern states lagging considerably behind their counterparts in the South and the West.

Human resource is the most precious wealth that India has. However, human resource becomes resourceful only if the basic necessities of life—food, clothing, housing, health, clean water, education, productive employment, and good natural and social environment—are met. No nation can become rich if the bulk of its human resources are poor. I have always wondered: If India has achieved so much with only a third of its population living reasonably well, how much more could it achieve when all its enviable resources are optimally utilised? Therefore, in my recent communications I have been repeatedly emphasising one point: For me, India Rising means the rise of every Indian and India's emergence as a developed nation means the opportunity of all-round development for every Indian.

Is this possible? Yes, it is. Can we make poverty history in India? Yes, we can. According to me, the key to success in this endeavour is not so much well-designed policies and programmes, which are no doubt important, but good governance. True, we must have policies that promote entrepreneurship and people's initiatives in a fairly regulated competitive environment; we must build good physical and social infrastructure; we must, especially, take necessary measures to rejuvenate our agriculture and rural economy; we must bring vibrancy to the informal sector that employs the largest number of people after agriculture; we must ensure quality education for all; we must appropriately employ scientific and technological resources, and create indigenous capabilities in frontier areas of knowledge and its applications; we must arrest the degradation of our environment, towards which our culture exhorts us to have a reverential attitude; and we must fully seize the opportunities that a rapidly changing world brings while protecting ourselves from the negative effects of globalisation.

It is equally true that we must not only achieve holistic development, but also ensure holistic security. Our concept of security should encompass India's external and internal security—namely, security of the country and the common man. Without reliable and comprehensive security, not only our developmental gains but also our very survival as a nation would be threatened.

However, to be able to achieve this objective, we must first of all ensure good governance. I firmly believe that it is honesty, probity, transparency, accountability, efficiency and devotion to duty among the people engaged in governance at all levels, which makes the greatest difference to the quantum and quality of a nation's progress. Without these attributes, our gains in development and security will be either inadequate or distorted and reversible. Which is why, after evaluating the experience of the various governments both at the Centre and in states during the past few decades, I have come to the firm conclusion that the present and future challenges before India can be effectively met only by reorienting our polity on the basis of three imperatives: Good Governance, Development and Security.

In my own humble way, I have been trying to popularise this new and much-needed reorientation of our polity both within my own party and among the people at large. For example, abstract terms like eight per cent or nine per cent GDP growth, important though they are, do not appeal to me—and they do not mean much to millions of common Indians either. If someone were to ask me 'What kind of GDP growth do you want?', I would say that kind in which 'G' stands for Good Governance at all levels from national to local; D' stands for Development for all regions and all Indians; and 'P' stands for Protection for every citizen.

I have also been making a related point in my political communication. 'All of us are proud that India has emerged as a vibrant and energetic democracy after 1947. However, as an observer of and a participant in the evolution of India's democracy over the last sixty years, I have also seen that a major shortcoming has crept in. Most political parties have come to believe that the politics of vote-banks is the surest way to winning elections and attaining power. They have also developed a skeptical attitude that good governance, democracy, security and probity in public life are not commitments that can win votes. Against this backdrop, the most significant aspect of the BJP's success in winning a renewed mandate in the 2007 assembly elections in Gujarat, under the leadership of Narendra Modi, is that it signalled the triumph of good governance, development and security over the politics of vote-banks. This is a welcome development for India.'[8]

NEED FOR POLITICS OF CONSENSUS

We are a thriving multi-party democracy. The diversity of our political system is a source of strength as well as vibrancy. Since the era of the Congress party's pan-Indian hegemony is long over, the configuration of India's contemporary politics has become essentially bipolar at the national level with the BJP and Congress as the two principal and stable poles. Apart from these two main national parties, there are many that identify themselves with specific regional or social aspirations. Coalitions have become the order of the day both at the Centre and in many states. Some of the coalition partners are also known to switch their allegiance from time to time.

This development in the last two decades has created a major challenge before our polity: how to ensure that a fragmented multi-party system, despite its inevitable pulls and pushes, can still maintain a core unity and continuity of purpose? Naturally, national parties have a greater responsibility in this regard than regional or sectional parties. Therefore, the need for a basic level of consensus amongst all parties, and especially between the two main national parties, has become paramount. Differences between the BJP and the Congress—as also between other parties—are bound to remain, since they profess different ideologies and have traversed different paths of evolution. Nevertheless, it is both possible and necessary for them to explore and expand the area of cooperation on issues of overriding national importance. For this, it is imperative that all parties inculcate the ethos of cooperation rather than confrontation, and maintain a basic level of dialogue which is not jettisoned for narrow considerations of competitive electoral politics.

For the BJP and the Congress to adopt a stance of consensus on critical national issues, it is essential for each to not look at the other as an 'enemy'. As far as the BJP is concerned, we view the Congress as an adversary, and not as an 'enemy'. Indeed, the very concept of 'enemy' in a democracy is unhealthy. Unfortunately, the Congress party's attitude to the BJP is far from healthy. The Congress leadership thinks the BJP is evil.[10] I earnestly appeal to Congress leaders to shun such an approach.

I had an occasion to discuss this matter with Rahul Gandhi, the young General Secretary of the Congress, during a chance meeting with him in the lounge at the Delhi airport one day in December 2007. He was leaving for his parliamentary constituency in UP and I was on my way to address an election rally in Gujarat. He walked up to me, greeted me warmly and said, 'Advaniji, I am pleased to meet you. I had never had an opportunity to formally introduce myself.' The natural courtesy and respect for age that he displayed was similar to how his father, the late Rajiv Gandhi, had greeted me in our first meeting after he became the Prime Minister. Rahul asked me about my 'medium-term' views on national politics. I said, 'I am concerned that the political space for our two mainstream national parties is shrinking, while regional parties are expanding and gaining political clout. If this continues, it will have serious implications for India in the future.' I then asked Rahul whether his own party was equally concerned about this development. His reply was in the affirmative. This prompted me to remark: 'The only way out is for the BJP and the Congress to view each other as "political adversaries" and not as "enemies". For this, the leadership of our two parties should have a line of communication open on important national issues.' Rahul seemed to agree with this suggestion.

18

In Pursuit of Meaning and Happiness in Life

To laugh often and love much; to win the respect of intelligent persons and the affection of children; to earn the approbation of honest critics; to appreciate beauty; to give of one's self; to leave the world a bit better, whether by a healthy child, a garden patch or a redeemed social condition; to have played and laughed with enthusiasm and sung with exultation; to know even one life has breathed easier because you have lived—that is to have succeeded.

—Ralph Waldo Emerson

I recently read a fascinating and widely acclaimed thriller, a genre I enjoy reading once in a while to keep my wits sharpened. *The Interpretation of Murder*[1] by Jed Rubenfeld, a law professor at Yale University, USA, is, however, less about a murder mystery and more about the mystery of life. The author, a student of Shakespeare and Sigmund Freud, in his debut novel, presents a psychoanalytical exploration of the two basic questions about human existence: happiness and meaning:

There is NO mystery to happiness.

Unhappy men are all alike. Some wound they suffered long ago, some wish denied, some blow to pride, some kindling spark of love put out by scorn—or worse, indifference—cleaves to them, or they do to it, and so they live each day within a shroud of yesterdays. The happy man does not look back. He doesn't look ahead. He lives in the present.

But there's the rub. The present can never deliver one thing: meaning. The ways of happiness and meaning are not the same. To find happiness, a man need only live in the present: he need only live *for* the moment. But if he wants meaning—the meaning of his dreams, his secrets, his life—a man must reinhabit the past, however dark, and live for the future, however uncertain. Thus, nature dangles happiness and meaning before us all, insisting only that we choose between them.

For myself, I have chosen meaning.

Although the novel claims that a man can either have meaning or happiness in life, I have had the good fortune of experiencing both, and in abundance.

Meaning comes with purpose, with a sense of mission, whatever be one's calling in life. It answers the question: 'Why should we live?' The answer takes us to our past—individual and collective—and also to our own dreams and goals about the future. It makes us realise that our life is meant to fulfill a duty, and the present provides both a field and an opportunity to carry out that duty to the best of one's abilities.

When I look back at my life of eight decades, I remind myself that I found my calling in life when, on a tennis court in Hyderabad in Sindh, I first heard the name of Rashtriya Swayamsevak Sangh and became a volunteer in 1942. I found meaning when I started attending Sunday evening discourses on the *Bhagavad Gita* by Swami Ranganathananda in Karachi. I found meaning when I left my home and family to work as a *pracharak* of the RSS, first in Karachi and later, after being uprooted by Partition, in Rajasthan. That meaning got further enriched when I embarked on a political journey fifty-five years ago, first as a worker of the Bharatiya Jana

Sangh and later of the Bharatiya Janata Party. It is a journey that has not yet ended. From the age of fourteen and a half years till now, only one duty has defined the purpose of my life: to serve my Motherland.

During the course of fulfilling this duty, my devotion, sincerity and commitment to my own cause and ideals have been tested many times, especially when I have faced any adversity in my life. I can say, with both humility and contentment, that I have not been found wanting in the eyes of my own conscience. Errors of judgement, I have committed many. I have also erred in the execution of my tasks. But I have never indulged in scheming or acts of opportunism for self-promotion nor have I compromised on my core principles for personal comfort or gains. I have stood my ground for the sake of self-respect and for what I believed was in the larger interest of the nation, even when doing so carried obvious risks. Whether I had to spend long stints in prison, as happened during the Emergency, or had to face a false charge of corruption in the Hawala case, or was labelled as a 'Hindu hardliner' for my role in the Ayodhya movement, or when I was misunderstood and castigated for having betrayed my ideology after my visit to Pakistan, I have followed the call of my conscience and stood firm. Besides fortifying my self-belief, it has given me happiness and imparted meaning to my life.

As this book mentions, I have been acutely, even painfully, aware of the fact that I chose to remain, all my life, in a vocation that has steadily fallen in public esteem since Independence. Politics, during the freedom movement was a mission. In the immediate aftermath of Independence, many people in politics still retained the missionary spirit. Politics, in many democracies, is a profession demanding a minimum degree of professionalism as in any other profession. While I would not assert that the ethos of mission and profession has altogether vanished in India, I am nonetheless anguished and alarmed at the rapidly spreading degeneration of politics into crass commerce, with the attendant ills of individualism, groupism, dynasticism, deceit and various forms of criminalisation. In this decadent environment, which has given rise to the image of the 'Ugly Indian Politician', I have striven to practice politics of service and probity as a mission. This, too, has given me satisfaction.

Occasionally, I have heard colleagues and acquaintances comment that I have never been *ziddi* (insistent). Perhaps true, but I have no regrets. However, I have been unabashedly ambitious for my party and my country. As this book attests, I have contributed my bit to the realisation of some of the larger goals that my party had set for itself and for India. I am proud of my participation in the struggle against the Emergency and my contribution to the restoration of democracy as the Minister of Information & Broadcasting in Morarji Desai's government. I am equally proud of my contribution to India's all-round development, and especially to the strengthening of its internal security paradigm and system, as Home Minister and Deputy Prime Minister in Atalji's government.

COLLEAGUES AND FRIENDS, PAST AND PRESENT

The achievements of my party or of the governments that I have worked in, were due to the determined collective efforts, in which I only played a part. I have had the privilege and honour of working with hundreds of outstanding colleagues in my own party, in the parties that allied with us from time to time, and in the two governments in which I had ministerial responsibilities. Working with them for common national objectives has also been a source of immense happiness.

In Morarji Desai's government, I admired the commitment and competence of H.M. Patel, Shanti Bhushan, Madhu Dandavate, Ravindra Varma, and, of course, the indomitable George Fernandes, who played a decisive role later in the formation of the NDA, also serving as its Convenor.

In later years, I have worked closely with a large number of leaders from other political parties who have made valuable contributions to India's development and to the maturing of its democracy—V.P. Singh, Devi Lal, N.T. Rama Rao, Biju Patnaik, Prakash Singh Badal, Gurcharan Singh Tohra, I.K. Gujral, Bal Thackeray, Ramakrishna Hegde, H.D. Deve Gowda, Sharad Pawar, Dr Farooq Abdullah, N. Chandrababu Naidu, Dr Jayalalithaa, Navin Patnaik, Nitish Kumar, Dinesh Goswami, Prafulla

Mahanta, Mamata Banerjee, Omprakash Chautala, Kanshiram, Mayawati, Dr M. Karunanidhi and Murasoli Maran.

In my own party, it has been my privilege to work with several generations of committed and highly talented colleagues. I must mention here the names of old-timers like Nanaji Deshmukh, Jagdish Prasad Mathur*, Sundar Singh Bhandari*, Krishna Lal Sharma*, Bhairon Singh Shekhawat, Kushabhau Thakre*, Sikandar Bakht*, Jana Krishnamurthy*, K.R. Malkani*, Kedarnath Sahni, Kailashpati Mishra, Murli Manohar Joshi, Jaswant Singh, Ved Prakesh Goyal, Keshubhai Patel, Madanlal Khurana, Vijay Kumar Malhotra, Sundarlal Patwa, Kailash Joshi, Shanta Kumar, Suraj Bhan*, and Appa Ghatate. Then came a new crop of leaders: Pramod Mahajan*, Kalyan Singh, Venkaiah Naidu, Sushma Swaraj, Rajnath Singh, K.N. Govindacharya, Arun Jaitley, Narendra Modi, Kalraj Mishra, Uma Bharati, Premkumar Dhumal and B.S. Yediyurappa. Now, another generation of leaders is contributing to the party's expansion. Amongst them are Gopinath Munde, Nitin Gadkari, Vasundhara Raje, Dr Raman Singh, Ananth Kumar, Sushilkumar Modi, Shivraj Singh Chauhan, Ravi Shankar Prasad, Manohar Parrikar, Shahnawaz Hussein, Dharmendra Pradhan, Balbir Punj and many others. The BJP also gained considerable strength by inducting some outstanding persons from a non-political and non-BJP background such as Jagmohan, Arun Shourie, Yashwant Sinha and Najma Heptulla. Harin Pathak, Ch. Vidyasagar Rao, I.D. Swami and Swami Chinmayananda worked with me as my deputies in the Home Ministry. I am aware that many of my former and present colleagues have gone unmentioned in this book, but my eyes become moist and my heart is filled with gratitude when I think of all of them.

I have great faith in the young blood of my party. The question 'Who after Vajpayee?' or 'Who after Advani?' never arises. The BJP is not like the Congress party in which the top slot is forever reserved for a member of the 'dynasty'. The BJP provides even an ordinary worker the opportunity to rise through the ranks and assume leadership responsibilities on the strength of his or her commitment, capability and record of service.

---

* These party colleagues are now no more.

This, among many other reasons, makes me proud and happy to belong to the BJP.

INTERACTION WITH MEDIA AND BUSINESS LEADERS

In a democracy, politics and media are inter-dependent. Politicians need the media to reach out to the people and the media, in turn, has a duty to convey the news and views about politics and other facets of national life to the people in a free, fair, impartial and credible manner, while functioning as a responsible critic and vigilant watchdog. Right from the beginning of my political life, I have taken great interest in the working of the Indian media; partly because I have myself been a journalist once and also because, as Information & Broadcasting Minister in the post-Emergency government of the Janata Party, I was called upon to play a crucial role in the restoration of press freedom as an integral part of reinstatement of democracy in India.

I treasure my association with many distinguished members of the media, both of yesteryears and today. I would like to mention some of them here: Ramnath Goenka, Girilal Jain, Khushwant Singh, Nikhil Chakravartty, R.K. Karanjia, B.G. Verghese, Vidyanivas Mishra, Dharmavir Bharati, M.V. Kamath, Vijay Chopra, M.J. Akbar, Aroon Purie, Prabhu Chawla, Aveek Sarkar, N. Ram, Cho Ramaswamy, V.K. Narasimhan, Shekhar Gupta, Manoj Sonthalia, Ramoji Rao, Devendra Swarup, Narendra Mohan, Ved Pratap Vaidik, Prabhash Joshi, Chandan Mitra, Tarun Vijay, Karan Thapar, Swapan Dasgupta, Vir Sanghvi, Achyutanand Mishra, Ram Bahadur Rai, Rahul Dev, Sir Mark Tully, Rajat Sharma, Tavleen Singh, Saeed Naqvi and Barun Sengupta. Several of those with whom I share a relationship of mutual respect have been critical of my party or me at some point or the other. This is natural, since freedom of thought is a prized attribute of journalists and media owners. I respect those who have this attribute and also an equally important quality, the courage of conviction.

I have always regarded India's business class as a prime mover of our country's development. Not having ever subscribed to the ideology that businessmen are an exploiting class, my party has consistently advocated a policy that encourages entrepreneurship. I have always enthusiastically lauded their achievements since these are, indeed our national assets, which benefit our economy, create employment, help improve the lives of people and, as is increasingly seen in recent years, raise India's stature internationally. A recent and most heartening feature of the Indian economy is the reversal in the phenomenon of 'Brain Drain'. Not only are hundreds of talented and highly educated Indians, settled abroad, returning to India, but many foreign professionals are turning to Indian companies for employment in India. Clearly, the wheel of history is moving in ways that is making more and more people in the world recognise India as a great economic power in the making. Few among them believed that India was capable of achieving what it has.

Among the Indian business houses, the one I admire the most are the Tatas. I cherish my interaction with the late J.R.D. Tata and his worthy successor Ratan Tata.* After he recently launched the Nano, I wrote a letter of congratulations to Ratan Tata saying: 'Despite its name, it is anything but a nano-scale achievement. It is yet another stupendous success from the Tata Group and, like all other successes in the past, both recent and distant, it has made India proud.... Keep it up. India expects more from a group that has always over-fulfilled its expectations.'

---

* Two things about the Tata Group have especially endeared it to me. Firstly, Swami Vivekananda, who was far removed from the world of business, was among those who encouraged Jamshedji Tata to set up India's first indigenous steel plant. Secondly, when Jamshedji had finalised his plans to establish the plant in what later came to be known as Jamshedpur in Jharkhand, and to supply its steel to the Railways, the then Chief of the Great Indian Peninsular Railway, Sir Frederick Upcott, mocked at him and said: 'Impossible. They just won't be able to do it. And if they do, I promise to eat every pound of steel rail the Tatas succeed in making.' I mentioned this in my speech at the annual general meeting of the Federation of Indian Chambers of Commerce and Industries (FICCI) in 2007, and added: 'History has kept no record of how many pounds of Indian steel this British gentleman ate after the Tatas' steel plant commenced production in 1912. But, surely, he would have turned in his grave after the media reported recently that Ratan Tata has made a (successful) bid to acquire Corus, the famous British steel company.'

The late Dhirubhai Ambani impressed me with his soaring vision about India's growth potential, and his two sons, Mukesh and Anil, have shown that it is indeed realisable. Another self-made first-generation businessman with impressive accomplishments is Sunil Mittal. Laxmi Mittal has made India proud by becoming the world's largest steelmaker. In the large clan of Birlas, I admired the late Aditya Vikram Birla for his farsightedness. His young son, Kumar Mangalam, has inherited both his father's ambition and ability. Venu Srinivasan is an old acquaintance whose commitment to quality and to the core values of business is something I have a high regard for. I admire Rajeev Chandrashekhar, now an independent Member of the Rajya Sabha, for his innovative suggestions on economic development.

In the eyes of the world, India has now become synonymous with excellence in information technology. I am happy that the BJP was the first among Indian political parties to devote an entire section to IT in its election manifesto in 1998. My own fascination with IT started quite early when, during my visit to the United States in 1990, I made it a point to see the headquarters of Microsoft near Seattle. Since then, India's own prowess in IT has grown enormously, partly due to the many bold steps that the Vajpayee government took to rapidly expand and modernise India's telecom and IT services. I try to keep abreast of the latest revolutionary advances in this field by talking to youngsters and also, whenever possible, by visiting the facilities of IT companies. I was greatly impressed, for example, when I went to see the Infosys campus in Bangalore some years ago. N.R. Narayana Murthy, the founder of Infosys, and his wife Sudha Murthy are a couple I admire very much for projecting an enlightened philosophy of business and philanthropy.

While I applaud the achievements of Indian business houses, I also believe that they exhibit the same shortcomings in ethical conduct that have unfortunately become the hallmark of other areas of national life, including politics. After all, if good governance is the ideal that we are striving for in India, good corporate governance has to be insisted upon. If good citizenship is what we expect from ordinary Indians, good corporate citizenship should be viewed as an even greater necessity. I have expressed my views on this matter on several business platforms. For example, while addressing a FICCI gathering in 2001 on probity in public life, I said: 'I must also say a strong word about the responsibility of businesses in combating corruption in the corridors of power. Do not violate or short-change established laws and policies for achieving short-term gains for your own individual businesses. Do not try to undercut each other through unhealthy corporate battles. By doing so, you harm the interests of Indian business as a whole. Good business practices will go a long way in creating a healthy atmosphere and building necessary social capital needed for promoting all-round national development.'

BOOKS, PLAYS, MOVIES, MUSIC

Books, theatre and cinema have been another source of immense happiness throughout my life. As I have described in these memoirs, my love for books started when I was still in my early teens. When I learnt Hindi after coming to Rajasthan, I read K.M. Munshi's *Jai Somnath* and, indeed, every single book written by him. It is this early habit that has enabled me to be with myself in the company of books throughout my hectic political life—whether I am campaigning for elections, travelling on my yatras or having a few solitary moments between meetings. Books take me into a world that is far removed from the limiting considerations of the here and now, a world of knowledge, ideas, emotions, adventure, imagination and even dreams. They introduce me to a dazzling variety of characters, each a unique manifestation of human nature, each a combination of strengths and weaknesses, and each grappling with the challenges of life in their own way, many failing, some succeeding.

I love a wide variety of books, but prefer books on politics, spirituality, history and futurology. C. Rajagopalachari's *Ramayana* and *Mahabharata* are my all-time favourites. Dr S. Radhakrishnan's books on Hinduism have influenced me deeply. I have immensely enjoyed reading Alvin Toffler's trilogy: *Future Shock*, *The Third Wave*, and *Power Shift*. Indeed, having read somewhere that I was a fan of his books, Toffler, during his visit to India in 2002, called on me at my residence. I have greatly admired Stanley Wolpert's many books on the history and politics of the Indian subcontinent. Stephen Covey's *The Seven Habits of Highly Effective People* and the many books by Paulo Coelho have inspired me. An important point Covey makes is that, for self-improvement or for becoming effective, one need not just sweet-talk or remember people's birthdays. These sophisticated things are fine, but what counts for more than anything else is one's basic honesty and integrity. So true.

Although I interact with Arun Shourie as a party colleague, I have also, independently, admired him as a writer with a crusading spirit. If I have to mention one writer on constititional matters who has not only inspired me but whose books have been a regular source of reference in my political and parliamentary work, it has to be Durga Das Basu. His *Introduction to the Constitution of India* and his eight-volume *Commentary on the Constitution of India* are works of extraordinary erudition.

While on the topic of books, I must express my appreciation of the long association I have had with Dina Nath Malhotra, the doyen of Indian publishing, and also Shyam Sunder, the founder of Prabhat Prakashan, a leading Hindi publishing house, and his two sons Prabhat Kumar and Piyush Kumar. Prabhat Prakashan published the Hindi edition of *A Prisoner's Scrapbook*, my book on the Emergency, and also reprinted its English edition in 2002, on the occasion of the twenty-fifth anniversary of the lifting of the Emergency. Its original publisher was the late Gulab Vazirani of Arnold Associates, who was, indeed, a fellow *swayamsevak* of the RSS in Karachi. He also wrote a small booklet[2] of his reminiscences during his years in Karachi. In 1980, I wrote a book titled *The People Betrayed*[3] on the rise and fall of the Janata Party's government. In 1995, Dr Atmaram Kulkarni, a Bombay-based political scientist, wrote my biography titled *The Advent of Advani*.[4] Although it had some factual inaccuracies, the author had done commendable research by talking to my colleagues and non-political associates.

I also like watching movies and plays, although I regret that I don't get enough time these days to satisfy this interest. In theatre, I have immensely liked the mono-act musical plays (*Kabir* and *Swami Vivekananda*) of Shekhar Sen. Satyajit Ray's movies have moved me deeply and so have those by Guru Dutt. I have liked the early movies of Raj Kapoor, and the strong patriotic theme in all the films made by Manoj Kumar. I admired

Sunil Dutt both as an actor and as a good human being, one who played a commendable role by undertaking a *pad yatra* for Hindu-Sikh unity when Punjab was rocked by terrorism. Some of the truly admirable movies I have watched recently with family and friends are Aamir Khan's *Taare Zameen Par*, Feroze Khan's *Gandhi, My Father*, Shahrukh Khan's *Chak De India* and *Lage Raho Munnabhai* by the duo of Vidhu Vinod Chopra and Raju Hirani. Among the foreign films, the ones I have liked the most are *The Bridge on the River Kwai*, *My Fair Lady* and *The Sound of Music*.

I should make a special mention of Amitabh Bachchan, whose versatility and almost limitless talent have never ceased to amaze me. His parents, the legendary Hindi poet Dr Harivanshrai Bachchan and Teji Bachchan, were closely known to me. Indeed, when Amitabh Bachchan's debut film *Saat Hindustani*, written and directed by K.A. Abbas, came out in 1969, Teji Bachchan arranged a special screening for me. Therefore, it was in some ways a journey down memory lane for me, too, when my daughter Pratibha did a lengthy, five-part interview with Amitji to mark the hundredth episode of her weekly *Namaste Cinema* programme on Zee TV. Though a legend, he encourages younger people. After the programme was telecast, he sent a text message to Pratibha: 'Thank you. It was such a joy talking to you. The quality of an interview is judged not by the person getting interviewed, but by the person interviewing, and you were marvellous.'

As a former movie critic and lifelong lover of films, I have closely watched the evolution of Hindi cinema. Since I was also once an avid lover of plays, I have often compared cinema and theatre as art forms. Theatre produces an intensity of artistic communication between the artistes and the audience that is unique to it. But it does not have the mass reach of cinema and television, whose impact is greatly enhanced by their visual richness, musical content and its ability to take the viewer on an odyssey in space and time. For as long as I have been watching Hindi movies, they have functioned as promoters of national integration.*

---

* In this context, I should make an appreciative mention of the joint efforts of film makers Bharat Bala and his wife Kanika, along with popular music director A.R. Rahman, to creatively render *Jana Gana Mana*, the national anthem, and *Vande Mataram*, the national song.

However, in recent decades, they have also emerged as India's powerful cultural ambassadors all over the globe. When I think of these twin-roles of Indian cinema (and I recognise the role of non-Hindi films also in this), my heart is filled with a sense of gratitude towards all the great artists, singers, music composers, producers, directors and others associated with our film industry. I am especially impressed by the young talent in Indian cinema, and would like to express a wish that they tap more into India's precious and inexhaustible inheritance of literature, arts, social reform, patriotic valor and spiritual exploration.

Music has always been a source of joy and relaxation for me. I used to play the flute when I was younger; indeed, I was a regular flutist in the RSS band in Karachi. I love film songs, both old and new, especially those with slow and soulful tunes. I have nearly 300 songs stored on my i-pod as well as in my MP3-installed mobile, and listen to them whenever I have some free time. Lata Mangeshkhar, India's Nightingale, is my all-time favourite among popular singers. I never tire of listening to her songs, especially her devotional numbers such as *Jyoti Kalash Chhalake*. I am grateful to Lataji because she has sung this song at my request at several public events where we have shared the dais. I find great solace in listening to *bhajans* by Anup Jalota and also to ghazals by Jagjit Singh, Mehdi Hasan and Mallika Pukhraj. Among classical dancers, I have been a fan of Sonal Mansingh and Raja Radha Reddy, who are also family friends. And among my family friends, who are also members of the BJP, are four renowned personalities from the film and TV world: Shatrughan Sinha, Vinod Khanna, Hema Malini and Smriti Irani.

*

In 1991, *Afternoon Despatch & Courier*, a Mumbai-based newspaper, carried an interview with me under the caption '20 Questions', which focused on my non-political life.

Q: What is your greatest weakness?
A: Books; at a grosser level, chocolates.

Q: Your most prized possession?

A: My books; and my wife's collection of Ganapati statuettes.

Q: How do you relax?

A: Whenever possible, go to a theatre to watch a play; or else occupy myself with books or TV.

Q: If you could change one thing about yourself, what would it be?

A: I think my temperament needs some wit and sparkle (which it presently lacks), and also some capacity to indulge in small talk.

Q: How would you describe yourself?

A: As a political activist earnestly exerting to make the BJP an instrument that can change today's image of the UGLY INDIAN POLITICIAN, steeped in corruption and opportunism.

Q: What do you consider your greatest accomplishment?

A: Through the Ram Rath Yatra, to be able to precipitate a vigorous national debate on the content of Indian Nationalism, and the true meaning of secularism.

Q: If you could be reborn, what would you like to come back as?

A: As I am, to complete the tasks remaining unfinished.

Q: If you were told that you had only twenty-four hours to live how would you spend them?

A: By forgetting that I had only one day left, and spending the day as normally as I otherwise do.

Q: Your favourite person?

A: My daughter, Pratibha.

Q: Your favourite city?

A: Karachi.

Q: How would you like to be remembered?

A: As a person who conscientiously strove to live up to his convictions.

In the same year, the *Telegraph*, a Kolkata-based newspaper, posed me a set of similar questions.

Q: *What is your idea of perfect happiness?*

A: Being at perfect peace with my own self, my own conscience.

Q: *What do you dislike most in others?*

A: Pettiness and Crudity.

Q: *What makes you most depressed?*

A: There was a time when criticism of my views hurt me. It bothers me no more. However, an attack on my bonafides does distress me deeply.

Q: *What is your favourite word?*

A: Credibility. In recent years, 'credibility' has become a key attribute whereby parties and politicians are judged.

Q: *On what occasions do you lie?*

A: There are occasions when telling the truth would cause needless hurt or anguish to a dear one. It is in such situations that I do try to lie. I do not know if I am able to get away successfully.

Q: *What is your greatest regret?*

A: That in spite of the fact that I adore Sanskrit, I did not study Sanskrit.

Q: *What brings tears into your eyes?*

A: Tears of joy or sorrow, immediately moisten my eyes. Even a moving piece of dialogue in a film, or, for that matter, fulsome praise showered on the BJP by an outsider, or news of some outstanding achievement by a near and dear one, makes me emotional.

Q: *How would you like to die?*

A: I would like death to come to me suddenly and abruptly, without notice, either to me or to anybody else.

✻

MY FAMILY, MY WORLD

If, in continuation to that interview, someone were to ask me today 'What is the source of greatest happiness in your personal life?' my answer, unhesitatingly, would be, 'My family'. Similarly, if I were asked, 'What is the source of greatest meaning in your political life?' I would say, 'Religion and Spirituality'.

Family is the mainstay of stability, strength and happiness in each person's life but it is especially so in the case of those who choose to enter public life. Family is where I have experienced boundless happiness, unfailingly and on every single day of my life. It is here that I have felt loved, anchored, protected, and cared for all through the inevitable ups and downs in politics. So much so, that when I come home after a meeting or an outstation tour, I feel that I have entered a private universe of my own, where I have no worries, no complaints, only a pure sense of contentment. Recently, my daughter Pratibha took the entire family—me, my wife Kamla, son Jayant and daughter-in-law Geetika—for dinner to a restaurant in Delhi. Each one ordered a dish of their choice and when all of them were placed on the table, Pratibha, the wittiest in our family, quipped, 'Ah, this is truly a global spread. We are true believers in *Vasudhaiva Kutumbakam* (The whole world is our family.)'

After a pause, I said, '*Vasudhaiva Kutumbakam* is fine. However, for some time now, my family has been my world.'

Ours is a close-knit family and Kamla has been, right from the beginning, in complete command of all the affairs of home, from finance to food. During the NDA rule, I used to jocularly say to my friends, 'I may be the Home Minister of India, but, within our family, Kamla is the Minister of Home Affairs.' I have never had to bother myself with the requirements at home. My aloofness often makes me a butt of banter in my family, with my wife chiding me for not knowing my own bank account number and for never visiting our own modest house that she bought in Delhi nearly twenty years ago. (We also own another house in Gandhinagar, my parliamentary constituency.) Jayant and Pratibha have been pursuing their own professional lives. By temperament, Jayant is reserved and reflective whereas Pratibha is outgoing, active and sociable. Apart from the *samskaras* that Kamla and I have been able to impart to them, they have taken two things from me: my childhood interest in cricket and movies. Jayant, who runs a small business in Delhi, is an avid follower of cricket and has many friends among India's Test players, both former and current. Pratibha, who anchors and produces television programmes, is passionate about films. She has specialised in producing thematic programmes based on Hindi cinema for TV channels. These have featured Ram, Krishna, Shiva, Ganesha and Hanuman, and festivals like Holi and Diwali, in Hindi cinema. She has also made a film on '*Vande Mataram*' in Hindi cinema. These have been widely appreciated for effectively presenting cultural and patriotic values. Among Pratibha's works are also films on my Swarna Jayanti Rath Yatra and Bharat Suraksha Yatra.

I am proud that my children are pursuing careers that are completely independent of my politics. For a long time, Pratibha did not even use the surname 'Advani' since she wanted to develop her own identity. This led to an interesting experience once when she had gone to interview the noted filmmaker, Vidhu Vinod Chopra. 'Are you happy with the government's steps to promote the film industry?' she asked him. 'Not really,' he replied. 'The biggest problem our industry is facing right now is piracy. But I don't think the Home Minister is even aware of it.' After the interview, someone told Chopra, 'Do you know who you were talking to? She is the Home Minister's daughter.' Chopra came up to Pratibha and said, 'Oops, I didn't know...' He became a good friend of our family thereafter. If Pratibha has any interface with my political life, it is that I have a fondness to show her films to select audiences at home and she frequently arranges special screenings of good movies for me, usually at the Films Division's auditorium at Mahadev Road.

'Pratibha' means talent, and she truely lives up to it. Even as a child she was very quick at picking up—be it studies or any creative pursuit, as can be seen from my caricature that she drew when she was *only* ten (reproduced in the book). Her thinking, more than anyone else's in the family, is a lot like mine. She has imbibed my likes, dislikes, my values and traditions that I believe in. I have a special bond with her because she is, indeed, my pillar of strength. She takes care of the smallest of my needs. I once gave her a book to read—*Don't Sweat the Small Stuff*. With her, however, it is always all the small stuff.

AT THE FEET OF SPIRITUAL PERSONALITIES

I am not a religious person in the conventional sense of the term. I do not do daily puja, nor do I have a regular routine of visiting temples. Nevertheless, religion and spirituality have had a profound influence on both my personality and my political life. It is easy to become conceited, arrogant and corrupt in politics. If I have been able to avoid these ills, it is because of my religious and spiritual upbringing. For the realisation that there is a Higher Power before which all other powers are insignificant, and to which we are all accountable for even the smallest of our actions, brings humility and perspective to our lives.

I have had the good fortune of interacting with many revered spiritual personalities such as Dada J.P. Vaswani, Satya Sai Baba, Dalai Lama, late Pandurang Shastri Athawale, late Dadi Prakashmani, head of Prajapita Brahmakumaris, Shri Jayendra Saraswathi Swamiji of Kanchi Math, Pramukh Swami Maharaj of Swaminarayan Sampradaya, Acharya Mahapragya, late Acharya Tulsi, late Acharya Sushil Muniji, Swami Vishveshteertha of Pejawar Math, Udupi, late Ramachandra Paramhamsaji of Ayodhya, Mata Amritandamayi, Sri Sri Ravi Shankar, Sant Morari Bapu, Shivkumar Swamiji of Siddhaganga Math, Tumkur, Sant Asaram Bapu, Rameshbhai Oza, Swami Ramdev, Baba Gurinder Singh Dhillon (Beas Guruji), Maharaj Rajinder Singhji, Swami Chidanand Saraswati and others. In this context, I must also mention my interactions with Mother Teresa and Maulana Wahiduddin Khan. I have learnt from and been blessed by each one of them.

With the passage of time, the influence of religion and spirituality (the two, in their true sense, are not different) on me has been deepening, and I now regard them to be the most important imparter of meaning to politics—indeed, to life in general. Here, religion should be understood not in its narrow denominational sense, but as Dharma, the universal moral order that sustains and guides human life in the right direction. In this sense, I disagree with those who say that politics should be divorced from religion. In the debate on the true meaning of secularism, I often quote Mahatma Gandhi's following seminal thought on this subject:

> For me, politics bereft of religion are absolute dirt, ever to be shunned. Politics concerns nations and that which concerns the welfare of nations must be one of the concerns of a man who is religiously inclined, in other words, a seeker after God and Truth. For me, God and Truth are convertible terms. Therefore, in politics also we have to establish the Kingdom of Heaven.[5] Many of my political friends despair of me because they say that even my politics is derived from religion. And they are right. My politics and all other activities of mine are derived from my religion.[6] Indeed, religion should pervade every one of our actions. Here religion does not mean sectarianism. It means a belief in ordered moral government of the universe. It is not less real because it is unseen. This religion transcends Hinduism, Islam, Christianity, etc. It does not supersede them. It harmonizes them and gives them reality.[7]

Of course, politics in India is far from being guided by the canons of dharma, and governance is a far cry from the ideal of dharma *rajya*, which both Mahatma Gandhi and Deendayal Upadhyaya advocated. However, even a sincere acceptance of the gap between the reality and the ideal can induce us to take a step towards bridging that gap. In my political as well as personal life, I have made sincere efforts to take some small steps in this direction. I may have faltered, but I have not stopped trying. This, too, has been a source of immense happiness in my life.

Epilogue

I am writing these lines at Parmarth Niketan, Rishikesh, an idyllic ashram located on the banks of the Holy Ganga, with the verdant mountains of the lower Himalayas towering behind it. It is run by His Holiness Swami Chidanandaji Saraswati, whose work for the reform and renaissance of Hinduism I have greatly admired. I had come to this place a year ago to experience the dawn of 2007, and am here again with my family to spend a few days in spiritual solitude. The air around is pure and the atmosphere sublime. But what has touched me the most is the *gurukul* established by Swamiji in which orphans and abandoned children are trained to become 'Rishikumars', receiving both traditional and modern education that helps each child to blossom with his own innate artistic and intellectual creativity. Participating in the elaborate *aarti* in the evening with Swamiji and these little angels, with the sacred waters of the Ganga flowing in front of me and the sky above illuminated by the full moon of *Paushya Poornima*, has had a purifying effect on me.

Swamiji discussed several ongoing and future projects of his ashram with me. Among these were the cleaning up the Ganga; making Uttarakhand, which is considered '*Dev Bhoomi*' (Divine Land), free of plastic and other litter; and renovating and beautifying of all the pilgrimage centres in the state. The idea strongly appealed to me because the ugly sight of pollution at Haridwar, Rishikesh, Mathura, Varanasi and other sacred places in India, which attract tens of millions of devotees from all over the country each year, always fills me with despair. Fortunately, the Chief Minister of Uttarakhand, Maj. Gen. (Retd.) B.C. Khanduri, also joined us in these discussions and it was decided that the government, civil society organisations and religious establishments should jointly undertake a massive and time-bound campaign to implement this project, first in Gangotri, where the Ganga originates, and subsequently thereafter in other places such as Yamunotri, Kedarnath, Badrinath, Uttarkashi, Hemkunt, Rishikesh and Haridwar. I feel confident of this project taking off for two reasons. Firstly, Khandurie has the reputation of being dynamic; as Minister of Surface Transport in the Vajpayee government, he had earned nationwide fame for implementing the ambitious National Highway Development Project. Secondly, there are several far-sighted religious leaders, both in Uttarakhand and elsewhere in the country, who are willing to contribute to make the vision of *Nirmal Ganga* (pollution-free Ganga) a reality.

Going forward, it is my dream to see that Ganga becomes free of pollution all along its course, right from Gangotri to Ganga Sagar, the place in West Bengal, where it merges into the ocean. Former Prime Minister, Rajiv Gandhi had launched a commendable project for this purpose, called the Ganga Action Plan, in the mid-1980s. Sadly, it did not yield the desired results because it was sought to be implemented in a bureaucratic way, without eliciting the enthusiastic involvement of what I might call the Ganga Parivar—the people living on both sides of the river, the pilgrims coming from different parts of the country, and, most importantly, the hundreds of religious establishments located along the course of the river. I have no doubt that a combined, determined and sustained effort of the society and the state would restore the Holy Ganga to its pristine purity. It may take decades to fully reach this objective, but it is a *maha yagya* (mega mission) worth undertaking. Indeed, it should be our long-term goal to make all the rivers, lakes and water bodies in India pollution-free. After all, they are not only the lifeline of our country's development, but also the symbols and sustainers of India's ancient and proud civilisation.

This endeavour is closely linked to how religion can make our politics more meaningful and transformative which I discussed in the previous chapter. The idea of cleaning up the Ganga inevitably made me contemplate about the pollution afflicting politics, governance and public life in India, and how adherence to a loftier, spiritually-inspired ideal could possibly help us get rid of it. And this contemplation found a voice when, at the end of the Ganga *aarati* a short while ago, Swamiji asked me to address the gathering of devotees who had congregated on the wonderful ghat that he has constructed on the river-bank. These were my impromptu remarks:

> I do not consider myself worthy of addressing a congregation of devotees because I am also, like many of you here, a devotee and a seeker. I have come here to receive some enlightenment and inspiration, and not to give it. However, if the idea is to let me share a few thoughts on the importance of spiritual guidance for politics and nation-building activities, I do have something to say on the matter.
>
> When I look back at the six decades that I have spent in public service—and this period has neatly coincided with the sixty years of India's Independence—I can identify three main achievements that have imparted strength to our nation and raised its stature internationally. Firstly, India not only adopted the democratic system of governance, but has zealously preserved it, belying the gloomy predictions of many foreigners that a country with a largely illiterate population and saddled with numerous 'divisive' diversities could remain neither democratic nor united. India has remained democratic essentially because of its Hindu ethos, just as it has remained secular because of its Hindu ethos. Our second greatest achievement is that India is now a nuclear weapons power, thanks to a courageous decision that our former Prime Minister Atal Bihari Vajpayee took in May 1998. Although some countries, ironically states with nuclear arsenals more lethal than ours, did criticise our government for this decision, it nevertheless made

every Indian proud, reassuring him that no evil power can dare attack or enslave a militarily strong India in the future, as had happened in the past for nearly a thousand years. Our third major achievement—and it is a recent phenomenon—is in the field of economic development. The entire world has now begun to view India as tomorrow's economic superpower. As a result, India and Indians are commanding the kind of attention and respect in the eyes of the international community, which was absent two or three decades ago.

As an Indian and as a political activist, these three achievements make me immensely happy and proud, especially because my party is privileged to have contributed to each of them. It is true that we still have many unfinished tasks and unfulfilled aspirations in the area of socio-economic development. Poverty and backwardness need to be fully eliminated. Every citizen needs to have security and an assured provision of education, healthcare, employment, housing, leisure and recreation so that he can live a happy life and realise his full potential as a human being. As I peer into the future, I have no doubt that all these tasks in India's material progress will be accomplished, sooner or later, although we would like it to happen sooner. But is material progress and prosperity the only ideal that India should aspire for? India has to live and strive for a much higher ideal. What is that higher ideal? How to understand it? Who can guide us to pursue it?

I do not normally talk about it in my political rallies, but since I am in the presence of the sacred Ganga, I am prompted to say that that ideal is India's spiritual progress, which can yield solutions to many of the vexed problems facing our own country and humanity at large. This thought has been expressed by all the great saints and seers of India, but here I would like to mention its most inspiring articulation on the eve of 15 August 1947 by Sri Aurobindo, who was requested by All India Radio to give a special message for India's Independence. It so happened that 15

August was also his birthday. I believe that his short message, which presents many bold themes of everlasting relevance for our country, deserves to be read and studied by every Indian who has chosen to be in public life.

Sri Aurobindo said that 15 August, the birthday of free India, 'marks for her the end of an old era, the beginning of a new age.' But was it of significance for India alone? No, said the great seer. 'We can also make it by our life and acts as a free nation an important date in a new age opening for the whole world, for the political, social, cultural and spiritual future of humanity.' He likened India's Independence to the beginning of realisation of a big dream, a grand project. 'The spiritual gift of India to the world has already begun. India's spirituality is entering Europe and America in an ever increasing measure.... Amid the disasters of the time, more and more eyes are turning towards her with hope.'

The yogi's inner eye, however, could see an even higher potential in India having become a free nation. As a visionary who believed that the human mind is destined to ultimately evolve into a Super-Mind, with infinite new possibilities that cannot fully be comprehended at the present stage of man's under-development, he described 15 August as 'a step in evolution which would raise man to a higher and larger consciousness and begin the solution of the problems which have perplexed and vexed him since he first began to think and to dream of individual perfection and a perfect society. This is still a personal hope and an idea, an ideal which has begun to take hold both in India and in the West on forward-looking minds.... Here too, if this evolution is to take place, since it must proceed through a growth of the spirit and the inner consciousness, the initiative can come from India and, although the scope must be universal, the central movement may be hers.'

Sri Aurobindo referred to the fact that 15 August was his own birthday 'I take this coincidence, not as a fortuitous accident, but as the sanction and seal of the Divine Force that guides my steps on the work with which I began life. Indeed, on this day I can watch almost all the world-movements which I hoped to see fulfilled in my lifetime.... In all these movements free India may well play a large part and take a leading position.' He concluded his inspiring message on a note of guarded optimism: 'Such is the content which I put into this date of India's liberation; whether or how far this hope will be justified depends upon the new and free India.'*

I have referred to Sri Aurobindo's message because each of us in politics and public life should realise the noble goals and soaring expectations that India's greatest minds have placed before the nation. We should measure our own activities, ambitions and life-goals against this higher ideal of nation-building. Are we demeaning ourselves with our selfish pursuits or are we ennobling ourselves by making our own modest personal contribution to India's march along the path of enlightenment and expansion shown by our spiritual giants?

Swamiji has taken up the cause of pollution of the Ganga. I can understand his agony. How can we say that we worship Mother Ganga when we pollute her waters and her environs? I was myself most distressed when, while coming to Rishikesh yesterday, I saw huge mounds of plastic and garbage on the roadside. All this must be changed. But it is not just the external environment that needs to be purified, but also the internal environment of our own lives. Without that, we cannot accomplish the big and challenging tasks of nation-building, nor can our accomplishments be enduring.

I have always believed that India has limitless potential for progress. We are blessed with rich resources, both human and natural, to realise that potential. Above all, we have an invaluable spiritual and civilisational heritage to guide us. I discussed with Swamiji how, using our resources properly, employing the power of modern science and technology, and being guided by our heritage,

---

* The full text of Sri Aurobindo's message on AIR on the eve of India's Independence is given in Appendix I.

can indeed create a *Swachcha Bharat* (Clean India), *Swastha Bharat* (Healthy India), *Saakshar Bharat* (Literate and Educated India), *Shaktishali Bharat* (Strong India), *Samruddha Bharat* (Prosperous India) and *Prabuddha Bharat* (Enlightened India).

What is needed is to contribute to nation-building with the same spirit of dedication that our forefathers displayed for making India free. I recall here the words of Swami Vivekananda, when he returned to India in 1897 after his hugely successful tour of Europe and America, during which he also delivered his historic address to the World Parliament of Religions in Chicago in 1893. Swamiji's ship landed in Madras, where he was accorded a rousing welcome. In his reply, he said something prophetic:

For the next fifty years…let all other vain gods disappear for the time from our minds. This is the only god that is awake, India, our own race…. All other gods are sleeping. What vain gods shall we go after and yet cannot worship the god that we see all around us, the Virat?… The first of all worship is the worship of the Virat—of those all around us. These are all our gods—men and animals; and the first gods we have to worship are our own countrymen.

It is interesting to note that Swami Vivekananda had given this clarion call 'for the next fifty years' in 1897. Exactly fifty years later, India won freedom from colonial rule. Should we not heed his call even now, with this difference that even as we follow our own faiths and worship our own gods, we all worship this *Virat* called India? Should we not see divinity in all its people, animals, rivers and oceans, environment, and work for its greatness and glory? Should we not imbibe the teachings of great men like Sri Aurobindo, Swami Vivekananda and others in our endeavour to build the India of tomorrow? I believe so. And this is the belief that gets reinforced when I come to a holy place like Rishikesh.

*

It so happened that I arrived in Rishikesh the same day that the NDA entrusted me with a new responsibility: to lead the alliance in the next

Lok Sabha elections. My party's Parliamentary Board had taken a similar decision a month earlier. This is indeed a challenging responsibility, and I shall do my utmost to discharge it successfully, seeking the support and cooperation of all my colleagues and countrymen, and seeking, above all, strength, guidance and grace from the Almighty. It shall be my unceasing endeavour to make good governance, development and security, both for the country and its citizens, the principal thrust of the NDA's election campaign and, if the people do give us the mandate, also the guiding objectives of our government.

India, I believe, has been expectantly looking for honesty in governance and strong leadership that is uncompromisingly committed to the nation's unity, integrity, security and progress. Our people want to see an end to 'pollution' at the Gangotri of Governance—at the nodal centres of power in New Delhi—so that the rest of the Ganga can become clean and life-supporting. And by 'pollution' I do not refer only to financial corruption and misuse of power in politics and administration. Of course, corruption of this kind is a foe of both national security and national development, and our people, who are being harassed and humiliated by it at all levels, want to see it eliminated. But 'pollution' also manifests in other poisonous forms: pseudo-secularism, minorityism, vote-bank politics, criminalisation, emasculation of institutions and insult to the sacred symbols of our nationalism, all of which are weakening India and making it vulnerable to grave threats.

No less worrisome is the fact that, even after sixty years of Independence, a majority of our population is receiving only the leftovers of economic growth, while the bulk of its fruits are allowed to be cornered by the rich and the privileged minority. The rich are becoming richer and the poor remaining poor. Our people want a government that cares equally for every section of our diverse society, especially for the poor and deprived. And they are looking for a leadership that genuinely respects democracy and is determined to safeguard its institutions from assaults inspired by selfish considerations.

Each of these expectations is legitimate, even urgent. And the future belongs to those in India's political class who hearken to the people's demands with a firm commitment to good governance, development and security.

I have performed every responsibility, minor or major, that has been entrusted to me from time to time in the course of my long political journey with honesty, devotion and commitment. This accounts for the credibility I have earned in public life. In future too, I shall perform any duty that Destiny may assign to me with the same aspiration: make my humble *seva* towards ensuring that India becomes more united, stronger and stands taller, with its Tomorrow brighter than its Today.

Parmarth Niketan
Rishikesh

Appendix I

Free India's Message to the World

Address by Maharshi Aurobindo, which was broadcast on All India Radio on the eve of India's Independence Day on 15 August 1947, which was also his birthday

August 15th, 1947 is the birthday of free India. It marks for her the end of an old era, the beginning of a new age. But we can also make it by our life and acts as a free nation an important date in a new age opening for the whole world, for the political, social, cultural and spiritual future of humanity.

August 15th is my own birthday and it is naturally gratifying to me that it should have assumed this vast significance. I take this coincidence, not as a fortuitous accident, but as the sanction and seal of the Divine Force that guides my steps on the work with which I began life, the beginning of its full fruition. Indeed, on this day I can watch almost all the world-movements which I hoped to see fulfilled in my lifetime, though then they looked like impracticable dreams, arriving at fruition or on their way to achievement. In all these movements free India may well play a large part and take a leading position.

The first of these dreams was a revolutionary movement which would create a free and united India. India today is free but she has not achieved unity. At one moment it almost seemed as if in the very act of liberation she would fall back into the chaos of separate States which preceded the British conquest. But fortunately it now seems probable that this danger will be averted and a large and powerful, though not yet a complete union will be established. Also, the wisely drastic policy of the Constituent Assembly has made it probable that the problem of the depressed classes will be solved without schism or fissure. But the old communal division into Hindus and Muslims seems now to have hardened into a permanent political division of the country. It is to be hoped that this settled fact will not be accepted as settled for ever or as anything more than a temporary expedient. For if it lasts, India may be seriously weakened, even crippled: civil strife may remain always possible, possible even a new invasion and foreign conquest, her position among the nations weakened, her destiny impaired or even frustrated.

This must not be; the partition must go. Let us hope that that may come about naturally, by an increasing recognition of the necessity not only of peace and concord but of common action, by the practice of common action and the creation of means for that purpose. In this way unity may finally come about under whatever form—the exact form may have a pragmatic but not a fundamental importance. But by whatever means, in whatever way, the division must go; unity must and will be achieved, for it is necessary for the greatness of India's future.

Another dream was for the resurgence and liberation of the peoples of Asia and her return to her great role in the progress of human civilisation. Asia has arisen; large parts are now quite free or are at this moment being liberated: its other still subject or partly subject parts are moving through whatever struggled towards freedom. Only a little has to be done and that will be done today or tomorrow. There India has her part to play and has begun to play it with an energy and ability which already indicate the measure of her possibilities and the place she can take in the council of the nations.

The third dream was a world-union forming the outer basis of a fairer, brighter and nobler life for all mankind. That unification of the human world is under way; there is an imperfect initiation organised by struggling against tremendous difficulties. But the momentum is there and it must inevitably increase and conquer. Here too India has begun to play a prominent part and, if she can develop that larger statesmanship which is not limited by the present facts and immediate possibilities but looks into the future and brings it nearer, her presence may make all the difference between a slow and timid and a bold and swift development. A catastrophe may intervene and interrupt or destroy what is being done, but even then the final result is sure. For unification is a necessity of Nature, an inevitable movement. Its necessity for the nations is also clear, for without it the freedom of the small nations may be at any moment in peril and the life even of the large and powerful nations insecure. The unification is therefore to the interests of all, and only human imbecility and stupid selfishness can prevent it; but these cannot stand for ever against the necessity of Nature and the Divine Will. But an outward basis is not enough; there must grow up an international spirit and outlook, international forms and institutions must appear, perhaps such developments, as dual or multilateral citizenship, willed interchange or voluntary fusion of cultures. Nationalism will have fulfilled itself and lost its militancy and would no longer find these things incompatible with self-preservation and the integrality of its outlook. A new spirit of oneness will take hold of the human race.

Another dream, the spiritual gift of India to the world has already begun. India's spirituality is entering Europe and America in an ever increasing measure. That movement will grow; amid the disasters of the time more and more eyes are turning towards her with hope and there is even an increasing resort not only to her teachings, but to her psychic and spiritual practice.

The final dream was a step in evolution which would raise man to a higher and larger consciousness and begin the solution of the problems which have perplexed and vexed him since he first began to think and to dream of individual perfection and a perfect society. This is still a personal hope and an idea, an ideal which has begun to take hold both in India and in the West on forward-looking minds. The difficulties in the way are more formidable than in any other field of endeavour, but difficulties were made to be overcome and if the Supreme Will is there, they will be overcome. Here too, if this evolution is to take place, since it must proceed through a growth of the spirit and the inner consciousness, the initiative can come from India and, although the scope must be universal, the central movement may be hers.

Such is the content which I put into this date of India's liberation; whether or how far this hope will be justified depends upon the new and free India.

Appendix II

Swami Vivekananda and the Future of India

Swami Ranganathananda

The 15th of August 1947, so far as India is concerned, may be, said to mark the end of one epoch and the beginning of another. Foreign domination which began with Plassey in 1757 ends today exactly 190 years later. This epoch of political slavery is but a short interregnum viewed against the background of India's long history. The real significance of this interlude in our history can be assessed only when we are at a little distance in time from it, when alone an objective consideration of events becomes possible. It is difficult for any but the greatest thinkers to view events dispassionately even while living them. Any such event, therefore, will appear to have a different value to such a thinker from what it will bear to an average person.

POLITICAL FREEDOM VERSUS POLITICAL SUBJECTION

Political slavery, to an average person, may mean nothing unusual, if it does not affect the routine within the little horizon of his daily life. But it becomes

---

* Swami Ranganathananda was President of the Ramakrishna Math and Mission when he passed away in 2005 at the age of 97. He was head of the Ramakrishna Mission in Karachi for six years (1942-48), before he had to close down the Math in the wake of Partion-related riots. This profound and preseient essay was written by Swamiji in Karachi on 15 August 1947.

galling when the same person becomes politically conscious—when its restrictions impinge upon his newly acquired sense of values of freedom and self-respect. With the dawning of the consciousness of these values, he becomes a political entity—a being who values freedom above mere material and physical security. This marks the emergence of a spiritual and moral value in the life of man and the evolution of a rudimentary moral and spiritual personality. It is this rudimentary personality that, later on, through political education in life, and through the intense pursuit of the value of freedom, grows into that finished social product, the citizen. The evolution of this citizen is the end of politics, as it is also the highest social end.

INDIA STANDS UP TO THE MODERN CHALLENGE

Political subjection in the nineteenth century, with its promise of an era of peace, was more or less accepted by the vast mass of Hindus and Muslims of this country, urged by considerations of physical and material security and as an escape from the uncertainties of the earlier centuries. But this was but a phase, and a short phase at that. Political slavery becomes a challenge, as much when it tends to uproot the cultural inheritance, as when it tends to restrict the scope of functioning, of a people. A people who possess inner reserves of vitality rise to meet this challenge, while those who are bereft of it take it easy and court extinction as a people, though continuing to live as individuals with new souls and new bodies. The history of the world is not without examples of the latter type. The challenge to India came from both the fronts—cultural as well as socio-political. India rose to meet the challenge first on the cultural front, then on the political—broadly speaking the second half of the nineteenth century evidenced the first, while this century up-to-date evidenced the second—thus demonstrating the abiding vitality of the people and their legacy. In the arresting story of this double process and the phenomenal successes it has attained even in so short a period lies the romance of recent Indian history and its significance to the world at large.

One noteworthy feature of India's rise to meet the new cultural challenge from the West needs to be well emphasized; for it contains a quality of dynamic synthesis, which has also imparted its tone to her response to the second challenge, namely, to her fight for political independence, and which contains promise of fruitful application in the spheres of her domestic and foreign relations as well. This striking feature is the note of affirmation and synthesis, inclusion and not exclusion, characteristic of new India's awareness and activity. What was but reactionary (used in the literal sense only) in the early phases, and often apologetic and negative, becomes transformed into a creative movement of thought, seeking to affirm and to synthesize any tested human value whether evolved in the East or in the West, whether scientific or religious, political or social.

VIVEKANANDA AND THE MODERN INDIAN RENAISSANCE

Swami Vivekananda stands as the most effective spokesman and representative of this phase of our cultural movement. He was one of those who found in the British connection a potent means for breaking our moribund society and civilization with a view to making it expansive. In his personality was fused the past and the present, ancient wisdom and modern knowledge; he knew the glory of our past; he felt intimately the degradations of our present day; he was a Hindu to the backbone; he loved and revered other religions as well; he was a lover of the social and spiritual gospel of Islam and Christianity and of their value to Indian life and thought. Above all, he was deeply imbued with the spirit of modern thought with its theoretical and practical contributions in the field of science, and political and economic contributions in the field of life and society. Last but not the least, he was fully aware of the international character of human relationships in the modern context. His was not the role of a reactionary patriot who would take his country away from the contamination of other peoples, or who would ride his chariot of nationalism roughly over the freedom of other nations. He loved India, but he loved humanity too, with equal passion. Says he in one of his letters affirming his faith in the glory of man as such, undivided by narrow domestic walls (*Complete Works*, vol. 8, Third Edition, p. 349,):

> 'What is India or England or America to us? We are the servants of that God who by the ignorant is called Man.'
> And we may as well add, whom the more ignorant call Hindu, Muslim, Christian, or Indian, Russian, American, etc.

Jawaharlal Nehru pays a tribute to this aspect of Swami Vivekananda's personality (*The Discovery of India*, p. 400):

> Rooted in the past and full of pride in India's heritage, Vivekananda was yet modern in his approach to life's problems and was a kind of bridge between the past of India and her present.

Himself an internationalist, he quotes with deep appreciation the following statement of the unity of mankind from Swami Vivekananda's lectures delivered in 1897 (quoted in *The Discovery of India*, pp. 401-2):

> Even in politics and sociology, problems that were only national twenty years ago can no longer be solved on national grounds only. They are assuming huge proportions, gigantic shapes. They can only be

solved when looked at in the broader light of international grounds. International organizations, international combinations, international laws are the cry of the day. That shows solidarity, ... There cannot be any progress without the whole world following in the wake and it is becoming every day clearer that the solution of any problem can never be attained on racial or national, or narrow grounds. Every idea has to become broad till it covers the whole of this world, every aspiration must go on increasing till it has engulfed the whole of humanity, nay, the whole of life, within its scope.

Applying this criterion to the recent past of India and pointing a lesson and a warning to his countrymen, both Hindu and Muslim, Swami Vivekananda affirms (quoted in *The Discovery of India*, p. 402):

I am thoroughly convinced that no individual or nation can live by holding itself apart from the community of others, and whenever such an attempt has been made under false ideas of greatness, policy, or holiness, the result has always been disastrous to the secluding one. 'The fact of our isolation from all the other nations of the world is the cause of our degeneration, and its only remedy is getting back into the current of the world. Motion is the sign of life.'

The words quoted above were uttered fifty years ago; they carry freshness and a vigour even today. In Swami Vivekananda's day, India was not an active factor in world affairs. Her past glory was a subject of sympathetic comment and study with several Western scholars. But the world in general pitied her in her plight. Her own children also felt a sort of self-pity for their aged and battered mother.

But all this quickly changed. The shock of conquest and the shame of subjection were a challenge which, far from extinguishing her inner fires, as happened in the case of many other nations and as was anticipated by many even in hers, on the contrary, led to her blazing forth in an outburst of thought and activity, initiating a real process of national rejuvenation. This awakening was a process, first, of self-discovery and, second, of self-expression.

The process of self-discovery on the part of India may be said to attain its culmination today—15th of August 1947—with the attainment by her of full political freedom; the energies so released will from now onward issue forth in a more intensified process of creative self expression.

VIVEKANANDA'S 'DOMESTIC POLICY'

Vivekananda as person led India into the current of world cultural forces. Vivekananda as idea seeks to guide India into the world community of nations after making her a well-knit people. In Vivekananda's conception, India had in her the requisite historically acquired capacity to function as the moral leader of nations. The new world situation also demands a strong moral guidance to the energies of nations. But India, he held, could not assume that role and discharge it effectively without first effecting certain vital changes within herself. Herein lies the scope of what he characteristically termed as 'domestic policy', leading to the assumption and discharge by her of that world responsibility which he called his 'foreign policy'.

Political freedom, economic advancement, and social solidarity are the three pre-conditions of effective Indian participation in world affairs. With the accomplishment of the first item today, the second and third remain to be tackled. Vivekananda, was the first to point out the harm that has been done to the spiritual and moral personality of our people by economic backwardness and social division. Involuntary poverty, to him, is unspiritual and immoral. Religion, he held, is not for empty bellies. Social inequalities and unwholesome hierarchies are a disease in the body-politic. In his wanderings through the length and breadth of India, he came into intimate personal contact with the emaciated and dismembered body and mind of India, as he had earlier come into contact with her undying and eternal unity of spirit through his contact with his master, Sri Ramakrishna, and through his own studies of her literature and history. He found the ideal and the real far apart; and he set his heart and hands to make the real approximate to the ideal. He wrestled through sorrow and anguish to lay bare the problem of modern India and to find its solution, and he worked himself to an early death in imparting to his countrymen his passion and his resolve. The mind and face of India today bear unmistakably the impress of Vivekananda's heart and resolve. To quote Sister Nivedita, Vivekananda's gifted Western disciple (*The Master as I Saw Him*, pp. 49-50):

> There was one thing, however, deep in the master's nature, that he never knew how to adjust. This was his love of his country and his resentment of her suffering. Throughout those years in which I saw him almost daily, the thought of India was to him like the air he breathed. True, he was a worker at foundations. He neither used the word "nationality", nor proclaimed an era of "nation-making". "Man-making", he said, was his own task. But he was a born lover, and the queen of his adoration was his motherland. Like some delicately-poised bell, thrilled and vibrated by every sound that falls upon it, was his heart to all that concerned her. Not a sob was heard within her shores that (did not find in him a responsive echo. There was no cry of fear, no tremor of weakness, no shrinking from mortification, that he had not known and understood. He was hard on her sins, unsparing of her want of worldly wisdom,

but only because he felt these faults to be his own. And none, on the contrary, was ever so possessed by the vision of her greatness!

DEMOCRACY IN FREE INDIA

Today, when the country is celebrating its day of deliverance from foreign subjection, it is well for us to remember Swami Vivekananda and his conception of the future of our country. He believed that our culture is a rich mosaic containing Hindu, Muslim and other elements. He also believed that the Hindus and the Muslims have certain things to learn from each other, which would make them not merely better Hindus and better Muslims, but, what is more important, better men. Since man-making was his religion, he exhorted his countrymen to discard narrow loves and hates and grow into that wholeness which is perfection of character. In the same vein, he exhorted the Hindus to discard the sectional loyalties of caste and sect and grow into that fullness and wholeness expressive of the Divine in man. It is as an effective help to this religion of man-making that he upheld the modern theory and practice of democracy with its faith in freedom and equality and the sacredness of personality.

DEMOCRACY AND THE TRAGEDY OF PARTITION

The strength of democracy lies in the citizen. Democracy in India seeks to turn Hindus, Muslims, Christians, Sikhs, Parsis, and others into citizens owing allegiance to certain fundamental values which are universal and human. This great process will derive ample sustenance from the inspiration of the great world religions. In fact, political, and even economic, democracy cannot go long, can also go wrong, without the guidance and inspiration that religion alone can impart. But that inspiration has to be sought not from the dogmas and creeds of religions, but from their inner core of essential truths. This work of elevating democracy to a moral and spiritual value is the task that awaits the energies of a Free India.

The above remarks may sound a bit strange, a bit too bold, in the context of present-day India. Our freedom has come to us with a good bit of sorrow in it; the voice that will proclaim freedom today will also be the voice that will proclaim our division into two political entities. But tragic as division is, we shall not make it more tragic by considering it as something more than political and administrative. Superficially, it appears to be a division based on cultural and religious grounds. But, on a close view, it reveals itself as a mere political division, based on political considerations only, but using cultural and religious badges. It has certainly roused religious and communal passion; it has left behind colossal material and human destruction.

SOCIAL FORCES TO UNDO THIS PARTITION ONE DAY

But all this does not prove that Islamic culture and religion require to be protected from the contamination of Hindu religion and culture in a separate sovereign state; all that it proves is that the Muslim intelligentsia has begun to think that it required a separate state to express its political and economic personality. If and when partition will fulfil this desire, it is bound to annul itself for want of a basic urge. The people are one whether under one sovereign state or two. And, as such, there will always be a large India looming behind the states of India and Pakistan. That India is bound to impinge itself on the social constitutions and on the political states of the two parts of divided India.

The social composition of the Indian population is bound to assert itself on her social constitution and on the political state. Whatever basic urge there is, therefore, is towards unity; the social forces can move only in this direction; the minority problem in both the states, in spite of division, is a powerful factor, in spite of appearances to the contrary, that will tend to eventual unity. And this unity will be on a higher and more enduring plane than on those of political expediency and manoeuvring through pacts and deals of the past few decades.

The pressure of politics has divided us; but the pressure of sociology will unite us; and culture reinforced by social and economic forces and the realities of the world situation will speed up the process. This process, which always goes on in a society, producing an ever-widening unity of types, had to reckon, in the case of India, with an incalculable third factor, the presence of a foreign power pursuing a policy of continual thwarting of healthy national forces in the interest of its own self-perpetuation. The elimination now of this incalculable third factor leaves the field free for the effective operation of social forces. This is the faith that sustains those who, though feeling the pang of partition, are yet not dismayed by it or confused by it. This section even now is large, comprising influential political parties and non-political groups and individuals both among the Muslims and among the Hindus. When the abnormalities of the present situation with its gushing passions and blinding hates will pass away, leaving the Indian sky clear, the country will recognize the correctness and cogency of the above faith and vision; the faith of a steady few will then become the enthusiasm of the many, leading to a reconciliation and reunion of the sundered parts, and the unsettling of a settled fact through popular will.

POLITICS: A PLAYTHING OF SOCIO-ECONOMIC FORCES

To work towards this glorious consummation silently and steadily is the task that faces the country today. We have to realize that politics is the plaything of social forces. Sociology is more fundamental than politics. In this healthy manipulation of social forces to make them tend towards social solidarity, the country will find inspiration and guidance from the personality and message of Swami Vivekananda.

Economic and cultural advancement of the Muslims and the Scheduled Castes will tend to establish a balance of social forces in the country. The impact of democracy on Hindu society will tend to the elimination of its inequalities, helping to put it on an even keel. Cultural and economic advancement will make the average Muslim less and less susceptible to communal and fanatical propaganda, and make him receptive to those aspects of his religion which are universal and human. The practice and preaching of a tolerant Islam is the task that awaits the Indian Muslim of tomorrow; its recently invoked divisive powers and negative and exclusive attitudes will have to be replaced by its sublime unifying attitudes and programmes. In short, Islamic democracy will have to grow into human democracy. The impact of this democracy on Hindu society will be wholesome for that society and the world. Vivekananda held the view that the beauty of Hindu religion has been marred by its social inequalities. In agony he cried in one of his letters written from America to a devoted worker in India (*Complete Works*, vol. 5, Seventh Edition, p. 15):

> No religion on earth preaches the dignity of humanity in such a lofty strain as Hinduism, and no religion on earth treads upon the necks of the poor and the low in such a fashion as Hinduism. The Lord has shown me that religion is not at fault, but it is the Pharisees and Sadducees in Hinduism, hypocrites, who invent all sorts of engines of tyranny in the shape of *paramarthika* and *vyavaharika* (absolute and relative truth). Religion is not at fault. On the other hand, your religion teaches you that every being is only your own self multiplied. But it was the want of practical application, the want of sympathy—the want of heart.

INTER-ACTION BETWEEN HINDUISM AND ISLAM: PAST AND PRESENT

The history of India and the character of Indian Islam and Hindu society would have been different if Islam had come to India as a friend and in peace. It would then have contributed its egalitarian social gospel to the purification of the social edifice of Hinduism—Hinduism would have gladly learnt these lessons from it, while imparting its own tolerant outlook to the sister faith. But the fact that Islam in its most effective forms came to India through the military conquerors who professed Islam but practised their own national savagery, and who ravaged India and battered Hinduism, made Islam an eye-sore to the Hindu mind. It is one of those sad chapters in inter-religious and intercultural contacts which yielded bitter fruits, but which, in a different form, would have been fruitful of great results for the religion and culture of mankind.

Yet, social forces override human frenzies and passions; for, once Islam got established in the land, the work of fusion and synthesis commenced, and the life and work of the great medieval saints of North India, both Hindu and Muslim, have added a brilliant chapter to our history. Their work, broadly speaking, bore the impress of Hinduism in the field of thought and religion, and of Islam in the field of social life. In the general framework of history the work of Kabir, Nanak, Dadu, Caitanya, Surdas and others may appear fugitive and forlorn, but they contain a moral and an inspiration for us of this age. If isolated individuals in unpropitious times could produce such glorious results, how much greater results in the direction of spiritual stability and social solidarity and the great end of, what Vivekananda called, 'man-making' could be achieved, if the forces of both the faiths could be canalized into constructive and creative channels through deliberate and self-conscious endeavour? This endeavour, aided by the theory and practice of modern democracy, and assisted by the impact of world forces, has for its glorious consummation the evolution of an Indian polity based on spiritual foundations, and endued with the moral passion of human welfare.

FREEDOM TO RELEASE THE SOCIOLOGICAL FACTOR OF MUTUAL EMULATION

Is this not the end and aim of all religions? Is this not what would please the hearts of the prophets and founders of the world's great religions? Is this not the natural issue of modern world forces when directed to human ends? Will not this consummation make India prosperous and powerful and the moral leader of nations? Cannot Indian Islam and Indian Christianity, like Hinduism, issue forth as distinct world forces with characteristic individualities of their own and a message to the other peoples of the world? Religion thrives best in the Indian soil, the Indian—whether Hindu, Christian, or Muslim—is deeply religious. Allied with narrow political passions, this religious feeling has exhibited the most brutal aspects. Allied with the passion for spirituality and human service, it has exhibited the most sublime aspects as well. It is up to the Hindus and Muslims and Christians to see that their religions exhibit this latter aspect. The average Muslim must learn to consider military conquerors and fanatics as human aberrations and abnormal types, who use the name of Islam to cover their own blood-thirstiness and egoism. They can at best be military heroes and not religious heroes. He must learn to venerate more the saints and sages of his religion who have imparted cheer and hope to man. This will, in turn, help the Indian Muslim to cultivate an attitude of reverence to other faiths, and their teachers and saints. The Prophet of Islam came as a warner to man; he came to unite; he came, as he has himself affirmed, as a blessing to mankind and not as a curse. Gentle as a lamb, but strong and courageous as a lion, he bent his energies to the moral and spiritual upliftment of his people. In his attitudes and activities, he has created a pattern of excellence which remains as a fund of inspiration to those who seek to follow him.

Mutual respect will lead to mutual emulation. We have suppressed this great sociological factor of emulation for long; it has led to a distortion of our religions and our personalities. It is time that we give free play to this compulsive factor of social evolution. That is the line of our future advance. It is a happy augury that Indian Christianity, overcoming its erstwhile temptations to the contrary—temptations engendered by political exigencies over which it had no control—has recognized this great truth and is consciously working towards this end. A glorious future for Indian Christianity is assured thereby. When will Indian Islam come to itself? When will Indian Muslims learn to impart their own genius to this great religion and produce a crop of saints and sages who will command the veneration of all men? The test of a living religion is this production of saints who bear witness to God and the highest in man. A too close and long association with 'real politics' can even destroy the soul of a religion.

Society expects this guidance from its leaders today. The nerves cannot stand the strain and tension of hatred and bickering for long. Free India, divided now into two sovereign states, calls for the burying of our hatchets; it demands the sending of a current of love all round.

VIVEKANANDA'S VISION OF EVENTUAL HINDU-MUSLIM UNITY

Swami Vivekananda believed in this glorious destiny for India and worked unceasingly to that end. He has left it as a legacy to us. He knew what blessings would flow from a junction of religions on the soil of India. Such significant attempts at what was then called *samudrasangam*, 'the confluence of the oceans', have been made by some of our far-seeking forbears in the far less propitious period of, the seventeenth century. Conditions are ripe today for its successful implementation in contemporary India. Referring to the interaction of Hinduism and Islam, Vivekananda has written, what Jawaharlal Nehru calls, 'a remarkable letter' to a Muslim friend, Mohammad Sarfaraz Hussain (*The Discovery of India*, p. 403, footnote). It is dated 10th June 1898. 1 cannot do better than quote this letter in extenso:

> My Dear Friend—I appreciate your letter very much, and am extremely happy to learn that the Lord is silently preparing wonderful things for our motherland.

Whether we call it Vedantism or any ism, the truth is that Advaitism is the last word of religion and thought and the only position from which one can look upon all religions and sects with love. We believe it is the religion of the future enlightened humanity. The Hindus may get the credit of arriving at it earlier than other races, they being an older race than either the Hebrew or the Arab; yet, practical Advaitism, which looks upon and behaves to all mankind as one's own soul, is yet to be developed among the Hindus universally.

On the other hand, our experience is that, if ever the followers of any religion approach to this equality in an appreciable degree in the plan of practical work-a-day life—it may be quite unconscious generally of the deeper meaning and the underlying principle of such conduct, which the Hindus as a rule so clearly perceive—it is those of Islam and Islam alone.

Therefore, we are firmly persuaded that, without the help of practical Islam, theories of Vedantism, however fire and wonderful they may be, are entirely valueless to the vast mass of mankind. We want to lead mankind to the place where there is neither the Vedas not the Bible nor the Koran; yet this has to be done by harmonizing the Vedas, the Bible, and the Koran. Mankind ought to be taught that religions are but the varied expressions of THE RELIGION, which is Oneness, so that each may choose the path that suits him best.

For our own motherland, a junction of the two great systems, Hinduism and Islam—Vedanta brain and Islam body—is the only hope.

I see in my mind's eye the future perfect India rising out of this chaos and strife, glorious and invincible, with Vedanta brain and Islam body.

Ever praying that the Lord may make of you a great instrument for the help of mankind, and especially of our poor, poor motherland, yours with love,

VIVEKANANDA

CONCLUSION

An India, spiritually united, economically strong, and socially stable, and imbued with ethical passion, will be a unique force in world affairs. This was Swami Vivekananda's dream of the future of our country. The world expects much from India. The stability of civilization depends upon the giving of a moral and spiritual direction to powerful world forces. The world calls. Will India listen and respond? Vivekananda believed that she can and will respond. Let Free India lay hold of that Faith and Vision and march forward. Arise! Awake! And stop not till the goal is reached!

Appendix III

(Reproduced here is one of the five pamphlets written by L.K. Advani while in prison in Bangalore Central Jail between June 1975 to January 1977. This literature was smuggled out of the prison and used by underground activists in their nationwide campaign against the Emergency rule imposed by Indira Gandhi's government.)

A Tale of Two Emergencies

A Detenu
(October, 1975)

> Autocratic power everywhere entrenches itself and tends to perpetuate itself in the name of public good; history records that abuse of constitutional despotism inevitably leads to absolute despotism.
>
> K. Subba Rao
> *Former Chief Justice of India*
> (At a New Delhi Seminar on
> 15–16 March 1975)

William Shirer's *The Rise and Fall of the Third Reich* is regarded as a monumental, definitive work on the history of Nazi Germany. Going through it a second time these days, I have been greatly struck by the remarkable, but disturbing similarity between the methodology of Adolf Hitler to make himself an absolute dictator and the steps being taken by Indira Gandhi here to decimate and destroy Indian democracy.

When the Weimar Constitution was adopted in 1919, it was hailed as the 'most liberal and democratic document of its kind the twentieth century had seen'. Shirer describes it as 'mechanically well-nigh perfect, full of ingenious and admirable devices which seemed to guarantee the working of an almost flawless democracy'.

But the Weimar Constitution, like our own, had its Emergency provisions, incorporated into it in good faith by the Founding Fathers with the confidence that they would be used only in times of grave crises, such as war.

Hitler became Chancellor (Prime Minister) of Germany on January 30, 1933; on February 28, he made President Hindenberg invoke Article 48 (Emergency Powers) and sign a decree 'for the protection of the people and the State'. Among other things the decree proclaimed:

> Restriction on personal liberty, on the right of free expression of opinion, including freedom of the Press; on the rights of assembly and association; and violations of privacy of postal, telegraphic and telephone communication; and warrants for home searches; orders for confiscations as well as restrictions on property, are also permissible beyond the legal limits otherwise prescribed.

The decree also authorized the Reich to take over complete power in the constituent states of the union, and prescribed harsh penalties for a number of crimes including 'serious disturbance of the peace'.

The excuse for this emergency was a fire in the Reichstag (German Parliament House) on February 27, just one day before the proclamation of the emergency. In India too, the Emergency was proclaimed on June 25, the avowed provocation being an opposition resolution of June 24. In both cases, obviously the decision had been taken earlier, and any pretext was deemed handy.

After the Reichstag fire, Hitler's Government issued a statement that they had unearthed 'a Communist conspiracy to burn down Government buildings, museums, mansions and essential plants' and that the burning of the Reichstag was to be a signal for a bloody insurrection and civil war.

Thirteen years later, in the historic Nuremberg trials it was substantially established that the Reichstag fire was the handiwork of the Nazis themselves; Goebbels had conceived the idea and had executed it under Goering's instructions.

Every other day, Indira Gandhi and her cohorts keep asserting that whatever they have done during these past months is 'within the four corners of the Constitution'. The charge being levelled against them by the opposition and by the Western Press that they have subverted democracy is therefore untenable, it is argued.

The history of Nazi Germany conclusively shows that doing anything constitutionally is not necessarily the same thing as doing it in a democratic manner. Hitler always used to boast that he had done nothing illegal or unconstitutional. Indeed, he made a democratic constitution an instrument of dictatorship. Shirer has noted:

> Though the Weimar Republic was destroyed the Weimar Constitution was never formally abrogated by Hitler. Indeed and ironically, Hitler based the legality of his rule on the despised republican Constitution.

A vigorous opposition, a free Press and an independent Judiciary are the three essential features of democracy. These are the institutional checks which a democratic polity possesses to restrain not only the Executive from going the authoritarian way, but also the Legislature from becoming a handmaid of an arbitrary tyrannical majority.

A myth assiduously propagated these days is that parliamentary imprimatur justifies everything, sanctifies even sin. With the German experience in mind, noted American columnist Walter Lippman had pertinently observed:

> Where the will of a majority of a people is held to be sovereign and supreme, that majority is bound by no laws because it makes the laws, that it is itself the final judge from which there is no appeal of what is right and wrong. This doctrine has led logically and in practice to the totalitarian state—to that modern form of despotism which does not rest upon hereditary titles of military conquest but springs directly from the mass of the people. This is the supreme heresy of our time, it masquerades as democracy.

Hitler had no use for the opposition: nor has Indira Gandhi, who never tires of referring to opposition parties as 'a minority seeking to subvert the wishes of the majority'. She conveniently forgets that even when her personal popularity was at its peak, as in 1971, her party could secure the support of only a minority of the electorate of 43 per cent (comparisons are odious, but it is interesting to note that Hitler was at the peak of popularity in 1933 and in the elections held that year his Nazi party polled 44 per cent votes).

On the eve of the Emergency, however, Indira Gandhi was at the nadir of her popularity graph. A gallup poll published around May had established this very clearly. With her popularity as a leader already at a low ebb the Allahabad verdict of June 12 suddenly stripped her of her legitimacy as a leader and as Prime Minister.

The opposition, on the other hand, successfully closed ranks, and under the inspiring leadership of Jayaprakash Narayan, formed themselves into a solid phalanx of alternative political power. The genesis of the Emergency lay in this situation. The so-called conspiracy 'to create internal disturbance' was even more phoney than the supposed conspiracy behind the Reichstag fire.

Shortly after the 1933 elections in Germany, Hitler decided to amend the Constitution so as to convert his forty-four per cent power into cent per cent power. He proposed an Enabling Act that would confer on Hitler's Cabinet exclusive legislative powers for four years.

A two-thirds majority in Parliament was required to carry out his amendment. The Nazis, together with the Nationalists who were supporting Hitler's Government, had a majority of only 16 in the Reichstag, and this was far short of the two-thirds needed.

So, at the very first meeting of Hitler's Cabinet held on March 15, 1933 the main item of business was how to procure this two-thirds majority. A plan was drawn up, and effectively put through. Some opposition parties, like the Catholic Centre, were 'managed', while others like the Social Democrats and the Communist were 'tamed'. Quite a few socialist members and almost all the 91 communists were put behind bars; they called it *Shutzaft*, or 'protective custody'.

The German Parliament met on March 23. Hitler had no difficulties in having it adopt the Enabling Act. The voting was 441 for, 84 against. Hitler proudly observed that it was Parliament, the representative body of the nation, which had by an overwhelming majority reposed such confidence in him. Shirer has commented:

> Thus was parliamentary democracy finally interred in Germany. Except for the arrests of the Communists and some of the Social Democratic deputies, it was all done quite legally, though accompanied by terror. Parliament had turned over its constitutional authority to Hitler, and thereby committed suicide, though its body lingered in an embalmed state to the very end of the third Reich, serving infrequently as a sounding board for some of Hitler's thunderous pronouncements.

The stratagem resorted to by Indira Gandhi to secure parliamentary approval for the Emergency proclamation, and for the series of constitutional amendments designed to place Indira Gandhi above the law provides a remarkable parallel. But there are some notable differences also.

Essentially the strategy was the same: manage some parties; tame the others. However, to force the Reichstag into submission Hitler had to jail only opposition Deputies; he did not have to put any Nazis behind bars.

Here, Indira Gandhi has had to imprison not only a host of opposition MPs but also two senior members of her own party's central Executive. One of them, Ram Dhan, had been elected the Secretary of the Congress Parliamentary Party only in May last.

Hitler is not known to have stopped the publication of parliamentary proceedings. Here, however, even the fact of the opposition expressing its strong disapproval of the Emergency, by staging of walkout and boycotting the rest of the session, was blacked out.

Incidentally, it is saddening to reflect that the presiding officers of the two Houses should have meekly acquiesced in this shameful, unheard of censorship of parliamentary proceedings. The Indian Parliament had seen a Speaker like Vitthalbhai Patel who forced even the British Viceroy to acknowledge that within the precincts of Parliament, only one writ could run—that of the Speaker. It is blasphemy to compare present day presiding officers to Vitthalbhai, let alone expect them to act like him.

The day the Reichstag passed the Enabling Act, abdicating its authority in favour of Hitler, Goebbels wrote in his diary: 'The German revolution has begun.' Shortly after the proclamation of Emergency in India, India's Ambassador in Washington told American newsmen that India was passing through 'something of a revolution'.

After having subverted the Parliament and subordinated the opposition, Hitler's revolution turned its attention towards the Press and the Judiciary, two other institutional roadblocks on his path to despotism. Censorship was, of course, peremptorily introduced. Goebbels was appointed Minister of Propaganda. On October 4, 1933 the subservience of the German Press to the wishes of the Government was formalized by enacting the Reich Press Law. Journalism was declared thereunder 'a public vocation'. Section 14 of the law ordered editors, to keep out of the newspapers anything which tends 'to weaken the strength of the German Reich, or the Common Will of the people.'

If one were to make a compilation of all the speeches made by Indira Gandhi ever since the Emergency with regard to the Press, the cardinal sin of the Indian Press, according to her, has been precisely this one over which Hitler had imposed an embargo under the Reich Press Law, namely, publishing material which tended to weaken the strength of the state, or the common will of the people.

Is the will of the people, or the strength of the state, weakened by criticism, or by exposure of its failings, or even condemnation of the follies of its high-ups? A totalitarian's answer to this poser would be an unhesitating 'Yes'. A democrat's reply would be an emphatic 'No'.

In the late thirties Winston Churchill carried on a vitriolic campaign in Parliament and outside, against his own party leader Chamberlain and his Munich approach, yet no one suggested that he was 'denigrating the institution of Prime Minister'.

When British Prime Minister Anthony Eden embarked on his ill-conceived Suez adventure, BBC offered its forum to the leader of the opposition, Hugh Gaitskell, and allowed him to administer a bitter tongue-lashing to the Tory Government. No one castigated the BBC for being unpatriotic even though the Labour Party's broadside was, without doubt, a serious damper for the Government's war effort.

Johnson's Vietnam policies provoked some of the biggest mass rallies America has witnessed in recent years. Youth and Negro organisations carried on a searing and raging campaign, characterized Johnson's policies as stupid and perverse and accused him of sacrificing the flower of America's youth at the altar of a senseless war. But no one accused these organisations of spreading sedition in the armed forces.

More recently, when a powerful campaign mounted by the *Washington Post* and other American newspapers against the Watergate crimes of Richard Nixon snowballed into a national outcry for his impeachment and ultimately led to his ouster from office, no one—Nixon and his cronies excepted, of course—thought that the American Press was doing something unpatriotic.

Looking at all these episodes of modern history in retrospect it would seem that if Winston Churchill, the BBC, the youth and Negro organisations of America and the US Press had not acted as forthrightly, as they did, the democratic conscience of the world certainly would have held them guilty of a grave sin, albeit of omission. Both these countries have emerged stronger as a result of these iconoclastic, anti-government activities.

Whether dissent or criticism by the opposition weakens or strengthens society is a moot question. The answer will depend entirely on the values to which one subscribes.

When Brezhnev asked Madhu Limaye and Indian opposition leader who met him at New Delhi, 'What is the need of an opposition,' the remark was not surprising coming as it did from a communist leader.

But when Indira Gandhi seeks to justify censorship of the Indian Press on the ground that its writings were weakening the nation's morale, democrats the world over fell baffled. Indira Gandhi's complaint that President Ford, the BBC and the Western Press criticise Indira Gandhi for authoritarianism but not Mao, is neither relevant nor fair—at least not while India continues priding herself as a parliamentary democracy.

Shortly after the proclamation of Emergency in June, the *National Herald* of New Delhi, which is very close to Indira Gandhi, editorially commended adoption of the African one party model. Following the bloody *coup* of Bangladesh of August 15, its enthusiasm for such one partyism seemed to diminish. In an editorial on the same subject on August 25, even while reaffirming its view that a one party setup was desirable, it said that this should not be forced, but should be allowed to emerge 'by natural evolution'—whatever that may mean.

It is difficult to say to what extent the *National Herald* was reflecting the official mind. It may have been a command performance, or merely a trial balloon.

Whatever that be, Indira Gandhi is on record saying that she has no intention of changing the democratic multi-party character of the Indian Constitution. In the same breath, however, she has been saying that there is no question of returning to the pre-Emergency period of licence and irresponsibility.

This charge of licence and irresponsibility has been levelled against Jayaprakash Narayan and the opposition parties on the one hand, and against the Press on the other.

In the case of J.P. and the opposition parties, Government can possibly dupe, or at least confuse public opinion by maintaining, that it has in its possession evidence to prove that they were conspiring to overthrow the Government by subversive means, but that it would not be in the public interest to reveal the evidence. Hitler had said just that with regard to the Reichstag fire.

But in the case of the Press, such chicanery is not possible. The role and performance of the Press is an open book.

Journalists the world over regarded the Indian Press as extremely sober and restrained.

In fact, opinion in the world of journalism has been inclined to regard the Indian Press as too sober, and too responsible bordering on timidity and docility.

It is, therefore, a travesty of truth to say, as some Ministers have been saying these days, that the Indian Press is sensation-mongering. Indira Gandhi too has been totally off the mark when she complained about the Press supporting the opposition and being against the Government.

The fact is that an overwhelming majority of newspapers in the country are dependent for their very existence on Government advertisements. They cannot, therefore, afford to be against the Government even if they want to. The main issue of political debate in the last eighteen months has been the movement led by Jayaprakash Narayan. Most papers have been critical of it even though, barring pro-CPI papers, all of them even pro-Congress dailies, have held him personally in high esteem.

The Press has divided the opposition parties. If they come together, they are a motley crowd. If they stress their respective stances, they are a weak and divided opposition.

One, therefore, wonders which newspapers Indira Gandhi has been talking about when she describes the Indian Press as anti-Government. In one of her speeches she went to the extent of saying that the Press has been so for nine and a half years, that is, ever since she became Prime Minister. Assuming, however, for a moment that this is so, is that a crime? For autocrats it may be so. But no democrat is going to buy this argument of Indira Gandhi's. The Britishers had democracy at home, but in their colonies they practised the worst form of autocracy. But even under the British rule never did the Indian Press suffer such draconian censorship orders as Indira Gandhi's Government has imposed.

When Gandhiji was arrested just before the 1942 *satyagraha*, Mirabehn (Margaret Slade) is said to have remarked: 'At the dead of night, like thieves they came to steal him away.'

On the night of June 25-26, 1975 Jayaprakash Narayan, the Mahatma Gandhi of today's India, was whisked away in an identical manner, with one difference.

The British Government never sought to prevent people from knowing that their beloved leader had been arrested nor did they suppress the news of even Bhagat Singh's hanging. Newspapers all over the country flashed the news of Mahatmaji's arrest with eight column banner headlines.

Under Indira Gandhi's rule, from June 26 onwards, J.P. and Morarji, Charan Singh and Vajpayee have just ceased to be. They have become 'non-persons'. That J.P. is in jail is today a top state secret and its publication would attract severe penalties. It is only under a Hitler or a Stalin that such stupidity can even be conceived of. In totalitarian countries, the media of mass communication have no role except to be subservient to the aims of authority. All media including the Press are virtually limbs of the state. But the function of the Press in a democracy is entirely different.

I remember a former press secretary of the US President, Bill Moyers, saying once:

> Government and Press are not allies, they are adversaries. One has the mandate to conduct the affairs of state, the other the privilege to find out all it can about what is going on. It is the nature of democracy to thrive upon this conflict without being consumed by it.

As has been already made out, the Indian Press has never been an adversary of Government, it has been an ally, albeit an unwilling one. Why then has it been so severely punished, it may be asked. The truth is that there is a very solid basis for Indira Gandhi's pique against the Indian Press.

It is a common characteristic of all despots that while they may be willing on occasion to condone criticism of Government, they cannot lightly overlook criticism of their person. The true reason for Indira Gandhi's wrath against the Indian Press is that after the Allahabad verdict, the Press showed a rare unanimity in holding that the verdict warranted her resignation till it was reviewed by a superior Court. Indira Gandhi is unwilling to forgive this.

Censorship has naturally made newspapers dull and drab. They read like official handouts, inane and insipid.

This happened in Nazi Germany also, following the imposition of censorship. At one stage, Goebbels himself told editors not to be too timid, and not to make their papers so monotonous.

A Berlin editor, Welke took Geobbels seriously. In his next issue, he came out with a sarcastic piece chiding the Propaganda Ministry for its red tape, and for the heavy hand with which it held down the Press and so made it dull. Within days of this publication, the journal was suspended, and the editor was carted off to jail.

Something similar has been happening these days in New Delhi.

Encouraged by repeated declarations by the Prime Minister that Press censorship had been relaxed, some pressmen, particularly foreign pressmen, have been trying to relay something other than the colourless Press notes of the PIB. But this has only landed them in trouble. During the past weeks, Reuters and U.P.I., both international news agencies, have had their telephone and teleprinter lines disconnected for alleged violation of censorship rules.

If one single attribute were to be identified as the hallmark of democracy, it is freedom of expression. Madison has very aptly said:

> A popular government, without popular information or the means of acquiring it, is but a prologue to a farce or a tragedy, or perhaps both. Knowledge will forever govern ignorance, and a people who mean to be their own governors must arm themselves with the power which knowledge gives.

Shortly after Hitler came to power, the Nazi leader Joachim Ribbentrop (who later became Hitler's External Affairs Minister) spoke of the need for a new legal system.

The old system, Ribbentrop said, needed to be replaced because under this earlier system, 'Adolf Hitler, too, like any other common mortal, could be tried under the same paragraph of the penal law.'

Addressing a convention of lawyers Dr. Hans Frank, Commissioner of Justice and Reich Law Leader said: 'There is in Germany today only one authority and that is the authority of the Führer.'

Is there much difference between Ribbentrop's and Dr. Frank's idolatry of Hitler, and Deva Kant Borooah's halleluja—chanting that 'Indira is India and India is Indira?' The outcome in both cases has been similar.

The Constitution and the Law were amended to mutilate the concept of the rule of law, and to place the Executive head of the country above the law. As part of the same process the judicial review was whittled down.

With regard to the position of judges in Nazi Germany, William Shirer has recorded:

> ...under the Weimar Constitution, judges were independent, subject only to the law, protected from arbitrary removal, and bound at least in theory by Article 109 to safeguard equality before law. Most of them were sympathetic to National Socialism (Nazism) but they were hardly prepared for the treatment they soon received under its actual rule.

The civil service law, relating to Government employees, empowered the Reich to remove any one 'who indicated that he was not prepared at all times for the National Socialist State'. This law was already being used to rid Government of Jews. On April 7, 1933, the law was made applicable to judges also.

In 1935, the orders and actions of the Gestapo (Hitler's secret police) were made 'not subject to judicial review'. The basic Gestapo law promulgated by Government on February 10, 1936, put the secret police organisation above the law. Courts were prohibited by law from interfering with its activities.

Indira Gandhi's attitude towards detenus held under MISA during the Emergency has been absolutely identical to his approach.

In 1937 the German Reich framed a new civil service law which provided for the dismissal of officials including judges for political unreliability.

Even a cursory look at the business transacted by the so-called Emergency Session of Parliament held in July and August 1975, would reveal that the primary target of most legislative measures undertaken was the Courts.

The President had already suspended enforcement of Fundamental Rights under Article 14 (Equality before law), Article 21 (Protection of life and personal liberty) and several clauses of Article 22 (Protection against Detention).

As if this was not bad enough, a series of constitutional and statutory amendments were effected. To recapitulate, these were as under:

(a) Courts were barred from pronouncing on the validity of a proclamation of Emergency of President's Rule or an ordinance.
(b) The MISA was amended to prevent Courts from giving relief to detenus even by virtue of common law or natural law.
(c) The Election Law was amended to bar Courts from adjudicating with regard to the date of appointment, resignation, dismissal, etc., of a Government employee.
(d) The judgment of the Allahabad High Court was declared null and void by 'Constitutional amendment'.
(e) Courts were stripped of their authority to deal with disputes relating to the election of President, Vice President, Speaker and Prime Minister.
(f) The Representation of People Act and MISA were included in the Ninth Schedule and thereby made immune to judicial review.
(g) The Maintenance of Internal Security Act was amended so as to provide that those detained during the Emergency need not be furnished the grounds of detention. They could be kept indefinitely in prison without having even the ghost of an idea why they had been jailed.

Some High Courts held the view that this bar on disclosure operated only between Government and the detenus. The Courts could not be precluded from examining the grounds and satisfying themselves that the detention was not arbitrary or *mala fide*. When Government still refused to give them grounds, as they did in editor Nayyar's case, the Courts struck down the detention.

Taking umbrage at this interpretation, the Government had issued a fresh ordinance on October 17 amending the Detention Law for the third time since the Emergency. The ordinance provided that the grounds of detention would be regarded as 'confidential' and so would not be available even to Courts for examination.

What do all these laws add up to? Firstly, an unabashed demonstration of the Executive's distrust of the Judiciary and, secondly, a determined bid on its part to attenuate the scope of judicial review, a concept which the Supreme Court has described as a basic feature of the Constitution.

The Emergency proclaimed in June 1975 is thus an Evil Trident with which Indira Gandhi has sought to suppress simultaneously all the three democratic institutions which have been obstructing her assumption of absolute power. The detention of tens of thousands of political activities is action against the opposition, censorship of the Press, arrest of critical editors (like Kuldip Nayyar and K.R. Malkani) and expulsion of almost all foreign correspondents (except those from Communist countries) are measures directed against the Press. The Presidential Order under Art. 359 and the string of laws passed recently are essentially anti-Judiciary measures.

It might embarrass many Congressmen to know that if Indira Gandhi is proud of her 20-point programme, Hitler was prouder still of his 25-point programme, which he used to call 'unalterable'. It was at first a kind of personal creed; later, it became the Nazi party's official programme.

Under Hitler's regime too, there used to be daily demonstrations of faith in his 25-point programme. The participants were not just common folk but leaders of opinion in various walks of life. At one such demonstration of loyalty held in the autumn of 1933, some 960 professors of the Berlin University, including some renowned scientists and academicians, participated.

Repoke, a senior professor, wrote later, 'It was a scene of prostitution that has stained the history of German learning.' Another teacher Julius Ebbing, wrote in 1945:

> The German Universities failed. While there was still time to oppose publicly with all their power the destruction of the democratic state. They failed to keep the beacon of freedom, and right, burning during the night of tyranny.

India too is passing through a night of tyranny. This razzle-dazzle talk of discipline cannot deceive anyone.

What we see in the country's climate today is not discipline. It is servile sycophancy and cowardly conformism. Indira Gandhi today commands awe, not respect. It is fear that holds sway, not duty or honesty.

Hitler had created even greater awe, and so was able to secure even stricter compliance with rules. He framed regulations providing that workers absenting themselves from work without satisfactory reasons would be imprisoned.

In Government offices today, under the pervasive umbrella of the Emergency, all safeguards against arbitrary action have been suspended. No one is in a position to assess in how many cases the action taken by superior authorities is justified, and in how many cases it is motivated by ulterior or collateral considerations.

Yet, all that this is known to have achieved is to make peons and *babus* scurry to office in time. It was Benito Mussolini, the Italian dictator, who had once boasted that trains had started running on time because of his fascism.

Well, if the cost of punctuality is democracy—and countries like the UK and Japan show that it is not—then this country would rather compromise with unpunctuality.

There can be no two opinions that the country needs to build up the virtue of discipline consciously and deliberately. But is it not ironic that an individual whose own spurt to political supremacy owes primarily to an act of gross and indefensible indiscipline, should be waving this rod of discipline at a person like Jayaprakash Narayan, steeped *manasa, vacha, karmana* (in thought, word, and deed) in the highest traditions of Gandhian discipline?

In fact, the indiscipline and irresponsibility that has been evident during the past few years not only in Government offices and industry but in all walks of life can be traced directly to the populist slogan-mongering initiated by Indira Gandhi herself in 1969.

On the institutional plane, if there is one organisation in the country which has made the maximum contribution towards character-building and discipline-building, it is the Rashtriya Swayamsevak Sangh. Literally millions of young men have imbibed their basic grounding in patriotism, integrity and discipline from this body. Yet, the RSS has been outlawed. Why? Presumably because its leader commended J.P.'s leadership and idealism and said that *swayam sevaks* were free to participate in the movement.

It ill behoves a Government which seeks thus to suppress the most efficacious non-official mechanism for inculcating discipline to talk about discipline.

Indira Gandhi's attitude to workers, to their right of collective bargaining and to trade unionism also bears a close resemblance to Hitler's.

One can appreciate conscious efforts being made to make trade unions more responsible and production-conscious. But what is being done now under cover of the Emergency is virtually to destroy the worker's rights of collective bargaining and in the name of production to give a free rein to the owners of industry.

Hitler banned strikes. He abolished trade unions. He replaced them by a governmental body, the Labour Front. The chronicler of Nazi Germany, Shirer, has commented:

> All the propagandists in the Third Reich, from Hitler on down were accustomed to rant in their public speeches against the *bourgeoisie* and capitalists and proclaim their solidarity with the workers. But a sober study of the official statistics revealed that the much maligned capitalists, not the workers, benefited most from Nazi policies....

No section has been more thoroughly exposed by the emergency than the CPI. They have meekly acquiesced in all the anti-labour misdoings of Government. Their supine surrender to the Establishment has proved, if any proof is necessary, that the CPI has no real concern for the workers.

As long as New Delhi-Moscow relations remain what they are, the CPI has no role in Indian politics except to act as a palanquin bearer of the ruling party.

To revert to the historic parallel which is our main theme here, it would be worthwhile to quote Shirer again on the role of Communists in Nazi Germany:

> The Communists, at the behest of Moscow, were committed to the silly idea of first destroying the Social Democrats, the Socialist trade unions and whatever middle class democratic forces there were on the dubious theory that although this would lead to a Nazi regime, it would be only temporary and would bring inevitably the collapse of capitalism, after which the Communists would take over.

Everyday we read in the papers and hear on the radio that so many officials or employees in the States have been sacked or compulsorily retired because of corruption or inefficiency.

Day in and day out the radio keeps blaring news about raids on industrialists and businessmen by income-tax officials. An impression is sought to be given that a relentless campaign has been launched by Government to root out corruption in the administration, in industry and in commerce.

In all these four months, have we heard of even one single Minister being sacked or one single Congress MP or MLA being proceeded against either on account of corruption, or tax dues, or any other?

This may be surprising, though significant. It is an undisputed fact that the roots of all corruption, administrative, industrial and commercial, lie in political corruption. The Santhanam Committee and the Administrative Reforms Commission have examined the problem in depth and suggested several sound measures to deal with political corruption. The main attack of J.P.'s movement was directed against this evil but Government stubbornly refuses to do anything about it.

Corruption among party colleagues has never bothered Indira Gandhi. Hitler too always showed supreme unconcern in this respect. Shirer has tartly remarked:

> He, who was monumentally intolerant by his very nature was strangely tolerant of one human condition, a man's morals. No other party came near to attracting so many shady characters as the Nazi party. Hitler did not care so long as they were useful to him...

The inescapable conclusion which can be drawn from this is that the seemingly strong arm measures adopted with regard to the bureaucracy, industry, business and workers are not honestly meant to clear society of its filth. They are essentially part of a political design to tighten the party stranglehold on the country. It is one more exercise in authoritarianism.

In the first few weeks of the Emergency there was a lot of talk about falling prices.

After a short while the claims became muted. Lately it is being admitted that prices are once again showing an upward trend.

Statistics and data apart, the man in the street knows that so far as his economic hardship is concerned, the Emergency has made not an iota of difference. Most opposition parties hold that the common man's lot cannot be improved except by a radical reorientation of policies to make them conform to a Gandhian framework of decentralised economics. Mere tinkering will not do.

The question raised by the Emergency is not what specific economic pattern would suit the country best. That can be left to contending political parties to canvas at the appropriate time.

The question really raised by the present situation and this extends far beyond the frontiers of political competition is: Are we going to permit this nation's constitutional commitment to social, economic and political justice, to liberty of thought and expression and equality of status and opportunity, to be thrown overboard all because a single individual suffers from the hallucination that he or she is indispensable?

The concept of a person's indispensability and democracy go ill together.

For the last two years or so, Jayaprakash Narayan and his associates have been warning the country that Indian democracy is in great peril and that only a proper mobilization of *Lok Shakti* can avert this danger.

A constant refrain of their campaign has been that the present regime will go to any lengths if it feels its own position is seriously threatened.

On June 12 last, two momentous events occurred. The Allahabad High Court unseated Indira Gandhi and disqualified her from contesting elections for a period of six years. The same day the people of Gujarat voted the ruling Congress out of power and installed in its place the Janata Front constituted by parties supporting the J.P. movement.

The Court verdict and the electoral verdict added up to a grave threat to Indira Gandhi's position as Prime Minister. It was this political threat and not any threat to state security, which has brought about this Emergency.

In his excellent analysis of the Watergate episode, 'The fall of Richard Nixon', Theodore H. White has made this perceptive observation:

> The true crime of Richard Nixon was that he broke the faith that binds America together and for this he was driven from power.
>
> The faith he broke was critical—that somewhere in American life there is at least one man who stands for law. The faith holds that all men are equal before the law and are protected by it; and no matter how the faith may be betrayed elsewhere by the ugly compromises of daily striving, at one particular point, the Presidency, justice is beyond the possibility of a fix.

Indira Gandhi has described the Emergency as 'a shock treatment', an objective totally alien to the purpose of Emergency conceived by our Constitution makers. But a shock it has no doubt been. It has shocked even sceptics into realizing the truth of J.P.'s prognostications. More sadly, however, it has shaken the faith of many in the future of Indian democracy.

Restoration of this faith is the task to which every thinking Indian needs to address himself. How to do this is a matter which each one of us has to decide for himself. But all of us can do one thing in common: shed fear and speak the truth as we see it. This in itself will be no mean contribution to the cause of democracy.

Appendix IV

BJP's Palampur Resolution on Ayodhya

The Bharatiya Janata Party's National Executive, meeting in Palampur in Himachal Pradesh in June 1989, passed the following historic resolution:

The National Executive of the Bharatiya Janata Party regards the current debate on the Ramjanmabhoomi issue as one which has highlighted the callous unconcern which the Congress Party in particular, and the other political parties in general, betray towards the sentiments of the overwhelming majority in this country—the Hindus.

...Though efforts have been continuing to persuade Muslims to respect the feelings of the Hindus and abandon their claim to the site, this site has also been subject matter of prolonged litigation.

Lately, the Congress Government has unleashed a virulent campaign against the BJP and the Vishwa Hindu Parishad, which has been representing the Hindu point of view in the negotiations with Government, alleging that while other sections of opinion have accepted reference of the dispute to the Allahabad High Court, the BJP and the VHP are unwilling to abide by a judicial verdict in this case. This propaganda is slanderous, and is based on a total misrepresentation of facts.

The BJP holds that the nature of this controversy is such that it just cannot be sorted out by a court of law. A court of law can settle issues of title, trespass, possession, etc. But it cannot adjudicate as to whether Babar did actually invade Ayodhya, destroyed a temple and built a mosque in its place. Even where a court does pronounce on such facts, it cannot suggest remedies to undo the vandalism of history. As far back as in 1885 a British Judge Col. F.E.A. Chamier disposing off a civil appeal relating to the site observed in a helpless vein: 'It is most unfortunate that a Masjid should have been built on land specially held sacred by the Hindus, but as that occurred 356 years ago it is too late to remedy the grievance...' (Dated 18th March, 1886, Civil Appeal No. 27 of 1885, District Court, Faizabad).

In this context, it should not be forgotten that the present turmoil itself stems from two court decisions, one of 1951 and the second of 1986. On March 3, 1951, in Gopal Singh Visharad versus Zabur Ahmad and others, the Civil Judge, Faizabad observed, inter alia, that...at least from 1936 onwards the Muslims have neither used the site as a mosque nor offered prayers there, and that the Hindus have been performing their Pooja etc. on the disputed site.

Then on 1st February, 1986, District Judge Faizabad referred to this 1951 order and directed that as 'or the last 35 years Hindus have (had) an unrestricted right of worship' at the place, the locks put on two gates in 1951 on grounds of law and order should be removed. (Civil Appeal No. 6/1986).

The 1951 order had provoked little reaction. Till then, secularism had not yet become a euphemism for Hindu-baiting, as it has become today. It is noteworthy that around this very time the Government of India, under the leadership of Pandit Nehru and Sardar Patel, and with the blessings of Gandhiji, had itself decided to undo a similar act of vandalism and to restore the great Somnath Temple at Prabhas Patan (Gujarat).

When the Jyotirling was formally installed at Somnath, the country's Rashtrapati, Dr Rajendra Prasad, participated in the ceremony.

However, by the time the second court order of 1986, came, secularism had come to be equated with an allergy to Hinduism and a synonym for minority appeasement. The Muslim League lobby in the country had acquired a new militancy and aggressiveness. The campaign launched by this lobby against the Supreme Court's judgment in the Shah Bano Case in 1985 had brought it rich dividends. A panic-stricken Government had amended the criminal law; the Supreme Court judgment was legislatively annulled. Having thus tasted blood, this lobby set up the Babri Masjid Action Committee, and mounted a vicious assault on the decisions of the Faizabad Court, and went to the length of boycotting Republic Day celebrations in protest against these orders. A rally organised by this lobby in front of Parliament House actually held out threats of violence unless these orders were reversed. It is significant that most of the members of the Babri Action Committee belonged to the Congress.

Against the above background, the reference made to the High Court is just an expedient device to sweep issues beneath the carpet. The move satisfied the Muslim League lobby, and so is electorally convenient. It certainly does not reveal any earnest desire on the part of Government to solve the problem.

The BJP believes that theocracy is alien to our history and tradition. It is, therefore, that in 1947 even though India was partitioned on religious grounds and even though Pakistan declared itself an Islamic state, India opted for the present Constitution, and guaranteed equality to all citizens irrespective of their religion.

Secularism, according to our Constitution-makers, meant *Sarva Pantha Sama Bhava*. It did not connote an irreligious state. It certainly did not mean rejection of our history and cultural heritage.

The National Executive records its appreciation of the attempts made by some Shia leaders to persuade the community that it was contrary to the tenets of Islam to have a mosque built upon a place of worship of another religion, and that, therefore, the site in dispute should be handed over to the Hindus and a mosque built at some other suitable place. The BJP calls upon the Rajiv Government to adopt the same positive approach in respect of Ayodhya that the Nehru Government did with regard to Somnath. The sentiments of the people must be respected, and Janmasthan must be handed over to the Hindus—if possible through a negotiated settlement, or else, by legislation. Litigation certainly is no answer.

Appendix V

Speech by L.K. Advani at a function organised by The Karachi Council on Foreign Relations, Economic Affairs & Law

KARACHI, 5 JUNE 2005

It is always a matter of pleasure when one goes abroad and gets an opportunity to interact with the intellectual elite of that country. But when the country one is visiting is Pakistan, and when the interaction with intellectuals is happening in a city which is one's birthplace, how can that experience be described? 'Pleasure'? 'Great pleasure'? 'Delight'?

I find these words trite on this occasion. The truth is that, I have no words to adequately capture the feelings that have welled up in me at this meeting in Karachi, which I have been able to visit only for the second time since I left it nearly six decades ago.

Karachi has changed beyond recognition, not only since I left in 1947, but also since I last came here in 1978. The city has of course become immensely more populous—its population in 1947 was a mere 4 lakh; today, I am told, it is nearly 1.4 crore. But Karachi has also become more developed and prosperous.

I compliment the people of Karachi for this achievement and hope that not only Karachi but the whole of Pakistan continues to travel rapidly on the path to prosperity and all-round development.

MY RETURN TO THE ROOTS

Friends, barring the dinner engagement later in the evening, this function happens to mark the conclusion of my weeklong visit to Pakistan. My visit had three parts. The first part, comprising two days in Islamabad, was largely political. The second leg, which meant two days in Lahore, was part political and part religious-cultural, since it included visits to the ancient Katas Raj Temples and to the Nankana Sahib Gurdwara.

But the last part in Karachi, again of two days, is purely sentimental. Before leaving for Pakistan, I had stated that the primary aim of my visit was to contribute, in my own humble way, to the ongoing peace process between India and Pakistan through my meetings with the leadership of Pakistan and also with representatives of various political parties and civil society organizations in this country. But I had added that the visit is also a kind of 'return-to-the-roots' for me and members of my family, who are coming to Pakistan for the first time.

My visit to the school where I studied, to the house where I lived (although it does not now stand in its original shape), to the Sindh Assembly building where I meet legislators belonging to the Pakistan People's Party (PPP), the reception and cultural programme organised by the Hindu Panchayat, and the lunch reception hosted by the Chief Minister of Sindh—all these will remain indelible memories in me.

JINNAH'S SPEECH ON AUGUST 11, 1947

I have many deeply engraved memories of the first twenty years of my life that I lived in Karachi. I shall recall here only one of them, because the person with which that memory is associated, and the philosophy that I learnt from him in Karachi, have a reverential place in my life.

In the last 3-4 years of my life in Karachi, I came in contact with Swami Ranganathananda, who was the head of the Ramakrishna Math here for six years from 1942 until it was closed down in 1948. I used to go to listen to his discourses on the *Bhagwad Gita*. In later years, I maintained regular contact with this great disciple of Swami Vivekananda, who went on to become the head of the Ramakrishna Math and Mission in India.

Swami Ranganathananda passed away in April this month. The last time I met him was in Calcutta last year. He was 96 but still very agile in mind and radiant in spirit. Our talk, among other things, turned to his years and my years in Karachi. He asked me, 'Have you read Mohammed Ali Jinnah's speech in Pakistan's Constituent Assembly on August 11, 1947? It is a classic exposition of a Secular State, one which guarantees every citizen's freedom to practice his or her religion but the State shall not discriminate between one citizen and another on the basis of religion.'

He asked me to send him the full text of the speech, which I did.

The reason for my recounting Jinnah's historic speech in the Constituent Assembly is two-fold. Firstly, as I said, it is associated with my last conversation with the Swamiji, who was one of the towering spiritual personalities in India. The second reason is that its remembrance was triggered by my visit to the ancient Katas Raj Temples in Chakwal district four days ago. The Government of Pakistan was kind enough to invite me to lay the foundation stone for a project to restore these temples, which are now in ruins but whose legend is rooted in the epic story of the Mahabharata.

I feel it appropriate to read out the relevant portion from Jinnah's speech.

> *'Now, if we want to make this great State of Pakistan happy and prosperous we should wholly and solely concentrate on the well-being of the people, and specially of the masses and the poor. If you will work in cooperation, forgetting the past, burying the hatchet, you are bound to succeed. If you change your past and work in a spirit that every one of you, no matter to what community he belongs, no matter what relations he had with you in the past, no matter what is his colour, caste or creed, is first, second and last a citizen of this State with equal rights, privileges and obligations, there will be no end to the progress you will make.*
>
> *I cannot overemphasise it too much. We shall begin to work in that spirit and in course of time all these angularities of the majority and minority communities, the Hindu community and Muslim community…will vanish. Indeed, if you ask me, this has been the biggest hindrance in the way of India to attain its freedom and independence and but for this we would have been free people long ago.*
>
> *Therefore, we must learn a lesson from this. You are free, you are free to go to your temples. You are free to go to your mosques or to any other places of worship in this State of Pakistan. You may belong to any religion or caste or creed; that has nothing to do with the business of the State…. You will find that in course of time Hindus will cease to be Hindus and Muslims would cease to be Muslims, not in the religious sense, because that is the personal faith of each individual, but in the political sense as citizens of the State.'*

What has been stated in this speech—namely, equality of all citizens in the eyes of the State and freedom of faith for all citizens—is what we in India call a Secular or a Non-Theocratic State. There is no place for bigotry, hatred, intolerance and discrimination in the name of religion in such a State. And there can certainly be no place, much less State protection, for religious extremism and terrorism in such a State.

I believe that this is the ideal that India, Pakistan as well as Bangladesh—the three present-day sovereign and separate constituents of the undivided India of the past, sharing a common civilisational heritage—should follow.

I hope that this ideal is implemented in its letter and spirit. The restoration of the Katas Raj temples is a good beginning.

TIME TO UNDO THE FOLLIES OF PARTITION

Esteemed friends from Karachi, people often ask me: 'Does this mean that you want to undo the Partition?'

My answer is: 'The Partition cannot be undone, because, as I said in Lahore at the SAFMA function, the creation of India and Pakistan as two separate and sovereign nations is an unalterable reality of history. However, some of the follies of Partition can be undone, and they must be undone.'

I dream of the day when divided hearts can be united; when divided families can be reunited; when pilgrims from one country—Hindus, Muslims, Sikhs—can freely go to holy sites located in the other country; and when people can travel and trade freely, while continuing to remain proud and loyal citizens of their respective countries.

Friends, at the end of my visit, if someone were to ask me to sum up the situation about Indo-Pak relations at present, I would, on the basis of what I have observed and experienced here since my arrival in Pakistan on the evening of May 30, say unequivocally that *'Fiza zaroor badli hui hai, bahut badli hui hai.'* (The atmosphere has definitely changed, it has changed a lot.)

Yes, it's true that there is tranquility on the border, which is no mean achievement in itself. True, there are greater people-to-people contacts, which too is a significant step forward. It is also true that the *awaam* (people) of both India and Pakistan have taken over the peace process.

But the peace and tranquility that exists is still tentative. It is also relative, in the sense that terrorist acts in Jammu & Kashmir have not come to an end. Only last month there was a terrorist strike in Srinagar aimed at innocent school children.

How do we convert this tentative peace into permanent peace? How do we remove all the irrational abnormalities in our bilateral relations to place

Indo-Pak ties on a completely normal footing based on the principle of mutual benefit?

I am posing these questions because these need to be discussed in-depth and with an open mind in both our countries. As I have reiterated on several occasions during my visit, I would like to emphasise that we need to seize this historic moment, which is pregnant with hope. We must convert this hope into confidence and resolve that we shall certainly find solutions to *all* the issues that have estranged our two brother-nations.

There should also be no going back on the realization that dialogue is the only way to resolve every single issue, including the issue of Jammu & Kashmir, between India and Pakistan. **Peace cannot be achieved through recourse to non-peaceful means. This must be clearly understood.**

IMPERATIVES OF WAGING PEACE

There is a phrase in English that has always intrigued me—**Waging Peace**. Normally, one comes across the phrase—**Waging War**. I have often wondered why the word 'wage' is used in the context of peace. It is probably because, if the resolve to win is the aim in any war, the same resolve to win has to be the aim of making peace.

However, there is a crucial difference. In war, strategists look for a quick victory. They have an impatience to achieve their goal. In waging peace, you cannot do that. We need patience. We need to realize that it takes time to minimize differences and to find a mutually acceptable solution, especially to longstanding problems.

It takes time—and I would urge all those who sincerely desire peace between India and Pakistan to realize this important truth—because not only the painful manner in which the Partition happened in 1947 but also subsequent hostilities have hardened feelings and rigidified mindsets in both India and Pakistan.

After all, the Partition resulted not only in unprecedented violence but also in the largest cross-migration in the history of mankind. In history, including in the history of undivided India, kingdoms and dynasties have come and gone. Power has changed hands either peacefully or violently. But in recent centuries these developments did not destabilize the society very much.

In contrast, when the British left in 1947, not only was there a change of power, but there was also human displacement on a massive scale. This has left behind a trail of tragedy. The wars that followed, the long period of terrorist violence and other events have contributed to the hardening of positions in certain sections of society both in India and Pakistan.

This is the reason why even well-intentioned moves for peace and normalization are often viewed with suspicion and met with disapproval on both sides.

I therefore strongly submit to one and all involved in the Indo-Pak peace process—to those in governments as well as to those in civil society organizations—that we should give due weightage to these critical viewpoints. Nothing can be achieved by either dismissing or disparaging these critical viewpoints.

This is because, firstly, those who view the peace process with suspicion both here and in India are not insubstantial in number. Secondly, in our endeavour to establish lasting peace between India and Pakistan, it is axiomatic that we should strive to carry with us all sections of society and public opinion in our two countries.

LET US MOVE ON ALL ISSUES IN TANDEM

I shall make one last point before concluding. For us to move towards peace and normalcy, it is necessary to move the dialogue process forward on all issues. This is the reason why we both have called it the Composite Dialogue process. I was happy to know that many people in Pakistan also believe that we should move in tandem on all issues. As I said in Lahore, it is not in the interest of the peace process to let slower progress on some issues become a hurdle in achieving faster progress on others.

Here I shall just flag off a few issues that show how the relations between India and Pakistan suffer from avoidable abnormality. For instance, since coming here I have not been able to watch any of the Indian news channels to see what is happening in India and also, secondarily, to know how my visit to Pakistan is covered. It is ironical that in Pakistan one can see American CNN, British BBC, Chinese CCTV but not Indian news channels.

The abnormality is also evident in other spheres. India and Pakistan have an official trade of about $ 250 million, which is meager by any standards in today's age of globalization. But the unofficial trade is at least 4-5 times larger. Isn't it ironical that we buy and sell our products of mutual demand by routing them through Dubai and Singapore, and thereby enriching those countries, but have not been able to regularize this trade right across our borders, thereby creating more employment and business opportunities for own people?

Take another example. Pakistan's economy, like the economies of any country today, has a lot of need for Information Technology solutions. And I am told that, in addition to being met by your local IT industry, you buy costly IT solutions from several western countries. But right across the border we in India have a flourishing IT industry, which is ready to cooperate with Pakistan and offer cheaper solutions. Ironically, the IT solutions that western companies sell around the world are produced in Bangalore, Hyderabad, Gurgaon and Pune.

I am making this point because Karachi is the commercial capital of Pakistan. And I may add that, historically Sindh was the incubator for global trade. In ancient times our forefathers from Sindh ventured forth to far off lands, in the same way as in modern times Sindhi businessmen have so successfully demonstrated their acumen in Hong Kong, Singapore, London and New York.

In the era of globalization, trade and business are not only about money and profit. They also bring another kind of profit—a stronger stake in peaceful, stable and cooperative relations between two countries.

It is heartening to know that soon we'll have a broad gauge rail link between Munabao and Khokrapar. I suggested to President Musharraf that we should also re-open the sea link between Karachi and Mumbai via Gujarat. He accepted the suggestion. The issue of re-opening of our consulate offices in Karachi and Mumbai is also on the cards.

All these are good signs. But much more can be done. And it should be our mutual resolve to do all the desirable things, and do them quickly.

With these words, I conclude my remarks. I sincerely thank the Karachi Council on Foreign Relations, Economic Affairs and Law for providing this opportunity of interaction with you.

Thank you.

Appendix VI

BJP: Past and Present

Statement by L.K. Advani at the BJP's National Executive, Chennai, 18-19 September 2005. Here he announced his decision to step down as party President in the wake of the controversy generated by his visit to pakistan earlier in the year.

The Bharatiya Janata Party is celebrating 2005 as the year of its *Rajat Jayanti* (Silver Jubilee). Since its inception in 1980, the BJP has been the beacon of hope for crores of Indians who cherish the ideals of cultural nationalism, national security, democracy and development. The people of India know that, during the six years of the NDA government at the Centre between 1998 and 2004, we made an earnest effort to take our country forward on the basis of these ideals, an effort in which we succeeded substantially. The NDA government laid the foundation and set direction for India's recognition as an important geo-political power centre of the world. On the political front, our greatest achievement in the past 25 years has been our emergence as one of the two principal poles in India's polity. We also proved that the BJP was capable of leading a stable non-Congress coalition that could not only impart dynamism to India's all-round development but also solve many problems that it inherited from the past.

Personally, I deem it a proud privilege that while the first session was presided over by Shri Atalji, the party's silver jubilee session being held this December at Mumbai is going to be presided over by me. I had accepted this responsibility as party President in October 2004 because Shri Venkaiahji had some personal problems. I have decided, however, that after the Mumbai session, I shall demit office, and the party's stewardship should be taken over by some other colleague.

BJP–RSS RELATIONSHIP

From time to time, and depending on the issue at hand, the BJP leadership has had no hesitation in consulting the RSS functionaries. After such consultations, the party takes its own independent decisions. Some of these decisions may differ—and have indeed differed—from the stated positions of the RSS and certain constituents of the 'Sangh Parivar'.

But lately an impression has gained ground that no political or organisational decision can be taken without the consent of the RSS functionaries. This perception, we hold, will do no good either to the party or to the RSS. The RSS too must be concerned that such a perception will dwarf its greater mission of man-making and nation-building. Both the RSS and the BJP must consciously exert to dispel this impression.

We feel that the RSS should continue to play its role to strengthen the ethical, moral and idealistic moorings of the workers as well as functionaries of the BJP, as in the past, and this is in the larger interest of the nation.

The BJP greatly appreciates the continuing interaction we have been having with the RSS and with other organisations in the Sangh Parivar. Their views provide valuable inputs for our decision-making process. But the BJP as a political party is accountable to the people, its performance being periodically put to test in elections. So in a democratic, multi-party polity, an ideologically-driven party like the BJP has to function in a manner that enables it to keep its basic ideological stances intact and at the same time expand itself to reach the large sections of the people outside the layers of all ideology.

It is in protecting the ideological moorings of the BJP and in articulating it in an idiom and language that the people understand that great care is needed. For us in the BJP, Pandit Deendayal Upadhyaya has been a model ideologue. We have seen him interpret the party's ideological commitments, as for example in respect of 'Akhand Bharat', with remarkable clarity and conviction, and yet with flexibility and finesse.

The RSS is a nationalist organisation whose contribution to character-building of millions and towards inculcating in them the spirit of patriotism, idealism and selfless service of the motherland has been incomparable. It is this organisation that has inspired tens of thousands of public-spirited persons to serve the nation through the medium of politics. Those in the political field and those who are serving the society in other fields have to function with unity and trust like a family to ensure that the country secures its rightful place in the comity of nations.

REFERENCES

PHASE ONE

Triumph of Freedom, Tragedy of Partition

1. Dr B.R. Ambedkar, *Pakistan or The Partition of India*, vol. 8 of *Writings and Speeches*, published by Government of Maharashtra, 1990 (1946), pp. 347-348.
2. Lata Jagtiani, *Sindhi Reflections,* Jharna Books, 2006, p. 214.

Sindh and India: An Unbreakable Bond

1. Jawaharlal Nehru, *The Discovery of India,* Penguin Viking, 2004, p. 70.
2. Kanhayalal Talreja, *Pearls of Vedas: Poetic Translation in Hindi, English and Urdu*, Rashtriya Chetana Sangathan, 2006, p. 48.
3. There is a reference to Shah Abdul Latif's *Ramkali* in M.J. Akbar's brilliant *Foreword* to Dr Rafiq Zakaria's book *Indian Muslims: Where Have They Gone Wrong?*, Bharatiya Vidya Bhavan, 2004, p. xi.
4. From Bhagwan S. Gidwani's speech at the International Sindhi Sammelan, Los Angeles, California on 13-15 July 2001.
5. From Bhagwan S. Gidwani's keynote address at the International Sindhi Sammelan, Toronto, July 1997.

My First Twenty Years in Sindh

1. Dennis Kincaid, *The Grand Rebel: An Impression of Shivaji, Founder of the Maratha Empire,* Collins Landon, 1937, pp. 51-52.

2. Dale Carnegie, *How to Win Friends & Influence People*, Pocket Books, a division of Simon & Schuster, Inc, 1982 edition, pp. 115-117.
3. Ibid., pp. 3-17.
4. Dr Rafiq Zakaria, *Price of Partition*, Bharatiya Vidya Bhavan, 1998, p. 174.
5. Dr Ajeet Jawed, *Jinnah: Secular and Nationalist*, Faizbooks.com, 2005, p. 372.
6. M.S.M. Sharma, *Peeps into Pakistan*, Pustak Bhandar, 1954, p. 135.
7. Sri Prakasa, *Pakistan Birth and Early Years*, Meenakshi Prakashan, 1965, p. 37. Also see Dr Ajeet Jawed, *Jinnah: Secular and Nationalist*, Faizbooks.com, 2005, p. 370.

PHASE TWO

Mahatma Gandhi's Tragic Assassination

1. Jawaharlal Nehru to Sardar Patel in Sardar Patel's Correspondence, vol. IV, 1973, ed. Durga Das, Ahmedabad, pp. 31-32. Reproduced in *Secular Politics Communal Agenda* by Makkhan Lal, Pragun Publication, 2008, p. 132. Makkhan Lal's book, which I released in New Delhi on 31 January 2008, has a wealth of well-documented material on the pseudo-secular politics of the Congress and Communist parties.

Dr Mookerjee and Formation of the Bharatiya Jana Sangh

1. Balraj Madhok, *Syama Prasad Mookerjee*, 1954, pp. 38-39.

PHASE THREE

Pandit Deendayal Upadhyaya: Thinker, Organiser, Leader Par Excellence

1. Excerpted from Mahesh Chandra Sharma, *Deendayal Upadhyaya: Kartrutva Evam Vichar*, Vasudha Publications, 1994, p. 106. Dr Sharma is a BJP member of the Rajya Sabha.
2. *Pandit Deendayal Upadhyaya: Vyakti Darshan*, Deendayal Research Institute, New Delhi, pp. 60-61.
3. Excerpted from Pandit Deendayal Upadhyaya, *Integral Humanism*, published by the BJP.

The Beginning of My Parliamentary Career

1. Lt. Gen. J.F.R. Jacob, *Surrender at Dacca: Birth of a Nation*, Lancer Publishers, 1997.

The Journey from Kanpur to Kanpur

1. M.G. Devasahayam, *JP in Jail: An Uncensored Account*, Lotus Roli, 2006, p. 302. This is an excellent book authored by a sensitive and honest officer who, as Deputy Commissioner and Inspector General-of-Prisons in Chandigarh, was responsible for JP during his incarceration at the Post-Graduate Institute of Medical Sciences from 1 July to 14 November 1975. Though a government servant, he developed great personal regard for JP and has faithfully recorded his anguished thoughts and feelings during the most trying period in his life.

PHASE FOUR

The End of the Darkest Period in India's History

1. Footnote: K.P. Krishnanunny, *Reporting Memoirs*, Kozhikode: Olive Publications.

The People Betrayed: The Fall of the Janata Government; Return of Indira Gandhi

1. L.K. Advani, *The People Betrayed*, Vision Books, 1980, p. 59.
2. M.G. Devasahayam, *JP in Jail: An Uncensored Account*, Lotus Roli, 2006, p. 302.
3. L.K. Advani, *The People Betrayed*, Vision Books, 1980, p. 97.
4. Ibid., pp. 97-98.
5. Ibid., p. 101.

The 1980s: the BJP's Phoenix-like Rise

1. *The Transformation of an Ideological Movement into an Aggregative Party: A case study of the Bharatiya Jana Sangh*, Ph.D. thesis by Hampton Thomson Davey Jr., an American scholar at the University of California, Los Angeles, 1969, UMI Dissertation Services; pp. x and xi.
2. N. Ram, 'Know your Bofors', *Frontline*, 13-26 November 1999.
3. B.M. Oza, *Bofors: The Ambassador's Evidence*, South Asia Books, 1997.

The Ayodhya Movement: When India's Soul Spoke

1. Ramesh Menon, *Siva: Siva Purana Retold*, Rupa & Co, 2006, p. xi.
2. Dr B.R. Ambedkar, *Pakistan or The Partition of India*, vol. 8 of *Writings and Speeches*, published by the Government of Maharashtra, 1990, p. 56.
3. Swami Vivekananda, *The Future of India*, in Selections from *The Complete Works of Swami Vivekananda*, 2003, p. 280.
4. K.M. Munshi, *Somnath: The Shrine Eternal*, Bharatiya Vidya Bhavan, 1965 (1951), p. 161.
5. Ibid., p. 167.
6. Makkhan Lal, *Secular Politics Communal Agenda: A History of Politics in India from 1860 to 1953*, Pragun Publication, 2008, pp. 150-154.
7. *The Shrine Eternal*, pp. 175-177.
8. K.M. Munshi, *Pilgrimage to Freedom*, Bharatiya Vidya Bhavan, 1967, p. 312.
9. Ibid., p. 288.
10. Reproduced in Dr Rafiq Zakaria, *Iqbal: The Poet and the Politician*, Penguin, 1993.
11. White Paper on Ayodhya and the Ram Temple Movement, published by the BJP in 1993.

The Trauma and Triumph of Punjab

1. South Asia Terrorism Portal, www.satp.org.
2. Satya Pal Dang, *Terrorism in Punjab*, Gyan, 2000, pp. 151-152.
3. Shekhar Gupta, 'Darra Adam Khel: Arms for the Asking', *India Today*, 31 July 1989.
4. Suneel Kumar, 'Sikh Ethnic Uprising in India and Involvement of Foreign Powers', South Asia Terrorism Portal, www.satp.org.
5. Khushwant Singh, *A History of the Sikhs 1839-1988*, vol. 2, New Delhi: Oxford University Press, 1999, pp. 303, 370.
6. K.P.S. Gill, *Knights of Falsehood*, Har-Anand Publications, 1997, p. 5.

Five Years of P.V. Narasimha Rao's Government

1. P.V. Narasimha Rao, *Ayodhya: 6 December 1992*, Penguin Viking, 2006, p. 1.
2. Ibid., p. 188.
3. Sudheendra Kulkarni, 'Advani in Hawala Scam: Finale of a frame-up',: the *Pioneer* 15 April 1997.
4. Kanchan Gupta, 'When Advani Declared Atal PM in 1995', the *Pioneer*, 11 December 2007.
5. Vir Sanghvi, 'Two Parties, Two Faces?', *Seminar*, 2001.

Three Prime Ministers in Two Years

1. *Frontline*, March 17-30, 2001.

PHASE FIVE

The Beginning of a New Era

1. *Sunday Indian Express*, 21 October 2007.
2. 'Venkataraman Speaks of an aborted N-test', PTI report carried in the *Indian Express*, 27 May 1998.
3. Manoj Joshi, 'Nuclear Shock Wave', *India Today*, 25 May 1998.
4. Ibid.
5. Praful Bidwai and Achin Vanaik, *South Asia on a Short Fuse: Nuclear Politics and the Future of Global Disarmament*, OUP, 2000.
6. The *Times of India*, 6 May 1999.

The Kargil War: A Decisive Victory for India

1. Interview with Nawaz Sharif in *India Today*, 15-30 July 2004.
2. Jaswant Singh, *A Call to Honour: In Service of Emergent India*, Rupa & Co, 2006, p. 212. For the full text of the transcript of the two conversations, see pp. 213-219.
3. Strobe Talbott, *Engaging India: Diplomacy, Democracy and the Bomb*, Brookings Institution Press, 2004, p. 160.
4. The *Asian Age*, 5 August 1999.
5. Dr Manmohan Singh, talking to reporters while returning from a visit to Nigeria and South Africa, the *Hindu*, 19 October 2007.
6. Harinder Baweja and Raj Chengappa, 'The War of Words', *India Today*, 9 August 1999.

The NDA Returns to Power

1. The *Economic Times*, 11 May 1999.

Review of the Working of the Indian Constitution

1. P.C. Alexander, *Through the Corridors of Power: An Insider's Story*, HarperCollins, 2004, p. 17.
2. Ibid., pp. 27-28.

At the Helm of the Home Ministry

1. Shishir Gupta, 'Terror crackdown Slackened in 2005', *the Indian Express*, 27 January 2006.
2. R.K. Raghavan, 'A Reverse for Police Reforms', *Frontline*, 7-20 May 2005.

Cross-Border Terrorism: A Pak-Jihadi Challenge and Our Response

1. 'India Will Have To Fight Its Own Battle', my interview to *Outlook*, 22 October 2001.
2. Jaswant Singh, *A Call to Honour*, Rupa & Co, 2006, p. 245.
3. Nisid Hajari, 'Fallout from Flight 814', *Time* weekly, 17 January 2000.
4. Rediff on the Net, 30 December 1999.
5. A good account of Pakistan's direct involvement in the hijack of IC 814 is given in the book by Zahid Hussain, *Frontline Pakistan: The Struggle With Militant Islam*, Penguin Viking, 2007, pp. 61-63. The author, a veteran Pakistani journalist, writes: 'The extent of Taliban/ISI/jihadist cooperation was revealed during the Indian hostage crisis of 1999, the resolution of which I witnessed first hand.'
6. In their book *Deception: Pakistan, the United States and the Global Nuclear Weapons Conspiracy*, British investigative journalists Adrian Levy and Catherine Scott-Clark write about a 'potentially devastating Intelligence' suggesting a link between Pakistan's ISI and the terrorists behind 9/11 (Atlantic Books, 2007, p. 317). This information endorses what the Vajpayee government had been saying all along: namely, that terrorism originating from Pakistan is a threat to the entire world, and not only to India.
7. The *Hindu*, 21 March 2000.
8. Purnima Tripathi, 'Terror in Parliament House', *Frontline*, 22 December 2001-4 January 2002.
9. Report by Ihtasham ul Haque in the Karachi-based *Dawn* newspaper, 15 December 2001.
10. My statement in Mumbai, as reported by the Indo Asian News Service, 5 October 2006.
11. 'Life bid on Advani foiled', *Tehelka*, 11 October 2001. It was a PTI report that said: 'Mumbai police have arrested six ISI operatives and aides of Chhota Shakeel who had planned to eliminate Union Home Minister L.K. Advani and some other key personalities and carry out major subversive acts, Police Commissioner M.N. Singh said today. The arrests were made in Mumbai, Chennai and Bangalore in the past week. He told reporters that the entire operation had been masterminded by some powers outside India at the behest of ISI.'

12. Interview in *India Today*, 11 October 2001.
13. The *Pioneer*, 19 November 2001.
14. Praveen Swami, 'Lashkar-e-Taiba, in Theory and Practice', the *Hindu*, 3 November 2005.

Pakistan's Proxy War How India engaged USA and the World

1. Ghulam Hasnain, 'Portrait of a Don', in *Newsline*, a Karachi-based monthly magazine, September 2001.
2. 'US Designates Dawood Ibrahim as a terrorist supporter, Indian Crime Lord has Assisted Al Qaida and Supported Other Terrorists in India', Press release by the US Treasury Department on 16 October 2003, http://www.treasury.gov/press/releases/js909.htm.
3. 'Indian stand vindicated,' says Advani, a PTI news report on Rediff.com, 17 October 2003.
4. Harish Khare, 'The "don" has been grounded', the *Hindu*, 17 October 2003. The report added: 'As Home Minister, Mr. Advani sprung the list on General Pervez Mushrraf at Agra; since then he has been at it, even at the risk of being misunderstood of wanting to indulge in a personalised agenda.' As a matter of fact, I did not—and could not have had—a 'personalised agenda'. Sadly, there were a few elements in the bureaucratic and media establishment who deliberately created the misunderstanding that I had one.
5. Rajeev Sharma, 'Pak to hand over Dawood: Powell', the *Tribune*, 20 January 2001.
6. Suman Guha Mozumder, 'Advani renews bond with Los Angeles', Rediff.com, 12 June 2003. The report said: 'The Indian American community of southern California gave a rousing reception in honour of the visiting deputy prime minister in Los Angeles. In a rare show of unity, over 72 Indian American organisations joined hands for the reception at Ambassador Lalit Mansingh's behest, something that Advani did not forget to appreciate. "What matters for me is not just the number of people present here tonight, but the fact that so many groups have united for this. This is laudable, he said."'
7. Shyam Bhatia, 'Advani's UK trip a diplomatic success', London, Rediff.com, 17 June 2003. The report said: 'L.K. Advani's trip to the United Kingdom is turning into a diplomatic triumph for India after the deputy prime minister was received at 10 Downing Street on Monday with the aplomb usually reserved for visiting heads of state. In political terms, this is almost an exact replay of Advani's experience in Washington, where he met President Bush and his key political aides.'

Dealing with the Kashmir issue

1. Jaswant Singh gives a detailed account of the events relating to Nehru's conduct of the 1962 war in his book *A Call to Honour*, Rupa & Co., 2006, pp. 153-181.
2. These questions have been posed, and answered convincingly, in a brilliantly researched book *War and Diplomacy in Kashmir 1947-48* (Sage Publications, 2002) by Chandrashekhar Dasgupta, India's former Ambassador to China and the European Union and one of the most erudite diplomats that I have met. The book brings out the perfidious role played by the British, especially Mountbatten, in shaping the course of the war to the detriment of India's interests. Dasgupta writes: 'The conflict which broke out between India and Pakistan in 1947 was unique in the annals of modern warfare: it was a war in which both the opposing armies were led by nationals of a third country. British generals commanded the armies of the newly independent states of India and Pakistan. In India, moreover, the Defense Committee of the Cabinet was chaired by Lord Mountbatten, not Prime Minister Nehru...' (p. 9) 'It was quite natural and proper that these British officers owed their primary loyalty to their King.... Mountbatten was in some ways a friend of India but he was in no sense a foe of Pakistan. The Governor-General's affection for India never interfered with his pursuit of the British interest. He left no stone unturned to dissuade or thwart the Indian government from extending its military operations right upto Jammu & Kashmir's border with Pakistan, going to the extent of sabotaging his government's plans for creating a *cordon sanitaire* along the border by aerial action.... He pressed for a reference to the UN.... The British side (thereafter) asserted that Kashmir was a "territory in dispute", pp. 200-205.
3. Tara Shankar Sahay, 'Acceptance of pre-1953 status for J&K would have set a dangerous precedent, Advani', Rediff.com, 4 July 2000.
4. V. Shankar, My Reminiscences of Sardar Patel, Macmillan, 1974.
5. Ahmed Rashid, 'EU condemns "flawed" Pakistan elections', Islamabad, *Telegraph*, UK, 14 October 2002. Commenting on the Army-guided polls, Pakistan's exiled former Prime Minister Benazir Bhutto said: *'Jo election general karvai voh kya election hai?'* (How could an election held by a General qualify to be called a general election?) *Frontline*, 26 October 2002.
6. Shekhar Gupta, 'Congrats, New Delhi, Thank You, Srinagar', the *Indian Express*, 11 October 2002.
7. 'Talks between Kashmiri separatists, New Delhi "milestone" on road to peace', *Agence France Presse*, 28 March 2004.
8. 'Mirwaiz praises Advani for his "sincerity"', the *Daily Times*, 29 January 2004.

9. Moulvi Abbas Ansari, chairman of the Hurriyat Conference, interviewed by Omkar Singh, Rediff.com, 23 January 2004.
10. *Poems of Mahjoor*, a centennial publication by Sahitya Akademi, tr. from Kashmiri into English by T.N. Kaul, 1988, pp. 124-129.

Vajpayee-Musharraf Summit in Agra

1. Anil Narendra, 'Driving home a point', the *Pioneer*, 26 July 2001.
2. 'No CBMs till Kashmir is solved: Musharraf', Excerpts of the press interaction reported by IANS on 16 July 2001.
3. Rediff.com, 17 July 2001, also in Jaswant Singh, *A Call to Honour*, Rupa & Co, 2006, p. 260.
4. The *Indian Express*, 17 August 2001.
5. Soon after the talks at Agra reached a dead end, Pakistan's spokesman Major General Rashid Qureshi, whose proximity to Gen. Musharraf was well known, suggested that a 'hidden hand' had scuttled the proposed joint statement. the *Tribune*, 19 July 2001.
6. B. Muralidhar Reddy, 'Musharraf blames it on Advani', reporting from Islamabad, the *Hindu*, 31 August 2001. The report said, 'For the first time since the Agra Summit one and half months ago, the Pakistan military ruler and President, Gen. Pervez Musharraf, has virtually accused the Union Home Minister, Mr. L.K. Advani, of blocking the joint declaration between India and Pakistan. In his address to the Northern Areas Legislative Council in Uiluil this morning, he maintained that the Prime Minister, Mr. A.B. Vajpayee, would have signed the joint declaration but for the pressure from the hard-liners within his Government. (He said) that on July 16, the last day of the two-day summit, Mr. Vajpayee had agreed on the draft declaration at 1.30 p.m. and was ready to sign it. But the hard-liners prevailed over the Indian Prime Minister.'
7. Pervez Musharraf, *In the Line of Fire: A Memoir*, Free Press, 2006, pp. 300-301.
8. Jaswant Singh, in his book *A Call to Honour* has refuted Musharraf's claims that Indian and Pakistani officials had produced a final and mutually acceptable draft declaration before the 2001 Agra summit collapsed, pp. 256-260.
9. Responding to Vajpayee's rebuttal of his claim in his memoirs, Musharraf maintained that 'What I have said in the book is final, and I stand by that.' 'Musharraf "deeply hurt" by Vajpayee's denial', by Nirupama Subramanian in Islamabad, the *Hindu*, 13 October 2006.

Securing Assam and North-East for the Future

1. Sanjoy Hazarika, *Rites of Passage,* Penguin Books, 2000, p. 60, 'Prime Minister Jawaharlal Nehru wanted the Assam Chief Minister, Bimala Prasad Chaliha, a Congressman himself, to go easy on deportations and even stop them. Chaliha refused, saying that the problem was so critical that Assam's demography and culture would be permanently changed.'
   It would not be out of place here to mention that Bhupen Hazarika, lyricist, singer and Assam's greatest living cultural icon, had given vent to his anguish in a song he composed in 1968: 'Today's Assamese must save themselves or else they will become refugees in their own land.' The lyric became very popular during the students' anti-foreigner agitation.
2. Seventy-third Report of the Committee of Petitions, Rajya Sabha, 22 March 1982.
3. Sanjoy Hazarika, *Rites of Passage,* Penguin Books, 2000, p. 70, Indrajit Gupta, former Union Home Minister stated in Parliament on 6 May 1997 that there were ten million illegal migrants residing in India. Quoting Home Ministry/Intelligence Bureau sources, *India Today*, in its issue of 10 August 1998, gave the statewise breakdown of illegal migrants (in millions): West Bengal (5.4); Assam (4.0); Tripura (0.8); Bihar (0.5); Maharashtra (0.5); Rajasthan (0.5); Delhi (0.3). Total: 10.83. The 2001 report of the Group of Ministers, which I headed, noted that nearly fifteen million illegal immigrants have entered India over the last five decades from Bangladesh, changing the demography of large parts of Assam, Meghalaya, West Bengal, Tripura and Bihar. 'Between 1983 to 2000, the sixteen tribunals in various districts…have located about 10,000 illegals (immigrants) of which a bare 1,400 have been deported.'
4. T.V. Rajeshwar 'Migration or invasion?', the *Hindustan Times,* 7 February 1996.
5. 'Flushing out ULFA', the *Hindu,* 18 December 2003.
6. Kalyan Chaudhuri, 'Promise of Peace', *Frontline,* 18 January 2003.
7. Subir Bhaumik, 'Church backing Tripura rebels', in Calcutta, BBC News, 18 April 2000. The report said: 'The government in India's north-eastern state of Tripura says it has evidence that the state's Baptist Church is involved in backing separatist rebels. Tripura Chief Minister Manik Sarkar said state police had uncovered details of the alleged link after questioning a church leader. Nagmanlal Halam, secretary of the Noapara Baptist Church in Tripura, was arrested late on Monday with a large quantity of explosives. Mr Sarkar said that allegations about the close links between the state's Baptist Church and the rebel National Liberation Front of Tripura (NLFT) have long been made by political parties and police.' The NLFT is accused of forcing Tripura's indigenous tribes to become Christians and give up Hindu forms

of worship in areas under their control. Last year, they issued a ban on the Hindu festivals of Durga Puja and Saraswati Puja. The NLFT manifesto says that they want to expand what they describe as the kingdom of God and Christ in Tripura.

Communal Violence in Gujarat: Propaganda versus Reality

1. 'Gujarat riot death toll revealed', BBC News, 11 May 2005. The information was provided by the Minister of State for Home Affairs in the UPA government, Sriprakash Jaiswal, in response to a question in the Rajya Sabha.
2. Rediff.com, 3 March 2002.

Defeat in Polls, Turmoil in the Party

1. Mungeri Lal is a North Indian fictional character who is prone to daydreaming.
2. In order to highlight the country's economic achievements during the NDA rule, the Ministry of Finance sponsored a high-visibility media campaign on the theme of 'India Shining' in 2003. We later realised that the campaign, conceptualised by a private advertising agency, made the government vulnerable to a politically costly attack from our adversaries, who propagated that the BJP was glossing over poverty and social inequality, which were mostly a legacy of the past.
3. 'Sonia Gandhi bows to India's xenophobes', the *Age*, Australia, 22 May 2004. http://www.theage.com.au/articles/2004/05.

My Pakistan Yatra

1. Raja of Mahmudabad, 'Some Memories', in *The Partition of India*, ed. C.H. Philips, p. 385.
2. Mohammed Currim Chagla, *Roses in December: An Autobiography* Bharatiya Vidya Bhavan, 2000 (1973), pp. 78-79.

I Have No Regrets

1. Lt. Gen. (Retd.) Surrinder Kochar, *Bhagavad Gita: Timelessly Pertinent*, Himalayan Books, 2005, p. xxxv.

A Statesman with a Poetic Soul

1. 'No parallel centres of power, says Advani', the *Tribune*, 30 June 2002.
2. Atal-Advani row, interview with Prabhu Chawla in *India Today*, 22 March 1999.

Reminiscences and Reflections

1. CNN-IBN, 9 December 2006. Dr Singh's exact statement was: 'We will have to devise innovative plans to ensure that minorities, particularly the Muslim minority, are empowered to share equitably in the fruits of development. *They must have the first claim on resources.*' (emphasis added)
2. Durga Das Basu, *Introduction to the Constitution of India*, Thirteenth edition, Prentice-Hall of India Private Limited, 1990, pp. 388-89.
3. Press conference held on 13 September 2007.
4. Donald Eugene Smith, *India: As a Secular State*, Princeton University Press, 1963.
5. Samuel P. Huntington, *Who Are We? The Challenges to America's National Identity*, Simon & Schuster, 2004.
6. Rabindranath Tagore, *Nationalism*, Rupa & Co, 2002, pp. 125-126.
7. From a document issued by the Bharatiya Janata Party on the occasion of my Swarna Jayanti Rath Yatra in 1997.
8. Dhananjay Keer, *Dr Ambedkar, Life and Mission*, Popular Prakashan, 1962.
9. My speech at the BJP's National Council meeting in New Delhi on 21 January 2008.
10. BJP-Congress relations formed a part of the interview that Shekhar Gupta, Editor-in-Chief of the *Indian Express*, conducted with me for his weekly 'Walk the Talk' programme for NDTV 24x7 channel on 15 March 2005. 'You don't see the Congress as an evil?' Gupta asked me. 'No, I don't,' I replied. He persisted: 'You wouldn't see the Gandhi family as an evil?' I said, 'I don't think the Gandhi family is an evil. But this conception that a Gandhi is alone fit to rule the country is basically undemocratic. It is totally unacceptable to any democrat. I am surprised the Congress has readily accepted it.'

In Pursuit of Meaning and Happiness in Life

1. Jed Rubenfeld, *The Interpretation of Murder*, Headline Review, 2006, p. 5.
2. Gulab Vazirani, *Lal Advani, the Man and His Mission*, Arnold Publishers, 1991.
3. Lal Krishna Advani, *The People Betrayed*, Vision Books, 1980.
4. Dr Atmaram Kulkarni, *The Advent of Advani*, Aditya Prakashan, 1995.
5. *Young India*, 18 June 1925.
6. *Harijan*, 2 March 1934.
7. *Harijan*, 10 February 1940.

Glossary

aarati	devotional offering
adharma	falsehood
agni pareeksha	trial by fire
ahimsa	non-violence
akhand paath	full and continuous reading from the Granth Sahib
angrez	the Britishers
antyodaya	welfare of the last person in society
atma gauravam	regional self-pride
bauddhiks	lectures
bawdi	water-hole
Bhagwa Dhwaj	saffron flag
bheda	divide your enemies
bhog	consecrated meal
charkha	spinning wheel
Chintan Shibir	camp for collective thinking
danda	(stick) show the stick to the recalcitrant
darshan	view
datoon	a thin *neem* stick used to brush teeth
Dharma Sansad	parliament of Hindu religious leaders from all parts of the country
dharma	truth
diksha	spiritual initiation
diya	lamp
gaddaar	traitor
gaon	village

gareeb	poor
gupt	hidden
gurbani	Guru Nanak's inspired word
haldhari kisan	plough-carrying farmer
halwa	a sweet dish
hukamnama	religious edict
janmasthan	birthplace
jathas	groups of pilgrims
jhanda	flag
jhoolas	large-sized cradles
kar sevaks	those doing voluntary service at religious places
karmabhoomi	area of work
Kartavya Path	the Path of Duty
Kartik Poornima	the night of the full moon as per the Hindu calendar in the month of Kartik
karyakartas	workers
khatas	the monthly diaries
kushasan	malgovernance
langar	community meal
maha yagya	mega mission
mandala	district
Maryada Purushottam	an exemplar among good human beings
mamas	maternal uncles
mausis	mother's sisters
mazdoor	worker
muhajirs	refugees
mukhiya	head
nani	grandmother
nar	man
nasbandi	the forcible sterilisation programme
neta	political leader
Netra	eye
nirguna puja	which is worship of the formless Him
Nirmal Ganga	pollution-free Ganga
pad yatra	journey on foot
paramarthis	generous patrons of spiritual activities
pati	husband
pavitrata	piousness
pinda	core
Prabuddha Bharat	Enlightened India
prana	life force

prant pracharak	full-time provincial organiser and motivator
pratah smaraneeya	persons worthy of being reverentially remembered every morning
puja	prayers
purusharthis	achievers owing to their own hard work
raagis	singers of Sikh *shabad*
rishi parampara	tradition of seers
rishis	sages
Saakshar Bharat	Literate and Educated India
saguna	puja in the Hindu tradition—worship of the Creator in His infinite forms
samata-yukt/ shoshan mukt	equality and freedom from exploitation
Sampoorna Kranti	Total Revolution
samrachana	constructive activity
Samruddha	prosperous
Samruddha Bharat	Prosperous India
samskaras	traditional values
sangathan	organisation
sangharsh	struggle
sanyas	retirement
sanyasi	hermit
sar karyawah	general secretary
sarpanch	head
sarva sparshi	having influence in, and drawing support from, all sections of our diverse society
sarva vyapi	present all over the country
seth	employer
seva	service
shakhas	daily assembly of Sangh volunteers
shakti	power
Shaktishali	strong
Shaktishali Bharat	Strong India
shanti	peace
sharanarthis	refugees
Shilanyas	laying the foundation
samajik samarasata	*social harmony*
swabhasha	national language
Swabhiman	national pride
Swabhimani	self-confident
Swachcha Bharat	Clean India

Swadesh	nation
Swastha Bharat	Healthy India
ulook dhwani	a conch-like sound, produced by the mouth, which is meant to blow evil spirits away
Vasudhaiva Kutumbakam	The whole world is our family.
vikas	development
Vishwa vandaneeya	deserving of being revered across the world
ziddi	insistent

List of Acronyms

AASU	All Assam Students Union
ABVP	Akhil Bharatiya Vidyarthi Parishad
AEC	Atomic Energy Commission
AGP	Asom Gana Parishad
AIADMK	All India Anna Dravida Munnetra Kazagham
AIBMAC	All India Babri Masjid Action Committee
AICC	All India Congress Committee
AIIMS	All India Institute of Medical Sciences
AIMPLB	All India Muslim Personal Law Board
AIR	All India Radio
APHC	All Parties Hurriyat Conference
ASEAN	Association of South-East Asian Nations
ASI	Archaeological Survey of India
ATR	Action Taken Report
BHU	Banaras Hindu University
BIMSTEC	Bay of Bengal Initiative for Multi-Sectoral Technical & Economic Cooperation
BJP	Bharatiya Janata Party
BLT	Bodo Liberation Tigers
BMS	Bharatiya Mazdoor Sangh
BOAC	British Overseas Airways Corporation
BoP	Balance of Payments
BSE	Bombay Stock Exchange
BSF	Border Secutiry Force
BTDA	Bodoland Territorial District Area

CAG	Comptroller and Auditor General
CBI	Central Bureau of Investigation
CBM	Confidence Building Measures
CCIT	Comprehensive Convention on International Terrorism
CCS	Cabinet Committee on Security
CDS	Chief of Defence Staff
CEC	Chief Election Commissioner
CFD	Congress for Democracy
CIA	Central Intelligence Agency
CISF	Central Industrial Security Force
CMG	Crisis Management Group
CMP	Common Minimum Programme
COFEPOSA	Conservation of Foreign Exchange and Prevention of Smuggling Activities Act
CPI	Communist Party of India
CPI(M)	Communist Party of India
CrPC	Criminal Procedure Code
CRPF	Central Reserve Police Force
CSC	Chiefs of Staff Committee
CWC	Central Working Committee
CWC	Congress Working Committee
DAE	Department of Atomic Energy
DIR	Defence of India Act
DMC	Delhi Municipal Corporation
DMK	Dravida Munnetra Kazagham
DONER	Development of North Eastern Region
DPSP	Directive Principles of State Policy
DRDO	Defence Research and Development Organisation
EEZ	Exclusive Economic Zone
EIC	East India Company
EU	European Union
FBI	Federal Bureau of Investigation
G8	Group of 8
GDP	Gross Domestic Product
GoM	Group of Ministers

HMG	His Majesty's Government
HuA	Harkat-ul-Ansar
HuM	Hizb-ul-Mujahideen
IAEA	International Atomic Energy Agency
IAF	Indian Air Force
IB	Intelligence Bureau
ICG	Intelligence Coordination Group
ICS	Indian Civil Service
IMDT	Illegal Migrants Determination by Tribunal
IMF	International Monetary Fund
INA	Indian National Army
INC	Indian National Congress
IPC	Indian Penal Code
IPKF	Indian Peace Keeping Force
IPS	Indian Police Service
ISI	Inter-Services Agency
ISS	Islamic Swayamsevak Sangh
ITBP	Indo-Tibetan Border Police
JeI	Jamaat-e-Islami
JeM	Jaish-e-Mohammad
JMM	Jharkhand Mukti Morcha
JMM	Joint Parliamentary Committee
KCF	Khalistan Commando Force
KLO	Kamtapur Liberation Organisation
LAC	Line of Actual Control
LCA	Light Combat Aircraft
LeT	Lashkar-e-Taiba
LJP	Lok Janashakti Party
LoC	Line of Control
LTTE	Liberation Tigers of Tamil Eelam
MCC	Maoist Communist Centre
MCOCA	Maharashtra Control of Organised Crime Act
MDMA	Multi-Disciplinary Monitoring Agency
MDMK	Marumalarchi Dravida Munnetra Kazhagam
MEA	Ministry of External Affairs
MISA	Maintenance of the Internal Security Act

MoD	Ministry of Defence
MP	Member of Parliament
MPLADS	MP's Local Area Development Scheme
MQM	Muttahida Quami Movement
NAC	National Advisory Council
NAG	National Agenda for Governance
NAM	Non-Aligned Movement
NCP	Nationalist Congress Party
NCRWC	National Commission to Review the Working of the Constitution
NDA	National Democratic Alliance
NDF	National Democratic Front
NEFA	North Eastern Frontier Agency
NF	National Front
NHRC	National Human Rights Commission
NLFT	National Liberation Front of Tripura
NPT	Nuclear Non-Proliferation Treaty
NSA	National Security Advisor
NSC	National Security Council
NSCS	National Security Council Secretariat
NTRO	National Technical Research Organisation
NWFP	North West Frontier Province
OBCs	Other Backward Classes
OIC	Organisation of Islamic Conference
OTC	Officers Training Camp
PDP	People's Democratic Party
PIP	Prevention of Infiltration from Pakistan
PLO	Palestinian Liberation Organisation
PMGS	Pradhan Mantri Grameen Sadak Yojana
PMO	Prime Minister's Office
PoK	Pakistan-occupied Kashmir
POTA	Prevention of Terrorism Act
PoWs	Prisoners of War
PPP	Pakistan People's Party
PTI	Press Trust of India
PWG	People's War Group
RAW	Research & Analysis Wing

RBI	Reserve Bank of India
RJD	Rashtriya Janata Dal
RSP	Revolutionary Socialist Party
RSS	Rashtriya Swayamsewak Sangh
SAARC	South Asian Region for Regional Cooperation
SAC	State Autonomy Committee
SAD	Shiromani Akali Dal
SAFMA	South Asian Free Media Association
SAFTA	South Asian Free Trade Area
SGPC	Shiromani Gurdwara Prabhandak Committee
SIMI	Students Islamic Movement of India
SLRs	Self-loading rifles
SRC II	Second States Reorganisation Commission I
SSB	Special Service Bureau
SVD	Samyukta Vidhayak Dal
TADA	Terrorist and Disruptive Activities (Prevention) Act
TDP	Telugu Desam Party
TRS	Telangana Rashtra Samithi
UAE	United Arab Emirates
ULFA	United Liberation Front of Assam
UN	United Nations
UNCIP	UN Commission for India and Pakistan
UNHRC	United Nations Human Rights Commission
UNI	United News of India
UNSC	United Nations Security Council
UP	Uttar Pradesh
UPA	United Progressive Alliance
VHP	Vishwa Hindu Parishad

Index

9th Lok Sabha election, 368
  Rajeev Gandhi ousted, 369
10th Lok Sabha elections, 455-456
  BJP's eye-catching performance in, 456
  results of, 455-456
11th Lok Sabha, 457-477, 511
  BJP as single largest part, 529
  elections to, 475-477
  third hung House, 477
12th Lok Sabha in 1999, 576
  dissolution of, 557, 558
  Rashtrapati Bhavan's communiqué on, 558
13th Lok Sabha,
  Congress lost in, 479
  dissolution of, 763
  elections to, 560, 578, 762
  NDA's victory in, 579
14th Lok Sabha, 92, 763-768
  elections to, 420, 586, 763
  four-phase schedule of polling, 763
  media predictions for NDA victory, 765
  results of, 766
  shocked defeat to NDA, 765-768
15th Law Commission, 167
1916 Lucknow Pact, 819
1971 elections, 187
  two-thirds majority to Indira Gandhi, 187
1977 Lok Sabha poll, 261-266
  announced, 261
  anti-Congress wave, 265
  Congress defeated, 265
  Janata Party's triumph in, 265-266, 267
  silent and peaceful ballot-box revolution, 264
1984 Lok Sabha elections, 318-319, 433
  BJP, poor performance of, 318-319, 320
  Congress won in, 319
  poor performance of BJP, 318-319, 320
1989 parliamentary elections, 339, 364, 371
  BJP's spectacular performance in, 339
  Congress thrown out, 339
1991 mid-term parliamentary polls, 453
1996 Lok Sabha elections, 529
  BJP as single largest party, 529
  Congress defeated, 529
  watershed in Indian democracy, 475-476
1998 Lok Sabha elections,
  BJP manifesto for, 530, 534, 601
  clear mandate for BJP-alliance, 600
  results of, 530
  share of votes in, 530
  victory to BJP, 530-531
3-Point Swarna Jayanti Pledge, 523-524

Abbas, Khwaja Ahmed, 111
Abdullah, Farooq (Dr), 566, 678, 683, 685
Abdullah, Omar, 683
Abdullah, Sheikh, 317, 413, 516, 676-680, 683
  Aatish-e-Chinar, 413
Abraham, Abu, 239
  Barefoot humour, 239
  Bathtub humour, 239
Acausal connecting principle, 194
Acharya, Mahapragya, 849
Acquisition writ petitions, 395

Index

Adhikari, R. (Major), 565
Adi Shankaracharya, 498, 692
Adiomal (founder of the Advani clan), 28
Advani, Dharamdas Khubchand, 28
Advani, Hashu, 40
Advani, Hiroo, 20
Advani, Hotchand, 121
Advani, Kishinchand, 28
Advani, L.K. (the Author),
  achievements as Home Minister, 664
  acquaintance with,
    Jai Prakash Narayan, 186, 263
    with film personalities, 282
  address at BJP's National Council meeting, 714
  admirable movies of, 885
  admiration for,
    Rajeev Gandhi, 327-328
    Rajpalji, 43 *see also* Rajpalji
  in Alwar jail, 75
  Anatomy of Fascism pamphlet, 228
  announcement of Atalji as Prime Minister, 837
  approach on Ayodhya, 540
  assessment of two visits to USA, 660
  columnist with multiple pseudonyms, 109-111
  detentions of,
    during emergency, 123, 204, 211-213, 877
    co-prisoners of, 216
    detention orders challenged, 212-220
    dramatic release of, 215
    legal battle from prison, 214-220
    letters to Appaji, 239-244
    life in jail, 211-213
    release from jail, 260
    in Rohtak jail, 219-220
    writing letters in prison, 238-239
    writ petition before Karnataka High Court, 214, 220
    writ-petitions filed again, 220, 221
    hearing of, 221
    at Massanjore, 380, 406, 449 *see also* Ram Rath Yatra
    at Mata Tila, 406
  assisting Atalji in Delhi, 835
  association with,
    business houses, 880
    colleagues and friends, 878-879
    film world, 281283
    leaders of other political parties, 878
    media members, 880
    new age leaders, 879
    non-political friends, 879
    party colleagues, 879
    spiritual personalities, 891-892
  atmosphere at home, 29-31
  beginning of parliamentary career, 155-174
  birth of, 27
  birthday celebrations of, 30
  bliss of family life, 119-127
  childhood days, 27-29, 155
  choice of Home Ministry, 600-601
    reasons of, 601
  close-knit family, 890
  contribution to India's development, 878
  deep respect for Gandhiji, 71
  and Deendayalji,
    effect of religion and spirituality, 891-892
    first meeting with, 148
    influence of,
    personal reminiscences with, 148-150
  as DMC chairman, 129-131
  early patriotic influences on, 40-42
  in earthquake-hit Gujarat, 743-746
  effect of Swami Ranganathananda on, 46-47
  elected president of BJP, 319, 320
  entry into Delhi Metropolitan Council, 128-136
  family atmosphere in Karachi, 109-110
  family of, 889
  fascination for,
    IT, 882
    Rajasthan, 66
  first entry into alliance politics, 104-105
  first lesson in secularism, 80-81
  first meeting with,
    Morarji Desai, 195
    with Musharraf, 698-700
  first presidential speech, 333-334
  first professional job of, 42
  first twenty years in Sindh, 27-51
  first visit to USA, 645-648
    purpose of, 645
  flurist in RSS band, 886
  Hawala charges on, 467-471, 837, 877
    charges quashed, 468-470
    Pioneer's comment on, 468-469
  Hindu hardliner, 688, 691, 837, 877
  homage to E.M.S. Namboodiripad, 538
  as Home Minister, 536, 580, 600-618
    first official duty, 536-537

last major initiative, 687-692
lesson learnt, 643
as I&B minister, 211, 270, 275, 276
early days, 275
first task as, 270
at international conference,
in Strasbourg, 462-464
on challenges before Emerging
Democracies, 462-464
at Karachi in 2005, 33
interactions with Dr Mookerjee, 90
interview on,
Aaj Tak, 697
GEO TV, 828-829
Jinnah controversy, 813-817
clarification given, 814-815
as journalist in *Organiser*, 107, 109-119
acting editor of, 112
movie critic in, *281, 283*
journey,
as a political activist started, 88
from Faizabad to Ayodhya, 386
from Kanpur to Kanpur, 175-192
journey from Karachi to Delhi, 12, 48, 51, 52-53, 58, 62
of life, 876-886
as a lawyer, 194
as linguistic interpreter, 106
last days in Sindh, 51
learning parliamentary work, 101-103
love for,
books, 41, 883-886
movies, 884-885
music, 886
meaning in life of, 876-877
meeting with,
British officials, 660
Congress delegation, 487-488
George Bush, 645, 655, 657
John Ashcroft, 656
Kamla, 120
marrage to, 120-121
Powell, 646, 650
Times of India report on, 651-652
Savarkar, 46 *see also* Savarkar, 45-46
Sheikh Abdullah, 683
Tom Ridge, 656
Tony Blair, 660-661
Yasser Arafat, 663
US officials, 646
memorable visits abroad, 283-285
to Karachi after Partition, 284

to communist-ruled East Germany, 283-284
to Moscow, 283
to re-unified Germany, 284
memories of Punjab, 436
at North Block, 603
new maker of the year 2005, 831
special interview of, 831-832
as party president, 185, 192, 175-178, 248, 324, 475-476, 774
a *pracharak* in Rajasthan, 148, 834
Pakistan yatra (2005), 783-806
departure from Delhi, 790
at Katas Raj temple, 804-806
meeting with PPP leaders, 799-803
meeting with President Musharraf, 793-795
reception by Hindu Panchayat, 811-812
visit to,
Jinnah's mausoleum, 785
controversy generated at, 785
Karachi, 809-812
Lahore museum, 808-809
Nankana Sahib, 809
St. Patrick's High School, 810
Takshasila and Nalanda, 796
political prisoner in Independent India, 406
prank played on grandmother, 37
prediction of exile for, 198-199
pre-Partition memories of Karachi, 15
A Prisoner's Scrapbook, 228, 884
presidential address,
at BJP Mahaadiveshan, 479
at BJP National Council in New Delhi, 324-325, 484, 714
at BJP *Rajat Jayanti* function, 776
at Calicut, 142
at Kanpur, 178-179
at Mumbai, 339, 472-473
at plenary session of Jana Sangh, 196-197
at Rohtak, 328
at Vijayawada session, 435-436
Rajasthan as *karmabhoomi*, 66-69, 100
from Rajasthan to Delhi, 100-107
lessons learnt at, 67-69
to Rajya Sabha, 131-132, 163-164
issues raised in, 163-164
Leader of House in, 276
reflections on,
Ayodhya events, 406-409
on tragedy of Partition, 56

relationship with Atalji, 106-107, 835-846
　　see also Vajpayee, Atal Bihari
resignation as Party President, 785, 825-826, 830
resignation withdrawn, 828
and RSS,
　　'alma mater', 303
　　entry to, 41
　　motivation to join RSS, 38-39
　　pracharak in Rajasthan, 4-5, 42-43, 58, 66-70, 109-110, 507, 521
　　swayamsevak, 37-40
schooling at St. Patrick's High School, 32-34
second visit to,
　　Karachi, 786
　　USA, 655-664
speech at,
　　Ganga ghat, 895
　　Karachi Council on Foreign Relations, Economic Affairs & Law, 815-817
　　Parliament, 449, 451
　　support to Congress on nuclear issue, 546
A Tale of Two Emergencies, 227
talks with Hurriyat leader, 687-692
　　Daily Times report on, 691-692
target of a terrorist act in Coimbatore, 602
The People Betrayed, 287, 884
training for OTC, 41-42
tribute to Rajeev Gandhi, 455
uncles of, 28-29
underground pro-democracy literature of, 226-229
views on non-political life, 886
visit to,
　　Ayodhya, 386
　　Britain, 660
　　Bulgaria, 423
　　Ground Zero, 645
　　Israel, 663
　　Ladakh, 113, 566
　　London, 860
　　Los Angeles, 659-660
　　other countries, 661-662
　　Qatar, 662
　　riot-hit Gujarat, 753-756
　　media report on, 753-754
　　Thailand and Singapore, 662-663
　　USA, 460
working relationship with Morarjibhai, 297-299
yatra from Varanasi to Ayodhya, 398

Advani, Sarla, 20
Advani, Sheela, 119
Afternoon Despatch & Courier, 886
Afzal, Mohammed, 630, 631
　　accused in Parliament attack, 630
　　death sentence awarded to, 631
　　death sentence stayed, 632
Aggregative Parties, 323
Agra summit (2001), 694-710, 789
　　announcement of, 697
　　biggest media event, 701
　　collapse of, 688
　　delegation-level meeting at, 701
　　delegations arrived, 700
　　end-of-the-summit press conference, 704
　　failure of, 704
　　joint declaration drafted, 702-703
　　　　India's rejection to, 702
　　　　Musharraf's comments on, 705-707
　　Musharraf's summit talks through media, 703
　　　　assertion about cross-border terrorism, 703-704
　　　　combative views on Kashmir expressed, 703
Agrani, 72
Ahle Hadis, 634
Ahmed, Fakhruddin Ali, 191, 193, 205
　　signing of Emergency Proclamation, 277
Ahmed, Shamshad, 568
Ahsan, Aitzaz, 798
　　The Indus Saga, 798
　　Making of Pakistan, 798
AICC 1961 session, 865
All India Radio (Akashwani),
　　Bhakti Sangeet programme on, 859
　　criticism of Hindi used by, 134-135
　　institutional autonomy to, 279
　　restoring credibility to, 278-279
　　under emergency rules, 211
Aiyer, Mani Shankar, 462, 487, 548
Ajatashatru, 144
Akal Takht, 429, 430
Akali Dal,
　　1984 Lok Sabha polls boycott, 434
　　alliance with BJP, 435-436 see also BJP-Akali Dal alliance, 435-436
　　single largest party in 1967 assembly polls, 426
Akbar, 41, 66, 506
Akbar, M.J., 285
Akhand Bharat concept, 147
Akhand path, 30, 31

Akhil Bharatiya Vidyarthi Parishad (ABVP), 182, 188, 499, 731
Aksai Chin, 666, 667
Akshardham temple,
  Gandhinagar, attack on, 633
  in Delhi, 806
Al Qaeda, 641, 649, 654
  terrorist attack in United States, 708
Al'Utbi, 344
Alamgir, Bahadur Shah Ibn, 356
Albright, Madeleine, 585
Alexander, 796
  invasion of India, 796
Alexander, P.C. (Dr), 598-599, 839
  candidature for presidentship proposed, 839
  dirty tricks' campaign against, 598
  Governor of Maharashtra, 598, 839
  reappointment of, 598
Ali, Aruna Asaf,
  first Mayor of Delhi, 104, 105
Alimchandani, Jairamdas Daulatram, 24
All India Anna Dravida Munnetra Kazagham (AIADMK), 295-296
All India Babri Masjid Action Committee (AIBMAC), 365, 371, 388, 390
All India Conference of Presiding Officers, 297
All India Institute of Medical Sciences (AIIMS), 214, 261
All India Muslim Personal Law Board (AIMPLB), 332
All India parties,
  recognition of, 96
All Parties Hurriyat Conference (APHC), 687-691
Allahabad case, 230
Allahabad High Court, 198, 203, 207, 231, 359, 364, 392
  challenge to Indira Gandhi's election petition in, 203, 208
  judgment on Indira Gandhi, 207, 208, 222, 230
  annulment of, 237,
  judgment on Ayodhya case,
    announcement of, 392, 396
    inexplicable delay in, 398
    postponement of, 395
All-India Civil Liberties Conference, 225
Alliott-Marie, Michele, 661
Al-Thani, Hamid Bin Khalifa Sheikh, 661
Amarnath pilgrimage, 687
  attack on pilgrims, 633

Ambedkar, B.R. (Dr), 2, 75, 238, 344, 494, 496, 506, 589, 591, 866, 868
  architect of the Indian Constitution, 238
  birth anniversary of, 589
  embraced Buddhism, 866
  Pakistan, 2, 344
  The Partition of India, 2, 344
  views on Article 32, 238
    explanation given for, 866
    as protest against untouchability, 866
America,
  folly in 2003, 657
  relations with India, 658-659
  support to Pakistan, 169, 172-173
  universalism of, 863
American Cultural Centre, in Kolkata, 632
  attack on, 632
American Jewish groups, 461
Amil community, 28-29
Amil Institute, 7
Amir, Ayaz, 571
Anand Bhavan, 505
Ananda Marg, 212
Anandpur Sahib Resolution, 434
Angrez, 39-40
Annadurai, C.N., 132
Ansari, Moulvi Abbas, 687, 692
Ansari, Z.R., 333
Anti-BJPism, 479, 512, 778
Anti-Defamation Bill of 1988, 336
  opposition to, 336
Anti-democratic Emergency rule (1975-77), 862
Anti-Hindi agitation in Tamil Nadu, 147
Anti-Nizam struggle in Hyderabad, 391
Anti-Rajiv wave, 337
Anti-Sikh carnage in Delhi in 1984, 250, 423, 431, 756
Antony, A.K., 537
Anushilan Samiti, 191
Anwar, Tariq, 583
Apang, Gegong, 728
Apte, S.S., 81
Arabian Sea, 604
Arab-Israel war, 147
Arafat, Yasser, 461
Archbishop Arulappa, S., 750
Archeological Survey of India (ASI), 347
Arjun Main Battle Tank project, 605
Armitage, Richard, 654
Around the World in Eighty Days, 35
Arunachal Pradesh, 666
  a part of Greater Assam, 728

China's territorial claim on, 728
ASEAN Summits, 732
Ashar, Premjibhai, 105
Ashcroft, John (General), 646, 656
Asom Gana Parishad (AGP), 437
Assam Accord of 1985, 717
Assam Gana Parishad (AGP), 713
Assam Rifles,
   manning the Indo-Myanmar border, 613
   shift to Home Ministry, 613
Assam,
   anti-foreigner movement, 717
   Bangladeshi infiltrators in, 716
   BJP's 3-D demands for, 722
   campaign to evict illegal immigrants, 716
   Congress governments in, 716
      ali, kuli and *Bengali* support to, 716
   conspiracy of muslim infiltrations in, 715
   danger of absorption in E. Pakistan, 715
   external aggression and internal disturbance in, 720
   foreign infiltrations in, 713, 714
   new era of peace in, 725-726
   students' movement, 716
   vote bank politics in, 716-718, 721
Association of South-East Asian Nations (ASEAN), 570
Atlee, Clement, 55
Atomic Energy Commission (AEC), 544
August Kranti Maidan, 494
Aulakh, Gurmit Singh, 428
Aurangzeb, 345
   mosques in Benaras, 372
Aurora, J.S. (Lt. Gen), 170
Awadh, abode of Ram, 3356
Awami League, 168
Ayaz, Shaikh, 22
Ayodhaya dispute, 341-421
   BJP resolution passed on, 367-368
   BJP support to, 367-368
   change in profile of, 362-363
   chief planks of election manifesto, 369
   Congress party's fluctuating attitude on, 364-365
   example of Poland, 372
   historical roots of, 357-359
   Nehru government views on, 360-361
   public meeting in UP for, 363
   resolution of, 360-362
   resurfaced in 1980, 362-363
   solution to, 419
   solution to, three options for, 419-421
   symbol of struggle, 367
Ayodhya movement, 250, 399, 779, 857
   and spirit of Somnath, 351
   criticism of, 409
   genesis of, *406*
   Hindu self-renewal and self-affirmation, 409
   sans political support, 367
   significance and impact, 406-409
   a historical watershed, 412, 415
Ayodhya,
   archaeological evidence of temple, 356-357
   arrival of Ram Bhakts, 398
   confrontation between VHP and UP Govt.,418
   construction of makeshift temple at, 352, 417
   happenings on 6 December, 400-402
      aftermath of, 403-409
      and Hindu awakening, 409
      attack on domes, 401, 475
      conspiracy theory, 404
      idols of Ram Lalla installed, 404-405
      makeshift temple erected, 404-405
      masjid demolished, 402
      public mood on, 402
   a hundred-day *purnahuti yagna* at, 418
   land acquisition by UP govt., 390
Ayyangar, Gopalaswamy, 680, 681
Ayyangar, M. Ananthasayanam, 103
Azad, Baba Prithvisingh, 502, 503
Azad, Chandrashekhar, 514
Azad, Maulana Abul Kalam, 347, 514, 680
Azam, Mohammed, 345
Azhar, Mohammad Masood, 622, 624-625
   release in bargain, 624
Aziz, Mohammed (Lt. Gen.), 568
Aziz, Sartaj, 567, 568
   India's demands to, 569
Aziz, Shaukat, 795

Babar, 355
Babbar Khalsa International, 431, 641
Babri Masjid, 352, 355-357
   demand to rebuild, 405
   demolition of, 352, 355, 361, 402, 466
      events leading to, 352-354
      aftermath of, 406
      arrest of leaders, 406
      ban on RSS, Bajrang Dal, VHP, 406
      dismissal of BJP governments, 406
      charge of conspiracy and pre-planning

on, 403
Babu Genu, 494
Babur, 66
Backward Classes Commission, 855
Badal, Prakash Singh, 426, 436, 517, 559
   imprisonment during Emergency, 426
   political incarceration of, 426
Badlani, Nand, 64
Bahuguna, Hemvati Nandan, 263, 304
Bakht, Sikandar, 310, 375
Balasubramnyan, P.K. (Justice), 719, 721
Balayogi, G.M.C., 629
Ballot-box revolution, 264-266
Banatwala, G.M., 332
Bandwagon Phenomenon, 95, 95
Banerjee, Mamata, 559
Banerjee, U.C., 758
Bangalore Central Jail, 205
Bangladesh,
   creation of, 713
   genesis of, 167-171
   infiltrations from, 438, 638, 670
   liberation of, 602, 712
   war in 1971, 195
Bank nationalisation, 157
Barbora, Golap, 717
Barnala, Surjeet Singh, 436
Baroda dynamite case, 244
Barooah, Devkant, 206, 257, 716
Barrington, Nicholas (Sir), 788, 790
Basu, Durga Das, 884
   Commentary on the Constitution of India, 884
   Introduction to the Constitution of India, 856, 884
Basu, Jyoti, 444, 482, 638
Basumatary, Hagrama, 725
Battle of Khanua, 66
Battle of Panipat, 574
Bay of Bengal, 605, 712
BBC, 212
Begum Zia, 724
Beijing Olympics, 2008, 672
Belur Math, 48
Bengal Partition in 1905, 714
Bengal State Prisoner's Act, 77
   a 'black law', 77
Bengal, division of, 820
Besant, Annie (Dr), 585
Best Bakery case, 755
Bhabha, Homi (Dr), 544
Bhagat Singh, 792, 809
Bhagat, P.S., 577

Bhagavad Gita, 6, 694, 830, 868
Bhagwat, Madhukar Rao, 42
Bhagwat, Mohan Rao, 42
Bhai Mahavir, 174, 177
Bhai Parmanand, 177, 424, 502
Bhai Pratap, 7
Bhan, Suraj, 310
Bhandari, Sundar Singh, 88, 124, 158, 178, 308, 836
Bharat Heavy Electricals Ltd., 508
Bharat Mata Sangham, 500
Bharat Suraksha Yatra, 739, 866
Bharat Uday Yatra, 764-765, 772
   response to, 764-765
Bharati, Subramania, *En Thai*, 500
   memorial museum of, 500
   Vande Mataram, 500
Bharati, Umashri (Sadhvi), 401, 492
Bharatiya Jana Sangh, 38, 40, 96, 115
   1964 CWC resolution of, 544-545
   formation of, 83-90
   founding session of, 87
   Kanpur session, 175-180
   symbol of, 87
Bharatiya Janata Party (BJP),
   1996 election manifesto, 481
   2004 elections lost, 768-771
      causes of, 766-771
      post election press conference, 768-769
   achievements of, 762-763
   adopted Gandhian Socialism, 322-323
   -Akali Dal alliance, 435-436, 517
      accusation of opportunism, 436
      made for each other, 436
   alliance with Shiv Sena, 337
   'anti-Ambedkar' and 'anti-dalit' propaganda, 589
   birth of, 306-319
   birth pangs of, 316-319
   Bombay session of, 314-316
      Atalji's presidential address in, 315
      historical significance of, 316
   at centre, 540
   clear majority winning of, 265
   commitment on Ayodhya, 416-418
   and Congress, political adversaries, 874
   constituent parties of, 262, 301, 308
   crucial meeting in Chennai, 830
   defeat in the 1980, 300
      factors responsible for, 300
   difference from Jana Sangh, 312
   difficulties faced by, 263
   disintegrated, 309-310, 315, 440

election symbol of, 264
electoral setback in 1993, 475
five basic commitments of, 322-323
five major accomplishments of, 777-779
flag of, 264
formation of, 122, 262
founding session of, 144, 310-31
Gandhian Socialism adopted, 312, 313
government,
 in Arunachal Pradesh formed, 728
 as 'khichdi sarkar', 307
 fall of, 286-305, 428
 reasons of, 288-305
growth of, 778
internal quarrels in, 294
issue of 'hidden agenda', 538-539
Jana Sangh members expelled from, 307-308
and Janata Dal, question of poll alliance, 337-338
-led alliance, 539
Maha Adhiveshan, 472
national executive meeting in Ranchi, 775-776
as New BJP, 541
and Opposition unity, 262
organisational character of, 323-324
outside support to V.P. Singh's government, 145
a party of yatra, 776
patriotic struggle in 1993, 497-498
performance in 1991 elections, 456
poor performance of, 318-319, 320
 recommendations of working group on, 322-323
 study of working group on, 321, 323
 two pertinent questions for, 320
Punjab Bachao Satyagraha, 431
Rajat Jayanti celebrations, 89
reason to join temple movement, 365
role in defending Hindu-Sikh unity, 432
satyagraha launched, 336-337, 430
self-created turmoil, 299
silver jubilee commemoration, 829
 end of celebrations, 830
special *Rajat Jayanti* session, 776-777
special session in Mumbai, 830
statement on Pakistan visit, 826-828
Swarna Jayanti Rath Yatra, 528
symbol and flag of, 311-312
three-pronged strategy for, 317
victoriy in,
 the assembly elections, 2003, 762

1993 Delhi Assembly elections, 475
1998 parliamentary elections, 416
 state assembly, 390
 UP Assembly polls, 456
Vision Document, 764
White Paper on Ayodhya, 369
Bharatiya Lok Dal, 308
Bharatiya Mazdoor Sangh (BMS), 40, 124, 182
Bharatiya Sindhu Sabha, 40
Bharatmata, 124
Bhartiya Jana Sangh,
 first plenary conference of, 88
 inspiring slogan of, 89
 RSS support to, 87
Bhat, Abdul Ghani, 687, 691
Bhatinda, bomb blast in a train, 518
Bhatt, Shankara (Chief Justice), 215
Bhattacharya, Buddhadeb, 638
Bhavnani, Santo, 120
Bhindranwale Tiger Force of Khalistan, 431
Bhindranwale, Jarnail Singh, 427, 437
Bhitai, Latif Shah, 21
Bhoomi Putra, 225
Bhutto, Bilawal, 804
Bhumi Putra, 273
Bhushan, Shanti, 223, 277, 313
Bhutan, anti-ULFA operations in, 723-724
Bhutto, Benazir, 17
 assassination of, 801
 described Kargil as Pakistan's biggest blunder, 570
 first meeting with author, 801
 relations of author with, 799-803
Bhutto, Shah Nawaz, 346
Bhutto, Zulfikar Ali, 17, 22, 169, 171, 285, 346
Bible, 43
Bihar Chhatra Sangharsh Samiti, 188
Bihar,
 a by-word for *kushasan*, 512
 students' agitation, 188
BIMSTEC, 732
Birkett, Norman, 252
Birsa Munda, 513
Blackwill, Robert, 622
Blair, Tony, 660
Blunkett, David, 660
Bodo Kocharis, 725
Bodo Liberation Tigers (BLT), 725-726
 peace talks with, 725
 surrender of, 725
Bodoland Territorial Council, 725
Bodoland Territorial District Area (BTDA),

725
Bodos, agreements with, 725
Bofors scam, 328-331, 369, 440, 451, 482, 585
   campaign against, 331
   cover-up operation in, 330-331, 465
   PC appointed for, 330
   question of payoffs in, 329-330
Bombay Presidency, 15, 30
   separation of Sindh from, 15
Bombay Stock Exchange (BSE), 464
Bomdila, 669
Bommai judgment of 1994, 535
Border Security Force (BSF), 67-68, 613
   water wing of, 613
Bordoloi, Gopinath, 715
Bose, Khudiram, 511
Bose, Subas Chandra (Netaji), 24-25, 39, 511, 521
Brahma, Upendra Nath, 725
Brain Drain, reversal of, 881
British Raj, 210
Brooks, Henderson (Lieutenant-General), 577
Brunton, Paul, 44
   A Search in Secret India, 44
Buddha Purnima, 542
Bukhari, Sajjat, 799
Bureau of Immigration, overhauled, 613
Burney, 280-281
Bush, George W., 645

Cairo conference, 545
Calcutta University, 84
Calcutta massacre, 54
Camus, Albert, 108
Capitalism, 150, 161
Carlsson, 330
Carlyle, Thomas, 156
Carnegie, Dale, 44
   How to Win Friends & Influence People, 43-44
Carter, Jimmy, 252
CBC television, 428
Cellular Jail in Andaman, 495
Censor Board, 281
   restoring powers of, 281
Central Bureau of Investigation (CBI), 467
   case filed in Hawala scandal, 467
   verdict challenged by, 470
Central Economic Intelligence Bureau, 613
Central Industrial Security Force (CISF), 613
Centre-State Relations, 596-597
Chablani, H.L., 215
Chagla *Roses in December*, 225
Chagla, Mohammed Currim, 221-223, 315-316, 821
   arguments of, 221-223
   Roses in December, 821
Chakravyuha, 480
Chakraborty, Subhankar, 729
Chakravartty, Nikhil, 257, 280
Chakravarty, Trailokyanath, 502
Chaliha, Bimala Prasad, 716
Chambers, Whittaker, 734
Chamier, F.E.A. (Col.), 358
Chandra, Naresh, 356, 397
Chandra, Satish, 610
Chandrachud, Y.V. (Justice), 143, 194
Chandrasekhar, D.M. (Justices), 221
Chandrashekhar, 296, 304, 337, 386, 434, 451-452
   as caretaker Prime Minister, 452
   campaign against the Emergency, 451
   defection from Janata Dal, 450
   government,
      Congress support to, 457
      Congress support withdrawn, 390
      fall of, 390, 453
      gold-pledging decision of, 459
   revolt against Indira Gandhi's authoritarianism, 451
   self-respecting political leader, 451
Chandraswamy, 464-465, 487
   link with CIA, 487
Chaphekar brothers, 494-495
Charan Singh, 264, 288-305
   and Atalji, 226
   as deputy Prime Minister, 270
   as Prime Minister, 287
   resigned, 287
   resurrected Bharatiya Lok Dal, 309
Charkha, 265
Charvaka, 867
Chatterjee, Bankim Chandra,
   Vande Mataram, 511
Chatterjee, Manini, 407
Chatterjee, Somnath, 446
Chattisinghpora, in Kashmir, 626
   Sikhs gunned down at, 626
Chaturvedi, Makhanlal, *Pushp ki Abhilasha* 561
Chaudhary, Tridib, 191

Chaudhuri, Nirad C., 409, 411
  6th December, a turning point in Indian history, 411
  Autobiography of an Unknown Indian, 409
  autobiography of, 411
Chauhan, Jagjit Singh (Dr), 426, 428
  self-styled 'President of Khalistan', 426
Chavan, S.B., 403, 483, 488
Chavan, Yashwantrao, 129, 278, 296, 309
Chawla, G.S., 251
Chawla, Prabhu, 831
Chhattisgarh, 508
  formation of, 741
Chicago Council on Foreign Relations, 658
Chicken's Neck, 604
Chidambaram, R., 542
Chief Ministers' conferences on internal security, 618-619
Chief of Defence Staff (CDS), 611
  necessity of, 611
Chiefs of Staff Committee (COSC), 611
China,
  border disputes with, 666-672
  cultural revolution in, 740
  factors responsible for, 666-668
  invasion of Tibet in 1950, 667
  nuclear test at Lap Nor, 544
  nuclear threat, 545
  occupation of Tibet, 112
Chinese aggression in 1962, 102, 103, 112-114, 135, 145, 181, 270, 543, 577, 613, 668, 728
  India's defeat in, 577, 677
    military defeat and loss of territory in, 543
Chintan Shibir at Gwalior, 151
Chishti, Khwaja Moinuddin Dargah, 704, 866
Chittagong, 712
Chittaranjan Locomotive Factory, 84
Chittorgarh Fort, 41, 66
Chittorgarh's Gora Badal Stadium, 506
Christian grievances, 747-750
Christianity, in India, 749
Churchill, Winston, 620
Chushul, 113
Citizenship Act, 1955, 746
Clinton, Bill, 569
  address to the Indian Parliament, 626
  visit to India, 625-628
    a diplomatic success, 626
  visit to Pakistan, 626
Clinton, Chelsea, 626

Clinton, Hillary, 626
Coalition dharma, 540
Coast Guard, 613
Coelho, Paulo, *Like the Flowing River*, 784
COFEPOSA, 212
Coffin scandal, 628
Coimbatore bomb blast, 482-483, 531-533, 602
  aim of, 532
  and a TV interview, 531-533
  handiwork of Al Ummah, 532
Cold War, 574, 657
Collective,
  consciousness, 306
  mind, 201
  subconscious, 347
Collins, 239
Commissions of Inquiry Act, 1952, 758
Common minimum programme, 197, 416, 533, 534, 555
Commonwealth conference, 228
Communal,
  Award of 1935, 848
  reservations, 848
    Congress' green signal to, 855
  violence, 10-11
Communalism *vs.* secularism, 759
Communism, 150
Communist extremism, 739
Communist Party of India, 96
Communists' saga of betrayals, 511
Complete Works of Mahatma Gandhi, 24
Comprehensive Convention on International Terrorism (CCIT), 664
Conference on fugitives, 650
Congress (I), 160, 300
  comeback of, 300
  decisive victory in 1971, 163
  trounced in Gujarat Assembly elections, 203
Congress (O), 160, 194, 195, 203, 264, 268, 313, 301, 308
  constitution of, 160
Congress,
  counter-productive policy in Assam, 437
  and CPI alliance, cracks in, 257
  crisis in, 158
  denouncing N-tests, 548
  division in 1999, 777
  -DMK electoral alliance, 488, 486
  encouragement to naxalites, 437
  for Democracy (CFD), 263
    formation of, 263

merger with Janata Party, 263
in 1967 general elections, 158
infighting in, 158-160
-led UPA government, 549
party's poll symbol, 265
president replaced, 482
pseudo-secular mindset of, 855, 858
rebel leaders, 581-583
role in appeasing militancy, 428
split in 1969, 160-162, 209, 249, 269, 440, 777
syndicate faction, 159
-TRS alliance, 742
united political action against monopoly of, 194-197
Constituent Assembly, 91, 229, 235, 238, 439, 590 591, 679, 681, 850-852
 Advisory Committee on Fundamental Rights, 850
 debate on communal reservations, 830
 of Jammu and Kashmir, 675, 676, 680
 of Pakistan, 813, 816,824-827, 831
Constitution of India, 132
 adoption of, 740
 amendments to, 588
  reasons of, 588
 Article 14 (Right to Equality before law), 205
 Article 19 (1) (o) and (g), 676
 Article 21 (Right to life and personal liberty), 205, 223, 224
 Article 22 (Protection against arrest and detention in certain cases), 205
 Article 51A, 593
 Article 75(5), 457
 Article 77, 206
 Article 83(2), 200
 Article 123 (Proclamation of Ordinances), 229
 Article 143, 193, 382
 Article 213, 229
 Article 341 of, 852
 Article 352 (Proclamation of Emergency), 304, 229
 Article 356 (Imposition of President's Rule in States), 229
 Article 359, 223, 224, 229
 Article 361, amended, 232
 Article 368, 236
 Article 370, 674-682
  abrogation of, 481
  demand to abolish, 517
  Nehru's statement on, 677
  oppositions to, 676-679
  provisions in, 675
  repeal of, 533
  retention and consequences of, 676
  and Sardar Patel, 679
  temporary provision of, 681
 atrocious mutilation of, 233
 basic structure,
  defence of, 237
  violation of, 235-237
 death-wish of, 237
 fiftieth anniversary of, 589
 dismantling of, 229-230
 preamble to, 587
 reservation for S/C and S/T in, 446
 review, 588-599
  criticism of, 589-592
  debate on, 589-592
  disinformation about, 591
  issue of hidden agenda for, 590
  president's comments on, 589-590
  reasons of, 588
Constitution 7th Amendment Act, 1956, 676
Constitution 41 Amendment Bill, 232
Constitution 44 Amendment Bill, 233
Constitution 38th Amendment, 229
Constitution 39th Amendment Bill passed, 229
Constitution 40th Amendment Bill, 231
 fastest amendment, 231
 obnoxious feature of, 231
 retrospectively validated, 231
Constitution 42nd Amendment, 233
 pernicious provisions of, 233
 undoing of, 277-281
Constitution, 44th Amendment Bill, 1978, 277-278
Constitution, 73rd and 74th amendments of, 595, 869
Constitutional safeguards, 278
Conversions, debate on, 747-750
Council Secretariat (NSCS), 610
CPI (M), 190, 482
 politics practiced by, 445
Creamy layer principle, 855
Criminal justice system, 606-607
 reforms in, 607
Criminal law, basic intent of, 639
Criminal Procedure Code (CrPC), amended, 230
Crisis Management Group (CMG), 621
Cross-border migrations,
 from Bangladesh, 724-725

Cross-border terrorism, 474, 562, 602, 603, 627, 639, 662, 670, 682, 709
  fight against,
    six-month 'ceasefire' announced, 696
    three-pronged approach to, 695-696
  India's battle against, 641-642
  Pakistan's acknowledgement to, 708
  a Pak-Jehadi challenge, 620-642
Cultural Nationalism, 367, 524, 525, 750, 863, 865-877

da Gama, Vasco, 497
Dada Chellaram, 30
Daily Gazette of Karachi, 50
Dalai Lama, 672
Dalit Christians, 853
Dalit Muslims, 853
Dandavate, Madhu, 190, 212, 269, 434, 443
  arrested, 205
  coded telegram of, 259
  detention, 214-215
  revoked, 259
Dang, Satya Pal, *Terrorism in Punjab*, 427
Dangerous Corner, a British play, 288-290
  mirroring India politics, 288-290
Das, K.K., 280
Das, Pulinm 502
Das, Shyam, 38
Davey, Hampton Thomson Jr., 323
Dawn, 571
Dayaram Gidumal National College, 35
D-Company, 649
De, Dinen, 729
De, Niren, 217, 223
Decentralisation, 595
Declaration of Press Freedom in India, 276
Ded, Lal (Lalleshwari), 665, 692
Deendayal Jayanti, 373
Deendayal Upadhyaya Research Institute, 198
Defections, 164
  demand for ban on, 164
Defence Acquisition Council, 612
Defence of India Bill, 577
Defence of India Rules, 210
Defence Procurement Board, 612
Defence Production Board, 612
Defence R&D Board, 612
Defence Research and Development Organisation (DRDO), 542, 605
Defence Technology Council, 612
Delhi Metropolitan Council, 297
Delhi Metropolitan Council Act, 129

Delhi Municipal Corporation (DMC), 104
  formation of, 104
Delhi,
  and Lahore, 792
    kinship between, 792
  statehood annulled, 128, 129
  Union Territory declared, 128
DeMille, Cecil B., 281
Demographic invasion, 604
Deodhar, D.B., 36
Deoras, Balasaheb, 304, 305
  third *Sarsanghchalak* of RSS, 263, 868
Deoras, Bhanurao, 338, 368, 461
Department of Atomic Energy (DAE), 542
Department of Information and Publicity, 220-221
  letter of, 220-221
Desai, Kanti, 290-293
  controversy of, 290-293
  corruption charges against, 291
Desai, Mahadev, 73
  Gandhiji's Secretary, 225
Desai, Morarji,
  an appraisal, 297-300
  arrest of, 203
  blind spot for son, 299
  consistent fight against Indira's leadership, 269
  as deputy prime minister, 158
  faith in God, 298
  fast unto death, 195
  fifth Prime Minister, 269, 270, 280, 290, 446
  government of, 210, 269, 289, 303, 878
    achievements of, 307
    collapse of, 295
  leader of the Congress (O), 194
  misgivings about the Jana Sangh, 195
  released from detention at Tawdu, 262
  resignation of, 287, 295, 298
  The Story of My Life, 298
Desai, Narayan, 225
  forfeiture of press under Emergency laws, 225
Deshmukh, C.D.(Dr), 160
Deshmukh, Nanaji, 88, 140, 158, 178, 186, 188, 199, 262, 369, 397, 781, 836
Deshpande, V.G., 171
Devi, Jogmaya, 89
Dewey, Thomas, 95
Dhan, Ram, 262
Dhar, D.P.(Prof.), 206
Dharma Rajya, 152, 880, 892

Dharma Sansad, 363, 392, 395, 418
Dhillon, Ganga Singh, 428
Dhillon, Gurinder Singh, 31
Dhudike, 518
Dickens, Charles, 36
   Tale of Two Cities, 36
Dikshit, Umashankar, 234
Dinesh Goswami committee (1990), 167
DIR, 1971, 230, 272
Directive Principles of State Policy (DPSP), 595
Directive Principles, 595
Disaster management, 745
   law on, 745
Divide and rule policy, 9, 54, 424, 715
Dixon, William, 847
DMK,
   government,
      demand for dismissal of, 502
   issue, 487-488
Doordarshan, 433
Dostoyevsky, Fyodor, 846
   Crime and Punishment, 846
Doval, Ajit, 614-615, 622
Dr Ram Manohar Lohia, 160
Dravida Munnetra Kazagham (DMK), 160
Dual membership issue, 300-305, 307, 309, 777, 836
   debate on, 300-305
   role of Limaye in, 300-305
   root cause of, 301
Dulat, A.S., 689
Dumas, Alexander, 36
   Three Musketeers, 36
Durant, Will, 91
   The Story of Philosophy, 91
Dutt, Sunil, 884-886
   pad yatra for Hindu-Sikh unity, 884-885
Dutt, Ullaskar, 502
Dutta, Shyamal, 621
Dvijas, 308
Dynastic succession, 318

East Bengal,
   influx of refugees into India, 169
   large-scale riots in, 146
   military operations in, 169
Economic Intelligence Council, 613
Economic, Social and Cultural Rights, 595
Eenadu, 531
Einstein, Albert, 71, 659
Ekatmataa Stotra, 73
Ekta Yatra, 474

Election Laws (Amendment) Bill, 230
Elections,
   basic realities of, 94-95
Electoral behaviour, 307
Electoral reforms, 164-167, 786, 592
   national debate on, 166-167
   role of Jana Sangh on, 166-167
Elst, Koenraad (Dr), 356, 379, 415
   Ram Janmabhoomi vs Babri Masjid, 371
   The Saffron Swastika, 379
Emergency Rule in India, 145, 185, 511
   arrest of journalists, 272
   atrocities committed during, 210
   ban on organisations, 212
   campaign against, 228
   debased character of, 225
   end of, 256-266
   events of, 205-207
   inquiry of excesses committed, 252
   lifted, 122, 266
   Lok Sabha term extended, 258
   physical torture to political prisoners, 244
   popular anger against, 244-245
   press censorship in, 210, 272
   tenth anniversary of, 251
   three categories affected by, 275-276
   unsavoury legacy, dismantling of, 276-277
   V.V. Giri's objections to, 208
Emerson, Ralph Waldo, 875
Estranged democracies to engaged democracies, 657-658
Ettayapuram, 500
European Union (EU), 570
Evangelical groups, 749
   conversion campaigns of, 749
Exchange of prisoners issue, 64
Exclusive Economic Zone (EEZ), 604
Executive and Public Administration, 594
External aggression, 713
External Emergency, 199,
   demand to revoke, 195, 199

Fernandes, George, 190, 239, 244, 269, 303, 382, 384, 443, 542, 555, 557, 566, 572, 573, 610
   visit to Kargil, 563
   arrest of, 239
   as defence minister, 542, 566, 572, 727
   demand of resignation, 628
   hero of the anti-Emergency battle, 244
   involvement in Coffin scandal, 628
Fernandes, Lawrence, 244
Feroze Gandhi Act, 275, 276

Films, 281
  blanket ban on shooting abroad lifted, 281
  recertification of ten-year-old films rule abolished, 281
First General Elections in 1952, 91-93, 174
  loopholes in, 93
First Lok Sabha, 101-102
First War of Independence, 1857, 15, 493, 495, 497, 502, 512, 786 see also India
Fodder scam, 484
Footprints, 470-471
Forcible sterilisations, 257
Ford, Gerald, 251
Foreign policy, 606
Foreigners (Tribunals for Assam) Order, 2006, 720-721
  struck down, 721
  Supreme Court's ruling on, 721
Foreign-origin issue, 580, 584, 593
Frankenstein, 35
Freedom at Midnight, 239
Freedom of expression, 273
Frere, Bartle (Sir), 15
Freud, Sigmund, 875
From the Earth to theMoon, 36
Frost, David, 251
Frost, Robert, 253
Fundamental Rights, 205, 224, 229, 233, 235, 277, 593

Gadgil, N.V., 64, 347
Gaffoor, Abdul, 188
Gaibi Aawaz, 20
Galbraith, John K., 669
Gallup, George Jr., 95
Ganashakti, 548
Gandhian Socialism, 312-314, 322
Gandhi, Devdas, 72
Gandhi, Feroze, 272
Gandhi, Indira,
  assassination, 250, 318-320-321, 331, 423, 431-434, 756, 777, 836
    aftermath of,
      massacre of Sikhs, 318
      Opposition's black out, 433-434
  back to power, 287
  broadcast to the nation, 204, 211
  and Congress split, 158-161
  comeback of, 316
  defeat in Raebareli, 266
  dictatorial regime of, 234-235
  dissolution of Lok Sabha announced, 260
  draconian rule in India, 199
  election,
    challenged in Allahabad High Court, 208
    declared void, 203, 222
    petition, hearing in Supreme court, 231
  Emergency imposed by, 173, 836
  Garibi Hatao slogan, 187, 761
  and her son Sanjay, 267
  insecurity and haughtiness in personality of, 249
  instinct for self-preservation, 209
  interview to *The Times of India*, 211
  like the Queen of England, 231
  as Minister of Information and Broadcasting, 131
  nuclear test on 18 May 1974, 546
  outrageous and outlandish lie of, 226
  policy of 'weapons' used by, 162
  praise from Atalji, 170
  repudiated, 230
  returned to power in 1980, 253, 286-305
  unpopularity of, 256
  victim of her own security, 248-250
  victory in 1978 by-election, 295
  winning slogan in 1980, 307
Gandhi, Mahatma,
  assassinated, 25, 71-82, 86, 148, 408
  birth centenary of, 160
  call of 'Do or Die', 6
  first visit to RSS camp, 73
  Hind Swaraj, 376
  Nagas respect to, 727
  power of religion used, 377
  Ram Rajya concept of, 860
  samadhi of, 268, 813
  Satyagraha movement, 23-24
  views on religious conversions, 749-750
  Vishwa vandaneeya, 73
  visits to Sindh, 25
Gandhi, Rajiv, 324, 363, 391, 432-434, 595, 598, 757, 761, 894
  assassination, 391, 452, 455, 461, 485, 486-489
    aftermath of, 455
    Jain Commission's interim report on, 485
    probe, Congress politicking behind, 486-489
    role of LTTE in, 454
  big blunders of, 332-336
  as General Secretary of Congress, 318
  historic visit to China, 671
  Mr. Clean image, 326-328

as Prime Minister, 318
severe blow on, 330
speech in AICC session in Mumbai, 326-327
speech on Mandal Commission report, 448
Sri Lankan policy of, 335
surrender to minorityism, 331-334
views on corruption, 327
views on reservations, 854 *see also* Mandal commission recommendations, 854
Gandhi, Rajeev government, 440, 454
downfall of, 440
IPKF policy of, 454
Gandhi, Rajmohan, 223
Gandhi, Samaldas, 346
Gandhi, Sanjay, 257
criticism of mother's economic policy, 257-258
death in airplane crash, 257, 318
defeat in Amethi, 266
Five-Point programme, 259
Gandhi, Sonia Maino, 329, 456, 535, 548, 555-559, 581-584
false claim to form Government, 555-556, 559
foreign issue of, 580-586
letter for Congress leaders, 581 583
reasons of, 583-584
resurfaced again in 2004, 586
status of a foreigner, 583-584
inner and outer voices, 554-560
prime ministership declined, 766-768
Ganesan, Sivaji, 501
Ganga Action Plan, 894
Ganga, 18
Gangotri, 894
Gao, Tapir, 729
Garibi Hatao, 159, 161, 162, 182, 761
Gates, Bill, 659
Gates, Robert, 428
Gaur, Babulal, 196
Gazetteer of Faizabad District, 358
Gazi Baba, 631
Geelani, Syed Abdul Rehman, 630, 632
Geelani, Syed Ali Shah, 689
Geeta Rahasya, 495
Geetika, 21, 787, 811
Gen. Jacob, 172
Surrender at Dacca: Birth of a Nation, 172
Genuine secularism, 367
George Bush (Jr.), 428
George Bush (Sr), 428

German Democratic Republic, 284
Get-rich-quick culture, 464
Ghatate, Appa, 238
Ghatate, N.M. (Appa), 124, 214
Ghazni, Mahmood, 344, 345
Ghosh, Aurobindo (Maharshi), 502
Ghosh, Barindrakumar, 502
Gidumal (of Gidwani clan), 28
Gidwani, Bhagwan S., 21-22
The Return of the Aryans, 21
Gidwani, Choithram (Dr), 7, 21, 23, 24, 25
Gidwani, Shamdas, 21
Gill, K.P.S., 437
Knights of Falsehood, 438
role in Punjab militancy, 437
Gill, Lachhman Singh, 426
Giri, Mohini, 340
Giri, V.V., 159, 193
Gita discourses, 47, 49
Global terrorism, 627, 628
Goa Freedom Fighters' Association, 497
Goa liberation from Portuguese rule, 496
Gobindram, Mukhi, 7
Godbole, Madhav (Dr), 610
Godbole, Rambhau, 203
Godhra, 418, 751-758
attacked on Karsevaks, 418, 842
investigations of, 757-758
and post-Godhra violence, 751, 753, 755, 758
Godse, Nathuram Vinayak, 72, 186
bitterness toward RSS, 72
Goebbels' doctrine, 80
Goenka, Ramnath, 273, 336, 369, 383
support to JP, 273
Gogoi, Tarun, 718, 725
Gokhale, Gopal Krishna, 230, 819
Golak Nath case, 235
Supreme court judgement in, 235
Golden Temple, in Amritsar, 430, 518
Golwalkar, M.S. (Shri Guruji), 7-9, 51, 63, 72-74, 77-81, 86, 87, 116, 125, 140, 142, 148, 175-189
all-Indian tour of, 78
aloofness from politics, 86-87, 184
arrest of, 77
best tribute to, 184
call for satyagraha, 77-78
commandment to RSS *swayamsevaks*, 181
condemnation of Godse's crime, 72
critical of separatist mentality, 183
demise of, 180
direct disciple of Ramakrishna

Paramahansa, 180
and Gandhiji, meeting between, 74
much-misunderstood personality, 180
personality of, 182-183, 185
sarsanghchalak of RSS, 7, 180
views on Indian Muslims, 183
visits to Sindh, 7
Gomango, Giridhar, 554, 557
    questionable vote of, 557
Gopal, S., 668
Gopalaswami, N., 656
Gopaldas, Khanchand, 51, 64
Goswami, Dinesh, 384, 443, 450
Govindacharya, K.N., 188, 325, 382, 492
Gowda, Deve, 190, 481-484, 492, 528
    Chief Minister of Karnataka, 492
    as prime minister, 481-484
    fall of government, 484, 528
    as India's eleventh Prime Minister, 482
Grand Alliance, 161
The *Great Game*, 667
Great Proletarian Cultural Revolution (1966-76), 740
Group Mind concept, 306
Group of 8 (G8) nations, 570
Group of Ministers (GoM), 609-610
    analysis and recommendations, 610-612
    members of, 610
    recommendations for police forces, 616
    setting up, 610
    Task Force,
        on Border Management, 610
        constitution of, 610
        on Intelligence, 610
        on Internal Security, 610
        on Management of Defence, 610
Grover, A.N., 208
Gujarat,
    communal violence in, 751-760
        action by centre, 752-753
        Congress description of, 752
        Godhra and post-Godhra violence in, 755
        saving life in, 755-756
        termed as 'genocide', 752
        three lies about, 752
    earthquake, 743-745
        destruction and loss of life, 743
        impact in Kutch and Bhuj, 743-744
        worst natural disasters, 743
    elections,
        announcement of, 195
        victory of Janata Morcha, 197
    fall of government, 529
Gujral, Inder Kumar, 163, 272, 283, 492, 528, 535, 573, 754
    as Prime Minister, 484-485, 528
    support withdrawn to, 485, 486, 529
Gupt, Maithili Sharan, 545
Gupta, Indrajit, 444
    interview to *Frontline*, 485
Gupta, Kanchan, 472
Gupta, Shekhar, 686
Gurbani, 30
Guru Gobind Singh, 41, 422, 424
Guru Granth Sahib, 28, 30, 424
Guru Nanak Dev, 28, 30, 424, 809
Guru, Afsan, 630, 632
Guru, Shaukat Hussain, 630, 632
Gurumurthy, S., 369, 381-385
    article in the *New Indian* Express, 488
    three-point solution to temple movement, 381
Gwalior case, 468

Habeas corpus petition,
    against detentions in emergency, 213-217
        dismissal of 217
    disallowed, 224
    hearing of, 214-215, 217-218
        in Supreme court, 223-225
    in Karnataka High Court, 221-224
Hai, Hakim Sayyid Abdul (Maulana), 389
Haji Pir, 117, 118, 171, 577
Haldhari kisan, 264
Haldighati, 41, 66
Happiness and meaning in life, 876
Haq, Mazrul, 822
Hari Singh (Maharaja of Kashmir), 673, 674
    signing the Instrument of Accession, 674
Harkat-ul-Ansar (HuA), 625, 641
Harkat-ul-Mujahideen (HuM), 625
Hastinapur, 791
Hawala scandal, 467-471, 474, 481, 785
Hedgewar, Keshav Baliram (Dr), 180, 521, 537
Hedgewar, K.B. (Dr), founder of RSS, 180, 191
Hegde, K.S. (Justice), 199, 208, 236
Hegde, N. Santosh, 214
Hegde, Ramakrishna, 190, 443
Henderson Brooks report, 577
Hendricks, Laurie, 261
Heptulla, Najma, 629, 755
Hidden agenda, issue of, 597
Highway Development Project, 894

Hijacking of IC 814, 621-625, 631
  advantages to hijackers in Kandhars, 623
  bargaining with hijackers, 624
  demand of hijackers, 622-623
  masterminded by ISI, 623
  officials sent to Kandahar, 622
  Pakistan's neck-deep involvement in, 625
  passengers and crew members released, 624
  rescue of passengers, 623-625
    risk involved in, 623
  three jailed terrorists released, 624
Hindi Chini Bhai Bhai, 113
Hindi,
  debate on, 132-136
  de-Sanskritisation of, 134-135
  vs. regional languages debate, 148
Hindi cinema,
  evolution of, 885
  India's powerful cultural ambassador, 886
Hindu,
  characteristics of, 415
  -Muslim division, 57-58
    difference in educational levels of, 32
  revivalism, 347
  and Sikhs, communal divide between, 431
  -Sikh unity, 436, 517
    rallies organised, 431
  society, reform and self-renewal of, 867
Hindu Mahasabha, 84
Hindu, 65, 328, 724
Hinduism, 378, 862, 867-868
  drawbacks of, 868
Hindustan Aeronautics, 84
Hindustan ki Masjidein, 389
Hindustan Times, 273, 479
Hindusthan Samachar, 279
Hindutva, 862
  and Bharatiyata, 863
  misrepresented, 863
  Supreme Court judgment on, 863
Hinglaj Temple in Baluchistan, 786
Hingorani, Ram (Dr), 64
History of idol breaking, 372
Hitabhilashi, 423
  killed in terrorist attack, 423
Hitler, Adolf, 227, 274
Hizb-ul-Mujahideen (HuM), 615, 635, 641
Holistic security, 871
Holland, Josiah Gilbert, 600
Hollywood films on biblical themes, 281
The House of Wax, 35
Howitzer guns, 328

Hugo, Victor, 329
Human bomb, 454
Human resource, 871
Humayun, 125
Hung Parliament, 369, 535, 766
Huntington, Samuel, 863
  Who Are We?, 863
Huseiniwala, 518
Hussain, Altaf, 811
Hussain, Shujjat, 805
Hussain, Zakir (Dr), 159
Hybrid bilingualism, 33
Hyde Act, 549-550
Hyderabad Fort, 14
Hyderabad, destruction and rebuilding of, 28

Ibrahim, Dawood, 602, 699, 729
  assets frozen, 649
  deportation of, 653
  'Fact Sheet' of, 649
  a global terrorist declared, 649-650
  Karachi's Osama, 649
  non-deportation of, 648-650
Ideological Parties, 323
Illegal Migrants Determination by Tribunal (IMDT) Act, 717
  flaws in, 717
  demand to repeal, 718-719
  Supreme Court's verdict against, 718-720
The Illustrated Weekly of India, 182, 481
India,
  adoption of Constitution, 91
  and America,
    as 'natural allies', 658
    cooperation between, 659
  and China,
    relations between, normalisation of, 671
    international land boundaries disputes with, 666, 667
    relations between, 670-672
  Balance of Payments (BoP) situation, 459
  became independent, 4
  border at North-East, 604
  challenge to, 636
  coastal border, neglect of, 604
  crisis-ridden economy, 459, 461
    root cause of, 459
  debate about Jinnah in media, 815-818
  demands against terrorism of, 647-648
  electoral system, major ills in, 164
  entry to nuclear club, 546
  excellence in IT, 881

First War of Independence, 15, 45, 493, 495, 497, 502, 512, 786
   150th anniversary of, 796
   freedom and partition of, 2-13, 202, 543
   gold reserves, mortgage of, 459
   human rights abuses in J&K propaganda, 462
   Independence golden jubilee, 491
   insecure and porous border, 604
   internal security of, 608
   international land boundaries disputes, 66
   a multi-religious country, 866
   a nuclear weapons state, 540, 579, 543
   national defence forces, 605
      combat preparedness of, 605
   nuclear deterrent, 543-548
      debate about, 549-550
   and Pakistan, border dispute with, 672-674
   Pakistan-supported terrorism, 645-648
   partition in 1947, 4, 8, 14, 53, 55, 100, 138, 709
      on communal lines, 14
      and communal violence, 65
      and cross-migration of populations, 53
      a *fait accompli*, 65
      error of judgment, 56-57
      role of Congress leadership, 56
      tragedy of, 10-12, 52-59
   philosophy on life, 150-151
   police forces,
      condition of, 616
      overall image of, 617
      process of modernisation, 616-619
   policy towards Israel, 460
   post Pokhran diplomacy, 546-547
   post-Partition scenario, 66
   PoWs issue, 170, 701
   proclamation as Republic, 91-92
   renaissance, 342
   resolution of border dispute, 671
   a Soft State, 601, 624, 670
   sad chapter in history of, 669-670
   safe haven for anti-national elements, 641
   as software superpower, 762
   security system in, 603-604
   state of Emergency in, 204-254
   subcontinent, map redrawn, 167-168
   three wars (1947-48, 1965, 1971), 709
   toughest challenge to, 870-873
   under Emergency Rule, 202
   victim of Pak-sponsored terrorism, 627
India Gate, 603
India Independence Act, 1947, 672
India Rising, 871
India Shining, 770
India Today, 546, 831
Indian & Eastern Newspapers Society, 275
Indian communists, extra-territorial loyalty of, 114
Indian Express, 273, 294, 303, 304, 336, 369, 686
   anti-government stance of, 273
   editorial, 479, 490
   owner of, 273
   stealing the show, 480
Indian Muslim, 10, 146, 147, 334
   four point appeal to, 525-526
Indian National Army (INA), 25
Indian National Congress, 22, 96
Indian Ocean, 604
Indian Parliament,
   building of, 603
   terrorist attack on, 628-632
      Pakistan's first reaction on, 630
      Prime Minister address to nation on, 630
Indian Peace Keeping Force (IPKF), to Sri Lanka, 334-335
Indian Penal Code (IPC), 230
Indian politics, 138-139
   major shortcoming in, 872
   role of caste in, 293
Indian Telephone Act of 1885, 352254
Indira-Mujib Accord (1971), 717
Indo-Bangla border, most fl uid borders, 718
Indo-French extradition treaty, 661
Indo-Lankan accord, 335
Indo-Pak,
   border, 613
   confederation, 145, 147
   war of 1947-48, 115
      Nehru's handling of, 576
   war of 1965, 116-118
      skirmish over Kutch, 116
   war of 1971, 167-171, 577, 602
      India's triumph in, 170, 575
      lessons taught, 172-174
Indo-Soviet Treaty for Cooperation, 173
Indo-Tibetan Border Police (ITBP), 114, 613
   creation of, 114
Indo-US Nuclear Cooperation Agreement, 549-550
Indo-US,
   nuclear deal, 549
   relations, 655

Indrajit Gupta committee (1998), 167
Indus civilisation, 17
    seat of the Sindhu-Saraswati civilisation, 17
    Vedic roots of, 17
Insurgency, 604
Integral Humanism, 120, 149-154, 312, 313, 322
Intelligence Bureau (IB), 614
    significance of, 614
Intelligence Coordination Group (ICG), 612
Interim Metropolitan Council, established, 129
International Monetary Fund (IMF), 459
International Sikh Youth Federation, 641
Inter-State Council, 164, 596
Invisible enemy, 614
IPKF, 454
    to Sri Lanka, 335, 346, 454, 489
    withdrawn from Sri Lanka, 446
Iqbal, Allama, 354, 791, 805
Irani, C.R., 273
Iraq war, 657
    issue of sending Indian troops to, 657, 660
    India's denial for, 657
ISI terrorist modules operations in India, 614-615
    at Chandipur-On-Sea, 614-615
    busting of, 615
    case of a blind madarasa teacher, 615
ISI-supported militant outfits, 631
Islam, Kazi Nazrul, 173
Islamabad Joint Statement (2004), 707-709, 800
Islamabad-backed proxy war, 697
Islamic extremist, and support to terror, 634-636
    Movement, 635
    Sevak Sangh, ban on, 406
    Swayamsevak Sangh (ISS), 532-533
Islamism, 634
Israel, diplomatic relations with, 461

Jacob, J.F.R. (Maj. Gen.), 170
Jacob, M.M., 598
Jagannath Puri Rath Yatra, 509
Jagdishpur, 512
Jaagirdari System, abolition, 95-96
Jagtiani, Gangadevi (Kamla's mother), 20-21
Jagtiani, Lata, *Sindhi Reflections*, 12
Jai Jawan Jai Kisan, 117
Jain Commission, 485, 486, 488
    report, 485-487
Jain, Girilal, 409, 414
    on Ayodhya movement, 412-414
Jain, J.K., 467
Jain, Kila Chand (Justice), 485
Jain, S.K., 467
Jaisalmer, 68
Jaish-e-Mohammad, 630
Jaiswal, Sriprakash, 718
Jaitley, Arun, 325, 382, 384, 688, 764, 774
Jaitley, Jaya, 555
Jallianwala Bagh, 518
Jamait-e-Islami Hind, ban on, 406
Jammu and Kashmir,
    1975 accord, 678
    accession to India in 1954, 676
    assembly elections in 2002, 685-687
    battle of ballot *versus* bullet, 685-683
    demand for plebiscite, 676
    four-pronged peace strategy for, 684
    legislative assembly,
        attack on, 631
        autonomy resolution, 678
        new problems added, 682-683
        suicide attack on, 628
    normalcy returning to, 687
    in Pakistan occupation, 674
    permit system in, 683
    terrorist attacks on HIndus, 684
    tradition of harmonious pluralism, 692
    unilateral ceasefire announced, 684
    Vajpayee government's success in, 686
Jan Morcha, 331
Jan, Mirza, *Hadiqa-i-Shahada*, 356
Jana Sangh,
    1953 Kashmir satyagraha, 517
    as alternative to Congress party, 139
    Calicut session, 142-144
    and CPI alliance, 105, 144-145
    Delhi unit of, 104
    distinguishing characteristic of, 106
    formation of, 140
    Hyderabad conclave, 189-190
    in 1957 Lok Sabha, 101
    National Council session of, 263
    National Executive meeting at Mount Abu, 198
    national session at Delhi, 192
    opposition to Tashkent talks, 117
    plenary session of, 196
    prophetic resolution of, 208
    rally against Kutch Agreement, 116
    resolution adopted in Udaipur session, 168

resolution of March 1971, 163
resolution passed in March 1972, 171-172
second-class treatment to, 309
a single non-communist political party, 262
triple-victory in the national capital, 129
Janata candidate, 196
Janata Dal (Secular), 386, 450
Janata Dal, 331, 440, 482
    formed, 337
    split in, 386
Janata Morcha, 195
Janner, Greville, 450, 860
    Speechmaker, 450
Jauhar, 66
Jawed, Ajeet (Dr), 50, 822-823
    Jinnah: Secular and Nationalist, 822-823
Jawed, Ajeet (Dr.), 50
Jayalalithaa, J. (Dr) 849
Jayant, 21, 121, 122, 214,215, 220, 226, 239, 260, 787, 811, 890
Jayewardene, J.R., 335
Jeelani, Saifuddin (Dr), 183
Jefferson, Thomas, 267, 591
Jethmalani, Ram, 17, 313
Jha, Adityanath, 131
Jhala, Jagat Singh, 95
Jharkhand Mukti Morcha (JMM), 464
Jharkhand, formation of, 741
Jiabao, Wen, 672
Jinnah, Mohammed Ali,
    ambition to be muslim Ghokhale, 819
    background of, 10
    birth of, 819
    comment in AICC Calcutta session, 1905, 820
    as defence counsel in Tilak's trial, 819
    Governor-General of Pakistan, 10, 25
    historic speech of, 48
    'homesickness' in Pakistan, 822
    Karachi visit of, 9
    last year in Pakistan, 50-51
    mausoleum of, 812
    opposition to Khilafat movement, 820
    principal architect of,
        Pakistan, 9
        Partition of India, 50
    the Quaid-e-Azam, 10
    role in India's freedom movement, 818
    speech in constituent assembly, 815

    vision of secular state, 814-815
Jintao, Hu, 672, 728
Jiye Sindh Movement, 18
Joint Parliamentary Committee (JPC),
    against defection, 203
    on electoral reforms, 165
    recommendations of, 165-166
Joint Task Force on Intelligence (JTFI), 612
Jois, Rama, 214, 217, 224, 238, 275
    arrested under MISA, 224, 275
Joshi, Jagannathrao, 158, 160, 178
Joshi, Murli Manohar (Dr), 325, 474-475
Joshi, Prabhash, 369
Joshi, S.M., 496
Journey to the Center of the Earth, 35
JP movement, 196, 199, 513
    goal of *Sampoorna Kranti*, 189
    invitation to Jana Sangh, 190
    protest march to Parliament, 191
Judicial Reforms, 594
Junagadh nawab, 346
    accession to Pakistan announced, 346
    fled to Pakistan, 346
    uncaring and decadent ruler, 346
Jung, Carl, 194
Justice Grover, 199
Jyotirlingam,
    concept of, 343
    twelve shrines of, 343

Kabir, 125
Kacchi phansi, 495
Kakodkar, Anil (Dr), 542
Kakori Conspiracy Case, 514
Kala Pani, 42, 502
Kalam, A.P.J. Abdul (Dr), 542, 599, 763, 768, 839
    hero of Pokharan II, 599
    most popular president, 599
    NDA presidential candidate, 599
    President of India, 839
Kalani, Hemu, 6, 506
Kalelkar, Kaka, 855
Kalidas, 520-521
Kaluchak Cantonment massacre, 632
Kamalnath,
    meetings on Ayodhya issue, 393-394
    unauthorised emissary, 394
Kamaraj, K., 158, 501
Kamath, H.V., 223, 233
Kamla, 20, 21, 31, 120, 121, 124, 131, 214, 215, 220, 226, 239, 260, 261, 373, 787, 809, 811, 787, 890

Kandahar, 621
Kant, Krishna, 380, 381, 629
Kapoor, Prithviraj, 111
Kapoor, Raj, 846
Kapur Commission, 79, 187
Kapur, J.L. (Justice), 79
Kar seva,
  commencement of, *381*
  for temple construction, 398-399,
    resumed, 392
  in Ayodhya, 373
  Samitis, constituted, 372
  stopped, *392*
Kar sevaks,
  arrests of, 418-419
  brutish confrontation on, 387
  burned in Gujarat, 418
  police attack on, 386
  police firing on, 390
  rushing to Ayodhya, 399
Karachi,
  rally, 8
  annual session of the AICC held, 24
  bomb explosion in, 51
  capital of Sindh, 14
  glory of the East, 14-16
  Kalachi-Jo-Goth, 14
  population of, 16
  Sindhi character of, 16
  visit of Prince of Wales to, 23
Karanjia, R.K., 184
  editor of *Blitz* weekly, 184
  tribute to Shri Guruji, 184
Karat, Prakash, 548
  'Pokharan II: BJP's Harmful Legacy'
    article, 548
Karbi-Anglong, 725
Kargil War (1999), 552, 560, 561-577, 609,
  620, 684, 695, 709, 789
  bitter blame-game, 571
  Cabinet Committee on Security (CCS)
    report on, 563
  deployment of Indian Air Force (IAF),
    564-565
  difference between India and Pakistan
    theory on, 570, 572
  no-crossing-the-LOC restraint, 566-567,
    570
  the Operation Badr, 563
  Pakistan false claims for, 567
  Pakistan,
    objective of, 563-564
    game plan in, 567-568
  and Pakistan's crisis, 570-572
    story of nuclear warheads, 571
    questions to Congress for, 576-577
  victory and Congress criticism, 575-577
  victory in, 564-565, 575-577, 578, 579
Kargil Review Committee, 572-575, 609
  recommendations, 575
  report of, 573-574
Kargil Victory Day, 565
Karnataka High Court, 214, 215, 220, 223
Karunanidhi, Dr, 487
Kashikar, S.G. (Prof), *Dialogue With
  Pakistan*, 824
Kashmir,
  invasion by Pathan tribes, 673
    cease fire resolution passed, 63
  issue of self-determination, 463-464
  satyagraha, 89
Kashmir dispute, 665-693, 672-674
  referred to UN, 673-674
  resolution of, 570
  UN resolution on, 673
Kashmiriyat, 692
Kasuri, Khurshid Mahmood, 786, 795
Katas Raj temple, 785-786, 804-806
  association with Mahabharat, 804-805
  restoration of, 785-786, 804-806
Katiyar, Vinay, 367
Katju, Vivek, 622
Kattabomman, Veer Pandya, 500-501
Kaushal, Swaraj, 467
Keamari, 15
Keerti Mandir, 505
Kennedy, John F., 668
  response to Nehru request, 669
Kesari Sitaram, 774
Keshavananda Bharati case, 236-238
  judgment on, 237
  review of, 237, 238
Kesri, Sitaram, 482, 483
  statement on bomb blasts, 483
  withdrawal of support to Gowda govt.,
    483
Khairabadi, Allama Fazlul Haq, 502
Khalidi, Omar, *Khaki and Ethnic Violence in
  India*, 850
Khalil Gibran, *Children*, 122
Khalil, Fazlur Rehman, 635
Khalistan,
  armed struggle for, 431
  demand of, 318
  Pakistan's support to, 431
  terrorism, 517

terrorist campaign, defeated, 438
Khalistan Armed Force (KAF), 431
Khalistan Commando Force (KCF), 431, 641
Khalistan Liberation Force, 431
Khalsa Panth, 424
Khan, Abdul Qadeer (Dr), 547
Khan, Anaulla, 502
Khan, Arif Mohammad, 330, 332, 333
Khan, Ashfaqulla, 514, 515
Khan, Imran, 798
Khan, Liaqat Ali, 85
Khan, M.P., 332
Khan, Muhammad Ayub (General), 117
Khan, Yahya, 168, 171
Khanduri, B.C. (Maj. Gen., retd.), 894
Khanna, Daudayal, 363
Khanna, H.R. (Justice), 191, 194, 237
   dissenting judgement of, 224
   role in defence of democracy, 238
Khaplang, S.S., 727
Kher, A.G., 80
Khilji, Allauddin, 66
Khuhro, Mohammad Ayub, 26
Khurana, Madan Lal, 435, 475
Khurshid, Salman, 548
Kincaid, Dennis, 41
   The Grand Rebel, 41
King Porus, 796
King, Martin Luther, 659
King, Martin Luther, Jr, 812
Kissa Kursi Ka, 281
Kissinger, Henry, 584
Kochar, Surrinder (Lt. Gen. Retd), 829
   Bhagavad Gita: Timelessly Pertinent, 829
Kolachee, Mai, 14
Kosygin, Alexei, 117, 118
Kotputli, 93
Kripalani, Acharya, 6, 8, 24, 223, 270
Kripalani, J.B., 223
Kripalani, Ram, 38
Krishak Praja Party, 84
Krishna Janmabhoomi, in Mathura, 358
Krishna Menon, V.K., 577
Krishnamurthy, Jana, 754
Krishnanunny, K.P., memoirs of, 266
Krishnappa, 216
Kulkarni, Dr Atmaram, *The Advent of Advani*, 884
Kumar, Jagpati, 513
Kumar, Nitish, 443
Kumar, Prabhat, 621
Kumar, Shanta (Dr), 516
Kumaramangalam, P.R., 393

Kumarmangalam, Mohan, 393
Kumbhalgarh, 506
Kundnani, K.M., 121
Kurukshetra, 519
Kutch satyagraha, 116

Laden, Osama bin, 635, 708
Lahore bus yatra, 550-552, 562, 620, 695, 684, 789, 808
Lahore Conspiracy Case, 59
Lahore Declaration (1999), 571, 695, 701, 709
   salient points of, 551-552
   signed, 551
   violation of, 566, 567
Lahore Fort, 791
Lahore peace initiative, denouncement of, 704
Lahoti, R.C. (Chief Justice), 719
Laila, Runa, 19
Lal, B.B. (Prof), 356
Lal, Bal and Pal, 499, 518
Lal, Devi, 337, 443, 454
   as Deputy Prime Minister, 446
   dropped from cabinet, 446
   kisan rally by, 446
Lal, Jhule, 19
Lal, Shanker, 216
Lal, Vihari, 517
Lala Hansraj, 80, 148
Lala Harichand, 62, 63
Land Acquisition Act, 390
language debate in the 1960s, 133-134
Lapierre, Dominique, 239
Larkana, 17
Larsen & Tourbo, 509
Lashkar-e-Taiba (LeT), 626
Latif, Shah Abdul 'Bhitai', 19-20
   Sur Ramkali, 19
Latur earthquake, 745
Lav Temple, 791
Lawful *hara-kiri*, 237
Left-wing extremism, 734, 736, 738
Legislative assembly's autonomy resolution, 378
   rejection of, 678
LeT, 630, 635
Liberation Tigers of Tamil Eelam (LTTE), 335
   role in Rajeev Gandhi's assassination, 454
   and Sri Lankan armed forces, clashes between, 335
   support of India to, 335

Liberhan Commission, 361, 398
License-permit-quota raj, 115, 162, 458
Light Combat Aircraft (LCA) project, 605
Limaye, Madhu, 190, 262, 496
   prejudice against Jana Sangh, 301
Line of Actual Control (LAC), 671
Line of Control, 564
   violation of, 563
Linguistic reorganisation, 425
Lohia, Ram Manohar (Dr), 56, 58, 118, 133, 145, 160, 514, 555-556
   The Guilty Men of Partition, 56
Lok Dal, 301, 337
Lok Sangharsh Samiti, 227, 262
Lok Virsa Museum, 796
Lone, Abdul Gani, 633, 685
   killed, 633, 685
Lone, Bilal Ghani, 687
Look East policy, 732
Lord Curzon, 820
Lowell, James Russell, 155

Macaulay (Lord), 133, 490
   colonising strategy, 133
Madame Cama, 494
Madarasas,
   along West Bengal's border, 638
   in India's border areas, 634
   misuse for terrorist activities, 634-635
Madhok, Balraj, 142, 157, 179-180
   disagreement with Atalji, 157
   expulsion of, 179-180
   shortcomings in personality of, 157
Maha Kumbh Mela, 18, 418
Maha Shivratri, 76
Mahabharata, 181, 281, 353, 791, 796, 862
Mahajan, Pramod, 325, 373, 375, 376, 401, 492, 542, 557, 764, 774, 843
   a meticulous organiser, 373
   suggestion of Rath Yathra, 373
Mahant Raghubardas, 358
Maharana Pratap, 41, 66, 506
Maharao of Kutch, 25
Maharashtra Control of Organised Crime Act (MCOCA), 637
Maharshi Aurobindo, 57-58, 125, 511, 521
Mahavir, Bhai, 233
Mahdani, Abdul Nasser, 532
   suspected role in blast, 533
Mahjoor, Ghulam Ahmad, 692-693
Mainstream, 257, 273
Maintenance of the Internal Security Act (MISA), 195

Malabar Congress, 537
Malaviya, Madan Mohan, 84, 514
Malhotra, Vijay Kumar, 129, 458
Malimath Committee, 618, 607
Malkani, K.R., 5, 24-25, 109, 130, 273
   fellowship at Harvard University, 112
   The Sindh Story, 24
Malkani, N.R. (Prof), 5, 7, 24
Mandal Commission, 449
   recommendations, 446-448
   debate on, 447-448, 854
   issue of creamy layer's exclusion, 855
   Rajeev Gandh's marathon speech on, 854
   set up of, 446
Mandal, Bindheshwari Prasad, 446
Maneckshaw, Sam (Field Marshal), 170
Mangeshkar, Lata, 375, 886
   India's Nightingale, 375
Mankad, Vinoo, 36
Mankekar, D.R., *Decline and Fall of Indira Gandhi*, 207
Manohar, Murli (Dr), 398, 406
Mansharamani, Rochaldas (Dr), 20
Mansingh, Lalit, 660
Manto, Saadat Hassan, 64, 792
   Toba Tek Singh 64
Maoist Communist Centre (MCC), 735
Maoist insurgents in Nepal, 738, 739
   and naxal outfits in India, link between, 738
Maran Murasoli, 557, 700
Marandi, Babulal, 735
Maruti car project, irregularities in, 187
Marx, Karl, 168
Marxist concept of socialism, 313
Mass awareness yatra, 363
Mass media, reforms needed in, 618-619
Mathur, G.P. (Justice), 719
Mathur, Jagdish Prasad, 106
Matsya Raj, 67
Maugham, William Somerset, 256
Mavalankar, G.V., Father of the Lok Sabha, 102
Mayawati, 516
Mazumdar, Abdul Muhib, 716
McMahon Line, 666
McMahon, Arthur Henry, 666
Mecca and Medina, 366, 416
Mega-cities, 596
Mehrotra, Lalji, 7
Mehta, Ashok, 313
Mehta, Harshad, 464

Mehta, Jamshed Nasarvanji, 47
Mehta, Manhar, 40
Mehta, Om, 207
Mekong-Ganga Cooperation, 732
Menon, Ramesh, *Siva: Siva Purana Retold*, 343
Menon, V.K. Krishna, 113, 669
Merchant, Vijay, 36
Ministry of Development of North Eastern Region (DONER), 731, 732
Minoritysm, 850, 856, 862
    mindset of, 850, 856
Minotity governments, 456-457
Minto-Morley reforms, 424
Mir Baqi, 356
Mir, Hamid, 828
Mira Behn, 73
MISA, 195, 210, 212, 214, 216, 217, 222, 225, 230, 261, 272, 275
    amended, 230
    Section 16A, 216
Mishra, Brajesh, 542, 622, 689, 700
Mishra, D.P., 222
Mishra, Dinanath, 584, 824, 844
Mishra, Kailashpati, 158
Mishra, L.N., 209
Mishra, Shyam Nandan, 203
Mobed, M.J., 36
Modi, Narendra, 325, 375, 492, 753, 758-760, 774, 842, 873, 879
    demand for resignation, 758, 842
    reelection of, 759
    resignation offered by, 843
    tenure as Chief minister, 759
    victim of vilification campaign, 758-760
Modi, Piloo, 264
Moga,
    act of terrorism in, 432
    Hindu-Sikh clashes in, 432
Mohan, Surendra, 262
Mohanta, Prafulla Kumar, 716
Mohatta Palace, 15
Mohatta, Shivratan, 7, 15
Mohenjo-daro, 22
Montessori, Maria, 229
Mookerjee, Ashutosh (Sir), 84
Mookerjee, Syama Prasad (Dr),
    demise of, 89, 143, 101,, 683, 835
    in Srinagar, 516
    defiance of 'permit system' in Kashmir, 683
    differences with Nehru, 84-85
    exit from Nehru's Cabinet, 86
    in first post-Independence Cabinet, 84
    Lion of Parliament, 85
    speech in the Lok Sabha, 85
Moscow Film Festival, 283
Mossad, 487
The Motherland, 273, 546
Mountbatten, Louis (Lord), 55, 179-180
    guilty for partition, 55
MP's Local Area Development Scheme (MPLADS), 593-594
    discontinuation of, 593
Mueller, Robert, 653
Muivah, Thuingaleng, 726
Mujib, Sheikh, 247
Mukherjee, (Justice), 236
Mukherjee, Hiren (Prof), 102, 191
Mukherjee, Nirmal, 280
Mukherjee, Pranab, 487, 827
Mukhi, Murli, 37
Mukti Bahini, 169
Multi-Agency Centre (MAC), 612
Multi-Disciplinary Monitoring Agency (MDMA), 487-489
Multi-party democracy, 873
Multi-Purpose Identity Cards, 746
Mumbai local train blasts, 633
Mumbai, serial bomb blasts in, 462, 602, 637, 699, 729
Munde, Gopinath, 475
Municipal Corporation of Delhi (MCD), 128
Munshi, K.M., 342, 346, 348-349, 351, 352819, 883
    Founder-Chancellor of Bharatiya Vidya Bhavan, 342
    I Follow the Mahatma, 819
    Jai Somnath, 342, 883
    letter to Nehru, 348-349
    Pilgrimage to Freedom, 346, 349
    Somnath: The Shrine Eternal, 349
Murlidhar, 51
Murphy's Law, 784
Murthy, N.R. Narayana, 881
Murthy, Sudha, 881
Musharraf, Pervez (Gen.), 33, 562, 568, 625, 694-710
    accusations on L.K. Advani, 688, 694, 705-706
    arrival in New Delhi, 698
    at Agra summit, 700-704 see also Agra summit, 694-710
    calling terrorism a freedom struggle, 710
    capture of power, 695, 580

court martial recommended for, 572
failed assassination bids on, 708
In the Line of Fire, 705
man behind Kargil war, 695
media interaction at Agra summit, 702
telling a white lie on Dawood, 698-699
visit to ancestral house, 698
Muslim League, 47, 50
call for Direct Action Day (16 August 1946), 54, 818
Week of the Long Knives, 818
conspiracy for Assam, 715
demand for separate Mislim nation, 9, 54, 714, 818
flaw in, 54
mission of, 65
Muslim *muhajirs*, 10, 16
Muslim Women (Protection of Rights on Divorce) Act, 1986, 333
Muslim Women's (Protection of Rights on Divorce) Bill in 1986, 334, 365

Nadimarg village, attack on, 633
Nadwatul-Ulama, 389
Nadwi, Abul-Hasan Ali (Ali Mian), 380, 389
Chairman of Muslim Personal Law Board., 389
Naga Hoho, 727
reconciliation campaign of, 727
Nagaland, 726
bilateral talks with Indian Prime Minister, 726
media report on, 726
insurgency in, 726
end of, 726-728
lasting peace in, 727
Nagalim, 727
Nagouri, Safdar, 635
Naidu, Chandrababu, 533, 580, 735, 763
Naidu, M. Venkaiah, 325, 417, 492, 763, 829, 830
naxalite attack on, 735
resignation as BJP President, 774
Naidu, Sarojini, 814
Naipaul, V.S. (Sir), 409, 414
An Area of Darkness, 410
Nambiar, Vijay, 700
Namboodiripad, E.M.S., 104, 127, 190
demise of, 537
homage to, 537
Nand Rishi, 692
Nanda, Gulzarilal, 363
Nandy, Ashis, article in *Quest*, 246-248

Naoomal, 36
Naoroji, Dadabhai, 494
Napier, Charles James (Sir), 14-15
mercenary nature of operations, 14
Napoleon, 14
Narain, Hukum Dev, 447
Narain, Lala Jagat, 429
of *Hind Samachar*, 429
Jagat, murder of, 429
Narain, Raj, 289, 290, 294, 303
Indian Mephistopheles, 294
'Vandal at Large', 294
Narasimhan, V.K., voices against the Emergency, 273
Narayan Guru, 498, 868
Narayan, Jayaprakash,
the Bhishma Pitamaha, 300
building bridges with Jana Sangh, 186
castigation of, 173
conscience-keeper of nation, 299
critic of RSS and Jana Sangh, 186, 187
demise of, 299-300, 836
detention of, 203, 222
hero of India's 'Second Freedom Struggle 122
organiser of India's Second Freedom Movement, 185
peace mission in Nagaland, 727-728
police assault on, 188-189
power politics renounced, 268
principal architect of Janata Party's triumph, 268 *see also* Bhartiya Janata Party
the Second Mahatma, 386
transformation in outlook, 186
Narayanan, K.R. (Dr), 529, 700, 838
activist President, 536
term ended, 598
played an 'activist' role, 555
Narayanan, V.N., 479
Nariman, Fali, 194
Nath sampradaya, 506
Nath, Kamal, 393-394
National Agenda of Governance (NAG), 533, 539-540
National Commission for Tribal Development, 738
National Commission to Review the Working of the Constitution (NCRWC), 587
broadbased composition of, 588
recommendations of, 592-597
setting up of, 588

National Committee on Disaster
    Management, 745
National Conference, 678, 683
    alliance with NDA, 683
National Council of Khalistan, 428
    letter to Pakistan President, 428
National Democratic Alliance (NDA), 416,
    534
    appeal to voters, 579
    call for stability, 579
    common manifesto of, 580
    Common Minimum Programme, 416, 534
    defeat in May 2004, 691
    election manifesto, 419-420
    formation of , 778
    hour of crisis for, 557-558
    return to power, 578-586
    size of, 579
    solidarity of, 559
    victory of, 579
National Democratic Alliance (NDA)
        government,
    achievements of, 553
    lost by one vote, 554
        aftermath of, 554-560
        aspects of destabilisation plot, 554
    stabilisation of, 502
    tragedy struck at, 553
    two-pronged policy towards Pakistan, 789
        vote of confidence debate, 553
        three main decisions for Nagaland, 726
        see also Nagaland, 726-728
National Democratic Front (NDF), 317, 534
National Development Council, 850
National Disaster Management Authority
    (NDMA),746
National Front (NF), 337, 440
    coalition, 369
    government, 440
        outside support to, 442
        seeking BJP support, 440
        declined, 440-442
National Herald, 211
National Human Rights Commission
    (NHRC), 588
National Information Board, 612
National Integration Council, 396, 861
National Judicial Commission, 594
National Liberation Front of Tripura
    (NLFT), 729-731
National parties, 93
National Security Advisor (NSA), 575, 612
National Security Council (NSC), 575, 609

National security,
    management of, 607, 608
    threats to, 601
National security system,
    blueprint for overhauling, 611
    issue of, 605
    obstacles in, 606
    organisational structure and working of,
        605
National Socialist Council of Nagalim (Isak-
    Muivah), 726
Nationalisation of banks, 159
Nationalist Congress Party (NCP), 583
Nav Nirman agitation, 188
Nav Nirman Samiti, 194
Naxalbari, 735
Naxalism,
    anti national slogan of, 735
    birth of, 735
    killing of ABVP activist, 736
    spread of, 734
        from 'Pashupati to Tirupati', 734
    three-pronged strategy for, 736
Nayanar, E.K., 537
Nayar, Kuldip, 251, 279, 310
    detained under MISA, 210
NEFA, 669
Neharwali Haveli, 698
Nehru, Arun, 330, 384
Nehru, Jawaharlal,
    address to nation on 19 November 1962,
        669-670
    approach on nuclear power, 544-545
        flaws in, 544-545
    blunder on Kashmir, 673
    contribution to parliamentary democracy,
        115
    endorsing cultural nationalism, 865
    era, end of, 114-115
    failure of, 115, 667, 668
    -Gandhi dynasty, 460, 765
    a great patriot, 1149
    India's ancient but self-renewing culture,
        865-
    Kashmir statement in Lok Sabha, 682
    -Liaqat pact (1950), 717
    most scholarly, 391
    personal prejudices, 115
    prejudiced view for Jana Sangh, 865
    seeking military assistance from USA and
        USSR, 668-670
    smug ostrich-like complacency, 544
    telegram to Pant, 360, 362

The Discovery of India, 17
   trust in Asian solidarity, 668
   trust in Chinese leadership, 667-668
   views on Hindi, 134
   views on reservations, 854
Nehrivian,
   past, legacy of, 671-674
   socialism, 187
Nepal, BJP's stand for, 739
Nerwa, 69
New Delhi Municipal Corporation (NDMC), 128
New Delhi's Raisina Hill, 603
News agencies,
   amalgamation of, 279
   revival of, 279
The New York Times, 224
Niazi, A.A.K.(Lt. Gen.), 170
Nij Thanw, 30
Nirankari sect,
   and Bhindranwale's followers, clashes between 429
   excommunication of, 429
Nirguna puja, 376
Nirmal Ganga, vision of, 894
Nishan Niketan Vachanalaya, 512
Nishkama karma, 126
Nixon, Richard, 169, 247, 251
Noakhali, 56
Non-Aligned Movement (NAM), 548
North-East, 711-714, 722-723
   area of strategic vulnerability, 712
   external aggression in, 713
   issue of national security, 722-723
   NDA's initiatives in, 723-724
   physical isolation of, 712
   present situation in, 712-713, 723
   security of, 711
   tribals in, 722
NSCN (I-M), 726-727
NSCN (K), 727
Nuclear disarmament, 546
Nuclear weapons programme, 626
Nuremberg trial, 289

Oak, Vasantrao, 62, 63, 496
Officers' Training Camp (OTC), 41
Ojha, Dhanraj, 64
One border one force concept, 613
Onlooker weekly, 316
Operation Blue Star, 430, 437, 445
   aftermath of, 431
   consequences of, 431

   success of, 431
Operation Ganesh, 484
Operation Parakram, 644-664
   peace-time deployment of troops, 644
Operation Shakti, 543
Operation Vijay, 563, 564-566
Opinion polls, influence on voter, 95
Organisation of Islamic Conference (OIC), 662
Organiser, 5, 107, 108-118, 120, 124, 128, 130, 186, 191, 273
Orwell, George, 250, 251
   Animal Farm, 251
   Nineteen Eighty Four, 250
Ottapidaram, 499
Ottoman Empire, 820
Overseas Friends of BJP conference, 460, 659
Oza, B.M., 330

Pachauri, Suresh, 487
Padgaonkar, Dilip, 410
   interview with Naipaul, 410-411 *see also* Naipaul
   interview with Nirad Chaudhry, 411-412 *see also* Chaudhuri, Nirad C., 409, 411
Padmanabhaiah, K., 726
Pai, Nath, 496
Pakistan,
   American arms aid to, 169, 172-173
   armed incursion into Kutch, 116-117
   as Muslim homeland, 54
   border dispute with India, 672-674
   creation of, 3, 168, 712
   defeat in 1971 war, 170, 427
   division of, 168, 712
   invasion of Kashmir by, 117
   military coup in, 580, 695
   mockery of elections in, 686
   nuclear weapons programme, 547
   proxy war against India, 422, 427, 574, 602, 606, 625, 643, 646, 708
      beginning of, 602
      'war through other means', 602
   resolution, 10
   support for the Khalistan movement, 427
   terrorist acts in, 708
   underground nuclear explosions in Chagai, 547
Pakistan Muslim League (N), 572
Pakistani, overstaying in India, 613
Pakistan-Occupied Kashmir (POK), 171
Pakistan Peoples Party, 169, 811
Pal, Bipin Chandra, 528

Palasi Raja, 498
Palestinian Liberation Organisation (PLO), 461
Palkhivala, Nani, 237, 238
Panchajanya, 834
Panchayati Raj, 595
   33% reservation for women, 507
   institutions, 588
Pande, Kamal, 653
Pandey, Mangal, 513, 514
Pandit, Vasant Kumar (Dr), 198, 203, 213
Pan-Islamic extremist groups, 634, 635
Pant, Govind Ballabh, 360
Pant, K.C., 688
Panthic Committee, 431
   declared the formation of 'Khalistan', 431
Pantulu, Tanguturi Prakasam, 503
Paramahamsa, Ramakrishna, 47, 48, 180, 511
Paramhans, Mahant Ramchandradas, 363, 417
Paris in the 20th Century, 36
Parliament,
   terrorist attack on, 644, 647, 789
   unfettered amending power for, 236
Parliamentary Proceedings (Protection of Publication) Act, 276
Parmarth Niketan, Rishikesh, 893
   future projects of, 893
Patel, Babubhai, 197
Patel, Chimanbhai, 188
Patel, Keshubhai, 475
Patel, Sardar Vallabhbhai,
   demise of, 80, 347, 349, 667
   the Iron Man of India, 505
   letter to Pantji, 360-361
Pather Panchali, 282-283
Patnaik, Biju, 220, 317, 484, 878
   comment on United Front, 484
   in Rohtak jail, 220
Patnaik, Naveen, 559
Patwardhan, Achyut, 303
   Janata, RSS and Nation article, 303
Pawar committee, 745, 746
Pawar, Sharad, 392, 397, 458, 581, 745
Peace bus, hijacked, 552
Penberthy, Jeff, 03
   article in *Asian Age*, 403
Pentangular Tournament, 36
People's Democratic Party (PDP), 532, 686
People's Rule, 202
People's War Group (PWG), 503, 735
   ban lifted from, 738

Perben, Dominique, 661
Peshwa, Nanasaheb, 46
Phanshi Cha Vad, 495
Phoenix, 12
Phone tapping, 251-252
   in Britain, 252
      Birkett committee for, 252
      inherently objectionable, 252
   legitimacy and limits of, 251
   in USA, 251-252
Phule, Jyotiba, 494, 868
Phule, Savitribai, 868
Pillai, Kesava Shankara, 273
Pillai, V.O. Chidambaram, 499
Pilot, Rajesh, 483
Pingle, Moropant, 396
The *Pioneer*, 403, 472
Plato, 306
Pluralist *samskaras*, 32
Pokharan I, 549
Pokharan II, 173, 541-543, 547-553
   criticism from Congress and Communist, 548
   matter of probe for BJP, 543
   political reaction to, 548
   Prime Minister's announcement on, 542-543
Poland,
   pulling down the Russian church, 372
   Russian occupation of Warsaw, 372
Police Modernisation Scheme, 737
Police reforms and modernisation, 616-618
Policy of lebensraum, 604
Political,
   earthquake in Delhi, 205-207
   leader, six basic qualities, 105-106
   party, three types of constituencies, 771
   stability, 592
Politics,
   of consensus, 873-874
   degeneration of, 877
   during freedom movement, 877
   and media, relation between, 880
   of vote bank, 872-873
Pot, Pol, 739
   of Khmer Rouge regime, 740
Poverty, curse of, 870-873
Powell, Colin, 646, 650
   journalist questions to, 650-651
   tour of India and Pakistan, 653
Power game, 554-557
Prabhas Patan, 342
Pradhan Mantri Gram Sadak Yojana

(PMGSY), 737-738
  inspiration for, 737
Praja Socialist Party, 96
Prakasa, Sri, 823-824
Prakash, A. Surya, 584
  Issue of Foreign Origin: Sonia Under Scrutiny, 584
Prakash, Baldev (Dr), 431, 436
Prasad, Rajendra (Dr), 115, 346, 350, 499, 513 591
Prasad, Thakur, 591
Prasar Bharati (Broadcasting Corporation of India) Bill, 279
  concept of, 279
Pratibha, 21, 31, 121, 122, 214, 215, 220, 226, 227, 239, 245, 260, 470, 787, 802, 803, 819
  anchor and produce TV programmes, 890-891
  interview with Amitabh, 885
Prescott, John, 660
Presidential election,
  2002, 838-839
  in August 1969, 159
Press censorship, 204
Press Council of India, constituted, 280
Press Trust of India (PTI), 258
Prevention of Corruption Act, 467, 470
Prevention of Infiltration from Pakistan (PIP) Act, 1964, 716
Prevention of Publication of Objectionable Matter Act, 276
Prevention of Terrorism Act (POTA), 636-641
  debate in Parliament, 639
  oppositions to, 636-638
  repealed, 640
  safeguards in, 640
Priestley, J.B., 288
Princely states, integration of, 88
Privy purses, abolition of 159
Proxy war, 422, 427, 574, 602, 606, 625, 643, 646, 708
Pseudo-secularism, 373, 379, 678, 862
  of Congress party, 857-862
PTI, 279
Punjab,
  accord, 434
  demand for Sikhistan, 425
  effects of terrorism in, 423
  history of militancy in, 437
  home to Ghadar revolutionaries, 424
  land of martyrs, 424
  militancy in, 423
    historical roots of, 424-426
    misuse of religious places, 429-430
    Pakistan's hands behind, 427-428
  some important lessons of, 437-438
  strategic location of, 425
  terrorism in 422
  trauma and triumph of, 422-452
Punjabi Suba,
  demand for, 425
  Pakistan's support to, 426
Punjab Kesari, 429
  fearless critic of Bhindranwale, 429
Punjabi *vs.* Hindi row, 183
Puri, Rajpal, 39, 42, 45, 51, 59, 62-64, 81, 82, 138
  influence on author, 138
  prant pracharak, 38, 39, 81, 138
Purie, Aroon, 831, 880
Pushkar, 866

Qalandar, Shahbaz, 19
Qasim, Mohammad Bin, 18
Qazi Nazar-ul-Islam, 84
Quattrocchi, Ottavio, 329, 331, 585
  agent of Italian multinational, 329
  flee the country, 165
  Involvement in Bofors scam, 329
Queen Padmini, 66
Quit India, 6, 23, 35, 104, 204, 503, 511
Qureshi, Fazal Haque 687
Qureshi, Rashid (Major-General), 630

Rabbani, Raza, 799
Radcliffe, Cyril, 55
Radhakrishnan, C.P., 531
Radhakrishnan, S. (Dr), 47, 103, 859
Radhakrishnan, T.I. (Dr), 49
Radhasoami sect of Beas, 31
Radio Moscow, 212
Raffarin, Jean-Pierre, 661
Raghavan, R.K., 617
Raghunath Temple, Jammu, fidayeen attack on, 632
Raghuramiah, K.V., 209
Raghuveera (Dr), views on HIndi, 134-135
Rahman, A.L.M. Fazlur (Gen), 730
Rai, Lala Lajpat, 424, 503, 518, 792
Railway Strike of 1974, 199
Raj Ghat, 268, 726, 813
Raj Path, 603
Raja Dahir, 18
Raja of Mahmudabad, 820

Rajeshwar, T.V., 718
Rajguru, 519, 792, 809
Raju, Alluri Sitarama, 503
Ram,
  a symbol of Indian cultural heritage, 421
  Gandhiji's devotion to, 355
    Muslim League criticism to, 355
  Imam-e-Hind, 354
  symbol of Indian culture, 352-355
Ram Navami, 356, 376
Ram Rajya, 353, 354, 365
Ram Rath Yatra, 341, 351, 368-385, 373, 374, 415, 493, 510, 524, 737
  calumny against, 378-380
  end of, 380
  huge response to, 378
  a mass-contact programme, 374
  propaganda by our adversaries, 379
  response to, 375-376
  rhetoric against, 381
  speech made from, 377-378
  starting of, 374
  stopped in Bihar, 380
Ram Setu issue, 858
Ram *shilas*, 364, 367
Ram Temple,
  construction of the, 376
  makeshift structure, 467
  Movement (1993), 369
Ram, Jagjivan, 158, 269, 296, 270
  Congress for Democracy (CFD) formed, 263, 301
  joined Congress (U), 309
  quit Janata Party, 309
  quit the Congress, 269
  resigned from Congress, 263
  a senior minister, 263
Ram, Kanwar (Bhagat), Tansen of Sindh, 20
Ram, Ladha, 502
Ram, Maryada Purushottam, 353
Ram, N., 328
Ramachandran, M.G., 295
Ramakrishna Mission, 46, 48
  in Karachi, 57
Ramana Maharishi, 44
Ramayana, 281, 353, 791, 792, 796, 858, 862
  story of, 353
  TV serial, 282
    popularity of, 282

Ramchand (author's uncle), 6
Ramjanmabhoomi, 353, 375, 386, 390, 393, 417, 466, 493, 533, 857

de facto temple and *de jure* temple, 259
Hindu effort to reclaim, 358-359
idols installed in 1949, 359
  puja allowed, 359
kar seva in, 370, 371
legal course sought, 358
make-shift Ram Temple at, 404-405, 466, 515
nyas, 393, 394, 417
opening of locks, 364, 415
reconstruction of temple at, 342
relocation of masjid suggested, 371-372
Shilanyas of Ram Temple, 364, 415
Ramjanmabhoomi Muktiyajna Samiti, 363
Ramprasad 'Bismil', 514
Rana Pratap, 41
Rana Sanga, 66
Ranade, Eknath, 81
  a hard taskmaster, 127
  a true karmayogi, 124-127
  death of, 127
  rock memorial mission of, 124-127 see also
Ranga, N.G., 134, 277, 503
Rani Chennamma, 497
Rani Laxmibai of Jhansi, 46, 497, 514
Ranji Trophy match, 36
Rann of Kutch, 116
Rao, B. Shiva, 851
  'Framing of the Indian Constitution' study, 851
Rao, C. Rajeshwar, 861
Rao, K. SUBBA, 193
Rao, N.T. Rama, 317, 337, 440, 447
  votary of Telugu *atma gauravam*, 443
Rao, P.V. Narasimha, 162, 352, 398, 456-462, 482, 557, 757, 774
  appreciations for, 458, 461-462
  approach to Ayodhya issue, 394, 465-467
  Ayodhya: 6 December 1992, 465
  disillusionments with, 464-465
  best Prime Minister, 391, 458
  fifth minority government of, 391, 398, 456-457, 488, 557
    relation during initial phase, 460
    three oddities of, 456-458
    White Paper on Ayodhya events released, 404, 405
  government of, 483
  proximity with Chandraswamy, 464-465
  on rebuilding of mosque, 466
  sworn in as Prime Minister, 391, 456-462

Rao, Subba K., 199
Rao, Varinder Chandrashekhar, 503
Rao, Venkata, 216
Rashtra Mandir, 515, 540
Rashtra Raksha Pratigya, 499
Rashtrabhakti Ki Teerth Yatra, 481
Rashtrapati Bhavan, 603
Rath yatra, genesis of, 372-385
Ray, A.N. (Chief Justice), 194, 223, 237
   as Chief Justice of Supreme Court, 208
Ray, Rabi, 199
Ray, Satyajit, 282, 884
Ray, Siddharth Shankar, 206, 207, 208, 235
Red Corridor, 604, 734
Red Fort, terrorist intrusion into, 631
Reddy, Brahmananda, 207
Reddy, Channa, 222
Reddy, Neelam Sanjiva, 130, 159, 287
   questionable role of, 294-297
Reddy, Snehalata, 244
Rehman, Maulana Fazlur, 797
Rehman, Sheikh Mujibur, 168-169
Rehman, Sherry, 799
Religion-based reservations, 848-850
   opposition to, 848-849
8Religious bigotry, 466
Representation of People Act, 1951, 167
   change in provisions of, 2,30
Research & Analysis Wing (RAW), 610, 689
Reserve Bank of India (RBI), 187
Revoke Emergency seminar, 198, 199
   speech in, 199-200
Revolutionary Socialist Party (RSP), 191
Rice, Condoleezza, 650, 656
Rightist reactionaries, 162
Rijiju, Kiran, 729
Rishi parampara, 57
Roosevelt, Eleanor, 824
Roy, Indubhushan, 502
Roy, M.N., *The Hindu Phenomenon* (1994), 409
Roy, Raja Ram Mohun, 868
RSS (Rashtriya Swayamsevank Sangh),
   in 1947, 6
   activities started in Sindh, 4
   alleged role in Gandhiji's assassination, 186
   ban lifted from, 77-79, 186
   ban on, 76, 78, 86, 148, 406
      demand for, 74-75
      reasons given for, 78-79
      following Mahatma Gandhi's assassination, 406

   and Congress, 39-40
   constitution, 81
   emerged from the *agni pareeksha*, 77
   and Gandhiji, a mututally respectful relationship, 73-75
   innocence in Mahatma's murder case proved, 78-80
   issue of written constitution of, 77-81
   Jodhpur camp, 63
   Mahatma as *pratah smaraneeya*, 73
   mission of, 4
   motto of, 119
   patriotic prayer of, 66
   pracharak system in, 119
   swayamsevaks,
      in Republic Day Parade, 181
      rescue and rehabilitation work, 65-66
   work of, 868
Rubenfeld, Jed, 875
   The Interpretation of Murder, 875
Rule of law, 224
Rumsfeld, Donald, 657
Rusk, Dean, 669
Russell, Bertrand, 751

SAARC summit, 647, 707-709, 789
   in Islamabad, 707-709, 789
      Vajpayee-Musharraf meeting, 688
      joint statement issued at, 688
Sabarmati Express, gutting of, 752
Sachal 'Sarmast', 21
Sachar committee, 849-850
   proposal of muslim head count in Armed forces, 849
Sachar, Rajinder, 849
Sadhu Vaswani, T.L., 3, 7, 8
Saeed, Hafeez Mohammad, 635
Safi ha Chahal Nasaih Bahadur Shahi, 356
Sagar, Ramanand, 282
Saguna puja, 376
Sahay, C.D., 622
Sahir Ludhianvi, 52
Sahni, Kedarnath, 105, 106, 325
Sai, Veer Surendra, 509
Saikia, Hiteswar, 716
Sain Noor Husain Shah, 21
Sain Qutab Shah, 20-21
Salem, Abu,
   close aide to Dawood, 654
   deported to India, 654-655
Samachar Bharati, 279
Samachar, 279
Samata Nagar, 314

Sami, 21
Samyukta Vidhayak Dal (SVD), 134, 145, 156, 157
Sangh Parivar, 399, 537, 773
Sanghvi, Vir, 474
Sangma, P.A., 483, 583, 593
Sant Longowal, 434
Santayana, George, 711
Santhanam, K. (Dr), 542
Saraswati river, 18, 21
Sardar Patel, 56
Sarkar, Jadunath, 41
   Aurangzeb and *Shivaji*, 41
Sarkar, Manik, 729
Sarkaria Commission, 164
   report, 535
Sarkozy, Nicolas, 661
Sarmast, Sachal, 20
Saryu river, 417
Sashastra Seema Bal, 613
Sathya Sai Baba, 260
Satpathy, Nandini, 263
Sattar, Abdul, 701, 794
Savarkar, Ganesh Damodar, 502
   India's First War of Independence, 502
   Swatantryaveer, 502
   Veer, 84
   Vinayak Damodar, *1857-The War of Independence*, 44-45
Save Democracy movement, 302
Save the Constitution Day, 5899
Saxena, Girish Chandra, 610, 684
Sayeed, Mufti Mohammad, 445
   daughter kidnapped, 445
   surrender before militant's demand, 445
Scheduled Castes and Scheduled Tribes reservations, 852
Scheduled Castes converts, 853
   Home Affairs circular on, 853
Schwarzenegger, Arnold, 585
Science of rigging, 93
Scindia, Vijayaraje (Rajmata of Gwalior), 176, 314, 322, 367, 375, 401,
   jailed during emergency, 176
Second Freedom Struggle, 262, 286
Second States Reorganisation Commission (SRC II), 742
Second World War, 170, 288
Secularism, 313, 349, 368, 892
   concept, 313
   Gandhi's thought in, 892
Security Council Resolutions 1269 and 1378, 664

Security,
   of airports, 613
   system in British India, 603
Seminar, 274
Sen, A.G., 216
Sen, Sukumar, 93
Sengupta, Shyamal, 729
Seshadri, H.V., 401, 738
Sethi, J.D., 313
Sethi, Najma, 806
Setusamudram Ship Canal Project, 858
Shabad, 31
Shah Bano case, 331, 365, 369
   government's somersault on, 332-333
   reaction of orthodox muslims to, 332
   Supreme Court's decision in, 332
Shah Commission, 210, 252-253
   report of, 253
   ban on, 253
Shah, J.C. (Justice), 252
Shah, Nawab Wajid Ali, 358
Shah, Noor Husain (Sain), 809
Shah, Viren, 239, 444
Shah-Nanavaty Commission, 758
Shahu Maharaj, 496
Shakdhar, S.L., 311
Shakespeare, 43, 875
Shamim, Mohammad (Justice), 468
Shankar, Mani, 206, 487
Shankar, V., 679-682
   My Reminiscences of Sardar Patel, 679
Shankar's Weekly, 273
Shankaranand, B., 330
Shantiniketan, 511
Sharada Peeth, 692
Sharia'h, the Muslim Personal Law, 332
Sharif, Nawaz, 551, 562, 571, 563, 695, 803
   arrested, 580
   asylum in Saudi Arabia, 571
   blamed Musharraf for Kargil, 570-571
   joint statement with President Clinton, 569
   meeting with Bill Clinton, 571
   official biography of, 570-571
   ouster of, 695
Sharma, Krishna Lal, 321, 325
Sharma, M.S.M., 50
Sharma, P.C., 653
Sharma, Rajendra, 124
Sharma, Shankar Dayal (Dr), 478, 535
Shastri, C.L.R., 273
   article 'On Saying No', 273
Shastri, Lal Bahadur, 116, 131, 181, 363, 391,

458-460
  death in Tashkent, 118, 158
  as prime minister, 181
  simplicity and modesty of, 116
  Tashkent Declaration signed, 117
Shastri, Prakash Veer (Dr), 102, 134
Shastri, Vishnukant (Prof), 521
Sheikh Noorudin, 692
Shekhawat, Bhairon Singh, 95, 392, 397, 475, 834
Shelat, J.M., 208
Shenoy, P.D. (Dr), 725, 731
Shih, Hu, 66
Shikarpuri Colony Bomb Case, 64
Shimla Accord (1972), 701
Shimla Agreement, 172, 551, 709
  summit, 171-172
  violation of, 566, 567
Simla conference, 1914, 666
Shinawatra, Thaksin, 662
Shirer, William, 226-227
  The Rise and Fall of the Third Reich, 226-227
Shiromani Gurdwara Prabhandak Committee (SGPC), 436
Shishu Mandir educational institutions, 182
Shiv Sena-BJP alliance, 475
Shiv Shanker, P., 487
  criticism of Rao govt. by, 487
Shivaji, 41, 140, 494
Shourie, Arun, 251, 369, 388, 556, 716, 731, 843, 884
Shukla, Vidya Charan, 272, 273
  new code of conduct for press, 273
Shyambabu, 212
Siachen Glacier, 564
Sibal, Kapil, 576
Sikh-is-a-terrorist slander, 433
Sikhs,
  and Hindus, bonds between, 424
  history, distortion of, 428
  demonisation of, 433
  massacre of, 434
Silent social revolution, 507
Silicon Valley, 659
Simon Commission, 503, 518
Sindh and India, 13-26
Sindh Times, 23
Sindh,
  and Partition, 7
  annexed to EIC, 14-15
  before Partition, 20
  before Qasim's invasion, 18-19
  bond between Hindu and Muslims, 22, 23
  cradle of the Indian civilisation, 11
  dark period of, 19
  divided, 11-12
  invasion of, 18
  invasion of, Post-Partition Pakistani historian's views on, 18
  massacre and migration of Hindus, 11-12
  religious tolerance in, 19
  role in freedom struggle, 23-25
  RSS activities started, 4
  separated from Bombay Presidency, 15 *see also* Sindh
  social fabric of, 4
  source of india's civilisational identity, 17-26
  treasures of, 14
Sindhi Hindus, 5
  and Congress, 6-7
  a double-edged tragedy for, 12
  influence of RSS on, 8-9
  migration of, 25
  Nanakpanthis, 30
  pain and suffering of, 17
Sindhri fertilizer plant, 84
Sindhu (Indus) river, 14
Sindhu Darshan festival, 566
Sindhu Resettlement Corporation, 25
Sindhu river, 9, 17, 21, 692
  origin of, 17
  Sindhu Sagar in Vedic period, 17
Singh, Charan, collapse of government, 440
Singh, Jaswant, 557
Singh, Manmohan, 487
Singh, Ajit, 337, 384, 487
Singh, Arun, 330, 610
Singh, Baba Gurbachan, murdered, 429
Singh, Beant, 318
Singh, Bhagat, 39, 275, 424, 516, 517, 519, 521,
Singh, Charan, 190, 262, 268, 269
  battle against Morarji, 291
  collapse of, 29
  collusion with Indira Gandhi, 289-290
  on Prime Ministerial *gaddi*, 294
  resigned, 295
  role of, 289-291
  war of letters with Morarjibhai, 292
Singh, Dara, 747
Singh, Darbara, 203
Singh, Fateh, 436
Singh, Giani Zail, 191, 318, 336, 429
  relationship with Rajeev Gandhi, 336

Singh, Gurnam (Justice), 426, 436, 502
Singh, Guru Gobind 436
Singh, Hira, 46
Singh, Inder Jeet, 218, 219
Singh, Jaswant, 324, 325, 567, 568, 573, 610, 700, 701, 843
   A Call To Honour, 668
   at plenary meeting in Vijayawada, 151
Singh, Joginder, removal of, 484
Singh, K.P., 653, 656
Singh, Kalyan, 352, 390, 395, 396, 401, 404, 515
   as chief minister, 456
   a hero of the Ayodhya movement, 515
Singh, Khushwant, 182, 249, 250, 432
   A History of the Sikhs, 432
   on Indira Gandhi's insecurity, 249, 250
   interview with RSS chief, 182
Singh, Mangej, 565
Singh, Manmohan (Dr), 31, 331, 458, 548, 576, 758, 768
   agenda of economic reforms, 459-460
   elected to Rajya Sabha, 458
   as finance minister, 459
   only election contested by, 458
   relations with, 460
   statement about muslim reservations, 850
Singh, Master Tara 425
Singh, Rajendra (Prof) (Rajju Bhaiyya), 396, 397
   Sarsanghchalak of the RSS, 839
Singh, Rajendra (Prof), 363, 369, 551
Singh, Rajnath, 325, 830
   as BJP President, 739
Singh, Ram Karan, 94
Singh, Raman (Dr), 508
Singh, Ranjit (Maharaja), 809
Singh, Roshan (Thakur), 514, 515
Singh, Satwant, 318
Singh, V.P.,
   attitude to Ayodhya, 449
   and BJP, mistrust between, 369-370
   a compromise formula, 380
   double standards of, 442
   expulsion from Congress, 330
   government,
      confidence vote lost, 386
      fall of, 385-389, 448-449, 555-556
      formation of, 440-441
      performance card of, 445-448
      support withdrawn, 385
      Vote-of-confidence debates in Parliament, 448
   Mandal card played by, 445-448
   as prime minister, 369, 442-443
   rebellion against Rajiv Gandhi, 482
   reservations for OBCs announced, 447
   resignation as Prime minister, 386
   revolt against Rajeev Gandhi, 330-331
   visit to Golden Temple, 445
   weekly dinner meetings, 444-445
Singh, Veer Kunwar, 512
Singh, Vir Bahadur, 363
Singh, Yashwant, 700
Singh, Zorawar, 436
Singhal, Ashok, 382, 386, 401, 418
Singhal, B.P., 397
Sinha, Jagmohanlal (Justice), 221
Sinha, S.B. (Justice), 721
Sinha, S.K. (Lt. Gen.), 718, 719
   report of, 719
Sinha, Satyanarain, 680
Sinha, Yashwant, 542, 552, 610
Sir Creek area, 613
Sir Ganga Ram Hospital, 792
Sister Nivedita, 585
Sleeping cells, 614
Smith, Donald Eugene, 861, 862
   India: As a Secular State, 861
Social diversity management, 105
Socialism concept, 161, 313
Socialist Party, 301, 308
Socio-economic development, 594-595
Solanki, Madhavsinh, 465
Somnath, 342-375
   accession to India announced, 346
   -to-Ayodhya Rath Yatra, stoppage of, 448
   battle of, 344
   destruction and pillage of, 344
   first *jyotirlinga*, 342
   historical background of, 342-351
   last assault on, 345
   location and architecture of, 344
   rebuilt, 346-351
   reconstruction of, 342-351
      condemnation in Pakistan, 351
      social reform aspect of, 348
   re-installation of *jyotirlingam*, 347-348
   restoration of, 861
   a symbol of national faith, 350
   target of foreign invasions, 344
Sonowal, Sarbanand, 719
Soomro, Allah Bux, 24
Soren, Shibu, 464
South Asian Free Media Association (SAFMA), 806

South Asian Free Trade Area (SAFTA), 806
Soviet Union, support during 1971 war, 173
Special Ayodhya Cell, 356, 397
Special Service Bureau (SSB),
    guarding the Indo-Nepal Border, 613
    transferred to the Home Ministry, 613
Spiritual Socialism, 313
Sriperumbadur, 454
St. Francis Xavier's Rock, 126
St. Patrick's High School, 285
Staines, Graham, 747
    and his sons burnt alive, 747
    involvement in missionary work, 748
Stalin, Joseph, 739
State Autonomy Committee (SAC), 678
State Reorganisation Commission, 128
Statesman, 116, 273
Statue of Liberty, 628
Stock market scandal, 464-465
Stop-the-BJP-at-any-cost mission, 482
Straw, Jack, 660
Students Islamic Movement of India (SIMI), 635, 641
Subrahmanyam, K., 572, 609
Subramaniam, Chitra, 328
Suez Canal, 15
Sufi tradition, 20
Sukhdev, 519, 792, 809
Sunday magazine, 285
Sunday Standard, 239
Sunni Waqf Boards, 388
Surjeet, Harkishan Singh, 444, 537, 554, 754
Swami Akhandananda, 180
Swami Chandrasekhara Saraswati of Kanchi, 126
Swami Chidananda Saraswati, 893
Swami Chinmayananda, 397, 725
Swami Dayananda, 505, 868
Swami Jayendra Saraswati of Kanchi Kamakoti, 380
Swami Ramanand, 391
Swami Ranganathananda, 7, 46-49, 57-58, 126, 815, 825
    biography of, 49
    Eternal Values for a Changing Society, 49
    head of the Ramakrishna Math, 815
    last meeting with, 48
    motto and mission of, 48
    The Charm and Power of the Gita, 49
Swami Shivanand, 761
Swami Vivekananda, 27, 47, 48, 49, 313, 511, 815, 868, 899
    historic speech on universal brotherhood, 124
    ideals of, 126
    a lion among men, 125
    on medieval iconoclasm in India's history, 345
    message of universal brotherhood, 658
    place of meditation, 125
    statement on religions, 377
    To the Fourth of July
Swaraj, Sushma, 325, 467, 492, 510, 700, 774, 869
Swarna Jayanti Rath Yatra, 481, 601
    in Andhra Pradesh, 503-504
        naxalite threat to, 503-504
    at Ayodhya, 515-516
    in Bihar, 512-513
        threat of naxalite attack on, 513
    to cellular jail in Andaman Islands, 501-502
    in Delhi, 519-520
    flag-off from Mumbai, 494
    in Goa, 496-497
    in Gujarat, 505-506
    in Haryana, 519
    in Himachal Pradesh, 516
    in Jammu & Kashmir, 516-517
    in Karnataka, 497-498
    in Kerala, 498-499
    at Lakhnow with Atalji, 515-516
    in Madhya Pradesh, 507-508
    in Maharashtra, 495-496
    in Orissa, 508-510
    planning of, 492-493
    in Punjab, 517-519
    in Rajastan, 506-507
    reasons of, 492-494
    schedule during, 520-521
    in Tamilnadu, 499-501
    theme of, 494
    in Uttar Pradesh, 513-515
    in West Bengal, 510-511
Swarup, Devendra, 76
Swedish State Radio broadcast, 328
    allegations of, 328-330
Swu, Isak Chisi, 726
Syed, G.M., 18
Syed, Mufti Mohammed, 686
Sylhet district, merger with East Pakistan, 715
Synchronicity, 194, 195

Tagore, Rabindranath, 173, 511, 860, 863
    essay on *Nationalism*, 863

Taj Mahal, 697
Taleyarkhan, A.F.S., 36
Taliban,
　creation of ISI, 623
　Pakistan's 'force multiplier', 646
Talreja, Kanayalal, 17
　Pearls of Vedas, 17
Tamil Nadu's Special Investigation Team, 532
Tandon, Bishan N., *PMO Diary*, 205-206
Tandon, Gopal, 205
Tandon, Purushottamda, 162, 514
Tankara, 505
Tarkunde committee (1974), 167
Tarkunde, V.M., 186
Tashkent, 117-118, 577
　Declaration, 171, 577
　Summit, 117-118
Tata, J.R.D., 881
Tata, Ratan, 881
Tatya Tope, 495
Tawang, 728
Telangana, 741-742
　demand for, 741-742
Telangana Rashtra Samithi (TRS), 742
Telegraph, 407
Telugu Desam party, 440
　launched, 317
　support to NDA, 763
Temples of Modern India, 508
The Ten Commandments, 281
Terrorism in India, 633-636
　administrative offensive against, 641-642
　ideological basis of, 634
　legal response to, 636
Terrorist and Disruptive Activities (Prevention) Act (TADA), 637
　lapse of, 638
　misuse of, 640
Terrorist groups, ban on, 641
Thackeray, Bal, 559
Thackeray, Balasaheb, 337
Thakre, Kushabhau, 158, 178, 538, 551, 836
Thakur, Janardan, 316
Thakur, Karpoori, 190
Thapar, Karan, 696
Thapar, Romesh, 274
Tharparkar district in Sindh, 712
Thengdi, Dattopant, 124
Thoreau, Henry David, 128
Tilak, Bal Gangadhar (Lokmanya), 13, 23, 419, 495, 499, 819
　imprisonment of, 23-24
　Kesari, 23
　sedition trial in 1905, 819
Tilak, Jayantrao, 495
Time, 283
Times of India, 294, 409, 410
Tithwa, 117, 118, 171
Tod, James (Colonel), 41
　Annals and Antiquities of Rajasthan, 41
Tohra, Gurcharan Singh, 436
Tom Ridge, 656
Tong, Goh Chok, 662
Top twenty terrorist list, 648, 650, 651
Tope, Tatya, 46
Tough Times Don't Last. Tough Men Do, 471
Toynbee, Arnold, 372
Tribals, proselytisation of, 749
Tricolour, 4
Trinity issues, 656
Tripathi, Kamalapati, 278
Tripura, 729-731
　activities of church organisations in, 730
　agonising episode in, 729-731
　Christian conversion mission in, 731
　development plus security approach in, 732
　killing of RSS *pracharaks* in, 729
Triveni Sangam, 18
Truman, Harry, 95
Tsunami, 745-746
　devastations in India, 745-746
Tully, Mark, 272
Tuticorin, 499, 500
Twenty Thousand Leagues Under the Sea, 35
Twenty-Point Programme, 259
Two Nation Theory, 3, 10, 40, 54, 169, 183, 438, 525, 819

Ugly Indian Politician, 877
Ugly Indian politician, image of, 522-523
UN Commission for India and Pakistan (UNCIP), 673
UN Counter Terrorism Committee, 664
UN SC Resolution 1373, 664
UN Security Council Resolution 1373 (2001), 643
Undivided and divided India, map of, 711-712
UNESCO conference, 284
UNI, 279
Uniform civil code, 334, 441, 481, 533, 539
Union Jack, 4
United Front (UF) government, 481-485,

529
  Congress support to, 481
  discord and disorder in, 483
  second time destabilised, 485
United Liberation Front of Assam (ULFA), 437, 723
United Nations, 639, 664
United Nations Human Rights Commission (UNHRC), 462
United Nations Security Council (UNSC), 673
United News of India (UNI), 258
United Progressive Alliance (UPA), 766
  -Left alliance, 104
United States' 1948 Presidential election, 195
Untouchability, 868
UP, President's Rule in, 404
Upadhayay, Deendayal,
  author of *Integral Humanism*, 150
  author's political Guru, 138
  birth of, 139
  column 'Political Diary' written by, 111
  creative and non-doctrinaire approach of, 145-146
  and Dr. Lohia, joint statement of, 146-147
  demise of, 174, 835
  economic thinking, 313
  homage to, 191
  joined RSS in 1937, 139
  murdered, 143-144
  on political untouchability, 145
  a powerful writer, 149
  as party president, 142
  personality of, 144-145
  presidential speech, 142-143
    at Calicut, 148
  principal architect of the Jana Sangh, 150
  as RSS *pracharak*, 141
  thinker, organiser and leader, 137-154
  tragic demise of, 156
Upendra, P., 382
US invasion of Iraq, 657
Uttarakhand, formation of, 741

V.R. Krishna Iyer committee (1994), 167
Vaddi, Nishan Singh, 512
Vaidya, Arun S., 461
  gunned down, 431
Vaidya, Chunibhai, 273
Vaiko, 559
Vajpayee, Atal Bihari,
  address to,
    Nation, 478-479

US Congress, 627
and Advani, L.K., 834-840 see also Advani, L.K.
  bringing BJP to power, 838
  constitution of NDA by, 837
  expelled from party on dual-membership issue, 836
  fellow traveller on political journey, 835-836
  fighting together during emergency, 836
  founding BJP in 1980, 836
  mutual trust and respect, 840-841
  relationship between, 840
  sahayatri in journey, 844
  some differences between, 841-844
  views on Gujarat issue, 842-843
  watching Hindi movies, 846
alternative to Indira Gandhi, 315
announcement as candidate for PM, 472-474
arrested during Emergency, 204
assertive diplomacy of, 708
best orator, 102
bus yatra to Lahore, 550-552, 562, 620, 695, 789, 808
comradeship with, 834
debate on vote of confidence, 480-481
  live telecast of, 480-481
defeated in Gwalior, 836
as External Affairs minister, 270
first government of, 579
first meeting with, 834
formed second government, 579
Founder-Editor of *Panchajanya*, 834
freed from jail, 261
government,
  in 1998, 682
  contributions of, 541-542
  destabilised, 440
  sworn in, 695
head of caretaker government, 560
hospitalised, 215
interview to *India Today*, 841
invitation to form govt., 478
invited to form Governement, 535
leader of Indian delegation to UNHRC conference, 462
leadership during Kargil war, 565-566
lost seat from Gwalior, 319
man of destiny, 835
meeting with Shastri, 117
Meri Ikyavan Kavitaayen, release of, 462
mukhiya of family, 841

as party president, 156-158
  challenges faced by, 156-157
poet at heart, 844-845
praise to Indira, 170
President of Bharatiya Janata Party, 310
presidential address in Bombay, 714
Prime Minister for thirteen days, 837
prime ministership third time (1998), 536, 580
public display of solidarity, 837
rare quality of, 705
re-energising Jana Sangh, 158
seventy-fifth birthday, 620
shifted residence, 542
thirteen day government, 205, 477-481, 492
tribute to, 833-846
views on evolution of balanced language policy, 132
visit to,
  China, 671
  Islamabad (2004), 707-709
  joint statement issued, 707-709
  Kashmir in 2000, 684
  Minar-e-Pakistan, 551
votary of *shanti* (peace), 550
We are all to blame article, 304-305
worshipper of *shakti* (power), 550
Valmiki, 353
Vama, 857
Vanavasi Kalyan Ashram, 182, 731
Vande Mataram, campaign against, 861
Vasudev, Uma, 248, 257
  Two Faces of Indira Gandhi, 248
Vatican, 366
Vazirani, Nihchaldas, 7
Veer Savarkar, 494, 495
  Kala Pani, 500
Veer Vanchi, 500
Veerapandia Kattabomman, film, 501
Venkatachalaih Commission, 597
Venkatachaliah, M.N. (Justice), 588
Venkataraman, R., 336, 535, 546, 557
Venkataswamy, B. (Justice), 215, 221
Venkatraman, R. 385, 386, 557
Venugopal, 223
Verghese, B.G., 273, 279
  sacking from the editorship of, 273
Verma, Brijlal, 304
  as Industries minister, 270
Verma, Motilal, 502
Verne, Jules, 35
VHP and AIBMAC meeting, 387, 392

evidences on mandir-masjid tendered by, 388
Vidarbha Congress, 537
Vidarbha, demand for, 741
Vidya Bharati, 182, 731
VIP security, 616-617
  issue of, 616
  trimming of, 616-617
Vishal Hindu Sammelan, 392
Vishwanath Temple in Kashi, 358
Vishwesha Teertha Swamiji (of Pejawar Math), 381
Vivekananda Education Society, 40
Vivekananda Rock Memorial,
  committee, 125
  construction of, 124-127 see also Ranade, Eknath,
  obstacles to, 124-125
Vohra, N.N., 610, 688
Voice of America, 212
Voice of Germany, 212
Vote-bank,
  politics, 367, 608, 713
  propaganda, 525

Wadhumal (of Wadhwani clan), 28
Wadhvani, Hemandas (Dr), 7
Wadhwa Commission, 747-748
  report, 748
Wadhwa, D.P. (Justice), 747
Wadhwani, Jhamatmal T., 40
Wagah border, 551
Waghela episode, 506
Waghela, Shankarsingh, 506
Wahab, Abdul, 20
Wahabism, 22, 634, 635
Wajed, Sheikh Hasina, 724
Wangchuck, Jigme Singye, 723
Warner Brothers, 35
Warraich, Suhail, 571
Watergate, 251
Watershed parliament elections, 529-531
Weimer Constitution, 227
Weimer Republic, 227
West Coast, 659
Westminster model, 211
White Paper,
  on Ayodhya events, 369, 404, 405
  on Chinese aggression, demand of, 103
  on misuse of mass media during Emergency, 270, 280
Wilde, Oscar, 844
Wilson, Herold, 450

Wolpert, Stanley, 54-55
  India, 54-55
    Shameful Flight: The Last Years of theBritish Empire in India, 54, 55
Women,
  in panchayats and municipal bodies, 869
  political empowerment, 869
    through reservation, 869
  reservation for, 869
World Affairs Council, 659
World Bank, 459
World Parliament of Religions, 125, 657
World Trade Centre, terror attack on, 627-628

Xiaoping, Deng, 671
Xinjiang, 666, 667

Yad Vashem, 663
Yadav, Laloo Prasad, 380, 385, 484, 512
Yadav, Mulayam Singh, 385, 390, 555-556, 559, 580
Yadav, Sharad, 196, 443
Yamuna, 18
Yashpal, 516
Young India, 23

Zam Zam, sacred well in Mecca, 17
Zardari, Asif, 801
Zardari, Hakim Ali, 811
Zedong, Mao, 666, 739, 740
Zia-ul-Haq (General), 285, 427, 428, 602
  strategy against India adopted, 427
    three objectives, 427